THE WORLD IN FLAMES

Columbia Studies in International and Global History

COLUMBIA STUDIES IN INTERNATIONAL AND GLOBAL HISTORY
Cemil Aydin, Timothy Nunan, and Dominic Sachsenmaier, Series Editors

This series presents some of the finest and most innovative work coming out of the current landscapes of international and global historical scholarship. Grounded in empirical research, these titles transcend the usual area boundaries and address how history can help us understand contemporary problems, including poverty, inequality, power, political violence, and accountability beyond the nation-state. The series covers processes of flows, exchanges, and entanglements—and moments of blockage, friction, and fracture—not only between "the West" and "the Rest" but also among parts of what has variously been dubbed the "Third World" or the "Global South." Scholarship in international and global history remains indispensable for a better sense of current complex regional and global economic transformations. Such approaches are vital in understanding the making of our present world.

Q. Edward Wang, *Staple to Superfood: A Global History of the Sweet Potato*
Pierre Singaravélou, trans. Stephen W. Sawyer, *Tianjin Cosmopolis: An Alternative History of Globalization*
James De Lorenzi, *Feasting on History: Ethiopia and the Orientalists*
Jie-Hyun Lim, trans. Megan Sungyoon, *Victimhood Nationalism: History and Memory in a Global Age*
Hale Eroğlu, *Muslim Transnationalism in Modern China: Debates on Hui Identity and Islamic Reform*
Sandrine Kott, *A World More Equal: An Internationalist Perspective on the Cold War*
Julia Hauser, *A Taste for Purity: An Entangled History of Vegetarianism*
Hayrettin Yücesoy, *Disenchanting the Caliphate: The Secular Discipline of Power in Abbasid Political Thought*
Anne Irfan, *Refuge and Resistance: Palestinians and the International Refugee System*
Michael Francis Laffan, *Under Empire: Muslim Lives and Loyalties Across the Indian Ocean World, 1775–1945*
Eva-Maria Muschik, *Building States: The United Nations, Development, and Decolonization, 1945–1965*
Jessica Namakkal, *Unsettling Utopia: The Making and Unmaking of French India*
Michael Christopher Low, *Imperial Mecca: Ottoman Arabia and the Indian Ocean Hajj*
Nicole CuUnjieng Aboitiz, *Asian Place, Filipino Nation: A Global Intellectual History of the Philippine Revolution, 1887–1912*
Mona L. Siegel, *Peace on Our Terms: The Global Battle for Women's Rights After the First World War*
Raja Adal, *Beauty in the Age of Empire: Japan, Egypt, and the Global History of Aesthetic Education*

For a complete list of books in the series, please see the Columbia University Press website.

The World in Flames

A GLOBAL HISTORY OF
THE SEVEN YEARS' WAR

Marian Füssel

Translated by Brian Hanrahan

Columbia University Press
New York

The translation of this work was funded by Geisteswissenschaften International—Translation Funding for Humanities and Social Sciences from Germany, a joint initiative of the Fritz Thyssen Foundation, the German Federal Foreign Office, the collecting society VG WORT, and the Börsenverein des Deutschen Buchhandels (German Publishers & Booksellers Association).

Columbia University Press
Publishers Since 1893
New York   Chichester, West Sussex

Der preis des ruhms
© 2020 Verlag C.H.Beck oHG, Munich
Translation copyright © 2025 Columbia University Press
All rights reserved

Library of Congress Cataloging-in-Publication Data
Names: Füssel, Marian author | Hanrahan, Brian (Translator) translator
Title: The world in flames : a global history of the Seven Years' War / Marian Füssel ; translated by Brian Hanrahan.
Other titles: Preis des ruhms. English | Global history of the Seven Years' War
Description: New York : Columbia University Press, [2025] | Series: Columbia studies in international and global history | Original title "Der preis des ruhms: eine Weltgeschichte des Siebenjährigen Krieges" published in 2020. | Includes bibliographical references and index.
Identifiers: LCCN 2025011345 | ISBN 9780231202404 hardback | ISBN 9780231202411 trade paperback | ISBN 9780231554541 ebook
Subjects: LCSH: Seven Years' War, 1756–1763
Classification: LCC DD411 .F94813 2025 | DDC 940.2/534—dc23/eng/20250515

Cover image: Detail of Bernardo Bellotto, *Rovine della Kreuzkirche di Dresda* (The Ruins of the Kreuzkirche in Dresden), 1765.

GPSR Authorized Representative: Easy Access System Europe, Mustamäe tee 50, 10621 Tallinn, Estonia, gpsr.requests@easproject.com

Contents

Translator's Preface vii

Preface: A Global Conflict in Close-Up 1

I Geopolitics Between Reich and Empire 21

II Sparking the Flame 57

III A War Without Fronts: The German Theater 90

IV 1757: The Year of Battles 113

V Everyday Life in Wartime 159

VI 1758: The Fighting Spreads 182

VII 1759: Annus Mirabilis 230

VII As Mighty As the Sword: The Media War 269

IX Urban Life in a State of Exception 297

x   1761: New Alliances, Missed Opportunities   336

xi   Mosquitoes and Monsoons: The Grab for Spain's Colonies   357

xii   A Second Miracle   381

xiii   1763: Peace at Last   390

xiv   Outcomes of the War   408

Epilogue   433

Acknowledgments   455
Notes   457
Bibliography   595
Index   679

Translator's Preface

One of the main features of Marian Füssel's history of the Seven Years' War is its inclusion of many lengthy passages from autobiographical, eyewitness, and other ego-documentary accounts, produced by kings, generals, naval officers, military medics, and ordinary soldiers, as well as civilian observers from many walks of life: priests, poets, nobles, and enslaved people, among many others. In linguistic terms, this produces a great variety of styles, a clamor of recovered voices.

The reader will notice that the many English-original texts among this material display an extraordinary variation of spelling, punctuation, and capitalization, often within individual texts. This was partly because English was far less standardized at this time and also because later editors have taken very different approaches, some modernizing their material completely, some maintaining all of the original idiosyncrasy. Füssel's book is a palimpsest as well as a panorama.

This heterogeneity informed my decision, in translating the foreign-language material, to sometimes use irregular capitalization and orthography, beginning with the book's opening set piece, a long quotation from Abelmann, the Hanover baker. This use was careful and deliberate, guided by the English-original material, seeking to avoid both anachronism and pastiche. I have, of course, attended to the different social roles of the authors and the different functions of the texts, attempting to fashion plausible enough

English equivalents for government decrees, plebian speech, satirical verse, threatening communiqués of condottieri, and so on.

The use of appropriately inconsistent orthography in translation is complicated by the gradual standardization of English usage and spelling over the course the eighteenth century. Not least because usage in the 1750s and 1760s was so diverse, with weak norms subject to rapid change, it would be incorrect to render every quotation from the period in this single style. I did not always use inconsistency and, when I did, not always in the same way. The specifics of each original mattered most; for various reasons, I found myself using it less with women's writing and texts translated from French. The overall effect is to amplify the book's linguistic heterogeneity, in keeping with the marked heterogeneity of mid-eighteenth-century English(es).

Where a previous published translation of a source existed, I used it, but many of these date to the late eighteenth or nineteenth century and come with peculiarities of their own. Occasionally—as with the reminiscences of the Swiss soldier Ulrich Bräker—published translations can be jarringly anachronistic, but they have been included largely as they are, another layer of difference. Wherever possible, material in Spanish, French, and Latin was translated from the original. Only very rarely did I resort to indirect translation: e.g., when the memoirs of Andrey Bolotov, a Russian officer serving in East Prussia, were available only in Russian and in German translation. In that case, I consulted other texts by Bolotov available in English before rendering the passages.

The long-term trend in the translation of proper names has been away from the various forms of Anglicization once prevalent; it has been many years since historiography in English has referred to "Leghorn" or "Lewis the Fourteenth." In the main text, I have mostly adhered to this, with some exceptions: where it was necessary to avoid anachronism, as with Königsberg or Madras, or where an Anglicized name is extremely familiar, as with Frederick II himself. (And if the king is Frederick, it makes sense for his much-overlooked brother to be Henry.)

A translation of this scope and complexity is made up of many, many thousands of small, interconnected decisions. They were all taken with care. I hope most of them are reasonably correct.

THE WORLD IN FLAMES

Preface

A Global Conflict in Close-Up

World History at Close Range

If in some future Moment, the History of our Time be presented, what Great Things shall be seen! The most powerful Peoples driven to impassionate War and Revenge, swords drawn by the hundred thousand, choking each other in Fury, as if to throttle Europe itself to Death. Rivers of Blood! Battles wherein ten and twenty thousand are slaughtered. Thirty such battles in Seven Years! Great victories of the few, against Armies thrice their size; the mightiest Peoples, and their Attacks of War, thwarted all! We ourselves assailed by all, assailed by all in vain. Our Majesty's pillars hurled down, but raised up once more, raised higher still. Remarkable events. But alas! How terrible this picture of War! Cities aflame, and smashed to Rubble! Wasted lands, their Villages vacant of people, Fields left unsown! Such fields as could be planted now overrun with vermin! Hands wrung in Fear! Pale faces, pale from fear and hunger, pale unto death with Sickness and Anguish! Weeping eyes! Bleeding wounds! Mutilated limbs in their thousands! Mouths that cry: Alas and Woe! Those forced to flee! Parents wandering abroad, their children in hand! The Fearful, blackmailed a thousand times by War's Violence, and their thousand sighs! The Abused, so barbarically Abused! Thousands looted and stripped bare! Their mouths cry out: Alas and Woe! Princes hounded from their own lands and peoples! Forced to flee hither and yon. Kings who face the assassin's outstretched hand. A horrifying case—a mighty Emperor, slain next his own Throne! A royal City, hurled by Earth-quake into the Abyss! More convulsions yet! The seething Sea, its flood tides flecked with human blood! Thunderstorms and torrents of hail! Rivers aflood, Fields drowned for Miles! What think we, looking upon such Scenes? These are yet no Pictures of Fancy. They are Events we have lived, and seen with our own Eyes. Our own Ears have heard them.[1]

This description of the Seven Years' War comes to us from Eberhard Jürgen Abelmann (1703–1765), a master baker in the city of Hanover. His account is a good example of a contemporary, close-up view of this enormous war. In addition to human suffering, he attends to what is distinct and memorable in his own historical experience. Narrative conventions in contemporary historiography tend to function differently. Explanation seeks, above all, to identify political causes; faced with individual experiences like Abelmann's, historians usually attempt to abstract from them. "The war began with an unsatisfactory peace" is thus a typical explanation given for the Seven Years' War. Frederick II's theft of Silesia leads to the Peace of Dresden, leaving Austria dissatisfied; Anglo-French rivalry is laid at the door of the 1748 Peace of Aachen.[2] Having invoked great-power competition, this approach explains the war's outbreak with one of two scenarios: Either it broke out in the Ohio Valley in July 1755, or it began with the Prussian invasion of Saxony in August 1756. Depending on one's national viewpoint, the war was a manifestation of one of two different eighteenth-century conflicts: on the one hand, Britain's ongoing struggle with France; on the other, the rivalry between Austria and Prussia. These two distinct conflicts intersect in Hanover, the city that was home to Abelmann, the master baker.[3]

The existence of radically different perspectives on the same war is itself a historical phenomenon. One of the basic insights of historical research is that events are constantly transformed as they are appropriated and reappropriated within different cultures of memory.

As the Seven Years' War has gone through cycles of remembrance over the last 250 years, distinct national cultures of memory have called it by different names and ascribed to it different meanings. In Germany and Austria, the war was long known as the Third Silesian War, putting the focus on how Frederick II desperately struggled to hold onto Silesia and, more generally, on how the war served to reinforce the dual Prussian-Austrian domination of Germany in the long term. In Britain and France, the war is remembered as a struggle for mastery in Europe and over the world's oceans, ultimately resulting in British imperial hegemony. In the United States, the conflict is known as the French and Indian War, regarded as a precursor to the American War of Independence. That term is also used in Canada, but there the war is additionally called La Guerre de la Conquête, the war of conquest that brought the colony of Nouvelle-France to an end.[4] For India, the war encompassed conflicts in Bengal and the Third Carnatic War and is seen as another chapter in its journey toward British colonial rule. In Spain, the Seven Years' War was the Fantastic War, a war against Britain and Portugal and another stage in Spain's decline from its position as the world's greatest power. Swedish history refers to the conflict as the Pomeranian War. For Russia, the war was another phase in its long historical journey to the West.

If we regard these various wars as interconnected, then the Seven Years' War was indeed a conflict of global proportions, with campaigns and theaters in Europe, North and South America, the Caribbean, Africa, and South Asia. However, against the backdrop of a continued boom in global history, labeling the Seven Years' War a *global conflict*—or, snappier still, a *world war*—has a dubious whiff of rebranding. In recent decades, historians of wars of earlier centuries have taken to searching for *the* first world war before the twentieth century. Candidates have included the Dutch War of Independence and the Wars of the Palatine, Spanish, and Austrian Successions, not to mention the Revolutionary and Napoleonic Wars.[5]

But, in fact, the use of *world war* to describe the Seven Years' War long predates contemporary allusions to the twentieth century and its wars. Or to be more precise, it predates the current wave of allusions to the world wars of the "Age of Extremes," to use Eric Hobsbawm's term. As early as 1881, Wilhelm Oncken (1838–1905) included a chapter in *The Age of Frederick the Great* titled "The World War for Prussia's Existence and Non-Existence."[6] Some decades later the tragedy of World War I provided historians with plenty of evidentiary material to compare modern and premodern world wars.[7] Published in 1957, in the wake of yet another global conflict, volume 3 of Churchill's *History of the English-Speaking Peoples* placed the Seven Years' War in a section titled "The First World War."[8] The same year a West German history textbook was even clearer, calling the conflict "the Second World War of the eighteenth century."[9] By 1968, the historian and theorist Reinhart Koselleck could cite, as a matter of course, the "global contexts" and "worldwide interdependencies" that meant the eighteenth-century conflict should be understood as "our planet's first World War."[10]

Deciding which war was the first truly global conflict is less important than identifying processes of global interconnection and then establishing their respective impacts.[11] We cannot label conflicts as world wars simply to boost their significance. It makes more sense to consider the global dimensions of the Seven Years' War—i.e., the conflicts subsumed under that name—in terms of the war's own historicization. Dieter Langewiesche makes an apt distinction between Europe's eighteenth-century "wars in the world" and the twentieth-century "world wars."[12] His coinage places the Seven Years' War within the broader process of European expansion, of which it unquestionably formed a part. However, the conflict also had its own specific effects of entanglement and disentanglement. Its globalizing outcomes operated on several levels. First, the causes of war went far beyond local contexts: Chains of causality extended from North America to Europe and back but also from Europe to the Caribbean and South Asia. Second, these causal connections prompted an increase in mobility: The war set armies and navies on the move, of course, but also clergymen and trading companies. Third, on the level of perception and interpretation, the conflict increased popular interest in news, engendering new demand in Europe for information from abroad. But the process was not a one-way street: It was matched elsewhere by an increased desire for news about European events.

The war's worldwide aspects were not the invention of modern global historians. Contemporaries repeatedly referred to the war's global nature, although often using concepts very different from ours, as discussed later. Moreover, this discourse varied from one place to another and between different historical actors.[13] We should avoid the anachronistic error of being overly hasty in projecting our conceptions of the world onto earlier centuries, using a framework formed by our own experience of globalization.[14] Instead, we should first ask, What did people in the eighteenth century know about processes we nowadays refer to as global entanglement? The sheer scale of the war's expansionary processes makes it particularly important to determine how contemporaries perceived and interpreted its events. To what extent could those involved in or affected by the war follow the course of events taking place beyond their own village, town, or territory?

To do methodological justice to this constitutive tension between the local and the global, this book takes a microhistorical approach to the Seven Years' War as a global conflict. For this reason, it includes accounts from around two hundred contemporary witnesses, drawn from all sides and all theaters of war. The depiction of the conflict interweaves event and structure; the war's own timeline is constantly intercut with broader questions of how it affected everyday life. This methodology, quite close to Robert Musil's idea of "world history [seen from] close up," was originally inspired by Hans Medick's everyday-life approach to the history of the Thirty Years' War.[15] Equivalent studies have convincingly proved the historiographical value of personal testimony as long as the analysis remains multiperspectival and goes beyond both naïve realism and quotation collage. However, unlike Musil reflecting on World War I in the Dolomites, I believe individual close-up views—the "invisibility" of the bigger picture notwithstanding—can cumulatively offer the historian a new image of everyday wartime life, one that comes close to historical reality as it was.[16] One great advantage of a microhistorical perspective is that it allows us to first examine individual practices up close and then reconnect them to the historical whole. In doing so, we can flatten out—in the sense of "flat ontology"—differences between micro- and macrosubjects.[17] In particular, we should pay attention to contemporaries' perceptions of what we would call entangled history, *histoire croisée*, connected history, or global history.[18] To refer to global interdependencies, for example, people in the eighteenth century often used metaphors of wildfires emitting sparks. Abbé Raynal (1713–1796), in his late-Enlightenment bestseller, *The History of the Two Indies* (1770), even called the Seven Years' War a "guerre universelle."[19] Others, by contrast, failed to perceive the entanglements and were amazed by attacks that seemed to come out of nowhere.

Forking Paths of Research

Scholarly literature on the Seven Years' War has reached near-unmanageable proportions. In fact, the study of the conflict began immediately after its conclusion.[20] Early British accounts of the war, published at this moment, continued to put distinct emphasis on its global dimensions. *An Impartial History of the Late War*, by John Almon (1737–1805), published in 1763, the war's final year, is divided into chapters reporting the "affairs" of America, Asia, Africa, and Germany. John Entick's (1703–1773) five-volume history, published in 1763 and 1764, was subtitled *Containing It's Rise, Progress, and Event in Europe, Asia, Africa, and America*.[21] The geographic extent of *Decadas de la Guerra* by Joseph Vicente de Rustant was equally broad. In the ten-volume narrative published in Spain in 1765, he primarily used newspaper reports for source material.[22] In 1764, chronological tables of the war's events around the globe were published in Germany.[23] The first substantial narrative accounts of the war appeared in the 1780s and 1790s, with the publication of *History of the Seven Years' War* (1783–1801) by Georg Friedrich von Tempelhof

(1737–1807) and a history by Johann Wilhelm of Archenholz (1743–1812) with an almost identical title, first published in 1788.[24] Tempelhof seems to have been the first to use the term *Seven Years' War* in print; previous authors largely referred to "the late war."[25] Like Tempelhof, Archenholz was a veteran of the conflict; his history places a clear, "patriotic" focus on Prussia and the Holy Roman Empire (sometimes referred to as the Reich or the Old Reich), the large swathe of central and western Europe still nominally governed by the emperor. By contrast, he treats British-French battles as a more marginal phenomenon.[26] But Archenholz actually did have considerable expertise on theaters of the war outside Europe. Some years previously he had produced a rather free German translation of Robert Orme's (1728–1801) record of British expansion into India.[27] In fact, some Prussian accounts did manage to present the conflict in its global dimensions, best exemplified by Johann Michael Friedrich Schulze's (1753–1817) *Historical Chart of the Seven Years' War*, published in 1792 by Christian Friedrich Himburg (1733–1801) in Berlin. Dedicated to King Friedrich Wilhelm II (1744–1797) and accompanied by "instructions for use," the chart was advertised as suitable for trade and commercial schools, offering a "handy synchronistic overview" structured along two axes (figure 0.1).[28] One axis presents a chronology of the individual war years, starting in 1755. The other is divided into four sections, for the four main theaters of war: the non-European world; the western Holy Roman Empire, Spain, and Portugal; Saxony, Thuringia, and Silesia; and, finally, Pomerania, the Mark of Brandenburg, and Poland.[29]

The nineteenth century saw the beginning of "professional history" but also the division of historiography along national lines. In terms of the Seven Years' War, the European, American, and South Asian theaters were now mostly approached separately. Above all, military-historical overviews flourished, typified by *The Wars of Frederick the Great*, an extensive project carried out by the Prussian General Staff.[30] However, works with a global perspective continued to be published, even during the late nineteenth-century heyday of national history.[31] Julian S. Corbett's two-volume *England in the Seven Years' War* (1907) and Richard Waddington's five-volume French study (1899–1914) are only two examples.[32] Lawrence H. Gipson's study, a monumental work of American imperial historiography, was published after World War II. However, for many years no new outline histories of the war were published in French or in German, let alone general histories with a global perspective.[33] Global aspects of the war played a very small role in the East German historiographical tradition, although in the early 1960s, Werner Krauss, a scholar

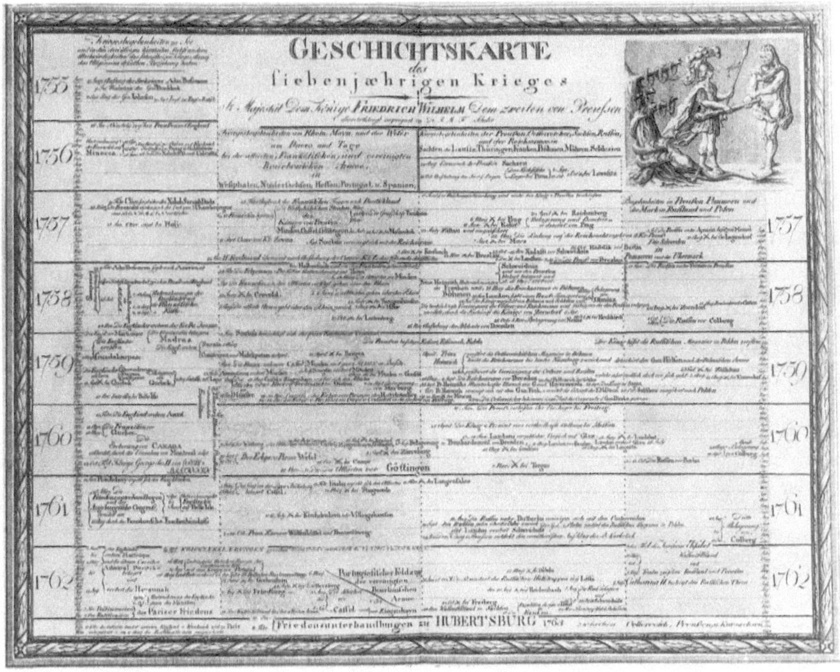

Figure 0.1 Historical chart of the Seven Years' War, 1755–1762. Johann Michael Friedrich Schulze (Berlin, 1792).
Source: bpk Bildagentur/Staatsbibliothek zu Berlin/Stiftung Preussischer Kulturbesitz, Berlin/Art Resource, New York.

of Romance languages, wrote about the "seven-year world war," the "New World theater of war," and the "connection" between the Seven Years' War and "the belligerent contradictions of colonialism."[34] In the 1980s, the "Prussian Renaissance" deepened the separation between the conflict's European and non-European dimensions. However, this period also saw increased research into the war's local manifestations in specific locations around the world.[35]

Today individual theaters of war have their own cycles of research, often driven by radically different preoccupations. The French and Indian War is a traditionally well-researched field.[36] In the past twenty-five years alone, more than a dozen overviews of this theater have been published, which build on Guy Frégault's classic 1955 Canadian study and on Fred Anderson's outstanding 2000 history, which also devotes attention to the war's other theaters.[37] In terms of Europe, Franz A. J. Szabo's 2008 synthesis takes a critical view of Prussia—or rather of Frederick the Great. Other recent overviews tend to only partially recount events within the Holy Roman Empire; even today, scholars must return to nineteenth-century narratives for details of the conflict in these areas.[38] For the South Asian theater, there have been specialist studies on regions like Bengal and actors like the East India Company. However, an up-to-date overview of the war in this region is still lacking.[39]

Only in the past couple of decades, with the increased importance of global history, has the Seven Years' War again come to be regarded as a worldwide conflict.[40] However, historians writing in English and French have tended to absorb German-language scholarship only partially or not at all. Conversely, the most recent German overview is not based on close work with primary sources and takes only a fragment of English-language scholarship into account.[41]

The war has also been reassessed in recent general histories of the Enlightenment and the eighteenth century.[42] The lifeworlds experienced during wartime are seen no longer as exceptions to eighteenth-century culture but as constitutive elements of it.[43] The Seven Years' War was not the Other of the century of Enlightenment; it was inseparably bound up with it. Factors in the complex relations between the war and the wider eighteenth century include mercantilist economic thought, new cultures of consumption, thriving media landscapes, the mathematization of warfare, and a new state-focused patriotism, stimulated by literature.

The approach of this book addresses two major problems in the current historiography of the war. First, globally oriented studies tend to concentrate almost exclusively on the British-French dimension, neglecting events in Europe and, above all, in the Holy Roman Empire. Conversely, narratives focused on Prussia tend to erase the British-French dimension. Second, very few new monographs use approaches from social or cultural history; their methodology is usually conservative, focused on traditional fields like diplomatic, military, and imperial history.[44] As a rule, synthetic overviews of the conflict present a grand narrative, either because they are based on existing secondary works or because they are written from the perspective of diplomats and royal cabinets. Moreover, these accounts often begin their explanations at the top, focusing on great men and big players, monarchs and senior ministers. The words of people outside the class of political decision-makers tend to be used for illustrative purposes only, which is surprising, given the extensive literature on the "experience of war."[45] Matt Schuman and Karl Schweizer's transatlantic history of the war alludes to aspects that could not be included and were to be addressed in later volumes, including "a treatment of individual soldiers and the experience of the civilian population; sensitivity to the plight of women, to ethnic and religious minorities and entire classes of people excluded from the formal exercise of political power; and suggestions as to the flow of information and perceptions of the war, not only in contemporaneous newspapers, pamphlets, and letters, but also in memory."[46] Precisely these questions play a central role in this book's analysis.

Witnesses and Witnessing

Friedrich Schiller (1759–1805) mocked the eighteenth century as "the ink-splattering century." Even in peacetime, the era was characterized by abundant self-reflection. In times of war, however, the corpus of relevant documents swelled still further. Thirty years of intense discussion around historiographical approaches to autobiographical writing—and the wider category of ego-documents—have established both its potentials and its limitations as historical source material.[47] Subjectivity, linguistic topoi (the "unspeakable") and site specificity are no longer regarded as defects in sources. Instead, these aspects are seen as typical of particular types of sources, potentially of great use to a critically self-conscious historiography of experience.[48] To date, personal accounts of eighteenth-century wars have been used to create longitudinal analyses, to probe the "motivations" of ordinary soldiers, to home in on particular actors, and to reconstruct the "ultimate experience" of battle between 1450 and 2000.[49] The approach in this book, by contrast, is to examine several warring parties within a tightly delimited timeframe while also expanding its purview to include all those affected by war, not just its military participants. By taking this approach, I am striving to emulate the broader perspectives of recent work addressing autobiographical writing from a transcultural perspective.[50] Scholarship on globe-spanning biographies—the subfield known as *global lives*—has taken on considerable importance within microhistorical approaches to global history. The best examples of the method include Emma Rothschild's wide-ranging history of the Johnstones, a Scottish family whose lives spanned the eighteenth-century British Empire, and Linda Colley's biography of Elizabeth Marsh (1735–1785), a much-traveled Englishwoman, the daughter of a ship's carpenter, whose adventures also made her a peripheral witness to the Seven Years' War.[51]

This book uses methodologies drawn from the historiography of experience but expands these to incorporate the history of knowledge and information in the Seven Years' War.[52] The central focus is always on the knowledge that contemporaries actually possessed, including knowledge of their local lived environment and of distant theaters of war. Drawing on Peter Burke's structuralist distinction between "raw" information and "cooked" knowledge, the analysis traces how globally circulating information units—for example, "the British have conquered Quebec"—became part of a broader body of knowledge, as evidenced by their inclusion, for example, in a war diary or in a biographical narrative. The epistemological "cooking" here largely results from the integration of this information into wider contexts.[53] Such contexts could include a particular campaign, the North American war, the war as a whole, or the history of Quebec's economic development.

Above all, this approach enables the writing of a history of perceptions and interpretations of the Seven Years' War, one that gives a say to as many actors as possible while representing the widest possible set of perspectives. This multiperspectival approach is the basic principle underlying the book's presentation of material, although at times it reaches a limit marked by the survival of some sources and not others. The primary sources are, above all, autobiographical writings (letters, diaries, memoirs), but these are sometimes brought together with media reports (newspapers, broadsides, sermons) and visual and material sources (engravings, paintings, artifacts).

The key pool of sources is thus a broad selection of autobiographical writings—what German historiography refers to as ego-documents—by around two hundred contemporaries. Of these, 95 percent are male, albeit with important exceptions. They are drawn from almost every side and every theater of war, although somewhat unequally so, a circumstance dependent on which sources have survived. In choosing this material, I have sought to include observers with varied social roles and different positions within the social hierarchy, thus occupying a broad range of vantage points. One limitation is that the great majority of published testimonies are by British soldiers or residents of the Holy Roman Empire. At least in terms of Britain, the victor's perspective continues to dominate academic publishing.[54] There is no single reason for the variation in the number of autobiographical documents published in different geographical areas; at least in terms of this war, substantially less autobiographical writing was produced in Catholic countries—including France and especially Austria—than in Protestant ones.[55] In addition, rates of literacy within the various armed formations should be taken into account.[56]

Autobiographical writings, personal testimonies, and, more broadly, ego-documents can include a wide variety of textual genres, with considerable differences in medium, content, and linguistic form.[57] Letters and diaries are characterized by a position very close in time to the events they address; journals, memoirs, and biographies are each respectively further away in temporal terms.[58] Even in the eighteenth century, something like a military postal system was available to ordinary soldiers and noncommissioned officers, including those serving in the field. However, far fewer of these letters survived and were published than in the nineteenth and twentieth centuries.[59] Journals and autobiographies were often published at the time or were at least written with publication in mind. This was also true, to some extent, for letters and diaries; although of a more private genre, they could make their way into the public sphere.

The particular moment of publication was crucial: Depending on circumstances, an autobiographical text could be a bestseller or a total flop. In 1757, the Scottish soldier Peter Williamson brought out his account of Indian atrocities, which quickly went through six editions. But by 1775, when Robert Kirkwood, another Scottish soldier, published his own "Adventures," public interest had moved on, and his book disappeared almost immediately.[60] Writers of personal testimony also varied widely in their social and personal backgrounds. Most self-published journals and diaries were written by soldiers or educated men of letters. The writings of both groups are marked by self-stylization and use strategies specific to their authors' class background. In the field of military theory, war experience could serve a further discursive function: It could supply a series of concrete illustrative examples. But other chroniclers of the war also had addressees in mind beyond their own family and relatives, although writing to one's kin remained a classic authorial device. Thus, Antonius Verhoeven, an ordinary locksmith from the village of Goch, south of Cleves, used the title *Memories for My Children and My Children's Children's Children's Children*.[61]

In many cases, accounts written by priests, artisans, or merchants would have served as a collective memory of times of upheaval. The eager chroniclers of the war years included large numbers of pastors, whose writings documented the sufferings of their communities. In some cases, they wrote chronicle entries into ecclesiastical registers, although strictly speaking these were meant to record only the sacraments of marriage, baptism, and burial (figure 0.2).[62]

A striking number of these chronicles begin with the outbreak of war and end with the coming of peace. Some of them include illustrations, images

Figure 0.2 Truthful Report of Events Taking Place in the Duchy of Weimar During the Great Wars of Frederick II, King of Prussia, and Maria Theresa, Queen of Hungary, Along with Their Allies, as Experienced by Johann Christian Becher, a Tailor of Weimar. Illustrated frontispiece depicting the fall of Phaeton (Weimar, after 1760).
© Klassik Stiftung Weimar, HAAB, Q 419.

that can also be read as a kind of ego-document. Examples of this include a two-volume work by Johann Christian Becher (1728–1781), a master tailor from the city of Weimar. Here the first volume contains the chronicle itself, while the other presents colored drawings of the uniforms of the armies passing through Weimar, as well as the costumes of their entourages. Other contemporary illustrations include watercolor sketches by George Hendrich Barfot, a Swedish sergeant who documented the 1758–1759 naval campaigns off Pomerania, and the drawings by Gottfried Gotsch from Elblag (now northern Poland) showing Russian troops.[63]

Some testimony resulted from historians and artists carrying out what was, in effect, witness surveying in the decades after the war. This protosurvey work was sometimes done with a specific aim in mind—for example, the reconstruction of a particular battle.[64]

Unfortunately, the popularity of autobiographical war stories, especially from the Seven Years' War, also led to the publication of fictional writings that were passed off as genuine accounts of the war. Some have passed into the historical record and are even today cited as authentic sources in scholarly literature. Two examples will illustrate the concern. Between 1937 and 1946, Ernest Gray published three fictional diaries, supposedly written by a British ship's doctor named John Knyveton, who never, in fact, existed.[65] The second volume bore a particularly convincing title: *Surgeon's Mate— The Diary of John Knyveton, Surgeon in the British Fleet During the Seven Years War 1756–1762*. Similarly, the biography of Jakob Friedrich Anton Logan Logejus was published in Breslau in 1934 under the title *My Experiences as a Cavalry Officer Under the Great King in the Years 1741 to 1759*. But Logejus was another semifictional author: The book is a new edition of a text first published in 1843, ascribed to an officer named Jakob Anton von Lojewsky.[66]

The fictionalization or outright counterfeiting of personal accounts of historical events also highlights the problem of texts' physical survival. Today many of these texts survive only as copies or in printed form. This is the case for the collection *Prussian Soldiers' Letters*, first published in 1901, as well as Ananda Ranga Pillai's voluminous diary from southern India.[67] When the original text does survive, its physical form can disclose useful information. The Prussian musketeer Johann Jacob Dominicus (1731–1775) kept his diary in a prayerbook and a Lutheran hymnbook, while Friedrich Freiherr von der Trenck (1727–1794) filled eight Bibles, some of them showing battle damage, with memoirs written in his own blood.[68] Both examples indicate a shortage of writing materials, as well as the formative influence of religious texts.

In Germany, Frederick II of Prussia (1712–1786) is, above all others, the name associated with the Seven Years' War. He expressed his interpretation of events in a wide variety of texts, producing large numbers of egodocuments, including political correspondence, poetry, and historiography.[69] However, in the words of Bertolt Brecht's poem "Questions from a Worker Who Reads," we might well ask, "Frederick the Second won the 7 Years War. / Who else won it?" Frederick's own accounts should be consciously decentered by giving equal consideration to subaltern figures—for example, Ulrich Bräker (1735–1798), a man who became the icon of common eighteenth-century soldiers.[70] Bräker, originally from Switzerland, deserted the Prussian army in 1756 and returned to his homeland, where he published his diary in 1789.[71] Olaudah Equiano (1745–1797), a subaltern figure of comparable fame, was an enslaved Igbo person, originally from what is today Nigeria, who bought his freedom a few years after the war's end and also published his autobiography in 1789.[72]

A German anthology titled *Traces of the Vanquished*, published in the 1980s, raised interesting questions on "resistance to the Seven Years War," asking if and how "ordinary" people defied or opposed the war or if they simply ran away.[73] We may perhaps leave aside the volume's ideological framing of its sources: Its tendency to ahistoricism is characteristic of its own time. However, the question of opposition to war, in thought and action, remains an important corrective to perspectives and conventions that are still current in military and political history. On this question, François-Marie Arouet is often given a say, and he is indeed an astute observer of the war, a decidedly critical and even pacifist one. Arouet, better known as Voltaire (1694–1778), spent most of the time between 1755 and 1760 in Geneva at the Propriété de Saint-Jean, an estate he came to refer to as Les Délices.[74] His relationship with Frederick II seems to have cooled during the war. However, they maintained a correspondent in common, Luise Dorothée von Sachsen-Gotha, who served as a sort of relay station between the two men, who both continued to write to her during the conflict.[75] In the world of British politics, the parliamentarian and writer Horace Walpole (1717–1797) is an important witness. For affairs at the Viennese court, we have the observations of the court chamberlain, Johann Joseph Fürst von Khevenhüller-Metsch (1706–1776), although his diaries for 1760 to 1763 unfortunately seem not to have survived.[76]

This war was characterized by the very large number of contemporaries who documented its events in chronicles, diaries, and other autobiographical writings, including many who did not serve in the military. In fact, many diarists—such as Andreas Georg Wähner (1693–1762), professor of Oriental languages at Göttingen University—never set foot outside their hometowns; nonetheless, they were privy to news as it took place on a global scale, although their interest tended to focus on events close to home.[77] Something similar was the case for Ananda Ranga Pillai (1709–1761), a merchant in the French service at Pondicherry, sometimes called the "Pepys of French India."[78] His private diaries for 1736 through 1761 were published in a twelve-volume edition.[79] The original diaries, written in Tamil, have now been lost, but they were the basis for a French translation and later an English one. Pillai apparently communicated with the French in a "bastard variant" of Portuguese, the contemporary lingua franca of India's southeast coast.[80] In North America, the German Protestant pastor Heinrich Melchior Mühlenberg (1711–1787), a resident in Pennsylvania since 1742 and an observant reporter of events, communicated between different worlds via his extensive correspondence.[81] He was born in Einbeck, in the Electorate of Braunschweig-Lüneburg (often referred to as Electoral Hanover), a territory that since 1714 had been joined with Britain in a personal monarchical union. He unhesitatingly referred to George II (1683–1760) as his king and to British troops as "our soldiers."

We know of very few autobiographical writings by women outside the nobility. The war featured three women operating at the highest political level—Empress Maria Theresa (1717–1780) in Austria, Tsarina Elizabeth Petrovna (1709–1762) in Russia, and Madame de Pompadour (1721–1764) in France[82]—which has led to the repeated representation of the war as a battle of the sexes.[83] Outside of Europe, testimony tends to come from the wives and daughters of governors, who helped to actively shape local events, as well as from nuns from religious orders engaged in charitable or pastoral work. One example is the diary of Charlotte Brown, matron of a military hospital in New York who later accompanied Edward Braddock (1694–1755) on his fatal expedition to the Ohio Valley.[84] Among "bourgeois" women writers in Prussia, the poet Anna Louise Karsch (1722–1791) stands out for her journalistic writing.[85] However, we tend to encounter the majority of women authors in private correspondence, in the role of mother or wife. Many editions of correspondence from this time include only letters by the male party in the exchange; women appear merely as addressees. Public attention, at least judicial attention, was also drawn to the rare cases of female soldiers, where women dressed as men to undertake military service, including Anna Sophia Dettloff in Prussia and Marguerite Goubler in France.[86] The memoirs written by Eleonore Juliane von Rehdiger (1713–1784) provide insights into conditions in Silesia throughout the conflict.[87]

In terms of personal mobility in wartime, officers and soldiers are somewhere around the middle of the scale. A typical example is Horace St. Paul, whose memoirs have led him to become known as the real Barry Lyndon. St. Paul fled Scotland after a duel and entered Austrian service; he was active in every theater of the Prussian-Austrian conflict, documenting his progress in several volumes of diaries.[88] Other soldiers traveled far more widely in the theaters of war of the Holy Roman Empire. These include the Brunswick sergeant Johann Heinrich Ludewig Grotehenn (1734–1786), the Prussian officer Christian Wilhelm of Prittwitz (1739–1807), the British officer William Todd (1724–1791), the French officer Antoine Rigobert Mopinot de la Chapotte (b. 1717), and the Russian officer Andrei Bolotov (1738–1833). Prittwitz, Mopinot de la Chapotte, and Todd all kept diaries and journals; Bolotov wrote an autobiographical account; and Grotehenn's letters survive.[89] For the North American theater of war, the journals of Louis Antoine de Bougainville (1729–1811) offer a similar source. He would later become better known as a naturalist and a circumnavigator of the earth.[90] Charles Bonin, known as Jolicoeur, published a memoir of his time as an enlisted soldier in the French and Indian War. On the British side, we have comparable accounts from officers, including John Knox (d. 1778) and John Grant (1741–1828).[91] These are illustrative examples chosen from a wider panorama of sources; all of the figures mentioned left behind extensive diaries or letters, now edited and published. However, their writings have rarely been analyzed systematically as historical sources for the war.

The evaluation of these autobiographical sources is based on an extensive analytic grid. To sum up the key criteria of the grid, great importance is given to direct experience of military violence, whether in battles, during sieges, or in irregular operations, including abuses against civilians in occupied cities and villages. Closely linked to this is sensory perception. How did the sounds of a city change over time? What did battles sound like? What new smells appeared? What things were made visible, and what things remained invisible? Wars also brought about changes in material culture. In this respect, what role was played by the armies' looting and plunder and their devastation of the land? What materials ran short? How were objects used in the creation of propaganda? These are just a few of the questions that address material culture, a subject as yet barely touched in scholarship on early modern wars.[92]

During the war, many people became extremely mobile, willingly or not, and thus witnessed several theaters of war. This fact raises other questions: How were the war's entanglements and its widening theaters perceived by its witnesses? How did they view foreign places and the people in them? During the war, ordinary Prussian soldiers encountered Cossacks and Kalmyks, British formations engaged with Native American fighters, and British colonial troops and sepoys came up against local opponents in India. Irregular operations took place in conjunction with classic battles in the field; sieges expanded to become complex amphibious operations. How did those present at the time view these dynamics and asymmetries? Combat always meant pain, suffering, and loss. But how did soldiers and civilians actually cope with the experience of violence, disease, and death?[93] And how did they perceive their own bodies?[94]

For most, religion had a central role in giving meaning to their experience. The Seven Years' War was not a war of religion, but religious arguments and patterns of interpretation nonetheless influenced people's thoughts and actions and the virtual propaganda war of religion.[95] Thus, the burning of besieged cities could be interpreted as divine justice; sectarian distinctions were rife in areas under occupation and among prisoners of war. The Indian and North American theaters, in particular, saw many moments of confrontation with non-Christian religions. Religious patterns of interpretation are encountered throughout these autobiographical writings.

The propaganda war of religion entailed the mobilization of public spheres, a process mediated by rumors, reading practices, and patterns of news communication. What information got through to whom? How were emotions stoked, and how were political loyalties activated? In addition to this media war, across Europe patriotism was turning into nationalism, accompanied by a politicization of the public sphere. How was national propaganda produced, and how was it received? Which camps emerged? And finally, how was peace staged and interpreted in these media? What were the experiences of those returning from war? And what were the consequences of the war, in both material and immaterial terms?

Events and Structures

The historical representation of every war faces the question of how events are related to structures, and vice versa. This problem has often been illustrated using the Seven Years' War and its individual battles as examples, as in the work of the historian and theorist Reinhart Koselleck and the sociologist Georg Simmel. Koselleck uses the Battle of Leuthen as an example of how "the before and after of an event" always retains its "own temporal quality," which "cannot be reduced to a whole within its longer-term conditions." Every event "produces more and at the same time less than is contained in its pre-given elements: hence its permanently surprising novelty."[96] Thus, Leuthen's "structural preconditions . . . are not sufficient to explain why Frederick the Great won this battle in the manner he did." Events and structures can be related to one another. All of the following contributed to the outcome of the battle: the recruitment and training of soldiers, the logistics of Frederick's way of war fighting, prior Prussian experience of the battlefield, and the tactic of arranging troops in an oblique line of battle. But the events of December 5, 1757, remain "unique within [their] immanent chronological sequence." How the battle unfolded, its effects, and its significance within the overall context of the war—all this, writes Koselleck, can "only be recounted in a chronological manner and in this way made meaningful." Nonetheless, the "outcome" of this particular battle can itself attain "structural significance," he argues. "The event assumed a structural status. Leuthen in the traditional history of the Prussian conception of the state, its exemplary effect on the revaluation of military risk in the military designs of Prussia-Germany (Dehio): these became lasting, long-term factors that entered into structural constitutional preconditions which had, in their turn, made the Battle of Leuthen possible."

Simmel's 1916 article "The Problem of Historical Time" is a useful methodological reflection on microhistory as a form of event-oriented history.[97] Simmel uses the Seven Years' War to discuss the "profound antinomy of historiography," framing the problem as a question: "How does an event become history?" How can the episodic images associated with a particular event—a battle, for example—be integrated into the event's overall historical unity? The "Battle of Zorndorf," Simmel goes on, can be seen as a "collective concept constituted in a special fashion from innumerable single processes. Suppose that military history attempts to discover all the details associated with the battle: every attack, every defensive maneuver, every episode, every specific engagement between different groups of troops, and so on. To the extent that this sort of knowledge is approached and a picture of the battle 'as it really happened' is approximated, the concept of a battle becomes atomized. It loses the continuity which is expressed in all these atoms of knowledge, the continuity which constitutes the single event that we call 'a battle.'"[98] This epistemological process affects any individual battle within any given war but also has an impact on the war itself, considered as a whole: "This same process is susceptible to further analysis. Suppose that the Seven Years' War is conceived as an integral whole that is constituted by battles, troop movements, and negotiations. Each of these battles may be analyzed into its respective stages according to the method indicated above. It seems that the pursuit of this method would lead to an atomistic construct of the event. In the final analysis, it seems that we would have only purely episodic images of moments."⁹⁹ The event that dissolves into "episodic images of moments"—snapshots in time—ultimately loses its historical particularity as an event. For Simmel, an individual clash within a battle like Kunersdorf does not rise to the status of "historic phenomenon," since it could have taken place in any other battle. Even if we could attain "knowledge of every nuance of the mental processes and physical movements that took place among the Russians, the Austrians, and the Prussians on August 12, 1759 [. . .], the aim of history cannot be realized by knowledge of this sort. On the contrary, its purpose is knowledge of the more comprehensive and abstract structure: the Battle of Kunersdorf."¹⁰⁰

In other words, the individuality of any historic event will eventually disappear as it is broken into progressively smaller components. The historian who does so, writes Simmel, will arrive at what he calls "a threshold of analytical reduction": "Knowledge of all the muscular movements of a soldier would destroy the coherent animation of the total process which correlates its beginning and its end into a temporal construct. The dimensions of the element of history must remain large enough so that individuality can still be ascribed to its content."¹⁰¹ Here he seems to support the approach taken by the official German military historiography of his time. This army history always presents an overview account of individual battles, embedding this within the continuity of the Seven Years' War as a whole, while giving little significance to well-known and well-respected testimony of events on the part of participants. In this way, battles are incorporated into a particular historical emplotment—Prussian troops were successfully deployed in oblique lines of battle, for example—which, in turn, helps to shape our overall image of the battle.

However, Simmel's observations can also be taken as neutral descriptions of the structural principles of historical representation, on both micro- and macroscales, which also outlines the constant difficulty of combining individual event images into historical synthesis. He warns against harboring any illusion that a close-up view could allow a naïve view of history "as it actually was" but also against subsuming events into historical ciphers like "the Miracle of the House of Brandenburg" or even using a priori generalizations like "a battle." Every event, including every battle, is first and foremost a product of construction, including the kinds of construction particular to specific media, to historiography, and to cultural memory. Microhistory has often used battles to reflect on the epistemological limits and possibilities of its own method, but it must not remain at the level of "snapshots."¹⁰² Instead, the close-up view should open up new contexts—contexts that have so often remained abstract—and render them concrete. The close-up view can allow us to work through the detail of the bigger picture while managing to avoid drowning in that detail.

This book makes no claim to be a *histoire totale* of the Seven Years' War and does not suggest that personal testimony should replace the study of official archival material.[103] Of necessity, many aspects of the war—including its economics, its diplomacy, and the internal communications of its militaries—are sketched in rather basic form. This is also true of adjacent fields, including the histories of law, medicine, and art, as well as cultures of remembrance. These fields have their own complex traditions and contexts of research, and for this reason, they receive only an occasional sidelong glance in the narrative.

Among the greatest challenges in writing the microhistory of a global conflict is structuring the material in terms of space and time. In this respect, three organizational models seemed possible: a structure that follows the lines of the geographical regions used in area studies (Europe, North America, South Asia, West Africa), one that proceeds by chronology, or one that is based on systematic themes, including diplomacy, violence, religion, and memory. I have already made use of the first, the area studies model, in a short general narrative of the war, where it proved quite successful.[104] One clear advantage of this model is that it allows a richer contextualization of specific regions, cultures, and historical actors. But its downside lies precisely in making processes of entanglement (and at times disentanglement) less visible, forcing these themes into separate synthetic chapters.

In this book, however, I present another model, one that better links structure and chronology. In doing so, I hopes to counteract additive conceptions of globalization, which posit the global as a simple summation of separate parts of the world, through either sequence or juxtaposition. In keeping with the idea of a close-up history of a global war, I intersperse the book's set pieces of structural analysis with close-up views of specific events, actors, and situations. This approach is not capable of illuminating all events in equal depth, and it does not claim to. The war saw more than twenty major battles in central Europe alone: A detailed appraisal of every one would make the book unmanageably long and would in any case be redundant. The same holds for sieges, which were even more common than battles. Instead, in this book I reserve detailed analysis for key events of the war, as well as for events that highlight particular characteristics of the conflict and its representation.

CHAPTER I

Geopolitics Between Reich and Empire

War and Globalization

What are the specific implications for narrative structure if we consider the Seven Years' War a global conflict?[1] The global nature of the war was ultimately an effect of overlapping regional conflicts. What must be decided then is which wars to examine with the lens of the Seven Years' War to avoid lumping in "every shot fired anywhere in the world" over the course of the 1750s and 1760s.[2] Examined more closely, the extent of the war, both temporally and spatially, remains a matter of dispute.[3] Its most immediately global aspect is the British-French imperial confrontation and the ways this confrontation was bound up with the Third Silesian War. Historians like Daniel Baugh have adopted this perspective, primarily a geopolitical one, thus granting greater importance to figures like William Pitt the Elder (1708–1778); Thomas Pelham-Holles, Duke of Newcastle (1693–1768); Frederick II; and the Duc de Choiseul (1719–1785).[4] Around this time, Britain had seen a debate between two geopolitical alternatives: *blue water policy* versus *continental commitment*.[5] The country's strategic calculations always incorporated its links to the European continent, not least because of its personal union with the Electorate of Hanover, which dated back to 1714. During the war, these continental ties would prove to have enormous consequences for Britain.[6] In 1762, the Franco-Spanish Pacte de Famille (Family Pact) dragged the Spanish colonial empire into the British-French imperial conflict. For its part, the Ottoman Empire—a key military actor on the margins of Christian Europe—stayed well clear of the conflict, although both Prussia and France repeatedly attempted to bring about an alliance, first with Osman III (1699–1757) and later with Mustafa III (1717–1774).[7] The sheer geographical range of the war's participants goes some way toward explaining the use of the term *world war* in this context.

When viewed through a global lens, the start of the war moves further and further back in time. German historiography traditionally dates the outbreak to 1756, but a more global perspective identifies its earliest phases as taking place between 1751 and 1754. In geographical terms, this means the war broke out in India (Arcot) and in North America (Ohio Valley). The most extreme version of this perspective claims that the war began in 1748, the year of the Peace of Aachen, a treaty that left many claims unresolved and many historical actors unsatisfied.[8] As early as 1899, the historian Georg Küntzel suggested that the Peace of Aachen "was in effect only a brief armistice," at least in terms of "settling the colonial and Silesian questions."[9] More recent scholarship has also complicated our understanding of the war's end, extending the conflict beyond 1763, the year of the Treaties of Paris and Hubertusburg. Suggested alternative endpoints include the Pontiac War (1763–1765) in North America and the fighting in India between the East India Company and the kingdom of Oudh (1764–1765).[10] Ever wider contexts can be added, extending the war further forward or further backward in time. Thus, the American historian Arthur Buffinton has suggested that the Seven Years' War be understood as part of a "Second Hundred Years' War" between France and Britain, lasting from 1689 to 1815.[11] This coinage, however, combines and homogenizes many different conflicts, often with no direct connection. Moreover, casting the conflict as a "Second Hundred Years' War" between Britain and France greatly restricts who can be seen as a significant historical actor in the war itself.[12]

The key lesson of postcolonial research, from India to North America, has been the importance of symmetrical, nonteleological approaches in investigating imperial conflicts.[13] Concretely, what this means is, first, not seeing British imperial triumphs as an inevitable historical endpoint. It means understanding that local actors potential possess powerful historical agency of their own and are not merely accessories to European entanglements. Recent work on Native American history has turned old perspectives on their head, narrating history from an Indigenous point of view, a perspective deeply influenced, above all, by the permanent colonial threat from the east.[14]

It is no simple matter to ground these symmetrical approaches in textual sources; the availability of documents varies greatly according to context. In terms of historical sources, we can draw on material evidence of Native American communication culture—for example, the wampum belts, made of pearls, seashells, and snail shells, which were used to confirm contracts and to make payments.[15] Other fields of inquiry suffer from similar shortages of material—there are few direct sources on the experience of ordinary soldiers in eighteenth-century armies, for example—but this has not led us to abandon the possibility of military history "from below."[16]

In terms of the war's global structure, local power structures and the interdependency of regional conflicts are more significant than the basic data of duration and spatial extent. Fighting broke out first in North America and India, followed the next year by war in Europe. But decisions made in Europe were what turned Africa and the Caribbean, for example, into theaters of the war. These connections between theaters pose the question of the war's globalizing *effect*. Global entanglement took place on several levels at once, significantly expanding the set of relevant geopolitical decision-makers. Global interaction took place in fields including the economy, religion, politics, military affairs, communications, and culture. Companies like the British East India Company (EIC) and the French Compagnie des Indes (CdI) were active around the world and exerted enormous influence on the conflict.[17] The CdI enjoyed very close links to the French crown, but the EIC was in a position to act far more autonomously. Nonetheless, the EIC remained dependent on military support from the British state, and the British crown maintained significant leverage because the company had to repeatedly apply for extensions of its privileges.

Many globally circulating trade goods played a role in the war, including furs from Canada, sugar and rum from the Caribbean, gum arabic from Africa, saltpeter from India, and stockfish from the waters off Newfoundland.[18] European trading companies were powerful military players, assuming the powers of territorial lords and creating extensive communication networks. After the death of Aurangzeb (1618–1707), emperor of the Mughal Empire, developments in India in some respects resembled those of the Holy Roman Empire, although colonial historiography has tended mostly to interpret Indian developments in terms of decay.[19] Rulers of former Mughal provinces formed alliances with trading companies, attempting to "mobilize their fiscal and economic resources to create their own state,"[20] a process Michael Mann has dubbed "segmentary state formation."[21] Mann's focus on South Asia leads him to identify these parallel state-building processes as the factor leading the Seven Years' War "to become, in fact, the first of the world wars." It would be a fallacy, he suggests, to reduce the war's global dimension solely to "intercontinental networks of resources, information and people."[22] Although we must continue the task of tracing and reconstructing these networks, we must, above all, chart the "fracture zones" of globalization, finding asymmetries and patterns of domination rather than smooth cross-border circulation.

Religious actors played a hugely important role in the war, creating channels of communication and directly impacting public events, whether this took the form of missionaries' correspondence or confessional and sectarian propaganda. For North America and India, the *Jesuit Relations*—the annual documents sent to Paris from the Society of Jesus—were an instructive source. In southern India, the reports issued by the Danish-Halle mission in Tranquebar play a similar role.[23] Even the Vatican became an actor in the war, albeit, as the title of one book on Vatican diplomacy suggests, as part of a "farewell to religious war."[24] In addition to the official churches, Freemasonry—the "invisible church"—played a role in extending imperial spheres of influence.[25] As the British armed forces increased in size, so did the number of military Masonic lodges, which offered a rare space for meaningful activity amid rampant boredom, a notorious problem for colonial soldiers.[26] Military lodges in the British army increased threefold between 1757 and 1764.[27]

In terms of military activity itself, situations on land increasingly involved intercultural encounters; this presented opportunities for learning but also highlighted the growing significance of naval forces.[28] "Small war," as irregular and guerrilla operations were called, was the exception in Europe but the rule in other theaters. Outside Europe, the war was marked by a permanent shortage of manpower, leading to the recruitment of allied units and the creation of hybrid formations like the Indian sepoys.[29] For this reason, among others, the list of relevant actors cannot be confined to Europeans. In North America and South Asia, local actors—Indigenous tribes on one continent and princely states in the territory of the former Mughal Empire on the other—enjoyed considerable autonomy, even if, in the long run, they were steadily being dragged into colonial dependency.

On the level of culture and communication, our main questions must concern perception, information, and knowledge.[30] Were the various actors aware of the globalizing effects of the war? If so, how did they articulate this knowledge? Information transfers—between Europe and North America and between South Asia and Europe but also between the Caribbean and South Asia—played a key role in military and political decision-making. But information traveled at different speeds in different places, speeds over which local actors had little direct influence. Contemporaries estimated the distance from Portsmouth to Madras at fifteen thousand miles. The journey out could last between four and a half and six months and the return journey at least six, with adverse winds increasing its length to eight or nine months. An exchange of military reports and orders between London and India took around a year. The land route was much shorter, passing via Marseille and Venice to the Mediterranean, then overland from Aleppo to Basra near the Persian Gulf, and finally to Bombay. But war with France and Austria effectively closed that route to the British.[31] Even within South Asia, French and British naval logistics were hampered by long distances, and there was a lack of shipyards suitable to repair ships in monsoon season. The French had to send ships in need of repair to Mauritius, while the British sent theirs to Bombay. In this way, space exerted its own unique influence over the course of events.

Aims and Interests

There has been lively historiographical discussion around the origins of the Seven Years' War for over a century now.[32] The specific dynamics of the war can be understood only in relation to previous conflicts, which, in turn, have often been subsumed into a discrete War of the Austrian Succession (1740–1748).[33] This earlier war was itself global in scope, fought in Europe, North America, South Asia, and the Caribbean. Among its component conflicts, distinctions are usually made among the First and Second Silesian Wars (1740–1742, 1744–1745) in Europe, the War of Jenkins' Ear (1739–1742) in the North American colonies, and the First Carnatic War (1746–1748) in southern India. The 1748 Peace of Aachen left many parties dissatisfied, and historians have repeatedly asked if that war ever really ended in some parts of the world. The evidence would suggest it did not, at least in North America and South Asia; in both regions, the conflict continued over zones of economic influence, rights of commercial access, and territorial control. In France and, above all, in Britain, arguments about colonial security were primarily couched in defensive terms, with slogans like "The colonies must be protected." In reality, the policies of both countries always contained expansionist elements.

In structural terms, Frederick II's ideology of preventive war was not dissimilar to this colonial outlook. His views of his opponents and rivals changed significantly in the years after the Peace of Aachen.[34] Prussian resources had been depleted by the War of the Austrian Succession, and for the first few years following the war, Prussia viewed Russia as a serious threat. However, by 1756 Prussia no longer regarded its eastern rival in this way.[35] For Frederick II, the Russian army was to be viewed with mild contempt, while France remained the most powerful country in Europe, despite its financial precarity. The Prussian king seems to have had little detailed knowledge of Britain. He recognized it as Europe's dominant sea power but thought it financially rather weak. On the latter point, he was enlightened by his London ambassador Abraham Louis Michell (1712–1782).[36] Frederick was also initially wrong in his assessment of France's commitment to a land war in Europe. After French naval success at the Battle of Menorca in 1756, the Prussian king thought Paris would favor a purely maritime conflict. He regarded Austria as his most aggressive opponent but had long thought that Maria Theresa lacked the financial wherewithal for war and would need time to develop her armed forces. By 1756, that Austrian buildup appeared to be underway, so the time seemed ripe for action.

Frederick's invasion of Saxony—ostensibly a preventive measure—has fueled centuries of debate about Prussian war guilt. The decades around the turn of the twentieth century saw a full-blown historians' debate on the subject, yielding empirical knowledge that has yet to be entirely absorbed.[37] Historians Leopold von Ranke (1795–1886), Albert Naudé (1858–1896), and Reinhold Koser (1852–1914) largely followed Frederick's own interpretation of events, suggesting that Prussia's war was a defensive one, with its territorial aims limited to taking Silesia.[38] Only with the work of Max Lehmann (1845–1929) were new sources brought to bear by a historian with the courage to interpret them.[39] Hans Delbrück (1848–1929), Lehmann's colleague at the University of Berlin, best known for the "strategy controversy," took a similarly critical approach to sources.[40] Frederick's "Political Testament," written in 1752, is the major bone of contention in the debate over Prussian war guilt.[41] This highly controversial document—more manifesto than testament—refers to Saxony, West Prussia, and Pomerania as future Prussian acquisitions, mentioned in Frederick's discussion of his desire to round out the territory of the Prussian state. On Saxony, the king is quite explicit: "Saxony would be the most useful."[42] In invading Saxony in August 1756, the king had more in mind than access to Bohemia; to get to Bohemia, he could simply have gone through Silesia. Between 1753 and 1756, Saxony's foreign policy, directed by Prime Minister Heinrich Count von Brühl (1700–1763), placed it in a weak, marginalized position.[43] Dresden had mediated the British-Russian subsidy agreement, but despite its efforts, it failed to win any French or British subsidies for itself. It ultimately failed even to join the coalition against Prussia. Its military, although significant compared to those of other polities in the Holy Roman Empire, offered little to trouble the Prussians at this time.[44]

Austria was prepared to pay almost any price to win back the vital province of Silesia, which Prussia had occupied since 1740. In the words of the Austrian State Chancellor Wenzel Anton von Kaunitz-Rietberg (1711–1794): "When we lost Silesia, a major organ of Austria's body was ripped away, not just an external limb."[45] Austria deployed hardline rhetoric against Prussia, calling for its "total destruction." But its real aim was to reduce its northern neighbor's status within the structures of imperial governance.[46] A 1778 memorandum by Kaunitz is blunt about this goal: "the reduction of the House of Brandenburg to its original state as a minor, thoroughly second-rate power."[47] The rhetoric of total destruction may have suited Prussia's own heroic self-image, but it was never a realistic option for the Habsburgs.[48] The objectives of Austria's allies were less clear. Russia sought to expand in the west, striving to assert supremacy over the Baltic region and reduce Poland to a relation of dependency.[49] But the poor health of the Russian empress and the intrigues of court factions prevented Russia from consistently pursuing its foreign policy agenda. The British were not displeased with the *renversement des alliances*, since France was increasingly its main adversary, particularly in the colonial arena, and presented an urgent threat to Electoral Hanover and the Austrian Netherlands. France had designs on the Austrian Netherlands, which had several major ports, but beyond this, it had no other expansionary aims in Europe, wanting, above all, to fulfill its existing treaty obligations.[50] France's entry into the war had something oddly unintended about it. However, one goal shared by most powers was the maintenance of the balance of power in Europe, something Prussia seemed now to threaten. This was why Prussian propagandists like the political economist Johann Heinrich Gottlob von Justi (1717–1771) used every possible argument to reject the "chimera of a European equilibrium," suggesting the idea was merely a "mask of power."[51]

In the case of Britain and Austria but also that of France and Prussia, we thus see confrontations between powers that did not regard one another as their primary opponent.[52] Saxony and Sweden both felt Prussia was the preeminent threat. For Sweden, this resulted in what at first may seem a paradox: rapprochement with Russia, its main adversary, done with a view to acquiring German possessions along the Baltic coast. The Netherlands and the Swiss Confederation, the two remaining neutral powers in northern and central Europe, enjoyed the economic benefits of neutrality. The Netherlands did well as a provider of maritime insurance and as a trading center for capital and weapons, while Switzerland offered an excellent recruitment pool for mercenaries.[53]

Armies and Other Resources

One way or another, every causal explanation of the "bellicosity of early modernity" comes back to problems of early modern state formation.[54] This link between warfare and state formation in early modernity has long been the subject of historiographical dispute. Johannes Burkhardt has suggested that European conflicts from the sixteenth century until the War of the Spanish Succession should be called "wars of state formation," stressing that the unfinished, in-progress nature of state formation acted as a particular catalyst for war.[55] European states had not yet been institutionally stabilized and were nothing close to the nation-states they would become. Rather, they were dynastic princely states, whose administrative apparatuses, economic systems, and military power were still being created. Some historians regard this incompleteness as the real driving force underlying these wars.

In English-language historiography, state formation is closely linked to taxation. Wars had to be paid for, meaning that questions of resource mobilization were always present. John Brewer has used the phrase "fiscal-military state" to refer to eighteenth-century Britain.[56] His memorable coinage refers mostly to the British state's capacity to efficiently raise taxes and borrow cheaply, thus laying the groundwork for a powerful army and navy. Some historians have even suggested using "fiscal-naval state" to make clear that British military dominance was ultimately about sea power.[57] Brewer's phrase has become indispensable in debates about the period and by now has been applied to almost all eighteenth-century states (as well as some from other eras).[58] The popularity of fiscal-military state as a concept is probably linked to a lack of consensus as to its definition, but at the heart of the model is a highly efficient tax-collection apparatus. Along with cheap loans, efficient tax collection allowed wars to be fought over the course of many years. With military-oriented taxation, the state largely existed to service its own war machine, while any gains from expansion, in turn, brought new taxes into state coffers. But the expansion of war zones also set limits on the process of accumulation. The questions that the phrase fiscal-military state was meant to answer—why Britain? and why only Britain?—should thus be addressed at a different level. It is less a matter of distinguishing the fiscal-military state from less efficient forms of government and more one of examining specific local constellations.

In terms of eighteenth-century conflict, *wars of state positioning* seems a preferable term, although state formation was still a work in progress at this time. In other words, these were wars involving hegemonic rivalries between European powers.[59] To explain the Seven Years' War, Heinz Duchhardt has helpfully divided the contemporary European power constellation into four ranked categories. At the top of the list come Britain, Prussia, Austria, France, and Russia—the "pentarchy" powers—followed by a second group of "relegated countries"—namely, Spain, Sweden, the Netherlands, and Poland. The Ottoman Empire, Savoy, and Denmark are considered "emerging powers," while Portugal, the Swiss Confederacy, and the minor German and Italian states are defined as "small and passive."[60]

Extended to the world outside Europe, this typology would have to include the Mughal Empire in India among the relegated powers; it had been mired in territorial disintegration since the death of Emperor Aurangzeb in 1707. Thus, Indian territorial history can be organized according to a different narrative frame: Mann's process of segmentary state formation, discussed earlier. However, one way or another, the main point is that Mughal supremacy was coming to an end. In this respect, structural parallels existed between the history of India and that of the Holy Roman Empire. Looking at North America and Canada, there was no equivalent of India's "wealthy native classes," but it would be incorrect to see alliances like the Six Nations Confederacy as being without a foreign policy or as having no status as actors in international law.[61] Europeans brought horses with them, as well as new kinds of textiles and metalworking. But they also brought firearms, gunpowder, alcohol, and—most devastating of all—disease. As a result, by 1700 the Indigenous population of North America had shrunk from somewhere between 5 and 10 million people to around 1.5 million.[62] European demand for furs led Indigenous people to neglect traditional subsistence, rendering them more and more dependent on trading with Europeans; the demand for furs also produced discord among the various tribes, hitherto uncommon. The Mohawk and Seneca—two nations within the Iroquois Confederacy—were increasingly encroaching on the hunting grounds of the Ottawa and Nipissing, tribes allied with the French, producing new conflicts and new treaties.[63] By 1701, with the Peace of Montréal, a "middle ground" developed: a zone of relatively peaceful trading relations. It would be this zone that was plunged into crisis by the French and Indian War.[64]

All standing European armies at the time were effectively mercenary forces.[65] That meant, first, that systems of general conscription barely existed, with the numbers of men under arms differing greatly between peacetime and wartime. Second, the motivation of each individual soldier could be a complex mixture of rationales.[66] National patriotism could sit alongside a desire for plunder or simply a struggle to survive; religious motivation could promote cohesion, as could the "familial" nature of some regiments. Historians' figures on the size of the different armies can vary greatly, prompting considerable confusion. This is partly the result of distinctions between the nominal strength of units and their actual manpower. Moreover, the size of an army could change considerably from one year to the next. The scale of mobilization varied greatly among European powers, depending on each state's political and economic makeup.

France had the largest land army; over the course of the seventeenth century, it had become the leading military nation in continental Europe.[67] During the Seven Years' War, the French crown had around 400,000 men at its disposal: 330,000 in regiments of the line, supplemented by some 80,000 militiamen.[68] Much contemporary military theory came from France, which served as a model in many areas of military endeavor. But by the time of the Seven Years' War, the country faced a backlog of necessary reforms, which was already having an impact on the army's efficiency. Foreign mercenary units, including the essential Swiss regiments, made up 25 percent of the French forces.[69] France maintained a principle of voluntary recruitment, and during the war, this meant the army had considerable difficulty quickly raising and deploying new troops. Despite its large population and its economic strength, France was burdened with huge public debts, and its administrative apparatus was plagued with venality and corruption. This added enormous extra cost, much of it going into the pockets of those holding public office.[70] All major military decisions were made at

Versailles, and as in Russia, court favoritism promoted hesitant, risk-averse decision-making by generals, since any "wrong" decision could result in personal downfall. These fears were not unfounded, as demonstrated by the many courts-martial at the end of the war. Structural deficits in administrative, military, and finance budgets drove French wartime costs to extraordinary levels, although peacetime military expenditures had been no more than 50 percent of the national budget, roughly the same as in Austria and Russia. Firearms and other equipment could be produced domestically, but strong regional differences resulted in a lack of standardization in arms procurement, meaning that regiments could not carry out their own repairs, for example. French artillery was hopelessly out of date, and the state was unable to implement innovative financial models, as Russia had done. Compared to Louis XIV's armies, France's military was in a parlous state, but the need for reform was not accepted, not least thanks to a historical belief in the country's superiority. Eighteenth-century wars did much to produce the disastrous conditions that culminated in the Revolution of 1789.

At the outbreak of the war in 1755, Britain's armed forces numbered approximately 43,000 men, with 31,000 in the army and 12,000 in the navy. Significantly, by 1756, the total in the navy had already risen to no less than 50,000. Britain would be the country that emerged as the strongest from the conflict, but it fought the war with the weakest land forces of all the major powers. Standing armies had been viewed skeptically in Britain since at least the civil wars of the seventeenth century. Nonetheless, the official number of soldiers in the army increased from 26,891 in 1738 to 76,516 in 1748 to 117,633 in 1762.[71] In Britain's navy, the complement of fighting men went from around 10,000 in 1752–1754 to 50,000 in 1756 to some 70,000 when the war ended in 1763.[72] Deployed to the Holy Roman Empire, His Britannic Majesty's Army in Germany formed part of a larger allied army consisting of troops from Brunswick, Hanover, and Hesse, among others.[73] The situation was very different in North America and South Asia.[74] In North America, British regulars fought alongside colonial militias. In South Asia, Britain's forces included EIC soldiers and British infantry and naval units, along with Indian sepoys. The British economy prospered thanks to overseas trade, but military costs remained reasonably stable. In any case, raising much larger armed forces would have come up against strong domestic opposition. Britain's consistent military policy, as well as its island geography, promoted relatively centralized arms production, which served the overlapping interests of the state and the commercial oligarchy. Those in the merchant class were well aware of how much they owed to the world's most powerful naval force. Arming the fleet was in the interest of the British crown—but not just the crown. The Bank of England regularly made loans to the government, which had, after all, proved itself sustainably creditworthy thanks to taxes on foreign trade. But continental commitment continued to place particularly onerous burdens on the British treasury, which had to pay for expensive subsidies for Prussia, as well as His Britannic Majesty's Army in Germany.[75]

Prussia's seizure of Silesia, which Frederick dignified as his own "rendezvous with fame," was motivated by both symbolic and material factors.[76] Beyond a larger population and increased economic strength for Prussia, the young Frederick sought fame, the "satisfaction . . . of his name in the newspapers and in future history books."[77] Prussia had an army that, as Bernhard Kroener puts it, was "too large for a medium-sized power, but too small for a great power."[78] From a mercantilist perspective, Prussia's grab for Silesia was a logical and consistent policy, since only by acquiring territory with economic resources and a large population could the country achieve the necessary growth. Silesia had around 1.3 million inhabitants when the war began.[79] The Prussian army increased from 80,000 men in 1740 to 166,000 in 1763; during the same period, Prussia's overall population grew from about 2.2 million to 4.7 million.[80] That amounted to one soldier for about every twenty-eight inhabitants. If soldiers' families were added to this total, Prussia's military population stood at around a quarter of the entire population by the mid-eighteenth century. This increase was also reflected in its public finances, with 70–80 percent of peacetime Prussian spending going to the military, while comparable countries averaged around 40–50 percent. In wartime, Prussian military spending rose to about 90 percent, compared to other countries' 80 percent.[81]

In 1756, the Prussian military had 143,000 men at its disposal.[82] This army was all that made Prussia competitive within the constellation of European powers. In other words, Prussia was just as much a fiscal-military state as Britain, but it had far fewer constraints on its tax-raising capacity.[83] Frederick was able to achieve 80 percent peacetime military spending because his government had less public debt and a tightly organized central administration, headed by the General Directorate. Moreover, he had the capacity to directly raise both rural land taxes (contributions) and urban consumption taxes (excises).[84] At the outbreak of the war, his "war treasury" held 15.5 million thalers, a very substantial figure. Prussian armaments production was supported by state protectionism. Its weapons were largely produced within its borders, primarily in Potsdam and Spandau, while key raw materials were imported via hubs like Hamburg and Amsterdam—and at times even procured from enemy countries.[85] Thus, Prussia imported ore from Sweden in wartime while the copper it needed was requisitioned from Saxony.

The calculus behind this full-scale mobilization of resources would pay off only if Prussia waged short, fast wars and fought them mostly in enemy territory.[86] For this reason, a crucial portion of Prussian defense investment went into fortifications. At least seven towns in Silesia were fortified, intended to serve as fortresses in wartime. By the outbreak of the war, Frederick had strengthened fortifications in these Silesian strongholds: Neisse (fortified in 1747–1748), Schweidnitz (1753–1754), Glogau (1754–1755), Glatz (1755–1756), and Kosel (1756).[87] Breslau and Brieg were considered less important and were at first not included (see figure 1.1).

Austria also had substantial armed forces, theoretically numbering 200,000 men. But its territory was larger and more fragmented than Prussia's, meaning it was slower in mobilizing its armed forces, which had to be pieced together from a large number of small garrisons.[88] A year before the war Maria Theresa's army had a paper strength of 126,272 men, but only 75,000 were mobilized at the outbreak of fighting in 1756.[89] Part of the reason for Austria's slow reaction was the fact that Frederick had not "given the least umbrage [offense]," as Kaunitz put it; the Prussian king had not wanted his arms buildup to grant Austria a pretext for war.[90] An Austrian Armaments Commission was established only on July 6, 1756, and met for the first time on July 8 and 9.[91] By the following year, Maria Theresa's army had a nominal strength of 170,000, but its strength in reality was no more than 80,000. Moreover, although we speak of an "Austrian" army, its armed forces were very much *k-und-k* (*kaiserlich und königlich*): in other words drawn from many parts of the Habsburg realms, not simply from Austrian lands. The Royal-Imperial army was extremely heterogeneous, composed of Germans, Bohemians, Hungarians, Italians, Croats, and Austrian Netherlanders.

Unlike Frederick, Maria Theresa inherited a large debt burden from her father. The privileges enjoyed by particularist interest groups put a brake on military spending. In the wake of the First and Second Silesian Wars, the Austrian administration had at last been restructured, with the emphasis put on centralization and a steady increase in tax revenue.[92] This resulted in better funding for the armed forces, whose budget rose from 6 million guilders in 1740 to around 10 million guilders in 1763. Like Prussia, Austria managed

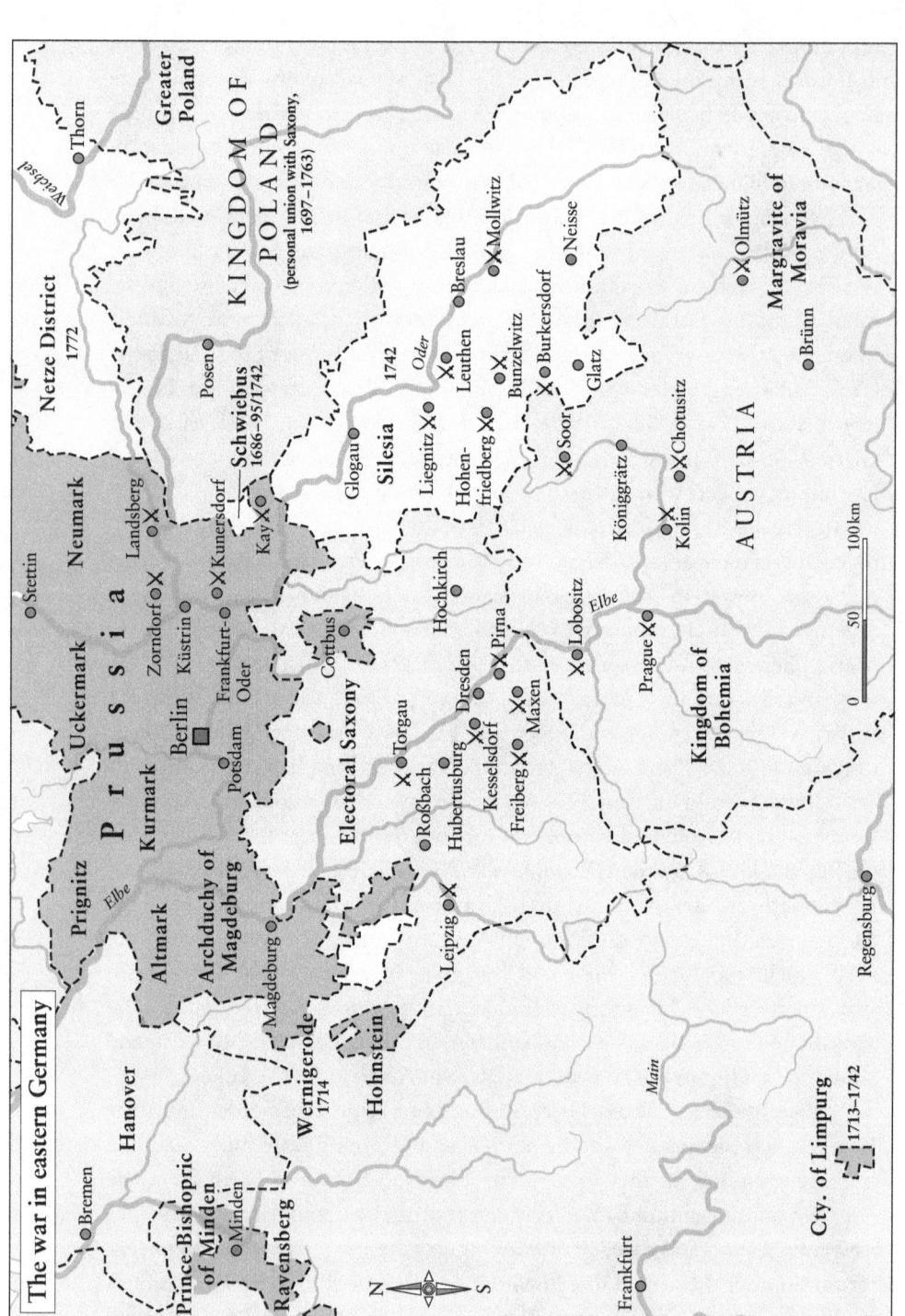

Figure 1.1 The war in eastern Germany.

to build up a domestic proto–armaments industry, reducing its dependence on foreign suppliers. Austria's artillery production was actually greater than that of Prussia, albeit with manufacturers often fronting much of the cost. But the Austrian government's shortage of funds proved fatal when it came to recruiting soldiers. Money was the key to recruitment.

Overall, what we see is an asymmetry of resource mobilization between Prussia and Austria, one that would favor Prussia both at the start of fighting and if the war was short. However, the longer the conflict went on, the more Austria's advantage would grow—but only as long the war was not fought in the Habsburg heartlands.[93] Austria's territories had substantial untapped capacity and numerous unused production sites, whereas Prussia was already close to its limit of production.

The Holy Roman Empire of the German Nation was a military force and a political actor in its own right. Although not a state in the modern sense, as a defensive alliance the empire sent its own armies into the field.[94] These forces were comprised of independent units raised by the various Imperial circles (*Reichskreise*), drawn from Franconia, Bavaria, Württemberg, the Electorate of Trier, and so on.[95] Political divisions within the empire meant only seven Imperial circles were in a position to supply troops. Some circles supplied none, including Upper and Lower Saxony, respectively dominated by the Electorate of Brandenburg and Electoral Hanover. This meant only 40 percent of the empire's nominal forces were available for mobilization, and barely half of these were actually mobilized, producing an effective force of about twenty-five thousand men.[96] A distinction must be drawn been the Imperial army itself and the contingents supplied by various imperial princes, including those of Würzburg, Württemberg, Saxony-Gotha, and Hesse-Cassel. These latter troops were often hired or subsidized by major powers, including France, Austria, and Britain. One example is the September 1756 subsidy agreement between Austria and the prince-bishop of Würzburg, which replaced Würzburg's deal with Britain and Hanover, made the previous year.[97] Karl Eugen von Württemberg's (1728–1793) policy of renting troops in return for subsidies was particularly ruthless toward the feudal estates but also toward soldiers and recruits. He concluded agreements with both France (1752, renewed 1756) and Austria (1760) and was able to mobilize a very large armed force, around sixteen thousand men, during the war.[98] The Württemberg royal family also provides a good example of how aristocratic siblings could end up fighting on opposite sides. The brothers Karl Eugen and Ludwig Eugen (1731–1795) both fought on the

French-Austrian side during the war. Ludwig Eugen was with the French army when it conquered Menorca in 1756 and later served under Austrian colors. However, a third brother, Friedrich Eugen (1732–1797), had a successful career in the Prussian army, where he was eventually promoted to the rank of general.[99]

Russia possessed powerful armed forces, with some three hundred thousand soldiers, but also had to contend with several structural problems.[100] Different parts of the administration got in one another's way, corruption fostered inefficiency and indecision, and overall tax revenues were too low in proportion to national resources.[101] Half of all government spending went to the armed forces; nonetheless, during the war Russia was dependent on Austrian subsidies of a million rubles a year.[102] Public finances and the business of raising armies could be mutually reinforcing, as when a bank specifically associated with artillery was founded in St. Petersburg. Pyotr Shuvalov (1710–1762) wanted the bank to finance Russian artillery manufacture, including the notorious secret "Shuvalov howitzers."[103] The tsarina had tightened up Russia's administration, establishing the Conference at the Highest Court, an imperial council that in exceptional circumstances could make military decisions, although this was officially the responsibility of the Council of War. The crucial figure on the new conference was Chancellor Alexey Petrovich Bestuzhev-Ryumin (1693–1766). Military leaders always had to seek approval for their decisions from higher authorities such as the Council of War. This contrasted sharply with Prussia, where the *roi connétable* (commander-king) held sole authority over military decision-making. The tsarina's death, a constant possibility during the war, hung like a sword of Damocles over Russia's political and military elites, further paralyzing their judgment. Some generals never traveled far from the capital and certainly never went overseas for any length of time in case events would suddenly require their presence in St. Petersburg.

At the time war broke out, the army had not seen active service in quite a few years. Among other things, this resulted in the complete failure of the Russian cavalry, which had to be reinforced or replaced with Cossack and Kalmyk auxiliaries.[104] The state of infantry training also left a great deal to be desired. There were massive logistical problems, making it impossible to supply the army over long distances. These problems were partly due to corruption, a notorious phenomenon, but poorly built infrastructure also played a role, canals being one example, along with a lack of peacetime quartermaster activity.[105] There was no shortage of raw materials essential for war. Iron production flourished, which benefited Shuvalov and his cannon makers more than anyone. This branch of industry was innovative but plagued with practical difficulties. The transportation of artillery, especially munitions, was too slow, and no sustainable system for training skilled workers had been developed.[106]

Spain was the most prominent of Europe's declining powers in the early eighteenth century: Its imperial status gave it a long way to fall.[107] The Spanish crown had held vast territorial possessions in the Americas and the Caribbean since the early sixteenth century, with further territories in the Far East that were smaller in scale but important nonetheless—most notably, the Philippines. But Spain's territorial extent and its substantial remaining prestige in Europe should not obscure the country's political, military, and economic weakness. The War of the Spanish Succession (1701–1714) had precipitated open crisis in the country. The Bourbon accession to the throne in 1713 prompted a comprehensive program of reform, including the establishment of four ministries of state along French lines, all directly responsible to the crown. As well as streamlining administration, Spain reformed its military structure. Its system of *quintas*, a method of military conscription comparable to the Prussian system of military cantons, had meant that around one in five male Spaniards served in the army. In 1734, a militia service was established, creating something akin to general conscription.[108] Spanish foreign policy was largely determined by its colonies, and Britain now became its greatest adversary, alongside Portugal, its traditional rival. Britain's maneuvers for strategic advantage received a boost in 1713, when it acquired Gibraltar and Menorca, while also agreeing to the Asiento, a thirty-year monopoly contract granted by Spain to trade African slaves to Spanish America. The Asiento came to an end in 1749–1750, but the Anglo-Spanish rivalry remained undiminished throughout this time, pushing Spain to develop closer relations with France, formalized in the three Bourbon Pactes de Famille of 1733, 1743, and 1761. The Spanish naval buildup consumed vast sums of money, pushing up domestic debt despite tax increases in Spain's overseas possessions. When Charles III came to the throne in 1759, he was a new monarch who appeared to offer hope, the first to do so in some time. During his reign, he would boost processes of domestic consolidation, but he could do little about overseas competition.

Within the constellation of European powers, Sweden was another country in clear, steep decline, its military strength and position severely weakening.[109] It remained an important maritime power, but ultimately this was of little consequence for the Seven Years' War. After the conclusion of the Great Northern War in 1721, Sweden had gradually been reduced to the status of a minor power. The Seven Years' War accelerated this process. Since the political reforms of 1720, the estates had dominated Swedish politics, with foreign and defense policy subject to parliamentary control by the Riksdag, comprised of representatives from the nobility, clergy, townspeople, and peasants. Two rival political groups dominated parliament: the stronger Hats faction and the more liberal Caps minority.[110] In the decades after the Great Northern War, Swedish statesmen negotiated a series of shifting alliances, seeking to regain some of the country's lost status. At times Sweden aligned with Prussia or Russia and at other times against them. By mid-century, however, the signs seemed to point toward neutrality as a policy. In July 1756, with the Seven Years' War barely underway, the country signed a treaty of neutrality with Denmark, with both countries agreeing to protect one another's merchant fleets against attack.[111]

With alliances forming, with Austria, France, and Russia on one side and Britain and Prussia on the other, the situation seemed favorable for Swedish intervention against the Hohenzollerns, with Sweden looking to acquire Prussia's Pomeranian provinces. The country's treaties with Austria and France guaranteed restitution of the Pomeranian territories it had lost to Prussia in 1679 and 1720.[112] This is why Swedish historiography refers to the Seven Years' War as the Pomeranian War. But Sweden also had colonial ambitions, and its representatives in Paris sounded out the possibility of obtaining a Caribbean island—possibly Tobago—as a reward for participation in an anti-Prussian alliance.[113] One way or another, French money would be needed: Sweden would intervene militarily only if granted French subsidies.[114] In addition, Sweden had deep institutional ties to the Holy Roman Empire, as Swedish Pomerania was formally part of the empire. This meant any intervention in Germany could be presented as Sweden taking action as a guarantor power of the Treaty of Westphalia. This argument would also serve to counter Prussian propaganda claims that it was the protector of Protestants within the empire. But support for war was low among the Swedish population, and the army was in its weakest condition in decades. The army that marched into Prussia in 1757 totaled 22,125 men, commanded by Field Marshal Matthias Alexander von Ungern-Sternberg (1689–1763).[115] In fact, Sweden's Council of the Realm, which was responsible for the country's entry into the war, had acted unconstitutionally and in subsequent developments often exhibited considerable indecision.

Prussia and Britain were thus the only European states to efficiently mobilize their economic potential as the basis for military expansion. Prussia and its army did so on land, whereas Britain did so mostly as a naval power. Many contemporaries tended to measure military power by population and territorial size. Seen in these terms, France would have seemed the heavy favorite to win a war, with the survival of Prussia looking distinctly improbable. However, what would prove decisive in this war was the capacity of powers to successfully mobilize their forces.

Becoming a Soldier: Motivations and Trajectories

Soldiers had many pathways to military service and a multiplicity of motivations.[116] Some were driven by material hardship, some by the promise of wealth, some by curiosity. Others were registered and conscripted into service through arrangements like Prussia's canton system. Happenstance could also play a role; very few soldiers just entering the service could have imagined the long journeys that lay ahead of them. Intensive sociohistorical research has largely rectified the old image of eighteenth-century armies as melting pots of petty criminals and desperate lower-class recruits. Those joining up often included trained craftsmen unable to find work in local labor markets. In the field, their skills could be of tremendous use, giving regiments autonomous capacity in shoemaking, tailoring, or carpentry.[117]

Aristocratic families also often had material factors in mind when sending their sons to make a career as an officer. For many young nobles, soldiering was the only way of making a living appropriate to their class status.[118] Soldiers in this position included Friedrich Rudolf von Barsewisch (1737–1801) and Christian Wilhelm von Prittwitz, two Prussian officers whose testimony will be frequently cited in this book. For officers like these, choosing the "correct" regiment was crucial in establishing and maintaining social networks.

To become an ordinary eighteenth-century soldier was to undergo a transformation with several phases. Men joined a unit either by enlisting in a canton system or by more or less directly applying on the "military job market." Acceptance was followed by a veritable ritual investiture, including the issuing of uniforms and weapons and the swearing of an oath, followed by a course of drill training in a garrison.

Ulrich Bräker (1735–1798) is probably the best known ordinary soldier of the Seven Years' War. He was born to a poor family in the region of

Toggenburg in Switzerland and went on to achieve literary renown much later, in the final decade of his life.[119] By his own account, Bräker's enlistment was somewhat hapless. Tempted by the false promises of a Prussian recruiting sergeant in the nearby town of Schaffhausen, he realized he had been taken on as a soldier rather than a domestic servant only when a corporal spread out a uniform in front of him, before adding a sixpence and saying "Well, this is what awaits you, son."[120] With this, his fate was sealed: "Now they led me into the dressing chamber, where I was fitted out with trousers, shoes, and half-boots, and given a hat, a neckerchief, stockings, etc."[121] The issuing of uniforms was in some respects an initiation ceremony, complete with oath taking:

> I had then to go, along with some twenty other recruits, to see Colonel Latorf. We were led into a Chamber as big as a church, they brought out a lot of flags with Holes in them, and ordered everyone to touch a corner of the Flag. An adjutant, or whatever he was, read out a whole sack of war articles and he spoke some words to us, most people repeated them in a murmur; I didn't move my mouth, instead I thought about what I wanted to do, I thought of Annie [Bräker's fiancé]; then they waved the flag over our heads and we were dismissed.[122]

A less well-known Swiss soldier, Markus Uhlmann, traveled from Switzerland to Westphalia to join the French army but later deserted and entered service on a Dutch ship, eventually ending up in Havana. "Go-betweens" like Uhlmann rarely left ego-documents behind, but their lives bore the traces of the war's enormous mobility and highlight the close connections between its various theaters. Uhlmann saw his own uniforming less as a boost in status and more as loss and subjection to control: "Once the uniforming was done, I was quartered in a tent with six soldiers, with drill in the afternoon, so I could not leave, and I came to realize that I did not want this ahead of me. I had to sell my coat, it would be impossible to drag it with me into the field; with great effort I got ½ a Crown Thaler for it."[123] The reasons for Uhlmann's desertion included the poor supply situation in his regiment and the lack of additional income as a field surgeon and barber, since most of the regiment's men did not need shaving and the wounded were taken to centralized infirmaries for treatment.[124]

Heinrich Ludewig Grotehenn, the son of a schoolmaster from the village of Wickensen in Lower Saxony, was at first quite disinclined to military service. According to his memoir, although his parents were of "slender means," they were both physically imposing, and he himself was of large stature, and by the age of eighteen, he was well capable of "carrying a musket with honor."[125] Having drawn the attention of General Philipp von Imhoff (1702–1768), Grotehenn went into hiding to escape conscription, but after a month, he went home and was subsequently arrested. He was transported to the town of Brunswick, albeit with some dignity intact: His hands were not bound, and the buttons of his breeches were not cut off. For Grotehenn, the decisive experience was that of being uniformed. The "Uniforming Chamber" contained so many uniforms and so much equipment that he thought himself in a royal armory: "I was kindly allowed to undress in this Chamber and be fitted for one of the splendid Uniforms, along with a hat. These Outfits gave me an entirely different appearance. In place of a simple green jacket, I put on a blue dress coat with white facings. A white waistcoat rather than red one, white breeches not black, short linen boots in place of my uncomfortable ones. I tried a hat with golden trim, then one with silver decoration. I now wanted to look at myself in a large Mirror." In fact, there was no mirror. Instead, Grotehenn was told there was more to come. "Barely able to think for Joy," he was shown a large number of "crooked Swords and Sabers" and was told to help himself. A white "enameled belt" was fastened around him, along with a leather ammunition pouch. "This all suited me marvelously. After all of this, I was also handed a long Musket, so that I was now fully armed."[126]

Charles Bonin joined the French military almost by accident. He was eighteen years old when he traveled from Paris to La Rochelle in 1751 in hopes that his uncle could find him a position with the City Guard. On arrival, he discovered his uncle was dead, so he entered service with a local commander on the Ile de Ré instead. Sometime later a desire to travel led him to join up for service in Canada, embarking on June 12, 1751. A five-month voyage brought him to Quebec City on November 5, where he was quartered with a tradesman.[127] He set about quietly exploring the city, which seemed to him like "an amphitheater built on a cliff."[128] By his estimate, Quebec had a population of about fifteen thousand, as well as a garrison of twenty-four hundred.[129] Short of money, he tried to join the artillery, only to be refused because of his small stature. But the wife of a captain vouched for him, along with two widows, and he was accepted as an artilleryman and given the nickname Jolicoeur ("Sweetheart").[130]

In the British context, James Miller, a private in the 15th Infantry Regiment, describes a more idealistic scenario, one of youthful patriotism.[131] From his earliest youth, he writes, the sound of drums had "set his heart on fire"; he imagined that a soldier must be "the first of mortals, because he is a guardian of his country."[132] He often sought the attention of soldiers, hoping they would notice him. In 1756, he was approached by a recruiting sergeant. The man sang the praises of the soldier's life while also offering cash in hand. Miller needed little persuasion. However, awakening from the "delirium of the first night," his enthusiasm gave way to grief, as he realized he had not even taken time to bid farewell to his relatives. But the farther he traveled from home, the more his sorrow seems to have evaporated.

A desire to escape the law drove Horace St. Paul, originally from Northumberland in the north of England, to join the Austrian army.[133] St. Paul had killed a man in a duel on May 24, 1751, prompting him to run away to France and then to Brussels. At the outbreak of the Seven Years' War, he was appointed aide-de-camp to a senior Austrian commander, Prince Charles Alexander of Lorraine (1712–1780). In 1757, St. Paul took on the same function for the Austrian Field Marshal Leopold Joseph von Daun (1705–1766).

The memoirs of John Grant, of the Black Watch Regiment, offer the viewpoint of a recruiting officer.[134] The Scottish labor market was particularly precarious in the mid-eighteenth century. After the pretender Charles Edward Stuart (1720–1788) fled to France following his defeat at Culloden in 1746, Scotland was put entirely under English rule, and its people were prohibited from carrying weapons and wearing traditional clothing. Poor harvests in 1755 and 1756 drove many young Scots into British military service, attracted by lavish promises of land, as well as the possibility of wearing Highland garb. Grant had considered signing up with the East India Company, but his relatives advised against it. In July 1758, at the age of seventeen, he was offered a commission as a lieutenant in the 42nd Royal Highland Regiment, which was at that time recruiting reinforcements for the North American campaigns.[135] Grant's new position obliged him to personally recruit twenty-five men for the regiment. He hired a bagpiper and four young men who could dance well and set up quarters in an ale house. There were mishaps along the way, but by September, he had gathered enough recruits together, and on November 19, they embarked at Greenock on the River Clyde estuary, bound for the Lesser Antilles.

Highlanders served in North America and in the Caribbean and would also later prove useful as settlers. Their former opponents also served on all fronts. Geoffrey Plank's revealing study has shown how the perceptions, thought processes, and patterns of behavior of many British officers were formed by service in Scotland with the Duke of Cumberland (1721–1765). These habits were transferred to new contexts in the "colonial" outposts of Europe and North America.[136] Veterans of the Scottish campaign included William Blakeney (1671–1761), who became lieutenant governor of Menorca; Humphrey Bland (1686–1763), later a governor of Gibraltar; Edward Cornwallis (1713–1776), who held commands in Nova Scotia, Menorca, and Gibraltar; John Campbell, Earl of Loudoun (1705–1782), the commander of the British army in North America; and James Wolfe (1727–1759), the leader of British forces against Quebec.[137] Although not of the same generation, these officers were united by their will to take firm action against "rebels and savages" and undertake a sort of cultural proselytism on behalf of the British Empire.

The reasons why soldiers deserted were as complex and varied as the reasons why they signed up. Of the witnesses whose testimony is presented here, only Bräker and Uhlmann deserted their units. But desertion was a major structural problem for all eighteenth-century armies.[138] Over the course of the Seven Years' War, the Prussian army lost some 80,000 men to desertion, the French 70,000, and the Austrians 62,000, while the small Hanoverian army lost 9,182 soldiers.[139] However, when Prussia tried to incorporate 10,000 Saxon soldiers into its army, the "loyal deserters" frustrated the plan by hurrying back to their own army. Soldiers "deserting" an army were sometimes simply changing paymasters rather than abandoning the profession. Deserters would sometimes later return to their regiment. Nonetheless, desertion could reduce the fighting strength of an army by anything from 30 to 50 percent.

War Making: Ethics and Practices

The image of "tamed Bellona" dominated accounts of eighteenth-century warfare for many years prior to the French Revolution.[140] Improved logistics, went the argument, had reduced the phenomenon of armies living off the land, thus sparing the civilian population, while large battles were deliberately avoided in favor of strategies of maneuver, which were less risky and ultimately caused fewer casualties. In other words, the eighteenth century had seen a general humanization of the customs of war. Wild Bellona had been tamed and had assumed a new form, that of a "rational domestic cat."[141] Phenomena offered as evidence for the thesis include prisoner exchange, the surrender of fortified places, medical service in the field, care for enemy wounded, billing systems and war booty, the rejection of unnecessarily cruel missiles, a rigidly linear system of a solely maneuvering strategy, and the general subjection of warfare to the rule of law.[142] In sum, a wide variety of "inhibiting factors," whether economic, political, or legal, stood in the way of "the expression of autonomous military initiative." Mid-eighteenth-century warfare did indeed differ markedly from that of the Thirty Years' War and also from that of the Coalition Wars of the Napoleonic era. However, the best phrase in this context is Bernhard Kroener's more recent formulation—a "regulated Bellona," a more open formulation that gives greater latitude to historians analyzing the forms, contexts, and effectiveness of military action.[143] The empirically unproductive discussion around the taming of Bellona can be set aside by pointing out the substantial difference between the discourse of war and warfare as it was actually practiced. Discourse and practice were undoubtedly governed by different logics. However, in one way they were connected: The concept of tamed Bellona shaped how war was viewed, at least within a middle-class public sphere. This view of war, in turn, rendered certain practices of warfare unacceptable.[144]

This book entirely discards the old idea of a tamed Bellona in favor of understanding contemporary perspectives through consistent methods of historicization: The idea that war was either tamed or let off the leash tends to get in the way of doing this. Eighteenth-century war theorists addressed these problems in terms of war discipline (*Kriegs-Zucht*). Significantly, this was described by the German writer and statesman Johann Michael von Loën (1694–1776) as "the *Policey* of soldiers"; at the time, the term *Policey* meant something like "good order."[145] According to von Loën, the concept includes "1) General morals and behavior of soldiers, 2) Obedience in regard of orders and regulations concerning military service, 3) Good order in regard of common security, 4) Good order in regard of provisioning troops and of the War Commissariat, 5) Punishments, 6) Rewards."[146] As with civilian Policey, in looking at war Policey, we should dispense with notions of war's taming and focus instead on how regulations were actually implemented. We should not assume that rules were issued only for symbolic effect or that war regulations were smoothly communicated from top to bottom in absolutist style.[147] Von Loen was taken hostage by the French at Lingen in 1757 and imprisoned for four years at Wesel, thus experiencing firsthand the effects of disordered war Policey.[148] If we take war discipline to be a specific case of Policey, applied in a belligerent context, it becomes clear how supposedly opposing phenomena can, in fact, coexist within a single cultural constellation. A specific regime of warfare existed during this period, one that should not be regarded simply as the disappearing remnants of Rococo war strategy or as Enlightenment beliefs restraining the excesses of war. This regime of warfare contained, at the same time, aestheticism and theories of efficiency, control failures and logistical blunders, and bloody battles and poor treatment of the dead and wounded.[149] Mid-eighteenth-century war exhibited a dialectic of Enlightenment, incorporating both the sociable culture of the officer's mess and the massacres carried out by irregular forces.

In terms of operational areas, warfare at this time can broadly be divided into land and naval operations.[150] Within each, we can distinguish three separate forms of combat, albeit with considerable overlap. In land warfare, the forms were battle, siege, and small warfare, for which the word *guerrilla* was later borrowed from Spanish. On sea, the three analogous forms were the naval battle, amphibious siege from the sea, and smaller raids, including privateering. In conflicts overseas—whether Canada, Cuba, the Philippines, or the coast of Africa—amphibious operations were frequent, combining land-based and naval modes of warfare. German-language research has long neglected naval operations as part of eighteenth-century warfare, but historians in both Britain and France have long traditions of research into the subject.[151] This work has particularly focused on recruitment, discipline, and operational issues.[152] For all three themes, there were significant differences between warfare on land and warfare at sea. The work of maritime warfare demanded different qualifications while ships themselves were a very particular and highly constricted social space. Moreover, the sea itself represented an autonomous environmental factor, impossible to control. Western European powers usually enjoyed dominance at sea, but both Prussia and Austria issued letters of marque, giving authorization to privateers. The war also saw a Prusso-Swedish naval battle, albeit a minor one.[153]

Today's historians agree that sieges were the dominant practice of eighteenth-century warfare on land. Contemporaries were of the view that battles should be exceptional events.[154] But they were a relatively common exception, to judge from the pattern of the war's large-scale land battles, even confining ourselves to those within the European theaters of war.

Looking solely at Anglo-French encounters, Jean-Claude Castex has counted fifty-six sieges and fifty-five battles, which include six naval battles, seven skirmishes, seven smaller attacks, and ten ambushes.[155] Prussian combat operations were more or less evenly divided between sieges and major battles.[156] But battles were generally much shorter than sieges, usually lasting a single day, whereas sieges could go on for weeks or months. Battles also offered far greater opportunity for individuals to make a name for themselves. For Frederick II, siege warfare had become purely a matter of skill, "like carpentry or watchmaking. Certain distinct rules have come about, so everything always goes the same way. [. . .] Everything is subject to accurate calculation, so that even a person not present can quite accurately calculate the day on which the fortress will surrender."[157] Compared to battles, sieges proceeded in accordance with rule-based processes and technical operations. They began with the digging of covered trenches, *saps*, which were used to make a slow approach to the city or fortress. In any siege, the overall supply situation was decisive for both sides, but so was the moment chosen to attempt a breach in the siege defenses.[158] If the defenders did not surrender, an attack would be carried out. Depending on its intensity and duration, this might be followed by a limited period of looting and destruction. Inside besieged cities, the gap between rich and poor grew wider than it already was. The wealthier classes had various options to protect their property and possessions, whereas the defenseless poor were directly exposed to violence.[159] Outside Europe, European armies attempted to conduct sieges using conventional European methods; depending on the context, this resulted in failure or in adaptation to local circumstances.[160] Bougainville's comparison between warfare in Canada and that in Flanders is telling: Unlike in Flanders, he suggested, war in Canada meant endless ordeals, with frequent marches to secure food and ammunition. This severely limited armies' room for maneuver.[161]

Even contemporary historians tend to focus on battles rather than sieges, although there is some disagreement as to whether or not battles played a decisive role in the war. Some scholars regard the mid-eighteenth century as an era of indecisive warfare, while for others, battle was a plausible way of forcing a decision, like a judge handing down a decision in a courtroom. It has even been suggested that battles may have reduced the number of atrocities committed against civilians.[162] But what actually was a battle? As an event, many prerequisites were needed for an early modern battle to come about. To understand the range of practices that made up any battle, distinctions must be made among infantry, cavalry, and artillery battle.[163] More complex forms of analysis are also possible, as in John Keegan's account of Waterloo, which describes various confrontation scenarios involving the three branches of land warfare: infantry vs. cavalry, cavalry vs. artillery, and so on.[164] Battle narratives themselves can be divided into three types. First, there is the general's perspective, recapitulating the confrontation like a game of chess that develops by virtue of various "moves." Then there is the simple soldier's perspective, the worm's eye view, that centers on a participant who perceives only their own immediate area of combat, with the focus on sense perceptions and acts of violence and injury. Third, there is the anecdotal mode, a narrative that condenses a battle into a series of key scenes.[165] Thus, every battle passes into memory culture through the recall of individual moments, usually associated with decisions made and crises exploited.

For both sides, a battle was a highly choreographed encounter but also an extremely contingent event, entailing considerable risks. Moreover, for a battle even to take place, both sides had to be reasonably determined to have one. If this determination was lacking, their meeting would be referred to as an encounter (*Treffen*), for which gains and losses were reckoned differently.[166] In English, a prearranged battle is referred to as a *pitched battle*. For some contemporaries, and for some modern scholars discussing the war, prearrangement meant battles were closely associated with legal decision-making processes and also with duels.[167] The term *rencontre* was often explicitly used for battles. Unlike duels, however, battles could involve anything up to 120,000 men and were fought on a battleground often extending over a couple of square miles. As a mass event, a pitched battle presented formidable logistical challenges, and it continues to pose epistemological difficulties. Armies marched to the battleground in columns, where they were then rearranged into lines. For this reason, the greatest challenges armies faced included provisioning their men and horses and positioning them correctly on the field.[168] Placing infantry soldiers in long lines—the origin of the term *linear tactics*—was carried out according to a well-defined *ordre de bataille*. The order of battle was structured by seniority, meaning the right and left and the front and rear were regarded as having different levels of prestige. The result was repeated disputes over rank and status.[169] A second formation was positioned in reserve 500 meters (about 550 yards) behind the first battle line, with a third line 200 hundred meters (about 220 yards) behind the second. Cavalry units were arranged in a similar manner.

Infantry lines were arranged by peloton, a unit about one-eighth the size of a battalion. The firepower of the infantry lines was considered crucial, so training drills focused on this. The centrality of firepower also underlay the quantitative growth of armies.[170] That of the Prussian army was widely praised, but a realistic assessment would suggest its rate of fire was closer to two shots a minute than to six. Prussian superiority in firepower was due, above all, to the material qualities of their muskets, flints, and gunpowder.[171]

In theory, military leaders retained an overview of every phase of a battle, with plans made and changed accordingly. In practice, this was rarely, if ever, the case. Battles were almost "invisible," since no one could have a complete overview of what was going on. Contingent outcomes were the classic problem of all military theories.[172] Eighteenth-century military theorists, in the spirit of rationalism, thus unanimously advised that battles should be avoided.[173] For strategists, the concern was that contingent factors would prove decisive in determining outcomes. The question of what would decide a battle was no easier to answer in practical military terms. Some historians even refer to the period between the Thirty Years' War and the Battle of Waterloo as an era of indecision.[174]

Since medieval times, possession of the battlefield had been the ultimate criterion for judging the outcome of a European battle. The key objective of any military leader was to capture the field of combat by the displacement of enemy troops. In the era of linear tactics, this was done by throwing the opposing lines into disorder, even forcing their complete disintegration. When sources say that formations were forced into disarray, it is usually a clear indication of impending defeat.[175]

However, things were not that simple. What constituted a battlefield, and its exact location, was open to question, since the definition could determine whether the battlefield had, in fact, been seized. Battles often developed a second layer of reality, becoming media events in which the confrontation was restaged in the form of competing validity claims. But battle rarely involved the complete physical destruction of the enemy: This kind of annihilation would have gone against the codes of conduct of the aristocratic officer culture, not to mention being close to impossible in technical and logistical terms. Defeated forces were not usually pursued in the aftermath of a battle. When they were, pursuit ended with nightfall.

The intensity of violence in any given battle depended on spatial, technological, and cultural factors. Ideally, a battle would take place on a wide plain offering plenty of opportunities for maneuver. If an army's lines were broken, an orderly retreat (*belle retraite*) would still be possible. Spatial constriction of the battlefield—thanks to a mountain, river, or swamp—almost always resulted in a massive escalation of violence, as seen at the Battles of Zorndorf, Hochkirch, and Kunersdorf. The effectively deployment of artillery was another way in which violence could escalate. Finally, violence could be ratcheted up by cultural differences and the prevalent image of the enemy, as strikingly illustrated by Russo-Prussian battles.[176]

Among the mass armies of absolutist states, some actors retained the capacity for autonomous violence: those responsible for "petty warfare," irregular operations carried out by light troops and volunteer *Freikorps*.[177] Light troops tended to conduct reconnaissance work and collect contributions, as well as protecting the van or rear guard. Other duties included "commando" actions, such ambushes, hostage taking, and the theft of cattle and horses.[178] The deployment of irregular forces epitomized a fundamental ambivalence about warfare during the Age of Enlightenment. On the one hand, irregulars were expected to show a high degree of "good discipline" (*guter Mannszucht*). On the other, the successful tactical use of these forces meant giving them substantial autonomy.[179] What became known as the *hussar's coup*—an independently undertaken feat of arms—was possible only because of this autonomy, but these actions could also offer leeway for unauthorized attacks and the harassment of the civilian population.[180] In other words, these independent military operations contrasted with the image of disciplined soldiers in an absolutist state machine.[181] Depending on the observer's perspective, irregular soldiering is described as being a throwback to traditional forms of warfare or as looking forward to modern ones, its historiographical image shifting between the mercenary rabble of the Thirty Years' War and the guerrillas of modern military history. In the Seven Years' War, irregular forces were everywhere subject to social stigma, overt or latent. They had a bad reputation, whether they were seen as fighting in ethnically coded auxiliaries—Russian Cossacks, Austrian Pandurs, Native American in the North American war—or they were presumed to be from marginalized social groups, including petty criminals, ex-convicts, day laborers, and the like.[182] One example of the cultural logic of European periphery is a pamphlet published during the war that drew a connection between "Kalmucks and Scottish Highlanders," each with their "hitherto unknown ways of life and customs."[183] Highlanders tended to be depicted as "good savages," whereas fighters from Europe's eastern regions were given exclusively negative characteristics. But no state could or would do without this kind of irregular fighting force. Frederick II of Prussia often spoke of irregular forces with contempt, once observing of a particular regiment, known for its blue insignia: "Thrice blue, and thrice damned, execrable vermin!" Nonetheless, during the war he established fourteen battalions of irregular infantry, along with eight *Freikorps* units composed of troops drawn from different military branches.[184]

Up to a point, naval warfare presents the same patterns in mirror image. The great naval battle is a traditional showpiece of historiography, but these were comparatively rare in this war, apart from the Battle of Quiberon in 1759. What were extremely frequent were pirate attacks, small raids on coastal facilities—raids on French facilities, above all—and amphibious siege operations, including those at Menorca, Louisbourg, Quebec, Guadeloupe, Gorée, Havana, and Manila.

It was customary in Europe for campaigning on land to last from spring until autumn, with armies then withdrawing to winter quarters.[185] There were exceptions to this, as with the Battle of Leuthen, which took place on December 5, 1757, and indeed some campaigns were entirely fought in winter.[186] This system also meant that contemporaries thought of the war's progress in terms of individual campaigning seasons. Accounts written at the time often include reviews of the year's events, in keeping with the temporal logic of seasonal campaigns.

Early modern warfare was characterized by the absence of fronts in the modern sense. The space in which war was waged—the theater of war or Theatrum Belli—was a broad zone crossed and recrossed by armies.[187] The itineraries described by war memoirs are eloquent testimony to this.[188] It is possible to speak of the northwest German or the Silesian theater of war but not of a western or an eastern front. Only with this in mind can we understand, for example, how Berlin could be captured twice in quick succession with no substantial strategic impact on the Prussian war effort. Things would have been different, of course, had Magdeburg, Prussia's actual center of operations, been captured. It was more important to capture territories and their main settlements *at the right moment* than to operate on a broad front. The ideal moment to seize key locations was just before armies retired to winter quarters: Captured territories could be important bargaining chips in a possible peace agreement. Non-European theaters of war likewise centered on key fortified locations that served as strategic focal points. This underlies an observation made by the Chevalier de la Pause, a French officer, who noted in his journal in 1759: "The whole science of war in Canada consists in attacking or defending posts that either open or close communications from one border to another."[189]

"For a Few Acres of Snow," or the World in Flames

At first glance, it seems as though the outbreak of fighting in the Ohio Valley pushed Britain and France unwillingly into war.[190] Closer examination reveals longer-term geopolitical calculation on both sides. The simmering North American conflict led France to disseminate an image of British aggression within the European public sphere.[191] One important French foreign policy goal was to keep the Netherlands out of any anti-French coalition.[192] This was why, beginning in September 1755, Jacob Nicolas Moreau (1717–1803) published *L'observateur hollandois*, a series of forty-six pamphlets. The pamphlets came with a fictional authorship: They were supposedly situation reports regularly sent from a Dutchman in Paris to a friend in the Netherlands.[193] France had political rivalries similar to those of England, with some voices advocating a focus on the continent and others pressing for colonial engagement.[194] On February 29, 1756, in a letter to his childhood friend Nicolas-Claude Thieriot (1697–1772), Voltaire wrote the famous words: "I do not know if the tableau contains much more shameful to the human race than the sight of two enlightened nations cutting one another's throats for a few acres of ice and snow in America."[195] He repeated the phrase in *Candide*, with the eponymous hero asking if people in England are as foolish as those in France and receiving this answer: "You know that these two nations have been at war over a few acres of snow near Canada, and that they are spending on this fine struggle more than Canada itself is worth."[196] Writing in January 1759 to Luise Dorothée, he linked both theaters of war: "One may grant that men fought over Helen, but not that all the world hack one another to pieces for the sake of Canada and Silesia."[197]

Voltaire's was only one position among many, albeit a relatively extreme one. Recent research has shown that the French political elite were by no means uniformly skeptical of colonial initiatives.[198] *L'observateur hollandois* was aimed at a French audience as well as a Dutch one.[199] While some in France demanded purely maritime campaigns, others pushed for the occupation of Hanover and the Austrian Netherlands. But proponents of colonial expansion were nowhere near unanimous. Some strongly favored a focus on Louisiana and the Mississippi Valley; others promoted Canada with equal determination. This was the context in which, in 1750, Rolland Michel Barrin, the Comte de la Galissonière (1693–1756), wrote a memorandum on the French colonies in North America.[200] He argued that it was no longer a question of whether it made sense to possess these colonies but rather one of how best to protect them against envious neighbors. This would involve "honor, glory, and religion," but ultimately Canada's greatest advantage would be as a strategic, if "barren," buffer against British Canada.[201] For this reason, he suggests, France should stop at nothing to strengthen its colonies, which must be regarded as an "American bulwark against the enterprises of the British." Ultimately, the colonies could not be left with only the forces currently at their disposal; to do so would be to abandon them to the British, since "mastery in America and the riches which result from the exclusion of other nations will unquestionably also ensure mastery in Europe."[202]

The fourth *L'observateur hollandois* letter, published in 1755, draws a telling parallel: "The balance of trade in America is akin to the balance of power in Europe," suggesting that, in fact, the two phenomena were one and the same.[203] Maps were used to heighten readers' identification with remote territories. The eponymous "observer" of *L'observateur hollandois* was a cartographic observer, inviting readers to join him on an imaginary tour of this geographic space.[204] Other rhetorical ammunition deployed included references to natural law and a refutation of territorial ownership claims based on the right of first discovery. In 1755, the Conseil d'Etat decided to avoid European entanglements in favor of an "Atlantic strategy," at least for the time being.[205]

Britain witnessed an even more pointed debate over colonial policy, which pitted supporters of blue water policy against those of continental commitment, although it took place within a public sphere differently structured than that of France. The crown held decision-making authority in Britain, but so did Parliament, and the press was far freer to report and comment on events; hence, the most radical statements and caricatures tended to come from Britain. The key social groups within public discourse were also different. In France, the court and its elites remained the dominant factor. In Britain, broad swathes of the "middling ranks" were already active in the public sphere.[206]

In Vienna, by contrast, there seems to have been little interest in North American colonies. "The American hostilities concern us not in the least," Maria Theresa wrote to her St. Petersburg envoy, Count Miklós Esterházy de Galántha (1711–1764), on May 22, 1756, shortly after the signing of the first Treaty of Versailles.[207] Many contemporary observers in Germany indicated they were aware of the global nature of the conflict but consciously preferred to concentrate on representing local events. A chronicle written in 1766 by Georg Schatz (1748–1783), a pastor from Wollbrandshausen, a village close to Göttingen, begins by presenting the war as a global Franco-British conflict:

> Anno 1755. French and English merchants inspected three of each other's ships and did find various contrebande goods, for which reason the kings of both nations declared war on each other by land and by sea. France is said to have taken the islande of minorca from the English on June 28 led by the duc de Richelieu, whereas the English took from the French the famous Fort Lovie and river S. Laurenty with all the colonies of America and was everywhere victorious, nevermind that Spaniards hurried for to help France, but soon Spain had to watch as, contrary to their will, their gold mines and the city of Havana in America were likewise taken from them.[208]

But then the perspective shifts: "I now shall leave these two powers to cruise the oceans and fight each other for 7 years, back and forth, in the meantime setting myself firmly down here in Germany."[209]

Contemporary historiography uses the term *entanglement* for long-distance global processes of exchange and interconnection.[210] In the eighteenth century, the term *network* was already a metaphor for complex relations, but the contagious effects of war images were more often described in terms of fire and sparks catching flame—a long-established metaphorical idiom. Moreover, it had strong experiential force in a society where urban conflagrations were a constant danger. The metaphor was already common during the Thirty Years' War.[211] In a letter of October 1755, sent from Providence to Einbeck, Henry Melchior Mühlenberg already applies the fire metaphor to the new conflict: "As for political conditions here, the flame of war is gradually spreading."[212] Images of fire were not confined to the German-speaking world—hence, the statement by the French ambassador to Mainz in October 1756: "Indeed, given the present situation of crisis in Germany, a single spark will suffice to set a conflagration ablaze."[213] The chronicle of Johann Georg Fülling (1721–1779), a pastor based in Isthar in Hesse, makes a similar argument. At the beginning of 1757, he notes:

"The flame of war, lit last year in all corners of Germany, has now burst into larger flames, and in this 1757th year has overtaken our own dear homeland [*Vaterland*]."[214] The spark, as an image of uncontrollable contingency, could also be used as a way of disclaiming responsibility. In "A Vindication of My Political Actions," a short text written in July 1757, Frederick uses the image to avoid responsibility for the outbreak of the war:

> Everyone is aware that the chaos now churning through Europe began in America and that the dispute between England and France over stockfish and uncultivated lands in Canada gave rise to the bloody war which has plunged our continent into mourning. The [North American] war was so far removed from the possessions of German rulers that it is difficult to see how the fire could spread from one continent to another, when they would appear to without connection. Thanks to the statesmanship of our era, there is at present no controversy in the world, however small, which is not very quickly capable of engulfing the whole Christian world and rending it in two.[215]

In 1759, the political economist and Prussian propagandist Johann Heinrich Gottlob von Justi anonymously published a pamphlet putting forward a peace proposal. This also uses fire imagery, lamenting the "unfortunate War whose Flames are engulfing the greater Part of Europe" while suggesting the conflict was "ignited" by the dispute between Britain and France. "American quarrels," it adds, served as "tinder for the current war."[216] The pamphlet concludes with a patriotic appeal: "For Germany's Honor and Welfare," readers should not permit "foreign Nations to choose Germany as the Battleplace wherein to conduct their own Affairs."[217] The same year, von Justi put the "American" perspective on Europe into fictional prose, in the form of another pro-Prussian propaganda pamphlet, entitled *An Investigation Into Whether Today's European Nations Have the Wish Some Day to Become Cannibals, or at Least Hottentots*. The author of the text, the pamphlet's subtitle suggests, is a "former European," now gone to America "so as not to one day see his own descendants Accoutered in the stinking guts of Sheep."[218] In the year 3759, this European's descendants live in North America, where "common sense and the Sciences will likely find their future Abode." One day a newspaper arrives, in which a Captain Bohn reports from a Europe now populated solely by savage peoples without higher culture, dressed in bearskins and feathers. Justi here enacts a clever switch in temporal and spatial perspective. Descendants of civilized Europeans look back from the New World to the Old, revealing a future where the ravages of the current European war have led to the disappearance of civilization. The account takes a Eurocentric view of Indigenous cultures, dismissed as a "primitive" Other. However, this is less striking than its shift in perspective, undertaken at a moment when many people in Germany felt the European war had been "ignited" from the American colonies.

Even in the war's final years, fire metaphors persisted in news media throughout the Holy Roman Empire. In Augsburg in 1762, the *Apotheker* (Apothecary) journal also identifies the conflict's roots in the North American clashes: "Through you [America] our states were set aflame / You turned peasants into soldiers / And forced citizens to take up arms / The fire, which came from you / Has sent fire across wide seas / and now rages here across my Germany."[219] The English artist William Hogarth (1697–1764) puts the metaphor into visual form (figure 1.2).[220] His 1762 engraving *The Times (Plate 1)* is clearly an illustration of political maneuvering around a peace agreement. William Pitt is shown operating a bellows to fan the flames

Figure 1.2 The Times, Plate 1. Engraving by William Hogarth (London, 1762).
Source: akg-images/UIG/GSINCLAIR.

engulfing an allegorical globe placed on a London house. All around, the city is already catching fire. Various figures are attempting to extinguish the blaze, while others feed the flames and sabotage attempts to put them out. A French cartoon from 1757 deploys similar imagery: The Gallic rooster uses a flaming torch to set Germany on fire while smoke is already rising in North America.[221] The cartoons make concrete reference to actors like Pitt and the Gallic rooster, but the image of flames can also be read as articulating something about the inherent logic of war.[222] When war itself becomes the object of enunciation, it is depicted as more than simply the continuation of politics by other means. War becomes an active figure, spinning further and further out of control.

CHAPTER II

Sparking the Flame

The Death of Jumonville

What was the exact moment when the war's first shots rang out? This was a much-discussed question among veterans and others who lived through the conflict.[1] Today we tend to date this highly symbolic event to July 9, 1755, the day when the French and their Native American allies routed a British force under General Edward Braddock at the Monongahela River in the Ohio Valley. This date serves as a significant symbolic punctuation mark in a long chain of violent interactions. However, it should not obscure the fact that the previous Franco-British war in North America—King George's War, which nominally ran from 1744 to 1748—in effect, never ended, despite the signing of the Treaty of Aix-la-Chapelle in 1748.[2] The subtitle of John Almon's very early account of the Seven Years' War acknowledges this continuity: *Deduced from the Committing of Hostilities in 1749, to the Signing of the Definitive Treaty of Peace in 1763.*[3] There were four latent zones of Franco-British conflict in North America, places where the cold war could turn hot at any time and where in some cases low-intensity fighting had never come to an end. These zones were located at the border between Nova Scotia and Canada, in the area south of Lakes Ontario and Champlain, in the valley of the Ohio River, and around the "neutral islands" of St. Lucia, St. Vincent, and Dominica.[4] In 1749, to better assert their territorial claims, the French buried lead plates bearing the royal seal at various key locations, intended to be proof of possession of the disputed lands.[5]

The second Logg's Town congress took place in May and June 1752, in what was known as the "Ohio country," the broad region north of the Ohio River and south of Lake Erie. At the congress, the 1744 Treaty of Lancaster was to be affirmed by the Ohio Company, Native American tribes, and merchants from Virginia. The treaty specified that the British would be allowed to build a fort at the fork of the Monongahela and Allegheny Rivers.[6] However, the word *fort* was not clearly defined in this intercultural communication, and British and colonial settlers were happy to use this vagueness to their tactical advantage. French attacks had continued while the negotiations were still under way, leading the Native Americans to demand the construction of a "strong house," understood as a fortified location for the storage of food and gunpowder.[7] But what the Virginia representatives had in mind was more like a settlement, including a garrison. Ultimately, the tribes signed the agreement, which guaranteed a halt to Indian attacks on British settlements south and east of the Ohio River. In agreeing to this, the tribes, in effect, paved the way for their own expulsion.[8] Their main representative at Logg's Town was the leader of the Iroquois Federation, Chief Tanaghrisson (d. October 4, 1754), who had been born into the Catawba tribe but had grown up with the Seneca. The British usually called him the Half-King. The interests of the British and the colonials in the situation were by no means clear-cut. The Ohio Company had already promised London it would build a fort, but it was reluctant to take on the costs involved.

The French and British were preparing for war, with both sides seeking to build and control forts along the Ohio Valley, which left both of them dependent on support from the Iroquois tribes. The same year, 1752, another French force began active fortification work, led by the Marquis Duquesne (1700–1778), and the tribes turned to the British colonists for help.[9] For their part, the British used the danger posed by the French to the Native Americans, as well as tensions between the tribes, to force through the construction of more forts.[10] Duquesne's response was to dispatch a force of over a thousand troops, led by Paul Marin de la Malque (1692–1753), that occupied Fort Venango (an existing British fort) and built several new ones of their own. In doing so, Duquesne was interpreting his mission very freely, since his orders had explicitly ruled out open confrontation.[11] On August 28, 1753, London ordered the royal council in Virginia to drive the French out of their recently taken positions, by force if necessary. Open conflict was merely a matter of time.

At this point, the young George Washington (1732–1799), then still a Virginia land surveyor, was tasked with guarding two forts under construction on the Monongahela River.[12] On April 16, 1754, laborers working on the fortifications were driven out on the orders of Claude-Pierre Pécaudy de Contrecoeur (1705–1775), a French naval officer. Washington and his men, including their Native American allies led by Chief Tanaghrisson, withdrew to temporary fortifications. Contrecoeur sent a scouting party under Joseph Coulun de Villiers de Jumonville (1718–1754), looking to establish whether British forces were already present in French territory. This party—consisting of Jumonville, an interpreter, four officers, and twenty-nine soldiers—was ambushed by Washington's men on May 28, although it is unclear whether Washington was under orders to do so. Washington's diary describes the incident:

> We formed ourselves for an Engagement, marching one after the other, in the Indian Manner: We were advanced pretty near to them, as we thought, when they discovered us; whereupon I ordered my company to fire; mine was supported by that of Mr. Wag[gonn]er's, and my Company and his received the whole Fire of the French, during the greatest Part of the Action, which only lasted a Quarter of an Hour, before the Enemy was routed. We killed Mr. de Jumonville, the commander of that Party, as also nine others; we wounded one, and made Twenty-one Prisoners, among whom were M. la Force, M. Drouillon, and two Cadets. The Indians scalped the Dead, and took away the most Part of their Arms.[13]

The other side saw events differently. In a letter to Duquesne, Contrecœur cited a French eyewitness, a Canadian named Monceau:

> At seven in the morning, he saw they were surrounded on one side by the English, and on the other by the Indians. The English fired two volleys, but the Savages did not fire. M. de Jumonville had an interpreter ask them to stop firing because he needed to speak with them. They ceased firing. Mr. Jumonville now had their orders read aloud. I had sent these orders, telling them to withdraw, of which I have the honor of enclosing a copy. During this reading, the aforementioned

Monceau saw all of our French draw closer to Mr. Jumonville in such a way that they all found themselves between the English and the Indians. During this time Monceau made his way back to the camp, passing through the woods and over rocky ground to the Mal-Enguelée River [Monongahela].[14]

One Native American warrior from the Tanaghrisson camp even told Contrecœur that "Mr. Jumonville was killed by a shot to the head while the orders were being read."[15]

Further light was cast on events by an illiterate Irish soldier, Private John Shaw.[16] In an oral affidavit given to the governor of South Carolina on August 21, Shaw reported that the French had been caught by surprise early that morning and that one of their soldiers had fired a shot, prompting Washington to order his men to fire in response. After several of the French had been killed, Shaw's narrative observed, the remainder of the force quickly surrendered with their weapons, asking for quarter. The soldier's testimony included details of the cruelty meted out to Jumonville:

> Sometime after, the Indians Came up, the Half King took his Tomahawk and Splitt the head of the ffrench Captain, having first Asked if he was an Englishman And having been told that he was a ffrench man, he then took out his Brains, and washed his hands with them, And then Scalped him All this he has heard and never heard it contradicted, But knows nothing of it from his own Knowledge, Only he has Seen the Bones of the ffrench Men who were killed in Number abt 13 or 14, And the Head of one Stuck upon a Stick; for none of them were Buryed, And he has also heard that one of our Men was killed at that time.[17]

Further detail is added by the account of another of Contrecœur's informants, a deserter named Denis Kaninguen. His version also has Tanaghrisson killing the wounded Jumonville, claiming that the Indian warrior uttered the words "You are not dead yet, my father" as he did so.[18] In this telling of events, the action serves both as a symbolic negation of French authority in general and as a projection of the killing of the French governor himself, known to Native Americans as Onontio, literally "big mountain." Fred Anderson's reading of events is that Washington entirely lost control of the situation and that Tanaghrisson may have wanted to raise his own profile among Native American warriors while also forcibly creating new "facts on the ground." In later years, Washington consistently sought to downplay the incident.[19]

By June 2, Washington and his men had hastily constructed a fortified redoubt they called Fort Necessity, but it was a small fort built on open ground and would be difficult to hold against attack. Clearly this was not Washington's plan. Instead he went on the offensive, with three hundred men moving out from the stronghold on June 16, headed in the direction of Fort Duquesne. Tanaghrisson unsuccessfully tried to convince the Delaware, Shawnee, and Mingo tribes to join him in making war against the French. The tribes let it be known they had no intention of leaving the Ohio Valley to support the British and preferred to join with the French. Tanaghrisson left the meeting with a few loyal followers, withdrawing to Aughwick, a trading post located at what is today Shirleysburg, Pennsylvania. Here the Half-King died of illness on October 4, 1754, although his followers believed he was killed by witchcraft.[20]

The following twelve months saw the escalation of the situation in the Ohio Valley, culminating in the outbreak of the French and Indian War in July 1755.[21] In other words, a long-simmering conflict finally escalated to a point where it could no longer be ignored by European political elites. In his autobiography, Benjamin Franklin (1706–1790), at the time a Pennsylvania provincial assemblyman, recalled growing fears of war: "In 1754, war with France [was] being again apprehended," with discussions conducted at Albany among the representatives from the colonies and from the Six Nations of the Iroquois.[22] The initiative for the talks had come from the London Board of Trade, which instructed Sir Danvers Osborne (1715–1753)—newly appointed as New York governor and about to leave for the colonies—to call a meeting at Albany with representatives from Virginia, Pennsylvania, Maryland, New Hampshire, Massachusetts, and New Jersey, as well as the Six Nations.[23] Osborne killed himself shortly after arriving in New York, so the invitations to the talks were sent by his deputy, James De Lancey (1703–1760). The discussions began on June 19, 1754, and raised the possibility of establishing a union of the colonies to function as a security alliance.[24] The representatives of the Six Nations were presented with wampum belts bearing the image of the seven governors and six Native American representatives connected with a heart, with all thirteen depicted as enjoying the protection of George II.[25] Various proposals circulated among the delegates, including Franklin's Short Hints Towards a

Scheme for Uniting the Northern Colonies. Ultimately, the Plan of Union was approved on July 10, 1754, and sent to the assemblies of the individual colonies for a vote. The head of the union was to be the president general; a Grand Council would be made up of representatives of the colonies. The British crown would have a right of veto, but financial decisions would remain with the colonies.[26]

This union never happened: It was rejected by every colony, as well as by London. A letter written in 1755 by William Shirley (1694–1771), governor of Massachusetts, reveals how political discourse was increasingly framed in terms of security: "Our colonies are all open and exposed, without any manner of security or defense. [The French] are protected and secured by numbers of Forts and Fortresses. Our men in America are scattered up and down the woods, upon their Plantations, in remote and distant Provinces. Theirs are collected together in Forts and Garrisons. Our people are nothing but a set of farmers and planters, used only to the axe or hoe. Theirs are not only well trained and disciplined but they are used to arms from their infancy among the Indians."[27] By now, everything pointed toward general escalation and increased armament on both sides. London decided to send regular troops to come to grips with the situation in the Ohio Valley, with General Edward Braddock as commander in chief. He had secret instructions to appoint a superintendent for Indian affairs, apparently in reaction to the Albany plan, and then to gradually expel the French from their forts, from the Ohio Valley to Lake Ontario.[28] When his force shipped out for North America in December 1753, it was accompanied by a number of women, the spouses or siblings of men on the expedition, including Charlotte Brown, who would later write a memoir of her time as a wartime nurse.[29] Faced with the British buildup, the French government did not stand idly by: On December 6, 1754, it sent its own squadron of eighteen ships to North America, with 3,150 soldiers on board.

Braddock's Defeat at the Monongahela River

On arriving in North America, Braddock called a meeting of the governors of all the colonies, to be held at Alexandria, in the colony of Virginia, in mid-April 1754.[30] The event was more an opportunity for Braddock to clearly transmit orders than any genuine process of consultation among equals. The general proposed an ambitious operational plan that involved four separate, simultaneous attacks on the French, with Admiral Edward Boscawen (1711–1761) additionally leading a fleet to block French supply lines at the mouth of the St. Lawrence River. Braddock himself would lead the 44th and 48th Regiments on an expedition against Fort Duquesne. At the same time, the 51st and 60th Regiments would advance on Fort Niagara from Albany under William Shirley, the second-in-command of British forces in North America. William Johnson (1715–1774), the recently appointed superintendent for Indian affairs, was to attack Fort Frédéric at Crown Point using Mohawk fighters and provincial troops from New England and New York. These provincial troops were not the same as the colonial militia: While financed by the colonies, they were usually recruited for a single campaign. A fourth advance would move out from Boston to attack French forts in Nova Scotia. Braddock's plan was ambitious and looked plausible on paper; whether it could be realized was another question. Moreover, details of the plan had already been published by the newspapers, giving the French good information about what was in store for them.[31]

Very few of those who devised these plans had any real idea of what it meant to take a large armed convoy across hundreds of miles of dense, roadless forest. They knew little of the uncertainties of fast river transport or whether there would be sufficient Native guides available to take the British through unfamiliar terrain. Military provisioning systems were by now relatively advanced in Europe, but in North America, they would have to be completely reorganized. Native American nations were quite prepared to enter into talks with the British, where they were represented by Chief Shingas of the Delaware and Chief Scarouady of the Oneida, and also the successor to Tanaghrisson as half-king. Shingas even gave Braddock a map of Fort Duquesne, drawn in secret by Captain Robert Stobo (1726–1770), who had been held as a hostage in the fortress. But Braddock managed to alienate the Delaware, whose warriors he regarded as neither a particular threat nor a significant ally. As a result, only Scarouady and seven Mingo warriors accompanied the British on the mission. Crucially, on the key question of settlements in the Ohio Valley after a British takeover, Braddock declared: "No savage shall inherit the land."[32] Many Native American fighters soon joined the French.

Braddock's 2,200-strong expeditionary army set out from Fort Cumberland for Fort Duquesne on May 29 and 30, 1754.[33] The march was agonizing for humans and animals alike, with many horses dying from exhaustion. The artillery train alone included four twelve-pounder ship's cannons, six

six-pounder fieldpieces, four eight-inch howitzers, and fifteen Coehoorn mortars.[34] A single twelve-pounder gun weighed over a ton. After just a week, Braddock decided to divide his force into a "flying van[guard]" and a supply force. In the course of the advance, the two parts of Braddock's force would be sometimes separated by a distance of sixty miles.

Early on July 9, the vanguard had advanced to within ten miles of Fort Duquesne. Contrecœur knew that the fort would be difficult to defend and that it could protect only two hundred of his sixteen hundred men, especially since his Native allies, who preferred raids and forays, could not be used for demanding defensive actions. But raiding tactics were, in fact, exactly what the situation called for: Braddock's force had to be tackled before he reached the fort. Captain Daniel Liénard de Beaujeu (1711–1755) was chosen to lead an ambush force of 36 officers, 72 marines, 146 Canadian militiamen, and 637 Native fighters.[35] The two sides engaged at around one o'clock in the afternoon of July 9. Scarouady spotted the enemy and firing began immediately, with Captain Beaujeu one of the first to be killed. The Native warriors on the French side were undeterred and kept the British under constant fire, shooting from behind trees. The close-packed British ranks made an easy target, and fifteen of the eighteen British officers were killed in the battle's opening minutes. The Native fighters moved skillfully on the terrain, prompting Philip Hughes, the British chaplain, to write: "I never saw one nor could I on Enquiry find any one who saw ten together."[36] Another eyewitness reported: "These Indians . . . kept an incessant fire on the Guns & killed ye Men very fast. These Indians from their irregular method of fighting by running from one place to another obliges us to wheel from right to left, to desert ye Guns and then hastily to return & cover them."[37] The fighting was unusually mobile and thus confusing, with several instances of friendly fire, where British troops shot at one another.[38]

The event came to be known as Braddock's Defeat. A letter written by Pastor Mühlenberg in October 1755 provides a vivid description, although he was not an eyewitness. His account presents the attack as, above all, a test of perception: "Before the savages launch an attack, they usually make terrible, howling war cries. These were enough to drive the Europeans nearly half out of their minds."[39] Mühlenberg's impression is confirmed in a letter written by Matthew Leslie, an eyewitness: "The screaming of the Indians is fresh upon my ear, and this terrible sound will haunt me until the hour of my death."[40] Mühlenberg's letter continues: "Thereafter, the bullets rained down on the vanguard from behind the trees as heavily as a hailstorm. The vanguard was congregated in one place like sheep and fell like flies. Our people saw nothing but trees and thick bushes, shot back at the trees, but got confused and fled to the general corps. The barbarians followed closely and attacked the general corps in the same manner."[41] Mühlenberg suggests the worst could have been avoided had Braddock been prepared to adopt local combat techniques:

> Two or three officers who were born in America and knew the savages' way of fighting entreated General Braddock to allow them to separate with some companies and fight against the savages in their own way. He did not permit it, however, but wanted to fight in the European manner and had his battalion grouped in square formation. It fired with cannons and muskets and the trees started trembling, which did not shock the enemies but gave them all the better opportunity to hit the whole crowd. In short time, they killed most of the officers, and the best of them, together with the large majority of enlisted men and four horses of General Braddock. They mortally wounded him, while the others fled in the greatest confusion. Some left the handsome cannons, the cash box and the remaining ammunition to the enemies and another part completely annihilated them on the run.[42]

Mühlenberg reiterates a criticism often made by contemporaries and participants in the war: The British troops failed to adapt European ways of fighting to American conditions. At times, this could lead to paradoxical situations. When the technique of platoon firing was used in confined spaces and confused situations, regular British units ended up shooting at one another and at American provincial soldiers, who were using Native American tactics and were mistaken for French troops. Fred Anderson has further suggested that the problem was not just the use of European combat techniques but also the way they were doggedly adhered to, regardless of circumstances.[43] Braddock's men had been strictly drilled in linear tactics, trained to hold their ground. They did so at the ambush at the Monongahela rather than adapting and seeking cover. Braddock was a courageous leader in this; he had several horses shot beneath him, until he was finally knocked from his horse after three hours of fighting, wounded by a bullet in the back. Washington, his aide-de-camp, vividly describes the night retreat that followed: "The dead, the dying, the groans, lamentations, and Crys of the wounded for help along the road . . . were enough to pierce a heart of adamant. The gloom and horror . . . was not a little encreased by the impervious darkness occasioned by the close shade of thick woods."[44] Braddock died some days later, on the road back to Fort Cumberland. The journal of a British soldier, batman to Captain Robert Cholmley, recounts his funeral: "Munday July ye 14. Early in the Morning we marched and after we had got a little distance from our old ground we halted till their was a grave dugg'd for the genll, where we Buried him in two Blankits in the high Road that was cut for the Wagons, [so] that all the Wagons might March over him and the Army [as well] to hinder any suspicion of the French Indiens. For if they thought he was Buried their, they would take him up and Scalp him."[45] The simple, anonymous funeral was hardly fitting for a general but was meant to safeguard both the corpse and the participants from Indian attack. The burial may also have carried some symbolic dishonor: Braddock had not covered himself in glory in the actions leading up to his death. While interpretations of dishonor must remain speculative, it is clear that Washington's presence at the funeral—he gave the funeral oration in place of the wounded chaplain—has significantly changed the event's meaning in retrospect.[46] In total, British losses from the operation came to 456 dead and 421 wounded, with the French and their allies suffering just 23 dead and 16 wounded. At the end of July, the remains of Braddock's force made a humiliating withdrawal to winter quarters in Pennsylvania.[47]

On July 11, word came to Fort Cumberland of the attacks suffered by Braddock. Charlotte Brown was among those who heard the news:

> [A]ll of us greatly alarm'd, a Boy came from the Camp and said that the General was kill'd 4 Miles from the French Fort and that almost all S'r Peter Hackets Regiment is cut off by a Party of French and Indians who were behind Trees. Dunbars Regiment was in the rear so that they lost but few Men it is not possible to describe the Distraction of the poor Women for their Husbands. I pack'd up my Things to send for we expected the Indians every Hour my Brother desired me to leave the Fort but I am resolv'd not to go but to share my Fate with him.[48]

The colonial press framed Braddock's Defeat more as a British failure than a French victory.[49] The news seems to have arrived in London six weeks later, on August 23. On September 4, James Wolfe wrote to his father from Southampton: "The accounts of Mr. Braddock's defeat are not yet clear enough to form a right judgment of the cause of it, but I do myself believe that the cowardice and ill-behaviour of the men far exceeded the ignorance of the chief, who, though not a master of the difficult art of war, was yet a man of sense and courage."[50] The *Berlinische Nachrichten* published news of Braddock's Defeat on September 4, citing a report published in London on August 26.[51] The paper carried another report on Saturday, September 6, this time citing news coming from The Hague on August 29. On Tuesday, September 9, it published a detailed account from Wills Creek, dated July 10.[52] The news from London was published in Vienna in the *Wienerisches Diarium* on September 10, about a week after the first Berlin report; the Viennese newspaper also printed a list of officers killed and wounded.[53] There is no great difference in the tone of the reports from Vienna and Berlin, although published on different dates. For the moment, peace still reigned in Europe.

As early as August 4, 1755, Frederick II wrote to Field Marshal Johann von Lehwaldt (1685–1768) in Königsberg: "After the rupture which has taken place between the English and French in America, war in Europe between France and England is now unavoidable, beyond all doubt, and since matters are somewhat confusing, I find it necessary to warn you, so that you may be somewhat on your guard over there. My will is therefore that no officer of regiments stationed in Prussia should be outside the province, and none shall have leave of absence."[54]

Frederick's allusion to the "confusing" nature of events was no exaggeration. Significantly, Austria clearly sought to disavow any connection with the situation overseas. Hence, Count Kaunitz made this argument at a ministerial conference on September 24, 1755: "On the one hand, the court here cannot in any way be expected to engage the question as to which power in America began these events, or to stand judge over them or to participate in them. On the other hand, Your Majesty has remained entirely peaceful toward the Most Christian King [of France] and inasmuch has given assurance that Your Majesty has no intention of spreading the flames of war in Europe."[55] On November 24, 1755, Mühlenberg wrote from Providence to Pastor Theophilus Arnold Krome (1696–1758) in Einbeck, telling him about the coming North American war: "The New England troops that invaded Chinecto in Nova Scotia were more fortunate than those of General Braddock, for they wrested several forts from the French. The third army, under General Major Johnson, that was on its way to the French Fort Crown Point, near Lac Sacrament, was fiercely attacked by a French army under the command of Baron von Dieskau, but it defended itself bravely, put the French to flight and captured General von Dieskau and a few eminent officers."[56] Mühlenberg even saw the naval situation as favoring the British: "Our fleet at sea between Nova Scotia and Cape Breton has also been somewhat fortunate, taking several warships and supply ships from the French. This is the present state of affairs in North America, which to all appearances is becoming a theater of war."[57]

The War in the Forests

The official declarations of war in May and June 1756 cleared the way for a realignment of power in North America. France was seeking, at the very least, to assert its possession of American colonies; for the British, the war offered a chance to be rid of their hated rivals at last.[58] The previous year the British had begun a form of ethnic cleansing in the territory of Akadie, driving French-speaking people out of parts of present-day Nova Scotia, New Brunswick, Maine, and Quebec. Between August 1755 and July 1764, the British deported between six thousand and twelve thousand Acadians to other colonies and to France. Many died as a result, in a series of events that came to be remembered as the Grande Dérangement.[59] A large group settled in New Orleans, where the Acadians eventually became known as Cajuns.

Perhaps even more than in Europe, the North American war was intensified by sectarian divisions—in this case, between French Catholics and British Protestants. But there were some Protestant denominations that reacted with ambivalence to the war. The Quakers remained largely pacifist. For Native Americans, the war became a struggle for survival; no European alliance would ever offer the Indigenous population a permanent guarantee of security. The Delaware, Shawnee, and Mohawk first made agreements with the British, but after 1758, they increasingly also looked to the French. A statement by Shingas, the Delaware chief, has been passed down indirectly through a report by Charles Stuart, a prisoner of the tribe for several years:

> Riseing up From his seat with Appearance of Deep Concern on his Countenance he address'd his Prisoners with Great Solemnity, Telling them that he was sorry For what had happened Between them and the English But that the English and not the Indians were the Cause of the Present War [. . .] Gen Braddock said that no Savage Should

inherit the Land [. . .]. After w'ch Shingas Proceeded to Say that they did not want to Carry on the War against the English and were now willing again To make Peace with them and restore all their Captives and Everything Else they had from them Provided the English wou'd Comply with the Following Proposals.[60]

Shingas's specific suggestions shed light on the interests of the Delaware. He proposed that the British send five men and their families to live and work with the Native Americans, who would take responsibility for their sustenance. The men would work making gunpowder and smelting lead out of ore. The Natives would help with developing mines for lead and other metals and would make firearms, with one man responsible for making iron. Together the two groups would promote weaving and other trades and live in love and friendship, becoming one people. Intermarriage would not be insisted on. Under these conditions, Native Americans were quite ready to make peace.

For Native Americans, going to war was an individual decision. Personal self-defense in moments of danger was seen as entirely normal. But this perspective was diametrically opposed to the "battle culture of forbearance" characteristic of well-drilled European infantry of the line.[61] The purpose of military action was also very different for Native Americans. Europeans tended always to be concerned with controlling space—possessing battlefields, capturing forts, securing supply lines. Native Americans aimed to capture booty, scalps, and prisoners while minimizing losses.[62] Mühlenberg describes the difference: "There is a peculiar manner of fighting here in America, which nobody understands better than the savages born here, known as Indians, and native-born New Englanders. Regular troops sent out to us from Old England are good enough at capturing and defending fortresses, but cannot match the barbarians in the deserts and forests."[63] In general, however, European observers misunderstood and disparaged Native American ways of waging war. In his memoir, the French soldier Charles "Sweetheart" Bonin reports that it was said of the Iroquois: "They arrive like foxes, attack like hares, and flee like birds."[64] Bonin took part in the 1754 Ohio Valley expedition led by Captain Michel-Jean-Hugues Péan (1723–1782) and chronicled the death of Jumonville, as well as Braddock's battles on the Monongahela.[65] European attitudes toward the "barbarians" are typified by those of George Schneider (1728–1796), a Hessian mercenary serving with the British.

Of the population around Fort Saratoga, he wrote: "The Savages or Indian People are strong, well-grown Men, black-brown in color and, like the Moors and the Tartar, a born bloodhound. These same people also cut off the Lobe of the ear, until only a little remains, and weave an iron or silver Trace around it. In their nose, it is usual for them to wear a silver Ring or a piece of Silver cut with figures. Around the arm or at the elbow they commonly wear a broad silver band, on which is Engrav'd the Name of their Nation and the deeds of its Heroes."[66] In Schneider's description, comparisons with other "alien" populations go hand in hand with typical descriptions of physiognomy and adornment, in an account comparable to contemporary Prussian and Saxon descriptions of Cossacks.[67] The war facilitated these encounters between people of different nationalities, skin colors, and religious denominations. Such meetings, whether voluntary or not, were a constant spur to mutual comparison. In other words, the war increased the likelihood of encounters, and these concrete instances then entered into a dialectical, mutually reinforcing relation with emerging practices of systematic comparative observation.

Irregular operations were the main form of combat in the North American theater (figure 2.1).[68] Europeans were constantly challenged to adapt their customary ways of fighting. Since 1722, the standard British infantry weapon had been the Brown Bess, a muzzle-loading flintlock rifle with low accuracy, available in a variety of models (referred to as patterns).[69] By 1756, British soldiers could use the Long Land Pattern musket, 159 centimeters (about 63 inches) in length, which came in several variants, first produced in 1730, 1742, and 1748. There was a major difference between Indian and European shooting techniques. Native Americans mainly used guns as hunting weapons, carving notches in them to better their aim. As hunters, they were used to hiding and approaching by stealth; the British referred to these tactics as "the sculking way of war."[70] On the European mainland, Jägerkorps (Hunter corps), equipped with rifle-barreled guns, were also regarded as particularly dangerous sharpshooters.[71] The eighteenth-century social logic prevailing in Europe's "cabinet wars" did not foresee that eventually hunter-soldiers would, like Native Americans, begin picking off enemy officers, who were clearly visible on horseback in their bright uniforms.[72]

A steady stream of horrifying reports allowed European soldiers to maintain their distance, at least discursively, from the "alien" practices of violence ascribed to Native Americans. In a letter of February 1, 1758, Mühlenberg recalled the battle for Fort Duquesne in 1755:

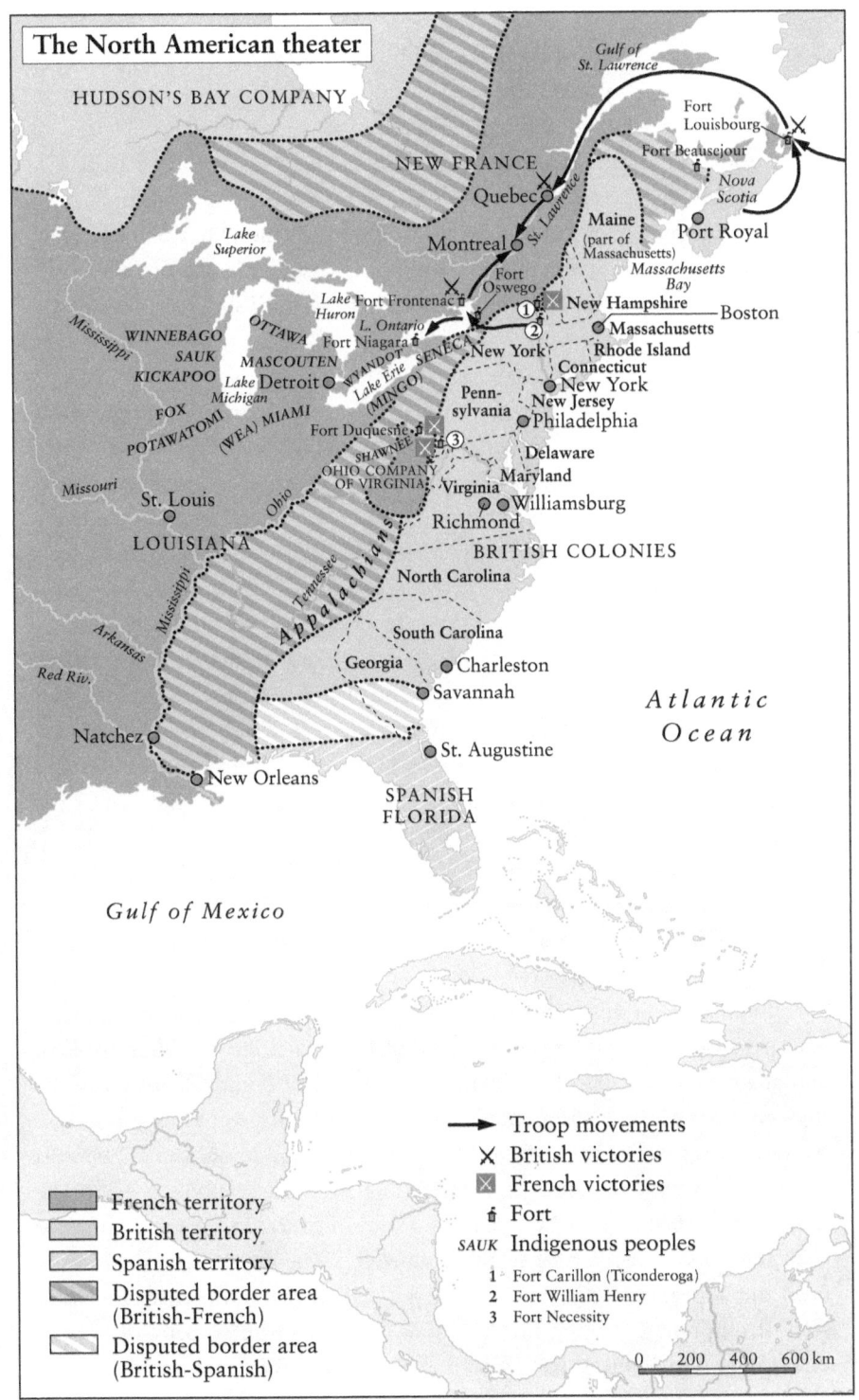

Figure 2.1 The North American theater.
© Peter Palm, Berlin/Germany.

> My neighbor watched the battle with his own eyes, in broad daylight. As a prisoner, he could only stand by and watch while the savages carried a buxom and attractive English woman, who was a lady of pleasure in the English camp, from the fort on horseback. They stripped her naked, tied her to a tree, lit a fire nearby, made a circle around her and danced around the tree. Then, one after the other, They cut a piece from the muscular parts of her living body, roasted it in the fire and ate it with great delight. They continued to do so until she was gradually consumed.[73]

Mühlenberg's anecdote weaves together manifold moral transgressions, combining several kinds of alterity: prostitution, nudity, and "pagan" dance, not to mention cannibalism.[74] Along with allegations of cannibalism, images of scalping were particularly disturbing.[75] Schneider, the Hessian mercenary, describes an ambush near Albany in June 1757: "In the Month of June there was another Skirmish, and 15 Men were scalbed, two of whom were still alive for a part of it. Among these, several of the Bodies were pitifully Mutilated. Some of their Heads had been hacked in, others were hacked on the body some 9 or 10 times, one had his Heart hacked out, and was beaten therewith around the mouth, and afterward they ate it quite raw, out of pure malice."[76] In fact, it had been the British who had put bounties on scalps, as shown by a list included in the declaration of war against the Delaware, signed on April 14, 1756, by Robert Hunter Morris (1700–1764), deputy governor of Pennsylvania. This offered 150 Spanish dollars for Native American prisoners over twelve, male or female; 130 dollars for a Native male scalp; 50 dollars for a Native female scalp; and 130 dollars for living Native prisoners under twelve.[77]

The population of the colonies soon became familiar with Native American ways of fighting. The French seem to have been more willing to learn and adapt than the British, evidenced by the many French-language writings on how to fight "la petite guerre."[78] The British colonists' response to Indigenous tactics took the form of the *ranger*, an autonomous guerrilla warrior. Although ranger-type soldiers had been successfully used in the Wars of the Spanish and Austrian Successions, it took quite some time for their role to stabilize and be institutionalized.[79] The situation changed only with the appearance of Robert Rogers (1731–1795), the commander of a sixty-strong unit known as His Majesty's Independent Company of American Rangers, or Rogers' Rangers. In 1756, Rogers' Rangers received orders to collect information, identify land routes, and "distress the French and their allies by sacking, burning and destroying their houses, barns, barracks, canoes, battos [. . .] and to way-lay, attack, and destroying their convoys of provisions by land and water."[80] The unit was highly successful, gaining a reputation of near legendary proportions. Nonetheless, regular commanders often continued to view ranger units, wrongly, as lazy, undisciplined criminal bands.[81] As a result, most ranger formations were disbanded at the end of the war.[82]

In general, London preferred to use local soldiers rather than British troops of the line. As Newcastle put it in 1755: "I have often heard from well-informed people that operations in these countries are best carried out by troops from within the country itself; these can best be used for this purpose and are best accustomed to the nature of this service."[83] He added that "regular troops should not be puff'd up." Instead, "Indians should be deployed if possible, and the Americans must take care of our business." American forces were incorrectly seen as something more akin to a people's army than part of Britain's "standing mercenary army." One parliamentarian described the New Englanders, unlike mercenary soldiers, as being closer to those who fought at Crecy and Poitiers in the Hundred Years' War.[84] As in Europe, local American formations struggled with the problem of desertion.[85] On this question, newspapers are an important source, since they regularly published "wanted profiles" with details of wanted deserters.[86] A particular feature of this phenomenon in North America was that deserters had the option of joining with Indian tribes to evade capture, as well as the possibility of defecting to European forces on the enemy side.[87]

The political culture of the colonies did not make a unified approach any easier. Mühlenberg makes a comparison with conflicts with the Ottomans in Europe: "The English Provinces have been put on alert, but their preparations are so lengthy, slow and lethargic that it seems more difficult than [having] the Roman Imperial Cities muster their common troops for a war against the Turks. At times, the governors and assemblies in our far-flung American provinces consider, deliberate and dispute for many months and years before reaching some conclusion and mobilizing some forces for defense."[88] Both in Europe and in the colonies, images of "Turks" and "American Indians" could function in either direction. Attacks in Europe were described as being like those of Native Americans in North America, but conversely, images of Muslims and Ottomans as "savages" helped form impressions of Native Americans.[89]

European soldiers' views of North America were dominated by the sheer fertility of the colonies on the Atlantic coast. Schneider, the Hessian mercenary, found the country around New York "highly Agreeable, in that it is blessed with beautiful fruit Gardens and Fruit under cultivation. We saw that the people lived in Abundance." He liked Philadelphia even better: "It is an entirely flat Land, highly cultivated with fruit gardens and land planted with Fruits. The city is larger than New York and is laid out like Manheim in the Palatinate. Most of its inhabitants are German."[90] There were a large number of German settlers in the "English" colonies—above all, in Pennsylvania but also in New York, Maryland, Virginia, and North and South Carolina, as well as the New England colonies.[91] The fact that some Germans could speak French was enough to make them suspicious in the eyes of many British settlers. An additional factor was the pacifism of many Protestant sects, which made it difficult to mobilize their German adherents for military operations. But attitudes gradually changed once fighting with the tribes began. Germans raised their own units or joined the Royal American Regiment. This has led some historians to identify a gradual Americanization of Germans in the colonies, with more and more making the British cause their own, which, in turn, eased their acceptance within colonial society. But this assimilation process could also mean cutting off contacts with the Old World.[92] These processes of disentanglement continued in parallel with intercontinental entanglements associated with the war.

The Westminster Convention and the Diplomatic Revolution

In Europe, opposing sides were beginning to cohere as the various actors began preparations for war. The Westminster Convention, agreed to by Britain and Prussia on January 16, 1756, was a treaty of neutrality and mutual security guarantees.[93] The first report about the treaty in the *Berlinische Nachrichten*, published on February 5, 1756, suggested that the kings of Prussia and Great Britain, "after full consideration," had agreed on a Convention of Neutrality, since the "unrest already existing for some time in America" meant "the resulting fires of war could ultimately even touch the lands of Europe."[94] The treaty claimed that its objective was to preserve peace in Germany. The second clause of the Convention of Neutrality was vital, stating that in the event of "foreign powers, under whatsoever pretext, march[ing] troops into Germany," the two nations would "combine their powers" to oppose the invasion.[95]

Initial signs seemed to point away from any swift British deployment to the continent. In fact, in the winter of 1755, there were growing British fears of a French invasion. On October 24, 1755, James Wolfe wrote to his mother: "I am something at a loss to conjecture whether this is a real or a political invasion."[96] Over six months later he regarded his early fears as almost ridiculous: "But what makes me laugh is our extravagant fears of an invasion at a time when it is absolutely absurd and almost impossible, unless we are to assume that the Danish fleet will come out of the Baltic on purpose to escort 10 or 12 French battalions to England."[97]

Preparations to defend against invasion included deploying thousands of Hanoverian and Hessian soldiers in southern England in May 1756. Jeffrey Amherst, later to command British forces in North America, was given responsibility for transporting Hessian subsidy troops to England and was present at their embarkation from the port of Stade, on the north coast of Germany.[98] The Hessians included a young ensign named Georg Ernst von und zu Gilsa (1740–1798). Like Amherst, he kept an extensive diary with his observations on his journey across England, including the sights of London.

At times, Gilsa's report makes the operations of "German" troops sound like an extended holiday, but the wider political ramifications were far less light-hearted.[99] One important incident took place on September 13, 1756, an event minor in itself but with substantial consequences.[100] In what became known as the Maidstone Affair, a Hanoverian soldier was accused of stealing two handkerchiefs from a shop in Maidstone, Kent. The soldier, apparently named Christoph Wilhelm Schröder, left no written testimony of his own.[101] He was accused of visiting a shop owned by Christopher Harris, where he selected eight good-quality handkerchiefs but paid for only six before leaving the premises. The shopkeeper accused Harris of theft, and he was brought before the local magistrate. Georg Ludwig Graf von Kielmannsegg (1705–1785), commander of the Hanoverian regiment, was outraged by the arrest of one of his men and insisted he had military jurisdiction over the case. Kielmannsegg sought assistance from Lord Holdernesse (1718–1778), secretary of state for the Northern Department, and Schröder was handed over to his regiment. The incident was quickly taken up by the press, which produced its own steady flow of reports and commentary. Pitt the Elder saw a chance to boost his own political ambitions and insisted that the controversy be addressed at the highest political levels. Holdernesse soon disappeared off the political map.

But why did the case prompt such public indignation in Britain? It seems that the presence of Hanoverian and Hessian troops touched off a persistent British distrust of standing armies. Moreover, these were foreign troops—and Germans at that. In this way, a minor dispute over military versus civil jurisdiction, a common occurrence across Europe at the time, gave rise to exaggerated scenarios of national peril.[102] The dispute was also framed as "the country versus the court," pitting rural rights against an unpopular Hanoverian monarch, British freedom against attempts to oppress it, and British masculinity against German effeminacy.[103] The authentic British patriot, a man of the people, was contrasted with Hanoverian soldiers, with their moustaches, fine clothes, and pigtails, in images that associated them with broader questions of militias and mercenaries (figure 2.2).[104]

Condemnations of foreign soldiery managed to reconcile apparent contradictions, with the Germans depicted as both effeminate and dangerously violent. There was no pro-Hanoverian camp as such, but some in the press

Figure 2.2 Law for the Out-Laws. Etching published by Matthew Darley and George Edwards (London, 1756).
© The Trustees of the British Museum/Art Resource, New York.

called for some moderation of criticisms of German forces. People should not, they suggested, "make an elephant of a fly" or show ingratitude to soldiers who had come to defend Britain. Nor should the matter be turned to party political advantage.[105] It was pointed out the Hanoverians were subsidy troops rather than amoral "mercenaries." But the loudest voices belonged to "patriots" claiming to speak on behalf of the country. Little is known about Schröder's ultimate fate. Some sources suggest he was sentenced to run the gauntlet three times and then issued a dishonorable discharge.[106] The "Germans" left England in May 1757, shipped back to Stade, where they were incorporated into the Duke of Cumberland's observation army.[107]

On May 1, 1756, France and Austria signed the Treaty of Versailles, a new defensive alliance, which historians have come to call the Diplomatic Revolution, a radical shift after centuries of Habsburg-French confrontation, either as tacit rivals or as open enemies.[108] The surprising diplomatic turn was masterminded by Count Kaunitz, the Austrian chancellor. He had been intent on recovering Silesia since the end of the War of the Austrian Succession in 1748 and was convinced that there would, sooner or later, be another war with Prussia. In early September 1755, Georg Adam Graf von Starhemberg (1724–1807), the Austrian ambassador, had opened secret negotiations in Paris, although at first the French refused to countenance breaking with Prussia.[109] Matters changed when the Anglo-Prussian Treaty of Westminster was agreed to, marking a radical change in the European constellation of powers. Previously the British had regarded Prussia, not France, as the greatest threat to Hanover. Anglo-Prussian rapprochement ushered in a complete reversal of antagonisms.[110] The British seem to have realized only quite late in the day that their new position would mean they would also have to break with Austria. For its part, Austria had no interest in a conflict with Hanover and wanted to either keep its imperial territories out of its conflict with Prussia or possibly secure their formal neutrality. However, Britain had made an offer of cooperation to Russia, including subsidy payments, and this had raised serious concerns in Vienna, encouraging the Austrian turn to France. In this way, the Westminster Convention inevitably had serious consequences for British-Austrian relations. The Franco-Austrian nonaggression pact had become a close alliance. Viewed through the lens of religion, the move may have seemed a long-planned one, but, in fact, it was the product of very recent diplomatic dynamics. France had no aggressive intent toward Prussia, but the Westminster Convention so enraged Paris that it concluded a defensive treaty with Austria, the aforementioned Treaty of

Versailles, an agreement that, as the historian Albert von Broglie (1821–1901) once put it, "had a smell of gunpowder about it."[111] The St. Petersburg Convention, agreed to by Britain and Russia in 1755, meant that Britain paid subsidies to maintain Russian troops along the border with East Prussia. But the convention had not yet been ratified and was revoked by the British in 1756, angering Tsarina Elizabeth and prompting her to join the anti-Prussia coalition in April of that year. This diplomatic maneuvering left Frederick II in dire straits. He wrote to Maria Theresa, requesting an Austrian statement clearly ruling out an attack on Prussia but received a very vague response. True to his maxim *praevenire quam praeveniri* (better to anticipate danger than be taken by surprise), he devised a plan for a preemptive strike against his adversaries' new alliance.[112] But before he could put this plan into practice, the first shots of the European war rang out elsewhere, far to the south.

Menorca Is Lost, and an Admiral Must Die

On April 21, 1756, fourteen thousand French soldiers landed at Ciudadela, the former capital of Menorca. In 1708, the Balearic island had been conquered by the British in the War of the Spanish Succession, with its capture later recognized in the Peace of Utrecht in 1713.[113] In 1722, the island's capital had been moved to the port of Maó (Mahón in Spanish), about thirty miles from where the French forces landed under the command of Louis François Armand de Vignerot du Plessis, third Duc de Richelieu and the Marshal of France (1696–1788). An arduous overland march brought the French to the plateau above Mahón, where they encamped and began bombarding the city on May 9. In technical terms, the siege was extremely difficult, since Fort St. Philip, the capital's defensive fortress, was built on bedrock, and the besieging force had to hack approach trenches out of bare rock. This problem would recur in similar operations outside Europe. On April 6, a fleet of ten British ships commanded by Admiral John Byng (1704–1757) was sent to relieve Mahón. Reaching Gibraltar on May 2, the British fleet quickly moved on to Menorca and by May 18 was positioned off the island. Byng had planned to take on seven hundred reinforcements at Gibraltar, but Thomas Fowke (1690–1765), Gibraltar's commander, refused him permission to do so, arguing that it would leave his own fortress too weak to defend. In what would prove a fatal error, Byng accepted Fowke's argument. Positioned off Menorca, Byng's fleet was reinforced by three ships from the

Mediterranean squadron, led by George Edgecumbe (1720–1795). On May 20, a naval battle began, which was more or less a stalemate in terms of actual losses, although Byng claimed it as a victory. Victory or not, Byng failed to carry out his mission. Unwilling to risk his fleet, he failed to communicate with the besieged British garrison at Máhon and landed neither troops nor materiel on the island.[114] He then commanded his ships to return to Gibraltar, where they docked on June 19 after a slow voyage, several days after the arrival of four British ships of the line under Rear Admiral Thomas Brodrick (1704–1769). On July 3, another British warship arrived, the *Antelope*, with Admiral Edward Hawke (1705–1781) on board, who relieved Byng, Fowke, and Vice Admiral Temple West (1713–1757) of their commands.

At eighty-four, Major General William Blakeney, the commander of the British fortress, was advanced in years, but the fortress had great advantages in both physical location and logistical organization. It boasted a garrison of three thousand men, organized in four regiments, equipped with over 240 cannons and 81mortars. On June 8, by contrast, the besieging French had just 41 guns and 18 mortars; Richelieu had to be as sparing with resources as the British. Ultimately, an assault seemed the only quick way to capture the fortress, since the British fleet might return at any moment.

The assault began at ten o'clock on the night of June 27. The French failed to take the fortress and suffered heavy losses, with around one thousand dead and eight hundred wounded. The situation seemed desperate, and the next morning Richelieu offered a ceasefire and honorable terms for the surrender of the fortress. Blakeney and his exhausted men accepted. Three weeks later Admiral Hawke's seventeen warships at last appeared off Mahón, at which point the French fleet, commanded by La Galissonière, immediately withdrew to Toulon. The loss of Menorca for the duration of the war was not strategically significant for the British. Italy was not a theater of war, so the island was not needed to harass Spanish troop movements. Moreover, the British Mediterranean fleet retained overall naval supremacy—not least because of its continued possession of Gibraltar, a key stronghold. Nonetheless, the loss of Menorca had highly significant political consequences in Britain. The public was outraged. Byng was arrested upon his arrival at Spithead on July 26, supposedly to protect him from the mob.

The unfortunate admiral was doomed. France had not made important strategic gains at Menorca, but the quick victory gave Paris early negotiating capital for any later peace talks. Nor should the boost to French patriotic mobilization be underestimated. Menorca became a byword for French military success and seemed to highlight the vulnerability of the supposedly all-powerful British Navy.[115] Byng was court-martialed and sentenced to death. On March 14, 1757, he was shot by a firing party on the deck of his flagship, the *Monarch*.[116] Byng's defeat had prompted a full-scale media campaign, which succeeded in mobilizing public opinion against him. Caricatures were published and his effigy burned in the streets.[117] In military and political circles, however, the king's insistence on execution was seen as disproportionate. Voltaire gave the episode literary posterity in *Candide*, which includes this much-quoted sentence: "In this country it is useful from time to time to kill one admiral in order to encourage the others."[118]

The Black Hole of Propaganda: Calcutta, June 1756

Several months previously, latent conflicts on the Indian subcontinent had escalated. Two weeks before Frederick's troops marched into Saxony, news arrived in Europe of the outbreak of Franco-British hostilities in southern India. On August 15, 1756, the merchant Ananda Ranga Pillai noted the arrival of news from the Dutch base at Mocha in his diary: "The chief of the Dutch factory at Mocha received news that war had been declared between England and France on February 23. He informed the French of it, and added that M. St. Georges, the Captain of the King's squadron, had left France with twelve men-of-war, before the declaration of war, and M. Dupleix with a few ships after it."[119]

In this way, India became another theater of war, albeit one given far fewer resources and much less attention than those on either side of the Atlantic. By the middle of the eighteenth century, several European trading settlements had been established on the coasts of India—at first mostly by the Dutch and Portuguese and later by the French and British. By the time of the Seven Years' War, there were British settlements at Bombay on the west coast, Fort St. George in Madras on the east coast, and Fort William in Calcutta on the Bay of Bengal. To the southeast was Fort St. David in Cuddalore, on what was known as the Carnatic coast. Here the French and British coexisted in particularly close proximity, with Pondicherry and Fort St. David almost within sight of one another. The Carnatic region, which stretched 800 kilometers (about 498 miles) from north to south and 130 kilometers (about 81 miles) inland, offered a relatively congenial theater of war for both sides (figure 2.3).[120] It lacked navigable rivers but had a road

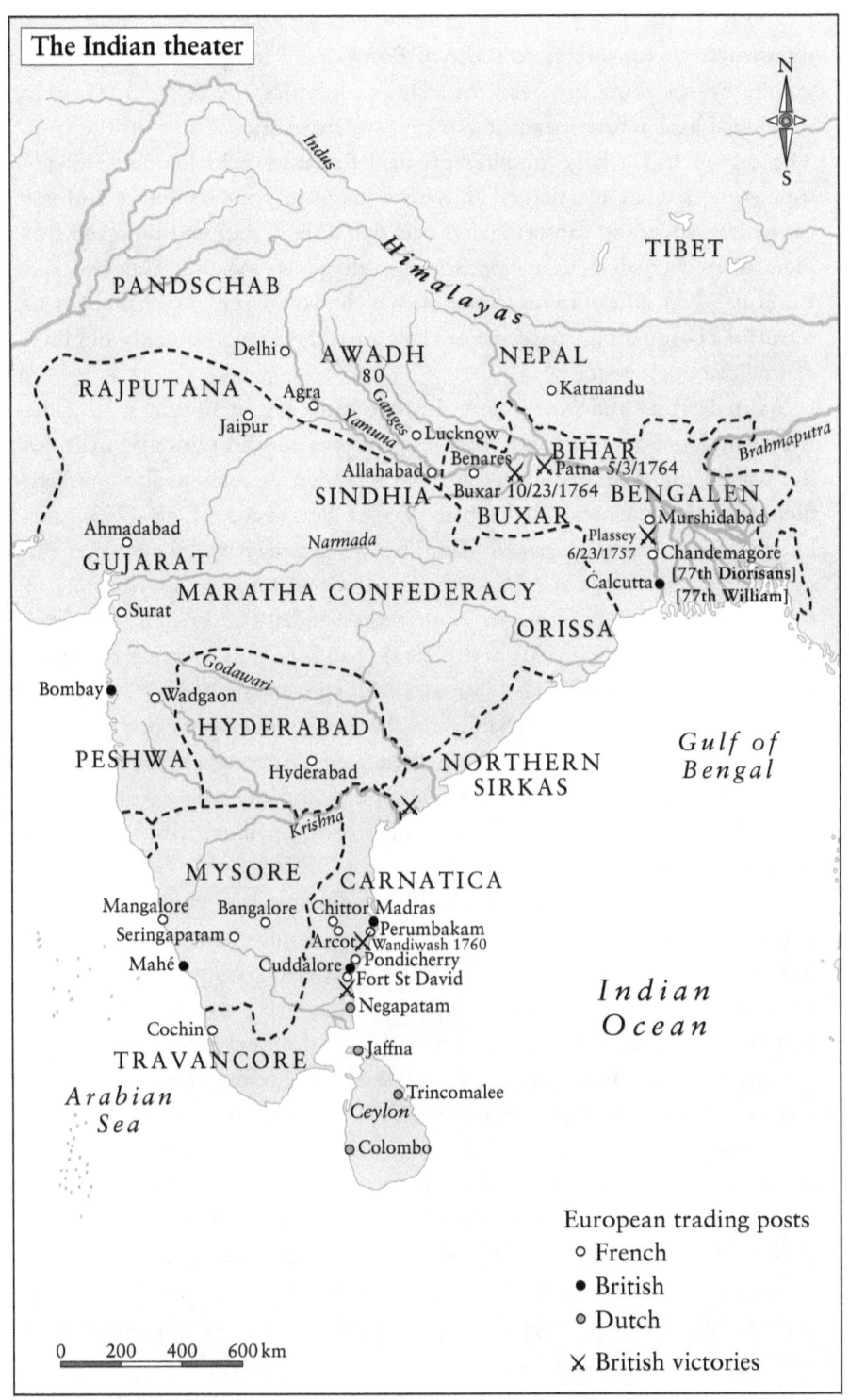

Figure 2.3 The Indian theater.
© Peter Palm, Berlin/Germany.

infrastructure comparable to those of Europe, and troops could be moved rapidly by sea along the coast. In terms of logistics, the region's relatively developed agriculture meant it was possible for armies to live off the land. The region had a large number of small fortresses, which offered disadvantages as well as advantages: They were often in poor condition and not easily defensible, and capturing and occupying them required time and soldiers. Moreover, all three major British settlements—Madras, Calcutta, and Bombay—had autonomous councils, which would present challenges in terms of coordinating strategy. For their part, the French quickly imposed centralized governance.[121]

As in Europe and North America, the outbreak of hostilities in India is best understood against the backdrop of previous hostilities.[122] In India, the War of the Austrian Succession had included various smaller conflicts, including the Carnatic-Hyderabad War of Succession (1748–1753), also known as the Second Carnatic War. This was a proxy war, focused on the struggle among rival claimants to become *subedar* (provincial governor) of the Deccan, a large territory in south-central India. The French supported Muzaffar Jang (c. 1715–1751) and Chanda Sahib (d. 1752), while the British backed Nasir Jung (1712–1750) and Muhammad Ali Khan (1717–1795). The French-backed Chanda Sahib was the early winner, but both sides also strengthened their defenses, with the French constructing a fortress at Arcot and the British building one at Trichinopoly. Both locations would suffer sieges during the Seven Years' War, which took up much time as well as substantial resources.

As a rule, war was unpopular with European trading companies, since it gave rise to unnecessary costs, which ultimately had to be solicited from company headquarters in Europe. European companies may have sometimes behaved like small states, but they were not actually states; nowhere was this difference clearer than on the question of war debts. Companies had obligations to shareholders, including the annual payment of dividends. They could not afford to carry debt on the scale of the European monarchies, so any wars they fought had to be waged off the land, financed using local resources. Nonetheless, the leaders of companies and trading outposts—figures like Joseph François Dupleix (1697–1763) and Robert Clive (1725–1774)—continued to wage war, driven by a desire for territorial expansion, which could, in turn, increase tax revenues. For this reason, tax privileges were the crux of contested sovereignty in India.

Both European and Indian rulers sought to reduce military costs by using foreign mercenaries, either hiring them for their own forces or renting them out to other actors. Indian princes also made use of European mercenaries. In doing so, they developed closer relations with the British and the French but also became more dependent on them. For their part, the Europeans filled the ranks of their armies with *sepoys*, a word derived from the Persian *sepahi*, meaning "soldier."[123] From the late 1740s on, the proportion of sepoys in the British armed forces grew rapidly. Fort St. David had more than three thousand Indian soldiers, while a unit of some two thousand sepoys was raised at Bombay, introducing sepoy recruitment to India's east coast regions. By 1756, the number of sepoys in the Carnatic had risen to around ten thousand, compared with two thousand European soldiers. Soon sepoys were also present in northern Bengal, where around two thousand Indian soldiers saw British service during the Seven Years' War.

By 1744, Anglo-French rivalries in India had escalated, prompting the French to capture Madras in 1746. British counteroffensives—at Pondicherry, Mahé on the west coast, and Chandannagar near Calcutta—coincided with the Peace of Aachen in 1748, a treaty that restored the prewar territorial status quo in India. However, this was not accompanied by disarmament, and both the French and the British East India Companies continued to maintain several thousand men under arms. The French-backed Chanda Sahib was unable to hold out in the conflict over the Hyderabad succession and was overthrown in what was, among other things, Robert Clive's first successful military engagement as a commander of the British East India Company (BEIC). An armistice was agreed to between the two companies at Pondicherry in 1754, but this proved a somewhat farcical "conclusion" to the conflict, since the British immediately sent out more troops from Europe, troops that might better have been sent to protect Electoral Hanover. Significantly, Paris did not ratify the Indian armistice.[124] Moreover, another factor seemed to point to war: Increasingly large amounts of saltpeter, the main component of gunpowder, were now flowing from South Asia to London.[125]

Even more than early modern Europe, India was a place of permanent dynastic quarrels and wars of succession. Primogeniture was not as firmly established as in Europe, and many potential royal successions were contested; rulers often had several wives, not to mention half-brothers, who were often reluctant to accept a rival's succession.[126] There were also constant external threats: Afghans in the north and the much-feared Maratha horsemen in the northwest. In the southwest, the warlord Haidar Ali Khan (1720–1782), the ruler of Mysore, had the best-organized Indian army of the time at his disposal. Relations between the BEIC and the rulers of Bengal took a dramatic turn in 1756 with the death of Nawab Alivardi Khan (1671–1756).[127] The young Siraj-ud-Daulah (1733–1757) emerged victorious in the struggle for succession as nawab, a ruler whom the older historical literature often describes as an ideal-typical "Oriental despot."[128] By now, economic rivalries between the company and the nawab had intensified, reaching the point of imminent crisis. This escalation was due to the long-standing abuse of the *dustucks*—a form of exemption from customs duties—and, more immediately, to the British actions at Fort William in Calcutta. The British had granted Krishna Das asylum at the fort; Das, a wealthy merchant and the son of the main Dacca tax collector, had already made substantial financial resources available to Siraj-ud-Daulah's rivals. The British had begun to modernize the fortifications in 1755, justifying the work with the possibility of renewed conflict with the French. By now, that conflict was looming.[129]

On May 15, 1756, less than a month after coming to power, the new nawab instructed the governor of Fort William to surrender Krishna Das and stop the expansion of the facilities. His request was ignored, and the messenger who delivered the letter was unceremoniously ejected from the fortress. On May 28, the nawab wrote another letter, this time to the ambassador in Calcutta: "It has been my design to level the English fortifications raised within my jurisdiction on account of their great strength. . . . If the English are contented to remain in my country they must submit to have their fort razed, their ditch filled up, and trade upon the same terms they did in the time of the Nabob Jaffeir Cawm."[130] A further exchange of letters followed, but no solution was reached. In early June, the nawab turned to force. A military campaign was launched, initially aimed at the British "factory" at Torei Kasimbazar (Cossimbazar). The factory had been the first BEIC settlement, established in 1658, close to Murshidabad, seat of the nawabs of Bengal. Now it was forced to submit to Siraj-ud-Daulah's powerful army of thirty thousand.[131] The French also maintained a trading post in the region at Kasimbazar, led by Jean Law de Lauriston (1719–1797), a nephew of the Scottish economist John Law. The younger Law's extensive *Mémoire* is among the most important chronicles of events in Bengal from a French perspective.[132]

At Fort William, the British condescendingly ignored Siraj-ud-Daulah's demands that they stop new fortifications, abide by trade restrictions, and hand over his political opponent.¹³³ The nawab, who by now had a force of 50,000 men, proceeded to attack the fort, which was garrisoned by 165 soldiers and 200 armed civilians. The siege lasted several days, during which time Roger Drake, the trading post's incompetent commander, secretly fled. Eventually the fortress fell and was sacked by the Indian forces. They then turned their attention to the city of Calcutta itself, which was captured on June 20, after four days of siege and heavy fighting. The nawab's attacking forces included a European artillery force led by a French renegade.

On the evening of the nawab's capture of Fort William, around seven o'clock, a large group of surviving Europeans had been imprisoned in a small guardroom in the fort. Estimates of the exact number vary between 39 and 146. The room would become known, infamously, as the Black Hole of Calcutta.¹³⁴ From inside the cell, the prisoners begged to be released or given relief, but the door was not opened until six o'clock the following morning, by which time between one-half and two-thirds of the captives were dead. Brijen K. Gupta suggests a death toll of either 18 or 43, with 21 survivors.¹³⁵ The sole contemporary source, a report by the survivor John Zephaniah Holwell (1711–1798), was published in English in 1758, with a German translation printed at Bremen the following year. This claimed 123 dead and 23 survivors.¹³⁶

Historical research has cast serious doubt on the authenticity of Holwell's report.¹³⁷ His text is very much a literary composition, incorporating arcs of tension and moments of suspense. Humiliation is piled on humiliation as the prisoners are stripped and imprisoned in a confined space, where they suffer terribly from heat and thirst, until ultimately the survivors are forced to remove the corpses from the room. "Before they knew the horrors of their situation," the prisoners were driven into the Hole, Holwell reports. "The number that entered this dreadful place was 146," he continues, including a woman, as well as "69 Dutch, English corporals, Soldiers, Moors, Whites, and Portuguese."¹³⁸ Within minutes of being placed in the Hole, the prisoners began to understand their terrible plight. "Within ten minutes after they were locked in, every one fell into a most profuse sweat, which soon brought on an intolerable thirst, that perpetually increased in proportion as the body was drained of its moisture." The prisoners immediately stripped off their clothes, desperately seeking relief from the heat. By Holwell's estimate, there was a surface area of just over two square feet per prisoner.¹³⁹ The first prisoners died when the group attempted to collectively sit down and stand up. Hats filled with water were passed through the window, but this only made things worse, with most of the water spilled as men fought bitterly to drink, giving rise to general uproar.[140] This lasted until around two o'clock in the morning, when things grew quieter. At around five o'clock in the morning, Holwell, who was standing close to a window, led an attempt to ask the viceroy (Siraj-ud-Daulah) to open the prison. But the viceroy hesitated, trying to find out if the group's leaders were still alive. A decision to free them was eventually made, but as the doors were about to be opened, another obstacle appeared: "As the door opened inward, and as the dead were piled up against it, and covered all the rest of the floor, it was impossible to open it by any efforts from without; it was therefore necessary that the dead should be removed by the few that were within, who were become so feeble, that the task, though it was a condition of life, was not performed without the utmost difficulty, and it was twenty minutes after the order came, before the door could be opened."[141] Holwell's account describes the grim scene that followed: "About a quarter after six in the morning, the poor remains of 146 souls, being no more than three and twenty, came out of the Black Hole alive, but in a condition which made it very doubtful whether they would see the morning of the next day. [. . .] The bodies were dragged out of the hole by the soldiers, and thrown promiscuously into the ditch of an unfinished ravelin, which was afterwards filled with earth."[142]

Holwell's account has been subjected to several critical readings and is now generally regarded as an exaggeration. A reenactment attempt, with students taking the place of the prisoners, demonstrated that it was physically impossible to squeeze the supposed number of prisoners into a space of that size. However, verification of Holwell's account is made more difficult by the fact that all thirteen known accounts of the incident can in one way or another be traced back to Holwell's original version. This has led some historians to argue that the entire story should be viewed as fictional, perhaps even as a hoax.[143] However, this does not alter the fact that the Black Hole of Calcutta became a highly effective popular myth, with substantial impact on British images of India and on government policy.[144] In purely phenomenological terms, the incident was not particularly extreme, compared to conditions on slave ships or on European battlefields. However, the narrative successfully condensed multiple layers of meaning and forms of cultural transgression into the story of a single night. First and foremost, from a European point of view, it was an outrage for Indians to use violence against European prisoners and civilians.

Second, cramming together people of very different social backgrounds represented a profound violation of social boundaries. The mixed confinement of gentlemen and common soldiers, not to mention people of different colors, must have been seen as an astonishing affront. The Black Hole of Calcutta myth promoted not only an image of the suffering prisoners but also an image of the decadent Mughal rulers. Thus, Siraj-ud-Daulah is depicted as sleeping, having asked not to be disturbed, while the prisoners are crushed to death. The guards are imagined as cruel thugs, taking delight in watching inmates kill one another for water. But Partha Chatterjee's recent close reading argues that the story is primarily meant to exemplify British self-discipline rather than to provide a straightforward indictment of the nawab and his guards.[145] As one of the few Englishmen in the cell, Holwell possesses an iron self-discipline that secures his survival. It is he who ultimately negotiates release with the nawab. Later this sense of moral superiority over Indians would underpin the ideology of a British "civilizing mission" on the subcontinent. The incident became one of the British Empire's main colonial *lieux de mémoire*, with its highly ambivalent images capable of interpretation in many ways. In the immediate aftermath, with the nawab's army's now openly threatening the British, the Black Hole of Calcutta story gave additional legitimation for taking Bengal by force, even if this aim was never made explicit.[146]

When the British retook Calcutta in January 1757, they immediately began strengthening its fortifications.[147] With the military situation now much changed, they were soon able to make aggressive demands of the nawab. A draft treaty they drew up on February 6 makes the following claims: "That we have Liberty to fortifye Calcutta in such manner as we may think proper and that our Bounds do extend the Whole Circle of the ditch dug upon the Invasion of the Morrattoes. That we be put in possession of the Thirty eight Villages Granted by the Phirmaund and be allowed to govern the same upon the Terms there expressed. Lastly That the Nabob do not erect any Forts or Fortifications below Calcutta within a Mile of the River Side, and that such as are now remaining be destroyed."[148] The BEIC, under Robert Clive's leadership, began construction of a new fort in Calcutta in 1758, but it was not finished until 1781. Ironically, this structure never saw a shot fired in anger during its entire existence.

Clive returned to Madras on May 25, 1756, now promoted to lieutenant colonel. In civilian terms, he was second-in-command, below the governor of Madras. By now, the BEIC Council in Madras was planning new operations against French forces, led by Marquis Charles de Bussy-Castelnau (1718–1785). Bussy was then in the Deccan plateau, undertaking a show of force against Salabat Jung (1718–1763), who had threatened to expel the French from his territories. The events that now ensued resulted from a complex interplay between news flows and frameworks of economic, military, and political calculation. Information about the Calcutta crisis and the nawab's threats arrived in Madras on July 14, prompting the immediate dispatch of two hundred European soldiers. But the British faced a dilemma: A confrontation with the French was looming, meaning they would have to divide their forces and conduct simultaneous operations in the north and the south. Calcutta was crucial in economic terms. The company earned 50 percent of its revenues through the settlement there, compared to 15 percent from Madras, 6 percent from Bombay, and the rest in China.[149] When news of Calcutta's fall arrived on July 20, the company decided to take action, since the monsoon would prevent French soldiers from arriving until early 1757, and in spite of the fact that no French declaration of war had yet arrived in Madras (it would not until November 13). After a lengthy debate on whether the army or the BEIC should lead the expedition to retake the company's Bengal possessions, command was finally given to Clive, who had twenty-five hundred European soldiers at his disposal, a very large force by the standards of the Europeans in India at this time.[150] Clive now held sole military and civilian command for the first time. The launch of the expedition proved a fiasco, with British forces making an arduous voyage by water up the Hugli River in Bengal. But the nawab's troops, commanded by Raja Manik Chand, the governor of Calcutta, continued to withdraw. The British went on to retake all their forts, and ultimately Calcutta, largely without a fight.

As the war continued, there were severe disagreements among the British, with commanders of the navy and regular infantry refusing to accept Clive's authority.[151] These bitter rivalries escalated further over who had the right to occupy Fort William.[152] The situation worsened with the arrival of news of the outbreak of war between Britain and France in Europe. The Seven Years' War in India had officially begun.[153]

The nawab reacted to Clive's provocations by marching on Calcutta, and Clive responded by attacking the enemy camp in an attempt to directly capture the nawab, an early example of the commando raids that made him famous. The attacked failed, but Clive was fortunate in his misfortune: His action caused such confusion in the enemy camp that the nawab eventually withdrew and agreed to a treaty with the British, allowing them to attack the French base at Chandannagar. By now, Bussy's continued campaign in the Deccan was having an impact elsewhere: His troops were not available to be sent to help Chandannagar, and after bloody fighting, the British took the settlement on March 23, 1757.[154] This victory more or less ended the French presence in Bengal, in what was a strong boost to the BEIC and its commercial interests.[155]

CHAPTER III

A War Without Fronts

The German Theater

Portents of War

The outbreak of war prompts demands for explanation. Some in the Holy Roman Empire saw omens of disaster in Nature's own disorders, much like their forebears in the previous century. The main omen in 1756 was an enormous plague of mice, experienced across a swathe of west-central Germany, including parts of today's Lower Saxony, Hesse, and the Rhineland.[1] In the village of Wollbrandshausen, Pastor Schatz noted in his chronicle: "There were Mice in such quantities throughout that the crops were damaged in the Fields, Flax razed to the ground, and what was picked was spoiled, and the Aftermath trampled and eaten away, even in wet Fields; God sent these mice in such great numbers, a forewarning for Germany, a herald of seven years of War and terrible Bloodletting and wretched Atrocities."[2]

The chronicle kept by Johann Gottlob Herr (1728–1765), pastor to the town of Hameln, made a similar argument: "Harbingers of the war's great Miseries were already seen in the year 1756, with a very large and considerable plague of Mice which caused no little Dearth."[3] In Bottendorf am Burgwald, a village in northern Hesse, the farmer Johann Daniel Geitz (1733–1802) began his own war chronicle thus: "And more often then were heavenly Signs, and at times large Earthquakes. Vermin of various kinds came onto the land, infesting the Fields, mice of all sorts—yellow, red, black, white."[4]

Commentators in contemporary print media tended to take a critical view of such correlations, which they called popular superstitions. The *Münchener Bott*, a Munich newspaper, addressed the plague of mice that affected Cologne the previous year: "Many could not be dissuaded that these small wild Animals were forerunners of the troops who were later to come and devastate and lay waste the Empire. Since the mice were of different colors, in their view this was a Reference to the many and different clothes and uniforms of the Soldiers. Such people even have recourse to Experience, and they cited earlier times as evidence."[5]

A Prussian invasion force of over sixty-two thousand men marched into Saxony on the night of August 28–29, 1756. Their right wing, led by Duke Ferdinand of Brunswick-Wolfenbüttel (1721–1792)—usually shortened to "Ferdinand of Brunswick"—advanced from the area around Halle-Aschersleben, moving toward Leipzig and Chemnitz and then on to Freiberg. Frederick II commanded the central thrust, which set out from close to Magdeburg, marching along the Elbe River via Dessau and Wittenberg, headed for the region around Döbeln. A third force, on the Prussian left, led by Duke August Wilhelm von Braunschweig-Bevern (1715–1781), marched from Guben to Fischbach via Bautzen.[6]

There was no official declaration of war, unlike when Prussia invaded Silesia sixteen years earlier[7] (see figure 3.1). However, on Saturday, September 4, the *Berlinische Nachrichten* devoted two pages to a text written by Frederick himself, the "Declaration of the Reasons Which Have Moved His Majesty to Advance Into Saxony."[8] In particular, the declaration deplores the "unjust" behavior of the Viennese court and its "dangerous intentions." This, the Prussian king writes, had presented him with the "unavoidable necessity [of taking] preventive action" against an "enemy unwilling [to come to] amicable agreement."[9] He had been compelled to take this step, he goes on, "forced [by] the laws of war, the unfortunate course of the times, and the safety of our own country."[10] He had no grievance with Saxony, Frederick continues, or its ruler. His troops, he insists, will maintain the strictest discipline.

The king was aware that his published justification was weak, and he soon wrote another, titled "The Causes Moving His Royal Majesty in Prussia to Stand Opposed to the Intentions of the Court in Vienna, and to Prevent Their Accomplishment."[11] This came closer to the desired effect, as observed by Prussia's representative at the Imperial Diet at Regensburg, Erich Christoph Edler Herr und Freiherr von Plotho (1707–1788). He wrote to

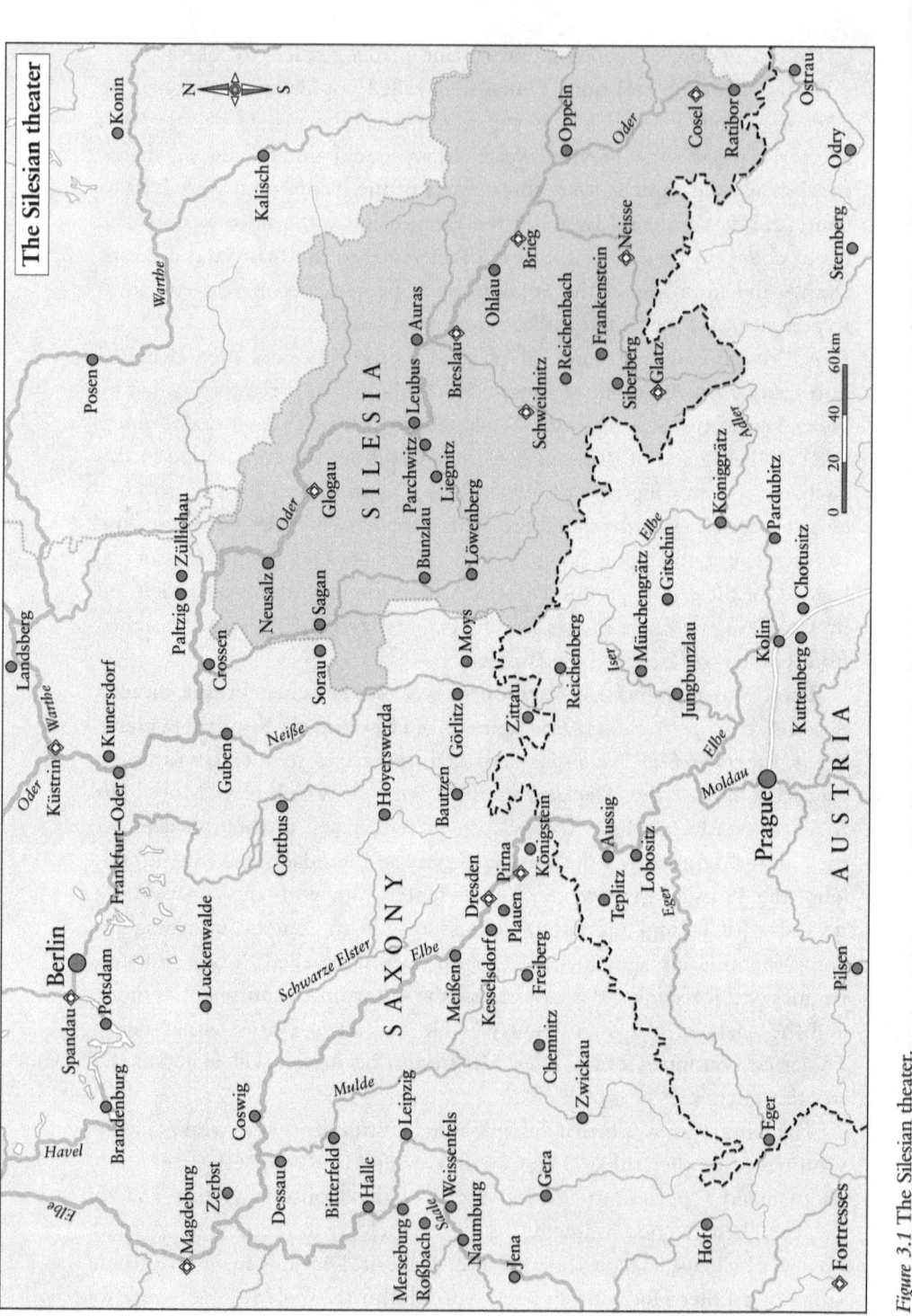

Figure 3.1 The Silesian theater.

Frederick that the general public was "astonished and overjoyed," the Catholic delegates stunned, and the Protestants delighted.[12] In London, over fifteen hundred copies of Frederick's second statement were printed in ten hours.[13] In Britain, this second statement was accompanied by a "diplomatic campaign of justification," actively supported by Frederick, who was seeking to shake off what he called the "disgusting title of aggressor."[14] The new justification had considerable success in winning over the British public to Prussia's preemptive war. The fact that Prussia was a Protestant country made it seem Britain's "natural confederate."[15] But the second statement enjoyed less success with the French public. Later the memoirs of the French envoy Louis Guy Henry de Valori (1692–1774) claimed that Frederick's writings had "acted as a microscope for the public, in conjunction with the facts as they stood," allowing the French people to see which alliance had truth and justice on its side.[16] "Public opinion, free of prejudice," he claimed, would see through Frederick's deceptions, identifying the Prussian king as the war's true instigator.

The Prussian capture of Dresden delivered more material to boost Frederick's claims to legitimacy. The king faced no resistance worth the name when he entered the Saxon capital at the head of his troops. One key early objective was to secure the royal archives; in particular, Frederick wanted to find "authentic pieces" revealing "machinations" conducted against him by the Saxon court. His orders regarding the archive were clear: "Original copies of such Saxon correspondence [should] be found in the Dresden archive and removed from it."[17] The material was to be published as quickly as possible, "everywhere in France, England, Holland, Poland, also in the Reich and other necessary places." The collection of documents was published on October 16, 1756, with the title "A Well-Founded Report of Unlawful Conduct and the Dangerous Attacks and Intentions of the Viennese and Saxon Courts Against His Royal Majesty of Prussia, as Proven with Written Documents."[18] This *mémoire raisonné* was intended for circulation throughout Europe, and after the original publication in German, versions were brought out in Latin, Polish, Dutch, and English. Reporting to the king from Regensburg, Plotho, the Prussian diplomat, advises that ambassadors at the Imperial Diet are saying the pamphlet has won as much for Frederick "as his most victorious battles," although at this early stage of the war, those victorious battles were purely notional.[19]

The autobiography of Ulrich Bräker, the Swiss private serving in the Prussian army, describes the route from Berlin to Pirna in some detail. On

August 22, 1756, the Prussian army, including Bräker's regiment, marched from Berlin, departing through the Köpenicker Gate. A twenty-day march brought them to Pirna on September 10, where they set up "a vast camp, almost as far as the eye could see."[20] The Saxon fortresses of Königstein and Lilienstein had been strengthened, and the Saxon army was nearby: "We could see straight across the valley into their camp, and below us in the valley of the Elbe lay Pirna, which was now similarly occupied by our men."[21] The Saxon army, commanded by Field Marshal Friedrich Augustus Graf Rutowski (1702–1764), the illegitimate son of former King Augustus II the Strong (1670–1733), had withdrawn to a camp in an almost unassailable position, below the Königstein fortress, close to the town of Pirna.[22] Until this point, the government of Saxony had harbored hopes that the Prussians might merely intend to make "friendly passage" through their territory en route to Bohemia.[23] The Prussian army was already a major burden on the country, ruthlessly living off the land as it went. Rutowski issued marching orders to the Saxon regiments just in time, and they withdrew at around the same speed as the Prussians advanced.[24] By early September, the Saxon army at Pirna amounted to about twenty thousand men.[25] Frederick demanded that Augustus III and his court evacuate Dresden and take shelter with the Saxon army, claiming he could not guarantee their safety if they remained. The court carried out his instructions on September 3, withdrawing to the military camp at Struppen, several miles southeast of Pirna. From there, the Saxon court crossed into Bohemia at Peterswald in the Erzgebirge Mountains, quietly implementing a plan to escape to safety in Poland.

The Prussian army had moved quickly, and by September 12, almost forty thousand men had completely surrounded the Saxons at Pirna. The Saxon camp was south of the Elbe River, situated in a triangle formed by the fortress of Sonnenstein near Pirna to the northwest, the Königstein fortress to the southeast, and the town of Langenhennersorf to the south.[26] It was a very large camp, and its defenders were too few in number to entirely secure it, but it was also impossible for the Prussians to completely cut off communications between the Saxons and the outside world. Moreover, the camp's location was excellent, with the Elbe River and the mountains offering protection: Any attempt to take it by force would be extremely risky. A Prussian assault was almost impossible, but so were any Saxon sorties, let alone a complete escape. Time now became the second great determining factor, after the camp's topographical situation. The longer the Saxons hung on, the more their supplies would dwindle.[27] Gottfried Zahn (1728–1791), a Saxon soldier trapped inside the camp, later wrote to his family, saying "Succour [reinforcement] was supposed to arrive, but there was no Succour, as every time it was Ambushed and beaten back. We had no Assistance, and were on duty Day and Night, almost as not to be borne. Cartridge Pouch and Weapon at all times to hand. Each man had 60 Cartridges [. . .], but very little Bread. It was almost no longer to be borne."[28] Hans Carl Heinrich von Trautzschen (1730–1812) offers an officer's perspective, describing the situation thus: "Frost and Hunger were thus our most powerful Enemies, and inevitable Death was our Expectation."[29] On September 22, Bräker witnessed a column of captured Saxon soldiers, which he interpreted—incorrectly, he later realized—to mean that the Saxon army had surrendered.[30] But the end was not yet in sight.

The besieged Saxons' great hope lay in a possible relieving force, an Austrian army led by Count Maximilian Ulysses Browne (1705–1757). Passing to the northwest of Bohemia, Browne advanced in the direction of Pirna. The Prussian king, leaving about a quarter of his men to maintain the siege at Pirna, headed southeast toward Bohemia, seeking to confront the approaching Austrians. Browne's army was ready for the fight and had taken up a waiting position on the other side of the Mittelgebirge, the low mountains of northern Bohemia.

Lobositz: The Experience of Battle

The war's first land battle on the European mainland took place near Lobositz—now Lovosice in the Czech Republic—on October 1, 1756.[31] Events began in thick fog, with an exchange of artillery fire. Once the fog had cleared, Frederick saw that large parts of the Austrian army were positioned behind a swamp and had been left largely undamaged by the bombardment. The Prussians had already suffered substantial losses, in particular to their cavalry, prematurely prompting Frederick to abandon the field. But then, between three and four o'clock in the afternoon, the Prussian infantry attacked Lobositz. This was the move that would ultimately decide the outcome of the battle. Browne ordered the Austrian forces to withdraw from the battlefield, allowing the Prussians to control the space.[32]

Perspectives on Lobowitz depend very much on the military status of the observer in question. Military commanders, including Frederick and Browne, take a broad general view of battles, recounting them in the manner of a chess game.³³ Mistakes are almost always attributed to officers or soldiers; in the case of Lobositz, blame was also put on the fog that lingered over the battlefield. Officers' accounts offer midrange observation, combining individual views of the battle with a broader overview. The viewpoint of the ordinary soldier brings us closest to violent practices as they were experienced by individuals, but their accounts often fail to relate these to the battle as an overall event.

Battle narratives likewise vary according to the author's rank and the genre of their testimony. Style and perspective differ among diaries, letters, and autobiographical writing. There is little difference among authors of different nationalities, however—Austrian and Prussian officers of similar rank might have more in common in their perception of events than a Prussian officer and a common soldier in the same army. There are overlaps between the various perspectives, of course. It is typical of the confusion of combat that the narrative overview often resumes only at the end of battle, reappearing in the discussion of consequences, including concern for those who had died. Lobositz was the first battle of the war and offers good examples of the different ways the various experiences of battle were articulated.³⁴

Let us first turn to the topography of the battlefield. As Christopher Duffy has aptly observed, the small area where fighting took place included "almost every conceivable variety of landscape." To the north, the battlefield abutted a bend in the Elbe, with the village of Lobositz to the south. The terrain here was characterized by "water-filled ditches, ponds, and the marshy banks of a trout stream."³⁵ To the west, in the direction of the Prussian advance, the plain became a valley, marked by "a chain of extinct volcanoes." On the Prussian left stood Lobosch Mountain itself, which Duffy refers to as the "ghostly cone," 420 meters (about 1,378 feet) tall and topped with a basalt summit; its slopes were planted with terraced vineyards separated by small walls. Across the valley lay the Homolka, another mountain not quite as tall as the Lobosch.

Battle began at six o'clock in the morning, with heavy artillery exchanges through the dense fog. Bräker describes the events in detail. He soon became aware of the hopelessness of his situation.³⁶ "Till then I'd still had hopes of escaping before battle was engaged; now I could see no way out, whether in front or behind, to right or to left." As his regiment advances, Bräker becomes more frightened: "Then all my courage sank into my breeches; my only wish was to creep into the bowels of the earth, and a similar fear, indeed deathly pallor, could soon be seen on all faces, even of those who'd always made out how tough they were." Brandy was the soldier's time-honored way of assuaging fear and instilling courage: "Emptied brandy-flasks (every soldier has one) were flying through the air amidst the general rain of bullets; most of the men had drained their meagre supply down to the last drop, on the principle of 'Today we need our courage: tomorrow we may be gone!'"[37]

Infantrymen found themselves particularly helpless in the ensuing confrontation with enemy artillery and cavalry: "Now we advanced under the shells to where we had to relieve the front line. Crimes! how those iron-cobs whizzed over our heads !-one minute driving into the earth before us, the next behind, sending stones and sods high into the air—now in amongst us, cracking men down right, left and center like straws." A letter written by the Prussian soldier Frantz Reiss offers another perspective on the artillery exchange: "Our Krumpholtz was standing close by me when the first cannonade shot off half his head; the ball blew Earth & bits of his brain & Skull into my face, tore my weapon from my shoulder, breaking it in 1000 pieces; by the grace of God I am unharmed."[38] He provides an astonishingly sober and explicit presentation of the deadly effects of shelling during battle, compared to Bräker's vivid but somewhat euphemistic language, and indeed compared to most testimonies of war.

Bräker, as an infantryman, also finds himself observing cavalry battles up close:

> All we saw was enemy cavalry on top of us, executing all sorts of movements, now stretching out in line, now forming a crescent, now contracting into a triangle or square. Then up came our cavalry; we opened a gap and let them through to gallop straight at the enemy cavalry. And what a clash! What a rattling and glinting, as they laid into them! It scarcely lasted a quarter of an hour, however, before our horsemen returned, beaten back by the Austrian cavalry, harried almost under the muzzles of our cannon. You never saw such a spectacle!—horses with riders banging from the stirrups, others trailing their guts along the ground. [. . .] Meanwhile we were still exposed to enemy cannon-fire until close on 11 o'clock, without our left flank engaging with small-arms, even though there was already fierce fighting on the right. Many thought we were bound to storm the imperial fieldworks.[39]

Bräker's fear seems to diminish as battle wears on: "By now I wasn't so frightened as at the beginning, although the culverins were carrying off men on both sides of me and the battlefield was already strewn with dead and wounded."[40] For a while, he thought himself safe, since the order to withdraw had been given, and they appeared to be heading back to camp. But another battle immediately followed the first, with Bräker's unit now facing Austrian Pandurs, once a much-feared border force, now a regular Hungarian infantry unit.[41] Bräker's regiment ran up the steep slopes of a vineyard, not yet realizing that the Pandurs were climbing the slopes on the other side, intent on occupying the pass at the summit so as to fall on the Prussian ranks from the rear. But the Prussians beat the Hungarians to the top: "Another couple of minutes and they'd have gained the heights from us and we wouldn't half have copped it! It now meant indescribable slaughter, dislodging the pandours from that wood. Our forward troops suffered heavily; but the rearguard followed up and got stuck in as well, until in the end we'd all gained the heights. We found ourselves stumbling over mounds of dead and wounded."[42]

Another description of the fighting in the vineyards was written by an anonymous sergeant in the Anhalt regiment: "Our left wing [. . .] marched down the steep vineyard slopes, and were faced with very bitter work indeed, the like of which you will not read in very many war stories. They marched freely into the guns of the enemy, who were concealed in hollow paths, deep trenches, and behind walls. Every yard of land was bought with precious Prussian blood. The work lasted from 8 in the morning till 2 in the afternoon, never stopping, under constant fire."[43] The Prussians seem to have fought with particular determination against the Pandurs. By this point in the battle, Bräker was close to losing his senses, firing off his ammunition almost at random. "Our true-blue Prussians and Brandenburgers pounced on the pandours like the furies; I slewed about all over the place like a mad thing, and immune to the slightest fear, in one burst I shot off well nigh all 60 of my rounds till my musket was pretty well red-hot and I had to drag it behind me by its strap; I don't believe I hit a living soul though—it all went into the air." Bräker's retelling here fits the pattern of the great majority of soldiers' accounts of action, in which they mostly suffer violence rather than actively inflicting it on others. The anonymous sergeant of the Anhalt regiment corroborates Bräker's observation about cartridges: "It seemed our left flank must now yield, having used the 60 cartridges they had each been issued, so they were sent 30 cartridges each from men on the right flank."[44] The shortage of ammunition meant using bayonets and rifle butts: "Prussians and Pandurs were lying mingled everywhere together, and where one of the latter still stirred, he was hit on the head with a butt or run through the body with a bayonet." Another important witness to this part of the battle is a Prussian musketeer named Dominicus, but he devotes just a single sentence to the "sharp clash with the Pandours," choosing mostly to write about the bad weather and his poor rations.[45] At the senior officer level, we find mention of the vineyard attack in a report by Duke von Bevern. Some battalions from the second line of troops still had ammunition "and so they fired at the enemy coming up the mountain; but since Bevern's regiment and Jung-Billerbeck's battalion had used most of their powder in 5 hours of constant firing, and since they were halfway up the hill, they went for the enemy's throats with bayonets, and so did the aforementioned battalions, hurling the enemy down the slope, bayoneting them in the ribs, clubbing them with muskets, running pêle mêle down the hill, and chasing them back to Lowositz."[46]

The diary of Lieutenant Jakob Friedrich von Lemcke (1738–1810) offers still another eyewitness account of Lobositz. He also describes the storming of the vineyard: "To the left, the vineyard slopes were all occupied by Pandours, and our Grenadiers had to climb over every terraced Wall in the vineyard. To the right, our regiment faced a steep hill. As we climbed it, we passed many thick Trees, where I sometimes wished we might stop, so that I could stand behind such Trees, because the endless shooting was most Terrible and unfamiliar to me."[47]

The next phase of the battle took place on level ground. By now, Bräker has almost no visual perception because of the large amounts of smoke and the great variety of noises, and he uses vivid onomatopoeia to give a sense of the cacophony of battle: "But who shall attempt to describe it?—the smoke and fumes that now went up from Lowositz, the crashing and thundering as if heaven and earth were about to melt away, the incessant rattle of many hundreds of drums, the clangour of martial music of all kinds, rending and uplifting the heart, the shouts of so many commanders and roars of their adjutants, the moans and groans from so many thousands of wretched, mangled, half-dead victims of this day: it dazed all the senses!"[48] Battle here becomes an almost entirely acoustic event.

As for the anonymous sergeant of the Anhalt regiment, the fighting on the plain prompts him to reflect on the disparity between the two armies:

> For our army was but a Handful, no more than 28,000 men strong, while the enemy had 66,000 men, and of select company, who had solemnly sworn to each other neither to Yield nor give Way; this was told us by all the wounded and Prisoners we took. On September 30, nearly all our infantry received no bread, and on top of that such hard marching, and then again on October 1 almost no bread at all, and yet fight we must. The cavalry horses had not been fed in 48 hours and given but a single watering. By contrast, the enemy was given wine on the 30 of September, and exhorted to courage by officers making grand Promises. Among others, the promise was made that they would soon be in Brandenburg, where everything could be plundered. In spite of all of this, our side was righteous and God was with us, and by means of our exhausted people He has laid our well-fed, much stronger enemy low.[49]

In other words, the victory of the numerically and qualitatively outmatched Prussians is explained by assistance from God. This original distinction is then loaded with a moralizing contrast, comparing "exhausted" Prussians to their "well-fed" enemies. However, unlike Bräker, the unknown Prussian is positively enthusiastic about participating in battle: "Fortune favored me with something that many Thousands desire, namely a distant view of a Battle." He includes a Latin sentence that translates as follows: "On this occasion I played a dual role; [my] Body, Appearance, and Weapons were military, but my mind lingered with the military deeds of Karl Gustav, as described by Pufendorff, and I recalled every defeat and every battle depicted there, as though cast in Brass."[50]

For Bräker, his desperate situation was an inducement to desert. An escape route was easily chosen: There was fighting everywhere except to his left. He hurried through the woods and vineyards, pretending to be "slightly wounded." When he encountered soldiers, he ignored their calls to return and fight.[51] Once out of sight, he gradually picked up his pace until he was sprinting away from the battlefield. Once at a safe distance, he could observe the "murdering and killing" from afar, the last time in his life he would witness anything of the sort.

Bräker was not the only Prussian deserter; another thirty members of his regiment were included in the lists of prisoners compiled at Budin, the Austrian headquarters.⁵² From there, Bräker made his way home to Toggenburg—today in the Swiss canton of St. Gallen—via Prague, Regensburg, and Bregenz. On October 26, he stood in front of his parents' house. Lobositz marked an existential turning point in his life. Images of battle were a popular metaphor in Pietism, which helped preserve his memories of battle to the end of his days. But how did Bräker manage to depict the battle with such unusual vividness and precision? During his time as a soldier, he seems to have carried a "writing tablet," taking notes to use later. On his journey back to Switzerland, he was already making money in taverns and monasteries with his colorful descriptions of the battle. Later he would recount his experience to friends and acquaintances. In 1788, he read Archenholz's history of the Seven Years' War.⁵³ For thirty years after Lobositz, these sources and these methods allowed him to keep the events of the day alive. Immediately after the battle, however, disputes raged over what its actual outcome had been.

A Disputed Victory

Prussian witnesses thought their own victory was obvious. Frederick's page, Georg Karl Gans Edler zu Putlitz, wrote: "They were set upon their retreat, and left the battlefield to us."⁵⁴ By eighteenth-century criteria, this would be considered a clear victory. However, some contemporaries insisted that it had been a victory for the Austrian side, and some nineteenth-century observers agreed.⁵⁵ The Austrian historian Alfons Dopsch (1868–1953), who was born in Lobositz, suggested the encounter was not a "battle" at all. Instead, he described it as an "encounter": a meeting of two armies by happenstance rather than a pitched battle assented to by both sides.⁵⁶

Days after the event, on October 6, 1756, the *Wienerisches Diarium* reported that the outcome had been undecided, as both armies returned to camp after the battle with "victory between the two Sides remaining in Doubt."⁵⁷ Meanwhile, the Prussians had sent messengers to spread news of their "complete Victory"; their reports reached Berlin and Dresden on October 3.⁵⁸ The Prussians could at least take credit for the hard fighting that pushed the Austrians out of the vineyards and forced their withdrawal from the town of Lobositz to Budin. A historical chronicle written in 1758 by Christoph Gottlieb Richter (1717–1774) makes this claim: "No sooner had the enemy fled than Browne let the Retreat be sounded, and stopped fighting, instead passing through the night quietly, and returning to his Camp at Buddin in the early morning. Thus the Prussians remained on the battlefield, from which they had driven the enemy. And it is the way of Nations that Victory is given those who take the battlefield. [. . .] And it is true that the battle did not decide the fortunes of the two Armies, and the Austrians deny that they lost, although the facts show things differently."[59]

The Austrians realized that the modest claims made in Browne's official dispatch had been an error, enabling Frederick to announce a Prussian victory. Retrospectively arguing against this Prussian claim, a dispatch sent by Kaunitz noted that the Austrians had gathered up wounded Prussians and buried the enemy's dead.[60] Since only a force in control of the battlefield is in a position to do this, the Viennese leadership regarded this as sufficient evidence to disprove a Prussian victory. On October 13, an official report in the *Wienerische Diarium* noted: "Our army remained all day on the battlefield, and through the night until the next morning, and ordered that the enemy's dead be buried."[61]

Here the claim to have held the battlefield is asserted in three separate ways: first, by performative practices that emphasize possession of the site; second, by a redefinition of space; and third, by representations in the media. Ultimately, everything depends on which battlefield is up for discussion—or rather which *part* of the battlefield. The Austrians had maintained control of parts of the battlefield near Sullowitz, and at these places, tending to the wounded would have been possible. It would have been far more difficult to do so at the scene of the fighting on the Austrian right. Claims to victory depended a great deal on who defined the battle space and who recognized those definitions.

Various performative practices were used to declare victory in the immediate aftermath of a battle. These included singing a Te Deum to give thanks for divine assistance and to document God's satisfaction with the outcome. A gun salute was also usually fired and a prayer service held. The diary of Dominicus, the Prussian musketeer, notes: "On the 17th we held a service of Thanks-giving, and on the 18th fired three times from all cannons. The Thanks-giving service at Lobositz was held on October 3rd, with the singing of the 152nd and 151st Psalms, but there was no sermon, for the preacher was among those wounded."[62] On the Austrian side, Jacob de Cogniazo (1732–1811), a veteran of the war, reports that the Prussians fired a "Victory" cannonade on the evening of the battle, while his own side had been content, "on the battlefield itself," to send a final "sharp parting shot

[*Retraitschuss*] into the victors' camp." The Prussians correctly celebrated victory, writes Cogniazo, while the Austrians "under a thunder of Cannon fire, took advantage of the great Emperor's name day to give thanks to the God of the army," thanking him that the "day had gone well." Cogniazo notes that "at the least, this time Frederick did not encounter the old Austrians, although we encountered the old Prussians, victorious in five pitched battles under their much-lauded leaders."[63]

Cogniazo's explanation is telling. The celebrations of the Austrian army had had a "somewhat ambiguous appearance," he observes. "Some claimed these to be victory celebrations—but this they could in no way be, although solemn worship was arranged at the main church of Prague to mark this unusual Day, and at Vienna nine days of prayer for officers and soldiers who fell in battle. Prince Piccolomini had given no orders for celebrations, and in his camp at Königgratz not a musket was fired to mark the Battle at Lowositz; this illustrates that the assertion that the Austrians claimed the victory was incorrect."[64]

Apart from actions on the battlefield itself, official reports on both sides claimed that they had been victorious or at least that the battle had been inconclusive. In this way, the site of contestation shifted from the site of battle to the broader European public sphere. By repeatedly reporting on victory celebrations, the Berlin newspapers steadily reiterated the original story of a Prussian victory. By early November, there had been reports of celebrations in Potsdam, Dresden, Wriezen, and Stargard, among other places.[65] In Cleves, the government petitioned the Prussian king to ban the *Gazette de Cologne*. It noted that while the *Gazette de Berlin* reported a clear Prussian victory and the *Gazette de Leipzig* was ambiguous, the *Gazette de Cologne* had reported an Austrian victory, apparently casting the king's subjects in Cleves into a state of "fear and horror." In this way, the battle became a second-order media event, in which contested reporting took the place of the original military encounter.

Reading the Battle

The dissemination of news about the battle via newspapers and pamphlets is well documented in a number of personal testimonies. Among the best-known sources is the correspondence of Meta Klopstock (1728–1758), letters that scholars have come to refer to as "iconic examples of reception."[66]

On October 16, 1756, Klopstock complains to her sister in Hamburg about the fuss made about the battle of Lobositz in the news media. She first describes domestic conditions of reception: "But there is here such Curiosity as to be beyond Description. Around the time when the post messenger comes, everyone here in the house a[nd] some of the neighbors are in my parlor, others have messengers waiting to take our newspapers once we have read them. What can have happened? In Bohemia? In Saxony?" Friedrich Gottlieb Klopstock (1724–1803), in particular, was "cheering them on" and holding forth on political affairs:

> Kl. [Klopstock] is always devising what Broune should do, a[nd] what he wishes for him not to do. The Saxons (the largest party here) will chasten themselves about what their country *might* do, and what it probably *will* not do. Amidst such noise, I at times go to the window and watch out for the messenger. When he comes; I run downstairs, hurl the newspaper into the crowd and go into the corner to read your letter. But now come the shouts: Prussia! Browne! Lobositz! and so on and so forth and who knows what's being shouted in the confusion, which all disturbs me, sometimes even while I am reading you telling me something about your children! They shout at me because I would rather read letters than newspapers. And I laugh at them because they have no letters to read. Last post day I was angry with Klopstock because when I wanted to read him the news of your [Hamburg] flood he said: Oh! Oh! Let me read about the battle first.[67]

But ultimately Meta also reveals her own emotional engagement: "By this you see which side Kl. is on. But to be honest, I did not like it myself when the King of Prussia lost a battle."

These passages offer not only extraordinary detail on the specific context of news reception but also information on representations of battle in the media. The Klopstocks here become virtual participants in the battle as an event, cheering things on in a way familiar today from media coverage of sporting events.

More well-known scenes of reception can be found in the autobiography of Johann Wolfgang von Goethe (1749–1832) and in some of his fictional works: "But scarcely had I completed my seventh year, on the 28th of August, 1756, than that world-renowned war broke out which was also to exert great influence upon the next seven years of my life. [. . .] The world, which saw itself appealed to, not merely as spectator, but as judge, immediately split into two parties; and our family was an image of the great whole."[68] As with the Klopstocks, great attention was paid to the war's early events, in the lead-up to Lobositz: "The occupation of Dresden, the moderation of the king at the outset, his slow but secure advances, the victory at Lowositz, the capture of the Saxons, were so many triumphs for our party." However, the family was divided into opposing camps: "Everything that could be alleged for the advantage of our opponents was denied or depreciated; and, as the members of the family on the other side did the same, they could not meet in the streets without disputes arising, as in 'Romeo and Juliet.'" Young Goethe, so his autobiography claims, was filled, above all, with admiration for the great king of Prussia: "Thus I also was then a Prussian in my views, or, to speak more correctly, a Fritzian; since what cared we for Prussia? It was the personal character of the great king that worked upon all hearts." Goethe's writing habits at the time—aged just seven—are also significant, in terms of both his emotional identification and his personal appropriation of war discourse: "I rejoiced with my father in our conquests, readily copied the songs of triumph, and almost more willingly the lampoons directed against the other party, poor as the rhymes might be."[69]

Even avowed nonreaders of newspapers, like James Wolfe, then still in England, celebrated the Prussian victory at Lobositz. On October 24, Wolfe writes to his mother: "I, who never read the news, never know what is doing, and my correspondents seem to have intelligence proportioned to my curiosity. Pray tell the General that I triumph in the King of Prussia's success."[70]

The German poet and cavalry officer Ewald Christian von Kleist (1715–1759) provides another report on the battle in the form of a letter to Johann Wilhelm Ludwig Gleim (1719–1803).[71] Gleim is so enthused by Kleist's depiction that he replies: "And thus I will long delight in our victories and long may you recount them to me, my dear Kleist! This time you have done so in such detailed and clear manner that one quite sees the battlefield before one, and fears for one's own safety thereon."[72] On October 24, 1756, another of Gleim's letters to Kleist addresses the question of victory at Lobositz: "The Austrians claim victory in the battle at Lowositz and write insolently, claiming they have Defended the field of Battle, and spent the night after the encounter on that Battlefield. I think her generals are spinning lies for the Empress. They also claim that our army was 50 or 60 thousand strong. But they are quite wrong about that, it was 130,000 strong.

With a hundred and thirty thousand men, Frederick attacked the Austrians. Because he alone was one hundred thousand men!"[73]

In Vienna, Maria Theresa and her husband frequently reacted to news of victory or defeat with great emotion. The empress often wept rivers of tears, according to Khevenhüller-Metsch, her lord chamberlain, who observed her constantly.[74] This was in keeping with the emotional tenor of a tear-stained era but also with the deeply religious sensibility of the Viennese court. Thus, the question of whether the tears were real or staged is not pertinent. When bad news was combined with a court culture of ceremony and celebration, a powerful emotional charge could be generated. News of Browne's unsuccessful mission to Saxony was brought by a "limping currier" on the evening of October 15, a day celebrated as Theresa Day. It was received with "great sensibility" by both of their imperial majesties, since this "latest and none-too-pleasing news-paper had arrived on what is both of their name days, a circumstance which petty minds might hold a malign omen pro futuro."[75] It should not be forgotten that the empress was pregnant with her sixteenth child at this time, a boy eventually born on December 8, 1756, and given the name Maximilian Franz.

Pirna: The Saxon Army Surrenders

Frederick's advance into Bohemia followed an operational strategy almost as contradictory as his political logic. As the historian Johannes Kunisch has pointed out, the king ran enormous risks by attacking the Austrians in Bohemia while leaving an undefeated Saxon army to his rear. For his part, Browne's retreat was well justified, intended to preserve men and materiel for an attempt to break the siege of the Saxon army.[76] However, Frederick's conduct of the war had a paradoxical effect. The calmness with which he seemed to make risky decisions made him an increasingly charismatic figure in the eyes of his opponents.

But the king was growing impatient. The Prussia supply situation was highly uncertain. On October 3, the king wrote to Lieutenant General Hans Karl von Winterfeldt (1707–1757) from the camp at Lobositz: "It is necessary to put an end to the Saxon forthwith, or I shall rightly be concerned that my affairs will suffer."[77] Given their own lack of supplies, the besieged Saxons would be able to hold out only until October 12. Browne, at the head of eight thousand men, set out on a forced march to relieve them. By October 11, he had reached the town of Schandau, close to the Koenigstein fortress. The Saxons stood ready to attempt a breakout. On the evening of October 12, they set out in the direction of a pontoon bridge across the Elbe. The Prussians discovered the bridge at around 2 o'clock in the morning. By afternoon on the following day, the Saxon army had crossed to the right bank of the Elbe, despite Prussian attacks. The pontoon bridge was then lost, falling into Prussian hands.[78] At this point, Browne decided to withdraw—possibly due to communication problems—in effect, leaving the Saxons to their fate.

By October 14, there were signs that the elector of Saxony was preparing to capitulate, as he sought to obtain official prisoner-of-war status for his soldiers to prevent their direct integration into the Prussian army. On October 16, the Saxons at last declared a surrender.[79] Gottfried Zahn, a soldier in the Saxon camp, complained: "The army was in the Lielienstern mountains, without Artillery, and we stayed on the mountain for three more days, without Bread. Then the whole Army had to surrender. We threw away all we had and had to lay down our weapons. There was not a single man with Courage or Sense. Pitiful it was." The next day ordinary Saxon soldiers were enlisted wholesale in the Prussian army. Again, Zahn reports on the scene: "We had to swear an oath to the King of Prussia on land and sea and we got a thaler of prest money. Afterwards we were brought to Berne [Pirna]. There were no shortages there."[80] The "subsuming" of the Saxon soldiers had significant consequences: Their patriotic spirit ultimately turned them into "loyal deserters" who abandoned the Prussian cause in large numbers at the first opportunity.[81] Of the high level of desertion among the Saxons, Zahn writes: "Many of us have deserted; but I do not wish to inflict this shame on you or on myself, I would rather be patient." With prophetic foresight, he adds: "They say this war will still be with us in six years' Time."[82] On October 20, Augustus III and his entire court moved to Warsaw, where they were received with artillery salutes on October 27.[83] From this point on, the elector of Saxony and the king of Poland were mostly "out of the game," largely reduced to observers of the war.

The Imperial Diet and the Politics of Procedure

It would be up to the Imperial Diet (Reichstag) to decide whether Frederick would be punished for breaching the peace of the Holy Roman Empire with his invasion of Saxony.[84] Since 1663, a "perpetual" Reichstag had been in existence, no longer dissolved after every session, with its permanent seat at Regensburg. Significantly, the seventeenth-century "settlement" that reformed the Reichstag meant that the imperial estates no longer attended the Reichstag in person but instead sent envoys who functioned as permanent representatives. Nor did the emperor attend in person; he was instead represented by a principal commissioner (*Prinzipalkommisar*). The Reichstag was a political forum in which religious questions could have a direct impact on political affairs. Prussia had long striven to assume leadership of the Corpus Evangelicorum, the subsidiary assembly of Protestant states. It now stood to benefit from concerns about possible Catholic hegemony in Germany, fed by rumors of plans for creating a Catholic Imperial League (Reichsliga) and possibly for increasing the "pro-Imperial majority" in the College of Princes (Reichsfürstenrat).[85]

The Seven Years' War was by no means a religious war.[86] At no time were the war aims or the motivations of the various parties determined by religious issues in any narrow sense. But we should not underestimate the role played by religious denominations in everyday life, propaganda, and political events. Religion served as a propaganda instrument on the political stage, intended to mobilize public opinion in Europe and the colonies. Important propaganda practices included not only pamphleteering but also the singing of a Te Deum after military success, a religiously infused "information ceremonial" that Frederick somewhat derisively referred to as "Te-Deum-ing."[87] The Anglo-Prussian diplomatic rapprochement included frequent invocations of the "Protestant interest," with Frederick hailed as a "Protestant hero." Likewise, the Catholic powers played the denominational card as what one historian has termed an "integrational argument in alliance politics."[88] On questions of religion, as in so many areas, there were stark contrasts between Frederick and Maria Theresa. While the empress celebrated a profoundly Baroque culture of Catholic piety, the "philosopher of Sanssouci"—as Frederick was sometimes called—took pleasure in ridiculing piety and organized religion.[89]

Frederick's personal relationship with religion was certainly more complex than his mockery. But religion was subordinate to politics during the war, becoming a significant political resource for the Prussian king. Prussia's opponents were well aware of this tactic—and none too pleased by it. But a paradoxical situation arose in Austria, where there was no political interest in recasting the war as a religious conflict.[90] This would have created too many problems at the Reichstag in Regensburg and would in any case have been highly unconvincing, not least because of Austria's alliance with Protestant Sweden. Nonetheless, on the level of broader religious culture, everything that happened in Vienna was profoundly shaped by Catholic practices and patterns of interpretation.

Plotho, an energetic ambassador known for his quick temper, was Prussia's envoy to the Imperial Diet from 1754 to 1766.[91] His unwavering commitment to the Prussian cause earned him several unflattering nicknames, including "Strangler of Truth."[92] Pamphlets published during this period clearly reveal what kind of "lobbying" was undertaken in and around the Imperial Diet.[93] The war's first battle, at Lobositz, also saw the beginning of rival media campaigns at Regensburg. The Austrian ambassador, Freiherr von Buchenberg (1701–1769), along with the ambassador of Electoral Bohemia, had the anonymous pamphlet titled *A Letter from Herr von *** to Herr von N. N, written at the Camp at Budin* published by the printer Heinrich Georg Neubauer (1742–1778).[94] The document's anonymous author plays down the supposed Prussian victory, insisting that the battle had, in fact, been indecisive.

In response, Plotho intervened with Regensburg's city council, which confiscated related materials from Neubauer. Buchenberg, the Austrian envoy, was outraged by the council's partisan action and offered protection to the printer, who went on to sell several thousand additional copies. Plotho did not manage to have the Prussian report on the battle printed in the newspapers, so he had it privately printed and distributed to the envoys at the Imperial Diet. The Austrians reacted by printing yet another pamphlet, sharply attacking Prussian claims of victory while also making explicit reference to Prussia's own propaganda about the event: "Since the King of Prussia intends to deceive the Publick, his ministers, press, and newspapers are all busy spreading the most curious Fictions and most downright Lies. But these voices, however noisy they be, are not enough for him. He must also make use of Post-horns to drown out common sense. Does a prince who won such Fame and Reputation in the last war require such a fictional Victory (une victoire postiche) to maintain his Repute?"[95]

For a time, Plotho produced pamphlets so diligently that even the Prussian government thought he had his own printing press. One text he distributed even prompted a charge of lèse-majesté, along with further official confiscations of printed materials, although Plotho's status as an ambassador was not affected.[96] Subjects that caught the local imagination included fictions about the war's religious aspects, including the rumors that Daun possessed a consecrated sword, as well as invective against the Imperial army and reports that the Austrian Netherlands might be ceded to Spain.[97]

Of the royal houses with electoral seats, Bavaria played a mediating role for the legal decisions still under review at Regensburg. Maximilian III Joseph (1727–1777), the elector of Bavaria, attempted two separate strategies of political deescalation in 1756. The Saxon royal family members were his relatives, after all: Augustus III was his father-in-law. Maximilian, along with the electors of Cologne, Mainz, Trier, and the Palatinate, cosigned a letter to George II, the king of England and also an elector, requesting that he intervene with Frederick to stop further action by Prussia against Saxony. King George, rather ungallantly, ignored their approach completely. A further attempt to forestall the war took the form of a combined intervention by the three Wittelsbach electors, with Maximilian bidding to bring Prussia to reason, supported by Karl Theodor (1724–1799), the elector of Palatine, and Clemens August I (1700–1761), the archbishop of Cologne. When this initiative also came to nothing, the Bavarian elector again wrote to Frederick on December 20, appealing for an amicable settlement and warning that he would be forced to act if one could not be reached.

On January 10, 1757, the Reichstag resumed its session after a Christmas break. A majority was quickly found in favor of a motion condemning the Prussian invasion of Saxony and adopting appropriate sanctions.[98] One week later, on January 17, 1757, the Reichstag issued an Imperial Declaration of War against Brandenburg-Prussia, which was ratified by Emperor Francis I (1708–1765) on January 29. Two days after that, the declaration of war was "dictated" in Regensburg, making it legally binding.[99] The Council of Electors voted five to one in favor, with Hanover casting the only dissenting vote. The representatives of Prussia and Austria abstained, as the parties immediately involved in the dispute. In the Council of Princes, the vote went sixty-two to twenty-six in favor of the declaration. States supporting the measure included some unequivocally Protestant territories, such as Ansbach and Mecklenburg-Güstrow.[100] This meant that Prussia had been found guilty of a breach of the imperial peace, so France and Sweden were called on to assume their role as guarantors of the Peace of Westphalia, which they accepted.

Enforcement measures now became necessary. First of all was the creation of an Imperial Army of Execution (Reichsexecutionsarmee), to be drawn from the individual Imperial Circles (Reichskreisen). Territories including

Bavaria, the Palatinate, Baden, and Württemberg were legally obliged to contribute a quota of troops directly to this Imperial army. But, in fact, all of these states formed part of the "neutral tendency."[101] In concrete terms, this meant their commitment vacillated, largely according to the fortunes of Prussia's war. Bavaria not only provided its territorial contingent to the Imperial army but also sent an auxiliary corps of four thousand men to serve with the French.[102] However, after Prussia's victory at Prague in 1757 and the subsequent incursions into the Bavarian-ruled Upper Palatinate by Prussian irregulars, Maximilian III Joseph of Bavaria chose to emphasize Bavarian neutrality.[103] Plotho suggested the actions of Lieutenant Colonel Mayr, the leader of a regiment of irregulars, would have the desired effect on the Bavarian elector and, in fact, "have already had a good and prompt Influence, so much so that he has himself declared Neutrality."[104] However, after learning of the Prussian defeats at Kolin and Grossjägersdorf and the British setback at Hastenbeck, Maximilian felt obliged to send his contingent to the Imperial army after all.[105] The following year, 1758, saw more Prussian attacks in the Upper Palatinate. Plotho conducted further negotiations at Regensburg, with the aim of having Bavaria's auxiliary corps withdrawn from the fighting. This was finally done in January 1759, much to Maria Theresa's displeasure.[106] Bavaria's involvement would be far less substantial in the remaining years of the war.

One incident at Regensburg quickly attained legendary status: namely, the ceremony at which Plotho was served with the official Imperial Order of Execution (Reichsexekution) against Frederick. The document was handed to the Prussian ambassador by the imperial notary Matthias Joseph Aprill on October 14, 1757.[107] It has often been claimed that Plotho then personally hurled the notary down a set of stairs. Although the incident is very probably apocryphal, there is evidence that Aprill, along with two companions, carried pistols and stones for their safety.[108] Plotho, in "violent anger and rage," is said to have shouted to his servants to "fling him down the stairs," but they did not do so.[109] Plotho also felt himself to be under real threat in Regensburg. When at one point a crowd appeared in front of his residence, he referred to it as a "storming of the building" and more generally described his stay in Regensburg as "torture."[110]

The next turn of political events came with Vienna's attempt to impose an imperial ban on Frederick, although delaying tactics and procedural errors at the Reichstag ultimately put paid to that initiative. Pro- and anti-Prussia camps accused one another of violating imperial custom (*Reichsherkommen*).

Neither France nor Sweden supported the proposed ban on the king of Prussia. One particularly significant factor was that the legal process made Hanover the coaccused, since it was an ally of Prussia. The Hanoverians persuaded the Corpus Evangelicorum to stop the process using what was known as the "itio-in-partes option."[111] This meant that in the event of a dispute on religious questions at the Reichstag, the Catholic and Protestant camps would split off (*itio in partes*) and vote separately. A decree could then be passed only if there was agreement between the two camps. Although some parties attempted to represent the Seven Years' War as a religious war, its religious aspects, in fact, remained largely "virtual" throughout, notwithstanding religion's remarkably tangible effects in everyday life. This diminished role of religion resulted more from the increasing power of procedure than from abstract processes of Enlightenment secularization. Legal arguments were what ultimately kept the fires of sectarianism in check, although both sides proved all too willing to pour oil on the flames.

CHAPTER IV

1757

The Year of Battles

"Battling, Only Ever Battling"

In 1757, troops advanced toward the Holy Roman Empire from both east and west. In April of that year, French soldiers marched into Prussian territory on the Lower Rhine.[1] In doing so, France was officially acting as an ally of Austria, "in the name of the Empress-Queen," but it captured Hesse and Hanover on its own behalf.[2] On April 19, Princess Luise Dorothée of Saxe-Meiningen (1710–1767) wrote to Voltaire, her regular correspondent: "The French are certainly very numerous, because by all accounts their army consists of more than a hundred thousand men. Very recently they have taken Cleves, with no further damage to its residents than a demand for contributions."[3] The French took Cleves, Wesel, Münster, and Lippstadt without a fight, commanded by Charles de Rohan, Prince of Soubise (1715–1787).

On April 20, Brunswick's army marched out from the city of the same name. Among its ranks was Johann Heinrich Ludewig Grotehenn, who reports: "Impossible even to describe the Crowds of People and On-Lookers, and among them some were seen who Congratulated our March, and some who offered Condolence, but for Myself, I was concerned with neither, but went calmly and confidently Forward toward my Fate, and contented myself not with any Fortune to come, nor was I troubled that Misfortune might trouble me."[4]

Some days later, on April 29, Russian regiments crossed the Daugava River and paraded through Riga. Among those marching in this "remarkable spectacle" was the officer and memoirist Andrei Bolotov:

> Impossible to describe the feelings awakened by this spectacle, not only in spectators, but also among ourselves, the participants. The thought that we were going to war, leaving our fatherland, setting off for foreign, distant, hostile countries, that we were starting out, and would suffer hardship, shed our blood, and die for the fatherland; the idea that very many of those marching would never return, but would leave behind their lives in the campaigns, and were now parting forever from where they were born and raised; the uncertainty as to whom would be accorded this unfortunate fate; these, and like considerations, thrust every man into gloom and lay heavy on every soul.[5]

On the other hand, Bolotov's heart was also filled with "fiery martial zeal," which could transcend all the hardship and danger.

The Russians deployed a new kind of artillery piece, Shuvalov's howitzer, named for its creator, General Peter Ivanovich Shuvalov.[6] The new gun struck terror in their Prussian adversaries but also provided a particular aura for Russian soldiers, since the gun's method of manufacture remained a close-guarded secret. Bolotov observes of the artillery pieces: "We were astonished when we saw these guns and utterly amazed at the copper pans which covered their muzzles, as if they were locked and sealed. Since anything that is hidden will arouse great curiosity, all of us desired to get to the bottom of this secret; but it was strictly maintained, with no one allowed near the cannon, and always a sentry on guard."[7]

A few weeks later the Allied armies mustered at Brackwede near Bielefeld.[8] Several eyewitnesses who have already been mentioned were now simultaneously present in the same Allied camp. Grotehenn, from Brunswick, was stationed at Brackwede between May 19 and June 13. Gilsa, a Hessian ensign in the German army returning from England, arrived at the camp on June 4 and left nine days later. Johann George Bess (1734–1810), a Hessian sergeant serving with the Hanoverian Jägers, arrived in early June.[9] Gilsa describes the army's composition: "This army consisted of 6 battalions of Prussian, Hanoverian, and Brunswick-Wolffenbüttelian troops, 1 battalion from Bickeburg [Bückeburg], 1 battalion each from Saxon-Gotha and Hesse, altogether 50,000 men."[10] Officers' accounts tend to have a strikingly different perspective than those of ordinary soldiers. Gilsa attempts to give an overview of troop formations and their commanders, whereas Grotehenn, a common soldier, focuses, above all, on his surroundings and his own body. Having slept in wet fields, he is now happy to lie down on "dry ground." Three hundred men from his unit, he adds, have already been taken ill, food is expensive, laundry is a problem, and there are outbreaks of vermin; every day three hundred men are assigned to entrenchment work at the camp. Bess mainly describes skirmishes with French hussars and the light troops of Fischer's Foreign Volunteers, close to the towns of Bielefeld and Herford. He is proud of the accuracy of his Jägers, who "shot the fellows up so much" that "it entirely knocked out their fire," thus "earn[ing] the respect" of the French. The Jägers' enemies had come to fear the very sound of their hunting horns: "on hearing our Half Moons (which they call 'the fatal music'), they start to run."[11]

By now, the French army was camped close to the town of Wesel; from April 27 on, it was commanded by Marshal d'Estrées (1695–1771).[12] By May, the French had moved on to Münster. On June 12, d'Estrées's forces arrived from Lippstadt and joined with Soubise's troops between Rheda and Neuenkirchen, creating a combined army of around 105,000 men. The following day the Duke of Cumberland ordered the Allies to retreat behind the line of the Weser, skirmishing with the French vanguard as they went. Their withdrawal allowed the French at last to capture the city of Bielefeld, which they proceeded to plunder.[13] Cumberland's reputation was still largely based on his brutal defeat of the Scots at Culloden in 1746, but here his actions were unusually defensive, and he did nothing to counter the French advance.[14]

France and Austria signed the Second Versailles Treaty on May 1, 1757, in which France promised to provide 129,000 soldiers and 12 million livres per year until Silesia was retaken.[15] Russia would contribute 80,000 troops to the alliance. The Holy Roman Empire, which was obliged to act by the decree of Reichsexekution against Frederick II, would send 25,000. Conflict across several theaters of war seemed inevitable. Frederick was clinging to the fiction of another "short and lively" war and now sought battle to force a decision.[16] In fact, the year 1757 saw more battles than any other year of the war (see map in figure 4.1).[17] The particularly large number of battles was remarked on by contemporaries, with Voltaire writing "Never have they given us as many battles as in this war."[18] A well-known formulation by Henry (1726–1802), Frederick II's brother, suggested a possible cause: "My brother always sought battle, it was his entire art of war."[19]

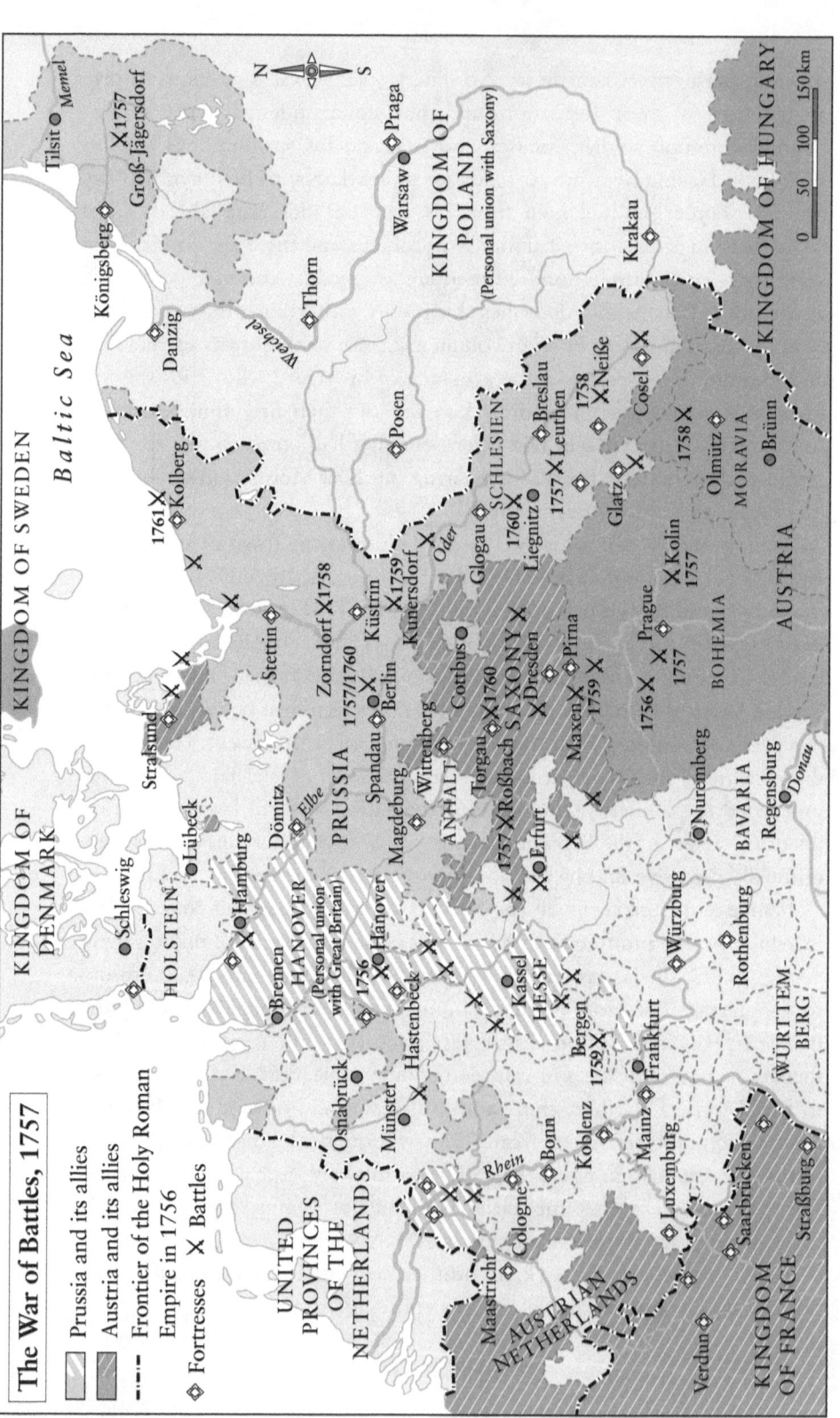

Figure 4.1 The war of battles, 1757.

For the Austrians, 1757 was the bloodiest year of the war. Based on total losses, we can estimate that over 22 percent of Austrian soldiers died in combat in that year.[20] In his autobiography, Goethe also comments on the eventful twelve months: "The year 1757, which we spent in perfectly civic tranquility, kept us, nevertheless, in great uneasiness of mind. Perhaps no other was more fruitful of events than this. Conquests, achievements, misfortunes, restorations, followed one upon another, swallowed up and seemed to destroy each other; yet the image of Frederick, his name and glory, soon hovered again above all."[21] Contemporaries took a keen interest in news of victories and defeats, with information tending to arrive at shorter and shorter intervals. The large number of battles also shaped how soldiers experienced the year, something all the more remarkable because wars of maneuver represented the contemporary strategic ideal.[22]

From Prague to Kolin

Frederick's actions were consistent enough: He had to take quick and determined action, making strategic decisions in order to preempt his opponents. Advancing into Bohemia seemed the best option, and a plan was worked out by staff at the Prussian army headquarters at Lockwitz, south of Dresden. Four army corps would advance into Bohemia and Moravia, joining forces to create two separate armies.[23] On April 18, the Prussians duly marched across the border and began moving through the mountains. On May 2, Frederick reached Prague, his first objective. Four days later one the biggest and bloodiest battles of the eighteenth century was fought very close to the Golden City.[24] The Austrians, fielding 72,600 men, established a long front on a plateau to the east of the city.[25] Frederick combined his own army with that of Field Marshal Curt Christoph von Schwerin (1684–1757) and now commanded around 80,000 men, granting him a slight numerical advantage. He would never again field as many soldiers in a single battle.[26] Frederick styled the momentous confrontation between the houses of Brandenburg and Habsburg as a new Battle of Pharsalus (Pharsalus was a famous battle between Caesar and Pompey in 48 BCE).[27] Lemcke, the Prussian lieutenant, commented critically: "The king absolutely wanted to give battle this day, although the Field Marshal was opposed to this because the troops were tired out from Marching."[28]

Some felt that even heaven took a side in the battle. At the Benedictine abbey of St. Procopius, an image of the eponymous saint, a patron of Bohemia, was said to have opened its eyes, which were "turned imploringly towards heaven."[29] The image of the saint was renowned for regularly performing a "Miracul" whenever disaster loomed; this time it was witnessed by priests at the monastery and by the faithful who had hurried to witness the saint's intervention.

Natural conditions played a crucial role. Underestimated or badly explored terrain could easily prove fatal. On the Prussian left, the cavalry was able to advance, but the Prussian heavy guns got stuck in the narrow streets of the village of Unter-Poczernitz and were unable to play any supporting role. Also on the Prussian left, the first line of infantry, closest to the enemy, discovered that its advance would not be across green fields but rather through half-empty fish ponds. Some soldiers sank to their waists in slime.[30] The infantry, commanded by Field Marshal von Schwerin, tried to advance onto higher ground, but sustained Austrian artillery fire from above caused substantial damage. This attack also saw the death of the field marshal, who was hit by several bullets and a round of canister shot. His death prompted many tributes, including one from the Norwegian officer Georg Friedrich von Krogh (1732–1818), a volunteer on the Prussian general staff, who noted in his diary: "However, the greatest loss was the death of Field Marshal General v. Schwerin, whose glorious career was ended in the seventy-fifth Year of his Life. Attempting to recompose our left wing, he took up a regimental Flag and marched toward the Enemy, but unfortunately came upon a Battery which shot him dead with canister, and thus he gave up his heroic Spirit."[31]

The Austrians were unable to take advantage of Prussian setbacks and also suffered the loss of an important commander. Ulysses Maximilian Browne sustained serious wounds in the battle and died on June 26.[32] The Prussians had more success in the second phase of battle and were able to push the Austrians back, creating and then exploiting a gap between the Austrians to the north and their forces fighting against Schwerin's men on their right, the Prussian left. At the same time, Lieutenant General Hans Joachim von Zieten (1699–1786) launched a cavalry attack from the south, taking on their counterparts on the Austrian right wing and forcing a further retreat. For a time, the Austrian position threatened to disintegrate, but at noon, the two sides were still locked in titanic clashes right across the field. Ultimately the Prussians won the day, with the Austrians withdrawing to Prague.

By now, the battlefield was shrouded in darkness. The scene was witnessed by a musketeer from the Anhalt regiment: "The beautiful and pleasant day was turned to great Darkness by powder smoke and also by the dust of so many people and horses, darkening the entire Air, so that People could scarce be made out, and it seemed quite as though the World was coming to its end that very day."[33]

By the end of the day, thirty-one hundred Prussians had died, with over eight thousand wounded and a further fifteen hundred missing or captured. Total Austrian losses were similar: between twelve and thirteen thousand men.[34] In other words, more than twenty-five thousand men were killed, were wounded, or went missing on May 6, 1757. The loss of Count Schwerin weighed particularly heavily on contemporaries' minds, highlighted by a remark by the Prussian officer Christian Wilhelm von Prittwitz: "We had indeed won the Battle, but it had no favorable consequences for us, especially since we lost Schwerin, a fine hero, in the process. The Imperials esteemed his death greatly, more even than Victory in the battle, and success proved them to have been quite right. After the death of this rare man, things began to deteriorate for us."[35] Schwerin's death would loom large in the memory culture associated with the Battle of Prague.[36]

The extraordinary scale of the battle was clear to those taking part. Prince Maurice of Anhalt-Dessau (1712–1760) wrote to his brother on the day of the battle: "The enemy was over 100,000 strong and the King of Prussia put his 70,000 men into the fire. It is probably the largest Bataille that there has ever been in this world."[37] One ordinary soldier recounted his impressions in a letter he wrote to his wife two days after the battle: "The 6th day sent us a Battel with the Austrians, quite beyond Description, indeed beyond all other Battels which a Person might name. The good Lord in His mercy has once more given us Victory, which although longed for by all was not possible for our side to win, but he helped us and now they are so shattered I do not believe that they will now stand against us again."[38] A few lines later the soldier again insists on the impossibility of communicating his experiences in writing: "I cannot describe it to you as it was even were I to fill three whole Sheets with writing."[39] He says he will tell his wife about the events in person: "My dearest wife should I ever retourn I will tel you myself of these Battels crueltey. This Battel was before Bragen [Prague] on the white mountains. But from now they may be call'd the red Mountains, since they are color'd with Blood."[40] Prittwitz also focuses on the heavy casualties: "[It was] one of the most terrible battles that ever has been. Our regiment remained in reserve with several others on the White Mountain and took no part in this bloodbath; but our grenadiers were there, with extraordinary suffering."[41]

Lieutenant Colonel Ivan Springer, a Russian liaison officer with the Austrians, was among those who analyzed the Battle of Prague from the losing side. Explaining the reasons for defeat, he writes: "A deroute [defeat] of this kind suffered by an army so mighty is to be found in almost no histories, except the battle of Pultawa. It could not have been otherwise, because where no firm disposition is given, things cannot possibly go well. [. . .] In a word, this bataille is more like a deliberate surprise attack than a normal field battle, since it was confusion from beginning to end."[42] No consideration was given to reserves, Springer adds, and every wounded soldier was carried from the field by two men, causing confusion. Above all, the Austrian staff failed to properly plan the deployment of their troops. Bolotov's unit was by now close to Kovno (Kaunas in present-day Lithuania) in the Polish-Lithuanian Commonwealth. A letter he wrote there comments on the high cost of the battle and its ultimate lack of consequences: "How bloody too was the [. . .] horrific battle between the Austrians and Prussians at Prague, and although in a few hours over thirty thousand men were slain and mutilated on both sides, it changed the state of affairs not in the least, did not diminish the violence of the war, and gave rise to no hopes for peace. This battle is all the more remarkable for the fact that, although all thought and expected it would have mighty consequences, this was not the case, and in fact it has had none."[43] Thus, there were contemporaries, even at a great distance from events, who were aware that while battles seem decisive, they may, in fact, prove otherwise, including those raising great expectations, which are difficult or impossible to fulfill. The *Berlinische Nachrichten* of Tuesday, May 10, reported a "great victory" at Prague. An official report on the battle was published at Vienna on May 14, prompting a Prussian reply that dismissed the Austrian version as a "tissue of sheer untruths."[44]

The bombardment of Prague began on May 12. The city's peacetime population was usually fifty-one thousand, but an additional fifty-one thousand Austrian soldiers had by now retreated behind its walls, with the situation becoming increasingly difficult in terms of food and supplies.[45] While Prussia unsuccessfully bombarded the besieged city, news arrived of the mobilization of an Austrian relief army. Frederick's initial response was to deploy an observation corps under the Duke of Braunschweig-Bevern, but he soon followed this with further reinforcements, combining these with

Bevern's troops to form an army of forty thousand.[46] His opponent, Count von Daun, led a much larger Austrian army, numbering around fifty-six thousand men.[47] The Kaiser-Strasse, the imperial highway running from Prague to Vienna, was the most important road linking the two armies. On the morning of June 18, Prussian troops advanced down this highway, moving out from Planian and toward the town of Kolin.

It was an extremely warm day. Prittwitz's account of the battle complains at length about the lack of water but speaks with appreciation of cooling ice blocks commandeered from an ice house close to the battlefield.[48] The Austrians were well positioned along a ridge. A number of Prussian generals, including Bevern and Zieten, informed Frederick that any attack on the Austrian position would be wildly risky. The king remained undeterred.[49] At two o'clock in the afternoon, the battle began, with an advance by the Prussian left, supported by Zieten's cavalry. Prittwitz recounts the scene: "Horse blankets were removed, the cannons were taken from their carriages, rifles were raised, sabers were bared, and the line of battle was formed. Then from all sides roaring voices resounded with the thunderous word: 'March, March!' After this, everything went to the beat of the drum and the music—although the latter did not last very long since the hautboists [oboists] quickly took themselves to safety—in a forward march straight toward where the enemy was expecting us, where they had established position in the correct manner."[50]

One hour later, at three o'clock, the Prussian center launched a frontal attack. After early success—notably, the capture of an oak wood on the Austrian flank—they nonetheless failed to achieve breakthrough. As at Prague, the many ponds in the landscape proved fatal for many Prussian soldiers. In his memoirs, the Austrian general Count Friedrich Georg zu Wied-Runkel (1712–1779) recounts how Count Franz Leopold von Nádasdy (1708–1783) lured a Prussian force of four thousand into a valley "where Farmers earlier had torn out the Ponds and thus the Prussians were left almost up to their necks in water, and our Croats shot them to pieces like wild ducks." Eyewitnesses emphasized the brutality of the artillery barrage. Wied-Runkel writes that the guns made "such terrible work of the Prussians" that he was "in fact moved to pity." He concludes: "The king will suffer the pain of this until this very Hour, for indeed our artillery opened the door to Hell, granting many slaves freedom from Prussian service, but for all Eternity."[51]

Frederick exhorted his men in person, and by around seven o'clock in the evening, they had breached the Austrian lines, briefly seeming to gain the upper hand. But the breakthrough was for nothing; there were no reserves to follow up. The battlefield could not be occupied, and the surviving Prussians flooded back along the Kaiser-Strasse toward Prague. On this day alone, the Prussian army suffered almost sixteen thousand dead and wounded, with the Austrians losing around eight thousand.[52] Under the circumstances, the siege of Prague could not be continued, and Bohemia could not be retained. On June 20, Frederick lifted the siege and withdrew to Saxony.

Kolin was the first Austrian victory over an army commanded by Frederick. Moreover, the victory was entirely unambiguous, prompting a correspondingly joyful response in Vienna.[53] Early on June 20, news reached the imperial court that Field Marshal Daun "had achieved a total Victori against the king of Prussia." The empress, "still in her night attire," gave the news personally to Chamberlain (Oberstkämmerer) Khevenhüller-Metsch, who kissed the royal hand in congratulations. Maria Theresa had only recently learned the news herself; here she was, "still in its first joy," with "tears in her eyes," the court chamberlain observed.[54] Around noon, an official delegation brought the "solemn Message" to the imperial couple at Schönbrunn, complete with trumpet blasts from postilions. The following day a Te Deum was sung at St. Stephen's Cathedral. Theater audiences were given free admission to comedies. Three days of prayer at the cathedral were decreed. Soon after, on June 22, came news of the Prussian withdrawal from Bohemia. On the same day, twenty-three enemy standards were brought into Vienna as trophies by the forces of Field Marshal Lieutenant Johann Benedikt Daun (no relation to Field Marshal Daun), an action celebrated with official festivities and several more Te Deums. On that day, the *Wiener Diarium* published an extra edition, which sent news of Kolin circulating across Europe.[55]

For its part, the *Berlinische Nachrichten* refrained from reporting the defeat at Kolin for some time: No detailed account of the battle and its heavy losses was published until July 14.[56] Reliable information remained difficult to come by, even within the Reich. Franz Rudolf Moll Ingersoll (1709–1789) was a high official (*Regierungsrat*) of the Landgraviate of Hesse-Darmstadt. In July 1757, while based with Imperial forces in Franconia, he complains repeatedly about the absence of reliable news from Saxony and Bohemia: "Then I await with quite burning desire to reliably discover from Your Majesty the actual state of things in Bohemia. Here, many quite astonishing things are told on this subject."[57] Three weeks later, clearly still frustrated, he writes: "It is quite incomprehensible that one cannot learn anything reliable of these regions."[58]

Bolotov, stationed in Kowno, also received word of the victory won by the "Imperials."[59] The Russian-Austrian alliance meant the news brought "almost as much joy [to the Russian army] as if it were a victory for our own troops." The Russian field marshal, he observes, had hastened to spread the news, summoning all of the regiment's clergy to headquarters. There, "amid the cannonfire, thanks was solemnly given to the Almighty. All of the generals were invited to luncheon with the Field Marshal, and the cannons kept up the salute all day long."[60] Two weeks later, on July 1, the Jesuits in Hamburg, together with the Austrian legation, sang "a solemn Te Deum in the Imperial chapel," thanking "God, the Lord of the Armies, from the bottom of their hearts, for the great victory won by the Austrians." "As well as a large crowd of Catholics, many Lutherans and Reformed people" were among those present.[61]

Austria's victory prompted much scornful mockery of the hitherto victorious Prussians. One target was the Te Deum composed for the Prussian victory at Prague by the Berlin court conductor Carl Heinrich Graun (1704–1759): "Providence didn't like the latest Protestant Composition as much as the last, and so the Battle was lost! The biggest threats to the Prussians are Browne, Daun, and Graun!"[62]

The usual solemn declarations of victory were not enough for the victory at Kolin. Henceforth, it was decreed, the battle would be celebrated as the "monarchy's second birthday," its memory to be celebrated in perpetuity by a monthly prayer service of "eternal remembrance."[63] Just four days after Kolin, on June 22, the empress founded the Military Order of Maria Theresa, with the date of the battle, June 18, established as its feast day. Daun was declared the order's first Knight Grand Cross. On the official decree sent to the field marshal, the empress added in her own hand: "Before the eyes of the entire army, you have proved yourself worthy of the Order, and thus you shall be its first Knight Grand Cross."[64]

While Vienna celebrated, soldiers' corpses lay unburied for weeks on the Kaiser-Strasse near Kolin, along with the carcasses of countless horses: There had been no one to bury them after the battle.[65] Epidemic disease was now a risk, severely affecting traffic on the highway. The army command angrily threatened tough sanctions after it was reported that nothing had been done about the horrific scenes.[66] War's "good Policey"—its ethical conduct—had failed. Typically enough, blame was shunted down the hierarchy of command, pinned solely on the authorities on the ground near Kolin.

Reactions to the Burning of Zittau

By the following month, Austria's brief glory had already been tarnished by another victory—more specifically, by its dramatic impact on the conquered civilian population. At the siege of the town of Zittau, close to the Saxon-Bohemian frontier, Austrian artillery set off one of the war's most devastating urban fires.[67] The burning of Zittau was well documented by contemporaries, and the subject was taken up in pamphlets and printed sermons.[68] These publications sought, so they claimed, to correct erroneous newspaper reports, foster "Christian sympathy" among the public, and provide precise information about the fire so that people might "form a true and clear idea."[69] An anonymous pamphlet titled *The Sad Remembrance of the Lamentable Fate Endured by the Good City of Zittau Endured on Julius 23rd 1757, as Well as on the Previous and Following Days* noted that the bombardment and the subsequent fire began shortly after nine o'clock in the morning and described how "by God's permission and providence," the "unfortunate time" came when "the good, beautiful, well-built city of Zittau had to be turned into a pile of Stones by the fire. The cannons' thunder was accompanied by a fire of bombs. Immediately when the first bombs hit the city's buildings, they did set fire to them. [. . .] All kinds of fire stations were established, and many vigilant, hardworking citizens risked their lives during the disaster, using all their strength to put out the first fire; in a mere quarter of an hour there were more than nine Fires."[70]

The anonymous observer is unsure of the precise fatality count. The number "found in cellars and other places cannot be determined with great exactitude. It is said to extend to one hundred, including a number of noble Families."[71] The author supplements his own remarks with extracts from published reports. In the *Erlangische Öffentliche Nachrichten*, one Zittau resident reports more than 180 "corpses pulled from the rubble," with 57 people found in one cellar alone. Some reports estimate the number of destroyed buildings at over five hundred, with only around sixty buildings left standing in the entire town.

Published a year after the fire, *Twenty-One Copperplate Engravings* by the artist Johann Daniel de Montalegre provides a particularly effective visual representation of the attack on Zittau. The architecturally precise images meticulously document the destruction of Zittau. Moreover, Montalegre's preface to the images explicitly addresses the emotional effect of realistic depiction, which he compares to the effect of the event on eyewitnesses. If it were possible, he writes, "to describe all the Pitiful Circumstances in detail, and actually depict all of the miserable Districts lying in terrible ruin, [spectators'] Hearts would be moved just as much as those who saw with their own eyes Zittau's wretched remaining Skeleton, in stone and heaps of Ash. They were prompted to Astonishment, and must often shed tears."[72]

Eyewitnesses described the fire's aftermath as a horrific spectacle: "The Dead, and the suffocated multitudes, were dragged from their Cellars and laid out before the burned-out Houses of the Freyer Gasse, and these bodies, along with the devastated City, presented a Spectacle such that even the most hardened of Dispositions were overcome with Dread and Horror."[73] But these more immediate impressions soon gave way to outrage at the bombing and questions as to its legitimacy.[74] Even the *Neueröfnete Historische Bilder-Saal*, a pro-Imperial publication in Nuremberg, found it difficult to justify the event: "It was merely the harsh Necessity of robbing the enemy of his accommodations which brought Misfortune on this good city, forcing the hand of our Imperial generals."[75] The bombing of Zittau made sense in terms of logistics: The capture of Zittau's stores of flour and ammunition by Allied forces was a heavy blow to the Austrians.[76] But even senior Allied officers were surprised at the destruction done to the city. Count zu Wied-Runkel relates the scene: "It was a miserable thing to see this fine Place reduced by the Fury of the Flames, which even Daun himself could not long watch or listen to, this city made into nothing, and the Cries and Weeping of the few remaining inhabitants."[77] Maria Theresa was said to have retrospectively donated 50,000 guilders in sympathy with the people of Zittau.[78] Nonetheless, the incident created substantial bad publicity for the Austrians, fracturing the propaganda image of "Saxony's liberators."[79]

Frederick continued to receive bad news throughout July. On the thirteenth of the month, he wrote in distress to his sister Wilhelmine (1709–1758), the Margravine of Bayreuth: "I am struck with so many blows that I am numb. The French have lately occupied Friesland and will cross the Weser. They have incited the Swedes to a declaration of war against me; they have sent 17,000 men to march into Pomerania. The Russians are laying siege to Memel, Lehwaldt has them in the rear and the flank. The Imperial troops will likewise march soon enough. As soon as all of these enemies attack me, I shall be forced to withdraw from Bohemia."[80]

The Russian Advance: Gross-Jägersdorf

The first Russian invasion of East Prussia took place in 1757, when forces under the command of General Stepan Fedorovich Apraksin (1702–1758) crossed the border in massive numbers.[81] The advance into Prussia began between July 20 and 22, setting out from the Polish town of Werbalow. The first notable incident took place at the village of Mikulen, around three miles from the town of Stallupönen (today Nesterov, in the Russian exclave of Kaliningrad).[82] A detachment of Russian dragoons, commanded by a French officer, Major De la Rois, failed to observe any Prussian troops. Presuming themselves safe, they got down to some drinking, but before long a detachment of Prussian black and yellow hussars advanced into the village, led by Colonel Malachowski (1713–1775).[83] A heated battle followed, in which forty Russian dragoons and several Cossacks were killed, with twenty-six Russians taken prisoner. The careless French major was demoted to private, placed in irons, and court-martialed.[84] Like the stolen handkerchief at Maidstone, the incident was minor in itself, but it had a substantial impact. As Bolotov put it:

> Outwardly, this seemed a meaningless incident: there are countless skirmishes of this kind in war and they are never what ultimately decides the outcome [. . .]. However, this was not so in the case of this incident; it was memorable for its great and terrible consequences and for the ill fortune it brought to many thousands of people. First, the whole Russian army was impressed by the courage of the Prussians, and this intensified the fear they already felt; second, the incident gave the enemy a highly unfavorable opinion of us [Russians] and our courage; third, and most importantly, the local inhabitants, as well as the Prussian troops, came to think of us as complete weaklings, capable of nothing at all.[85]

The battle led Prussian villagers to fight as partisans, shooting at the Russian invaders from the windows of their houses.[86] This, in turn, prompted the Russian field marshal to order that "no mercy be shown to residents anywhere that something of this kind takes place; places where this occurs are to be pillaged."[87] For Bolotov, this marked the beginning of the Cossack atrocities that continued throughout the war, which earned Russian soldiers a lasting reputation as "barbarians."[88]

On July 26, the Russian army, including Bolotov, reached the royal city of Gumbinnen. By the beginning of August, it had advanced to a position between Insterburg and Georgenburg, heading west in the direction of Königsberg. Bolotov's memoir repeatedly criticizes the behavior of Cossacks and Kalmyks, whose scorched earth policies did permanent damage to the reputation of the Russian army.[89] The actions of Russian auxiliaries meant Russia's overall force enjoyed something like an abundance of food, but they also left behind a steady trail of devastation: "Of all the villages we saw, not one was inhabited—they were all of them empty, entirely robbed. Not a house was spared from looting, our soldiers had even discovered those dwellings which had been very carefully concealed, covered with twigs or dung. Every last thing had been looted."[90]

The two Russian armies, led by Apraksin and General Wilhelm Graf von Fermor (1702–1771), had a combined strength of fifty-five thousand men. A Prussian army of thirty-two thousand was dispatched to oppose them, under the command of Field Marshal Lehwaldt. He had orders to attack the Russians at the first opportunity, in an effort to force a swift peace agreement in which Prussia would annex Polish West Prussia.[91] In a letter to Lehwaldt of June 23, 1756, Frederick played down the danger: "This much I can predict: that they have the worst Generals, and Apraksin, now given command, is as bad a general as it is possible to be, so you shall have little enough to fear."[92] Furthermore, Frederick continues, the strength of Austrian regiments had been "advertised as very much greater" than it, in fact, was, so Lehwaldt could expect to deal with considerably fewer enemy soldiers in reality.

On August 30, 1757, the two sides met in battle at Gross-Jägersdorf, fifty kilometers (about thirty-one miles) east of Königsberg.[93] Like many of his fellow officers, Bolotov was fond of theatrical metaphors, and his battle report reads as if he was watching a play. In a favorable position on the Russian left, concealed behind a thick overgrowth of bushes, he could imagine himself and his comrades as "mere spectators of the bloody battle which now loomed."[94] The two sides began to exchange fire in uninterrupted barrages. Writing in retrospect, Bolotov notes that "with regard to the bloody spectacle," he is now unable to "describe the shock suffered to the soul." Poor visibility soon clouded the gruesome scene: "Soon lost too was the pleasure of observing it all; the incessant firing rendered the smoke so thick we could no longer view the two armies, only hear the crack of muskets and the thunder of cannon."[95] Chaotic fighting held a fascination for observers at the time, as Bolotov never tires of emphasizing: "In a word, everything presented a pitiful image to the tender heart, and those of us who saw all of this could never see enough, so strange and striking it was."[96] In the same breath, he notes a "certain military amusement." The artillery position nearest to the group of Russian officers who were observing was instructed to fire a bomb directly at an equivalent group of officers who were observing on the Prussian side: "He carried out our wish, and the shot was so good that the bomb fell directly by the willow tree, exploding a foot above the ground. What that did to my good sirs, the Prussian officers! All fled wildly, except for three who would remain at that place for all Eternity."[97] The Russians ultimately won the day, albeit with heavy losses of around six thousand dead and wounded, with the Prussians losing around forty-five hundred.[98] The victory was the result, above all, of highly effective Russian artillery and the staunchness of their infantry in the face of heavy fire.

After the victory at Gross-Jägersdorf, the tsarina's army quite unexpectedly withdrew to Russia. Bolotov professed profound shock:

> August 29, however, saw the bleak and memorable day on which we witnessed the end of our hopes, with our hearts filled with grief, emasculated, covered in shame and dishonor. To cut a long story short, on this unforgettable day we turned our backs on the enemy, and took off back to the fatherland, so filled with shame we could barely look each other in the eye. [. . .] Even today, I am filled with rage when I think of the uproar in the entire army. [. . .] There was muttering everywhere, and furtive cursing of our senior commanders.[99]

Apraksin's defensive approach was not without consequences: He was removed from his command at the end of October, imprisoned in St. Petersburg, and put on trial.[100] He died of a heart attack in August 1758 while still in investigative custody and was succeeded by Count Fermor.[101]

By early September, Prussian forces had set out in pursuit of the withdrawing Russians, which slowed their retreat while also giving rise to still more misery for the local population. As Bolotov explains: "Their light forces kept us under constant harassment, attacking our foragers and our sentries, and we had to drive them off by burning every village and settlement to the ground as we went, so they could find no shelter. This inflicted much suffering on the innocent rural population."[102] Typical of these cruelties were the actions of Cossack and Kalmyk troops that devastated the town of Ragnit on the Memel River in the days after September 24, 1757.[103]

Some weeks previously the nearby city of Tilsit had been captured by Russian troops. The town council and clergy immediately surrendered to the approaching army, swearing an oath to their new occupiers. But the occupation escalated after another nearby skirmish between Prussian hussars and a large force of Cossacks.[104] Several hundred Cossacks were now moved into Ragnit and proceeded to commit violence on a large scale against the civilian population. An impression of the events can be found in reports written by Theodor Werner, the vice burgomaster, as well as other eyewitnesses, including the royal bailiff and the city cantor.[105] Beginning at eight o'clock in the evening, attacks were carried out by a "huge uncountable Swarm of Cosaques and Kalmucks [. . .], like a raging Stream," involving widespread plunder and acts of violence.[106] The looting lasted three days, during which time residents were forced to strip naked and were "chased Bloodthirsty around the streets, with Whippings, Pikings, and Saber-blows." Werner includes fourteen individual accounts of violence, listing the dead and wounded. In the course of the rampage, many women were raped, houses looted and set on fire, and cattle slaughtered.[107] Sources report between twenty and twenty-six fatalities.[108] Among the victims, particular attention was paid to the killings of Mayor Boltz and the pastor Martin Lindenau, as well as those in the service of the town council, the clergy, and the royal authorities.

The reports use recurring stereotypes in their description of the Cossacks. Their heavy armaments are mentioned—in particular, their "five instruments of death"—as well as their prodigious drinking, robust physical constitution, and "depraved temperament." These elements made up an image of a "terrible enemy of mankind."[109] Cossacks were depicted as significantly more cruel than Kalmyks.[110] Taken as a whole, the reports suggest that the Russian irregulars, above all, wanted money, clothes, and livestock and would use any and all means to get them. Despite the brutality of the attack on Ragnit, some contemporaries viewed it as an exception to otherwise exemplary behavior on the part of Russian troops. Thus, Georg Albrecht Donalitius (1719–1792), the royal bailiff, writes: "Were it not for this incident, I could truthfully say that I had known Russian troops only to be kind and compassionate."[111]

Eyewitnesses compared the sacking of Ragnit to the "massacre of the Innocents of Bethlehem," the key historical point of reference for war atrocities since medieval times. The destruction of the city now became a veritable media event; it was cited in, among others, *Patriotic Letters*, written by the military chaplain Adolph Dietrich Ortmann (1718–1781).[112] Bolotov also comments on these events, largely focusing on the damage caused to Russia's public image and quoting the Prussian press as saying "The Russians went forth from Prussia and will leave no favorable memory. The city of Ragnit was reduced to ashes, along with surrounding villages."[113]

Correspondence published in the *Danziger Beyträge* about "atrocities committed by Russian light troops" is a rich source of information on the public legitimation of the events at Ragnit.[114] The letters present clear differences of opinion on the use of Cossacks in irregular operations. In one letter, General Apraksin, the Russian commander, informs the Prussian Field Marshal Hans von Lehwaldt that he has "never taken the least pleasure in the Scorching and Burnings Down done by irregulair Troops [. . .]." However, he does not think it possible to end these measures until "the crazed peasants in some way cease their outrageous Actions, which are more than Hostile." He leaves it to Lehwaldt to judge whether "the Peasants themselves did not provoke the Cossacks and Callmucks to their utmost Rancour; Thusly, they are themselves the true Cause of the disaster that befell them."[115] Acts of violence by Russian light troops, he adds, were "not always by premeditation, but largely come about through Contingency." The Cossack atrocities would end only when the rural population observed good order, as had been demanded of them. In other words, Russia's military leadership here acknowledges that the violence is unusual but places the blame on continued resistance by the rural population. A document included with the letter again refers to rural resistance, listing its various forms. Noting that "it is not true that the Nation in question [Russia] does not observe military discipline," it suggests that it was already an "established truth" that local resistance had been "the initial cause of disorderly conduct" among the Russian forces.

The correspondence illustrates a key military problem of the time: the supplying of troops. The rural residents drove their cattle into the forest, trying in any way possible to keep them out of the hands of Russian troops. This meant, writes Apraksin, that his troops had to take the cattle by force. This could not, he adds, "occur without excesses," since the "stubborn peasant will turn to violence to defend his cattle." Lehwaldt's reply acknowledges that the Russian general took no pleasure in the "Cruauties" committed but claims the Prussians had given no reason for the Russians to commit them. He describes the behavior of the Russian irregulars as a "kind of revenge," quite out of keeping with the "profession of a virtuous soldier."

Their actions might perhaps be explained by the high losses among regular Russian forces, but they were unusual even among heathen peoples.[116] In response to Apraksin's argument that earlier actions by Prussian hussars had provoked a Cossack reaction, Lehwaldt says that his hussars had not been active in these areas and that the Cossack actions had been intended to cut off supplies to his own troops. The Cossacks, he writes, had indeed intentionally burned the places mentioned by Apraksin "and in this way did take from the Enemy army the Subsistence they found there. These Actions, contrary to all Customs of war and of Humanity, have continued until the present Day."[117] There were critical comments on the Russian side too, suggesting the Cossacks' actions had been counterproductive. For his part, Lehwaldt emphasized the dishonor inherent in this kind of warfare, "which is Condoned by their Army, although it brings so little Honor, and even be to their Disadvantage, and which must bring the country people to the most extreme Desperation. [They] should punish it most severely, and put an end to it in the name of Decency, since there are many means by which even furious people can be kept under control."[118] As propaganda, Lehwaldt's letter was intended to discredit Russian troops, but it also questions the basic ability of the Russian command to control its own army.

In the mid-nineteenth century, Xaver von Hasenkamp, editor of the newspaper *Neue Preussischen Provinzialblätter*, wrote about the atrocities at Ragnit and attempted to explain their cause. Referring to them as a "scene of horror," he suggested it was no "occasional outbreak, [with] Russian military discipline too weak to contain the notorious lawlessness of the savage hordes."[119] Rather, he says, the violence was a "well-considered, well-planned operation." The actions against Ragnit and its residents should be seen as a "strategic measure," a "means of moral terror" (*moralisches Schreckmittel*). In short, the action had essentially been a message directed to the citizens of Tilsit, since the Russians were already on the point of abandoning the city.[120]

Does all of this amount to a Russian version of "shock and awe"? Or was it simply a loss of military control? The threat embodied by irregular troops can be seen in statements like that of Apraksin, who justified the use of Kalmyks by saying "[the enemy] will take fright at the very name alone."[121] All in all, the sources suggest that the Russians exercised poor control over their irregulars, who were in an angry mood because of the difficult supply situation. However, there are also indications that the attack on Ragnit had a particular tactical purpose, aimed at securing the Russian retreat.[122] This withdrawal would prove particularly costly for the Kalmyks, thousands of whom fell victim to smallpox, then known as blackpox, a disease they had never before faced.[123]

From Hastenbeck to Kloster-Zeven

On July 26, 1757, the same day that the Russians reached Gumbinnen, a significant battle took place between an Allied army of thirty-six thousand under the Duke of Cumberland and sixty thousand French troops commanded by Marshal d'Estrées.[124] The encounter took place at Hastenbeck, today a suburb of the German city of Hamelin. It began at six o'clock in the morning with a two-hour "artillery duel."[125] By late morning, the battle line was nearly four miles long. By noon, very heavy fighting had developed, centered on Hastenbeck. Then something quite unusual happened. Both commanders incorrectly assessed the situation, and at about one o'clock in the afternoon, each gave the order to retreat, more or less simultaneously.[126] Confusion, contradictory reports, and a desire to avoid risking their armies had led both generals to break off the battle. Losses were relatively light for an encounter involving around ninety thousand soldiers: twenty-three hundred Allied soldiers dead and wounded, with fourteen hundred casualties on the French side. In effect, Hastenbeck was neither won nor lost, which led the Prussian general staff to conclude, 150 years later, that the battle "would permanently occupy a peculiar position in the history of warfare."[127] There have been many occasions on which both sides have claimed to have taken a battlefield, retrospectively proclaiming victory, notes the official war history. But it was highly unusual—in fact, unprecedented—for both sides to do so, "beat[ing] the retreat almost at the same time, for fear of being outflanked and brought to catastrophe, only for he who first noticed the opponent's departure to again advance, occupy the abandoned battlefield, and in this way—and solely in this way—emerge the winner."[128] Hastenbeck is exceptional for this reason, but it also serves to illustrate two general phenomena. First, it featured a maneuver aimed at protecting troops from impending destruction or from inadequate possibilities for retreat. Cumberland carried out this maneuver, moving his men across a single bridge and through marshy lowlands watered by the Hamel and Remte Rivers.[129] Second, here again we see the importance of the performative occupation of the battlefield, which was a way for one side to claim victory.

But Hastenbeck cannot, in fact, be regarded as having been undecided, especially if we examine subsequent events more closely. The French have to be regarded as the winners, since they now had their opponents on the run. But they would be forced to pursue them without Marshal D'Estrées, their victorious general, who fell victim to court intrigues at Versailles just a week after the battle, to be succeeded by the Duc de Richelieu, hero of the capture of Menorca.[130] After the setback at Hastenbeck, Cumberland's army withdrew beyond the Weser River and headed for the fortress at Stade.[131] Meanwhile, on September 8, Richelieu and Cumberland concluded a peace accord, the Convention of Kloster-Zeven, through the mediation of Count Rochus Friedrich zu Lynar (1708–1781), a Danish diplomat.[132] The convention was comprised of four primary and four ancillary articles.[133] The first article ordered a cessation of hostilities within twenty-four hours, while the second arranged for the repatriation of auxiliary troops from Hesse, Brunswick, Saxe-Gotha, and Lippe-Bückeburg. The third limited the size of the Stade garrison to between four and six thousand troops, while the remainder of the observation army would retreat across the Elbe to the Duchy of Lauenburg. The fourth article stipulated the withdrawal of a "detached corps" of the Hanoverian army to Stade within twenty-four hours.

The following day in Göttingen, Andreas Wähner, the professor of Oriental languages, recorded that a ceasefire had been "signed at Closter Zeven." In the town of Celle, on September 11, the garrison auditor Johann Philipp Schowart noted news of the convention in his diary.[134] However, neither the French nor the British government ratified the agreement made by Richelieu and Cumberland. The French felt their flank would be left under permanent threat, while Britain faced radical change in foreign policy under its new prime minister, Pitt the Elder, a critic of the country's military operations in Hanover. The convention as it had been agreed to was seen as a failure, with Cumberland relieved of his command. By now, the British attempt to secure Hanover was floundering, with the French posing a serious threat to the capital of Electoral Hanover while the Russians and Austrians menaced Berlin and Potsdam, the two centers of Prussian government.

A Daring Raid on Berlin

On Sunday October 16, 1757, the city of Berlin witnessed an audacious feat of arms, for once doing justice to the phrase.[135] As the residents were attending church services that morning, they were met with sudden and shocking news: The enemy stood at the gates of the city. A Hungarian general, Count András Hadik (1711–1790), had arrived at the head of a raiding party of five thousand, including eleven hundred hussars and twenty-one Grenzers, light infantry troops originally used to patrol the southern military frontier of the Habsburg lands. Rumors of troop movements had reached the city two days previously, but the only reaction had been to double the guard on the gates. The force commanded by Hadik, who was celebrating his birthday that Sunday, had set out from Elsterwerda on October 11 on a quick and well-concealed march. At this time, the city of Berlin had a population of around one hundred thousand, having undergone a recent phase of rapid urban development.

Hadik called on the city to surrender. The city council (*Stadtrat*) answered with a written statement: "Unconvinc'd of the correctness and authenticity of the Command, the Magistracy is all the less Able to impart an Answer."[136] A chronicle kept by the Berlin master baker Johann Friedrich Heyde offers a concise description of events: "On the 16th day of Octobris, under the command of General Hadik, we in Berlin were confronted by several thousand Austrians, prompting great horror. In the afternoon at 2 o'clock a Skirmish took place leading to the shooting dead or the wounding of some 150 on both Sides."[137] That morning Hadik's men had captured Köpenick, on the outskirts of the city, but he hesitated to advance on Berlin itself, unsure how many soldiers were stationed in the city and reluctant to facilitate uncontrolled looting.

Captain Baron von Walterskirchen presented a second capitulation demand to the city authorities. The response was one of meek submission: "The Magistracy, along with the whole city, lays itself at your feet, imploring Mercy, and quite willingly agrees to the Fire Charge, in as much as their present unfortunate Circumstances will allow."[138] Within eight hours, the city had paid a ransom of 160,000 thalers in cash and made out a bill of exchange worth another 50,000 talers, the payment being listed as a "Fire Charge." An additional 25,000 talers were donated to Hadik's troops as a "gift." Reporting the payment, Heyde's chronicle sounds almost relieved: "As agreed, this time the guests did not enter the city, but withdrew on the morning of October 17, taking with them 200 000 talers, as well as gifts for Officers. They have left behind one of their best Generals, a man named Babecini, on the battlefield at Cottbusser Tor."[139] In a moment of magnanimity, the departing Hadik left letters certifying that Berlin need quarter no more soldiers for the duration of the war and sparing the city from any further payments.[140]

One description of the raid can be found in a letter written jointly on October 18 by the Berlin poet Karl Wilhelm Ramler (1725–1798), known as the German Horace, and the composer Christian Gottfried Krause (1719–1770). The letter's recipient was the poet Johann Wilhelm Ludwig Gleim, sometimes called the German Anakreon. Ramler and Krause describe how the raiders blew up a city gate and threatened to set the city ablaze, and they recount the brave resistance of the garrison—in particular, a battalion from Christian Hemming Von Lange's (1688-1760) regiment 7. These defenders of Berlin killed a top enemy general, they report, and seemed to take down an Austrian soldier with nearly every round they fired. But thereafter, they write, "such a capitulation was made, that we paid them off with two tons of gold to keep the royal Residence from being looted. Our enemies departed immediately thereafter, on Monday morning at 5 o'clock, after looting & killing, and devastating the area around the Schlesisches Tor, the gate through which they had made their Entry to the city." Now, they continue, all hopes rested with the great king: "By the hour, we expect Friederich, our great avenger. This day has already seen several regiments march in; Berlin is returning to life." The letter exhibits plentiful rage. The enemy stirred "so much anger" in Ramler's heart, it goes on, that with "just this rage and a dozen guns, he might have driven the Austrians quite out from the whole city." Ramler complains that the defenders had won the "Bataille within the city Walls," with Krause adding that cannons had been available inside the city, along with "some 1,000 men," but they had not been used, while the court and garrison commander fled to Spandau with five hundred men: "God will know who is responsible [*cujus culpa*]." They lament what the king will see on arrival: "O great Friederich, how we sorrow that the news you receive from your dear Berlin is not otherwise! The king arrives this evening, the court is already come from Spando." The Prussians have recaptured a coach full of gold looted from Berlin, they add, and captured a troop of Austrian soldiers: "God grant that, should we not recover the rest of the gold, at least we may kill as many Austrians as we can."[141]

Vienna received the news of Hadik's raid eagerly. Khevenhüller-Metsch describes the arrival, on October 22, of the "first news of the Berlin Surprise, undertaken so boldly and successfully by General Haddick. Since the Événement could only be regarded as truly a glorious feat of our arms, I immediately took the opportunity to kiss the Empress's hand during the meeting of the Cabinet."[142] Hadik's attack had revealed a vulnerability at the political heart of Prussia. Frederick's response was to move the entire court, including his ministries and the state treasury, to the safety of the city of Magdeburg. This would not be the last visit by foreign troops to Berlin during the war.

Rossbach: A Strange Battle

Hadik and his men left Berlin in hectic flight, pursued by Prussian troops as far as Hoyerswerda.[143] By now, the combined French and Imperial army was close to Gotha, operating somewhat "indecisively" along the Saale River.[144] Frederick continued to seek a decisive battle. With surprising rapidity, he melded the various units at his disposal into a larger army, although numerically still far inferior to that of his opponents. The French were not offensively disposed, as shown by their defensive destruction of a bridge near Weissenfels, an action intended to stave off Prussian attacks across the Saale. However, the Prussians eventually managed to cross on November 3. Two days later the French-Imperial army marched out, attempting unsuccessfully to bypass the Prussian camp close to Rossbach. Soubise wanted to establish camp rather than go on the attack, but Prince Joseph of Saxe-Hildburghausen, his cocommander and head of the Imperial army, urged him to take the offensive.

The afternoon of November 5, 1757, saw a memorable battle take place at Rossbach.[145] The encounter seems to have begun spontaneously, but its progress was affected by an incident that later became legendary. Georg Karl Hans Edler zu Putlitz, the king's personal attendant (*Leibpage*), has left one account. He describes Frederick's own viewpoint on the battle as he surveyed the field from a nearby manor house while also dining quietly with his generals. From this building, the *roi connétable* (commander-king) could look down and observe the battlefield: "From the house's attic window could be seen the enemy's entire Position. The king himself went up and saw them and believed that everything was as it had been on the 4th of November, since the imperial army was on the [Prussian] right wing." An officer, Captain von Gaudi, was ordered to remain on the roof and observe the situation. As Frederick and his staff lunched below, news arrived of an enemy advance. The king ordered his forces to hold fast to their positions. The young officer on the roof sent another report, saying that the enemy's position had shifted, with their lines moving apart. Now the king himself went up onto the roof "and did not think anything had changed. However, as he descended the stairs, the entire enemy Army hove into view, lined up before the Prussian headquarters, visible through a sitting room window."[146] Around half past two, Frederick realized that the Prussians were vulnerable to an attack against the advancing forward units of his left wing. On the king's orders, at half past three, Friedrich Wilhelm Seidlitz (1721–1773) launched a cavalry charge against the encircling French force. The move caught the attacking force by surprise: The French-Imperial tactical maneuver seemed to have been successfully fought off.

The second line of Prussian infantry was deployed in oblique order; this arrangement meant that when it advanced, it forced the troops of the French and their allies into a ravine, in a fateful turn of events. Around five o'clock, Seydlitz ordered the Prussian cavalry forward in another flanking attack. The battle then soon drew to a close, with the French and Imperial armies falling back in disarray, their disordered units losing contact with one another. It was already early November, so dusk fell early that day, allowing the French and Imperial forces to escape. Putlitz describes the situation: "A pitch black night had come. Our Enemies could not be pursued, as would otherwise have happened. And thus all had to remain as it was at Battle's end. [. . .] No one could much tell Friend from Enemy. And thus the Enemy enjoyed a fine Stroke of luck."[147]

Franz Rudolf Mollinger, secretary to Prince Georg of Hesse-Darmstadt, was present at Rossbach as part of the Darmstadt regiment allotted to the Imperial army. In the days following the battle, he continually wrote letters reporting to a government official in Darmstadt.[148] "At last, on the fifth [of the month] came the unfortunate day when fate had determined we would become a Spectacle, a day the Holy Roman Empire can justifiably wish it to 'disappear from memory' (*excidat ille dies aevo* etc.), as Thuanus wished of the massacres of St. Bartholomew's Day."[149] Early in the battle, around two o'clock in the afternoon, the Prussian army managed to break camp at great speed, completing the action in just a few minutes. This led the Imperial army to believe that the Prussians were on the run, heading for Merseburg. "But heavens, how wrong we were!" laments Mollinger. An artillery barrage from the Prussian left began while Imperial units were still forming on the right of the French and Imperial lines and before the French could fully deploy their artillery. "At the same time, his cavalry struck ours like lightning, without warning. In less time than it takes me to write this, they had piled them all in heaps, Imperials, French, and [their] German allies, all without exception. And after that, you've never seen running like it! Here I should stop my description, and thus have described the Bataille as quickly as we lost it, and completely."[150]

Mollinger does not, in fact, end his description here, well aware of his audience's curiosity. He notes that he "had the pleasure" of viewing the entire proceedings from a hill overlooking the battlefield. Nonetheless, the unmasterable complexity of the battle means even the best views cannot provide explanations: "In spite of all this, it is not possible for me or anyone in this world to present the whole process from life; I have difficulty still in persuading myself that this was not a Dream that I had witnessed." Of course, the Battle of Rossbach was not a dream, but should we even think of it as a battle? Mollinger's descriptions give valuable hints as to contemporary definitions:

> [Rossbach] certainly was a Bataille. Two enemy armies were drawn up in order to Strike against the Other, with encounters down the Entire Length of the Line. Thus this bataille had all the requisita of any true bataille. However, one may in vain search History for its like. Since the Flood there has been not one single example of this, with an army like ours being so horribly and entirely Knock'd out of the field by an army barely half of its strength, and then chased into Flight, and in so short a time, but with so little loss of men.[151]

Rossbach had the fewest casualties of any large battle in the war's European theaters: 550 dead and wounded on the Prussian side and 3,000 French and Imperial casualties, along with 7,000 prisoners. Despite this, the dead were treated no better than usual.[152] Johann Christian Meier (1732–1815), a pastor from the town of Schneverding, published his memoirs in 1811. He writes of a visit to the battlefield on November 6, 1757, the day after Rossbach. At the time, Meier was a student in Halle; having heard news of the battle, he felt "curiosity for a tragedy I had never Witness'd" and set out with friends to visit the scene:

> In the Night and early morning, peasants from the surrounding villages had stripped the dead entirely and laid them out, stiff as they were, on their faces. The living and the wounded were no longer on the battlefield. About four hundred Prussians remained, but all had

been buried already, and we could not find a single one. The dead lay far and wide, all across an immeasurable plain; but time was too short on that winter day to wander the whole battlefield. As far as the eye could see, all was full of dead men, sometimes in heaps, sometimes scattered, although many were already buried. The position of many of the corpses prompted me to shudder, especially when cannonballs had hit their Body or Head, or their Bodies had been cut with sabers, and lacerated to shreds. It had rained a little that night and their backs were as white as bones in a cooked fish. Most of the dead bore residues of gunpowder in their hair, even where their heads had been cut apart and split open. The heavy cavalry and hussars attacking the cannons had wreaked horrific devastation, yet they said this battle was easy, a mere hare hunt.[153]

The degradation meted out to corpses from the defeated armies is notable: "The dead had been dragged with bent Dung-Hooks, pulled onto a wall and kick'd back down. This had prompted hearty laughter and there was much jesting about them and mock funeral sermons were said over them, the words of which I do not care to repeat. How great is human impudence and insensitivity! It was the peasants who had to do these burials, but they were supervised by others, and those people did most of the joking." Thus, it seems there was military involvement in the burials. At the end of his battlefield visit, Meier writes: "We departed the battlefield, our curiosity for such things now sated for life."[154]

Soubisiades: Reactions to Rossbach

Filled with fresh confidence, Frederick wrote to his beloved sister Wilhelmine: "It is said that 20,000 Prussians have defeated 50,000 French and Germans. Now I may go to my grave in peace, with the glory and honor of my nation saved. We may know misfortune, but never again dishonor."[155] Frederick's victory at Rossbach stopped the French advance eastward: This would be his last direct confrontation with the French in this war. Across Europe, his reputation for outstanding generalship had been strengthened. He had inflicted an embarrassing defeat on Europe's major military power while boosting his own standing. The king of Prussia was now something more than merely the major player in the Third Silesian War; the battle meant he was now a key figure in Europe as a whole.[156] One contemporary pamphlet depicted Frederick and Gustavus Adolphus as Protestant heroes; Rossbach was close to the battlefield of Lützen, where Gustavus had been fatally wounded in 1632, and by this time, it was already a resonant site of historical memory.[157]

The defeat at Rossbach also received widespread coverage in French media, with the losing general subject to particular ridicule.[158] Barbier, a Parisian writer, comments on the abuse that made the rounds in France: "Much Mockery was made of the Prince of Soubise on the subject of the Battle of Rossbach. It was no longer observed that one had been 'broken by the North wind (*bise*)' but rather 'by the *Sou-bise*.' It is also said that Soubise Palace is up for rent, since the Prince had to stay behind at cadet school; it is also rumored that he was relieved of his command, although this is not true. In this way the public takes its revenge in verse and song."[159] Mocking songs and verses quickly came to be known as Soubisiades.[160] One well-known verse went: "His lantern in his hand, Soubise says, I've searched and searched but just can't find it, where the devil is my army? It was there just yesterday morning. Did someone steal it from me? Did I misplace it? Oh I lose everything, what a fool I am! But let's wait until day, let's wait till the noonday sun. So, what do I see? Oh my heavens! My heart's delight! O blessed miracle, there it is, over there. Oh no, bloody hell, what's all this, over here? Oh no! I was wrong! It's the *enemy's* bloody army!"[161] The Soubisiades had their roots in popular tradition. There had already been Mazarinades, songs ridiculing Cardinal Jules Mazarin (1602–1661), and Poissonades, which targeted Madame de Pompadour, originally known as Jeanne-Antoinette Poisson. Now a royal mistress and a clergyman were again caught in the crossfire of criticism, with Madame Pompadour and the Abbé Bernis (1715–1794), until recently France's foreign minister, blamed for the appointment of the inexperienced Soubise.[162]

It was one thing for a general to have his reputation tarnished, although not even very badly: Soubise was made marshal of France the next year. The reputation of the French crown was quite another matter. Increasingly open criticism was voiced by philosophers and Enlightenment thinkers, who held up the Prussian king, or at least characteristics popularly attributed to him, as a mirror to the French court. Favoritism, court intrigues, and courtesans' whisperings were now major features of the decrepit French political system. Rossbach may even have prompted the phrase "Après nous le deluge" (After us, the deluge), said to have been uttered by Madame de Pompadour when news of the defeat arrived during a ball at court. France's rulers now had to choose whether to prioritize the continental war or the colonial war. The war in Germany had been planned as a short campaign and had already dragged on too long with no end in sight. However, success in Europe was by now top priority, with the colonial theaters forced to take a back seat.

In Britain, opinion among political leaders had shifted radically. Early on, various military disasters in Germany prompted skepticism toward continued continental commitments. But the course of events radically changed this, and news of victories on the continent was enthusiastically received.[163] In his diary, Thomas Turner (1729–1793), a shopkeeper from East Hoathly in Sussex, regularly documents his reading of newspapers. The entry for May 23, 1757, recording the Prussian victory at Prague, is relatively short and sober. In November of the same year, Frederick's victory at Rossbach earns a detailed commentary:

> In reading The Gazette for the 22nd instant I find the King of Prussia, with about 20,000, has beat the combined forces of the empire and France, which were 60,000; he having totally routed them and taken almost or quite all their cannon, baggage, etc., taking and killing in the field of battle and the pursuit 10,000 men. Oh, could England boast of such warlike P------and to have such a true heroic courage diffused through all its martial men (as must evidently appear to have been in this small host)! But how can we expect to find such courage in the poor degenerated people of England, when it is virtue, and that alone, that constitutes the true hero and inspires courage into the breast of the warrior (which at this time seems almost to be extinguished in the British nation). For dissoluteness of manners, a spirit of effeminacy and self-interest, together with an intolerable share of pride and luxury, seem almost to over-spread the whole face of this kingdom. And I presume when such are the vices of a nation, they must inevitably be ruined without a speedy reformation.[164]

Turner was right that the moment did not appear bright for the British cause. Its troops had lost Fort William Henry and had not yet conquered Louisbourg. The amphibious operations against Rochefort had come to little.[165] In addition, the Convention of Kloster-Zeven was regarded as unfavorable to British interests; several days after Frederick's victory at Rossbach, the agreement was unilaterally repudiated by the British and their allies.

Fresh Wind in the West

As the commander who had signed the Convention of Kloster-Zeven, Cumberland was disgraced and relieved of his command. His replacement was Duke Ferdinand of Brunswick, appointed as head of the observation army in November 1757.[166] The appointment of Ferdinand, one of Frederick's generals, strengthened Prussia's ties with the British and Allied army, which was now vital to the survival of the Prussian state. Moreover, the repudiation of Kloster-Zeven was equally in the interests of Britain and Prussia.[167] Ferdinand took care to put himself under the direct orders of the British crown, although he was paid by Frederick. As far as Frederick was concerned, the British had merely "borrowed" Ferdinand.[168] The new commander was granted extensive decision-making powers, giving him room to maneuver comparable to that of the Prussian *roi connétable* himself.

Grotehenn's diary notes that Ferdinand's appointment did more than simply change the mood. With a "sharpshooter" and a "master hunter" now in command, he observes, the army was truly "on a hunt for Frenchmen." The Duke of Brunswick took over as soon as the "Duke of Cummerland"—as Grotehenn calls him throughout—had bid farewell and received the gratitude of his troops. Ferdinand, writes Grotehenn, immediately won his soldiers' hearts: "This Lord seems most dear to many People and appears to possess great Wisdom; at our first Parade ground inspection, he saluted us with a Good Morning and called all us his compatriots, until we were quite afire with fear and love."[169]

Ferdinand's army hurriedly set out from Magdeburg on November 21, 1757, marching to confront a French force positioned near Stade. The main advance began on December 1 but suffered various problems, including supply issues and the tricky position of Duke Charles of Brunswick-Wolfenbüttel, Ferdinand's elder brother. Brunswick-Wolfenbüttel itself had been occupied by the French, and it seemed unlikely that Charles would send troops to campaign against his occupiers (see map in figure 4.2).[170] At the end of November, Ferdinand formally repudiated Kloster-Zeven and laid siege to the town of Harburg.[171] With Ferdinand marching against Richelieu, the French evacuated Lüneburg and tried to muster at Celle. The Allies took the town of Uelzen on December 6, but there was little direct contact between the two sides; the French withdrew quickly, while the Allies advanced slowly.[172] Everything seemed to point to a major confrontation at Celle. Richelieu prepared for battle, one in which Celle would suffer greatly.

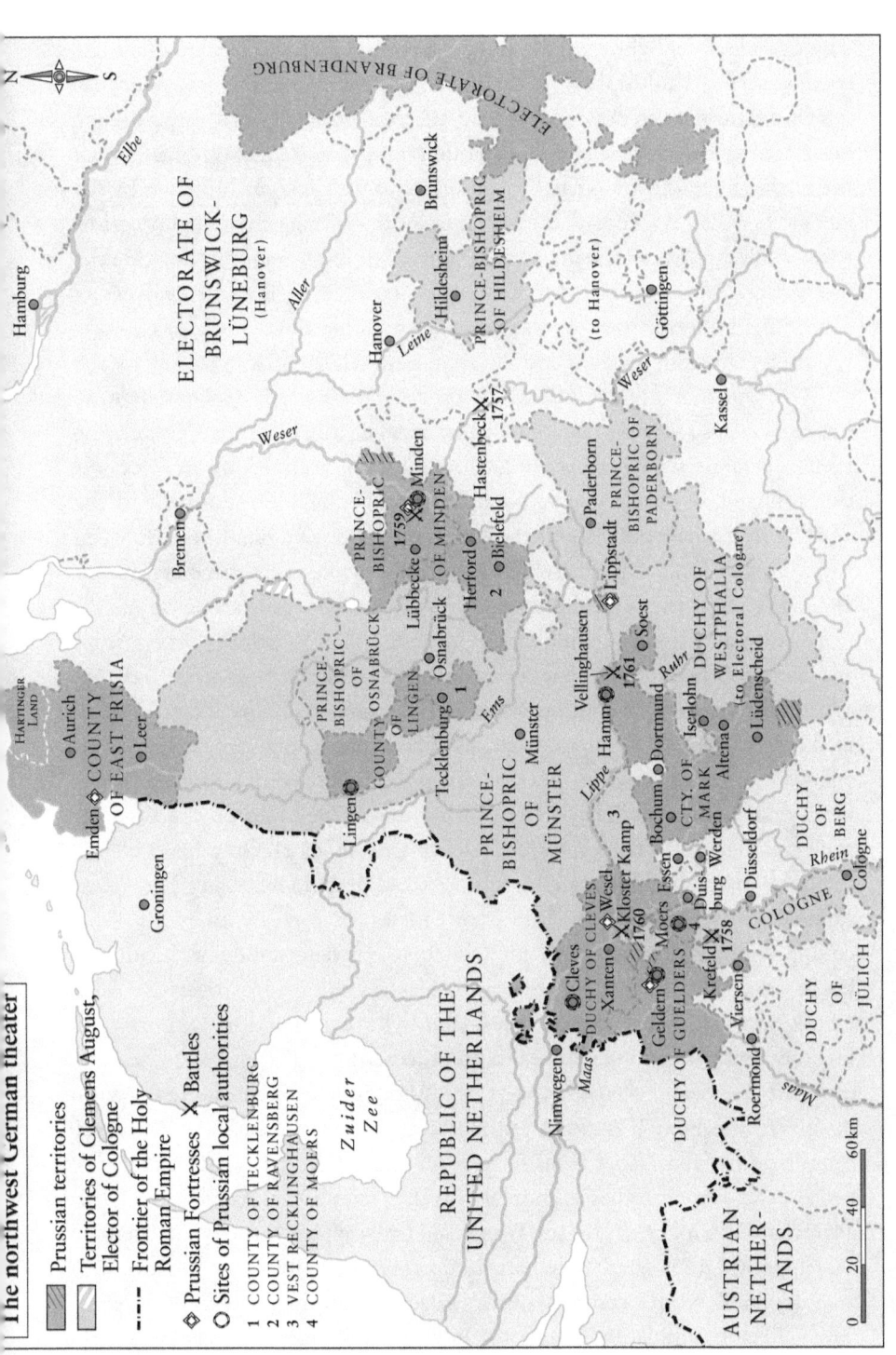

Figure 4.2 The northwestern German theater.
© Peter Palm, Berlin/Germany.

The diary kept by Schowart, the town's garrison auditor, offers eloquent testimony to this hardship. He describes December 13 as "this wretched day which, centuries from now, people may still recall with sadness."[173] The French bombardment of the town began at around noon, lasted for two hours, and set fire to the street known as the Fritzen Wiese, as well as some buildings by the city gates, which Richelieu's men claimed were blocking their field of vision. Many buildings were looted and then burned to the ground. To describe the destruction, Schowart turned to a familiar topos: "There is no pen capable of describing the terror these operations created within the town."[174]

Jacques Emmanuel Roques de Maumont (1727–1805), pastor to the town's Huguenot population, was another witness inside Celle, where he was now acting as a kind of mediator between the townspeople and the French occupiers.[175] Roques de Maumont also comments on the devastation inflicted on the city, always emphasizing his own commitment to the city.[176] He has no doubt about the looming battle: "We stand here between two fires, and if the Bataille, which I think inevitable, takes place before our Gates, as cannot happen otherwise, then may God have Mercy upon us."[177]

Looting and arson continued the next day. The French set fire to ships and storehouses to make any crossing of the Aller River more difficult, apparently unaware that the storehouses held grain that could have been of vital help to their own forces. To attack, Ferdinand would somehow have to effect a crossing of the Aller, but various attempts between December 15 and 17 all ended in failure. The lateness of the season, well beyond the time for campaigning, took a toll on both sides. On December 21, Grotehenn writes: "Because of continuing and increasing Cold and Snow, many here have suffered in their Health, and the poor Horses are even dying, partly from cold, partly from hunger."[178] But Richelieu was determined and gathered his forces to hit back at the Prussians. He had the bridges over the Aller rebuilt and sought battle with Ferdinand, who continued to withdraw. At one moment, everything seemed to point to battle on December 25, but the moment passed, and no battle took place. With both armies heading for winter billets, the French surrendered Harburg on December 27.[179] A formal capitulation of the Hanoverian fortress was signed on the night of December 29, and French forces withdrew two days later. On the other hand, the Maréchal de Broglie (1718–1804) managed to capture the city of Bremen on January 15, 1758, a valuable bargaining chip in any future negotiations.[180]

Ferdinand's winter campaign thus ended without major territorial gains. The suffering population in territories repeatedly crossed by armies seems to have had ambivalent feelings about the war. In late 1757, Johann Christoph Cuntz (1718–1804), a pastor from Kirchditmold near Kassel, writes: "Thus we had our first visit from the French in this year of 1757, and this quite tolerable invasion was held, by those who know no better, to bring great misery upon the Hessenland, which it could no more endure. In fact, in this year many subjects of Hesse have drawn greater benefit from selling food and provisions than they suffered harm. In brief: no full-scale War was here to be seen."[181]

After victory at Rossbach, Frederick could withdraw his troops from the Saale, turning his attentions to the Silesian theater, where events had turned to the Austrians' advantage.[182] An Austrian assault on the fortress at Schweidnitz had forced its surrender on November 12. A Prussian force under the Duke of Bevern concentrated on defending the Silesian city of Breslau, which was under severe threat. On November 22, battle was joined in front of the gates of the city: Bevern's army amounted to twenty-nine thousand men, outnumbered by a combined Austrian force of around eighty thousand, commanded by Duke Charles of Lorraine, Leopold von Daun, and Franz Leopold von Nádasdy. Historians have generally regarded the battle as an Austrian victory.[183]

However, when the fighting ended, it was not at all clear who the victor was, as had also been the case at Hastenbeck and would be later at Torgau. The Silesian noblewoman Juliane von Rehdiger was an eye- and earwitness to the battle:

> At 9 in the morning, we heard cannonfire, which shook our House, and in this way received news of the Bataille taking place before our Gates. The Imperial troops had attacked the Prussian fortifications, and thus we could watch from our own homes, where I myself watched the sad spectacle with tears in my eyes. Villages were burning, guns flashing, bullets whistling, and thus we became aware that we were likewise in danger in our own homes. The battle lasted until 5 o'clock in the evening, and we were ignorant of which side had taken Victory, until at 4 in the morning I received news that the Prussians had been defeated and that very night had passed through the city and across the Oder.[184]

Christian Taege (d. 1804), a military chaplain, offers a similar account: "As the sun was setting, we saw the Prussians withdraw to Breslau in disorderly retreat. [. . .] The Austrians in the meantime moved not a single foot forward, barely realizing that the Prussians were pulling back, and at dawn they were amazed to see the field abandoned after a battle that was in no way decisive."[185] On the Austrian side, Giuseppe Gorani (1748–1819) had words of appreciation for Bevern's "very beautiful retreat," which took advantage of nightfall.[186] After the battle, Breslau proved incapable of withstanding an Austrian siege, which was more strategically damaging to the Prussians than the battle itself. Terror and chaos were rampant in the city, and the Prussian army experienced severe disciplinary problems with its soldiers, not to mention an increasingly hostile civilian population.[187] It is telling that although those in the garrison was allowed to leave with their arms and regimental colors, only six hundred of the forty-two hundred Prussians withdrew, as arranged, in the direction of Glogau. The remainder simply deserted.

Reports of success at Breslau put Vienna in a triumphant mood. Emotions were running high, and the eagerly awaited news of victory prompted breaches of court etiquette. The Emperor Francis was so elated by reports of victory that on November 25, "on the conclusion of his Repast, he betook himself in person to Lange-Enzerstorff," several miles from Vienna, in order "to speak directly to the messengers." The emperor's gesture received some criticism at court, since it was felt it "would have been both more natural and more decent had he bid the officer bearing messages to come to him incognito, rather than to travel out to meet him."[188] However, spirits in the imperial capital would soon change, the rampant euphoria shifting to a far darker mood.

Leuthen: The Victory of Experience

Frederick's army now advanced into Silesia in a forced march, setting out from Leipzig in Saxony and arriving on November 28 at the town of Parchwitz, northwest of Breslau. At Parchwitz Castle, on the morning of December 4, the king addressed his generals and regimental commanders.[189] Frederick's battle exhortation, which he gave in German, has come to be known as the Parchwitz Address, later a key element in Prussian and German military mythology. The king told his audience that the impending battle would be extremely risky and that he would rely to an unusual degree on his soldiers' discipline: "I will, against every rule of the art, attack an enemy almost twice as strong, an enemy which is dug in on high ground.

I must do this, or all is lost. We shall defeat the enemy or be buried before his batteries. This is what I believe, and this is how I shall act."[190] Having stated this, he offered those present the option to leave: "If there is one or other among you who does not think as I do, I demand that he leave immediately, and I will grant him this with not the slightest reproach."[191] The rhetorical device used by Frederick—an appeal to his soldiers' sense of honor—is said to have won them over entirely. Georg Fridrich von Tempelhof, a chronicler of the war, noted: "Who could be unmoved by the King's speech? Who would not wish to be taken forth immediately to face the enemy, to take actions such as might do justice to the faith he had placed in every man."[192] Putlitz, the king's personal attendant, reports Frederick as saying "Any man preferring to take his leave, may now go home," whereupon Major Konstantin von Billerbeck (1713–1785) replied: "Yes indeed, the time would be now, for a shameless poltroon [*infamer Hundsfott*]!"[193] Adolph Menzel depicted the scene in visual form in a painting he began in 1859, but he stopped work and then abandoned it unfinished in 1867.[194]

If Frederick had failed to defeat the Austrians in the field, he would effectively have been granting them Silesia to use as winter quarters, an excellent starting point for the next summer campaign. There was no choice but to take the initiative. The resulting confrontation, the Battle of Leuthen, was fought on December 5, 1757. It remains perhaps the most famous battle of the European war, at least in a German context.[195] The battle was not decisive, and its fame is not due to important strategic consequences. Nor was it seen as a crucial battle at the time; Rossbach was regarded as far more significant. Instead, Leuthen owes its reputation to Frederick's almost unique deployment of troops in oblique order and also to the way key scenes were later exaggerated and elevated to near-mythical status.[196] These include the aforementioned Parchwitz Address and the fighting in the Leuthen churchyard, as well as the image of victorious Prussian soldiers singing the "Hymn of Leuthen" on the evening of the battle.

The battlefield of Leuthen lay about eleven miles west of Breslau. Frederick knew the area from peacetime maneuvers after 1748. But some opposing officers were also familiar with the terrain, including Ferdinand Friedrich von Nicolai (1730–1814), a general in the Württemberg army, who had been a guest at Prussian maneuvers in the area.[197] The Austrian and Imperial forces were deployed along a north-south axis on a line about six miles long, stretching from Nippern to Sagschütz, commanded by Prince Charles of Lorraine. Shortly before the battle, Frederick was largely unaware of the actual strength of the forces lined up against him: The *roi connétable* was under the impression the Austrians had about thirty-nine thousand men when, in fact, they had close to fifty-five thousand.[198] The Austrian leadership thought the outnumbered Prussian army would not dare to attack in December; their forces took up a defensive position in front of Breslau as a "show of strength" rather than with an intention of battle.[199]

But the Prussians attacked nonetheless! The first assault was directed at the so-called Kiefernberg, a fortified position south of Sagschütz.[200] This was another possibility the Austrians had barely considered: They regarded a frontal attack on their fortifications as ill-advised and thus highly improbable. Terrible road conditions made a Prussian attack on their right seem equally unlikely. Then, in the southern part of the battlefield, the Prussian right wing, hitherto hidden almost unnoticed behind a hill, swiveled toward the Austrian left, an action that would develop into a fight for the village of Leuthen, the decisive combat of the battle. At the same time, the Prussians feigned a direct assault at Gross Heida, further distracting the Austrians from Frederick's crucial oblique tactics. Despite being outnumbered overall, the Prussians' oblique attack—which focused their strength almost entirely on the Austrian left—gave them the advantage at a crucial juncture. The Leuthen churchyard was the site of particularly bitter fighting, since its stone walls offered soldiers some protection. But the Prussian cavalry, commanded by Zieten, finally broke the Austrian line, leaving the men no choice but to flee.

Ernst Friedrich Rudolf von Barsewisch, a Prussian officer, is one of the battle's few eyewitness sources. During the night before the battle, he writes, he was "afflicted by a terrible dream," in which he seemed to have "been severely wounded by the Imperial forces [. . .], so badly that the blood was flowing out of my body." In the dream, he is afraid he will "bleed to death."[201] Upon awakening, he was so disturbed that he asked Wohlgemuth, the company field surgeon to tend to him personally if he was left wounded on the battlefield. Early in the afternoon, Barsewisch's dream almost became bitter reality when he was hit by musket fire during the attack on Kiefernberg Hill: "With the flag in my hand, I was hit by a musket ball in the left side of my neck, which went through the flesh, avoiding my throat and large artery—the *arteria carotis*—and ending up between my shoulder blades. I fell to the ground as though dead."[202] An hour later a regimental drummer found Barsewisch lying face down on the mud and carried him to safety, although he was wounded again en route, grazed on the calf by another musket ball. Taking cover on the other side of the hill, the drummer cleaned the officer's wounds and bandaged his neck.[203] In a nearby village, the two men found Wohlgemuth, who tended to Barsewisch before sending him by horse to the field hospital at Neumarkt.[204] That night he was operated on by a captured Dutch surgeon, who had been serving with the Austrians' Modena regiment. With a small, spring-bladed knife, the surgeon cut out the musket ball, which Barsewisch kept as a treasured souvenir of the battle.[205] In the days that followed, he was an observer of the great suffering underlying the "great Victoria" at Leuthen, as many wounded soldiers arrived at the hospital where he lay: "some 20,000 wounded from both Armies, [. . .] with much and great Agony on all sides."[206] Wound fever kept the Prussian officer out of action for several weeks. He eventually returned to his regiment on January 22, 1758, "with a twisted neck, and my wound not entirely healed."[207]

Not everyone would enjoy such good fortune. Leuthen had a very high casualty rate, but as with many battles, the toll was unequally distributed. The Prussian side suffered around six thousand killed or wounded, while Austrian and Imperial forces lost more than twenty thousand men, including twelve thousand taken prisoner. Regiments from Bavaria and Württemberg were particularly hard hit, something that did little to encourage these states' future participation in the Imperial Army of Execution.

Frederick's Parchwitz Address had begun the battle with pathos. Things ended on a similar note. On December 27, writing from Berlin, the Swiss philosopher Johann Georg Sulzer (1720–1779) told his compatriot Johann Jakob Bodmer (1698–1783) about a scene by then already passing into myth: "When the last of the enemy had fled, the King began to call out 'Victoria!' in a loud voice, and was then echoed by his victorious Army. And when the halt was called, the soldiers, of their own volition, fell to singing 'Now Thank We All Our God.'"[208] In this way, the old German hymn "Nun Danket Alle Gott" passed into history as the "Hymn of Leuthen."[209] Two weeks after the battle the Prussians retook Breslau.[210]

Successive waves of joy and sorrow swept across the court in Vienna. Maria Theresa tried to keep the mood in the city under control: On December 8, she instructed the post office to delay delivery of the *Journalière-Estaffette* for twenty-four hours so that "the same sorrowful newspaper will not again arrive on the Kaiser's gala day." The courier bearing "the first news of the unfortunate Bataille near Lissa" arrived at around 11 o'clock the following morning. Dinner was immediately canceled, and the imperial couple withdrew from public view for the remainder of the day. Khevenhüller-Metsch's memoirs recount the scene: "The Empress could do naught but weep and was nigh-on inconsolable, yet went forthwith to the chapel, where she made her prayers through unceasing tears."[211] The court chancellor acknowledged that "accounts of the circumstances published by the Enemy" were "on this occasion not exaggerated" and had, in fact, "far underestimated the unhappy truth. Posterity will find it hard to believe that a way could have been identified to lose 40,000 of one's finest troops in a single action. And yet such a way was found."[212] Nonetheless, Khevenhüller-Metsch would also later complain that "this unfortunate battle has been deliberately embellished."[213]

He was not wrong about the embellishment, as a glance at Frederick's political symbolism reveals. The Austrians cast a medal to commemorate the victory at Kolin in June 1757, with one side showing Emperor Francis I and Maria Theresa and the other showing a seated Minerva, her right hand pointing at an obelisk that has been struck by lightning. Above her can be seen the inscription Frangit Deus Omne Superbum (May God punish the prideful).[214] Days after Leuthen Frederick took symbolic revenge, striking a medal that bore the same motif but was larger by five millimeters (about one-fifth of an inch). It also bore his own likeness, along with the inscription Fridericus Borussorum Rex.[215]

There was more humiliation to come in the imperial capital. As Paris had mocked Soubise after Rossbach, Vienna gave expression to its contempt for Charles of Lorraine, the defeated commander at Leuthen, in song and caricature. One image depicted Charles, Daun, and the Hungarian commander Nádasdy, each general uttering his own sentence. Daun cries, "With Sword and Blood!" Nádasdy says, "With Acuity and Courage." Charles notes, "The wine is good." The court was appalled, not least because Charles was the empress's brother-in-law. The government clamped down hard on the slanderous slogan, which was even scrawled on the doors of the Hofburg and St. Stephan's Cathedral. A reward of 500 ducats was offered to anyone identifying its author, to which an anonymous wit responded: "We are four in all: myself, my Ink, my Pen and my Paper; but None will betray the Others, and I do ____ on your five hundred ducats!"[216]

In the wake of the dramatic events in Silesia, the information situation in December was extremely fluid and unclear in many parts of Germany. The chaotic conditions were strikingly illustrated by the diary of Professor Wähner in Göttingen. He records eleven separate rumors, each of which he introduces with the Latin term *Fama*. On December 5, he notes that the Austrians have been "totally defeated" at Lissa; however, this may be a retrospective entry, since news of the battle was not published in the *Frankfurter Zeitung* until December 9.[217] On December 13, a Göttingen student was said to have been told by his father, a senior courtier in Hanover, that "everything in Silesia has been Redressed"; in other words, order had been restored.[218] On December 15, Wähner noted, with some impatience, that there had been "not a Word in the Frankfurter Zeitung" about the victory at Leuthen.[219] Instead, the deluge of negative rumors continued. On January 3, there were rumors that Frederick was dead: "Fama: The King of Prussia has died, either of a Wound he had before Breslau, or else by Poison, may God have Mercy upon Him."[220] Success stories were urgently needed to shore up support for Frederick, and as with Rossbach, news of the Prussian victory was received enthusiastically in Britain, albeit also prompting more complaints about a general lack of news. The Earl Temple, writing to his brother George Grenville, made a direct analogy with Rossbach: "The Austrians were Soubised, and I waited with impatience to enjoy all the Gazette particulars of last Saturday. No Gazette! But behold a d—d extraordinary one from Brussels: lying, impudently false as that paper is generally; I am a little staggered from so many circumstances, and wait in the most painful anxiety 'till to-morrow night, unless some charitable Parson in the neighbourhood should relieve me from my doubts by his intelligence, before."[221]

Prussia was successful in the final months of 1757, although in many places information on its success, and the rest of the war, was patchy and uncertain. Seen from the court at Vienna, the situation looked entirely different. In late December, Khevenhüller-Metsch summed up the military situation: "In *militaribus*, we have had no month so fatal as this month now is for us, a catastrophe all the more painful since it was not expected, and could not have been expected, after so recently receiving such positive news."[222] In the autumn, the Austrians had seemed on the verge of retaking Silesia. Now suddenly all appeared lost. Not long after Breslau, Liegnitz also fell to the Prussians. In April 1758, the fortress of Schweidnitz would likewise be conquered. By Christmas 1757, the Prussians, under the leadership of General Heinrich August de la Motte Fouqué (1698–1774) and the cavalry general Zieten, pushed the remaining Austrian formations into Bohemia. Silesia was once again a Prussian province.

At the end of the year of battles, many of our eyewitness soldiers and officers were simply glad to have survived. Over the course of 1757, Dominicus, the Prussian musketeer, had witnessed the slaughter at Lobositz, Prague, and Rossbach. Of the Prussian officers, Barsewisch had been at Rossbach and Leuthen, while Prittwitz served in the Battles of Prague and Kolin. In Brunswick, Grotehenn fought at Hastenbeck, while Bolotov was a participant observer at Gross-Jägersdorf.

Writing in the summer of this year of battles, Voltaire drew grim conclusions about the first two years of war: "For two years now this best of all possible worlds has been quite ugly, but it has been tending that way for quite some time. This latest shock does not yet resemble those of past centuries; but in due course it will be a match for all of the misery and horror of more heroic times. It would indeed be a great misfortune should the Prussian, Austrian, Russian, Hanoverian, French, and other armies not ruin at least half a hundred cities, beggar at least fifty thousand families, and send four or five hundred thousand men to their deaths."[223]

A Disputed "Massacre" at Fort William Henry

John Campbell, the Earl of Loudoun, arrived in New York on July 22, 1756, to take up his new position as commander in chief of all British-American forces.[224] He had been given substantial military and civilian powers, meant to allow united and decisive action on the part of the British colonies. After Braddock's death at the Monongahela in July 1755, command of the British forces had initially been given to William Shirley, the governor of Massachusetts. However, the new responsibilities proved too much for him, and his tenure was short-lived; he was relieved of command on January 20, 1756, six months before Loudoun's arrival.

The change in British leadership gave the French space and time for maneuver during 1756.[225] On August 14, the French commander, General Louis Joseph de Montcalm (1712–1759), succeeded in conquering Fort Oswego on Lake Ontario. Attacks by the Shawnee and Delaware tied down colonial forces in the hinterland.[226] Both sides quickly tried to raise more forces, with varying degrees of success. Together, the individual British colonies raised 8,000 men, although the contingents were of very different sizes, ranging from New Hampshire's 350 men to the 1,800 sent by Massachusetts.[227] French reinforcements mostly had to come directly from France, since their local militias were far weaker. In terms of naval activity, in May and June 1757, the French again managed to get reinforcements, forcing a total of eighteen ships of the line and three frigates through to their port at Louisbourg, Nova Scotia. July saw the arrival of a British fleet with seventeen warships under Admiral Sir Francis Holburne (1704–1771). Loudoun originally had a plan to capture Louisbourg to prevent further French landings, but this seems to have been abandoned because of poor weather and insufficient troop numbers.

French attacks continued to focus on the Great Lakes and the surrounding region. In March 1757, Fort William Henry, a British fort located at the head of Lake George, was attacked by fifteen hundred French Canadians and allies. The British managed to fend off the four-day attack, largely because the French lacked artillery. But the mission was not without success, as the French managed to destroy enemy boats on Lake George in what was a severe blow to British logistics.[228] Montcalm's first assault on the fort was followed, five months later, by a second, beginning on August 3, 1757. This second attack would become a question of vital public interest across North America, when the six-day confrontation ended in what was depicted as a bloody massacre of British forces.[229] The August assault on Fort William Henry saw some twenty-five hundred British and colonial troops defending the fort against a force of around eight thousand French troops and their Native American allies. The attack is recounted in the memoir of the Hessian mercenary Georg Schneider (1728–1796), then serving with the Royal American Rifles at Fort Edward, fourteen miles to the south. Schneider reports that after Montcalm had taken the fort, the British commander, Lieutenant Colonel George Monro (1700–1757), agreed to capitulation terms, assisted by Lieutenant Colonel John Young, who had arrived with reinforcements prior to the defeat. Under these terms, defeated British troops would keep their arms and could march to Fort Edward but could not be deployed again for eighteen months.

The next day, however, events took an unexpected turn. As the departing British marched out through Fort William Henry's outer fortifications, they passed a large group of Native American warriors, who began to seize soldiers' backpacks and confiscate swords and watches from the officers. According to Schneider, they also began to take guns and equipment as they attacked with greater and greater ferocity, striking "the British in the Head with their Axes, and Scalping them alive, then and there, and they would have killed all 11,000 had they not run away. Four Hundred souls had this Cruelty to Suffer, not counting those which the Indians took away as Prisoners. The rest came to Fort Edward on August 10, without a Rifle between them, some even without Clothing to cover their bare skin."[230]

How did this happen? The composition of Montcalm's troops provides some initial insight. Along with roughly sixty-two hundred regular soldiers, Montcalm had a very large force of Native Americans, around eighteen hundred fighters from many regions of the country, including the Atlantic coast and the Great Lakes.[231] In total, the Native American force had fighters from thirty-three different nations—even some Iowa who had made the long journey to Canada. All had been encouraged by news of the French capture of Fort Oswego the previous year. This recruitment success would prove problematic for Montcalm, since the heterogeneous group of fighters was not really under his "command"—or under anyone's command—as the term would be understood in a European military context. Despite potential problems of control, the siege began with a traditional exchange of courtesies, with Montcalm writing to Monro to request his surrender: "Humanity obliges me to warn you that once our guns have been placed and the cannons are firing, there may be no time to prevent the cruelty of a mob of savages from so many different nations, nor may it be any more in our power."[232] As expected, Monro refused capitulation. Trenches were dug on August 4, and the fort was besieged in the classic European manner. By August 7, half the British cannon had already burst from continuous firing. The French barrage did not let up, and the situation of the fort's defenders grew steadily worse. Monro called a council of war for the evening of August 8, where his officers advised him to surrender. The capitulation was agreed to on the afternoon of the following day. Montcalm negotiated using as a guideline the articles of surrender agreed to at Menorca the previous year, which offered relatively generous conditions.[233]

The deal may have been "honorable" by European standards, but it was agreed to entirely over the heads of France's Native allies, who learned of the terms only after they had been settled. Moreover, the terms meant that the Native Americans who had fought in the siege would receive nothing—neither booty nor prisoners. Was everything they had done for nothing? Had they been swindled? Faced with this risk, Native American warriors went ahead and took what was legally theirs according to Native custom. Inside the fort, on the afternoon of August 9, Native American fighters searching for booty attacked seventy wounded British soldiers within the fortress, scalping many of them as they went. French control over the fort was restored only at around nine o'clock in the evening.[234]

There was still more chaos to come. As described above by Schneider, the surrendered garrison and other inhabitants marched out of the fort in a long column in the early morning hours of August 10. But the undefended rear of the line was soon attacked by Native warriors, who seized weapons and other possessions, killing anyone who resisted. Panic broke out, causing even more deaths. Once the French had reestablished order, Fort William Henry was a scene of devastation. One hundred eighty-five soldiers and civilians had been killed, with between three hundred and five hundred more taken hostage. The rest of the British and colonial forces had fled. Even most of the Native American fighters had disappeared, taking advantage of the early morning light, with only some three hundred Abenaki warriors remaining with Montcalm's army. The French immediately began to secure the release of the remaining British hostages and were able to have around two hundred returned by the end of August.[235] The final two hundred hostages were held until the end of the war in 1763. Montcalm's efforts to free these people should be understood more in terms of his personal responsibility for French compliance with the surrender agreement rather than humanitarian concern. Had the French general failed to do his utmost to protect British hostages, he could expect little mercy in similar situations in future. However, the Native Americans felt deeply betrayed, and France could not afford to further alienate them. Too late the Native Americans realized that the hospital at Fort William Henry had contained smallpox. The booty they had seized—blankets, clothing, and the like—was contaminated with the virus, against which they had no immune defenses.[236]

Eyewitnesses on the French side included Pierre Roubaud (1724–1789), a Jesuit priest who wrote a long report on the events.[237] His account insists that the terrible incident will, without question, echo loudly across "every corner of Europe." His reading of events places the blame squarely on the Native Americans, ascribing it to their "insatiable ferocity" and their "independence." In his own words: "The Savages, then, are alone responsible for this infringement of the law of Nations."[238] Roubaud describes in detail how he saved a small child from certain death and did all he could to stand up for the British victims.

Within weeks, the events at Fort William Henry had become a media event, first in the colonial public sphere and later in Europe.[239] Reports of the siege and its aftermath first appeared in New York on August 19, followed three days later by an account in the *Boston Gazette*, in which the author complained of contradictory eyewitness testimony.[240] The earliest reports speak of marauding "bloodhound" Indians, killing all who displayed resistance. By August 29, the term *massacre* was explicitly used; the word was repeated on September 5. Reports from New York were republished in the London papers on October 12 and 13.[241] The news had first arrived on the continent slightly earlier, on October 9, when a Canadian merchant ship brought news of the fort's capture. This, in turn, was the basis for a relatively neutral account published in the *Berlinische Nachrichten* on October 29.[242] However, the newspaper's next issue, published on November 1, took a very different tone, speaking of "Savages" who carried out "revolting cruelties," citing as evidence a report in a London newspaper of October 18.[243]

For Montcalm, the capture of Fort William Henry was a genuinely Pyrrhic victory. He lost his Native allies while massively damaging the image of French conduct in war. Now, in addition, catastrophic harvests forced him to withdraw most of his forces so his men could be sent to help bring in the harvest. In the meantime, Monro's cries for help from Fort William Henry eventually had an impact, with some five thousand new recruits joining the colonial militias.

Plassey: Clive of India

In southern India, initial signs pointed toward French success. On June 5, 1757, the Pondicherry merchant Ananda Ranga Pillai noted in his diary: "By the Hindu science of astrology, it was foretold that in the year Îswara, all the English ports would pass into the hands of the French who would hoist the white flag in them. Accordingly the English forts and ports are falling into French hands, and all may rest assured that all places, from England in Europe to Madras and Fort St. David in India, will pass into French hands. I am sure that this will happen."[244] The French governor-general had asked whether he knew of the war between the English and the French. Pillai replied: "Formerly when they seized our ships, Madras was lost. The astronomer had predicted this, and I informed M. Dupleix [the former governor-general] of it. They have now captured Bengal, but all their factories are about to pass into your hands, the astrologers say."[245]

Having largely eliminated the French presence in Bengal, the next step for Clive and the East India Company was to cleverly engineer a conspiracy to bring down Siraj-ud-Daulah, still the ruling nawab of Bengal.[246] Clive concluded a secret agreement with Mir Jafar (1691–1765), one of Siraj's generals, and an Indian merchant named Omichund (d. 1767).[247] The battle of Plassey, close to what is today the village of Palashi in West Bengal, would be the final test of Clive's conspiracy, on which success or failure would rest.

Clive was taking a great risk in seeking battle; he was greatly outnumbered, and his position in front of a rapidly rising river blocked any retreat. Battle was finally joined on June 23, 1757, although in truth it was more a cannonade than a battle, with the British suffering just twenty-five soldiers killed. Clive benefited from various factors and fortunate contingencies. Heavy rain played an important role, dampening the powder of the nawab's forces, but Clive also held a solid defensive position and was lucky in the deaths of several enemy commanders, as well as in the reaction of the nawab, who panicked and ultimately fled.[248] On the evening after the battle, Clive wrote to "Charles Watson and the Gentlemen of the Council of Fort William [Calcutta]." He describes the situation thus:

> Gentlemen—This morning at one o'clock we arrived at Placis Grove, and early in the morning the Nabob's whole army appeared in sight and cannonaded us for several hours, and about noon returned to a very strong camp in sight, lately Roydoolup's, upon which we advanced and stormed the Nabob's camp, which we have taken with all his cannon, and pursued him six miles, being now at Doudpoor and shall proceed for Muxadavad to-morrow. Meer Jaffeir, Roydoolup and Luttee Cawn gave us no other assistance than standing neuter. They are with me with a large force. Meer Muddun and five hundred horse are killed and three elephants. Our loss is trifling, not above twenty Europeans killed and wounded.[249]

Clive's victory at Plassey could be said to have put a great empire at his mercy. Mir Jafar was installed as the new nawab in Murshidabad, the capital from which Siraj-ud-Daulah had fled. Clive's British forces extracted financial tribute from the old nawab's palace treasury,[250] and the new nawab paid Clive around 230,000 pounds.[251] In Calcutta, every member of the East India Company Council received 27,000 pounds; army subalterns got 3,000 pounds each. The British navy was awarded 400,000 pounds. The latter payment was so large that it almost prompted rebellion, given the comparatively minor naval contribution to key events of the war.[252] In all, some 3 million pounds were paid to the British by Mir Jafar during his years on the throne. At the time, plunder on such a scale was not regarded as problematic, although it would later become so for Clive. Siraj-ud-Daulah was captured after Plassey and executed shortly thereafter. Clive proceeded to simultaneously provide aid to the new nawab and his opponents, weakening the nawab and helping secure British supremacy in Bengal according to the logic of *divide et impera*.

Further south, in the Carnatic region, events were developing more slowly. Both sides had sent large troop contingents in 1756, but the monsoons brought further reinforcement to a halt. The French were under orders to wait until fresh soldiers arrived from Europe, and new operations began only in the spring of 1757.[253] British tax collection officials fanned out across their territories, looking to raise revenues to pay off the debts of their ally Muhammad Ali, the nawab of the Carnatic, and to finance their own military campaigns. In Pondicherry, the French saw a chance to march on the city of Trichinopoly (now Tiruchirappalli in Tamil Nadu), sending Major d'Auteuil (1714–1774) at the head of a strong force of four thousand.[254] The British garrison in the city amounted to just nine hundred men, commanded by Joseph Smith, as well as another thousand provided by Muhammad Ali. Of these, a considerable number were needed to guard five hundred French prisoners. Smith held out successfully until the arrival of a relieving force under Major Caillaud. The British now began their own operation, sending a force to advance on Wandiwash, a key French fortress between Madras and Pondicherry; the mission would ultimately fail to achieve its objective. For the remainder of 1757, action was confined to minor raids, giving neither side decisive advantage.

Seen from London at the end of 1757, the situation did not look particularly favorable, especially since news from Plassey had yet to arrive in the British capital.[255] On October 6, First Lord of the Admiralty George Anson (1697–1762) wrote to his father-in-law, the Earl of Hardwicke (1690–1764), lamenting that "there seems to be a fatality in everything we undertake and nothing succeeds." Anson arrived from a meeting of the war council shortly before writing the letter and declares himself "heartily tired with the reflection that not one event from the beginning of the war has come before us, that has not been unfortunate."[256]

CHAPTER V

Everyday Life in Wartime

The war was not simply a matter of battles and sieges. The everyday experience of war also consisted of social, material, and cultural elements, which form part of religious and material history, as well as the history of consumption and communications. Religion was a political resource as much as it was as a source of personal or collective meaning. However, the personal testimonies we hear in this book are, above all, expressions of *physical* experience. It was this physicality—whether experiencing heat, cold, hunger, or thirst or being rendered speechless—that was the bearer of everyday experience. Communication with others was essential in order to live and survive, so language became conspicuous as a crucial factor in the history of experience. The ability to speak a foreign language could determine survival. Religion, the body, and language were also fields where communities could form and where social boundaries were drawn; all three became important factors in determining inclusion and exclusion. French, for example, was an essential lingua franca for the aristocratic officer corps, enabling a caste solidarity that transcended national boundaries.[1] On the other hand, religious motivation could be decisive in securing, or failing to secure, the loyalty of ordinary soldiers. Shortages of food or clothing could drag down morale and even induce desertion. Sayings like "You are what you eat" took on entirely different meanings during wartime than they had in ordinary civilian life. In a society like early modern Europe, characterized by "limited goods," wartime conditions presented a constant series of new challenges.²

A Religious War?

At one point in his chronicle, the Hanoverian master baker Eberhard Jürgen Abelmann writes: "As this latest War has continued without end, many were overcome by no small Fear that the War would become a Religious War, although this has been most graciously averted by the great Ruler of this World."³ To make the threat of confessional conflict more plausible, he invokes "The 30 Years' Religious War," a conflict to which he devotes an extended digression late in his chronicle. That contemporaries made direct historical comparisons with the Thirty Years' War, by then over a century in the past, rather than with the more recent Wars of Succession suggests that confessional tensions had reached levels not seen for a long time. As argued previously, the Seven Years' War was not a war over religion. Although at first glance the Prusso-Austrian and Franco-British conflicts appeared to fit the template of a sectarian conflict, any reading of the Seven Years' War as a religious war was rendered absurd by the Franco-Swedish alliance, if not before.⁴ But denomination and religion did continue to play a role, one that should not be underestimated. Religion served as a resource for emotional mobilization, which could be put to use in everyday life, in propaganda, and in political practice. This is even more the case if we look beyond Christianity and toward non-European contexts.

If Prussia had successfully concluded an alliance with the Ottomans, it would have meant the entry of an Islamic state into the European war. For Prussia to make common cause with Christendom's "archenemy" would certainly have created scandal. However, it would also have underlined how, even in the eighteenth century, the foreign policies of European states were highly nuanced and ultimately based on considerations of sovereignty. Critical perspectives on the practices of Catholic piety can be found in the reports sent by the Ottoman envoy Ahmed Resmi Efendi (1694/95–1783) during his visit to Vienna in March and April 1757. At the time, the city's inhabitants lived in constant dread of a Prussian advance, "fearing the King might arrive before the gates of Vienna. Besides their Armor of War, they also implored the Assistance of Saints and holy images. Every day saw solemn Petitions made in the churches, with the most exalted images, and prayers were said for the defeat and annihilation of the King of Prussia."[5] The translation here omits an ironic jibe in the original Turkish, which invokes not "saints" in general but rather "Lat" and "Menat," statues of pre-Islamic gods mentioned in the Koran, which at the time were an Islamic symbol for an "era of ignorance."[6]

In accounts of the war, Jewish people mostly appear as traders and financiers, playing an important role in supplying the various armies.[7] Reports of celebrations marking victory and peace in Jewish communities of the Holy Roman Empire are a testament to their varied political sympathies. For example, after the Battle of Leuthen in 1757, David Hirschel Fränkel (1707–1762), the chief rabbi of Berlin, offered thanks for the Prussian victory in a synagogue, suggesting that Frederick II was an instrument of God's will. The text of his sermon was published the following year in Erlangen and Philadelphia. An English translation printed in London also reached a colonial audience via its publication in Boston and elsewhere.[8] Religious antagonisms undoubtedly hit Native Americans the hardest, as they were collectively marginalized as "heathens," a category used to legitimate the ruthless violence used against them.[9] Even Native American settlements that had converted under the influence of missionaries could expect little mercy, given the overall policy of driving Indians from their lands, which had an overwhelming impact. Religious questions were also at issue in India, most typically with regard to the sepoys, Indian soldiers, mostly Muslims and Hindus, in European service. In this context, there were cases that presented a wide range of conflicts and obstacles.[10] There were instances when Hindu sepoys cited religious reasons for refusing to storm a temple or serve on a ship at sea. In the British-Spanish confrontations at Havana in Cuba and Manila in the Philippines, sectarian antagonisms aggravated the looting of religious institutions, but otherwise they had little impact after the surrender, since the treaties made guaranteed free practice of religion. The impact of religion and sectarian identity was thus global. These identities could create communication networks through, for example, the reports and letters of missionaries and clergy. But they also served to demarcate new boundaries of identity and helped transport existing identities from the Old World to the other parts of the globe.

Georg Wilhelm Friedrich Hegel, lecturing on the philosophy of world history in the winter of 1830–1831, said this of the politics of religion in the Seven Years' War: "The Seven Years War was indeed in itself not a war of religion; but it was so in view of its ultimate issues, and in the disposition of the soldiers as well as the potentates under whose banner they fought. The Pope consecrated the sword of Field-Marshal Daun, and the chief object of the Allied Powers proposed to themselves, was the crushing of Prussia as the bulwark of the Protestant Church."[11] Today we are better informed than Hegel on the "consecrated sword" supposedly given to the commander of Austria's forces. The anecdote of the pope's gift to Field Marshal Daun is a reminder of the personal efforts undertaken by Frederick to foment religious war.[12] The story of the pontiff sending a message to Daun, giving profuse thanks for successes "against the heretics," was Frederick's own invention, created to be used in pamphlets that were fighting a "virtual religious war."[13] Frederick sent the French original of his text to Voltaire and to his close confidant Jean-Baptiste de Boyer, the Marquis d'Argens (1703–1771), who translated it into Latin. Other translations and reprints quickly followed. Later in the century, Johann Wilhelm Archenholz became aware of the story of the sacred sword, which he took to be fact, suggesting the consecration was "conduct quite unworthy of the eighteenth century, if not of this war."[14]

Hegel was not entirely wrong as far as "disposition of the soldiers" went. Religious meaning was crucially important for the morale of the troops, who were constantly putting their lives in danger. Military chaplains were meant to ensure good morale among the men, whom they served as confessors. Many military preachers were also very active chroniclers of the war.[15] Clerics rarely saw active combat: Figures like the Prussian military chaplain Karl Andreas Friedrich Balke (d. 1779), who saw action near Rossbach, were the exception.[16] The centrality of religious meaning became particularly evident in conflict situations, including sectarian confrontations, as well as more extreme examples like pitched battles. In 1759, the Berlin garrison preacher Carl Friedrich Wegener (1734–1787) published *The Christian in Times of War*, a devotional book with an entire chapter on "Thoughts of a Christian in the Line of Battle."[17] Individual soldiers took their own religious precautions as they saw fit. Thus, the Swiss officer Dominique Dubois-Cattin (b. 1733) describes in a letter to his brother how, before the Battle of Bergen, he prayed to the Mother of God for support, promising a pilgrimage and two devotions.[18] After surviving the battle, he instructed his brother to arrange for masses to be sung at home in Switzerland.

For civilians affected by the war, religious patterns of interpretation were just as important in coping with suffering. Sieges, in particular, prompted religious interpretations among the populations of cities and towns affected.

In 1758, Andreas Belach (1717–1779), a senior Prussian tax official in Breslau, published *The Christian in War and Under Siege*, a Christian interpretation of the siege of the city.[19] In the wake of the Battle of Leuthen, the siege of Breslau by Imperial forces began on December 7; six days later the city was bombarded with heavy artillery. Belach comments: "The Fire Works which our Citizens would send into the Air on News of good Fortune, were now replaced by real Fire-Works, which would have been a feast for the eyes were not the sight of them combined with such Risks."[20] He is here quite contemporary in his aesthetic preferences, akin to Hogarth's "line of beauty"—the English artist held that the serpentine line was the most beautiful line of all—in his rhapsodies on "how the Fire-balls drew behind them manifold Tails of sparks: snake-like, wave-shaped, shooting in spirals."[21] The whole spectacle was "terribly beautiful," he added. While Belach could draw aesthetic pleasure from the fire, elsewhere the flames fueled sectarian hatred. The Zittau fire of 1757 angered the Saxon population, exacerbating existing religious misgivings about the Austrian liberators. Prince Elector Friedrich Christian (1722–1763) notes in his diary: "The Saxons have been screaming with all their might against the Austrians since the sad fire of Zittau, which increased their long-held Hatred of them, to which religion has contributed a substantial Quantity."[22]

Nearly all of the war's armies were mixed in terms of religion. This could give rise to a number of problems, from the award of medals to the rights of military chaplains. Thus, Dubois-Cattin, a recruiting officer in the French service and a member of the Swiss Reformed Church, reports with satisfaction to his brother the news from Paris that "His Majesty is bestowing honors of distinction on officers of the [Reformed] religion, in imitation of the cross for the Catholics."[23] In 1762, the Cologne city council prevented members of a Swedish regiment in French service from holding Reformed church services in the city.[24] The German regiments that embarked for England in 1756, and left the following year, included a substantial number of troops from principalities like Hanover and Hesse. The annual reports of the Jesuit order in Hamburg repeatedly document the pastoral care they offered to Protestant armies: "In addition to the usual annual journeys, the Hanoverian army offered a vast field in which to practice apostolic zeal and Christian love, as it left its winter quarters and took to the field. Soon [the town of] Harburg called for a missionary from the order, and soon after Stade did the same, then Horneburg, then again Stade." Around Easter, "as the army was planning its march into the Field," a Jesuit missionary spent ten days at the places mentioned, "busy with apostolic work; he counted 700 common soldiers given strength by the Lamb."[25] The author notes with great concern that a lack of funds meant missionaries were unable to travel to Celle to minister to souls in that city, leaving many Catholic soldiers without a "Catholic military pastor."

Although sectarian tension alone was not grounds for the war, even the appearance of it could nonetheless create problems of military loyalty. Questions of loyalty and sectarian identity were a repeated issue for mixed-denomination units in the Imperial armies. Johann Caspar Schiller (1723–1796), the father of the famous author, was present on the march of the Württemberg corps from Swabia to Austria in September 1757: "Both at Geisslingen and at the camp near Linz, many in the regiments of General von Spiznass and Prince Louis revolted, because of the fear of a religious War spread by malicious-minded persons."[26] Something similar happened in 1758, when Protestant inhabitants of Swabia tried to appeal to the "confessional conscience" of a Saxon regiment en route to serve with the French.[27]

Within the military, we can also see an unmistakable long-term trend toward secularization. In 1810, Joseph Ferdinand Dreyer, then ninety-two years old, published a description of his life and times: He had been a regimental drummer and a Prussian "partisan" in the three Silesian Wars and the War of the Bavarian Succession. His portrayal of the Prussian military in the mid-eighteenth century is almost entirely glorifying; he clearly belonged to a generation that was highly skeptical of Prussia's later armed forces. Much of his reporting of the Seven Years' War is of the genre "everything was better in the past"—in particular, with reference to obedience and discipline—with later generations accused of "softness" in comparison to their forebears.[28] In the case of Dreyer, the lament for lost glory is, above all, a response to Prussian losses in the Napoleonic Wars.[29] He identifies newer soldiers' lack of religiosity as a key illustration of a shift in mentality between generations: "There was cursing at God and laughing at the Devil, and the soldiers thought themselves fine because they did not think or believe like other Christians. In this, the officers set an example, and Field-preachers sat down with Ensigns to play cards and drink. The increasing Occurrence of this has brought Disobedience, more and more common. In our day, we went to Battle singing 'A Fast Fortress is Our God,' etc. and ended it with 'Now Thank We All Our God,' etc. We defeated the Enemy for duty and obedience to our King."[30]

Confessionalization had resulted in the physical separation of different religions within the Holy Roman Empire, but the war, however unintentionally, brought together those of different religious faiths. This often created everyday situations of sectarian confrontation: for example, around the billeting of troops, their transit through particular territories, and the presence of prisoners of war. Questions touching on problems of religious topography were particularly polarizing: Where should the war dead be buried? Who could celebrate the service, and where? These issues affected Protestant British soldiers in Catholic Westphalia as much as Catholic French troops in Protestant states like Prussia, Saxony, and Electoral Hanover. They had an effect on Protestant prisoners in Austria and Catholic prisoners in Prussia, on French prisoners in British camps, and vice versa, and on British marines raiding Brittany.

The Prussian ensign Christian Wilhelm von Prittwitz, recounting his imprisonment at the Austrian town of Krems, says he would prefer to say nothing of the follies committed there. But as an "honest narrator," he nonetheless provides a detailed description. The poor behavior of prisoners of war is acknowledged, but it is quickly linked to a general Catholic immorality and in this way partly relativized: "If its lavish and superstitious Clergy had not already placed the city of Krems into Immorality, the Quartering [of prisoners] would have done the same. But everywhere the same sad Observation was to be made. Black-coats consorted with red-coats [priests consorted with officers], the latter only intensifying an Iniquity begun before their time."[31] His remarks on perceptions of religious practices in Krems are also informative: "The pure, unadulterated word of God was simply not to be heard, also there were no Bibles, nor other Christian devotional literature. From the pulpit, the most tasteless nonsense imaginable was oft propagated as true Doctrine, which could not be heard without revulsion and Disgust. Hence we were left with neither Guidance nor Admonition, and thus the moral scourge was all the more."[32] The experience of difference prompts Prittwitz to perceive the advantages of his own denomination all the more clearly: "Just as one appreciates the Benefit and True Value of a well-organized Government only when one is in Lands either with None at all, or only the appearance thereof, so too was it here with regard to Religion and the Worshipping of God. Because everything given that venerable Name was here nothing but Fiction and Fable. But this permitted one to see the advantages of true and unadulterated Protestantism over the silly and sinister ways of Catholicism." Very concrete conflicts could arise from this kind of confessional hostility, as Prittwitz goes on to explain:

> Whenever the [eucharistic] Sanctuary was carried in the streets and we happened to come upon it, we would customarily stop and remove our Hats. But this gesture of Reverence was declared to be Unsatisfactory, and it was demanded that we prostrate ourselves, no less, something we could not rest easy with, and thus a dispute arose which came to the ears of Empress Maria Theresia in Vienna and she herself decided that we must either genuflect the Knee, or else go away immediately when the Bell announcing the Blessed Eucharist was heard. Of course, we chose the latter, although no doubt it was amusing to observe how one approaching such a Procession would turn and hurry to his Quarters with long strides. However, this Procedure did indeed eliminate the previous dispute, satisfying the town's devout Citizens.[33]

With conflict thus avoided, Prittwitz strikes a conciliatory note, going so far as to admit a slight admiration for the piety of other believers:

> Had the ceremony of worship not been a mere *opus operatum*, in which one thought either nothing at all or thought of unedifying things, then the immense devotion observed on every occasion related to it would without Doubt have caused some benevolent Sensation in us. Because when the monstrance was carried about, Every-one, no matter how noble or how lowly, fell down upon the stones of the street, and the Guardsmen were ordered to shoulder arms, and then the officer would command: 'Kneel on your right knee, remove your hats' and so on, which, since it was done at a military Pace, was not an unimpressive sight. The Priest also usually had several soldiers of the Guard gathered about him, who accompanied him, carrying their muskets in their right hands.[34]

The passage makes clear how military ceremony could diminish sectarian difference or at least render it more tolerable in aesthetic terms. However, for the Prussians, Catholic behavior could easily pass over into absurdity, as when Jesuits performed a military-style salute: "It appeared Comical indeed, when the Jesuits came out to Publicize with thundering Cannon the Victory of their peoples [at Breslau in 1757], operating the guns in their black monk's habits as if they were actual Artillery-men."[35]

Death and funeral services, in particular, were situations where a foreign religiosity could become problematic. Prittwitz finds the idea behind the "passing-bell" used to announce death's approach "highly commendable" but thinks it fails to achieve what it intends: "Then, as a Fellow Christian lies in his final Moments, they mutter out a couple of Ave Marias or Paternosters and the matter has been dealt with." Prittwitz even expresses a desire to introduce a similar bell to his local congregation of Moravian Brethern.[36]

Such confessional and national divisions are vividly illustrated by two engravings produced by William Hogarth in 1756, each titled *The Invasion*: One shows a scene in France (figure 5.1), the other a scene in England (figure 5.2).[37] On the French side of the English Channel, Hogarth depicts an inn named The Royal Clog. Symbolizing an impoverished France, it sells only watery soup, while hungry French soldiers grill frogs over a fire. This, suggests Hogarth, is the French army that is preparing to invade Britain. In the background, French women work in the fields while soldiers dream of revenge, as well as England's fine beer and beef. The threat of Catholicism

Figure 5.1 The Invasion I. Engraving by William Hogarth (London, 1756). *Source*: akg-images.

Figure 5.2 The Invasion II. Engraving by William Hogarth (London, 1756).
Source: Heritage-Images/The Print Collector/akg-images.

is personified by a monk checking an executioner's ax for sharpness, having already readied several symbols of religious intolerance to bring on the campaign, including a statue of Saint Anthony, plans to build a Dominican abbey, implements of torture, and a wheel on which to "break" and execute Protestants.

The English side presents a very different scene, with well-fed British soldiers in front of an inn named Duke of Cumberland, which promises "roasted and boiled foods" every day, an ironic jab at the duke, echoing contemporary public criticisms made of him. A broad-shouldered soldier paints a caricature on the wall, depicting Louis XV with a gallows in his hand. Meanwhile, the words of "Rule Britannia" have been placed on the table, with "beef and beer" available in large quantities. The British women gaze at the well-dressed soldiers while to the right of the picture a young man stands on tiptoe to fulfill the army's height requirement. Britain, the picture tells us, is as well supplied in patriots as it is in other resources, its "lions" set to confront the "hungry French slaves."

Religion had a significance in the everyday lives of British soldiers similar to that in other European armies.[38] In large parts of the Emsland, Westphalia, and the Sauerland—all regions of northwestern Germany—the Catholic majority did not welcome the British with open arms. In a city like Münster, the population regarded itself as being under some threat from the British and Allied occupiers, since troops from Brunswick and Hesse were no less of a social burden than the French troops. In late 1759, the population of Münster would have particular reason to dislike the Allied forces: They had laid siege to the city, at the time under French occupation, culminating in a heavy bombardment that set off substantial fires within the city.[39] Grotehenn, the soldier from Brunswick, spent considerable time in the Catholic city of Telgte, near Münster; his account is particularly informative about everyday perceptions of other religions. Telgte was a well-known site of Marian pilgrimage, and he thus came into repeated contact with the local culture of piety.[40] On his first day in the city, he was taken to see the image of Mary, where he politely marveled at the magnificently decorated pilgrimage site, complete with crutches left behind by those cured at the shrine. He was told stories of the Virgin's miraculous power of healing. He had been billeted in a garden house with broken windows and soon came down with a heavy cold and "chest fever." He called for a surgeon to have himself bled, although his landlady had insisted that he take her horse and ride to the Marian shrine to be healed. Grotehenn's refusal represented a choice in favor of "rational" medical treatment: This was how he himself saw his bloodletting, and it was generally regarded as such by contemporaries.

If taken to extremes, unbidden religious coexistence could end in sacrilege and abuse. At the very least, it caused confusion and prompted questions. These patterns of perception and behavior also appeared outside Europe, as seen in the treatment of the property of Roman Catholic orders in Manila, Havana, and Canada. In North America, religious confrontations were even more complex than in central Europe: here there were divisions among different Christian denominations, but these also distinguished themselves from Indigenous people, whom they regarded as pagans.[41] One example of mutual sectarian jibing can be found in an account written by John Knox in Annapolis in April 1758. While the "better sort" of French behaved with civility, this was not necessarily the case with servants or workers, who took any opportunity for impertinence. If they met a British officer or official while driving oxen in the area, they would immediately "shout at the cattle, calling them 'Luther' or 'Calvin' or 'Cranmer.' The poor animals were then beaten mercilessly with whips and clubs, as if their owners really did have these famous Protestants at their mercy."[42] These were small incidents and situations, but they could create resentments and, with them, a breeding ground for religious outrage.

Generating hype and scandal around sectarian attacks was an important way of mobilizing religion as an emotional resource. Outrage could spread via media reports, in this way bringing events and habits to public attention across Germany. The case of Frederick II, Landgrave of Hesse-Cassel (1720–1785), who converted to Catholicism as heir to the throne in 1749, is a good example of how conversions within royal houses could be used for sectarian propaganda.[43] Frederick had become a major general in the Prussian army in 1741 and was promoted to lieutenant general in 1744. Despite being courted by Vienna, he reentered active Prussian service in April 1756 and remained in the army of the Prussian king for the entirety of the war, serving as governor of the Wesel fortress and vice governor of the Magdeburg fortress. In May 1760, when he acceded to the throne as landgrave, he was awarded the rank of field marshal.

At the very beginning of the war, sectarian emotions had run high in Erfurt, a city with a mixed religious population, thanks to the execution on October 1, 1756, of three criminals who had recently converted from Protestantism to Catholicism. At the execution, Father Beckmann, a Jesuit priest, spoke out fiercely against Protestantism, only to be spontaneously slapped in the face by the executioner's assistant.[44] Protestants in the watching crowd reacted by beginning a riot, and the Jesuits present were saved from death only by the intervention of soldiers from the Mainz garrison. The French envoy in Mainz viewed the event as a dangerous one, which the Prussian king could easily have used to intensify the climate of sectarian conflict.

In the run-up to the Battle of Rossbach in 1757, the actions of the French in Saxony likewise stirred emotions. *Acta Publica*, a Strasbourg newspaper, reported: "In Weischütz, a French colonel made Mr. Schren, the local Pastor, bend over so he could step on him to mount his Horse. Even the churches have not been spared from the plunder. In Zeuchfeld, Branderode, and many other places, altars, pews, and pulpits have been hacked apart and ruined. All will learn to their disgust, that in Baumersrode they even dishonored Chalices and the vessel of the Sacrament, in which they relieved themselves before setting them back upon the altar. In short, may God have mercy on this wretched State of things!" The report mobilizes classic cultural topoi of impurity, which were inevitably bound to rouse Protestant emotions. The standard comparison with the Turks is duly made: "The combined army, which came to the aid of the Saxons, showed itself worse than the Turks; in many places they treated the people in a most cruel manner, and made their filth upon the Altars and Pulpits of the Churches."[45] Descriptions of provocative behavior on the part of the French could serve to divert attention from the actual enemy, the Prussians, who were at the time occupying Saxony.

On November 5, 1757, the day of the Battle of Rossbach, Frederick's sister, the Margravine Wilhelmine, wrote to him from Bayreuth: "The bitterness our Catholic neighbors hold against us is incomprehensible. The priests' sermons are so filled with impudence and stupidity, they claim that you want to exterminate religion. [. . .] I have constant fears that this rancor will lead to religious war. If I were inclined to laughter, I would tell you that you will have a place of honor in Paradise as a defender of the faith, at least on the same level as Calvin and Luther."[46] Frederick's unrelenting policies—above all, his treatment of the primarily Catholic province of Silesia—fueled rumors of religious repression. On December 30, 1757, the Catholic chaplain Andreas Faulhaber (1713–1757) was executed at Glatz in Silesia, in what became a veritable religious media event.[47] The killing of Faulhaber, who had been convicted of aiding and abetting a Catholic soldier to desert, attracted much attention across the entire empire. The chaplain had heard the soldier's confession, and it was assumed that he had approved of his desertion, although he refused to divulge the content of the conversation. Faulhaber was posthumously celebrated as a martyr to the secrecy of the confessional.

The religious practices of other denominations were a regular subject for mockery. Pastor Cuntz of the town of Kirchditmold, near Kassel, reported that in 1761 two French soldiers carrying "half a slaughtered cow on a long pole" had followed a funeral procession through the entire village, all the way to the cemetery gate.[48] There seems to have been an outbreak of mock executions in the Fulda area in 1757 and 1758, with either political or sectarian motivation. On one occasion, an effigy of Frederick II was hanged on a gallows; on another, a straw doll representing him was set alight, accidentally starting a larger blaze.[49] Fearing a media scandal, the authorities in both Fulda and Hesse-Darmstadt tried to sweep the incidents under the carpet, with some success. Both territories were allies of the Reich and the emperor, although Fulda was Catholic and Hesse-Darmstadt was Protestant.

Territories of mixed denominations were particularly prone to excesses of sectarian agitation. In Cleves, one of Prussia's provinces in western Germany, repeated edicts were promulgated against "insults to religion" because young people had rioted or elaborate religious processions had prompted sectarian confrontations.[50] Social inequalities could exacerbate tensions, as in Cleves, where the Catholic majority was ruled by a Protestant administrative elite. Religious affiliations could also influence specific espionage activities; Catholics often passed information to the French, whereas members of the Reformed church were typically loyal to Prussia. Contemporary accounts suggest Lutherans tended to indifference.[51] The climate was particularly tense in Switzerland, where some feared an imminent religious civil war; some cantons had subsidy contracts with France, whereas in evangelical cantons, Frederick was hailed as the savior of the Protestant cause.[52] Prussia even possessed territory in Switzerland, holding sovereignty over the town of Neuchâtel between 1707 and 1857.[53]

Propaganda invocations of religious war became a kind of post hoc rationalization of the great diplomatic *renversement des alliances* (reversal of alliances) in the run-up to the war. These invocations offered evidence that explained the connection between the two great rivalries of the war, the Franco-British and Austro-Prussian rivalries. With everyday life still profoundly shaped by confessional affiliation, political machinations that mobilized religious emotion proved consistently effective. For Prussia, creating sectarian scandal in the media was a tactic used to gain a hearing for its case while framing itself as an underdog, something it never was in reality. This created a steady supply of new evidence that the war was a religious conflict.

This social logic of media scandals highlights the Seven Years' War as an early modern media war. War by media was by no means new, but this conflict gave it a new scope and new dimensions. Prussia certainly made numerous attempts to, as Maria Theresa put it, "adopt a religious disguise." However, Prussia's fanning of the flames of sectarian war had an apparently paradoxical result, at least at first glance, setting in motion a "farewell to the wars of religion," as Johannes Burkhardt would later put it. The Roman Curia explicitly avoided the term *guerra de religione* during the conflict: a semantic shift that went hand in hand with a change in practice. Frederick's media tactics were successful, but they were also quite legible as stunts and tricks on his part. Moreover, the success of their emotional appeal made clear the need for separation of religion and politics at an imperial level. Religious capital could still be mobilized as a political resource, but it was no longer dominant across the entire political field. The religious card could still be played, but it was not a guaranteed trump. In this way, the Seven Years' War proved to be a kind of cultural laboratory for working out the relation between religion and politics, in which old and new practices coexisted, working both with and against one another. By the mid-eighteenth century, contradictions became possible: For example, a sure faith that one was defending God's cause could coexist with the belief that the current war was not a religious war.

Warmth and Cold

Two fundamental experiences of soldiering were being subjected, first, to a variety of climatic conditions and, second, to shortages of food and drink. Weather and provisioning are central topics in the historical anthropology of war; during the conflict itself, they could have a very concrete influence on decisions and could even become a decisive factor in the wider war. It was no coincidence that campaigns ideally took place in spring and summer, with armies retiring to winter quarters in the fall.[54] The Battles of Leuthen, which took place on December 5, and Torgau, fought on November 3, demonstrate that the principle was not always followed to the letter. Soldiers slept in tents or in the open air; a billet in a household was considered a great stroke of luck.[55] Reminiscing in 1791, the father of the writer Friedrich Schiller tells a somewhat tall tale about the cold following the Battle of Leuthen. He had fallen asleep by the fire, he writes, but during the night, everything began to freeze: "When I woke and sought to rise, I found that my foot had been frozen in mud up to my knee; so as not to damage my boots, I had to use warm water to break myself loose."[56] For his part, Archenholz describes the winter of 1759–1760 in Saxony as a "campaign [which] cost the king more men than two battles would have done."[57] Ordinary soldiers had only a few lean-tos and, in some cases, not even these, meaning that "poorly-clad soldiers froze their limbs every day." Ordinary soldiers, he writes, had "run around the Camp like madmen, [seeking] to liquify blood made solid by the cold." Others crawled into tents, "where they lay on top of each other, to warm at least some parts of their own bodies against the bodies of their comrades."[58] This single winter campaign, concludes Archenholz, cost the king more men "than would have two great battles."[59]

"After enormous hardships amid the mountains, the forests, and the ice, fog, and snow in this country, which the barbarian character has left in its state of chaos, on our way to the sources of the Ruhr, where we found that accommodation, bread, and guides were all lacking, fearing we were surrounded by a superior Enemy, one who sought to revenge Himself upon us, we at last arrived at Werl in a sad state of decay." The description is not of Canada but rather of Westphalia in western Germany—specifically, the region south of the town of Hamm—as described by Mopinot de la Chapotte, a French officer, in a letter of October 29, 1758.[60] He served with the dauphin's cavalry regiment in campaigns across northwestern Germany in 1757–1758 and again in 1761–1762, eventually attaining the rank of lieutenant colonel. Among other places, he saw action at the siege of Wesel (1757) and the Battles of Hagenbeck (1757), Lutterberg (1758), Krefeld (1758), and Vellinghausen (1761). On campaigns like the one just described, precise scouting of the terrain was strategically vital, but the descriptions it produced often activated cultural stereotypes, as in Mopinot's account.[61]

Pastor Cuntz, observing from his home near Kassel, gives an impressive description of a gigantic French army camp in the winter of 1760, holding some seventy thousand men, who were a burden on the entire region for fourteen weeks. "Cold weather seemed set to take hold, and the whole army [. . .] had to dig down into the earth. They turned our fields into a true desert, turning up the Soil from the bottom upwards. They made what was called Braken [barracks], so the whole 80,000 men had Lodgings in the Earth, and there was barely a tent to be seen, but rather small houses built next each other, so the camp resembled very much a City."[62] Large amounts of wood were needed to heat these "earth-huts," leading to widespread deforestation in the surrounding areas. In 1757, Prittwitz, the young Prussian officer cited earlier, makes reference to his own side seizing wood for firewood near Prague, calling it an "Abomination of Desolation": In some villages every house was destroyed to get hold of the wood. "They carried off roofing Shingles, Planks, long Spars and wood bundles to their Camp, and finally took an entire village, a method which caused much Screams and Howling among the unhappy residents, and also much Begging and Pleading."[63] In addition to the cold, rain caused a great deal of trouble for soldiers. Dubois-Cattin reports of a march to Paderborn where they saw so much rain that tent pegs could not be hammered down into the mud.[64] The climate seemed to grow milder as peace drew closer in the winter of 1762–1763. Johann Daniel Geitz, from Bottendorf in the north of Hesse, writes of "a Miracle, unlike any held in people's Memories: not a single flake of Snow fell all Winter long, so the cattle could graze all the Winter long, including also the Horses, Oxen, Cows, and Sheep. Behold once more the Miracle of the Lord."[65]

Available sources repeatedly emphasize the inadequate uniforms worn by soldiers in cold and wet weather.[66] One particularly vivid episode, which shows soldiers' pragmatism in bad weather, is reported in the memoir of the Scottish officer John Grant, where he writes about the Highlanders of the Black Watch who were deployed to Canada in the winter of 1760–1761. The Highlanders marched in traditional kilts until late autumn, when Grant's men changed them "for leggings of green cloth like the backwoodsmen." However, they continued to suffer from the cold, since they possessed only *plaids* (Scottish cloaks) to keep them warm. Relieved and proud, Grant notes that nonetheless they did not have a single man missing due to illness during the whole winter. His own ears were frozen, since his hat had no earflaps; he also made temporary repairs to his own house by nailing a French tent to its badly damaged roof, pitching his own soldier's tent within, and putting curtains around his bed. Although the space was heated by a fire and a stove in the evening, it got so cold at night that icicles hung from the ceiling in the morning. The men had to be inventive on their journey: When it snowed, Grant and his soldiers would set up branches to mark the next day's route. He also mentions the food situation: Spruce beer, flavored with the resins of spruce trees, was the main drink, along with plentiful schnapps and wine. Vegetables were in particularly short supply; there were only small amounts of cabbage, onions, and garlic. The soldiers' daily meal was a piece of pork, "boiled in a pile of cabbage, with a few extra slices of bread."[67]

Hunger and Thirst

Stable food supplies for both humans and animals have always been a cornerstone of military logistics. In Europe, soldiers' main food was bread.[68] In 1757, the Prussian army placed a provisioning order with the supplier Heinrich Carl von Schimmelmann (1724–1782). The order highlights the scale and composition of food supplies that were required. It included a typical range of foods: almost 6,000 tons of wheat, barley, and oats; 100 hundred tons of wine; 200 tons of brandy; 25 tons of tobacco; 15 tons of cheese; 250 tons of rice; 33 tons of bacon; and around 26 tons of herring, salted cod, and roach.[69]

The type and quality of food were constant issues for both officers and ordinary soldiers. For common soldiers, the main issue was a shortage of food, but officers frequently indulged in luxuries, making an effort to live up to their social status while in the field. Fine dining is a common theme in the letters of the Swiss officer Dubois-Cattin to his brother and in the letters of Baron Louis Joseph de Castelnau (1728–1793). On several occasions, for example, Dubois-Cattin orders rare mushrooms; he also writes about a group of eight officers, each of whom, in turn, invites the others to dine, simply as a way of passing the time.[70] Making and receiving gifts of food was "simply what one did," forming a key social link between officers, and could be found in all armies.[71] The Baron de Castelnau liked to spend his time hunting and quotes menus that run for entire pages.[72] In the final year of the war, Frederick's beloved greyhounds still enjoyed their own luxuries. Staying at Dahlen Castle before the signing of the peace treaty, the dogs received a cooked chicken daily, along with five pounds of roast veal and a quart of warm milk. They also had their paws bathed in milk.[73]

By contrast, Hans Carl Heinrich Trautzschen, the Saxon officer encamped near Pirna in 1756, reports on malnutrition among the soldiers, who were living, almost literally, a dog's life: "Few had any Food now other than roots of trees of which the fruit was long since eaten; boiled hair-powder salted with gunpowder was a meal; horses chewed on wood for Fodder."[74] For Grotehenn, food was a constant preoccupation. In October 1757, he reports from the town of Rotenburg an der Wümme that salt had become very rare, until there was no more to be had for any price, and every man had exhausted his stock, so then "the first meals were salted with Gunpowder, of which the taste was better than its appearance." In his tent, soldiers were boiling up herring with carrots and potatoes to create something vaguely tasting of salt. Camp followers then sold that broth as a salt substitute, alongside their own herring. The second scarce commodity was tobacco. This was not a problem for nonsmokers like Grotehenn, but he had comrades "for whom this was so painful, given their habit of Puffing away incessantly, that the absence of Salt was as nothing in comparison."[75] Responding to the shortage, the Duke of Cumberland arranged for a supply of large barrels of tobacco, albeit containing strong and even "semi-raw" tobacco leaves, which the "particularly keen adherents" of tobacco nonetheless smoked heavily, "as if to make up for lost time. [. . .] But some became quite unwell, and became Intoxicated and rather foolish, strengthening still further my aversion to the smoking of Tobacco."[76]

For soldiers in the field, the heaviest burden of all was the lack of drinking water.[77] Most first-person accounts include complaints about water shortages.[78] Prittwitz, for example, reports on the march from Pomerania to Posen in the summer of 1759: "The most oppressive of several evils was that we frequently suffered from a lack of water and were sometimes forced to search for and dig up springs ourselves. When this happened, I was amazed how several wells could be dug in a short time, but it was likely also the case that many hands brought the work to a swift end."[79]

For many mercenaries, local food encountered while "living off the land" also took some getting used to. The Swiss soldier Markus Uhlmann joked that some Westphalian farmers gave him nothing to eat because he "talked Churman," since they "had to give everything to the French"; he also mentioned a bread that was clearly inedible to the Swiss palate, which he refers to as "pump perniggel": "I could not learn to eat this, it was as black as the Earth, quite sour, and since it can weigh from 4 to 25 lb, it is not baked through, and in the chewing it is like enough to Dough, and sticks fast in the Teeth."[80] Trautzschen, the Saxon officer, also had an aversion to "Bumpernickel," observing in a letter from Unna that the bread was "as contrary to the stomach" as the "language of the locals" was to his ears.[81]

By contrast, even in a besieged city like Kolberg, a wide range of foodstuffs could be maintained, despite blockades. As one witness recalled: "Wine, Brandy, Vinegar, Beer, Bread, Herring, Sugar, Tea, Cofeee etc. could always be had. Only that in the 6th week of siege, Brandy and Sugar became scarce, and in the 8th week the Heering, but when the roads were open, brandy and sugar came once more. Butter, Bacon, Peas and Holstein Cheese were so plentiful in our stores that at first they were sold to citizens of the town."[82] It was only after the situation changed, with the sudden quartering of Russian soldiers, that everything became more expensive, with many goods in short supply.[83] Sources contain repeated reference to the substitute foods people turned to when faced with shortages. Thus, Pastor Cuntz reports shortages in Kassel in 1762, when a "wretched bread" was baked from acorns, and the "grandest lords" were forced to cook with the cheapest cooking oils.[84]

Ubiquitous alcohol consumption presented all armies with massive disciplinary problems.[85] Surviving sources suggest very frequent charges of alcohol abuse in the British and Russian armies in particular.[86] Soldiers' appetite for schnapps had particularly disastrous consequences during the Battle of Zorndorf: The Russian General Count Saint-André reports that scattered bands of Russian soldiers took possession of "the waggons of camp

Followers, laden with Brandy." They "got so drunk they shot and bayonetted each other, not sparing their own Generals, but rather cursing them tremendously, in the harshest of terms, even attacking some with Muskets, saying it was they who had brought them to this Misfortune."[87]

Alcohol fulfilled a number of social functions: It lent soldiers courage before battle, added calories to the meager food supply, and could be used as a gift or a reward. But despite its reputation as "the cheapest pay," it could come at a heavy price.[88] Alcohol is perhaps the dominant theme in Corporal William Todd's diary entries on everyday life in the war's northwestern German theater. He mentions "geneva" (gin) or simply "liquor" almost daily, frequently because of disciplinary problems of some kind. The importance of alcohol is also reflected in the testimonies of the German civilian population. In 1760, Johann Conrad Lütgert (1730–1764) writes of the British infantry regiments billeted in his hometown of Isselhorst in Westphalia: "They kept excellent discipline, had many Ducats and drank much Brandy."[89] British forces kept a particularly sharp eye out for alcohol when attacking or besieging towns occupied by the French. In October 1758, various Münster chronicles complained of the English practice of plunder: "The engelish were Masters of this [looting], and this in all places, because the engelish were also most inclin'd to stealing."[90] Around the same time, a different chronicle reports the fears of Münster smallholders: "Many shops and Brandy Houses remained closed to the English who did not pay."[91] Excessive drinking on the part of British soldiers became a key factor in their contacts with civilians, contributing to the image of Britain left behind in northwestern Germany. Alcohol probably had the worst long-term consequences for Native Americans, who died en masse from its effects, either directly from the drink supplied by Europeans or indirectly from the poverty associated with it.[92]

Language and Its Limits

In all of the aforementioned ways, both the weather and the patterns of consumption played a decisive role in the waging of the war. But linguistic competence also played a role, especially in obtaining provisions, a context where it functioned alongside money and violence. We should not underestimate the question of linguistic communication or the challenge it presented, not least given the wide range of warring parties.[93] Language was essential in getting through many social situations. Not to understand something could have literally fatal consequences when, for example, coercing contributions or foraging locally for supplies. Today even a few words of English serve as a lingua franca; in the eighteenth century, that role was played by French and, to a lesser degree, Latin. For many officers, the acquisition of languages could be an important element in success.[94] Particularly in colonial contexts, translators played a central role, acting as cultural intermediaries of a sort.[95] In North America, language itself was part of Europe's expansionist policies, as when misleading translations of terms like *fort* and *property* were used as a stratagem to obtain Native American assent to treaties.

We also have examples of linguistic ability being beneficial to civilians in Europe. In 1761, Johann Philipp Zellmann (1712–1774), from Herzberg in Brandenburg, records in his diary: "I seemed to make friends with whomever I spoke with in Latin. It was precisely my use of the Latin language which caused a respected officer to be so well-inclined in my Direction, that he had me go with him to the palace, to be presented to General Grandmaison."[96] Billeted in Oftersheim in the Electoral Palatinate, the French officer Baron de Castelnau complained of boredom: No one in the village spoke French, and he had no opportunity to learn German.[97] The city of Cologne had a pragmatic policy of bilingual publication, in German and French, for edicts and theater advertising.[98] Communication problems were particularly severe for the British in northwestern Germany, since very few people spoke English in rural areas and active speakers were rare even in the cities.[99] Major Richard Davenport (1719–1760) of the 10th Dragoon Regiment records a stay in the town of Bramsche, where he shared a lavish dinner with a convent of nuns. His accounts give insight into how communication functioned: "I placed Knigge [Bodo Knigge, a second lieutenant] next to the old woman, who was well over 70, to talk German to her, and I sat myself next to the fat friar and talked Latin to him, with a bottle always between us. And in this Manner, we all became great friends."[100] For Davenport, language appears, above all, to be an obstacle to his "gallant" contacts with women, rendered still more difficult, he emphasizes, by denominational difference:

> In these damned Protestant villages, there is a kind of regularity of morals and a fear of their pastor among the young women, that is a great check to intrigue. They are never clear of the fear of the

consequences of their sins. In Catholic villages, and especially towns, they are "smoaky" and know that they can settle accounts once a month or so. They dread the time a little as it approaches, but after Confession the heart is as light as feathers. Besides these defects in the people, there is in us an ignorance of the language and from thence an impossibility of employing to any purpose, the art of persuasion. A man who can only say, "Will you?" and one word more, must not expect the answer to his question to be always "Yes", yet sometimes, these few words joined with the glittering appearance of a ducat, will have a good effect, but less here than in any quarter I have been.[101]

Civilians affected by billeting repeatedly complained about the British soldiers' lack of language ability. Franz Goswin von Michels, a former mayor of Soest, another Westphalian town, notes: "Almost no officer speaks any German or French, which is very *incommode*, but they keep good discipline and punish [their men] very harshly with whips."[102] The personal union between the British and Hanoverian monarchies at least meant there were considerable numbers of English-speaking Germans in those parts of the country, which went some way to balancing out the situation. Three years later in Portugal, however, the British encountered a far more difficult situation: Of the entire British officer corps and general staff, only three could speak Portuguese.

Communications were just as difficult for Russian soldiers, both with allies and with enemies. Many Russian officers could speak German or French, but it was a very different story with common soldiers, especially Cossack and Kalmyk auxiliaries. When Christian Täge, a military chaplain, was taken prisoner by the Russians, he was quickly assigned to interpret for Count Fermor, the Russian general.[103] As a translator, he also performed the blessing of the Cossacks and Kalmyks before they crossed the Vistula River.[104] "But I speak not a word of Russian!" Täge tells his captors, who reply: "It matters not if you are understood by no-one. Russians are fond of any preacher whom they know has done the blessing proper to his office." The chaplain got to work and seems to have been quite taken with the success of his own performance: "I became aware of some emotion among the officers, and the common men crossed themselves at least at the name of Jesus, Abraham etc. For my part, I could not help being affected by profound emotion during my own address."[105] The writer Andrei Bolotov also benefited from a knowledge of German. While in Tilsit, he recorded this in his journal: "In this case also, my German helped me a great deal. It can be said of the Germans to the credit that they are very benevolent to foreigners who are capable of speaking in their language."[106] At the bakery, he is unexpectedly given ten bread rolls. "In this way I managed to make this purchase and all others with incomparably more success than those unable to speak German."[107]

Buying bread was one thing, but battle was quite another, where communications could not be left to chance. Commands had to be comprehensible to all, including in a markedly polyglot context like the Austrian army. The Prince Charles-Joseph of Ligne (1735–1814), a young Austrian officer in this war and later a general and statesman, commanded that all his orders be translated in such a way as to be actually "understood by the various nations which make up this army, and then the translation must be checked for correctness. I have met many people who claimed to speak German, who, from sheer force of habit, come to believe that they in fact can so do."[108] In this way, language became an important resource of war, whether in communications within any given army, as a way of speaking to civilian populations, or in contacts with non-European cultures.

CHAPTER VI

1758

The Fighting Spreads

An Ottoman Alliance?

Seeking to avoid encirclement, Frederick II was always on the lookout for possible new alliances. The solution seemed to be located on the Straits of the Bosporus. As early as the 1740s, he had repeatedly put out diplomatic feelers toward the Ottoman Empire.[1] Even before the war, he had sent an envoy to Istanbul: "Karl Adolf von Rexin," a Silesian whose real name was Gottfried Fabian Haude (b. 1714). Haude arrived in the Ottoman capital in 1755.[2] His first contacts in Constantinople were meant only to explore the possibility of a treaty of trade and friendship, although he had no plenipotentiary powers to finalize any agreement. This first mission was unsuccessful, and by November 1755, Haude had returned to Potsdam. In 1756, again using the name of Rexin, Haude undertook a second mission to the Sublime Porte, this time with more explicit instructions regarding Austria and Russia. Sultan Osman III (1699–1757) died in October 1757 and was succeeded by Mustafa III (1717–1774). "The Turk is shifting his ground," Frederick was assured, which raised his hopes of a Turkish alliance.[3] Throughout 1757, the Prussian king pushed for an alliance with the Ottomans, seeking to force Austria to fight against a new enemy; he became convinced that the Turks would "enter the field with a considerable army."[4] Frederick's unshakable hopes for an Ottoman intervention—which were pure conjecture—ultimately became a guiding principle, which seems frequently to have influenced tactical decisions on the ground.

However, Koca Ragib Pasha (1698–1763), who was the Ottoman grand vizier, a role something like a prime minister, understood brilliantly how to draw out negotiations and in this way repeatedly held off the advances of both Prussia and France.[5] The Austrians were also making active diplomatic advances to the Ottomans. During his stay in Vienna in March and April 1757, while Prussian troops were approaching the city, the Turkish envoy Ahmed Resmi Efendi found himself "continually embarrassed" by Austrian attempts to "demand rapprochement" with Constantinople.[6] Resmi did not undertake a mission to Berlin until the fall of 1763.

Frederick's hopes for an Ottoman alliance permeated right down to the level of common soldiers, as evidenced by a letter written by Johann Heinrich Zander in Dresden on April 11, 1757. He reports that deserters "coming from the Austrians" were saying that "the TURCK stood at THE FRONTIERS OF HUNGARY" and an Austrian army would have to be sent to fight them. He further reports that the king of Prussia was rumored to have said over dinner, "My Lords I have a new RECRUIT who is more to me than 3 times one hundred thousand others," adding "by which he is thought to have meant the TURCK." It was also said that Frederick, in the last war, had freed the sultan from the prisons of the queen of Hungary, which meant he owed a duty of loyalty to the Prussians. Nonetheless, Zander remains ultimately perplexed at the overall situation: "But where things will go with the war, only God knows."[7] For now, Frederick's hopes were disappointed; news of Ottoman troops coming to his aid remained mere rumor and speculation. However, hopes of bringing the Ottomans into the war had not at all been extinguished.

The War in Pomerania

On September 13, 1757, at the Imperial Diet at Regensburg, Johann August Greiffenheim (1712–1789), the Swedish representative, announced that Sweden would invade Prussia, citing the country's responsibilities as a guarantor of the Peace of Westphalia. As he was making his announcement in Regensburg, Swedish forces were crossing the Peene River into Prussian territory, where they captured the city of Anklam. In this way, yet another country entered the Seven Years' War, albeit without an official declaration of war.[8] By the mid-eighteenth century, Sweden was one of Europe's declining powers, still suffering from its losses in the Great Northern War (1700–1721). The country's main foreign policy goal in the current war was to regain control of the Baltic. Strategically, after its advance into Prussia, Sweden had only two realistic options: It could march south to attack Berlin, which was poorly protected, or head eastward to Stettin, where it could join forces with the Russian armies (figure 6.1).

During what in Sweden is called the Pomeranian War, large swathes of the contemporary German state of Mecklenburg–Western Pomerania and parts of Poland became a theater of operations, affecting an arc stretching from Damgarten in the west to Stettin in the east.[9] The most significant cities to be involved in the fighting were Stralsund, Greifswald, and Wolgast.[10] In the mid-eighteenth century, this part of Europe was not generally under arable cultivation; instead, it was dominated by forests, lakes, swamps, and canals, none of which made military maneuvering any easier. Living off the land was also a challenge: Agricultural infrastructure was not comparable with that in Sweden or in much of the Holy Roman Empire. The Peene River was a key strategic feature of the region, and both armies operated along its banks.

In 1755, the Swedish army numbered around forty-six thousand men. It consisted of two kinds of regiments: the regiments with conscripted professional soldiers and the "allotted regiments" of the Indelta, a kind of part-time militia that had expanded gradually since the 1680s.[11] In Sweden, as in England, there were two competing political camps. The Swedish commander, Field Marshal Matthias Alexander von Ungern-Sternberg (1689–1763), was a member of the Cap party but was appointed by the ruling Hat faction to force the opposition to share responsibility for the war. However, the sixty-eight-year-old field marshal fell ill and could assume field command only in October 1757. Swedish troops also suffered delays: They arrived in Pomerania in August 1757 but were not fully operational until mid-September.[12] By that point, it had become clear that the Swedish armed forces had been suffering from considerable material deficiencies since the time of the Great Northern War. Some of its equipment was inadequate, and its logistics were poorly coordinated. At times, wheels for the baggage train were sent on different ships than the wagons themselves.[13] An army of over twenty-two thousand men was deployed in Pomerania; the Swedes could also make use of their fleet, which was administered by the army and thus known as the Arméns flotta.

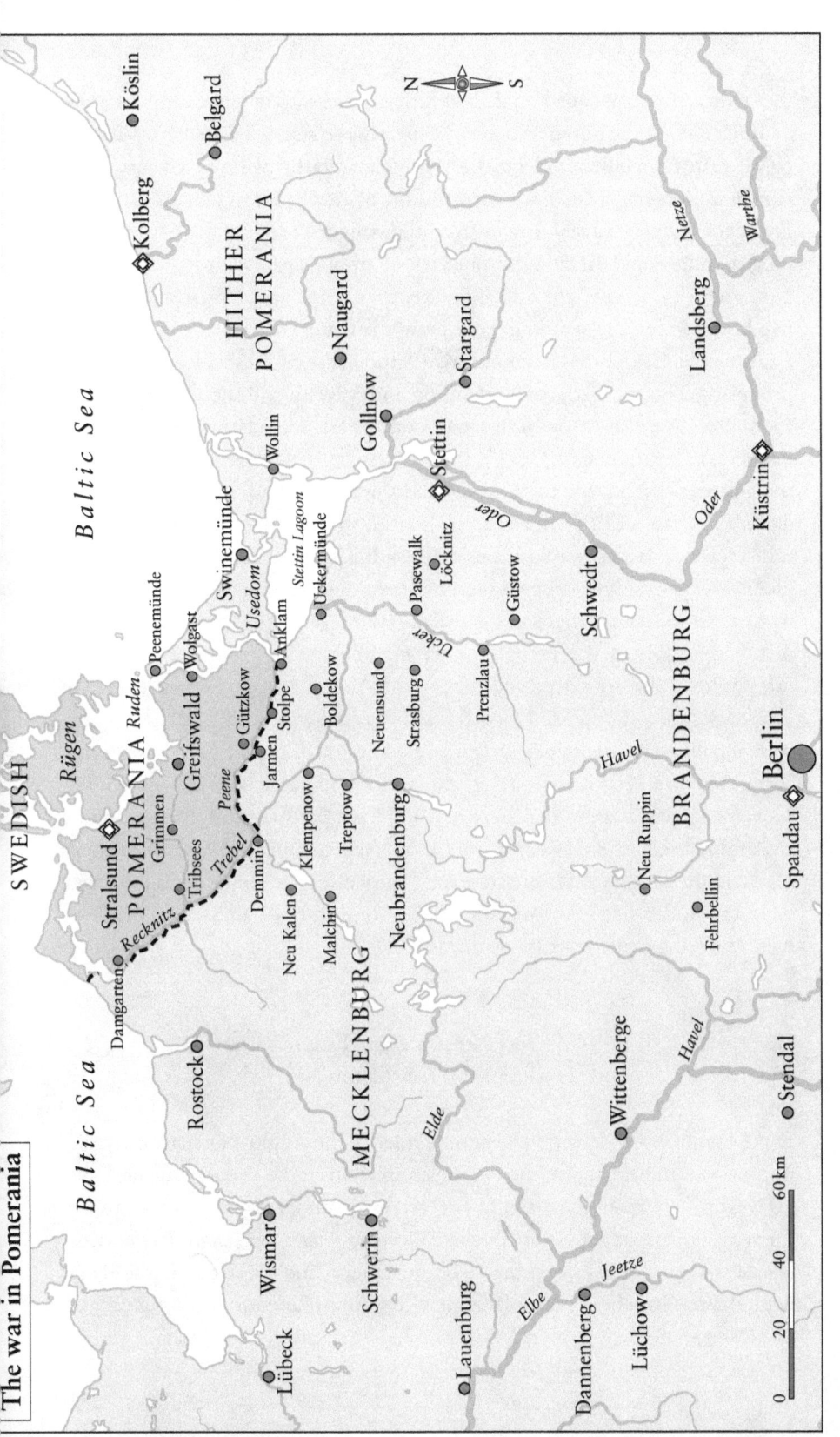

Figure 6.1 The war in Pomerania.
© Peter Palm, Berlin/Germany.

At first, the Prussians could field little in the way of opposition. A total of ninety-seven hundred Prussian soldiers were stationed in its territories of Western Pomerania and Further Pomerania, but this included just three regular regiments, with the rest made up of newly recruited militia units. Frederick retrospectively downplayed the danger posed by the Swedes: "As long as one could field some number of troops against them, one could keep them in check without difficulty; even a thousand infantrymen and five hundred hussars would greatly draw their respect."[14]

At first, in late September and early October, the Swedish advance seemed promising: The army captured Demmin and Anklam and then Swinemünde soon after. Swedish troops also landed on the islands of Usedom and Wollin, and on September 23, 1757, they laid siege to Peenemünde. Although the city was taken after a few hours and the Swedish advance continued as far as Prenzlau and the outskirts of Stettin, the advance bogged down by mid-October. By now, two thousand Swedish soldiers were suffering from illness, weakening the force and leaving their commander with two options: to turn to the east, where the Russians were advancing, or to move west of the Elbe, where the French, under Richelieu, also seemed to be making progress. But in early November came the disastrous French defeat at Rossbach, quickly followed by a Russian withdrawal. Suddenly the Swedes were left alone in the field.[15] Ungern-Sternberg withdrew behind the Peene River, but the Prussians went on the counteroffensive, and by the end of November, the Swedes had been pushed back to Stralsund. Swinemünde, Demmin, Anklam, and Wolgast were all retaken, making Swedish Pomerania available for use as winter quarters for Prussian forces. Stralsund and Rügen were put under siege. At this point, nearly one-third of all Swedish soldiers were suffering from sickness or disease.

"We're Hunting Frenchmen": Ferdinand's 1758 Campaign

Duke Ferdinand of Brunswick, commander of the Anglo-German army, did not succeed in his plan to liberate the country from the French during 1757. However, the Allies did expand the territory under their control, giving them a better starting point for the following year's campaign. Before this, however, they would have to make improvements, including to their soldiers' equipment. Grotehenn complains that "I would like enough to march had

I only had a pair of full Shoes, so far it is not Uncommon for some to walk on the leather of their own feet, as is done by a Dog," highlighting what was a serious problem for the whole army.[16] In late January, to cover the most pressing requirements, Ferdinand ordered that 13,500 pairs of stockings and 9,000 pairs of shoes be shipped from Hamburg and Magdeburg.[17] In addition to arranging material improvements, the commander's main task remained that of increasing the army's overall numerical strength. By mid-February 1758, Ferdinand's army numbered around thirty-four thousand men.[18] On the French side, little had changed: No new recruits were sent from France, and there were no shipments of shoes or any other equipment.

In addition to material shortages, the French army suffered from corruption on the part of Richelieu and his officers, which, in turn, fueled indiscipline and abuse. Charles Louis Auguste Fouquet de Belle-Isle (1684–1761), appointed as minister of war in 1758, undertook a number of reforms aimed at combating corruption.[19] In Paris, Foreign Minister Bernis—soon to be replaced by the Duc de Choiseul—came up with a plan to establish Hanoverian neutrality and withdraw French armies from the Rhine and the Weser, turning them into an army of observation. But Vienna immediately declared the proposal completely unacceptable.[20] Richelieu was relieved of his command of operations in northwestern Germany, replaced by Louis de Bourbon, Count of Clermont (1709–1771). Clermont was a member of the royal family, a great-grandson of le Grand Condé, one of France's most famous seventeenth-century generals. Despite his illustrious military ancestor, he had first been destined for the priesthood and was mocked for being neither one thing nor another: "half plumed helmet, half clerical collar, unsuited for one as for the other."[21] Arriving at Hanover on February 14, he faced a very poor situation: The French army was desperately short of men and materiel, and its units were scattered across the northwestern area of the Holy Roman Empire, from Bremen in the north to Frankfurt in the south, from the Oker, Aller, and Weser Rivers in the east to the Rhine and Maas Rivers in the west. It would be difficult for Clermont to concentrate his forces ahead of the coming campaign, so he came up with a plan to evacuate the northern territories in large part, concentrating his forces in Hesse. The plan was never carried out. A withdrawal from Hanover was unacceptable to Versailles, which granted Clermont permission only to withdraw his forces from Celle.

On February 18, Ferdinand set his Anglo-German army on the march. Divided into several army groups, his forces had retaken Rotenburg, Verden, and Hoya by the end of the month.[22] Bremen also soon surrendered, as did Brunswick, Wolfenbüttel, Goslar, and Göttingen. Soon the French were left controlling only Hameln, Rinteln, and Minden.[23] Nienburg fell on February 28, followed by Minden on March 13, with the remaining French forces withdrawing to the Rhine. Rather than using scorched earth tactics, they gave gifts to the local population during their retreat and sold them cheap grain, although this often had to be repeatedly demanded by locals, who feared that available resources would otherwise be destroyed.[24] We can read similar reports in accounts by Abelmann, the master baker in Hanover, and by Schowart, the garrison auditor in Celle.[25] A story mentioned by Schowart on February 20 sums up the downbeat mood among the French. He reports hearing an officer of the dauphine's regiment at the pharmacy saying that they had "three armies: one buried, a 2nd in the hospital, while the 3rd seems about to hang its head in despair."[26] Reports in Hanover claimed that hardship was rampant among French forces, who were calling Germany the "graveyard of the French."[27] By March 1758, Grotehenn was at Nienburg, on the Weser River, where he witnessed the "French hospital" and its cemetery. He counted over four hundred men who "appeared very close to Death," as well as many whose hands and feet "seemed quite entirely Frozen" or whose frozen limbs had already been amputated.[28] The cemetery was a pit, "as large in Extent as a large house," containing the remains of around a thousand men, "thrown upon the other until the Pit was quite Filled-up." Some soldiers were said to have been buried alive: When the burial wagons were loaded at the hospital, some "were so close to Death, they were loaded on alive, along with the others, and then thrown into the Pit." According to the bookbinder in whose house Grotehenn was billeted, the burial wagons had been driven out to the burial ground late one evening, "and there were yet living men among them, so that in the Night one of them returned to the Gates, quite Naked, and he had to be let in by the Guard."[29] The fear mobilized in this anecdote, that of being buried alive, was a profound eighteenth-century anxiety. In Hameln, Pastor Herr recounts a similar scene, along with the precautionary measures taken: "But it did so happen that a Frantzos [Frenchman] was revived in the graveyard. After this, the dead were first laid out, for twice 24 hours, in the small garden at the market Church."[30] A 1757 letter written in Soest by the head of a French military hospital offers an internal perspective on the work of the hospital, describing the staff, the supply situation, and the never-ending quantities of work.[31]

In March and April 1758, Ferdinand's Anglo-German army encamped in Westphalia to regroup and recover. The Duke of Holstein, the Prussian general whose cavalry had tracked the French retreat, wrote to Ferdinand on March 30: "A shame, a shame, my gracious Lord, that we should be quartered in cantonments, with fears that we will never get at the French again!"[32] By early April, the only bridgeheads across the Rhine that the French occupied were at Düsseldorf and Wesel: The bulk of their forces had been safely withdrawn to the left bank of the river.[33] Without fighting a single battle, Ferdinand's six-week campaign had been a complete success. But this would change as spring turned to summer.

At first, Ferdinand's strategy was primarily defensive. He ordered that Hameln, Lippstadt, and Kassel be fortified, seeking to protect the Upper Weser region against any French advance.[34] On April 11, Britain and Prussia signed a new subsidy agreement, guaranteeing substantial payments to Frederick, totaling around 3.6 million thalers.[35] A supplementary declaration to the agreement provided for an increase of around sixty-five hundred men in Ferdinand's Allied army, taking it to a total nominal strength of fifty-five thousand. In London, Pitt advocated crossing the Rhine and launching an offensive against the French. Ferdinand initially felt this was too risky. But by late April, he regarded the situation as adequately secure and sought to cross the Rhine near Rees, with the aim of retaking Wesel and then pushing the French back across the Maas River. His forces crossed into Dutch territory at Herwen on the night of June 2–3. The Dutch reacted with anger but were assuaged by a rapid payment of compensation for the action, which was described as an accidental incursion.[36] The Allies took Cleves without a fight when the French withdrew to concentrate their forces around Kalkar. The two sides first met in battle at Kloster Kamp on June 12: here the Allies emerged victorious, with only minor losses.[37] Soubise's army was originally due to march on Bohemia, but Belle-Isle, the French minister of war, managed to have it undertake diversionary maneuvers on the east bank of the Rhine. Belle-Isle further urged Clermont to seek battle: Even a lost battle would better than none, he is said to have told him. Clermont positioned his troops in a strong defensive position along the medieval fortifications near Krefeld.

The Battle of Krefeld took place on June 23, with Ferdinand's army of 30,500, attacking the French, who could field around 47,000.[38] Ferdinand envisioned a three-pronged attack, seeking to confuse the enemy as to which was the main advance. The French duly concentrated on clashes on their own right flank, while Ferdinand, in fact, targeted their left. On this side of the field, French reinforcements arrived too slowly, and Ferdinand's troops won the day. Ferdinand's success here seemed to closely follow the strategic example set by his brother-in-law Frederick. Victory had been achieved with an extremely risky plan, not entirely popular with his generals. It required the skillful exploitation of enemy mistakes and a numerically inferior attack on a well-defended position, all while maintaining close contact with his own soldiers. Ferdinand personally coordinated the decisive cavalry attack. After the battle, he paid great attention to his soldiers, seeing that they were rewarded with money and alcohol and that the dead were buried and the wounded cared for.[39] Although the battle brought Ferdinand new fame as a general, it did not have any great "operational significance."[40] The French suffered heavy losses but quickly made up for these, and Ferdinand did not manage to drive their forces from the Lower Rhine. Instead, Clermont's army dug in at Cologne, a city known throughout the war as the "great lodging house" of the French army.[41] The unsuccessful Clermont was forced to resign, to be replaced by Louis Georges Contades (1704–1795), the French army's longest-serving general.

But what had happened to Soubise's army? Its ultimate objective hung uncertainly in the balance: It would either head east to Bohemia or go west to conduct operations in Hesse. On the day the Battle of Krefeld was fought, a decision was made in Versailles to send Soubise to Hesse, with the intention of tying down Ferdinand's army in that region. Maria Theresa agreed to the plan, allowing the march on Bohemia to be postponed for several weeks, although her army urgently required support at this time, given Frederick's maneuvers near Olmütz.

For the 1758 campaign, Frederick first adopted a strategy of tying down Austrian forces on the Danube, seeking to create space to confront the Russians later on.[42] The capture of the fortress of Olmütz was the main operational goal of the Prussian units now advancing on Moravia.[43] The town was defended by around seventy-five hundred soldiers of the Austrian and Imperial armies, led by Lieutenant General Ernst Dietrich Marshal von Burgholzhausen (1692–1771). The attacking Prussian force, numbering eleven thousand men, was commanded by Field Marshal James Keith (1696–1758). On May 4, the Prussians arrived at Olmütz. The Prussian officer Friedrich Rudolf von Barsewisch, whose account of being wounded at Leuthen was cited earlier, gives a brief summary of the progress of fighting at Olmütz. Siege entrenchment began on May 26. Three days later Prussian outposts were attacked by the enemy, but Frederick's forces nonetheless began their bombardment on May 31. On the same day, the king moved his headquarters to Latein, but the following month a fire broke out in the village, and the commander's camp was moved to Schmirsitz. Another attack on Prussian forward positions was fought off on June 24.[44] For some time, Keith's forces failed to encircle the city completely, leaving two city gates open through which supplies could enter.

The decisive turning point in the campaign occurred at the village of Domstadtl, about sixteen miles northeast of Olmütz.[45] Here Austrian General Ernst Gideon von Laudon (1717–1790) lay in wait for a Prussian supply convoy, said to have consisted of three thousand vehicles, including "many wagons with ammunition, equipment, tents, money, and bread." There was skirmishing between the two sides at Gundersdorf, followed by an Austrian ambush of the convoy at Domstadtl on June 28 and again two days later. Barsewisch reports that Laudon was "so fortunate as to capture 100 wagons, including two which contained Money, and in this way gathered rich Booty."[46] As a result of this "unexpected incident," Frederick called off the siege of Olmütz on July 2, by which time part of the city had already been burned. The memoirs of the Austrian officer Giuseppe Gorani recount the incident in some detail.[47] "Led by one such as Laudon," Gorani writes, they were capable of "nothing short of miracles," which is, he insists, what they performed on that "memorable day."[48] "Our successes were so brilliant, so decisive, and so complete, the Prussian king was deprived of all his resources, and the siege of Olmütz could no longer continue."[49] The day also proved to be a successful one for Gorani personally, albeit not as profitable as it might have been. The colonel of his regiment plundered three hundred gold ducats, part of which he intended to use to buy land at home. Gorani was given a purse full of ducats but ended up with only seven, "throwing away [the remaining money] on Follies, at restaurants, with girls, and also with playing Pharao and at dice."[50] Gorani was at least promoted to *sous-lieutenant surnuméraire* (acting second lieutenant). Laudon was promoted to the rank of lieutenant general.

News of the relief of Olmütz arrived at the court in Vienna at around nine o'clock on the morning of July 3; by eleven o'clock, Major von Voit had reached the palace at Schönbrunn, accompanied by an escort of postillions, bringing "Détail" about the "fortunate events."[51] The empress was offered compliments; the victorious generals were awarded diamond rings and promotions. The day was also Khevenhüller-Metsch's birthday, who noted the compliments paid him in his diary, no doubt with some pride. On July 2, the same day he had called off the siege at Olmütz, Frederick ordered a general Prussian retreat from Moravia, with his forces pulling back into Bohemia. Gorani, observing the withdrawal from the Austrian side, called it "truly a masterpiece of military science," since not a single wagon or a single soldier was lost in the process.[52]

Dangerous Descents: British Raids on the French Coast

In 1757 and 1758, the British navy undertook repeated raids on French port cities, operations that were referred to by contemporaries as *descents*. The most significant of these was an attack on Rochefort in September 1757, along with attacks on St. Malo in June 1758 and Cherbourg in August 1758.[53]

Rochefort, the first major target, was the largest naval arsenal in France, located to the south of La Rochelle.[54] Although the city had been fortified in 1689 and boasted a strategic location at the mouth of the Charente River, it had a garrison of only three thousand men. One calculation made by the British was that the crypto-Protestant) Huguenot population around Rochefort might launch a religious uprising when the Protestant British arrived. The prediction ultimately proved incorrect but nonetheless indicates how confessional factors could influence tactical reasoning.[55] A British expeditionary army of eighty-five hundred was sent, commanded by the experienced General Sir John Mordaunt (1697–1780). This force included James Wolfe as quartermaster general and Corporal William Todd.[56] Todd, whose diary documents the action, went aboard the warship *Lark* on September 6. By September 23, the fleet was close to its destination, with Todd noting that the British troops had taken the Île d'Aix in the bay off Rochefort.[57] The island garrison's guns were either captured or put out of use. But this small action was the only immediate operation planned by the British. Although they enjoyed vastly greater numbers, they thought the weather too risky to land and felt there was little chance of taking Rochefort's arsenal without a siege. Only Wolfe had the initiative to investigate the situation more closely, climbing the highest tower of the island fortress to observe the coast for an hour. He suggested that a landing might be feasible if Fouras, a fort on the mainland, could be destroyed; other British generals were not convinced. The French used campfires on the coast to give the impression of being a much larger force than they actually were.[58] A landing on the coast to the north of Rochefort was rejected because of reports of French reinforcements. On September 29, the British fleet weighed anchor and headed back to Spithead, where it arrived on October 5. The operation was a failure. Mordaunt was made the scapegoat, and he was court-martialed on December 14.[59] The tribunal acquitted him of disobedience, but he had fallen out of favor with the king, which put an end to his hopes of preferment. This was not the case for Wolfe, the young quartermaster general who had displayed courage as well as loyalty to his commander.[60]

The following year the focus of British amphibious operations turned to targets in Brittany, which was host to ten French infantry regiments, supported by dragoons, along with two battalions of provincial militia. For the French civilian population, these raids marked a rare appearance of the enemy within France itself—if we discount occasional encounters with prisoners of war.[61] However, this did not in itself lead to a general patriotic mobilization. In fact, both the intensity of French patriotism and its main focus—whether king, fatherland, or local region—differed considerably, depending on social status and local circumstances.

The British had a three-part strategic goal. They wanted to relieve the pressure on Prussia, tying down French forces in the west of their country without having to actively intervene in Germany. They also sought to reduce the threat to British ships from French privateers while diminishing France's international creditworthiness.[62] Thomas Bligh (1685–1775) was given command of the descents in 1758; his orders appeared in British pamphlets and magazines the same year.[63] In some cases, they contained very specific detail, as when he was instructed to land at Cherbourg and "attack the batteries, fortifications, and city." If that was successful, he should continue, "demolishing and destroying the port and basin, together with all the ships, naval stores and works, batteries, fortifications, arsenals and magazines, thereunto belonging, you are to use all possible means, effectually to demolish and destroy the same." When that mission was completed or if it could not be carried out, the government ordered Bligh to proceed "to carry a warm alarm along the coast of France, and to make descents upon any part or parts thereof; and attack any place, that may be found practicable, from the easternmost point of Normandy as far westward as Morlaix inclusive."[64]

The first raid was undertaken near Cancale in June 1758, commanded by the Duke of Marlborough. It had no significant outcome, succeeding only in destroying a few French ships and stores. Corporal Todd reports that his ship anchored off Cancale on June 5.[65] The landing took place the following day, with British officers apparently fearing their men would fatally gorge on oysters and other rich seafood. Soon the first soldier was executed for desertion: William Cross, a tailor who was reported to have run away from the company.[66] In fact, the sentence was a terrible miscarriage of justice. Having heard screams from a wood, Cross found a French woman being raped by another soldier, who ran away when confronted. But Cross was soon arrested. The woman, Todd continues, confirmed that he had, in fact, been her rescuer and then burst into inconsolable tears on learning that his execution had already taken place. On June 7, the British captured St. Servan, a town close to St. Malo, where they burned ships and destroyed port facilities, although residents and their homes were spared.[67]

The attack set off an enormous conflagration. Faced with the tremendous noise of masts collapsing and guns exploding, Todd draws on the rhetoric of the indescribable: "The great Conflagration that all this made is to any ones thinking that was not here incredible, neither can one Describe it in any reasonable form, but this we may well suppose that no one ever beheld any thing so Dreadfull in the Memory of Man. It was also Expected that amany Sailor's Suffer'd by being asleep in the Ships when they were fired etc."[68] The British advanced on St. Malo on June 8. They immediately offered negotiations, but the garrison refused to surrender. By now, the French had opened nearby floodgates, submerging many roads and making provisioning more and more difficult for the besieging force. Matters were not helped by a series of violent thunderstorms. In his journal, Sergeant John Porter of the Royal Welsh Fusiliers comments: "I never saw more Rain in the space of 16 Hours in my life."[69] Todd and the rest of the British contingent withdrew to Cancale. The embarkation of troops to the fleet began the next day, but it would take five more days before anchors could be weighed and another three before the winds and tides brought them to the open sea. Not until July 3 would the ships drop anchor at Spithead.[70]

Later that summer the British undertook two further landings, the first at the bay of Cherbourg in August and the second at Saint-Briac in September, with Bligh commanding the land forces and Admiral Anson and Commodore Howe in charge of the naval elements. The British sent a substantial force: twenty-seven ships of the line and nineteen frigates, a large number of sloops, and supply and transport ships, with ten thousand infantrymen and around thirty-two thousand sailors. But once the landing had been accomplished, the British could at first only maneuver aimlessly amid the bocage of northern Brittany.

Corporal Todd was in the British raiding party at Saint-Briac,[71] his unit having landed at the bay of Cherbourg on August 7.[72] The port city surrendered the following day, with French troops allowed to leave unmolested without surrendering their arms, although some prominent local figures were taken to Britain as hostages. Todd was in high spirits, looking forward to plentiful booty in the "great and populous city of Cherbourg."[73] Here, too, ships were set ablaze and port facilities demolished, but British forces were under instructions not to interfere with the general population. In his diary, Todd regularly complains about the price of salt and tobacco, but this aside, he revels in the abundance of foods on offer in the Breton port.[74] He is particularly impressed by the devastation wreaked on the harbor and the garrison buildings, including adjoining houses, but justifies the destruction by claiming it would keep British shipping safe from the swarms of French privateers previously based in the port.[75]

French units approached British positions on August 15. Todd recounts how the British deployed along the coast in fighting order and notes the unhealthy stench at the rear of their camp, where animal carcasses were left unburied in the hot August weather. The stench of putrefaction was produced by the seven thousand cattle, pigs, and sheep slaughtered during the British occupation, with correspondingly large amounts of discarded bones, offal, and the like.[76] The embarkation of British forces from Cherbourg took place without problems the following day, and the fleet sailed up and down the English Channel for several days before anchoring the majority of its ships at St. Lunaire. Here troops were onshore from August 26 to September 2, pillaging the local countryside. The operation was officially to collect contributions, but these could rarely be raised in full; the next step was almost always direct plunder. Corporal Todd is quite affected by fate of the population, observing that the treatment of civilians is "more shocking" than "stand[ing] in 10 Fights with the Enemy," since all have the same chance in battle, but these "poor, Defense-less people" have no chance at all.[77] French chroniclers of the time particularly recall British attacks on local clergy and church buildings, as well as the more usual kinds of looting and violence.[78]

One event well remembered locally is the battle at Le Guildo, at the mouth of the Arguenon River, on September 8, 1758. Here Bligh's men, en route to the village of Saint-Cast, where they were due to be reembarked, were ambushed by local volunteers and delayed for almost two days.[79] The small incident has taken on great importance in local memory culture, since it contributes to the myth that Breton action alone successfully repelled the British invaders without the help of the king's army.

As in other theaters of war, contacts between invaders and locals varied according to social status. Officers and local dignitaries chatted in French over bottles of wine, while common soldiers, seen as marauding "foreigners," had few positive contacts with the Breton population. Todd often refers to opposing forces as "only Malitia," his consistent use of the spelling possibly underlining his low opinion of this relatively harmless opponent.

This view of the French changed only on September 11, 1758, at the beaches of the bay of Saint-Cast.[80] Here Bligh's soldiers were trapped onshore by the forces of the governor of Brittany, the Duc d'Aiguillon (1720–1788), in engagements that saw their entire rear guard wiped out.[81] Around seven o'clock in the morning, French forward units began to fire at the British rear guard, which had been established to defend the embarkation. British forces moved slowly out along the coastal road, setting up in battle order on open ground at around eleven o'clock.[82] However, the full French attack did not come until the afternoon, by which time most of Bligh's men had already embarked. British ships cannonaded the French from the sea (figure 6.2); nonetheless, the attacking force managed to drive the remaining British troops slowly into the sea. After the devastation caused by British forces in the previous weeks, Todd expected no quarter from the French and was surprised when a French general offered pardon while British soldiers were still in the water, eventually taking some three hundred prisoners.[83] Overall British losses were considerable, with no less than three thousand dead and wounded and eight hundred captured. The French lost no more than three hundred in total. On September 15, the British fleet sailed for home, anchoring in Spithead three days later.[84]

Thanks to his book *Journal de ma vie*, Jacques-Louis Ménétra (1738–1812) is among the best-known ordinary French people of the eighteenth century.[85] As a young glazier, he undertook a journeyman's wandering passage around France between 1757 and 1763; in 1764, he began writing down his impressions in a journal that was later edited for publication. Having arrived at St. Malo shortly before the Battle of Saint-Cast, Ménétra found work with a privateer but, in fact, never went on board. Instead, as his journal recounts, he decided to enter service with a local citizen militia in the town of Dinan, where he commanded seven other soldiers who were guarding a small cannon on a nearby hill. Unfortunately, one of the soldiers was found sleeping on guard duty, resulting in Ménétra being relieved of his

Figure 6.2 Battle of St. Cast, September 11, 1758. Copper engraving by Nicolas-Marie Ozanne (undated).
Source: Gallica/Bibliothèque nationale de France, Département Estampes et photographie, RESERVE QB-201 (103)-FOL.

minor command. In the aftermath of the Battle of Saint-Cast, he returned to St. Malo and then went to sea aboard a privateer. After a few months of this, he deserted while on the Ile d'Yeu, off the French Atlantic coast, and returned to the mainland to restart his journeyman wanderings. Without ever straying far from France, Ménétra became a kind of privileged spectator to the war.

After victory at Saint-Cast—called a battle, although the term might be questioned—celebrations began in Paris and soon spread across the north of France, as if the action had, in effect, won the war for France.[86] A Te Deum was sung at Notre Dame on October 1, followed by another a week later at St. Malo and a third a week after that at Nantes. In Paris, buildings were illuminated, and there was a great deal of celebratory fireworks, dancing, and music; pamphlets and food were distributed free of charge. Many broadsheets and popular songs circulated among the people, and there were dances and costumes *à la Saint-Cast*, while Brittany itself attracted an increasing number of battlefield tourists.

Saint-Cast brought an end to the British raids. The attacks had caused some damage to French shipping but failed to achieve their strategic goal: to tie down troops in France that would otherwise be deployed in the German theaters of war. Moreover, the raid operations appeared very similar to traditional pirate and privateer expeditions, and it was increasingly difficult to publicly justify them as an appropriate means of war.

Deep in Western Germany

The British failures in Brittany were indirectly beneficial to Ferdinand of Brunswick, since they meant the new resources Pitt had secured would now go directly to support his campaign in Germany.[87] In search of new targets on the Channel and the North Sea coast, the British devised a plan to send troops to Emden, where they landed a force of eight thousand men on August 3, 1758, joining with Ferdinand's army on August 21. Some weeks previously, on July 7, Düsseldorf had surrendered to Allied forces under Wangenheim, but a plan for Ferdinand's forces to follow this up by taking Wesel was soon thwarted. Frederick's failure in Moravia, which had culminated in his retreat from Olmütz, meant that Soubise could now threaten Hesse and the Allied line along the Weser. On July 23, the French achieved a total victory at Sandershausen, forcing Ferdinand to abandon plans to advance farther west.[88] He thus recrossed the Rhine, coming back to the east bank to regroup near Coesfeld and organize resistance to the advancing French armies. His hopes that the Dutch might enter the conflict did not materialize. Once more, the tides of war appeared to be on the turn, and now Hanover again seemed to be in danger. After the defeat at Sanderhausen, the Allied General Johann Casimir von Isenburg managed to gather his units around Einbeck and by September had restored them almost to their former strength.[89] But the French advance proved slower and less determined than expected, with neither Soubise nor Contades thinking to unite their armies.[90] Ultimately, the French made no major coordinated push forward.

The French won another victory near Lutterberg on October 10, witnessed by, among others, Trautzschen, the Saxon officer whose report from the camp at Pirna was cited earlier.[91] Trautzschen recounts the unfolding of the battle and the moment of victory, while also describing the horrors of the battlefield.[92] Fifteen Saxon battalions—nine thousand men in total, commanded by Franz Xaver (1730–1806), a Saxon prince—joined with the

French army at Castrop. These Saxon units had been "subsumed" into the Prussian army after the capitulation at Pirna, but most units had defected back to the other side over the winter of 1756–1757.[93] Regaining their honor after this series of events seems to have been a strong motivating factor for these Saxon regiments, who now faced their "baptism of fire" at Lutterberg. Trautzschen was full of enthusiasm: "Our Prince [Soubise] has always fought at our head of our Ranks, the fire of Heroism burns within his breast, and under his Leadership we have had the honor of winning the most compleat victory."[94]

By the end of the year, the two sides had again separated. Under Contades, most of the French took up winter quarters on the west bank of the Rhine, with only Soubise's troops quartered on the other side, between Giessen and Hanau. Ferdinand's army set up camp in Münster, while Isenburg's force took up quarters in Kassel.[95] By September, Belle-Isle, the French minister of war, had realized that losses overseas would require a renewal of attempts to conquer Electoral Hanover. He wrote to Contades on September 19: "We cannot flatter ourselves that we can offer great resistance to the English on sea or in America; only by taking possession of all that the King of England has in Germany, can we compel these princes to make peace."[96] But what had happened on the other side of the Atlantic to lead Belle-Isle to this conclusion?

Lions and Pineapples: Fort Ticonderoga and the Capture of Louisbourg

The British were determined that their North American setbacks of 1757 would not be repeated the following year. Pitt was particularly firm on this point and relieved Loudoun, his commander in chief, of his duties, along with General Webb, the commander of Fort Edward. Overall British military numbers were increased by eight thousand men. Rather than continuing with a single commander over all British territory, some division of labor was introduced, with James Abercromby (1706–1781) taking charge of the Great Lakes area, John Forbes (1710–1759) commanding the Ohio region and other central territories, and Colonel Jeffrey Amherst (1717–1797) taking responsibility for New England and the advance on Louisbourg.[97] Amherst was to be assisted by three newly appointed brigadier generals, one of them being James Wolfe, now promoted from colonel to brigadier.[98]

With the increase in troop numbers, Abercromby now commanded over ninety-five hundred men, with Forbes commanding seven thousand and Amherst fourteen thousand. On the naval side, the North American fleet was placed under the leadership of Admiral Edward Boscawen (1711–1761). Its task, like British naval units off the French coast, was to prevent French ships from reaching land. In other words, in operational terms Britain now had three autonomous land armies, all receiving directives centrally from London. Pitt held all threads in his hand. The autonomy of these armies increased their individual capacity to act but left them dependent on long lines of communication between Europe and America.

Abercromby's first advance was against Fort Carillon, a French fort later known as Fort Ticonderoga. The main attack on the fort began on July 8, 1758. At the time, the expeditionary force consisted of sixteen thousand men, the largest British military force ever assembled in North America.[99] The soldiers had been put on boats to go north three days before the assault itself, and they soon established a fortified camp close to the fort to serve as their base. Inside the French positions, Montcalm had only about thirty-five hundred men and enough food for about nine days. He could not afford to leave the initiative to the British and was forced to improvise, building fortifications on a spur of rock lying upstream from the fort itself. The tree-and-sandbag fortifications were referred to as *abatis*, from the French terms for felled trees (*arbres abattus*) and perhaps for slaughterhouse (*abbatoir*).[100] Montcalm's men were said to have built them in a single day. The French commander was taking a big risk: Field fortifications were highly effective against infantry but useless against artillery, of which Abercromby had a large quantity.[101] However, the British reconnoitered the situation carelessly, and the council of war decided to push ahead with an unaccompanied infantry attack, leaving their artillery at the boats' original landing point. British forward units—skirmishers and snipers, including Robert Rogers and his rangers—were well adapted to local conditions, but Abercromby's overall plan of attack made no concessions to the immediate context. Eight British battalions, arrayed three rows deep, were to attack the French position head-on. The assault was launched just after half past twelve in the afternoon and ended in a terrible bloodbath. One soldier, Joseph Nichols of Massachusetts, watched the action from a flank, noting that the soldiers were "mowed down" like grass.[102] Abercromby would accept only written reports; he continued to order attack after attack. The British charged against the *abatis* for eight hours but without success.[103] As night fell, two thousand

British soldiers lay dead or wounded. A withdrawal was finally ordered at nightfall, followed by a panicked escape early in the morning of July 9, with men rowing for their lives.[104] Reflecting on the debacle later, witnesses described the operation as an "ignominious retreat," leaving little doubt of Abercromby's utter failure. At first, the French could not believe their own success and suspected the withdrawal to be a ruse. But after two days, their scouts found only a long trail of wounded soldiers, abandoned equipment, broken boats, and even lost shoes. There could be no doubt as to what had happened, and on July 12, a Te Deum was sung at the French fort.[105] On August 21, Montcalm had a large cross built over the fortifications, bearing the Latin inscription Quid dux? Quid miles? Quid strata ingentia ligna? En signum! En victor! Deus hic, Deus ipse triumphat (Which general? Which soldier? What mighty woods upright? Behold the sign! Behold the victor! This God, God himself, has triumphed).[106]

The transmission of news about the Ticonderoga disaster offers another example of the slow pace of transatlantic communications. On August 31, Johann Philipp Schwoart, auditor of the garrison at Celle in Electoral Hanover, noted the unsuccessful attack on the French fort and the heavy British losses, citing a report in the *Whitehall Evening Post*. On September 2, Andreas Georg Wähner, professor of Oriental languages at Göttingen, learned from a Hamburg newspaper that "General Abercrombie has sought to attack the French in an entrenched en-campment and was given a bloody nose."[107]

On June 2, 1758, some weeks before the attack on Fort Carillon, Amherst's men had made a landing on the rocky terrain close to Louisbourg. Among them was Georg Schneider, the Hessian mercenary serving with the Royal American Rifles. His account underlines the practical challenges faced by this kind of amphibious siege operation, particularly on difficult terrain. It describes how the British force had to spend two days on the "desert land," without tents or provisions, until supplies finally arrived by boat on June 10. "After we had taken these Things onto Land, we pitched our Camp about an Hour away from the Fortification, close by several swampy Valleys, which we had to approach using bundles of Wood, and building Paths, which we finished at the beginning of July amid great Toil and Danger."[108]

The landing marked the beginning of the siege of Louisbourg, a confrontation that included, among other things, a remarkable exchange of gifts.[109] On June 17, under a white flag of truce, Amherst sent a present of two West Indian pineapples to Madame de Drucour, wife of the French governor, to apologize for the inconvenience the siege was likely causing her.[110] The following afternoon around two o'clock, Madame de Drucour returned the compliment, sending Amherst fifty bottles of wine, brought by the French officer Marquis Desgouttes on a boat flying the white flag. The logic of gift and countergift was clearly insufficient. On June 24, Amherst took advantage of an exchange of messages about prisoners to send two more pineapples. Madame de Drucour rewarded the drummer who brought them with a tip but did not send more wine in exchange, since the Chevalier de Drucour complained angrily that the British general appeared to want to "exchange [his] entire wine cellar for pineapples."[111]

This anecdote crops up in every account of the conquest of Louisbourg, usually without a full explanation of its symbolic content. The curious exchange is left as an indicator of the exchange of courtesies typical of aristocratic officer culture in eighteenth-century wars.[112] However, pineapples were also a common colonial status symbol, a marker of luxury consumption that distinguished the haves from the have-nots. But the large amount of wine—some authors say it was champagne, ramping up its value still more—is a reminder of conspicuous consumption on the part of those suffering siege, meant to demonstrate to their enemies that they could hold out indefinitely.[113] However, the French governor's patience seems to have been exhausted by the constant British shelling. Any polite exchanges would soon come to an end, especially with British attempts to finally take the French port.

Violence escalated as the grueling siege dragged on, with the Europeans quite willing to use cruel practices against those they regarded as savages. Olaudah Equiano, the enslaved valet of a British naval officer, reported: "I had that day in my hand the scalp of an indian king, who was killed in the engagement: the scalp had been taken off by an Highlander. I saw this king's ornaments too, which were very curious, and made of feathers."[114] Louisbourg surrendered on July 27. It was agreed that the civilian population would be shipped to France, but military personnel would be made prisoners of war. A total of 5,637 captured French soldiers were brought to England. The region's new ownership structure was symbolically marked by renaming the island known as St. Jean to Prince Edward Island.

Among the British commanders, James Wolfe had shown particular dedication during siege operations.[115] On the day of the surrender, he wrote letters to his mother, father, and uncle. In the letter to his mother, he recounts the situation of frightened and starving Frenchwomen, says he tries to avoid violence as much as possible, and reports on the lightly wounded son of Mrs. Bell, telling his mother she should tell her of her son's exemplary conduct.

Wolfe's letter to his father describes the various operations and losses in more detail, calling the Native Americans "veritable canaille" and, above all, mourning the death of Lord Howe. The letter to his uncle Walter also describes operations briefly; complains at greater length about the Natives, "the most contemptible canaille on earth"; and proudly elaborates on the violence used: "We cut them to pieces wherever we found them." He also grieves again for death of Howe, the "spirit of that army," to be mourned as one of the "greatest losses that could befall the nation."[116] The three very different letters, written on the same day about the same event, clearly demonstrate how messages could be tailored for different addressees.

An entry from John Knox's journal underlines the slow pace of communications within North America itself. In May 1758, he expresses considerable indignation:

We are credibly informed, that upwards of forty letters for the Officers and Soldiers of the 43d regiment lately lay at the Post-Office at Halifax, and the Postmaster, not knowing how he should be repaid the Postage of them, or where to forward them to, transmitted them back to New-York, by which means it is not improbable but they may all miscarry; it is an unlucky Circumstance that some Regulation is not set on Foot, to prevent such Disappointments happening to the Troops throughout America, and those particularly who are doomed to Exile in the miserable Fortresses of this remote Province.[117]

It was well-known, Knox adds, that during the last war in Flanders, the postal system functioned very well under the responsibility of the army's postmaster general, with letters delivered on time. "It is almost incredible what Sums have been paid for single European Letters by Officers and Soldiers, and the unnecessary extravagant Expense that has been incurred by the letters travelling over almost every part of British America, before they reached their proper Owners."[118] At Annapolis, on September 6, 1758, he reports the arrival of a sloop from Boston. As the boat comes into earshot, Knox cries out: "What news from Louisbourg?" The boat's captain replies: "Nothing strange."[119] With the soldiers present already turning back to the fort in disappointment, one calls out: "Damn you Pumpkin, is not Louisbourg taken yet?" Now the captain replies: "Taken! Ay, above a month ago, and I have been there since: but, if you have never heard it before, then I have a good parcel of letters for you now!" This prompts thirty minutes of hurrahs and cheering, with hats hurled into the air. Similar scenes would soon also be seen in Britain, where celebrations sought to outdo one another with illuminations, salutes, and other festivities.[120] The army's image had changed, with the Highlanders now seen as celebrated war heroes, bravely confronting the French with their broad swords. Scalpings of the kind described by Equiano were no doubt spoken of less widely.

On the French side too, people waited a long time for news. In November 1758, Bougainville wrote: "It is long now since new messages have come from Europe. All winter long we have counted on peace, but none now count on this."[121] In France, attempts were made to downplay, or distract from, the news of Louisbourg's loss.[122]

A month after the conquest of Louisbourg, Lieutenant Colonel John Bradstreet succeeded in taking Fort Fronténac, another French stronghold at the mouth of the St. Lawrence River, which fell on August 27, 1758. Compared to Louisbourg, this was a small operation, since the fort was defended by just 110 French soldiers. But its location, guarding access to the Great Lakes, was of crucial importance. Its capture meant the British now controlled the important supply line to Fort Duquesne: Soon there was a crisis of provisioning at the French fortress, leading to the defection of the French forces' Shawnee, Delaware, and Mingo allies. A British expedition against Fort Duquesne itself added to French problems; led by General Forbes, it managed, above all, to construct a new road, three hundred miles long, known as the Forbes Road.[123] The French commander of the fort, General de Lignery (1703–1759), could hold out no longer, and he surrendered in November, although his forces destroyed the fort before handing it over. Forbes, the new commander of the fort, died several months later, in March 1759. The unexpected success of the Forbes expedition, which had learned from Braddock's errors at the Monongahela River, marked a decisive turning point for the events of 1759.

Charles Bonin, the French soldier known as Sweetheart, seems to have lived at Fort Duquesne from the official start of the war until 1758. He also seems to have worked as a shopkeeper, apparently a lucrative enough position, since he received many orders for army supplies.[124] In addition, he observes the fatal effects of alcohol on the Native American population. He incorrectly cites the "massacre" of Fort William Henry as having taken place in 1758, the year when he had to leave Fort Duquesne, after three years in which he claimed to have earned 32,400 francs.[125] Returning to Quebec, Bonin took great pleasure in his social life, enjoying numerous balls and sleigh rides. Now a man with a certain degree of wealth, he married and bought a house but broke off the marriage after just a few months and concerned himself, above all, with recovering his furniture. The winter had cost him some 15,000 francs, he claims.[126]

Close to Fort Duquesne, the British built Fort Pitt, a new stronghold located where Pittsburgh is today. This moment may perhaps be taken to mark the beginning of the end of Nouvelle-France. In any case, the British had put themselves in a strategically favorable position for the coming year, having closed off access to Quebec from the sea and mobilized a very large number of troops. Paris was clearly losing interest in Canada, which is obvious from the risibly small number of reinforcements approved, just four hundred men in total.[127] Moreover, France's Native allies had lost their appetite for war against the British, and their withdrawal would have much more serious consequences.[128] At Fort William Henry, the French could still call on eighteen hundred Indigenous fighters; at the defense of Ticonderoga, there were just fifteen. Although 1758 did not see many spectacular events, it nonetheless was the year in which the Seven Years' War in North America was decided.[129]

Zorndorf: Violence Unleashed

In January 1758, the Russian army occupied East Prussia. In June, it marched through Poland to Posen, moving farther and farther west. Frederick, still in Bohemia, was forced to act. On August 11, he ordered his forces north at a forced march, heading for the lower reaches of the Oder River. Near Küstrin, his force joined with the army commanded by Count Christoph II of Dohna-Schlodien (1702–1762), which had arrived from Pomerania. Russian troops had bombed and destroyed Küstrin, with the *Berlinische Nachrichten* accusing them of "not inten[ding] to conquer the Fortress, which is not easily done by bombardment. Rather, they wanted for themselves, and for the Prince of Saxony, the cruel spectacle of a burning city, since neither Trenches were dug nor Breaches shot out, there was only firing over and into the unfortunate City, and the Bombs and Fire Balls were directed solely at the Buildings."[130] An escalation of violence had begun that would reach its first sorrowful climax at the Battle of Zorndorf on August 25.

The battle merits close attention for several reasons.[131] It was one of just two direct confrontations between Frederick and the Russian army;

contemporaries regarded it as one of the most violent battles of the war, and its unclear outcome produced a veritable second battle across the media. Afterward, one Russian officer wrote: "More a Butchery than a Battle" (C'etoit plutôt une Boucherie qu'une Bataille).[132] Zorndorf was called a slaughterhouse by contemporaries, but it was "heated" in more than one sense, since it was fought in the last days of August, in extreme summer heat.[133]

The Prussian army of thirty-seven thousand crossed the Oder at the village of Alt-Güstebiese, moving south with a view to pinning down the Russians, commanded by Count Fermor. On August 24, they came across the Russian vanguard, camped near marshy ground. The following day the Prussian left flank launched a powerful attack, including a massive artillery barrage, while the right held back. But their use of a classic oblique order of battle did not pay off. The Prussians could not outflank the Russian right and were thrown back. This meant that the two armies collided head-on, a constellation of battle that usually produced extremely high casualties.

The battle memoir of a Prussian musketeer named Hoppe describes how Frederick's army fought with bayonets when they ran out of ammunition, killed enemy artillerymen with the butts of their muskets, and drove others into the marsh.[134] Spatial constriction on the battlefield made it almost impossible to escape, resulting in tremendous bloodshed. The intervention of the Prussian right wing turned the battle in favor of Frederick. This, along with a successful cavalry attack on the Russian right, commanded by Seydlitz, put an end to the fighting. Both sides ceased fire in the evening, with the Russians withdrawing to the village of Zorndorf. The Prussians bivouacked adjacent to the battlefield, a fact that would soon be reflected in media reports of the battle.

This bloodbath resulted in over 30,000 dead, wounded, or captured: 12,800 on the Prussian side and 20,000 on the Russian side.[135] Various factors contributed to this escalation of violence, ranging from the spatial logic of the combat site to direct violations of battle norms—i.e., atrocities. Frederick, angered by the destruction of Küstrin, had issued an order to "give no quarter." When the Russians found themselves in a hopeless position in front of the marshes, their only alternatives were thus to fight or "be put down."[136] "Because," explains the Prussian officer Christian Wilhelm von Prittwitz, "the river Mietzel, whose bridge they had destroyed, and the Marsh, which had offered them protection in their first position, now in the second position blocked any possibility of a retreat en bon ordre, and now they also learned, that they faced an enemy who would offer them no pardon."[137]

Archenholz's *History of the Seven Years War* deploys images of cannibalism to illustrate the utter brutality of the fighting: "The animosity on either side was beyond all bounds; even severely wounded Prussians forgot their own position, and thought only of the destruction of their enemies. It was the same with the Russians; some of these, mortally wounded, lay on the Prussians who were dying, and tore their flesh with their teeth and these had to bear this agony, until their companions came up, and dispatched these cannibals."[138] The extent of destruction at Zorndorf eventually became public knowledge. Our information about the situation after the battle comes from reports written by the magistrate of the town of Neudamm and by two clergymen: the senior pastor of Neudamm and Christian Abraham Seidel, the pastor of Grüneberg.[139] The Neudamm pastor describes how, two days after the battle, at the burial of bodies, wounded Russian soldiers were "battered around the head or shot by Jägers—the same troops charged with the burial—then buried with the rest. The Method may have seemed harsh, but it was done out of consideration. Because Russians have such a hard Life, for the seriously wounded there was no manner and no hope of a cure, so they had to be dealt with in this way." Some were even buried alive: "Before this, some of them had actually come to their Senses once more in the cold Earth, and had worked their way through and lay there with their upper Bodies sticking up from out of the Earth, shouting at astonished passers-by: 'kliba' (*bread*), 'biba' (*drink*), 'krusulki' (*brandy*). They added: 'stuppey, stuppey' (*quickly*)."[140]

Prittwitz also offers a detailed description of the battlefield: "Shudders and Horror were my Companions on my Walk through this Valley of Misery and Death. Just as I had seen the Living arrayed in Ranks, I now also saw the Dead struck down, lying in similar Order. To the right of me Prussians, to the left of me Russians. With the Latter, it could be seen that they had fed well on the Fat of the Land, while the former had endured Hunger and Hardships of all sorts, even naked you could distinguish which Army the Bodies belonged to."[141] The sight of the battlefield ultimately prompts Prittwitz, who had a Pietist background, to deeper reflection: "How can one who was the cause of these sad Phenomena remain calm and relaxed at the sight, had his Conscience not been convinced already that he has been forced to do so by Others? Who can calculate the number of victims who have given up their spirit on similar occasions, and those who in future will continue to expire, for as long as this terrible War continues?" He evinces particular compassion for the fate of the wounded, "of whom there are such a great Multitude, which no one can care for, nor take them in, in the circumstances, nor ease their fate in any way." Struggling to justify the suffering, Prittwitz invokes his God and his king,

> for although one must immediately acknowledge oneself an Instrument of this, it took place by Necessity and Duty only, because we have never had a Dispute with each other, and we have never done anything to the other in our whole Lives that would merit such a terrible Punishment. Yet what Mortal can here be a Judge? This must be left to the Judge of Worlds, who knows all Contexts, our Duty is to obey Authorities, protect our Fatherland from Attack, and not think about who is right or wrong, that this may be decided by God and the King.[142]

Prittwitz's conscience is clearly burdened by the horror and devastation, as he seeks ways to rationalize the incomprehensible. First, he disposes of his own responsibility, since he was "forced to do so by Others," serving as an "Instrument," acting out of "Necessity and Duty." Instead, he delegates responsibility to God and king; he depicts himself as entirely in their power. He even explicitly absolves himself from passing "judgment" on what occurred. The suffering seems pointless, since he holds no particular personal grudge against the adversary. In this way, the lack of meaning associated with extreme violence is rerationalized, assigned to superior agents like God, king, and fatherland.[143]

The Media Battle and Its Audience

For weeks after Zorndorf, a different kind of post hoc rationalization preoccupied the European public sphere—namely, which army had actually won the battle. Tradition has it that, a month after Zorndorf, a Prussian raiding party from Neu-Stettin captured a Russian courier with a bag of official correspondence, confiscating a hundred private letters.[144] Sometime later, at the royal chancellery in Potsdam, selections were translated by Leonhard Euler (1707–1783), a Swiss mathematician and a member of the Prussian Academy of Sciences, to be used in pamphlets in the aftermath of the battle. Zorndorf was refought in the media to a degree almost unparalleled among all the battles of the Seven Years' War.[145] Across Europe, a wide-ranging interpretative dispute broke out about the outcome of Zorndorf, primarily involving political journalists but also including newspaper readers and diarists in large numbers. The argument encompassed four topics: (1) which army had conquered the battlefield, (2) the extent of each side's losses, (3) the question of plunder, and (4) the issue of Russian cruelty. Of these four points, we will consider only the first in detail.

Luise Dorothée of Saxe-Gotha wrote to Voltaire on September 16:

> Another unique thing about this victory is that it has been reported so differently by the journalists in Vienna and Berlin. The former say the Russians were defeated on August 25, but the battle went so much better for them the following morning that they recaptured territory, with only eight thousand men and a few cavalry units saved from the entire Prussian army. The Berliners leave twenty thousand Russian dead on the battlefield, with the Prussians capturing one hundred and three cannon, with twenty-seven standards, the entire Russian field treasury, all their ammunition, two thousand prisoners; as far as they are concerned it was a complete victory.[146]

Voltaire, in his reply, suggests that the matter is quite clear: "The latest victory of the King of Prussia at Küstrin is only being contested in writing, it appears to me. That the Russians were beaten overall seems entirely clear, because they have not made an appearance. Were they the victors, they would be in Berlin, and the King of Prussia would not be at Dresden."[147] On the Russian side, assessments of the media war were very similar. In his memoirs, Andrei Bolotov sums up the media war: "Never has so much been written about a battle as about Zorndorf or, as it was also called, Küstrin. Since both sides sought to claim victory, at first they both lied through their teeth, either through concealment, or by making claims, and this prompted both sides to issue multiple and various replies, explanations, and displays of evidence. And this is why newspapers at the time were extremely interesting."[148]

An eager discussion of false claims of victory and defeat had followed not long after the first appearance of newspapers in the seventeenth century. In this context, one particularly influential treatise was "Dissertation sur les libelles diffamatoires" (A dissertation concerning defamatory libels), by Pierre Bayle (1647–1706), the French Enlightenment philosopher, printed as an appendix to his well-known *Dictionnaire*.[149] Here he discusses questions of media politics in terms of raison d'état: "Besides the fact that ruses are permitted in war, we must excuse the artifices of the writers of news; for the care they take to counteract the relations of the enemy is also a kind of warfare, and thus their writings have been counted among the weapons of the pen."[150] A partial German translation of Bayle's text was later included in the entry for "Newspaper" in the *Zedler-Lexicon*, the most important German encyclopedia of the eighteenth century. It also became the subject of an anonymous pamphlet during the Seven Years' War, addressing the question *Whether It Is Advisable, by the Rules of Statecraft, to Deny the Loss of a Battle, or to Spread False Victories and Advantages*.[151] The author of the pamphlet was Johann Heinrich Gottlob von Justi, a well-known German cameralist (teacher of political economy). He produced an extensive series of political pamphlets, mostly anonymously, and later included this text in his *Collected Writings on Politics and Finance*.[152] The pamphlet assumed that readers fundamentally shared Bayle's opinion that "sixty years ago, the newspapers were already true to what they are, namely a mixture of truth and lies, although most newspaper writers cannot much be held responsible for this."[153] In his subsequent reflections, von Justi takes a position slightly different from that of Bayle, pleading for a (media) politics tailored to any given situation, although fundamentally adhering to a principle of honesty.

Information on actual historical processes of news reception becomes far more sparse once we look beyond the intellectual elite. But there are occasional hints to be found in contemporary testimonies. Thus, the Silesian noblewoman Juliane von Rehdiger notes: "Both sides are agreed that they alone had victory, I will thus not pass judgment, but this much is certain: many humans were left behind [on the battlefield], and much humanity was set aside."[154] In Krefeld, the Mennonite bookseller Abraham ter Meer (1729–1804) was another avid reader of newspapers, with repeated references in his diaries to information gleaned from them.[155] On September 1, he notes: "News has come that the king has entirely defeated the Russians at Zorndorf, on August 25."[156] This kind of certainty would not last long.

The Berlin newspapers were openly partisan in the Zorndorf media war:

> One would find it hard in all of History to find an Example of the Invention of so many untruths to obscure so great an event. But they will enjoy no Success in their claims among reasoning Men. The position of both Armies after the day of the 25th, the retreat of the Russians to Landsberg, the Quantity of Prisoners, and the Number of

Signs of Victory, [. . .] and finally the Commanding-General's own Admission, does provide such Evidence as to make Doubt impossible for an unbiased Mind. Let us leave our Opponent to their Pleasures, such that, incapable of winning Victories in the Field, they instead seek Victory through the Authors of their News-papers, who seek to cloud the Vision of Common People."[157]

A Königsberg newspaper offered an entirely different interpretation: "How little cause have the Prussians to claim a Victory and to have it trumpeted by many postillions can readily be understood from [what has been printed] above, since unquestionably the Russian-Imperial forces claimed the Battlefield, and thus had more reason to Celebrate a Thanksgiving for vanquishing the enemy, than had that enemy cause so to do."[158]

The *Berliner Zeitung* was indignant, suggesting "that the Russian side not only wants to contradict the account of the Battle of Zorndorf that has been Published in these pages, but takes its impudence so far as to claim the Russian Army had command of the battlefield."[159] The Russians, it goes on, had exaggerated numbers to their own benefit while also misrepresenting the actions of individual units. The Prussian report on the battle argues vehemently that there was no Russian capture of the battlefield, but in doing so, it reveals that the actual location of the battlefield was by no means clear. In the early part of the battle, the Russian army was positioned between Quartschen and Zorndorf. The Prussians then drove them into marshy ground, pushing them back as far the forest that stretched from Zorndorf to Küstrin. Therefore, the actual battlefield, it argues, must be considered to be the site "where the Russian army was positioned at the beginning of the action, between Quartschen and Zorndorf. It was entirely driven out of this place, and by evening was half a mile away. Whereas His Royal Majesty [Frederick] pitched camp in the midst of the battlefield, spending the night in that place."[160] In this case, the symbolic occupation of the battlefield, and therefore also victory, clearly depended on who managed to define the site of battle. On its own, the performative act of occupation was clearly not enough.

Even the dead participated in this debate. A pamphlet titled *Conversation Between a Prussian Black Hussar and a Muscovite Cossack About the Bloody Battle at Zorndorf* features a dead Prussian hussar, now in the underworld, complaining of the spread of so many contradictory rumors about the battle: "One might go quite mad if one tried to be the judge of it. This past 25th day of August, I fell in battle under the bayonets of your infantry, and I fell with this proud thought: that we were the Victor. And see, since then there have been reports published that either Diminish'd, or even Deny'd, that victory we received. Cursed newspapermen! You think yourselves justified in deluding the underworld public, just as you have done in the world above!"[161] In his *Life Story*, Christian Täge, the Prussian chaplain who ended up in Russian captivity, attempts to retrospectively adopt the middle ground: "An impartial Observer will be forced to conclude, that both Parties had a certain justification in claiming Victory, since this was in fact what Took place."[162]

Hochkirch: A Night Raid

After the bloody fighting at Zorndorf, Frederick turned straight away to Saxony, arriving at Dresden with his army on September 11, 1758. There he combined his forces with those of his brother Henry. What followed was a series of classic outmaneuvering attempts on the part of both the Prussians and the Austrians. Frederick ran out of patience first, and in late September, he marched his forces east, in the direction of Bautzen. An advance force under Wolf Dietrich von Retzow failed to reach on Strohmberg. Heading southeast through the Oberlausitz region, the Prussian army of thirty thousand made camp at Hochkirch, close to a sprawling forested area. The Austrian army was almost twice the size of Frederick's force. It was still under the command of Daun, and he took advantage of his numerical superiority to launch a nighttime attack on Frederick's forces.[163] The assault was made before dawn and involved several corps, each attacking from a different direction. The Prussians were left with little room for maneuver, and the fighting bogged down in and around the village of Hochkirch.

The Prussian military chaplain Carl Daniel Küster (1724–1804) witnessed the Austrian assault. He opens his description with a sonic portrait: "Meanwhile the Earth shook with the crash of heavy munitions from our great Batteries and from the enemy's murderous Guns. Howitzer grenades fell like hailstones. The air rang with the buzz and rattle of musket balls. Our ears were filled with Hungarian battle cries—Hudry, Hudry, Hudry [March! March! March!]—with the mingled commands of Prussian and Austrian officers, the squelch of bullets and sabers hitting home, and familiar cries of survivors among the fallen, lying wounded on the ground."[164]

The most memorialized part of the battle is undoubtedly the defense of the Hochkirch churchyard by the 2nd Battalion of the 19th "Margrave Karl" Infantry Regiment, led by Major Simon Moritz von Lange and Lieutenant von der Marwitz. Küster, who described the churchyard as a "little spiritual fortress," later included an episode featuring these two "heroes" in his *Officier-Lesebuch* (Officers' reader), an anthology he edited, which was aimed at a readership of serving officers but also used for the edification of later generations.[165] The story recounts how "the brave Major [. . .] had just brought the second battalion, the Margrave Karl's, onto guard duty in the churchyard that night, which as usual was well set-up for defense, as one could easily shoot over the wall; the entrance was also closed and always well-manned."[166] The Austrians allegedly launched their attack on the churchyard with a ruse, sending soldiers claiming to be deserters to the entrance. This was followed by "the carelessness of an unnamed person," who, "contrary to all customs of war, allowed a large number of supposed defectors to enter the churchyard, while keeping sidearms [daggers, bayonets, swords]. Several armed Austrians had already penetrated the churchyard, killing the guards on the gate, when the Major rushed to the gate with a few platoons of men, recaptured it, and had it closed and Barricaded. Thus, in darkness, began the battle for the little churchyard."[167] Several waves of Austrian attacks followed: "At first there was hand to hand fighting, soon but then the Major gave the order to the small force of Prussian defenders to withdraw until they had their backs to the wall, firing rapidly, until they were free of treacherous infiltrators. In all of this, the Major sustained several heavy saber wounds, while the brave Lieutenant von Marwitz was severely wounded, and several soldiers lost their lives. But the courage of the rest of the defenders was not diminished in the least." But then the Austrian cannons fired a breach in the wall, seriously wounding the major, and barely a quarter of an hour later, the Austrians "managed a final breakthrough," storming the cemetery. "We bravely defended the attack, while the actual battle was taking place all around the village," concludes Küster.[168]

Around this point in the battle, Count Jacob de Cogniazo, an eyewitness on the Austrian side whose observations on the Battle of Lobositz are cited earlier, was badly wounded and carried from the field.[169] Meanwhile, a massive Austrian artillery bombardment had immediately and definitively turned the tide of battle in their favor. Inside the churchyard, Küster observed the Austrian attack: "A failed attack by the enemy produced deadlock for quite a time; but then they advanced with Cannon, blowing a breach in the wall. Our troops defended the breach manfully, and the enemy only took it after a brutal fight, when the valiant Major, fighting at the head of his Troops, was felled with two mighty blows of an Austrian saber."[170] The chaplain's account stresses, above all, the victors' fair and gallant behavior, which prevented the Prussians from falling victim to a total bloodbath: "A brave Austrian officer stemmed the rage of the victors, ensuring they did not hack down the few [Prussians] left alive. With great nobility, he called out: 'Stop! Stop! They are our prisoners; a courageous Warrior does not kill without Reason.'"[171]

For contemporaries, this small "battle of the cemetery" was a striking reminder of the fighting at Leuthen the previous year, when it was Austrian and Würzburg troops that had held out in a churchyard for many hours.[172] The stout defense of such places against a numerically superior enemy was very suited to heroic rewriting on both the attacking and the defending sides. The defeat at Hochkirch was a result of the determination of the Austrians, who urgently needed success after the substantial defeats of the previous year. But they were helped by Frederick's stubborn preconceptions, verging on blindness, that left the Prussian king unable to grasp the situation on the ground until far too late.[173]

Frederick suffered a double loss that October 14: the defeat at Hochkirch and the death of his beloved sister Wilhelmine, the Margravine of Bayreuth, although the king would not learn of her passing until four days later. On November 23, the king wrote from Dresden to George Keith, pretender to the title of Earl Marishal of Scotland, whose brother, Field Marshal James Keith, had died at Hochkirch: "Nothing remains for us, my dear Lord, but to weep together for our common loss. If my head were a basin of tears, it would never be large enough to contain my grief."[174]

The campaign continued after Hochkirch but without producing a decisive breakthrough, which merely succeeded in exacerbating Frederick's misery. He writes: "Our campaign is at an end. Neither side could record success other than the loss of many good men, many poor misfortunate soldiers now forever crippled, the ruin of many provinces and the robbery, looting, and burning of several prosperous cities."[175] But Austria's continued failure to liberate Saxony had likewise plunged Maria Theresa into increasing despair. On December 21, 1758, she wrote to Elector-Princess Maria Antonia of Saxony: "You can be sure of my continued rage against this monster, and that I will use every possible means, and fight to the last man, to free you from this slavery."[176]

Frederick sank into a profound depression, with repeated suicidal thoughts. Nonetheless, during the winter of 1758–1759, he composed something akin to an interim report, titled "Reflections on Tactics and on Certain Parts of War," in which he sums up his military actions to date and subjects them to powerful analysis. For example, he ponders the situation of stalemate in the face of numerically superior adversaries, the constellation later glorified as a Prussian miracle: "These much superior forces, these nations which have invaded us from all four corners of the earth: what they have achieved? Should it be allowed to do so little with so many resources, forces, and armaments? Is it not clear that, were these forces to have cooperated and attacked simultaneously, they could have crushed us, one corps after another, and then by constantly advancing towards the center, could have forced our troops to focus solely on the defense of our capital?" Frederick does more here than simply identifying the problem as a lack of coordination. He suggests that the sheer number of his adversaries had led to delegation in decision-making, producing paralysis: "But it is precisely their large number that has been harmful to them. Each must rely on others, the leader of Imperial forces depends on the Austrian general, who depends on the Russians, who depend on the Swedes, who ultimately depend on the French. Hence the carelessness in their movements, and their slowness in executing plans." To this could be added fatally poor time management and exaggerated self-confidence: "Lulled by delusional hopes and confidence in their future success, they believed themselves masters of their time. How many favorable moments have they let slip, how many good opportunities have been missed! In short: to what monstrous errors do we owe our salvation!"[177] Most of the problems that Frederick here identifies among his adversaries could be observed in the Pomeranian theater, which regularly displayed these characteristics in particularly intense form.

Pomeranian Maneuvers

In early January 1758, Field Marshal von Ungern-Sternberg, commander of the Swedish army, asked to be relieved of his command. In fact, the decision had already been made in Stockholm the previous month. The Swedish armed forces would have another four commanders during the war, none for longer than two years. None of them managed to coordinate their efforts with the French army in northwestern Germany or to jointly occupy Berlin with the Russians and the Austrians, although one of them, Count Gustav David Hamilton (1699–1788), got as far as Fehrbellin, fifty miles away, in September 1758.[178] In tactical terms, the Prussians held an advantage, since they could deploy hussars and hunting troops, functioning as a mobile guerrilla force. In response, King Adolf Frederick established a new Swedish hussar regiment, commanded by Friedrich Ulrich Count zu Putbus (1734–1764).[179] The Pomeranian war did not see a single major battle; it consisted entirely of maneuvering and irregular operations.

Von Ungern-Sternberg's replacement, Gustaf Fredrick von Rosen (1688–1769), was already seventy years of age when he assumed command. His time in command was relatively uneventful. On March 13, 1758, the Prussians captured the town of Peenemünde after a brief siege. Another siege, that of the city of Stralsund, was abandoned after six months on June 18. Then eight thousand Swedish reinforcements arrived at Stralsund, raising expectations for some new initiative on the part of the Swedes.[180] Nonetheless, General von Rosen submitted his resignation and was succeeded by Hamilton, who began his tenure by occupying the towns of Demmin and Anklam. On July 27, he retook Peenemünde, and in mid-August, he began slowly moving in the direction of Prussian territory at the head of sixteen to seventeen thousand men. On September 1 came the order from Stockholm to take Berlin. Following the Battle of Zorndorf, the Prussian capital had been left practically undefended, with no troops available to guard the city. But Hamilton was slow in advancing, and by late September, he had only reached Neuruppin, almost fifty miles from Berlin. In the meantime, a Prussian corps had taken up a position to defend the city. This Prussian force, commanded by General Carl Heinrich von Wedel, amounted to no more than six thousand men but immediately began attacking Swedish advance parties. On September 28, the armies met in battle at the town of Fehrbellin, which had been the scene of a decisive victory for the Great Elector in 1675. Inside the town, the eight hundred men in the Swedish garrison managed to defend their positions until other Swedish troops could arrive. The defense prompted Wedel's Prussian force to withdraw. Not long after, the Swedes also withdrew: Hamilton felt his extended supply lines were in danger. This was as far south as Swedish forces advanced at any point during the war. Another round of occupation and reoccupation followed. From 1758 on, cities like Stralsund, Rostock, and Greifswald became places of payment and plunder, subject to a series of demands for billeting and military contributions.[181] However, the eighteenth century was not called the "century of sociability" for nothing: Organizations like the Freemasons could act as mediators, and social contacts with local dignitaries were partly organized by Masonic lodges within the Swedish military.[182]

One good source for the everyday nuisances associated with billeting is the daily register compiled between 1757 and 1759 in Loitz, a Swedish-Pomeranian town on the Peene River.[183] The record was maintained by Mayors Georg Christian Almer and Johann Gottfried Mehl and notes the daily burdens endured by the town's population. Billeting, hostage taking, and marauding groups of hussars were some of the main misfortunes they suffered, but the register also documents attempts at war profiteering and a lack of solidarity on the part of some of Loitz's inhabitants, who raised rents, drove up the prices for food, tried to pass costs on to their fellow citizens, and in general took advantage of their feudal privileges as town councillors or clergymen.[184]

In all of this campaigning, the Swedes come across as astonishingly passive. This was possibly due to a lack of reconnaissance and the comparatively light weapons of their troops. Missing pension rights may have contributed to individual soldiers' lack of motivation.[185] In the autumn of 1758, the Swedes withdrew from the Mark Brandenburg, taking up winter quarters on the far side of the Peene. Hamilton was criticized by the Swedish leadership for his withdrawal from Fehrbellin, but he had by now also submitted his resignation.[186] Jacob Albrecht von Lantingshausen (1699–1769) was appointed his successor, taking up his duties on December 19, 1758. For his part, Frederick was preoccupied with raising contributions to pay for the defense of Pomerania. On April 4, he wrote to Lieutenant General von Dohna-Schlodien, the new Prussian commander in the theater:[187] "Regarding the Mecklenburg payments, nota bene: take hostages and threaten the Duke's bailiffs with arson and looting, that will force them to pay punctually!"[188]

As for Swedish accounts of the war, we have testimony, in both words and images, from George Hendrich Barfot, as well as other autobiographical sources, including the diary of the regimental chaplain Olof Langelius (1716–1782).[189] Langelius's unit set out for Silesia on November 30, 1758, where he recorded close observations of the region, including its population, customs, and eating habits and, of course, the events of the war. On December 19, 1758, they landed on the Wittow peninsula on the Baltic island of Rügen, before moving on to Stralsund and then to Greifswald, where Langelius arrived on December 24.[190] He comments pointedly on the local population on Rügen, calling them "lordly types, among them many stupid and arrogant people."[191] At first, battle had seemed inevitable, but no battle came; in January, the Prussians managed to capture Greifswald, and the Swedes withdrew to Stralsund.[192]

The Coast of West Africa

In 1758, the British came up with a plan to send an expedition to Africa, the underlying logic of which was primarily economic.[193] Thomas Cummings, a Quaker businessman from New York, had convinced Pitt to try to wrest the gum arabic trade away from the French.[194] *Gummi arabicum*, a resin harvested from the sap of African acacia trees, was used in the eighteenth century in, among other things, paint manufacture, calico printing, and silk processing. Today it is as a key ingredient of Coca-Cola.

On March 9, 1758, a fleet of four warships set sail from Plymouth with two hundred marines on board. They were headed for Fort St. Louis, a French fortress on the estuary of the Senegal River. The British reached the estuary on April 23 and were soon approached by representatives of the French, coming out from the mud-built fort to offer surrender.[195] Spurred by this early success, the British hazarded another advance, moving on to the French port of Gorée, one hundred miles south. Originally named Goete Reede by the Dutch, it was a highly symbolic center of the slave trade. But the British attack was a failure, and the fleet returned to England. Pitt resolved to send a more powerful fleet, not least because of the four hundred tons of gum arabic the mission brought back to London, a tempting cargo of booty.[196]

In September, the British formed a new fleet, this time under the command of Captain Augustus Keppel (1725–1786), with four ships of the line, a warship with fifty guns, three frigates, and two gunboats (bomb vessels). It put to sea from Spithead on October 22, 1758.[197] On November 29, the *Litchfield* was shipwrecked off the coast of Morocco, with 130 men drowned; 220 survivors were taken prisoner by the Moors. The disaster was partly the result of the inability to calculate longitude while at sea, a problem ultimately solved, in large part, by the work of Tobias Mayer (1723–1762), a German mathematician. Mayer himself was yet another victim of the Seven Years' War: He died of typhoid, infected by French soldiers who had been billeted in his home in Göttingen.

On December 28, 1758, the remainder of the British fleet anchored in the Bay of Dakar. Operations against Gorée began the following morning (figure 6.3). The French had little with which to oppose the British bombardment and quickly hoisted the white flag. Sixteen British and thirty French troops were killed in the operation, with three hundred French soldiers captured and subsequently shipped to France in a prisoner exchange.

News of the conquest reached Germany in late January 1759. But the majority of personal testimonies mention Gorée with, at most, a single sentence. In Krefeld, Abraham ter Meer notes: "The Haarlem newspaper reports that the British have taken the island of Gorée and its fortress."[198] The reports of Professor Wähner in Göttingen and Pastor Fülling in Hesse mention Gorée very briefly as part of broader summaries. For example, "the conquest of the island of Gorea is strengthened by t[he] L[ord] v[on] Werpup." Another report was published a day later, as reflected in the accounts of the diarists: "Gorea is conquered; and with it, three hundred French taken prisoner, not counting the many Negroes, and also ninety-four cannons, eleven stoneshooters [outsized cannons], and four mortars. Reported by the court newspaper on January 29."[199] Without exact contextual knowledge, information on West Africa no doubt remained rather thin, as indicated by a

Figure 6.3 Attack on *Gorée*, December 29, 1758. Painting by Dominic Serres (late eighteenth century).
© National Maritime Museum, Greenwich, London.

short sentence from Eberhard Jürgen Abelmann, the Hanover master baker: "Expedition against the Fortress and Island of Gorre in Africa, commanded by the leader of the Keppel Squadron: a happy ending."[200] The newspaper *Hanoverrische Beyträge* included a piece on Gorée as part of a series of articles on overseas locations in May 1759.[201] In 1759, *The Bold Sawyer*, a London broadsheet, published a rhyming poem to praise the "true British boys" who managed to capture Gorée: "Commander Keppel with his good design / Commanded the squadron, five sail of the line."[202] Having proved himself, Captain Keppel would be given command of further important missions, including against Belle-Île-en Mer and Havana.

In the Caribbean: Burning Sugar and Tropical Disease

The West Indies assumed greater importance in Pitt's strategic thinking after the capture of Louisbourg in 1758 (see map in figure 6.4). In the long term, the importance of Martinique to France meant it might be suitable for an exchange, possibly for Menorca.[203] Plans for further raids on the coast of France had been shelved, freeing up the necessary men and ships for an expedition to the West Indies. Peregrine Thomas Hopson (1696–1759) was placed in command, although he had not been Pitt's first choice, given his advanced age.

At the time, the population of Guadeloupe was around fifteen thousand, of which about 15–20 percent were European or of European extraction.[204] The island was late in organizing its defense: Only in 1759 were two or three companies of militia established, recruited from slaves, but these numbered no more than 100 to 150 men because white residents were reluctant to arm the enslaved Blacks on the island. Confrontation was constant between the islands' plantation owners and the government in Paris. In 1757, the newly appointed governor, Charles François Emmanuel Nadau du Treil (1703–1786), declared the island to be in "a kind of anarchy."[205] Others, like the novelist Jacques Cazotte (1719–1792), who came to Martinique as a ship's paymaster, later condemned the governor and his administration as incompetent.[206]

Our knowledge of the British expedition to Martinique and Guadeloupe between 1758 and 1759 comes from, among other sources, journals kept by George Durant (1731–1780), the operation's deputy paymaster, and Francis Downman, an explosives expert in the Royal Artillery.[207] The financial resources of the British army were administered by the Pay Office,

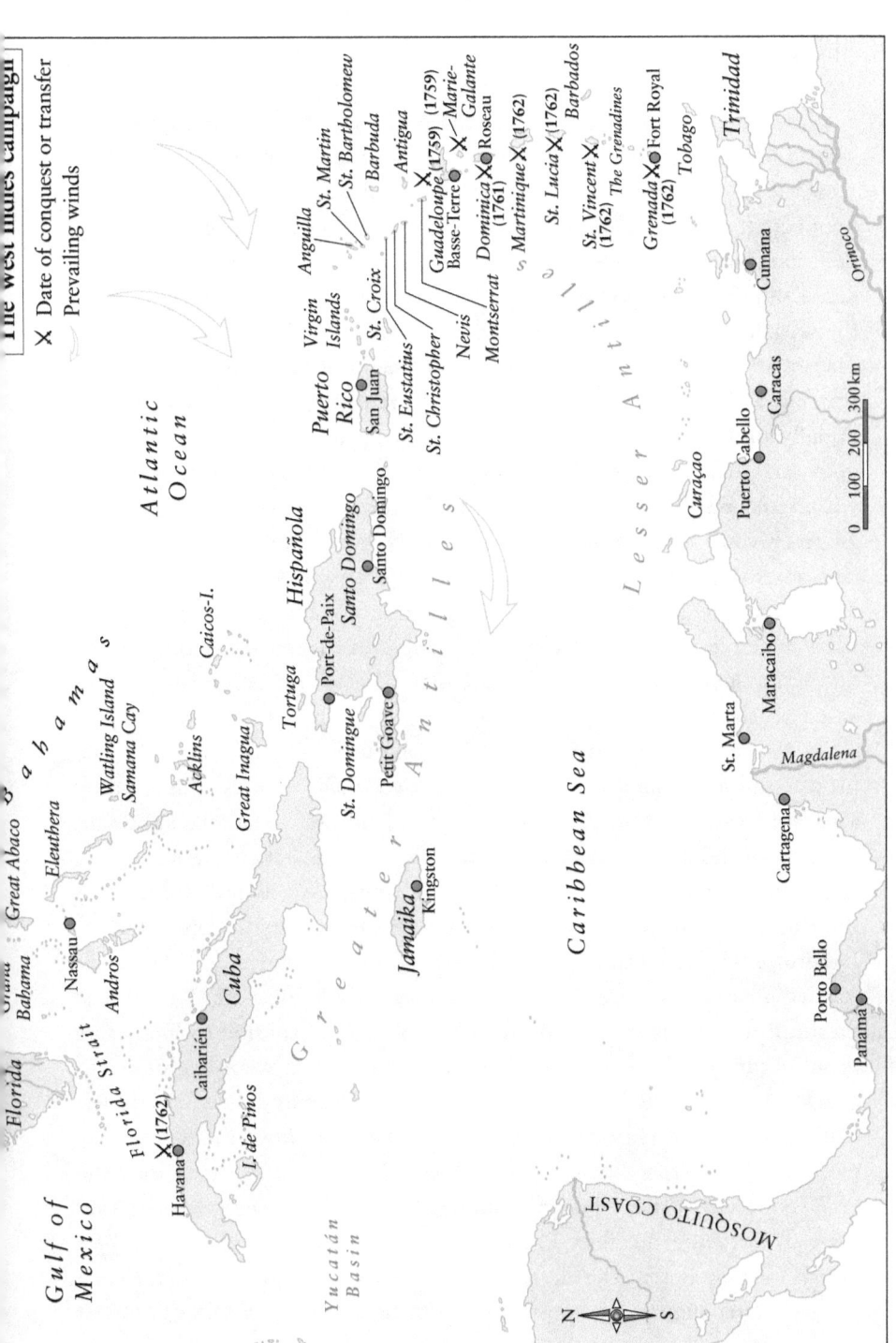

Figure 6.4 The battle for the West Indies.
© Peter Palm, Berlin/Germany.

headed by the paymaster general, who distributed the funds approved by Parliament to the troops, either directly or via a deputy paymaster like Durant. Durant had worked for the Pay Office since 1757; he was not a soldier, so his reports are less euphemistic about the sufferings of the war. He set sail from Portsmouth on October 25, 1758, on board the *St. George*, one of a fleet of nine warships (men of war), accompanied by four gunboats (bomb vessels). Before long, poor weather conditions forced the fleet to return to England, but on November 14, 1758, the *St. George* finally sailed out from Plymouth, headed for the West Indies.[208] On January 3, they reached Barbados, a British possession since 1625. They left the island on January 13, sailing close to the French island of St. Lucia before finally arriving at Martinique on January 15.[209] Here they came under fire and initially moved out of range, but the following day the *Bristol*'s sixty-four guns launched a fierce bombardment of the port, which was occupied within an hour by marines and the ship's crew. Other British troops went ashore, bivouacking not far from Point de Negrès. On October 17, clashes began with French militiamen, and an attempt was made to take the citadel. This was unsuccessful, and the entire operation was abandoned on the same day. On the morning of October 19, a single ship, the *Rippon*, bombarded St. Pierre, the economic center of the island, before the entire British fleet sailed north to Guadeloupe.[210]

The expedition arrived at Guadeloupe on the evening of January 22. The main island of the archipelago consists of two smaller islands connected by a narrow isthmus. Basseterre, the western island, was the more important of the two, despite its mountainous terrain; its main settlement, also called Basseterre, contained the main French fortress, Fort Royal. Grandterre, the eastern island, was flatter and smaller.[211] On January 23, an attack on Basseterre was launched around half past eight in the morning.[212] The ships formed a battle line—for the British, "a most Noble Prospect" but a "most dreadful one" for island's unfortunate population. According to Durant, as soon as the people of Guadeloupe realized that "we were beginning to attack, many of the Religious broke from their convents & flew up into the Mountains, the Peasants drove their Cattle from the shore, the Slaves were removing their little Properties & and the Plantater raised Fires along the Hills, collected all their Force, & either thro' wild Despair or in the vain hope of terrifying our fleet, Crowded along the Shore, & in vast numbers pour'd into the Forts." The alarm was sounded within the city. Eight French ships were set alight in the port and sent to float into the English fleet. But the attacking force kept its distance, and by nine o'clock, it had found a nearby anchorage. From then until seven o'clock in the evening, the majority of the British ships were in action: "The Island seemed to shake & the very Seas to roll back" with the constant thundering of their guns.[213] Since the first broadside, everything had been enveloped in the smoke of gunpowder. By seven o'clock, every gun in the city had been silenced, except for the ones in the citadel. With the fall of darkness, four British gunboats sailed in close to shore, bombing the city and the fortress with mortars. Soon the city's stores of gunpowder exploded, and a conflagration began. Disorder and confusion broke out within the fortress, and the defending forces fled. Durant reports 150 dead and 200 wounded on the British side.[214] But the French Governor Nadau du Treil still refused to surrender; the remaining French forces were now positioned around the mountain of Dos D'Âne, protected by the difficult terrain.

Durant reports that by January 25, the island offered "a continual scene of widespread Desolation."[215] Some streets had only the skeleton frames of buildings left, with flames blazing from their doors and windows, precipitated by the vapors of distilled spirits.[216] The destruction of the city was greatly exacerbated by the large quantities of alcohol and sugar in storage there: "In one part of the Town (where the Merchants kept their valuable Liquors in vaults) the pavement was absolutely red hot, & in others where the Warehouses stood you was often intercepted by Streams of liquid Sugar, which generally run about 50 or 60 yards & appeared like o'erflowing Rivers of melted Pitch:—the only Building of Consequence which I found intire was the Church, which indeed had a great appearance." Durant gives a detailed description of the church's interior, left in enormous disorder: "The Isles [sic] were full of Trophies and Relicks, the Pews were every where scattered with Beads & Books: the vesteries on each side [of] the Chancel, were a foot deep in Papers, Prayer Books, Musick, wax Lights, massy Candlesticks & ten thousand nameless Trinkets & all within the communion rails was crowded with those gaudy trifles which are held most sacred; so it was impossible to stir a Step without trampling on the blessed Virgin Mary or kicking before you a wooden apostle or a maimed crucified Jesus." Departing this "Strange Scene of Folly & Confusion," he headed for the outskirts of the city. But there he was even more greatly moved by the sufferings of the "Destructive War." Spared the flames, these places were nonetheless "almost as much destroyed by the barbarous Plundering & mischiefous wantonness of the Soldiery & Sailors."[217]

Durant describes the citadel and the garrison, as well as the construction and furnishings of the town's buildings. Arriving at some villas outside the city, he enters a garden and comes across another gruesome scene: "The out Houses stained with Blood, & strew'd with the warm carcasses of Dogs, Cats, Pigs, Sheep, Goats & all sort of Domestick Animals, which the Soldiers or Sailors had killed or wounded & were not able to carry away, being laden, I am afraid, with richer plunder." Along with dead animals, he is confronted with a panorama of destruction, including furniture, fabrics, glassware, pictures, porcelain, all "shiver'd to atoms" by the plundering soldiery.[218] Discouraged and exhausted, Durant made his way back to the *St. George* in the hope of getting some rest. But here he is presented with another a scene of destruction, with the quarterdeck soaked in blood and many men torn to pieces by cannonballs.

Tropical diseases became the most dangerous enemy faced by the British invaders.[219] Hundreds now fell sick with dysentery, and two thousand men had to be evacuated to Antigua, which reduced the effective British strength to thirty-three hundred troops.[220]

For Durant, the early part of February was marked by boredom. His account describes his daydreams, while also freely reporting on his sexual relationships. On February 17, he notes: "Made love to French Negress, & found a Black at Gardaloup & a white in Drury Lane differ'd only in Complexion, as their Sentiments & winning ways seem'd pretty much the same."[221] In the eighteenth century, Drury Lane, in London's Covent Garden, was a part of town notorious for prostitution and gambling.

In mid-February, the British attempted another advance, managing to establish a bridgehead between Basseterre and Grandterre. On February 22, 1759, news of the capture of Gorée on the West African coast reached Guadeloupe, where it was celebrated with a bonfire. Durant reports: "General rejoicing for the taking of Gorée—the whole fleet was man'd &a saluted the Fort, the Fort discharged all her Cannon, the Walls were lined & gave three Volies, each of which was returned with the greatest exactness from all the other Regiments in their several Encampments."[222] For the island's population, this was a "most dreadful sight": They not only saw huge clouds of fire but also witnessed the destruction of four of their main fortifications in the course of the celebrations. Victory celebrations not only were visual and acoustic expressions but also could serve as a kind of threatening gesture.

Hopson, the British commander, died of tropical fever on February 27 and was succeeded by General John Barrington (1722–1764). The French

Governor Nadau du Treil faced a more and more difficult situation: He felt himself entirely abandoned. On March 13, he wrote to the Marquis de Beauharnais, governor-general of the French Antilles: "There are so unjust as Men [. . .], none so insubordinate as Militias, none so unreasonable as Officers in Command, and none as unhappy as a Governor placed at the Head of such a people."[223]

Barrington finally succeeded in capturing the island in April, and the articles of surrender were signed on May 1, 1758.[224] French officers and officials were assured they would be treated with military honor, but they were also forced to leave Guadeloupe. The island's remaining inhabitants were given thirty days to decide whether to leave or to stay. Their religion and system of government would be preserved, as would internal taxes and property rights. Free Black residents were not to be enslaved, and the island would be granted a lucrative privilege: permission to export products to Britain on the same terms as British subjects.

By the time the British completed the island's capture, Durant was laid low with intestinal cramps, sweating, and vomiting, from which he suffered for nearly three months.[225] Around the same time, Lieutenant Downman, the artillery officer, complains in his diary about the supply situation but is pleased to report that he has "not the slightest illness."[226] By then, more than eight hundred British soldiers had died of tropical diseases, compared to the small numbers killed during the actual fighting.[227] Durant remained in the West Indies until the end of 1759, enjoying success in his work as deputy paymaster.[228] It was gradually becoming clear that the British were getting the upper hand in the battle for colonial spheres of influence.

India 1758–1759

Few places in Germany were better informed about conditions in southern India than the city of Halle an der Saale. Pietist missionaries from Halle had run an overseas mission at the Danish trading colony of Tranquebar since 1706, with the mission later expanded to Madras (in 1728) and Cuddalore on the Carnatic coast and to Calcutta in Bengal. This produced a dense network of information exchange connecting London, Copenhagen, and Halle; missionaries would send letters to both London and Copenhagen, to be more certain that their message would get through.[229] The information that was sent was collected and processed in Halle and then published in a journal, usually referred to as *Hallesche Berichte* (Reports from Halle). There was a publication lag of several years, meaning that reports on the conflict in India came out only after the war had ended.²³⁰ But newspapers were published several times a week in Halle and often printed letters from India during the war.

For the Halle missionaries, the conflict bore all the signs of a religious war:

> In April 1758, Lieutenant General Lally came to this coast with his Army, which can be called Terrible in respect of these regions, so as to bring all of these Lands under his Rule. And even before the Army's arrival (of which they had learned news from France), the Fathers in Pudutseri (Pondicherries) prophesied from the pulpit that the Religion of the Heretics on this coast would soon be cast down. But this did not occur. All that Mons. Lally did to his supposed advantage was to capture Fort St. David. Immediately thereafter, his Power had already commenced to wane.²³¹

Information was transmitted from India to Europe, but also from Europe and North America to India. One example of the distortion possible when a paucity of basic information was filled by the imagination can be found in a confusing entry from Ananda Ranga Pillai's diary on February 26, 1758:

> At 9 A.M. a number of Officers arrived, saying that Messengers had come from Surat with the news that, because the king of Kannadhâ—a country inhabited by coffrees—had allied with the English, the French king had sent Troops to take this place; the Englishmen, with the help of the King of Prussia, had opposed them, but when his Son and many of his troops were killed along with many of the English, the King of Prussia could no longer maintain his Position and he fled, and the English sought Peace. But it is not known if peace has in fact been made, or not.²³²

Kannadhâ undoubtedly refers to Canada, although a homophonous Indian word can denote a Dravidian language in southern India; the entry is correct in its description of the structure of alliances: France versus Prussia and Britain. The claim that Canada was inhabited by *coffrees*—a word used for enslaved African workers in India—may result from confusion between conditions in different parts of the Americas. What is meant by the son of the king of Prussia remains completely unclear.

Similar confusion clouded news of Cumberland's surrender at Kloster-Zeven, which had taken place almost exactly a year previously. In the second week of September, Pillai seized on information from conversations with several Frenchmen, who spoke of Dutch rumors about newspaper reports that claimed "the French King had sent one of his Cousins with 10,000 Cavalry and 30,000 infantry, which had surrounded the son of the King of England in his fortress, and bombarded it so long that the British surrendered. Then the Prince, with his 25,000 men, was brought to Paris, the capital, as a prisoner."[233] The capture reported here is already a fiction, but the story then takes an even wilder turn, suggesting that the current English king had ruled for fifty years and, before that, had been in possession of "Fort Hanover." Pillai thus merges two Hanoverian kings, George II and George I (1660–1727), who assumed the English throne in 1714. He goes on to suggest that the Hanoverian succession had taken place because the previous English king was killed by his people, in an apparent reference to Charles I, executed in the seventeenth century. The French, he writes, sent an army against Hanover, led by the grandson of the murdered king, while the Netherlands (Nidadâni), belonging to the king of Prussia, were conquered by the French. The allusion to a grandson here refers to Charles Edward Stuart, the Young Pretender, grandson of James II (1633–1701), not Charles I.

The reception of rumors could clearly produce its own form of knowledge—in Pillai's case, serving to render dynastic entanglements plausible across cultures. Comparing his entries from 1757 with those of 1759, we see hope and confidence in French success slowly give way to skepticism and concern. Pillai here is old and not as mobile as he once was, and he becomes an armchair observer of events, overwhelmed by the sheer number of rumors and false reports. But French decline was clearly evident on the ground in Pondicherry. French troops' discipline was fraying, leading to an increasing number of clashes with the civilian population.[234] Conditions were increasingly anarchic.[235]

Information received in Bombay in July 1758 by the British gunner James Wood seems to have been more reliable than many of the rumors reported by Pillai. On July 25 and 26, two British ships, the *Revenge* and the *Drake*, brought news from Persia, including the following: "That General Mordaunt was under arrest for neglect of duty in regard to Rochefort, that the King of Prussia had beat an army belonging to the French consisting of 80.000 men, that his army consisted of 35,000, that he had taken and killed above 30,000 and that Lord Loudoun was greatly distressed in North America; that he has written for England for 10,00 men, and it is thought that if he does not speedily get them, he will resign, not being able to do anything with the forces he has now with him."[236] In fact, the combined French and Imperial army at Rossbach consisted of forty-one thousand men, with Prussian forces amounting to twenty-two thousand, so the comparative strength is relatively accurately reproduced, although French losses amounted to ten thousand men rather than thirty thousand. The reinforcements demanded by Loudoun did ultimately arrive from Britain.

Meanwhile, the East India Company Council in Madras was concerned that Clive had not yet withdrawn from Bengal. For some, these concerns verged on rage; the mood on the council was ultimately altered only by news of Clive's spectacular successes. Long-awaited French reinforcements, commanded by Thomas Arthur, the Comte de Lally-Tollendal (1702–1766), did not arrive in the Carnatic until April 1758, by which time the southern Indian campaigning season was already half over. The voyage from Europe usually took six months, but Lally had taken an entire year to reach the subcontinent. In response, Admiral Pocock, commander of British naval forces in the East Indies, again sailed his fleet south from Bengal, leading to two inconclusive sea battles on April 29 and August 3. In June, Lally succeeded in taking Fort St. David on the Coromandel coast but was unable to transport his men by sea to Madras because the French naval commander d'Aché had already sailed his fleet to Mauritius for repairs to his badly damaged ships.

Lally himself lacked vital skills for his new position. He disregarded local customs, which turned the population against him, while also managing to offend Bussy by ordering him to return to the Carnatic from the Deccan plateau. At the end of October, lacking money and resources, Lally began a desperate advance on Madras and Fort St. George, with a fighting force of twenty-three hundred Europeans and five thousand sepoys. The British fortress was commanded by Stringer Lawrence (1697–1775), an experienced officer who had fought at Culloden in 1746, among many other engagements. He was well prepared for a siege of several months. The French reached Madras on December 12, plundering the city's "black town," the unfortified neighborhoods mostly inhabited by the native population. The British unsuccessfully launched a sortie to take advantage of the situation, attacking the French while they were looting. The French began a classic siege operation with entrenchment and mines, aiming to breach the city's defenses. But before the French could break through, Pocock arrived from Bombay on January 16, bringing supplies for the beleaguered city. Lally was forced to retreat to Arcot. Losses on both sides were heavy, with 486 dead and wounded, 122 captured, and 20 desertions among the British. Some 322 sepoys were killed or wounded, with 440 desertions. The French reported 1,500 dead or wounded.[237]

Meanwhile, Clive had sent an expeditionary army under Lieutenant Colonel Francis Forde to the Northern Circars (a territory on the east coast, between Bengal and the Carnatic), where it successfully attacked French forces commanded by the Comte de Conflans. On April 7, Forde took the French fortress of Masulipatam, leading the local *subahdar* (provincial governor) to renounce his agreement with the French. Lally's primary problem was a shortage of money, which prompted increasing levels of desertion. The British adopted a strategy designed to make the situation worse: They drove the French out of areas where they might have obtained fresh financial resources or territorial bargaining chips for an unexpected peace in Europe.

Despite these British territorial gains, the conflict in India saw no decisive conclusion in 1759. On December 18, 1759, Pillai received news from Europe via Goa that raised his hopes. It was reported that the French East India Company had borrowed 40 million livres in silver from merchants and that thirty or forty ships were soon to arrive, carrying supplies and a new governor who would impose order. This "happy news" that French fortunes were prospering everywhere in Europe suggested that the Dutch would soon switch allegiance from the British to the French and that the king of Prussia had been weakened by the loss of much territory and many soldiers.[238]

CHAPTER VII

1759

Annus Mirabilis

The Shifting Winds of War

The year 1759 looked set to be a remarkable one. Britain's fortunes were soaring, with the country on its way to becoming "master of the world." But Prussia was staring into the abyss.[1] At first glance, the North American situation seemed promising for the British: They had forty-five thousand regular soldiers under arms, including General Hopson's force, by now already in the West Indies. On February 27, 1759, the pastor Heinrich Melchior Mühlenberg wrote from Providence, Rhode Island, to his colleague Theophilus Arnold Krome in Einbeck, looking back on the progress of the war: "Our political affairs were miserable and dangerous in the summer of 1757, for we had lost two important strongholds [Fort Oswego and Fort William Henry]. [. . .] Last year, in 1758, we clearly experienced the most gracious help of God, with the capture of Cape Breton Island and the adjacent areas, Fort Frontenac on Lake Ontario and Fort Duquesne on the Ohio River. [. . .] However, the good success of the other expeditions since then has outweighed the damage."[2] In Bombay, James Wood of the Royal British Artillery had a similar impression. On May 16, 1759, a ship from Persia brought him news of the taking of Louisbourg and Gorée and the expulsion of the French from Hanover. More information followed on June 3, via the crew of the schooner *Diligence*, that confirmed Louisbourg's capture. There was also news from France that the "famous pier" of the port of Cherbourg had been destroyed, along with some ships; from Germany came word that the French army under De Clermont and St. Germain had been defeated at Krefeld on June 23, 1758.[3] Three days later Wood received news of the decisive British victory at the siege of Masulipatam in the Deccan region of India.

For the French-Imperial forces, the situation was difficult but not hopeless. The Duc de Choiseul and Marshal Belle-Isle had developed a daring French plan to invade England, which might have shifted the situation back in France's favor.[4] The idea of an invasion awakened fundamental anxieties in British foreign policy, but at first, its operational feasibility seemed dubious. But French planners were thinking not of conquest in the classical sense but of a landing in Scotland, followed by a march on London. French military control over London would have dealt a massive blow to the British Empire as a whole, with far more serious consequences than if something similar had happened to Berlin. British government creditworthiness would have collapsed—and with it, the country's entire system of colonial logistics.[5] A rapid peace agreement would have been the most likely result. Apart from immediate fears of invasion, the British government was primarily concerned about its budget. The national debt was rising, and public credit had to be stabilized.[6] Any new taxes would be unpopular; the most likely tax to be imposed would be on beer—specifically, on malt.

On April 13, 1759, Good Friday, "profound stillness" reigned in the Goethe family in Frankfurt, a harbinger of the "approaching storm." Young Wolfgang "ascended to the garret" of the house. Although he could see nothing, he "could very well hear the thunder of cannon and the general discharge of musketry."[7] The first wagons bearing the wounded were already arriving in the city, their "various sad gestures and mutilations" indicating the sufferings endured on the battlefield. Goethe's father was confident of an Allied victory and ventured out onto the Bornheimer Heide to take a look. Only then did it dawn on him that the French had won the battle, a fact quickly confirmed by others present. The event in question is remembered as the Battle of Bergen.[8] The engagement marked the failure of Ferdinand of Brunswick's attempt to defeat the Duke of Broglie before his army joined with a separate French force under Contades. The Anglo-German army had been slightly weaker in numbers, with its twenty-four thousand soldiers facing around thirty thousand French. It had attacked in three waves but did not manage to overcome the enemy, prompting Ferdinand to withdraw.[9]

The mood of the leadership in London revived only with the arrival of news of the capture of Guadeloupe in mid-June 1759.[10] Fears of invasion were still acute, and Admiral Anson discussed the recall of some ships with Pitt, but the prime minister felt that British national defenses remained adequate. Just three large ships were recalled from the Caribbean to support Admiral Hawke's fleet, which had been observing French activities at Brest since May, operating from its base at Torbay on the south coast of England. This observation of possible French invasion preparations soon turned into a total blockade of the French navy, one that also impeded French merchant shipping.[11]

The naval blockade represented an unprecedented humiliation for the French. But in Germany, Ferdinand had been forced onto the defensive against Contades. The situation grew worse for the Allies when the French took Minden on July 11, putting pressure on Electoral Hanover, including the city of Hanover itself. The French move opened the way to Magdeburg, the site of the Prussian court, where thousands of French prisoners of war were also being held.[12] Magdeburg represented the "strategic center of the Prussian monarchy," its massive fortress acting as Prussia's logistical hub on the Elbe. In 1757, Frederick had transferred the royal family and the state archives to the city, both of which he felt were in urgent need of protection.[13] It is significant that neither the French nor the Austrians managed to reach or to besiege this great central fortress at any point during the war; over the course of the conflict as a whole, this would prove crucial in spatial and strategic terms.

Guns and Roses: The Battle of Minden

In early August, a battle was fought close to the city of Minden, about thirty-five miles from Hanover.[14] Ferdinand's army numbered about forty thousand men; the French army under Contades had initially been around the same size, but its ranks had swelled with an additional fifteen thousand men from Broglie's corps.[15] The French, in other words, had a clear numerical advantage.[16]

Again several figures we have encountered in this narrative were witnesses to the fighting, including the Saxon officer Hans Carl Heinrich von Trautzsche and Grotehenn and Cleve, all soldiers for the forces of Brunswick.[17] After the Battle of Bergen in April, Grotehenn's regiment had been ordered in June to move on Lippstadt and then on Minden. But Minden was in the hands of the French, so his unit ended up close to Osnabrück, where he wrote to his father on July 28. This would be his last letter for a month, when he wrote again from Breitenkamp, cheerfully confirming his experience at the Battle of Minden on August 1: "Our wish has finally been fulfilled, namely our shared desire to attack and overcome our proud enemy." Grotehenn's letter notes that skirmishing began between the forward units of the two armies at around six o'clock in the morning, followed sometime later by the "main Bataille," which "only ended at 12 noon." The French cavalry withdrew across the Weser River while the infantry retreated through the city of Minden. As far as Grotehenn was concerned, the Allied victory was unequivocal: He estimated twelve thousand dead and wounded in total, including six thousand on the Allied side. He clearly had a sense for symbolic as well as material capital: He puts particular emphasis on the precise numbers of "trophies" captured, including cannons, standards, flags, kettledrums, and trumpets, with his own regiment capturing no fewer than six cannons. But he remembers to mourn the loss of a relative: "The first of our Regim[ent] to be shot and killed was my Cousin and compatriot, Conrad Meyer from Kirchbrack [Grotehenn's home village]. At about 7 o'clock he had his Shoulder entirely shot away by a Cannonball, so that he was killed instantly."[18] The numerical losses cited by Grotehenn are greatly exaggerated for both sides; they nonetheless bear witness to the very strong impression made by the battle's destructiveness.

The battle had developed unusually in operational terms, something noted by Grotehenn when he cites the remarkable inferiority of the French cavalry in the face of combined Hanoverian infantry and cavalry. Initially, the Hanoverian Guards Regiment, an infantry unit, had been "Hack'd down" by French "gendarmerie on horseback (which are all Noblemen and Armored)." But the regiment re-formed its ranks after the French had surged through. Behind them, the Allied cavalry "bravely set upon" the French horsemen, leaving "the Gendarmerie . . . trapped between Cavalry and Infantry, and a large part of them were slain, along with their Horses." In addition, the Hanoverian Guards captured the French cavalry's kettledrums and silver trumpets. In an unprecedented turn of events, British infantry also prevailed against French cavalry units in an incident reported by the Hessian soldier Barthold Koch: "Now the English fought well, driving back the French cavalry, until little was left of it." Koch also notes physical objects that bore witness to the French defeat: "On the battlefield were over 20 carts filled with cuirasses and boots. French horses were running through the Field with English bayonets in their bodies. And so the French cavalry attacked four Times, but was each time repulsed."[19]

Writing in 1787, Georg Friedrich von Tempelhof regards it as well established that Minden was "without question one of the most strangest [battles] in the history of war, [. . .] not solely because of its remarkable and unusual arrangement of battle, but also because of the preparations for this, and the conduct of the generals and the troops throughout the battle."[20] Minden offers a particularly drastic example of how battlefields could become sites for the performance of aristocratic etiquette and ideas of social hierarchy. For many officers, war was an affair for gentlemen, who often placed greater value on ceremonial rank than on military efficiency in a modern sense.[21] Probably the most famous episode from the Battle of Minden largely resulted from an assertion of aristocratic claims to recognition, although it is impossible to completely disentangle decisions made for symbolic reasons from those following instrumental logic.

Koch describes the scene:

This was the moment to destroy the entire French army, whereupon Lord Sackville, an English general, saved it from Destruction. By now, our Infantry had done everything possible. It was the Cavalry's turn to complete the Battle and make an End to it. Duke Ferdinand thus sent an Adjutant to General Sackville [with orders] to crush them. But he refused, demanding a written Order from the Duke. Three adjutants, two of them English, brought him the Order to crush the Enemy. But he did not, and [thus] within a few Moments a great Defeat for the French had not come to pass.[22]

The nonintervention of the British cavalry, under the orders of General Lord George Sackville, is among the most striking moments of insubordination in the entire Seven Years' War.[23] Sackville, positioned behind a grove of trees and unable to directly observe the situation, took no action, despite repeated demands from Ferdinand's messengers. The immediate reason for Sackville's inaction was a dispute with Ferdinand over the chain of command: It seems he was not prepared to accept orders from his nominal Prussian superior. Interpretations vary, and the precise reason is not important. Ferdinand's policy of secrecy may have been an issue, with Sackville feeling he had not been sufficiently informed. After he had returned to England, Sackville was subject to a full-fledged media campaign against him; the general began court proceedings, intending to establish the truth, but they ended disastrously for him.[24]

Before the battle, tensions had also arisen within the Brunswick forces. Ferdinand had entrusted Count Wilhelm of Schaumburg-Lippe with command of the artillery positioned to defend the redoubts in front of the village of Todtenhausen. But Wilhelm came into conflict with General Wangenheim "about the arrangement and use of the Guns, how they would be brought into the Entrenchments, the firing of Volleys of Retreat, etc. [. . .] Each took it on themselves to give Commands to Lieutenant Colonel Huth (the leader, so to speak, of the artillery corps) [. . .]—each with opposing Wishes."[25] Ferdinand attempted to mediate the dispute, as is clear from his agitated correspondence, but it was ultimately ended only by the onset of the battle itself. On the day of the battle, Count Wilhelm's stubbornness enjoyed success, winning praise from Ferdinand and the king of England.

Coordination between units on the French side was likewise anything but smooth, with a notable dispute between Marshal Contades and Lieutenant General Broglie about how the attack should be launched.[26] Contades wanted to go on the offensive only after Broglie had launched his assault on Wangenheim's corps. Broglie seems to have left a request from Contades unanswered, which won the enemy valuable time. Contades claimed Broglie's inaction played a crucial role in the battle's overall development, ultimately enabling Ferdinand's successful attack on the French center. Like Sackville, Broglie was subject to court-martial; unlike his English counterpart, he was eventually acquitted. The French could barely comprehend their defeat. Later Broglie would write a report on the battle: "As I already had the honor to report to you, in this way 8 to 10 Battalions [4,000–5,000 men], on a flat heath, defeated 61 French escadrons [approximately 7,320 men]: had I not seen it, I should not believe it!"[27] Given these numbers, the loss at Minden certainly demanded explanation. The Paris public learned of the defeat from the *Gazette* of August 18, 1759.[28]

Over the years, various attempts were made to explain the defeat in military-historical terms. In 1847, another layer of local context became available with the publication of an account by Jobst Hinrich Lohrmann.[29] He was a former sailor who on July 30, two days before the battle, had been ordered by Contades to ride to the Duke of Brissac in the neighboring town of Herford. He was to carry with him a pair of shoes, ostensibly the model for a much larger production order, but, in fact, they contained the French battle plan. Lohrmann had reason to suspect the ruse and allegedly took a roundabout route, going by way of moors and hills, before handing the shoes to Ferdinand's forces. The shoes were taken apart and the French battle plan revealed, pressed between the soles. This allowed Ferdinand to prepare very precisely for the battle. The anecdote has at least three noteworthy aspects. First, it connects the fate of the battle to decisive action on the part of a Minden resident, helping to anchor the event in local memory. Second, it provides a more straightforward explanation for the confusing military maneuvers undertaken by both sides, which had appeared quite odd even to contemporary observers. Finally, the incident is very much in keeping with the historical outlook of the French armed forces, since—if correct—it explains military defeat in terms of betrayal rather than failure or contingent events.

Among the most important trophies captured by the Allies at Minden was the correspondence between Contades and Belle-Isle. This contained highly controversial statements on a French plan to implement a scorched earth strategy in Westphalia, which caused particular concern because of its suggestion of massive forest clearances. The correspondence was rapidly published; in Germany, the strategy stirred up dark memories of the French devastation of the Palatinate during the Nine Years' War (1688–1697).[30] Indeed, the reaction to the leaked plans ultimately prevented their implementation; the incident marks a moment when public opinion becomes a key factor in constraining the conduct of war.

Viewed retrospectively, victory at Minden is one of a series of British successes in 1759; it can thus undoubtedly be considered important in world history.[31] This was given contemporary visual expression in a 1759 print titled *The Applied Censure, or Coup de Grace*, showing the English lion battling a Gallic rooster, helped by a Hanoverian horse (figure 7.1).[32] With a backward kick, the horse forces the French king to withdraw his army from Hanover, Hesse, and Westphalia. This gives the lion room to hold down the rooster with his claws, forcing it to concede colonial territories, including Louisbourg; Forts Duquesne, Crown Point, and Niagara; the Senegal estuary; and Gorée. A clear reference to Minden can be discerned in the figure of Lord Sackville prone beneath the lion; the general is attempting to justify himself while the horse complains that victory could have been clearer had the unnamed general followed his orders. The lion thanks him with these words: "O Pretty! O pritty! Thou hast save[d] me a great deal of labour & trouble, I have crush'd the Cock & secured America."[33]

However, even when examined more closely, the significance of the battle remains minor: It prevented a French advance into Electoral Hanover but did not stop France from continuing the war in that theater or from

Figure 7.1 The Applied Censure or Coup de Grace. Anonymous copper engraving (London, ca. 1759).
© The Trustees of the British Museum, released as CC BY-NC-SA 4.0.

using the territory thus gained as a result in the peace negotiations of 1761.[34] The significance granted the battle by the British seems more like a post hoc rationalization of their generally successful campaign in northern Germany. Above all, Prussia profited from the Allied victory, since it stopped a French march on Magdeburg: Its benefit to Frederick would be revealed in dramatic fashion in the following two weeks. On the whole, the battle did not have a direct global impact but rather functioned as a kind of "connecting link" between the different interests involved in the war and between its various theaters.[35]

The victory over the French and Saxons by Allied forces—British, Hanoverians, Prussians, Brunswickers, and Hessians, as well as troops from Schaumburg-Lippe and Saxony-Gotha—has made Minden an important commemorative event in British military history, although the victorious general was a German.[36] Every year on August 1, Minden Day, acts of commemoration are performed by British army units drawn from nine of the regiments involved in the battle. On this day, soldiers decorate their headgear with roses, since British soldiers fighting at Minden apparently wore wild roses on their uniforms.

Since 1748, a Masonic lodge, part of the Grand Lodge of Ireland, had been associated with the XX Regiment of Foot. After the regiment's excellent performance at Minden, it was renamed Minden Lodge.[37] It initially returned home with the regiment in 1762 before being transferred to Quebec in 1775, returning to England in 1783, and being stationed later in Egypt, Malta, and elsewhere, thus carrying the name of Minden around the world with it. Military lodges of this kind created local structures of sociability, serving as meeting places for colonial elites and in this way acting as "builders of the Empire."[38]

Candide on the Battlefield

Before long, the Battle of Minden even found its way into the canon of world literature. The best-known victim at Minden may have been a fictional one, Dr. Ralph, mentioned in the subtitle of Voltaire's well-known *Candide or, Optimism: Translated from the German of Doctor Ralph, with the Additions Which Were Found in the Doctor's Pocket, When He Died at Minden in the Year of Our Lord 1759*.[39] The title led the Vatican astray, as it listed *Candide* in the *Index of Prohibited Books* under the authorship of Dr. Ralph. Voltaire's satirical novel was undoubtedly the most important literary work of 1759; to this day, thanks to the premise of its authorship, it remains linked with the East Westphalian town after which the battle was named.

After the young Candide has been sent away from his home castle in Westphalia because of a love affair with Princess Cunégonde, he embarks on an adventurous journey across Europe and much of the rest of the world, having experiences that, piece by piece, deconstruct Leibniz's notion of the "best of all possible worlds." Whether the Lisbon earthquake, the Inquisition, the slave trade, or the war—everywhere it is clear that the world as it is offers precious little cause for optimism. In graphic style, Voltaire describes Candide's adventures on the battlefield of Bulgars:

> Nothing could have been so fine, so brisk, so brilliant, so well-drilled as the two armies. The trumpets, the fifes, the oboes, the drums, and the cannon produced such a harmony as was never heard in hell. First the cannons battered down about six thousand men on each side; then volleys of musket fire removed from the best of worlds about nine or ten thousand rascals who were cluttering up its surface. The bayonet

was a sufficient reason for the demise of several thousand others. Total casualties might well amount to thirty thousand men or so. Candide, who was trembling like a philosopher, hid himself as best he could while this heroic butchery was going on. Finally, while the two kings in their respective camps celebrated the victory by having Te Deums sung, Candide undertook to do his reasoning of cause and effect somewhere else.[40]

Voltaire here captures the acoustic horror of battle as a true "concert in hell" and ultimately has Candide climb over mountains of dead soldiers, only for him to witness still more atrocities, this time directed against the civilian population.

After Candide escapes unnoticed from the bloody turmoil of battle, he comes to

a nearby village which had been burnt to the ground. It was an Abare village, which the Bulgars had burned, in strict accordance with the laws of war. Here old men, stunned from beatings, watched the last agonies of their butchered wives, who still clutched their infants to their bleeding breasts; there, disemboweled girls, who had first satisfied the natural needs of various heroes, breathed their last; others, half-scorched in the flames, begged for their death stroke. Scattered brains and severed limbs littered the ground. Candide fled as fast as he could to another village; this one belonged to the Bulgars, and the heroes of the Abare cause had given it the same treatment.[41]

The battle and the massacre suggest both parties were equal in their cruelty. War turns into senseless slaughter; its framing by law and religion only renders it all the more absurd. With the concert of battle and the Te Deum in the first example and with international law in the second, Voltaire shows, with bitter irony, how instruments of norm establishment had already been entirely perverted. After the war, the article "War" in Voltaire's *Philosophical Dictionary* excoriated the cynicism of those who lent religious significance to the war:

What is marvelous about this infernal undertaking is that each chief of murderers has his banners blessed and solemnly invokes God before he sets off to exterminate his neighbors. If a chief has had the good fortune to have only two or three thousand men butchered, he does not thank God for it. But when about 10,000 have been exterminated by fire and sword, and, by a crowning grace, some town has been destroyed from top to bottom, then they sing a rather long four-part song [a Te Deum], composed in a language unknown to all those who fought, besides being crammed with barbarisms. The same song serves for marriages and births, as well as murders: which is unpardonable, especially in the nation most famous for new songs.[42]

Kunersdorf: The Miracle of the House of Brandenburg

By 1759, four years of war had left the Prussian army exhausted, so Frederick ceded the initiative in that year's campaigning to the Russians and Austrians.[43] Under Daun, the goal of the Austrian army was to join forces with the Russians and defeat the Prussians together. Frederick tried to prevent this by maneuvering his forces, but ultimately he could do nothing to stop an Austrian corps under Laudon, which was on its way to meet the Russians.

The Russians, led by Pyotr Saltykov, were also on the move, headed southeast in the direction of the Austrian force. On July 23, at Kay, not far from the Oder River, they encountered a Prussian army led by Lieutenant General Wedel. Wedel's forces were defeated in the ensuing battle.[44]

After the battle at Kay, the Russian and Austrian armies finally combined. Meanwhile, Frederick marched his own force to join Wedel's army, and on August 6, the two armies met at Müllrose. By now, the Prussian army had increased in size, containing between forty and fifty thousand men. It crossed the Oder on August 11 and the following day faced a Russian-Austrian army of around seventy to eighty thousand men.[45] Frederick again attempted to use the oblique battle order, which had proved so successful at Leuthen, but his plan was a failure, thanks to a series of undoubted mistakes. The battle that ensued, known as the Battle of Kunersdorf, turned out to be one of Prussia's worst defeats.[46]

The first in a series of interconnected errors was Frederick's inadequate reconnaissance of the terrain and the enemy positions.[47] He had observed the enemy from high ground near Trettin and had come to the conclusion that a substantial attack would have to be directed against their left flank.[48] This meant he had to regroup his army in the woods that morning, a time-consuming maneuver, and then march off to the left in three columns.[49] He positioned his right wing, eight battalions of grenadiers, close to the Hühnerfliess, a small stream running along the northern edge of the battlefield. They were to take the Mühlberg, one of the low hills north of the village of Kunersdorf, and then push forward to attack the enemy's left. Meanwhile, in a diversionary measure, General Finck's corps was to attack the enemy on the heights in front of Trettin. Frederick wrongly assumed the opposing front line would be positioned to his north, along a line between Kunersdorf and the town of Frankfurt-an-der-Oder. But in reality, Russian-Austrian forces were distributed along a line running southeast that was heavily fortified in its southern parts, so the Prussian outflanking move encountered massive resistance. Moreover, given their long march into the battle area, the Prussians enjoyed no element of surprise. Nonetheless, supported by a massive artillery bombardment, Prussian grenadiers managed to take the Mühlberg by around half past twelve that afternoon, leaving the Russians in disarray. But in the absence of artillery or cavalry support, the advantage could not be used as Frederick had hoped. Nearly all the Prussian cavalry had been positioned on the left wing, on what was supposed to be level ground.[50] The Mühlberg had sandy soil, and moving guns into position, especially the heavy twelve-pounders, took time.

The delays gave the Russians time to re-form their defensive line in the small sandy valley known as the Kuhgrund. This was the scene of some of the "most murderous Combat," as Friedrich August von Retzow put it, with both sides advancing to the fight without hesitation. The Prussian infantry was almost wiped out.[51] Finally, the Russians withdrew to the Judenberge, another of the low hills in the area. Frederick was so sure of his success that he dispatched a messenger to Berlin with a provisional message of victory.[52] His generals tried to persuade him to end the battle there. But Frederick felt the enemy had not yet been decisively beaten and allowed the fight to go on. Some historians regard this decision as the battle's turning point—and thus its true crisis—which determined its ultimately devastating outcome from a Prussian point of view.[53] Archenholz's *History of the Seven Years War*, for example, says this: "In a few hours he had been precipitated from the glory of an undoubted victory to the distress of a complete defeat."[54]

On the Prussian left, General Finck's corps received orders to take the Spitzberg, while Frederick himself attempted to push the Russians back from the fringes of the Kuhgrund. Both attempts failed. In a watery landscape, faced with lakes and wet ground, Finck's men found it extremely difficult to advance in columns, leaving them exposed to heavy artillery fire. The Prussian right, still facing off against the Russians at the Kuhgrund, took heavier and heavier casualties.[55]

Among the Prussian infantry battalions advancing from three sides was the von Hauss infantry regiment, commanded by Major Ewald Christian von Kleist. Although his right hand was already injured, Kleist fought at the front line until he was hit again by heavy fire, leaving him wounded on the field. Two desperate cavalry attacks on the left wing, under Seydlitz and Prince Friedrich Eugen von Württemberg (1732–1797), were too late to turn the tide.[56] The cavalry was bombarded with Russian canister shot, attacked in the flank by Russian and Austrian cavalry, and finally forced to retreat. In this way, every single Prussian formation was put in disarray, and the entire Prussian army fled.

The autobiography of the Prussian officer Christian Wilhelm von Prittwitz reports on Kunersdorf in great detail, as does the diary of the musketeer Johann Jacob Dominicus.[57] Both were in the first wave of the attack on the Prussian left, part of Wedel's forces. On the Austrian side, Giuseppe Gorani recounts the battle in his memoirs.[58]

Contemporary research suggests the Prussian side lost more than eighteen thousand men, while the Russians lost around fourteen thousand and the Austrians around twenty-three hundred.[59] However, commemoration of the battle focused on just two of the thirty-five thousand men wounded or killed on August 12, 1759: the apparently indestructible Prussian king himself, who narrowly escaped from grave danger, and the poet-officer Ewald von Kleist, who died of his wounds on August 24 at the house of the Frankfurt professor Gottlob Samuel Nicolai (1725–1765). The heroization of Kleist's death in battle began immediately afterward, partially prompted by the close connections he had with the leading intellectual personalities of the pro-Prussian literary world.[60]

The battle contribution of Prussia's general-king was even more dramatic than that of its dead poet. As Retzow reports, Frederick made every effort to keep soldiers in formation: "The king shrank from no Danger, risking his life like a common Soldier, doing everything he could to get some Battalions to stand firm; everything around him, exhausted by the heavy bloodshed and seized by Panic, was deaf to his commands, since all were seeking, as best they might, to come to safety at the bridges on the Oder." But the king, who often presented himself as being on the verge of heroic suicide, remained on the field: "Frederick II, abandoned by his otherwise devoted army, accompanied only by a few adjutants, remained on the battlefield, precisely at the place where enemy fire was at its fiercest. In vain he was asked to betake his royal person to safety. It appeared that he wished not to survive the Misfortune he had inflicted upon himself; because in his great desperation for the great losses suffered, he was heard to exclaim 'N'y a-t'il donc pas un b . . . de boulet qui puisse m'atteindre?' [Is there no d★★★ed bullet that will strike me?]"[61] The king continued undaunted, giving commands amid "large numbers of slain and wounded." Retzow emphasizes Frederick's double role as a commander but also as one who fought and suffered alongside his soldiers. Putting one's own life in danger marks, as it were, the fine line between the rationality of command and the emotional gesture of sacrificial death. The battle now drew close to the king's own body: "Of those who were around him, some were killed and some wounded by his side. One of his horses had already been shot on its underside, now a second was shot in the chest and was about to fall when von Götz, his aide-de-camp, and a sergeant helped him from the horse before it fell. Götz gave him his own animal." But the king had scarcely remounted "when he was hit by a musket ball, which struck him at the hip pocket of his uniform, its progress stopped only by a golden case he carried with him." After the king's life had been saved by sheer chance, his soldiers made a final intervention to bring him to safety: "At almost exactly that Moment, enemy Cavalry appeared, and the king would have been in danger of Death or Capture, had not von Prittwitz, a cavalry captain, hurried over with a troop of hussars to stop the Enemy and shield their Monarch. His adjutants took advantage of this Moment; they grabbed the reins of his horse and dragged him unwillingly from the Fray."[62]

The fact of the defeat, and its scale, left Frederick in no doubt. He wrote to Count Finckenstein in Berlin:

At last I was almost taken prisoner myself and had to leave the battlefield. Shots pierced my coat and two horses were killed beneath me. My misfortune is that I am still alive. Our losses are very considerable: from an army of 48,000, I have not now as I write 3,000 remaining. All of that and I am no longer the master of my forces. In Berlin, you will do well to think of your own safety. It is a great calamity. I will not survive it. The consequences of the battle will be worse than the battle itself. No more resources are left to me and, to tell the truth, I consider everything to be lost. I will not survive the destruction of my country. Farewell forever.[63]

Frederick's uniform coat, pierced by enemy fire, and his golden tobacco case, which was struck by the bullet, later became relics of Prussian military remembrance culture.[64]

Saltykov's report on the battle arrived in St. Petersburg on August 24: "Your Imperial Majesty's victorious army, with God's blessing etc. has achieved a victory over the Prussian Army, led by His Majesty the King. This was such a brilliant victory that the Lord's almighty hand has evidently blessed the valor and manliness of Your Imperial Majesty's troops."[65]

However, the hoped-for turning point did not materialize for the Russians and Austrians. Prussian forces gradually regrouped, and Frederick was able to write to his brother Henry on September 1, 1759: "I have received your letter of the 25th and announce to you the Miracle of the House of Brandenburg! When the enemy had already crossed the Oder and needed only to hazard a second battle to end the war, he has now gone to Lieberose via Müllrose."[66]

In fact, the real miracle was worked by Henry himself from his camp in Schmottseifen, where, during the weeks between Kunersdorf and the end of September, he conducted operations to tie down the Austrian forces.[67] The Russians had veered south of the direct line between Frankfurt and Berlin, and Henry ordered his army to undertake sweeping marches across Lusatia, first pinning down the Austrians and then repeatedly leading them around by the nose. This ingenious strategy saved his brother from a second and perhaps decisive defeat while at the same time revealing his opponents' indecision: They could not decide whether to prioritize a further battle, a retreat to winter quarters in Silesia, or the securing of their supply lines.[68] The Russians and Austrians did not manage to join forces; instead, both were pressured to retreat to safe areas for the winter. The situation forced the Austrian army to return to its home quarters via Poland for the first time.[69]

Meanwhile, news of Frederick's defeat at Kunersdorf and Ferdinand's victory at Minden had traveled around the world.[70] As early as November 10, Mühlenberg notes in his diary: "In the evening, we saw in the *New-York Gazette* the sad news of the loss suffered by His. M[ajesty] in Prussia at Cunersdorf."[71] News of the event had taken around three months to reach Pennsylvania. But in late November, Mühlenberg received good news about the successful outcome of the year's campaign, forwarded to him in

Philadelphia from Gotthilf August Francke in Halle: "God has helped again, as this campaign has been largely advantageous to the king of Prussia. Things are at least more favorable for him since the Russians have retreated to Poland to take up winter quarters. The king then returned with a part of the army from Silesia to Saxony, together with Prince Henry and forced the numerically superior Austrian army, under the command of Field Marshall Daun, to retreat below Dresden."[72] On October 22, Sir Andrew Mitchell, the British envoy to Prussia, wrote: "The King of Prussia lives, and while he lives he will continue to perform miracles."[73] The year 1759 would indeed be a year of miracles, especially on the British side.

Quebec: The Fall of New France

The winter of 1758–1759 was one of the coldest in Canadian history. The harvest of 1758 was the worst of the war. With neither people nor food arriving from France, the fall of the city of Quebec was a matter of time.[74] But the city was ideally situated for a long defense: It was sited on a promontory on the St. Lawrence River, close to where the river divides into two channels; the channels merge farther downstream, forming a river measuring several miles across. On its eastern side, the city was bordered by the smaller St. Charles River, across from Beauport, where French defensive constructions stood on the bank of the northern channel of the St. Lawrence. To the west of the city lay a flat plateau known as the Plaines d'Abraham, so named because it had once been settled by Abraham Martin, a scout for Samuel de Champlain (1567–1635), the "discoverer" of Canada in the early seventeenth century.[75] The Plains of Abraham was a plateau with steep slopes on all sides and a single point of entry, L'Anse au Foulon, where a narrow ravine allowed access from the river. Besieging the city, or even attacking it directly by land, was almost impossible, and given the distances involved, bombarding it from the opposite bank of the St. Lawrence would not be easy.

In the long run, even the best location is of no use without supplies. In late April 1759, a small fleet of French frigates and transport ships managed to sail up the St. Lawrence and reach the city. Among the passengers was Louis Antoine de Bougainville, a veteran of the fighting at Forts William Henry and Carillon, now promoted to colonel, who was returning to Canada with important orders from the French court at Versailles.

But before examining the French plans, let us consider those of the attacking side. Pitt's strategy called for Amherst to occupy the French forts of Carillon (Ticonderoga) and St. Frédéric (Crown Point) and then march on Quebec with twelve thousand men. James Wolfe had the task of advancing upriver to Quebec with a force of eleven thousand New England troops, a fleet of forty-nine ships, and thirteen thousand marines, commanded by Charles Saunders. Wolfe departed Louisbourg on June 4, already late in the campaigning season.[76] After Montcalm ordered all French troops to withdraw to Quebec, Carillon fell to the British on July 24, and St. Frédéric followed on August 4. But the British advance still had several obstacles to overcome.

The first hurdle was to safely cross the St. Lawrence; here the young James Cook (1728–1779) excelled, providing precise measurements of the shallows.[77] Just before the fight for Quebec, we see young Bougainville and Cook facing off. Almost the same age, they would later become famous antagonists in the context of global circumnavigation. The two men embodied archetypal contrasts between Britain and France: Cook the disciplined bourgeois, Bougainville the aristocratic bon vivant. This clash of cultural stereotypes was paralleled in the Quebec campaign in the contrast between Wolfe and Montcalm—respectively, the attacker and the defender of the city.

In every respect, things looked grim for Wolfe, who was further plagued by fever and kidney stones. At first, none of his actions had much effect in reaching the overall strategic goal. Not until June 28 could he manage to land his eighty-five hundred troops on the Ile d'Orléans, downriver from Quebec. A bombardment of the city began on July 12, but it proved unsuccessful, as was a frontal attack on Beauport on July 31, which the French fought off with heavy British losses. In this situation, how could Wolfe lure the enemy into battle? His initial choice, a cruel one, was to implement a policy of terror and scorched earth, although in doing so he was merely reacting to the constant pinprick tactics of the Canadians, who used the same methods.[78] The area around Quebec was burned to the ground, its valuables plundered, and its inhabitants raped and scalped. No fewer than fourteen hundred farmhouses were reported to have been devastated.[79] By early August, the tactics had instilled horror and helplessness among the local population.

The instructions that Bougainville carried from France were intended to end the ongoing disputes on strategy between Vaudreuil and Montcalm. Vaudreuil favored gradual withdrawal and guerrilla tactics using allied Native

American tribes. Rather than holding Quebec at any price, he believed the concentration should be on Montreal and its neighboring region, known as the Pays d'en Haut. Montcalm had a diametrically opposed strategic plan. He thought it would be fatal to disperse French forces and wanted all professional units—he did not include Native allies in the plan—to gather at Quebec. In his view, defending the city was key to the defense of all of Nouvelle-France. The two men agreed on one thing only: The enemy must be prevented from taking control of all of Canada so that France could regain all of its North American territory in future peace negotiations. The arrival of Bougainville lent the weight of royal authority to Montcalm's plan. He mobilized anyone who could be mobilized, bringing the total defensive force to between twelve and fifteen thousand men, including five regular French regiments, several militia companies, some companies of sailors and refugee Acadians, and a few hundred Native Americans, including Cree warriors from the north and converts to Christianity from Quebec. From boys to old men, every available male in the vicinity of the city was enlisted into Montcalm's motley army, including thirty-five Jesuit seminarians. Given the composition of his forces, a pitched battle on open ground was not Montcalm's preferred option.

Wolfe, in a letter to his mother, describes the situation: "My antagonist has wisely shut himself up in inaccessible entrenchments, so that I can't get at him without spilling a torrent of blood, and that perhaps to little purpose. The Marquis de Montcalm is at the head of a great number of bad soldiers, and I am at the head of small number of good ones, that wish for nothing so much as to fight him—but the wary old fellow avoids an action doubtful of the behaviour of his army."[80] At the end of August, Wolfe convened a council of war with his three senior brigade officers. They advised him that rather than attempting another attack at Beauport, he needed to find a way in through the cliffs to the west of the city. Wolfe was by now in very poor health, and when he collapsed on September 4, he was very weak and rumored to be on the point of death. Moreover, with the onset of winter looming, time was of the essence. Seeking further counsel, Wolfe turned to Captain Robert Stobo, a Scotsman who had been a prisoner of war in Quebec between 1755 and 1759 and who knew the city very well. In all probability, it was Stobo who alerted Wolfe to the path leading from L'Anse au Foulon up to the Plains of Abraham.[81]

At first, nothing happened. Wolfe ordered that thirty-five hundred soldiers positioned upriver to the west be made ready, but he gave his leading officers no further details. On September 10, stormy weather made any new operation impossible. Wolfe finally revealed his plan to his officers at half past eight on the evening of September 12. Thirty minutes later two lanterns were hoisted on the mast of the HMS *Sutherland*: the signal to set out for L'Anse au Foulon. Wolfe put on a fresh uniform and gave his will and personal papers to a trusted lieutenant. He was ready to die.

It was a calm, moonlit night, and the boats headed upriver in ideal weather.[82] They were spotted by sentries on shore, but French-speaking soldiers on board persuaded the Canadians that the boats were a supply convoy.[83] The first vessels made land half an hour before sunrise, disembarking the light infantry, which quickly scaled the steep path to the heights, led by Lieutenant Colonel William Howe (figure 7.2).

A small French outpost was swiftly taken, and its commanding officer, Vergor, was wounded. Prior to this, he had had just enough time to send a messenger to Montcalm. Unfortunately, the French commander did not believe the terrified messenger: "We knew all too well the difficulties of breaking through our lines at this point, as long as they were defended, and so we did not believe a word of the man's story, thinking that fear must have addled his mind."[84]

By around four o'clock in the morning, Wolfe had reached the Plains of Abraham with just two hundred men; below, boats carrying the next wave of British troops were taking artillery fire from a French battery on the heights. Howe's men managed to quickly subdue the French guns, and by daylight, no less than seven British battalions had reached the plateau. Had the British intended to slowly besiege the city in the classic manner, they would now have begun entrenchments on the hill known as the Buttes à Neveau. But they did nothing of the sort, instead forming battle lines in front of the city.

Montcalm had been deceived by British diversionary actions at Beauport, where they installed buoys and sent various boats on ostentatious maneuvers. He was expecting another frontal attack at this point in the river and thus focused on consolidating its defenses. However, at around seven o'clock in the morning, after a sleepless night, the French commander arrived at the Plains of Abraham to be confronted with an unexpected sight: the enemy laid out before him in full battle formation—a shocking vista, no doubt, made all the more so, since the British lines were virtually untouched by scattered fire from Canadian militiamen and Native allies. Montcalm positioned four French infantry battalions in front of the walls

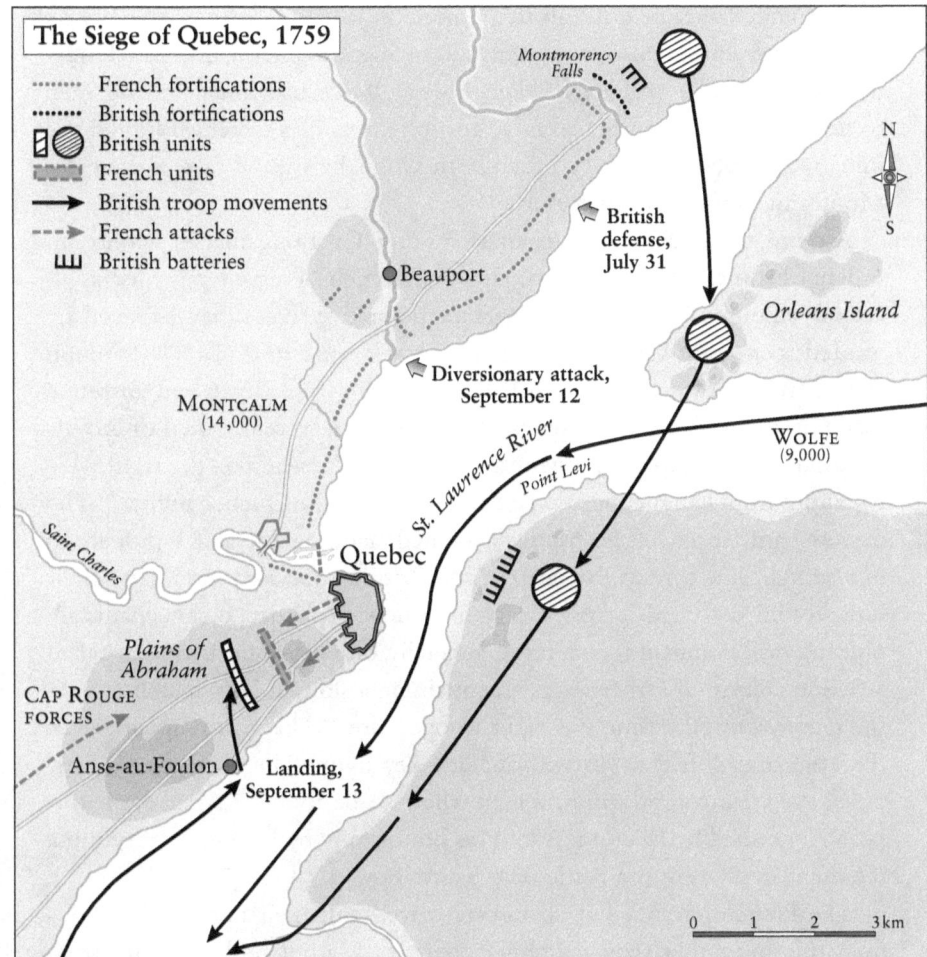

Figure 7.2 The siege of Quebec, 1759.
© Peter Palm, Berlin/Germany.

of the city and attempted to bring in reinforcements from Beauport, but he could not mobilize more than forty-five hundred men all told. Bougainville's two thousand soldiers were seven miles away at Cap Rouge and very unlikely to arrive in time. By half past nine, Montcalm's patience was at an end: He informed his artillery commander it was time to take action. The enemy had already succeeded in carrying two artillery pieces up from the river, he explained, and their entrenching work would soon make a French frontal attack impossible, given the troops available. "How can it be that

Bougainville has not heard all this noise?" he added.[85] In fact, the British were neither entrenching nor boldly advancing into enemy fire, which now included a French artillery barrage. Instead, Wolfe had instructed his men to lie down, to conserve energy and to offer less of a target. Although the initiative seemed to be very much with Wolfe, he was, in fact, waiting for Montcalm to make his next move.

Around ten o'clock, rather than waiting for Bougainville, Montcalm ordered his men to advance, which some French observers regarded as an act of "ambition" in the contemporary, pejorative sense; they believed he wanted to prevent Vaudreuil from having any hand in a possible triumph and so went ahead without him.[86] Regular units from Béarn and Guyenne made up the center of the French line; on the left were the men of Royal-Roussillon and militias from Montreal and Trois-Rivières; on the right were battalions from Languedoc and La Sarre, as well as the Quebec militia.[87] The narrow battle space left no room for refined tactics, so the attack proceeded in a straight line toward the enemy. The British stood two rows deep, their line around 850 yards across. Everything now depended on mechanically obeying drill commands and, more generally, on what John Lynn has called a "battle culture of forbearance": maintaining a slow, orderly march toward the enemy until the time was right to open fire.[88] That morning, however, the Highlanders had to do without one key figure. Their regimental bagpiper, essential to motivation, was nowhere to be found.[89] After the battle, he was shunned by all and restored his honor only by helping to regroup a regiment in disarray at a battle near Sainte Foy.

The French advanced at an uneven pace, with their untrained militiamen running rather than marching; their battle front broke up into scattered lines. What followed was the shortest battle of the Seven Years' War.[90] Wolfe's men stood immobile in a dense line, with orders to wait until the enemy was at about 45 yards before firing. The French advanced in chaotic formation and fired from various points between 120 and 150 yards from the British lines.[91] General Wolfe was among the first to be hit, a musket ball shattering his wrist. His wound was tied up with a handkerchief, and he continued to lead his men. In reloading, French units acted according to their training, with line regiments maintaining their formation and the militiamen crouching on the ground for cover. This proved to be the battle's turning point, as the French line broke apart. When the French were about 60 yards from their line, the British opened fire from the flanks, while the British center waited, as ordered, until the enemy was at 40 yards before unleashing a hail of deadly fire. John Knox witnessed the barrage, comparing it to one mighty cannon shot.[92] Its effect was similarly devastating, and the French turned and fled into the city. Beginning the pursuit, the British seemed to lose their order for the first time; they were still coming under accurate fire from Canadian and Indian riflemen at the edge of the battlefield. As a French officer reported: "The rout was total only among the Regulars; the Canadians, accustomed to falling back in Indian-fashion (and like the ancient Parthians) and then to turn on the enemy with more confidence than before, rallied in some places, and under cover of the brushwood, by which they were surrounded, forced divers corps to give way, but at last were obliged to yield to the superiority of numbers. The Indians took scarcely any part in the affair."[93]

On the British right, Wolfe was leading the Louisbourg Grenadiers and the 28th Regiment when he was hit in the stomach and chest. He retained consciousness long enough to learn that the French were falling back in disarray. The fighting had lasted no more than fifteen minutes.

One observer of the event was a young nun, her name unknown, who watched the bloodbath from the windows of the Quebec hospital.[94] Here, in a district outside the city walls, the nuns of Quebec's three orders had gathered to take care of the poor who had sought refuge, as well as sick and injured soldiers.[95] At the busiest times, up to six hundred people filled the hospital.

The battle itself had ended with British control of the field, but there was still a possibility that Bougainville might arrive and make one last attempt at resistance.[96] By now, Wolfe was bleeding to death, with his brigade officers also largely out of action. Only Brigadier General George Townshend was in a position to stem the disorderly pursuit of the French and regroup the British forces. He did so just as Bougainville arrived, still with hopes to supporting Montcalm. But his attack was repulsed, with Townshend again succeeding in preventing a disorderly pursuit.[97]

Around noon, the British soldiers could at last have something to eat and take care of their dead and wounded. Losses on both sides were approximately equal: 658 British dead and wounded, compared with 644 French. But this was not known on the French side, where a lack of leadership added to the overall uncertainty. Montcalm himself was among those seriously wounded, hit with canister shot in the leg and stomach. He succumbed to his wounds around four o'clock the following morning and was buried in a shell crater in the Ursuline Chapel in Quebec.[98] His two most senior officers also suffered fatal wounds. With Bougainville's force now positioned to the west of the city, Vaudreuil called a council of war at Beauport late that afternoon. In line with his overall strategy, he decided to abandon Quebec, leading his troops to the settlement of Jacques Cartier, some thirty miles upstream. Perhaps the city could hold out until he had regrouped his forces and joined them with troops from Montreal, commanded by the Chevalier de Lévis.

Vaudreuil and his men moved out of Quebec at around nine o'clock in the evening, leaving their artillery, ammunition, and food stores unprotected at Beauport. The only defense for the city's four thousand residents and refugees was about twenty-two hundred militiamen and sailors. There were enough supplies for only three days. The British began digging siege trenches on September 14 but did not begin firing for several days.[99] On September 17, with the British preparing a heavy barrage from guns on land and water, the demoralized garrison gave up, dispatching an envoy at around four o'clock in the afternoon to negotiate surrender. Relatively generous terms were agreed to the same night, and Mayor Ramezay signed the surrender agreement on the morning of September 18.[100] By afternoon, the British flag was flying over the Citadelle de Québec. The unnamed nun reports with relief that the articles of surrender guaranteed religious tolerance and the protection of the hospital under international law. From now on, British and French soldiers had to be cared for equally. The "greatest misfortune," she writes in a report to her superiors, is that the British continued to talk during mass.[101] She believed the defeat was due to a deserter's betrayal.

Only when the fighting was over was the full extent of the destruction visible. One British soldier's journal summarizes the devastation at the end of the siege: "During the whole Siege from first to last, 535 Houses were burnt down, among which is the whole eastern Part of the lower Town (save 6 or 8 Houses) which make a very dismal Appearance. We also destroyed upwards of Fourteen Hundred fine Farm-Houses in the Country, &c."[102] The city was bombarded no less than four times, and he notes: "General Monckton set the Town on Fire, (being the 4th Time) and the Flames raged so violently, that 't was imagin'd the whole City would have been reduced to Ashes."[103]

The series *Twelve Views of the Principal Buildings in Québec* (1761) by Richard Short, a naval officer, stands out among the various visual representations of the fall of Quebec.[104] His images document the destruction of the city's main buildings, including the damaged interior of the Jesuit Church,

Figure 7.3 Ruins in Destroyed Québec, in the Center the Church of Notre Dame de la Victoire. Copperplate engraving by Antoine Benoist (London, 1761).
© The British Library Board, from the British Library Collection: Maps K.Top.119.39.a.9; akg-images/Manuel Cohen.

the ruins around the bishop's house, and the destruction visited on the Church of Notre Dame de la Victoire (see figure 7.3, engraved by Benoist after Short). Many of Short's engraved images include the words "taken on the spot," underlining the authenticity of his visual evidence. By the time Short's drawings appeared as engravings on the London market, they had gone through several transformations: The London maritime painter Dominic Serres (1719–1793) used oils to produce versions of Short's images, which, in turn, served as templates for engravers like Pierre Canot, before the Quebec images were finally published under Short's name. Serres completed four paintings based on Short's Quebec series, each approximately twelve by eighteen inches, largely focusing on the representation of ruins.

Taking and destroying the city was one thing; holding it was quite another. The poor harvest and the onset of winter now caused problems for the new occupiers, who had to billet their soldiers in the ruins. No reinforcements would arrive before the river froze, and the British faced the consequences of Wolfe's scorched earth tactics. The precarity of their situation affected how they dealt with the French in defeat: Their emphasis now was on cooperation and leniency rather than on a severe approach. Soldiers could surrender with military honor and be allowed to return to France rather than being held as prisoners of war. Militiamen had to surrender their weapons but could return to their families when had they had done so. The practice of Catholicism was not hindered, and anyone swearing an oath of loyalty to the occupiers was treated according to their rights. British common law was not initially introduced to Quebec, not least because there were no lawyers to apply it; this led to a long tradition of provincial autonomy within the Canadian legal system.[105]

It quickly became clear that the military situation was by no means settled. The Chevalier de Lévis had reached Jacques Cartier by September 17; shortly afterward he advanced on St. Augustin, just a day's march from Quebec. He quickly realized the futility of attacking the British when he had neither artillery nor functioning supply lines, but he was determined to reconquer the capital of New France as soon as he had resources to hand.

Charles Bonin was another witness to the French withdrawal. His memoirs include a report on the retreat from Fort Carillon (Ticonderoga) in June 1759.[106] His unit fell back in the direction of Montreal, building a new fortress, Fort Levis, on the island of that name. News of the fall of Quebec arrived while the work was still under way. Although the situation in Quebec itself remained quite precarious, the capture of the city was celebrated extensively across the American colonies. Philadelphia, New York, and Boston all saw sermons from the pulpit, fireworks displays, bell ringing, and window lights.[107] The most extensive celebrations seem to have taken place in Boston, where the acoustic spectacle included the ringing of bells all day and the firing of salutes by the militia, as well as artillery barrages launched from within the city and from ships in the harbor. In the evening, a "Concert of Music" took place in the concert hall, along with a parade, a celebratory feast, various sermons and speeches, and, finally, a vast quantity of fireworks, the "largest number of rockets ever seen, on any occasion."[108] Printed sermons contained millenarian interpretations of victory over the Catholics, suggesting it was a harbinger of the millennium. The "whore of Babylon"—meaning France—had been defeated; Spain and Portugal would soon follow, alongside a general turning away from Roman Catholicism.[109] The chosen people, having endured so many trials, were at last seeing signs of divine grace, it was suggested. A sermon of thanksgiving given on October 16 by Reverend Samuel Cooper (1725–1783) of Boston contains interpretive patterns characteristic of Protestant clergy: "We have received a Salvation from Heaven, greater perhaps than any since the Foundation of the Country."[110]

The British victory on the Plains of Abraham was as brilliant as it was risky, but it was by no means a decisive battle, although it was retrospectively styled as such in cultures of remembrance after the final fall of New France.[111] Nonetheless, the immediate reaction was enormous on both sides of the Atlantic. The year 1759 was declared an *annus mirabilis*.[112] On Tuesday, October 16, news of the capture of Quebec reached London, where it was published in the *Gazette Extraordinary*.[113] On October 18, there were extensive celebrations across the country. James Woodforde (1740–1803), at this time a student at Oxford and later a cleric, notes in his diary: "Very great Rejoycings this night on the taking of Québec."[114] In a letter to George Montagu dated October 21, Horace Walpole comments: "Our bells are worn threadbare with ringing for victories."[115]

In Sussex, Thomas Turner was even more elated at the British achievements in Canada than he had been about victory at Rossbach in 1757. On Saturday, October 20, he read the *Gazette Extraordinary* of the previous Wednesday. In his journal for that day, he briefly recapitulates the outcome of the siege, along with news of the deaths of Wolfe and Montcalm and the wounding of General Monckton. He enthuses: "Oh, what a pleasure is it to every true Briton to see with what Success it pleases Almighty God to bless His Majesty's arms with, they having Success at this time in Europe, Asia, Africa and America, and I think in this Affair our generals, officers and common men have behaved with uncommon Courage and Resolution, having many and great Difficulties to encounter before they could bring the City to surrender."[116] Already it was clear that Wolfe's death would be the dominant image associated with the conquest of Quebec.[117]

The news took longer to reach Germany and to be confirmed. On the same day that news of victory arrived in London, Professor Wähner in Göttingen received the *Frankfurter Zeitung*, which contained a contradictory report, published in Paris on October 5, that cited letters from North America saying "the English had been beaten by the French at Québeck and their fleet scattered by a strong storm wind on the Laurenz river."[118] News of the actual victory only arrived nine days later, on Thursday, October 25, when a courier from "our army" reported: "Quebeck is gone to the English." More detailed information arrived two days later. On Saturday, October 27, Wähner notes a report in the *Altonaer Zeitung* that confirmed it was "entirely correct" that Quebec had been conquered by Wolfe's troops on September 18, with both Wolfe and Montcalm killed in the process.[119] It is typical of Wähner's careful scrutiny of information for its authenticity that he spends as much time tracing the route of the news as he does considering the event reported. He describes in detail how the message was dispatched by an officer to Pitt, arriving in London on the sixteenth of the month, before being forwarded the following day to The Hague, where it arrived on October 19 or 20. At this point, the English language teacher John Thompson (1693–1768) makes a significant appearance: He is a trusted informant who had "half an hour before received a letter from Hanover, and also the Eng. newspapers, with reliable news that Quebec was captured on Sept. 18. God be praised!"[120]

On Wednesday, October 24, Abraham ter Meer, the Mennonite book dealer from Krefeld, read about the British victory while at Emmerich on the Lower Rhine. His information came from the *Harlem Gazette*.[121] On the same day, Johann Philipp Schowart, the garrison auditor in Celle, received the news from an English courier who had conveyed the information to Hanover: "Quebec was over. We learned afterwards that it had happened through a Capitulation on the 18th, after a bloody Encounter nearby on the 13th, which the English won despite the enemy's greater strength, but lost their brave General Wolff, as the French lost General Montcalm, so both commanding Generals remained behind at the battle."[122]

The news from Quebec raised Frederick's hopes that peace might soon be achieved. On October 28, he wrote to the Marquis d'Argens: "Two or three days ago news came of the capture of Quebec. So now all of North America is lost to the French, and the English can bring some ten thousand men and more than thirty warships back to Europe this winter, and they will be left with sufficient for the taking the island of Martinique in March. Believe you me sire, by this winter the French will forsake all their allies, and hence there will be peace in the spring."[123] The same day, he wrote to Prince Henry about the victory, saying it would give the British an opportunity to make peace on their terms.[124] On October 30, he reiterated this view in a letter to Finckenstein in Magdeburg and again on the following day in a letter to Ferdinand of Brunswick: "I think the taking of Quebec and the battle won in America is very important news: all information suggests the French will be willing to make peace; they shall be forced to do so because of the deterioration of their trade and the depletion of their finances, and I would bet my head that we will happily conclude this campaign when the Great Alliance begins to disintegrate this winter."[125]

Unsurprisingly, the news was worst received in France, where it triggered a financial crisis.[126] Confirmation was published in the *Gazette* of November 3, citing reports from London of October 20. In fact, the news had reached France as early as October 15.[127] By this stage of the war, the French government was having substantial difficulty paying its creditors, who faced payment demands of their own. Large companies like Beaujon and Goosen & Co., which were very important for the navy, were forced to declare bankruptcy. Etienne de Silhouette (1709–1767), who had been appointed *contrôleur général des finances* just six months earlier, was fired after popular protests and replaced with Jean-Baptiste Bertin (1720–1792), a protégé of Madame de Pompadour.[128] De Silhouette's brief tenure in the role would come to have a substantial effect, albeit indirectly.[129] He was rumored to be so miserly that he decorated his chateau with paper cutouts, not paintings, so his name was given to *silhouettes*, very popular in the late Enlightenment. Louis XV's response to the financial crisis was to melt down the royal table silver to mint coins. The gesture had some symbolic effect but could not avert the crisis. The French defeat in North America inspired mocking words from one person who had never been in favor fighting a war for Canada or its fish and furs. On December 8, 1759, Voltaire wrote to Luise Dorothée von Sachsen-Gotha: "I have no new news about public affairs since the French lost their tableware and their fleet. And now good Catholics have no fish for their fasting and no beaver fur to cover their heads, once reputed so light, but which now weigh so heavy."[130]

For French troops stationed in Germany, like the Baron de Castelnau, bad news was now piling up, with Quebec taken, Madras lost, and Pondicherry perhaps under siege and with no news from the Imperial army or the Russians. But perhaps the French navy could break the blockade and escape the port of Brest. Might that be a new turning point?[131]

Unequal Sea Battles: From Stettin Lagoon to Quiberon

In early 1759, Swedish forces were again cut off inside the city of Stralsund.[132] A Prussian army of thirteen thousand had marched from Saxony to Damgarten, passing through Mecklenburg territory en route, and was now advancing on the Swedes from the west; meanwhile, over the course of January other

Prussian units captured the cities of Anklam, Demmin, and Peenemunde.[133] The events of the Pomeranian War take up little space in contemporary accounts from other parts of the Holy Roman Empire, although Professor Wähner in Göttingen, for example, repeatedly makes note of information from the Pomeranian theater. Thus, for example, on January 7, 1759: "The Newspapers of Altona say the Swedes will not move from Stralsund, but will remain holed up in their camp near Greifswald. Now the Prussians are on the move; so a Bataille may still take Place there."[134] But no battle took place, as had been the case in every other year of Pomeranian campaigning. The Prussians who had marched north included Christian Wilhelm von Prittwitz.[135] He reports on the relationship with the Swedes: "The Swedish army was always in a most wretched Condition, especially their cavalry, by and large they were more Friends than Enemies to us, but in spite of this, they had to be removed from the country."[136] He and his fellow soldiers were particularly troubled by the cold: "But since it was a harsh winter, we suffered much from Frost and Cold. We marched the whole day with nothing warm to enjoy. The Snow was very deep and in the evenings we either crawled into a Village or we made a large fire in the fields. This was because at that time, at least in our Regiment, there was no such thing as Hats or Furs."[137]

Several months later, on May 15, the Prussians broke off the siege of Stralsund and withdrew. The Swedes were too weak to pursue them but needed to demonstrate some kind of initiative in order to justify the subsidies they were receiving from France, which was expecting Swedish support for an invasion of Britain—specifically, Scotland.[138] In return, Sweden was to receive the Caribbean island of Tobago in any postwar settlement.

The Swedish strategy was to recapture Stettin, which would mean taking Usedom and Wollin first. The account left by Olof Langelius, the Swedish military chaplain, reports arduous marches undertaken in the direction of Demmin, during which he found the population disturbed by the constant passage of different warring parties. One miller tells him that if he had flour, he would rather "feed it to the pigs" than sell it to the Swedes.[139] At Schmarsow, Langelius and the other Swedes found an abandoned Prussian field camp, which made their stay easier.[140] As might be expected of a military chaplain, Langelius pays great attention to churches in the areas the army passes through; in his account, he provides detailed descriptions of churches in Demmin, Pasewalk, Prenzlau, and Wolgast.

The overland route to Stettin was open, but as yet there was no passage by river, since the Dievenow was not deep enough and the Swine was blocked with sunken ships. But finding a navigable route remained of the utmost importance for Swedish supply lines. On September 2, the Swedes captured Swinemünde for a second time. Now the Prussians' main concern was to block Swedish access to the sea. A memorable event took place in September 1759: a sea battle between Prussia and Sweden on the Stettiner Lagoon—more precisely, on a shoal within the lagoon, known as the Repziner Haken.[141] Until now, Prussian involvement in maritime warfare had been very limited, although until March 1760 it continued to issue its own letters of marque, which authorized the bearers to engage in privateering.[142] Because of Prussia's lack of naval resources, in June 1756 Frederick had asked the British to move its fleet to the Baltic Sea. The British consistently refused to do so.[143]

Under Duke August Wilhelm von Braunschweig-Bevern, governor of Stettin, the Prussians had established a small "lagoon flotilla," comprised of merchant ships, galleys, galiots, and fishing boats, to which were now added two captured Swedish *espings* (barges).[144] Prittwitz had a chance to observe the fleet and was very impressed with both its symbolic and its operational values: "The Esquadron of Ships may have seemed insignificant to the Inhabitants of Wolgast, most of whom were Sailors, but it protected us inasmuch as it kept us safe from Enemy Attack by Sea. We officers were very much impressed by the Fleet since its Appearance was something quite new to us. As it drew near, we went On-board to examine it more closely."[145] News of the new flotilla reached a European audience via a report in the *Berlinische Nachrichten* of April 14, 1759, which suggested that maritime threats to Prussia were greater than they actually were.[146] The Prussians faced the Swedish "archipelago fleet," a naval force operated by the Swedish army to support land forces.

In late August, the Prussian fleet, commanded by Captain Ernst Mathias von Köller (b. 1719), tried to prevent the Swedes from sailing from the Peene River into the Stettin Lagoon.[147] The Swedes fired artillery from the shore, helping thwart Prussian attempts to stop the Swedish fleet. Under the command of Admiral Captain Karl Rutensparre, the Swedes seemed to have the numerical advantage, although the Prussians had more guns overall.[148] On September 10, a windless day, the Swedish galleys confronted the Prussian ships at nine o'clock in the morning. Artillery barrages lasted for two hours before the Swedes boarded and captured two Prussian galleys, which they then used to fire on the other Prussian ships. After three hours of fighting, the Swedes emerged victorious, having captured nine ships and taken 481 prisoners.[149] The Prussian lagoon fleet suffered around 30 dead; sources give wildly different figures for Swedish casualties, fluctuating between 30 and 420.[150] Only a small number of Prussian *espings* managed to escape. In addition, some of the Prussian prisoners who were being shipped to Karlskrona succeeded in capturing the ship transporting them and used it to make their escape to Kolberg.[151] This would be the last appearance of a Prussian naval force for another century.[152] Nonetheless, German historiography has never tired of emphasizing the heroic Prussian resistance against an overwhelming and well-trained enemy. Georg Hendrich Barfot, a Swedish naval artillery officer who witnessed the battle, created a series of watercolors that serve as visual documentation of the clash on the lagoon.[153] These illustrations, numbering around fifty, are lovingly detailed, documenting ships, fortifications, landscapes, and battles. In 1760, Barfot had them bound and presented them to the Swedish statesman Baron Nils Palmstierna, probably in hopes of publication. Instead, Barfot's visual chronicle of the battle was placed in a regimental library, where it remained.

The occupation of Wollin, with the capture of 1,750 prisoners and 130 artillery pieces, marked the highpoint of Swedish operational success.[154] But winter was again approaching. Lantingshausen, the Swedish commander, offered battle to the Prussians, but they refused to accept the challenge.[155] The Prussians began withdrawing from Anklam at the beginning of November, and by the end of the year, the Swedes had again advanced north of the Peene River. Manteuffel led a Prussian advance that sought to force the Swedes back as far as Stralsund, but it was unsuccessful, and the Swedes settled into winter quarters in their part of Pomerania.

British naval blockades forced French naval forces to remain inactive, confined to the ports of Brest on the Atlantic and Toulon on the Mediterranean. In Brest, Hubert de Brienne, the Comte de Conflans (1690–1777), waited with his twenty-one ships of the line. At Toulon, Admiral Jean François Bertet, Comte de la Clue (1696–1764), commanded a Mediterranean squadron consisting of twelve ships of the line and three frigates.[156] But thirteen British ships of the line, led by Admirals Edward Boscawen and Thomas Brodick, cruised off the coast of southern France, ruining all French initiatives. La Clue was the first to venture out of port, on August 5, 1759, while the British ships were at Gibraltar for repair. After twelve days at sea, La Clue set a course for Cadiz and managed to pass through the Strait of Gibraltar, but shortly thereafter he divided his fleet in two. The breakout had quickly come to the attention of the British fleet, which set off in hot pursuit. A first battle ended with the loss of the French *Centaure*, but La Clue managed to escape, heading in the direction of Cape St. Vincent in southern Portugal. Then the wind subsided, and La Clue took shelter in a bay close to the small Portuguese town of Lagos. Here a battle took place in which the French lost four ships, including their flagship. Two French ships escaped to Rochefort, but the remainder of La Clue's fleet was trapped in Cadiz.[157]

Olaudah Equiano, the fourteen-year-old personal servant of Henry Pascal, a British naval officer, witnessed the events. He served on the middle deck of the *Namur*, a ship with ninety guns and a crew of 780, under the command of Matthew Buckle. Equiano's responsibility on the middle deck was, "with another boy, to bring powder to the aftermost gun." Here he saw how "many of my companions, in the twinkling of an eye, were dashed in pieces, and launched into eternity."[158] His biggest concern was that the ship might explode, since the powder he had to carry from one end of the deck to the other was constantly spilling onto the deck. But "the reflection that there was a time allotted for me to die as well as to be born" banished his fear and allowed him to do his job "with alacrity." Equiano's perspective on the battle does not extend beyond the cannon deck. At the end of the engagement, he reports only on the condition of the ship: "Our ship suffered very much in this engagement; for, besides the number of our killed and wounded, she was almost torn to pieces, and our rigging so much shattered, that our mizen-mast and mainyard, &c. hung over the side of the ship; so that we were obliged to get many carpenters, and others from some of the ships of the fleet."[159]

At the end of August 1759, Admiral Hawke was ordered to light a festive bonfire at sea, off the port of Brest, to publicly celebrate the victory of the Anglo-German army at Minden.[160] A gun salute at sea to symbolically declare victory was also ordered. At first, the weather was not suitable, but shortly thereafter Hawke was delighted to comply with the request, somewhat further west at St. Mathieu. The salute was carried out within sight of a French naval squadron, clearly suggesting that the *feu de joie* was intended to symbolically communicate with their opponents, as well as to boost British morale.

Despite the unfavorable strategic situation, the Duc de Choiseul stuck to his plan for an invasion of England. News of the fall of Quebec seems, in fact, to have encouraged him to take a chance on an operation that could radically change the overall war situation. Seventy transport ships were brought to the Bay of Morbihan, off Brittany, and twenty thousand soldiers were stationed at the port of Vannes. Six ships of the line were to sail from Brest to safeguard the convoy, but Conflans was eager to deploy his entire fleet to break Hawke's blockade. On November 9, westerly winds forced Hawke to make for Torbay, on the south coast of England. For Conflans, it seemed his moment had come. A few days later he ordered twenty-one ships of the line and five frigates to sea. On the evening of November 19, the French fleet approached Cape Quiberon, off the Bay of Morbihan, where a British blockade squadron was cruising. It seemed feasible to break through this small force, which consisted of five ships of the line and nine frigates under Robert Duff. But Duff divided his squadron in two, one fleeing fled north and the other south. Conflans followed in pursuit but soon realized that Hawke was approaching at high speed. He withdrew to the northern part of Quiberon Bay.

At dawn, William Spavens (1735?–1799), a seaman on board the *Vengeance*, clearly foresaw the decisive battle: "The day now cleared up, and exhibited a grand and awful sight: A powerful French fleet drawn up in fighting position, ready for action; and a British fleet with well-appointed officers, and properly manned, bearing down upon it with crowded sail, and each breast glowing with ardor to decide the grand dispute betwixt the two nations, which should have the sovereignty of the seas."[161] What followed was a chaotic sequence of maneuvers, no less clouded in gunsmoke than any crowded encounter on land, in a naval battle that continues to puzzle historians. Hawke launched his attack at nine o'clock in the morning. From then until the fall of darkness, at five o'clock in the afternoon, the British undertook various pursuit maneuvers, slowly but surely decimating the French fleet. The ships were laid out in keel line, their main battle formation. As with a battle line on land, this was designed to generate maximum firepower. On land, the formation was subject to the contingencies of unknown terrain and surprise cavalry attacks; at sea, the battle line and ships' maneuvers were at the mercy of the currents and the winds.

There was no doubt about the result of the encounter on the morning of November 21: Conflans's fleet was thrown into complete disarray, losing about one-third of its ships and twenty-five hundred sailors, compared to Hawke's loss of just two ships. The *Heros* and the *Soleil Royal*, flagship of the Marquis de Brienne, ran aground and were burned; the *Théssée* and the *Superbe* were sunk; the *Formidable* was captured by the HMS *Resolution*; and the *Juste* and the *Inflexible* were shipwrecked or lost.[162] Eight French ships of the line escaped to Rochefort,[163] while five more sailed up the Vilaine,

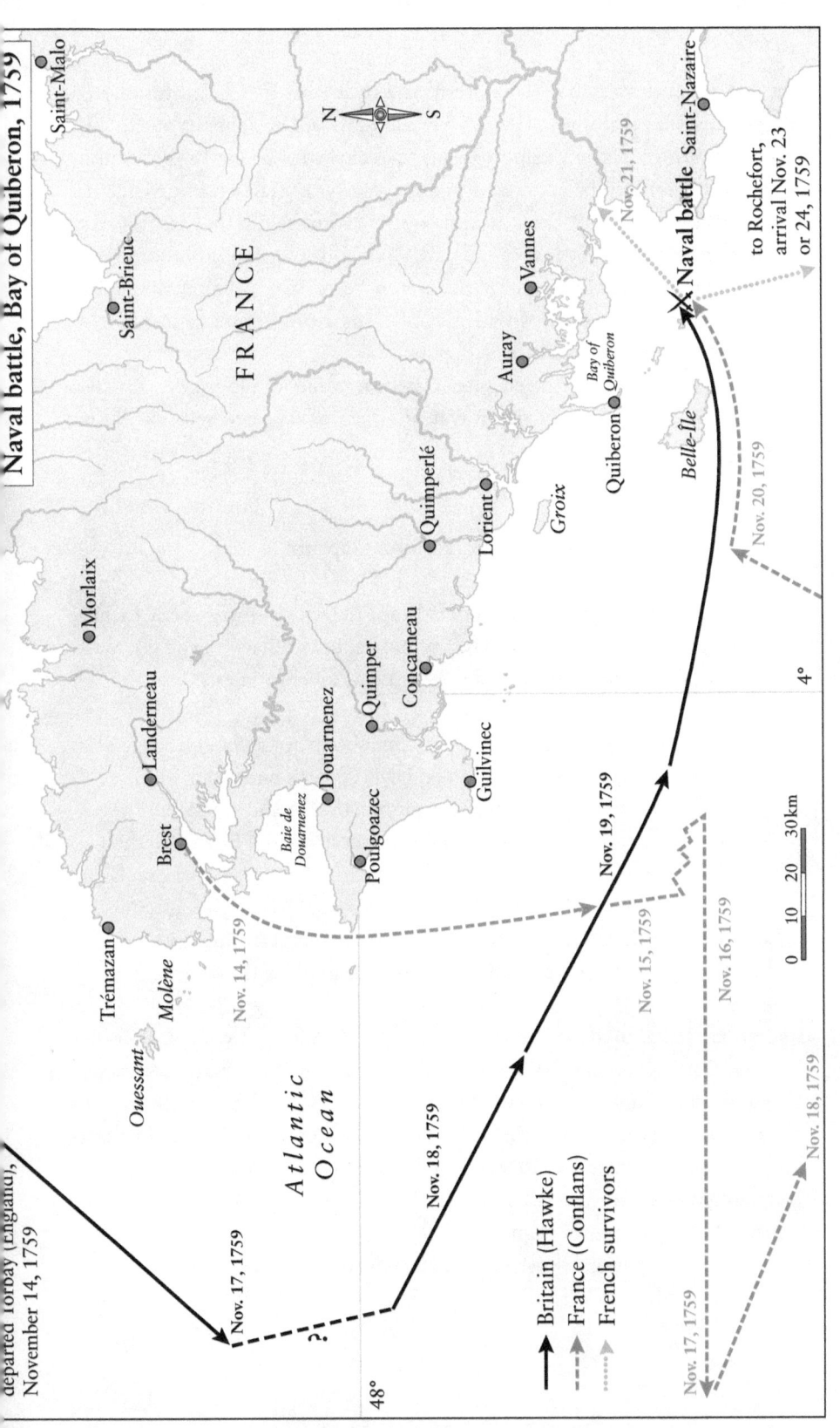

Figure 7.4 Naval battle in the Bay of Quiberon, 1759.
© Peter Palm, Berlin/Germany.

the river that flowed into the eastern part of the bay.¹⁶⁴ On November 25, French invasion plans were definitively abandoned. The captains of the ships now sheltering on the Vilaine refused to make a break for Brest, resulting in the most senior commander serving a two-year prison term, while the others were relieved of their commands.¹⁶⁵ Nonetheless, their refusal very likely prevented further loss of life and ships. Today Quiberon is considered by many to be the Trafalgar of the Seven Years' War, a battle that sealed British maritime supremacy, with serious long-term consequences for the supply of the French colonies.

Although 1759 had turned into a British annus mirabilis, the Prussian miracle was simply that of survival in the face of repeated setbacks. There was great longing for peace.

Maxen and Finck's Capture

Five weeks after the defeat at Kunersdorf, Frederick's spirits seem to have recovered, or at least he managed to put on a confident face to Voltaire, writing to him on September 22, 1759, from Eckersdorf in Silesia:

> My situation is not so desperate as is put about by my enemies. I will yet bring this campaign to a good end. My spirit is unbroken, but I see that it is about peace. [. . .] The battles of Minden and Cadix, and the loss of Canada, are arguments which may yet bring the French to their senses, after they had been confused by toxic Austrian hellebore. All I ask for is peace, but I desire no shameful peace. After fighting against all Europe with success, it would be all too shameful a thing if I should lose by the stroke of a pen what I have claimed with the sword."¹⁶⁶

For the Prussian army, the miracle year of 1759 ended with yet another disaster. On November 20, Prussia and Austria fought a battle at Maxen, about fourteen miles from Dresden, which ended in the capture of over eleven thousand Prussian soldiers.¹⁶⁷ The Prussian commander was Lieutenant General Friedrich August von Finck (1718–1766), whose name came to be synonymous with the failed undertaking, later derisively dubbed Finckenfang (Finck's Capture) (figure 7.5).

Among the prisoners taken that day were two important witnesses: the Prussian officer Carl Wilhelm von Hülsen and the Prussian musketeer

Figure 7.5 Finck Lays His Sword Before Daun After the Battle of Maxen. Painting by Hyacinth de La Pegna (between 1759 and 1762).
© Heeresgeschichtliches Museum, Wien.

Johann Jacob Dominicus, also a chronicler of Lobositz, Rossbach, and Kunersdorf. The latter reports on his capture: "We had to step Forward. Then we were told that we were Prisoners, that we could keep our Knapsacks and our things, but we would have to lay down our Firearms and sabretaches. Major Iselstein gave the command: 'Attention, present arms!' and we threw them down, along with our Sabers and Sabertaches." Because of the cold weather, Field Marshal Friedrich Herzog von Zweybrücken (1724–1767), commander of the Imperial forces, ordered that tents and curtains be distributed to the prisoners. Austrian mockery of the prisoners ensued: "When that was done, we had to turn to the right, and then the Austrians had formed a square, into which they drove us. The Austrians were so happy, laughing out loud and saying: 'Ha ha! This is how we guard you; had the day been longer, we would have driven you into the Elbe.'"[168] Hülsen describes surrender in terms of profound dishonor: "I embraced Lieutenant von Gaudy, and we wept bitterly, each clasped to the other: 'Farewell, honor! Fortune, adieu!' we exclaimed in profound despair."[169] At Dresden, the first stop on the prisoners' journey, Hülsen realized he would not soon see his homeland again, since he was to be transported to a far-off prison camp: "What a prospect lay before me! To be brought as a prisoner to an entirely foreign and superstitious country rendered my soul miserable, and yet I would come to experience that everywhere I go, God is with me!"[170] The "foreign and superstitious" country mentioned is Austria. Both of the prisoners would return at the end of the war, unlike very many others. "Hundreds, if not thousands," of prisoners taken at Maxen died of dysentery while passing through Lower Styria to Croatia and were buried in mass graves at the Rannerhof, close to Zagreb.[171]

Frederick regarded the defeat as an affront, for which he would not forgive his men. On November 22, he wrote to the Marquis d'Argens: "I am so numbed by the disaster that befell General Finck and simply cannot seem to recover from it. I am quite overcome, it cuts me to the core."[172] On the same day, he wrote to Finckenstein, his minister: "You must attempt, with regard to the public, as much as possible to gloss over this disaster."[173] This contrasted with the scene in Vienna, where the news was received with great enthusiasm. Khevenhüller-Metsch's diary notes that Colonel Reizenstein and Major Prince Leopold Lobkowicz arrived at court on Saturday, November 24, accompanied by twenty-four postilions blowing trumpets, to deliver news of "first, the happy events at Maxen, and second, the unexpected and glorious Consequences of the same." The imperial couple entered the Hall of Mirrors, where they allowed "all present—foreigners and natives—to enter and kiss the hand to congratulate them."[174] A Te Deum was sung that Sunday in celebration of the victory.

Peace at Last? A Missed Chance at Augsburg

That same Sunday, November 25, 1759, at Rijswijk Castle, close to The Hague, Great Britain and Prussia delivered a proposal to France and Austria for a peace congress to be held at Augsburg. The message was delivered through Duke Louis Ernest of Brunswick-Lüneburg (1718–1788), captain general of the Netherlands.[175] Prussian diplomats in London had been discussing the suggestion at length since June, prompted by Frederick's increasingly desperate situation.[176] But the proposal still came too early for the British; the situation in the North American theater remained uncertain and would need to be improved in order to negotiate a peace agreement from a position of superiority. There were no serious discussions of a peace proposal until the end of September, when the Prussian diplomats Dodo Heinrich zu Knyphausen (1729–1789) and Abraham Louis Michell met with Pitt, Lord Holdernesse, and the Duke of Newcastle in London.[177] Maria Theresa, strengthened by Finck's Capture, likewise hoped that further military success would improve her bargaining position, since Prussia was offering only the status quo ante bellum. For Austria, the return of Silesia was essential.[178] Assessing the expectations of the various parties, the veteran Danish foreign minister Johann Hartwig Ernst, Count von Bernstorff (1712–1772), proved particularly shrewd. In a letter to Choiseul of December 18, 1759, he writes: "The King of England wants to win, the King of Prussia wants not to lose, because if he does not lose, he will have won everything."[179]

One particularly illustrious eighteenth-century figure now made an appearance as a possible diplomat at peace talks. Thanks to the intervention of a Portuguese friend, Giacomo Casanova (1725–1798), the Venetian "adventurer," was to represent the kingdom of Portugal at the planned conference in Augsburg, where, in fact, he sojourned from August until December 1761.[180] The previous year Casanova had visited Voltaire at Geneva. While at Augsburg, Casanova may well have conversed with Gottfried Achenwall (1719–1772), a prominent German jurist and statistician, one of many others also awaiting the hypothetical conference.

As one of the most resolutely antiwar intellectuals of his time, Voltaire had repeatedly articulated the desire for peace. In this vein, he had written to Luise Dorothée von Sachsen-Gotha on May 26, 1758:

> May it come soon, this peace that is so desirable for peoples and even for princes! War ruins great and small to enrich those who rob courts and armies in the guise of serving them. Europe laments while merchants of food, fodder, and hospitals grow fat on public misfortune. It is said that the army known as the Imperial Army died of exhaustion and nothing was left of it; most soldiers returned home to become workers or gardeners: I wish that all the soldiers in the world should take that road. The earth needs cultivation more than it needs drenching in blood.[181]

In a letter of October 7, Luise Dorothée explicitly addresses Voltaire's criticism but also references the global dimension of the war, which otherwise plays little role in their correspondence: "One might bet at one hundred to one, that none of the belligerent powers will be the victor in this turmoil, the only benefit will be to various dishonorable characters, such as food suppliers and moneylenders. It is really a sin that so many regions are devastated for the love of these wretched people, with weapons and the fire of war carried into all four regions of the world, to bring grief to peoples and render destruction and despair universal."[182] The "dishonorable characters" mentioned here would likely include men such as Pierre de Rigaud de Vaudreuil (1698–1778), François Bigot (1703–1778), Joseph Michel Cadet (1719–1781), Carl Heinrich von Schimmelmann, Franz Balthasar Schönberg from Brenkenhoff (1723–1780), David Splitgerber (1683–1764), Peter Taylor (1714–1777), and Richard Oswald (1705–1784)—all figures to whom we will return later in this book.[183] Seen from a diachronic perspective on history, it is worth noting that both Voltaire and Luise Dorothée considered the current war far more terrible than the Thirty Years' War, which Voltaire describes as "infinitely less murderous" and Luise Dorothée as "a mere farce compared to this."[184]

The Augsburg Peace Congress never took place. The *Hamburgische Correspondent* reported from Paris on January 8, 1761: "Although peace is spoken of here, at the same time one witnesses very great preparations for a bloody campaign." Among others, the Spanish ambassador to London let it be known that his Catholic majesty was well inclined "at any time to offer the hand to all powers, in order to put out the fire that has consumed almost all four continents." But for the moment no end to the fighting was in sight: "Therefore, in the War, this year's Campaign at least will indeed take place."[185]

CHAPTER VIII

As Mighty As the Sword

The Media War

The greatest media event of 1755 was unquestionably the Lisbon earthquake, which took place on November 1, several months after the Seven Years' War had begun in the faraway forests of North America.[1] The earthquake triggered a tsunami and set off an enormous fire that raced through the Portuguese capital, killing between thirty and one hundred thousand people. The disaster profoundly disturbed European society, prompting, among other things, a renewed philosophical interest in questions of theodicy. But just two years later the war in the Holy Roman Empire had almost completely supplanted the earthquake as the media's main preoccupation, as can be traced by the catalogs issued for the Leipzig trade fair.[2] War reporting was an essential driver of eighteenth-century "structural transformation in the public sphere."[3]

A New Carthage?

In August 1756, the French *Journal encyclopédique* observed: "It may be difficult to fathom in years to come, that the war between the English and French is fought in just as lively a fashion on paper as it is on the high seas."[4] The main news publication of the French crown was *La Gazette*; it was also the oldest newspaper in France, in existence since 1631 (the name was changed to *Gazette de France* in 1762).[5] As was generally the case at this time, its reporting was categorized by place of origin. Significantly, its information on North America and India always came via London, since direct communication by sea was impeded by the British naval blockade. For this reason, its coverage of North America was comparatively rare and reports from India even more so.[6] In general, the *Gazette*'s reporting was characterized by a lag of between four and eleven days, and it tended to run shorter articles than the equivalent *Gazettes* elsewhere in Europe: the *Gazettes d'Utrecht, de Cologne, d'Amsterdam*, and *de Bruxelles*.[7]

Journalistic analogies between the war and the Roman-Carthaginian conflict were very popular—above all, in France. The analogy cast Britain as Carthage: commercially successful but doomed to defeat and destruction.[8] The main stereotype applied to the British was not sectarian but rather invoked an image of "barbarians," suggesting they were alike in nature to Native Americans.[9] In 1760, this was vividly expressed in *Les sauvages de l'Europe*, a novel by Robert-Martin Lesuire (1737–1815), published in English translation in 1764.[10] But the decisive change in this conflict's modernization of political propaganda was that the entire British nation was identified as France's antagonist, where previously the focus would have been on a specific foreign monarch.[11] The war was thus presented as a kind of patriotic competition between nations.

In terms of the colonies, the content of French pamphleteering had three phases, which also apply to the image of France's Native American allies. At first, writers still had some French successes to celebrate—for example, the capture of Fort Oswego. In this context, Indians were described as particularly dangerous—and thus valuable as partners.[12] In the years that followed, as defeat followed defeat, the main focus shifted to British wrongdoing, which served to reinforce old resentments. In a third phase, after the loss of Quebec, reports declined in frequency and more often depicted France's Native American allies as unreliable turncoats, the real culprits in French defeats. The British were certainly not the only targets of French propaganda. On April 21, 1757, Voltaire wrote to Luise Dorothée von Sachsen-Gotha: "There are more diatribes against the King of Prussia in prose and verse than regiments marching against him."[13] Louise Dorothée replied on May 3, suggesting she "doubted that the king pays any attention to the diatribes against him. He is concerned with too many things of importance for these idiocies to make an impression, or do harm to his spirit."[14]

More than any other European country, eighteenth-century Britain enjoyed a wide range of journalism, with writers benefiting from the continent's greatest freedom of expression.[15] Publications used a variety of formats during the war: "essay journals" like *Test*, *Contest*, and *Monitor* were significant, as were "moral weeklies" and gazettes like the *London Gazette*.[16] Texts published in essay journals were often recirculated in the gazettes. The timeliness and reliability of information took on extra significance during wartime. To obtain information quickly, many newspapers kept a network of correspondents, which very likely included British envoys overseas, who wrote regular reports on the situation. These included Andrew Mitchell in Prussia, Robert Keith in Austria, and Hanbury Williams in Russia.[17]

Between 1756 and 1758, Britain completed its foreign policy transformation from the "old system," involving the alliance with Austria, to the "new system," which switched its allegiance to Prussia. Journalism played an essential role in this process, with a first high point seen in the coverage of the second Treaty of Westminster, signed on April 11, 1758.[18] The treaty guaranteed Britain would pay Prussia annual subsidies of some 670,000 pounds; we might also understand this as a way to convert Frederick II's symbolic capital—his renown within the British public sphere—into hard cash.

On the other hand, Israel Mauduit's (1708–1787) 1760 pamphlet *Considerations on the Present German War*, which made the case against further involvement in Germany, also exerted considerable influence on public opinion. Mauduit, a London merchant and the representative in Britain of the commonwealth of Massachusetts, sold fifty thousand copies in a few months, going through no fewer than six editions.[19] It was one of the most effective British political pamphlets of the eighteenth century and continued to influence attitudes toward Prussia right up to the end of the conflict.[20] It was in Britain's interests to support a German civil war, Mauduit argued, but, in fact, France was Britain's real enemy and would remain so. If subsidies were paid to Prussia, this could best be described as "tribute money." Frederick was merely "the Newspapers' hero." Any notion that Britain was fighting for the Protestant cause was empty propaganda, nothing more. With great clarity, his argument separates the "German war" from the "English war." For Britain, he suggests, the only solution was what would later be termed "splendid isolation," along with a stronger navy.

News of overseas victories regularly prompted waves of enthusiastic public celebration across Britain.[21] These celebrations took on a new quality during this period—above all, because they emerged spontaneously from the population at large rather than being prompted by the authorities. Public celebrations were primarily the work of the emerging, ambitious urban middle class: traders, merchants, manufacturers, and civil servants.[22] But the popular appropriation of war news and the creation of public heroes were greatly fueled by the popular press, manufactured artifacts, and public celebrations. Thomas Turner—a Sussex shopkeeper who has become an iconic figure in eighteenth-century British media reception—read both the local *Sussex Weekly Advertiser* and the *London Gazette*.[23] The war events recorded by Turner range from the loss of Menorca in 1756 to the Battle of Krefeld in 1758 and the conquest of Montreal in 1760.[24] But two news items stand out clearly: Prussia's 1757 victory at Rossbach and the conquest of Quebec in 1759.

However, the cosmopolitan ideals of the European scholarly republic continued to exert some influence in Britain, ubiquitous Francophobia notwithstanding. The primary example was the *Critical Review*, published by the Scottish writer and doctor Tobias Smollett (1721–1771), a periodical that showed it was possible for British reviewers to provide balanced, even laudatory, accounts of French literature, despite the many failings of the British press.[25]

Edward Gibbon's diaries assiduously record news from theaters of war around the world, including diaries for the years he spent in England, 1758–1763. Better known as one of the great historians of his era, he observed that his understanding of Roman military history had benefited greatly from his time in the Hampshire militia in the early 1760s, as evidenced by his enormous *Decline and Fall of the Roman Empire*. While in service, he noted the regular gun salutes fired for British victories, including the victory at the Battle of Vellinghausen in 1761 and the capture of Havana in 1762.[26]

The year 1760 saw broad public debate in Britain over the fate of Canada and Guadeloupe in any peace agreement.[27] The discussion was usually structured in terms of a choice of alternatives, an either/or, and is thus very revealing about contemporary economic mentalities, as well as fantasies of imperial order. In a nutshell, the debate came down to "Sugar or Furs?" The discussion began in earnest in January 1760, with the pro-Canada essay *Letter Addressed to Two Great Men, on the Prospect of Peace, and on the Terms Necessary to Be Insisted Upon in the Negotiation*, attributed to John Douglas (1721–1807), a protégé of Lord Bath and later a bishop.[28] The counterargument came in *An Answer to the Letter*, which made the case for Britain simply retaining all territories it had conquered in the Americas.[29] A third position was to be found in *Remarks on the Letter*, which went through several editions and made the case for the unconditional retention of Guadeloupe.[30] The debate grew more heated with the appearance of still another pamphlet, *A Letter to the People of England*, which called for Britain to hold onto Canada, even if it meant giving up all its West Indian holdings. Benjamin Franklin responded to the last intervention with his own essay, which has come to be known as the Canada Pamphlet.[31]

By the time peace was made in 1763, about forty more pamphlets had been published on this subject. What were their arguments? One major point made in support of the West Indies was that they could supply all of Britain's growing daily sugar needs, while Canada produced only "a few fur Hats," a phrase echoing Voltaire's barbs against Canadian fields yielding rich harvests of snow.[32] The pro-Canada faction argued that the sugar trade could function without Guadeloupe, whereas Canada was essential to the fur trade. Moreover, it was said, the Canadian territories would produce more useful goods in the future, and if a "general empire" could be established in all of North America, the sugar islands could be picked off at a time of Britain's choosing. Supporters further claimed the climate of a northern colony would be more suited to the development of the "white race."[33] Other arguments included possible movements toward independence among the American colonies and the question of the British Empire's economic independence. Ultimately, the pro-Canada lobby prevailed in 1763, leaving the empire, for the moment, rich in forests and agricultural land but short of sugar.[34]

Developments in journalism went hand in hand with the emergence of new kinds of patriotism. Media-driven patriotic feeling was a phenomenon across Europe, affecting France as much as it did Britain and Prussia.[35] Russian soldiers could be moved by a concept like Fatherland (*Otečestvo*), which also served to shore up political legitimation.[36] However, there was no personified focus for popular Russian patriotism at this point, no one to fill the role played by Frederick in Prussian patriotic sentiment. The Fatherland was without its empress.

The "King of Press-ia" Fights a Newspaper War

Fredericks "Political Testament" of 1768 suggested that in the century of Enlightenment, journalism had become something akin to the war's true reality: "Had we not been forced to fight against all of Europe, we would be able to protect our borders, so that peaceful citizens could be left calm and undisturbed in their homes and would not be aware that their nation is involved in fighting, if they did not learn it from war reporting."[37]

The sentence—or more precisely, the second half of the sentence—has been cited many times as exemplifying the eighteenth-century "tamed Bellona," meaning the population was supposedly spared much of the suffering of war, especially compared to the Thirty Years' War. As the German historian Gerhard Ritter put it: "Here the triumph of technical virtuosity was blended with the victory of humanitarianism. Bellona, the furious goddess of war, was to be rendered tractable, tamed like a kitten on the hearth."[38] But the quotation also refers to a specific media culture, boosted by massive demand for war information, in which journalism itself became a key part of fighting a war. Many collections of essays, reports, and pamphlets were published during the Seven Years' War, which today provide important sources for historians. The most important of these collections include the *Teutsche Kriegs-Canzley*, published in Regensburg by Leopold Montag (1709–1783); the *Danziger Beyträge*, edited by Gottlob Naumann (1718–1798), a regimental quartermaster in Berlin; and *Acta Publica*, published in Vienna by Johann Thomas Trattner (1717–1798).[39] Of these, the *Kriegs-Canzley* covers the war only in and around the Holy Roman Empire, whereas the *Danziger Beyträge* is genuinely global in its reporting.

Focusing solely on developments within the empire, we can roughly divide newspapers and other media into three categories.[40] First, there were the official organs of the press in both Prussia and Austria, including the *Berlinische Nachrichten*, the *Magdeburgische Zeitung*, and the *Wiener Diarium*.[41] The second category consisted of nonofficial newspapers published in any given territory, which by law had to model their coverage on the carefully vetted content in official publications. In a place like Halle, a provincial city in Prussia, a royal decree of November 30, 1759, specified: "News shall not be Published of our own war Operations nor those of the Enemy, nor of any such Undertakings, except those already Published in our local Newspapers, which have been Censored with care."[42] The third category was made up of publications from the autonomous cities of the empire. These publications were subordinate to neither of the two alliances and thus were both difficult to control and in a better position to publish particularly controversial material. In this context, it is worth mentioning the *Hamburgische unpartheyische Correspondent* in Hamburg and the *Reichs Post-Reuter* in nearby Altona, as well as the *Gazette de Cologne*. Austria immediately banned all Berlin newspapers at the outset of the war in 1756, but Prussian reaction was considerably slower. In 1759, the Prussian government banned newspapers from Vienna, Prague, Frankfurt, Cologne, Regensburg, Brussels, and other cities in the Holy Roman Empire, the only exceptions being the newspapers from Hamburg and Altona.[43] By the mid-eighteenth century, the North American colonies had developed their own media landscape;[44] here cruelties inflicted by Native Americans were a central theme.[45] But the gaze of the colonial press extended far beyond local events, also reporting on the latest developments in Europe. The *Pennsylvania Gazette*, in particular, carried wide coverage of European affairs.[46]

The rapid dissemination of news became a crucial political instrument; Frederick grasped this better than almost any of his contemporaries.[47] Significantly enough, a joke doing the rounds in Hamburg in 1757 claimed it was said in Berlin that Frederick should be called "King of Press-ia [. . .] because he has kept the printing presses in constant motion, and because it was he who said 'I have ranged against me several kings and many newspapermen.'"[48] But Frederick knew very well that the media could not win a war on their own. On February 19, 1760, he wrote to the Marquis d'Argens, with whom he maintained a regular correspondence about his poems and pamphlets: "Alas the war will be decided with the saber, not the pen. Were it a matter only of the written word, we would have long since have hunted down these Austrians, Russians, Imperials, and Swedes."[49]

A Writers' War

The war had a substantial impact on Europe's various public spheres, including its literary, artistic, and scholarly milieus. Among other things, it served as a catalyst for patriotic discourse.[50] Many authors of the German Enlightenment who spoke out about the war had themselves been involved in it, whether as victims or profiteers or in some other respect.[51] They often had astonishingly detailed military knowledge, and in keeping with their Enlightenment values, they wrestled intellectually with the war they saw all around them.[52] Literary scholarship has tended to address this material in terms of the long-term "emergence of a sense of nationhood," whereas historiographical perspectives tend to focus more on the war's mobilization effects.[53] Historical approaches also differentiate between the degrees of chauvinism in different territories and specific local constellations of friend and enemy.[54] The conflict obliged people to take a position. Almost everyone was forced to make some kind of statement; several figures from the German Enlightenment, otherwise peacefully minded, came out with strikingly aggressive rhetoric during the war. This sentiment found expression in plays, pamphlets, and sermons, as well as in music and poetry.[55] Sermons hailing victories and expressing gratitude sounded from the pulpit, with many clergymen offering euphoric accompaniment to the war. Thus, August Friedrich Wilhelm Sack (1730–1786), preacher to the court at Berlin, repeatedly sang the praises of Prussia's "Old Testament victories."[56] Voltaire directed his undiluted scorn at pastors whose sermons trumpeted victory in kitsch Old Testament language: "Everywhere a certain number of haranguers are paid to celebrate these bloody occasions. [. . .] They all talk at length and cite, apropos of a battle in the Wetterau, something that happened in Palestine a long time ago."[57]

German writers associated with the war include Ewald von Kleist, Gotthold Ephraim Lessing, Moses Mendelssohn, Christian Fürchtegott Gellert, and Johann Wilhelm Ludwig Gleim, all of whom were close followers of events. Gellert (1715–1769) was reputed to be "unworldly and quite unwarlike."[58] Nonetheless, he wrote the following to an unnamed friend on September 21, 1757: "For your political News I thank you indeed. Never in forty years have I read so many News-papers as in the last 4 weeks: and I will readily go to [the nearby village of] Meineweh and wait my time in the Tavern until the arrival of the Post."[59] The Berlin philosopher Mendelssohn (1729–1786) described the aesthetic fascination of battles, with the unnamed battlefield most probably referring to Kunersdorf: "After the bloodbath at ★★★ all our citizens hurried to view the corpse-strewn battlefield. Even the wise man, who previously would happily have given his life to prevent the outrage, now wades through human blood, and feels an awful shudder of delight from this most terrible place."[60]

Gleim's *Grenadier Songs* caused a particular sensation. Published in 1758, the book's full title was *Prussian War Songs by a Grenadier in the Campaigns of 1756 and 1757*.[61] The songs attempt to recreate the "authentic" language of a simple grenadier; the project drew more or less direct inspiration from actual letters sent by soldiers through the military mails. This was supposedly done with the help of Count Christian Ernst zu Stolberg-Wernigerode (1691–1771),[62] who had copies made of letters written by warrant officers in the Anhalt-Dessau and Hülsen regiments. Gleim, who was secretary of the Halberstadt Cathedral Chapter and a close associate of the count, gained access to these copies. In this way, the Prussian writer turned soldiers' interpretations of the war into poetry, although the process was less likely to work in reverse. Thus, in 1766 Thomas Abbt writes in *Vom Verdienste*

(Of merit): "Had Gleim managed to put these War Songs of the Prussian Grenadier into the hands of the common soldier, then he would, at least in the Prussian states, have received the highest rank among the edifying poets."[63] However, Abbt suggests that only Gellert's poetry has had this effect across "all of Germany."

Gleim's war songs did enjoy some popular success, not least because they transformed the Pietist soldiers of his letters into chauvinist warmongers. For the literati, the songs also highlighted the brutalization of ordinary language already taking place. Thus, Gleim's "Battlesong at the Launch of the 1757 Campaign" (Schlachtgesang bei Eröffnung des Feldzuges 1757) includes these words: "From your skulls / We shall soon drink / Your own sweet / Hungarian wine! / Bottled shall it be / in our field panniers."[64] His "Victory Song After the Battle of Prague" (Siegeslied nach der Schlacht bei Prag) is no less bloody: "Red his sword was / and with every step / flowed thick Pandur blood / so through the seven trenches / we hunt the bearskin caps / and there Frederick / your Grenadiers piled corpses high."[65] In the early part of the war, it was mainly Hungarians and Pandurs who were described with this language of brutal slaughter. But Adolph Ortmann's *Patriotic Letters* of 1758 also includes images of the Russians and their irregular auxiliaries, Cossacks and Kalmyks.[66] It is no surprise that Ortmann's text was republished in 1943 as part of Nazi war propaganda.[67] In 1758, his principles were entirely clear; he believed Russians were barbarians because they lacked Christian religion: "But whence the cursed rages of these human Monsters? What source this Anger?—A void, nothing more, a void where the true and living knowledge of God should be! This deficiency makes them a people without Feeling. And for just this same reason, a Hottentot is a Hottentot, a Cannibale a Cannibale."[68] In the same year, Gleim writes lines like these: "Eat that, Kalmucks and Cossacks! / [. . .] Your Empire's Tyrants, its Executioners / not Human yet, the Kalmucks and Cossacks, are sent / to the land of humans / there to Rage against them / and to be the devils of your armies."[69]

Major battles often served to crystallize patriotically tinged poetry and other literary works. Several writers celebrated the Battle of Zorndorf in the service of Prussian propaganda. In early September 1758, Gleim wrote to Johann Peter Uz, lamenting that newspaper coverage of Zorndorf made the victory seem "not nearly as large as it actually is."[70] Gleim himself hymned the battle in a poem titled "The Grenadier to the Muse of War, Written After the Victory at Zorndorf on August 25, 1758."[71] In 1759, publication began of the review journal *Letters on Recent Literature* (Briefe, die neueste Literatur betreffend), purportedly edited by an officer wounded at Zorndorf but, in fact, published by the Berlin writer and bookseller Friedrich Nicolai (1733–1811). The officer was Nicolai's fictional creation: The figure supplied a fictional frame story and a means of preserving Nicolai's own anonymity but also reveals how profoundly the battle had been anchored in contemporary consciousness, becoming a byword for military heroism.[72] Another hint of this can be found in Gellert's well-known "Hussar Letter," in which the writer recounts a curious visit from a Prussian hussar who had fought near Zorndorf and who wanted Gellert to share in his plunder.[73] Abbt's well-known tract "On Dying for the Fatherland" (Vom Tode für das Vaterland), published in 1761, invokes the battle thus: "How holy our Descendants shall hold the fields of Zorndorf and Kunersdorf! Trembling sorrow and shudders of awe shall pass through them, when their foot treads upon the fallen gravestones, whereunder lie these heirs of Epaminondes."[74]

Anna-Louise Karsch (1722–1791) was an anomaly in the male-dominated literary world of the time. She seemed to achieve fame almost overnight in 1761, becoming a highly fashionable literary figure in Berlin, Magdeburg, and Halberstadt.[75] Her poem "Victory of the King at Torgau," published in the *Magdeburgische Zeitung* on February 7, 1761, prompted a letter to the same newspaper one week later: "The recently published victory Poems, written by the wife of a Glogau Tailor, had a quite unexpected Effect on the sensibility of various Magdeburg patriots of good taste. The Poetess should be aware, that she is read here with Admiration and applause."[76] Karsch was in regular correspondence with Gleim, who published a selection of her poems in 1764, permitting her to participate more directly in patriotic literary circles.

Within the Holy Roman Empire, a clear cultural disparity existed between Protestant Prussia and Catholic Austria in terms both of propaganda and war poetry.[77] The majority of propaganda texts and martial poetry were written by Protestants from northern and central Germany, thus the corpus of pro-Prussian works is larger.[78] The Austrian side had a much smaller number of writers—notably, Michael Denis (1729–1800), a Viennese Jesuit.[79] He railed against foreign troops in his collection *Poetic Images of Most Warlike Events in Europe Since the Year 1756*, which serves as a kind of counterpart to Gleim's grenadier poems, although Denis's texts contain fewer diatribes against the enemy. His poems sometimes operate on a metalevel, as when he condemns enemy war propaganda: "I am not alone in laughing / at Prussia's lust for fame / the victory at Lowositz they dreamed up. / Little by little, truth dawns on the clever world / those for whom the Postman's bell / heralds emotions of deception and betrayal."[80] He mocks the victories claimed by Prussia, citing their high casualties: "The Austrian gave way / And what forced him so to yield? / Was it Frederick's Cavalry, who so quickly lost their Bearings? / If the king was victorious, where are his victory signs? / [. . .] You Braggarts! [. . .] Clearly most of you / Remained on the Field of Battle."[81]

The global Franco-British confrontation was put into musical form in the work of Georg Philipp Telemann (1681–1767), the probable composer of a 1763 cantata (TWV 13:20) entitled "Hannover siegt, der Franzmann liegt" (Hanover is victorious, the Frenchman lies prostrate).[82] Music historians previously believed the work to have been written in response to one or more of the Battles of Krefeld (1758), Minden (1759), and Vellinghausen (1761), but, in fact, it was probably not composed until 1763 to mark the final peace treaty. The cantata contains seven parts; of these, the final movement—titled "Gassenhauer" (Popular song)—makes the clearest reference to British victories: "Senegal and Cape Breton / have given France's realm / two deep wounds indeed."

It is also possible to discern a kind of "cold war," running in parallel to the actual fighting, in the translations of theoretical texts on war. Anton Leopold von Oelsnitz, a Prussian lieutenant, translated into German a well-known book of commentary on the Greek historian Polybios, authored by the French military theorist Chevalier Jean-Charles de Folard (1669–1752). Oelsnitz used his preface to boast of being a "Royal Prussian officer," claiming that the Prussian military had elevated "the art of war to its highest Extent."[83] In 1757, soon after the publication of the third volume, Oelsnitz's elder brother, Wilhelm Ludwig von Oelsnitz, died of wounds he suffered at the Battle of Prague. This prompted Johann Theobald Bion, an Austrian artillery captain, to begin his own translation, apparently thinking the translator had died and left the work unfinished. Bion took the opportunity to tweak Oelsnitz's self-description, noting sardonically that the Prussian author could rest assured "he shall indeed be remembered, and at less expense, in the Elysian fields."[84]

Andreas Belach, author of a Christian interpretation of the siege of his home city of Breslau discussed earlier, was an outsider in this field of war literature. In 1760, he published a much darker work, *Nachtgedanken bey einer gefährlichen Reise in Kriegszeiten* (Night thoughts on a dangerous journey in wartime), a cross between a travelogue and a didactic poem that takes the reader through the ruins of Silesia.[85] Religious pamphlets that admonished their readers to do penance used dramatic pictures of battlefield casualties, invoked death as the great equalizer, and demanded that the deaths of common soldiers be respected: "Learn here! Ye princes and generals! Here worldly greatness is no help, nor the boasting of such: here what counts is the common Man, he is what counts in Fights and Battles; he deserves not your Scorn."[86] With a couple of major exceptions, the art, music, and literature of the time contained no real antiwar aesthetic as we would understand it today. Neither Lessing nor Chodowiecki nor Telemann saw the rightness of wartime violence to be an issue as such, at least not while the war was still going on. This is another reason why Voltaire's *Candide* is such a striking exception within contemporary artistic production.[87]

The War of Images

The Seven Years' War also did not see the production of antiwar art as we might understand it today. A noticeable gap lies between Jacques Callot's *Les Grandes Misères de la Guerre* from the Thirty Years' War and Goya's *Los Desastres de la Guerra*, created in response to the Napoleonic campaigns. But the mid-eighteenth century was never short of visual interpretations of contemporary events.[88] William Hogarth in Britain and Daniel Chodowiecki (1726–1801) in Prussia both created important visual representations of the war and its protagonists, although sometimes this work was published considerably later, as with Chodowiecki.[89] British caricatures circulated during the war itself, and some seem quite modern in their radicalism,[90] taking aim, above all, at leading London politicians like William Pitt and Lord Bute. Francis Hayman (1708–1776) created four large images for the rotunda of Vauxhall Gardens in 1760 or 1761, of which two depicted recent military successes, the victory at Plassey in 1757 and the surrender of Montreal in 1760.[91] However, many large-format pictures that even today shape the memory of the British Empire's global successes were created after the war had ended—most importantly, Benjamin West's *The Death of General Wolfe* (1770).[92]

There were many images of contemporary events published in Germany, including numerous allegorical representations, with a very wide range of audiences in terms of political loyalty. One particularly popular genre was the game allegory, used to portray the coexistence and rivalry of the European powers. Although later literary and historiographical works would depict Frederick and Maria Theresa as perfect opposites, media representations during the war itself were far more asymmetrical. The later images pitted the nonreligious Prussian king against the deeply religious Habsburgs, the childless Frederick against the fecund Maria Theresa, the battlefield *roi connétable* against the immobile queen of Hungary, aggression against passivity, cool rationalism against baroque emotionality, and so on.[93] But during the war itself, these dichotomies were not yet so clearly entrenched. When the two were juxtaposed in pictures or song, images of play and competition tended to dominate. Allegories of games illustrated the ups and downs of the fortunes of war, its uncertain outcome, and the complex web that linked the warring parties. The particular game referred to in such images could be a political masquerade ball, a tournament, a chess match, a card game like faro, or a game of dice or billiards.[94] The image of Frederick and Maria Theresa dancing together was particularly popular: The trope seems to have circulated primarily orally, but it was noted in the writings of several contemporaries.[95] On November 14, 1757, an anonymous diarist from Freiberg in Saxony noted: "Fritz was dancing recently at Collin, and fell over in the dance, but did not fall entirely, he's still on his feet and he's dancing again: at Rossbach he danced a Menuet, at Lissa a ballet. Theresia fell down, and has not danced since. Theresia is delicate, willing, and clever, but for all that, is but a Woman."[96] The diary quickly moves on to Tsarina Elisabeth and Madame de Pompadour: "Elisabeth is mild, assiduous, and quick / but an old Virgin. The Bombadour is chaste, oft betimes saying stupid things / Tres faciunt collegium." A year later we find the same rhymes quoted in the correspondence of Landgravine Caroline von Hessen-Darmstadt and in a letter from Georg Friedrich Meier, a Halle philosophy professor, to Gleim of September 15, 1758. Meier encloses the text of the rhyme with his letter, also thanking Gleim for sending him a copy of his *Songs of a Prussian Grenadier*.[97]

In terms of engraving, Catholic countries had very few artists to compare with Hogarth or Chodowiecki; even today, this substantial asymmetry exerts significant influence on our own visual memory of the Seven Years' War. But some large oil paintings of key battles were commissioned, both during the war and shortly afterward, especially in Austria. August Querfurt's (1696–1761) paintings of the Battle of Kolin in 1757 should be mentioned in this context,[98] as well as a series of paintings by Hyacinth de la Pegna (1706–1772), depicting the Battle of Hochkirch and the Prussian surrender of arms at Maxen in November 1759 (see figure 7.5). Franz Paul Findenigg (1726–1771) created paintings of Hochkirch burning on the morning after the battle,[99] of Finck's Capture at Maxen,[100] and of the raising of Prussia's siege of Olomouc on July 2, 1758, while Johann Christian Brand (1722–1795) painted a notable representation of the Battle of Hochkirch.[101] Kolin, Hochkirch, and Maxen clearly played a particularly important role in Austrian battle iconography. Querfurt's representation of Kolin is typical of what might be called topographical-analytical battlefield painting. However, the way in which the two armies line up geometrically, receding deep into the landscape, is somewhat atypical of Querfurt's style, which tends to be more focused on individual scenes. This painting, however, is intended to provide an overview of the battle as a whole; it bears some relation to battle plans and maps, thanks to the additional geometric figures and letters inserted into the image. We know little about the painting's commissioning and ownership—only that it was originally the property of Field Marshal Daun himself. In 1763, an entire room in the Austrian castle of Hainfeld, forty miles west of Vienna, was painted with images celebrating Laudon, including representations of events at Landeshut, Glatz, Hochkirch, Schweidmitz, Kunersdorf, and Domstadtl.[102]

The example of Maxen allows us to survey the sheer range of contemporary visual representations. De la Pegna, *peintre extraordinaire* to the court of Maria Theresa, painted two battle representations for Daun himself between 1759 and 1762. The first of these is an image of the Battle of Hochkirch, while the other focuses on Finck's Capture at Maxen, centering on the defeated Prussian general handing over his sword in surrender. Although de la Pegna's painting is relatively accurate in terms of the event itself, other contemporary images of the battle discard almost all specificity of location, which is identified solely by a caption or accompanying text. With the mass reproduction of prints and pamphlets, artists used many ready-made iconographic elements, meaning that any representation could become an interchangeable signifier.[103] A print depicting the battle of Maxen is almost identical to a representation of Lobositz produced three or four years earlier.[104] In this case at least, there is little difference between the iconography of victory and defeat.

On the Austrian side, there are thus clearly plenty of representations of victorious battles, but victory painting appears not to be present as a genre in Prussia, despite there being no shortage of victories to represent. There were, it seems, just two contemporary Prussian oil paintings of this kind, both displayed at the Royal Palace in Breslau. Today both are lost, probably destroyed.[105] One depicted the Battle of Leuthen; the other showed Austrian prisoners marching away after their defeat at Breslau on December 21, 1757. The fighting between Austrian cavalry and Zieten hussars is recognizable in the left foreground of the Leuthen painting, but the center of the picture is dominated by long rows of platoons exchanging fire, extending the pictorial space into the depths. All in all, the painting is a highly conventional representation of little artistic value.

Given the paucity of research on this topic, one can only speculate about the reasons for such very different strategies of representation in Austria and in Prussia. With his tight budget, perhaps Frederick did not care to spend money on this type of image, especially since he had neither a court audience to appreciate such images nor a court painter who could realize them adequately (if we disregard Antoine Pesne). In addition, buildings like Potsdam Royal Palace were already full of other paintings, mostly inherited. Last but not least, the iconophobic Calvinist mentality may have precluded taking one's own military endeavors as a subject for visual representation. However, the visual material discussed next suggests that this representational reluctance was largely confined to court painting, not to other visual media.

Consuming the War, Remembering the War

The eighteenth century is often said to have experienced a "consumer revolution," with the mass production of some commodities and the emergence of new forms of identity largely shaped by practices of consumption.[106] The coffeehouse may be the most notable example of the consumption of novel beverages leading to new kinds of sociability and communication. The war saw a boom in several forms of craft manufacturing, which could be anachronistically seen as a kind of early "fan merchandising."[107] Popular items included Iserlohn tobacco cases, silk *Vivat!* ribbons, inn signs, porcelain tableware, and decorative "box thalers" (double-sided coins used to hold messages or images) with war-related motifs.[108] Tobacco cases (figure 8.1) allowed any consumer to carry war-related merchandise in their coat pocket, at a price of a thaler. When offering a friend tobacco, the decorative case would call to mind the event in question, perhaps functioning as

Figure 8.1 Tobacco box commemorating the Battle of Zorndorf (Iserlohn, northwest Germany, ca. 1758).
Source: akg-images.

a conversation starter. Individually made enamel snuffboxes could represent complex scenes on both sides of the lid, as well as around the sides. Typical scenes included the Russian capture of Berlin and the battle of Torgau, both from 1760.[109]

Vivat! ribbons were mostly made of "linen or plain-weave fabric," some six to twelve inches in length and one or two inches in width.[110] As with serially produced tobacco cases, nearly all celebrate victory in battle. These ribbons could be bought outright or rented for a fee. Worn on the exterior of one's clothing, they would advertise a wearer's point of view even more clearly than a tobacco case. On December 11, 1757, shortly after the Prussian victories at Rossbach and Leuthen, the writer Karl Wilhelm Ramler wrote to Gleim in Halberstadt: "For a night and day now, the young people have not ceased to let off Victory Salutes, they are still shooting all around us as I write. Various merchants have had silk Ribbons made up to celebrate both Victories, which we all now wear on our Waistcoats, Muffs, swords, hats, and other Head coverings."[111] The ribbons are partially self-referential, with inscriptions alluding to their visibility on the wearer's body: "This ribbon shall adorn our brow, like garland leaves of Victory."[112] Johann Christian Becher's "Uniform Notebook" is a visual record of the war in the Duchy of Weimar, maintained by the Weimar tailor as a companion volume to his written chronicle. As well as a ring commemorating the conquest of Breslau, Becher includes no fewer than five colored *Vivat!* ribbons in his notebook—some as painted representations, some physically stuck onto the pages. One commemorates Leuthen in 1757, two are from Rossbach in 1757, and there is one each from the victories at Domstadtl and Zorndorf, both in 1758.[113] It is significant that ribbons commemorating Rossbach, Leuthen, and Zorndorf seem to have been awarded individually to Prussian troops or handed out to "young ladies and gentlemen," as with the queen's ring. By contrast, a manufactured taffeta ribbon honoring victory at Domstadtl appears to have been sold in Erfurt on July 26, less than four weeks after the battle, at a price of 4 groschen. Becher refers to the ribbons as "medals" or "service ribbons," clearly placing them within a context of institutional military awards.

What we see is the emergence of an entire protoindustry devoted to celebrating Frederick II, both within the Holy Roman Empire and across Europe, finding expression in everything from poems to inn signs, from *Vivat!* ribbons to teacups. By comparison, use of Maria Theresa's image was largely confined to the Habsburg lands. To some degree, these popular media also reflect global interconnections among theaters of war, although European events remain very much the dominant subject. Only occasionally did tobacco tins show military scenes from overseas—for example, the British conquest of Martinique in February 1762.[114] However, one 1758 *Vivat!* ribbon clearly alludes to global interconnections, its slogan invoking both the Battle of Zorndorf and the conquest of Louisbourg: "George has yonder quelled the French / As Frederick here does Russian rages quench" (Dort hemmt George Frankreichs Muth / Hier dämpfet Friedrich Rußlands Wuth) (figure 8.2).[115] Soldiers' powder horns often tended to include motifs drawn from overseas, including maps, places, weapons, insignia, and protagonists. These were mostly taken from the French and Indian War but also include, for example, Britain's capture of Havana in 1762. As with the tobacco cases, memory and identification here combine in the form of a ubiquitous everyday object.[116] Many of these engravings seem to have been produced by soldiers themselves, perhaps made by regimental colleagues who had a knack for this kind of handiwork.

Another example of a soldier's personal memory object can be found in one of Grotehenn's letters to his father, written after a skirmish near Bielefeld in June 1757: "A Round of Canister-shot blew off the upper 1/4 of my weapon's barrel. I send herewith the iron piece, asking that you keep it as a Souvenir. It shows how by the grace of God the Ball, passing close to my Head, crushed my weapon's iron, and not my Bones."[117] Georg von Szent-Ivány, a captain of the Austrian grenadiers, mentions a silver gorget

Figure 8.2 Vivat! ribbon commemorating the Battle of Zorndorf and the siege of Louisbourg in 1758.
CC-BY-NC-SA © Museum Weißenfels—Schloss Neu-Augustusburg.

that one of his men removed from a dead Prussian officer on the battlefield near Prague: "And I Sayd to Grenadier Bogdan: listen here before you send that off, keep it by you, and I'll pay you what the Silver is worth, I want that for an Eternal Keepsake."[118]

Wall blakers, wall-mounted candle holders, were another example of the combination of handicrafts and an impulse to preserve. A large number of grenadier caps bearing brass shields were left behind on the battlefield at Kolin in 1757. Craftsmen in the town's Jewish quarter used them to make large numbers of brass candle holders.[119] Military artifacts, in particular, were repeatedly recycled in the early modern era.[120] But looted items could also become objects of civilian remembrance. Johann Philipp Zellmann, the wine merchant from Hertzberg, reports that "Just Heinrich and the servant Daniel [. . .] have got some Loot [. . .] an unsheathed Saber, likely lost by some French Carabiniers they met near Hildesheim, which I shall keep in eternal Remembrance of these terrible Times of War."[121] Capturing loot and collecting souvenirs went hand in hand. Corporal Todd, for example, tells how he appropriated a framed map during the attack on Cherbourg in 1758: "I got a fine map of France & all the Sea Coast of England with the names of Portsmouth, Plymouth etc. It was in a fine frame in a Gentlemans House that was quite ruinated of all etc."[122] Looting was explicitly forbidden for British forces, but Todd clearly sees this as a case of finders keepers. The map was obviously functional, as well as aesthetically pleasing, and two days later Todd gave it to the steward of his ship.

In purely practical terms, it was impossible for soldiers to carry around their plunder for long, especially any bulky items, so they tried to quickly convert loot into money or some other form of exchange. There are repeated descriptions of flea market scenes. Grotehenn reports from Fulda in December 1759: "Today in the city of Fulda there are Auctions on almost every Street, and the Hussars and Cavalry are selling their plundered Carriages, Horses, and Baggage-carts. Quite almost Anything is to be found there."[123] Many people seem to have used such auctions to recover their own property: "Many former Proprietors [. . .] bought back their own Possessions from the Hussars."[124]

The plunder was particularly luxurious when General Seydlitz's Prussian forces surprised Soubise's French officers at dinner at Gotha: "There were only a few French soldiers taken, but a number of servants, cooks, hairdressers, mistresses and actors, who always formed part of the train of a French army. The baggage of several generals fell into the hands of the

Prussians, with a number of cases of perfumery and luxuries of the toilet, which Seydlitz made over to his hussars; but he sent back the mistresses without ransom."[125] Archenholz's retrospective account of the war suggests these "luxuries of the toilet" symbolize, in material form, an emasculated French military culture, whose defeat at Rossbach should thus come as no surprise.[126]

By contrast, the official contents of a Prussian soldier's knapsack were modest: "one Knife, one Spoon, one fork, one brush for Shoes and sweeping, 1 Powder bag, 1 comb, 1 tallow rag, one field hat, 2 undershirts, 2 collarets (with bib), 2 sleeve sets, 1 pair stockings, 1 Bandage for bloodletting, & 2 pair linen trousers."[127] Material culture could bear many interpretations and allowed a wide range of expressions of identity. It was, in other words, a political medium. Personal consumption could align very well with one's preferred political cause.

News as Commodity

Craft items were not the only objects of consumption; news itself—and war reports, in particular—also became a lucrative commodity at this time. The contemporary hunger for news and war images was fed by historical works published while the war was still going on; for example the lawyer and journalist Christoph Gottlieb Richter published a six-volume history, which he wrote "in a Jewish style" under the pseudonym Simeon Ben Jochai.[128] The individual volumes of Richter's history were bound with numerous engravings, many of which survive separate from the books and continue to have a strong influence on the visual memory of the war. Another popular example of fictionalized war reporting was the series *A French Soldier Speaks with a Saxon Peasant About the Current War*, a weekly paper published for fifteen months between 1757 and 1758.[129] The series features dialogues between the eponymous soldier and peasant, each speaking in their own dialect; the conversations between the two served as a way of disseminating the latest stories and news from the war.

Like engravings, maps were another popular consumer item during the war, ideal for armchair generals and political windbags (*politische Kannegieszer*). Both groups were easily enough mocked, as in this derisive description by General Johann Anton von Tilliers (1721–1761) in Vienna, although it may be meant in good spirits: "People speak of nothing but war. Even women take a war map from their nightstand every night, rather than a prayerbook. And all have their ideas, and imagine themselves in command of our own Forces, or of the Russian or Prussian armies."[130] Tilliers's phrase "even women," along with his allusion to waning devotional energies, is clearly striving to symbolically ratchet up the image of war euphoria. But this kind of behavior was by no means absurd: We need only think back to Meta Klopstock's eager reading of news from Lobositz. The word *Kannegiesser* literally means "can maker" but came to be applied more generally to those fond of talking about politics while knowing little on the subject. In contemporary English, they might be called armchair politicians. The term came from a Danish play titled *The Political Tinker/The Pewterer Turned Politician*, written by Ludvig Holberg (1684–1754), which had its first performance in 1722. In the city of Gotha, Johann Georg Pleissner, a prominent political commentator, composed a handwritten *History of the War in Thuringia* but angered the authorities by including details about the war in the region.[131] Since he was a *Zinngiesser* (tinsmith) by profession, local wits mocked him with the fashionable insult *Kannegiesser* (political tinker).

The city of Hamburg offers a clear example of the links among war, consumption, and partisan emotion.[132] Frederick installed a network of Prussian residents in the most important city for newspapers within each Imperial Circle. For Hamburg, the role went to Johann Julius Hecht (1721–1792), who supplied the press with official information for the duration of the war, actively influencing coverage.[133] Austria had its own resident in Hamburg, Karl Joseph Graf Raab zu Rauenberg (d. 1775), but he seems to have clearly lost the battle of media influence to his Prussian counterpart. Their rivalry was such that Klefeker, the Hamburg censor, documented their disputes in files labeled "Generalia of the Newspaper Wars, durante Bello inter Imperatorem et Regem Borussiae a 1756 ad 1760."[134] Disputes over specific victory celebrations are also well documented—most notably, in the annual reports of Jesuit missionaries in Hamburg. When the Hamburg Senate announced "public Prayers from the pulpit for the Fortune and Progress of Prussian arms," Count Raab, the Austrian diplomat, made it clear to them, "in a forceful but friendly manner," that "the Emperor is head of this City, Hamburg is an Imperial city, protected by the Imperial Eagle's mighty Wings."[135] The warning seems to have given the Lutherans pause, but Reformed Anglicans living in Hamburg seem to have gone ahead with their prayers. The intense interest elicited by these issues in Hamburg and elsewhere was quite understandable. Reports and celebrations of victory could annoy opponents and delay or weaken the exercise of imperial sovereignty over Prussia. These reactions within the city could help or hinder subsidies from key allies like Britain and even induce foreign soldiers in the city to desert.

Johann Matthias Dreyer was a journalist active in Hamburg and also the press representative of the bishopric of Lübeck. He complained of media-driven emotion in the city: "There can have been no War wherein such intense partisanship have occurred among distant readers as in Hamburg in the current War. People otherwise sensible have rendered themselves ridiculous. Should I wish to compose a work on this *enthusiasmo politico*, I should have new material every Day." At the risk of anachronistic exaggeration, Dreyer's comments here seem to sketch out an investigation into political emotion, with particular attention to communication over large distances. Within the city, spaces of consumption were also spaces of political sociability: "Town Hall, Tavern, Stock-market, and Wine-cellar are all alike filled with political Pundits, and these being jurists or soldiers or nightwatch-men."[136] Such social mixing threatened social boundaries for well-off and publicly minded citizens. Christian Ludwig von Griesheim, a legal theorist resident in Hamburg, complained: "Even Day-laborers and their dependents hang around by the News-stalls, more so indeed than at stalls for Bread, and there they await the Arrival of the Newspapers. Then they wait not at all, not even so as to repair to an Ale-house, but rather stand on streets and bridges and read the news, and often thus block the Publick way. And they find listeners of their own kind; their Judgments are most frequently risible. One would think Hamburg's rabble composed of none but Statesmen!"[137] Alcohol and billiards had traditionally stirred up emotions; now politics did too. A *Vivat!* ribbon worn on a coat made one's sympathies quickly legible. Disputes sometimes spilled over into scenes reminiscent of modern-day soccer matches: "While at Billiards, talk of battles lost and won has precipitated many small confrontations in Hamburg, and human Blood has been shed, although the Battle-field be many hundreds of miles away."[138] Even in Venice, skirmishes broke out between monks or gondoliers taking Frederick's or Maria Theresa's side. As mentioned earlier, factional tensions in Switzerland prompted widespread fears of civil war between Catholic and Reformed cantons.[139]

The official tolerance for "reckless Disputation" by the lower orders quickly reached its limits. The Margrave of Baden issued warnings on the matter as early as October 1756, commanding that "every Man shall refrain from passing Judgment on the Actions of High Princes, and from any untimely Reasoning or Chatter on matters of War and Religion, either in inns or other Places in Public Society, as well as from the carrying around of News[papers], for the most part ungrounded in Truth; and all should behave, as in any case befits Christian persons, with peace toward their Neighbor; and should this be breached, then We shall be minded to rigorously exact Punishment for such Imprudence."[140]

A True Presentation of the Current Times, an Augsburg engraving from 1760, offers a panoramic view of a society agitated by war coverage (figure 8.3).[141] One figure, Historicus, seen at the desk to the left of the picture, attempts to filter truth from the incoming messages. Lower down, tipsy patrons of an inn are at each other's throats, and the city watch has arrived to keep them apart. To the right, "argumenters" (*Räsonierer*) are punished with beatings, imprisonment, and the pillory. It seems as though time is out of joint: Messengers from the gods approach from heaven, carrying an endless stream of newspapers and rumors. News reports were often unreliable, producing the information uncertainty characteristic of wartime societies with a high demand for news.[142]

Figure 8.3 A True Presentation of the Current Times. Copper engraving by Johann David Nessenthaler (Augsburg, ca. 1760).
Source: bpk Bildagentur/Deutsches Historisches Museum, Berlin/Art Resource, New York.

The war thus brought about a major boom in the reading of newspapers, which, in turn, prompted a critical backlash. Among our key sources, even the likes of Andreas Wähner and Abraham ter Meers were ultimately drawn into the outcry, although both were themselves avid readers of news. In a journal essay published in 1758, the theologian Christoph Gottfried Jacobi (1724–1789) criticized contemporary reading culture: "A disorderly hunger for the latest Newspapers has contributed much to disordered Conduct during the current War. Many are now so accustomed to the Receipt and Taking-in of new and various Particulars that they feel done without, if they do not receive fresh war News every day."[143] Jacobi thinks it impossible to keep up with the complexity of events in the various theaters of the supraregional war: "It cannot be otherwise than that large and varied Undertakings of war will produce much and varied News, and this will be brought from one Place to another. To pay attention to each, and to fully concern oneself with their investigation, the mind would needs be multiplied, and needlessly alarmed, and particularly it would, by occupation with small and minor events, be distracted from the Important and the Whole." The ability to distinguish between what is important and what is not suffers as a result, he writes, and the demand for news produces much that is simply useless: "Is this disordered Demand for much News not to blame for the Dissemination of so many unfounded and contradictory News-papers?" Using news of the Battle of Rossbach as an example, Jacobi discerns two categories of people "with regard to the news messages they receive": first, cautious skeptics and, second, those who will believe anything, however improbable. The latter have no desire "seriously to [. . .] approach the Truth, but rather merely want access to new Information as it arrives."[144]

In this way, the contemporary news economy could prompt a fundamental media critique. Exaggerated reports of victory were often the subject of sardonic caricature. In 1760, Johann Martin Will, an Augsburg draughtsman, produced *The All-Too-Hasty Courier*, a print showing a messenger on horseback holding a piece of paper bearing the words "The enemy is defeated, all is conquered" (figure 8.4) The lengthy rhymed verses that caption the drawing explain: "Hereby the Courier gives us many things to understand, things which may indeed never have taken place in this world. The secretary puts news into his hand, whether truth or lie he does not know. The courier in slippers dashes quickly as he can. Where news be loved, it has been invented; only the truly gullible take their Pleasure therein. Meanwhile Lies are often scarce perceived, and the fool limps along behind, following the

Figure 8.4 *The All-Too-Hasty Courier*. Etching by Johann Martin Will (Augsburg, ca. 1760). *Source*: Herzog August Bibliothek Wolfenbüttel: Graph. A1: 2820.

Opposite of truth. If you are Wise, give not your Credence easy, and keep your Silence to the end."[145]

One newspaper, the *Münchnerisches Wochen-Blat in Versen* (Munich weekly paper in verse), published by Mathias Etenhueber, consisted almost entirely of second-order media coverage, including commentary on news and on rumors doing the rounds, as well as satirical commentary on the widespread craving for news itself. The paper's first edition, published on January 1, 1759, proclaims its credo: "These days, the loser in the field is the winner on paper / He who write the news makes his fabulous images / And shows the smallest victory in splendid form / Because his partisanship stands by his side."[146]

Publishers did very well in this news environment, and they made no bones about it. In 1757, Johann Matthias Dreyer announced the appearance of his new paper, *Staats- und Gelehrten Neuigkeiten* (State and scholarly news), published in Altona: "In these times of War, the most advantageous and profitable Matter, is to be a Hussar or Put out a News-paper."[147] The New Year's reflections published by the *Erlangener Zeitung* in 1757 read similarly: "For our part, armies can persist in attacking, winning, losing, scorching and burning as long as they so wish. Should both at the same time think themselves Victors, and each claim to have taken the Field, we too are well suited. The longer the Game continues, the more content we are, and the more it brings in. Let it merely not approach too close, but rather give us a fine wide Berth."[148] For the reader, war reporting could mediate between proximity and distance; in doing so, it also brought home the threatening reality of war, something experienced as part of everyday life by hundreds of thousands of people.

Knowledge of the World? Global War as Media Event

Within the Holy Roman Empire, at least the literate public was well aware that the war was being fought across four continents. A range of news publications already provided much information on non-European cultures, but the war now meant that this knowledge was additionally framed as "current affairs."[149] The year 1762 saw the publication in Nürnberg of the thirteenth volume of the *Neueröffneter Historischer Bilder-Saal* (Newly opened historical hall of pictures), a book series that regularly described the war's events using a visual vocabulary of spreading flames. The Franco-British war, under way since 1755, "which concerned only a few disputes in Acadia and America, has most unfortunately spread to Europe, creating Sparks in Germany which would burst into Flames."[150] The *Historischer Bilder-Saal* offered its readers an entire chapter on Britain's overseas campaigns, a method sometimes also used by private chroniclers like Eberhard Jürgen Abelmann, the Hanoverian master baker.[151] His chronicle, the *Hannoverisches Kriegesdenkmal* (Hanover war memorial), has a separate chronological chapter on "England's Conquests Overseas."[152] Like many of his contemporaries, Abelmann was a diligent reader of newspapers; his sources of information included *Hannoverische Beyträge zum Nutzen und zum Vergnügen* (Hanover essays, for utility and pleasure), a forerunner of the popular *Hannoverisches Magazin*. He frequently refers his readers to other sources, citing articles on Caribbean islands and the "Nature of and Actions Toward of the City of Quebec."[153]

Abelmann's sources suggest a basic deficiency in his knowledge. The preface of a 1762 German account of Britain's occupation of Guadeloupe tellingly states: "The present violent War was first kindled in the American Colonies, and thus in almost all the Papers we read of events of War which cannot be understood without correct Knowledge of those lands."[154] As well as providing metacommentary on the burgeoning field of colonial reporting, the anonymous author suggests a need for increased knowledge of these places, in effect promoting his own work. During the war, *Hannoverische Beyträge* published a series of articles informing its Hanoverian readers about new British conquests. In 1758, the paper's *Nützliche Sammlungen* (Useful miscellany) section contained articles on Cape Breton and Louisbourg, followed in subsequent years by pieces on Gorée (1759); Quebec (1760); Grenada, St. Vincent, and St. Lucia (1762); and Florida, New Orleans, and Manila (1763).[155] Abelmann's perspective was clearly formed by the articles he read in the *Beyträge*; his attitude toward the overseas territories focused, above all, on economic utility: "America largely belongs to Spain and has many Mines of Gold and Silver. There are no richer mines in the world than those at Potosi."[156] However, he clearly believes the war's greatest British victory occurred when "the courageous British brought the island of Cuba under its Sway."[157]

Inhabitants of the Hanoverian territories often had a closer connection to London than other territories of the Reich, as shown by the *Göttingische Anzeigen von gelehrten Sachen* (Göttingen advertiser of learned matters), which regularly reported on British publications.[158] In 1761–1762, while the war was still ongoing, the paper published a short review of the *London Magazine* series "History of the Origin and Progress of the Present War." The reviewer sums up the main value of the series: "At least for a German, they can serve to round out our ideas of Wars on other Continents. There are many things about such things which a German reader cannot know from the News-papers here."[159] The reviewer's sympathies are not with the London author, who makes a clear argument against the continental commitment: "a clever, discontented Englishman who does not know Germany has here passed some miserable hours."[160] The two decades after the war saw the publication of crucial British books about India, including Robert Orme's *A History of the Military Transactions of the British Nation in Indostan* (1763) and Edward Ives's *A Voyage from England to India, in the Year 1754*

(1773), as well as their dissemination to a German audience via translations by Enlightenment historians, including Archenholz and Christian Wilhelm Dohm (1751–1820).[161] Among British writers like the poet and historian Richard Owen Cambridge (1717–1802), who published an account of the Anglo-French War on the Coromandel coast in 1761, it was widely agreed that only the war had prompted Europeans in India to extend their knowledge of the country: "This war alone has taught them the Geography of the lands for a hundred miles around their Settlements."[162] In this way, the war became what one historian has called a "catalyst for the development of imperial space."[163] Here we learn something specific about the history of knowledge and about contemporary perceptions of global interdependence. Contemporary observers, like Abelmann, Wähner, and ter Meer, may record the capture of Gorée or Havana in their diaries, but this by no means guarantees any substantial knowledge of these places. The secondary knowledge contained within articles, imparting "the basics," gave them the context required to turn "raw" information into "cooked" knowledge.[164]

CHAPTER IX

Urban Life in a State of Exception

Corruption and Cooperation in Occupied Cities

Occupation was an almost ubiquitous experience of the Seven Years' War. Nearly every warring party occupied the territory of some other polity during the conflict, even for a short time. France occupied Hanover, Russia occupied East Prussia, and Austria occupied Prussia's western provinces. Prussia occupied Saxony, and Britain and its allies occupied the ecclesiastical territories of Münster and Hildesheim.[1] Paradoxically, Silesia, the province that had so often triggered European conflicts, experienced comparatively few periods of long-term occupation. In southern Europe, Spanish troops occupied parts of Portugal in 1762, while outside of Europe, Britain occupied Canada (1760–1764), as well as Havana (1762–1764) and Manila (1762–1764), both ports in Spanish-ruled territories.

Occupiers' behavior toward local rulers and the wider population was largely governed by whether the occupation was intended to be temporary or quasi-permanent. The spectrum of occupation styles ranged from the Russian occupation of East Prussia under Nikolaus Friedrich von Korff (1710–1766) to the French occupation of Electoral Hanover under Richelieu.[2] Richelieu's troops extorted millions from cities and other communities across northern Germany, both by coercing contributions and by issuing *sauvegardes* (letters of protection that exempted the bearer from billeting obligations, etc.).[3] However, corruption among French officers and war commissioners meant only about one-third of the money raised actually went toward the French war effort. War commissioners were responsible for provisioning and partly for paying troops; to do this, they drummed up contributions within occupied areas.[4] An important indicator of whether an occupation was intended to be permanent or near-permanent was the demand that the population pay homage to the new rulers. The Russians demanded homage, while the French did not. The British did so in Canada but only after 1764. For his part, Frederick II imposed an oath of loyalty on Saxony but did not do so until 1758—and only then as a reaction to Russian provocation.[5]

One characteristic of eighteenth-century wars is the way aristocratic habitus and military rationality could work at cross-purposes.[6] Chains of combat command were subverted by competing claims of rank and authority. Family politics could stand in the way of raison d'état and could also interfere with rational performance criteria. This was particularly the case when it came to patronage and corruption. Patronage was a relatively unproblematic concept at the time; client-patron relations shaped both the actions and the thought processes of many people involved in the war. But corruption was a different matter. In both the premodern and the modern eras, corruption could affect a wide range of activities, which were, in turn, associated with very different normative evaluations and punitive possibilities.[7] The modern military undoubtedly frowns on practices identified as corruption, but the premodern military, with its private economic arrangements, often offered greater leeway.[8] Moreover, there was a direct link between patronage and corruption. One need only look at appointment procedures for France's war commissioners, who were selected from within networks of the bourgeois economic elite.[9] The case of Richelieu shows how individuals pushed the limits of the leeway afforded them. Citizens of Paris saw corruption take on direct architectural expression in the form of the Pavillon de Hanovre, Richelieu's city palace, designed and built by the eminent architect Jean-Michel Chevotet (1698–1772) at a reputed cost of 2 million livres.[10] Construction was begun in 1758; early the same year a shortage of funds had forced the French to withdraw from Hanover. Corrupt behavior had direct, visible consequences for French military operations.[11] Richelieu was recalled to Paris to be confronted with corruption allegations.[12] The Richelieu scandal, and later ones like that involving the war commissioner Antoine-François Dumouriez, led the French crown to launch a veritable anticorruption campaign, which used a kind of questionnaire to encourage local civilian authorities to report illegally collected contributions.[13]

The Russian military presence in East Prussia had something paradoxical about it. The occupation regime in Königsberg, as implemented by the general staff and other Russian officers, was generally civilized and tolerant, while Russian irregulars in the surrounding countryside were simultaneously committing atrocities and exhibiting a total lack of discipline.

Along with foraging and forced contributions, billeting was one of the major burdens that weighed on civilian populations.[14] The inequalities of a hierarchical, estate-based society intensified the impact of these practices. In 1761, Johann Daniel Geitz, a farmer in Bottendorf, recorded the local effects of occupation: "This was truly an Affliction: sometimes the French billeted themselves, and sometimes assigned billets to others. So rather than receive the largest number [of billeted soldiers], the rich had (only) 1 or maybe 2 Officers, something of that kind. But those in the middle, and even the poor, had to take Soldiers in large numbers into their Homes, which in this way were entirely ruined."[15]

The social gap between rich and poor grew still wider in times of war. The war had particular impacts on urban life, with the population experiencing devastating fires, sieges, and marauding bands of soldiers. In this context, the particular experience of university cities was shaped by their own social constellation, as was the experience of towns that hosted large numbers of prisoners of war.

1760—Restricted Space

In Germany, the campaigning season began comparatively late in 1760, getting under way only in June. Frederick felt forced to divide his battered army into several independent formations. A small force held Silesia, while Prince Henry led another to harass the Russians east of the Elbe. Frederick himself turned to Saxony, looking to recapture Dresden. In strategic terms, this meant both sides later had to attempt to concentrate their forces. The Russians and Austrians sought to join their separate armies; later in the year, Frederick and Henry would do the same. Of course, both sides were also working to thwart their opponents' strategic maneuvers.

The Austrian general staff, commanded by Franz Moritz von Lacy (1725–1801), initially developed a cautious campaign plan, aiming only to push the Prussians out of Saxony.[16] This was not enough for Kaunitz, the state chancellor, who looked to Laudon as a replacement commander, hoping he would prove more aggressive. Laudon's new strategy was to push on without waiting for the Russians, mobilizing an army of seventy-five thousand to operate in Saxony while another force of forty thousand would attack Silesia. For his part, the Russian commander Saltykov hesitated to take the offensive; the only campaign objectives formulated were to attack Pomerania, penetrating as far as Rega, and then to besiege the city of Kolberg.

One of Laudon's major objectives was to recapture the fortified city of Glatz in Silesia. He thus advanced on the city with his force of forty thousand men; the encirclement and siege began on June 7. A few days later Laudon sent twenty-eight thousand men from this force to attack a smaller Prussian force, numbering around twelve thousand, commanded by General Fouqué. The armies met in battle at Landeshut in Silesia on June 23, 1760, and the Prussians suffered something like a repeat of the debacle at Maxen the previous November. As they had at Hochkirch in 1758, the Austrians launched a surprise nighttime attack, advancing on the Prussians from several directions. Thrown into increasing disarray, the Prussian force used up its entire stock of ammunition against the numerically far superior enemy.[17] Prussian infantrymen who tried to surrender were mercilessly cut down by the Austrian cavalry, an action that contemporaries condemned as a "disgrace to all human feeling."[18] Rampaging Austrian soldiers even managed to attack their own commanding general. The looting of Landeshut began at two o'clock that morning and continued for nine hours, with the civilian population the victims. On December 1, 1760, the town council, the *Bürgerschaft*, sent a report to Frederick, describing how the city had been "utterly ruined."[19] The plundering by Austrian troops left 12 of the town's residents dead, 43 seriously injured, and "more than 300 badly Assaulted and Abused in the most extreme Degree."[20] Several women had been "Debauched" and "Defiled."[21]

In his memoirs, Count Cogniazo—the Austrian officer seriously wounded at Hochkirch—makes telling comparisons with regard to the "Massacre" carried out by his own side. Austrian soldiers, he writes, should have "better customs of war than the Tatar and the Kalmuk"; it was inexcusable to commit "Inhumanities" akin to "scalping the hair from the scull like the Illinoises do."[22] For Cogniazo, Kalmyks and Native Americans could be invoked as ideal or typical perpetrators to emphasize the transgression committed by what today might be called "the alien in one's own."[23] Contemporaries saw Landeshut as particularly outrageous because it was the work not of irregular auxiliary forces but of Catholics, who even committed atrocities against other Christians.[24] The sectarian anger of the Austrians seems, in part, to have been provoked by the figure of Fouqué. The Prussian general, son of a Huguenot refugee, had served as fortress commander of Glatz for the previous eighteen years and was a notorious authoritarian. During his time in charge, he had abolished many Catholic holidays and had hanged the priest Andreas Faulhaber in 1757. Faulhaber became a prominent Catholic martyr, and his remains were still hanging outside the city when the Austrians conquered the fortress almost three years later.[25]

After the crushing defeat at Landeshut, the Prussian cavalry managed to retreat toward Schweidnitz, but most of the infantrymen—around eight thousand—were captured by the Austrians. After several substantial defeats the previous year, this was another major setback for Frederick and his attempts to reconstruct his army. At Glatz, Laudon's men pressed home the advantage, continuing with the siege and ultimately capturing the fortress on July 26. Meanwhile, Frederick had started a siege of his own at Dresden in mid-June. Although this Prussian action would ultimately prove unsuccessful, it left lasting traces.

Dresden in Flames

Dresden, the capital and royal seat of Saxony, had been captured by Imperial and Austrian troops some weeks after the Prussian defeat at Kunersdorf in August 1759. The following summer Frederick began his siege, hoping to regain the city in a quick and effective operation. But even as he did so, Daun's Austrian army was headed in his direction. After just eight days, the Prussian king was forced to break off the siege.[26] Despite the short duration of the siege, in its last days the Prussians subjected the city to very heavy bombardment, with devastating consequences. Suspicions circulated that Frederick, aware he would soon have to break off the siege, deliberately decided on this policy of destruction. Thus, the brief siege became a prominent media event, sparking a propaganda debate in which the legitimacy of Prussian tactics was discussed in great detail.[27] For example, four Troncks—devices used to shoot fireworks on festive occasions—had been installed on the tall spire of the Kreuzkirche (Church of the Holy Cross), one of the city's main churches. The Prussians used this as an excuse to target the church, claiming the pyrotechnic devices had been used to fire on them.[28]

Gustav Klemm (1802–1867), a chronicler of the city, itemized the bombardment's effects: "The siege of Dresden cost 1478 dead and wounded among the Prussians, 416 houses were burned in the City of Dresden. 20 people were killed within the City."[29] Before the end of year, the theologian Johann Joachim Gottlob am Ende (1704–1777), pastor and dean of the Kreuzkirche, published a series of sermons in which he suggested that divine judgment had been visited upon the church, a classic mode of interpretation of such events.[30] Specifically, he claimed that the faithful had been insufficiently penitent, leading God to send his wrath upon them in the form of a "terrible Fire."[31] But he invoked mercy and consolation, as well as punishment. Pious Christians, he preached, would be safe from God's inextinguishable "fire of Rage," which would inflict still greater pain, incomparably worse than the city had just suffered.[32] One of his sermons addressed the Kreuzkirche's congregation as "living Corpses," divested of their "Life-force."[33] He then turned his gaze from the church to the city of Dresden, his dramatic words painting a picture of death and destruction: "The beautiful city, the precious, the excellent, the much-populated Royal City of Dresden, has it not been—if I may put it like this—suddenly made a Corpse? Dead bodies scattered in the streets, in the city and its outlying Districts; some Shot to death, others killed by Buildings as they fell. Many most beautiful Palaces and Buildings are burned to the ground. The Marckt-Platz [marketplace] and streets are deserted and empty, and where People do walk, their Appearance is of Bodies divested of their Souls."[34] The city's famous Kreuzkirche lies "as a Corpse laid low, lain in Ashes."[35] Time and again, he continues, he has been reduced to tears. He also makes direct reference to his own experience of the bombardment:

> But for me, the most Horrific was that I, with God's help, decided I should leave my official Residence only when it was on fire or when the Creuz-kirche, directly adjacent, was itself in Flames. The latter happened more quickly than expected, and any quenching of the Fire was made impossible by the constant deadly Bombardment. And so it was time that I also must think of how to save myself and mine own. [. . .] And so, as God bade us, we went out together. The embers from the burning Creuz-kirche struck our Faces, and fiery bullets hissed as they passed above our heads and all around us.[36]

This element of personal experience, interspersed throughout the sermons, allows them to be read as ego-documents.

In addition to the visually evocative language of diaries and sermons, paintings and copperplate engravings offer direct visual representations of the burning of Dresden. One particularly well-known set of images is the near-photorealist depictions of the destroyed city produced by Bernardo Bellotto (1721–1780), nephew of the more famous Canaletto.[37] After three years away, Bellotto had returned to Dresden at the end of 1761. His wife, son, and three daughters were all unharmed, but his house in the Pirnaische Vorstadt district had been entirely destroyed, with the loss of works of art and furnishings worth around 50,000 thalers.[38] In the wake of this experience, he made an etching and a painting of the ruins of the Pirnaische Vorstadt. These works have long been considered lost, but another of his ruin paintings does survive, which depicts the Kreuzkirche in ruins, although already undergoing reconstruction (figure 9.1). A similar fate befell Gottlieb Wilhelm Rabener (1714–1771), sometimes called the "German Swift," whose books and manuscripts fell victim to the flames. He documented his loss in a letter to his friend Ferber in Warsaw, but to his dismay, the letter was soon made public in an unauthorized pirate version.[39]

Figure 9.1 Ruins of the Kreuzkirche in Dresden. Painting by Bernardo Bellotto, sometimes known as Canaletto, the same name as his better-known uncle (1765).
Source: akg-images.

After his losses at Landeshut and Glatz, Frederick moved toward Silesia, where his twenty-four thousand Prussians would face ninety thousand troops commanded by Daun, Laudon, and Lacy. The Austrians, sensing their superior strength, came up with a plan to surround the Prussians and force the *roi connétable* to capitulate. The end of the war seemed close at hand. Frederick tried to escape the trap by withdrawing his army to the northeast, but he encountered Laudon's force near Liegnitz, where the two sides fought a nocturnal battle.[40] Fighting began at around four o'clock in the morning on August 15, 1760, and lasted no more than two or three hours, during which time sixteen thousand Prussian soldiers won out against an Austrian force twice its size. A Prussian chaplain from Seydlitz's regiment of Cuirasseurs describes the scene: "By 7 o'clock we had occupied the Champ de bataille, and the enemy was on the run. [. . .] Our army remained in place on the Champ de bataille until 11 A.M.. The Infantry fired a Victory Salute, whereupon we continued our march to Parchwitz. For all that it was brief, and caused us few losses, this Action has been glorious for us, and greatly to our Benefit."[41]

The chaplain's account unquestionably minimizes Prussian losses; with half the Austrian numbers, they suffered around thirty-four hundred dead and wounded, in comparison to thirty-eight hundred on the Austrian side.[42] But a further forty-eight hundred Austrians were unaccounted for, either captured or missing. More significant than the raw numbers, however, was the fact that Frederick had escaped the Austrians' attempted encirclement and posted a victory in battle, his first in quite some time. On this occasion, night had proved treacherous for the Austrians. Lacy's force had become disoriented in the darkness and made slow progress; moreover, it took some time for Daun to realize that Laudon had been defeated. Prussian campfires, still burning on the battlefield, helped contribute to the disorientation. By August 29, Frederick had brought his army together with that of his brother, Prince Henry.[43] Now he took the initiative, turning to pursue Daun's forces into southern Silesia. However, while all this took place, Russian and Austrian units were again threatening Berlin. In October, they raided the city, prompting Frederick to change direction once again, this time moving north into Saxon territory.

A Second Berlin Surprise

The war's second raid on Berlin (figure 9.2) took place in October 1760, almost exactly three years after the surprise attack launched by General

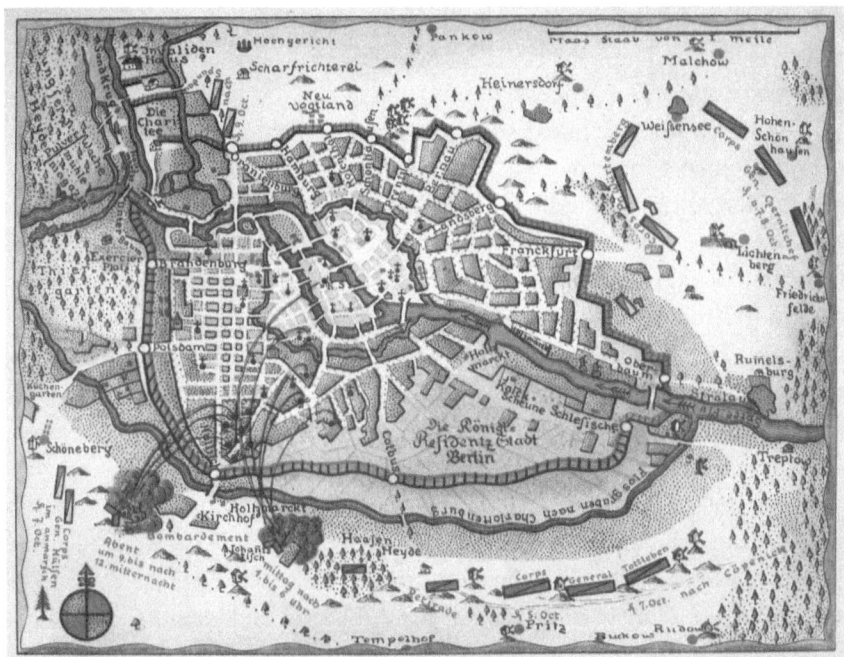

Figure 9.2 The royal residence city of Berlin in 1760. Colored print (ca. 1760).
Source: bpk Bildagentur/Dietmar Katz/Art Resource, New York.

Hadik. This time the Prussian capital was raided jointly by Russian forces commanded by Gottlob Curt Heinrich von Tottleben (1715–1773) and Austrian troops under Lacy.[44] Johann Peter Süssmilch (1707–1767), a Protestant pastor in Berlin, described the events in detail in a report he submitted to August Friedrich von Eichel, a senior Prussian privy councillor.[45] Since early October, Cossack troops, the traditional Russian vanguard, had frequently been spotted in the countryside around the city. On Friday, October 3, the moment arrived: "The day was very beautiful, but they were rather like the sultry days of Jul[ius], which so often can bring a sudden Storm. Around 10 o'clock there was a terrible Moving-about in the streets, and much murmuring, and it was said about that the Cossacks were already by the Gates, at the Hallesches Tor and the Ricksdorfer Tor, and this was also alas all too true, and those experienced in matters of war thus concluded that the main Body of the enemy would arrive at noon, and this also came to be."[46] The Prussian General von Seydlitz was in Berlin at this time recovering from wounds suffered at the Battle of Kunersdorf, and it fell to him to prepare the city's defense. At one o'clock in the afternoon, the city received a formal demand of surrender. At two o'clock, the Russians opened fire with two batteries of artillery.

The initial bombardment had little impact, with no buildings set alight and only three people injured. After Hadik's invasion in 1757, bastions had been added to the city walls, which allowed counterfire to be directed at an enemy outside. But that evening the situation changed, as another attack was launched, this time with more serious effects. Around nine o'clock, "enemy fire from Cannons and Howitzers was redoubled, and continued with the greatest possible violence until a Quarter past Ten O'Clock. Bombs, fires, bullets, burning bullets, Shuvalov ovals [oval-bore howitzers] were fired in terrible numbers, along with other bombs not known to our artillerymen, and sundry Burning Matter, more than would have been imagined possible for such a small number of guns."[47] The first buildings began to go up in flames, and then "around 11 o'clock a Raid itself began, as we had suspected." Pastor Süssmilch's account stresses, above all, the contrast of noise and silence, recalling how the infantry and "dismounted Dragoons and Cossacks" approached with "a terrible shriek [. . .] which could be heard in buildings in the middle of the city, in the still of night, as well as many individual shots from small firearms."[48]

The following day, Saturday, was quiet. On Sunday, Prince Friedrich Eugen of Württemberg engaged with Cossack units close to the city, forcing them to retreat beyond the town of Köpenick. Monday saw a few minor skirmishes. The following day—Tuesday, October 7—turned out to be another "warm and fearful day,"[49] with Cossack units storming Schöneberg, another outlying district, with artillery deployed on both sides. But once again, Süssmilch ultimately records a lack of conclusive action, noting that "even this Tuesday, so terrible for Berlin, was not a decisive Day, and towards Evening we observed both armies in the same place they had been this Morning."[50] The next day brought poor visibility and other sensory impairments: "A storm Wind blew up out of the west in the afternoon, and then nothing could be heard within the city, nor could much at all be seen, because of the Rain that followed behind."[51] That night the Prussian commanders ordered the garrison to withdraw to Spandau and directed the city government to surrender to Tottleben's Russian command.[52] The formal terms of surrender were reasonably favorable to the ordinary population: No troops would be billeted in the city and no Cossacks would be posted inside the city. In fact, the city did not escape so lightly: "In the confusion of the Troops entering the city, all was quiet, and we heard of no disorder, except for the Hussars and Cossacks who entered the Invalidenhaus, beyond the city's Palisades, looted everything, and did vile deeds as always, and they also penetrated through the Palisades, to the buildings of the Charité, the large Sick and Poor House." This was no isolated incident of disorder. Moreover, the promise not to billet troops turned out to apply only to Russian troops, not to Austrian troops, leading Süssmilch to observe that "the part [of Berlin] occupied by Russians was more orderly than that under the Austrians' control."[53]

Berlin's newspapermen were the only group singled out for direct punishment by the occupying powers. In an addendum to his report, Süssmilch notes that the editors of two Berlin newspapers, the *Haude-Spenersche Zeitung* and the *Vossische Zeitung*, were sentenced to run a gauntlet of a thousand soldiers at the Neumarkt, a large public square in the city. The previous year they had published a Prussian government report dishonoring General Tottleben, who now sought satisfaction for the insult he had suffered. Specifically, on Tuesday, October 2, 1759, reports from Pomerania and the Neumarck had suggested that a lieutenant named Brincken had "been ordered" to "raise contributions from these territories." The order, it was claimed, had been given by Tottleben, described as a turncoat famous for his cruel tactics but also as a "well-known avanturier [adventurer]."[54] At the very last minute, the two editors were pardoned: The order arrived as they were already standing in the public square, chests bared, awaiting the command to run the gauntlet.[55]

The punishment of the editors was an unusually symbolic action. For the most part, occupiers' interests were quite material. The city received an initial demand for a compulsory contribution of 4 million thalers, a figure negotiated down to 1.5 million by Johann Ernst Gotzkowsky (1710–1775), a Berlin merchant who had already helped to arrange the terms of surrender.[56] Gotzkowsky was a major supplier to the court and also responsible for acquiring paintings for Frederick's collection. He was in direct communication with the king. Later, Berliners were said to have called him "the patriotic merchant," in recognition of his services to the city. As to the contribution, the city paid over 700,000 thalers in silver, with the remainder in bills of exchange supplied by local merchants. The bills of exchange issued to Hadik in 1757 had all been paid, and this financial reliability proved an advantage for the city in 1760, since it meant the occupiers did not take hostages. Süssmilch observes: "How advantageous are Trust and good Faith in human society, even in war, and in negotiations with the Enemy?"[57] In addition to the cash, many other items were directly taken from the city, with militarily significant resources destroyed, including the city foundry and the mint. The gunpowder mill was "blown up" and Prussian army equipment "sold off cheaply" to citizens, since the occupiers had no way to transport it.[58] Johann Friedrich Heyde, the master baker and chronicler who also recorded Hadik's raid, on this occasion notes: "It is possible to buy a uniform [Mondur] for a few Groschen, a rifle for 3 or 4 Groschen. There was also some thousand Barrels of salt stored in the Zeughaus, and some of those Barrels sold for 8 to 16 Groschen."[59] The City Palace was only partly looted. Süssmilch claims "six crates of old silver" and the contents of the palace treasury were taken; the palaces at Schönhausen and Charlottenburg received rougher treatment. The loss of several hundred horses may ultimately have been a more painful blow for the royal household.[60]

On Sunday, October 12, foreign troops left Berlin after just four days of occupation. According to Süssmilch, Berliners were thankful that their own troops had withdrawn to Spandau, since this largely saved the city from destruction.[61] The pastor regards the issue as quite clear and the actions of the Prussian military as entirely rational. Heyde, the baker, was less sympathetic: "There was No-one to help from the 4th October to the 15th, our Superiors were not here. We knew not where was our King with his Army. All sorts of hot air was spoken, supposedly to console us, but on closer inspection, it was merely wind, nothing more."[62]

The brief capture of the Prussian capital had limited strategic benefit, but the psychological effects should not be underestimated. Once more, foreign powers had succeeded in occupying Berlin; this time it also involved a Russian advance far into the west. Russian occupation was associated with particular suffering, especially for those in surrounding villages who fell victim to bands of marauding Cossacks. Süssmilch documented events outside the walls, observing that while the city "enjoyed extensive peace and protection," Cossacks and hussars carried on "their usual business in the Countryside." Barns were emptied, cattle and sheep were driven away, and anything that could not be removed was smashed to pieces. "The Womenfolk, old women and young girls, married women and daughters, were raped in front of their Parents and husbands, and many died from the Violence they endured; in short, they stopped at nothing which Inhumanity could conceive, and which will cause Horror and Disgust to Humanity." Two aspects of Süssmilch's account are notable, going beyond his stereotypes of atrocity. First, he makes a direct connection between the level of violence applied in any given region and the possibility of publicity, noting that the generals of the occupying army at first flattered themselves that atrocities seen elsewhere would not here be "carried out before the eyes of so many, impartial Witnesses." Second, as with many Russian sources, Süssmilch notes that the "ordinary Russian soldier [. . .] also very much complained about this Rabble," since the Cossacks would often destroy other Russian soldiers' corn and foraged produce.[63] The Cossacks' actions were not hidden from the public, as is confirmed by several contemporary pamphlets.[64] Even in Britain, pamphlets were published on "Russian cruelty," including one by the evangelist preacher George Whitefield (1714–1770) and the Lutheran Court Chapel in London, which sought to raise money for regions affected in Prussia: an early form of transnational "media entanglement" that succeeded in raising substantial funds.[65]

Wittenberg, another city in Electoral Saxony, also suffered a devastating fire during the conflict.[66] On October 13, 1760, while under Prussian occupation, the city was bombarded and set ablaze by Austrian and Imperial artillery.[67] The fire broke out at half past six in the morning, and before long, the conflagration had consumed large swathes of the city. The besiegers had previously cut off water supplies, blocking ditches and the city's medieval water pipes, to make it harder to extinguish the flames. The city surrendered the same day.

The destruction was very serious: One-third of Wittenberg's buildings were destroyed, 132 buildings in the center and some 200 in outlying districts, with another 181 badly damaged.[68] Fortunately, loss of life was limited, with just two fatalities.[69] Wittenberg Castle, the castle church, and the law faculty of the university, along with various monastery buildings and chapels, were destroyed in the fire. The city's fate prompted several reflections by local theologians, which are, above all, significant for their wide-ranging theological interpretations of the event. The account by the Wittenberg theology professor Christian Siegismund Georgi (1702–1771) also includes three powerful engravings that document the destruction. He explains that he wrote his text to offer "adequate concepts of God's just and punitive Judgment" to the faithful and to explain the miraculous preservation of his own house when all around it were destroyed. He also mentions "various outsiders" who had asked him about "the terrible condition of our destroyed Wittenberg, especially our sacred Places." To address those inquiries and to inform those who wish to "afford [Wittenbergers] assistance in their Suffering," he declares that he will "depict our Fate in a public Letter rather than a private one, while presenting this fire as an Example of God's Anger."[70] He primarily interprets the conflagration as divine judgment on the sinful lives of Wittenberg's citizens,[71] and he also links the destruction of the Schlosskirche to the burning of Dresden and Zittau: "This mother of the Evangelical Zion would all too soon follow her unfortunate daughters, the Protestant Kreuzkirche in Dresden, and God's house in Zittau."[72] A deacon of the town, Christian Ernst Meerheim (1720–1762), wrote a penitential sermon in reaction to the fire titled "The Wittenberg Taberah." The reference to Taberah placed the sermon in a long theological tradition of interpreting urban conflagrations: Many early modern "fire sermons" invoked God's burning of the camp of the Israelites who had spoken out against Moses.[73] Meerheim directly compares the dissatisfied Israelites to his own Saxon compatriots but also offers words of comfort to his congregation, noting the comparatively few deaths that occurred. He goes on to suggest the destruction might have been much worse if, for example, the fire had reached the large quantity of gunpowder stored under the castle.[74]

By now, Frederick's opponents were advancing ever deeper into the Prussian heartland. Although forced onto the defensive, the king was still determined to face his enemies and defeat them in battle. An opportunity soon arrived. By early November, Daun had reached Torgau, on the Elbe River in northwestern Saxony, where the two sides met in battle on November 3, 1760.[75] Frederick's approach was tactically innovative: He divided his forces, with Zieten's troops in the south and his own to the north, where he attacked in three columns. The early Prussian waves were all repulsed, at high cost to the attacking force. Around half past four in the afternoon, the battle seemed to reach a turning point—its *crisis*—when Frederick was struck by a musket ball and fell unconscious from his horse.[76] At the southern end of the battlefield, Zieten was enjoying more success, with his forces pushing through to take the high ground from the Austrians. But could they claim to have actually *won* the battle? Torgau was the final example of a battle without a clear outcome during the Seven Years' War. Archenholz describes the scene: "The soldiers of both armies [. . .] appeared to have decided upon a cessation of hostilities, and congregated together round the numerous fires in the forest of Torgau, where they patiently awaited the return of day, as neither party was aware of the result, and each had determined to give themselves up to those who had been victorious."[77] Things became much clearer when the sun rose over the "field of Corpses," at least to contemporary eyes. Frederick realized that "there remained no more Austrians to fight. He was possessed of the entire Battlefield; Victory was entirely decided, and Saxony reclaimed."[78] Juliane von Rehdiger, the Silesian noblewoman, also heard about the conflicting interpretations of Torgau: "Both parties claim Victory, but the Imperials withdrew across the Elbe in the night, leaving Torgau and the battlefield to the King."[79] The two sides lost almost thirty thousand dead and wounded between them.[80] Frederick downplayed the losses, attempting to conceal the battle's true casualty figures. Military leaders on both sides were under pressure to justify their actions; in response, they tended to blame others or complain about the shortage of capable subordinates.[81] The overall strategic situation, like the battlefield at Torgau, was evenly balanced. Frederick had by no means succeeded in retaking Saxony, where the Austrians remained doggedly present, with Daun able to withdraw his forces to Dresden.

Frederick wintered at Leipzig, where he wrote many letters excoriating his situation. On September 30, he wrote to his brother Henry: "This campaign seems even more unbearable than the previous. No matter what care and trouble I take, in large matters I cannot make a single step forward, only in small matters do I enjoy success."[82] The great monarch had also been physically affected by the campaigns of the previous years; he had turned into "Old Fritz." To Countess Sophie Karoline de Camas, a confidante and an influential courtier, he wrote on November 18: "I swear this is a dog's life, which none have known excepting myself and Don Quixote. All this upheaval, all this disorder, has made me so old you will barely know me. The hairs on the right side of my head are entirely grey; my teeth are breaking off and falling out; the wrinkles on my face are like the folds of a woman's skirt, my back is as bent as a fiddle, my mind as sad and melancholy as a Trappist monk."[83]

The Fighting in Northwestern Germany

After the defeats of 1759, the French leadership set ambitious goals for the new campaigning season. Hesse and Hanover were to be retaken: This would, wrote Broglie, the marshal of France, put "France in a position to dictate peace terms by next October."[84] The fortresses of Wesel, Düsseldorf, Cologne, and Koblenz were to be held, while the main army would operate in the Frankfurt area. To achieve these aims, the French deployed an enormous force, totaling 156,200 troops.[85] On the other side, Ferdinand commanded 98,000 men and held the fortresses of Münster, Lippestadt, Kassel, and Hameln. Both Broglie and Ferdinand planned to divide their forces, deploying smaller armies in Westphalia while retaining their main force in Hesse.

Included among the British troops sent to reinforce Ferdinand was Corporal William Todd, the soldier-diarist last seen with British forces in northern France in 1758. By the spring of 1760, Todd had transferred from the 30th to the 12th Infantry Regiment, which meant a redeployment from garrison service in England to the war in northwestern Germany. His unit landed at Emden and set out for Osnabrück, arriving there on April 20, 1760.[86]

Several weeks later Todd traveled via Paderborn to Fritzlar in the north of Hesse, where, on May 20, Ferdinand concentrated the main part of his army. Grotehenn was also in this troop concentration, with the Brunswick soldier noting proudly that "we will indeed put a sizeable Army in the Field this Year."[87] Todd's account of his time in northern Germany covers a variety of incidents but mainly focuses on his drinking schnapps and the general lack of available resources. Another British witness, Major Richard Davenport (1719–1760)—whom we last saw in 1758, when language barriers thwarted his sexual ambitions—also writes reports from this theater of war, but his testimony comes with a significantly different emphasis. Davenport, a cavalry officer, focuses, above all, on his horses and equipment—in particular, his uniform—occasionally digressing to discuss the weather or the local delicacies. Unlike the infantrymen who appear in Todd's diary, cavalry officers drink red wine—and only that. Davenport takes up his winter quarters at Bramsche in early 1760 and writes to his brother: "I am much better lodged than I was last Winter and my Horses are tolerably well put up. We are but three Leagues from Osnabruck, which is a very good Town, from whence we can be supplied with wine at a reasonable Rate."[88]

Davenport's final letter, dated July 12, 1760, is written from the camp at Sachsenhausen: "I never was in better health and spirits."[89] His only complaint is the lack of sleep and regular meals. He experienced his first skirmishes with the enemy at Butzbach at the end of May; by the end of June, the French had managed to cross the Ohm River and were planning to cross the Eder. After a minor encounter near Korbach, the Anglo-Hanoverian force instigated the first major battle of the year, fought close to Warburg on July 31.[90] The following letter was sent to Davenport's brother not by Davenport himself but by "Eliott," his friend and fellow officer. Writing on August 1, 1760, after the battle, Eliott addresses Davenport's brother: "Dear

Davenport, prepare yourself for the greatest shock. Our dear friend, your brother, was killed upon the spot, instantaneously, in Yesterday's action."[91] Major Davenport had been killed in a cavalry attack, an action that endures in British cultures of military remembrance thanks to an incident involving John Manners, the Marquess of Granby (1721–1770). The Brunswick writer and historian Jakob Mauvillon describes the moment: "This was the attack where Lord Granby, the commander of the Royal Horse Guards, charged at the head of troops. In the heat of battle, his hat flew from his head, now all the more visible for its large bald pate. Regardless, he rode on, showing clearly that had he led the English cavalry at Minden, it would most certainly not have remained behind [a reference to Sackville's cavalry failing to charge at Minden]."[92] In Mauvillon's account at least, the performance of genuine gallantry trumps the codified meanings of aristocratic military attire. The anecdote became so well-known that, to this day, many British pubs still bear the name of the cavalryman-aristocrat.

Ferdinand had fought the battle at Warburg as part of his broader operation to secure a line along the Diemel River, but that line was now crossed by Prince Franz Xaver of Saxony, a French ally, leading his battalions north on a foray across the territory of Hesse. The Saxon advance took the cities of Kassel, Münden, and, finally, on August 5, Göttingen. Here their move north was brought to a temporary halt by overextended supply lines, which stretched all the way back to Frankfurt.[93] Once again, all of Hesse was in French hands. In September, Ferdinand tried to push French forces across the Diemel, but the attempt was unsuccessful, so he sent his nephew, the Duke of Brunswick, to lay siege to the fortress of Wesel with thirty thousand men. Arriving at Wesel on September 30, they first spent several days preparing the siege train.[94] A French force with fresh troops, commanded by the Marquis de Castries, Belle-Isle's nephew, was sent to relieve the besieged fortress. But the young Duke of Brunswick reacted quickly, sending twenty thousand troops to face Castries's advancing force. This led to the bloody Battle of Kloster Kamp, fought during the night of October 15, which ended in a narrow French victory, forcing Brunswick to lift the siege of Wesel three days later.[95] However, Castries did not have the resources to pursue the Anglo-German armies, and Ferdinand soon launched new counteroffensives, including a siege of Göttingen, a particularly arduous action that lasted from November 21 to December 12 but that nonetheless proved unsuccessful.[96] This marked the end of the 1760 campaigns, and both sides withdrew to winter quarters.[97] Frederick was appalled at Prussia's poor return on the campaign and deluged Ferdinand with reproaches and lists of lessons to be learned. His commander replied dryly: "The impatience which Your Majesty displays with me cannot change the season nor can it supply foodstuffs. It seems profoundly unfair that you make me responsible for things over which I have no control."[98] In Britain, support was also wavering for the unsuccessful German war.[99] Had it been completely pointless to send British reinforcements for the Allied army? More generally, the war in Germany was becoming less important to Britain, largely because of the conquest of Canada, a process completed when Montreal fell in September 1760.

Montreal Capitulates

In 1760, the challenge for the British in Canada was to hold Quebec while also moving to capture Montreal. For the French, the task was nothing less than preventing the looming loss of Nouvelle-France. In April and May 1760, they made an attempt to retake Quebec, with the Chevalier de Lévis leading an army of seven thousand men from Montreal.[100] James Murray (1721–1794) was the British military commander tasked with defending the city. In addition to the French threat, his men faced extreme cold and a shortage of supplies. On April 28, the French force took the initiative and engaged the British close to the Plains of Abraham in a battle even bloodier than the first they fought there. This time the contest was between two numerically balanced armies, each with about thirty-eight hundred men. The French managed to push the British back behind the city walls and lay siege to them—an almost exact reversal of the events of the previous September, when the French had been forced to retreat into the city. One clear difference this time around was the atrocious weather, which saw British artillery sink deep into wet slush. The battle raged for several hours; at its conclusion, the French had 193 dead and 640 wounded, while the British had 259 dead and 829 wounded.

The French, in the wake of this victory, nonetheless could not recapture the city of Quebec. The failure demanded explanation. For the French soldier Charles Bonin, it could, in part, be ascribed to a moment of bad luck. He reports that during the French landing, two artillerymen had fallen into the river. One was drowned, while the other found refuge on an ice floe. But the floe drifted into the British-occupied city, where the surviving soldier was rescued from the ice and revived. He died shortly thereafter—but not before revealing the French plans to his captors, giving the British a clear advantage in the battle.[101] As far as the siege was concerned, however, success or failure would depend on the supply situation. A tense period of waiting followed, with both commanders standing by for their respective supply convoys to sail up the St. Lawrence. It was simply a question of who would arrive first. The answer came two weeks later when loud cheers rang out from Quebec, as the British occupying force welcomed the appearance of the naval frigate *Leostoff*. The soldiers' hurrahs lasted for almost an hour, with hats hurled repeatedly in the air, and an artillery salute added to the acoustic performance. In his journal, the British officer John Knox reaches for a historical analogy: "I believe I may venture to advance, that the garrison of Vienna, when closely besieged, and hard pressed, above Fourscore years ago, by the Turks, were not more rejoiced on sight of the Christian army, under the famous Sobieski, marching to their Relief, than we of Québec were upon the arrival of the Leostoff, with the agreeable intelligence of a British fleet being masters of the River St. Lawrence, and nigh at hand to sustain us."[102] The British again had the upper hand. An exchange of prisoners followed, conducted under a flag of truce. Various goods were also exchanged, including newspapers, in what was, in fact, a subtle act of intimidation directed toward the French. The accounts of Knox and the Chevalier de Lévis both mention that newspapers were passed across the lines to the French generals. Knox recounts how "London News-papers, fraught with the defeat of Conflans, Thurot, and many other interesting events, were sent to the French Generals, early in the evening, by a flag of Truce."[103] Nonetheless, by May 11, Lévis was in a position to begin the bombardment of Quebec.[104]

As for Montreal, by early 1760, the conquest of the city was Pitt's top priority in the North American theater. Precise instructions had been issued to provincial governors in a circular dated January 7.[105] But the situation on the ground was less clear. Amherst, the British commander in chief in North America, was receiving conflicting reports about events at Quebec, 160 miles downriver from Montreal.[106] On May 28, news came from Oswego suggesting that the French had retaken the city. But a new report arrived on the same day, via two prisoners who had escaped from Montreal. This suggested that "the French have retir'd from Quebec with great Losses, and given up the Siege."[107]

In August 1760, the British lay siege to Fort Levis, the new French fortress downriver from Montreal. Bonin soberly reports the heavy bombardment while praising the finesse of his commander, Pierre Pouchot (1712–1769), who realized that further resistance was futile. On August 25, Pouchot ordered the firing of multiple gun salutes, ostensibly to mark the king's birthday but, in fact, to use up the remaining stores of gunpowder and thus prevent them from falling into British hands. Pouchot surrendered after the final shot was fired; among other things, this resulted in Bonin being taken to New York as a prisoner.[108] However, the young French soldier led a very free life in the city, which he describes in detail—especially his concerns regarding his hoard of cash, which amounted to 13,500 Canadian francs. He exchanged some of this money for guineas, obtaining a poor rate, and sold his gold watch and other valuables.[109] The end was approaching fast, both for Bonin's sojourn in North America and for the entire project of Nouvelle-France.

In military terms, what followed was a coordinated effort by three armies on a scale never before seen in this theater. Advancing on Montreal, Amherst led over ten thousand men across the St. Lawrence, with General William Haviland (1718–1784) taking his thirty-three hundred men across Lake Champlain and Murray arriving from Quebec with twenty-five hundred troops. Between September 3 and September 6, the three armies joined forces before the city of Montreal, fielding a combined force of seventeen thousand men. (By this point, Murray's force had grown to four thousand.) The British siege of Montreal could begin. John Grant, the Highland officer of the Black Watch regiment, describes how, in the early morning of September 6, boats full of Amherst's soldiers approached the island of Montreal, landing at the settlement of La Chine, nine miles from the city: "At daybreak therefore the whole Army were embarked with 2 days' provisions in their haversacks but without their baggage. Marshalled in divisions, Colours displayed, drums beating, pipes playing, the River was like glass, the morning beautiful, it was a glorious sight." After landing, the British moved out at a quick march in the direction of Montreal. At this point, the mood changed. In Grant's words: "Our situation was not pleasant as we expected an attack every moment and we were not sure of a support."[110] After sundown, he and his fellow soldiers slept outside without tents, their bodies warmed by the hard march in hot weather. Many of them caught fever as a result, including Grant.

For the French, the situation inside Montreal was hopeless. Their erstwhile Native American allies were withholding support, and Governor Vaudreuil felt forced to agree to an immediate surrender. Having been ordered to seek a cessation of hostilities until it could be established whether peace had been agreed to in Europe, Bougainville was sent out to speak with Amherst under a flag of truce. Amherst replied to him in French: "I have come to take Canada and I will take nothing less."[111] What followed surprised even the soldiers present, including Grant and his comrades of the Black Watch: "The next day we stood to our arms, but the Capitulation of the Canadas was signed. Our tents arrived and I retired to mine in a high fever."[112] The agreement of surrender was signed on September 8, guaranteeing property rights and freedom of religion, as well as the right to freely return to France.[113] In his journal, Amherst proudly notes: "I believe never three Armys setting out from different & very distant Parts from each other joined in the Centre, as was intended, better than we did, and it could not fail of having the effect of which I have just now seen the consequences."[114] Back in England, the Sussex shopkeeper Thomas Turner noted victory celebrations taking place on October 7: "In the evening there was a rejoicing at Halland and bonfire for our armies under the command of General Amherst having taken Montreal and all Canada from the French. All the Neighbours were regaled with a supper, wine punch and strong beer."[115]

In Berlin, detailed information on the fall of Canada was published in an omnibus edition (*Sammeledition*) of the *Berlinische Nachrichten*, carrying news from October 11 to 21.[116] In Krefeld, the Mennonite bookseller Abraham ter Meer learned the news on October 15, through a French newspaper published at Cologne. Grotehenn, by now with Anglo-German forces near Warburg, was made aware of the news when he heard a victory salute fired on October 14.[117] People within the Holy Roman Empire were certainly aware of the fall of New France, although their daily lives must have presented more pressing problems.

Charles Bonin's memoir reflects on the loss of Canada in general, as well as his own more personal losses. Bonin ends the account of his North American years by outlining, with clear satisfaction, later legal proceedings begun against fifty colonial officials who had returned to France, in what became known as the *affaire du Canada*. Court proceedings lasted twenty-three months (although Bonin's memoir cites a figure of eighteen). Nineteen of the defendants tried were imprisoned in the Bastille, with eight ultimately ordered to pay restitution of sums totaling 11 million livres.[118] The *affaire du Canada* was one of the most famous trials in eighteenth-century France. It focused on money, above all, with defendants including the former Governor-General Vaudreuil; François Bigot (1703–1778), the intendant of Nouvelle-France; Joseph Michel Cadet (1719–1781), a major supplier to the army; and Michel-Jean-Hugues Péan, aide-major of the French navy.[119] After almost two years, judgment was handed down on December 10, 1763, in a final sentencing document that at times reads like a novel.[120] Bougainville managed to extricate himself from any association with the affair, as did Bonin's commander, Pierre Pouchot.[121] Pouchot's *Memoirs of the Recent War in North America* was published in 1781, one of the few personal accounts of the French and Indian War to come out in France. In fact, Pouchet had died some years before its republication, but a new war in the British colonies had prompted renewed French interest in the history of Canada.[122]

In January 1761, Bonin went aboard a British ship, the *James*, to be sent home to France. He reached Portsmouth on February 15 and by the end of the month had voyaged on to Le Havre. Here he was paid several years of wages, which he immediately exchanged for gold, along with his money from New York. This marked the end of Bonin's ten-year journey to the provinces of New France, now forever lost to his mother country.[123] Back in Paris, he began drafting his memoirs, a process that, including revisions, probably took him until the 1780s. Later the turmoil of the revolutionary period prevented their publication, and they were never made public in his lifetime.[124] Bonin's writing contains many descriptive passages about the Canadian landscape and its inhabitants. These are clearly written partly from a sense of ungraspable loss, as Bonin tries to make palpable for his readers all that had been abandoned by the French government.

Boom to Bust: Boston, New York, Philadelphia

The economic consequences of the war affected ports in the northeastern part of British North America, including Boston, New York, and Philadelphia.[125] The early years of the conflict helped reverse an economic slump that had afflicted the colonies between 1750 and 1754. The war boosted the shipbuilding industry, craft work flourished, and unemployment fell. In New York alone, the number of ships built increased from 157 in 1749 to 477 in 1762.[126] Military demand for bread and uniforms brought boom times in the bakery and tailoring trades. Real estate development accelerated steadily; the construction trade enjoyed good times as never before. Privateering and raiding activities also made their contribution to the prosperity of these port cities, although the popularity of privateering had paradoxical consequences for the government, slowing the supply of naval recruits and new soldiers for land-based forces. Moreover, the benefits were spread unequally across the cities of the northeast. Boston's brief economic growth spurt withered away when the war turned south toward the Caribbean. These conditions pushed more recruits from Boston joined the military than from any other part of the American colonies, an enlistment rate boosted by the rhetoric of religious war. Boston also suffered a disproportionally high number of casualties, a demographic hemorrhage worsened by the effects of a 1760 city fire. In 1756, Boston's population had stood at 15,680, Philadelphia's at 14,895, and New York's at 13,045. To compare the situation with Germany, at this time Göttingen was around half Boston's size, while Leipzig was roughly twice as big. But Boston's population stagnated during the war, while Philadelphia and New York enjoyed exponential demographic growth.[127]

The years 1759–1760 were ones of great military triumph, but they also marked an economic turning point for all three cities, as military spending diminished. Free-spending soldiers left the army and became veterans flooding into the labor market. Boston had less to lose than the other cities, and Philadelphia's recession was softened by continued activity in the construction industry. But New York was the main port for British military operations, and it was hit particularly hard by the army's departure. John Watts (1715–1789), Scottish-born but now one of New York's major businessmen, commented laconically that recent operations in the Caribbean meant soldiers now could drink their rum in a warmer climate, directly where it was produced.[128]

Prices for food and wood had been driven up over the course of the conflict, hitting the poor particularly hard. At the same time, taxes rose to previously unimagined levels. Almshouses were full, which affected Boston worse than Philadelphia, since the latter city had a longer history of institutions caring for the poor. But as the simultaneous construction boom in Philadelphia might suggest, there were also profiteers at the other end of the social ladder. Social inequalities in the city widened as a result of the war. On the whole, the conflict was preparing the ground for the movement, soon to appear, for political emancipation within the colonies. As economic tensions with Britain became more and more serious in the years following the war, a series of milestones marked the deterioration of their relations: the Sugar Act of 1764 and the Stamp Act of 1765 were only the first moves in what would be a long dispute over taxes and customs. Time and again, not coincidentally, these tensions would crystallize in Boston, location of the Boston Massacre in 1770 and the Boston Tea Party in 1773.

The Fischer Corps on the Rampage

Guerrilla fighting and other forms of small warfare created units that were, in effect, "confraternities of violence," including hussars, Freikorps volunteers, and other irregular formations. These units have been called a "practical corrective" to the slower, more large-scale war of maneuver, taking on important tactical functions. However, the autonomy they enjoyed presented a massive threat to "good Policey"—i.e., the ethical conduct of war.[129] Voices promoting good military discipline (*Kriegs-Zucht*), above all, criticized these "irregular Troops, to whom most of the Debauchery can be attributed," as one anonymous observer put it.[130] One notorious unit in the army of Electoral Hanover was the hussars led by Lieutenant General Johann Nicolas von Luckner (1722–1794). Their equivalent in the Prussian army was a "free battalion," commanded by Johann von Mayr (1716–1759), which regularly caused violent mayhem, especially in Franconia.[131] Of all the units under French command, the Freikorps led by Jean Chrétien Fischer (1713–1762) attracted particular public notoriety for its wartime atrocities. Fischer, a German Protestant originally from Württemberg, led a unit of French irregular forces in Hesse during the War of the Austrian Succession. By 1755, he was a colonel in the French service, based at Pondicherry in India.[132] His Fischer Corps was notorious and is frequently mentioned in personal testimonies from residents of Hesse, Westphalia, the regions of the Lower Rhine, and other parts of northern and eastern Germany, from the North Sea coast to Thuringia. Taken together, these various records trace a partial itinerary of the corps' movements during the war.

At the outbreak of the European war in 1756, the Corps des Chasseurs de Fischer had some five hundred men but continued to recruit, and over the next two years, it increased its strength to around two thousand troops. An entry in the register of a parish near Minden in northern Germany provides the following description of the Fischer Corps:

> It consists of 4 classes of soldiers—hussars, Mousquetirs, Grenadirs on horseback and Jäger, and is about 1,500 men strong. It was established by General Fischer during the last Brabant War, in which it endured its

first Tests. No Tests of courage or Fearlessness these, rather Tests of Rage, Inhumanity, Cruelty, and Robbery. During the war they were distinguished from other enemy soldiers by these hateful Vices, so improper to the Character of any true, upright Soldier. For this Corps is a rabble of oath-breakers, without Religion or Conscience, which commits Deeds such as ordinarily are done by Creatures most Hideous.[133]

One of the earliest references to Fischer's hussars and dragoons places them at Goch, near Cleves, on March 30, 1757.[134] In August 1758, the pastor Johann Georg Fülling reports that Fischer's men have been demanding contributions at Kassel. In mid-September, they appeared briefly before the city of Hanover.[135] They were thwarted by the city's fortifications and were unable to take hostages or extort contributions, but their appearance before the city walls temporarily paralyzed urban administration, with councilmen fleeing the city in terror. On September 26, 1758, Pastor Cuntz of Kirchditmold near Kassel witnessed fighting involving the "Fischersche Corps."[136] In January 1759, Mayor Geiss of Felda in Upper Hesse recorded the onerous billeting imposed by the "Fisser Kor"; in August 1759, they again appeared at Kassel.[137] Their extortion tactics—"mafia-style," we might say today—are described in detail in a letter written by Fischer in March 1760 to the governing council of Cleves: "I am glad indeed . . . to see that you Gentlemen have brought your Affairs sufficiently in order such that I am not forced to be difficult, since I do seem to be such a Terrible Bearer of Ill Fortune, and my Troops are light Troops, whom, despite my most arduous Efforts, I cannot always entirely maintain in Order; wherever we go, they do insist on having their Executions, at the very least. If I take a mere 800 men to some Country, I cost that Place some 10,000 livres a Day."[138]

In the summer of 1760, the Fischer Corps made its way across northwestern Germany: in May, it was reported to be at Elberfeld; on June 13, at Duisburg and Ruhrort; and by August, at Freudenberg, near Siegen.[139] In late April 1761, Fischer was appointed to lead the French army's espionage activities and gave up his position as leader of the corps. In July 1761, the Fischer Corps was still operating in the region. Now under the command of Marquis Louis-Henri-Gabriel de Conflans d'Armentières (1735–1789), it is recorded as attempting blackmail in the town of Soest.[140] Fischer died of a fever on July 1, 1762, at Landwehrhagen near Kassel, where he was buried under the church tower.[141] His gravestone is inscribed with these words: "Hic jacet ille Fischer; milites dolor, Ducis amicitia, Hoc sine arte monumentum, magno Gallorum Iuctu, posuerunt. Anno Domini MDC-CLXII. The prima Mensis Julii" (Here lies Fischer; the pain of soldiers, the friend of the duke, here the French erected this monument without art, in great sadness. In the year of the Lord 1762 on the first day of July).

Neither Fischer's resignation nor his death led to the disbanding of his eponymous corps, and news of its activities continued to fill the chronicles. On August 10, 1762, Johann Daniel Geitz, from Bottendorf in northern Hesse, reported that the "Fischersche Corps" had arrived at Frankenberg, taken the fortress, and imprisoned its garrison, and then it "fell upon the Town" and "plundered the People." Corps soldiers were billeted with citizens who "had to obtain for them as much Wine and Brandy as they could."[142] In the autumn of 1761, elements of the Fischer Corps were involved in a spectacular action in East Friesland, where their atrocities provoked a genuine peasant uprising.[143] Their new commander, Conflans, at twenty-six years of age, was young and inexperienced and apparently quite unable to maintain discipline within the ranks. The East Friesland case is notable because it involves sexual violence, otherwise mentioned relatively rarely in chronicles: "A company of Hussars [. . .] was not content with Plunder. It also wanted to violate Maids of the Village, shameful Treatment which The Village could not endure. The peasants took up Arms, killed five Hussars, and chased the Remainder as far as Hezel."[144] This kind of resistance only accelerated the spiral of violence, since the corps' soldiers could then claim a legitimate right of defense. At Loga, an actual battle took place between the corps and the peasants, who now totaled some three thousand men under arms.[145] One officer, Colonel Camfort, seems to have behaved with particular brutality. In *Ostfriesische Geschichte*, his history of East Friesland, published in the 1790s, Tileman Dothias Wiarda writes: "Discipline was the worst imaginable. No Lock or Bolt could put a limit to the greedy Hands of this band of Robbers, no Chastity could keep a Woman or Girl safe from the voluptuous Urges of such Monsters."[146] A French officer, Antoine Mopinot de la Chapotte, mentions events in East Friesland in a letter to Paris written on September 29, 1761. He was optimistic, however, that "all that takes place in this land will not damage our country's reputation, and a little too much zeal in plundering does not stop the substantial and useful contributions this country would have given, had they have been treated with a little less vigor."[147]

Events in East Friesland became as much of a media event as the Russian rampages in Ragnit in September 1757.[148] Clearly influenced by Ragnit and events of its kind, remarks by one anonymous diarist in the city of Soest are revealing about how French war atrocities were perceived. The entry for November 18, 1761 reads: "So far we have had no Frenchmen here, but there is most sad News from Lingen, Tecklenburg, Osnabrück, and especially East Friesland, where they comport themselves in the Turkish and Russian manner, exorbitant acts of Arson being the least thereof; every house Loot'd and Burn'd, especially those on the plain, and the Earth flattened; people Strangled and Beaten to Death, not a young Woman left Unviolated, so that finally Prince Soubise came to hear of it, and sent two noble Commanders to the Bastille."[149] It is notable that French violent practices regarded as particularly excessive are referred to as Turkish and Russian, inscribed within a semantics of Otherness that was used for an entire spectrum of violent acts. Even rape is placed within this category. Statements by the anonymous diarist are certainly not an entirely reliable source on this issue: He cites no comparable cases, even within the same region. The actions of irregular forces are thus here used to represent a very specific dynamic of violence. Irregular forces did not fit into the Enlightenment image of "limited" warfare, but in tactical terms, they very much represented a modernization of war fighting. This sort of structural paradox was also present in the case of prisoners of war, who also had a considerable effect, but in a different way, on the urban environments in which they found themselves.

Prisoners of War: Guests of the Enemy

Imprisonment is a particularly useful lens with which to examine what constituted "good Policey" in eighteenth-century warfare.[150] Placing enemy soldiers in long-term captivity—making them prisoners of war—was by no means the rule. Rather, in any situation, decisions were made on the ground by local military leadership. Whether an enemy was granted quarter in battle was a matter of tactics as much as humanity: This was seen clearly at Zorndorf, where no quarter was given. Only a pardon, communicated verbally or through signs, could performatively grant the status of prisoner of war; this was also a guarantee that the prisoner would not be physically harmed.[151] For example, if a garrison surrendered following a siege, it might be allowed to freely retreat if the soldiers took a solemn vow to return to their homeland and not fight again in the current war against the victor of the battle. There were many examples of this practice, including in Germany and North America. In an era of standing mercenary armies, it was also relatively common to "incorporate" individual captured soldiers into one's own army, as Frederick did with considerable unscrupulousness. But the approach failed radically with the Saxon army after the Battle of Pirna. Entire Saxon regiments were declared now to be part of the Prussian army, with their noncommissioned officers named as officers, but the Saxons, it turned out, were "loyal deserters" and collectively ran away.[152] If we compare Frederick's tactic with Native American practices of incorporating European prisoners into their tribe, we can see structural parallels across cultures on questions of "human resources."[153] In the North American context, these parallels are quite one-sided, since Europeans rarely took Native American prisoners: An Indian scalp brought almost as much money as a living male prisoner. During Pontiac's War, the war against Native American tribes launched by the British in 1763, General Amherst gave explicit orders to "take no Prisoners."[154]

Another way to avoid the expense of prisoners of war was through cartel agreements, which were made in order to enable prisoner exchanges.[155] Prussian, Austrian, Russian, British, and French prisoners were exchanged in various permutations via the cartels of Hadmersleben (1757, an exchange of Prussian and Austrian prisoners), Sluys (1759, French and British), Bütow (1759, Prussian and Russian), Brandenburg (1759, Prussian and French), and Dorsten (1760, French and British/Allied).[156] The value of prisoners was calculated according to their place in social and military hierarchies, using tables specially compiled for the purpose, akin to modern exchange-rate tables. These quoted the value of a prisoner in terms of either "heads" or cash, referred to as *ranzion*. Under this system, a Prussian infantry general was worth 10,000 guilders, or around two thousand "heads."[157] One example of lower-value prisoners was Croats serving in the Austrian military, who were imprisoned in very poor conditions in the Prussian fortress of Küstrin and who made various spectacular escape attempts as a result.[158] At first, the number of prisoners returning to serve in armies was very high. In the spring of 1758, 12,487 men returned to the Prussian army; the following year the figure was even higher, at 18,494.[159] But this happened much less, if at all, after about the midpoint of the war. A large number of soldiers were held in captivity for long periods.[160] Over the course of the war, 62,889 Prussian soldiers were held prisoner by the Austrians, who lost 78,360 men to imprisonment.[161]

In England and Scotland, French prisoners of war were held at a large number of prisons, including London, Portchester, Portsmouth, Exeter, Liverpool, Southampton, Sissinghurst, and Edinburgh. Only one prison was reserved solely for prisoners of war: Millbay in Plymouth.[162] In addition to prisons on land, the British relied to a greater degree on prison ships, known as "hulks." In 1756, the British had 7,261 prisoners of war in their custody; by 1763, the number had increased, according to some sources, to around 40,000. Other sources put the total figure at 65,000, with around 25,000 held on British soil.[163] The capture of prisoners had its greatest impact in the naval context: By the spring of 1758, 10,000 French sailors were held in British captivity, compared with total French naval manpower of 60,000 and total British naval manpower of 84,000. Unlike soldiers on land, sailors needed complex training and could not be recruited at short notice. In France, British soldiers were imprisoned at Brest, Dinan, and Morlaix, among other locations.

The treatment of prisoners was a key political issue in the propaganda war.[164] The Black Hole of Calcutta and the "massacre" at Fort William Henry were particularly striking examples of this. Some prisoners published testimony of their experience after their return home; in a North American context, these were referred to as captivity narratives, which amplified individual fates within the public sphere.[165] No less adventurous is a captivity narrative left by Johann Ludwig Wagner (1735–1820), a postmaster from the city of Pillau on the Baltic Sea. The city—modern-day Baltiysk in Russia's Kaliningrad exclave—had been taken by the Russians; Wagner plotted against the occupiers and was caught and sentenced to death by quartering, a sentence subsequently commuted to exile. Sent to a prison camp in Siberia, Wagner managed to return after several years and wrote a detailed account of his time in Russia.[166] Other prisoners produced artifacts while in captivity—for example, carvings in wood—thus bequeathing material evidence of a very particular kind.[167] One striking example of prisoner experience, encompassing several kinds of difference, happened in Montreal in 1759 and 1760, when twenty-seven Protestant British soldiers in the care of Catholic nuns were made to work in the order's hospital and almshouse.[168]

Prisoners had to live somewhere, but they also had to be guarded, which could tie down a substantial number of troops.[169] This became a particularly pressing issue for Ferdinand of Brunswick after the French advanced into northern Germany in late summer 1758. After capturing seven thousand

French prisoners of war, Ferdinand had to ensure that the captive population would not use up too many of his own forces at a moment when he urgently needed men to garrison the fortresses on the Weser.[170] By January 1760, the Austrians held 19,400 Prussian prisoners, distributed across eighteen small towns, in groups of 600 to 1,200.[171] Several accounts by Prussian soldiers held in the Austrian town of Krems channel their distaste for Catholic culture into descriptions of general moral decline, as discussed in chapter 5 on confessional conflict during the war.[172] The Imperial army also took Prussian prisoners of war.[173] Prussian soldiers from the garrison at Wittenberg, captured when the Imperial army took the town in 1760, spent over two years as prisoners in the Swabian town of Memmingen.[174]

In September 1758, considerable interest was aroused in Berlin by the passage of a large number of Russian prisoners of war on their way to Magdeburg (see the picture by Chodowiecki in figure 9.3).[175] The Swiss mathematics professor Johann Georg Sulzer writes in a letter of September 26: "Yesterday we enjoyed the Pleasure of witnessing 1,200 Russian prisoners led through here. It is impossible to give an adequate Idea of the Barbarism in the faces and Manners of these People, taking so many ugly Forms. A Callot could spend half a Lifetime drawing such bizarre Figures; I would

Figure 9.3 Russian prisoners of war in Berlin. Etching by Daniel Chodowiecki (Berlin, 1758). *Source*: akg-images.

have given a Finger from my hand that you could have seen this Appearance."[176] There was, in fact, a Prussian "Callot" creating such drawings at this time: Daniel Chodowiecki, who depicted a scene with Russian prisoners, including crypto-portraits of himself and his wife as almsgivers.[177] In the same letter, Sulzer mentions Swedish prisoners: "Our streets and Pathways are teeming with walking Battle-trophies; we shall soon have Prisoners of every Nation here."[178] In Sulzer's eyes, Berlin has become a kind of cabinet of curiosities, containing exotic specimens from all nations.

In November 1758, just days after Finck's Capture at the battle of Maxen, the Austrian officer Giuseppe Gorani was taken into Prussian captivity after a minor skirmish.[179] He would remain a prisoner until the end of the war; this initially meant a journey that took him through Berlin, Spandau, Magdeburg, Stettin, and Tilsit before he ultimately arrived at Königsberg. On December 24, 1759, he arrived in Berlin, where a brusque reception awaited. As the column of Austrian prisoners entered the city, crowds of locals cried out "Rossbach, Rossbach," mistakenly thinking them French because of their white uniforms. One courageous Austrian officer shouted back: "Kollin, Kollin!, Hochkirch, Hochkirch!, Breslau! Maxen!"[180] Names of battles had become slogans to be hurled at the enemy with pride or contempt. Upper-class life also saw its fair share of everyday polemical discourse. Gorani's fond account of Berlin society includes an anecdote in which a lady-in-waiting asks a French officer his thoughts on Berlin.[181] "Oh, it is a big village," he answers. "Indeed," she retorts, "and all the more so with these French peasants wandering about." In Berlin, Gorani, who was nineteen years old, was introduced to Samuel Formey (1711–1797), a Huguenot philosopher and a senior member of the Berlin Academy. Later he would describe his stay in the city as the happiest time of his life. After almost a year in Berlin, Gorani was moved to Neuruppin in November 1760 and from there to Magdeburg, where he seems to have led a libertine life, busy with games, balls, and love affairs.

A very large number of prisoners of war, from several armies, were detained at Magdeburg. The city had also been the refuge of the Prussian court; it was considered relatively safe and indeed proved to be so, since at no point in the war was it captured. But the city's most famous prisoner was not a prisoner of war. Friedrich Freiherr von der Trenck (1727–1794), an eighteenth-century adventurer, had been imprisoned as an Austrian spy in 1755 and was held for eight years in close captivity in the Magdeburg citadel. During his imprisonment, he wrote his memoirs. Trenck's recollections bear witness to his unusual life, even in the materiality of their production: He wrote them on Bibles, using his own blood, filling no less than eight volumes in this way.[182] The life of Magdeburg prisoners of war highlights the strict distinction between officers and ordinary soldiers, a central characteristic of the eighteenth-century military system. Prisoners of war inhabited different worlds, depending on their rank. This social distinction found many forms of expression, including living quarters, the carrying of weapons, and the preferred forms of sociability. The philologist Johann Christoph Adelung, in his book *Memoir of the Reign of Our Current King Frederick II*," claims that the POW population in Magdeburg amounted to one thousand officers and fifteen to twenty thousand common soldiers. Officers, he writes, "wore Sidearms and enjoyed the city's every Liberty," whereas "common Soldiers" suffered "greater Restrictions."[183] The liberty enjoyed by captive officers is highlighted in the brisk activity of the Masonic lodges that arrived with the captured regiments.[184] Another rich source on conditions for Magdeburg prisoners of war is the memoir written by Friedrich Eberhard Boysen (1720–1800), preacher at the city's St. Johanneskirche.[185] He estimates the prisoner population at around nineteen thousand, including Austrians, Russians, and Swedes, whom he judges "in respect of order, cleanliness, and manners" to be largely the same as French or Imperial soldiers. "And thus the judge's Sword and the doctor's Artistry were seldom called into use."[186] Boysen is also well placed to correct the media cliché of the Pandur militia as particularly immoral. Among the Austrians, "the Pandours took precedence, [as they had been] much decried by the News-papers for Immorality and Barbarism. A shortage of Accommodation led to their being quartered at the Grammar school. [. . .] Thus a seat of learning [Musensitz] was transformed into one of incarceration, but these Pandours did not desecrate the place, as the French had done in the guildhalls, but rather they treated it properly, in a way unexpected, for those supposed coarse men with beast-like ways."[187]

Even civilians could end up as prisoners: "One notable event in Magdeburg was the arrest of several respected councilors from Leipzig as hostages, who had to spend some time in the Citadel, and yet it was under honorable conditions."[188] An epidemic, first observed on June 18, 1759, took a heavy toll on the prison population, as well as on Magdeburg civilians.[189] Boysen counted over fifty dead in a single month in his own parish. The situation was made worse as those working in the hospital themselves gradually succumbed to the disease. As a pastor, Boysen's experience of the epidemic was mostly at the hospital for prisoners of the Imperial army. One revealing detail that emerges from his work is the fact that many soldiers changed their names when recruited, "for fear of Discovery by people in their home Regions." If they died, this could make it difficult to contact their places of origin. But the presence of prisoners of war in such numbers—all aristocratic courtesy and social pleasantries notwithstanding—was ultimately also a very serious security risk. Here Adelung's *Memoir* reports plans for an uprising on September 7, 1761, a day when the garrison would be undermanned: The plot was eventually discovered through the interception of prisoners' correspondence.[190] The plotters had apparently already "acquired a Supply of Arms and Munitions." Given the "dangerous Conspiracies" revealed in prisoners' subversive correspondence, the confidentiality of the mails was suspended, and prisoner communications more closely monitored.[191]

From 1760 on—in particular, after the capture of Fouque at the Battle of Landeshut—contacts between Prussian and Austrian officers grew more tense. The Prussian general so constantly mocked his conditions of detention in Vienna that he was transferred to military custody.[192] This set off a worsening of conditions of imprisonment on both sides, as each side responded to the other's actions. Eventually, Austrian officers in Magdeburg were transferred to the citadel. In late 1762, many Austrian prisoners, Gorani among them, were taken from Magdeburg and sent first to Stettin in September and then to Tilsit in November before eventually ending up at Königsberg in East Prussia. Gorani arrived there on February 28, 1763, two weeks after the signing of the Treaty of Hubertusburg, which ended the war between Prussia and Austria/Saxony. While in Königsberg, Gorani made the acquaintance of Immanuel Kant and was an active Freemason. As a whole, his imprisonment reads more like a Grand Tour than a period of incarceration, as Gorani becomes acquainted with wartime life in educated and university milieus, which provided their own very specific experiences of the war years.

Mars and the Muses: Universities at War

The war affected a number of university towns across the Holy Roman Empire, whose particular social structures led to specific circumstances of occupation. Conditions of occupation were often better in these towns, not least because of social contacts between army officers and people associated with the university. However, there were specific risks: Relations between students and soldiers, for example, were tense at the best of times. Student-soldier friction was most pronounced in universities in central Germany and Prussia, including Duisburg in the west, but there were also incidents in Göttingen, Erfurt, Halle, Wittenberg, Leipzig, Greifswald, Frankfurt an der Oder, and even as far east as Königsberg.[193] The situation was somewhat different in every case: Each university town had its own occupying power, which had its own particular status within the city. Nonetheless, there was a certain similarity in the structural challenges and opportunities universities faced. Universities were privileged corporations with their own legal jurisdictions, as well as the capacity to recruit new members. For this reason, their main concern was the issue of legal and ceremonial recognition. The presence of many scholars, some renowned far beyond their own universities, could be a risk or an opportunity. Learned men could serve as a form of entertainment for occupying forces, who were notoriously easily bored. The principal risk was that academics might have greater value as hostages if push came to shove.

Leipzig and Wittenberg were among the first university towns to be occupied. Prussian soldiers moved into Leipzig, then with a population of around thirty thousand, on the night of August 29–30, 1756, although most had had left the city by September 1.[194] Lieutenant Jakob Friedrich von Lemcke, the Prussian officer last seen fighting at the Battle of Lobositz, reports in his diary: "The inhabitants, who had not thought an enemy at hand, were entirely taken Aback by our sudden arrival. We marched through the beautiful city and stopped in front of the Town-hall, where we stood at the ready. The Prince of Braunschweig and his Uncle [the Duke of Brunswick and the overall Prussian commander Ferdinand of Brunswick], and some others, were all there at the Town-hall, ordering supplies and billeting for the troops."[195] Unfortunately for the people of Leipzig, this was merely the beginning of demands for contributions. On June 13, 1757, hostages, including the mayor and various city councillors, were taken from Leipzig to Magdeburg, where, as we have already seen, they were held as hostages at the Magdeburg citadel. They were to be imprisoned there until Leipzig paid its contributions, and they were ultimately released at the end of October.[196] In the early years of the war, members of the university were exempt from paying Prussian contributions.[197] On August 19, 1757, violent riots broke out during what students called an *Abend-Music* (evening music), a concert held to mark a professor's wedding. The Prussian commander, Major

General von Hauss, ordered his soldiers to beat the young students as they illegally paraded to the professor's house shouting "Vivat!" in his honor.[198]

Leipzig repeatedly changed hands over the course of the war, liberated by Austrian and Imperial forces only to be quickly reoccupied by Prussian troops, who proved to have an unrelenting passion for squeezing resources out of wealthy merchants. On October 13, 1758, the Leipzig writer Luise Gottsched (1713–1762) wrote to a friend about the Prussians' repressive measures, put in place that fall to force a payment of 600,000 thalers in unpaid contributions:

> Even from afar, you will have already suffered at news of the terrible days Leipzig has faced, which have been a stern test for sensitive souls. Imagine, if you will, the terrible tumult of soldiers on the first Sunday of the trade fair, with hussars swarming about, the silent fear of the population, the looming threat of an horrific destiny. With hearts pained, we saw the church service cut short, the bells left unrung, the gates locked, terrible preparations made to burn down our outlying districts, many unfortunates fleeing to the churchyards, children weeping, parents desolate, the old trembling in the belief they had seen their children and possessions for the final time, with only the salvation of their bare lives to outweigh the loss of all they possessed.[199]

Gottsched's summary of the effects of occupation on civilians is vivid and emotional. The soundscape of the city was changed by the occupation, as was the environment; access through the city gates was made more difficult, and there seemed to be soldiers at every turn. Residents perceived the occupation regime as a threat to life and limb, with churchyards becoming places of refuge. Gottsched's details are highly concrete and specific but nonetheless articulated with the use of classic topoi, including the sufferings of children and the old.

Frederick himself spent time in Leipzig during two successive occupation winters, in 1760–1761 and 1761–1762. The city's total contributions to Prussia during the occupation came to around 12 million thalers, as estimated by the nineteenth-century historian Ernst Kroker.[200] One intriguing figure who makes an appearance in Leipzig during the occupation is Johann Ernst Gotzkowsky, the "patriotic merchant" who helped negotiate contributions during the first brief occupation of Berlin in 1760, a figure who was much praised at the time but who did not act entirely out of altruism. Frederick initially demanded 1.1 million thalers from Leipzig, but Gotzkowsky, acting for the city council, managed to negotiate this down to 800,000 thalers. But the city was late in making its payments, which caused serious problems for Gotzkowsky. He ended up responsible for the debt, which was still not paid off long after his death in 1775. In 1762, Gotzkowsky again provided assistance to Leipzig after Frederick had demanded another 3 million Reichstalers, a figure Gotzkowsky negotiated down to 1.1 million, which he once more paid on behalf of the city. This time, however, he paid in poor silver coin, with lower precious metal content, whereas the bond itself had been denominated in "real" gold currency.[201] Depending on the specific terms of each repayment, Gotzkowsky's profit amounted to between 30 and 50 percent. Total war damage to Saxony in the Seven Years' War is thought to have come to between 250 and 300 million Reichstalers.[202]

Around the same time troops entered Leipzig on August 30, 1756, another Prussian force occupied Wittenberg, this one commanded by Prince Moritz von Anhalt-Dessau. Among the Saxon soldiers who had been evacuated from the city shortly beforehand was Moritz's brother, Friedrich Heinrich Eugen von Anhalt-Dessau (1705–1781), a senior officer in the army of Electoral Saxony.[203] One important witness to life in Wittenberg under Prussian occupation is Hans Carl Heinrich von Trautzschen, a Saxon army officer whose letters report on his stay in the city in the spring of 1757. Wittenberg was one of four locations to host captured Saxon officers after the surrender at Pirna.[204] Trautzschen was bright and keen to learn about the university town but could only mock the martial demeanor of some of its students: "Nothing seems more Horrible to me, and at the same time more Ridiculous, than the bellicose Spirit of the Students. If they think such affected Bravery mimics military men, then they do considerable Injustice in ascribing such a Quality to us."[205] Wittenberg recovered slowly from the damage of the war, especially the devastating city fire caused by Austrian bombardment in 1760. It was not helped in this by the debt of 159,665 thalers that it now additionally owed to Prussia.[206] The town's attractiveness as a place to study suffered noticeably as a result.

The university city of Duisburg, in Prussia's Rhenish provinces, was first confronted with French military forces in early April 1757.[207] Although it enjoyed some legal privileges, the university bickered constantly with the city's ruling magistracy, which meant it was not well placed to protect faculty and students from demands for billeting and contributions. The authorities at least decreed that professors' houses would have soldiers billeted only if there were no spaces in the homes of ordinary citizens.[208] The city saw repeated disturbances between students and soldiers. Moreover, many students left Duisburg for fear of forcible recruitment; this was a problem for professors, since students provided their main source of income. New student registrations fell from forty-eight in 1755 to twenty-one in 1760.[209]

On Saturday, July 16, 1757, French troops marched into Göttingen, another German university town placed under occupation.[210] The arrival of the French put the city under extreme pressure simply in terms of population, with seventy-five hundred soldiers now added to its ordinary population of eighty-three hundred. The autobiography of Johann David Michaelis (1717–1791), a professor of theology at Göttingen, looks back fondly on the French as the "best Enemies anyone might have."[211] His benevolent interpretation is perhaps unsurprising; a record of Göttingen billets for 1761 and 1762 registers his home as vacant, the only house in the city listed as such.[212] After the war, many cities that had undergone a siege, including Leipzig, Hanover, Kassel, and Münster, turned their city walls into promenades. Göttingen also did so, repurposing its fortifications into open green spaces.[213]

On October 29, 1757, another university town, Halle an der Saale, was briefly raided by French units looking to extort protection money.[214] After a deal had been negotiated, city councillors and other dignitaries were taken hostage and did not return until November 17. Two days after the French attack, on October 31, there was another raid on the town, this time by elements of the Imperial army, which plundered and burned buildings. On this occasion, Johann Friedrich Striebritz (1707–1772), a philosopher and the university prorector, was called to act as negotiator. Imperial troops raided the town again in August 1758 and yet again one year later, leading to further hostage taking. Among those taken on this occasion were the professors Johann Tobias Carrach (1702–1775) and Johann Ernst von Flörcke (1695–1762).[215] The hostages from Halle were held at Nuremberg, where some—including Flörcke—died before Prussian troops liberated the group in 1762. On October 8, 1760, Andreas Elias Buechner, a professor of medicine at Halle, wrote to Christoph Jacob Trew in Nuremberg, mentioning two "very hard enemy Invasions," each of which "lasted close to one Month, and caused extraordinary unrest. Our *fata* at the University is more tolerable, since both General Lusinsky and the Duke of Württemberg exempt professors from billeting and its arduous Consequences; but the merciless Imperial war commisarii treated us all the worse as a result, and the Corpus Professorum alone had to supply some 4000 Reichsthalers for the Contribution demanded."[216] There were rumors that Catholic occupying forces would convert the Francke Foundations, a prominent Pietist educational institution, into a Jesuit college. This turned out not to be the case, but Halle was particularly hard-hit among the university towns of the empire because of frequent raids, albeit usually short-lived, by mobile cavalry units, especially hussars and Croats.[217] The sums demanded by the raiders increased steadily, and Halle was less fortunate than other university cities—for example, the eastern Prussian city of Königsberg—in negotiating special academic status.

Russian troops occupied Königsberg, the traditional royal seat of East Prussia, on January 22, 1758. Two days later city officials swore an oath of allegiance to Tsarina Elizabeth, and members of the university did so the following day.[218] Academic freedom and university finances were left untouched. In fact, the Russian occupation provided a boost for the social status of professors, who were invited to receptions at the palace, while officers attended university ceremonies and public disputations in large numbers.[219] While he was based at Königsberg, the Russian officer and diarist Andrei Bolotov was tasked with keeping an eye on two students, one a young relative of his own general and the other the son of another general. He clearly maintained good contacts with local academics: "All of this made me known within the university, earning me the particular esteem and respect of the professors, so that they would invite me to every university celebration, alongside famous men, thus shewing me exceptional honor and courtesy. In this manner I came know the ways and habits of the university, and familiarize myself with what was taught there."[220] In addition to Bolotov's account, the diary of Johann George Bock (1698–1762), a professor of poetry, gives a detailed overview of the situation in the city.[221]

Königsberg remained under occupation until August 1762, with the greatest impact perhaps being a wave of cultural modernization. Russian officers brought money into the city but also a lifestyle that went beyond the prevailing limits of class and religion. The pietistic university town became a place of "balls, masquerades, sleigh rides, illuminations, fireworks, plays," and much more. Women now also attended these events, accompanied by military officers.[222] Bock notes that the Russians had "observed perfect discipline." After one year of occupation, he comes to this conclusion: "If we are truthful, we have experienced nothing hostile except the contributions imposed. Excellent military discipline has been observed, salaries are paid correctly, there have been no affronts, and most things have been left as they were."[223] However, reports from the countryside surrounding Königsberg stand in stark contrast to such urban civility. Bock's diary does make some reference to conditions in rural areas, but reports on these were subject to censorship within Königsberg.[224]

At the University of Greifswald, on the Baltic coast, professors were squeezed hard by the Prussian army's contribution demands, which highlighted underlying conflicts between the estates and the "Academie." The estates could not accept benefits or special privileges for academics. The diary of Augustin von Balthasar (1701–1786), a Greifswald lawyer, offers a close-up view of tensions in the city's society, as well as the basic attitudes toward the university. In a striking anecdote, Landrat von Bähr—a *Landrat* was a minor public official—loses control of himself at a meal attended by officers and academics, exclaiming that, as Balthasar phrases it, "no Professor and no Academy were of any use to the Country, and once Peace had come, we should locate a Wagon and seek the Highway that leads from here, etc. etc." Landrat von Bähr then announces that he had studied three years at Greifswald and learned precisely nothing. This was going too far even for Balthasar, who responds in kind, making his antipathy clear, noting that "a professor is of greater use than a Landrat" and suggesting that Bähr's failure to learn was no one's fault but his own. Had the landrat spent ten years at university, Balthasar quotes himself as saying, "he would in any case have learned nothing."[225] This is an example of how the war could highlight social and hierarchical tensions; the pressure it brought to bear could force individuals to take up public positions. Nonetheless, as in Göttingen and Königsberg, professors like Balthasar here moved in the same social circles as army officers and were on friendly terms with them.

The overall problems faced by universities were similar everywhere, but the way they were dealt with differed in each specific case. In all university towns, homes and university spaces were occupied and sometimes destroyed, contributions were demanded, there was conflict between students and soldiers, and the possibility of being taken hostage loomed over professors and town officials. Moreover, the permanent presence of soldiers in university towns brought its own problems: Wounded soldiers could be a source of disease, for example. Social divisions widened still further. Marginalized social groups often fared particularly badly, while professors, with their many privileges, often got on rather well with officers from the occupation forces. In some places, foreign officers even had a culturally modernizing impact, as when their presence brought theater to Göttingen.[226] But latent tensions between different social institutions, each with its respective privileges, frequently now emerged in the form of open confrontation.

CHAPTER X

1761

New Alliances, Missed Opportunities

British Gains and the Pacte de Famille

In September 1761, Johann Philipp Zellmann, a wine merchant from Herzberg am Harz in Lower Saxony, noted in his journal: "Meanwhile, as our country is so Mistreat'd, the English exult in their conquests; while we are deprived of our sausages, they take everything from the French in Asia, Africa and America."[1] He distances himself from the British, warning of overconfidence even as he notes their joy in victory. The wine merchant had suffered at the hands of Herzberg's French occupiers, and he takes more satisfaction in French losses than in British victories. The year 1761 would see more British progress toward victory in India and the Caribbean, while the war in Germany seemed mired in stalemate.

George II had died in October 1760, leading to an escalation of long-simmering rivalries among British leaders, exacerbating the fragility of the Pitt-Newcastle administration.[2] Pitt belonged to the camp of the late monarch, while the Earl of Bute belonged to a faction supported by the new king, George III. In January 1761, with the monarch's support, Bute demanded ministerial office. The three Whig ministers—Newcastle, Devonshire, and Hardwicke—declared themselves in favor of his appointment as secretary of state, knowing this would be unacceptable to Pitt.

The Duke of Belle-Isle, the French secretary of state for war, died on January 26, 1761, with Foreign Minister Choiseul temporarily taking over his responsibilities. In October, his cousin, César Gabriel de Choiseul-Praslin (1712–1785), was named as a replacement foreign minister.[3] During Choiseul's last months as foreign minister, he had pushed for a peace treaty, while, at the same time, as war minister, continuing to plan the next campaign in Germany. In diplomatic terms, this meant France extended a relatively generous offer to Britain. According to the logic of *uti possidetis* (possession as of the current moment), France sought to guarantee the possessions of both sides, based on the status quo as of May 1 in Europe, July 1 in the Americas, and September 1 in India.[4] Significantly, "Europe" here did not include the Holy Roman Empire, where things were left deliberately vague. The British refused, demanding that possession be assessed from the date of any peace treaty.

In August 1761, the two Bourbon kingdoms of France and Spain concluded their third family pact.[5] The agreement was based partly on common political interests but primarily on shared economic ones.[6] British hegemony over foreign trade was a constant thorn in Spain's side; one possibility for Spain might be to invade Portugal, challenging the British domination of an important market. The British got wind of the Franco-Spanish pact the following month: Pitt wanted to take swift military action against Spain, but the majority of his ministers favored negotiations.[7] At a meeting of ministers on October 2, Pitt declared: "You are now at war with the House of Bourbon; but, for open war with Spain, you are prepared and she is not."[8] But other ministers remained unconvinced, and three days later Pitt handed in his resignation.[9] Pitt had offered Gibraltar to Spain in exchange for an alliance against France, but the Spanish king had not been tempted. Pitt's departure brought Bute to power, who initiated a change in policy, culminating in a clear statement made in September: "If we have a war with Spain we must give up the German war; it is not possible to carry on both."[10] As a result, the Anglo-Prussian subsidy agreement was not renewed.[11]

As early as October 1760, Pitt had worked out a plan to capture Belle Île, an island off the coast of Brittany, roughly opposite Saint-Nazaire, to tie down French forces that might otherwise be deployed to Germany. In March 1761, the plan, still a controversial one, was approved.[12] On April 8, British naval forces under Augustus Keppel and Studholme Hodgson attacked the island with fifty landing craft, but the operation rapidly descended into disaster. The bay where British forces sought to land, near Port Andro, resembled a walled amphitheater, complete with a thousand well-entrenched French troops. After suffering heavy losses, the British managed to withdraw under massive fire. But this was a very large expeditionary force, and its leaders did not abandon the plan. On April 22, the British made another attempt at landing. As at Quebec in 1759, a bold amphibious operation succeeded thanks to surprise and favorable weather conditions. The island's commander, Gaetan Xavier Guilhelm de Pascalis de Sainte-Croix (1708–1762), withdrew his forces to the citadel of Le Palais. The British prepared for a siege. The enslaved teenager Oloudah Equiano, last seen at the naval battle of Lagos, off the coast of Portugal, was part of the British force that landed on Belle Île. On May 5, the British began bombarding the citadel, a fortress built by Vauban. A month later they began their assault, breaching the fortress's walls on June 6. The following day the white flag flew over the citadel. Equiano reports: "During the siege I have counted above sixty shells and carcases in the air at once. When this place was taken I went through the citadel, and in the bomb-proofs under it, which were cut in the solid rock; and I thought it a surprising place, both for strength and building: notwithstanding which our shots and shells had made amazing devastation, and ruinous heaps all around it."[13] Terms of surrender were signed that evening, with two thousand French soldiers transported to the mainland. The *Gazette de France* had reported the successful defense of Le Palais on April 8, but now the paper went silent on the island's fate. There were attempts to turn defeat into victory: On July 9, de Pascalis Sainte Croix was feted as a hero in Paris.[14] Although the British operation had been successful, reaction at home was mixed. Success had come at an enormous cost, and it was unclear how much the diversionary action would, or could, influence the French army in Westphalia.

At this point, the British held so many trump cards they could afford to resolutely refuse peace offers based on *uti possidetis*. In June, after the capture of Belle Île, the British offered to exchange Menorca for Guadeloupe and Marie Galante in the Caribbean, as well as the West African island of Gorée, while demanding that France give up its claims in India and abandon Canada except for Cape Breton (Isle Royale).[15] In response, Choiseul offered to withdraw from Hesse and Westphalia, as well as to demilitarize Louisbourg, which would become purely a fishing port. But the British held firm and now sought to exchange Belle Île for Menorca, insisting that all of Canada be given up, including Cape Breton, as well as Gorée. The British might return Guadeloupe and Marie Galante, according to this offer, but only if there was a total French withdrawal from all German territories. By the middle of 1761, both sides had hardened their demands. Meanwhile, the

British position continued to improve, with news arriving in Europe of the capture of Dominica and Pondicherry.

By early 1761, Ferdinand of Brunswick's Anglo-German army had been greatly weakened and now barely numbered 30,000, while it faced a French force that had swelled to a combined total of around 160,000. North of Ferdinand's army, Broglie had 60,000 troops holding Göttingen and Kassel, while a second French army of 100,000 men under Soubise occupied the Lower Rhine. But their strategic goal had changed: They now sought to capture Westphalia, not Hanover. Within a few months, Ferdinand managed to increase his force to 80,000, but he was still too weak to face the combined French armies, so he instead aimed to fight them separately. However, his maneuvering failed. On July 8, 1761, Broglie and Soubise joined forces close to the Westphalian city of Soest.

The two French generals did not see eye to eye. Broglie, undefeated in the field, resented his subordination to Soubise, whose reputation had been badly damaged by his embarrassing defeat at Rossbach. On July 15, Ferdinand managed to bring the French to battle near Vellinghausen, east of the town of Hamm, in Westphalia.[16] The battle began in the afternoon. By evening, an advance by Broglie put Ferdinand in great danger, but nightfall brought a halt to the fighting, giving the Anglo-German army time to reinforce. By morning, their combat strength was roughly equal to that of the French. At this point, Broglie gave way, breaking off the battle. This forced Soubise to follow suit, and the two French armies separated. Soubise would now pursue a plan to advance on Westphalia and take the city of Münster, while Broglie's army tied down Allied forces along the line of the Weser River. This strategy put Ferdinand's forces under palpable strain, but, in fact, little changed in the status quo for the remainder of the year. Broglie's encampment near Einbeck was recaptured by Ferdinand's troops on November 11, while Soubise retired to winter quarters on the Lower Rhine. A busy campaigning season, with heavy losses on both sides, had changed almost nothing in the balance of power in the northwestern German theater.

Seen in global perspective, the situation was very different. In November 1761, Pitt made his much-quoted observation: "America was conquered in Germany." However, as Richard Middleton has shown, this was more a retrospective rationalization than a consistent geopolitical strategy.[17] It is also doubtful whether France could ever have posed a serious naval threat to the British or whether New France ever had much of a chance compared to the

British colonies farther south. But Pitt's clear, simple claim was popular with the British public.[18] In 1762, there was a definitive rift between Soubise and Broglie, with Broglie returning to France and Soubise taking over as sole commander, to be advised by Marshal d'Estrées. Numerically, things were now relatively evenly balanced, prompting Ferdinand to take the initiative once more. On June 24, 1762, he again drew the French into battle, this time near Wilhelmsthal, north of Kassel.[19] Ferdinand's army won the day, but for now, there was no sign of a lasting French retreat.

In the other German theater of war, Frederick had remained at Leipzig until the spring of 1761, while Kaunitz, the Habsburg state chancellor, urged his generals to force a decisive battle in Silesia. For the moment, both sides were playing a waiting game. In talks with London about possible peace terms, Frederick remained adamant: He would countenance no ceding of territory.[20] On August 18, Frederick wrote to the Marquis d'Argens, saying that, in view of the very large Russian-Austrian formations in the field, "I believe things will come to a decision in the coming days."[21] Unusually for him, Frederick now sought, above all, to avoid confrontation. Balke, the Prussian field chaplain, noted: "The king was minded to be on the defensive; small war came to the fore."[22]

In concrete terms, this first meant constructing defensive positions. The Prussians built a fortified encampment at Bunzelwitz in Lower Silesia, northwest of Schweidnitz, comparable to the fortified Saxon camp at Pirna in 1756 or Bevern's camp at Breslau in 1757.[23] They began entrenchment work on August 20, 1761. Frederick's fifty-thousand Prussian soldiers faced Laudon's Austrian force of nearly seventy-two thousand, as well as forty-seven thousand Russians under Field Marshal Alexander Borissovitch Buturlin (1694–1767). Prussian forces were divided into two separate groups to complete the entrenchments, with both groups working day and night. Within three days, a defensible camp was in place. Four hundred and sixty cannons, some brought from Schweidnitz, were deployed in defensive positions. In front of these were trenches mined with so-called *Fladderminen* (flying mines), which could be blown up in the event of an attack.[24] The Prussian encampment at Bunzelwitz was closely associated with myths of Frederick as a "great king": first, because it symbolically stood for many instances of stoic Prussian endurance against superior opponents during the Seven Years' War and, second, because here Frederick, even more than usual, put himself on the same level as the common soldier. He "was content with the meager fare" provided to the army, sleeping on straw in the open air on a fortified position known as the Pfaffenbergschanze.[25] The *roi connétable* faced the possibility of enemy attack with great composure, a self-confidence that was clearly not lost on the soldiers. Tempelhof, the historian of the war, was himself present at the camp: "The vast encampment of the Austrians and Russians seemed to embrace the Prussian camp like the arms of the crescent moon, and daily reminded the soldiers of the enemy's superior numbers. But it made not the slightest impression upon Frederick. On the contrary, his spirits rose when he realized he had waited in vain for an attack, every night and for some Hours after the sun rose. [. . .] Then he willingly took a pick and shovel and worked on the perfecting of the entrenchments, which every day were improved incessantly."[26]

On August 25, the Russian army reached Bunzelwitz, followed a day later by the Austrians. Almost immediately, the Russian leadership under Buturlin rejected any idea of an assault. But Laudon remained undeterred, presenting a joint plan of attack for September 1.[27] Buturlin refused to agree, but Frederick, whose spies had informed him of the plan, constantly expected an attack in the days that followed. On September 9, the Russians finally broke camp, withdrawing to Posen at a quick march. On September 26, Frederick's forces left Bunzelwitz and marched east. By now, the mood in Vienna had turned gloomy. On October 6, in a letter to Maria Antonia, Electoral Princess of Saxony, Maria Theresa wrote: "Peace seems farther away than ever; alas, misfortune rules over us, which affects the courts with their ministers and generals, although they do have the best of intentions! We succeed in nothing and our enemies in everything."[28] This was an exaggeration: Five days previously Laudon had taken the fortress at Schweidnitz in a spectacular assault, thus gaining an important bargaining chip for Austria.[29]

The Three Sieges of Kolberg

Kolberg, a port and fortress in western Pomerania, was one of the most bitterly contested locations in the entire war. For the Russians, capturing the city could bring two strategic benefits: A base in Pomerania would make cooperation with the Swedish army easier while also offering comfortable winter quarters, a base for operations early in the year.[30] This resulted in no fewer than three separate Russian sieges of the city during the war.[31] The first siege lasted from October 4 to November 1, 1759, and was abandoned without success. A second siege, this time accompanied by amphibious operations, began in August 1760, although "formal" entrenchment started only on September 7.[32] The bombardment caused substantial material damage to the city, but on September 22, unexpected relief came in the form of a Prussian corps commanded by Hans Paul von Werner (1707–1785), which arrived before the Russian trenches could extend as far as the fortress itself.[33] Only with the third siege, from August 22 to December 16, 1761, did the Russians succeed in taking the city. Two months after the Russians launched the operation, Prussian units, short of supplies, evacuated their fortified camp in front of the fortress on the east bank of the Persante River. The fortress held out for another month before it fell.[34]

All three sieges were well documented by witnesses inside the city. The first siege is described in the *Memoirs* of the Kolberg pastor Johannes Rau (1701–1760) and the following two by Johann Christian Kneisel, rector of the city school.[35] Typically for the time, Kneisel frames the siege in terms of divine judgment; the severity of the punishment suggested the "mountainous Guilt borne by the Inhabitants." The fact that the city was not completely destroyed was due to the prayers of "God's children" living within the city.[36] The bombardment seems to have come as a complete surprise to residents of "Sodom's Sister," the name Kneisel uses for the town.[37] He then lists off individual incidents; the list is striking for the frequency with which bombs fell vertically down through buildings, reaching the cellar without exploding.[38] The impact of a "Shuvalov firebottle" is recorded in great detail.[39] During the bombardment, the sonic space of the city was shaped, in turn, by silence and by the thunder of guns. Deaths increased as fighting reached the city itself. Familiar patterns of behavior now also appeared in Kolberg: The Russians refused to rescue the dead and injured, with Kneisel suspecting that many wounded soldiers died as a result.[40] However, officers were buried in a city churchyard "with all possible war decorations."[41] As at Louisbourg in 1758, besiegers and besieged alike seem to have found time for a polite exchange of fruit and wine. On November 28, Kneisel reports: "From 10 A.M. to 12 noon, the Russian officer appeared again, with Trumpeter. He brought 2 Pommeranzes and 2 Oranges and received 2 bottles of Rhenish wine."[42]

Voltaire and Luise Dorothée von Sachsen-Gotha took an active interest in the siege's progress. On November 9, 1761, Voltaire writes: "I am surrounded by Russians who say they will take Kolberg, and by Germans who assure me that the siege will be lifted."[43] But he believes neither. Luise Dorothée's reply, written on November 21, maintains hope: "The fate of

Kolberg is not yet settled, but one begins to hope that this place will remain in the hands of its legitimate owner."[44] Russian troops marched into Kolberg less than a month later. By December 6, the Russian attack trenches had already approached dangerously close to the city.[45] The Prussians signed a capitulation on December 16; the following day the Russians moved into the city, led by Count Pyotr Alexandrovich Rumyantsev-Zadunaisky (1725–1796).[46] In Kneisel's eyes, God had nonetheless acted in a "paternal" way, since the city was neither burned down nor taken by assault.[47] During the occupation, contact with the Russian occupiers was repeatedly complicated by the language barrier: "It was not possible to speak with these Foreigners, which prevented friendly Intercourse between the occupation Force and City Residents."[48] Although peace was agreed to on May 5, the last Russian troops did not leave the city until August 10, 1762, when the Prussians once more assumed the "scepter."[49]

Kneisel has high praise for Rumyantsev, whom he describes as the "philanthropic General," as well as for Wesemsky, the Russian quartermaster general. Any "Outrages," he suggests, were the work of Russian light forces, including hussars and Cossacks. But the material suffering that the city had undergone became clear once the occupation forces had withdrawn. The enormous demand for firewood had taken a particular toll. Merchant shipping was destroyed, and the city's population fell by 20 percent. It would be decades before Kolberg recovered.

The Last Days of the Pomeranian War

January 1760 was cold in the north of Germany, with most waterways frozen over. Although the balance of power had swung back toward the Swedes, the year began with a surprise Prussian attack on Swedish winter quarters.[50] The Prussian advance was halted, however, at the key river crossings of Anklam and Stolpe, and their surprise offensive failed. By the end of January, the Swedes had reconquered Anklam and captured the wounded General Heinrich von Manteuffel (1696–1778), but they soon abandoned the town, withdrawing again to their winter quarters.[51] Olof Langelius, the Swedish military chaplain and diarist, clearly had time on his hands in the following months: He managed to pen a detailed comparison of Swedish and German church law, as well as to record local customs and take plant samples. A vine leaf and a sprig of mulberry were pressed between the pages of his diary.[52]

Momentum now seemed to be with the Swedes. By the summer, the Prussians had deployed 6,250 men along the Peene River under Major General Joachim Friedrich von Stutterheim. On the opposite bank, the Swedish commander, Albrekt Lantingshausen, had gathered a force of 14,800, and the Swedish advance began on August 15, 1760. Under General von Fersen, a diversionary Swedish force advanced on Demmin and threatened Anklam, while the main force, commanded by Lantingshausen, took up positions to the west, close to Malchin. The Prussians then once again withdrew, moving back from Anklam and Demmin and opening the way for Lantingshausen to advance to Prenzlau by September 6. But the Swedish were forced to advance over difficult terrain: The Prussians used a kind of scorched earth tactic, setting barns on fire and felling trees to block roads and paths. One very young participant in this theater of the war had a great military future: The nineteen-year-old Gebhart Leberecht von Blücher (1742–1819), famous for leading the Prussians at Waterloo, was serving with the Swedish hussars. He was taken prisoner in August, near the Pomeranian village of Kavelpass. Colonel Wilhelm Sebastian von Belling (1719–1779) soon persuaded him to join the Prussian service, making him his adjutant.

For his part, Langelius's quiet pursuit of horticulture and ecclesiastical jurisprudence was interrupted on a notable day in mid-September, when Prussian hussars disrupted a religious service he was leading for 250 soldiers of his regiment. The hussars, he wrote, seemed to "swarm like Crows on the wing," like "bothersome Flies," seeming to be everywhere, beyond all control.[53] In early October, the Prussians launched a more general counterattack, this time led by General von Werner von Pasewalk, but it did not succeed. At the end of that month, Lantingshausen again moved his Swedish army into winter quarters north of the Peene River. At this point, Prince Friedrich Eugen von Württemberg offered Lantingshausen an armistice until April 1, 1761, which was gladly accepted. As for Langelius, his diary for 1761 began with a prayer for peace, but the soldiers in his unit had no faith in the ceasefire and remained on constant alert.[54]

Like his predecessors as Swedish commander, Lantingshausen soon submitted a request to be relieved of command, which was accepted on February 16. His replacement was the artillery officer Augustin Ehrensvärd (1710–1772), who did not get around to assuming his responsibilities in the field until July 1761. By now, rates of sickness in the Swedish army had fallen below 5 percent, and their forces had remedied previous defects in light cavalry, mobile infantry, and artillery. A Swedish army crossed the Peene on July 19 under Ehrensvärd's command, quickly advancing as far as Boldekow in Brandenburg. All seemed set for a promising campaigning season, especially after the Swedes won a minor battle between light formations at Neuensund in the Uckermark region on September 18, an encounter that Langelius thought was the greatest Swedish victory of the whole war.[55] Nonetheless, on October 8, the Swedes retired to winter quarters at Usedom, once again withdrawing behind the line of the Peene River. Langelius compares the army's withdrawal to the biblical exodus from Egypt.[56]

The last battle of the Pomeranian War was fought close to the town Malchin in Mecklenburg on January 2, 1762. The Swedes won the battle and marched into the town. According to Langelius, Swedish and Prussian soldiers were buried together in a mass grave, with many prisoners taken. Ehrensvärd, like his predecessors, took his leave of the war quite rapidly, marching his victorious army back to winter quarters. On April 7, an armistice was signed at Ribnitz.[57] Ehrensvärd was, in turn, replaced by Erik Lybecker (1698–1766), who briefly became Swedish commander, the very last of the war. By now, peace negotiations had begun in earnest, leading to a separate peace between Prussia and Sweden, agreed to in Hamburg on May 22. Negotiating speed was of the essence for the Swedes: After the death of Tsarina Elizabeth, there was considerable risk that Russia might turn from an ally to an enemy. The peace was brokered by the Swedish queen consort, Luise Ulrike of Prussia (1720–1782), the fifth of Frederick's six sisters. Langelius expressed disappointment at the lack of religious gratitude shown with regard to the peace but acknowledged the thankfulness of some Freemasons he met at Greifswald on Midsummer's Night.[58] On September 6, he arrived home to his rectory at Söderköping, "happy and in good health."[59] The Pomeranian War was a disaster for Sweden and has since been largely omitted from national cultures of remembrance: no wonder, since it brought devastating results for the country.[60] The war resulted in around thirty thousand dead, diseased, or wounded Swedish soldiers and cost between 59 and 62 million thalers, a sum equal to the entire Swedish national debt. Not an inch of territory was gained, while the economy suffered a substantial wave of inflation. Sweden simply lacked the financial means for territorial expansion at the expense of Prussia. It had chosen a low-intensity war of attrition, but this came at a high price, after initially promising gains in both European diplomacy and international trade.

Controlling the Caribbean

By 1761, Canada was completely in British hands, and planning began for an operation against French possessions in the Lesser Antilles.[61] Pitt sent six thousand men to capture Martinique and another two thousand to attack Dominica. But bad weather delayed the procurement of transport vessels, and the fleet did not leave New York until November 19, 1761, commanded by General Monckton. On Christmas Day, sixty-four transport ships reached Barbados, with seventy-four hundred British regulars aboard. This was only a small part of a large expeditionary fleet that was joined by, among others, British ships from off the French Atlantic coast, commanded by Rear Admiral Rodney. Ultimately, the British expeditionary force sent to the Caribbean amounted to some twenty-five thousand men. French forces on Martinique were led by a new governor, Captain LeVassor de la Touche (1745–1804). Any reinforcements from France would amount to only a fraction of the British numbers, so his defense of the island would be reliant on natural topography and the readiness of local militias to fight.

A first British attempt at landing took place on January 6 but was quickly abandoned in the face of difficult terrain and tenacious defenses. Eleven days later, on January 17, a second landing took place, this time without significant resistance, and some fourteen thousand British troops came ashore. La Touche's hopes now rested entirely on the prompt arrival of a relief fleet from Brest. But while he was waiting, he committed tactical errors that allowed the British to capture the island within a few weeks. On February 15, he signed the terms of surrender. As was by now usual, the British transported French regulars back to France, while local militia and privateers were made prisoners of war. The capture of Martinique set off a chain reaction of French surrender as the islands of the Lesser Antilles capitulated, one after another: first, St. Lucia, followed by Grenada on March 5, and then a week later, St. Vincent. On April 4, on the other side of the Atlantic, in Hamelin in Electoral Hanover, "a Te Deum was sung for the felicitous Conquest of Martinique. Cannons were fired from the city Walls and from Klüt-mountain, with the garrison 3 times setting off Wild-fires."[62] Two days previously, in London, news from the Caribbean had prompted the Earl of Hardwicke to write enthusiastically to Newcastle: "This is really important News in the superlative degree, for if Admiral Rodney is right, It gives the King the key to the West-Indies, as much as Gibraltar does that for the Mediterranean; & it certainly might give England, in effect, the whole

Sugar-Trade of the World, except what remains in St. Domingo."[63] Things seemed set for a new round of debate on British peace objectives, a rehash of the Canada vs. Guadeloupe discussions of previous years. What was different this year was that both London and Versailles wanted to agree to a rapid peace, but France was all the more reluctant to concede its remaining prized possessions, the sugar islands of the West Indies.

The Road to British Supremacy in India

By late 1759, conflict was again stirring in the Carnatic region of southern India.[64] The British had appointed Eyre Coote (1726–1783) as their new commander in chief in southern India; his 84th Infantry Regiment had reinforced Madras in November.[65] Farther north in Bengal, Clive deployed a powerful force to counter an offensive launched from Delhi by the son of the Mughal emperor. Now Coote went on the offensive, at last able to take on the French with significant numerical advantage. After several feints, he attacked the fortified town of Wandiwash (Vandavasi) near Madras, taking the fortress on November 29, 1759, after a short siege. The arrival of fierce monsoon rains brought further movement to a halt. The two sides could not leave their positions in January. When the rains eased, they fought a decisive encounter at Wandiwash.[66] In numerical terms, the Battle of Wandiwash was considerably smaller than battles in Europe. The two sides were relatively evenly balanced: Lally, with around 1,500 European troops, 1,800 sepoys, and 3,000 local Maratha cavalry, was opposed by Coote, with 1,900 Europeans and 3,350 sepoys. Lally was aware of low morale among his poorly paid troops and seems to have sought to avoid open warfare, preferring to recover Wandiwash by siege. Nonetheless, Coote managed to force him into battle.

The French general positioned his European forces in a single long line, with his sepoys held back as a reserve and the Marathas deployed as skirmishers ahead of the line. A few French sailors with a couple of cannons were placed close to a water hole, covering Lally's left flank. Coote, by contrast, placed his men in four staggered lines and attempted to encircle Lally's line in a roughly semicircular movement.[67] His first line had four European infantry battalions and twelve field guns, flanked by sepoys. Coote himself was in this line. The second line was made up of three hundred European grenadiers, also flanked by sepoys; the third contained the combined European and Maratha mercenary cavalry; and the fourth had the rest of the sepoys. Lally launched a cavalry assault around noon, which was repulsed, and then Coote's infantry marched forward, supported by artillery, until the two sides met in a face-to-face bayonet battle.

Just when the British pincer movement was about to force the French to give way, a lucky British cannon shot blew up a cart at the French water hole position, panicking their entire flanking force. The British took advantage of the moment, rolling through the French forces on that flank and sending them into disarray. French morale, already fragile, was definitively broken when Lally was taken prisoner after his horse was been shot from under him. The sepoys took no action, and around two o'clock in the afternoon, the French sounded a general retreat. Coote had shown himself a brilliant military leader, but that single "lucky shot" was, in fact, the battle's crucial turning point.

The French suffered 400 soldiers killed and wounded, with 150 taken prisoner, compared to 183 European soldiers and 70 sepoys dead or wounded on the British side. The French also lost their artillery pieces and their siege positions around Wandiwash. On January 29, 1760, the Halle missionaries reported that they had reliable news of a battle fought between the British and the French a week previously, on January 22: "Not far from Wandawashy there was an Encounter between the English and the French, with the Former gaining complete Victory over the Latter." The missionaries' thoughts were, above all, with their brothers in Madras: "We have thus Reason all the more to exalt the Ways of the Lord, because, had the Former been vanquished, the misery of our brothers in Madras would greatly increase. Already they have been forced to flee from Wöpery for fear of the Maratti. That God in his Mercy guide this War and put an End to the Shedding of Blood!"[68]

At Madras, the British East India Company Council was now expecting Coote to take swift action against Pondicherry. But the two sides were still relatively evenly matched, and Coote hesitated. Rather than attempting a decisive move, he adopted a strategy of attrition, including a scorched earth policy. By May 1760, however, he was at last ready for action and surrounded Pondicherry with a broad swathe of British forces. A relieving force sent by Haider Ali failed to break through, and the French fleet made no appearance. The systematic siege of Pondicherry began on September 4 and lasted until January 15, 1761. In a letter of January 1 to Luise Dorothée von Sachsen-Gotha, Voltaire comments on the impending loss of the town: "It is said the English now control Pondichéry: I suffer some loss thereby, but if peace comes of it, I shall draw comfort from it."[69] The British began a heavy bombardment on January 10. Inside the city, Ananda Ranga Pillai, diligent chronicler of events in the region, died on January 12, just before Pondicherry was captured by the British.[70] Three days later the starving garrison surrendered.

News of Pondicherry's capture did not arrive in Europe until May. On May 29, 1761, Frederick wrote to Finckenstein, saying he still doubted "the reality of the Pondicherry affair."[71] The Halle missionaries also reported on the event, noting that on January 15, 1761, hunger had compelled the French "to pass Disposition [over the fort] to the English: since then the French Lieutenant-General Mons. Lally, along with the entire Governorate, Garrison and the entire White Population have been made Prisoners of War." The British, in their "Affability," the report continues, permitted no plundering, left property intact, and had surely fed the "half-starved Soldiers." By now, the British were at the point of destroying Pondicherry, and its "Tamil inhabitants" had been given instructions to settle in Cuddalore. But the French were said to have been transported to Europe, according to the report, "along with their Clerics," a fact that likely had particular significance for the missionaries.[72] At Pondicherry, it soon became clear what it meant to destroy a fort in a struggle of colonial rivals, in both material and symbolic terms. The city's fortifications were razed to the ground. In due course, all French property was destroyed, and the majority of prisoners of war were shipped to Europe. On the British side, John McLean—who in our time might be called an embedded artist—documented the destruction in an engraving that includes an image of himself drawing the scene (figure 10.1). He dedicated the piece to George Pigot, president of the Council of Fort St. George. Some years later the French astronomer Guillaume le Gentil (1725–1792) also made a visual record of the ruins of Pondicherry, by now back in French hands, in his famous account of a *Voyage Among the Indian Seas*.

The British were determined to make any French military recovery in India as difficult as possible. They considered capturing and destroying the crucial French base at Mauritius, but the plan would have required too many resources, and it was rejected. Thus ended, for the moment, the Franco-British war in India. The two sides initially enjoyed rough parity in military forces, and French failure can ultimately be attributed to financial inferiority. The French may have had a strong fleet, better relations with the local population, and a solid strategic approach, but in the end, all this was outweighed by a constant lack of funds.[73]

Figure 10.1 Ruins of the Citadel at Pondicherry. Pen and ink drawing by John McLean (1762).
© The British Library Board, from the British Library Collection.

News of the European peace reached Madras on May 19, 1763. Two years later the British East India Company obtained *diwani* rights, allowing it to collect taxes on behalf of the Mughal emperor in some provinces of India. With this, the way was open for the company's transformation from a trading company to a territorial sovereign.

No Peace for Native Americans

The French had been defeated militarily in North America, but relations between the British and the Indigenous nations remained to be clarified. Records of this process almost always cite Native American voices at second hand, via reports by whites who had contact with them.[74] Thus, our record of a 1761 speech by Minavavana (c. 1710–1790), an Anishinabe (Chippeway) chief, comes from the fur trader Alexander Henry (1739–1824), who encountered the Anishinabe while hunting for furs. Initially, he had pretended to be French but was quickly exposed and taken captive. The

Anishinabe had an alliance with the Ottawa and Potawatomi, known as the Council of Three Fires, which allowed them to hold their own against the rival Six Nations. Minavavana's speech addresses the captive and, in doing so, gives us information about relations between Britain and the tribes:

> Englishman! We are informed that our father, the king of France, is old and infirm, and that being fatigued with making war on your nation, he is fallen asleep. During his sleep, you have taken advantage of him, and possessed yourselves of Canada. But his nap is almost at an end. I think I hear him already stirring, and inquiring for his children, the Indians. And when he does awake, what must become of you? He will destroy you utterly! Englishman! Although you have conquered the French, you have not yet conquered us. We are not your slaves. These lakes, these woods and mountains were left to us by our ancestors. They are our inheritance, and we will part with them to none.[75]

Minavavana then observes that as yet there had been no formal peace talks between the tribes and the British: "Englishman! Your king has never sent us any presents, nor entered into any treaty with us. Wherefore he and we are still at war; and, until he does these things, we must consider that we have no other father, nor friend, among the white men than the king of France." But Henry himself was in no danger, the chief emphasizes, stressing his people's desire for friendship: "But, for you, we have taken into consideration that you have ventured your life among us, in the expectation that we should not molest you. You do not come armed, with an intention to make war. You come in peace, to trade with us and supply us with necessaries, of which we are much in want. We shall regard you, therefore, as a brother; and you may sleep tranquilly, without fear of the Chippewas. As a token of our friendship, we present you with this pipe to smoke."[76]

The Fantastic War

Events in the Spanish-Portuguese theater of war are collectively known as the Fantastic War, since it involved no major battles at all.[77] However, although less spectacular than the conflicts in other regions, the fighting on the Iberian Peninsula was no less important in the war's late phase. The term *fantastic* might also be applied to the Bourbons' strategic illusions about what war with Portugal would involve.[78] At first, it seemed a British-Spanish confrontation could be avoided, with cautious rapprochement the order of the day. The Spanish offered to swap Gibraltar for Menorca; even a settlement of rivalries in Honduras was on the table. But the succession of the "Anglophobic" Charles III to the Spanish throne in 1759 set off a dynamic likely to lead to open confrontation.[79] The Spanish were laboring under the illusion that they could drive the British out of the Caribbean by direct confrontation. This idea was probably motivated by fear, rarely the best adviser: Choiseul had deliberately fueled Spanish anxieties about a British trade monopoly and possible attacks on Florida or Mexico. In response, the Spanish developed a plan to block British ships' access to Atlantic ports and to directly attack British trading stations in Honduras (wood), Jamaica (sugar), and West Africa (slaves).[80] After Pitt's resignation in October 1761, all signs from Britain suggested the country wanted peace with Spain. But even Bute was forced to change course when, late in the year, the Spanish suddenly began seizing British goods and expelling their merchants, bankers, and diplomats. Britain declared war on Spain on January 4, 1762. Several British regiments were immediately dispatched to Portugal, as any Spanish occupation of its Iberian neighbor would disrupt the Atlantic trade, especially in port wine and in gold from Brazil.[81] A Spanish victory there would mean massive trading losses for Britain.

Portugal itself had little room for maneuver. Joining the Franco-Spanish "pacte de famille" would mean becoming a mere appendage to its larger neighbor; having Britain as a trading partner was far more lucrative. The country was still suffering the consequences of the terrible Lisbon earthquake of 1755 while also undergoing the reform policies of Sebastião José de Carvalho e Mello, later the Marquês de Pombal (1699–1782). Pombal had a firm grip on power, using it, in particular, against the opposition nobility, which also affected the officer corps. Within Europe, Portugal was uniquely ill-suited for war, with a poorly equipped army, ramshackle roads, and precarious supplies of food and forage.[82] The British appointed the Irishman James O'Hara (1681?–1773) as commander in chief: He was an experienced military man who had twice served as ambassador in Lisbon and spoke fluent Portuguese. But Pombal was reluctant to cede effective command to the British officer and forced O'Hara to wear civilian clothes so as not to provoke a Spanish attack. The British had even less to work with in terms of logistics and infrastructure; the fortresses at the Spanish frontier were in a wretched state. Eventually, Pombal's failure to give O'Hara a free hand caused a scandal, but Portugal had no capable candidate to take his place as overall commander. Eventually, the job was given to Wilhelm Friedrich Ernst Count von Schaumburg-Lippe (1724–1777), a German prince who would play a crucial role in Portuguese history. He had already won plaudits as a Prussian artillery general—in particular, as an artillery commander under Ferdinand of Brunswick in the northwestern German theater, where he played a leading role at Krefeld (1758); at Lutterberg, Minden, Kassel, Marburg, and Münster (all 1759); and, most recently, at Vellinghausen (1761).[83] Wilhelm's staff was nothing if not inventive: To cut communication times to Portugal, an inventor in the count's service designed a miniature fish-shaped submarine, the so-called Steinhuder Hecht (Steinhude Pike), intended to take messages to Lisbon in just six days. The plan came to nothing at the time, although a limited prototype was eventually built after the war.

On May 5, 1762, Spanish troops crossed into Portugal from Zamora, advancing on the mountainous province of Trás-os-Montes and briefly threatening the city of Porto (see map in figure 10.2.). Although the Spanish had to temporarily withdraw, the Portuguese royal family regarded themselves as being in great danger, and preparations were made for them to escape to Brazil. King Joseph I formally declared war on Spain on May 18, 1762, although Lippe did not arrive in Lisbon until July 3. The same day, he was appointed commander in chief of the Portuguese army.[84] His mission was not easy: He had just fifteen thousand men at his disposal to face forty-two thousand Franco-Spanish troops under the leadership of Nicolás de Carvajal y Lancaster Marqués de Sarriá (1696–1770).[85]

The new Portuguese commander patched together garrison forces and dispatched them to the border fortresses. He positioned his main force at Abrantes, more or less in the middle of the country, with seven thousand men situated in defensible positions, as he hoped to rely on a strategy of maneuver. In this, he proved entirely successful: There was not a single major battle in the field before the final withdrawal of Spanish forces from Portugal in November 1762.

The Spanish strategy was to capture the cities of Porto and Lisbon, and its troops attempted to do so in three successive offensives. The opening advance took place in the north and quickly captured frontier fortresses, including Miranda and Chaves. Logistical problems, along with a partisan war fought by peasants under the leadership of O'Hara's son Charles, brought the advance to a temporary standstill, preventing the Spanish from crossing the Douro. Meanwhile, the British-Portuguese leadership was

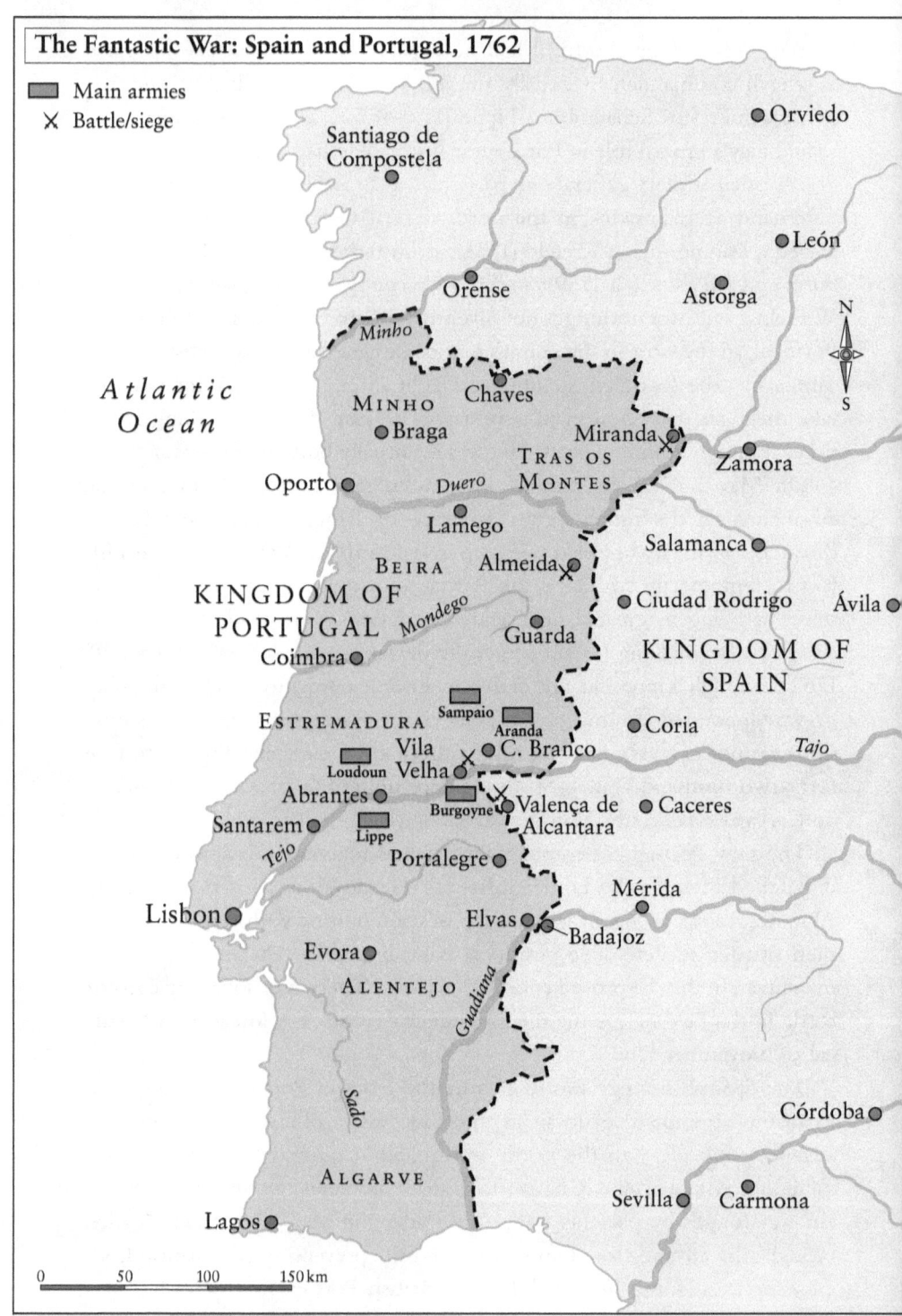

Figure 10.2 The Fantastic War: Spain and Portugal, 1762.
© Peter Palm, Berlin/Germany.

suffering from problems of rank and hierarchy. John Campbell, the Earl of Loudoun, had been relieved of the British North American command in 1757 after his inaction had contributed to the loss of Fort William Henry. Five years later he was considered a good choice to take over from O'Hara as British commander in the Portuguese theater. Among his many challenges were ongoing disputes over seniority in the British and Portuguese officer corps. British officers had been inserted into the Portuguese military hierarchy, often affording them superior status to their colleagues. In one case, a British officer was promoted over the heads of 133 of his Portuguese colleagues. Loudoun himself squabbled with Lippe over how he should be correctly addressed. The role of language in all of this should not be underestimated. Pombal did not understand English, and when Loudoun, worn out by unfulfilled logistical promises, announced he would no longer write to him in French, it was rightly construed as an insult.[86]

The Spanish began no new initiative until August 1762. Sarriá was relieved of his command, replaced by Pedro de Pablo Abarca Bolea, the Conde de Aranda (1719–1798). At the time, Aranda was serving as Spanish ambassador to the Saxon court in Warsaw and had had no direct war experience for many years. He seems to have been chosen solely because he was the protegé of Ricardo Wall (1694–1777), Spain's chief minister and its foreign minister. Aranda's forces advanced into the province of Beira, south of Trás-os-Montes, and laid siege to the city of Almeida, which fell on August 25. This greatly threatened Lippe's plans for an offensive, but then a surprise British raid on the Spanish border town of Valencia d'Alcántara successfully left the Spanish forces in disarray, cutting them off from their key supply base at Badajoz.

The British elite displayed an increasingly negative attitude toward their Portuguese allies, as evidenced by the correspondence of Lady Elizabeth Montagu (1718–1800), who expressed her contempt in no uncertain terms. In response to an August 28 letter from the Earl of Bath, outlining his son's experience in Lisbon and his vehement verdict on the Portuguese, Montagu replies:

> Certainly I could not help lamenting much that he should run any hazards for the sake of such a vile scurvy people as the Portuguese. In the whole nation there is not a single spark of that virtue which animated him to go in their defence, and it is hard for a hero to fight, as for a prophet to interceed, for a city that has not a righteous man in it. I never heard of a nation saved by the virtue of its allies when its

own spirit was totally extinct. I believe the Portuguese were the lowest of the human race before the earthquake; but that since this great calamity they are still more, as their superstition is still more deep and gloomy than before.[87]

She was by no means alone in her opinion. Linguistic and confessional differences on the ground also helped to sour good British-Portuguese relations. The poor relationship is highlighted by one extraordinary fact: During the Fantastic War, more British soldiers—twenty-three in total—were killed by their Portuguese hosts than by the Spanish, who managed to kill only fourteen.[88]

The war in Portugal ended in stalemate. Clashes at Vila Velha de Rodão on the Tagus in early October played a crucial role in bringing conflict in the theater to an end. Aranda had marched his forces toward Lippe's camp at Abrantes, attempting to draw him into open battle. In doing so, they crossed the Tagus at Vila Velha at the end of September. They had secured the crossing point when they were met with an unexpected British-Portuguese night attack, which stopped their advance in its tracks. In fact, the timely intervention ended the Spanish march on Abrantes, preventing any further risk to Lisbon.

But why were the Spaniards so late in marching toward the Portuguese capital? The answer may well lie in a somewhat different "family pact," with King Charles III, seeking to protect the Portuguese queen, his sister Maria Anna Viktoria, who had married Joseph I in 1729. A final Spanish advance through the southern province of Alentejo also stalled before fighting ended with a preliminary peace agreement, signed at Fontainebleau on November 24. In January 1763, all Spanish forces withdrew from Portuguese territory. The British and Portuguese had lost very few men in combat, but many hundreds died of starvation, fever, and heat stroke. The war in Portugal was a classic war of maneuver, a textbook campaign if judged according to the ideals of contemporary war theory. Not a single major battle was fought in the field. Nonetheless, the campaign left a bitter aftertaste, inflicting a heavy toll on the Spanish and on their Anglo-Portuguese opponents. Both sides were badly affected by a disastrous supply situation, which decimated the Spanish attacking force and fueled British resentment toward a mission that rapidly came to be seen as pointless. Of the forty thousand Spanish soldiers who marched into Portugal, only twenty-five thousand marched home at the end of the campaign. For the Spanish, strategic illusions about fighting a continental war against the British had now become bitter reality.

CHAPTER XI

Mosquitoes and Monsoons

The Grab for Spain's Colonies

Havana, 1762: The Key to the New World

War between Spain and Britain had military consequences for Spain's colonies, as well as the Iberian Peninsula. Above all, Cuba and the Philippines became strategic objectives for the British.[1] The Spanish crown regarded Havana as the "key to the New World"; the British also prized its geostrategic position, giving it names like "the Gibraltar of the West."[2] Spain could not do without a powerful fleet to effectively protect its colonial empire. In the aftermath of the War of the Spanish Succession, the Spanish administration had invested in a naval buildup, but the navy's budget had been cut under Ferdinand VI (1746–1759), leaving the Spanish fleet with little to put up against a British navy almost twice its size. In 1759, Spain had fifty-nine thousand seamen on paper; in fact, only about twenty-six thousand were available and ready for service. Likewise, the navy notionally possessed fifty ships of the line, as well as thirty-eight Spanish ships attached to the French fleet. These ships were also somewhat hypothetical: Of the fifty, only twenty were available for immediate deployment.

The situation in Cuba was somewhat better. Seven Spanish ships had arrived at Havana on June 29, 1761, expanding the island's naval complement to twelve ships. By June 1762, the garrison had been increased to forty-five hundred soldiers,[3] in addition to another sixty-three hundred men in the naval forces, including seamen, gunners, and marines.[4] The city had adequate supplies: Between 1758 and 1761, 153 artillery pieces, 5,000 muskets, 40,000 pounds of gunpowder, and 78,244 musket balls had been shipped to the Cuban capital.

On Pitt's orders, the British sent an expeditionary fleet to take up a position near Barbados. The force, including nineteen ships of the line and between eight and ten thousand soldiers, arrived in the Caribbean in September 1761. On January 6, 1762, at Horse Guards House in London, a meeting was held by a secret committee of admirals and senior cabinet ministers, including Bute, Newcastle, George Grenville, Egremont, Anson, Ligonier, and the Duke of Devonshire. A memorandum by Devonshire sums up their discussion: "After some conversation about taking the most effectual methods of distressing and attacking the Spaniards, which ended in the resolution of attacking Havana, Lord Bute threw down the idea of recalling the British troops [from Germany]."[5] Newcastle and Devonshire remained vehemently opposed to any such recall. Nonetheless, the fact of its proposal reveals both Britain's fraught financial circumstances and the zero-sum conception of how theaters of war were linked, whereby forces deployed in one place would have to be withdrawn elsewhere. The British already had a rough plan of attack, based on a report by Admiral Charles Knowles (1704–1777), the governor of Jamaica. He had visited Cuba in 1756, coming away with erroneous impressions of the island's defenses. The admiral had already published a description of the port of Havana in 1741 and now put together further plans, which gave the impression that the island could be captured relatively easily. These plans, as far as the British were concerned, simply awaited implementation.

From the start, conquering Cuba was seen in terms of temporary occupation rather than permanent acquisition. Temporary possession of the island would disrupt trade and the Spanish economy and could be used as a negotiating chip to exchange for other territories. For Newcastle, the planned operation was "a very expensive and risky expedition, a wild goose chase." Overall command was given to the experienced Vice Admiral Sir George Pocock, with Commodore Augustus Keppel to assist him as senior naval commander.[6] Keppel was accompanied by two of his brothers: the eldest, George, third Earl of Albemarle (1724–1772), was appointed commander of the land forces, while William Keppel (1727–1782), youngest of the three, was made major general, with command over elements of the naval force.[7] George Durant, who had accompanied the expedition against Guadeloupe, again served as paymaster general.[8] He eventually pocketed substantial private profits from the Cuban expedition, becoming a wealthy man almost overnight.

The Spanish forces were led by Field Marshal Don Juan de Prado (1716–1770), governor of Havana since 1761, with José Antonio Manso de Velasco (1688–1767) serving as infantry commander and Marqués de Real de Transporte Admiral Gutierre de Hevia (1704–1772) commanding the fleet.

Simply in terms of logistics, it was highly ambitious to transport sixteen thousand men from three widely separated locations (four thousand in England, four thousand in New York, and eight thousand in the Caribbean) to attack a heavily fortified location like Havana.[9] The urgency of the operation made the challenge all the greater. The hurricane season, due to begin in August, loomed large in the planning, but this was not the only temporal constraint: The British fleet had to reach Cuba before news of the declaration of war reached the island.[10] The plan was not a secret in London and was even reported in the newspapers.[11] The Havana expedition set sail from Spithead on March 5, led by Pocock and Albemarle. Their first aim was to reach the Lesser Antilles and join with the forces of Major General Monckton and the naval squadron of Rear Admiral Rodney. The expeditionary fleet would then head toward an area north of the island of Santo Domingo, where it would rendezvous with a troop contingent arriving from New York. On April 20, the fleet reached Barbados, where Pocock and Albemarle learned that most of Monckton's British troops, by now around nine thousand men, had already captured Martinique. Having collected these forces from the captured French island, on May 25 the fleet was joined by a third British naval squadron under Sir James Douglas. The combined British fleet now lay off Cape St. Nicolas on Santo Domingo, directly opposite the eastern tip of Cuba. It comprised twenty ships of the line, one fifty-gun ship, five frigates, three bomb vessels, a sloop, a cutter, and around two hundred transport, supply, and food ships, along with eleven thousand soldiers. It was impossible for a force of this size to go unnoticed as it sailed along the north coast of Cuba.

One eyewitness to the siege of Havana was the young Swiss deserter Markus Uhlmann, who had abandoned the French service near Münster in July 1759. Having escaped to Holland, he went on to serve on a number of ships. In 1761, in the Spanish port of Cádiz, he was hired as ship's doctor on the Dutch ship *Vrouw Clara Magdalena*, at that time in the Spanish service. He arrived at Havana on December 19.[12] For a man of his time, Uhlmann had an astonishingly modern sense of global distances and used latitude and longitude to work out the time in Zurich compared to Havana.[13] On February 27, he writes: "The newspaper here says the King of Spain has declared war on Great Britain. I will not recount the terrible shock of the Inhabitants, who all believe themselves to be as good as already in English hands." On April 5, he notes a report from a French ship, communicating the British capture of Martinique.[14] Also the Cuban merchant Martin de Araña, who returned to Havana from Jamaica on May 21, had seen Rodney's troops and heard from Jewish merchants of a British plan to attack the Cuban capital.[15] De Araña even had good estimates of British troop numbers and naval strength, but was refused admittance when he went to speak to Governor Prado about the situation; in fact, the governor's secretary threatened to have him thrown in prison if he continued to spread panic in the city.

The British fleet appeared off Havana on Sunday, June 6 (see map in figure 11.1). Governor Prado was awakened and told of their arrival but initially assumed the ships must be a friendly convoy. Undisturbed, he and the Spanish ruling elite attended mass at Havana Cathedral in celebration of Trinity Sunday. Only that afternoon did the governor realize the seriousness of the situation, hastily convening a council of war. Troops were hurriedly deployed to Chorrera and Guanabacoa to prevent enemy landings, and three ships of the line were sunk at the entrance to the harbor, creating a barrier to protect the heavily laden merchant ships at anchor.

El Morro, Havana's fortress, had an Achilles heel, a fact known to its Italian architect Battista Antonelli (1547–1616) in the late sixteenth century and quickly grasped by Knowles, whose maps were the main British source of information in planning the attack. Whoever took both the fortress at the harbor entrance and the high ground at La Cabaña would control the entire city.[16] The wooded heights at La Cabaña overlooked the fortress from the southeast, close to the port's eastern entrance. The Spanish had left the location unfortified, although El Morro itself could be bombarded from there, as could parts of the city and harbor. Laying siege to the city was impossible with the forces available to the British. Based on poor information about the city's fortifications, Patrick Mackellar, Albemarle's chief engineer, wrote a memorandum proposing a landing some miles along the coast to the east, at Cojímar, or the same distance to the west, at Chorrera.[17] One way or another, El Morro would have to be taken first, before Havana itself, in order to threaten the city and port.

Archibald Robertson (1745–1813) was one of Mackellar's men, a Scot serving with the Royal Corps of Engineers, whose diary describes the Havana

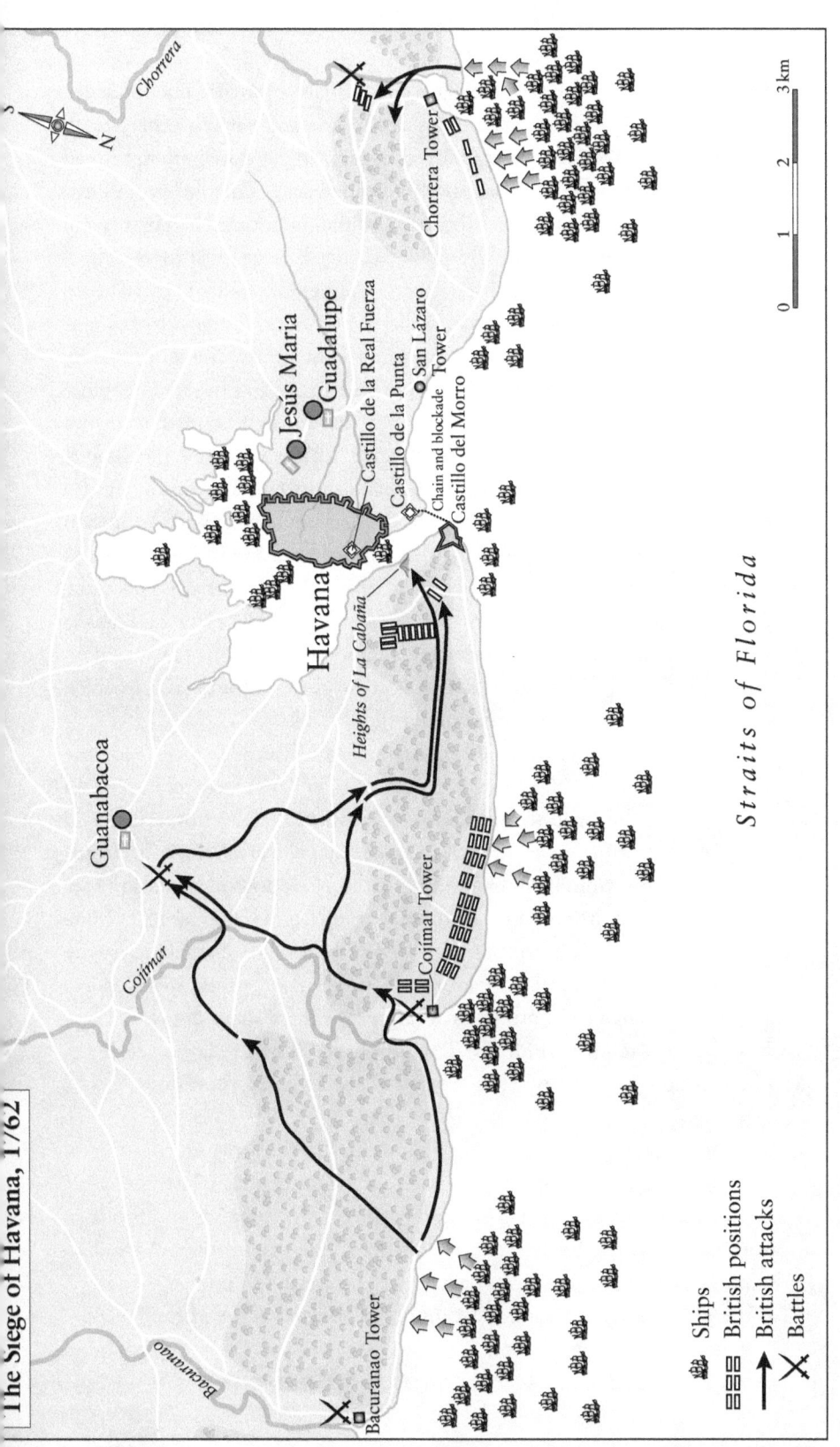

Figure 11.1 The siege of Havana, 1762.
© Peter Palm, Berlin/Germany.

landings in objective, technical language, as if it were a job like any other. On June 7, Pocock sailed with twelve ships of the line and various other vessels to Chorrera in a diversionary maneuver, hoping to tie down enemy forces there.[18] Meanwhile, the main British force landed at Cojímar, where Augustus Keppel went ashore with four thousand soldiers at around half past ten in the morning. Rather than immediately attacking the small fort there, which was held by six hundred Spanish soldiers, Keppel decided to soften it up with a naval bombardment. After an hour of bombing, the Spaniards abandoned the fort, retreating to La Cabaña. The following day the British easily captured Guanabacoa, some miles south of El Morro, and began to explore the area around the fortress. By now, panic was rising among the Spanish authorities, who ordered women and children to leave the city. On June 9, the decision was made to abandon La Cabaña to its fate. The following day British forces surrounded La Cabaña on the landward side; with confusion and disorder already taking hold in Havana, the British also began a naval bombardment of the city itself to distract from the La Cabaña operation, while simultaneously capturing the abandoned fort at Chorrera. La Cabaña was ultimately captured with almost no resistance on June 11.[19] The attack on El Morro could begin. Commanded by William Keppel, the British installed artillery on the high ground overlooking the fortress.

Up to now, everything seemed to have gone according to plan for the besiegers. The capture of Havana's crucial fortress appeared to be within their grasp. But the Spanish still had two important allies: hurricanes and mosquitoes.[20] As time wore on, those under siege were helped by tropical storms and the tropical diseases transmitted by yellow fever mosquitoes (*Aedes aegypti*). The importance of natural resources for the siege became obvious when the British captured the area around Chorrera, including the nearby river, the only local source of fresh water. By contrast, siege operations at Cojímar had to transport drinking water from some distance, along with wood and sand (for sandbags). The supply situation in Havana itself was also increasingly precarious, if we are to believe Uhlmann's account:

> How bad, sad, and miserable Things appeared in the Town during this time surpasses any telling, there was scarcity and starvation. There were no Supplies and for a time the pass was cut off, stopping any foods from the Country. Twelve men on duty got 2½ pounds of bread and 6 pounds of meat a day for 14 days. But the situation improved as soon as the pass was opened, as a great supply of Oxen was then brought to

the city, which filled up the Churches. But even these animals became so thin that many of them died of hunger, for they had nothing to feed on, I can testify that back home better Animals than this would be brought to the Knackers-Field, to get any meat from them at all would be a great blessing.[21]

For a while, the Spanish had time on their side. By the end of June, the British had nearly completed their preparations at the La Cabaña battery and along the coast at Cojímar. The Spanish decided to take the initiative and launch a counterattack, with 500 Spanish regulars attacking the British coastal battery and another 260 landing at the bottom of the heights at La Cabaña. Both attacks came up against well-entrenched, vigilant British defenses, resulting in seventy-three casualties on the Spanish side and just a handful for the British. The British completed their batteries, and the bombing could begin.[22]

The British naval bombardment of El Morro's northern side on June 11 had already shown how difficult it would be to inflict significant damage on the fortress. That action had almost ended in disaster, but it did force the Spaniards to focus their artillery on attacking ships rather than tackling the British land batteries. Environmental factors also hit the British preparations: In early July, a large artillery battery caught fire and was quickly engulfed in flames; after two weeks with no rain, the wooden floor had dried out, leaving it highly flammable.[23] The shortage of water made putting out fires very difficult and was also affecting more and more soldiers as disease spread quickly. James Miller, the British infantryman whom we saw enlisting enthusiastically as a teenager in 1756, describes the scene: "The fatigues on shore were excessive, the bad water brought in disorders, which were mortal, you would see the men's tongues hanging out parched like a mad dog's, a dollar was frequently given for a quart of water; in short by dead, wounded, and sick the army were reduced . . . it was supposed that we should be obliged to re-embark without taking the place."[24] Miller by now had plenty of military experience, having participated in the Rochefort expedition of 1757, the taking of Louisbourg the following year, the fall of Quebec in 1759 and its subsequent defense, the capitulation of Montreal in 1760, and the capture of Martinique in 1762.[25]

British forces on Cuba were waiting for reinforcements from the American colonies, but none came. Amherst in New York had received his orders to embark only on April 1, and his troops would likely not arrive until

August.²⁶ Meanwhile, Albemarle even had to evacuate Guanabacoa because he was short of men for the assault on El Morro.²⁷ On July 17, the fortress had been sufficiently bombarded that the British could begin the last stage of trench digging: the creation of *approches*, linear trenches going toward the siege objective. But conditions in Cuba were unlike those usually found in European sieges: These soldiers were digging not through earth but through solid rock. Inadequate scouting prior to the operation now also came back to haunt the British, as the sheer scale of the moat surrounding the fortress now became clear. How could the fortress be stormed under these conditions? After careful review by engineers, on July 17 the British began to build a barricade-like structure that extended right up to the walls of one of the bastions. Under cover of the structure, they began to undermine the fortress, ultimately aiming to blow a breach in its defenses. Another Spanish counterattack was repulsed on July 22. A week later the mining operations were at last completed.

Two days before the attack the long-awaited reinforcements from New York arrived, providing 3,188 fresh troops. Their voyage had been very difficult, with several transports running aground on reefs and another five coming under French attack.²⁸ But Albemarle needed every single healthy soldier he could get.

Prior to the attack, two of the Keppel brothers disagreed over the deployment of marines. Major General Keppel, who favored the use of land forces, prevailed in the argument. In keeping with the etiquette of officers and gentlemen, Albemarle approached the fortress's Spanish commander, Don Velasco, a final time, offering to accept his surrender and explaining that in the event of an assault, he would have difficulty preventing his soldiers from committing a massacre. Velasco replied with equal courtesy, observing that his situation was not as desperate as his lordship supposed.²⁹ At two o'clock in the afternoon on July 30, the British exploded the mines they had positioned under El Morro, opening a breach in the wall of the western bastion (see figure 11.2). The attacking force would have preferred to see more destruction, but Keppel and Mackellar decided to risk an immediate attack. Their 268 infantrymen, along with 150 sappers, began to climb the fortress. After an hour of fierce hand-to-hand fighting, El Morro was in British hands, with Velasco himself badly wounded and taken prisoner. The British suffered 12 dead and 28 wounded, while the Spanish had 137 dead and 37 wounded. Another 326 Spanish soldiers surrendered, while 213 fled, many of whom were drowned. Uhlmann comments on the fighting: "On

Figure 11.2 Defense of the Castillo de los Tres Reyes Magos del Morro in Havana, 1762. Painting by José Rufo (1763).
Source: akg-images/Album/Oronoz.

the afternoon of July 30, the English stormed the upper Castel, the next day they began a Bombardment of the City. It is unknown how many of the garrison fell. But we may glean the Spanish losses from the following: there were 1,400 men in the castel, of whom 600 were taken captive, with quite a few more jumping from the Walls into the water whence they were fished out. The rest remained through fire and sword, including the Commandant of this staunch Fortress."[30]

Surrender negotiations were conducted between August 9 and 13. The usual courtesies was shown: Albemarle wrote directly to Governor Prado on August 9, asking him to submit proposals for Havana's surrender in order to avoid the "fatal calamities which always accompany the storming of a city."[31] Prado's reply, sent the following day, was that his duty as a servant of the Spanish crown forbade him to surrender and he was determined to maintain the city's defense with hopes of a good outcome.[32] The next day the British launched an intense bombardment of Havana and the forts La

Punta and La Fuerza, rapidly proving their superior firepower. It took just hours to breach the city wall and launch the assault. Around two o'clock in the afternoon, Don Prado recognized the hopelessness of the situation and asked for a twenty-four-hour truce to prepare articles of surrender.[33] But Albemarle and Pocock were unimpressed by the articles eventually submitted, declaring them so "contrary to the customs of Warfare" that they had to be returned for revision.[34] Among other things, Prado had refused to include ships in the port in the city's handover.

But on August 13, the engineer Mackellar could at last note in his diary: "This day the capitulation was signed and sealed; the long time it took to be settled is said to be owing to an unreasonable earnestness in the enemy to save their shipping, which they at length gave up."[35] The next day British troops marched through the city gates and officially took possession of Havana. No further acts of violence were committed against the city or its civilian population during the capture of the city. The terms of surrender were comparatively moderate, given the dramatic struggle that preceded the city's capture. However, resistance continued in the Cuban interior; a complete conquest of the island was out of the question.[36]

For British soldiers, their victory marked the beginning of much suffering. There were more British deaths from yellow fever and other tropical diseases than from fighting.[37] By August 13, the day the British took Havana, 988 of their men had died. By October 4, another 4,295 had died, of which 3,788 had succumbed to disease. The "Empire of the Mosquito" had taken a brutally relentless toll.[38] By October, of the 7,225 British soldiers on the island, only about 900 were fit for service.[39] John Grant, for example, complained: "The flies also, and venomous reptiles when we could not get shelter, also tormented us—and the want of good water."[40] Further insight into their suffering can be found in the journal of John Graham, chaplain to the 1st Connecticut Regiment. On September 28, 1762, he wrote: "The last night as well as the preceding day, Sultry Hott, had but little rest—my Ears constantly acosted with the groans and outcrys of the Sick and distressed: that the Camp is no other than a constant Scene of Woe, and misery opened, where the actors are a Collect Society of the most unhappy and unfortunate, forlornly wretched."[41] The sick soldiers looked awful: "Not unlike walking ghosts just come from the Shades—but viewing more narrowly find them to be men. Crawled out of their Tent, wasted with Sickness: their flesh all consumed, there bones looking thro the Skin, a Mangie and pale Countenance, Eyes almost Sunk into there heads, with a dead and downcast look—hands weak, knees feeble. Joints Trembling—leaning upon Staves like men bowed and over loaded with old age, and as they Slowly move along Stagger and Reel, like drunken men—pity-full objects."[42] The funerals continued, as Graham reports: "There is one, two, three Graves open'd, here they come with as many Corps, there blankets both there winding sheet and Coffins; scarce have they finished the interment of these, but a messenger comes in hast to tell them they must open a grave or two more, for Such a one is dead, and another is dying."[43] Far more British and American soldiers died of disease in Cuba than were killed in action during the entire French and Indian War.

News of the conquest of Havana reached London on August 17, 1762, but did so via a circuitous path.[44] En route to Georgia, the merchant vessel *Betsy* encountered British warships near Cape Holmes, which passed information about the capture of El Morro. The *Betsy*, in turn, passed the news to the *Nelly*, which was sailing from the Carolinas to Dover. Official news of the victory arrived in London on September 27, sparking joyful responses across the country.[45] On October 3, the Oxford student James Woodforde notes news of the capture of Havana in his diary, and on October 11, Heinrich Ludewig Grotehenn reported artillery salutes in his Brunswick regiment "because of the conquest of Havana Island."[46] In Germany, the news prompted the Augsburg journal *Der Apotheker* to reflect on the risks of global British supremacy: "For the size of your works / the earth seems almost too small." More specifically, it continues: "Even Havana has fallen / Humbled before you / This brings you wide Renown / But to me it bring concern / This was a coup too grand / Too rich by far, and envy-filled / England, you are become too powerful / to be borne!"[47]

The siege of Havana was documented in forms other than the written word: The events were also illustrated with an extraordinary series of images: twelve engravings entitled *Britannia's Triumph*, published in 1765 by the English artist Philip Orsbridge.[48] For embedded artists with the British military, it was particularly important to emphasize one's own status as eyewitness, so the series was advertised with the words "Taken by an Officer on the Spot."[49] Orsbridge's drawings have a marked "documentary realist" aesthetic, a style that grew in importance during the Seven Years' War; we might recall the images of the ruins of Quebec by the London painter Dominic Serres (1719–1793) or the paintings of the destruction of Dresden by Bellotto. Serres created a series of oil paintings based on Orsbridge's images, and these, in turn, served as templates for engravers like Pierre Canot, meaning

Figure 11.3 The Storming of the El Morro Fortress in Havana in 1762. Painting by Dominic Serres (between 1770 and 1775).
© National Maritime Museum, Greenwich, London.

the engravings come with correspondingly complex authorship attribution: "Pierre Canot after Dominic Serres after Philip Orsbridge" (see figure 11.3).

Although many media representations of victory in Cuba were published and there were widespread public celebrations, not until 1800 was a historiographical appraisal of the risky venture undertaken, with the publication of David Dundas's (1735–1820) "Memorandum on the Capture of Havana."[50] Dundas had been an eyewitness to the events, and by 1800, he was a well-respected military theoretician. His sober account of the operation showed how close to disaster the mission had come, saved only by very good luck. The navy acted in an exemplary manner, Dundas suggests, while the land forces committed several important errors.

Spanish-language accounts of the conflict at first tended to emphasize outstanding heroic combatants, including Don Luis de Velasco. More recently, attention has primarily focused on the consequences of free trade for the economic history of the island.[51] Cuba went through a brief economic boom, but the prestige of the Spanish empire suffered a severe setback, especially regarding its defensive capacities. Cuban goods like tobacco and sugar could now find their way to British markets, while British commodities—especially enslaved African people whose labor was used in plantation agriculture—became much cheaper in Cuba. Once the conflict ended, both the Spanish and British world empires, turned to reform, which ultimately led to the independence of their North American colonies.[52]

Looting for the Empire: Manila, 1762

By 1762, the British were planning the capture of Manila, the capital of the Spanish-ruled Philippines. The operation would involve British land and naval forces, along with British East India Company troops, with the naval forces led by Vice Admiral Samuel Cornish (1715–1770) and the land forces led by Brigadier General William Draper (1721–1787). By now, this kind of combined operation was almost routine.[53] Prior to the operation, as was customary, a memorandum was drawn up, laying out the strategic importance of the target to be attacked. In this case, in autumn 1761 Draper supplied the memorandum to Lord Egremont, Pitt's successor as secretary of state for the Southern Department. The text opens with a mention of what today might be called securitization. In other words, Draper describes a threat scenario that appears to demand action,[54] suggesting that Spanish possession of Manila allows "the Spaniards [. . .] to fit out large galleons to cruise upon our China trade and may by taking positions at the Mouth of Canton totally interrupt our commerce unless our India ships go there under convoy of men of war which has never yet been done. The capture of this settlement will disable them from such attempts and entirely remove the seat of war from the East Indies."[55] The next sentence supplies the actual argument, which is primarily about economic expansion: "Our possession of Manila would provide our East India Company with a very convenient storage facility and a port, not only to continue its trade with China, but also put it in a position to expand their business to this whole part of the world."[56] The British were accustomed to victories, and their self-confidence was close to an all-time high. Draper concludes his memorandum with a question in Latin: "Virtus Britannica quid non donat?" (What cannot British valor achieve?).[57]

In fact, the situation was by no means as straightforward as this. There was no accurate map of the passage from Madras to Manila, and the company's ships suffered greatly en route. But there was a favorable opportunity. Draper already had the required troops at hand, in the form of the 79th Regiment. Even before Britain actually declared war on Spain on January 4, 1762, plans were afoot for simultaneous attacks on Havana and Manila. Both operations relied on the element of surprise and were supposedly strictly confidential, but this did not stop the London press from reporting on the project. On January 16, the *St. James Chronicle* mentioned a fleet possibly bound for Manila and repeated the claim two weeks later. Then on February 12, it reported a "great expedition" bound for Havana and, on the same day, published the following verse: "Let's away to Manila, the pride of Old Spain / Where with gold silk and diamonds, great plenty doth reign."[58]

On June 27, 1762, Draper arrived in Madras aboard the *Argo*.[59] However, assessments of the Manila situation offered by British officers in India differed radically from those put forth in London. Major General Stringer Lawrence, commander of British land forces in India, was concerned about a French counterattack and was not prepared to furnish as many troops as had been planned in London, as he feared for the security of his territory. In addition, Indian sepoys under British command had their own cultural and religious perspectives. Among other things, some refused to undertake voyages by sea, another reason why Draper ultimately got far fewer troops than he had been promised.[60] The soldiers that Lawrence did supply were a mixed bunch, consisting of around 600 regulars, 100 artillerymen, 300 East India Company troops, 600 sepoys, 50 Indian irregulars from the nawab, and 314 seamen. This group included many mercenaries and deserters.[61] On July 27, Draper described the European troop contingent in a letter to the secretary of war: "Exclusive of my own Battalion & the Artillery, The Rest are a Composition of Deserters of all nations, whom I take with me more to Ease the Fears & apprehensions of the People of Madras, than from any Service I can expect from them, But I have no choice: Those or none; such banditti were never assembled since the time of Spartacus."[62] It was no surprise when, shortly before the expedition got under way, relations between the military and the East India Company deteriorated still further. Tensions were set off by negotiations over war plunder. Draper was prepared to offer the company only one-third of plundered gains, citing a law forbidding the company from profiting from prize money acquired at sea.

Manila was a major missionary and trading center, with a population of around one hundred thousand, including Spaniards, Chinese, and Filipinos.[63] In Spanish, the city bore the appropriate nickname *Almacén de la Fé*

(Warehouse of the Faith).[64] Half of the city's Spanish population belonged to one of the religious orders—primarily the Jesuits but also the Dominicans, Franciscans, Augustinians, and Poor Clares. By the mid-eighteenth century, trade was no longer as significant as it had been; nonetheless, a galleon full of silver arrived annually from Acapulco, to be exchanged for Chinese goods, primarily silk.[65] Local laws specified that if a governor died in office, his authority would be assumed by the archbishop, which is why at the time of the 1762 invasion the city was governed by Archbishop Don Manuel Antonio Rojo del Rio (1708–1764).[66] The city of Manila itself was relatively compact, less than three miles in circumference.[67] In theory, it was well fortified, protected by twelve bastions and six gates. In fact, its defenses were not in optimal condition. The artillery was in particularly poor shape, with one-third of its 130 guns defective.[68] Rojo had about six hundred Spanish regulars and three hundred militiamen available but thought he would need about four thousand men to effectively defend the fortress.[69] One anonymous diarist suggests that the majority of the soldiers in the garrison—mostly "Mexicans," like the archbishop—were inexperienced and "undisciplined."[70] Since Manila had no port of its own, maritime traffic came through Cavite, a few miles away. Although an entire regiment had been assigned to the fortress, only a few hundred men were directly available for its defense, with the remainder scattered across the archipelago. People felt safe in the city.

Draper and the British fleet raced to arrive in the Philippines ahead of the news of the declaration of war between Spain and Britain. They succeeded: When their ships appeared in the Bay of Manila on September 23, it came as a complete surprise to the Spanish—so much so that they initially thought the ships might be seeking refuge in Manila (see map in figure 11.4). That day Rojo wrote to the commander of the fleet, expressing his disappointment that he had not stated the reason for its visit before anchoring offshore.[71] If they were in search of protection, he added, he was quite prepared to grant it. Things became clearer the following day when a letter arrived, in Spanish, from Draper and Vice Admiral Cornish: "The conduct of the Spanish crown has induced His Majesty of Great Britain, Our Royal Highness and Lord, to declare war on that crown; said king has sent us to wage war against said crown, to conquer Manila and the Philippines, and convince the Spaniards that the most distant subjects of their sovereign are not safe from the power and might of our king or beyond the reach of his most legitimate discontent."[72] Citing British principles of "moderation

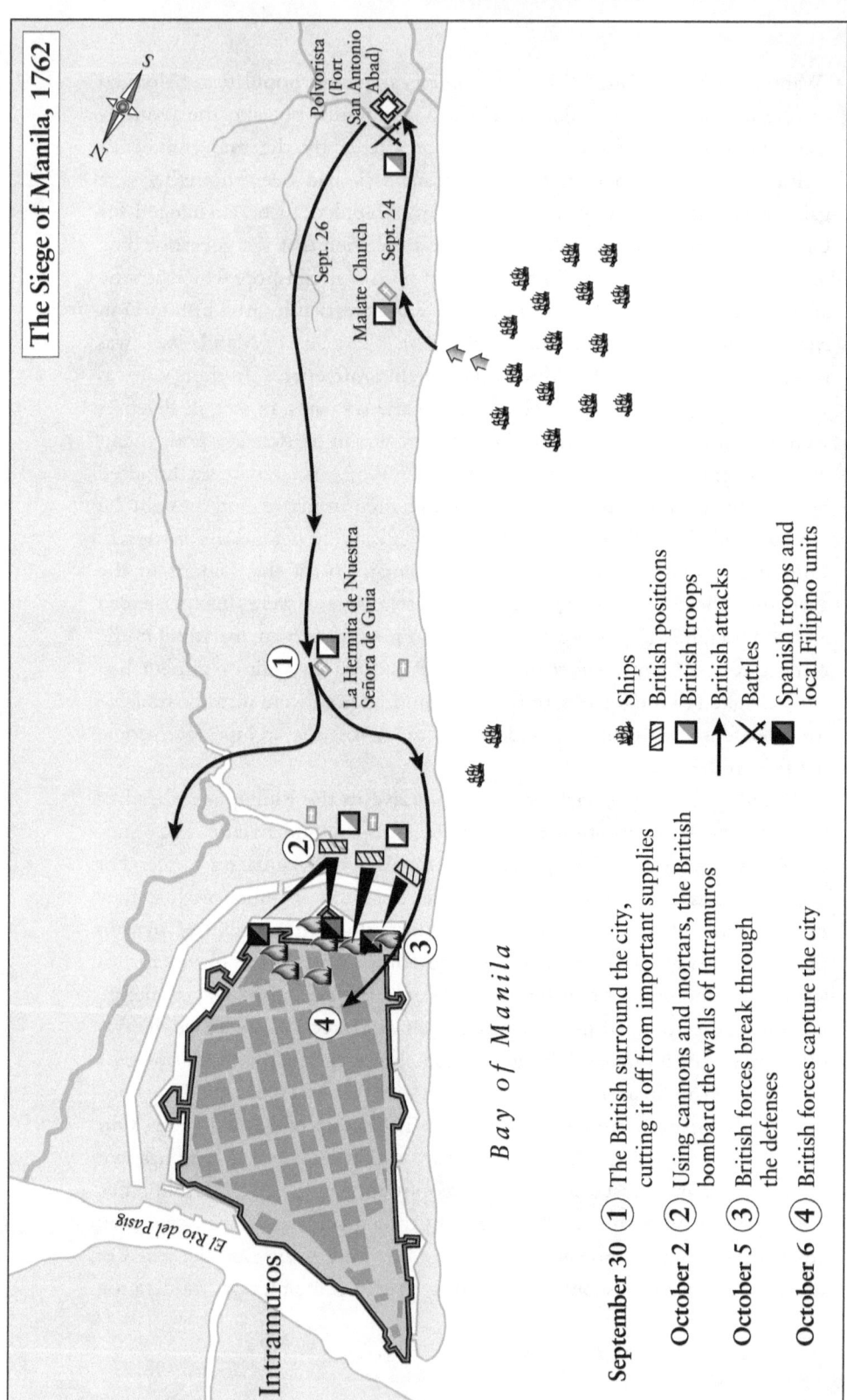

Figure 11.4 The siege of Manila, 1762

and humanity" and the severe consequences of any "fruitless resistance," they demanded the immediate capitulation of the city and its fortress. Rojo replied that day, stating that as a loyal vassal of his Catholic majesty, he would do everything in his power to defend the city to the last drop of blood.[73] That evening, September 24, the British effected a largely unchallenged landing, close to the city but out of range of its defensive artillery. By the next day, Draper had landed about one thousand European troops and eight hundred sepoys; seamen and other naval forces increased the total European force to around two thousand.[74] The Spaniards attempted a small sortie with around four hundred men and two guns, commanded by a Swiss officer named Cesar Faillet (or Fayette) but soon retreated without success.[75] Draper repeated the ultimatum originally sent in response to Rojo's first communication. On September 26, threatening massive force, he called on Rojo to reconsider his position, suggesting that his soldiers were a violent and dangerous lot, whom he could probably not control in the event of delays: "I have a multitude of most Fierce People, who are unacquainted with the more Humane Parts of War; it will not be in my Power to restrain them, if you give us more trouble."[76] Rojo summoned the council of war and advised surrender. But the officers on the council remained opposed; in the end, a unanimous vote was taken to continue the fight.[77]

The British situation was not an easy one. Time was of the essence, since they did not have enough troops to surround and besiege the city. Replying to Draper's threat, Rojo said he was sure the British auxiliaries were well under control, as were his own. But escalation was not long in coming. On September 25, the British had captured a small galleon belonging to the main Spanish treasure ship from Acapulco. Rojo's nephew, Antonio de Sierra Tagle, was one of the prisoners taken; as a gesture of courtesy, the British decided to send him to the city bearing small gifts. Under a white flag, a small group, including a drummer and Draper's secretary, Lieutenant Frayer, approached the city gates.[78] But the group was spotted by Filipino irregulars, known to Europeans as "Indians," who attacked, killing both Frayer and the governor's nephew.[79] In response, Draper threatened to hang all Spanish prisoners, whereupon the governor told the British General he had no control over his own irregular forces.[80] When questioned by Rojo, the irregulars insisted they had been fired on first by British sepoys and had merely responded in kind. The sepoys, they claimed, continued to shoot as Lieutenant Frayer and the governor's nephew approached.[81] Both sides thus attributed responsibility for the escalation to uncontrollable Indigenous auxiliaries. This allowed commanders to exchange courtesies while laying sole blame for extreme violence on their irregular forces.

Despite various difficulties at sea, the British managed to use their ships—the *Elizabeth*, the *Falmouth*, and the *Southsea Castle*—to position adequate materiel and siege artillery on land and offshore.[82] But as they had with the yellow fever mosquito in Cuba, the Spanish again found an unexpected natural ally—this time the monsoon rains. However, heavy monsoon seas also offered advantages to the British—for example, as acoustic camouflage: "The roaring of the waves prevented the enemy from hearing the noise of our workmen in the night."[83]

The British bombardment began on October 3, using heavy siege guns, including several mortars and eight twenty-four-pounders. Within hours, they had put the Spanish guns out of action. On the night of October 4, the Spanish attempted a counterattack with around two thousand Filipinos (Pampangans), but the operation failed because of a lack of artillery, as the British hit back with close salvo fire. The following day the British breached the city walls and now stood ready for the final assault.

Inside the city, another council of war was convened. This time military officers voted to surrender, but the heads of the religious orders demanded continued resistance. The Franciscans reported that an old woman named Mother Paula, venerated as a holy woman by the group of religious women she led, had had a vision of St. Francis defending the breach in the city walls.[84] On October 5, the British restarted their bombardment, this time hurling 2,244 twenty-four-pound rounds, 64 eighteen-pound rounds, and a variety of mortar bombs at the city and its defenders, using some thirty-four thousand pounds of gunpowder.[85]

The assault on the city began on October 6 around four o'clock in the morning.[86] In his journal, Draper noted: "We met with little resistance, except at the Royal gate, and from the galleries of the lofty houses which surround the grand square. In the guard-house over the Royal gate one hundred of the Spaniards and Indians, who would not surrender, were put to the sword. Three hundred more, according to the enemy's account, were drowned in attempting to escape over the river, which was very deep and rapid."[87] After the success of the initial attack, what remained of Spanish forces holed up in the citadel of Santiago. Rojo realized soon enough that further resistance would be futile. At eight o'clock in the morning, he raised the white flag and sent a messenger to Draper, requesting that surrender negotiations begin. Draper then came to the citadel, where the two men exchanged courtesies in a mixture of French and Latin. By half past eleven that morning, the British flag was at last flying over the citadel. The Spanish had lost several hundred men, but the British had successfully taken the city with a very low death toll: Just five British officers, sixteen other Europeans, and five Indian sepoys were killed, and about one hundred were wounded.[88]

Violence in the city continued for many hours after the surrender. Even while negotiations were under way, Draper's initial threats became bitter reality for Manila's population. The British had put together a heterogenous coalition of violence, which Draper now gave three hours to loot the city. But things rapidly got out of hand, and the plunder, in fact, continued for almost forty hours, until order was eventually restored by the 79th Regiment of the line.[89] Events in the city are vividly documented by the anonymous diarist, as well as by Don Francisco Leandro Viana, a senior Spanish tax official.[90] Religious orders were particularly hard-hit. The Dominicans complained of the loss of 7,870 pesos and the theft of sacred vestments and church ornaments by British seamen; the Jesuit College of San Ignacio was also looted, with 3,836 pesos stolen, while the Augustinian monks suffered the looting of San Nicolas, with the loss of some 70,000 pesos.[91] British soldiers also stole bells from a number of Franciscan churches and then sold them back to their owners.[92] Looters took clothes, jewels and devotional objects valued at between 7,000 and 8,000 pesos from the house of Josepha Augustiana de Larraguiver.[93] Draper captured one of the robbers and personally killed him. Many people were executed without trial: Augustin de Santa Maria reports corpses hanging together in front of the windows of houses, like bunches of bananas.[94]

Draper was later called on to justify these excesses, which he explained in terms of his men's uncontrollability:

> It is a known and universal rule of war, amongst the most civilized nations, that places, taken by storm, are subject to all the miseries that the conquerors may chuse to inflict. [. . .] We entered Manila by Storm, on the 6th of October 1762 with an Handful of Troops, whose Total amounted to little more than Two Thousand; a motley Composition of Seamen, Soldiers, Sepoys, Cafres, Lascars, Topasees, French and German Deserters. Many of the Houses had been abandoned by the frightened Inhabitants, and were burst open by the Violence of Shot or Explosion of Shells. Some of these were entered and pillaged. But all military Men know, how difficult it is to restrain

the Impetuosity of Troops in the first Fury of an Assault, especially when composed of such a Variety and Confusion of People, who differed as much in Sentiments and Language as in Dress and Complexion. Several Hours elapsed, before the principal Magistrates could be brought to a Conference; during that Interval, the Inhabitants were undoubtedly great Sufferers. But, my Lord, this Violence was antecedent to our Settling the Terms of the Capitulation, and by the Laws of War, the Place, with all it's Contents, became the unquestionable Property of the Captors, until a Sufficient Equivalent was given in Lieu of it. That several Robberies were committed, after the capitulation was signed, is not to be denied; for Avarice, Want, and Rapacity, are ever insatiable: But that the place was pillaged for Forty Hours, and that pillage authorized and permitted by me, is a most false and infamous Assertion.[95]

The situation was made considerably worse for civilians when Spain's Filipino auxiliaries also began to plunder the city. In 1814, the Spanish historian Joaquín Martinez de Zuñiga compared the British invaders with the Filipinos (which he referred to as Indians): "The Indians were far worse than they, for they found out the location of their masters' riches, so that they too might participate in plundering. The Indians who had been sent out of the town, with those who lived in outlying districts, along with prisoners whom the English had the imprudence to liberate from the prisons, now spread through the quarters of Santa Cruz and Binondoc and plundered them, exercising the rights of conquerors, murdering all who resisted, ravishing the women, committing every kind of atrocity."[96]

The Spanish capitulation was signed on October 7. As in Cuba, the Spanish were left free to practice their religion, but Manila was placed under British administration—in other words, under military rule.[97] In addition, the city had to pay a sum of 4 million Spanish dollars as protection from further looting, with the first half payable immediately and the second at a later date.[98] The excesses of irregular troops on both sides created an uncertain situation that inevitably worked to Draper's advantage. The Spanish administration had little choice but to accept the extortionate terms, which seemed the only way to restore public order. Draper could present himself and the regular British army as those who brought back order and, more generally, as representatives of clean, honorable warfare.

Draper was not the only figure under pressure to justify their actions. Archbishop Rojo was severely criticized in print, to which he extensively responded, claiming he had worked tirelessly for a surrender with military honor and had at least arranged that those capitulating would be allowed to keep their swords.[99] Addressing the British bombardment of the city, he writes that the attacking force would have reduced Manila to rubble, were it not for his assiduous management of the situation.[100] Things were seen very differently by the diarist Fiskal Viana, as well as by many other witnesses, including the Jesuit Agustin Maria de Castro y Amuedo (1740–1801).[101] Rojo, writes Castro y Amuedo, had "surrendered, throwing himself at the feet of the British with the keys of the citadel in his hand." Along with the keys, he continues, Rojo had "handed over . . . the Philippines, and the freedom, glory and honor of Spain." The British commander, he alleges, recognizing the unprecedently easy handover, had patted Rojo on the shoulder, saying "My Lord Patriarch, you are simple indeed." For Castro y Amuedo, the events were nothing short of catastrophic: "This account must be written through tears of Blood. All of this took place in fewer than 3 hours."[102]

Britain's problems in the Philippines only now began in earnest. As in India, they faced the difficulties of establishing a new administration and especially of dividing the spoils of war.[103] Draper saw his mission as completed, although a Spanish guerrilla army remained in the field, commanded by Simón de Anda y Salazar (1709–1776). It had withdrawn into the depths of the jungle, taking with it the silver from the Acapulco treasure ship. The British appointed Dawsonne Drake, a civilian East India Company official, as the new governor of Manila.[104] There was much recrimination between the governor and Admiral Cornish, who did not regard the military mission as over and was unwilling to submit to the company's civilian authority.[105] Both men tried to make the occupation of Manila as lucrative as possible. The military authorities frequently did so with violence, while Drake took a different approach, aiming to develop Manila as a prosperous trading base for the company. But both military and civilian authorities sought to accumulate as much capital as they could as quickly and directly as possible.[106] The East India Company had taken part in the operation as a private actor and now demanded that the British government pay it 163,243 British pounds to cover ship repairs, salaries, hospital costs, garrison provisions, the purchase and care of horses, the expansion of fortifications, the maintenance of prisoners from Manila in Bombay, and many other items.

On November 2, 1762, the company accepted an initial payment of 28,365 British pounds, which ultimately proved to be all that the British government paid to the company.

However, this figure does not come close to representing the immense wealth that actually accrued to the East India Company in prize money and war booty, thought to amount to 636,514 Spanish dollars. The company divided this profit in three equal parts, with one-third going to the company itself, and the remaining two-thirds divided in eight. Cornish, Draper, and Tiddeman each received payments of 17,681 Spanish dollars. Any money remaining after x were paid was divided among other officers and soldiers. In addition to this direct prize money, the company received other funds, including from confiscated Spanish ships and their cargo. It was unsurprising that the Spanish crown, at the end of the war, refused to pay the second half of the 4 million Spanish dollars, since the British had arguably plundered at the same time they were demanding payment for protection against plunder, a tactic that allowed them to lay their hands on far larger sums.[107] Chinese merchants were the main group caught between the two sides and were the biggest victims of the British capture of Manila. They did business with the British during the occupation and afterward were subjected to numerous attacks and eventually expelled from the Philippines in 1766.[108] Six thousand Chinese merchants are thought to have been killed in 1766 alone while suffering financial losses greatly exceeding those of the Catholic Church in Manila.[109]

The British also took plunder with more symbolic value. Draper personally acquired nine Spanish flags, which he later donated to King's College at Cambridge University.[110] The East India Company formed the acting government of Manila between 1762 to 1764, which continued to battle with Anda y Salazar for overall supremacy in the Philippines.[111] On July 23, 1763, the *Houghton*, a British merchant vessel, arrived in Manila from Madras, bringing the first news of the end of hostilities in Europe. Actual copies of the peace treaty arrived only on October 15.[112] The question now arose as to whether Britain would retain long-term control of the archipelago, but a decision was made in Europe in favor of Spain, and the company gave Manila back to the Spanish in early April 1764.[113] The last British troops left the city in early June. Historians have come to mixed conclusions about Britain's brief rule over the Philippines. Some regard it as having brought about greater structural interdependence between the Spanish and British empires; others suggest it marked the beginning of explicit Anglophobia.[114]

The War in Latin America

Havana and Manila were not the only places to see fighting after Spain's entry into the war. Conflict also broke out in four separate parts of Latin America, with the Spanish mostly having the upper hand.[115] In Nicaragua, the British attacked the fortress of Immaculata Concepción. The Spanish also fought the British and Portuguese on the Rio de la Plata, close to Buenos Aires, while in Brazil there was fighting between the Spanish and Portuguese in the province of Mato Grosso and around the Colonia del Sacramento.

In Nicaragua, a combined force of British regulars and fighters from the Miskito Sambu, a local ethnic group of mixed African and Indigenous ancestry, laid siege to Immaculata Concepción, which guarded the strategically important San Juan River. The attack began on the morning of July 26, 1762, with the British facing a Spanish garrison of only about a hundred troops, in what came to be remembered as the Battle of Rio San Juan de Nicaragua. The garrison had been commanded by José de Herrera y Sotomayor (ca. 1700–1762), but he had died unexpectedly on July 15, and the successful defense of the fortress was largely inspired by his nineteen-year-old daughter Rafaela de Herrera y Torreynosa (1742–1805), who personally fired the cannon shot that killed the commander of the British force. A new Spanish commander, Juan de Aguilar y Santa Cruz, then oversaw a successful defense, with fighting continuing for six days before a final British withdrawal on August 3.

In October 1762, Don Pedro de Cevallos (1715–1778), governor of Buenos Aires, led the Spanish conquest of Colonia del Sacramento, a Portuguese colony on the Rio de la Plata, located across from Buenos Aires in what is today Uruguay, in an action that also captured twenty-six British ships and 4 million pounds.[116] Private interests also became involved in the conflict over the settlements at the mouth of the Rio de la Plata. Late in 1762, Captain John McNamara, a former officer of the East India Company, led three frigates—the *Lord Clive*, the *Gloria*, and the *Ambuscade*—on a private mission from Plymouth to the Colonia del Sacramento. McNamara's small fleet took on five hundred Portuguese soldiers at Rio de Janeiro, but on January 6, 1763, the Spanish successfully defended the fortress against the British ships. A lucky shot from the fortress made a direct hit on the *Lord Clive*. McNamara's flagship caught fire, killing him and 271 others, including most of the ship's crew.[117] In June 1763, far to the north, in the inland Brazilian province of Mato Grosso, Spanish and Portuguese forces fought over the Fort do Principe da Beira on the Rio Guapore, unaware that peace had been agreed to some time earlier in Europe.[118] The battle ended unsuccessfully for the Spanish, whose sick and starving troops were forced to retreat. Spain's actions in defense of its fortresses in Nicaragua and Uruguay were its only military successes in the Seven Years' War.

CHAPTER XII

A Second Miracle

The Tsarina Dies

In just two days in January 1762, the Seven Years' War underwent two radical turning points. On January 5, Tsarina Elisabeth of Russia died; on the following day, Britain declared war on Spain. Elisabeth's death prompted very different reactions across Europe. In Königsberg, Andrei Bolotov responded with shock: "Hardly had the new year of 1762 begun, when a messenger on horseback from St. Petersburg brought news which struck us all like a thunderbolt, throwing us into great restlessness, agitation, and confusion. Tsarina Elisabeth had died and entered the light of eternity."[1] By contrast, the news put Frederick in triumphant spirits, and he dedicated a derisive epitaph to the late tsarina: "O wanderer, here lies Messaline / to Russians and Cossacks a concubine / Exhausting them all, of these shores she takes leave / Seeking new lovers in the realm of the dead."[2]

The new tsar, Peter III (1728–1762) of the house of Schleswig-Holstein-Gottorf, was an ardent admirer of Frederick who liked to dress in Prussian uniforms and recruited German soldiers as his bodyguards. On February 11, Frederick wrote to the Marquis d'Argens with palpable relief: "You will already know that the Emperor of Russia is taking care of our interests like the best citizen of Berlin, and we shall immediately conclude a peace, and perhaps an alliance, which will at a stroke free us from this infamous horde of barbarians who have devastated us, as well as from the Swedes, of whom we shall also be rid."³

An armistice was concluded with Russia on March 16. Four days later the Swiss mathematician and Berlin resident Johann Georg Sulzer wrote to Ludwig Gleim, the Prussian war poet: "Here, everything is revived after the armistice was made public. Peace with Russia will soon follow. Everything one hears about the new emperor indicates a prince who thinks with vision and determination. What a beautiful prospect when two such monarchs as Friedrich and Peter combine their forces and their offensives!"⁴ Peace between Prussia and Russia was agreed to on May 5.

In talks leading to a peace agreement with Sweden, Frederick is said to have revealed his disdain for the Baltic theater of war when he asked the Swedish negotiator: "Did I have a war with the Swedes?" Answered in the affirmative, he replied: "Ah now I recall, my Colonel Belling has had dealings with you," reducing the conflict with Sweden to the guerrilla warfare conducted by cavalry and local militias under Wilhelm Sebastian von Belling.⁵ Prussia concluded a separate peace with Sweden on May 22.

Another poet, Anna Luise Karsch, described the peace celebrations held at Halberstadt Cathedral on June 9, 1762. In a letter to Commandant von Reichmann, she writes: "I have the pleasure, my dear friend, to enclose one of the ribbons that he distributed. You will know yourself that Gleim composed the inscription, but I tell you anyway, with my best recommendation."⁶ Karsch is referring to one of the *Vivat!* ribbons used to commemorate battles (discussed in chapter 8), which were an ideal size and shape to enclose with a letter. In the Pomeranian city of Kolberg, at this point still under Russian occupation, peace was celebrated on July 11, "without secular celebrations" and without any "Russian participation."⁷ For many at the time, this "miracle" could only be an expression of divine intervention. This underlies comments by the Prussian officer Christian Wilhelm von Prittwitz, who was deeply influenced by Pietism:

> Without higher assistance, of course, the many dogs would have killed the hare, but when the need was at its greatest and we knew not what to do, the good Lord had the Empress Elisabeth die, a Death which turned a terrible Enemy into a wealthy Friend, one who helped to broker Peace and who returned the Lands he had conquered. This unexpected, indeed barely imagined, Assistance came at a moment when our King knew not which way to turn, so hounded he was

by his large number of Enemies. This shews that it was God indeed, and God alone, who arranged the Circumstances such as to keep the Dynasty of Prussia on its feet, even as it had begun to decline.[8]

The situation at the Russian court was precarious. Peter's "German" mentality and reformist politics went against the general situation in Russia. The royal marriage was shattered. Peter's wife, Sophie Auguste Friederike von Anhalt-Zerbst (1729–1796), was also the daughter of a German prince. Later better known as Catherine the Great, in 1762 she had had a son by her lover Grigory Orlov (1734–1783). For his part, Peter was thought to be planning to crown his mistress Elizaweta Romanova Vorontsova (1739–1792) as tsarina. It was only a matter of time before the royal couple's relationship devolved into open conflict. The peace signed by Peter, and the alliance he subsequently agreed to with Prussia, initially made very little difference on the ground in East Prussia, although it had substantial impact in Mecklenburg-Schwerin,[9] where war loomed between Denmark and Russia.[10] In June and July, Danish troops advanced via Hamburg and Lübeck as far as Lake Schwerin, while Russian troops marched on Rostock and Güstrow.

In East Prussia, Governor Suvorov was replaced by Lieutenant General Panin, and Russia's subjects now swore an oath to Peter, as they had previously done to his aunt Elisabeth.[11] As they withdrew, Cossack units demanded more money from the local population, inflicting yet more suffering. East Prussia was handed back to Frederick on July 5, 1762; four days later Prussian government officials returned to Königsberg. On the same day, Peter's wife ascended to the throne of Russia, having deposed her husband with Orlov's help. Peter died not long after, during a palace revolt on July 17, 1762, in circumstances that have never been fully clarified. At exactly this moment, the Russians withdrew from Mecklenburg, as did the Danish two weeks later. There was no last-minute outbreak of renewed fighting.

By now, there had been three different rulers on the Russian throne in six months. Catherine, the new incumbent, had no intention of returning to the country's previous alliance with Austria and sought to make peace with Denmark. Neither was there a general retreat, however; on July 16, the Russians reoccupied East Prussia. But this new takeover proved very short-lived. By August 6, the Prussians had retaken the province and restored it to rule from Berlin. Ultimately, the Russian evacuation of East Prussia would take months to be completed; the last Russian soldier did not leave until the end of the year.[12]

Alliance on the Bosporus: An Enduring Mirage

Prussia had long harbored the hope of a potential alliance with the Ottomans, a deal that might tie down Russian and Austrian forces in southeastern Europe. In hopes of reaching such an agreement, every year Frederick increased the money available to Karl Adolf von Rexin, his envoy in Constantinople. In late December 1758, the amount was 400,000 thalers; by February 1760, it has risen to 500,000.[13] In military terms, Frederick had little faith in the Turks, instead hoping they could adopt guerrilla tactics to terrorize the Austrians.[14] His plans were quite specific about this, as suggested by the following message to Rexin: "You must make this plan quite clear to the Grand Vizier, and have a map of Hungary with you, so as to point things out with your finger, so to speak."[15] However, the Ottomans still wanted British approval for any plan, which delayed things still further; news of the Prussian defeat by the Austrians at Landeshut in June 1760 did not help. Rexin asked for details of the plan so he could "mute the Viennese trumpet of lies."[16]

On April 2, 1761, Prussia and the Ottoman Empire finally agreed to a treaty of friendship, which was ratified in July. Although the new accord gave Frederick some sense of security, he was also forced to justify his action. An alliance with Christianity's archenemy was widely seen as a monstrous act.[17] Frederick defended himself on this matter to Johann von Grant, one of his generals:

> I have now agreed and signed an alliance with the Ottoman Porte, in this way I am thinking of the future of the war, how to conduct it, if not with superiority, at least with more equality. The animosity of my enemies, who have made bloody war on me, has compelled me to enter into an alliance with the Turks. I have found more bonnes fois, justice, loyalty and faith with them, than with the Christian powers warring against me, who, while I was engaged with them in the holiest of negotiations, sought to undermine my power and honor and promote my downfall. Thus the whole world and all of Christianity will approve of the step I have taken. If my enemies, albeit too late, repent of their thoughtless, illegal actions, it is no longer up to them to make comparisons between themselves and me."[18]

The letter was, in fact, addressed to Vienna as much as to Grant; the message was intended to make its way to the Austrian capital.

The Prussian-Turkish deal addressed only trade issues and had little real impact on the strategic situation, since the war was already coming to an end. At this point, Frederick had no illusions about the "brilliant chimera" of a possible alliance with Turkey.[19] Nonetheless, in 1762 he continued to collaborate with the Ottomans on drawing up campaign plans, although the situation became increasingly delicate after the death of the tsarina. In a letter to Lieutenant General Werner on April 13, Frederick outlined a plan involving twenty-six thousand Crimean Tatars, which frankly suggested a possible strategy of terror: "But were the Turks to act, they can be far more brazen and carry out several ravages. To force the Austrians to cover Vienna, they can simply have the Tatars commit far more excesses in Austria than elsewhere; how they would then burn some villages near Vienna, and those belonging to the most distinguished gentlemen, so they can see the flames from Vienna; whereupon they will scream mightily that all is lost."[20] None of this ever came to pass.

By now, Frederick was making peace with Russia while sticking to the project of a Turkish alliance, with the Ottomans to be used solely against the Austrians.[21] But negotiations with the Ottomans dragged on for so long that eventually the fall of Tsar Peter again changed the situation in Russia. In spite of the 1761 treaty, a military alliance with the Turks did not come about, and Frederick gradually began to worry that Rexin was "shredding and squandering" his money.[22] His concerns were not unjustified. According to most observers in Constantinople, Rexin's diplomatic efforts were anything but professional. By the end of the war, Prussian machinations on the Bosporus had swallowed up around a million thalers.[23]

Last Skirmishes

What of France in all this? Could Paris reverse the fortunes of war? Ubiquitous false reports prompted a Munich paper, the *Wochen-Blat in Versen* (*Weekly news-paper in verse*), to apply a new slogan to the French cause: "The dead live longer." The newspaper's first edition of 1762 argued: "How often yet stands France defeated? Her Coffers emptied? Her Court, her Regiments, and her Warmaking gone awry? Yet every time she surges once more. Do not believe that Franckreich will so easily be brought Low. If seaborne Luck is sleeping, perhaps it will wake on Land. Perhaps the War's own Fire will burn down now, and burn out."[24] The French leadership was convinced that the island of Newfoundland had great strategic importance: It was thought to be indispensable in the reconstruction of French sea power and potentially an important bargaining chip in peace negotiations, so an expedition was launched to capture the island. In May 1762, the French Admiral Chevalier de Ternay sailed from Brest with a fleet that managed to break through the British blockade. On June 27, French forces under Comte Louis Joseph d'Haussonville (1737–1806) took the British settlement at St. John, occupying it with fifteen hundred French regulars. The British recapture of the town was to be the final battle of the French and Indian War.[25] Led by William Amherst (1732–1781), a brother of Jeffrey Amherst, the British landed at Torbay, north of St. John, on September 13. The French had sent an advance unit to secure Signal Hill, a strategically important elevation, but the British launched a surprise attack on September 15 and took the hill by storm. With great difficulty they hauled artillery to the high ground and then began to bombard St. John. The French gave up three days later.[26]

Almost simultaneously, on September 21, the war's western German theater saw one of its final battles, fought close to the village of Amöneburg in Hesse.[27] Duke Ferdinand's Allied forces laid siege to Kassel, and took the city on November 4.[28] In fact, a preliminary peace between Britain and France had already been signed the previous day at Fontainebleau. On November 15, at the Brücker Wirtshaus—an inn at Amöneburg—a ceasefire was signed between the Allies and France, with Ferdinand signing for the former and Marshals d'Estrees and Soubise for the latter.[29] Grotehenn's diary records the event with delight, noting that this "Confession" meant there would be "no more Hostilities exercised" since "all Hostilities are at an End."[30] The French began withdrawing their forces as early as November 16. Five days later Grotehenn's unit departed for its winter quarters in the Prince-Bishopric of Hildesheim.

Before the peace had been finalized, the Prussians kept up the pressure with small-scale guerrilla operations. General von Kleist led a foray into Franconia, an action that prompted the imperial estates to declare their neutrality. In the war's final years, an increasing number of violent incidents had damaged the Prussian's army's reputation for discipline and "gutes Manneszucht." Prussian violations of the norms of war had affected both the aristocracy and the general population and would be long remembered. One particularly inglorious strategy was the Prussian forays against the castles of aristocratic families on the opposing side. This tactic, used by

Frederick himself, was a clear breach of the unwritten code of conduct governing warfare at the time.[31] As early as 1757, the Prussian king had ordered the destruction of Grochwitz Castle near Herzberg, north of Dresden, which belonged to Count Brühl, the prime minister of Saxony. Two more castles belonging to Brühl were attacked in 1758 and 1760: Pförten Castle near Forst in Lausitz and Oberlichtenau Castle near the Saxon town of Kamenz.[32] The Prussian attacks could, in turn, be traced back to the Austrian and Russian raid on Berlin in October 1760, when Frederick's own palaces at Charlottenburg, Schönhausen, and Friedrichsfelde had been plundered, with the alleged participation of Brühl's Light Horse Regiment cavalry. This chain of deliberate provocations culminated in the devastating looting of another of Brühl's palaces, a hunting lodge at Hubertusburg near Wermsdorf, by a Prussian "free battalion." Between January and May 1761, the building was damaged to the point of complete destruction. We owe our knowledge of the destruction to the careful documentation of the palace caretaker, George Samuel Götze (1692–1767).[33] The officer in charge of the looting was Colonel Karl Theophil Guichard (1724–1775), to whom Frederick had given the official nickname Quintus Icilius, following a debate on Roman military history. According to Count Ernst Ahasuerus Heinrich von Lehndorff (1727–1811), chamberlain to Frederick's wife, Elisabeth Christine (1715–1797), Guichard now received another nickname thanks to "[his] plundering of the Palace in such mean fashion." After personally selling off the "Floors and the Copper from the Roof," Guichard became known as the "Hubertusburg Decorator."[34]

Addressing how the conflict altered armies' room for maneuver in wartime, Frederick said: "I began the campaign as a general; I will end it as a partisan."[35] The phrase applies in the limited sense to military tactics but also to his increased ruthlessness toward territories through which armies moved and toward civilian populations in general. Among Frederick's most senior generals, confidence in the king had been substantially eroded; some officers called him "the gravedigger" behind his back. Many of his old generals, like Winterfeldt and Schwerin, were long dead. Younger generals often had little esteem for the aging king and would grimace after he had passed by on his horse.[36] But Frederick was not about to give up.

In Silesia, the fortress of Schweidnitz and the county of Glatz remained in the hands of the Austrians while peace negotiations were conducted elsewhere. Both sides knew that control over Schweidnitz could determine the peace terms that would end the Third Silesian War.[37] Daun's Austrian army was numerically stronger than Prussian forces, but Frederick made a daring attempt to lure his opponent into the field. In late June, he received unexpected help from his former adversary, with the appearance of General Zakhar Grigoryevich Chernyshev (1722–1784) and twenty thousand Russian troops close to Breslau. Together the Prussians and Russians marched against Daun's army, which was encamped near Burkersdorf. But on July 18, 1762, fortune took another sudden turn, with the arrival of news from St. Petersburg of Peter III's downfall, along with orders to the army to immediately depart Silesia. Once again, Frederick staked everything on a single card. He asked Chernyshev to stay three days longer, without participating in the fighting; the ruse succeeded, and the Prussian king defeated Daun at the Battle of Burkersdorf on July 21.[38] In return for his cooperation, Chernyshev was given 15,000 ducats and a sword inlayed with diamonds. Today the name of Burkersdorf is almost unknown, unlike Rossbach or Leuthen. Still the battle was the site of important tactical innovation: As at Krefeld and Torgau, Frederick attacked in two independent columns.

Moreover, Bunkersdorf had a significant impact on the war's outcome. Victory opened Frederick's path to Schweidnitz; the siege of the town began in August but dragged on until October.[39] The fortress, with its Austrian garrison of ten thousand, held out until a bomb hit its powder magazine on October 7, in an incident similar to one during the 1759 siege of Münster. Two days later came the surrender. The nearby city of Breslau, however, had little appetite for celebration; hunger and deprivation weighed too heavily on the population, as Juliane von Rehdiger noted in her memoir. One of her poems reflects the city's situation: "Were it myrtle, with merely wreaths of peace to weave / The city would of poets have no need / But war endures, and misery at every turn."[40] Daun was forced to withdraw to Glatz, while Frederick turned to Saxony, looking to capture Dresden if he could, to be used as a bargaining chip to exchange for Glatz.

In 1761, Frederick's brother Henry had again taken command of Prussian forces in Saxony; the two brothers' strategic approaches now at last appeared to be converging.[41] Henry wanted to fight a decisive battle for control over Saxony, thereby securing it for his winter quarters.[42] On October 29, 1762, the last battle in the central European theater was fought close to Freiberg in Saxony.[43] On difficult terrain, Henry proved tactically superior, dividing his army into four groups; the Prussians had won the encounter by midday. The Imperial army and its Austrian allies lost a total of seven thousand men, including those killed, wounded, and taken prisoner, compared to the

Prussian casualties of just fourteen hundred.[44] Ultimately, the Austrians were not entirely driven from Saxony—they continued to hold Dresden—but this final Prussian victory increased Vienna's willingness to conclude the peace. On November 29, the Saxon Privy Councillor Thomas Freiherr von Fritsch (1700–1775) appeared at Frederick's headquarters at Meissen, looking to begin peace negotiations. At first, Frederick harshly rebuffed his approach, but further talks were facilitated by the intervention of the tsarina. This time the conversation made progress, opening the way for a final peace accord.

CHAPTER XIII

1763

Peace at Last

Fontainebleau and the Path to Peace

The war ended as gradually as it began. The dates given for peace treaties may suggest clear punctuation marks in the historical narrative, but the transition between war and peace was, in fact, comparatively fluid.[1] This was certainly true on a global scale, since communications could take many months; there could be no question of peace instantaneously breaking out around the world. But even in Europe, processes of demobilization and diplomatic reorientation dragged on for months. Plans for a peace congress at Augsburg, which ultimately never took place, confirm that the initial idea was to settle both of the great casus belli at the same time. In the end, separate solutions to the Franco-British and the Austro-Prussian wars were worked out at Paris and Hubertusburg, respectively, as the two major conflicts began to disentangle.[2]

Peace talks in Paris lasted from September 14 to November 3, 1762.[3] However, the French government needed Spain's consent before it could conduct binding negotiations with Britain. Once Charles III of Spain agreed to the exchange of diplomats, Louis-Jules Mancini-Mazarini, the Duke of Nevers (1716–1798), traveled to London, while John Russell, the fourth Duke of Bedford (1710–1771), made his way to Paris. Russell's diplomatic correspondent in London would be Charles Wyndham, second Earl of Egremont (1710–1763). Bedford was thought to be disposed to make peace, and the French tested his willingness to compromise, despite the fact that, in military terms, France was on the defensive in every theater of the war.[4] At the end of September, Choiseul increased pressure on the Spanish. For their part, Bute and Egremont wanted to have a peace agreement in place before the British Parliament returned to session: The return of Pitt was an outcome Choiseul also sincerely hoped to avoid. At this point, news of the capture of Havana arrived in London (September 29) and shortly thereafter in Paris (October 3). Madrid learned of the fall of the Cuban capital on October 9; nonetheless, the Spanish government announced itself ready to continue the fight. To placate its Spanish ally, France offered to cede Louisiana to the Spanish crown, with Spain exchanging Florida for Cuba.[5] Charles III agreed to the proposal, although Choiseul initially kept Spain's acquiescence a secret from the British while he, almost at the last minute, negotiated more favorable conditions for Newfoundland fisheries.

A preliminary peace was signed at Fontainebleau on November 3 and thereafter ratified by George III. The approval of Parliament was also required, although it had no power to make changes to the articles. Hardwicke spoke against the peace in the House of Lords, but his intervention made no difference; the agreement was approved by acclamation.[6] But how would the House of Commons react? Pitt was the most important opponent of the peace deal. On December 9, despite gout and a weak voice, he gave a fiery three-and-a-half-hour speech, seeking to dissuade the Commons from supporting the peace.[7] As Hardwicke had previously argued in the Lords, Pitt contended that the return of the West Indian sugar islands and Newfoundland fishing rights would restore French maritime power and might even nullify British successes in India. With victory close in the German territories, he suggested, this peace would sacrifice Frederick II, thereby alienating him, and it ill-rewarded Britain for its strong position. But in the end, the Commons voted overwhelmingly in favor of the deal, with 319 votes for and 65 against. The Nos included Robert Clive, who thought the agreement a danger to interests of the British East India Company. But a clear majority of parliamentarians had reasons enough to vote in favor: The public was yearning for peace, Britain had already enjoyed victories, no one knew how the king would react to a refusal, and Pitt and Newcastle could not establish a common position against the deal.[8] The parliamentary vote cleared the way for a formal proclamation of peace, scheduled for Paris in February.

The Peace of Paris

The Peace of Paris has never enjoyed the historiographical status of the Peace of Westphalia in 1648 or the Congress of Vienna in 1815. It remains curiously neglected, less researched than even the three treaties—Utrecht, Rastatt, and Baden (1712–1714)—that ended the War of the Spanish Succession.[9] At the time, however, people understood that the agreement would involve massive territorial changes.

Fred Anderson has demonstrated how a futuristic novel written in 1763 can help to shed light on British thinking about the long-term consequences of the peace.[10] The anonymously published *The Reign of George VI, 1900–1925* presents a scenario far in the future, in the early twentieth century.[11] The book's counterhistorical narrative suggests that Britain, by granting far too generous a peace in 1763, unintentionally helped France and Russia become leading nineteenth-century world powers. In the early twentieth century, the reign of George VI is thus dominated by Britain's worldwide struggle to reestablish its position as a global power. The conflict ends with Britain imposing peace in Paris in 1920, after British troops have "liberated" France, with George, the "philosopher king," hailed as the bringer of freedom. At the time the book was written in 1763, its primary target was clearly the British negotiators in Paris: The Duke of Bedford, the main British envoy, is one of the book's major historical villains. Many contemporary satires poked fun at Bedford's supposed naivete, diplomatic inexperience, and inclination to peace: "Brave in the field, in council they are tools / Make war like lions, and make peace like fools."[12]

The central negotiating trio comprised Bedford, Choiseul for France, and Jerónimo Grimaldi, the first Duke of Grimaldi (1710–1789), for Spain.[13] Bedford argued that France should be treated fairly, with his letters to Pitt and Bute suggesting that to ensure a lasting peace, France should not be subjected to excessively harsh terms. Too harsh a peace, in other words, would inevitably lead to France seeking revenge as soon as it could.

The treaty was signed on February 10 at the British ambassador's palace. It contained twenty-seven main articles and three ancillary ones.[14] The first three articles deemed the agreement of peace to mean the end of fighting (article 1), affirmed the foundational validity of previous peace treaties since 1648 (article 2), and agreed on the exchange of hostages and prisoners (article 3). Article 4 had particularly important consequences for territorial possessions, since it specified the cessation of French territories in Canada and elsewhere in North America. It noted that the French crown renounces all claims "to Nova Scotia or Acadia in all its parts, and guaranties the whole of it, and with all its dependencies, to the King of Great Britain," as well as all claims to "Canada, with all its dependencies, as well as the island of Cape Breton, and all the other islands and coasts in the gulph and river of St. Lawrence."[15] The treaty's reference in article 4 to France's "sovereignty, property, possession, and all rights, acquired by treaties or otherwise" in Canada had a surprisingly large impact on international law. But as the historian Hermann Wellenreuther has correctly pointed out, Native American tribes did not use these type of "treaties," which were, in fact, a "legal projection of Eurocentric concepts about the relationship of the tribes to the colonies and to the mother countries."[16] In this way, Native American nations were denied "any autonomous standing in international law."[17] In return for the French crown's renunciation of claims, French residents of Canada were awarded freedom of religion and "the liberty of fishing and drying on a part of the coasts of the island of Newfoundland" (article 5). In addition, France was given the islands of St. Pierre and Miquelon, "to serve as a shelter to the French fishermen" (article 6).[18] Furthermore, the border would now run down the center line of the Mississippi, with everything on the eastern side ceded to Britain, other than the city of New Orleans (article 7).

In the Caribbean, the islands of Guadeloupe, Maria-Galante, Desirade, Martinique, and Belle-Île were all restored to France. Grenada was ceded to Britain, which also kept St. Vincent, Dominica, and Tobago (articles 8 and 9). On the African coast, Gorée was returned to France, while the British were granted Senegal (article 10). In southern India, the French had their factories and settlements restored to them, according to the status quo of 1749, with the British returning everything they had conquered after that date (article 11). France was forbidden to maintain any form of military presence in Bengal. Some of the wording of the article differed clearly from that in the preliminary agreement, the result of informal lobbying by the East India Company, which had no official representative at the peace talks.[19] The company's aims were to exclude the French completely from Bengal and to set the reference date for restitution as far back as possible so as to negate the gains made by Dupleix. All of this resulted in an internal rift in the company between Lawrence Sullivan and Robert Clive, more about the manner of the negotiations than about any specific content.

Article 12 of the peace agreement returned Menorca to Great Britain. The French fortress at Dunkirk was to be demolished (article 13), and

French troops were to withdraw from all territories in the Holy Roman Empire (articles 14 and 15).

Agreements between Britain and Spain were listed after the Franco-British accords. These articles addressed prize moneys arising from the war (article 16), British logging operations in Honduras (article 17), fisheries (article 18), the restitution of Cuba to Spain (article 19), and Spain's compensatory cession of Florida to Britain, with its inhabitants granted freedom to practice their Catholic religion (article 20). They were followed by provisions dealing with the withdrawal of all French and Spanish troops (article 21); the mutual restitution of archives and documents from conquered territories (article 22); the mutual restitution of occupied territories not specified (article 23); the respective deadlines for evacuating occupied territories, taking into account the distances involved (article 24); and a guarantee that the treaty provisions applied to Electoral Hanover (article 25), where French occupying forces were to leave, as they also would from Prussian territories on the Rhine. A separate agreement confirmed that these territories would not simply be reoccupied by Austrian troops.[20] In conclusion, the various monarchs solemnly vowed to comply with the treaty (article 26), stipulating that the signatory parties would exchange final copies, including confirmation of ratification, as soon as possible (article 27).

For France, the terms were worse, all in all, than those negotiated by Choiseul in August 1761. Spain's war had lasted barely a year, yet the country suffered disastrous consequences, although its long-term territorial losses were not particularly large. The biggest territorial gains were made by Britain, which had won "half a continent with the scratch of a pen," in the words of Francis Parkman (1823–1893).[21] The British, increasingly now the inhabitants of an empire, thus faced a new challenge: "the problem of having acquired too much power too quickly over too many people."[22] But overall, despite critical voices at home, the Peace of Paris proved to be an enormous success for Britain. Its success is made all the more clear if it is compared to the parallel Treaty of Hubertusburg.

The Peace of Hubertusburg

Negotiations among Prussia, Austria, and Saxony were held from December 30, 1762, to February 15, 1763, at the palace of Hubertusburg in Saxony, originally a royal hunting lodge.[23] On the Prussian side, the chief negotiator was Ewald Friedrich von Hertzberg (1725–1795), head of the secret cabinet archive. The Saxon envoy was Thomas von Fritsch, a senior public official, while Austria sent Heinrich Gabriel von Collenbach (1706–1790). The negotiators were accompanied by various diplomatic secretaries; there were usually about ten men seated at the negotiating table. Fritsch had already conducted preliminary negotiations with Frederick at Meissen in November 1762.[24] On December 16, Frederick wrote from Leipzig to Luise Dorothée von Sachsen-Gotha: "Perhaps we will have peace this winter. Their Lordships of the Imperial Circles wish to withdraw their troops. Already the Lord [Prince-Bishop] of Bamberg, and the Electors of Bavaria and of Mainz have so decided. The flammable material must be pulled out of the conflagration, then perhaps the fire will go out. The Austrians will remain the last fighters in the arena, as they have done in all wars. Perhaps this will mean a worse peace for them."[25]

But why Hubertusburg?[26] Frederick had his headquarters in Leipzig and proposed to conduct negotiations in that city. The Saxon side had no problem with this; in fact, they hoped it might accelerate the process. Moreover, they initially persuaded Collenbach to negotiate at Leipzig. The Habsburg envoy had traveled halfway to Leipzig, reaching the village of Strauchitz in Saxony, before being overcome by grave doubts about the arrangement. He communicated these to Fritsch and broke off his journey. His reluctance was understandable: Accepting negotiations in Leipzig could easily have been seen as the Austrians suing for peace at the Prussian's king's headquarters and thus could have been interpreted as weakness on their part. But the Austrian headquarters at Dresden was also unsuitable—for the same reason. So it was decided to meet at Hubertusburg, near the Saxon town of Wermsdorf, roughly halfway between the Prussian and Austrian commands. Frederick agreed, issuing a decree that the town had neutral status.

The palace at Hubertusburg offered plenty of space, but the interior was in terrible condition, having been looted in 1761 by Prussian soldiers who had taken even the copper roof and parquet flooring of the main building.[27] To avoid precedence disputes, equal accommodations were assigned to the Prussian and Austrian plenipotentiaries: Each side was given ancillary buildings associated with one of the palace's two curved wings, which usually housed the chamberlain and the castle inspector. The apartments of the chamberlain, Gustav Lebrecht, were used as conference rooms, probably on account of their size.[28] The negotiators agreed to conduct their exchanges in a relatively informal manner, deliberately eschewing ceremonial pomp and dining together at a common table. There were no festive events held at Hubertusburg that winter; without balls, banquets, or excursions, there was no courtly spectacle to get in the way of intensive work. Messengers traveled daily from Leipzig and Dresden to Hubertusburg and back. Negotiations were not particularly quick—there were twenty-three sessions in six weeks—but progress was significantly faster than at other eighteenth-century peace congresses; in 1748, the Peace of Aachen had taken nearly six months to negotiate. On January 31, Frederick wrote to Luise Dorothée: "We really are concluding a peace. That means negotiations, which means piles of documents, trickeries to be thwarted, ambiguities to be cleared up, subterfuges to be forestalled."[29] This was, no doubt, the case for all the negotiators involved. One particularly vexing question was the Prussian demand for the return of the Silesian county of Glatz, then still under Austrian occupation.[30] Frederick ratcheted up the pressure on Saxony with tough demands for financial contributions. Toward the end of January, the electoral government waived all claims for compensation, paving the way for a Prussian-Saxon treaty. When Collenbach, the Austrian representative, relented on the Glatz issue, the way was also open to a final Prussian-Austrian deal. On February 15, 1763, the various documents of the peace were drawn up, and the Prussian-Austrian and Prussian-Saxon treaties were sent to the various royal courts for ratification.[31] This took some time, not least because Augustus III of Saxony was still in exile in Warsaw. On March 1, negotiators met again at Hubertusburg, this time for the formal exchange of documents. Frederick had expressed his own view of the treaty two weeks earlier; when he visited Hubertusburg on February 17, he told Von Hertzberg, his main negotiator: "This peace we have concluded is without doubt a good thing, but let us not make this obvious."[32]

Europe Celebrates the Peace

Across Europe, news of a final peace agreement was greeted with feverish enthusiasm. In Krefeld, Abraham ter Meer was in a particular state of excitement. Starting on January 2, 1763, he noted every rumor and every piece of news about a possible peace. On February 23, he at last could write: "Today (February 15), the Peace was signed—and thus the other Rumors had been premature—between our lord the King and Elector, along with the Empress-Queen, and the King of Prussia. [. . .] The same News-paper reports also that the final Peace between the crowns of England and Portugal, and also between those of France and Spain, was signed on the 10th of the month in Paris. And thus is Peace general. [. . .] How can I find Expression such as might leave Posterity even a mere image of our joy?"[33]

Peace was celebrated in many places across Europe; in the Holy Roman Empire, celebrations were largely concentrated in the cities of northwestern and central Germany.[34] Festivities began early in the territories of Electoral Hanover; already in January 1763, the territory saw festivities marking the preliminary peace of Fontainebleau and the coming Peace of Paris. In the city of Hanover itself, master baker Abelmann kept detailed accounts in his chronicle: "Our city and the whole of Hanover held a Festival of Thanks and Peace on January 6 of this year, to celebrate the peace so long wished for [. . .]."[35] In the city of Celle on January 13, he reports, a gathering was held of "all of the city's merchants [. . .], who long celebrated their joy in the Victory now achieved." At Celle's town hall, "the following lines were presented, in a fine frame: 'Good King George the Third / Has now here Made a Peace / God made strong his arm / So cry out Celle: Long live the king! / Let your hearts extol! / As all we Merchants do.'"[36]

Festivities marking the Peace of Hubertusburg did not all happen on the same day or even in the same week. Events took place across the Reich from early March to the end of May. Some territories announced a specific date for celebration; in other polities, it was left to localities to decide. Thus, Hanau, a county in Hesse, celebrated on March 9; in Silesia, Westphalia, and the Lower Rhine region, festivities took place four days later, on March 13. The Prussian city of Magdeburg marked the occasion on March 17, while Leipzig in Saxony held its peace celebrations on March 21. For Wetzlar in Hesse, the date was March 27, but for the Thuringian imperial city of Nordhausen, it was April 10. The free imperial city of Hamburg was among the last to celebrate, giving official expression to its civic joy on May 15.[37] In some localities, each particular corporation, society, and guild held its own separate celebration. In the city of Halle, for example, almost twenty different peace celebrations took place between March 7 and May 28.[38]

While some territorial authorities issued central decrees regarding prayers and sermons in the regions they controlled, celebrations at a local level took very different forms, sometimes going far beyond officially ordained modes of festivity. Many descriptions of local events were published in print, in this way making them available to a wider audience.[39] The main focal points for celebrations were church ceremonials and nocturnal illuminations. Tensions could arise, however, between religious devotions and other modes of celebration, as when one celebratory sermon nonetheless condemned, as abhorrent to the Lord, a large variety of "sinful, mad, lavish, invidious expressions of joy."[40] Sunday was often maintained as a day of rest and prayer, with more exuberant forms of public joy diverted to Mondays.[41]

Cities sought to outdo one another with public decorations. In Duisburg, a group of forty-three wealthy citizens, most of them merchants or professors, decorated their own houses with images and sayings, including "And thus does a Patriot give thanks to the State." The texts were later republished in a city newspaper, the *Duisburg Intelligenz-Zettel* (*Duisburg intelligence notes*).[42] In some locations, a complex iconography of peace developed, which expanded on the usual visual repertoire of civic-heraldic animals. There was a boom in craft-made peace "merchandise," including everything from *Vivat!* ribbons to elaborately designed peace carpets.[43] Some printed engravings illustrate these local *Vivat!* ribbons and festive decorations.[44] One print, in particular, by placing the Peace of Hubertusburg and the Peace of Westphalia on the same level, highlights the significance that contemporaries attributed to the peace.[45] Once again, the Thirty Years' War is posited as a benchmark for the later war.

Some descriptions of peace festivities reveal details of wartime sufferings in the place in question. At Nordhausen, for example, official celebrations were scheduled for April to allow the city's hostages time to return from Magdeburg, which they finally did on March 31, 1763. They had been captured three years previously, on March 4, 1760.[46] In Jena, student fraternities used peace celebrations as an opportunity to parade wearing their colors while participating in an official university festival on the Landveste, a stretch of land along the river.[47] In many places, local Jewish communities held their own peace and victory celebrations.[48]

The happy news of peace found expression in cantatas and bell ringing but also in cannon fire, with the ominous thunder of artillery fire turning into a pleasant "sound of joy."[49] Abraham ter Meer rendered the soundscape of festivities particularly clearly in his diary, which contains detailed sonic descriptions. After the news of peace had been confirmed in Krefeld, celebrators began firing the first volleys, which were accompanied by shouting and joyful cries of "Vivat!" The sounds of rejoicing—*les bruits de rejouissants*—continued day and night, suggests Ter Meer: "One becomes almost accustomed to hearing Gunfire; the firing is as if to remove all Gunpowder from the World, thereby to end the Making of War; even those of the Fairer Sex fire rounds of the musket."[50]

The news was announced in Berlin on March 5, the name day of the Prussian king: "With Trumpets and Drums, a Herald in fine Uniform, accompanied by a detachment of Gendarmes, was announced the Peace made between Brandenburg, Austria and Saxony, and thereafter on the Sunday of the 6th, a thanksgiving Sermon was preached on the 14th chapter and 27th verse of the Gospel of John."[51] Frederick himself did not return to the city until March 30, arriving sometime between eight and nine o'clock in the evening.[52] The Berlin merchant Johann Ernst Gotzkowsky, who had helped arrange Berlin's forced contributions in 1757, described how citizens of the city eagerly awaited the king's arrival: "When the day of H[is] Maj[esty]'s arrival was known, not a soul remained at home, all swarmed the streets, and from half a mile outside the city wall as far as the Royal Palace, loyal citizens, each in his finest holiday attire, from early morning 'till late at night lined the way along down which the King would make his entry."[53]

Among the waiting crowd was Johann Kaspar Lavater (1741–1801), later well-known as a writer and the popularizer of physiognomy. Here in the streets of Berlin, the young Lavater was already reading faces, paying close attention to those waiting for the king:

> Thus we awaited the King and the morning passed in the tedious Perusal of citizens as they pass'd by. If they are to be even slightly judg'd by their Physiognomy, their general Character seems very poor, disorderly, slavish, wild, or proudly voluptuous. [. . .] All afternoon long we awaited the King, but in vain! Our hopes were trampled upon the ground. Night fell. The torches were too few by far; the procession of Merchants, Crafts-men and clerks was interrupt'd and scatter'd. We caught no sight at all of the King, and knew not even whether he had pass'd our spot, or gone by some other route to his Palace.[54]

Gotzkowsky was also briefly left in the dark: "As fate would have it, H[is] Maj[esty] could only pass through here very late, in darkness, and thereby the joy of his reception wasted, and the reception could not proceed in the order planned, as had been prepared. A large portion of the citizenry were equipped with torches. From far away the arrival of the King was heard, the clatter of his carriage wheels, and there came a general shout of joy: Long live the King!"[55]

Johann Friedrich Heyde, the Berlin master baker, also took note of events, observing that the king's eventual arrival "greatly moved the citizens."[56] Frederick received the congratulations of the magistracy at the Frankfurt Gate, but he refused the gilded carriage offered to him, instead choosing to return to the palace via backstreets.[57] The poet Anna Luise Karsch expressed particular disappointment: "I see three thousand torches moving, I do not see the King's coach, I do not see him, the cause of all this pomp. He disappoints the expectations of a hundred thousand people, he goes through a different part of the city, he goes to a different gate of his royal residence: at this moment he seems to me a smaller person. He beats down all of these flaming hearts, as if a sudden downpour had extinguished before us the flame on an altar of sacrifice: it is unfair, it is halfway cruel . . ."[58] The Marquis d'Argens, a close friend of Frederick, was also extremely angry: "I wrote to him to say he owes it to his people to accept their love! It is unforgivable that he does not come!"[59]

The following morning Frederick received individual delegations, each presenting congratulatory verses: merchants, the French colony, the guilds of butchers and of marksmen, and so on. On April 12, Lavater finally succeeded in catching a glimpse of the great king:

> Just as I was writing, the King himself came riding along, slowly, wearing an old blue coat, accompanied by some Generals, the Prince Henry and the Crown Prince. [. . .] I watch'd him closely, for a long time. The form of his face strikes me as quite different to the various Portraits sold of him, it is heroic above all, the Forehead is slanted and continues the same line as the Nose. A small, purs'd Mouth, of which only the upper lip be visible. His eyes are small, positioned under delicate Brows, but not fiery. His Cheeks appear somewhat sunken. He seemed more courteous than any of his Companions. He doffed his Hat to the worst of those who bowed to him, and before every occupied window, and made inquiries about the new Buildings and their Inhabitants.[60]

These voices express and echo disappointment in a king who insisted on withdrawing from the public sphere. Others, however, harbored far more substantial grievances against Frederick. Andrew Mitchell, the British envoy to Prussia, reported to London that he had seen posters on the major thoroughfares of Berlin calling for the death of the tyrant-king, with allusions to the violent death of Tsar Peter III.[61] That same month Frederick began writing his own account of the lately completed war, which was published posthumously as the *Histoire de la Guerre de Sept Ans*.[62]

On returning to Berlin, a visibly aged Frederick seemed reluctant to celebrate. This reluctance was shared and surpassed by his counterparts in Vienna, where there was indeed "little cause for celebration" in political terms.[63] The occasion was dominated by ceremonies of religious thanksgiving. On March 5, the Saturday edition of the *Gazette de Vienne* reported news of the ratification of the Peace of Hubertusburg, including details of all the treaty articles.[64] On Wednesday, March 9, a brief report on the newspaper's final page noted that "[last Monday] 3 days of public Prayers and processions began in the capital to give thanks for the Peace the Almighty has been pleased to grant to Europe, and tomorrow, on the 10th of March, a Te Deum will be sung in formal Thanksgiving."[65] The next edition of the paper reported more extensively on the solemn Te Deum at St. Stephen's Cathedral, which was attended by the imperial couple, the court, the papal nuncio, the clergy, members of the university, the city council, and the entire military garrison.[66] The courtier and diarist Karl Graf von Zinzendorf was also present at the service; because he did not arrive at the cathedral until ten o'clock that morning, his view was restricted. His account gives little impression of euphoric reaction to the peace: "I sat on a pew across from the chamberlains. I could see little—many heads, and the tips of the bailiffs' halberds. I observed the brightly colored panes in the church's large cross windows. I heard music coming from the dais."[67]

Two years later the *Neueröfnete Historische Bilder-Saal* (*Newly published historic hall of images*) retrospectively reported in detail on Vienna's three-day "festival of thanksgiving" in 1763, during which "Both Imperial Majesties" went to St. Stephen's, "where the Cardinal and Archbishop of Vienna himself was celebrating high Mass."[68] The report includes a significant detail omitted by the *Gazette de Vienne*: "Prussian prisoners of war who had been at Crems and other Places came to Vienna around this time and saw the testimonies of joy prompted by the festival of peace. The following day they were granted an audience with the Empress, who had given orders that they be shown every-thing worthy of seeing." The description goes on to outline the customary commemorations: "The Day was given palpable Solemnity by the presence of the Imperial Court and other prominent Persons, including the Papal Nuncio and the entire clergy, the military, members of the university and the city council with the city and district courts. At the place known as the Freyhof, a battalion formed on the parade ground, with its battle music, firing a triple volley; the threefold firing of the cannon marked the closing of the first Day."[69]

Almost two weeks later, on March 22, heralds in London officially proclaimed the Peace of Paris.[70] Even now there was skepticism among the population, as the French astronomer Jérôme Lalande (1732–1807) reports in his journal while in England: "On the 22nd, the peace was proclaimed at five sites in London. In the evening there were illuminations on the Whitehall side, &c. But in a rather petty fashion the English called out curses like: 'You are as stupid as peace.'"[71] Londoners officially celebrated the Peace of Paris with a jubilee day on May 5. Lalande notes that sixty-one cannons were fired from the tower. Public prayers were printed and sermons preached.[72] In his journal, James Boswell (1740–1795) notes laconically: "This was a Thanksgiving day for the Peace. But I did not go to Church."[73] To the south of London, in Sussex, Thomas Turner took even less interest in the celebrations. On May 5, he writes: "We had no kind of rejoicing in this place though it is the day for proclamation of peace and general thanksgiving throughout the nation. I think almost every individual seems to be dissatisfied with the peace, thinking it an ignominious and inglorious one."[74] The British public sphere was awash with criticism of the peace; during the winter of 1762–1763, more than eighty critical broadsheets circulated, excoriating the terms as too generous.[75] One caricature, entitled *The Proclamation of Proclamations*, depicts a herald riding a horse with donkey's ears; above him hovers Fama, demonic looking, with a wooden leg to symbolize sufferings already endured and a riding boot meant to indicate the peace forced through by Bute.[76] At the center of the image, Bute himself is depicted, receiving congratulations from the French and Spanish. At the left-hand edge, a crippled sailor cries out in protest, thus completing the image of national tragedy.

In Paris, the peace was not celebrated until June, when festivities lasted from the twentieth to the twenty-second of the month.[77] On June 23, the Duke of Croy noted succinctly in his diary: "The peace, the celebrations of which ended yesterday, brought to an end a sad, unfortunate war."[78] Edmond Jean François Barbier (1689–1771), a Paris lawyer and chronicler of his time, offers more extensive comments on the celebrations in his *Journal historique et anecdotique*.[79] On June 20, a new equestrian statue of the king was unveiled after a long procession. The glazier and diarist Jacques-Louis Ménétra was present at the unveiling, although his diary mentions it only in passing.[80] In the evening, a "grand concert" was held in the Tuileries

Garden, which was illuminated for the occasion. As if to symbolize the decline of French power, a fifteen-minute rainstorm destroyed all the decorations after just half an hour, extinguishing the artificial lights. Barbier notes critically that the *Gazette*, a week after the events at the Tuileries, reported the event to have been a lavish festival that passed without incident, with crowds happily dancing through the night.[81]

On June 21, a group of army officers and municipal dignitaries journeyed through the streets of Paris for nine hours, enacting the decree that commanded "the publication of peace in all public places and markets of the city."[82] The following day a huge bonfire was lit in the Place Louis XV, which was also illuminated for the occasion.[83] The various dignitaries—including nobility, members of the urban upper class, and foreigners of distinction—gathered at noon, only to be caught up in another unfortunate thunderstorm. By evening, the sky had cleared, allowing "un fort beau spectacle" to take place.[84] The event began with a joust between the boatmen of the Seine, followed at six o'clock by the singing of a Te Deum in Notre-Dame, and concluding with a spectacular Franco-Italian fireworks display at half past nine. This event also had its problems: The French fireworks went off without a hitch, but the Italian fireworks had been dampened by the midday downpour and failed to ignite. Overall, the French celebrations were something of a mixed bag. In a letter of June 30 to Luise Dorothée von Sachsen-Gotha, Voltaire wonders what the French could possibly have to celebrate: "They venture to hold celebrations in Paris; I really do not know why. In my view, the British are entitled to have celebrations, and a few of the German princes."[85]

Precarious Promises

The French and Indian War is generally regarded as a turning point in relations between white settlers and Native Americans, marking the end of the "middle ground" and the start of racially based policies of expulsion and killing.[86] In September 1763, the Ottawa sent the following message to the Illinois:

> The English tell us incessantly What ye Indians dare ye speak, see what we have done; we have [conquered] your Father [the French king] and the Spaniards; We are masters of these lands and of all of which

belonged to your Father, for we have beat him & we possess all these countrys even to the Illinois—The Delawares told us this Spring, that the English sought to become Masters of all, and would put us to Death, they told us also "Our Brethren let us Die together, seeing the Design of the English is to cutt us off, we are Dead one way or another."[87]

More and more European settlers were advancing west of the Appalachians and north of the British colonies. In this context, the treaty agreed to at Paris created new realities in terms of property law and international law, all decided entirely over the heads of the Native Americans.[88] The Native nations remained firmly convinced that they had ceded no lands to France and thus had no obligation to cede any to the British.

A rebellion was launched by an alliance of tribes led by the Ottawa under Chief Pontiac, prompting the colonists to refer to the new conflict as "Pontiac's Uprising" or "the Pontiac War."[89] Even before the rebellion had broken out, Native Americans had been making plans for resistance, prompted by the French surrender in 1760 and preliminary peace plans in 1762. Actual fighting began in early May 1763 when the Native alliance laid siege to Fort Detroit, west of Lake Erie. Up to nine hundred Indian fighters from different tribes took part in the siege, although it was eventually broken off in June. In late July, the British, commanded by James Dalyell, Amherst's aide-de-camp, launched a counterattack on Pontiac's encampment, but this resulted in a costly defeat for the attacking forces. In a separate offensive in June 1763, the Native Americans had also attacked Fort Pitt, the newly built British fort close to the present-day city of Pittsburgh. The main attack on the fort failed, but the tribes at least managed to capture eight smaller forts (Sandusky, St. Joseph, Miami, Michilimackinac, Ouiatanon, Presque Isle, Le Bœuf, and Venango), located mainly to the south of the Great Lakes. The siege of Fort Pitt saw the use of what is perhaps the best-remembered tactic of the Pontiac War, whereby soldiers under Amherst's command "gifted" smallpox-infected blankets to members of the Delaware, Shawnee, and Mingo, resulting in many fatalities among the tribes.[90] Historians now generally believe that Amherst did not personally give the order to pass on the infected blankets, although he may well have welcomed the strategem.[91] However, these British tactics were considerably less unusual than the usual focus on Amherst as an "Indian hater" might suggest. For one thing, we must consider the sheer "material availability" of the virus locally:

The disease was rampant in Fort Pitt, where victims were treated in the lazaretto. Second, this technique of biological warfare was quite widespread in North America in the eighteenth century.[92] Native American tribes seem to have used equivalent practices, although they were particularly vulnerable to the tactic.[93] They lacked immunity to the variola viruses brought by Europeans and had highly inadequate medical treatment, so they suffered the fatal consequences of smallpox epidemics.

The Cuban campaign had taught the British and Americans another lesson about the disastrous consequences of infectious disease. The extremely high losses in that campaign had lasting consequences in the North American colonies. Hundreds of emaciated and wounded soldiers were shipped to New York hospitals, where they died.[94] Much of the army was still not operational at the outbreak of the Pontiac Rebellion. The delay in response to the Native American uprising ultimately led the British administration under George Grenville (1712–1770) to introduce difficult measures, from new taxes to the billeting of troops, all of which helped to usher in the American Revolution. Unpaid wages and poor living conditions prompted several mutinies among soldiers under British command, eventually forcing concessions from the army leadership.[95]

In October 1763, the Potawatomi, Anishinabe, and Wyandot agreed to peace terms with the British. On October 7, the delineation of a new royal border was proclaimed, the Proclamation Line, with European and Indian lands separated along the watershed line of the Alleghenies and Appalachians.[96] The war was ended by two successive British expeditionary forces, one led by John Bradstreet (1764) and the other by Henry Bouquet (1765), that persuaded most of the tribes to conclude peace treaties. Pontiac himself surrendered to Sir William Johnson (1715–1774) at Oswego on July 25, 1766. The following year the Six Nations and a significant number of other tribes negotiated a peace treaty that adapted article 4 of the Peace of Paris to their own legal concepts. George Croghan, assistant superintendent for Indian affairs, briefed Thomas Gage, the British commander in chief, about the agreement. In terms of territorial ownership, articles 3 through 5 of the agreement are particularly revealing: "Thirdly They Agreed, that HIS Britannick Majesty's Troops might, when ever they thought proper, Occupy such Posts, where the French had before, or make others; for the Security of Trade whereever His Majesty Judged best."[97] Article 4 confirmed the sale of land to the king of France and the right of French subjects to build "forts or posts." It was agreed, reports Croghan, that "the King of France had a right to cede to the King of Great Britain.—But denied, That he had any right to cede any other part of their Country, to his Britannick Majesty."[98] It was acknowledged that French settlers had been granted the right to settle, and this might now, for "a proper consideration," be granted to English settlers: "They sayd, that the Great Giver of Life, had given them that Country and the wild Beasts thereon, for their Support, and that their Forefathers, had come thro' that Land, many hundred years before any white Man had crossed the great waters, wherefore, they looked upon themselves, as the sole Owners of it. And expected, that no part of it, Should be taken from them, before they were paid for it."[99] These negotiations mark the actual end of the Seven Years' War in North America. However, the settlers had no intention of sticking to the agreements made; they felt themselves cheated out of the war's "profit" and regarded Native American territory as "unused lands."[100] The settlers increasingly found themselves in opposition to the British crown, which by the royal proclamation of October 1763 stood as guarantor of the border between Native and settler territories, roughly along the line of the Appalachians.

The Pontiac Rebellion was relatively limited in military terms, but it had lasting consequences. For Native Americans, royal border guarantees notwithstanding, it marked the beginning of a more aggressive expulsion policy by European settlers. For the American colonies, it marked a new escalation in relations with the British mother country.[101]

In India, the Seven Years' War resulted in consequences for the Franco-British rivalry, as well as confrontations between Britain and powerful local actors. In 1764, near Buxar, in the border area between Bengal and Oudh, a momentous battle was fought between British East India Company troops and an alliance of three Indian sovereigns: the Mughal Emperor Shah Alam II; Mir Quasim, who had worked with the British as nawab of Bengal until 1763; and the nawab of Awadh. As was often the case in India, the balance of forces was very lopsided. The company force, commanded by Hector Munro (1726–1805), a Scotsman, consisted of around seven thousand men, including over five thousand sepoys. They faced some forty thousand soldiers of the Indian alliance. But the three Indian armies were ill-coordinated, and the British won the day, paving the way for the Treaty of Allahabad. The agreement was signed by Shah Alam II and by Robert Clive for the company at a solemn ceremony on August 12, 1765. The treaty granted the company the rights of *diwani* as a civil administration. Specifically, this meant the company could raise taxes in the province of Bengal;

Figure 13.1 Alam Conveying the Grant of the Diwani to Lord Clive. Painting by Benjamin West (1818).
© The British Library Board, from the British Library Collection: Fsoter 29; akg-images/ British Library.

this step was crucial in transforming the British presence in India from a collection of trading outposts to a territorial sovereign. This process had been carefully planned since 1754; it was in no way a chance occurrence.[102] Benjamin West, already the painter of an impressive depiction of Wolfe's death at Quebec, was commissioned by Clive to record the event in a painting titled *Alam Conveying the Grant of the Diwani to Lord Clive* (figure 13.1).

CHAPTER XIV

Outcomes of the War

The Empire at Home:
Repercussions for European Society and Culture

The visual representation of Clive at Allahabad prompts questions about the long-term effects of global entanglements on European societies. The influence of these entanglements can be traced across a number of fields, including journalism, cultural styles, military learning processes, and cultures of remembrance.[1]

Some former officials of the British East India Company and some returning military officers brought substantial wealth back with them to Britain, often distinguishing themselves through their lavish lifestyles and overt social climbing, They were sometimes mocked as British "nabobs," with their female equivalents dubbed "nabobinas."[2]

The most famous of the nabobs was Clive himself, who departed India on February 21, 1760, with his wife, Margaret, and arrived in England in early July, where his ostentatious public displays of wealth immediately caused a sensation. The diary of the Duchess of Northumberland presents an inimitably direct observation of the British nabob:

> Col. Clive arrived in town from India, July 5th. He and his Lady dined that day at the White Hart in Guildford. He had 4 Post Chaises and a numerous retinue with him. The populace assembled in vast numbers;

and he may be said to have dined in public, as the Doors and Windows were all thrown open that every ones curiosity might be satisfied. His complexion bears a near resemblance in colour to Mahogany; and had his dress been Oriental he might easily have been taken for the Nabob himself. It's reported that the wealth he amassed infinitely exceeds what common Fame with her usual Liberality had endowed him with, and that he has in his possession a Diamond worth upwards of £100,000.[3]

From this point on, Clive worked steadily to expand his grand properties, adopting the lifestyle of an aristocratic gentleman, a social class he hoped soon to join. He rented a number of houses in London and the countryside, as well as funding several candidates for Parliament. In 1761, he bought seventy-five hundred acres of land from Lord Montfort, paying 70,000 pounds. Two years later he acquired Walcot Hall, a six-thousand-acre estate, for 92,000 pounds.[4] He took up residency in a sumptuous house in London's fashionable Berkeley Square.[5] In 1771, within just a few months, he acquired an extensive collection of paintings. Although he acknowledged he had not the slightest knowledge of art, he hoped to be recognized as an aristocratic connoisseur; his forms of ostentatious consumption were bound to be scoffed at by established masters of distinction. Once again, Horace Walpole was on hand to mock, sneering at "those learned patrons of taste, the Czarina, Lord Clive or some Nabob," who paid inflated prices for worthless art.[6]

Clive faced the enormous challenge of making his lifestyle acceptable to British aristocratic society, at this time very much a closed milieu. In the eyes of the nobility, he was disqualified by his strange manners and taste in clothing, as well as the poor figure he cut on the dance floor.[7] Clive's plans to make political conquests in Britain went more slowly than planned thanks to a recurrence of his severe stomach problems. Although he had initially sided with Pitt, he reoriented his loyalties when the political situation changed with the death of George II, choosing instead to ally with the Duke of Newcastle. His reward was an Irish peerage, by which he became Baron Clive of Plassey; in 1764, he was promised membership in the Order of Bath, although he became only a knight of the order in 1772.[8] On this occasion, Walpole observed: "My Lord Clive could not conquer the Indies a second time without becoming a Knight of the Bath."[9] In 1764, Charles Clive created a visual representation of his cousin Robert's newly acquired noble status, painting the Baron of Plassey arrayed in robes of deep red, lined with ermine.[10] A crown on a table next to him and a portrait of Mir Jafar in the background make reference to his newly acquired rank and to his most important ally in the battle for Bengal.

The Peace of Paris had enraged Clive by restoring France's Indian possessions as they had stood in the year 1749. He turned against the government, seeking to safeguard the interests of British colonists in India. Within the East India Company, he fought bitterly with a new adversary, Laurence Sullivan, who questioned the continued payment of Clive's Indian salary as a nawab of Bengal. This affected Clive's public image, giving the impression that he was concerned solely with securing his own income.[11] As early as 1760, Walpole had scoffed: "General Clive is arrived, all over estates and diamonds. If a beggar asks charity, he says 'Friend, I have no small brilliants about me.'"[12] In Britain, the old system of royal patronage had been weakened, but a system of political power based solely on capital was not yet in place. In this context, Clive represented a new social type: the middle-class colonial nouveau riche, characterized by coarse manners. The rapid rise of this class, epitomized by Baron Clive, called existing social hierarchies into question. Although seen as a threat by some, the emergence of this new middle class represented a step in the cultural modernization of British society.

The military experience of returning officers was instructive for the British army, not least in the field of small warfare. These tactics had, of course, previously been used in Europe, but experience from outside Europe could help to expand or modify specific practices in irregular warfare. In another effect on the armed forces, military cultures of remembrance became increasingly global as they came to be associated with the wars of empire. The momentum toward empire created abundant symbolic forms, whether memorials to General Wolfe and naval war heroes in Westminster Abbey or the many landscaped English gardens designed with global expansion and the blue water policy in mind.[13]

Occasionally this influence also extended to Germany, as in the Royal Navy Room created by Leopold III Frederick Franz, the Duke of Anhalt-Dessau, at his seat at Wörlitz Palace. The room contained a collection of engravings honoring British naval success in the war.[14]

Walpole again gives crucial testimony in this context, confirming the new imperial self-confidence that developed during Britain's rise to world power, a confidence displayed even by those, like Pitt, who were critics of expansionist imperial policies. Some suggested that Britain's global empire now put the Roman Empire in the shade, as Walpole did in a letter of March 22, 1762, to George Montagu, commenting on the capture of Martinique: "Do you think Demosthenes or Themistocles ever raised the Grecian stocks two per cent, in four-and-twenty hours? I shall burn all my Greek and Latin books; they are histories of little people. The Romans never conquered the world, till they had conquered three parts of it, and were three hundred years about it; we subdue the globe in three campaigns; and a globe, let me tell you, as big again as it was in their days."[15]

These increasingly globalized contexts, and the processes that gave rise to them, did not affect all European societies equally. In the Holy Roman Empire, for example, global experience remained essentially a media phenomenon, rarely making an appearance in the field of politics or popular culture.

Winners and Losers: Profits, Losses, and Reparations

Once the treaties had been signed, the damage assessed, and the soldiers returned home, historians set about narrating the history of the conflict. But what had the war achieved? What were its immediate and its long-term consequences?

There were human losses in every theater of the war. In Europe alone, historians estimate the military dead at between 550,000 and 800,000, with total worldwide military fatalities somewhere between 850,000 and 1.2 million.[16] It is difficult to establish precise figures for eighteenth-century wars, and it is telling that current estimates are still based on Frederick's *History of the Seven Years' War*, along with calculations made in the 1930s by the Russian American sociologist Pitirim Sorokin (1889–1968).[17] Frederick estimated that the Prussian army had lost 180,000 dead; the Prussian officer corps had 5,500 men at the beginning of the war: by the end of the conflict, 1,500 of these had died and 2,000 had been wounded. In one aristocratic family in Pomerania—the Bellings of Ueckermünde—23 male members served in the army at some point during the war; 20 of them died. The Berlin geographer Anton Friedrich Büsching (1724–1793) traveled through the Mark of Brandenburg in 1775, where he found many aristocratic estates occupied by widows. He also observed a town where the war had reduced the general population by one-third, including 100 male inhabitants killed or captured at Landeshut in 1760.[18]

Russia lost around 120,000 soldiers, France about 200,000, and Britain 160,000 (20,000 according to Sorokin's figures). For Sweden, the figure was 30,000 soldiers, while Spain lost 3,000. The smaller German principalities fighting with the Imperial army may have lost around 25,000.[19] Christopher Duffy reckons total Austrian losses—both military and civilian—at 303,595; of these, 36,622 were battlefield casualties, with an additional 93,408 soldiers dying of wounds or illness.[20] Some estimate Prussian civilian losses at around 320,000, with an equivalent figure of 90,000 for Saxony. All told, this would suggest a total far in excess of 1 million dead for the war, since victims outside of Europe must also be added to the total. These include 1,500 fatalities among North American settlers, for example, with another 1,000 captured by Native tribes.[21]

Prussia budgeted 169,250,000 thalers for the war, but some 29,400,000 were left unspent by the end of the conflict, suggesting an actual total expenditure of around 140,000,000 thalers.[22] In comparison with some, the Prussian situation was not too bad. Total British spending may have amounted to 161 million pounds (1,932 million livres), with French spending around one-third of that, 700 million livres.[23]

Many contemporaries regarded Frederick's survival without territorial losses in a "world of enemies" as something approaching a miracle. On February 19, 1763, a few days after the conclusion of peace, Luise Dorothée de Saxe-Gotha wrote to Voltaire: "The centuries to come will have difficulty in believing that a small kingdom like Prussia could withstand so many terrible enemies. Each one of these hostile powers was superior in terms of funds and people [to Prussia], which seemed in all probability about to be subjugated, annihilated, and crushed. And yet it is the King of Prussia who drew himself from the affair in the most glorious way in the world, without losing the least fleck of land. Should we not call this a miracle?"[24]

The classic view is to see Prussia and Britain as the war's winners. Britain is thought to be the winner in a more active sense, with the country now well on its way to global hegemony, while the Prussian victory is implicitly more passive, in that it successfully preserved the status quo. But Frederick clearly did not win the war; he should instead be seen as having survived a hard-fought draw.[25] He achieved none of his secret war aims; he was a "victor without spoils."[26] France was a clear loser: dispossessed of much territory, burdened with huge debts, and militarily discredited.[27] Other, less obvious actors must also be included in the war's total reckoning, including some who were also clearly among the losers. Along with France, Austria, and Sweden, these included Poland and Saxony, at this time still joined in monarchical union. Lesser winners of the conflict included Portugal, Russia, and the Holy Roman Empire.[28] The German historian Johannes Burkhardt long propounded the thesis that the Holy Roman Empire was the European war's "real victor." In his view, the Reich was the only European player that genuinely achieved its war aims: Electoral Saxony was liberated, the prewar order was restored, and the functioning of the imperial "constitutional order" was preserved.[29]

The authorities strove to get an accurate overview of total losses as quickly as possible in order to supplement anecdotal reports of loss and subjective perceptions of suffering. It is no coincidence that the end of the Seven Years' War coincided with a more general rise in the gathering of population statistics.[30]

German provinces that were directly affected, like Minden-Ravensberg in western Germany, the County of Mark, and the Duchy of Kleve, all had to reckon with population losses of between 10 and 15 percent.[31] In eastern Germany, Prussian provinces recorded still greater depletion; for example, Pomerania lost 20 percent of its population, and Neumark lost 27 percent.[32] By contrast, East Prussia recovered relatively quickly from Russian occupation, although the city of Königsberg was damaged again in November 1764—this time by a devastating fire.[33] Under these conditions, it was not easy to repay the loans the city had taken out to settle Russian claims.[34] As far as looting was concerned, cities in the west got off relatively lightly, with some exceptions, including Bielefeld (1757) and Minden (1759). However, the rural population suffered serious losses in its livestock holdings: Horses, cattle, and sheep were confiscated in large numbers by transiting troops, to be used for food or transport. Cattle diseases had had a negative effect on numbers even before the war, and this trend continued.[35] We have more precise numbers for military animals: Austria alone recorded enormous total losses, with 47,168 horses killed, wounded, or sold.[36] As late as 1783, the Prince-Bishopric of Paderborn was still disputing the costs of damage caused by both French and Allied soldiers, claiming it was owed compensation for providing a contingent of troops to the Imperial army.[37] Costs for damage caused by the French amounted to over 1 million thalers for the County of Lippe alone, not a penny of which was seen until the 1790s, despite the best efforts of its government.[38] Erfurt was burdened with war debts of nearly 1.5 million thalers, which seem not to have been fully paid until 1793.[39]

Economies of War

The economy was a major area in which the local and the global were entangled. The war gave rise to new modes of monetary and material circulation, from public finances to soldiers' pay and plunder; conversely, the course of the war was itself shaped by financial flows. At the start of the conflict, Frederick had a huge war treasury at his disposal, but it proved to be enough for only two or three years of campaigning. Thereafter, he was highly dependent on British subsidies.

Individual testimonies, which bemoan rising food prices, looting, and plunder, allow us to perceive the war's microeconomics more clearly. For all armies, plunder was an important means of motivating soldiers. Looting was a constant source of violence, deployed against victims but often also breaking out among the plundering soldiers themselves.[40] Plunder had a social logic, with the distribution of goods highly dependent on social class and hierarchy. But basic material circumstances also played a part: For example, large objects were difficult to transport and thus needed to be sold or swapped quickly.

In terms of individuals, the war's biggest financial winners included Heinrich Carl von Schimmelmann, a grain supplier to the Prussian army; Franz Balthasar Schönberg von Brenkenhoff, another businessman who supplied horses and grain to the military; and David Splitgerber, a banker and manufacturer.[41] Schimmelmann, a highly colorful entrepreneur, landed his first major coup by paying 120,000 thalers for shares in the Meissen porcelain factory, which had been confiscated by the Prussians. In 1758, he auctioned that holding in Hamburg for many times its original price and opened his own trading house on the proceeds. He entered the Danish service in 1761 and went on to become a slave trader. In 1763, his acquisition of four cotton and sugar plantations in the Danish West Indies was said to have made him the richest man in Europe. John Kennion (1726–1785), from Liverpool, was another wealthy slave trader who obtained his starting capital during the war.[42] By the 1750s, he had acquired shares in slave ships, as well as sugar plantations in Jamaica. During the British expedition to capture Havana, he served as a commissary, responsible for supplying food, clothing, and war materiel.[43] While in Cuba, he secured a concession from Albemarle to supply the north of the island with slaves, which seems to have been another profitable business venture.[44] While slave traders made a profit, enslaved Africans were among the big losers of the Seven Years' War, along with North American Natives: for both groups, possibilities for resistance shrank further with growing British-American hegemony.[45] The war's outcome weakened the Native Americans and the French, two possible allies for enslaved Africans. As white settlers moved westward, they made more and more use of African slaves. The fact that Black soldiers had fought the French and Indians alongside British units and American militias did very little to advance their emancipation.[46] On the contrary, armed slave revolts were a crucial threat scenario used to justify new securitization measures. In 1760, Tacky's War, one of the largest revolts by enslaved people in the eighteenth century, took place in Jamaica, dealing a serious long-term blow to imperial confidence.[47]

The Seven Years' War had its direct financial beneficiaries, but it also offered indirect advantages to many others: for example, poets and composers who obtained work and patronage as a result. This type of war profiteer included German authors like Johann Gottfried Herder (1744–1803), Johann Friedrich Reichardt (1752–1814), Johann Joachim Bode (1731–1793), and Emer de Vattel (1714–1767).[48] In 1758, Vattel published a multivolume legal compendium that would decisively shape modern international law. The previous year he had criticized Frederick's invasion of Saxony but generally kept a lower political profile in his published work.[49] In the wake of the war, Saxony restructured its administration, a process that saw Vattel rise to become a privy councillor.

Success in war could bring profits and commercial privileges, as well as more direct rewards of both a symbolic and a material kind. The Portuguese government, for example, was generous in its appreciation of its foreign defenders. In 1763, the *Danziger Beyträge* reported that the British generals had recently been awarded an "ample pension," with officers granted swords bearing the Portuguese coat of arms and the inscription "True Loyalty and Courage are the Protection and Safety of Portugal." Count Wilhelm of Lippe, the organizer of the highly successful Portuguese defensive campaign, was rewarded with specifically devised gifts and honors, including a monthly salary of 2,000 moidors and splendid silver tableware. He was also awarded the Order of the Black Eagle, with diamond-encrusted insignia, and—a special honor for an artillery commander—six miniature "golden cannon," each weighing thirty-two pounds.[50] The most important symbolic honor of all was the award of the title Altezza, otherwise permitted only to the crown prince.

Wartime manipulations of the coinage had a lasting impact on the economic cycles of many different states and territories, although the effects varied radically from one case to the next.[51] In 1763, there was a huge financial crisis. Poland was affected particularly severely by Frederick's fiscal tactics.[52] Debasing the coinage led to inflation. This was also fueled by increased demand from occupying armies, leading to huge price increases, a phenomenon repeatedly discussed by diarists and chroniclers.[53] The public placed put much of the blame for price increases on Jewish currency dealers such as Daniel Itzig (1723–1799), Moses Isaac (1710–1776), and Veitel Heine Ephraim (1703–1775), who became the subject of mocking verses. Debased coins became colloquially known as *Ephramiten*, prompting rhymes such as "The outside is silver, inside's a sham / outside Frederick, inside Ephraim!"[54] In fact, the main culprit behind rising prices was the Prussians' own "royal protector."[55] As the historian Horst Carl has pointed out, the groups hardest hit by inflation were wage-dependent members of the urban underclass, who had to cope with rising food prices, as well as falling wages.[56] The result was rising tensions and local unrest, especially in East Friesland. Overall existing class inequalities were exacerbated, particularly in the western provinces of Germany, but serious popular disorder did not materialize. The war also had a particular financial impact on Brittany, where General Duc d'Aiguillon, a victorious wartime general, attempted to impose a tax increase in 1764, giving rise to a regional crisis of royal authority known as the "affaire de Bretagne."[57]

Electoral Saxony, the territory that Frederick had taken "into safekeeping," was particularly hard-hit by the war.[58] One unusually close-up perspective on sufferings in Saxony can be found in the *Gemayne Buch* (common book) of the small village of Schmannewitz, in northern Saxony, about fifteen miles from Leipzig. This record of events, maintained by the village mayor, Hanss George Ehrlich (1722–1784),[59] reveals that between September 1, 1756, and November 24, 1762, the village was affected by an incident of war about every 3.5 days, including expropriations, billeting demands, conscription, and the confiscation of animals and vehicles. These actions were carried out by Prussian, Austrian, and Imperial forces alike.[60] The sober accounting presented by the *Gemayne Buch* offers particularly impressive testimony to the sufferings of ordinary rural people, even if the village was largely spared direct combat operations and physical violence.

A few months after the war ended, Saxony appeared to be on the brink of a genuine turning point. Augustus, the elector of Saxony—and also King

August III of Poland—died on October 5, 1763, followed three weeks later by the death of Brühl, his chief minister. The king's death brought the personal union between Saxony and Poland to an end. August's successor, Friedrich Christian, died just ten weeks later, on December 17, 1763; his son Friedrich August (1750–1827) was thirteen years old and not yet capable of governing. Much-needed changes in government were largely determined by officials like Thomas von Fritsch.[61] Late Baroque administration gave way to a more sober style of governance, including a newly established Department for Lands, Economy, Manufacturing, and Commerce, which had responsibility for pressing issues of economic development. However, the new administrative moves for the most part amounted to a restoration rather than a reform—in effect, a "restoration of the pre-war state."[62]

Russian political life also lost prominent figures shortly after the end of hostilities. Peter Shuvalov died on January 15, 1762, and Count Bestuzhev on April 21, 1766; Shuvalov's brothers, Ivan (1727–1797) and Alexander (1710–1770), had been favorites of Tsarina Elisabeth, and their careers ended with her death.

Prussia's *rétablissement* was less successful than Saxony's.[63] The country struggled to pay down debts run up during the conflict: Some Prussian municipalities were said to be paying debts from the Seven Years' War in the mid-nineteenth century. Within Prussia's boundaries, Pomerania and Silesia were the main theaters of war operations; these regions were also the hardest hit by population decline.[64] Archenholz attempted a comparison with the situation in America: "The hitherto highly cultivated fields of Germany on the Oder and the Weser offered to the view the same appearance as the American wastes of the Ohio and the Orinoko."[65] Frederick compared the situation in Silesia with that of Brandenburg after the Thirty Years' War and, among other things, earmarked 3 million thalers to repair war damage there. The Prussian king also exempted residents of the province from all taxes for six months, had grain and horses from military stocks sold cheaply or given away, and released soldiers to work in civilian professions, seeking to counteract a fall in the civilian population. In addition, he ordered the reconstruction of buildings destroyed in the war (reportedly eight thousand in Silesia as a whole), organized a reduction in contribution debts, and commissioned a reform of the coinage.[66] Thus, the city of Halle an der Saale received 40,000 thalers from the king in 1764 and again in 1766.[67] Population losses were higher in Pomerania and the Mark, but Frederick seems to have focused more of his attention on Silesia, a relatively newly acquired province. In the summer of 1763, the king even launched a state lottery in Prussia to cover some of the costs of reconstruction.

In 1763, Prussia was overwhelmed by a financial crisis, a self-inflicted one, although it first made its appearance in Amsterdam. This led to a complex combination of bank failures and grain speculation, which then affected large numbers of Prussian merchants, including war profiteers like Splitgerber. Frederick's debasing of the Prussian coinage was by now taking its toll.[68] The chamberlain, Count von Lehndorff, noted in his diary: "People speak only of Bankruptcies, which are everywhere the order of the day. In Hamburg, 56 merchants have felt its Effects, and Amsterdam, Gdansk and even London have suffered greatly. Some of these men contributed much to this through their excessive Luxury, especially in Berlin, where even merchants have acquired gilding, statues, paintings and large homes."[69] Nonetheless, the currency was debased again in 1764, prompting a further crisis two years later.

The Production of Heroes

The war produced plenty of dead men, but it took political aesthetics to make heroes of them.[70] Military hero worship had a very long tradition; it was not the invention of the Seven Year' War, although the conflict did see some early changes.[71] Ordinary soldiers were still not the subject of remembrance, but there was journalistic hero worship aplenty during this war; it was a typical feature of the conflict's journalistic style. While the war was still going on, the Halle historian Carl Friedrich Pauli (1723–1778) compiled *The Life of Great Heroes of the Current War* (1758–1764), a nine-volume work presenting a new canon of war heroes—mostly generals, of course.[72] His preface takes up the question of what makes a hero. He freely acknowledges that "the perfected traits which make up heroes are not found solely at the head of an army. [. . .] A statesman can attain the true greatness of a warrior, both can be heroes: but the general has the opportunity to make his greatness shine brighter than the statesman. The deeds of a soldier are more noticeable than those of an ordinary citizen."[73] In other words, a specific audience already exists for wartime feats, and this significantly contributes to the production of heroes. Pauli lists the qualities that make up a war hero: Courage, humanity in the field, good physical condition, education, experience, and virtue are among the most important. Each volume in the series has a preface highlighting specific aspects of the heroic: Volume 3 is devoted to "Causes of a Heroic Death," while volume 4 addresses "The Hero in Adversity, or in the Lands of the Enemy." Many of the book's heroic officers are long forgotten, but several are still closely connected with memories of the war, including Kurt Christoph Graf von Schwerin, Hans Karl von Winterfeldt, August Wilhelm Prince of Prussia (1722–1758), and James Francis Edward Keith. In the ninth and final volume of the series, Pauli had intended to recount the death of Ewald von Kleist near Kunersdorf, in similarly heroic fashion. But in the end, the volume was comprised entirely of death announcements, listing fallen heroes whose bodies had been, with great effort, recovered from the battlefields and laid to rest in their respective capital cities or at their aristocratic estates.

After his death at the Battle of the Plains of Abraham, James Wolfe was embalmed and, on September 23, 1759, his body was put on ship to England. On November 17, his remains were received in London with full military honors.[74] Wolfe's final resting place was a private grave at Greenwich, but an elaborate memorial to him was also erected in Westminster Abbey, placing him in a long line of British war heroes.[75] After the Battle of Prague in 1757, the body of Kurt Christoph von Schwerin was recovered and taken to a nearby monastery. From there, his remains were transported to his estate in Pomerania, in what became an elaborate ceremonial journey.[76] Among the most important of the many stops en route were those at Dresden and Frankfurt an der Oder, where Schwerin's regiment formed part of the garrison and where his body was accorded military honors. Schwerin's body eventually arrived in Pomerania, and he was buried at the village church of Wussecken, on his estate; his grave later became something of a military shrine.

France also saw the postwar construction of war heroes—in particular, the idolization of Chevalier Louis d'Assas du Mercou (1733–1760), an officer killed just before the Battle of Kloster Kamp in October 1760. The person most responsible for this particular heroization was probably Voltaire: In the second edition of *Précis du siècle de Louis XV* (*Outline of the century of Louis XV*, 1769), the writer quoted the chevalier's last words as being "To me, Auvergne! It is the enemy!" Directly after shouting this heroic warning to his regimental comrades, D'Assas was run through with British bayonets. The chevalier was honored with monuments, and his name was given to many streets; his descendants continued to receive a pension until 1960.

The best-known war hero in the Spanish overseas service was the naval commander Luis Vicente de Velasco e Isla (1711–1762); he was struck by a bullet while defending Havana on July 31, 1762, and died despite being treated by British military surgeons.[77] King Charles III named a Spanish warship after Velasco, and this tradition continued for centuries; a Spanish naval vessel was named in his honor as recently as 1994. The king also had a memorial built for Velasco, and medals were struck in his honor. One particularly unusual honor was the grant of the title Marqués de Velasco de Morro to his brother, Iñigo José. Similarly, the title Vizcondado del Asalto del Morro (Viscount of the Attack on the Morro) was awarded to Francisco González y Bassecourt (1726–1793), brother of Captain Vicente González de Bassecourt (1712–1762), who also died defending Havana, in this way directly embedding the name of the siege in the annals of Spanish nobility.[78] Velasco was also honored by the British with monuments at Westminster Abbey and the Tower of London. Until the early twentieth century, British warships continued to fire a salute whenever they sailed close to his birthplace at Noja in the Basque Country.

The war introduced the secularized pietà as an important visual motif in commemorating heroic death, a convention that soon spread throughout Europe and even across the Atlantic. The hero—whether James Wolfe, Louis-Joseph de Montcalm, Ewald von Kleist, or Kurt Christoph von Schwerin—dies a "beautiful" death, surrounded by appreciative comrades. A renowned painting by Benjamin West, *The Death of General Wolfe at the Battle of Québec* (1770) (figure 14.1), elevated the motif to a genre, prompting a series of analogous depictions, including an engraving of the death of Montcalm by François-Louis-Joseph Watteau the Younger (1783) (figure 14.2), which was quickly followed by drawings by Chodowiecki (1786) and many other Prussian artists.[79] Johann Christoph Frisch's painting of von Schwerin's death (figure 14.3) features an interesting element of intercultural mirroring, with a Prussian hussar taking the place of the contemplative Iroquois seen in West's painting of Wolfe's death.

Thomas Abbt's text "Vom Tode für das Vaterland" ("On dying for the fatherland," 1761) helped to create a new cultural discourse, both textual and visual, centering on the idealized and heroic "soldier's death."[80] He makes explicit reference to the deaths of Schwerin and Ewald von Kleist, the poet-soldier; in 1761, Bernhard Rode (1725–1797) painted a memorial image of Kleist, Schwerin, and Winterfeldt in Berlin's Garrison Church. A year later this was followed by a memorial to Field Marshal Keith, another

Figure 14.1 The Death of General Wolfe. Oil painting on canvas by Benjamin West (1770). Source: World History Archive. © 2024 Image Content Collections Ltd; akg-images/WHA/World History Archive.

Figure 14.2 The Death of the Marquis de Montcalm in the Battle of the Plains of Abraham at Québec. Copperplate engraving after François-Louis-Joseph Watteau (ca. 1783). © RMN-Grand Palais/Art Resource, New York.

Figure 14.3 The Death of Field Marshal Schwerin. Oil painting on panel by Johann Christoph Frisch (1787).
Source: bpk Bildagentur/Stiftung Preussische Schlösser & Gärten Berlin-Brandenburg, Berlin/Art Resource, New York.

Prussian hero of the Seven Years' War.[81] Historians have long wondered how Kleist came to have such a place of honor, the young writer memorialized alongside Prussian generals. It was once thought that Frederick had personally intervened to have him commemorated in this way, but it is now clear that the initiative came from Johann Wilhelm Ludwig Gleim, Kleist's close friend and fellow poet.[82] After the war, patriotic fervor cooled distinctly among the literati and was regarded by some with retrospective embarrassment.[83]

Courts-Martial

At the other end of the reputational spectrum are those who were disgraced in the war, including those put on trial when peace finally came. Commanders were court-martialed by nearly every one of the war's participant monarchies—during the war but especially in its immediate aftermath. The charges made against senior commanders ranged from losing battles and failing to defend fortified towns to engaging in military disobedience and high treason.

In March 1763, Frederick ordered that General Finck and Major General Johann Karl von Rebentisch (1710–1765) be immediately arrested on their return from captivity so they could be held accountable for Finck's Capture, the surrender of an entire army corps at the Battle of Maxen in November 1759.[84] In May of that year, investigations were launched involving Major General Leopold von Zastrow (1702–1779), Lieutenant Colonel Johann Bartholomäus d'O (b. 1708), Colonel Friedrich Wilhelm Quadt zu Wickrath (1720–1765), and Carl Friedrich von Wrede (1702–1764), all accused of surrendering the fortresses at Glatz and Schweidnitz.[85] Finck was sentenced to two years' imprisonment; after his release, he became a general in the Danish army. Rebentisch was sentenced to a year and afterward served with the Portuguese military. After his two years in prison, Wrede chose to serve with the army of Hesse-Kassel. Quadt was sentenced to four years, while d'O was sentenced to life imprisonment in the fortress of Neisse. In addition to these real cases of courts-martial, a fictitious Prussian military defendant achieved fame on German stages in the aftermath of the war. In Gotthold Ephraim Lessing's comedy *Minna von Barnhelm* (begun in 1763, completed in 1767), Major Tellheim faces accusations of bribery associated with the Seven Years' War. In the play, Tellheim's regiment had been stationed in Thuringia, where his lenient treatment of the civilian population raised suspicions that he was corrupt.[86]

The "affaire du Canada," in which several dozen military and civilian officials were accused of corruption, came to trial in Paris in 1761, with proceedings continuing until December 1763. With the end of the war, legal consequences loomed for "losers" in other colonial territories. Lally-Tollendal, the Irish-born lieutenant general who had been governor of France's possessions in the East Indies, was captured in 1761 and taken to Britain as a prisoner of war. On his return to France in 1764, he was imprisoned in the Bastille for two years before being condemned to death, with the sentence carried out on May 9, 1766. Lally's illegitimate son Gérard (1751–1830) discovered the secret of his paternity on the day of the execution and thereafter worked with Voltaire to restore his father's name. The campaign took some time: It was 1778 before the king finally annulled Lally's decree of condemnation.

José Antonio Manso de Velasco, the former governor of Chile who was appointed to lead Havana's council of war, was another official to experience a steep fall from grace. With the capture of the Cuban capital, the British took Velasco prisoner and shipped him to Cadiz, where he was court-martialed by the Spanish crown, which held him responsible for the articles of surrender in Cuba. He was imprisoned in Granada and suspended from military service for a hundred years; he eventually died in exile in the Andalusian town of Priego de Córdoba in 1767. Juan de Prado, the colonial governor of Cuba, suffered a similar fate.[87] The court hearing his case was headed by Count Aranda, who publicly demanded the death penalty for the disgraced official. The sentence was ultimately reduced to ten years' imprisonment, along with the confiscation of Prado's private fortune. In 1770, he died in prison in the town of Vitigudino in western Spain.

However, the Spanish crown understood that punishing scapegoats would not solve underlying problems. A new Junta de Ministros (Ministerial Council) was established, with specific responsibility for colonial affairs; its members included the Marqués de Grimaldi, the former Spanish ambassador to Paris. A cousin of Aranda's was chosen to be the new governor of Havana, and Alejandro O'Reilly (1723–1794), an Irish-born general, was tasked with reforming the military. O'Reilly had acquired up-to-date military expertise fighting for the Austrians against the Prussians. A commission of experts was also appointed to investigate how Cuban trade had increased while the island was under British occupation.

Home from the Wars

As fighting came to a close in 1762 and 1763, ordinary soldiers began returning from the various theaters of war. In the western German town of Isselhorst, Johann Conrad Lütgert noted that between December 10 and 13, "all Engl. Troups set out from Osnabrück passing through Münster and so to the Frontier of Holland to be embark'd for Engeland. Mr. Macullock came to Isselhorst to take Leave, and depart'd once again on 17th Dec. [. . .] At the Year's commencement, all Hanoverian Troups march'd to their standing Quarters, tho' garrisons remained in Munster, Paderborn and some other Places."[88] The peace was formally announced in nearby Bielefeld on February 19, and peace celebrations were held there on March 13. Nonetheless, some military formations still posed a real threat to the civilian population.

Thus, Lütgert reports the appearance, on March 20 and 21, of,: "a Compagnie of infanteri and a Esquadron of Cavalry of the cursed Turken-Corps which Lived off the masses, and thus Maltreated people as was not done by Friend or Foe at any time in the Course of the War, and no matter to them that there be now Peace, and these Villains called themselves Prussian Troups."[89] The "Turken-Corps" was a unit of the *Volontaires auxiliaires*, apparently integrated into Ferdinand's army only in May 1762. It was largely made up of deserters and was disbanded soon after the war.[90]

The departure of occupying forces varied greatly according to local circumstances. In Frankfurt am Main, the city council had enjoyed a consistently good relationship with the French occupation commander, Comte François de Théas de Thoranc (1719–1794). When the French took leave of the city on February 26, 1763, Johann Christian Senckenberg (1707–1772) noted in his diary: "Today, C[om]te de Thoranc is gone forever. M[ar]q[ui]s des Salles is leaving tomorrow. [. . .] Thoranc was very courteous and when the city offered him a payment as recognition, took not one penny, thankful for all the kindness he enjoyed here. Both made quite tender farewells, and both said that they were sorry they must be leaving here."[91] In the town of Meinbrexen on the Weser River, the jurist Christian König recorded positive reports of the French in the church register: "At the Withdrawal of the French from Meinbrexen on 17 Oct, it is to be recalled that a certain officer, out of his particular Pitie, gave to the preacher at that time 2 Shields of louis d'Or [two gold coins], with one to be Distribut'd in Lauenförde, the other in Meinbrexen, among those who had known the most Suffering. A sad but strange Alms-giving from an enemy who may have contemplated, and with mov'd Heart lamented, the Devastations caused by this war."[92] In stark contrast to König's emotional comments in Meinbrexen are the observations of Pastor Schatz of Wollbrandshausen, near Göttingen, who even condemns French excrement, which he regards as worse than any other human excrement. He prefaces his comments with the words "Paradoxum, ad verum est, quod pagina huic inseritur" (paradoxical, yet true, that which is inserted on this page), before making his scatological claim: "The excrementa of the French, *salva venia* [with all due respect], were not like the Crapp of German folk, neither dog nor pig did care to smell such French Crapp, still less taste it, the Crapp does lie in piles in Gardens & Meadows and has made them not Fertile nor fecund but Barren."[93]

The fate of returning soldiers also varied greatly. Some had made their fortune; some were facing a death sentence. Some were recognized; others were ignored. Their circumstances were particularly drastic in Britain, where an army with a nominal strength of 120,000 now had to be quickly reduced to 45,000.[94] A sudden influx of 75,000 unemployed soldiers into Britain's cities and villages would not be easy to manage, and there was a marked increase in crime after peace was declared. However, as Stephen Brumwell has shown, the apparent correlation is, in fact, deceptive. Actual British military manpower was significantly lower than the nominal figure. Moreover, contrary to popular belief, eighteenth-century armies were not roving bands of career criminals. In fact, only volunteers and conscripts who had served their term were demobilized at this point, along with wounded and injured soldiers, who were invalided out. Many British soldiers also decided to remain in the American colonies.[95] Those taking that option continued to receive official support after the war in the form of untaxed land leases for veterans.

Back in Britain, unemployment among veterans was a serious problem—and not made easier by the army's profoundly unequal severance arrangements. On leaving service, an army commander received 70,000 pounds, while a sergeant got 80 and a common soldier was paid just 2 pounds and 2 shillings.[96] According to one 1772 calculation, the Havana expedition alone captured about 737,000 pounds in prize money. James Miller, the common soldier whose diary is quoted earlier, saw just 11 Spanish dollars of this, whereas the three Keppel brothers—a commander in chief, a deputy commander in chief, and a major general—could each look forward to substantial shares.[97] Likewise George Durant, the paymaster on the British expeditions to Guadeloupe and Havana, returned to England a rich man. He made no bones about his newfound wealth: In 1764, he paid 44,000 pounds for Tong Castle in Shropshire and then had the largely ruined property extensively renovated. He also acquired a townhouse in Portman Square, married the eighteen-year-old daughter of a London merchant, and became a Member of Parliament for the Evesham constituency, where he served from 1768 to 1774.[98]

Not all Havana veterans enjoyed such successful homecomings. The diary of the Scottish writer James Boswell reports a visit to the theater at Covent Garden in London on December 8, 1762. As the overture began, two "highland officers" walked into the theater, whereupon the "mob" in the upper gallery howled "No Scots! No Scots!" and pelted them with apples. Boswell rushed to the aid of his compatriots, who told him they were from the 42nd Royal Highland Regiment, under the command of General Lord John Murray (1711–1787), just returned from Havana. Such is the gratitude shown to returning soldiers, notes Boswell, quoting one of the officers as saying "If it was french what could they do worse?"[99] Seeking to alleviate exclusion and social misery, journals such as *The Gentleman's Magazine* printed articles like "An Address to the Public in Favour of Disbanded Soldiers"; some aristocratic landowners donated 5 pounds for every soldier in units drawn from their local region.[100] Very few veterans had the opportunity to enjoy retirement at Chelsea's Royal Hospital, although the overall number of British war pensioners increased from 6,514 in 1757 to 14,700 seven years later.[101] Men suffering from, to use a modern phrase, post-traumatic stress disorder were placed in an institution very far from pleasant Chelsea: London's Bethlem Royal Hospital, where the mad were incarcerated, would become ever more notorious as the century went on.[102]

Another eyewitness to the war in Cuba only returned to Europe nine months after the end of the war. Markus Uhlmann, the Swiss deserter and ship's doctor, landed in the Netherlands at the end of September 1763, docking at Dordrecht. On October 9, he left Amsterdam and headed home to Switzerland, where he died the following year, on December 20, 1764, of causes not recorded, at the age of twenty-six.[103] Despite having deserted the Prussian army at Lobositz, Ulrich Bräker proudly wore his uniform to church: "On Sunday morning, I cleaned my uniform, as in Berlin, to go to the Church parade. Everyone I knew welcomed me; the others stared at me like I was a Turk."[104] For many prisoners of war, the peace meant a long walk home. The Prussian musketeer Johann Jacob Dominicus notes in his diary: "February 25th was the happy day when we first heard with certainty about peace."[105] A seemingly endless journey followed. He set out from Villach in Carinthia on April 16, 1763, and walked for several weeks, passing through Bratislava, Breslau, Frankfurt an der Oder, Berlin, and Minden before finally arriving at his home village of Harhausen, about twenty-five miles from Cologne. Grotehenn, the Brunswick subofficer, had a much shorter walk, and by January 26, 1763, he had already reached the city of Brunswick: "Henceforth can it be sung with bright voice, all enmity now is done: On said 26th Jan[uary], for we had our Triumphant Entry, out some long Way to meet us came not only General-Lieutenant von Imhoff, chief of our Regiment, but a fair number of women and children; the former welcomed his regiment with joy, the others embraced with pleasure their husbands and fathers; Only I was abandon'd, as I was 6 years ago when not one of my relations came to take Leave of me, this tyme none did come welcome me at the arriving march."[106]

Grotehenn may have had a sad and lonely homecoming, but things could have been far worse. For Olaudah Equiano, the Seven Years' War ended with bitter disappointment. On returning to Portsmouth in 1762, he was suddenly sold by his owner and put on a ship bound for the West Indies.[107] After four more difficult years at sea, Equiano was finally able to purchase his freedom in July 1766.[108] Now both whites and Blacks addressed him with a "new appellation," the "the most desirable in the world"—that of freeman.[109] Equiano later traveled widely, including to the Arctic (1772–1773), the Mediterranean, and Central America. In the 1780s, he campaigned for Black rights in London, becoming a leading figure in the abolitionist movement.[110] His autobiography, published in 1789, was primarily intended to draw attention to the inhumane living conditions suffered by enslaved people. It made him the most important Black author in Britain and North America in the eighteenth century.[111]

Many returning soldiers harbored literary ambitions. The Saxon officer Hans Carl Heinrich von Trautzschen returned to Dresden, where he swapped the soldier's life for that of a scholar, declaring "I have of late turned my horses into books, and I am assured they will give me more pleasure in this form than in their previous one."[112] In 1764, he retired to Ernstthal to devote himself entirely to a life of writing and learning. Beginning in 1772, he published his own plays, but they were mostly panned by critics, and in 1778, he reentered Saxon military service, rising to the rank of colonel by 1798.[113]

Often a military homecoming made clear just how many men had been lost. In late March 1763, the Prussian officer Ernst Friedrich Rudolf von Barsewisch, who had been badly wounded at Leuthen, returned to Berlin, where he was subjected to a "most close inspection" by "their Royal and Princely Highnesses": "The citizens of Berlin frequently came to meet us and expressed particular joy at our arrival. Unfortunately, after seven years, few of the soldiers who once marched out from the Garrison now remained. Of the Von Linden regiment, only 50 old soldiers were left. According to lists of the departed, our Regiment alone had lost 5,000 men, for the most part either fallen before the enemy or taken by disease."[114] Another Prussian officer regularly cited in this book, Christian Wilhelm von Prittwitz, was discharged in 1762, having been shot in the foot at Kunersdorf and left permanently disabled.[115]

In addition to wounded soldiers, returnees included the doctors who had treated them. War, with its many different wounds and illnesses, presented medical professionals with a broad field of observation. More soldiers had died of disease than on the battlefield, and the war produced a surge of empirically based studies in military medicine. In this context, particularly important works were written by John Pringle (1707–1782), Donald Monro (1727–1802), Ernst Gottfried Baldinger (1738–1804), and Johann Ulrich von Bilguer (1720–1796).[116] Pringle, whom many consider to be the father of modern military medicine, published a very successful work titled *Observations on the Diseases of the Army*. The original edition, published in 1752, was based on observations during the War of the Austrian Succession, but later editions were expanded to include material drawn from the Seven Years' War. By contrast, Monro's treatise on diseases suffered by British troops between 1761 and 1763 is entirely composed of observations made during the war. Using this material, the Scottish military doctor provides detailed descriptions of over twenty conditions, ranging from typhoid to scabies, before moving from the descriptive to the prescriptive, addressing various "means of preserving the health of soldiers on service."[117] The measures discussed range from dietary prescriptions to instructions on setting up field hospitals. The Monro family of Edinburgh produced an entire dynasty of physicians: George Monro (1721–1793) also served as a physician during the Seven Years' War, both in Europe and overseas. Initially stationed in North America in 1757, George accompanied the British expedition to Martinique in 1761, from where he reported to Donald about the development of fever on the island.[118] Baldinger, a Prussian military doctor, wrote *On the Diseases of an Army, Written on the Basis of Direct Observations*, a study published in Latin in 1763 (titled *De militum morbis*) and in German translation in 1765. In the book's first section, he focuses on the suffering of the civilian population ("burghers' [diseases]") before moving on to a general discussion of diseases affecting soldiers. Finally, he analyzes illnesses of "the most recent campaign"—above all, scurvy, diarrhea, dysentery, and scabies, as well as the disease later called "trench fever."[119] In other fields too, personal war experience could be put to good use—for example, in the agricultural theories of Otto von Münchhausen (1716–1774), which made a connection between the war and developments in environmental history.[120]

The War's Impact on Politics and Culture

While spurring progress in specialist fields, the conflict also fueled more-general learning processes, some of them with very far-reaching consequences. In the Atlantic world, the period from 1763 to 1789 is known for the crises of the ancien régime, as well as for attempts at reform. Both of these processes can be traced to trends emerging from the Seven Years' War, a connection confirmed by recent research.[121] The crises fueled by the war found concrete expression in coups and peasant revolts in Russia, reform programs like that of the Marquês de Pombal in Portugal, and revolutions like those in France and in North America. These revolutions are only the most important of the historical processes and events that have their roots in the Seven Years' War.[122] However, the relationship should be conceived in terms of mutually impacting long-term processes rather than direct causal progression.[123]

Clear continuities existed on the level of individual historical actors. Many soldiers from the Seven Years' War went on to fight in the American War of Independence, with considerably greater levels of individual career continuity than with either the Culloden generation (1746) or those who fought in the War of the Austrian Succession. Even if soldiers were fighting on a different side, they brought their experience from the French and Indian War to the next major conflict when it began thirteen years later. These included not only "Americans" like Washington and Robert Rogers but also British commanders and soldiers, including Charles Cornwallis (1738–1805); Robert Abercromby (1740–1827); Augustus Keppel, one of the conquerors of Havana; and Lord Sackville, the "coward" of Minden. To these can be added German mercenaries like Barthold Koch from Hesse and Prussian officers like Friedrich Wilhelm von Steuben (1730–1794), a former adjutant to Johann von Mayr, the Prussian Freikorps commander. Johann Ewald (1744–1813), another Hessian, fought in several battles of the Seven Years' War and again served with British forces in the Revolutionary War. He eventually became a major theorist of asymmetric guerrilla warfare.[124] The list should also include the many French officers and men who fought as allies of the Americans in the later war: Among them were Bougainville, by then a rear admiral, and the legendary military Methuselah, Jean Thurel (1698–1807), a soldier for seventy-five years, who served under Louis XVI as he had under Louis XIV and was eventually awarded the Legion of Honor by Napoleon.

Even during the Seven Years' War, frictions had repeatedly arisen between Britain and its North American colonies, prompted by insufficient resources, lack of coordination between the colonies, and a local army that was inadequate, compared to British troops. All of this created suspicions in London ministries, as well as among British commanders on the ground. For their part, the colonists regarded Britain's demands as excessive impositions.[125] Victory in the French and Indian War changed attitudes among the colonists, who grew in confidence and came to see themselves as a powerful arm of the British Empire, one that must be taken seriously. This new political perspective went hand in hand with a desire for a greater say in government.[126] This brought into play the knowledge and experience not only of individual American soldiers and parliamentarians but also of those who had witnessed European reforms at first hand. A widespread feeling emerged that colonial militiamen had made an active contribution to the empire and that this justified claims to greater political participation. This view was not shared in London. British decision-makers and the wider British public had consistently been presented with negative images of the colonists, depicting them as too weak or simply unwilling to stand up to the French and the Indians.[127] As a result, London politicians became firmly convinced that the future of the colonies would be secured only by rigid and firmly enforced reform measures. The war that broke out in the 1770s and 1780s was kindled by this tension between colonials' newfound self-confidence and Britain's continuing view of them as the empire's "problem child."

One paradox of war is that losers often learn more cogent lessons than victors. Time and again, war's losers have had to address these questions: How could this happen? How can we prevent this from ever happening again? To use Wolfgang Schivelbusch's much-quoted phrase, these learning processes are also expressions of a "culture of defeat."[128] France introduced extensive military reforms in the aftermath of the war: The Prussian army, now considered state of the art, became the new military yardstick for the French.[129] By contrast, Prussia itself seems to have rested on its military laurels, a phenomenon often invoked in explanations of the "catastrophe" of 1806.[130] In the long term, the Austrian military emerged strengthened from its conflicts with Prussia; at the latest by the end of the War of the Bavarian Succession (1778), the Habsburg state possessed a modernized army, with powerful artillery, efficient administration, and fortresses along its northern frontier.[131]

French colonial policy presents geopolitical questions that have only recently been intensively addressed by historians.[132] Choiseul sought to establish

French Guiana as a South American counterpoint to British-dominated North America.¹³³ As many as fifteen thousand potential colonists were recruited for that purpose, primarily from Catholic regions of southwestern Germany. But the project ended disastrously: Most of the colonists, who also included many French and Maltese, died of malnutrition, fever, and epidemics. We do not have precise casualty figures, but an 80 percent fatality rate would mean something on the order of ten thousand deaths. In the nineteenth century, French Guiana came to enjoy a notorious reputation as a penal colony.

Another consequence of the war was that France paid greater attention to Africa, which came to be seen as the "key to commerce," a central tenet of French colonial policy under both the ancien régime and the nineteenth-century governments.¹³⁴ The experience of defeat also prompted learning processes in Spain.¹³⁵ The temporary loss of Havana and Manila was a wake-up call for the Spanish government, which launched processes of military and administrative reform, enabling the country to maintain control of Cuba and the Philippines until 1898, when both colonies shook off Spanish rule.¹³⁶

In our own time, direct legacies of the Seven Years' War may at first glance seem limited to cultures of remembrance. However, the Canadian historian Denis Vaugeois has demonstrated the long-term influence of the war on Canadian legal history—in particular, in disputes over the legal status of Indigenous Canadians.¹³⁷ His remarkable case study makes the connection between a British letter of safe conduct from the Seven Years' War and a number of lawsuits brought in the 1990s by Indigenous Canadians (R. v. Sparrow, R. v. Sioui), who sought protections based on treaties made with their Huron ancestors. In 1760, James Murray, the British general and then governor of Quebec, issued a letter of safe conduct to the Huron-Wendat tribe, guaranteeing their safe return from Montreal. This document is known as the Murray Treaty, since it has subsequently been granted treaty status, amounting to a British-Indigenous agreement with ongoing legal validity.¹³⁸ In this respect at least, the Seven Years' War continues to have an immediate impact to this day.

Epilogue

The Seven Years' War established a new pentarchy in the constellation of European powers, consisting of Britain, France, Prussia, Austria, and Russia, all states that would significantly affect European history in the decades to come.[1] This moved the center of gravity of the European great power system distinctly eastward.[2] Spain and the Netherlands continued to lose influence, while Prussia and Russia were now unquestionably major powers on the continent.[3] For its part, France lost its status as Europe's hegemonic power.[4] The aftermath of war also made visible important shifts in trade patterns. British trade with the Netherlands declined in importance, while its trade with Russia grew, resulting in the renewal of the Anglo-Russian trade agreement in 1766. British exports to Europe fell by 9 percent between 1750–1751 and 1772–1773, while its exports to North America, the Caribbean, and India more than doubled.[5] For France, the situation was almost the opposite: Exports to its colonies fell by 21 percent, while its exports within Europe increased, compared to Britain's. In terms of economic effects, the war had different short-, medium-, and long-term consequences.[6] In the short term, after an initial boom in armaments, the war brought recessionary tendencies to Britain, whereas France experienced more of an upswing. But British long-term gains were unmistakable. The war and its aftermath also revealed the fragility of overextended empires stretched around the globe, which in the long term also had an impact on Britain.

Historians have attributed several long-term structural effects to the Seven Years' War, in addition to its immediate political and economic consequences. The war has been dubbed the "father of the modern age," a claim with perhaps too unambiguous a genealogy. On the other hand, the conflict is sometimes reduced to the prehistory of the Atlantic revolutions of 1776 and 1789 or seen simply as an intensifier of Austro-Prussian dualism in Germany. However, making this kind of connection is not always helpful in consistently historicizing the war. The historical significance of a war that was fought across four continents and that resulted in over a million fatalities does not have to depend on how it enabled later, "more significant" events. Nor does the war need labels like "world war" to lend it modernity—and thus greater relevance. But neither does historization consist of saying "this only ever happened here" or "this appeared here for the very first time," although many historians misunderstand it as such. Counterexamples from earlier or later wars are never difficult to identify. Instead, what is really at stake here is what Walter Benjamin called the "temporal nucleus" of a historical phenomenon, which I understand to mean its specific constellation of social, political, and economic conditions; material cultures; patterns of cultural interpretation; and modes of thought and behavior.

Anyone seeking to typologize the war, to define it as this or that kind of conflict, will at first find only unsatisfactory answers. In the past, eighteenth-century wars were often referred to as "cabinet wars,"[7] although the term has now been widely deconstructed and rightly rejected for its Eurocentrism.[8] The grand cabinet tables of European capitals were not the only places decisions were made: Many local actors, in Europe and overseas, also had agency in the events. If the term *world war* is problematic, so are others, like *total war*, which is generally reserved for mass industrial warfare in the twentieth century, although historians have recently used it, not entirely incorrectly, to characterize the Napoleonic Wars.[9] In terms of the Seven Years' War, it is perhaps possible to posit Prussia as a society totally given over to war. For other parties, however, this was always a limited war, not a total one.[10] The real problem with the term *total war* in this context is not that it can never be applied to mid-eighteenth-century circumstances but rather that it reintroduces a teleological perspective, implying a progression from "tamed Bellona" to "Bellona unleashed." This is a perspective long since discarded by historical research.[11] Moreover, overemphasizing the rupture represented by late eighteenth-century revolutionary wars tends to obscure some very real continuities. It is important to establish the historical characteristics of eighteenth-century wars without setting them rigidly into frameworks of "no longer this" and "not yet that."

Of course, historical events—wars, above all—are always retrospectively situated in history's before and after. The Seven Years' War, in particular, has often been characterized as a transitional moment that saw the encounter of old and new. In an earlier account of the conflict, I chose the phrase "laboratory of modernity" to capture the war's transformational characteristics.[12] The metaphor clearly has its limits; the war had neither the confined space nor the controlled procedures of a real laboratory. But the phrase captures something of the war's experimental character.

The Seven Years' War certainly had many characteristics we would today tend to label either modern or premodern. Territorial patriotism, for example, which was encouraged in every theater of the war, already contained elements of modern nationalism.[13] The *merchandising* of war—to use a deliberately anachronistic term—reached hitherto unknown levels, whether in the form of memorabilia, tobacco boxes, or *Vivat!* ribbons. Armaments technology also reached new heights, for example, in the development of artillery; technological improvements began to change the relation between military efficiency and aristocratic culture, albeit more as a gradual shift than a radical realignment.[14] Private trading companies like the British East India Company took on the role of territorial state actors, drastically changing the concept of political economy. But long-established practices and modes of interpretation also remained in effect. Examples include not only the interpretation of mouse plagues but also the way the conflict's constellations were instrumentalized in terms of religious or sectarian war. Moreover, despite all attempts to "tame Bellona," logistics presented overwhelming structural demands; this meant armies fell back on "living off the land," a familiar pattern of the ancien régime.[15]

Some aspects of the media war certainly seem to transcend the epoch. In media-historical terms, the Seven Years' War was a phase of enormous consolidation; that said, media had also been extremely important in previous conflicts, especially during the Thirty Years' War.[16] On this issue, personal testimonies reveal an astonishing range of media subjects, not least of which was the presence of female readers. A reused version of an image of battle was not considered a fake, as a modern war photograph torn from its original context would be; aesthetic conventions of the period meant an image of that kind could be regarded as an adequate representation of reality. In terms of information history, there was no sudden acceleration of the news circulating among Europe, Asia, and the Americas, but its frequency increased sharply during the war. When guerrilla-style operations—small war, in the parlance of the day—are seen in a long-term context, they seem more the rule than the exception. In other words, most ascriptions of newness or oldness appear very flawed on closer inspection. In what follows, I will instead discuss specifics of the Seven Years' War on three levels: political and military decision-making, characteristic patterns of violence and entanglement, and the perception of the conflict by contemporaries.

A War of Miracles

Contemporaries were clearly aware of two crucial questions about the war and its history: First, how had Prussia managed to hold its own against far superior enemies? And, second, how could Britain have defeated France, the greatest European power in 1756 in terms of both population and land forces?[17] Two distinctly different strategic models are in play here, not least since Britain fought both land and naval campaigns, while Prussia had to fight only on land. Their respective land wars also differed, with Frederick II's unified command structure contrasting with the delegation of authority widely practiced by the British. In the German theaters of war, Britain maintained control over His Britannic Majesty's Army in Germany but otherwise preferred to pay others to do its fighting. This delegation of responsibility freed up resources for naval warfare, where Britain enjoyed a distinct advantage. After the uncertainties of the war's first three years, British maritime capacity was eventually built up to such a degree that the country became the world's leading naval power. France placed all its hopes on the land campaign against Electoral Hanover, but its efforts failed because its military leaders were incapable of cooperation. Both Prussia and Britain were far better at mobilizing military manpower and economic resources than their opponents: This would prove decisive in the South Asian theater, among others. In military terms, the British developed unique competence in amphibious operations, with their naval and land forces combining in a highly efficient manner.

But how did contemporaries view the war's outcome? Frederick himself, with typical sarcasm, blamed the "divine folly" of his enemies.[18] Others discerned God's hand at work in the outcome, while later observers, including Thomas Mann, put the result down to fate.[19] Individualistic approaches dominated the historiography of the nineteenth and early twentieth centuries, emphasizing the "heroic will to self-assertion" displayed by political and military "genius."[20] The 1970s saw the emergence of structuralist interpretations, of which the most convincing was perhaps the work of Johannes Kunisch.[21] He regarded the real "miracle" of the war as being the combination of the *roi connétable*'s particular freedom of action and the "structural limits" of Prussia's eighteenth-century army.[22] However, his approach must be supplemented by cultural factors, allowing us to find answers to the "miracle" question in a diverse set of economic, political, military, media, and individual factors.

Frederick inherited a strong army, which he then made even stronger. He invested in light troops, field artillery, and infantry drill training, meaning his troops had better weapons and better gunpowder than their opponents, as well as a higher rate of fire.[23] His conquest of Silesia represented a wise investment of his inheritance: The region was rich in natural resources, with fortresses that would prove difficult for the Austrians to capture. Possession of the province made Prussia's strategic position considerably more comfortable. The country's overall geography bestowed a further structural advantage. Frederick's armies could make use of internal lines of operation; he thus enjoyed shorter supply lines—i.e., faster and safer ones—and could use winter quartering to more effectively strengthen his forces.[24] The strategic doctrines of Prussia's enemies were another reason for their failure. They constantly attempted diversionary tactics, seeking to divide Prussian forces in order to establish clear superiority before defeating each of them in turn.[25] This approach was time consuming, with much energy given over to coordination and deployment, and it hindered any long-term planning other than a precisely coordinated move-by-move strategy. The job of leading a war coalition proved to be challenging, and this played into Frederick's hands. The Prussian monarch put his faith in the decisive power of battles; although his choice would delight later military strategists in the nineteenth and twentieth centuries, it was far from mainstream strategic thinking during the Age of Enlightenment.[26]

Although Frederick had read widely in military history and was steeped in heroic military culture, his strategy was primarily the result of sheer necessity: Material circumstances meant he was simply not in a position to conduct a long-term strategy of exhaustion. All armies of the period were strongly influenced by the doctrine of maneuver, a defensive mindset in which battle was something to be avoided. Moreover, although all armies faced constraints in terms of weapons technologies and logistics, these factors weighed less heavily on Frederick. As a semiofficial Austrian pamphlet put it in 1761, the king of Prussia could "undertake bold, daring, and dangerous plans, and risk his fortune in a manner which a commanding General dependent on Cabinet orders would not trust himself to do, given the Possibility he would risk too much, and Events would turn out badly."[27] The Prussian general-king held unified decision-making powers in his own hands. In Choiseul's much-quoted words: "We must not forget that we are dealing with a prince who is at once his own commander in the field, chief minister, logistical organizer and, when necessary, provost-marshal."[28] In contrast to Frederick's freedom in decision-making—which repeatedly led the risk-minded king to the brink of the abyss—there was leadership discontinuity in many opposing armies, especially those of the French, Russians, and Swedes, which began almost every campaign with new commanders and often also suffered internal disputes over competencies.[29]

This action-theoretical argument about leadership styles posits that Frederick productively accumulated different roles and was thus empowered to make quick decisions. There is much to be said for this, and, indeed, it was already noted by Frederick's contemporaries. But it has not gone unchallenged.[30] The king of Prussia was by no means a general of genius. Unlike his brother Henry, he regularly made serious mistakes, as at Kolin, Hochkirch, and Kunersdorf. What he did not do, however, was give up. Where others sought security, Frederick dared to take further risks.[31] As Tim Blanning has aptly noted, he was "an indifferent general but a brilliant warlord."[32] He managed to win the trust of others, particularly through skillful self-presentation in the media. In ways barely matched by other monarchs, generals, and ministers (perhaps only Pitt in Britain came close), he knew how to conduct politics using people's emotions.[33] By the end of the war, Prussian survival had been secured, ultimately thanks to the economic and mental exhaustion of his enemies. This debilitation must, in turn, be understood against the backdrop of divergent war aims and the difficulties of coalition warfare, as well as Frederick's capacity for risk-taking, which he maintained to the last.

There has been similar historiographical discussion, albeit less polarized, around British success, focusing on the question of individuals versus structures. In the British case, Pitt, Hardwicke, and Newcastle made an efficient political leadership team, able to make consistent use of Britain's superior military and economic resources—above all, its navy and its superior financial structures.[34] In the French context, Choiseul was not inactive as a leader, but he was too dependent on court patronage from the king and Madame de Pompadour, especially on military questions. Court favorites were frequently appointed to France's highest military offices, where they displayed little competence and, even worse, little willingness to cooperate with rivals. But unity was also in short supply at the courts in St. Petersburg and Stockholm. In St. Petersburg, this was dramatically revealed in the drama surrounding the death of Tsar Peter III, while the queen of Sweden, Louisa Ulrika of Prussia, could hardly approve of the war waged against her brother.[35] By the end of the war, only the British still possessed adequate financial resources. Whether or not to pay subsidies to Prussia was a political question, decided by Parliament, but British solvency played no role in the considerations. For four years, the British paid Prussia 675,000 pounds a year, a figure close to Prussia's entire annual tax revenues.[36] Looking back, Stanislaus II August Poniatowski (1732–1798), who was crowned king of Poland in 1764, pondered how Prussia managed the seemingly impossible: "that an Elector of Brandenburg could, for seven years, resist the united countries of Russia, Austria, France and Sweden."[37] He concluded that Prussian survival was possible only through British subsidies, the financial plunder of Saxony, and the systematic debasement of its own currency. More specifically, Prussia's war costs amounted to around 140 million thalers, which was funded by about 50 million in coerced contributions, 30 million in currency debasement, and 27 million in British subsidies. In other words, around two-thirds of Prussia's war costs were borne by someone else.[38] In both financial and military terms, Frederick was a master of resource mobilization. The situation was different with French subsidies paid to Austria and with Austrian subsidies paid to Russia. In both cases, the punctuality of payments varied during the war, as did their motivation. Unlike their opponents, the governments of Prussia and Britain largely managed to win over public opinion to the patriotic cause; in the case of Britain, this had a positive influence on Parliament but also on the financial markets.

Security-Driven Politics

Securitization is the most apt term, albeit a somewhat awkward one, to describe many of the war's politico-military initiatives and their broader legitimation.[39] A key example of the politics of insecurity appears very early in the war, with the idea of preventive war, Frederick's famous legitimizing topos. Securitization required the development of a threat scenario—whether it was real or not mattered little—in order to depict certain political and military actions as imperative. For this reason, the Austrians constantly declared "conditions of total security" to be one of their key war aims.[40]

Europeans in North America, South Asia, and elsewhere built trading posts that they then gradually fortified, creating a situation involving both insecurity and protective measures. An environment described in terms of insecurity was contrasted with the safety of fortified locations; in this way, the promise of security was literally set into stone, a promise that was also extended to Native trading partners. The utopian French project of building a border wall across North America ultimately fitted into this framework, as did the establishment of local sepoy regiments in India. But there was one striking difference between Europe's "wars in the world" and twentieth-century world wars: non-European auxiliaries were not deployed in Europe itself, unless Cossacks and Kalmyks are included in the category.[41]

The dynamic of colonial expansion during the war has often led historians to draw comparisons between the metropolitan leadership of the warring polities—whether in London, Paris, or Madrid—and the "men on the spot," making decisions out in the colonies themselves. There has been quite justified skepticism about the degree of geopolitical control exercised from colonial headquarters; apart from anything else, the sheer distance involved imposed massive limitations on this control. In the case of India, attention has shifted toward the actions of local European representatives, leading to a kind of "robber baron" thesis, focusing on figures like Clive. This has also led to the minimization of the violence deployed against local rulers, as if a preexisting power vacuum meant that authority simply fell into British hands. The latter thesis, at least, has no basis in reality. In fact, there was coalescence between the interests of European metropoles and those of local colonial leaders who enjoyed a fairly wide scope of action, given the distances involved. The audience for securitization scenarios included actors and states within India itself but also those who wielded power in London. A risky military action could be justified as absolutely essential; this was all the easier when those lobbying for action also controlled the information required to assess the situation. The East India Company pursued its economic interests by military means, but the company became obsolete at the moment when economic monopoly was converted into political power. It is no paradox that the company's power weakened as the colonial state established its own authority. The company lost its trading monopoly in 1833; in 1858, its tasks of political administration were transferred to the British government.

The cruel effects of colonial policy were even worse for Native American tribes than for the population of the Indian subcontinent. Attacks on and violent expulsions of Native Americans now took on genocidal proportions; time and again European settlers depicted themselves as vulnerable and under threat, although, in fact, they were the most dangerous element in the situation.[42] By 1765, it was clear that settlers also posed a threat to British rule, with ever-louder protests breaking out in the ports of the Atlantic coast. As the colonial historian Daniel Baugh put it: "The concern for security shifted from the wilderness to the populated seaboard."[43] But 1763 was not a decisive turning point for local non-European forces in South Asia or in North America. Instead, the end of the war served to reinforce processes already begun, with wars everywhere continuing to be waged. Later wars fought in India include the Mysore conflict (1766–1799) and the Anglo-Maratha wars (1779–1818), while in the United States, the various wars with Native Americans continued well past the middle of the nineteenth century. The close-up view of history repeatedly reveals how major consequences can spring from small measures and from localized events driven by securitization policies. In Calcutta, for example, British concerns initially focused on the depth of a single fortified trench and the protection of a single merchant. These modest beginnings, however, marked the first steps toward territorial takeover. The particular value of a threat scenario lies in its capacity to legitimize new possibilities for decision-making and action. Threats clearly demand responses. But not all historical actors enjoyed the same room for maneuver or for decision-making.

Disease and Violence

Given the extensive discussion of combat operations during the war, it may come as a surprise to learn that the majority of soldiers died of disease rather than in battles. Infectious diseases, including smallpox, yellow fever, and dysentery, claimed hundreds of thousands of victims. In the long term, Native American tribes were hardest hit, but the Kalmyks were also very badly affected in 1757. Over ninety thousand Russian soldiers are said to have died of illness, compared to eighteen thousand killed in action.[44] The Swedish army suffered huge losses to illness while failing to fight a single major battle in the field. As mentioned earlier, the British lost more men to yellow fever in Cuba than in all the battles of the French and Indian War. Diseases also traveled with armies, infecting civilian populations. Death by infectious disease is difficult to glorify; it has played little role in the war's official memory cultures. Nonetheless, the Seven Years' War—whether viewed in close-up or in statistical terms—was primarily a war of disease. Its defining characteristic was not the taming of Bellona but the continued powerlessness of Asclepius.

The war's highly differentiated topography becomes clear if we adopt a spatial mode of analysis, focusing on presences and absences, proximities and distances. In London, Paris, Madrid, Vienna, St. Petersburg, and Copenhagen, the war remained largely a virtual experience. The general public learned of it through the ringing of bells, services of thanksgiving, or the entry of foreign ambassadors, as well as through information arriving by courier or in newspapers. This was also the case in German cities like Munich, Augsburg, Stuttgart, Hamburg, and Regensburg, as well as in North American colonial cities like Boston, New York, and Philadelphia. In addition to media reports, prisoners and wounded soldiers returning home could convey the presence of war to cities—whether Boston, Magdeburg, or Graz. But the situation was very different in those parts of the Holy Roman Empire located north of Frankfurt and south of Emden. Here hundreds of urban and rural localities were affected by the passage of troops, both from their "own" side and from their enemies. These places often suffered serious damage, as seen in Münster in Westphalia; Dresden, Wittenberg, and Zittau in Saxony; Küstrin in Prussia; and Prague in Bohemia, among many others. The war directly affected the capital cities of three of its warring polities: Berlin, Dresden, and Hanover. In France, the conflict had a direct impact on towns on the coast of Brittany, as with the siege of St. Malo, for example. Quebec and Montreal were key sites fought over in Nouvelle-France, as were Havana and Manila in the Spanish colonies. On the Indian subcontinent, a similar distinction can be made between places directly touched by the war and those that remained at peace. Bombay in the west of the subcontinent was not directly affected, while Calcutta and Madras—and more broadly, Bengal and the Carnatic coast—became theaters of war. This meant that specific physical experiences of the war—hunger, epidemics, billeting, hostage taking, captivity, looting, and fire—were quite unevenly distributed, as were media representations of those experiences. But this topography of war makes it clear that contemporary images of a "world in flames" were not without foundation. A grasp of the war's geography also reveals that the war did damage to civilian life on a global scale; the conflict went far beyond a cabinet war, a category to which it has often been reduced in diplomatic and political histories. Still, with knowledge of the conflict's global dimensions, this experience of civilian disruption was not universal. Many people remained spectators of the conflagration engulfing parts of the globe.

A close-up view of history rapidly reveals the limits of classic interpretative frameworks, including the trope of a "tamed Bellona."[45] Eighteenth-century warfare may have consciously turned away from battles—regarded as too risky and too costly in human terms—in favor of a strategy of constant maneuvering. Paradoxically, however, the costs of this more "enlightened" strategy were borne by the civilian population, as they had been in previous strategic paradigms.[46] Huge armies, up to seventy thousand men strong, were constantly on the move, putting enormous pressure on the land and its inhabitants.[47] There was no question of any far-reaching humanization of war. Moreover, as shown in individual testimonies, the longer the conflict went on, the more suffering it inflicted on the population.[48] In 1757, the second year of the European war and the first in western Germany, many peasants did well, since armies were still paying for provisions and forage.[49] But when soldiers returned a second, third, or fourth time, they found fewer resources available, and they were less able and less willing to pay anything at all.[50] It scarcely mattered whether these troops were friends or enemies. Mounted troops brought the greatest distress to local populations, especially when the raiders were fast and mobile, like hussars or Freikorps. At times, rural populations were attacked by several different raiding parties in a single week.

It is almost impossible to overestimate the importance of logistics in how the war unfolded.[51] An event that seemed to "miraculously" affect a battle's outcome could merely be the result of the structural necessities of resupply. Armies could not be enlarged without also increasing the logistical structures on which they depended. We see striking examples of this in campaigns fought by the French and Russian armies in which logistics, war atrocities, and propaganda interact, a typical combination for the time.[52] Poor supply systems led to the escalation of violence against civilian populations. Media coverage meant this violence, enhanced with particular images and stereotypes of the enemy, could transcend the local and have more long-lasting effects.

Prussia's success was largely due to its logistical capacity: It managed to mobilize its own resources while simultaneously destroying enemy supplies.[53] A logistical perspective also highlights the centrality of maritime activity in the Franco-British conflict, even for the parts of the war fought on land. Although only a limited number of sea battles were fought, waterways and maritime routes remained crucially important.[54] Rivers were vital in North America, where roads hardly existed, but also in the German regions of Westphalia and Hesse, for example: There the British managed to bring in supplies from the north via the Ems and Weser Rivers, whereas the French had few waterways suitable for their advances. Almost all of Prussia's main magazine depots were linked via the Oder River, a waterway that Frederick called the "army's foster mother." Austria relied heavily on the Danube as a logistical thoroughfare.[55] Oceans and seas became a key factor in the war, capable of opening up spaces but also of shutting them down. On an individual level, crossing the sea was an important experience for many participants in the war. Space became a crucial determinant of the nature and intensity of violence. Constriction and logjams, whether on battlefields or in cities, could lead to an escalation of violence. Mobility and speed had a similar influence on the violence of irregular operations. The final few years of the war provide particularly sad evidence of this.

The idea of a "tamed Bellona" must be revised in terms of both time and space. For several reasons, the European war was fought with more ferocity after 1759–1760 than in its earlier years. The effects of this can be seen in the treatment of prisoners of war but also in raids carried out by irregular forces. Warfare also saw competition between different norms, a process typical of early modernity. Thus, older customs could exist side by side with new norms of international law.[56] The Austrian attack on Landeshut in 1760 and British violence in Manila in 1762 were legitimized with reference to so-called customs of war, including the right to plunder a city after storming it. In Manila, this controlled excess was supposed to be limited to three hours. Controlled excess—the very notion is paradoxical—represented a kind of "measured" violence, a form ultimately produced by norm competition.[57]

In terms of the social spaces where this violence occurred, distinctions must be made between town and country, as well as between the actions of different occupying powers. The assumption that violence was always unleashed without limit does as little justice to historical circumstances as the idea that violence had been brought under control.

However, it would also be ahistorical to deny any change in the conduct of war. Officers and war commissioners were subject to a different framework of legitimacy when dealing with civilian populations than were the colonels of the Thirty Years' War. A key area in which warfare was transformed was weaponry. Many technical improvements were made, although they could not always be adequately financed; neither were they easy to legitimize with contemporary values. A few examples will suffice: Frederick negotiated with an English inventor to manufacture a flamethrower; accurate firearms with rifled barrels became a threat to highly visible officers on horseback; Shuvalov howitzers were constructed and put to use; and poisoned blankets were used as a kind of biological weapon.[58] The flamethrower was never built, and the rifles proved to be economically too expensive, aesthetically too short, and operationally too slow to load. Nevertheless, the reactions of contemporaries make clear the tensions between what was technically possible and what was culturally acceptable.

The expansion of operations beyond Europe presented further challenges to prevailing practices, including practices that were firmly embedded in existing institutions. Besiegers in North and South America and South Asia often faced very different conditions than in Europe. The usual practices and temporal rhythms—digging trenches, blowing breaches, and making assaults—here faced new challenges, including a different pattern of seasons and a different natural environment. Trenches could not be dug through rock in the same way as through soil. Amphibious sieges required landings. The relatively small numbers of available troops often made it impossible to fully surround a besieged object. Time pressure arose in Europe too, of course—for example, when relieving forces were known to be en route, although starvation among besiegers was less common in more densely populated operational areas. Monsoons, hurricanes, and bitter Canadian winters presented the warring parties with different challenges than taking up winter quarters in Europe, where retreat was usually easier to accomplish.

Strategies of maneuver placed a heavy burden on civilian populations, but we should not presume that more direct modes of armed combat were fairer or more humane.[59] This does not correspond to historical reality: Battles were very frequently *not* decisive and yet still demanded an extortionate price in blood. Moreover, they in no way shortened the war, as evidenced by the conflict's bitterly fought final battles.[60] What, if anything, was actually decided by the war's great battles is a complex question. In attempting to answer it, we should maintain distinctions among levels of decision-making. Victory and defeat were determined on the ground by the action of claiming the battlefield, a crude simplification. If that question remained in doubt, however, it could be disputed in media coverage, as seen in the aftermath of Lobositz, Zorndorf, and Hastenbeck. On another level, we can ask about the impact of a given victory on a particular campaign and finally on the entire war. With almost no exceptions, fighting continued after every battle in the war's European theaters, albeit sometimes after a pause for the winter break. What happened after Kunersdorf was a clear example of the capacity of armies to regenerate. In the case of Rossbach, the battle's media afterlife eclipsed its actual strategic importance, the moment when Prussia stopped the French advance to the east.

As with sieges, battles in the conflict's later stages were especially significant as a way of laying claim to territory, looking to give negotiators the strongest possible hand at the peace table. This phase of the war saw no truly decisive battles along the lines of Hastings or Waterloo. Nonetheless, some historians have granted such status to various events in the war. The siege of Quebec is regarded as marking the demise of Nouvelle-France, the cannonade at Plassey is framed as a foundational event for the British Raj, and Rossbach lived on until revenge was taken at Jena in 1806.

Entanglements and Disentanglements

Although recent historiographical discourse on globalization may claim otherwise, it is not the case that everything was connected to everything else in the eighteenth century.[61] When considering whether the Seven Years' War was a global conflict, and if so, how, a close-up view of history reveals ambiguity at every level, from individual testimonies to the final peace congress. As we have seen, Markus Uhlmann tried to calculate the time difference between Havana and Zurich, while in southern India, Ananda Ranga Pillai reflected on the children of Frederick of Prussia. These were merely two individual attempts to make sense of interconnected theaters of war and do not lend themselves to generalization. That said, comparisons formed a key part of contemporaries' efforts to interpret their situation: The sources provide a steady stream of examples. Comparisons were made between religious denominations, past wars (e.g., the Thirty Years' War) and present ones, different kinds of fighting men (Turks, Indians, and Cossacks), women, prisoners, and foodstuffs. Analogies and comparisons could bring together far-flung actors, places, and practices, rendering them visible as separate parts of an overall process. In this way, entanglement was a precondition for comparison, as well as an effect of it.[62]

The conclusion of the Seven Years' War produced no great event like the peace congresses at Westphalia in the seventeenth century and at Vienna in the nineteenth. The large number of theaters of war and parties to the conflict and their highly varied interdependencies, not to mention the greatly differing distances between them, gave rise to a whole series of separate peace agreements. In Europe, the agreements of St. Petersburg and Hamburg should be listed along with Paris and Hubertusburg. In North America, we can mention the British treaties with the Cherokee, agreed to at Long-Island-on-the-Holston in 1761 and Charlestown in 1762. Other simmering conflicts with Native nations remained entirely unresolved.[63]

The northeastern part of the Holy Roman Empire was one region in which the war's fundamental Austro-Prussian and Franco-British conflicts were decisively entangled. Although the Anglo-Prussian alliance was primarily a matter of subsidies, Ferdinand of Brunswick—a Prussian general leading a British and Allied army—acted as a kind of personification of the coalition. The Baltic Sea was another region where the two conflicts might have interconnected, but here the British refused active involvement, despite Frederick's numerous entreaties.[64] From this perspective, the Baltic region represents a *disentangling* of the two major subconflicts of the war rather than their intensified entanglement.

Statements by Frederick and Maria Theresa reveal little agreement on the war's global entanglements. There are clear differences between the two monarchs' positions, although there are limits to how much they tell us about the conflict's global nature: Their statements are drawn from different contexts and sought to justify different things. In 1757, Frederick claimed it was entirely clear "that the turmoil which has engulfed Europe had its beginnings in America"; by contrast, the previous year Maria Theresa remarked that the "American disputes have not affected us in the slightest."[65] For the Austrian empress, the war was basically all about Silesia, while Frederick was keen to justify his "preventive" attack on Saxony. Nonetheless, both statements are typical of the mid-eighteenth-century view that global relations had broken down. For some, the entire world was ablaze; for others, the fire was limited to their own village or town.

Britain and Electoral Hanover were linked by personal union, and their residents paid attention to the war outside Europe. This seems to have been the case in both polities and across boundaries of class. An awareness of global connections is present in the testimonies of Turner, the Sussex shopkeeper; Abelmann, the master baker in Hanover; Schowart, the garrison auditor in Celle; and Wähner, the Göttingen linguist, although we should not neglect processes of dissociation and mutual incomprehension between the two countries, a phenomenon rightly highlighted by the historian Hermann Wellenreuther.[66] The Seven Years' War saw an intensification of communications on a global scale but also clearly revealed the limits of common ground between the king's subjects in the Holy Roman Empire and those in the nascent British imperial polity. The Göttingen philosopher Samuel Christian Hollmann (1696–1787) puts this very clearly in *In Praise of the War*, a book written during the conflict but published after it ended: "The king's German Subjects have thus, along with their Allies, the poor Hessians, had in part to pay for the Engellish, and pay with skin and blood. How little would it thus cost, that they too should share in the great Assets the Engellish have conquered in this war! They, who had no other concern with this War, than that their sovereign was alike the King of the Engellish, who began this merchants' war in America, and they had thus also to carry it on."[67] The "merchants' war," launched as part of British blue water policy, met with incomprehension among Hanoverians, who saw themselves exposed to unnecessary suffering for the sake of imperial calculations that were largely foreign to their concerns.[68] Emphatic patriotism was not to be expected in Electoral Hanover; to the degree that this emotion had any role in the imperial territories of northwestern Germany, it was focused on Ferdinand of Brunswick and his victories over the French. This coolness toward the merchants' war should not lead us to overlook the economic aspects of the Seven Years' War in the Reich. The struggle for Silesia was essentially a struggle over economic resources.

Apart from the peasantry, awareness of the global nature of the conflict seems to have been determined less by social stratum than by place of residence and political sentiments. Cities like London, Hamburg, Cologne, and Augsburg, all centers of media production and consumption, had different approaches to news than places more remote from media circulation. Paris was a special case. In terms of media, the French capital was, in effect, more "remote" than other cities, but this was the result not of economic geography but of control by the government, which kept a tight rein on information about France's Canadian losses.[69]

In terms of the war overseas, the focus of media attention in Europe was very much concentrated on the Atlantic world, with news from South Asia distinctly less important. It was only in the final quarter of the eighteenth century that news from India became a more prominent subject in the

British and the German media, by which time the North American colonies were well on their way to independence.[70]

There were, as we have seen, some people who carefully recorded world events as they took place. But we should not forget the large number, quite possibly the majority, who were concerned solely with their own monarch and their territory and with the specific place where they lived. It thus makes sense to speak of "fracture zones of globalization," understood as those "spaces, moments, and arenas of historical globalization" that witnessed a "struggle for the production of new spatial relationships."[71] Underlying this concept is the assumption that "globalization is characterized by a permanent dialectic of deterritorialization (through entanglement, mobility, acceleration of communications, etc.) and reterritorialization (via efforts to dominate, as much as possible, options for action and processes of identification)." The focus on entangled histories has been and remains an important corrective to narrow national conceptions of the Seven Years' War. Works with titles like *Prussia Moves the World* continue to be published, clearly indicating the ongoing necessity of a corrective global focus.[72] Global history as a whole has long been characterized by a search for connections, border crossers, contact zones, and modes of circulation and appropriation. But these actors, spaces, and processes must be regarded as historical objects of empirical study, and studied and tested as such, rather than simply being assumed a priori.

We can thus observe new boundaries and new forms of separation emerging alongside growing entanglements. In North America, the French and Indian War marked the end of the "middle ground"; in India too, some existing connections were severed as new ones were established.[73] New processes of circulation prompted new practices of control—for example, the British blockade of the French Atlantic. News circulated more intensely but was also censored.[74] The huge number of surviving *prize papers*—private letters that were on board ships seized by the British, today a valuable historical source—shows that news did not always reach its addressees.[75] In the aftermath of the war, Frederick himself acted as a gatekeeper of depictions of the conflict.[76] In fields of knowledge, we also encounter ignorance. Some channels of knowledge became denser and more consolidated—between Britain and Hanover or between Britain and its colonies—but we also encounter historical actors who were barely aware of developments on a global scale. There were thus clear limits to *soziale Trägerschaft des Diskurses* (social carriers of discourse) in the eighteenth century, to use a phrase coined in recent globalization discourse.[77] Moreover, this was the case on all rungs of the social ladder, including educated circles. Nonetheless, contemporary perceptions of global entanglement were widespread: They moved between, as well as within, the separate communication zones of Britain, France, and Hanover, on the one hand, and Prussia, the Holy Roman Empire, and Habsburg lands, on the other. The globalism created by the war contained ruptures. Entanglement went hand in hand with disentanglement. The flammability of this "glocalized" world would remain a liability within the modern world system.[78]

Writing the War

The ways the war was written about are as varied as those who did the writing.[79] For this reason, the sources reveal a few striking trends rather than any fixed patterns. The genre in which people were writing could also affect their mode of expression. Sometimes a writer's diary entry describes an event differently than their later autobiography. In the eighteenth century, texts could be produced privately or publicly, regardless of genre; this was as true for diaries as it was for letters. Many authors cited in this book—including Bräker, Cogniazo, Equiano, Küster, Täge, and Trautzschen—published their war experiences during their lifetimes—but long after the end of the conflict. For some (Bräker, Casanova), the war was just one episode in a longer life story, whereas others (Dominicus, Wähner) described only their experience of the war years. Some (Prittwitz, von Hülsen) explicitly addressed their own offspring, while others (Barsewisch, Dreyer, Tempelhof) addressed a public interested in the history of the war.[80] Some testimonies resulted from pragmatic considerations. James Miller, for example, wrote to legitimize his own participation in the war. In 1792, he sent his memoirs to his former commander, Jeffrey Amherst, as part of an attempt to win promotion and a higher pension while serving with a unit of Chelsea Hospital Invalids on the island of Jersey.[81]

Mobility or immobility could also have a lasting impact on how narratives were written. Many highly mobile figures—including Bolotov, Bonin, Grotehenn, Langelius, Prittwitz, Uhlmann, and Todd—wrote accounts that read almost like travel reports, with descriptions of countries, peoples, local customs, buildings, and foods, painting a multifaceted picture of their interactions with the civilian population.[82] Writers who stayed in one place—including Khevenhüller-Metsch, Pillai, Wähner, ter Meer, and the various German pastors cited—tended to register local occurrences alongside reports of outside events. For some, like Wähner, this can lead to a sparse style of information accountancy; in other cases, as with Abelmann, this can produce a sort of chronicle. While Turner in Sussex remained purely a consumer of war coverage, other contemporaries—like Cuntz, Geitz, Schowart, and Zellmann, all of whom lived in the Holy Roman Empire—were affected more directly—in particular, by billeting—and could compare their own experiences with what they read of others elsewhere. We see these writers, as consumers of news, struggle to verify new information, reflecting the widespread use of false reporting for propaganda purposes. All this added up to a particularly uncertain climate of information.

The testimonies of both officers and fighting men bear witness to their experience with tactics and weapons technologies. If we take these authors at their word, they very rarely used violence against other people. This can be explained partly by authors' moral filtering of their own texts but also by factors like the machine-like nature of linear tactics and peloton firing, which subordinated individuals to a larger killing machine, thus possibly reducing perceived individual responsibility. The situation was different with combatants who were in cavalry units or who became isolated from their units, as their narratives tend to depict a greater degree of agency.[83]

In letters sent directly from the field, combat often prompted images of indescribability, followed by detailed information about friends and relatives who were wounded or killed.[84] Concern with one's own body is another key theme.[85] Emotional excitement that overwhelmed the entire body in combat was usually indicated with terms like *heat*.[86] In the work of Küster, the Prussian military chaplain whose descriptions of the Battle of Hochkirch were cited previously, we can see early stirrings of combat psychology, including the use of the word itself, as when he uses his own experience to reflect on "fighters' psychological experiences of pleasure and displeasure in the tumult of battle."[87]

Diaries that would now be considered private often overlapped with regimental diaries. Sometimes first-person narrators speak for a collective, especially in the case of common soldiers and noncommissioned officers.[88] Later accounts, which often come with the generic descriptor *Journal* or *Mémoire*, are usually concerned with justifying the author's actions and use the sober language of military professionalism (as did Prince Charles-Joseph of Ligne and Count Wilhelm von Schaumburg-Lippe).[89] This does not undermine the value of these documents for cultural histories of the war, since they offer insight into the "sociology of command," conveying ideas of honor, as well as perceptions of their own troops and of foreign fighters.[90] Objectivity and abstraction helped create an ordered narrative of deeply disordered events. Some combatants—often British but sometimes German-speaking—deployed an arsenal of euphemisms and diminutives, writing of the "play" of gunfire or the "caress" of bullets. This language made violence describable but could also trivialize it.[91] Thus, Henry Montgomery, a British platoon leader at the Battle of Minden, describes in a letter how a musket ball entering his leg caused only "as much pain, as would a tap of Miss Mathew's fan."[92]

The influence of religious socialization is palpable in the writings of many of these authors. Prittwitz's Pietism, for example, helped him both reflect on and distance himself from the brutality of battle.[93] God and king became the main devices used to lend significance to and thus cope with the incomprehensible suffering of war. A writer's gender could determine both access to literacy and frequency of writing, but it also had an impact on the narrative forms and devices used, including images of masculinity and femininity and the ascription of gender roles.[94] These might include not only notions of martial honor or courage in the face of the enemy but also a clergyman's depiction of himself as an assiduous servant of his community, his church, and his princely state. Reports from quite different fields of experience sometimes used very similar narrative models, such as captivity and reverse captivity narratives: stories, respectively, by Europeans and Native Americans about their capture and experience as prisoners of war.[95]

A Sensory War

Wartime conditions affected every one of the human senses. As well as new things to see, there were new smells and tastes and, above all, altered soundscapes, both rural and urban. Food substitutes—gunpowder used a condiment, for example—could produce unusual experiences of taste. On the eve of what historians have called the "olfactory revolution," observers of the war noted the conspicuous smells of animal carcasses and charred human flesh, both on the battlefield and in the aftermath of looting.[96]

Nonetheless, visual and acoustic perceptions dominate personal accounts of the war. The range of visual perspectives runs from a complete lack of vision, enveloped in fog or smoke from the guns, to the panoptic fascination of a battle viewed from the proverbial "general's hill." Courtly aesthetics could frame not only perceptions of uniforms and battle lines but also the fascination or horror provoked by the sight of a burning city. The sources offer evidence of acoustic perceptions, as well as visual ones. Bells and cannons were two main devices used to produce very loud sounds in early modern soundscapes. These two, among the loudest media of the period, constantly reappear as shapers of the war's sonic space: Bells could communicate victory or danger, while cannonades conveyed threat or celebration. Depending on the context, the same acoustic signal could be evaluated in many different ways. During peace celebrations, the martial sound of gunfire was recoded as the joyous annunciation of peace. Onomatopoeia became a popular stylistic device in many personal testimonies of the war. The distinction between noise and silence, and their specific pattern of alternation, also served to represent the shifting moods and circumstances of war and peace. Silence by no means always connoted peace. It could indicate the calm before a storm or stand for dejection after defeat. Along with references to familiar sounds and media, personal testimonies sometimes note entirely new perceptions, as in 1757, when Schowart reports of the "wonderful harmony" resulting from the interplay of French bagpipes with thundering cannons.[97]

Like the ringing of bells, soldiers' experiences of heat, cold, and constant thirst were not exclusive to the Seven Years' War; the specific experiences of this conflict arose from the various ways soldiers dealt with them. Were garments changed for different weather conditions, or did the traditional aesthetics of military uniforms take precedence? The honor of a regiment was to some degree dependent on its uniforms, so these questions could touch on existential issues rather than mere irrational vanity. When Grotehenn and his regiment returned to their base at Brunswick, which was also his hometown, he experienced profound embarrassment at their appearance. After several years in the field, they were bearded and wearing patched and discolored uniforms and hats stolen from peasants. He compares their appearance to French religious "emigrants," describing them as "halfway Hottentot."[98] Thus, even the most quotidian wartime experiences contain their temporal nucleus, no matter how timeless they may at first appear.

Problems with language barriers and false news used for war propaganda were not peculiar to eighteenth-century wars. But they took on specific forms in that context. Only three senior British officers are said to have spoken Portuguese during the Fantastic War. Knowledge of English was not yet widespread in the northwestern area of the Holy Roman Empire. Latin was regularly used as a lingua franca. Translators gained in importance during the war, although their work often goes unmentioned in the testimonies left by participants.

From the perspective of the general population, seven years of war brought suffering but almost no political change. Georg Schatz, the pastor from near Göttingen, sums up the outcome: "After this War which cost so many millions and all its horrific Shedding of blood had finally come to its End, and all Lands and Subjects came to the same Lords as before the War, there is nothing more to observe than that great Lords quarrel, but their Subjects will pay with their Necks, also the fine bride named Silesia, around whom the Imperials danced for 7 long years, making fine warlike steps, and which also cost many Thousands their throats, will remain in the hands of Prussia, just as she had been ceded in 1742."[99] This was not at all a radical position. Count von Lehndorff, one of Frederick's most senior courtiers, came to similar conclusions: "And thus all our miseries come to an end. If now we consider the innumerable victims claimed by this war, how many provinces have been devastated, how many families ruined, and all this so as to see the rulers go back to the status quo ante, one should wish to cry aloud at the lunacy of mankind."[100] Even Frederick himself, one of those mainly responsible for this lunacy, having seen the war at close-up, changed his verdict on the price of glory: "Considered at a distance, our military glory is beautiful indeed; but whoever witnesses the misery and woe by which such glory is won, by what physical pains and hardship, in heat and cold, in hunger, filth and nakedness, will learn to judge 'glory' in an altogether different manner."[101]

Acknowledgments

The idea of writing about the Seven Years' War in terms of global history originally sprang from a conversation with Jürgen Luh on August 25, 2006. I fleshed out this monograph in conceptual terms as a habilitation project, but there was not the same institutional urgency to complete the project after 2011. It disappeared into the desk drawer for several years, although I continued to write a number of essays on the subject. The book would never have been completed without the award of a senior fellowship at the Fritz Thyssen Foundation at the Historisches Kolleg in Munich in 2017–2018. I would thus very much like to thank the Fritz Thyssen Foundation, the Kolleg's board of trustees, and, above all, Karl-Ulrich Gelberg and Elisabeth Hüls, who were an ever-reliable source of advice and support, making a great contribution to the success of my stay.

I have presented various aspects of the research in courses and colloquia over the years: I would like to thank my interlocutors at Göttingen, Berlin, Paris, Jena, Munich, Bielefeld, and Freiburg for stimulating critical discussion, among other things. Among my colleagues at Göttingen, I am especially grateful to Rebekka Habermas, Hans Medick, and Hermann Wellenreuther for their valuable conversations and research advice. I would also like to thank Daniel Hohrath (Ingolstadt) for his valuable information on eighteenth-century military history and close critical reading of the manuscript. I would like to express my gratitude to my editor Stefan von der Lahr of the book's German publisher, C. H. Beck, who provided great support and invaluable advice during the publication process, along with his colleagues Angelika von der Lahr and Andrea Morgan. I would also like to thank my student assistants Johanna Hausmann and Kathrin Ullmann, who created the index. The most important person to thank is my partner, Stefanie Rüther, who has accompanied this project since its earliest stages, repeatedly reading, correcting, and commenting on my texts.

Notes

Preface: A Global Conflict in Close-Up

1. Eberhard Jürgen Abelmann, *Hannover im Siebenjährigen Krieg: Hannoverisches Kriegsdenkmal; Das Kriegsgeschehen in Stadt und Kurfürstentum, dokumentiert von einem Bäckermeister*, ed. Hans Hartmann (Niemeyer, 1995), 215–216.
2. Hans-Wolfgang Bergerhausen, "Nur ein Stück Papier? Die Garantieerklärungen für die österreichisch-preussischen Friedensverträge von 1742 und 1745," in *Menschen und Strukturen in der Geschichte Alteuropas*, ed. Helmut Neuhaus and Barbara Stollberg-Rilinger (Duncker & Humblot, 2002); Thomas R. Kraus, *"Europa sieht den Tag leuchten . . .": Der Aachener Friede von 1748* (Aachener Geschichtsvereins, 1998).
3. Oskar Ulrich, "Die Stadt Hannover im siebenjährigen Kriege," *Zeitschrift des historischen Vereins für Niedersachsen* 59 (1894).
4. See Catherine Desbarats and Allan Greer, "The Seven Years' War in Canadian History and Memory," in *Cultures in Conflict: The Seven Years' War in North America*, ed. Warren R. Hofstra (Penguin, 2006); Jacques Mathieu, "Les rappels mémoriels de la guerre de sept ans au Canada," in *La guerre de Sept ans en Nouvelle-France*, ed. Laurent Veyssière and Bertrand Fonck (Septentrion, 2011).
5. Marian Füssel, "Global Wars in the Eighteenth Century: Entanglement—Violence—Perception," in *The War of the Spanish Succession: New Perspectives*, ed. Matthias Pohlig and Michael Schaich (Oxford University Press, 2017).
6. Wilhelm Oncken, *Das Zeitalter Friedrich des Grossen: Allgemeine Geschichte in Einzeldarstellungen*, 2 vols. (Berlin: Grote, 1881), vol. 2, bk. 7.

7. Albert Schoch, *Siebenjähriger Krieg und Weltkrieg: Ein geschichtlicher Vergleich* (Deutscher Wille, 1922).
8. Winston Churchill, *A History of the English-Speaking Peoples*, 4 vols. (Cassell, 1956–1958; see vol. 3 (1957).
9. Heinrich Walle, "Der Siebenjährige Krieg zwischen Anekdote und Klischee," *Historische Mitteilungen* 18 (2005): 101.
10. Reinhart Koselleck, "Chance as Motivational Trace in Historical Writing," in *Futures Past: On the Semantics of Historical Time*, trans. Keith Tribe (Columbia University Press, 2004). For other early statements on the Seven Years' War as a global conflict, see Winfried Baumgart, "Der Ausbruch des Siebenjährigen Krieges: Zum gegenwärtigen Forschungsstand," *Militärgeschichtliche Mitteilungen* 11 (1972): 163; Kurt Peball, "Aspekte der Forschung zum Kriegswesen der Zeit Maria Theresias und Josephs II," in *Österreich im Europa der Aufklärung: Kontinuität und Zäsur in Europa zur Zeit Maria Theresias und Josephs II—Internationales Symposion in Vienna, 20–23. Oktober 1980*, ed. Richard Georg Plaschka, 2 vols. (Österreichischen Akademie der Wissenschaften, 1985), 1:607f.
11. See Christopher Duffy, "Die Dynamik eines Weltkrieges im 18. Jahrhundert," in *Formen des Krieges: Vom Mittelalter zum "Low-Intensity-Conflict,"* ed. Manfred Rauchensteiner and Erwin A. Schmidl (Styria, 1991); Helmut Bley and Hans-Joachim König, "Globale Interaktion," in *Enzyklopädie der Neuzeit*, vol. 4 (Metzler, 2006).
12. Dieter Langewiesche, *Der gewaltsame Lehrer: Europas Kriege in der Moderne* (Beck, 2019), 31–34.
13. Langewiesche, *Der gewaltsame Lehrer*, 48.
14. Jan Eckel, "'Alles hängt mit allem zusammen': Zur Historisierung des Globalisierungsdiskurses der 1990er und 2000er Jahre," *Historische Zeitschrift* 307 (2018).
15. Benigna von Krusenstjern and Hans Medick, eds., *Zwischen Alltag und Katastrophe: Der Dreissigjährige Krieg aus der Nähe* (Vandenhoeck & Ruprecht, 1999); Hans Medick, *Der Dreissigjährige Krieg: Zeugnisse vom Leben mit Gewalt* (Wallstein, 2018).
16. "This is how world history looks close up: you see nothing." Robert Musil, "Das hilflose Europa (1922)," in *Gesammelte Werke*, vol. 8 (Rowohlt, 1978), here 1076.
17. Theodore R. Schatzki, "Practice Theory as Flat Ontology," in *Practice Theory and Research*, ed. Gert Spaargaren et al. (Routledge, 2016).
18. Sidney Mintz, *Sweetness and Power: The Place of Sugar in Modern History* (Viking, 1985); Sanjay Subrahmanyam, "Connected Histories: Notes Towards a Reconfiguration of Early Modern Eurasia," *Modern Asian Studies* 31, no. 3 (1997); Michael Werner and Bénédicte Zimmermann, "Vergleich, Transfer, Verflechtung: Der Ansatz der Histoire croisée und die Herausforderung des Transnationalen," *Geschichte und Gesellschaft* 28 (2002); Sebastian Conrad et al., eds., *Jenseits*

des Eurozentrismus: Postkoloniale Perspektiven in den Geschichtsund Kulturwissenschaften, 2nd ed. (Campus, 2013).
19. Guillaume-Thomas Raynal, *Histoire philosophique et politique des établissemens & du commerce des les deux Indes*, vol. 6 (Amsterdam, 1770), 406.
20. See Hamish M. Scott, "The Seven Years' War and Europe's Ancien Régime," *War in History* 18, no. 4 (2011): 449–455; Patrick J. Speelman, "Father of the Modern Age," in *The Seven Years' War: Global Views*, ed. Mark Danley and Patrick Speelman (Brill, 2012), 533–536.
21. John Almon, *An Impartial History of the Late War: Deduced from the Committing of Hostilities in 1749, to the Signing of the Definitive Treaty of Peace in 1763* (London: Johnson and Curtis, 1763); John Entick, *The General History of the Late War: Containing It's Rise, Progress, and Event in Europe, Asia, Africa, and America . . .*, 5 vols. (London: Dilly, 1763–1764). For an early French account of the war, see Jean-Baptiste Targe, *Histoire d'Angleterre depuis le Traité d'Aix-la-Chapelle en 1748, jusqu'au Traité de Paris en 1763: Pour servir de continuation aux histoires de MM Smollett et Hume*, 5 vols. (London: Desaint, 1768).
22. Joseph Vicente de Rustant, *Decadas de la Guerra de Alemania, e Inglaterra, Francia, España, y Portugal: Con Reflexiones Politico-Militares sobre sus acontecimientos*, 10 vols. (Madrid: Ortega, 1765).
23. Anonymous, *Summarischer Auszug der neueren Kriegsgeschichte von 1756 bis 1763 oder Chronologische Tabellen, darinnen die wichtigsten Kriegsbegebenheiten die zu gleicher Zeit, zwischen denen im Krieg verwickelt gewesenen Hohen Machten, der Zeit-Ordnung nach, bis zu denen erfolgten Friedensschlüssen und deren Vollziehung, kürzlich und unpartheyisch beschrieben werden* (Frankfurt, 1764); see also Heinrich von Bünau's survey, apparently published after the author's death, covering the war between 1756 and 1761: Heinrich von Bünau, *Detail De La Guerre oder Umstaendliche Historie Des Krieges zwischen den Cronen Frankreich und Engelland Und Dero Alliirten in Teutschland*, 5 vols. (Ratisbonne: Bader, 1763–1767).
24. Georg Friedrich von Tempelhof, *Geschichte des siebenjährigen Krieges in Deutschland zwischen dem Könige von Preussen und der Kaiserin Königin mit ihren Alliierten*, 6 vols. (Berlin: Unger, 1783–1801; repr., Bibliotheca Rerum Militarium XXIX, 1986); Johann Wilhelm von Archenholz, "Geschichte des siebenjährigen Krieges in Deutschland von 1756 bis 1763," in *Aufklärung und Kriegserfahrung: Klassische Zeitzeugen zum Siebenjährigen Krieg*, ed. Johannes Kunisch (Frankfurt, 1793; repr., Deutscher Klassiker, 1996); an English translation was published in 1843: Johann Wilhelm von Archenholz, *The History of the Seven Years War in Germany*, trans. F. A. Catty (Jugel, 1843); on the context and publication history of Tempelhof's account, see Kunisch, *Aufklärung und Kriegserfahrung*.
25. Scott, "Seven Years' War," 450, 454.
26. Stephan Jaeger, "Die historiographische Inszenierung nationaler Identität: Johann Wilhelm von Archenholz, 'Geschichte des siebenjährigen Krieges,'" in

Performative Geschichtsschreibung: Forster, Herder, Schiller, Archenholz und die Brüder Schlegel (De Gruyter, 2011).

27. Robert Orme, *A History of the Military Transactions of the British Nation in Indostan, from the Year 1745 to Which Is Prefixed a Dissertation on the Establishments Made by Mahomedan Conquerors in Indostan* (London: Nourse, 1763; 2nd ed., 2 vols., London: Nourse, 1778); Johann Wilhelm von Archenholz, *Die Engländer in Indien nach Orme*, 3 vols. (Leipzig: Deutsche Buchhandlung, 1786–1788).

28. Johann Michael Friedrich Schulze, *Von dem Gebrauch der Geschichtskarte des siebenjährigen Krieges* (Berlin: Himburg, 1792).

29. Schulze, *Von dem Gebrauch der Geschichtskarte*, 11.

30. Großer Generalstab, ed., *Die Kriege Friedrichs des Grossen*, Dritter Teil, *Der Siebenjährige Krieg*, 12 vols. (Mittler, 1901–1913). See also the posthumously published Eberhard Kessel, *Das Ende des Siebenjährigen Krieges: Torgau und Bunzelwitz 1760–1763*, ed. Thomas Lindner (Schöningh, 2007). On "official" historiography, see also Martin Raschke, *Der politisierende Generalstab: Die friderizianischen Kriege in der amtlichen deutschen Militärgeschichtsschreibung 1890–1914* (Rombach, 1993); Bernhard R. Kroener, "'Den Krieg lernen': Die Feldzüge Friedrichs des Grossen in der amtlichen Geschichtsschreibung des Kaiserreiches," in *Archivarbeit für Preussen*, ed. Jürgen Kloosterhuis (Geheimen Staatsarchiv Preußischer Kulturbesitz, 2000).

31. See, for example, Arnold Schaefer, *Geschichte des siebenjährigen Kriegs*, 2 vols. (Berlin: Hertz, 1874); Arnold Schaefer, "Urkundliche Beiträge zur Geschichte des siebenjährigen Krieges," *Forschungen zur deutschen Geschichte* 17 (1877).

32. Julian S. Corbett, *England in the Seven Years' War: A Study in Combined Strategy*, 2 vols. (Longman, 1907; repr., Greenhill, 1992); see also Christopher Duffy's introduction to the 1992 reprint: "Corbett and His England in the Seven Years' War"; in chapter 11, I quote from the 1907 edition of Corbett's work. See also Richard Waddington, *La guerre des sept ans: Histoire diplomatique et militaire*, 5 vols. (Paris: Firmin-Didot et Cie, 1899–1914).

33. Lawrence H. Gipson, *The British Empire Before the American Revolution: Provincial Characteristics and Sectional Tendencies in the Era Preceding the American Crisis*, vols. 6–8 (Caxton, 1946–1954); on Gipson, see John Shy, "The Empire Remembered: Lawrence Henry Gipson, Historian," in *A People Numerous and Armed: Reflections on the Military Struggle for American Independence* (Oxford University Press, 1976).

34. Werner Krauss, "Über die Konstellation der deutschen Aufklärung," in *Studien zur deutschen und französischen Aufklärung* (Rütten & Loening, 1963), 317. I am grateful to Astrid Ackermann (Jena) for this reference.

35. Good examples of this are the source editions published in Cuba since the 1960s. For an overview of research on the Seven Years' War in West Germany after 1945, see Marian Füssel, "Zwischen lokalem Gedächtnis und kollektivem

Vergessen: Der Siebenjährige Krieg in der Erinnerungskultur der Bundesrepublik Deutschland," in *Umwelten: Ereignisse, Räume und Erfahrungen der Frühen Neuzeit—Festschrift für Manfred Jakubowski-Tiessen*, ed. Sven Petersen et al. (V&R unipress, 2015).

36. On literature published prior to 1986, see John Gavin Lydon, *Struggle for Empire: A Bibliography of the French and Indian War* (Garland, 1986); as a reference work, see Bud Hannings, *The French and Indian War: A Complete Chronology* (McFarland, 2011); Donald E. Stoetzel, *Encyclopedia of the French and Indian War in North America 1754–1763* (Heritage, 2008); Jean-Claude Castex, *Dictionnaire des batailles terrestres franco-anglaises de la Guerre de Sept Ans* (Les Presses de l'Université Laval, 2006).

37. Guy Frégault, *Canada: The War of the Conquest* (Oxford University Press, 1969; originally published in French in 1955). Selected relevant works include Frank W. Brecher, *Losing a Continent: France's North American Policy, 1753–1763* (Greenwood, 1998); Fred Anderson, *Crucible of War: The Seven Years' War and the Fate of the Empire in British North America, 1754–1766* (Knopf, 2000); William M. Fowler, *Empires at War: The Seven Years' War and the Struggle for North America 1754–1763* (Douglas and MacIntyre, 2005); Walter R. Borneman, *The French and Indian War: Deciding the Fate of North America* (HarperCollins, 2006); Warren R. Hofstra, ed., *Cultures in Conflict: The Seven Years' War in North America* (Penguin, 2007); Jacques Mathieu and Sophie Imbeault, *La Guerre des Canadiens, 1756–1763* (Septentrion, 2013); Christian Ayne Crouch, *Nobility Lost: French and Canadian Martial Cultures, Indians, and the End of New France* (Cornell University Press, 2014); William R. Nester, *The French and Indian War and the Conquest of New France* (University of Oklahoma Press, 2014); Bertrand Fonck and Laurent Veyssière, eds., *La Chute de la Nouvelle-France: De l'affaire Jumonville au traité de Paris* (Septentrion, 2015); Richard Hall, *Atlantic Politics, Military Strategy and the French and Indian War* (Palgrave Macmillan, 2016).

38. Franz A. J. Szabo, *The Seven Years War in Europe, 1756–1763* (Pearson Longman, 2008); Szabo's devastating judgment on Frederick is found on page 427. On Prussia's western provinces, see Horst Carl, *Okkupation und Regionalismus: Die preussischen Westprovinzen im Siebenjährigen Krieg* (Zabern, 1993); on the operational history of the northwest German theater, see Walther Mediger, *Herzog Ferdinand von Braunschweig-Lüneburg und die alliierte Armee im Siebenjährigen Krieg (1757–1762)*, prepared for publication and completed by Thomas Klingebiel (Hahnsche Buchhandlung, 2011); among older studies, see William von Hassell, *Die schlesischen Kriege und das Kurfürstenthum Hannover, Insbesondere die Katastrophe von Hastenbeck und Kloster Zeven: Mit Benutzung archivalischer Quellen* (Hanover: Hahn, 1879); for the war in the eastern provinces, see Xaver von Hasenkamp, *Ostpreussen unter dem Doppelaar: Historische Skizze der russischen Invasion in den Tagen des siebenjährigen Krieges* (Königsberg: Theile, 1866).

39. Michael Mann, *Bengalen im Umbruch: Die Herausbildung des britischen Kolonialstaates 1754–1793* (Steiner, 2000); Penderel Moon, *The British Conquest and Dominion of India* (Duckworth, 1989); James M. Vaughn, *The Politics of Empire at the Accession of George III: The East India Company and the Crisis and Transformation of Britain's Imperial State* (Yale University Press, 2019).
40. Tom Pocock, *Battle for Empire: The Very First World War 1756–63* (O'Mara, 1998); William R. Nester, *The First Global War: Britain, France, and the Fate of North America 1756–1775* (Praeger, 2000); Matt Schumann and Karl W. Schweizer, *The Seven Years War: A Transatlantic History* (Routledge, 2008); Daniel A. Baugh, *The Global Seven Years War, 1754–1763: Britain and France in a Great Power Contest* (Pearson, 2011); Sven Externbrink, ed., *Der Siebenjährige Krieg (1756–1763): Ein europäischer Weltkrieg im Zeitalter der Aufklärung* (Akademie, 2011); Danley and Speelman, *The Seven Years' War*; Frans De Bruyn and Shaun Regan, eds., *The Culture of the Seven Years War: Empire, Identity, and the Arts in the Eighteenth-Century Atlantic World* (University of Toronto Press, 2014); Edmond Dziembowski, *La Guerre de Sept Ans* (Septentrion, 2015); Klaus-Jürgen Bremm, *Preussen bewegt die Welt: Der Siebenjährige Krieg 1756–63* (Theiss, 2017).
41. See Bremm, *Preussen*.
42. Steffen Martus, *Aufklärung: Das deutsche 18. Jahrhundert—ein Epochenbild* (Rowohlt, 2015), 632–686.
43. Johannes Birgfeld, *Krieg und Aufklärung: Studien zum Kriegsdiskurs in der deutschsprachigen Literatur des 18. Jahrhunderts*, 2 vols. (Wehrhahn, 2012); Stefanie Stockhorst, ed., *Krieg und Frieden im 18. Jahrhundert: Kulturgeschichtliche Studien* (Wehrhahn, 2015).
44. Exceptions include the collected volumes: Externbrink, *Weltkrieg*; Danley and Speelman, *Global Views*; De Bruyn and Regan, *Culture*.
45. I will mention only research group SFB 437, active at Tübingen between 1999 and 2008; see Georg Schild, ed., *Kriegserfahrungen: Krieg und Gesellschaft in der Neuzeit; Neue Horizonte der Forschung* (Schöningh, 2009).
46. Schumann and Schweizer, *The Seven Years War*, 2.
47. Fabian Brändle et al., "Texte zwischen Erfahrung und Diskurs: Probleme der Selbstzeugnisforschung," in *Von der dargestellten Person zum erinnerten Ich: Europäische Selbstzeugnisse als historische Quellen 1500–1850*, ed. Kaspar von Greyerz et al. (Böhlau, 2001).
48. Joan Wallach Scott's well-known critique of the category of experience has significantly influenced my methodological reflections on how the category has been shaped in linguistic and discursive terms. Joan Wallach Scott, "The Evidence of Experience," *Critical Inquiry* 17, no. 4 (1991).
49. Christy Pichichero, *The Military Enlightenment: War and Culture in the French Empire from Louis XIV to Napoleon* (Cornell University Press, 2017); Ilya Berkovich, *Motivation in War: The Experience of Common Soldiers in Old-Regime Europe*

(Cambridge University Press, 2017); Yuval Noah Harari, *The Ultimate Experience: Battlefield Revelations and the Making of Modern War Culture, 1450–2000* (Palgrave Macmillan, 2008); Katrin Möbius and Sascha Möbius, *Prussian Army Soldiers and the Seven Years' War: The Psychology of Honour* (Bloomsbury Academic, 2020).

50. Claudia Ulbrich et al., eds., *Selbstzeugnis und Person: Transkulturelle Perspektiven* (Böhlau, 2012).

51. Emma Rothschild, *The Inner Life of Empires: An Eighteenth-Century History* (Princeton University Press, 2011); Linda Colley, *The Ordeal of Elizabeth Marsh: A Woman in World History* (HarperCollins, 2007).

52. For an overview of historiography of experience informed by the sociology of knowledge, see Nikolaus Buschmann and Horst Carl, "Zugänge zur Erfahrungsgeschichte des Krieges: Forschung, Theorie, Fragestellung," in *Die Erfahrung des Krieges. Erfahrungsgeschichtliche Perspektiven von der Französischen Revolution bis zum Zweiten Weltkrieg*, ed. Nikolaus Buschmann and Horst Carl (Schöningh, 2001). For a history of science approach to the Seven Years' War, see Ewa Anklam, *Wissen nach Augenmass: Militärische Beobachtung und Berichterstattung im Siebenjährigen Krieg* (LIT, 2007); for military knowledge in contemporary literary production, see Birgfeld, *Krieg und Aufklärung*; for information history, using the example of the War of the Spanish Succession, see Matthias Pohlig, *Marlboroughs Geheimnis: Strukturen und Funktionen der Informationsgewinnung im Spanischen Erbfolgekrieg* (Böhlau, 2016).

53. Peter Burke, *A Social History of Knowledge: From Gutenberg to Diderot* (Polity, 2000), 11.

54. For a listing of English-language testimonies for the period 1755–1763, see Christopher Sampson Handley, *An Annotated Bibliography of Diaries in English*, vol. 3, *Diaries 1745 to 1779* (Hanover, 2002). There are several existing anthologies of first-person accounts for the French and Indian War: see Anonymous, Narratives of the French and Indian War, 4 vols. (Leonaur, 2008–2019); Timothy J. Shannon, *The Seven Years' War in North America: A Brief History with Documents* (St. Martin's, 2014).

55. On Austria, see Christopher Duffy, *Sieben Jahre Krieg: 1756–1763; Die Armee Maria Theresias* (öbv and hpt, 2003); Christopher Duffy, *By Force of Arms: The Austrian Army in the Seven Years War*, vol. 2 (Emperor's Press, 2000). Duffy's assessment suggests that in the case of Austria, equal roles were played by backwardness in the publishing industry and Austrian generals' reluctance to recount the war in written form. For a helpful research overview, see Michael Hochedlinger, "'Bella gerant alii . . .'? On the State of Early Modern Military History in Austria," *Austrian History Yearbook* 30 (1999).

56. On literacy, tradition, and publishing, see Berkovich, *Motivation in War*, 39–54.

57. Winfried Schulze, ed., *Ego-Dokumente: Annäherung an den Menschen in der Geschichte* (Akademie, 1996); Benigna von Krusenstjern, "Was sind Selbstzeugnisse?

Begriffskritische und quellenkundliche Überlegungen anhand von Beispielen aus dem 17. Jahrhundert," *Historische Anthropologie* 2, no. 3 (1994).

58. Yuval Noah Harari, "Military Memoirs: A Historical Overview of the Genre from the Middle Ages to Late Modern Era," *War in History* 14, no. 3 (2007); Michael Epkenhans et al., eds., *Militärische Erinnerungskultur: Soldaten im Spiegel von Biographien, Memoiren und Selbstzeugnissen* (Schöningh, 2006).

59. Correspondence from common soldiers is usually found in the form of individual letters. See Christian F. Zander, ed., *Fundstücke. Dokumente und Briefe einer preussischen Bauernfamilie (1747–1953)* (Kovač, 2015); Rolf Dieter Kohl, "Ein Brief des Wiblingwerder Bauernsohnes Johann Hermann Dresel aus dem Siebenjährigen Krieg," *Der Märker* 28 (1979); Eduard Schulte, "Aus Westfälischen Feldpostbriefen des Siebenjährigen Krieges," *Westfalen* 9 (1918); Hans Müller-Brauel, "Alte niedersächsische Feldbriefe," *Niedersachsen* 20, no. 9 (1914/15).

60. [Peter Williamson], *French and Indian Cruelty; Exemplified in the Life and Various Vicissitudes of Fortune . . .* (York: Nickson, 1757); Ian McCulloch and Timothy Todish, eds., *Through So Many Dangers: The Memoirs and Adventures of Robert Kirk, Late of the Royal Highland Regiment* (Purple Mountain Press, 2004), 21.

61. Heribert Teggers, ed., "Der 7jährige Krieg im Klevischen: Aus dem Tagebuch eines Gocher Schlossermeisters," in *Heimatkalender für das Klever Land* (1958), 85–88, here 85.

62. Klaus Dittmann, "Notizen des Pfarrers im Weiterstädter Kirchenbuch während der Schlesischen Kriege und dem 7jährigen Krieg," *Hessische Familienkunde* 27, no. 1 (2004); Karl Betz, *Der Siebenjährige Krieg in den Kirchenbüchern von Ettingshausen und Queckborn* (Schriftenreihe der heimatgeschichtlichen Vereinigung Reiskirchen, 1994).

63. [Johann Christian Becher], *Wahrhaftige Nachricht derer Begebenheiten so sich in den Herzogthum Weimar bey den gewaltigen Kriege Friedrichs II Königs von Preusen mit der Königin von Ungarn Marien, Theresien sammt ihren Bundsgenossen zugetragen/patriotisch aufgeschrieben von Johann Christian Becher* (handwritten manuscript), Herzogin Anna Amalia Bibliothek, Weimar, Q 419, n.d.; Günter Lanitzki, *Galeeren auf dem Peenestrom: Die preussisch-schwedische Seeschlacht 1759 oder wie die Kartoffel nach Skandinavien kam* (Edition Ost, 2000); Tomasz Karpinski, "Unknown Iconographic Sources for the History of the Russian Army: The Russian Garrison in Elblag During the Seven Years' War Through the Observation of Eyewitnesses," *History of Military Affairs* 11 (2020), http://www.milhist.info/2020/09/14/karpinski.

64. For Major Georg von Szent-Ivány's account of the Battle of Prague, see Major Sommeregger, "Die Schlacht von Prag im Jahre 1757: Nach den Erinnerungen eines Augenzeugen," *Mitteilungen des k.u.k. Kriegs-Archivs* 7 (1911); Jürgen Kloosterhuis, "Der Husar aus dem Buch: Die Zietenbiographie der Frau von

Blumenthal im Kontext der Pflege brandenburg-preussischer Militärtradition um 1800," *Jahrbuch für brandenburgische Landesgeschichte* 52 (2001).

65. See documentation by Martin H. Evans and Geoffrey Hooper, "Three Misleading Diaries: John Knyveton, MD—from Naval Surgeon's Mate to Man-Midwife," *International Journal of Maritime History* 26, no. 4 (2014); see rather Anonymous, "Journal of a Naval Surgeon 1758–1763," in *Naval Yarns: Letters and Anecdotes, Comprising Accounts of Sea Fights and Wrecks, Actions with Pirates and Privateers, from 1616 to 1831*, ed. William Henry Long (London: Gibbings, 1899).

66. Götz von Lojewksi reconstructs the work's complex textual history: http://www.sonicduck.de/wappenkunde/?p=345, accessed November 17, 2017. The account is taken as contemporary in, for example, Bernhard R. Kroener: "Die Geburt eines Mythos—die 'schiefe Schlachtordnung': Leuthen, 5. Dezember," in *Schlachten der Weltgeschichte*, ed. Stig Förster et al. (Beck, 2001).

67. Hans Bleckwenn, ed., *Preussische Soldatenbriefe* (Biblio, 1982). At the time of first publication in 1901, originals of the letters seem still to have been held at the Fürstlich Stolbergschen Hausarchiv in Wernigerode.

68. Dietrich Kerler, *Aus dem siebenjährigen Krieg: Tagebuch des preussischen Musketiers Dominicus* (Munich: Beck, 1891; repr., Biblio, 1972), x–xi; Werner Vogel, ed., *Die Blutbibel des Friedrich Freiherr von der Trenck (1727–1794)* (Böhlau, 2014). It has been established that the handwriting is in blood but not as yet whether this is Trenck's blood.

69. Friedrich II, *Die politische Correspondenz Friedrichs des Großen*, ed. Johann Gustav Droysen et al., 48 vols. (Berlin: Duncker & Humblot, 1879–2015); Gustav Berthold Volz, ed., *Die Werke Friedrichs des Grossen*, 10 vols. (Hobbing, 1913–1914).

70. Gayatri Chakravorty Spivak, "Can the Subaltern Speak?," in *Marxism and the Interpretation of Culture*, ed. Cary Nelson and Lawrence Grossberg (Macmillan, 1988).

71. Ulrich Bräker, *Sämtliche Schriften*, vol. 4, *Lebensgeschichte und vermischte Schriften* (Beck, 2000). For an English translation of Bräker's memoir, see Ulrich Bräker, *The Life Story and Real Adventures of the Poor Man of Toggenburg*, trans. David Bowman (Edinburgh University Press, 1970).

72. Olaudah Equiano, *The Interesting Narrative of the Life of Olaudah Equiano*, ed. Brycchan Carey (Oxford World Classics, 1990). For further sources, see Vincent Carretta, ed., *Unchained Voices: An Anthology of Black Authors in the English-Speaking World of the Eighteenth Century* (University Press of Kentucky, 1996).

73. Hellmut G. Haasis, *Spuren der Besiegten*, vol. 2, *Von der Erhebung gegen den Absolutismus bis zu den republikanischen Freischärlern 1848/49* (Rowohlt, 1984); on this, see also Michael Sikora, *Disziplin und Desertion: Strukturprobleme militärischer Organisation im 18. Jahrhundert* (Duncker & Humblot, 1996), 19; for the English-speaking world, see Peter Way, "Class and the Common Soldier in the Seven Years' War," *Labor History* 44, no. 4 (2003): 473–481.

74. Sven Externbrink, "Voltaire zwischen Candide und Roi-Philosophe," in Externbrink, *Weltkrieg*.
75. Bärbel Raschke, ed., *Der Briefwechsel zwischen Luise Dorothée von Sachsen-Gotha und Voltaire (1751–1767)* (Leipziger Universitätsverlag, 1998); Günter Berger and Julia Wassermann, eds., *Vetternwirtschaft: Briefwechsel zwischen Friedrich II. und Luise Dorothea von Sachsen-Gotha* (Duncker & Humblot, 2012); on the relay station, see page 12 and, for an example, pages 44–45.
76. Horace Walpole, *The Yale Edition of Horace Walpole's Correspondence*, ed. Wilmarth Sheldon Lewis, 48 vols. (Yale University Press, 1937–1983); Johann Joseph Khevenhüller-Metsch, *Aus der Zeit Maria Theresias: Tagebuch des Fürsten Johann Joseph Khevenhüller-Metsch; Kaiserlichen Oberhofmeisters*, ed. Rudolf Khevenhüller-Metsch and Hanns Schlitter, 8 vols. (Holzhausen, 1907–1925). The relevant volumes are volume 3, *1752–1755* (1910); volume 4, *1756–1757* (1914); and volume 5, *1758–1759* (1911).
77. Andreas Georg Wähner, *Tagebuch aus dem Siebenjährigen Krieg*, ed. Sigrid Dahmen (Universitätsverlag Göttingen, 2012); on Wähner's life, see Sigrid Dahmen, "Andreas Georg Wähner (1693–1762): Professor für morgenländische Sprachen in Göttingen," *Göttinger Jahrbuch* 60 (2012).
78. John Frederic Price and Henry Dodwell, eds., *The Private Diary of Ananda Ranga Pillai, Dubash to Joseph François Dupleix . . . : A Record of Matters Political, Historical, Social and Personal from 1736 to 1761* (Government Press of Madras, 1904–1928). Price edited volumes 1 through 3, and Dodwell edited volumes 4 through 12. On Pillai, see Chidambaram S. Srinivasachari, *Ananda Ranga Pillai, the "Pepys" of French India* (Varadachary, 1940).
79. Price and Dodwell, *Diary of Pillai*. Volumes 10–12 are relevant.
80. Price and Dodwell, *Diary of Pillai*, 12:126 and n1.
81. Heinrich Melchior Mühlenberg, *The Correspondence of Heinrich Melchior Mühlenberg*, ed. Timothy J. Wengert and Wolfgang Splitter, vol. 3, *1753–1756*, and vol. 4, *1757–1762* (Picton, 2010).
82. Friedrich Walter, ed., *Maria Theresia: Briefe und Aktenstücke in Auswahl*, 2nd ed. (Wissenschaftliche Buchgesellschaft, 1982).
83. Marion Kobelt-Groch, "Friedrich II. und Maria Theresia: Der Siebenjährige Krieg—Ein Kampf der Geschlechter?," *Historische Mitteilungen der Ranke-Gesellschaft* 18 (2005); on Pompadour's diplomacy, see Eva Kathrin Dade, *Madame de Pompadour: Die Mätresse und die Diplomatie* (Böhlau, 2010).
84. [Charlotte Brown], "The Journal of Charlotte Brown, Matron of the General Hospital with the English Forces in America, 1754–1756," in *Colonial Captivities, Marches and Journeys*, ed. Isabel M. Calder (Macmillan, 1935).
85. On Karsch, see the section "A Writer's War" in chapter 8 in this volume.
86. Marian Füssel, "Between Dissimulation and Sensation: Female Soldiers in Eighteenth Century Warfare," *Journal for Eighteenth-Century Studies* 41, no. 4 (2018).

On the role of women in the war in the Holy Roman Empire, see Marian Füssel, "Unsichtbare Zeugen: Frauen im Siebenjährigen Krieg," in *Karrieren in Preussen—Frauen in Männerdomänen*, ed. Susanne Brockfeld and Ingeborg Schnelling-Reinicke (Duncker & Humblot, 2020).

87. Paul-Ulrich Flashar, ed., *Familienbuch Michaelis von Tschirschky*, vol. 2, *Memoiren der Eleonore Juliane von Rehdiger verw. Freifrau von Lüttwitz geb. von Falkenhayn 1713–1784; Das Tagebuch der Urahne; Ein Lebensbild aus dem 18 Jahrhundert* (self-published by Gottfried Michaelis, 1996).

88. Neil Cogswell, ed., *Horace St. Paul: Journals 1756–1760*, 8 vols. (Gralene, 1996–2007).

89. Andrew Cormack and Alan Jones, eds., *The Journal of Corporal Todd 1745–1762* (Sutton, 2001); Jean Lemoine, ed., *Sous Louis le Bien-aimé: Correspondance amoureuse et militaire d'un officier (Antoine-Rigobert Mopinot de la Chapotte) pendant la guerre de sept-ans 1757–1763* (Calmann-Lévy, 1905); Andrei Bolotov, *Leben und Abenteuer des Andrej Bolotow von ihm selbst für seine Nachkommen aufgeschrieben*, 2 vols. (Beck, 1990); Christian Wilhelm von Prittwitz, *"Ich bin ein Preusse . . .": Jugend und Kriegsleben eines preussischen Offiziers im Siebenjährigen Krieg* (Hüttemann, 1989); Marian Füssel and Sven Petersen with Gerald Scholz, eds., *Johann Heinrich Ludewig Grotehenn, Briefe aus dem Siebenjährigen Krieg: Lebensbeschreibung und Tagebuch* (Militärgeschichtliches Forschungsamt, 2012).

90. Louis Antoine de Bougainville, *Écrits sur le Canada: Memoires—Journal—Lettres* (Septentrion, 2003); on this, see also Sven Externbrink, "Europäische gegen amerikanische Kriegskultur: Louis-Antoine de Bougainville und der French and Indian War (1756–1760)," in *Das ist Militärgeschichte! Probleme—Projekte—Perspektiven*, ed. Christian Th. Müller and Matthias Rogg (Schöningh, 2013).

91. The first French edition was prepared by Henri Raymond Casgrain, ed., *Voyage au Canada dans le nord de l'Amerique Septentrionale, fait depuis L'An 1751 a 1761 par J. C. B.* (Quebec: Brousseau, 1887); for a more recent, annotated edition in English, see Andrew Gallup, ed., *Memoir of a French and Indian War Soldier Jolicoeur Charles Bonin* (Heritage, 2007). John Knox, *An Historical Journal of the Campaigns in North America: For the Years 1757, 1758, 1759 and 1760*, 3 vols. (London: Johnston, 1769; repr., Books for Library Press, 1970). John Knox, *An Historical Journal of the Campaigns in North America: For the Years 1757, 1758, 1759 and 1760.* Ed. Arthur G. Doughty, 3 vols. Toronto: Champlain Society, 1914. Earl John Chapman and Ian Macpherson McCulloch, eds. *Dangerous Service: Memoirs of a Black Watch Officer in the French and Indian War—John Grant, 1741–1828.* Robin Brass Studio, 2017.

92. See Marian Füssel and Sven Petersen, "Ananas und Kanonen: Zur materiellen Kultur globaler Kriege im 18. Jahrhundert," *Historische Anthropologie* 23, no. 3 (2015).

93. See Sascha Möbius, "'Von Jast und Hitze wie vertaumelt': Überlegungen zur Wahrnehmung von Gewalt durch preussische Soldaten im Siebenjährigen Krieg," *Forschungen zur Brandenburgischen und Preußischen Geschichte*, n.s., vol. 12 (2002); Pichichero, *Military Enlightenment*.

94. Martin Dinges, "Soldatenkörper in der Frühen Neuzeit: Erfahrungen mit einem unzureichend geschützten, formierten und verletzten Körper in Selbstzeugnissen," in *Körper-Geschichten*, ed. Richard van Dülmen (Fischer, 1996).
95. See Antje Fuchs, "Der Siebenjährige Krieg als virtueller Religionskrieg an Beispielen aus Preussen, Österreich, Kurhannover und Grossbritannien," in *Religionskriege im Alten Reich und in Alteuropa*, ed. Franz Brendle and Anton Schindling (Aschendorff, 2006).
96. See the chapter "Representation, Event and Structure" in Koselleck, *Futures Past*, 110 (translations of quotations were occasionally modified). For recent historiographical discussion of structure and event, see Andreas Suter and Manfred Hettling, eds., *Struktur und Ereignis* (Vandenhoeck & Ruprecht, 2001).
97. Georg Simmel, "The Problem of Historical Time," in *Essays on Interpretation in Social Science*, ed. and trans. Guy Oakes (Manchester University Press, 1980), 144; on the context, see the editor's comments, 523f.; on its reception in the contemporary sociology of violence, see Wolfgang Knöbl, "Jenseits des situationistischen Paradigmas der Gewaltforschung," in *Narrative der Gewalt: Interdisziplinäre Analysen*, ed. Ferdinand Sutterlüty et al. (Campus, 2019).
98. Simmel, "Problem of Historical Time," 139.
99. Simmel, "Problem of Historical Time," 140–141.
100. Simmel, "Problem of Historical Time," 142 (translation modified).
101. Simmel, "Problem of Historical Time," 142, 143.
102. On this, see Carlo Ginzburg, "Microhistory: Two or Three Things That I Know About It," trans. John Tedeschi and Anne C. Tedeschi, *Critical Inquiry* 20, no. 2 (1993).
103. The archives in London, Paris, Vienna, and Berlin are by far the most important. On the precarious condition of Prussian records as a result of losses in World War II, see Jürgen Kloosterhuis et al., eds., *Militär und Gesellschaft in Preussen: Quellen zur Militärsozialisation 1713–1806; Archivalien in Berlin, Dessau und Leipzig*, pt. 1, vol. 1, *Geheimes Staatsarchiv Preussischer Kulturbesitz* (Geheimes Staatsarchiv Preußischer Kulturbesitz, 2015).
104. Marian Füssel, *Der Siebenjährige Krieg: Ein Weltkrieg im 18. Jahrhundert*, 2nd ed. (Beck, 2013).

1. Geopolitics Between Reich and Empire

1. The problem is well framed in terms of global history in Mark H. Danley, "The 'Problem' of the Seven Years' War," in Danley & Speelman, *Global Views*.
2. Danley, "The 'Problem,'" xxx.
3. On the temporality of the conflict, see Danley, "The 'Problem,'" xxv–xxix.
4. Baugh, *Global War*, 1–33.

5. Daniel A. Baugh, "Great Britain's Blue Water Policy, 1689–1815," *International History Review* 10, no. 1 (1988); John Brewer, *The Sinews of Power: War, Money and the English State 1688–1783* (Hutchinson, 1988); Daniel Robinson, "Giving Peace to Europe: European Geopolitics, Colonial Political Culture, and the Hanoverian Monarchy in British North America, ca. 1740–63," *William and Mary Quarterly* 73, no. 2 (2016); Marie Peters, "Early Hanoverian Consciousness: Empire or Europe?," *English Historical Review* 122, no. 497 (2007).
6. Tony Hayter, "England, Hannover, Preußen: Gesellschaftliche und wirtschaftliche Grundlagen der britischen Beteiligung an Operationen auf dem Kontinent während des Siebenjährigen Krieges," in *Europa im Zeitalter Friedrichs des Großen: Wirtschaft, Gesellschaft, Kriege*, ed. Bernhard R. Kroener (Oldenbourg, 1989); Uriel Dann, *Hanover and Great Britain 1740–1760: Diplomacy and Survival* (Leicester University Press, 1991); Hermann Wellenreuther, "Die Bedeutung desSiebenjährigen Krieges für die englisch-hannoveranischen Beziehungen," in *England und Hannover: England and Hanover*, ed. Adolf M. Birke and Kurt Kluxen (Saur, 1986); Jeremy Black, *Continental Commitment: Britain, Hanover and Interventionism 1714–1793* (Routledge, 2005).
7. Virginia H. Aksan, "The Ottoman Absence from the Battlefields of the Seven Years' War," in Danley and Speelman, *The Seven Years' War*; Rudolf Otto Karl Porsch, *Die Beziehungen Friedrichs des Grossen zur Türkei bis zum Beginn und während des siebenjährigen Krieges* (Marburg: Ehrhardt, 1897).
8. On the "interwar period" in the Franco-British conflict, see François Ternat, *Partager le monde: Rivalités impériales franco-britanniques, 1748–1756* (Presses de l'Université Paris Sorbonne, 2015).
9. Gustav Berthold Volz and Georg Küntzel, eds., *Preussische und Österreichische Acten zur Vorgeschichte des siebenjährigen Krieges* (Leipzig: Hirzel, 1899), lxvii.
10. Danley, "The 'Problem,'" xxix and n13.
11. Arthur H. Buffinton, *The Second Hundred Years' War, 1689–1815* (H. Holt, 1929).
12. François Crouzet, "The Second Hundred Years War: Some Reflections," *French History* 10 (1996): 432; François Crouzet, *La guerre économique franco-anglaise au XVIIIe siècle* (Fayard, 2008).
13. See Füssel, "Global Wars," 394.
14. Daniel K. Richter, *Facing East from Indian Country: A Native History of Early America* (Harvard University Press, 2001). On terminology: Although *Indian* has less negative connotations in German than in English, I will use the term *Native American* in these pages. Tribal names, which are often used in its stead, like Iroquois and Delaware, are often pejorative, and the names used by the tribes themselves—Haudenosaunee (Iroquois) and Lenni Lenape (Delaware)—will be recognized by few readers. Hence, I use the term *Indian* in these pages. For a balanced treatment of the question, see Aram Mattioli, *Verlorene Welten: Eine Geschichte der Indianer Nordamerikas 1700–1910* (Klett-Cotta, 2017), 31–32;

Michael A. McDonnell, *Masters of Empire: Great Lakes Indians and the Making of America* (Hill & Wang, 2016).

15. Fred Anderson, *The War That Made America: A Short History of the French and Indian War* (Viking, 2005), 59, 160.
16. Wolfram Wette, ed., *Der Krieg des kleinen Mannes: Eine Militärgeschichte von unten* (Piper, 1992); Way, "Class and the Common Soldier."
17. On the Compagnie des Indes, see Philippe Haudrère, *La Compagnie française des Indes aux XVIII siècle*, 2 vols., 2nd ed. (Les Indes Savantes, 2005); for a shorter, popular account, see Philippe Haudrère and Gérard Le Bouedec, *Les compagnies des Indes* (Ouest France, 2015); on the East India Company, see Philip Lawson, *The East India Company: A History* (Longman, 1993); Huw V. Bowen, *The Business of Empire: The East India Company and Imperial Britain, 1756–1833* (Cambridge University Press, 2007).
18. On the permanent trade war between Britain and France, see Crouzet, *La guerre économique*.
19. Michael Mann, "Der ungeliebte Krieg: Compagnie des Indes und East India Company als Kombattanten in einem globalen Konflikt, 1742–1763," in Externbrink, *Weltkrieg*, 102.
20. Mann, "Der ungeliebte Krieg," 101.
21. Michael Mann, *Geschichte Südasiens: 1500 bis heute* (WBG, 2010), 10 and 61.
22. Mann, "Der ungeliebte Krieg," 103. See also Mark Häberlein and Michaela Schmölz-Häberlein, *Halles Netzwerk im Siebenjährigen Krieg: Kriegserfahrungen und Kriegsdeutungen in einer globalen Kommunikationsgemeinschaft* (Franckeschen Stiftungen, 2020).
23. Reuben Gold Thwaites, ed., *The Jesuit Relations and Allied Documents*, vol. 70, *All Missions: 1747–1764*, and vol. 71, *Lower Canada, Illinois: 1759–1791—Miscellaneous Errata* (Pageant, 1959); Mark Häberlein and Michaela Schmölz-Häberlein, "Der Siebenjährige Krieg und das Kommunikationsnetz des Halleschen Pietismus," in *Der Siebenjährige Krieg: Mikro- und Makroperspektiven*, ed. Marian Füssel (De Gruyter, 2021).
24. Johannes Burkhardt, *Abschied vom Religionskrieg: Der siebenjährige Krieg und die päpstliche Diplomatie* (Niemeyer, 1985).
25. Jessica L. Harland-Jacobs, *Builders of Empire: Freemasons and British Imperialism, 1717–1927* (University of North Carolina Press, 2007); Andreas Önnerfors, "Freimaurerei und Offiziertum im 18. Jahrhundert," *Militär und Gesellschaft in der Frühen Neuzeit* 14, no. 1 (2010) (on the Seven Years' War, see 237–238).
26. Harland-Jacobs, *Builders of Empire*, 58. On coping with boredom, see John Knox, *An Historical Journal of the Campaigns in North America: For the Years 1757, 1758, 1759 and 1760*, 3 vols. (London: Johnston, 1769; repr., Books for Library Press, 1970), 1:182–183.
27. Önnerfors, "Freimaurerei," 237.

28. Marian Füssel, "Lernen—Transfer—Aneignung: Theorien und Begriffe für eine transkulturelle Militärgeschichte," in *Waffen—Wissen—Wandel: Anpassung und Lernen in transkulturellen Erstkonflikten*, ed. Birthe Kundrus and Dierk Walter (Hamburger Edition, 2012), 34–49.
29. See Kaushik Roy, "The Hybrid Military Establishment of the East India Company in South Asia: 1750–1849," *Journal of Global History* 6 (2011); Gerald James Bryant, "Indigenous Mercenaries in the Service of European Imperialists: The Case of the Sepoys in the Early British Indian Army, 1750–1800," *War in History* 7 (2000).
30. On the cultural repercussions of the war in Britain, see Carol Watts, *The Cultural Work of Empire: The Seven Years' War and the Imagining of the Shandean State* (Edinburgh University Press, 2007).
31. Baugh, *The Global Seven Years War*, 283.
32. Baumgart, "Ausbruch"; Joseph Weiss, "Der Streit über den Ursprung des siebenjährigen Krieges," *Historisches Jahrbuch* 18 (1897); Patrice Louis-René Higonnet, "The Origins of the Seven Years' War," *Journal of Modern History* 40 (1968); Karl W. Schweizer, "The Seven Years' War: A System Perspective," in *The Origins of War in Early Modern Europe*, ed. Jeremy Black (John Donald, 1987).
33. The two standard accounts are Reed Browning, *The War of the Austrian Succession* (St. Martin's Press, 1993), and Matthew Smith Anderson, *The War of the Austrian Succession, 1740–1748* (Longman, 1995).
34. Ferdinand Wagner, "Die europäischen Mächte in der Beurtheilung Friedrichs des Grossen 1746–1757," *Mitteilungen des Instituts für Österreichische Geschichtsforschung* 20 (1899).
35. Wagner, "Die europäischen Mächte," 403–415; Peter Hoffmann, *Friedrich II. und Russland: Die erste Periode seiner Regierung bis zum Hubertusburger Frieden 1763* (NORA Verlagsgemeinschaft, 2019).
36. Wagner, "Die europäischen Mächte," 417–418.
37. Johannes Kunisch, "Der Historikerstreit über den Ausbruch des Siebenjährigen Krieges (1756)," in *Friedrich der Große in seiner Zeit* (Beck, 2008); Johannes Burkhardt, "Wie ein verlorener Krieg zum Sieg umgeschrieben wurde: Friedrich der Große, der Siebenjährige Krieg und der Friede von Hubertusburg," in *Sprache, Macht, Frieden: Augsburger Beiträge zur Historischen Friedens- und Konfliktforschung*, ed. Johannes Burkhardt et al. (Wißner, 2014), 270–284.
38. Leopold von Ranke, *Geschichte von Österreich und Preußen zwischen den Friedensschlüssen von Aachen und Hubertusburg* (Leipzig: Duncker & Humblot, 1875); Albert Naudé, "Friedrich der Große vor dem Ausbruch des Siebenjährigen Krieges," *Historische Zeitschrift* 55 (1886) and 56 (1886); Reinhold Koser, "Zum Ursprung des Siebenjährigen Krieges," *Historische Zeitschrift* 74 (1895).
39. Max Lehmann, *Friedrich der Große und der Ursprung des Siebenjährigen Krieges* (Leipzig: Hirzel, 1894).

40. Hans Delbrück, "Der Ursprung des Siebenjährigen Krieges," in *Erinnerungen, Aufsätze und Reden*, ed. Hans Delbrück (Stilke, 1902).
41. Frederick II, "Political Testament," 1752, in C. A. Macartney, ed., *The Habsburg and Hohenzollern Dynasties in the Seventeenth and Eighteenth Centuries* (Harper & Row, 1970); for the original French text, see *Politische Correspondenz: Ergänzungsband: Die politischen Testamente Friedrichs des Grossen*, ed. Gustav Berthold Volz (Reimar Hobbing, 1920).
42. Frederick II, "Political Testament," 341.
43. René Hanke, *Brühl und das Renversement des alliances: Die antipreußische Außenpolitik des Dresdener Hofes 1744–1756* (LIT, 2006).
44. Stefan Kroll, *Soldaten im 18. Jahrhundert zwischen Friedensalltag und Kriegserfahrung: Lebenswelten und Kultur in der kursächsischen Armee 1728–1796* (Schöningh, 2006).
45. Reiner Pommerin and Lothar Schilling, "Denkschrift des Grafen Kaunitz zur mächtepolitischen Konstellation nach dem Aachener Frieden von 1748," in *Expansion und Gleichgewicht: Studien zur europäischen Mächtepolitik des Ancien Régime*, ed. Johannes Kunisch (Duncker & Humblot, 1986), 205. See also Johannes Kunisch, "Die militärische Bedeutung Schlesiens und das Scheitern der österreichischen Rückeroberungspläne im Siebenjährigen Krieg," in *Kontinuität und Wandel: Schlesien zwischen Österreich und Preußen*, ed. Peter Baumgart and Ulrich Schmilewski (Thorbecke, 1990); Christopher Duffy, "Militärische Aspekte Schlesiens im Siebenjährigen Krieg," *Jahrbuch der Schlesischen Friedrich-Wilhelms-Universität zu Breslau*, vol. 42–44 (2001–2003).
46. On this quote, see Michael G. Müller, "Russland und der Siebenjährige Krieg: Beitrag zu einer Kontroverse," *Jahrbücher für Geschichte Osteuropas* 28 (1980).
47. Barbara Stollberg-Rilinger, *Maria Theresa: The Habsburg Empress in Her Time* (Princeton University Press, 2021), 404.
48. Bernhard R. Kroener, "Herrschaftsverdichtung als Kriegsursache: Wirtschaft und Rüstung der europäischen Großmächte im Siebenjährigen Krieg," in *Wie Kriege entstehen: Zum historischen Hintergrund von Staatskonflikten*, ed. Bernd Wegner (Schöningh, 2000), 149.
49. Walther Mediger, *Moskaus Weg nach Europa: Der Aufstieg Russlands zum Europäischen Machtstaat im Zeitalter Friedrichs des Großen* (Westermann, 1952); Herbert H. Kaplan, *Russia and the Outbreak of the Seven Years' War* (University of California Press, 1968); Müller, "Russland"; Hamish M. Scott, *The Emergence of the Eastern Powers, 1756–1775* (Cambridge University Press, 2001).
50. Eckhard Buddruss, *Die französische Deutschlandpolitik 1756–1789* (P. von Zabern, 1995), 70–119.
51. Johann Heinrich Gottlob von Justi, *Die Chimäre des Gleichgewichts von Europa: Eine Abhandlung, worinnen die Nichtigkeit und Ungerechtigkeit dieses zeitherigen Lehrgebäudes der Staatskunst deutlich vor Augen gelegt* (Altona: David Iversen, 1758);

Quote from Johannes Kunisch, *Das Mirakel des Hauses Brandenburg. Studien zum Verhältnis von Kabinettspolitik und Kriegführung im Zeitalter des Siebenjährigen Krieges* (Oldenbourg, 1978), 38n48.

52. Kroener, "Herrschaftsverdichtung," 151.
53. Marc Höchner, *Selbstzeugnisse von Schweizer Söldneroffizieren im 18. Jahrhundert* (V&R Unipress, 2015), 25–35; Alice Clare Carter, *The Dutch Republic in Europe in the Seven Years' War* (Macmillan, 1972), 103–152; Paul Meyer, *Zeitgenössische Beurteilung und Auswirkung des Siebenjährigen Krieges (1756–1763) in der evangelischen Schweiz* (Helbing & Lichtenhahn, 1955), 118–135.
54. Johannes Burkhardt, "Die Friedlosigkeit der Frühen Neuzeit: Grundlegung einer Theorie der Bellizität in Europa," *Zeitschrift für Historische Forschung* 24 (1997).
55. Burkhardt, "Die Friedlosigkeit."
56. Brewer, *Sinews of Power*, 21. See also Larry Neal, "Interpreting Power and Profit in Economic History: A Case Study of the Seven Years' War," *Journal of Economic History* 37 (1977).
57. Patrick Karl O'Brien, "Fiscal and Financial Preconditions for the Rise of British Naval Hegemony, 1485–1815," Working Paper No. 91/05 (London School of Economics, November 2005), 37.
58. Rafael Torres Sánchez, ed., *War, State and Development: Fiscal-Military States in the Eighteenth Century* (Ediciones Universidad de Navarra, 2007); Christopher Storrs, ed., *The Fiscal-Military State in Eighteenth-Century Europe: Essays in Honour of P. G. M. Dickson* (Ashgate, 2009).
59. Kroener, "Herrschaftsverdichtung," 146.
60. Heinz Duchhardt, *Balance of Power und Pentarchie: Internationale Beziehungen 1700–1785* (Schöningh, 1997), 233. Duchhardt goes so far as to call India a "quantité négligeable" in "state-political terms."
61. Duchhardt, *Balance of Power*, 234.
62. Mattioli, *Verlorene Welten*, 36–37.
63. Mattioli, *Verlorene Welten*, 40–41.
64. Richard White, *The Middle Ground: Indians, Empires, and Republics in the Great Lakes Region, 1650–1815* (Cambridge University Press, 1991).
65. Marian Füssel, "Stehende Söldner-Heere? Europäische Rekrutierungspraktiken im Vergleich (1648–1815)," in *Soldgeschäfte, Klientelismus, Korruption in der Frühen Neuzeit: Zum Soldunternehmertum der Familie Zurlauben im schweizerischen und europäischen Kontext*, ed. Kaspar von Greyerz et al. (V&R Unipress, 2018).
66. Berkovich, *Motivation in War*.
67. Lee Kennett, *The French Armies in the Seven Years' War: A Study in Military Organization and Administration* (Duke University Press, 1967); Rafe Blaufarb, *The French Army, 1750–1820: Careers, Talent, Merit* (University of Manchester Press, 2002).

68. Kennett, *French Armies*, 77.
69. Kennett, *French Armies*, 72–87.
70. James C. Riley, *The Seven Years' War and the Old Regime in France: The Economic and Financial Toll* (Princeton University Press, 1986).
71. Stephen Conway, "The Mobilization of Manpower for Britain's Mid-Eighteenth-Century Wars," *Historical Research* 77, no. 197 (2004): 378f.; Way, "Class and the Common Soldier."
72. Conway, "Mobilization of Manpower," 379.
73. Reginald Savory, *His Britannic Majesty's Army in Germany During the Seven Years War* (Oxford University Press, 1966); Hamish D. Little, "The Treasury, the Commissariat and the Supply of the Combined Army in Germany During the Seven Years War (1756–1763)" (Doctoral thesis, University of London, 1981).
74. Stephen Brumwell, *Redcoats: The British Soldier and War in the Americas, 1755–1763* (Cambridge University Press, 2002); Way, "Class and the Common Soldier."
75. Carl William Eldon, *England's Subsidy Policy Towards the Continent During the Seven Years' War* (University of Pennsylvania, 1938).
76. Johannes Kunisch, *Friedrich der Große: Der König und seine Zeit* (Beck, 2004), 167.
77. Kunisch, *Friedrich*, 159. On Frederick's longing for glory, see Jürgen Luh, *Der Große: Friedrich II. von Preußen* (Pantheon, 2014), 9–111; on the Silesian wars, 49–76.
78. Kroener, "Herrschaftsverdichtung," 149.
79. For an overview, see Peter Baumgart, "Schlesien als eigenständige Provinz im altpreussischen Staat (1740–1806)," in *Schlesien*. ed. Norbert Conrads (Siedler, 1994); Peter Baumgart and Ulrich Schmilewski, eds., *Kontinuität und Wandel: Schlesien zwischen Österreich und Preussen* (Thorbecke, 1990).
80. Kroener, "Herrschaftsverdichtung," 154; Marcus Junkelmann, "Der Militärstaat in Aktion: Kriegskunst im Ancien Régime," in *Friedrich der Große in Europa: Geschichte einer wechselvollen Beziehung*, ed. Bernd Sösemann and Gregor Vogt-Spira, 2 vols. (Steiner, 2012), 2:169.
81. Junkelmann, "Militärstaat," 169.
82. Christopher Duffy, *Friedrich der Große und seine Armee*, 2nd ed. (Motorbuch, 1983), 252.
83. Peter H. Wilson, "Prussia as Fiscal-Military State, 1640–1806," in Storrs, *The Fiscal-Military State*.
84. Kroener, "Herrschaftsverdichtung," 155.
85. Volker Schmidtchen, "Der Einfluss der Technik auf die Kriegführung zur Zeit Friedrichs des Großen," in *Friedrich der Große und das Militärwesen seiner Zeit*, ed. Militärgeschichtliches Forschungsamt (Mittler, 1987); Paul Rehfeld, "Die preussische Kriegsindustrie unter Friedrich dem Grossen" (Diss., University of Berlin, 1942).
86. Kroener, "Herrschaftsverdichtung,", 156–157.

87. Volz and Küntzel, *Acten zur Vorgeschichte*, xviii–xxiii.
88. Volz and Küntzel, *Acten zur Vorgeschichte*, 157–161.
89. Duffy, *Armee Maria Theresias*, 125–132; Michael Hochedlinger, *Thron und Gewehr: Das Problem der Heeresergänzung und die "Militarisierung" der Habsburgermonarchie im Zeitalter des Aufgeklärten Absolutismus (1740–1790)* (Steiermärkisches Landesarchiv, 2021).
90. Max Lehmann, "Urkundliche Beiträge zur Geschichte des Jahres 1756," *Mitteilungen des Instituts für österreichische Geschichtsforschung* 16, no. 3 (1895): 480–481.
91. See transcript in Lehmann, "Urkundliche Beiträge," 487–491.
92. Michael Hochedlinger, "The Habsburg Monarchy: From 'Military-Fiscal State' to 'Militarization,'" in Storrs, *The Fiscal-Military State*; Peter George Muir Dickson, *Finance and Government Under Maria Theresia: 1740–1780*, 2 vols. (Clarendon, 1987).
93. On Prussia's "superiority in the transport sector, combined with the distribution situation in central operations space," see Marcus Warnke, *Logistik und friderizianische Kriegführung: Eine Studie zur Verteilung, Mobilisierung und Wirkungsmächtigkeit militärisch relevanter Ressourcen im Siebenjährigen Krieg am Beispiel des Jahres 1757* (Duncker & Humblot, 2018), 208.
94. Helmut Neuhaus, "Das Reich im Kampf gegen Friedrich den Großen: Reichsarmee und Reichskriegführung im Siebenjährigen Krieg," in *Europa im Zeitalter Friedrichs des Großen: Wirtschaft, Gesellschaft, Kriege*, ed. Bernhard R. Kroener (Oldenbourg, 1989). An overview of the older literature can be found in Ulf-Joachim Friese, ed., *Die Reichsarmee: Studien unter besonderer Berücksichtigung ihrer Beteiligung am Siebenjährigen Kriege 1756–1763* (LTR, 2008).
95. Heinrich von Eicken, "Die Reichsarmee im siebenjährigen Krieg: Dargestellt am kurtrierischen Regiment," *Preußische Jahrbücher* 41 (1878); Hermann Helmes, "Kurze Geschichte der Fränkischen Reichstruppen 1714–1756 und ihrer Teilnahme am Feldzuge von Rossbach 1757," *Darstellungen aus der Bayerischen Kriegs—und Heeresgeschichte* 16 (1907).
96. Neuhaus, "Das Reich im Kampf," 218.
97. Lothar Freiherr von Thüna, *Die Würzburger Hilfstruppen im Dienste Österreichs 1756–1763: Ein Beitrag zur Geschichte des Siebenjährigen Krieges; Nach archivalischen Quellen* (Würzburg: Stuber, 1893), 1–6, 241–244.
98. Peter H. Wilson, *War, State and Society in Württemberg, 1677–1793* (Cambridge University Press, 1995), 209–246.
99. See Daniel Hohrath, "'Verwandte—Freunde—Vorbilder': Aspekte der militärischen Beziehungsgeschichte Preußens und Württembergs im 18. Jahrhundert," in *Preußen, Deutschland und Europa 1701 bis 2001*, ed. Jürgen Luh et al. (INOS, 2003).
100. John L. H. Keep, "Die russische Armee im Siebenjährigen Krieg," in Kroener, *Europa im Zeitalter Friedrichs*. For the history of military operations, the standard

work remains Dmitrij F. Masslowski, *Der siebenjährige Krieg nach russischer Darstellung: Mit Autorisation des Verfassers übersetzt und mit Anmerkungen versehen von A. von Drygalski*, vols. 1–3 (Berlin: Eisenschmidt, 1888–1893); on the political history, see Mediger, *Moskaus Weg*. For a collection of Russian sources, see Nikolai Korobkow, ed., *Semiletnjaja woina: Materialy o Dejstvijach russkoj armii I flota v 1756–1762* (Voennoe Izdatel'stvo Ministerstva Vooruzennych Sil Sojuza SSR, 1948).

101. Janet Hartley, "Russia as a Fiscal-Military State, 1689–1825," in Storrs, *The Fiscal-Military State*.
102. Dieter Ernst Bangert, *Die Russisch-Österreichische Militärische Zusammenarbeit im Siebenjährigen Kriege in den Jahren 1758–1759* (Boldt, 1971), 24.
103. Günter Dirrheimer and Friedrich Fritz, "Einhörner und Schuwalowsche Haubitzen: Russische Geschützlieferungen an die Österreicher im Siebenjährigen Krieg," in *Maria Theresia: Beiträge zur Geschichte des Heerwesens ihrer Zeit*, ed. Johann Christoph Allmayer-Beck (Hermann Böhlaus Nachfolger, 1967).
104. Marian Füssel, "Die Aasgeier des Schlachtfeldes: Kosaken und Kalmücken als russische Irreguläre während des Siebenjährigen Krieges," in *Die Rückkehr der Condottieri? Krieg und Militär zwischen staatlichem Monopol und Privatisierung: Von der Antike bis zur Gegenwart*, ed. Stig Förster et al. (Schöningh, 2010).
105. On logistics, see Keep, "Die russische Armee," 153–159; Bernhard R. Kroener, "Wirtschaft und Rüstung der europäischen Großmächte im Siebenjährigen Krieg," in Militärgeschichtliches Forschungsamt, *Friedrich der Große*, 159–162.
106. Kroener, "Wirtschaft und Rüstung," 160–161.
107. Duchhardt, *Balance of Power*, 166–172.
108. Christina Borreguero Beltrán, *El reclutamientio militar por quintas en la España del siglo XVIII: Origines del servicio militar obligatorio* (Universidad de Valladolid, 1989).
109. Teofran Säve, *Sveriges deltagande i sjuåriga kriget åren 1757–1762* (Beijer, 1915); Klaus-Richard Böhme, "Schwedens Teilnahme am Siebenjährigen Krieg: Innen- und außenpolitische Voraussetzungen und Rückwirkungen," in Kroener, *Europa im Zeitalter Friedrichs*; Gunnar Åselius, "Sweden and the Pommeranian War," in Danley and Speelman, *The Seven Years' War*; Patrick Winton, "Sweden and the Seven Years' War: War, Debt, and Politics," *War in History* 19, no. 1 (2012).
110. Böhme, "Schwedens Teilnahme," 200–201.
111. Gunner Lind, "The Making of the Neutrality Convention of 1756: France and Her Scandinavian Allies," *Scandinavian Journal of History* 8 (1983): 171–192; Ole Tuxen, "Principles and Priorities: The Danish View of Neutrality During the Colonial War of 1755–63," *Scandinavian Journal of History* 13 (1988): 207–232; Mathilde Breiholz, "Preußen und Dänemark während des Siebenjährigen Krieges (1756–1763)" (Diss., Erlangen, 1930).

112. Åselius, "Sweden and the Pommeranian War," 143.
113. Winton, "Sweden and the Seven Years' War," 13.
114. Winton, "Sweden and the Seven Years' War," 15; Svante Norrhem, *Mercenary Swedes: French Subsidies to Sweden 1631–1796* (Nordic Academic Press, 2019).
115. Böhme, "Schwedens Teilnahme," 207.
116. See Berkovich, *Motivation in War*, 128–164.
117. Füssel, "Stehende Söldner-Heere," 268–270.
118. Frank Zielsdorf, *Miliärische Erinnerungskulturen in Preußen im 18. Jahrhundert: Akteure, Medien, Dynamiken* (V&R unipress, 2016), 113–117.
119. See Jürgen Kloosterhuis, "Donner, Blitz und Bräker: Der Soldatendienst des 'armen Mannes im Tockenburg' aus der Sicht des preußischen Militärsystems," in *Schreibsucht: Autobiographische Schriften des Pietisten Ulrich Bräker*, ed. Alfred Messerli and Adolf Muschg (Vandenhoeck & Ruprecht, 2004).
120. Bräker, *Poor Man of Toggenburg*, 119.
121. Bräker, *Poor Man of Toggenburg*, 121.
122. Bräker, *Poor Man of Toggenburg*, 122.
123. Markus Uhlmann, *Das abwechselnde Fortün oder das veränderte Schicksal eines Jünglingen: Ein Reisebericht aus der Zeit des Siebenjährigen Krieges*, ed. Jean-Pierre Bodmer (Schulthess, 1980), 15.
124. Uhlmann, *Das abwechselnde Fortün*, 14–30.
125. Füssel and Petersen, *Grotehenn Briefe*, 140.
126. Füssel and Petersen, *Grotehenn Briefe*, 141.
127. Casgrain, *Voyage au Canada*, 29.
128. Casgrain, *Voyage au Canada*, 30.
129. For an extensive description of the city and its inhabitants, see Casgrain, *Voyage au Canada*, 30–37.
130. Casgrain, *Voyage au Canada*, 37f.
131. On Miller, see Peter Way, "Memoirs of an Invalid: James Miller and the Making of the British-American Empire in the Seven Years' War," in *Rethinking U. S. Labor History: Essays on the Working-Class Experience, 1756–2009*, ed. Donna T. Haverty-Stacke and Daniel J. Walkowitz (Continuum, 2010).
132. Way, "Memoirs of an Invalid," 31.
133. Cogswell, *Horace St. Paul*.
134. Earl John Chapman and Ian Macpherson McCulloch, eds., *Dangerous Service: Memoirs of a Black Watch Officer in the French and Indian War—John Grant, 1741–1828* (Robin Brass Studio, 2017), 96–99.
135. On the Highlanders in North America, see Ian M. McCulloch, *Sons of the Mountains: The Highland Regiments in the French and Indian War, 1756–1767*, 2 vols. (Purple Mountain Press, 2006).
136. Geoffrey Plank, *Rebellion and Savagery: The Jacobite Rising of 1745 and the British Empire* (University of Pennsylvania Press, 2006), 5–6, 130–180.

137. Stephen Brumwell, *Paths of Glory: The Life and Death of General James Wolfe* (Hambledon Continuum, 2006).
138. Sikora, *Disziplin*; Berkovich, *Motivation in War*, 55–94.
139. Bernhard R. Kroener, "Die materiellen Grundlagen österreichischer und preußischer Kriegsanstrengungen 1756–1763," in Kroener, *Europa*, 56; on Hanover, see Isabelle Pantel, *Die hamburgische Neutralität im Siebenjährigen Krieg* (LIT, 2011), 135 and n14; Berkovich, *Motivation in War*, 56, 70–71, 74.
140. On the "tamed Bellona," see Gerhard Ritter, *The Sword and the Scepter: The Problem of Militarism in Germany*, vol. 1, *The Prussian Tradition 1740–1890* (University of Miami Press, 1969).
141. On customs of war, see Sascha Möbius, "Kriegsbrauch," in *Enzyklopädie der Neuzeit*, ed. Friedrich Jaeger, vol. 7 (Metzler, 2008).
142. Ritter, *The Sword and the Scepter*, 40; on contemporary legal norms, see the informative compendium of international law by the Swiss jurist Emer de Vattel, published during the war. Emer de Vattel, *Völkerrecht; oder: Gründliche Anweisung wie die Grundsätze des natürlichen Rechts auf das Betragen und auf die Angelegenheiten der Nationen und Souveräne angewendet werden müssen*, 3 vols. (Frankfurt: Schulin, 1760), 3:1–384.
143. Bernhard R. Kroener, "Krieg," in Jaeger, *Enzyklopädie der Neuzeit*, vol. 7, cols. 145–146.
144. Ralf Pröve, "Der delegitimierte Gegner: Kriegführung als Argument im Siebenjährigen Krieg," in Externbrink, *Der Siebenjährige Krieg*.
145. Johann Michael von Loen, *Der Soldat oder Abhandlung vom Kriegs-Stand*, 3rd ed. (Frankfurt: Fleischer, 1752; originally published in 1738), 326; on this, see Christiane Büchel, "Der Offizier im Gesellschaftsbild der Aufklärung: Die Soldatenschriften des Johann Michael von Loen," *Aufklärung* 11, no. 2 (1999).
146. Loen, *Soldat*, 326.
147. For an overview of the extensive research on the subject, see Andrea Iseli, *Gute Policey: Öffentliche Ordnung in der Frühen Neuzeit* (Ulmer, 2009).
148. Birgfeld, *Krieg und Aufklärung*, 1:232–233.
149. Also relevant here are reflections on a calculating Bellona. See Martin Wrede, "'Zähmung der Bellona' oder Ökonomie der Gewalt? Überlegungen zur Kultur des Krieges im Ancien régime," in *Theatrum Belli—Theatrum Pacis: Konflikte und Konfliktregelungen im frühneuzeitlichen Europa; Festschrift für Heinz Duchhardt zu seinem 75. Geburtstag*, ed. Irene Dingel (Vandenhoeck & Ruprecht, 2018).
150. For the best overviews on the eighteenth century, see Jürgen Luh, *Kriegskunst in Europa 1650–1800* (Böhlau, 2004); Armstrong Starkey, *War in the Age of the Enlightenment 1700–1789* (Praeger, 2003); Christopher Duffy, *The Military Experience in the Age of Reason* (Routledge and Kegan Paul, 1987).
151. For an overview, see Christian Buchet, *The British Navy, Economy and Society in the Seven Years War*, trans. Anita Higgie and Michael Duffy (Boydell, 2013);

A. B. McLeod, *British Naval Captains of the Seven Years' War: The View from the Quarterdeck* (Boydell, 2012); David Syrett, *Shipping and Military Power in the Seven Years War: The Sails of Victory* (University of Exeter Press, 2008); James S. Pritchard, *Louis XV's Navy, 1748–1762: A Study of Organization and Administration* (McGill-Queen's University Press, 1987); Jonathan R. Dull, *The French Navy and the Seven Years' War* (University of Nebraska Press, 2005).

152. Stephen F. Gradish, *The Manning of the British Navy During the Seven Years' War* (Royal Historical Society, 1980); Timothy J. A. Le Goff, "Problèmes de recrutement de la marine française pendant la Guerre des Sept Ans," *Revue historique* 283 (1990); Markus Eder, *Crime and Punishment in the Royal Navy of the Seven Years' War, 1755–1763* (Ashgate, 2004).

153. Dieter Hartwig, "Maritime Aspekte im Denken und Handeln Friedrichs des Großen," in *Deutsche Marinen im Wandel: Vom Symbol nationaler Einheit zum Instrument internationaler Sicherheit*, ed. Werner Rah (Oldenbourg, 2005).

154. Luh, *Kriegskunst*, 81–83; Höchner, *Selbstzeugnisse*, 238; Daniel Hohrath, "Bastionen statt Schlachtfelder? Die schlesischen Festungen und ihre Belagerungen im Siebenjährigen Krieg," in Füssel, *Der Siebenjährige Krieg*.

155. Castex, *Dictionnaire*.

156. See Günther Gieraths, *Die Kampfhandlungen der Brandenburgisch-Preussischen Armee 1626–1807* (De Gruyter, 1964).

157. Gustav Berthold Volz, ed., *Die Werke Friedrichs des Großen*, 10 vols. (Berlin: Hobbing, 1913–1914), vol. 6, 55.

158. Christopher Duffy, *Siege Warfare*, vol. 2, *The Fortress in the Age of Vauban and Frederick the Great 1660–1789* (Routledge and Kegan Paul, 1985); Luh, *Kriegskunst*, 81–128.

159. Daniel Hohrath, "Der Bürger im Krieg der Fürsten: Stadtbewohner und Soldaten in belagerten Städten um die Mitte des 18. Jahrhunderts," in *Krieg und Frieden: Militär und Gesellschaft in der Frühen Neuzeit*, ed. Bernhard R. Kroener and Ralf Pröve (Schöningh, 1996).

160. Michel Thévenin, *Changer le système de la guerre: Le siège en Nouvelle-France 1755–1760* (Les Presses de l'Université Laval, 2020); Elizabeth Bartlett Hornor, "Besieged: British-American Forts, Families, and Communities in the Seven Years' War, 1755–1763" (Diss., Stony Brook University, 2011).

161. Bougainville, *Écrits*, 360.

162. Marian Füssel, "Die Krise der Schlacht: Das Problem der militärischen Entscheidung im 17. und 18. Jahrhundert," in *Die Krise in der Frühen Neuzeit*, ed. Rudolf Schlögl et al. (Vandenhoeck & Ruprecht, 2016).

163. See Duffy, *Armee Maria Theresias*, 443–457; Sascha Möbius, "Kriegsgreuel in den Schlachten des Siebenjährigen Krieges in Europa," in *Kriegsgreuel: Die Entgrenzung von Gewalt in kriegerischen Konflikten vom Mittelalter bis ins 20. Jahrhundert*, ed. Sönke Neitzel and Daniel Hohrath (Schöningh, 2008), 189–196.

164. John Keegan, *The Face of Battle* (Jonathan Cape, 1976).
165. Marian Füssel and Michael Sikora, "Einführung: Schlachtengeschichte als Kulturgeschichte," in *Kulturgeschichte der Schlacht*, ed. Marian Füssel and Michael Sikora (Schöningh, 2014).
166. For example, see the account of the Battle of Lobositz in chapter 3 of this book.
167. James Q. Whitman, *The Verdict of Battle: The Law of Victory and the Making of Modern War* (Harvard University Press, 2012).
168. Duffy, *Armee Maria Theresias*, 441; on supplies for horses, see Warnke, *Logistik und friderizianische Kriegführung*, 126–134.
169. Max Plassmann, "Bikonfessionelle Streitkräfte: Das Beispiel des Schwäbischen Reichskreises (1648–1803)," in *Militär und Religiosität in der Frühen Neuzeit*, ed. Michael Kaiser and Stefan Kroll (LIT, 2004), 41.
170. Möbius and Möbius, *Prussian Army Soldiers*, 39–43.
171. Warnke, *Logistik und friderizianische Kriegführung*, 73–75.
172. Füssel, "Krise der Schlacht," 322–326.
173. Füssel, "Krise der Schlacht," 324–325.
174. Russell F. Weigley, *The Age of Battles: The Quest for Decisive Warfare from Breitenfeld to Waterloo* (Vintage, 1993).
175. Herfried Münkler, *Gewalt und Ordnung: Das Bild des Krieges im politischen Denken* (Fischer, 1992), 184.
176. See Duffy, *Armee Maria Theresias*, 443–457; Möbius, "Kriegsgreuel."
177. On irregular operations, see Johannes Kunisch, *Der kleine Krieg: Studien zum Heerwesen des Absolutismus* (Steiner, 1973); Martin Rink, *Vom 'Partheygänger' zum Partisanen: Die Konzeption des kleinen Krieges in Preußen 1740–1813* (Lang, 1999); Sandrine Picaud-Monnerat, *La petite guerre au XVIIIe siècle* (Economica, 2010).
178. On the various tasks assigned to irregular forces, see Johann von Ewald, *Abhandlung über den kleinen Krieg* (Kassel: Cramer, 1785).
179. The ideal of good individual discipline should be seen in the context of wider demands for specific military discipline. On this, see Georg Dietrich v. der Gröben, "Versuch von der Kriegs-Zucht," in *Kriegs-Bibliothek oder gesammelte Beyträge zur Kriegs-Wissenschaft, Erster Versuch*, ed. Georg Dietrich v. der Gröben (Breslau: Korn, 1755).
180. Stephanie Schwarzer, *Zwischen Anspruch und Wirklichkeit: Die Ästhetisierung kriegerischer Ereignisse in der Frühen Neuzeit* (Meidenbauer, 2006), 235–257.
181. On military machine metaphors, see Rink, '*Partheygänger*,' 46ff.
182. Marian Füssel, "Panduren, Kosaken und Sepoys: Ethnische Gewaltakteure im 18. Jahrhundert zwischen Sicherheit und Stigma," in *Söldnerlandschaften: Frühneuzeitliche Gewaltmärkte im Vergleich*, ed. Philippe Rogger and Benjamin Hitz (Duncker & Humblot, 2014); Pröve, "Gegner," 279–280.
183. Anonymous, *Besonderes Gespräch eines Rußischen und Englischen Officiers von der bisher unbekannten Lebensart und Sitten der Kalmucken und Bergschotten, von welchen*

sich ein Theil bey denen Rußischen und Hannöverischen Armeen im Felde befinden/aus dem Rußischen und Englischen übersetzt (Frankfurt, 1760).

184. Frank Wernitz, Die preußischen Freitruppen im Siebenjährigen Krieg, 1756–1763: Entstehung, Einsatz, Wirkung (Podzun-Pallas, 1994), 42; Curt Jany, *Geschichte der Königlich Preußischen Armee bis zum Jahre 1807*, vol. 2, *Die Armee Friedrichs des Grossen 1740 bis 1763* (Siegismund, 1928), 679–688; on British units, see Frank Wernitz, "'They Have Been Blooded and Behaved Very Well'—britische leichte Truppen in der Armee des Herzogs Ferdinand von Braunschweig 1760–63: Ein Beitrag zur Geschichte des kleinen Krieges im 18. Jahrhundert" (Diss., Ludwig Maximilian University of Munich, 1993).

185. Hans Schmidt, "Der Einfluss der Winterquartiere auf Strategie und Kriegführung des Ancien Régime," *Historisches Jahrbuch* 92 (1972).

186. Thomas Lindner, *Die Peripetie des Siebenjährigen Krieges: Der Herbstfeldzug 1760 in Sachsen und der Winterfeldzug 1760/61 in Hessen* (Duncker & Humblot, 1993).

187. Marian Füssel, "Theatrum Belli: Der Krieg als Inszenierung und Wissensschauplatz im 17. und 18. Jahrhundert," *Metaphorik* 14 (2008).

188. On northwest Germany, see, e.g., Füssel and Petersen, *Grotehenn Briefe*.

189. Thévenin, "Guerre," 53.

190. On conflicts of interest in the Ohio Valley, see Eric Hinderaker, *Elusive Empires: Constructing Colonialism in the Ohio Valley, 1673–1800* (Cambridge University Press, 1997).

191. John Shovlin, "Selling American Empire on the Eve of the Seven Years War: The French Propaganda Campaign of 1755–1756," *Past & Present* 206, no. 1 (2010).

192. Carter, *Dutch Republic*.

193. Shovlin, "Selling American Empire," 121; Edmond Dziembowski, "Transparence ou désinformation? La perte du Canada dans la presse gouvernementale française," in Fonck and Veyssière, *La Chute*.

194. See Armin Reese, *Europäische Hegemonie und France d'outre-mer: Koloniale Fragen in der französischen Außenpolitik 1700–1763* (Steiner, 1988). On communication with the colonies, now becoming an important issue, see Kenneth Banks, *Chasing Empire Across the Sea: Communications and the State in the French Atlantic, 1713–1763* (McGill-Queen's University Press, 2002).

195. Quoted in Externbrink, "Voltaire," 145.

196. Voltaire, *Candide or, Optimism: The Robert M. Adams Translation, Backgrounds, Criticism*, 3rd ed. (Norton, 2016), 113.

197. Voltaire to Luise Dorothée, Tornay Castle, on the road to Geneva, January 25, 1759, in Raschke, *Briefwechsel*, 151.

198. Shovlin, "Selling American Empire," 123; William James Newbigging, "Propaganda, Political Discourse and the Battle Over French Public Opinion in the Seven Years' War," *Proceedings of the Nineteenth Meeting of the French Colonial History Society* 19 (1994).

199. Shovlin, "Selling American Empire," 124.
200. Roland Lamontagne, ed., *Aperçu structural du Canada au XVIIIe siècle* (Leméac, 1964), 93–112.
201. Lamontagne, *Aperçu structural du Canada*, 96–97.
202. Lamontagne, *Aperçu structural du Canada*, 112.
203. Jacob N. Moreau, ed., *L'observateur hollandois [. . .]* (The Hague: François, 1755), no. 4, 21.
204. Moreau, *L'observateur hollandois [. . .]*, 10–11; Shovlin, "Selling American Empire," 133–135.
205. Shovlin, "Selling American Empire," 130.
206. Bob Harris, "'American Idols': Empire, War and the Middling Ranks in Mid-Eighteenth-Century Britain," *Past & Present* 150 (1996).
207. "Maria Theresia an Esterházy, Vienna, May 22, 1756," in Volz and Küntzel, *Preussische und Österreichische Acten*, 374.
208. Willi Bode et al., "Das Eichsfeld im Siebenjährigen Krieg: Die Chronik des Pfarrers Schatz aus Wollbrandshausen," *Eichsfeld-Jahrbuch* 13 (2005): 130.
209. Bode et al., "Das Eichsfeld im Siebenjährigen Krieg, 130.
210. Mintz, *Sweetness and Power*; Subrahmanyam, "Connected Histories"; Werner and Zimmermann, "Vergleich, Transfer, Verflechtung."
211. Medick, *Der Dreißigjährige Krieg: Zeugnisse*, 14–15.
212. Mühlenberg, *Correspondence*, vol. 3, *1753–1756*, 300 (translation modified).
213. Quoted in Sven Externbrink, *Friedrich der Große, Maria Theresia und das Alte Reich: Deutschlandbild und Diplomatie Frankreichs im Siebenjährigen Krieg* (Akademie, 2006), 120.
214. Johann Georg Fülling, *Die Isthaer Chronik des Pfarrers Johann Georg Fülling: Zur Geschichte Niederhessens im siebenjährigen Kriege*, ed. Gerhard Bätzing (Bärenreiter, 1957), 3.
215. Frederick II, "Rechtfertigung meines politischen Verhaltens," in Volz, *Werke*, 3:210; for a partial English translation, see Theodor Schieder, *Frederick the Great* (Routledge, 1999), 116–117; see similar verbal images in [Montag], *Teutsche Kriegs-Canzley*, vol. 2, no. 83, 537.
216. [Johann Heinrich Gottlob von Justi], *Wohlgemeynte Vorschläge eines die jetzigen unglücklichen Zeiten beseufzenden Menschenfreundes auf was vor Bedingungen die jetzo in Krieg befangenen Mächte zu einem dauerhaften und ihrem allerseitigen Interesse gemäßen Frieden gelangen könnten zur Aufmunterung gantz Deutschlands* (Friedensnah, 1759), 38; on this text, see also Schaefer, *Geschichte des siebenjährigen Kriegs*, 2:724 and n2.
217. Justi, *Wohlgemeynte Vorschläge*, 39.
218. [Johann Heinrich Gottlob von Justi], *Untersuchung, ob etwa die heutigen europäischen Völker Lust haben möchten, dereinst Menschen-Fresser, oder wenigstens Hottentotten zu werden [. . .]* (Philadelphia in Pensilvanien [i.e. Schwerin]: Lowe,

[1759]), 7f. The broadside prompted a rapid response: Anonymous, *Beweis daß derjenige, der schon ein Hottentotte ist, nicht erst einer werden dürfe, zur Antwort auf das Pensilvanisirten Preußen witzige Frage: Ob etwan die heutigen Europ. Völker Lust haben möchten, dereinst Menschen-Fresser, oder wenigstens Hottentotten zu werden [. . .]* (Frankfurt: Simon Hallers, 1760); on this text, see also Manfred Schort, *Politik und Propaganda: Der Siebenjährige Krieg in den zeitgenössischen Flugschriften* (Lang, 2006), 392–395.

219. "Sehnsucht nach einem allgemeinen Frieden," *Der Apotheker*, 1762, no. 16, 242, quoted in Nicole Waibel, *Nationale und patriotische Publizistik in der Freien Reichsstadt Augsburg: Studien zur periodischen Presse im Zeitalter der Aufklärung (1748–1770)* (Lumière, 2008), 315.
220. Douglas Fordham, *British Art and The Seven Years' War: Allegiance and Autonomy* (University of Pennsylvania Press, 2010), 18–19, 91–94.
221. Paris, Musée Carnavelet, no. G.24 357; Gerda Mraz and Gottfried Mraz, *Maria Theresia: Ihr Leben und ihre Zeit in Bildern und Dokumenten* (Süddeutscher, 1980), 124.
222. See Herfried Münkler's reading of Clausewitz. Herfried Münkler, *Die neuen Kriege* (Rowohlt, 2004), 61–63.

2. Sparking the Flame

1. In 1806, for example, Johann Wilhelm von Archenholz published a short article in the journal *Minerva* with the title "The First Shot of the Seven Years War." He wrote it in response to an article in the journal *Der Freymüthige* (no. 191) about Charles Emmanuel Warnery's claim that the war's first shot was fired during the storming of Stolpe, a Saxon mountain fortress. See Johann Wilhelm von Archenholz, "Der erste Schuß im siebenjährigen Kriege," *Minerva* 4 (1806).
2. Crouch, *Nobility Lost*; Ternat, *Partager le monde*.
3. Almon, *Impartial History of the Late War*.
4. Hermann Wellenreuther, *Ausbildung und Neubildung: Die Geschichte Nordamerikas vom Ausgang des 17. Jahrhunderts bis zum Ausbruch der Amerikanischen Revolution 1775* (LIT, 2001), 268.
5. Fowler, *Empires at War*, 14; Paul R. Misencik, *George Washington and the Half-King Chief Tanacharison: An Alliance That Began the French and Indian War* (McFarland, 2014), 22–28.
6. Anonymous, "The Treaty of Logg's Town, 1752: Commission, Instructions &c, Journal of Virginia Commissioners, and Text of Treaty," *Virginia Magazine of History and Biography* 13 (1905–1906); Francis Jennings, *Empire of Fortune: Crowns, Colonies and Tribes in the Seven Years War in America* (Norton, 1988), 42; on this, see Marian Füssel, "Die Politik der Unsicherheit: Versicherheitlichung,

Gewalt und Expansion in den britischen Kolonien im Siebenjährigen Krieg," in *Sicherheit in der Frühen Neuzeit*, ed. Christoph Kampmann and Ulrich Niggemann (Böhlau, 2013).

7. Anonymous, "Treaty of Logg's Town," 168.
8. Anderson, *Crucible*, 18.
9. His full name was Michel-Ange Duquesne de Menneville, Marquis Duquesne.
10. Jennings, *Empire of Fortune*, 52–70.
11. Wellenreuther, *Ausbildung und Neubildung*, 271–273.
12. On this, see recent accounts: Colin G. Calloway, *The Indian World of George Washington: The First President, the First Americans, and the Birth of the Nation* (Oxford University Press, 2018); Misencik, *George Washington and the Half-King*.
13. George Washington, *The Diaries of George Washington 1748–1799*, vol. 1, *1748–1770*, ed. John C. Fitzpatrick (Mifflin, 1925), 87.
14. Jacob Nicolas Moreau, ed., *Mémoire contenant le Precis des faits, avec leurs pieces justificatives, Pour server de Réponse aux Observations envoyées par les Minstres d'Angleterre dans les Cours de l'Europe* (Paris: Imprimerie Royale, 1756), 106; a modern edition can be found in Fernand Grenier, ed., *Papiers contrecœur et autres documents concernant le conflit anglo-français sur l'Ohio de 1745 à 1756* (Les Presses Universitaires Laval, 1952); see also Anderson, *Crucible*, 53–54.
15. Moreau, *Mémoire*, 107–108; Anderson, *Crucible*, 54.
16. Jennings, *Empire of Fortune*, 68–70.
17. John Shaw's affidavit in William L. McDowell Jr., ed., *Colonial Records of South Carolina: Documents Relating to Indian Affairs, 1754–1765* (University of South Carolina Press, 1970), 4–5.
18. [Joseph-Gaspard Chaussegros de Léry], "Journal de Joseph-Gaspard Chaussegros de Léry, lieutenant des troupes, 1754–1755," in *Rapport de l'archiviste de la province de Québec pour 1927–1928* (L.-Amable Proulx, 1928), 372–373; Crouch, *Nobility Lost*, 47 and n28.
19. Anderson, *Crucible*, 58–59.
20. Anderson, *Crucible*, 61.
21. Hinderaker, *Elusive Empires*.
22. Benjamin Franklin, *Autobiography* (Boston: Houghton Mifflin, 1906 [1791]), 138.
23. Wellenreuther, *Ausbildung und Neubildung*, 274–278; Anderson, *Crucible*, 77–85; Jennings, *Empire of Fortune*, 71–108; Michael J. Mullin, "The Albany Congress and Colonial Confederation," *Mid-America* 72, no. 2 (1990).
24. On the debate in the newspapers of the colonies, see David A. Copeland, *Debating the Issues in Colonial Newspapers: Primary Documents on Events of the Period* (Greenwood, 2000), 165–175.
25. Anderson, *Short History*, 59.
26. Wellenreuther, *Ausbildung und Neubildung*, 277.

27. Charles Morse Stotz, *Outposts of the War for Empire: The French and English in Western Pennsylvania; Their Armies, Their Forts, Their People, 1749–1764* (University of Pittsburgh Press, 2005), 8.
28. Stanley McCrory Pargellis, ed., *Military Affairs in North America, 1748–1765: Selected Documents from the Cumberland (William Augustus, Duke of) Papers in Windsor Castle* (Archon, 1969), 53–54.
29. On the journey across the Atlantic, see [Brown], "The Journal of Charlotte Brown," 169–174; on the context of military care carried out by women, see Sarah Fatherly, "Tending the Army: Women and the British General Hospital in North America, 1754–1763," *Early American Studies* 10 (2012).
30. On this, see Anderson, *Crucible*, 86–107; Jennings, *Empire of Fortune*, 157–160; Stanley McCrory Pargellis, "Braddocks Defeat," *American Historical Review* 41 (1935–36); Robert L. Yaple, "Braddock's Defeat: The Theories and a Reconsideration," *Journal of the Society for Army Historical Research* 46 (1968); Paul Edward Kopperman, *Braddock at the Monongahela* (University of Pittsburgh Press, 1977); Thomas E. Crocker, *Braddock's March: How the Man Sent to Seize a Continent Changed American History* (Westholme, 2009); David L. Preston, *Braddock's Defeat: The Battle of the Monongahela River and the Road to Revolution* (Oxford University Press, 2015).
31. Mühlenberg, *Correspondence*, 3:310.
32. Jennings, *Empire of Fortune*, 154.
33. For a vivid source text, see Douglas R. Cubbison, *On Campaign Against Fort Duquesne: The Braddock and Forbes Expeditions, 1755–1758, Through the Experiences of Quartermaster Sir John St. Claire* (McFarland, 2015).
34. Anderson, *Crucible*, 759 and n4. The small, portable Coehoorn mortar was named after its Dutch inventor, Menno van Coehoorn (1641–1704).
35. Anderson, *Crucible*, 99.
36. Charles Hamilton, ed., *Braddock's Defeat: The Journal of Captain Robert Cholmley's Batman, the Journal of a British Officer [and] Halkett's Orderly Book* (University of Oklahoma Press, 1959), 29; on the authenticity of the source, see Paul E. Kopperman, "An Assessment of the Cholmley's Batman and British A Journals of Braddock's Campaign," *Western Pennsylvania Historical Magazine* 62, no. 3 (1979).
37. Hamilton, *Braddock's Defeat*, 50; see also Bernd Horn, "Only for the Strong of Heart: Ranging and the Practice of la Petite Guerre During the Struggle for North America," in *Show No Fear: Daring Actions in Canadian Military History*, ed. Bernd Horn (Dundurn, 2008), 25.
38. Anderson, *Crucible*, 102.
39. Mühlenberg, *Correspondence*, 3:300.
40. Anderson, *Crucible*, 102.
41. Mühlenberg, *Correspondence*, 3:300.

42. Mühlenberg, *Correspondence*, 3:300. See his similar comments in a letter of November 24, 1755, 3:314ff.
43. See Anderson, *Crucible*, 103.
44. Cited in Anderson, *Crucible*, 104.
45. Hamilton, *Braddock's Defeat*, 32.
46. James Wolfe, *The Life and Letters of James Wolfe*, ed. Beckless Willson (Heinemann, 1909), 274. See also William M. S. Rasmussen and Robert S. Tilton, *George Washington: The Man Behind the Myths* (University of Virginia Press, 1999), 63. From 1800 on, there were also memorials (built in 1804 and 1913), paintings, and engravings that represented and memorialized the event, turning it into an American *lieu de mémoire*.
47. Anderson, *Crucible*, 105.
48. [Brown], "Journal of Charlotte Brown," 183–184.
49. N. Darnell Davis, "British Newspaper Accounts of Braddock's Defeat," *Pennsylvania Magazine of History and Biography* 23 (1899).
50. Wolfe, *Life and Letters*, 274.
51. *Berlinische Nachrichten*, no. 106, Thursday, September 4, 1755, 444–445.
52. *Berlinische Nachrichten*, no. 107, Saturday, September 6, 1755, 448–449; *Berlinische Nachrichten*, no. 108, Tuesday, September 9, 452–453.
53. *Wienerisches Diarium*, no. 73, Wednesday, September 10, 1755.
54. Volz und Küntzel, *Preussische und Österreichische Acten zur Vorgeschichte*, 26.
55. Volz und Küntzel, *Preussische und Österreichische Acten zur Vorgeschichte*, 177; see also Maria Theresia to Starhemberg, in Volz und Küntzel, *Preussische und Österreichische Acten zur Vorgeschichte*, 180.
56. Mühlenberg, *Correspondence*, 3:312–313.
57. Mühlenberg, *Correspondence*, 3:313.
58. Wellenreuther, *Ausbildung und Neubildung*, 281.
59. Wellenreuther, *Ausbildung und Neubildung*, 269; John Mack Faragher, *A Great and Noble Scheme: The Tragic Story of the Expulsion of the French Acadians from Their American Homeland* (Norton, 2005); on the Francophone view, see Ronnie-Gilles LeBlanc, ed., *Du Grand Dérangement à la Déportation: Nouvelles perspectives historique* (Université de Moncton, 2005).
60. Beverly W. Bond Jr., ed., "The Captivity of Charles Stuart, 1755–1757," *Mississippi Valley Historical Review* 13, no. 1 (1926); also printed in Shannon, *The Seven Years' War in North America*.
61. See John A. Lynn, *Battle: A History of Combat and Culture* (Westview, 2003), 128–129.
62. Horn, "Only for the Strong of Heart," 23.
63. Mühlenberg, *Correspondence*, 3: 299–300 (translation modified).
64. Casgrain, *Voyage au Canada*, 54.
65. Casgrain, *Voyage au Canada*: on the expedition, see 66–84; on Jumonville, 101–104; on Braddock's defeat, 134–138.

66. Holger Th. Gräf, "Vom Hirtenjungen um Grossbrit: Capitaine—George Schneider und seine Tagebuchnotizen zu den Jahren 1744–1764," *Archiv für hessische Geschichte und Altertumskunde* 73 (2015): 89.
67. Füssel, "Aasgeier des Schlachtfeldes."
68. Horn, "Only for the Strong of Heart"; Daniel J. Beattie, "The Adaptation of the British Army to Wilderness Warfare, 1755–1763," in *Adapting to Conditions: War and Society in the Eighteenth Century*, ed. Maarten Ultee (University of Alabama Press, 1986); Florian Panissié, "La petite guerre à l'épreuve des colonies, de la théorie à la pratique: Le cas du siège de Québec en 1759," in *La France face aux crises et aux conflits des périphéries européennes et atlantiques du XVIIe au XXe siècle*, ed. Éric Schnakenbourg and Frédéric Dessberg (Presses universitaires de Rennes, 2010).
69. Ryan R. Gale, *"A Soldier-Like Way": The Material Culture of the British Infantry, 1751–1768* (Track of the Wolf, 2007).
70. Patrick Malone, *The Skulking Way of War: Technology and Tactics Among the New England Indians* (Johns Hopkins University Press, 1993).
71. Luh, *Kriegskunst in Europa*, 147–149; Ernst Friedrich Rudolf von Barsewisch, *Von Rossbach bis Freiberg 1757–1763: Tagebuchblätter eines friderizianischen Fahnenjunkers und Offiziers; Nach dem wortgetreuen Erstabdruck von 1863 neu herausgegeben, kommentiert und bearbeitet von Jürgen Olmes* (Rühl, 1959), 112.
72. Horn, "Only for the Strong of Heart," 21–22.
73. Mühlenberg, *Correspondence*, 4:42.
74. Cannibalism was, in fact, a ritual practice among several tribes, although culturally biased accounts by Europeans largely prevent us from understanding the way in which these practices were actually used. For a trenchant overview of the literature, see Daniel Morley Johnson, "Cannibalism," in *The Encyclopedia of North American Indian Wars, 1607–1890: A Political, Social, and Military History*, ed. Spencer Tucker et al., vol. 1 (ABC-CLIO, 2011), 119–120.
75. On the origins of this practice, see James Axtell and William C. Sturtevant, "The Unkindest Cut, or Who Invented Scalping," *William and Mary Quarterly* 37 (1980).
76. Gräf, "George Schneider und seine Tagebuchnotizen," 91.
77. Claus Biegert, ed., *Die Wunden der Freiheit: Der Kampf der Indianer Nordamerikas gegen die weiße Eroberung und Unterdrückung; Selbstzeugnisse, Dokumente, Kommentare* (Lamuv, 1994), 36–37.
78. Hall, *Atlantic Politics*, 129–134.
79. Horn, "Only for the Strong of Heart," 31–39; Beattie, "Adaptation of the British Army," 69.
80. Horn, "Only for the Strong of Heart," 40.
81. Horn, "Only for the Strong of Heart," 41–42.
82. Horn, "Only for the Strong of Heart," 43.

83. Newcastle to Holdernesse, August 26, 1755, quoted in Peter James Marshall, "The Thirteen Colonies in the Seven Years' War: The View from London," in *Britain and America Go to War: The Impact of War and Warfare in Anglo-America, 1754–1815*, ed. Julie Flavell and Stephen Conway (University of Florida Press, 2004), 77.
84. Marshall, "The Thirteen Colonies in the Seven Years' War," 77.
85. See Thomas Agostini, "'Deserted His Majesty's Service': Military Runaways, the British-American Press, and the Problem of Desertion During the Seven Years' War," *Journal of Social History* 40, no. 4 (2007).
86. Agostini, "'Deserted His Majesty's Service,'" 957–968.
87. Agostini, "'Deserted His Majesty's Service,'" 973.
88. Mühlenberg, *Correspondence*, 3:309–310.
89. See Nabil I. Matar, *Turks, Moors and Englishmen in the Age of Discovery* (Columbia University Press, 1999).
90. Gräf, "George Schneider und seine Tagebuchnotizen," 88.
91. Glenn Weaver, "The Germans of British North America During the French and Indian War," *Social Studies* 48 (1957).
92. Weaver, "The Germans of British North America," 233.
93. Manfred Schlenke, *England und das friderizianische Preussen: 1740–1763; Ein Beitrag zum Verhältnis von Politik und öffentlicher Meinung im England des 18. Jahrhunderts* (Alber, 1963), 225–227; Georg Küntzel, "Die Westminsterkonvention," *Forschungen zur Brandenburgischen und Preußischen Geschichte* 9 (1897).
94. *Berlinische Nachrichten*, no. 16, Thursday, February 5, 1756, 61; reprinted in *Danziger Beyträge*, vol. 1, 56–58.
95. *Berlinische Nachrichten*, no. 16, in *Danziger Beyträge*, vol. 1, 59.
96. Wolfe's letter to his mother, October 24, 1755, in Wolfe, *Life and Letters*, 279.
97. Wolfe's letter to his father, written at Devizes, July 17, 1755, in Wolfe, *Life and Letters*, 295.
98. Reginald Savory, "Jeffery Amherst Conducts the Hessians to England, 1756," *Journal of the Society for Army Historical Research* 49 (1971); see also Christoph Flucke (ed.), *Die litterae annuae: Die Jahresberichte der Gesellschaft Jesu aus Altona und Hamburg (1598–1781)—Zweiter Halbband: 18. Jahrhundert* (Aschendorff, 2015), 1072–1073.
99. [Georg Ernst von und zu Gilsa], *Adliges Leben am Ausgang des Ancien Régime: Die Tagebuchaufzeichnungen (1754–1798) des Georg Ernst von und zu Gilsa*, ed. Holger Th. Gräf et al. (Hessisches Landesamt für geschichtliche Landeskunde, 2010), 3–15.
100. Matthew McCormack, "Citizenship, Nationhood, and Masculinity in the Affair of the Hannoverian Soldier, 1756," *Historical Journal* 49, no. 4 (2006): 971–993; M. John Cardwell, *Arts and Arms: Literature, Politics and Patriotism During the Seven Years War* (Manchester University Press, 2004), 108–112.

101. McCormack, "Citizenship," 973.
102. For an overview, see Jutta Nowosadtko et al., eds., *Militär und Recht vom 16. bis 19. Jahrhundert: Gelehrter Diskurs, Praxis, Transformationen* (V&R unipress, 2016).
103. McCormack, "Citizenship," 977–982.
104. See the caricature "Law for the Out-Laws," in McCormack, "Citizenship," 991.
105. McCormack, "Citizenship," 983–987.
106. McCormack, "Citizenship," 976.
107. On the return to Germany, see Gilsa, *Adeliges Leben am Ausgang des Ancien Régime*, 14–15.
108. Lothar Schilling, *Kaunitz und das Renversement des Alliances: Studien zur außenpolitischen Konzeption Wenzel Antons von Kaunitz* (Berlin: Duncker & Humblot, 1994); Richard Waddington, *Louis XV et le renversement des alliances: Préliminaires de la Guerre de Sept Ans 1754–1755* (Paris: Firmin-Didot, 1896).
109. On the French point of view, see Externbrink, *Friedrich der Grosse*, 244.
110. Karl H. Schneider, "Die Schlacht bei Minden—lokales Ereignis mit globaler Bedeutung," *Zeitschrift für Weltgeschichte* 14, no. 2 (2013): 37.
111. Adolf Beer, "Zur Geschichte des Jahres 1756," *Mitteilungen des Instituts für Österreichische Geschichtsforschung* 17 (1896): 115.
112. The formulation can be found in a later letter from Frederick to Pitt, written at Kunzendorf on July 3, 1761, in Friedrich II, *Politische Correspondenz*, vol. 20, no. 13,018, 508; for the context, see Michael Salewski, "Praevenire quam praeveniri: Zur Idee des Präventivkriegs in der Späten Neuzeit," *Historische Mitteilungen* 18 (2005).
113. Dziembowski, *La Guerre de Sept Ans*, 136–143; Dull, *The French Navy and the Seven Years' War*, 50–54; Janet Sloss, *A Small Affair: The French Occupation of Menorca During the Seven Years' War* (Bonaventura, 2000); Desmond Gregory, *Minorca, the Illusory Prize: A History of the British Occupations of Minorca Between 1708 and 1802* (Fairleigh Dickinson University Press, 1990); Raoul de Cisternes, *La campagne de Minorque d'après le journal du commandeur de Glandevez et de nombreuses lettres inédites* (Paris: Calmann-Lévy, 1899); Herbert W. Richmond, ed., *Papers Relating to the Loss of "Minorca" in 1756* (Navy Records Society, 1913).
114. Baugh, *Global Seven Years War*, 189.
115. Dziembowski, *La Guerre de Sept Ans*, 168–179; Dull, *The French Navy and the Seven Years' War*, 54.
116. Anonymous, *Zuverläßige Lebens-Geschichte des grosbritannischen Admirals von der weissen Flagge, Johan Byng, welcher am 14. März 1757 nach Urtel und Recht am Boord des Kriegs Schiffes der Monarch erschossen worden: Nebst einem kurzen Vorbericht von der jetzigen Verfassung der grosbritannischen See Macht* (Frankfurt, 1757); Brian Tunstall, *Admiral Byng and the Loss of Minorca* (Allen, 1928); Dudley Pope, *At Twelve Mr Byng Was Shot* (Lippincott, 1962); Joseph J. Krulder, *The Execution of Admiral John Byng as a Microhistory of Eighteenth-Century Britain* (Routledge, 2021).

117. Pocock, *Battle for Empire*, 32f.
118. Voltaire, *Candide*, 114.
119. Price and Dodwell, *Diary of Ananda Ranga Pillai*, 10:176–177.
120. Gerald James Bryant, "The War in the Carnatic," in Danley and Speelman, *Global Views*, 90.
121. Bryant, "The War in the Carnatic," 79.
122. Mann, "Der ungeliebte Krieg," 104–114; Bryant, "War in the Carnatic."
123. Channa Wickremesekera, *Best Black Troops in the World: British Perceptions and the Making of the Sepoy, 1746–1805* (Manohar, 2002); Dirk H. A. Kolff, *Naukar, Rajput and Sepoy: The Ethnohistory of the Military Labour Market in Hindustan 1450–1850* (Cambridge University Press, 1990); Bryant, "Indigenous Mercenaries."
124. Mann, "Der ungeliebte Krieg," 111.
125. On the trade in saltpeter, see Mann, *Bengalen im Umbruch*, 45–47; David Cressy, *Saltpeter: The Mother of Gunpowder* (Oxford University Press, 2013), 143–151; on Prussian saltpeter production, see Warnke, *Logistik und friderizianische Kriegführung*, 140–141; James W. Frey, "The Indian Saltpeter Trade, the Military Revolution, and the Rise of Britain as a Global Superpower," *The Historian* 71 (2009).
126. Bryant, "War in the Carnatic," 76.
127. On events in India, see also Marian Füssel, "Händler oder Krieger? Robert Clive, die East India Company und die Kapitalisierung des Siebenjährigen Krieges in Indien," in *Die Kapitalisierung des Krieges: Kriegsunternehmer im Spätmittelalter und in der Früher Neuzeit*, ed. Matthias Meinhardt and Markus Meumann (LIT, 2021), 133–153.
128. See Brijen K. Gupta, *Sirajuddaullah and the East India Company, 1756–1757: Background to the Foundation of British Power in India* (Brill, 1962).
129. See the "narrative" by Governor Drake in Samuel Charles Hill, ed., *Indian Records Series: Bengal in 1756–1757; A Selection of Public and Private Papers Dealing with the Affairs of the British in Bengal During the Reign of Siraj-Uddaula*, 3 vols. (Murray, 1905), vol. 1, 124; see also the letter of September 17, 1756, from the Council to the Court of Directors in London, in Hill, *Indian Records Series*, vol. 1, no. 89, 214–215.
130. Hill, *Indian Records Series*, vol. 1, no. 5, 3.
131. Jean Law de Lauriston, *Mémoire sur quelques affaires de l'Empire Mogol 1756–1761*, ed. (Champion, 1913), 63–66.
132. Lauriston, *Mémoire*.
133. See The Nawab to Coja Wajid, June 1, 1756, in Hill, *Indian Records Series*, vol. 1, no. 6, 4; Mann, *Bengalen im Umbruch*, 48f.
134. Noel Barber, *The Black Hole of Calcutta: A Reconstruction* (Collins, 1965); Gupta, *Sirajuddaullah and the East India Company*, 70–80.
135. Gupta, *Sirajuddaullah and the East India Company*, 78.

136. John Zephaniah Holwell, *A Genuine Narrative of the Deplorable Deaths of the English Gentlemen and Others Who Were Suffocated in the Black Hole* (London: Millar, 1758), 2. Another variation appeared in *Gentleman's Magazine* and was also translated into German: "A Genuine Narrative of the Sufferings of the Persons Who Were Confined in the Prison Called the Black Hole, in Fort William at Calcutta," *Gentleman's Magazine* 28 (1758), reprinted in John Walker, ed., *A Selection of Curious Articles from the Gentleman's Magazine*, vol. 3 (London: Longman, 1814); [John Zephaniah Holwell], "Zuverlässige Nachricht von den Drangsalen, so diejenigen Personen erlitten haben, welche in dem Gefängnisse, das schwarze Loch genannt, im Fort William zu Calcutta im Königreiche Bengalen eingesperret worden [. . .] aus einem Briefe von J. Z. Holwell und William Davis," *Bremisches Magazin zur Ausbreitung der Wissenschaften, Künste und Tugend* 3 (1759).
137. Iris Macfarlane, *The Black Hole or the Makings of a Legend* (Allen & Unwin, 1975); Kate Teltscher, "'The Fearful Name of the Black Hole': Fashioning an Imperial Myth," in *Writing India 1757–1990: The Literature of British India*, ed. Bart Moore-Gilbert (Manchester University Press, 1996); Jan Dalley, *The Black Hole. Money, Myth and Empire* (London: Collins, 2006); Ian Barrow, "The Many Meanings of the Black Hole of Calcutta," in *Tall Tales and True: India, Historiography and British Imperial Imaginings*, ed. Kate Brittlebank (Monash University Press, 2008); Ian David Shovlin, "Overseas Violence and the Seven Years' War: Alleged Atrocities Committed by Non-Europeans as a Subject for Public Discussion in British News Commentary, 1754–1764" (PhD diss., Durham University, 2018).
138. "Genuine Narrative of the Sufferings," 312.
139. "Genuine Narrative of the Sufferings," 313.
140. "Genuine Narrative of the Sufferings," 315.
141. "Genuine Narrative of the Sufferings," 319.
142. "Genuine Narrative of the Sufferings," 319–320.
143. Gupta, *Sirajuddaullah and the East India Company*, 72–73.
144. Dalley, *Black Hole*; Partha Chatterjee, *The Black Hole of Empire: History of a Global Practice of Power* (Princeton University Press, 2012).
145. Chatterjee, *Black Hole of Empire*, 25–26.
146. Dalley, *Black Hole*, xi.
147. See Charles Robert Wilson, ed., *Indian Record Series: Old Fort William in Bengal; A Selection of Official Documents Dealing with Its History*, 2 vols. (Murray, 1906), 2:100–104.
148. Wilson, *Indian Record Series*, 2:104.
149. Bryant, "War in the Carnatic," 89.
150. Mann, *Bengalen im Umbruch*, 52f.
151. Mann, *Bengalen im Umbruch*, 54.

152. On the negotiations over booty, which soon after prompted passage of a new law in Britain, see Mann, *Bengalen im Umbruch*. 56f.
153. Peter James Marshall, "War and Its Transformations: India 1754–1765," in *The Making and Unmaking of Empires: Britain, India, and America c. 1750–1783* (Oxford University Press, 2005).
154. See Lauriston, *Mémoire*, 105–137; Mark Bence-Jones, *Clive of India* (Constable-Associates, 1974), 115–118.
155. See Sushil Chaudhury, "The Imperatives of the Empire: Private Trade, Sub-Imperialism and the British Attack on Chandernagore, March 1757," *Studies in History* 8, no. 1 (1992).

3. A War Without Fronts: The German Theater

1. See a record from a convent in Jülich in Otto Dresemann, "Aus einer Chronik des Karthäuserklosters Vogelsang bei Jülich," *Annalen des Historischen Vereins für den Niederrhein inbesondere das Alte Erzbistum Köln* (1895): 92.
2. Bode, Rexhausen, and Wehking, "Das Eichsfeld im Siebenjährigen Krieg," 130.
3. Johann Daniel Gottlieb Herr, *Wohl und Wehe der Stadt Hameln während des Krieges von 1757 bis 1763 zusammengestellt von Manfred Börsch* (Stadtarchiv, 1986), unpag. [9].
4. Gustav Hammann, ed., *Die Bottendorfer Chronik des Johann Daniel Geitz: Der Siebenjährige Krieg von 1756–1763 im Frankenberger Land* (Pfarramt, 1974), 9.
5. Anonymous, "Das erfreuliche Ungewitter," in *Der Münchner Bott [. . .] auf das Gnadenreiche Christ-Jahr 1757* (Munich, 1757), 64.
6. Marcus von Salisch, *Treue Deserteure: Das Kursächsische Militär und der Siebenjährige Krieg* (Oldenbourg, 2008), 66–68.
7. Anuschka Tischer, *Offizielle Kriegsbegründungen in der Frühen Neuzeit: Herrscherkommunikation in Europa zwischen Souveränität und korporativem Selbstverständnis* (LIT, 2012), 37–38.
8. Otto Krauske, ed., *Preussische Staatsschriften aus der Regierungszeit König Friedrichs II.*, vol. 3, *Der Beginn des Siebenjährigen Krieges* (Berlin: Duncker, 1892), 121; Schort, *Politik und Propaganda*, 42–43.
9. The *Danziger Beyträge* published French and German versions of the text; see *Danziger Beyträge*, vol. 1, 1756, 191.
10. *Danziger Beyträge*, vol. 1, 1756, 193.
11. Krauske, *Preussische Staatsschriften*, 133–188; Schort, *Politik und Propaganda*, 43–48.
12. Krauske, *Preussische Staatsschriften*, 137.
13. Krauske, *Preussische Staatsschriften*, 139.
14. Schlenke, *England und das friderizianische Preussen*, 229; Hans Marcus, "Friedrichs des Großen literarische Propaganda in England: Eine Sammlung bisher

unveröffentlichten Archivmaterials," *Archiv für das Studium der Neueren Sprachen und Literaturen*, vol. 151 (1927): 161–243.
15. Schlenke, *England und das friderizianische Preussen*, 230.
16. Krauske, *Preussische Staatsschriften*, 140.
17. Frederick to Podewils and Finckenstein, Sedlitz, September 12, 1756, in Friedrich II, *Politische Correspondenz*, vol. 13, no. 8019, 377.
18. Krauske, *Preussische Staatsschriften*, 318–389; Schort, *Politik und Propaganda*, 58–72.
19. Krauske, *Preussische Staatsschriften*, 332.
20. Ulrich Bräker, *The Life Story and Real Adventures of the Poor Man of Toggenburg*, trans. Derek Bowman (Edinburgh University Press, 1970), 134; see also the letter by Christian Friedrich Zander in Zander, *Fundstücke*, 28.
21. Bräker, *Poor Man of Toggenburg*, 134.
22. On the events at Pirna, see the detailed account in Salisch, *Treue Deserteure*, 55–137.
23. Salisch, *Treue Deserteure*, 69–70.
24. Salisch, *Treue Deserteure*, 72.
25. Salisch, *Treue Deserteure*, 74.
26. On the spatial disposition of the battle, see Salisch, *Treue Deserteure*, 78–83.
27. Salisch, *Treue Deserteure*, 90–96.
28. Max Könnecke, "Ein Soldatenbrief aus der Zeit des siebenjährigen Krieges," *Mansfelder Blätter: Mitteilungen des Vereins für Geschichte und Altertümer der Graffschaft Mansfeld zu Eisleben* 9 (1895): 76.
29. Hans Carl Heinrich von Trautzschen, *Militärische und literarische Briefe des Herrn von T.: Die Feldzüge von 1756 bis 1763 betreffend* (Leipzig, 1769), 42.
30. See Bräker, *Poor Man of Toggenburg*, 137, on the misinterpretation; see Kloosterhuis, "Donner, Blitz und Bräker," 141–142.
31. Of the wide literature on the battle, see Christopher Duffy, *The Military Life of Frederick the Great* (Atheneum, 1986), 102–108; Duffy, *By Force of Arms*, 22–31; Kunisch, *Friedrich der Grosse*, 351–352. Of the older literature, see Großer Generalstab, *Der Siebenjährige Krieg*, vol. 1, *Pirna und Lobositz*, 262–285; Franz Quandt, "Die Schlacht bei Lobositz, 1. Okt. 1756" (Diss., Berlin: Max Pfeiffer, 1909); Max Immich, "Zur Schlacht bei Lobositz," *Forschungen zur Brandenburgischen und Preußischen Geschichte* 6 (1893): 355–376; Hermann Granier, *Die Schlacht bei Lobositz am 1. Oktober 1756* (Diss., Berlin, 1889).
32. On Browne, see Christopher Duffy, *Feldmarschall Browne: Irischer Emigrant—Kaiserlicher Heerführer-Gegenspieler Friedrichs II. von Preussen* (Herold, 1966), 280–301.
33. On Frederick's reports immediately after the battle, see Friedrich II, *Politische Correspondenz*, vol. 13, 479–487.
34. On this, see Möbius, "'Von Jast und Hitze.'" Jürgen Kloosterhuis has compiled other, hitherto unknown sources on Lobositz, including a letter by First Lieutenant Friedrich von Mengede. See Jürgen Kloosterhuis, "Zwischen Garbeck

und Lobosit: Ein westfälisch-märkischer Beitrag zur militärischen Sozial- und Ereignisgeschichte in der Zeit Friedrichs des Großen," *Der Märker* 45 (1996): 84–97; Kloosterhuis, "Donner, Blitz und Bräker," 173–181; finally, see also Neil Cogswell, ed., *Lobositz to Leuthen: Horace St. Paul and the Campaigns of the Austrian Army in the Seven Years War 1756–67* (Helion, 2017), 32–37.

35. Duffy, *Military Life*, 103.
36. Bräker, *Poor Man of Toggenburg*, 138–141; see the detailed account in Kloosterhuis, "Donner, Blitz und Bräker," 174–181.
37. Bräker, *Poor Man of Toggenburg*, 138.
38. Bleckwenn, *Preußische Soldatenbriefe*, 30.
39. Bräker, *Poor Man of Toggenburg*, 138–139.
40. Bräker, *Poor Man of Toggenburg*, 139.
41. Füssel, "Panduren, Kosaken und Sepoys," 187.
42. Bräker, *Poor Man of Toggenburg*, 139–140.
43. Bleckwenn, *Preußische Soldatenbriefe*, 2.
44. Bleckwenn, *Preußische Soldatenbriefe*, 3.
45. Kerler, *Tagebuch des preußischen Musketiers Dominicus*, 4–5.
46. "Bericht des Herzogs von Bevern von der am 1. Oct. 1756 vorgefallenen Schlacht bei Lowositz," in Anonymous, *Sammlung ungedruckter Nachrichten, so die Geschichte der Feldzüge der Preussen von 1740 bis 1779 erläutern*, 3 vols. (Dresden: Walther, 1782–1785; repr., LTR, 1983), 564. Citation to LTR edition.
47. Reinhard Walz, ed., "Kriegs- und Friedensbilder aus den Jahren 1754–1759: Nach dem Tagebuch des Leutnants Jakob F. von Lemcke," *Preußische Jahrbücher* 138 (1909): 25.
48. Bräker, *Poor Man of Toggenburg*, 140.
49. Bleckwenn, *Preußische Soldatenbriefe*, 4–5.
50. Bleckwenn, *Preußische Soldatenbriefe*, 7.
51. Bräker, *Poor Man of Toggenburg*, 141.
52. Kloosterhuis, "Donner, Blitz und Bräker," 179.
53. Kloosterhuis, "Donner, Blitz und Bräker," 136, 142, 172.
54. Curt Jany, "Aus den Erinnerungen eines Leibpagen des Großen Königs," *Hohenzollern-Jahrbuch* 16 (1912): 76.
55. See Bernhard Jahn, "Die Medialität des Krieges: Zum Problem der Darstellbarkeit von Schlachten am Beispiel der Schlacht von Lobosit (1.10.1756) im Siebenjährigen Krieg," in *"Krieg ist mein Lied": Der Siebenjährige Krieg in den zeitgenössischen Medien*, ed. Wolfgang Adam and Holger Dainat (Wallstein, 2007), 88–110.
56. Alfons Dopsch, *Das Treffen bei Lobosit, sein Ausgang und seine Folgen* (Graz: Styria, 1892).
57. *Wienerisches Diarium*, no. 80, Wednesday, October 6, 1756; Schort, *Politik und Propaganda*, 264f. and 412–416.

58. See Hans Jessen, "Die Nachrichtenpolitik Friedrichs des Großen im 7jährigen Krieg," *Zeitungswissenschaft* 15, nos. 11–12 (1940): 635.
59. [Christoph Gottlieb Richter], *Die Historie des Kriegs zwischen den Preussen und ihren Bundsgenossen und den Österreichern und ihren Bundsgenossen von dem Einfalle in Sachsen an bis zu dem Friedensschlusse zu Hubertusburg von R. Simeon Ben Jochai*, 6 vols. (Nürnberg, 1758–1763), 1:42–43; quoted in Lindner, *Die Peripetie des Siebenjährigen Krieges*, 16.
60. Alfred Ritter von Arneth, *Geschichte Maria Theresias*, vols. 5 and 6, *Maria Theresia und der siebenjährige Krieg, 1756–1763* (Vienna: Braumüller, 1875), 5:472 and n26.
61. *Wienerisches Diarium*, special edition, no. 82, October 13, 1756.
62. Kerler, *Tagebuch des preußischen Musketiers Dominicus*, 6–7. Psalm 151 is "Herr Gott dich loben wir" (We praise you lord God) and Psalm 152 is "Nun danket alle Gott" (Now all gives thanks to God).
63. Jacob de Cogniazo, *Geständnisse eines österreichischen Veterans in politisch-militärischer Hinsicht auf die interessantesten Verhältnisse zwischen Oestreich und Preußen, während der Regierung des Großen Königs der Preußen Friedrichs des Zweyten mit historischen Anmerkungen gewidmet den königlich preußischen Veteranen von dem Verfasser des freymüthigen Beytrags zur Geschichte des östreichischen Militär-Dienstes* (Breslau: Löwe, 1788–1791; repr., 4 vols., LTR, 1982), 2:238. All citations refer to the LTR edition.
64. Cogniazo, *Geständnisse eines österreichischen Veterans*, 238–239 in the note. On this point, see also Archenholz, "In Vienna for nine days prayers were offered up for those who had fallen in the battle, which was called by the wits, 'a thanksgiving that it was no worse.'" *History of the Seven Years War*, 20.
65. Jessen, "Die Nachrichtenpolitik," 635.
66. See Martin Welke, "Die Legende vom 'unpolitischen Deutschen': Zeitungslesen im 18. Jahrhundert als Spiegel des politischen Interesses," *Jahrbuch der Wittheit zu Bremen* 25 (1981): 176f.
67. Hermann Tiemann, ed., *Meta Klopstock geborene Moller Briefwechsel mit Klopstock ihren Verwandten und Freunden*, vol. 2, *1754–1758* (Maximilian-Gesellschaft, 1956), 529f.
68. Johann Wolfgang von Goethe, *The Auto-Biography of Goethe: Truth and Poetry—from My Own Life*, trans. John Oxenford (London: Bohn, 1848), 32.
69. Goethe, *Auto-Biography*, 33.
70. Wolfe, *Life and Letters*, 305.
71. Letter from Kleist to Gleim, from the camp at Pirna, October 3, 1756, in August Sauer, ed., *Ewald von Kleist's Werke*, theil 2, *Briefe von Kleist* (Herbert Lang, 1968), no. 197, 340–344.
72. Letter from Gleim to Kleist, at Halberstadt, October 6, 1756, in Sauer, *Kleist's Werke*, theil 3, *Briefe an Kleist*, no. 57, 152f.
73. Letter from Gleim to Kleist, October 24, 1756, in Sauer, *Kleist's Werke*, theil 3, *Briefe an Kleist*, no. 58, 155–156. Later, Gleim's *Grenadier Songs* included a

victory song for the Battle of Lobositz, with these lines: "And brothers, clever Braun [Browne] took flight, in envy of the heroes! He left the battling-field behind, to Frederick and to us!" Fritz Brüggemann, ed., *Der Siebenjährige Krieg im Spiegel der zeitgenössischen Literatur* (Reclam, 1935), 102.

74. For example, after the Prussian invasion of Saxony and after the defeat at Leuthen. Khevenhüller-Metsch, *Aus der Zeit Maria Theresias* 4:42, 137.
75. Khevenhüller-Metsch, *Aus der Zeit Maria Theresias* 4:47.
76. Kunisch, *Friedrich der Grosse*, 352–353.
77. Friedrich II, *Politische Correspondenz*, vol. 13, no. 8148, 483.
78. Salisch, *Treue Deserteure*, 116–119.
79. Salisch, *Treue Deserteure*, 128–130.
80. Könnecke, "Ein Soldatenbrief," 77.
81. Salisch, *Treue Deserteure*.
82. Könnecke, "Ein Soldatenbrief.", 77.
83. Salisch, *Treue Deserteure*, 136–137.
84. Max Koch, "Der deutsche Reichstag während des Siebenjährigen Krieges" (Diss., University of Bonn, 1950).
85. Schort, *Politik und Propaganda*, 99; Schlenke, *England und das friderizianische Preussen*, 231; Burkhardt, *Abschied vom Religionskrieg*, 66–99; Hermann Meyer, *Der Plan eines evangelischen Fürstenbundes im Siebenjährigen Kriege* (Celle: Schweiger & Pick, 1893).
86. See Siegfried Fitte, *Religion und Politik vor und während des siebenjährigen Krieges* (Berlin: Gaertner, 1899); Burkhardt, *Abschied vom Religionskrieg*; Johannes Burkhardt, "Religious War or Imperial War? Views of the Seven Years' War from Germany and Rome," in Danley and Speelman, *Global Views*, 107–133; Fuchs, "Der Siebenjährige Krieg als virtueller Religionskrieg."
87. In a postscript in a letter written to Count von Podewils, a senior Prussian minister, after the Battle of Hohenfriedeberg, Frederick notes: "Have the Te-Deum-ing etc. done, as you see fit." Frederick to Minister of State Count von Podewils in Berlin, June 6, 1745, in Friedrich II, *Politische Correspondenz*, vol. 4, 187. On the ceremonial of information, see Michèle Fogel, *Les cérémonies de l'information dans la France du XVIe au milieu du XVIIIe siècle* (Fayard, 1989).
88. Johannes Burkhardt, *Vollendung und Neuorientierung des frühmodernen Reiches 1648–1763*, 6th ed. (Klett-Cotta, 2006), 406.
89. Wolf-Dieter Hauschild, "Religion und Politik bei Friedrich dem Großen," *Saeculum* 51 (2000): 191–211.
90. Stollberg-Rilinger, *Maria Theresa*, 436–438.
91. Michael Rohrschneider, *Österreich und der Immerwährende Reichstag: Studien zur Klientelpolitik und Parteibildung (1745–1763)* (Vandenhoeck & Ruprecht, 2014), 143ff.

92. *Das Preußische A.B.C. oder Lob-Gedicht auf den Königl: Preußischen Minister Freyherrn von Plotho* (Vienna, 1760), cited in Rohrschneider, *Österreich und der Immerwährende Reichstag*, 146.
93. Schort, *Politik und Propaganda*, 264–274.
94. Reproduced in [Eckstädt], *Die Geheimnisse des Sächsischen Cabinets: Ende 1745 bis Ende 1756*, 2 vols. (Stuttgart: Cotta, 1866), 177–182; the full name of the Austrian directorial envoy (*Direktorialgesandter*) was Marquard Paris Anton Freiherr von Buchenberg zu Ullersdorf.
95. Eckstädt, *Geheimnisse*, 177.
96. Eckstädt, *Geheimnisse*, 266–267.
97. Eckstädt, *Geheimnisse*, 268–274.
98. Alois Schmid, *Max III. Joseph und die europäischen Mächte: Die Außenpolitik des Kurfürstentums Bayern von 1745–1765* (Oldenbourg, 1987), 358–359.
99. For details of the events, see Sven Düwel, *Ad bellum Sacri Romano Germanici Imperii solenne decernendum: Die Reichskriegserklärung gegen Brandenburg-Preußen im Jahr 1757; Das Verfahren der 'preußischen Befehdungssache' 1756/57 zwischen Immerwährendem Reichstag und Wiener Reichsbehörden*, 2 vols. (LIT, 2016), 2:599–664.
100. Düwel, *Ad bellum Sacri Romano Germanici Imperii solenne decernendum*, 2:616–617; these figures are sometimes given as sixty-one to twenty-three rather than sixty-two to twenty-six.
101. The older study by Theodor Bitterauf, *Die kurbayerische Politik im siebenjährigen Kriege* (Beck, 1901), should be supplemented by Schmid, *Max III. Joseph*, 348–475; and Hans Gerspacher, *Die badische Politik im Siebenjährigen Krieg* (Carl Winter, 1934).
102. Schmid, *Max III. Joseph*, 359–365.
103. Schmid, *Max III. Joseph*, 373–378.
104. Schmid, *Max III. Joseph*, 379.
105. Schmid, *Max III. Joseph*, 384–386, 393–396.
106. Schmid, *Max III. Joseph*, 424–430.
107. [Montag], *Teutsche Kriegs-Canzley*, vol. 4, 946–951.
108. Rohrschneider, *Österreich und der Immerwährende Reichstag*, 143 and n246.
109. [Montag], *Teutsche Kriegs-Canzley*, vol. 4, 950.
110. Rohrschneider, *Österreich und der Immerwährende Reichstag*, 146.
111. Burkhardt, *Vollendung und Neuorientierung des frühmodernen Reiches 1648–1763*, 415; for more on the context, see Andreas Kalipke, *Verfahren im Konflikt. Konfessionelle Streitigkeiten und Corpus Evangelicorum im 18. Jahrhundert* (Aschendorff, 2015); Stollberg-Rilinger, *Maria Theresa*, 434–436; Meyer, *Plan eines evangelischen Fürstenbundes*, 75–79.

4. 1757: The Year of Battles

1. See Max Braubach, "Politik und Kriegführung am Niederrhein während des siebenjährigen Krieges," in *Diplomatie und geistiges Leben im 17. Und 18. Jahrhundert: Gesammelte Abhandlungen* (Röhrscheid, 1969); Leopold Henrichs, *Das Fürstentum Moers im Siebenjährigen Krieg* (Kaltenmeier & Verhuven, 1917).
2. Carl, *Okkupation und Regionalismus*, 61.
3. Luise Dorothée to Voltaire, Gotha, April 19, 1757, in Raschke, *Briefwechsel*, 107.
4. Füssel and Petersen, *Grotehenn Briefe*, 31.
5. Bolotov, *Leben und Abenteuer*, 1:203–204.
6. Dirrheimer and Fritz, "Einhörner und Schuwalowsche Haubitzen."
7. Bolotov, *Leben und Abenteuer*, 1:204.
8. Ferdinand von Westphalen, ed., *Geschichte der Feldzüge Herzog Ferdinands von Braunschweig-Lüneburg*, 5 vols. (Berlin:Verl. d. Königl. Geheimen Ober-Hofbuchdr., 1859–72), 1:247–248; on Westphalia, see Hans Donalies, "Der Anteil des Sekretärs Westphalen an den Feldzügen des Herzogs Ferdinand von Braunschweig (1758–62)," *Forschungen zur Brandenburgischen und Preußischen Geschichte* 8 (1895); Otto Weerth, *Die Grafschaft Lippe und der siebenjährige Krieg* (Detmold: Meyer, 1888), 9–11.
9. Füssel and Petersen, *Grotehenn Briefe*, 34–36; [Gilsa], *Adeliges Leben am Ausgang des Ancien Régime*, 16–17; George Beß, "Aus dem Tagebuch eines Veteranen des siebenjährigen Krieges: Mitgetheilt durch den Obersten z. D. Wilhelm Beß," *Zeitschrift des Vereins für Hessische Geschichte und Landeskunde* 12 (1878).
10. [Gilsa], *Adeliges Leben am Ausgang des Ancien Régime*, 16.
11. Beß, "Aus dem Tagebuch," 195. "Half Moons" is a reference to the Jägers' crescent-shaped hunting horns.
12. D'Estrées's full name was Louis-Charles-César Le Tellier, Chevalier de Louvois, Marquis de Courtanvaux; in 1763, he became Duc d'Estrées.
13. Theodor Weddigen, "Bielefeld und das Haus Milse im siebenjährigen Kriege," *13. Jahresbericht des Historischen Vereins für die Grafschaft Ravensberg* (1899): 29–31.
14. Evan Edward Charteris, *William Augustus Duke of Cumberland and the Seven Years' War* (Hutchinson, [1925]).
15. Christopher Clark, *Iron Kingdom: The Rise and Downfall of Prussia, 1600–1947* (Harvard University Press, 2009), 477; Szabo, *Seven Years War*, 48–51.
16. "Die Generalprinzipien des Krieges und ihre Anwendung auf die Taktik und Disziplin der preußischen Truppen (1748)," in Volz, *Werke Friedrichs*, 6:77.
17. From the older historiography, see Johann von Heilmann, *Beitrag zur Geschichte des Feldzugs von 1757* (Berlin: Mittler, 1854); Warnke, *Logistik und friderizianische Kriegführung* provides a more recent, detailed account.
18. Sven Externbrink, "'Que l'homme est cruel et méchant!' Wahrnehmung von Krieg und Gewalt durch französische Offiziere im Siebenjährigen Krieg," *Historische Mitteilungen* 18 (2005): 51.

19. Theodor von Bernhardi, *Friedrich der Große als Feldherr*, 2 vols. (Berlin: Mittler, 1881), 1:4; on Henry as a commander, see Richard Schmitt, *Prinz Heinrich von Preussen als Feldherr im siebenjährigen Kriege*, 2 vols. (Greifswald: Abel, 1885–1897); for details of his life, see Eva Ziebura, *Prinz Heinrich von Preußen* (Stapp, 1999), 93–158.
20. Duffy, *Armee Maria Theresias*, 133.
21. Goethe, *The Auto-Biography of Goethe*, 55.
22. See Johannes Kunisch, "Friedensidee und Kriegshandwerk im Zeitalter der Aufklärung," in *Fürst—Gesellschaft—Krieg: Studien zur bellizistischen Disposition des absoluten Fürstenstaats* (Böhlau, 1992), 131–159.
23. Kunisch, *Friedrich der Grosse*, 359.
24. Friedrich Amann, *Die Schlacht bei Prag am 6. Mai 1757: Quellenkritische Untersuchungen* (Heidelberg: Petters, 1887); Großer Generalstab, *Der Siebenjährige Krieg*, vol. 2, *Prag*; Maximilian von Hoen, "Die Schlacht von Prag am 6. Mai 1757," *Streffleurs militärische Zeitschrift* 1 (1911): 11–44, 369–404, 581–612, 773–796, 939–958; Stefan Hartmann, "Zur Geschichte der Schlacht bei Prag am 6. Mai 1757," *Jahrbuch preußischer Kulturbesitz* 27 (1991); Duffy, *By Force of Arms*, 46–51; Möbius, "Kriegsgreuel in den Schlachten des Siebenjährigen Krieges," 196–199.
25. Warnke, *Logistik und friderizianische Kriegführung*, 277.
26. Hartmann, "Zur Geschichte der Schlacht bei Prag," 362.
27. Andrew Bisset, ed., *Memoirs and Papers of Sir Andrew Mitchell. K. B.: Envoy Extraordinary and Minister Plenipotentiary from the Court of Great Britain to the Court of Prussia, from 1756 to 1771*, 2 vols. (London: Chapman and Hall, 1850), 325. Julius Caesar won a decisive victory over Pompey at Pharsalus in 48 BCE.
28. Walz, "Kriegs- und Friedensbilder aus den Jahren 1754–1759," 27.
29. Khevenhüller-Metsch, *Maria Theresia*, 4:113–114; Stollberg-Rilinger, *Maria Theresa*, 418.
30. Duffy, *Military Life of Frederick the Great*, 116–117.
31. Caspar Aubert, ed., "Prag und Kolin: Ein glücklicher und ein unglücklicher Tag aus dem Kriegsleben des Grossen Königs; Nach dem Tagebuch eines norwegischen Offiziers [Georg Friedrich v. Krogh] während des Feldzuges in Böhmen 1757," *Militär-Wochenblatt* 1913, supp. 6 (1913): 176; see also Duffy, *Military Life of Frederick the Great*, 117.
32. Duffy, *Feldmarschall Browne*, 340–348.
33. Bleckwenn, *Preußische Soldatenbriefe*, 51.
34. Warnke, *Logistik und friderizianische Kriegführung*, 283, which corrects the numbers provided by the General Staff, Prague, Annex 5, 9*–10*; Duffy, *Military Life of Frederick the Great*, 120; Hartmann, "Zur Geschichte der Schlacht bei Prag," 367.
35. Prittwitz, *Jugend und Kriegsleben eines preußischen Offiziers*, 47.
36. Marian Füssel, "Der inszenierte Tod: Militärische Sterbe- und Beerdigungsrituale im Kontext des Siebenjährigen Krieges," in *Übergänge schaffen: Ritual und*

Performanz in der frühneuzeitlichen Militärgesellschaft, ed. Ralf Pröve and Carmen Winkel (V&R unipress, 2012), 139–143.

37. Albert Naudé, "Berichte des Prinzen Moritz von Anhalt-Dessau über die Schlachten bei Prag, Kolin, Roßbach, Leuthen und Zorndorf," *Forschungen zur Brandenburgischen und Preußischen Geschichte* 5 (1892): 236. Two weeks later, in a letter written on May 21, Maurice repeated the claim with more specificity: "On the 6th of May took place probably the greatest Bataille in two lifetimes [2 letzten Seculis]." Naudé, "Berichte des Prinzen Moritz von Anhalt-Dessau, 237.
38. Bleckwenn, *Preußische Soldatenbriefe*, 6ff.
39. Bleckwenn, *Preußische Soldatenbriefe*, 7.
40. Bleckwenn, *Preußische Soldatenbriefe*, 7f.
41. Prittwitz, *Jugend und Kriegsleben eines preußischen Offiziers*, 45.
42. Reproduced in Hartmann, "Zur Geschichte der Schlacht bei Prag," 369.
43. Bolotov, *Leben und Abenteuer*, 1:210.
44. *Berlinische Nachrichten*, No. 56, Tuesday, May 10; Amann, *Schlacht bei Prag*, 14.
45. Warnke, *Logistik und friderizianische Kriegführung*, 309–317; on the figures, see 310–311. On the situation in Prague, see also the letter of June 7, 1757, from Luise Dorothée to Voltaire, in Raschke, *Briefwechsel*, 112.
46. Warnke, *Logistik und friderizianische Kriegführung*, 324.
47. Warnke, *Logistik und friderizianische Kriegführung*, 325.
48. Prittwitz, *Jugend und Kriegsleben eines preußischen Offiziers*, 53–56.
49. A large proportion of the older literature is now available in a collection of documents: Ulf-Joachim Friese, ed., Die Schlacht bei Kolin am 18. Juni 1757 und die Tage davor und danach in preußischer und österreichischer Darstellung, 2 vols. (LTR, 2006). From more recent historiography, see, above all, Peter Broucek, *Der Geburtstag der Monarchie: Die Schlacht bei Kolin 1757* (Österreichischer Bundesverlag, 1982). For an account of an eyewitness on the Austrian side, see Charles Joseph de Ligne, *Mon journal de la guerre de sept ans: Textes inédits introduits, établis et annotés par Jeroom Vercruysse et Bruno Colson* (Champion, 2008), 64–67, 251–255; Cogniazo, *Geständnisse*, 2:347–368; for the Austrian perspective, see Duffy, *By Force of Arms*, 51–56.
50. Prittwitz, *Jugend und Kriegsleben eines preußischen Offiziers*, 56; on the musicians, see Sascha Möbius, "'Ein feste Burg ist unser Gott . . .!' und 'das entsetzliche Lärmen ihrer Trommeln': Preußische Militärmusik in den Schlachten des Siebenjährigen Krieges," in *"Mars und die Musen": das Wechselspiel von Militär, Krieg und Kunst in der Frühen Neuzeit*, ed. Jutta Nowosadtko and Matthias Rogg (LIT, 2008).
51. Franz Martin Mayer, "Zur Geschichte des siebenjährigen Krieges," *Mitteilungen des Instituts für Österreichische Geschichtsforschung* 7 (1886): 385.
52. Großer Generalstab, *Der Siebenjährige Krieg*, vol. x, Kolin, 87–88, corrected in Warnke, *Logistik und friderizianische Kriegführung*, 333–337.

53. On explanations given for the defeat, see Duffy, *Military Life of Frederick the Great*, 130–131.
54. Khevenhüller-Metsch, *Maria Theresia*, 4:98.
55. *Wienerisches Diarium*, special edition, No. 50, June 22, 1757; *Gazette de Cologne*, June 28, 1757.
56. *Berlinische Nachrichten*, No. 84, Thursday, July 14, 1757, 333–336.
57. Letter written by Ingersoll at Bischofsheim, July 1, 1757, in Karl Brodrück, *Quellenstücke und Studien über den Feldzug der Reichsarmee von 1757: Ein Beitrag zur deutschen Geschichte im 18. Jahrhundert* (Leipzig: Dyk, 1858), 76.
58. Letter written by Ingersoll at Fürth, July 23, 1757, in Brodrück, *Quellenstücke*, 82.
59. Bolotov, *Leben und Abenteuer*, 1:212–213.
60. Bolotov, *Leben und Abenteuer*, 1:213.
61. Flucke, *Die litterae annuae*, 1094–1095.
62. See Alfred Dreyer, "Hamburgische Stimmungsbilder aus den ersten Jahren des Siebenjährigen Krieges," *Hamburgische Geschichts- und Heimatblätter* 4 (1929): 64.
63. Cogniazo, *Geständnisse*, 2:369–374, Arneth, *Maria Theresias*, 5:199–200; Broucek, *Der Geburtstag der Monarchie*, 135–144; Stollberg-Rilinger, *Maria Theresa*, 421.
64. Arneth, *Maria Theresias*, 5:199.
65. Marian Füssel, "Ungesehenes Leiden? Tod und Verwundung auf den Schlachtfeldern des 18. Jahrhunderts," *Historische Anthropologie* 23, no. 1 (2015): 37–39, which draw on Gottfried Uhlig von Uhlenau, *Erinnerungen an die Schlacht von Kolin und die damalige Zeit: Nach authentischen Quellen bearbeitet und zur Säkular-Feier am 18. Juni 1857 herausgegeben* (Vienna: Braumüller, 1857), 212–227.
66. Ibid.
67. See Marian Füssel, "Zwischen Schauspiel, Information und Strafgericht: Visualisierungen und Deutung von brennenden Städten im Siebenjährigen Krieg," in *Urbs incensa: Ästhetische Transformationen der brennenden Stadt in der Frühen Neuzeit*, ed. Vera Fionie Koppenleitner et al. (Deutscher Kunstverlag, 2011), 307–310; see also Zittauer Geschichts- und Museumsverein e. V., ed., *Macht und Ohnmacht: 250. Jahrestag der Zerstörung Zittaus am 23. Juli 1757* (Zittauer Geschichts- und Museumsverein, 2007); Duffy, *By Force of Arms*, 61–62. From the older literature, see Gottlieb Korschelt, "Das Bombardement von Zittau," *Neues Lausitzisches Magazin* 62 (1886).
68. Johann Daniel de Montalegre, *Die vormahls in ihrem Flor stehende nunmehro aber in Ruin und Asche liegende Königl. Pohlnische und Churfürstl; Sächsische Sechs-Stadt Zittau in der Ober-Lausitz in XXI. Kupffer-Platten* (Zittau, 1758; repr., Neisse, 2000).
69. For example, see Christian Gottlieb Cunitius, *Das höchst betrübte Schicksal der in der Oberlausiz gelegenen Churfürstl. Sächsischen Sechsstadt Zittau, Bey deren am 23. Julii dieses jetzt laufenden 1757. Jahres durch die Kayserl. Königl. Armée erfolgten Einnahme [. . .]* (Zittau, [1757]), 4.

70. Anonymous, *Das traurige Andenken des bejammernswürdigen Schicksals, welches die gute Stadt Zittau am 23sten Julius, 1757: Wie auch vorhergehende und nachfolgende Tage ausgestanden; Nebst einigen Beylagen* (n.p., 1757), 3 recto.
71. Anonymous, *Das traurige Andenken*, 4 [n.p.]. As an appendix to his report, Cunitius published a list specifying "persons shot and burned to death in Zittau on July 23, 1757" (Specification Derer durch Schuß und Brand am 23. Juli 1757 verunglückten Personen in Zittau), naming a total of seventy-three victims who were "suffocated in cellars and found dead"; see the documentation of the dead in Cunitius, *Das höchst betrübte Schicksal*, 21–24.
72. Montalegre, *Die vormahls in ihrem Flor stehende*, unpag.
73. Cunitius, *Das höchst betrübte Schicksal*, 15.
74. On the controversy surrounding of the bombardment of Zittau, see, in particular, Schort, *Politik und Propaganda*, 402f.; see also various texts in [Montag], *Teutsche Kriegs-Canzley* vol. 3, no. 64–66, 371–386.
75. Andreas Lazarus von Imhof, *Des neueröfneten Historischen Bilder-Saals Dreyzehnder Theil* (Nürnberg: Buggel & Seitz, [1762]), 87–88. This contains an image of the bombardment. On the negative media coverage, see also [Richter], *Die Historie des Kriegs*, 162.
76. Warnke, *Logistik und friderizianische Kriegführung*, 374–376.
77. Mayer, "Zur Geschichte des siebenjährigen Krieges," 413–417.
78. Arneth, *Maria Theresias*, 5:206.
79. This is made clear in the correspondence of Duchess Maria Antonia, electress of Saxony. See Woldemar Lippert, ed., *Kaiserin Maria Theresia und Kurfürstin Maria Antonia von Sachsen: Briefwechsel 1747–1772; Mit einem Anhang ergänzender Briefe* (Teubner, 1908), 312.
80. Gustav Berthold Volz, ed., *Friedrich der Große und Wilhelmine von Baireuth*, vol. 2, *Briefe der Königszeit: 1740–1758*. (Koehler, 1926), 361f.
81. Georg von Frantzius, "Die Okkupation Ostpreußens durch die Russen im siebenjährigen Krieg mit besonderer Berücksichtigung der russischen Quellen" (Diss., University of Berlin, 1916).
82. Bolotov, *Leben und Abenteuer*, 1:215–217.
83. The colonel's full name was Paul Joseph Malachow von Malachowski.
84. Bolotov, *Leben und Abenteuer*, 1:216.
85. Bolotov, *Leben und Abenteuer*, 1:217.
86. For details of peasant resistance, see Ernst A. Legahn, "Preußische Partisanen," *Wehrwissenschaftliche Rundschau* 18 (1968).
87. Bolotov, *Leben und Abenteuer*, 1:217.
88. Möbius, "Kriegsgreuel in den Schlachten des Siebenjährigen Krieges"; Füssel, "Die Aasgeier des Schlachtfeldes."
89. Bolotov, *Leben und Abenteuer*, 1:221. For local perceptions of Russian soldiers, see Friedrich Pastenaci, "Fragmente aus dem Tagebuch des Hospital Predigers

Pastenaci über die im Jahr 1757 vorgefallene Invasion des russischen Heeres ins Königreich Preußen, die Stadt Gumbinen betreffend," *Neue preußische provinzial Blätter*, vol. 11(1866).
90. Bolotov, *Leben und Abenteuer*, 1:225.
91. Frederick to Lehwaldt, in Friedrich II, *Politische Correspondenz*, vol. 12, no. 7601, 448–457.
92. Frederick to Lehwaldt, in Friedrich II, *Politische Correspondenz*, vol. 12, no. 7601, 451.
93. Großer Generalstab, *Der Siebenjährige Krieg*, vol. 4, *Groß-Jägersdorf und Breslau*, 47–115.
94. Bolotov, *Leben und Abenteuer*, 1:236.
95. Bolotov, *Leben und Abenteuer*, 1:237.
96. Bolotov, *Leben und Abenteuer*, 1:238.
97. Bolotov, *Leben und Abenteuer*, 1:239.
98. Großer Generalstab, *Der Siebenjährige Krieg*, vol. 4, *Groß-Jägersdorf und Breslau*, 98.
99. Bolotov, *Leben und Abenteuer*, 1:256.
100. Masslowski, *Der siebenjährige Krieg nach russischer Darstellung*, 1:266.
101. Masslowski, *Der siebenjährige Krieg nach russischer Darstellung*, 2:2–3.
102. Bolotov, *Leben und Abenteuer*, 1:261.
103. See Hasenkamp, *Ostpreußen unter dem Doppelaar*, 211ff.; [Johann George Bock], "Die Occupation Königsbergs durch die Russen während des siebenjährigen Krieges," [ed. F. W. Schubert], *Neue preußische Provinzial-Blätter, dritte Folge* (1858): pt. 1, 1:71.
104. See the report by Cantor Rosenbaum in "Nachrichten von der den 24. September 1757 von den Russen und Cosacken verübten Plünderung und Einäscherung der Stadt Ragnit in Preußen," *Beiträge zur Kunde Preußens*, n.s. vol. 1 (1837): 153–162.
105. Theodor Werner, "Beschreibung von Vice-Bürgermeister Werner über Verwüstung Ragnits," *Preußische Provinzialblätter* 14 (1835): 417–420; [Rosenbaum], "Plünderung und Einäscherung der Stadt Ragnit."
106. Werner, "Beschreibung," 417.
107. However, accounts of rape may have been embellished: According to one eyewitness report: "It was also said that the Cossacks and Callmucks raped women violently, of which I have no certainty. This much is certain, however, that no bastard child was baptized, as shown here by the German and Lithuanian baptismal registers." [Rosenbaum], "Plünderung und Einäscherung der Stadt Ragnit," 140.
108. [Rosenbaum], "Plünderung und Einäscherung der Stadt Ragnit," 129.
109. [Rosenbaum], "Plünderung und Einäscherung der Stadt Ragnit," 129f.
110. Thus, Hasenkamp already makes distinctions between the humanity of Cossacks and that of Kalmyks, Hasenkamp, *Ostpreußen unter dem Doppelaar*, 215.

See, for example, the report of Donalitius, an eyewitness: "In general, the Kalmucks, most of whom were Mahomedans but who also included some pagans, proved much more humane and compassionate than the Cosacks in all incidents, although the latter all claimed the name of Christians." [Rosenbaum], "Plünderung und Einäscherung der Stadt Ragnit," 169.
111. [Rosenbaum], "Plünderung und Einäscherung der Stadt Ragnit," 169.
112. Ortmann's eighteenth letter quotes extensively from news reports on the ongoing war in Prussia. See Adolph Dietrich Ortmann, *Patriotische Briefe zur Vermahnung und zum Troste bey dem jetzigen Kriege* (Berlin: Voß, 1758), no. 18, 285–291.
113. Bolotov, *Leben und Abenteuer*, 1:268.
114. See *Danziger Beyträge*, vols. 31–34, 1758, 69–80 (Apraksin to Lehwald and enclosure; Lehwald to Apraksin and enclosure).
115. According to Masslowski, Ragnit was burned to the ground because "the inhabitants had fired upon the Cossacks as they marched away," Masslowski, *Der siebenjährige Krieg nach russischer Darstellung*, 1:260.
116. *Danziger Beyträge*, vols. 31–34, 1758, 75f.
117. *Danziger Beyträge*, vols. 31–34, 1758, 76.
118. *Danziger Beyträge*, vols. 31–34, 1758, 76.
119. Hasenkamp, *Ostpreußen unter dem Doppelaar*, 219.
120. Hasenkamp, *Ostpreußen unter dem Doppelaar*, 219f.
121. See Masslowski, *Der siebenjährige Krieg nach russischer Darstellung*, 1:35. On how Kalmyks were perceived by western armies, see also Ernst von Frisch, *Zur Geschichte der russischen Feldzüge im Siebenjährigen Kriege nach den Aufzeichnungen und Beobachtungen der dem russischen Hauptquartier zugeteilten österreichischen Offiziere vornehmlich in den Kriegsjahren 1757/58* (Winter, 1919), 28.
122. See, for example, the account given by Hans Heinrich von Weymarn in *Über den ersten Feldzug des Russischen Kriegsheeres gegen die Preußen im Jahr 1757: Aus Archivalnachrichten, welche der unlängst verstorbene Russ. Kaiserl. General en Chef und Ritter Herr Hans Heinrich von Weymarn, auf erhaltenen Befehl der Kaiserlichen Conferenz zu St. Petersburg 1758 überreicht hat; Ein merkwürdiger Beytrag zur Geschichte des siebenjährigen Krieges; Nebst einem Plan der Bataille bey Groß-Jägerndorf, herausgegeben von August Wilhelm Hupel*, ed. August Wilhelm Hupel (Riga: Hartknoch, 1794), 53–62.
123. Archenholz, *History of the Seven Years War*, 96; repeated almost verbatim in Carl Wilhelm von Hülsen, *Unter Friedrich dem Großen: Aus den Memoiren des Aeltervaters 1752–1773*, ed. Helene von Hülsen (repr., Biblio, 1974), 48; for context, see Hasenkamp, *Ostpreußen unter dem Doppelaar*, 227.
124. Moritz Oppermann, *Die Schlacht bei Hastenbeck: Zum 250. Jahrestag am 26. Juli 2007* (Niemeyer, 2007), 25–29 first edition published 1957; citation is to 2007 edition. Olivier Lapray, *Hastenbeck 1757: The French Army and the Opening Campaign of the Seven Years War* (Helion, 2021).

125. Oppermann, *Die Schlacht bei Hastenbeck*, 22.
126. On the French view, see Pierre-Victor de Besenval, *Mémoires de M. le Baron de Besenval écrits par lui-même, imprimés sur son manuscrit original, et publiés par son exécuteur testamentaire: Contenant beaucoup de particularités et d'anecdotes sur la Cour, sur les ministres et les règnes de Louis XV et Louis XVI, et sur les événemens du temps*, 4 vols. (Paris: Buisson, 1805), 1:81–92; for witnesses on the Allied side, see Füssel and Petersen, *Grotehenn Briefe*, 38–40.
127. Großer Generalstab, *Der Siebenjährige Krieg*, vol. 5, *Hastenbeck und Rossbach*, 108.
128. See also Gerhard Niemann, "Die Operationen im Westen während des Siebenjährigen Krieges bis zur Schlacht von Hastenbeck und die Schlacht bei Hastenbeck am 26. Juli 1757," *Wehrwissenschaftliche Rundschau* 11 (1961): 596.
129. See Oppermann, *Die Schlacht bei Hastenbeck*, 26.
130. Oppermann, *Die Schlacht bei Hastenbeck*, 37–38.
131. Walther Mediger, "Hastenbeck und Zeven: Der Eintritt Hannovers in den Siebenjährigen Krieg," *Niedersächsisches Jahrbuch für Landesgeschichte* 56 (1984): 137–166.
132. "Lettre à ✳✳✳ concernant la convention de Kloster-Seven," in Rochus Friedrich von Lynar, *Hinterlassene Staatsschriften und Andere Aufsätze Vermischten Inhalts*, 2 vols. (Hamburg: Benjamin Gottlob Hoffmann, 1793–1797), 1:585–593, and the entire second volume.
133. Reprinted in Lynar, *Hinterlassene Staatsschriften*, vol. 2, 138–143, 146–150; a German version appears in [Montag], *Teutsche Kriegs-Canzley*, vol. 3, no. 102, 634–638.
134. Wähner, *Tagebuch aus dem Siebenjährigen Krieg*, 8; Jens Mastnak and Michael-Andreas Tänzer, eds., *Celle im Siebenjährigen Krieg: Das Tagebuch des Garnisonsauditeurs Johann Philipp Schowart* (Celle: Bomann-Museum, 2010), 93.
135. Maximilian Ritter von Thielen, "Des k.k. Feldmarschall-Lieutenants Andreas von Hadik Zug nach Berlin 1757," *Oestreichische militärische Zeitschrift* 2 (1835); Albert Naudé, "Die Einnahme von Berlin durch die Österreicher im Oktober 1757 und die Flucht der Königlichen Familie von Berlin nach Spandau," *Märkische Forschungen* 20 (1887); Tibor Simányi, *Die Österreicher in Berlin: Der Husarenstreich des Grafen Hadik anno 1757* (Amalthea, 1987); Duffy, *By Force of Arms*, 67–70.
136. Thielen, "Hadiks Zug nach Berlin," 133.
137. Helga Schultz, ed., *Der Roggenpreis und die Kriege des großen Königs: Chronik und Rezeptsammlung des Berliner Bäckermeisters Johann Friedrich Heyde 1740 bis 1786* (Siedler, 1988), 58. See also Friedrich Holtze, ed., "Chronistische Aufzeichnungen eines Berliners von 1704 bis 1758," *Schriften des Vereins für die Kechiche Berlins* 36 (1899): 106.
138. Thielen, "Hadiks Zug nach Berlin," 139.

139. Schultz, *Der Roggenpreis*, 58. This appears to refer to the hussar general Farkas Babocsay. See Simányi, *Die Österreicher in Berlin*, 114, 142.
140. Simányi, *Die Österreicher in Berlin*, 118.
141. Carl Schüddekopf, ed., *Briefwechsel zwischen Gleim und Ramler*, 2 vols. (Litterarischer Verein, 1899), vol. 2, no. 310, 297–298.
142. Khevenhüller-Metsch, *Maria Theresia*, 4:124.
143. Simányi, *Die Österreicher in Berlin*, 119–127.
144. Kunisch, *Friedrich der Grosse*, 375.
145. Johann Elieser Theodor Wiltsch, *Die Schlacht von nicht bei Roßbach oder Die Schlacht auf den Feldern von und bei Raichardtswerben den 5. November 1757, und was ihr voranging, und nachfolgte* (Halle: Anton'schen Sortiments-Buchhandlung, 1858) is an essential depiction of the battle; for operational history, see Großer Generalstab, *Der Siebenjährige Krieg*, vol. 5, *Hastenbeck und Rossbach*, 195–235; Christopher Duffy, *Prussia's Glory: Rossbach and Leuthen 1757* (Emperor's Press, 2003); Duffy, *By Force of Arms*, 79–81; on the contending interpretations of the battle, see Thomas Nicklas, "Die Schlacht von Roßbach (1757) zwischen Wahrnehmung und Deutung," *Forschungen zur Brandenburgischen und Preußischen Geschichte*, n.s., vol. 12, no. 1 (2002); see also Alexander Querengässer, ed., *The Battle of Rossbach 1757: New Perspectives on the Battle and Campaign* (Helion, 2022); Jean-Pierre Bois, *Rossbach 1757: La Prusse devient une puissance militaire* (Economica, 2021).
146. Jany, "Aus den Erinnerungen eines Leibpagen," 83.
147. Jany, "Aus den Erinnerungen eines Leibpagen," 84.
148. The first brief message arrived from Freyburg (Unstrut) on the evening of the battle, followed by the second from Erfurt on November 7, followed by a third, longer message from Anstadt later the same day. On November 8, Mollinger continued his report from headquarters at Teichel. Brodrück, *Quellenstücke*, 111.
149. Brodrück, *Quellenstücke*, 114. The reference is to the historian Jacques-Auguste de Thou (1553–1617), speaking of the St. Bartholomew's Day Massacre in Paris on August 24, 1572.
150. Brodrück, *Quellenstücke*, 115.
151. Brodrück, *Quellenstücke*, 116.
152. Großer Generalstab, *Der Siebenjährige Krieg*, vol. 5, *Hastenbeck und Rossbach*, 222.
153. Manfred Heinecker and Heiner Wajemann, eds., *Ein Leben zwischen Schule und Pfarrer: Die Memoiren des Schneverdinger Pastoren Johann Christian Meier 1732–1815* (Ludwig-Harms-Haus, 2011), 89–90.
154. Heinecker and Wajemann, *Ein Leben*, 90.
155. Friedrich II, *Politische Correspondenz*, vol. 16, no. 9489, 8.
156. Kunisch, *Friedrich der Grosse*, 377–378.
157. Anonymous, *Der Hohe Geist Gustav Adolphs des Grossen, Königs in Schweden, wie Er Sr. Königl. Majestät Friedrich dem Andern, König in Preußen [et]c. [et]c. kurz vor dem Siege bey Roßbach in dem Lüzner Schlacht-Felde erschienen* (n.p., 1758).

158. See Dziembowski, *La Guerre de Sept Ans*, 255–257; on textual and visual reportage on Rossbach, see also Pierre Rétat, "Aux confins de la presse: Information graphique et information écrite; Récits et plans de batailles," in *Le journalisme d'Ancien Régime: Questions et propositions*, ed. Pierre Rétat (Presses Universitaires de Lyon, 1982).
159. Edmond-Jean-François Barbier, *Journal historique et anecdotique du règne de Louis XV*, 4 vols. (Paris: Renouard, 1847–1856), 4:244–245.
160. Friedrich Schlachter, "Spottlieder in französischer Sprache, besonders auf die Franzosen aus dem Beginne des siebenjährigen Krieges" (Diss., Friedrich-Alexander University of Erlangen, 1901); Emmy Allard, *Friedrich der Große in der Literatur Frankreichs: Mit einem Ausblick auf Italien und Spanien* (Karras, 1913).
161. For a German translation of the mocking verses, see Wilhelm Oncken, *Das Zeitalter Friedrichs des Großen*, 2:185; see also Schlachter, "Spottlieder in französischer Sprache," vi.
162. On Bernis, see François-Joachim de Pierre de Bernis, *Mémoires et lettres de François-Joachim de Pierre cardinal de Bernis (1715–1758)*, ed. Frédéric Masson, 2 vols. (Paris: Plon, 1878).
163. On the reception of Prussian victories in Britain, see Schlenke, *England und das friderizianische Preussen*, 234–253.
164. David Vaisey, ed., *The Diary of Thomas Turner 1754–1765* (Oxford University Press, 1985), 99, 124f.
165. Dziembowski, *La Guerre de Sept Ans*, 258.
166. Mediger, *Herzog Ferdinand von Braunschweig-Lüneburg*, 45–47; "Vorläufige Anzeige der Ursachen, welche Ihro Königl. Majestät von Großbritannien, als Churfürst zu Braunschweig und Lüneburg . . . zu Wiederergreiffung der Waffen gegen die aufs neue im Anzuge begriffene Französische Armee bewegen, de dato Stade den 26. Nov. 1757," in [Montag], *Teutsche Kriegs-Canzley*, vol. 4, no. 22, 558–562; for other key sources, see the diary of Adjutant-General Johann Wilhelm von Reden (1717–1801), edited by his son-in-law, Wilhelm August von der Osten, *Feldzüge der alliierten Armee in den Jahren 1757 bis 1762 nach dem Tagebuche des Generaldjutanten, nachmaligen Feldmarschalls von Reden, Hamburg 1805–06* (LTR, 2005); and the observations of state secretary Christian Heinrich Philipp von Westphalen (1723–1792), in Westphalen, *Geschichte der Feldzüge Herzog Ferdinands von Braunschweig-Lüneburg*; Thomas Klingebiel, *Feldherrn der Aufklärung: Ferdinand von Braunschweig und Friedrich der Große* (Appelhans, 2022).
167. See Schneider, "Die Schlacht bei Minden," 46.
168. Mediger, *Herzog Ferdinand von Braunschweig-Lüneburg*, 49.
169. Füssel and Petersen, *Grotehenn Briefe*, 44; Mediger, *Herzog Ferdinand von Braunschweig-Lüneburg*, 55–56.
170. Mediger, *Herzog Ferdinand von Braunschweig-Lüneburg*, 58–61.

171. Burghardt Schmidt, "Die Kämpfe um die Festung Harburg im Siebenjährigen Krieg: Ein Beitrag zur Militärgeschichte des 18. Jahrhunderts," *Harburger Jahrbuch* 21 (2000).
172. Mediger, *Herzog Ferdinand von Braunschweig-Lüneburg*, 73–77.
173. Mastnak and Tänzer, *Tagebuch des Garnisonsauditeurs Johann Philipp Schowart*, 118.
174. Mastnak and Tänzer, *Tagebuch des Garnisonsauditeurs Johann Philipp Schowart*, 119.
175. Jacques Emmanuel Roques de Maumont, *Briefe an einen Freund während des Aufenthalts der französischen Truppen in Zelle, in den Jahren 1757 und 1758: Aus dem Französischen übersetzt* (Braunschweig: Waysenhaus, 1780).
176. Roques de Maumont, *Briefe an einen Freund*, 72–87.
177. Roques de Maumont, *Briefe an einen Freund*, 77.
178. Füssel and Petersen, *Grotehenn Briefe*, 45.
179. Mediger, *Herzog Ferdinand von Braunschweig-Lüneburg*, 92. "Capitulation bey der französischen Uebergabe des Schlosses zu Harburg an die Hannoverischen Truppen d. d. 29. Dec. 1757." [Montag], *Teutsche Kriegs-Canzley*, vol. 4, no. 42, 813–815.
180. See "Accords-Puncte zwischen dem Herzog von Broglio und der Stadt Bremen bey Einrückung der Französischen Trouppen in diese Stadt, d. d. Bremen den 17. Jan. 1758," in [Montag], *Teutsche Kriegs-Canzley*, vol. 1, no. 17.
181. Hugo Brunner, "Aufzeichnungen des Pfarrers Johann Christoph Cuntz zu Kirchditmold aus der Zeit des siebenjährigen Krieges (1757–1762)," *Zeitschrift des Vereins für hessische Geschichte und Landeskunde* 25 (1890): 144.
182. See Colmar Grünhagen, ed., "Journal bey Belagerung der Vestung Schweidnitz Anno 1757," *Zeitschrift für Geschichte und Alterthum Schlesiens* 7, no. 1 (1866): 57–69. Julius Schmidt, ed., "Diarium von der ersten und zweiten Belagerung der Festung Schweidnitz, was sich unter derselbigen in der Stadt und Vorstadt zugetragen. Aus einer Handschrift mitgetheilt," *Schlesische Provinzialblätter*, n.s., vol. 6 (1867): 514–526, 598–591, 645–655.
183. Großer Generalstab, *Der Siebenjährige Krieg*, vol. 4, *Groß-Jägersdorf und Breslau*, 195–221; Cogniazo, *Geständnisse*, 2:401–415.
184. Flashar, *Familienbuch Michaelis von Tschirschky*, vol. 2, *Memoiren der Eleonore Juliane von Rehdiger*, 124.
185. [Christian Täge], *Christian Täge's ehemaligen russischen Feldpredigers Lebensgeschichte, herausgegeben vom Verfasser der Novellen von Doro Caro* [i.e., August Samuel Gerber] (Königsberg: Goebbels und Unzor, 1804), 112–113.
186. Giuseppe Gorani, *Mémoires de Gorani* (Gallimard, 1944), 72.
187. Colmar Grünhagen and Franz Wachter, eds., *Akten des Kriegsgerichts von 1758 wegen der Kapitulation von Breslau am 24. November 1757* (Breslau: Max, 1895).
188. Khevenhüller-Metsch, *Maria Theresia*, 4:130.
189. For a detailed study, see Jürgen Kloosterhuis, *Menzel Militaris: Sein "Armeewerk" und das "Leuthen"-Bild im militärhistorischen Quellenkontext* (Geheimes Staatsarchiv Preußischer Kulturbesitz, 2015), 96.

190. Koser gives a synopsis of three eyewitness accounts of the speeches— by Tempelhof, Retzow, and Kaltenborn. Kaltenborn's version is cited here. Reinhold Koser, "Vor und nach der Schlacht bei Leuthen: Die Parchwitzer Rede und der Abend im Lissaer Schloß," *Forschungen zur Brandenburgischen und Preußischen Geschichte* 1 (1888): 607f.
191. Koser, "Vor und nach der Schlacht bei Leuthen," 608.
192. Koser, "Vor und nach der Schlacht bei Leuthen," 609.
193. Koser, "Vor und nach der Schlacht bei Leuthen," 611; Jany, "Aus den Erinnerungen eines Leibpagen des Großen Königs," 84.
194. Kloosterhuis, *Menzel Militaris*, 98–99.
195. Paul Gerber, *Die Schlacht bei Leuthen* (Ebering, 1901); Großer Generalstab, *Der Siebenjährige Krieg*, vol. 6, *Leuthen*; Duffy, *Prussia's Glory*; Duffy, *By Force of Arms*, 84–88; Thomas G. Otte, *Leuthen* (Oxford University Press, 2024).
196. Kroener, "Geburt eines Mythos."
197. On this, see Hohrath, "Verwandte—Freunde—Vorbilder."
198. Information on this is somewhat unclear in Kroener, "Geburt eines Mythos," 174; for a more detailed breakdown, see Duffy, *Prussia's Glory*, 134–136.
199. Kroener, "Geburt eines Mythos," 175.
200. Stefan Felleckner, *Kampf: Ein vernachlässigter Teil der Militärgeschichte; Augenzeugen aus dem Siebenjährigen Krieg (1756–63) und dem Ersten Weltkrieg (1914–18) berichten über Gefechte* (Westarp, 2004), 13–27.
201. Barsewisch, *Tagebuchblätter eines friderizianischen Fahnenjunkers und Offiziers*, 31.
202. Barsewisch, *Tagebuchblätter eines friderizianischen Fahnenjunkers und Offiziers*, 40.
203. Barsewisch, *Tagebuchblätter eines friderizianischen Fahnenjunkers und Offiziers*, 48.
204. Barsewisch, *Tagebuchblätter eines friderizianischen Fahnenjunkers und Offiziers*, 49.
205. Barsewisch, *Tagebuchblätter eines friderizianischen Fahnenjunkers und Offiziers*, 51–52.
206. Barsewisch, *Tagebuchblätter eines friderizianischen Fahnenjunkers und Offiziers*, 52.
207. Barsewisch, *Tagebuchblätter eines friderizianischen Fahnenjunkers und Offiziers*, 57.
208. Gustav Berthold Volz, *Friedrich der Große im Spiegel seiner Zeit*, vol. 2, *Siebenjähriger Krieg* (Hobbing, 1927), 120f.
209. Bernhard R. Kroener, "'Nun danket alle Gott!' Der Choral von Leuthen und Friedrich der Große als protestantischer Held: Die Produktion politischer Mythen im 19. und 20. Jahrhundert," in *"Gott mit uns": Religion, Nation und Gewalt im 19. und 20. Jahrhundert*, ed. Hartmut Lehmann and Gerd Krumeich (V&R unipress, 2000); Siegmar Keil, "Der Choral von Leuthen—ein preußisch-deutscher Mythos," *Die Tonkunst* 4 (2007).
210. "Capitulations-Punkte von der Uebergabe der Stadt Breßlau an Se. Königliche Majestät in Preußen, de dato 20. Decemb. 1757," in [Montag], Teutsche Kriegs-Canzley, vol. 4, no. 40, 806–809.
211. Khevenhüller-Metsch, *Maria Theresia*, 4:137.

212. Khevenhüller-Metsch, *Maria Theresia*, 4:140. On the Viennese reception of Leuthen, see also "Kaiserlich-Königliche Relation von der den 5. December 1757 zwischen Neumark und Lissa vorgefallenen Bataille," in [Montag], *Teutsche Kriegs-Canzley*, vol. 4, no. 57, 1059–1062.
213. Khevenhüller-Metsch, *Maria Theresia*, 4:143.
214. See Elke Bannicke, "Die Wiederherstellung der allgemeinen Glückseligkeit: Kolin und Leuthen—zwei Medaillen von 1757," *Numismatisches Nachrichtenblatt* 61, no. 9 (2012); Friedrich Benninghoven et al., eds., *Friedrich der Grosse: Ausstellung anläßlich des 200. Todestages König Friedrichs II. zu Preußen* (Geheimes Staatsarchiv Preußischer Kulturbesitz, 1986), 177, 187–189.
215. Manfred Olding, *Die Medaillen auf Friedrich den Großen von Preußen 1712 bis 1786; Anhang: Medaillen mit Bezug auf Preußen aus der Zeit von 1740 bis 1786* (Gietl, 2003), 114–115.
216. Schlachter, "Spottlieder in französischer Sprache," ix.
217. Wähner, *Tagebuch aus dem Siebenjährigen Krieg*, 23–24.
218. Wähner, *Tagebuch aus dem Siebenjährigen Krieg*, 24.
219. Wähner, *Tagebuch aus dem Siebenjährigen Krieg*, 25.
220. Wähner, *Tagebuch aus dem Siebenjährigen Krieg*, 26.
221. Earl Temple to Mr. Grenville, Tuesday, December 13, 1757, in William James Smith, ed., *The Grenville Papers: Being the Correspondence of Richard Grenville Earl Temple K. G., and the Right. Hon. George Grenville, Their Friends and Contemporaries [. . .]*, 4 vols. (London: Murray, 1852), 1:230–231.
222. Khevenhüller-Metsch, *Maria Theresia*, 4:140.
223. Letter from Voltaire to Luise Dorothée, June 24, 1757, in Raschke, *Briefwechsel*, 113.
224. Stanley McCrory Pargellis, *Lord Loudoun in North America* (Yale University Press, 1933).
225. Wellenreuther, *Ausbildung und Neubildung*, 283–284.
226. Anderson, *Crucible*, 150–157.
227. Wellenreuther, *Ausbildung und Neubildung*, 284; David Syrett, "American Colonial Governments and the Raising of Provincial Troops During the Seven Years' War," *Journal of the Society for Army Historical Research* 81, no. 326 (2003).
228. Anderson, *Crucible*, 186.
229. Ian K. Steele, *Betrayals: Fort William Henry and the "Massacre"* (Oxford University Press, 1990).
230. Gräf, *Schneider*, 91.
231. [Louis Joseph de Montcalm], *Journal du marquis de Montcalm Durant ses campagnes au Canada de 1756 à 1760*, in Casgrain, *Collection des manuscrits du maréchal de Lévis*, 7:264–269.
232. [Montcalm], *Journal du marquis de Montcalm*, 7:278; Anderson, *Crucible*, 192; [Louis Antoine de Bougainville], *Adventure in the Wilderness: The American Journals of*

Louis Antoine de Bougainville, 1756–1760, ed. Edward Pierce Hamilton (University of Oklahoma Press, 1964), 159.
233. Anderson, *Crucible,* 195–196.
234. [Montcalm], *Journal du marquis de Montcalm,* 7:292.
235. [Montcalm], *Journal du marquis de Montcalm,* 7:299.
236. [Montcalm], *Journal du marquis de Montcalm,* 7:199.
237. "Lettre du Père ★★★, Missionaire chez les Abnakis," in Thwaites, *Jesuit Relations and Allied Documents,* 70:174–198.
238. "Lettre du Père ★★★," Thwaites, *Jesuit Relations and Allied Documents,* 70:174, 196.
239. Steele, *Betrayals,* 149–154; Armand Francis Lucier, ed., *French and Indian War Notices Abstracted from Colonial Newspapers,* 5 vols. (Heritage, 1999), 2:288–296.
240. A better-sourced report appeared in the *New York Gazette* on August 29 and was reprinted in the *Boston Gazette* on September 5. See Steele, *Betrayals,* 150.
241. Steele, *Betrayals,* 154. On the trans-Atlantic circulation of information, see Will Slauter, "Le paragraphe mobile: Circulation et transformation des informations dans le monde atlantique du XVIIIe siècle," *Annales: Histoire, Sciences sociales* 2 (2012).
242. *Berlinische Nachrichten,* no. 130, Saturday, October 29, 1757, 523.
243. *Berlinische Nachrichten,* no. 131, Tuesday, November 1, 1757, 527.
244. Price and Dodwell, *Diary of Ananda Ranga Pillai,* 10:397.
245. Price and Dodwell, *Diary of Ananda Ranga Pillai,* 10:400.
246. Clive's participation in the conspiracy was later judged severely by Victorian historiography. See Robert Harvey, *Clive: The Life and Death of a British Emperor* (Hodder & Stoughton, 1998), 192–204. Current research is, above all, divided on the question of whether the British were conducting subtle protoimperial tactics or a more ad hoc exploitation of Indian divisions. See Sushil Chaudhury, *The Prelude to Empire: Plassey Revolution of 1757* (Manohar, 2000).
247. On Mir Jafar Ali Khan Bahadur, see Atul Chandra Roy, *The Career of Mir Jafar Khan, 1757–65 A.D.* (Das Gupta, 1953).
248. See Orme, *History of the Military Transactions of the British Nation in Indostan,* 2nd ed., 2:172–178; German translation: Johann Wilhelm von Archenholz, *Die Engländer in Indien nach Orme* (Leipzig: Dykische Buchhandlung, 1786), 2:219–226. For more modern accounts, see Michael Edwardes, *Plassey: The Founding of an Empire* (Hamish Hamilton, 1969); Peter Harrington, *Plassey 1757: Clive of India's Finest Hour* (London: Osprey, 1994); Stuart Reid, *The Battle of Plassey 1757: The Victory That Won an Empire* (Frontline, 2017); Sudeep Chakravarti, *Plassey: The Battle That Changed the Course of Indian History* (Aleph, 2020).
249. No. 481, in Hill, *Indian Records Series,* vol. 2, 429–430.
250. Roy, *Career of Mir Jafar Khan.*
251. Harvey, *Clive,* 227.

252. On organizational conflicts over resources after Plassey in 1757, see Forrest, *The Life of Lord Clive*, 2:15–17; there had been conflicts of this type even before the relief of Calcutta, which even prompted legislation in London. Mann, *Bengalen im Umbruch*, 56f.
253. Compare Bryant, "War in the Carnatic," 91.
254. His full name was Louis Hubert de Combault d'Auteuil.
255. Bremm, *Preußen bewegt die Welt*, 204.
256. Philip Chesney Yorke, ed. *The Life and Correspondence of Philip Yorke, Earl of Hardwicke, Lord High Chancellor of Great Britain*, 3 vols. (Cambridge University Press, 1913), 3:186.

5. Everyday Life in Wartime

1. Ewa Anklam, "Siebenjähriger Krieg," in *Frankreich und Deutschland im Krieg (18.–20. Jahrhundert): Zur Kulturgeschichte der europäischen "Erbfeindschaft" (chronologische Darstellung)*, Ute Daniel et al. (Technische Universität Braunschweig, 2004), 36, 45.
2. George M. Foster, "Peasant Society and the Image of Limited Good," *American Anthropologist* 67 (1965).
3. Abelmann, *Hannover im Siebenjährigen Krieg*, 245.
4. For a contemporary point of view, see "Gründlicher Beweiß, daß das teutsche Reich dermalen keinen Religions-Krieg zu befürchten: Nebst einigen Erinnerungen über das ohnlängst zum Vorschein gekommene Schreiben eines Brandenburgers," in [Montag)], *Teutsche Kriegs-Canzley*, vol. 4, no. 8, and "Vorstellung derjenigen Gründe, welche auf das gewisseste erweißlich machen, daß die Gefahr eines Religions-Krieges in dem Teutschen Reiche voritzo keinesweges vorhanden," in [Montag], *Teutsche Kriegs-Canzley*, vol. 4, no. 17.
5. [Ahmed Resmi], *Des Türkischen Gesandten Resmi Ahmet Efendi Gesandtschaftliche Berichte von seinen Gesandtschaften in Wien im Jahre 1757, und in Berlin im Jahre 1763* (Berlin: Nicolai, 1809), 18.
6. Abdullah Güllüoglu, "Die Wahrnehmung des Anderen in den Berichten des osmanischen Gesandten Ahmed Resmi Efendi (1694/95–1783)," in *Orientalische Reisende in Europa—Europäische Reisende im Nahen Osten: Bilder vom Selbst und Imaginationen des Anderen*, ed. Bekim Agai and Zita Agota Pataki (EB-Verlag, 2010), 68–69.
7. For a case study of trading by Christian and Jewish war suppliers, see Mark Häberlein, "Waffen, Monturen, Getreide: Geschäfte fränkischer Kaufleute im Siebenjährigen Krieg," *Jahrbuch für Regionalgeschichte* 32 (2014).

8. [David Hirschel Fränkel], *Dankpredigt über den grossen und herrlichen Sieg* (Erlangen: Tetzschner, 1758): "Eine Danck-Predigt wegen des wichtigen und wundervollen Siegs welchen Sr. Königl. Maj. in Preussen am 5ten December, 1757, über die, der Anzahl nach ihm weit überlegene, gesamte oesterreichische Armee in Schlesien, preisswürdig erfochten." It was published the same year in English translation: "A Thanksgiving Sermon, for the Important and Astonishing Victory Obtain'd on the Fifth of December, 1757, by the Glorious King of Prussia, Over the United, and Far Superior Forces of the Austrians in Silesia" [David Hirschel Fränkel], (London: Green and Russell, 1758; Philadelphia: Anton Armbrüster, 1758).
9. David S. Lovejoy, "Satanizing the American Indian," *New England Quarterly* 67, no. 4 (1994).
10. Wickremesekera, *Best Black Troops in the World*, 15, 83–84, 102–105, 126.
11. Georg Wilhelm Friedrich Hegel, *Lectures on the Philosophy of World History*, trans. J. Sibree (Bell, 1902), 456.
12. Burkhardt, *Abschied vom Religionskrieg*, 220–225. "Thinking that such holy weapons might do good service in Silesia, [Clement] sent Fieldmarshall Daun a consecrated hat and sword, in order that he might more effectually overcome the heretics." Archenholz, *History of the Seven Years War*, 187.
13. Schort, *Politik und Propaganda*, 269–271, 304, 336; Fuchs, "Virtueller Religionskrieg."
14. Archenholz, *History of the Seven Years War*, 187.
15. Angela Strauß, "Kollektive Kriegserfahrung preußischer Feldprediger: Vaterlandsliebe und Nutzbarkeitsgedanken in Handbüchern," in *Geistliche im Krieg*, ed. Franz Brendle and Anton Schindling (Aschendorff, 2009); Michael Francis Snape, *The Redcoat and Religion: The Forgotten History of the British Soldier from the Age of Marlborough to the Eve of the First World War* (Routledge, 2005).
16. Emil Buxbaum, ed., "Das Tagebuch des Feldpredigers Balke vom Seydlitz'schen Kürassierregiment aus den Jahren 1759–1762," *Internationale Revue über die gesamten Armeen und Flotten*, Hannover, 3, no. 2 (1885): 15, 142–150, 251–258, vol. III/3: 37–43, 139–146, vol. III/4: 29–34, 126–134, 250–255 and vol. IV/2 (1886): 151–165; Karl Andreas Friedrich Balke, "Materialien zur Geschichte des Siebenjährigen Krieges: Tagebuch des Feldpredigers des Kuirassier-Regiments von Seydlitz [1759–1760]," *Zeitschrift für Kunst, Wissenschaft und Geschichte des Krieges* 96 (1856): 17–45, 117–146, 191–211. The identity of Balke (alternatively spelled *Balk*) is unclear; it may be Elias Gottlob Dominici (1730–1791); see Helmut Eckert, "Dominici—nicht Balke: Das Tagebuch des Feldpredigers beim Kür.-Rgt. von Seydlitz," *Zeitschrift für Heereskunde* 245 (1973): 39ff.; Angela Strauß, *Freigeister und Pragmatiker: Die preußischen Feldprediger 1750–1806* (V&R unipress, 2022), 52–53.

17. Carl Friedrich Wegener, *Der Christ in Kriegszeiten* (Berlin: Birnstiel, 1758 [1759]).
18. Dominique-Hubert-Joseph Dubois-Cattin, "Correspondance du capitaine Dominique-Hubert-Joseph Dubois-Cattin pendant la Guerre de Sept-Ans," in *Soldats Suisses au Service Etranger*, Huitième Série (Jullien, 1919), 162f. See also Höchner, *Selbstzeugnisse von Schweizer Söldneroffizieren*, 125.
19. Andreas Belach, *Der Christ im Kriege und in der Belagerung* (Breslau: Pietsch, 1758). See also Daniel Hohrath, "'Von der wunderbahren Würkung der Bomben': Protestantische Theologen als Zeugen von Festungsbelagerungen des 18. Jahrhunderts," in Kaiser and Kroll, *Militär und Religiosität*, 310–312; on Belach's life and work, see Johannes Birgfeld, "Kriegspoesie für Zeitungsleser oder Der Siebenjährige Krieg aus österreichischer Sicht: Michael Denis' *Poetische Bilder der meisten kriegerischen Vorgänge in Europa seit dem Jahre 1756* im Kontext des zeitgenössischen literarischen Kriegsdiskurses," in Adam and Dainat, *Der Siebenjährige Krieg in den zeitgenössischen Medien*.
20. Belach, *Christ im Kriege*, 183. The German term *Ernstfeuerwerk* (serious fireworks) was used in contrast to *Lustfeuerwerk* (pleasure fireworks); see Medick, *Zeugnisse*, 198 and n10.
21. Belach, *Christ im Kriege*, 184.
22. Horst Schlechte, ed., *Das geheime politische Tagebuch des Kurprinzen Friedrich Christian 1751 bis 1757* (: Böhlau, 1992), 435. The prince's full name was Friedrich Christian Leopold Johann Georg Franz Xaver von Sachsen.
23. Letter of February 2, 1759, from the camp at Oberursel, in Dubois-Cattin, "Correspondance," 150.
24. Gerd Schwerhoff, *Köln im Ancien Régime, 1686–1794* (Greven, 2017), 245–246.
25. Flucke, *Die litterae annuae*, 1086–1087; 1088–1089.
26. Johann Caspar Schiller, *Meine Lebens-Geschichte* (Selbstverlag, 1993), 7; for broader context on Schiller, see Johann Jacob Bäbler, "Aus dem Tagebuch eines württembergischen Regimentsarztes im siebenjährigen Krieg," *Euphorion: Zeitschrift für Litteraturgeschichte* 7 (1900).
27. Salisch, *Treue Deserteure*, 224.
28. Joseph Ferdinand Dreyer, *Leben und Taten eines preußischen Regiments-Tambours* (Breslau: Korn, 1810; repr., Biblio, 1975), 19ff.
29. On this, see the chapter in Dreyer's *Leben und Taten* titled "Guter Rath an meine Cameraden," 56f.
30. Dreyer, *Leben und Taten*, 22.
31. Prittwitz, *Jugend und Kriegsleben eines preußischen Offiziers*, 75.
32. Prittwitz, *Jugend und Kriegsleben eines preußischen Offiziers*, 75–76.
33. Prittwitz, *Jugend und Kriegsleben eines preußischen Offiziers*, 76.
34. Prittwitz, *Jugend und Kriegsleben eines preußischen Offiziers*, 76.
35. Prittwitz, *Jugend und Kriegsleben eines preußischen Offiziers*, 77.

36. Prittwitz, *Jugend und Kriegsleben eines preußischen Offiziers*, 76f.
37. See Fordham, *British Art and the Seven Years War*, 72–75; Fuchs, *Virtueller Religionskrieg*, 336–340.
38. Snape, *Redcoat and Religion*, 7–68.
39. Aegidius Huppertz, *Münster im siebenjährigen Kriege insbesondere die beiden Belagerungen des Jahres 1759* (Coppenrath, 1908), 183–245.
40. Füssel and Petersen, *Grotehenn Briefe*, 50–52.
41. See Robert Emmett Curran, "'[Catholics,] by the Very Principles of That Religion . . . Can Never Be Faithful Subjects': The Peaking of Anti-Catholicism and the Seven Years' War," in *Papist Devils: Catholics in British North America, 1574–1783* (Catholic University of America Press, 2014). Patrick Griffin, "The Last War of Religion or the First War for Empire? Reconsidering the Meaning of the Seven Years' War in America," in *Multiple Reformations? The Many Faces and Legacies of the Reformation*, ed. Jan Stievermann and Randall C. Zachman (Mohr Siebeck, 2018). Thomas Cranmer (1489–1556) was archbishop of Canterbury and a key figure in the English Reformation.
42. Knox, *Historical Journal of the Campaigns in North America*, 1:160.
43. Theodor Hartwig, *Der Uebertritt des Erbprinzen Friedrich von Hessen-Cassel zum Katholicismus: Ein Beitrag zur Geschichte der katholischen Propaganda aus der Zeit des siebenjährigen Krieges; Nach den Acten des Hessischen Staatsarchivs* (Kassel: Kay, 1870); on this, see also Arnold Schaefer, "Zur Geschichte der katholischen Propaganda in der Zeit des siebenjährigen Krieges," *Historische Zeitschrift* 25 (1871): 108–118.
44. Constantin Beyer, *Neue Chronik von Erfurt oder Erzählung alles dessen, was sich vom Jahr 1736 bis zum Jahr 1815 in Erfurt Denkwürdiges ereignete* (Erfurt: Der Renserschen Buchhandlung, 1821; repr., Rockstuhl, 2002), 33–37. The event is also depicted in the memoir of Becher, the Weimar tailor: [Becher], *Wahrhaftige Nachricht derer Begebenheiten*, 26–28.
45. Letter to a friend, written by an officer of the Imperial army, in *Beyträge zu denen bisher bekannt gemachten Nachrichten von der am 5ten November 1757 bey Roßbach vorgefallenen höchst merkwürdigen Schlacht und einigen hieher gehörigen Umständen. Nebst einem in Kupfer gestochenen accuraten Plan* (Leipzig, 1757), cited in Anklam, "Siebenjähriger Krieg," 230.
46. Volz, *Friedrich und Wilhelmine*, 2:333.
47. Michael Hirschfeld, "Ein Justizmord im Siebenjährigen Krieg: Der gewaltsame Tod des Glatzer Priesters Andreas Faulhaber (1713–1757) im Kontext der Eroberungs- und Kirchenpolitik von Friedrich II. von Preußen," *Archiv für schlesische Kirchengeschichte* 72 (2014).
48. Brunner, "Aufzeichnungen des Pfarrers Johann Christoph Cuntz," 241–242.
49. Thomas Notthoff, "Strohfeuer oder Symbolakt? Executio in effigie im Hessen des Siebenjährigen Krieges," *Hessisches Jahrbuch für Landesgeschichte* 62 (2012): 149–167.

50. Carl, *Okkupation und Regionalismus*, 368–369.
51. Carl, *Okkupation und Regionalismus*, 370–371.
52. See Meyer, *Zeitgenössische Beurteilung*, 75–78, 113–118, 135–141.
53. See Nadir Weber, *Lokale Interessen und große Strategie: Das Fürstentum Neuchâtel und die politischen Beziehungen der Könige von Preußen (1707–1806)* (Böhlau, 2015).
54. Schmidt, "Der Einfluss der Winterquartiere."
55. See Ralf Pröve, "Der Soldat in der 'guten Bürgerstube': Das frühneuzeitliche Einquartierungssystem und die sozioökonomischen Folgen," in Kroener and Pröve, *Krieg und Frieden*; Dinges, "Soldatenkörper in der Frühen Neuzeit," 77.
56. Hans Jessen, ed., *Friedrich der Große und Maria Theresia in Augenzeugenberichten* (Rauch, 1965), 324.
57. Archenholz, *History of the Seven Years War*, 298.
58. Archenholz, *History of the Seven Years War*, 267.
59. Archenholz, *History of the Seven Years War*, 268.
60. Lemoine, *Sous Louis le Bien-aimé: Correspondance amoureuse et militaire d'un fficier*, 252, cited in Externbrink, "Wahrnehmung von Krieg und Gewalt," 50; see also Anklam, "Siebenjähriger Krieg," 36, 39.
61. Uta Krüger-Löwenstein, "Hessen im Siebenjährigen Krieg: Berichte französischer Offiziere," *Zeitschrift für hessische Geschichte und Landeskunde* 87 (1978/80).
62. Brunner, "Aufzeichnungen des Pfarrers Johann Christoph Cuntz," 226.
63. Prittwitz, *Jugend und Kriegsleben eines preußischen Offiziers*, 44–45.
64. Dubois-Cattin, "Correspondance," 181. See Höchner, *Selbstzeugnisse von Schweizer Söldneroffizieren*, 80.
65. Hammann, *Die Bottendorfer Chronik des Johann Daniel Geitz*, 42.
66. Dinges, "Soldatenkörper in der Frühen Neuzeit," 74–76, 81–83; Luh, *Kriegskunst in Europa 1650–1800*, 178–194.
67. Chapman and Macpherson, *Memoirs of a Black Watch Officer*, 149.
68. Warnke, *Logistik und friderizianische Kriegführung*, 113–126.
69. Warnke, *Logistik und friderizianische Kriegführung*, 235.
70. Dubois-Cattin, "Correspondance," 170, 219, 221; on the cycle of mutual invitations, 155.
71. On the Russian army, see Denis Sdvižkov, "Landschaft nach der Schlacht: Briefe russischer Offiziere aus dem Siebenjährigen Krieg," *Forschungen zur Brandenburgischen und Preußischen Geschichte*, n.s., vol. 22, no. 1 (2012): 44.
72. Louis Joseph Castelnau, *Lettres du Baron de Castelnau de 1728–1793* (Champion, 1911), 150–151, 208 (hunt), 157–158 (menu); for contrast, see the letters of a lower-ranking soldier in Maria Louise Puech-Milhau, "La Campagne d'allemagne (1756–1762) d'après les lettres de militaries castrais," *Revue du Tarn* 11 (1945).
73. Claus Legal and Gert Legal, *Friedrich II: Preußens König, Sachsens Feind, Regent auf Schloss Dahlen* (Burghügel, 2011), 232–234.

74. Trautzschen, *Militärische und literarische Briefe des Herrn von T.*, 42.
75. Füssel and Petersen, *Grotehenn Briefe*, 41.
76. Füssel and Petersen, *Grotehenn Briefe*, 41–42.
77. According to Warnke, *Logistik und friderizianische Kriegführung*, 94, this "rarely presented a problem," a judgment possibly due to his concentration on administrative files.
78. [?] Hoppe, "Wahrhafte Schilderung der blutigen Schlacht bei Zorndorf, von einem alten preußischen Soldaten, welcher 34 Jahr gedient und jetzt (1793) noch lebt," in *Officier-Lesebuch historisch militärischen Inhalts*, ed. Carl Daniel Küster, 3 vols. (Berlin: Carl Matzdorff, 1793), 1:183–184; Archenholz, *History of the Seven Years War*, 333.
79. Prittwitz, *Jugend und Kriegsleben eines preußischen Offiziers*, 114–115.
80. Uhlmann, *Das abwechselnde Fortün*, 21.
81. Trautzschen, *Militärische und literarische Briefe des Herrn von T.*, 92–93.
82. Johann Christian Kneisel, *Denkwürdigkeiten der zweyten Rußischen Belagerung von Colberg im Jahr 1760* (Berlin: Real-Schule, 1761), 349–350.
83. Kneisel, *Denkwürdigkeiten der zweyten Rußischen Belagerung*, 353.
84. Brunner, *Aufzeichnungen des Pfarrers Johann Christoph Cuntz*, 256–257.
85. Dinges, "Soldatenkörper in der Frühen Neuzeit," 79–80.
86. On the Russian army, see Sdvižkov, "Landschaft nach der Schlacht," 44 and n47; on the situation in the British army, see Paul Edward Kopperman, "'The Cheapest Pay': Alcohol Abuse in the Eighteenth-Century British Army," *Journal of Military History* 60, no. 3 (1996).
87. Saint-André's account is cited in Frisch, *Geschichte der russischen Feldzüge*, 114.
88. On British soldiers and alcohol in general, see Kopperman, "'The Cheapest Pay.'"
89. Hans Georg Baumeister, ed., *Annotation von meinen Lebens-Laufe Johann Conrad Lütgerts aufgesetzet im Frühjahr 1751* (Gütersloh-Isselhorst, [2000]), 36.
90. See the city chronicles cited in Huppertz, *Münster im siebenjährigen Kriege*, 123 and n3.
91. Anonymous, "Münsterische Chronik oder Begebenheiten im siebenjährigen Krieg in Münster," *Zeitschrift für vaterländische Geschichte und Altherthumskunde* 36 (1878): 122.
92. Peter C. Mancall, *Deadly Medicine: Indians and Alcohol in Early America* (Cornell University Press, 1995).
93. Helmut Glück and Mark Häberlein, eds., *Militär und Mehrsprachigkeit im neuzeitlichen Europa* (Harrassowitz, 2014), is essential on this question.
94. See Höchner, *Selbstzeugnisse von Schweizer Söldneroffizieren*, 55.
95. Edward G. Gray, ed., *The Language Encounter in the Americas, 1492–1800: A Collection of Essays* (Berghahn, j2003); Nancy Hagedorn, "'A Friend to Go Between Them': The Interpreter as Cultural Broker During Anglo-Iroquois

Councils, 1740–1770," *Ethnohistory* 35 (1988); James H. Merrell, *Into the American Woods: Negotiators on the Pennsylvania Frontier* (Norton, 1999).

96. Johann Philipp Zellmann, "Aus schwerer Zeit: Tagebuch des Johann Philipp Zellmann zu Herzberg am Harz aus der Zeit des siebenjährigen Krieges: Mitgeteilt aus einer Familienchronik von Dr. K. Zellmann," reprinted in *Zeitschrift des Harzvereins für Geschichte u. Altertumskunde* 33, no. 2 (1900): 50–51; for further examples, see Anklam, "Siebenjähriger Krieg," 52, 60–61.
97. Castelnau, *Lettres*, 151.
98. Schwerhoff, *Köln im Ancien Régime*.
99. See comments by Franz Goswin v. Michel, the mayor of Soest, in Friedrich Menneking, *Victoria by Vellinghausen 1761: Spaziergänge in die Geschichte des Siebenjährigen Krieges in Westdeutschland* (Hüttemann, 1989), 196.
100. Charles Walter Frearson, ed., *"To Mr. Davenport": Being Letters of Richard Davenport (1719–1760) to His Brother During Service in the 4th Troop of Horse Guards and 10th Dragoons, 1742–1760* (Gale & Polden, 1968), 76–77.
101. Frearson, *Letters of Richard Davenport*, 78.
102. Eduard Vogeler, "Beiträge zur Geschichte von Soest während des siebenjährigen Krieges," *Zeitschrift des Vereins für die Geschichte von Soest und der Börde* 9 (1891/92): 31.
103. [Täge], *Täge's ehemaligen russischen Feldpredigers Lebensgeschichte*, 138.
104. [Täge], *Täge's ehemaligen russischen Feldpredigers Lebensgeschichte*, 139–142.
105. [Täge], *Täge's ehemaligen russischen Feldpredigers Lebensgeschichte*, 141; on the religiosity of Russian officers, see Sdvižkov, "Landschaft nach der Schlacht," 52–54.
106. Bolotov, *Leben und Abenteuer*, 1:262–263.
107. Bolotov, *Leben und Abenteuer*, 1:263.
108. Ligne, *Mélanges militaires*, vol. 1, 229f.; also cited in Duffy, *Armee Maria Theresias*, 440.

6. 1758: The Fighting Spreads

1. See Carl Adolf Bratter, *Die preussisch-türkische Bündnispolitik Friedrichs des Grossen* (Kiepenhauer, 1915); Porsch, *Die Beziehungen Friedrichs des Grossen zur Türkei*; Szabo, *Seven Years War*, 401.
2. Karl Pröhl, *Die Bedeutung preußischer Politik in den Phasen der orientalischen Frage: Ein Beitrag zur Entwicklung deutsch-türkischer Beziehungen von 1606–1871* (Lang, 1986), 84–105. On Frederick's instructions, see Friedrich II, *Politische Correspondenz*, vol. 11, no. 6589, 7f.; no. 6598, 16–17; no. 6602, 21–24.
3. Friedrich II, *Politische Correspondenz*, vol. 16, no. 9642, 133; Porsch, *Beziehungen*, 35.
4. Friedrich II, *Politische Correspondenz*, vol. 17, no. 10,330, 241; Porsch, *Beziehungen*, 38.

5. Aksan, "The Ottoman Absence," 172.
6. [Resmi], *Resmi Ahmet Efendi Gesandtschaftliche Berichte*, 22.
7. Zander, *Fundstücke: Dokumente und Briefe einer preußischen Bauernfamilie*, 52.
8. Åselius, "Sweden and the Pommeranian War," 135; Arnold, "Schwedens Teilnahme am siebenjährigen Kriege," *Beihefte zum Militärwochenblatt* 12 (1908); for recent research in German, see Robert Oldach, ed., *Schwedens Beteiligung am Siebenjährigen Krieg im Spiegel des Tageregisters der Stadt Loitz 1757–1759* (Ernst-Moritz-Arndt-Universität Greifswald, 2014), 24–57; still the most detailed account is Säve, *Sveriges deltagande*.
9. Anonymous, *Geschichte des preußisch-schwedischen Krieges in Pommern, der Mark und Mecklenburg 1757–1762: Zugleich als Beitrag zur Geschichte des siebenjährigen Krieges; Nach gleichzeitigen Preußischen und schwedischen Berichten* (Berlin: Mittler, 1858); Karl von Sulicki, *Der Siebenjährige Krieg in Pommern und in den benachbarten Marken* (Berlin: Mittler, 1867); W. von Schulz, "Mecklenburg und der 7-jährige Krieg," pts. 1 & 2, *Jahrbücher des Vereins für Mecklenburgische Geschichte und Alterthumskunde* 53 (1888); 54 (1889). For various military diaries from the Pomeranian theater, see Anonymous, *Sammlung ungedruckter Nachrichten*, vol. 3.
10. On Stralsund, see Robert Oldach, *Stadt und Festung Stralsund: Die Schwedische Militärpräsenz in Schwedisch-Pommern 1721–1807* (Böhlau, 2018). For a contemporary chronicler in that city, see Johann Christian Müller, *Meines Lebens Vorfälle und Neben-Umstände*, teil 3, *Pastor in Stralsund (1755–1766)*, ed. Katrin Löffler (Lehmstedt, 2020).
11. Åselius, "Sweden and the Pommeranian War," 145.
12. Böhme, *Schwedens Teilnahme am Siebenjährigen Krieg*, 208.
13. Åselius, "Sweden and the Pommeranian War," 145.
14. Volz, *Werke Friedrichs des Großen*, vol. 4, *Geschichte des Siebenjährigen Krieges*, II: 27. For an English translation, see *Posthumous Works of Frederic II*, 2 vols. (London: Robinson, 1789).
15. Åselius, "Sweden and the Pommeranian War," 152.
16. Füssel and Petersen, *Grotehenn Briefe*, 47.
17. Mediger, *Herzog Ferdinand von Braunschweig-Lüneburg*, 107.
18. Mediger, *Herzog Ferdinand von Braunschweig-Lüneburg*, 110–115.
19. André Dussauge, *Le ministère de Belle-Isle: Études sur la guerre de sept ans* (Fournier, 1914).
20. Mediger, *Herzog Ferdinand von Braunschweig-Lüneburg*, 128–129.
21. Mediger, *Herzog Ferdinand von Braunschweig-Lüneburg*, 130.
22. Mediger, *Herzog Ferdinand von Braunschweig-Lüneburg*, 134–141.
23. Mediger, *Herzog Ferdinand von Braunschweig-Lüneburg*, 142.
24. Mediger, *Herzog Ferdinand von Braunschweig-Lüneburg*, 149.
25. Abelmann, *Hannover im Siebenjährigen Krieg*, 107; Mastnak and Tänzer, *Tagebuch des Garnisonsauditeurs Johann Philipp Schowart*, 146.

26. Mastnak and Tänzer, *Tagebuch des Garnisonsauditeurs Johann Philipp Schowart*, 150. For similar statements by Clermont, see Szabo, *Seven Years War*, 135; Archenholz, *History of the Seven Years War*, 211.
27. Mediger, *Herzog Ferdinand von Braunschweig-Lüneburg*, 126. See also Abelmann, *Hannover im Siebenjährigen Krieg*, 94–96; Sebastian Pranghofer, "Der Umgang mit Krankheit und Seuchengefahr im Kriegsalltag in Nordwestdeutschland, 1757–1763," in *Krank vom Krieg: Umgangsweisen und kulturelle Deutungsmuster eines Zusammenhangs von der Antike bis zur Gegenwart*, ed. Gundula Gahlen et al. (Campus, 2022).
28. Füssel and Petersen, *Grotehenn Briefe*, 48. For casualty figures, see Louis Heinrich Friedrich von Sichart, *Geschichte der Königlich-Hannoverschen Armee*, vol. 3, *Vierter Zeitraum 1756–1789* (Hanover: Hahn'sche Hofbuchhandlung, 1870), 324. There figures are suggested for the French of 100 dead, 250 hospitalized, and 420 captured or otherwise wounded. See also Patricia Berger et al., *Ruhe süße Ruhe schwebe: Historische Friedhöfe in Nienburg* (Nienberger Stadtarchiv, 1993), 27.
29. Füssel and Petersen, *Grotehenn Briefe*, 48.
30. Herr, *Wohl und Wehe der Stadt Hameln*, unpag. [14].
31. Jean Bouvier, ed., "Le fonctionnement d'un hôpital militaire pendant la Guerre de Sept Ans," *Revue d'Histoire de la Pharmacie Année* 180 (1964): 56.
32. Mediger, *Herzog Ferdinand von Braunschweig-Lüneburg*, 157.
33. Mediger, *Herzog Ferdinand von Braunschweig-Lüneburg*, 158.
34. The objections of Wilhelm VIII, Landgrave of Hesse-Kassel, meant this was not carried out in the case of Kassel. Mediger, *Herzog Ferdinand von Braunschweig-Lüneburg*, 162–163.
35. Mediger, *Herzog Ferdinand von Braunschweig-Lüneburg*, 166–167.
36. Mediger, *Herzog Ferdinand von Braunschweig-Lüneburg*, 187.
37. Füssel and Petersen, *Grotehenn Briefe*, 54–57.
38. Großer Generalstab, *Der Siebenjährige Krieg*, vol. 7, *Olmütz und Crefeld*; Werner Hermkes, "Die Schlacht bei Crefeld am 23. Juni 1758" (Diss., Eschweiler, 1906); Ernst von Schaumburg, "Die Schlacht bei Crefeld am 23. Juni 1758," *Annalen des Historischen Vereins für den Niederrhein* 5 (1875).
39. Mediger, *Herzog Ferdinand von Braunschweig-Lüneburg*, 223.
40. Mediger, *Herzog Ferdinand von Braunschweig-Lüneburg*, 224.
41. On Cologne during the Seven Years' War, see Schwerhoff, *Köln im Ancien Régime*, 234; Wilhelm Hamacher, "Die Reichsstadt Köln und der Siebenjährige Krieg" (Diss., University of Bonn, 1911); Konstantin Becker, "Von Kurkölns Beziehungen zu Frankreich und seiner wirtschaftlichen Lage im Siebenjährigen Krieg 1757–1761," *Annalen des Historischen Vereins für den Niederrhein* 100 (1917).
42. Otto Hermann, "Der Feldzugsplan Friedrichs des Grossen für das Jahr 1758," *Historische Vierteljahresschrift* 15 (1912); Heinrich Köhler, *Friedrichs Mährischer Feldzug 1758* (Thomas & Hubert, 1916).

43. Josef August Bartsch, *Olmütz im Jahre 1758 und seine frühere Kriegsgeschichte: Denkschrift zur hundertjährigen Jubiläumsfeier des Entsatzes am 2. Juli 1758* (Olmütz: Slawik, 1858); Otto Hermann, "Olmütz (1758)," *Forschungen zur Brandenburgischen und Preußischen Geschichte* 23 (1910).
44. Barsewisch, *Tagebuchblätter eines friderizianischen Fahnenjunkers und Offiziers*, 60–61.
45. Otto Schier, "Die Kämpfe bei Gundersdorf und Domstadtl am 28. u. 30. Juni 1758," *Zeitschrift des Deutschen Vereines für die Geschichte Mährens und Schlesiens* 12 (1908); Duffy, *Military Life of Frederick the Great*, 159–161; Duffy, *By Force of Arms*, 105–113.
46. Barsewisch, *Tagebuchblätter eines friderizianischen Fahnenjunkers und Offiziers*, 61.
47. Gorani, *Mémoires*, 96–100.
48. Gorani, *Mémoires*, 99; for Laudon's own view, see his letter of July 4, in Karl Buchberger, ed., "Briefe Loudon's: Beiträge zur Charakteristik Loudon's und der Geschichte des Siebenjährigen Krieges," *Archiv für österreichische Geschichte* 48 (1872): 389–394.
49. Gorani, *Mémoires*, 99.
50. Gorani, *Mémoires*, 100.
51. Khevenhüller-Metsch, *Maria Theresia*, 5:46–47.
52. Gorani, *Mémoires*, 100.
53. David Hopkin et al., "The Experience and Culture of War in the Eighteenth Century: The British Raids on the Breton Coast, 1758," *French Historical Studies* 31, no. 2 (2008); Richard Middleton, "The British Coastal Expeditions to France, 1757–1758," *Journal of the Society for Army Historical Research* 71 (1993); André Corvisier, "La Défense des côtes de Normandie contre les descentes anglaises pendant la guerre de Sept Ans," *Revue Internationale d'Histoire militaire* 35 (1976).
54. Baugh, *Global War*, 262–270; Dull, *The French Navy and the Seven Years' War*, 84–85; Richard Middleton, *The Bells of Victory: The Pitt-Newcastle Ministry and the Conduct of the Seven Years' War 1757–1762* (Cambridge University Press, 1985), 26–31; William Kent-Hackman, "The British Raid on Rochefort, 1757," *Mariner's Mirror* 64 (1978).
55. Dull, *The French Navy and the Seven Years' War*, 84–85.
56. Wolfe, *Life and Letters*, 323–333.
57. See Cormack and Jones, *Journal of Corporal Todd*, 28–34.
58. Cormack and Jones, *Journal of Corporal Todd*, 33.
59. Middleton, *Bells of Victory*, 42–43.
60. Middleton, *Bells of Victory*, 43.
61. Hopkin et al., "The Experience and Culture of War," 195.
62. Hopkin et al., "The Experience and Culture of War," 195.
63. *A Letter from the Honourable L-----t G-----l B---gh, to the Rt. Hon. W-m P-t, Esq Se-----y of S---te. Together with His M-y's Instructions for the Late Expeditions on the Coast of France* (Dublin, 1758).

64. "The following taken from Gen. Bligh's instructions clearly shews the genuine intention of our late expeditions to the coast of France," *The Gentleman's and London Magazine*, October 1758, 608.
65. On the subsequent operation, see Cormack and Jones, *Journal of Corporal Todd*, 46–56; John Porter, "An Account by an Eye-Witness of the Expedition Against St. Malo in May and June, 1758," *Royal United Services Institute Journal* 58 (1914): 758–763.
66. Cormack and Jones, *Journal of Corporal Todd*, 47.
67. Cormack and Jones, *Journal of Corporal Todd*, 48–49.
68. Cormack and Jones, *Journal of Corporal Todd*, 49.
69. Porter, "An Account, " 761.
70. Cormack and Jones, *Journal of Corporal Todd*, 62; on problems with the cross-Channel passage, see also Porter, "An Account, " 761–763.
71. Cormack and Jones, *Journal of Corporal Todd*, 68–102.
72. Cormack and Jones, *Journal of Corporal Todd*, 68–69.
73. Cormack and Jones, *Journal of Corporal Todd*, 73.
74. Cormack and Jones, *Journal of Corporal Todd*, 75.
75. Cormack and Jones, *Journal of Corporal Todd*, 80.
76. Cormack and Jones, *Journal of Corporal Todd*, 82.
77. Cormack and Jones, *Journal of Corporal Todd*, 94.
78. Hopkin et al., "The Experience and Culture of War," 210.
79. Hopkin et al., "The Experience and Culture of War," 203.
80. For sources, see Sigismond Ropartz, ed., *Saint-Cast: Recueil de pièces officielles et de documents contemporains relatifs au combat du 11 septembre 1758* (Saint-Brieuc: Prud'homme, 1858); for a narrative account, see Yann Lagadec et al., *La Bataille de Saint-Cast (Bretagne, 11 septembre 1758): Entre histoire et mémoire* (Presses universitaires de Rennes, 2009).
81. See also the report by a private soldier of the 68th Foot, named Jonas (b. 1743): Anonymous, *A Soldier's Journal Containing a Particular Description of the Several Descents on the Coast of France Last War: With an Entertaining Account of the Islands of Guadaloupe Dominique, &C. and also of the Isles of Wight and Jersey; To Which Are Annexed, Observations on the Present State of the Army of Great Britain* (London: E. and C. Dilly, 1770), 38–40.
82. Cormack and Jones, *Journal of Corporal Todd*, 96–97.
83. Cormack and Jones, *Journal of Corporal Todd*, 99.
84. Cormack and Jones, *Journal of Corporal Todd*, 101–103.
85. Jacques-Louis Ménétra, *Journal of My Life*, ed. Daniel Roche (Columbia University Press, 1986), 43–44.
86. Hopkin et al., "The Experience and Culture of War," 215.
87. Mediger, *Herzog Ferdinand von Braunschweig-Lüneburg*, 231.

88. Franz von Geyso, "Das Korps des Prinzen Johann Kasimir zu Ysenburg-Birstein unter Besonderer Berücksichtigung des Gefechts bei Sandershausen am 23. Juli 1758," *Zeitschrift für hessische Geschichte* 45 (1911); Mediger, *Herzog Ferdinand von Braunschweig-Lüneburg*, 263–267.
89. Mediger, *Herzog Ferdinand von Braunschweig-Lüneburg*, 268–270.
90. Mediger, *Herzog Ferdinand von Braunschweig-Lüneburg*, 286.
91. Dussauge, *Belle-Isle*, 359–363.
92. Trautzschen, *Militärische und literarische Briefe des Herrn von T.*, 93–97.
93. Mediger, *Herzog Ferdinand von Braunschweig-Lüneburg*, 287; Salisch, *Treue Deserteure*, 212–215.
94. Trautzschen, *Militärische und literarische Briefe des Herrn von T.*, 96.
95. Mediger, *Herzog Ferdinand von Braunschweig-Lüneburg*, 314–315; Hugo Brunner, *Kassel im siebenjährigen Kriege: Ein Beitrag zur Geschichte der Stadt* (Kassel: Hühn, 1884), 70.
96. Brunner, *Kassel im siebenjährigen Kriege*, 285.
97. See Wellenreuther, *Ausbildung und Neubildung*, 286.
98. Wolfe, *Life and Letters*, 347.
99. Anderson, *Crucible*, 240–241.
100. Mühlenberg, *Correspondence*, 4:73.
101. Anderson, *Crucible*, 242.
102. Anderson, *Crucible*, 244. For a further witness account, see "The Journal of Rufus Putnam—Provincial Infantry," in Anonymous, *Narratives of the French and Indian War* (Leonaur, 2008), 107–108.
103. Bougainville, *Écrits sur le Canada*, 277–280.
104. Mühlenberg, *Correspondence*, 4:74.
105. Bougainville, *Écrits sur le Canada*, 286.
106. Bougainville, *Écrits sur le Canada*, 303.
107. Mastnak and Tänzer, *Tagebuch des Garnisonsauditeurs Johann Philipp Schowart*, 166; Wähner, *Tagebuch aus dem Siebenjährigen Krieg*, 41. On Ticonderoga, see Ian M. McCulloch, "'Like Roaring Lions Breaking from Their Chains': The Battle of Ticonderoga, 8 July 1758," in *Fighting for Canada, Seven Battles, 1758–1945*, ed. Donald E. Graves (Robin Brass Studio, 2000); William R. Nester, *The Epic Battles for Ticonderoga, 1758* (State University of New York Press, 2008); on the press in Hamburg, see Holger Böning, *Periodische Presse: Kommunikation und Aufklärung; Hamburg und Altona als Beispiel* (Lumière, 2002).
108. Gräf, *Schneider*, 95.
109. Hugh Boscawen, *The Capture of Louisbourg, 1758* (University of Oklahoma Press, 2011).
110. Francis Parkman, *Montcalm and Wolfe* (Boston: Little, Brown, 1884; repr., Da Capo, 1995).

111. René Chartrand, *Louisbourg 1758: Wolfe's First Siege* (Osprey, 2000), 57.
112. See Starkey, *War in the Age of the Enlightenment*, 93–98.
113. One reading of this incident interprets the pineapple as a symbol of hospitality; however, this connotation appears to be a 1930s invention. See Fran Beauman, *The Pineapple: King of Fruits* (Chatto & Windus, 2005), 130–132.
114. Equiano, *The Interesting Narrative*, 41. The preferred German term for Highlanders in the eighteenth century was *Bergschotte*, or "mountain Scots."
115. Wolfe, *Life and Letters*, 363–398.
116. Wolfe, *Life and Letters*, 382–385.
117. Knox, *Historical Journal of the Campaigns in North America*, 1:171.
118. Knox, *Historical Journal of the Campaigns in North America*, 1:171–172.
119. Knox, *Historical Journal of the Campaigns in North America*, 1:204.
120. Marshall, "The Thirteen Colonies in the Seven Years' War," 82.
121. Bougainville, *Écrits sur le Canada*, 333.
122. Dziembowski, "Transparence ou désinformation?," 185–187.
123. Douglas R. Cubbison, *The British Defeat of the French in Pennsylvania, 1758: A Military History of the Forbes Campaign Against Fort Duquesne* (McFarland, 2010).
124. Casgrain, *Voyage*, 139–149.
125. Casgrain, *Voyage*, 166–167.
126. Casgrain, *Voyage*, 171–172.
127. Wellenreuther, *Ausbildung und Neubildung*, 290.
128. Fred Anderson, "1759—Year of Decision?," in De Bruyn and Regan, *The Culture of the Seven Years War*.
129. Anderson, "1759—Year of Decision?"
130. *Berlinische Nachrichten*, no. 99, Saturday, August 19, 1758, 430; see also the account by Musketeer Hoppe in Hoppe, "Wahrhafte Schilderung der blutigen Schlacht bei Zorndorf," 181–184.
131. Kunisch, *Friedrich der Grosse*, 387–392. From the extensive literature on the battle, see, in particular, Max Immich, *Die Schlacht bei Zorndorf am 25. August 1758* (Berlin: Speyer and Peters, 1893); Großer Generalstab, *Der siebenjährige Krieg*, vol. 8, *Zorndorf und Hochkirch*; Otto Herrmann, "Zur Schlacht bei Zorndorf," *Forschungen zur Brandenburgischen und Preußischen Geschichte* 24 (1911); Stefan Hartmann, "Eine unbekannte Quelle zur Schlacht bei Zorndorf," *Zeitschrift für Ostmitteleuropa-Forschung* 34 (1985); Marian Füssel, "Das Undarstellbare darstellen: Das Bild der Schlacht im 18. Jahrhundert am Beispiel Zorndorf (1758)," in *Kriegs/Bilder in Mittelalter und Früher Neuzeit*, ed. Gabriela Signori and Birgit Emich (Duncker & Humblot, 2009). For a selection from the older literature, see Ulf-Joachim Friese, ed., *Die Schlacht bei Zorndorf am 25./26. August 1758 und die Tage davor und danach in preußischer, russischer und österreichischer Darstellung*, 2 vols. (LTR, 2010–2011).
132. Sdvižkov, "Landschaft nach der Schlacht," 40.

133. Hoppe, "Wahrhafte Schilderung der blutigen Schlacht bei Zorndorf," 186.
134. Hoppe, "Wahrhafte Schilderung der blutigen Schlacht bei Zorndorf," 190.
135. For the figures in detail, see Großer Generalstab, *Der siebenjährige Krieg*, vol. 8, *Zorndorf und Hochkirch*, 161.
136. Hülsen, *Aus den Memoiren des Aeltervaters*, 86; see also Möbius, "Kriegsgreuel in den Schlachten des Siebenjährigen Krieges," 201–202.
137. Prittwitz, *Jugend und Kriegsleben eines preußischen Offiziers*, 93.
138. Archenholz, *History of the Seven Years War*, 167.
139. The report by the pastor of Neudamm was published with the title *Besondere Merkwürdigkeiten und Anekdoten aus Neudamm in der Neumark und der herumliegenden Gegend von der unglücksvollen Gegenwart der russisch-kaiserlichen Armee* (Salzwedel, 1765 [possibly published as early as 1758]); Georg Wartenberg, "Bericht des Neudammer Magistrats über die Schlacht bei Zorndorf," *Die Neumark* 3 (1926); Paul Schwartz, "Aufzeichnungen über die Schlacht von Zorndorf," *Schriften des Vereins für Geschichte der* Neumarck 8 (1899).
140. Schwartz, "Aufzeichnungen über die Schlacht von Zorndorf," 93.
141. Prittwitz, *Jugend und Kriegsleben eines preußischen Offiziers*, 100f.
142. Prittwitz, *Jugend und Kriegsleben eines preußischen Offiziers*, 102; see also Hoppe, "Wahrhafte Schilderung der blutigen Schlacht bei Zorndorf," 195.
143. See Stefan Kroll, "'Gottesfurcht' und 'Vaterlandsliebe': Zwei Triebfedern zur Motivierung und Disziplinierung im Krieg? Das Beispiel Kursachsen im 18. Jahrhundert," in Kaiser and Kroll, *Militär und Religiosität*, 225–248.
144. Sdvižkov, "Landschaft nach der Schlacht," 33–34.
145. For details, see Füssel, "Das Bild der Schlacht im 18. Jahrhundert am Beispiel Zorndorf," 330–335.
146. Luise Dorothée to Voltaire, Gotha, September 16, 1758, in Raschke, *Briefwechsel*, 141.
147. Voltaire to Luise Dorothée, Aux Délices, September 26, 1758, in Raschke, *Briefwechsel* 142.
148. Bolotov, *Leben und Abenteuer*, 1:310f.
149. See Pierre Bayle, *Dictionnaire historique et critique: Nouvelle Édition*, vol.15 (Paris: Desoer, 1820), 148–189.
150. Bayle, *Dictionnaire*, 179.
151. See Johann Heinrich Zedler, *Grosses vollständiges Universal-Lexicon aller Wissenschafften und Künste*, vol. 61 (1749), col. 901f.; see also Anonymous, *Zwey Abhandlungen von der Kriegs-Zucht, und Ob es nach den Regeln der Staats-Kunst rathsam ist, den Verlust einer Schlacht zu läugnen, oder falsche Siege und Vortheile auszubreiten* (Berlin, 1760), which had already been published in 1757 in Göttingen and included in [Montag], *Teutsche Kriegs-Canzley*, vol. 3, no. 67, 392f.
152. Johann Heinrich Gottlob von Justi, *Gesammelte politische und Finanz-Schriften: Über wichtige Gegenstände der Staatskunst, der Kriegswissenschaften und des Kameral- und Finanzwesens*, 3 vols. (Copenhagen: Rothenschen, 1761; repr., Scientia,

1970), 1:33–46. According to Justi, most of these writings had previously appeared in Johann Heinrich Gottlob von Justi, *Deutsche Memoires, oder Sammlung verschiedener Anmerkungen, die Staatsklugheit, das Kriegswesen, die Justiz, Morale, Oeconomie, Commercium, Cammer- und Polizey-auch andere merkwürdige Sachen betreffend, welche im menschlichen Leben vorkommen, von einigen Civil- und Militairbedienten, auch von andern gelehrten und erfahrnen Personen aufgezeichnet und hinterlassen worden* (Leipzig, 1741–1744). However, some texts contain references to contemporary events in the Seven Years' War; there must thus have been some editing for republication. On Justi's work as a "political writer," see Ferdinand Frensdorff, "Über das Leben und die Schriften des Nationalökonomen J. H. G. von Justi," *Nachrichten der Königl. Gesellschaft der Wissenschaften zu Göttingen: Philologisch-historische Klasse*, no. 4 (1903): 391–412, 417–438; Viktor Heydemann, "Deutsche und Französische Broschüren aus der Zeit des Siebenjährigen Krieges," *Zeitschrift für Bücherfreunde*, n.s., vol. 20 (1928): 95–97.

153. Justi, *Gesammelte politische und Finanz-Schriften*, 41.
154. Flashar, *Memoiren der Eleonore Juliane von Rehdiger*, 129.
155. Abraham ter Meer was clearly a keen reader of Cologne's French-language newspaper—the *Gazette de Cologne*—as well as papers from Lippstadt and Harlem. Gottfried Buschbell, ed., *Das Tagebuch des Abraham ter Meer (1758–1769)* (Zelt, 1936), 41f., 45, 49, 53; see also Miriam Müller, "On dit: Die Nachrichtenrezeption des Krefelders Abraham ter Meer im Siebenjährigen Krieg," *Annalen des Historischen Vereins für den Niederrhein insbesondere das alte Erzbistum Köln* 215 (2012).
156. Buschbell, *Das Tagebuch des Abraham ter Meer*, 27.
157. *Danziger Beyträge*, 1759, Nos. 55–58, 436f.
158. *Danziger Beyträge*, 1758, Nos. 45–48, 394. On the situation in Königsberg, see [Bock], "Occupation Königsbergs," pt. 2, vol. 1, 213–215.
159. *Berlinische Nachrichten*, no. 109, Tuesday, September 12, 1758, 470; [Montag], *Teutsche Kriegs-Canzley*, vol. 2, no. 134, 1051–1052,.
160. [Montag], *Teutsche Kriegs-Canzley*, vol. 2, no. 134, 1053.
161. Anonymous, *Gespräch zwischen einem preuß. Schwarzen Husaren und einem Moscowitischen Cosacken über die blutige Schlacht so den 2. Augusti 1758 bey Zorndorf ohnweit Cüstrin vorgefallen* (n.p., 1758), 5.
162. Täge, *Täge's ehemaligen russischen Feldpredigers Lebensgeschichte*, 175.
163. Paul Hohenemser, "Kritik der Quellen zur Schlacht bei Hochkirch 14. Oktober 1758" (Diss., Heidelberg University, 1899); Großer Generalstab, *Der Siebenjährige Krieg*, vol. 8, *Zorndorf und Hochkirch*; Norbert Robitschek, *Hochkirch: Eine Studie* (Verlag von Teufens, 1905); Karl Ernst Berger, *Hochkirch: Schicksalstage in der Oberlausitz während des siebenjährigen Krieges* (n.p., c. 1999); Andreas Bensch, *Der Kampf um Hochkirch 1758: Ein militärhistorischer Tatsachenbericht*, 3rd ed. (Bensch, 2000); Duffy, *By Force of Arms*, 129–147.

164. Carl Daniel Küster, *Bruchstück seines Campagnelebens im siebenjährigen Krieg*, 2nd ed. (Berlin: Matzdorff, 1791; repr., Archiv, 1998), 36.
165. "Beispiel außerordentlicher Tapferkeit des Majors v. Lange und des Lieutenant von Marwitz, in Vertheidigung des Kirchhofs bey dem nächtlichen Ueberfall bey Hochkirch," in Küster, *Officier-Lesebuch*, pt. 3, vol. 2, 117–131.
166. "Beispiel außerordentlicher Tapferkeit," vol. 2, 123f.
167. "Beispiel außerordentlicher Tapferkeit," vol. 2, 124. Großer Generalstab, *Der Siebenjährige Krieg*, vol. 8, *Zorndorf und Hochkirch*, 492f., dismisses the rumor as having no basis in fact.
168. "Beispiel außerordentlicher Tapferkeit," vol. 2, 125.
169. Cogniazo, *Geständnisse*, 43.
170. "Beispiel außerordentlicher Tapferkeit," vol. 2, 125–126.
171. "Beispiel außerordentlicher Tapferkeit," vol. 2, 126.
172. "In this way had the Austrians also heroically defended the churchyard at the Battle of Leuthen, giving their largely defeated army the time to withdraw in good order." "Beispiel außerordentlicher Tapferkeit," vol. 2, 127. See also Cogniazo, *Geständnisse* 3:42: "The Austrians made the same mistake with this churchyard as the Prussians had made with the churchyard at Leuthen."
173. Kunisch, *Friedrich der Grosse*, 394.
174. Jessen, *Friedrich der Große und Maria Theresia in Augenzeugenberichten*, 342.
175. Jessen, *Friedrich der Große und Maria Theresia in Augenzeugenberichten*, 342.
176. Walter, *Maria Theresia*, 147.
177. "Betrachtungen über die Taktik und einige Teile des Krieges oder Betrachtungen über einige Veränderungen in der Art der Kriegführung (27. Dezember 1758)," in Volz, *Werke Friedrichs*, 6:125.
178. Carl-Gustav von Wrangel, "Der siebenjährige Krieg in Vorpommern," *Acta Wrangeliana* (1934): 59, 61.
179. See Felicitas Spring, "Aus dem Leben des schwedischen Husaren David Ginow (um 1740–1803): Unterwegs zwischen Litauen, Schwedisch-Pommern und Mecklenburg," *Genealogie* 59, no. 2 (2010): 98ff.
180. Oldach, *Stadt und Festung Stralsund*, 275–286.
181. Oldach, *Stadt und Festung Stralsund*, 275–286; Karl Ernst Hermann Krause, "Rostock im siebenjährigen Kriege," *Beiträge zur Geschichte der Stadt Rostock* 7 (1913); Müller, *Meines Lebens-Vorfälle*, 69–75, 99–108, 166–167, 194–195, 208–209, 238.
182. On prosperous times for Swedish military lodges, see Önnerfors, "Freimaurerei und Offiziertum im 18. Jahrhundert," 238–246.
183. Oldach, *Schwedens Beteiligung am Siebenjährigen*.
184. Oldach, *Schwedens Beteiligung am Siebenjährigen*, 59–66 (billeting), 70–71 (hostage taking), 71–72 (hussars), 80–83 (profits).
185. Oldach, *Schwedens Beteiligung am Siebenjährigen*, 72–73.
186. Winton, "Sweden and the Seven Years' War," 19.

187. On Dohna, see Anonymous, "Journal der Campagne des Generallieutenant, Grafen von Dohna, gegen die Rußen und Schweden, in den Jahren 1758 und 1759," *Bellona* 11 (1783).

188. Friedrich II, *Politische Correspondenz*, no. 9892, 354.

189. Extracts from Langelius's diary were published in Swedish in Harald Tigerström, ed., *Olof Langelius drar i fält—Utdrag ur en östgötaryttares dagbok åren 1758–1762* (Tigerström, 1989). There were plans for a Swedish-German edition, but this seems unlikely to take place for the foreseeable future. On this, see Dirk Schleinert, "Der Siebenjährige Krieg in Vorpommern in kulturgeschichtlicher Perspektive," *Mare Balticum: Kultur-Geschichte-Gegenwart* x (2001); Dirk Schleinert, "Altvorpommern im Siebenjährigen Krieg: Aus dem Tagebuch des schwedischen Regimentspfarrers Olof Langelius, in *Die Demminer Kolloquien zur Geschichte Vorpommerns: Ausgewählte Beiträge 1995–2011*, ed. Henning Rischer and Dirk Schleinert (Sardellus, 2012); Dirk Schleinert, "Grimmen während des Siebenjährigen Krieges im Tagebuch des schwedischen Feldpredigers Olof Langelius," in *Die Marienkirche in Grimmen und ihre Gemeinde. Beiträge zur Kirchengeschichte einer pommerschen Stadt*, ed. Norbert Buske et al. (Ludwig, 2015).

190. Tigerström, *Langelius*, 20–22.

191. Tigerström, *Langelius*, 30.

192. Sulicki, *Der Siebenjährige Krieg in Pommern*, 186–197.

193. See James F. Searing, "The Seven Year's War in West Africa: The End of Company Rule and the Emergence of the *Habitants*," in Danley and Speelman, *Global Views*; Baugh, *Global War*, 330–332; Léonce Jore, "Les établissements français sur la côte occidentale d'Afrique de 1758 à 1809," *Revue Française d'Histoire d'Outre-Mer* 51 (1964); A. J. Marsh, "The Taking of Goree, 1758," *Mariner's Mirror* 51 (1965).

194. James L. A. Webb Jr., "The Mid-Eighteenth-Century Gum Arabic Trade and the British Capture of Saint-Louis du Sénégal, 1758," *Journal of Imperial and Commonwealth History* 25 (1997).

195. Baugh, *Global War*, 331.

196. Frank McLynn, *1759: The Year Britain Became Master of the World* (Jonathan Cape, 2004), 99.

197. The only British casualties were incurred two months later, in an attempt to capture an emir. See Baugh, *Global War*, 331.

198. Buschbell, *Das Tagebuch des Abraham ter Meer*, 49.

199. Wähner, *Tagebuch aus dem Siebenjährigen Krieg*, 71–72; Fülling, *Chronik des Pfarrers Johann Georg Fülling*, 36.

200. Abelmann, *Hannover im Siebenjährigen Krieg*, 207.

201. [Johann Hinrich Pratje], "Nachricht von der Insel Goree, und von dem derselben abhängenden Handel," *Hannoverische Beyträge* 36, Friday, May 4, 1759, cols. 569–600. The article was based on information found in the first volumes

of Johann Joachim Schwabe's collection of travel writings. Johann Joachim Schwabe, *Allgemeine Historie der Reisen zu Wasser und zu Lande: Oder Sammlung aller Reisebeschreibungen [. . .]*, 21 vols. (Leipzig: Arkstee &. Merkus, 1747–1774).
202. Cardwell, *Arts and Arms*, 229.
203. Marshall Smelser, *The Campaign for the Sugar Islands, 1759: A Study in Amphibious Warfare* (University of North Carolina Press, 1955); Jean Barreau, "La Campagne de 1759," in *Les Guerres en Guadeloupe aux XVIIIe siècle* (1703, 1759, 1794; repr., x, 1976), 37–91; also published in *Bulletin de la société d'histoire de la Guadeloupe* 25, no. 3 (1975), 27, no. 1 (1976), and 28, no. 2 (1976); citations here are to the separate printing. On this, see also Baugh, *Global War*, 377–385, Dull, *The French Navy and the Seven Years' War*, 138–139; Richard Pares, *War and Trade in the West Indies, 1739–1763* (Clarendon, 1936); Trevor Burnard and John Garrigus, "The Seven Years' War in the West Indies," in *The Plantation Machine: Atlantic Capitalism in French Saint-Domingue and British Jamaica*, ed. Trevor Burnard and John Garrigus (University of Pennsylvania Press, 2016).
204. Barreau, "La Campagne de 1759," 46.
205. Barreau, "La Campagne de 1759," 47.
206. See Edward P. Shaw, ed., "An Episode in the Seven Years' War: A Memoir of Jacques Cazotte Concerning the Capture of Guadeloupe by the English," *Hispanic American Historical Review* 28, no. 3 (1948).
207. Alan J. Guy, "George Durant's Journal of the Expedition to Martinique and Guadeloupe, October 1758–May 1759," in *Military Miscellany I: Manuscripts from the Seven Years War, the First and Second Sikh Wars and the First World War*, ed. Alan J. Guy et al. (Sutton, 1996); Francis Arthur Whinyates, ed., *The Services of Lieut.-Colonel Francis Downman, R. A. in France, North America, and the West Indies Between the Years 1758 and 1784* (Woolwich: Royal Artillery, 1898), 5–13. Another report on the expedition was published directly after it had taken place. See Richard Gardiner, *An Account of the Expedition to the West Indies, Against Martinico: With the Reduction of Guadelupe, and Other the Leeward Islands, Subject to the French King, 1759* (London: Baskerville, 1759). See also Anonymous, *A Soldier's Journal*, 61–168.
208. Guy, "George Durant's Journal," 17.
209. On the battle for Martinique, see Smelser, *Campaign for the Sugar Islands*, 39–69.
210. Smelser, *Campaign for the Sugar Islands*, 59–69.
211. On the garrison, see Boris Lesueur, "La garnison de la Guadeloupe sous l'Ancien Régime," *Bulletin de la Société d'Histoire de la Guadeloupe* 154 (2009): 29–58.
212. Barreau, "La Campagne de 1759," 53.
213. Guy, "George Durant's Journal," 34.
214. Guy, "George Durant's Journal," 35.
215. Guy, "George Durant's Journal," 35.

216. Guy, "George Durant's Journal," 35–36.
217. Guy, "George Durant's Journal," 36.
218. Guy, "George Durant's Journal," 38.
219. Erica Michiko Charters, *Disease, War, and the Imperial State: The Welfare of the British Armed Forces During the Seven Years' War* (University of Chicago Press, 2014).
220. Baugh, *Global War*, 381.
221. Guy, "George Durant's Journal," 43.
222. Guy, "George Durant's Journal," 44; see also Gardiner, *Account of the Expedition to the West Indies*, 39.
223. Barreau, "La Campagne de 1759," 69.
224. Barreau, "La Campagne de 1759," 81–88; Whinyates, *Services of Lieut.-Colonel Francis Downman*, 6; Baugh, *Global War*, 383.
225. Guy, "George Durant's Journal," 46–47.
226. Whinyates, *Services of Lieut.-Colonel Francis Downman*, 7.
227. Dziembowski, *La Guerre de Sept Ans*, 288.
228. Guy, "George Durant's Journal," 14.
229. See Häberlein and Schmölz-Häberlein, "Kommunikationsnetz des Halleschen Pietismus"; Häberlein and Schmölz-Häberlein, *Halles Netzwerk im Siebenjährigen Krieg*.
230. Gotthilf August Francke, ed., *Der Koeniglich-Daenischen Missionarien aus Ost-Indien eingesandter Ausfuehrlichen Berichte Achter Theil, Von der LXXXV bis LCV-Isten Continuation: Darinnen die Fortsetzung des Missionswercks bis auf das Jahr 1761 umstaendlich beschrieben wird [. . .]* (Halle: Waisenhaus, 1765), iv–v.
231. Francke, *Der Koeniglich-Daenischen Missionarien*, 893.
232. Price and Dodwell, *Diary of Ananda Ranga Pillai*, 11:114–115. See also the report on page 87 of the same volume of Pillai's diary, which is clearly based on the Battle of Kolin.
233. Price and Dodwell, *Diary of Ananda Ranga Pillai*, 11:275–276.
234. Price and Dodwell, *Diary of Ananda Ranga Pillai*, 11:95.
235. Price and Dodwell, *Diary of Ananda Ranga Pillai*, 11:318.
236. Rex Whitworth, ed., *The Diary of James Wood R. A. 1746–1765* (Cooper, 1988), 118–119.
237. Bryant, "War in the Carnatic," 96.
238. Price and Dodwell, *Diary of Ananda Ranga Pillai*, 11:457.

7. 1759: Annus Mirabilis

1. McLynn, *1759: The Year Britain Became Master of the World*.
2. Mühlenberg, *Correspondence*, 4:88–89.
3. Whitworth, *Diary of James Wood*, 134–135.

4. This was not the first or last plan of this kind. See Pierre Coquelle, "Les Projets de descents en Angleterre d'apres les archives des Affaires Étrangères," *Revue d'histoire diplomatique* 15 (1901).
5. Middleton, *Bells of Victory*, 107.
6. Middleton, *Bells of Victory*, 113–119.
7. Goethe, *The Auto-Biography of Goethe*, 78.
8. For a detailed account, see Ingo Beringer, *Blutiger Karfreitag 1759: Die Schlacht bei Bergen und Vilbel* (Bad Vilbeler Verein für Geschichte und Heimatpflege, 2009).
9. On the Allied side, eyewitnesses to the battle included several figures who have already made an appearance in these pages, including Dubois-Cattin, the Swiss officer, on the French side, and Grotehenn, Brunswick diarist Heinrich Urban Cleve (1733–1808), and Johann George Bess, a noncommissioned officer in the Hanoverian Jäger corps, on the Anglo-German side. Dubois-Cattin, "Correspondance," 159ff.; Füssel and Petersen, *Grotehenn Briefe*, 67–68.
10. Middleton, *Bells of Victory*, 120.
11. Middleton, *Bells of Victory*, 119, 121.
12. On the city of Hanover, see Ulrich, "Die Stadt Hannover im siebenjährigen Kriege."
13. Duffy, *Military Life of Frederick the Great*, 91; on the history of the city during the war, see Ingelore Buchholz, "Leben in der Festungsstadt," in *Magdeburg: Die Geschichte der Stadt 805–2005*, ed. Matthias Puhle and Peter Petsch (Stekovics, 2005).
14. For an overview, see Martin Steffen, ed., *Die Schlacht bei Minden: Weltpolitik und Lokalgeschichte* (Bruns, 2008); Stuart Reid, *The Battle of Minden 1759: The Impossible Victory of the Seven Years War* (Frontline, 2016).
15. On Broglie, see Victor François, Duc de Broglie, *Correspondance inédite de Victor-François, duc de Broglie, maréchal de France, avec le prince Xavier de Saxe, comte de Lusace, lieutenant général, pour servir à l'histoire de la guerre de sept ans (campagnes de 1759 à 1761)*, ed. Albert de Broglie, 4 vols. (Albin Michel, 1903–1905).
16. Großer Generalstab, *Der Siebenjährige Krieg*, vol. 11, *Minden und Maxen*, 24f.
17. Marian Füssel, "Ansichten des Krieges: Deutsche Augenzeugenberichte zum 1. August 1759," in Steffen, *Schlacht bei Minden*, 97–108, 231–234.
18. Füssel and Petersen, *Grotehenn Briefe*, 73.
19. Barthold Koch, *Kurze Kriegsgeschichte des siebenjährigen deutschen, des achtjährigen englisch-amerikanischen, die Begebenheiten zwischen Hessen und Bückeburg nebst anderen Vorfällen in Hessen und zuletzt des französisch-russischen Krieges (1758–1815)* (Verein für Hessische Geschichte und Landeskunde, 2007), 17.
20. Tempelhof, *Geschichte des siebenjährigen Krieges*, 3:201.
21. See Luh, *Kriegskunst in Europa 1650–1800*.
22. Koch, *Kurze Kriegsgeschichte*, 17.

23. See Charles Winslow Elliott, "The Men That Fought at Minden," *Journal of the American Military Institute* 3, no. 2 (1939).
24. On the media debate surrounding the Sackville scandal, see Viktor Link, "Geschichte in der Literatur: Drei Darstellungen der Schlacht von Minden und Herzog Ferdinands von Braunschweig und Wolfenbüttel in englischen Romanen des 18. Jahrhunderts," *Wolfenbütteler Studien zur Aufklärung* 1 (1974); Philip J. Kluckoff, "Smollett and the Sackville Controversy," *Neuphilologische Mitteilungen* 69 (1969); Piers Mackesy, *The Coward of Minden: The Affair of Lord George Sackville* (St. Martin's, 1979).
25. Westphalen, *Geschichte der Feldzüge Herzog Ferdinands von Braunschweig-Lüneburg*, 3:469; Hans H. Klein, *Wilhelm zu Schaumburg-Lippe: Klassiker der Abschreckungstheorie und Lehrer Scharnhorsts* (Biblio, 1982), 98f.
26. See Carl Renouard, *Geschichte des Krieges in Hannover, Hessen und Westfalen von 1757 bis 1763* (Kassel: Fischer, 1863–64), 2:252–258. See also Luh, *Kriegskunst in Europa 1650–1800*, 209f.
27. Leopold Kulke, "Die Schlacht bei Minden 1759 und ihre Folgen aus französischer Sicht," *Mitteilungen des Mindener Geschichtsvereins* 43 (1971): 82.
28. *Gazette* [*de France*], no. 34, August 18, 1759, 399–402. On the British reception of news of the battle, see, in particular, George Ridpath, *The Diary of George Ridpath of Stitchel, 1755–1761*, ed. Sir James Balfour Paul (Edinburgh University Press, 1922), 264, 266.
29. Klaus Marowsky, "Jobst Hinrich Lohrmann und die Schlacht bei Minden," in *Die Schlacht bei Minden: Ein Erinnerungsbuch zum 200. Gedenktag der Schlacht bei Minden am 1. August 1759* (Bruns, 1959), 131–138.
30. [Montag] *Teutsche Kriegs-Canzley*, vol. 1, no. 2–3, 20–107; Archenholz, *History of the Seven Years War*, 232–233; Carl, *Okkupation und Regionalismus*, 226.
31. Schneider, "Schlacht bei Minden."
32. Frederic George Stephens, *Catalogue of Prints and Drawings in the British Museum—Division 1: Political and Personal Satires*, vol. 3, pt. 2, 1751–1760 (London: British Museum, 1877), no. 3686, 1200–1201.
33. Cardwell, *Arts and Arms*, 246–247.
34. Schneider, "Schlacht bei Minden," 49.
35. Schneider, "Schlacht bei Minden," 50.
36. See Hans Nordsiek, "Immer auf der Siegerseite: die Schlacht bei Minden 1759: Realität und Interpretation," *Mitteilungen des Mindener Geschichtsvereins* 71 (1999).
37. John Clarke, *History of the Minden Lodge, No. 63, Held in the XXth Regiment of Foot: On the Registry of the Grand Lodge of Ireland, with an Account of the Celebration of Its Centenary, 27th December, 1848* (Bermuda, 1849).
38. Jessica L. Harland-Jacobs, *Builders of Empire: Freemasons and British Imperialism, 1717–1927* (University of North Carolina Press, 2007).

39. Gerd Voswinkel, "Der nicht verstandene Vorsatz von Voltaires 'Candide' und die Schlacht von Minden," in *Die Kunst des Vernetzens: Festschrift für Wolfgang Hempel*, ed. Botho Brachmann et al. (Verlag für Berlin-Brandenburg, 2006), 211–222.
40. Voltaire, *Candide*, 27.
41. Voltaire, *Candide*, 27f.
42. "War," in Voltaire, *Philosophical Dictionary* (Penguin, 1979), 346.
43. Marian Füssel, "Zwischen Kriegserfahrung und Heldenmythos: Ewald von Kleist und die Schlacht von Kunersdorf am 12. August 1759," in *Ewald von Kleist: Zum 250. Todestag*, ed. Lothar Jordan (Königshausen & Neumann, 2010), 137–159, 137.
44. On Kay, see Großer Generalstab, *Der Siebenjährige Krieg*, vol. 10, *Kunersdorf*, 149–184; Masslowski, *Der siebenjährige Krieg nach russischer Darstellung*, 3:1–66.
45. Großer Generalstab, vol. 10, *Kunersdorf*; Masslowski, *Der siebenjährige Krieg nach russischer Darstellung*, 3:67–121; Manfred Laubert, *Kritik der Quellen zur Schlacht bei Kunersdorf (12. August 1759)*; Stefan Hartmann, "Eine neue Quelle zur Schlacht bei Kunersdorf," *Jahrbuch für brandenburgische Landesgeschichte* 42 (1991); Werner Benecke, ed., *Kunersdorf 1759, Kunowice 2009: Studien zu einer europäischen Legende, Studium pewnej europejskiej legendy* (Logos, 2010). On Kleist at Kunersdorf, see also Füssel, "Zwischen Kriegserfahrung und Heldenmythos"; Duffy, *By Force of Arms*, 165–171; Grzegorz Podruczny and Jakub Wrzosek, "Lone Grenadier: An Episode from the Battle of Kunersdorf, 12 August 1759," *Journal of Conflict Archaeology* 9, no. 1 (2014).
46. See Robert Pois and Philip Langer, "Frederick the Great at Kunersdorf, August 12, 1759," in *Command Failure in War: Psychology and Leadership* (Indiana University Press, 2004).
47. Anklam, *Wissen nach Augenmaß*, 20, 96–110.
48. Tempelhof, *Geschichte des siebenjährigen Krieges*, 3:209.
49. Archenholz, *History of the Seven Years War*, 252.
50. Tempelhof, *Geschichte des siebenjährigen Krieges*, 3:217.
51. Friedrich August von Retzow, *Charakteristik der wichtigsten Ereignisse des Siebenjährigen Krieges*, 2 vols. (Berlin: Himburg, 1802), 2:106.
52. Retzow, *Charakteristik der wichtigsten Ereignisse*, 2:106.
53. Tempelhof, *Geschichte, des siebenjährigen Krieges*, 3:219; Retzow, *Charakteristik der wichtigsten Ereignisse*, 2:107ff.; Archenholz, *History of the Seven Years War*, 255ff.
54. Archenholz, *History of the Seven Years War*, 259.
55. Retzow, *Charakteristik der wichtigsten Ereignisse*, 2:112.
56. Reinhold Koser, "Seydlitz in der Schlacht von Kunersdorf," *Historische Zeitschrift* 87, no. 1 (1901).
57. Prittwitz, *Jugend und Kriegsleben eines preußischen Offiziers*, 121–128; Kerler, *Tagebuch Dominicus*, 58–61 (diary), 61–66 (letter).

58. Gorani, *Mémoires*, 123–124.
59. For a detailed accounting of the dead and wounded, see Johann Ludwig Kriele, *Ausführliche und zuverlässige historisch-militärische Beschreibung der Schlacht bei Kunersdorf und Frankfurt am 12ten August 1759: Mit beigefügtem genauen Situations-Plane nebst verschiedenen Nachrichten der Schicksale Frankfurts und der umliegenden Gegend in damaliger Zeit* (Berlin: Maurer, 1801; repr., LTR, 2001), 58–127.
60. See Füssel, "Zwischen Kriegserfahrung und Heldenmythos."
61. Retzow, *Charakteristik der wichtigsten Ereignisse*, 2:112f.
62. Retzow, *Charakteristik der wichtigsten Ereignisse*, 2:113f.
63. Friedrich II, *Politische Correspondenz*, vol. 18, no. 11,335, 481; for a German translation, see Max Hein, ed., *Briefe Friedrichs des Großen*, vol. 2 (Hobbing, 1914), no. 44, 52.
64. Benninghoven et al., *Friedrich der Grosse*, 205f.
65. Masslowski, *Der siebenjährige Krieg nach russischer Darstellung*, vol. 3, no. 14, 412.
66. Friedrich II, *Politische Correspondenz*, vol. 18, no. 11,393, 510.
67. Duffy, *By Force of Arms*, 171–178.
68. On this, see, for example, Laudon's correspondence: Buchberger, *Briefe Loudon's*, 400–404.
69. Duffy, *By Force of Arms*, 178–180.
70. For the correspondence between Walpole and Mann in late August, see Walpole, *Walpole's Correspondence*, vol. 21, *With Sir Horace Mann*, 21:317–321.
71. Mühlenberg, *Corresondence*, 4:180 with n362.
72. Mühlenberg, *Corresondence*, 4:107.
73. Bisset, *Memoirs and Papers of Mitchell*, 2:107.
74. For a fundamental edition of source material, see Arthur George Doughty and George William Parmelee, eds., *The Siege of Québec and the Battle of the Plains of Abraham*, 6 vols. (Dussault & Proulx, 1901); see also Jacques Lacoursière and Hélène Quimper, eds. *Québec ville assiégée 1759–1760: D'après les acteurs et les témoins* (Septentrion, 2009). Frégault, *Canada: The War of the Conquest*, 233–276, is a classic account. Of more recent work on the campaign, see Charles Perry Stacey, *Québec, 1759: The Siege and the Battle*, ed. Donald E. Graves (Robin Brass Studio, 2002 [1959]); Gordon Donaldson, *Battle for a Continent: Québec 1759* (Doubleday, 1973); Stuart Reid and Gerry A. Embleton, *Québec 1759: The Battle That Won Canada* (Osprey, 2003); Matthew C. Ward, *The Battle for Quebec, 1759* (History Press, 2005); D. Peter McLeod, *Northern Armageddon: The Battle of the Plains of Abraham* (Douglas & McIntyre, 2008); Phillip A. Buckner and John G. Reid, eds., *Revisiting 1759: The Conquest of Canada in Historical Perspective* (University of Toronto Press, 2012); Phillip A. Buckner and John G. Reid, eds., *Remembering 1759: The Conquest of Canada in Historical Memory* (University of Toronto Press, 2012); Malcolm Fraser, "The Capture of Quebec: A Manuscript

Journal Relating to the Operations Before Quebec from 8th May, 1759 to 17th May, 1760," *Journal of the Society for Army Historical Research* 18 (1939).
75. Anderson, *Crucible*, 348.
76. Anderson, *Crucible*, 344.
77. John Robson, *Captain Cook's War and Peace: The Royal Navy Years, 1755–1768* (Seaforth, 2009).
78. Matthew Ward, "Crossing the Line? The British Army and the Application of European 'Rules of War,'" in Buckner and Reid, *Revisiting 1759*.
79. Anderson, *Crucible*, 344.
80. Letter from Wolfe to his mother, August 31, 1759, in Wolfe, *Life and Letters*, 469.
81. Robert Stobo, *Memoirs of Major Robert Stobo, of the Virginia Regiment* (Pittsburgh: Skirven, 1854), 66–71. On the battle on the Plains of Abraham, see among others Ward, *The Battle for Quebec*, 171–200.
82. See Donald W. Olson et al., "Perfect Tide, Ideal Moon: An Unappreciated Aspect of Wolfe's Generalship at Québec 1759," *William and Mary Quarterly* 59 (2002).
83. [James Moncrief], *A Short Account of the Expedition Against Québec Commanded by Major-General Wolfe in the Year 1759* (Nuns of the Franciscan Convent, 1901), 36–37. Moncrief's authorship remains uncertain; Patrick MacKellar (1717–1778) is regarded as another possible author.
84. [Montcalm], "Journal du marquis de Montcalm," 7:611.
85. [Montcalm], "Journal du marquis de Montcalm," 7:612; Anderson, *Crucible*, 357.
86. Edmund Bailey O'Callaghan and Berthold Fernow, eds., "Journal Kept in the Army Commanded by the Late M. de Montcalm, Containing the Operations Before Québec from the 23 May to October," in *Documents Relative to the Colonial History of the State of New York*, 15 vols. (Albany: Weed, Parsons, 1853–1887), 10:1039; Ward, *The Battle for Quebec*, 186.
87. Ward, *The Battle for Quebec*, 185.
88. Lynn, *Battle: A History of Combat and Culture*, 128.
89. Earl John Chapman and Ian Macpherson McCulloch, eds., *Bard of Wolfe's Army: James Thompson, Gentleman Volunteer, 1733–1830* (Robin Brass Studio, 2010), 185–186.
90. On the temporality of the event, see Sven Externbrink, "Der kürzeste Vormittag—Québec 13. September 1759," in *Der Siebenjährige Krieg: Mikro- und Makroperspektiven*, ed. Marian Füssel (De Gruyter, 2021).
91. [Moncrief], *A Short Account*, 42.
92. Anderson, *Crucible*, 361.
93. O'Callaghan and Fernow, "Journal Kept in the Army Commanded by the Late M. de Montcalm," 10:1039.
94. Anonymous, *Siege of Québec in 1759. Tr. from the French: Narrative of the Doings During the siege of Québec, and the Conquest of Canada; by a Nun of the General Hospital of Québec* (Quebec: Mercury Office, 1858), 9.

95. On the dead, see Jean-Yves Bronze, *Les morts de la guerre de Sept Ans au Cimetière de l'Hôpital-Général de Québec* (Presses de l'Université Laval, 2001).
96. [Moncrief], *A Short Account*, 43.
97. [Moncrief], *A Short Account*, 44.
98. Montcalm's body was exhumed in 2001 and reburied in the cemetery of the Old Hospital in Quebec, where soldiers are also buried. See Fowler, *Empires at War*, 290.
99. [Moncrief], *A Short Account*, 45.
100. [Moncrief], *A Short Account*, 45–50.
101. Anonymous, *Siege of Québec*, 11–12.
102. "A Journal of the Expedition up the River St. Lawrence: Containing a True and Most Particular Account of the Transactions of the Fleet and Army Under the Command of Admiral Saunders and General Wolfe, from the Time of Their Embarkation at Louisbourg 'til After the Surrender of Québeck, Boston 1759," reprinted in *Magazine of History with Notes and Queries* Extra number, no 24 (1913): 113; see also the reprint in Doughty and Parmelee, *The Siege of Québec*, vol. 5, app. 2, 11.
103. "A Journal of the Expedition up the River St. Lawrence," 108. On the condition of the buildings, see [Moncrief], *A Short Account*, 50. For specific details of the destruction, see also Doughty and Parmelee, *The Siege of Québec*, vol. 3, 267f.
104. Richard Short, *Twelve Views of the Principal Buildings in Québec: From Drawings, Taken on the Spot, at the Command of Vice-Admiral Saunders by Richard Short, Purser of His Majesty's Ship the Prince of Orange; Engraved by Mssrs Grignion, Canot, Elliot, and others [. . .]* (London, 1761); for context, see John E. Crowley, "'Taken on the Spot': The Visual Appropriation of New France for the Global British Landscape," *Canadian Historical Review* 86, no. 1 (2005): 13f.
105. Jacques Viget, ed., *Règne militaire au Canada ou Administration Judiciaire de ce Pays par les Anglais de 8 Septembre 1760 au 10 Aout 1764* (Montreal: La Minerve, 1872); Horst Carl, "Mikro- und Makroperspektiven auf eine standardisierte Situation—Okkupationserfahrungen im Siebenjährigen Krieg im Vergleich," in Füssel, *Der Siebenjährige Krieg: Mikro- und Makroperspektiven*.
106. Casgrain, *Voyage au Canada*, 172–184.
107. See Anderson, *Crucible*, 373–376.
108. Anderson, *Crucible*, 374.
109. Anderson, *Crucible*, 375.
110. Anderson, *Crucible*, 374.
111. Anderson, "1759—Year of Decision?"
112. See McLynn, *1759: The Year Britain Became Master of the World*.
113. Huw V. Bowen, "British Conceptions of Global Empire, 1756–1783," *Journal of Imperial and Commonwealth History* 26 (1998): 22 and n1.

114. James Woodforde, *The Diary of a Country Parson 1758–1802*, ed. John Beresford (Canterbury Press, 1999), 2.
115. Letter to Mantagu, Strawberry Hill, October 21, 1759, in Walpole, *Walpole's Correspondence*, vol. 9, *With George Montagu*, 9:251.
116. Vaisey, *Diary of Thomas Turner*, 191. The identification as a "Briton" rather than an "Englishman" is worthy of note. See Stephen Conway, "War and National Identity in the Mid-Eighteenth-Century British Isles," *English Historical Review* 116, no. 468 (2001): 872, 874.
117. On the history of media representations of Wolfe as a hero, see Alan McNairn, *Behold the Hero: General Wolfe and the Arts in the Eighteenth Century* (Liverpool University Press, 1997).
118. Wähner, *Tagebuch aus dem Siebenjährigen Krieg*, 114.
119. On the same day, Frederick's Prussian subjects learned of their ally's conquest of Quebec from the pages of the Berlin press: see *Berlinische Nachrichten*, no. 129, Saturday, October 27, 1769, 537–539. By contrast, in Vienna the *Wiener Diarium* confirmed news of the French defeat only on November 7 (as late as October 31, the newspaper had carried a report claiming the contrary). See *Wiener Diarium*, no 87, Wednesday, October 31, 1759, and Wednesday November 7, 1759.
120. Wähner, *Tagebuch aus dem Siebenjährigen Krieg*, 115.
121. Buschbell, *Tagebuch des Abraham ter Meer*, 78–79. On Ter Meer as a reader of newspapers, see Müller, "On dit."
122. Mastnak and Tänzer, *Tagebuch des Garnisonsauditeurs Johann Philipp Schowart*, 184–185. The following Monday Schowart noted further details of the victory: "In the battle near Québec on the 13th, the French lost 1500 men, but the English barely half as many, and the English also lost 348 men [. . .] including 14 Officers taken prisoner in Québec. The English took some 241 Guns [. . .] Mortars and Howitzers" (185).
123. Hans Schumann, ed., *Friedrich der Grosse: Mein lieber Marquis: Sein Briefwechsel mit Jean-Baptiste d'Argens während des Siebenjährigen Krieges*, 2nd ed. (Manesse, 1986), 161–162.
124. Friedrich II, *Politische Correspondenz*, vol. 18, no. 11,553, 609.
125. Friedrich II, *Politische Correspondenz*, vol. 18, no. 11,558, 613–614.
126. Dull, *The French Navy and the Seven Years' War*, 158–163.
127. *Gazette*, no. 45, November 3, 1759, 543–547.
128. John Francis Bosher, "Financing the French Navy in the Seven Years' War: Beaujon, Goosens et Compagnie in 1759," *Business History* 28 (1986); Arnaud Orain, "Soutenir la guerre et réformer la fiscalité: Silhouette et Forbonnais au Contrôle général des finances (1759)," *French Historical Studies* 36, no. 3 (2013).
129. Thierry Maugenest, *Étienne de Silhouette (1709–1767): Le ministre banni de l'histoire de France* (La Découverte, 2018).

130. Voltaire to Luise Dorothée, Aux Délices, December 4, 1759, in Raschke, *Briefwechsel*, 168.
131. See Castelnau's letter, written close to Gießen, October 28, 1759, in Castelnau, *Lettres*, 131.
132. Oldach, *Stadt und Festung Stralsund*.
133. Ulrich van der Heyden, "Die erste preußische Seeschlacht auf dem Stettiner Haff im Jahre 1759," *Baltische Studien* 103 (2017): 122; Sulicki, *Der Siebenjährige Krieg in Pommern*, 197–201.
134. Wähner, *Tagebuch aus dem Siebenjährigen Krieg*, 66.
135. Prittwitz, *Jugend und Kriegsleben eines preußischen Offiziers*, 106–115.
136. Prittwitz, *Jugend und Kriegsleben eines preußischen Offiziers*, 107. See also Müller, *Meines Lebens Vorfälle*, 85–86.
137. Prittwitz, *Jugend und Kriegsleben eines preußischen Offiziers*, 107.
138. Winton, "Sweden and the Seven Years' War," 19.
139. Tigerström, *Langelius*, 33.
140. Tigerström, *Langelius*, 34–35.
141. van der Heyden, "Die erste preußische Seeschlacht"; Lanitzki, *Galeeren auf dem Peenestrom*; Sulicki, *Der Siebenjährige Krieg in Pommern*, 242–245.
142. van der Heyden, "Die erste preußische Seeschlacht," 112.
143. Karl-Heinz Ruffmann, "Der Ostseeraum im Siebenjährigen Krieg," *Zeitschrift für Ostforschung* 5 (1956): 501–504.
144. van der Heyden, "Die erste preußische Seeschlacht," 114–117; Sulicki, *Der Siebenjährige Krieg in Pommern*, 235–237.
145. Prittwitz, *Jugend und Kriegsleben eines preußischen Offiziers*, 114.
146. *Berlinische Nachrichten*, no. 45, April 14, 1759, 178; van der Heyden, "Die erste preußische Seeschlacht," 117–118.
147. van der Heyden, "Die erste preußische Seeschlacht," 124.
148. van der Heyden, "Die erste preußische Seeschlacht," 123–125.
149. van der Heyden, "Die erste preußische Seeschlacht," 128.
150. van der Heyden, "Die erste preußische Seeschlacht," 128–129.
151. van der Heyden, "Die erste preußische Seeschlacht," 131–132.
152. There was a second flotilla on the Haff, but it was never used and was disbanded on May 29, 1762: see van der Heyden, "Die erste preußische Seeschlacht," 134.
153. Lanitzki, *Galeeren auf dem Peenestrom*.
154. Sulicki, *Der Siebenjährige Krieg in Pommern*, 237–242.
155. Tigerström, *Langelius*, 41.
156. This was the number of ships La Clue had when he left Toulon. See Dull, *The French Navy and the Seven Years' War*, 137.
157. Sam Willis, "The Battle of Lagos, 1759," *Journal of Military History* 73 (2009).
158. Equiano, *The Interesting Narrative*, 51.
159. Equiano, *The Interesting Narrative*, 51–52.

160. Ruddock F. Mackay, ed., *The Hawke Papers: A Selection; 1743–1771* (Routledge, 1990), 271–272.
161. See William Spavens, *Memoirs of a Seafaring Life: The Narrative of William Spavens, Pensioner on the Naval Chest at Chatham*, ed. Nicholas Andrew Martin Rodger (Folio Society, 2000), 50. See also Nicholas Tracy, *The Battle of Quiberon Bay 1759: Hawke and the Defence of the French Invasion* (Pen & Sword, 2010); Ruddock F. Mackay and Michael Duffy, *Hawke, Nelson and British Naval Leadership, 1747–1805* (Boydell, 2009); Mackay, *Hawke Papers*; Ruddock F. Mackay, *Admiral Hawke* (Clarendon, 1965); Geoffrey Marcus, *Quiberon Bay: The Campaign in Home Waters, 1759* (Hollis & Carter, 1960).
162. Dull, *The French Navy and the Seven Years' War*, 162.
163. The *Orient*, the *Dauphin Royale*, the *Solitaire*, the *Tonnant*, the *Intrépide*, the *Northumberland*, the *Magnifique*, and the *Bizarre*.
164. The *Glorieux*, the *Robuste*, the *Dragon*, the *Eveillé*, and the *Brillant*.
165. Dull, *The French Navy and the Seven Years' War*, 162.
166. Hein, *Briefe Friedrichs des Großen*, vol. 2, 58–59.
167. On the capitulation at Maxen, see Georg Winter, *Die kriegsgeschichtliche Überlieferung über Friedrich den Grossen kritisch geprüft an dem Beispiel der Kapitulation von Maxen* (Berlin: Gaertner, 1888); Ludwig Mollwo, *Die Kapitulation von Maxen* (Marburg: Sömmering, 1893); Großer Generalstab, *Der Siebenjährige Krieg*, vol. 11, *Minden und Maxen*; Marcus von Salisch, "Zwei 'unerhörte Exempel': Die Kapitulationen von Pirna 1756 und Maxen 1759 im Vergleich," *Neues Archiv für sächsische Geschichte* 84 (2013). For contemporary accounts, see Johann Gottlieb Tielcke, *Beiträge zur Kriegskunst und Geschichte des Krieges von 1756 bis 1763*, 6 vols. (Freyberg: Barthel, 1775–1786), 1:1–40; Friedrich Wilhelm Ernst Gaudi, *Journal vom Siebenjährigen Kriege*, ed. Jürgen Ziechmann, vol. 6, *1759* (LTR, 2009), 327–349; Tempelhof, *Geschichte des siebenjährigen Krieges*, 3:346–370; Duffy, *By Force of Arms*, 197–209.
168. Kerler, *Tagebuch Dominicus*, 77.
169. Hülsen, *Aus den Memoiren des Aeltervaters*, 105.
170. Hülsen, *Aus den Memoiren des Aeltervaters*, 106.
171. Duffy, *Armee Maria Theresias*, 233.
172. Schumann, *Briefwechsel mit Jean-Baptiste d'Argens*, 165.
173. Friedrich II, *Politische Correspondenz*, vol. 18, no. 11,617, 656.
174. Khevenhüller-Metsch, *Maria Theresias*, 5:137.
175. Baugh, *Global War*, 456–458; Middleton, *Bells of Victory*, 135–136; Alois Schmid, "Der geplante Friedenskongress in Augsburg 1761," in *Land und Reich, Stamm und Nation: Probleme und Perspektiven bayerischer Geschichte. Festgabe für Max Spindler zum 90. Geburtstag*, ed. Andreas Kraus, vol. 2 (Beck, 1984); Carter, *Dutch Republic*, 27–30; Zenab Esmat Rashed, *The Peace of Paris 1763* (Liverpool University Press, 1951), 30–33.

176. Friedrich II. *Politische Correspondenz*, vol. 18, no. 11,395, 510–511; no. 11,533, 592.
177. Middleton, *Bells of Victory*, 135.
178. Schmid, "Der geplante Friedenskongress in Augsburg," 236f.; Peter D. Brown and Karl W. Schweizer, eds., *The Devonshire Diary: William Cavendish, Fourth Duke of Devonshire Memoranda of State of Affairs 1759–1762* (Royal Historical Society, 1982), 35.
179. Johann Hartwig Ernst von Bernstorff and Étienne-François de Choiseul, *Correspondance entre le Comte Johan Hartvig Ernst Bernstorff et le Duc de Choiseul: 1758–1766* (Copenhagen: Gyldendal, 1871), 112.
180. Giacomo Casanova, *History of My Life* (Everyman, 2006), 748. The German edition of Casanova's memoir contains more detail on the visit to Augsburg. See Giacomo Casanova, *Geschichte meines Lebens*, vol. 8 (Beck, 1986), 28, 33–46, and n95.
181. Voltaire to Luise Dorothée, Aux Délices, May 26, 1758, in Raschke, *Briefwechsel*, 129.
182. Luise Dorothée to Voltaire, Gotha, October 7, 1758, in Raschke, *Briefwechsel*, 143.
183. See the section "Winners and Losers: Profits, Losses, and Reparations" in chapter 14.
184. Voltaire to Luise Dorothée, Aux Délices, September 26, 1758, in Raschke, *Briefwechsel*, 142; Luise Dorothée to Voltaire, Gotha, December 12, 1758, in Raschke, *Briefwechsel*, 147.
185. *Hamburgischer Correspondent*, no. 12, January 8, 1761, 37, cited in Jessen, *Friedrich der Große und Maria Theresia in Augenzeugenberichten*, 376.

8. As Mighty As the Sword: The Media War

1. Gerhard Lauer and Thorsten Unger, eds., *Das Erdbeben von Lissabon und der Katastrophendiskurs im 18. Jahrhundert* (Wallstein, 2008).
2. See Ulrich Löffler, *Lissabons Fall—Europas Schrecken: Die Deutung des Erdbebens von Lissabon im deutschsprachigen Protestantismus des 18. Jahrhunderts* (De Gruyter, 1999), 517–525, 631–647.
3. See Andreas Gestrich, *Absolutismus und Öffentlichkeit: Politische Kommunikation in Deutschland zu Beginn des 18. Jahrhunderts* (Vandenhoeck & Ruprecht, 1994), 221–234; Jürgen Habermas, *The Structural Transformation of the Public Sphere: An Inquiry Into a Category of Bourgeois Society*, trans. Thomas Burger (MIT Press, 1991).
4. *Journal encyclopédique, par une societé des gens de lettres*, August 15, 1756, 78, cited in David A. Bell, "Jumonville's Death: War Propaganda and National Identity in Eighteenth-Century France," in *The Age of Cultural Revolutions: Britain and*

France, 1750–1820, ed. Colin Jones and Dror Wahrman (University of California Press, 2002), 37.

5. Gilles Feyel, *L'annonce et la nouvelle: La presse d'information en France sous l'Ancien Régime (1630–1788)* (Voltaire Foundation, 2000), 720–777; on its wartime distribution, see especially 727–744.
6. Jacinthe De Montigny, "Le Canada dans l'imaginaire colonial français (1754–1756)," *French History and Civilization* 7 (2017): 87.
7. François Souchet, "Gazettes et journaux face à l'actualitè (été 1757)," in *Les Gazettes européennes de langue française (XVVe-XVIIIe siècles)*, ed. Henri Duranton et al. (Université de Saint-Étienne, 1992); Pierre Rétat, *Gazette d'Amsterdam: Miroir de l'Europe au XVIIIe siècle* (Voltaire Foundation, 2001).
8. Séran de la Tour, *Parallèle de la conduite des Carthaginois, a l'égard des Romains, dans la seconde guerre punique, avec la conduite de l'Angleterre, a l'égard de la France, dans la guerre déclarée par ces deux puissances, en 1756: Où l'on voit l'origine, les motifs, les moyens, & les suites de cette guerre, jusqu'au mois de décembre 1756* (n.p., 1757).
9. Bell, "Jumonville's Death," 39.
10. Robert-Martin Lesuire, *Les sauvages de l'Europe* (Berlin, 1760). See also *Die europäischen Wilden* (Frankfurt, 1770); Jacques Rustin, "Un pamphlet romanesque contre les Anglais dans la guerre de Sept ans: Les Sauvages de l'Europe (1760) de R.-M. Lesuire," *Recherches et travaux* 49 (1995).
11. Bell, "Jumonville's Death," 46–50.
12. See Newbigging, "Propaganda, Political Discourse and the Battle Over French Public Opinion."
13. Voltaire to Luise Dorothée, Aux Délices, Geneva, April 21, 1757, in Raschke, *Briefwechsel*, 108.
14. Luise Dorothée to Voltaire, Gotha, May 3, 1757, in Raschke, *Briefwechsel*, 110.
15. Stephen Botein et al., "The Periodical Press in Eighteenth-Century English and French Society: A Cross-Cultural Approach," *Comparative Studies in Society and History* 23, no. 3 (1981); Jeremy Black, *The English Press in the Eighteenth Century* (Croom Helm, 1987).
16. Egbert Donald Spector, *English Literary Periodicals and the Climate of Opinion During the Seven Years' War* (Mouton, 1966); Matt Schumann and Karl W. Schweizer, "Anglo-American War Reporting, 1749–1763: The Press and a Research Strategy," *Canadian Journal of History* 43 (2008): 269.
17. Schumann and Schweizer, "War Reporting," 270; on Mitchell, see Patrick Francis Doran, *Andrew Mitchell and Anglo-Prussian Diplomatic Relations During the Seven Years War* (Garland, 1986).
18. Schlenke, *England und das friderizianische Preussen*, 225.
19. Karl W. Schweizer, "Foreign Policy and the 18th Century English Press: The Case of Israel Mauduit's Considerations on the Present German War," *Publishing History* 39 (1996).

20. Schlenke, *England und das friderizianische Preussen*, 253–265.
21. For example, on the reception of news of the taking of Cape Breton in 1758, see Harris, "American Idols," 115–118. On the celebration of successes in 1759, the annus mirabilis, see Bowen, "British Conceptions of Global Empire," 1–3; see also McLynn, *1759: The Year Britain Became Master of the World*, 312–313.
22. Harris, "American Idols," 112; Bob Harris, *Politics and the Nation: Britain in the Mid-Eighteenth Century* (Oxford University Press, 2002), 113ff.; Nicholas Rogers, *Whigs and Cities: Popular Politics in the Age of Walpole and Pitt* (Clarendon, 1989); Kathleen Wilson, *The Sense of the People: Politics, Culture and Imperialism in England, 1715–1785* (Cambridge University Press, 1998). Cf. Friedrichs Donald Gibson, ed., *A Parson in the Vale of White Horse: George Woodward's Letters from East Hendred, 1753–1761* (Sutton, 1982), 104–105 (Prussia: Frederick and Ferdinand), 111–112 (Louisbourg), 122 (Quiberon Bay).
23. Vaisey, *Diary of Thomas Turner*, 347.
24. Vaisey, *Diary of Thomas Turner*, 55 (Minorca, 1756), 99 (Prague, 1757), 124f. (Rossbach, 1757), 155–157 (Krefeld, 1758), 161 (Louisbourg, 1758), 191–192 and 194–195 (Quebec, 1759), 212 (Montreal, 1760).
25. Valerie Wainwright, "'Fellow-Citizens in Science and Brothers in Humanity': Anglo-French Rivalry and the Discursive Practices of the 'Critical Review' 1756–1763," *Journal of European Studies* 44, no. 4 (2014).
26. Edward Gibbon, *Gibbon's Journal to January 28th, 1763: My Journal I, II & III and Ephemerides* (Norton 1929), 29 (Vellinghausen), 154 (Havana).
27. William L. Grant, "Canada Versus Guadeloupe: An Episode of the Seven Years' War," *American Historical Review* 17, no. 4 (1912); François Ternat, "Les enjeux géopolitiques intercontinentaux dans les négociations franco-britanniques entre 1760 et 1763," in Fonck and Veyssière, *La Chute*.
28. Grant, "Canada Versus Guadeloupe," 735.
29. Anonymous, *An Answer to the Letter to Two Great Men, Containing Remarks and Observations on That Piece, and Vindicating the Character of a Noble Lord from Inactivity* (London: Henderson, 1760).
30. William Burke, *Remarks on the Letter Addressed to Two Great Men, in a Letter to the Author of That Piece* (London: Dodsley, 1760).
31. Anonymous, *A Letter to the People of England, on the Necessity of Putting an Immediate End to the War, and the Means of Obtaining an Advantageous Peace* (London: Griffiths, 1760); Benjamin Franklin, *The Interest of Great Britain Considered with Regard to Her Colonies and the Acquisitions of Canada and Guadeloupe: To Which Are Added, Observations Concerning the Increase of Mankind, Peopling of Countries, Etc.* (London: Becket, 1760).
32. Anonymous, *Reasons for Keeping Guadaloupe at a Peace, Preferable to Canada, Explained in Five Letters from a Gentleman in Guadaloupe to His Friend in London* (London: Cooper, 1761).

33. Anonymous, *A Detection of the False Reasons and Facts, Contained in the Five Letters [. . .]* (London: Hope, 1761); Grant, "Canada Versus Guadeloupe," 740.
34. Grant, "Canada Versus Guadeloupe," 742.
35. Linda Colley, *Britons: Forging the Nation 1707–1837* (Yale University Press, 1992); Edmond Dziembowski, *Un nouveau patriotisme français, 1750–1770: La France face à la puissance anglaise à l'époque de la guerre de Sept Ans* (Voltaire Foundation, 1998); Mathias Persson, "Mediating the Enemy: Prussian Representations of Austria, France and Sweden During the Seven Years War," *German History* 32, no. 2 (2014).
36. Sdvižkov, "Landschaft nach der Schlacht," 51.
37. Richard Dietrich, ed., *Politische Testamente der Hohenzollern* (dtv, 1981), 268; Friedrich der Große, "Testament Politique [1752]," in *Die politischen Testamente Friedrich's des Grossen*, ed. Gustav Berthold Volz (Berlin: Hobbing, 1920), 48; for an English translation of the 1752 testament, see C. A. Macartney, ed., *The Habsburg and Hohenzollern Dynasties in the Seventeenth and Eighteenth Centuries* (Harper & Row, 1970), 332–346.
38. Ritter, *The Sword and the Scepter*, 1: 41; Pröve, "Der delegitimierte Gegner," 282; Wrede, "Zähmung der Bellona," 221–222.
39. [Montag], *Teutsche Kriegs-Canzley*; Gottlob Naumann and Carl Friedrich Wernich, eds., *Beyträge zur neuern Staats- und Kriegesgeschichte*, 19 vols. (Danzig: Schuster, 1756–1764). Historians continue to disagree as to whether the newspapers were actually produced in Danzig and Berlin. See most recently Gaudi, *Journal vom Siebenjährigen Kriege*, 10:15–16.
40. On circulation figures, see estimates in Pröve, "Der delegitimierte Gegner," 278 and n14.
41. Andreas Gestrich, "Kriegsberichterstattung als Propaganda: Das Beispiel des 'Wienerischen Diarium' im Siebenjährigen Krieg 1756–1763," in *Augenzeugen: Kriegsberichterstattung vom 18. zum 21. Jahrhundert*, ed. Ute Daniel (Vandenhoeck & Ruprecht, 2006).
42. Ernst Consentius, "Friedrich der Große und die Zeitungs-Zensur. Mit Benutzung der Akten des Geheimen Staats-Archivs," *Preußische Jahrbücher* 115 (1904): 236.
43. Consentius, "Zeitungs-Zensur," 220–249.
44. See David A. Copeland, *Colonial American Newspapers: Character and Content* (University of Delaware Press, 1997); Copeland, *Debating the Issues*. For a comprehensive compilation of reports on the French and Indian War, see Lucier, *French and Indian War Notices*.
45. Copeland, *Debating the Issues*, 180–191; Chris Kostov, *Terror and Fear: British and American Perceptions of the French-Indian Alliances During the Seven Years' War* (PublishAmerica, 2005); Shovlin, "Overseas Violence and the Seven Years' War."
46. Schumann and Schweizer, "Anglo-American War Reporting," 274.

47. For example, see Hedwig Pompe, "Im Kalkül der Kommunikation: Die Politik der Nachricht," in Adam and Dainat, *Der Siebenjährige Krieg in den zeitgenössischen Medien*. Frederick himself had become proficient in waging "newspaper war" during the first two Silesian wars. See Hans Jessen, "Die Anfänge der friderizianischen Nachrichtenpolitik," *Zeitungswissenschaft* 15, no. 7 (1940); Karl Kurth, "Grundzüge der friderizianischen Nachrichtenpolitik im 1. und 2. Schlesischen Kriege," *Zeitungswissenschaft* 15 (1940). For more detail, see Patrick Merziger, "Der öffentliche König? Herrschaft in den Medien während der drei schlesischen Kriege," in Sösemann and Vogt-Spira, *Friedrich der Grosse in Europa*.
48. Dreyer, "Hamburgische Stimmungsbilder," 62. Dreyer's 1929 study evaluates the "reports on public mood" written by Johann Matthias Dreyer to Alardus von Canthier, the "legation councillor" responsible for external affairs for the bishop of Eutin. See also Alfred Dreyer, *Johann Matthias Dreyer 1717–1769: Ein Hamburger satirischer Dichter und Holstein-Gottorper-Diplomat* (Christians, 1934).
49. Letter from Frederick to the Marquis d'Argens, Freiberg, February 19, 1760, in Schumann, *Briefwechsel*, 194.
50. For a nuanced account, see Birgfeld, *Krieg und Aufklärung*; see also Hans-Martin Blitz, *Aus Liebe zum Vaterland: Die deutsche Nation im 18. Jahrhundert* (Hamburg: Hamburger Edition, 2000), 145–280; Klaus Bohnen, "Von den Anfängen des "Nationalsinns": Zur literarischen Patriotismus-Debatte im Umkreis des Siebenjährigen Kriegs," in *Dichter und ihre Nation*, ed. Helmut Scheuer (Suhrkamp, 1993); Hans Peter Herrmann, "Individuum und Staatsmacht: Preußisch-deutscher Nationalismus in Texten zum Siebenjährigen Krieg," in Hans Peter Herrmann et al., *Machtphantasie Deutschland: Nationalismus, Fremdenhaß und Patriarchalismus im Vaterlandsdiskurs deutscher Schriftsteller des 18. Jahrhunderts* (Suhrkamp, 1996). In older historiography, see Karl Schwarze, *Der siebenjährige Krieg in der zeitgenössischen deutschen Literatur: Kriegserleben und Kriegserlebnis in Schrifttum und Dichtung des 18. Jh.* (Junker und Dunhaupt, 1936).
51. Reimar F. Lacher, *"Friedrich, unser Held"—Gleim und sein König* (Wallstein, 2017), 84–100; Birgfeld, *Krieg und Aufklärung*, 1:232–286, 2: 853–854.
52. Birgfeld, *Krieg und Aufklärung*, 1:18–20.
53. For a comparative overview, see Jörn Leonhard, *Bellizismus und Nation: Kriegsdeutung und Nationsbestimmung in Europa und den Vereinigten Staaten 1750–1914* (Oldenbourg, 2008), 119–131, 181–207, 285–289, 316–318.
54. Thus, it is relatively rare to see dehumanization in the confrontation between Prussian and Austrian or French troops of the line, whereas hatred was aggressively stirred up against "foreign" forces, including Pandours, Cossacks, and Indians.
55. See, for example, an older collection of "folk ballads": Franz Wilhelm von Ditfurth, *Die historischen Volkslieder des siebenjährigen Krieges, nebst geschichtlichen und sonstigen Erläuterungen* (Berlin: Lipperheide, 1871); on sermons, see Curt Horn,

"Die patriotische Predigt zur Zeit Friedrichs des Großen," *Jahrbuch für Brandenburgische Kirchengeschichte* 19 (1924); for poetry, see the overview by Christoph Deupmann, "Der Siebenjährige Krieg in der deutschsprachigen Lyrik," in *Geschichtslyrik: Ein Kompendium*, ed. Heinrich Detering et al., vol. 2 (Wallstein, 2013).

56. Mark Pockrandt, *Biblische Aufklärung: Biographie und Theologie der Berliner Hofprediger August Friedrich Wilhelm Sack (1703–1786) und Friedrich Samuel Gottfried Sack (1738–1817)* (De Gruyter, 2003), 530–535.
57. Voltaire, "War" in Voltaire, *Pocket Philosophical Dictionary* (Penguin, 2011) 346.
58. Klaus Bohnen, "'Was ist ein Held ohne Menschen liebe!': Zur literarischen Kriegsbewältigung in der deutschen Aufklärung," in *Lessing und die Toleranz*, ed. Peter Freimark et al. (Text und Kritik, 1986), 26.
59. *Christian Fürchtegott Gellerts sämmtliche Schriften, sechster Theil* (Carlsruhe, 1774), 459, quoted in Bohnen, "Zur literarischen Kriegsbewältigung," 26; on Gellert, see also Wolfgang Fink, "Précepteur ou aumônier? Christian Fürchtegott Gellert et la guerre de Sept Ans: Les lettres à Grabowski," in *Soldats et civils au XVIIIe siècle: Échanges épistolaires et culturels*, ed. François Genton and Thomas Nicklas (Presses Universitaires Reims, 2016).
60. Moses Mendelssohn, "Rhapsodie oder Zusätze zu den Briefen über die Empfindungen," *Schriften zur Philosophie, Aesthetik und Apologetik*, ed. Moritz Brasch (Leipzig: Voss, 1880; repr., Olms, 1968), 100.
61. Lacher, *Gleim und sein König*, 16–83; Blitz, *Aus Liebe zum Vaterland*, 145–280; Jörg Schönert, "Schlachtgesänge vom Kanapee, oder: 'Gott donnerte bei Lowositz' u den 'Preußischen Kriegsliedern in den Feldzügen 1756 und 1757' des Kanonikus Gleim," in *Gedichte und Interpretationen*, vol. 2, *Aufklärung und Sturm und Drang*, by Karl Richter (Reclam, 1983); Uwe-K. Ketelsen, "Ein Ossian der Hohenzollern: Gleims 'Preußische Kriegslieder von einem Grenadier' zwischen Nationalismus und Absolutismus," in *Exile and Enlightenment*, ed. Uwe Faulhaber et al. (Wayne State University Press, 1987); Uwe-K. Ketelsen, "Warum wollte 1757 der Preuße aus des Ungarns Schädel süßen Tokayer trinken? Ein Beispiel symbolischer Organisierung von Feindschaft am Beginn des bürgerlichen Zeitalters," in *Feindschaft*, ed. Medardus Brehl and Kristin Platt (Fink, 2003).
62. Karl Schwarze, "Gleims 'Preußische Kriegslieder von einem Grenadier' und Soldatenbriefe als ihre Quelle," *Germanisch-romanische Monatsschrift* 25 (1937).
63. Thomas Abbt, *Vom Verdienste*, 2nd ed. (Goslar: Hechtel, 1766), 300.
64. Brüggemann, *Der Siebenjährige Krieg*, 103.
65. Brüggemann, *Der Siebenjährige Krieg*, 106.
66. Ortmann, *Patriotische Briefe*.
67. Adolf Friedrich Ortmann, *Im friderizianischen Geist: Briefe aus dem Siebenjährigen Kriege für unsere Zeit*, ed. Johannes Priese (Jungland, 1943).

68. Ortmann, *Patriotische Briefe*, 296 (letter 18).
69. Brüggemann, *Der Siebenjährige Krieg*, 134.
70. Letter from Gleim to Uz, September 8, 1758, in Carl Schüddekopf, ed., *Briefwechsel zwischen Gleim und Uz* (Tübingen: Litterarischer Verein, 1899), 318.
71. Johann Wilhelm Ludwig Gleim, "Der Grenadier an die Kriegsmuse nach dem Siege bei Zorndorf den 25. August 1758," in *Preussische Kriegslieder von einem Grenadier* (Heilbronn: Henninger, 1882; repr., Kraus, 1968).
72. See Gotthold Ephraim Lessing, *Briefe, die neueste Literatur betreffend*, ed. Wolfgang Albrecht (Reclam, 1987), 11.
73. Christian Fürchtegott Gellert, *Briefwechsel*, ed. John F. Reynolds, vol. 2 (1756–1759) (De Gruyter, 1987), no. 440/441, 193–197.
74. Thomas Abbt, "Vom Tode für das Vaterland," in Kunisch, *Aufklärung und Kriegserfahrung*, 621. Epaminondas was a Theban military leader who established Theban hegemony in Greece in the fourth century BCE.
75. Guido Heinrich, "Leibhaftige Ästhetisierung und mediale Endverwertung: Die Rezeption der Kriegslyrik Anna Louisa Karschs in Berlin, Halberstadt und Magdeburg," in Adam and Dainat, *Der Siebenjährige Krieg in den zeitgenössischen Medien*, 144–147.
76. Guido Heinrich, "Leibhaftige Ästhetisierung," 165–166.
77. On the archival documentation of propaganda texts, see Kloosterhuis et al., *Militär und Gesellschaft*, 177–178.
78. For a poem on the Hessian theater of war by the Württemberg ensign Friedrich Zimmetshäuser, see Bäbler, "Aus dem Tagebuch eines württembergischen Regimentsarztes," 153–157.
79. Johannes Birgfeld, "Kriegspoesie für Zeitungsleser."
80. Michael Denis, *Poetische Bilder der meisten kriegerischen Vorgänge in Europa seit dem Jahr 1756*, vol. 1 (Augsburg: Wegner, 1768), 18.
81. Denis, *Poetische Bilder*, 18–19; see also Johannes Birgfeld, "Kriegspoesie für Zeitungsleser," 223.
82. Carsten Lange, "Telemann und England," in *Aspekte der englisch-deutschen Musikgeschichte im 17. und 18. Jahrhundert*, ed. Friedhelm Brusniak and Annemarie Clostermann (Studiopunkt, 1997), 131–134; Werner Menke, *Das Vokalwerk Georg Philipp Telemann's: Überlieferung und Zeitfolge* (Noske, 1941), 114f.
83. *Geschichte des Polybius: Mit den Auslegungen und Anmerkungen des Ritters Herrn von Folard [. . .]. Uebersetzt von Anthon Leopold von Oelsnitz Lieutenant bey dem Königlichen Preußischen Infanterieregiment von Haack*, vol. 1 (Berlin: 1755–1756), 8 (translator's preface).
84. [Jean Charles de Folard], *Geschichte des Polyb: Mit den Auslegungen und Anmerkungen des Ritters Herrn von Folard, französischen Obersten [. . .]*, trans. Jean Thibault Bion, 7 vols. (Vienna: Trattern, 1759–1760), vol. 1, preface, unpag.

85. Andreas Belach, *Nachtgedanken bey einer gefährlichen Reise in Kriegszeiten: Vom Verfaßer des Christen im Krieg* (Breslau, 1761); for a comprehensive treatment of this, see Birgfeld, *Krieg und Aufklärung*, vol. 2, 750–810, 877–878.
86. Anonymous, *Die Abbildung eines Schlacht-Feldes und die Buße eines hart bleßirten sterbenden Soldaten samt einem Anhang zum Lobe der Dreyeinigkeit Gottes* (n.p., 1758), unpag. [7].
87. See also Voltaire, "War" in *Pocket Philosophical Dictionary*.
88. Bernd Roeck, "Fabrizio auf dem Schlachtfeld von Waterloo oder Zur Entstehung der 'Schrecken des Krieges' als Thema der Kunst," in *Die Schrecken des Krieges: Kriegs- und Revolutionsdarstellungen aus fünf Jahrhunderten* (Ausstellungskatalog) (Galerie Mäder, 1987).
89. Gerhild H. M. Komander, *Der Wandel des "Sehepuncktes": Die Geschichte Brandenburg-Preußens in der Graphik von 1648–1810* (LIT, 1995); Doris Schumacher, "Der Siebenjährige Krieg in der bildenden Kunst: Von den Anfängen durch Johann Wilhelm Ludwig Gleim und Friedrich II. bis zu den populären Illustrationsfolgen des späten 18. Jahrhunderts," in Adam and Dainat, *Der Siebenjährige Krieg in den zeitgenössischen Medien*.
90. Cardwell, *Arts and Arms*; Fordham, *British Art and the Seven Years War*.
91. Fordham, *British Art and the Seven Years War*, 119–120.
92. McNairn, *Behold the Hero*.
93. See Stollberg-Rilinger, *Maria Theresa*, 9–11.
94. Stollberg-Rilinger, *Maria Theresa*, 446 and n183.
95. See Marian Füssel, "'Theresia fiel nieder und tanzt seitdem nicht wieder': Mediale Repräsentationen der 'Königin von Ungarn' während des Siebenjährigen Krieges," in *Die Repräsentation Maria Theresias: Herrschaft und Bildpolitik im Zeitalter der Aufklärung*, ed. Werner Telesko et al. (Böhlau, 2020).
96. Eduard Heydenreich, "Ein Volkslied des Siebenjährigen Krieges," *Archiv für Litteraturgeschichte*, vol. 11 (Teubner, 1882): 447–448.
97. Documented in Füssel, "Mediale Repräsentationen."
98. Illustration in Benninghoven et al., *Friedrich der Grosse*, 177–178.
99. Benninghoven et al., *Friedrich der Grosse*, 200.
100. Illustration in the catalogue Gerda Mraz/ Gottfried Mraz, *Maria Theresia. Ihr Leben und ihre Zeit in Bildern und Dokumenten* (Residenz-Verlag, 1980), 172.
101. See illustration and commentary in x, *Maria Theresia und ihre Zeit*, 159.
102. Hans Bleckwenn, "Das Laudon-Zimmer in Schloß Hainfeld," *Waffen- und Kostümkunde* 33, no. 1/2 (1991).
103. On the phenomenon of battlefield image recycling, see also Thomas Weißbrich, "'Eigentliche Abbildung': Zum Verhältnis von Ereignis und Graphik in frühneuzeitlicher Bildpublizistik," in *Unvergessliche Augenblicke: Die Inszenierung von Medienereignissen*, ed. Graduiertenkolleg Transnationale Medienereignisse (Societäts, 2006), 38ff.

104. See "Plan von der Gefangen Nehmung der Königlich Preußischen Armee bey Falckenstein und Maxen bey Dresden" [Plan to capture the Royal Prussia Army under Falckenstein and Maxen at Dresden], in Komander, *Wandel des "Sehepuncktes"*; and also the broadsheet "Deutliche Abbildung und Beschreibung von der großen und hitzigen Schlacht bey Lowositz in Böhmen den 1. October 1756" [Clear representation and description of the great and heated battle at Lowositz in Bohemia on October 1, 1756], in Kloosterhuis, "Zwischen Garbeck und Lobositz," 91.
105. As early as 1911, the art historian Paul Seidel noted: "It is a particular aspect of the great monarch's character that he did nothing to glorify his martial deeds through art." See Paul Seidel, "Schlachtendarstellungen aus der Zeit Friedrich des Großen," *Hohenzollern-Jahrbuch* 15 (1911): 297.
106. Neil McKendrick et al., eds., *The Birth of a Consumer Society: The Commercialization of Eighteenth-Century England* (Indiana University Press, 1982).
107. See Füssel and Petersen, "Ananas und Kanonen."
108. Wolf-Dieter Könenkamp, *Iserlohner Tabaksdosen: Bilder einer Kriegszeit* (Westfälisches Museumsamt, 1982); Paul Seidel, "Vivatbänder oder Seidenbänder im Hohenzollern-Museum," *Hohenzollern-Jahrbuch* 16 (1912); Konrad Vanja, ed., *Vivat—Vivat—Vivat! Widmungs- und Gedenkbänder aus drei Jahrhunderten* (Museum für Deutsche Volkskunde, 1985); Ernst Preßler, *Schraubtaler und Steckmedaillen: Verborgene Kostbarkeiten* (Münzen und Medaillenhandlung, 2000); Johannes Weidner, "'Der Alte Fritz' in der deutschen Volkskunst," *Schlesien* 26 (1981); Sandra Hertel, "Ein Bild von Freund und Feind: Die Iserlohner Tabaksdosen im Medienkrieg zwischen Friedrich II. und Maria Theresia," *Der Märker* 67/68 (2019).
109. For the "Berlin" tin, see Jürgen Wilke, "'Umstände Nachricht von dem Ueberfall der Königl. Residentz, Berlin von Rußisch Kaiserl. Truppen unter dem Commando He. Generals und Graffen von Totleben': Probst Süßmilch schildert seine Erlebnisse im Herbst 1760," in *Berlin in Geschichte und Gegenwart: Jahrbuch des Landesarchivs Berlin* (Siedler, 1990), 26, 34.
110. Vanja, *Vivat—Vivat—Vivat!*, 18.
111. Schüddekopf, *Briefwechsel zwischen Gleim und Ramler*, 2:307. The second victory mentioned in the letter refers to the Battle of Prague. For similar reports from Switzerland, see Meyer, *Zeitgenössische Beurteilung*, 146–147.
112. Vanja, *Vivat—Vivat—Vivat!*, 19, 48.
113. [Becher], *Wahrhaftige Nachricht derer Begebenheiten*, digitized, unpag., (item 14), p. 8 (item 28), p. 201 (item 418), p. 207 (item 422).
114. See Könenkamp, *Iserlohner Tabaksdosen*, 74f. Another tin with a naval motif depicts the British naval victory at Cartagena.
115. Seidel, "Vivatbänder," 141–142.
116. Stephen V. Grancsay, *American Engraved Powder Horns: A Study Based on the J. H. Grenville Gilbert Collection*, exh. cat. (Metropolitan Museum of Art, 1945); R.

Scott Stephenson, *Clash of Empires: The British, French and Indian War 1754–1763* (Senator John Heinz Pittsburgh Regional History Center, 2005), 31, 43–44, 65, 70, 78.
117. Füssel and Petersen, *Grotehenn Briefe*, 37.
118. Sommeregger, "Die Schlacht von Prag," 18.
119. See Fritz Waltermann, "Mützenblech als Wandblaker," *Zeitschrift für Heereskunde* 67 (2003): 82f.
120. Donald Woodward, "'Swords Into Ploughshares': Recycling in Pre-Industrial England," *Economic History Review* 38, no. 2 (1985): 177.
121. Zellmann, "Tagebuch des Johann Philipp Zellmann," 20.
122. Cormack and Jones, *Journal of Corporal Todd*, 82.
123. Füssel and Petersen, *Grotehenn Briefe*, 79.
124. Füssel and Petersen, *Grotehenn Briefe*, 80.
125. Archenholz, *History of the Seven Years War*, 106.
126. On this topos of perception, see Anklam, *Krieg*, 45–47, 53–54.
127. See Warnke, *Logistik und friderizianische Kriegführung*, 143.
128. [Richter], *Die Historie des Kriegs*. See Lindner, *Die Peripetie des Siebenjährigen Krieges*, 16.
129. Lutz Voigtländer, *Krieg für den "gemeinen Mann": "Der mit einem Sächsischen Bauer von jetzigem Kriege redende Französische Soldat"; Eine neue Form der Berichterstattung in einer Wochenschrift des 18. Jahrhunderts. Zugleich eine kleine Geschichte des Siebenjährigen Krieges zwischen Kolin und Zorndorf* (Lumière, 2006).
130. Arneth, *Maria-Theresias*, 6:432.
131. Johann Georg Pleißner, *Kriegs-Geschichte von Thüringen von Anno 1756 bis 1763: Besonders, was unser Hertzogthum Residentz Stadt Gotha dabey merkwürdiges betroffen als ein Diarium verfasset* ([Gotha], 1763), Forschungsbibliothek Gotha, Sign. Chart. B No. 1127; Johann Georg Pleißner, *Ausführlicher und wahrhafter Bericht von dem Feldzuge und Kriegshändeln welche zwischen der Reichs-Executions- und Französischen combinirten Armee, imgleichen der Königl. Preußischen Kriegsmacht vorgefallen insonderheit, was die Stadt und das Fürstenthum Gotha hiebey an Durchzügen und Einquartierungen betroffen, aus was sich bey dieser Gelegenheit merkwürdiges ereignet, in Form eines Diarii verfasset von einem in Gotha sich aufgehaltenen Passagiere* (Erfurt, 1759).
132. Schort, *Politik und Propaganda*, 122.
133. See Martin Welke, "'. . . zu Österreichs Gloria durch Publicität mitzuwürcken': Zur Pressepolitik des Kaiserhofes im Reich im 18. Jahrhundert," in *Mediengeschichte. Forschung und Praxis: Festgabe für Marianne Lunzer-Lindhausen zum 65. Geburtstag*, ed. Wolfgang Duckowitsch (Böhlau, 1985).
134. Welke, "'. . . zu Österreichs Gloria," 180; on the situation in Hamburg, see also Dreyer, "Hamburgische Stimmungsbilder"; Pantel, *Die hamburgische Neutralität*.
135. Flucke, *Die litterae annuae*, 1082–1083.

136. Dreyer, *Johann Matthias Dreyer*, 53.
137. Christian Ludwig von Griesheim, ed., *Verbesserte und vermehrte Auflage des Tractats: Die Stadt Hamburg in ihrem politischen, öconomischen und sittlichen Zustande*, 2 vols. (Hamburg: Drese, 1760), 2:243–244.
138. Griesheim, *Verbesserte und vermehrte Auflage*, 2:243.
139. Duffy, *Military Life of Frederick the Great*, 243; Meyer, *Zeitgenössische Beurteilung*, 135–157.
140. Karlsruhe, Generallandesarchiv, Dept. 74, no. 6273, quoted in Haasis, *Spuren der Besiegten*, 547.
141. Engraving by Johann David Nessenthaler, Augsburg, c. 1760, in Ingrid Mittenzwei and Erika Herzfeld, *Brandenburg-Preußen 1648 bis 1789: Das Zeitalter des Absolutismus in Text und Bild* (Pahl-Rugenstein, 1987), 340–341.
142. On the Thirty Years' War, see Medick, *Zeugnisse*, 272.
143. Christoph Gottfried Jacobi, "Anmerkungen bey dem jetzigen Kriege," in *Nützliche Samlungen*, pt. 4 (1758), cols. 732ff.
144. Jacobi, "Anmerkungen," col. 732.
145. Reproduced in Mittenzwei and Herzfeld, *Brandenburg-Preußen 1648 bis 1789*, 337.
146. *Münchnerisches Wochen-Blat in Versen—Kriegs- Friedens-, und in- und ausländische Begebenheiten und Zufälle betreffend, verfertiget, verlegt und herausgegeben von Mathias Etenhueber (1759–1777)*, January 20, 1759 (no. 1), cited in Anklam, *Wissen nach Augenmaß*, 213.
147. Böning, *Periodische Presse*, 63ff.
148. Richard Fester, "Die Erlanger Zeitung im siebenjährigen Krieg," *Forschungen zur Brandenburgischen und Preußischen Geschichte* 15 (1902): 183.
149. See additionally the bibliography in Susanne Zantop, *Kolonialphantasien im vorkolonialen Deutschland (1770–1870)* (Schmidt, 1999), 268–272.
150. Von Imhof, *Historischer Bilder-Saal* 13, 1.
151. Abelmann, *Hannover im Siebenjährigen Krieg*, 42–43. For a detailed study of Abelmann's chronicle and sources, see Marian Füssel, "Zwischen Empire und Reich: Zur Kommunikation des globalen Siebenjährigen Krieges im Raum der Personalunion," in *Kommunikation and Kulturtransfer im Zeitalter der Personalunion zwischen Großbritannien und Hannover: "To Prove That Hanover and England Are Not Entirely Synonymous,"* ed. Arndt Reitemeier (Universitätsverlag Göttingen, 2014).
152. Abelmann, *Hannover im Siebenjährigen Krieg*, 149–154.
153. Abelmann, *Hannover im Siebenjährigen Krieg*, 151, 153.
154. Anonymous, *Historisch-geographische Beschreibung der in diesem Krieg von den Engländern eroberten französischen Antillischen Inseln: Besonders von Guadaloupe und Martinique etc. zur Erläuterung der gegenwärtigen Kriegs-Staats- und Handlungs-Geschichte* (Stuttgart: Mezler, 1762), 2v.

155. *Nützliche Sammlungen* appeared from 1755 to 1758, succeeded by the *Hannoverischen Beyträge* from 1759 to 1762, followed by the *Hannoverische Magazin* from 1763 to 1790. See J[ohann] H[inrich] Pratje, "Nachricht von Kap-Breton und Louisbourg, und von dem Stockfischfange daselbst," *Nützliche Sammlungen*, 1758, cols. 1105–1116; [Johann Hinrich Pratje], "Nachricht von der Insel Goree, und von dem derselben abhängenden Handel," *Hannoverische Beyträge* 36, Friday, May 4, 1759, cols. 569–600 (article based on the first volumes of Schwabe, *Allgemeine Historie der Reisen*); Joh. Franz Wagner, "Nachricht von Quebek," *Hannoverische Beyträge* 6, Monday, January 21, 1760, cols. 81–96; J.[ohann] T.[obias] Köhler, "Kurze Beschreibung der von der Großbrittanischen Seemacht in America ohnlängst eroberten Inseln Grenada, St. Vincent und St. Lucia," *Hannoverische Beyträge* 52, Monday, June 28, 1762, cols. 817–832, and 53tes Stück, Friday, July 2, 1762, cols. 833–848; J.[ohann] T.[obias] Köhler, "Beschreibung des Landes Florida in dem nördlichen Amerika, welches durch den neulichen glorreichen Frieden von Spanien an Großbritannien abgetreten worden," *Hannoverisches Magazin* 27, Monday, April 4, 1763, cols. 417–460; Anonymous, "Beschreibung von Neu-Orleans, welches den Franzosen im Frieden verbleibet," *Hannoverisches Magazin* 41, Monday, May 23, 1763, cols. 649–654; J.[ohann] T.[obias] Köhler, "Beschreibung der philippinischen oder manilischen Eylande in Ostindien, besonders aber von Manila, der vornehmsten unter denselben und ihrer Hauptstadt, wie auch von dem reichen Handel, der von daraus mit den Gallionen nach Acapulco getrieben wird," *Hannoverisches Magazin* 46, Friday, June 10, 1763, cols. 721–766.
156. Abelmann, *Hannover im Siebenjährigen Krieg*, 152. Potosi, in modern-day Bolivia, was a symbol of Spain's silver wealth in the early modern period. In the seventeenth century, it was one of the largest cities in the world.
157. Abelmann, *Hannover im Siebenjährigen Krieg*, 153.
158. See Jennifer Willenberg, *Distribution und Übersetzung englischen Schrifttums im Deutschland des 18. Jahrhunderts* (Saur, 2008), 144–145.
159. See [Johann David Michaelis], review of "History of the Origin and Progress of the Present War," from *London Magazine* (June 1761), *Göttingische Anzeigen von gelehrten Sachen* 1 (1761/1762): 171.
160. [Michaelis], review of "History of the Origin," 172.
161. Orme, *History of the Military Transactions of the British Nation in Indostan*; Archenholz, *Die Engländer in Indien nach Orme*; Edward Ives, *A Voyage from England to India, in the Year MDCCLIV: And an Historical Narrative of the Operations of the Squadron and Army in India* [. . .] (London: Edward and Charles Dilly, 1773); Eduard Ives, *Reisen nach Indien und Persien/in einer freyen Übers. aus dem englischen Orig. geliefert, mit historisch-geographischen Anm. . . . Welcher die Reise nach Indien, und einen Theil der Zusätze des Uebersetzers enthält*, 2 vols. (Leipzig: Weidmann, 1774–1775).

162. Richard Owen Cambridge, *An Account of the War in India, Between the English and French, on the Coast of Coromandel, from the Year 1750 to the Year 1760* (London: Jefferys, 1761), vi.
163. See Leonhard, *Bellizismus und Nation*, 288.
164. Burke, *Social History of Knowledge*, 11.

9. Urban Life in a State of Exception

1. Carl, *Okkupation und Regionalismus*, 17.
2. Frantzius, "Okkupation Ostpreußens"; Francine-Dominique Liechtenhan, "Sollte Ostpreußen ins russische Reich integriert werden? Zur Geschichte der deutsch-russischen Beziehungen im Siebenjährigen Krieg," in *Deutsch-russische Beziehungen: Politische, wirtschaftliche und kulturelle Aspekte von der frühen Neuzeit bis zum 20. Jahrhundert*, ed. Frantisek Stellner (Set Out, 2007); Mediger, *Herzog Ferdinand von Braunschweig-Lüneburg*, 126–127.
3. Abelmann, *Hannover im Siebenjährigen Krieg*, 88; Horst Carl, "'Pavillon de Hanovre': Korruption im Militär im 18. Jahrhundert," in *Integration—Legitimation—Korruption: Politische Patronage in Früher Neuzeit und Moderne*, ed. Ronald Asch et al. (Lang, 2011).
4. On the war commissioners, see Carl, *Okkupation und Regionalismus*, 148–171; on British and Hanoverian commissioners, see Hayter, "England, Hannover, Preußen," 179–181; Mediger, *Herzog Ferdinand von Braunschweig-Lüneburg*, 910–971; Stephen Conway, "Provisioning the Combined Army in Germany, 1758–1762: Who Benefited?." in *The Contractor State and Its Implications, 1659–1815* (Universidad de Las Palmas de Gran Canaria, 2012).
5. [Montag], *Teutsche Kriegs-Canzley*, vol. 1, no. 33, 175–176 and no. 69, 619–620.
6. Luh, *Kriegskunst in Europa 1650–1800*, 214f.
7. Jens Ivo Engels, *Die Geschichte der Korruption: Von der Frühen Neuzeit bis ins 20. Jahrhundert* (Fischer, 2014).
8. Carl, "Korruption im Militär," 240–243.
9. Carl, "Korruption im Militär," 246.
10. Carl, "Korruption im Militär," 233.
11. Horst Carl, "Unter fremder Herrschaft: Invasion und Okkupation im Siebenjährigen Krieg," in Kroener and Pröve, *Krieg und Frieden*, 336.
12. Mediger, *Herzog Ferdinand von Braunschweig-Lüneburg*, 127.
13. Carl, "Korruption im Militär," 234.
14. Pröve, "Der Soldat."
15. Hammann, *Die Bottendorfer Chronik des Johann Daniel Geitz*, 37.
16. Szabo, *Seven Years War*, 276–277.

17. Retzow, *Charakteristik*, 2:191–205; Archenholz, *History of the Seven Years War*, 329–331; Großer Generalstab, *Der Siebenjährige Krieg*, vol. 12, *Landeshut und Liegnitz*, 99–113; Duffy, *By Force of Arms*, 232–240.
18. Retzow, *Charakteristik*, 2:203; Möbius and Möbius, *Prussian Army Soldiers*, 132.
19. Volker Laube, *Die Katastrophe von Landeshut in Schl. am 23. Juni 1760*, ed. Alfred von Klützow, (Landeshut: Ernst Rudolph, 1861), 38–43, 79–81. I am grateful to Professor Jürgen Kloosterhuis (Berlin) for suggesting this source.
20. Laube, *Katastrophe von Landeshut*, 41, 80.
21. Cogniazo, *Geständnisse*, 3:159–160; see also Möbius and Möbius, *Prussian Army Soldiers*, 167.
22. One anonymous diarist who was present in Hirschberg, a nearby town, makes an explicit comparison with "Calmukks, Cosacks and Tattars." Laube, *Katastrophe von Landeshut*, 80.
23. Laube, *Katastrophe von Landeshut*, 80.
24. Duffy, *By Force of Arms*, 239–240.
25. Duffy, *By Force of Arms*, 223–232.
26. See Ulrich Rosseaux, "Die Belagerung Dresdens im Jahr 1760 als Medienereignis des 18. Jahrhunderts," *Dresdner Hefte* 68 (2001); Gestrich, "Kriegsberichterstattung als Propaganda," 34–36.
27. See Alfred Heinze, *Dresden im Siebenjährigen Kriege* (Dresden: Tittmann, 1885), 153 and n4; Schort, *Politik und Propaganda*, 406f.
28. Gustav Klemm, *Chronik der Königlich Sächsischen Residenzstadt Dresden*, 3 vols. (Dresden: Grimmer, 1837), 2:438.
29. Johann Joachim Gottlob Am Ende, "Christliches Denkmahl des am 19den und 20ten Jul. dieses Jahres über Dreßden gebrachten schrecklichen Feuers," in *Dreyen Predigten, Welche theils in der Kirche zu Neustadt bey Dreßden, theils in der Frauen-Kirche zu Dreßden, gehalten, und nebst einer historischen Nachricht von der zugleich mit eingeäscherten Kirche zum heiligen Creuz [. . .]* (Dresden: Gerlach, 1760).
30. Am Ende, "Christliches Denkmahl," 3.
31. Am Ende, "Christliches Denkmahl," 18.
32. Am Ende, "Christliches Denkmahl," 5.
33. Am Ende, "Christliches Denkmahl," 6.
34. Am Ende, "Christliches Denkmahl," 7.
35. Am Ende, "Christliches Denkmahl," 8f.
36. See Stefan Kozakiewicz, *Bernardo Belloto, genannt Canaletto*, 2 vols. (Bongers, 1972) 1:136f., 2:238–242; Fritz Löffler, *Dresden im 18. Jahrhundert. Bernardo Belloto genannt Canaletto*, exh. cat. (Weidlich, 1985), 69f.; Alberto Rizzi, *Bernardo Belloto: Dresda Vienna Monaco (1747–1766)* (Canal & Stamperia, 1996), 144ff.
37. Kozakiewicz, *Belloto*, 1:131.

38. See Gottlieb Willhelm Rabener, *Schreiben an einen seiner Freunde in Warschau, die Belagerung Dresdens betreffend* (Vienna: Schulz, 1761).
39. Großer Generalstab, *Der Siebenjährige Krieg*, vol. 12, *Landeshut und Liegnitz*, 199–226.
40. Buxbaum, "Das Tagebuch des Feldpredigers Balke," 3, no. 4 (1885): 129.
41. Großer Generalstab, *Der Siebenjährige Krieg*, vol. 12, *Landeshut und Liegnitz*, 215–216.
42. Buxbaum, "Das Tagebuch des Feldpredigers Balke," 3, no. 4 (1885): 131–132.
43. Duffy, *By Force of Arms*, 265–273; Hermann Granier, "Die Russen und Österreicher in Berlin im Oktober 1760," *Hohenzollern-Jahrbuch* 2 (1898): 113–145.
44. Wilke, "'Umstände Nachricht,'" 17–60.
45. Wilke, "'Umstände Nachricht,'" 21.
46. Wilke, "'Umstände Nachricht,'" 23.
47. Wilke, "'Umstände Nachricht,'" 24.
48. Wilke, "'Umstände Nachricht,'" 27.
49. Wilke, "'Umstände Nachricht,'" 29.
50. Wilke, "'Umstände Nachricht,'" 30.
51. Wilke, "'Umstände Nachricht,'" 30–31.
52. Wilke, "'Umstände Nachricht,'" 33.
53. *Berlinische Nachrichten*, no. 118, Tuesday, October 2, 1758, 485.
54. Wilke, "'Umstände Nachricht,'" 44–45. See also the report in Granier, "Die Russen und Österreicher in Berlin," 140–141; Archenholz, *History of the Seven Years War*, 371–372.
55. Nina Simone Schepkowski, *Johann Ernst Gotzkowsky: Kunstagent und Gemäldesammler im friderizianischen Berlin* (Akademie, 2009), 261–265.
56. Wilke, "'Umstände Nachricht,'" 36.
57. Wilke, "'Umstände Nachricht,'" 38–39.
58. Schultz, *Roggenpreis*, 81.
59. Thomas Fischbacher, "Die Residenz im Kriege: Graf Heinrich von Brühl, Friedrich II. von Preußen und König August III. von Polen und die symbolische Zerstörung von Schlössern im Siebenjährigen Krieg in Sachsen und Brandenburg," in *Zeichen und Medien des Militärischen am Fürstenhof in Europa*, ed. Peter-Michael Hahn and Matthias Müller (Lukas, 2017), 201–204.
60. Wilke, "'Umstände Nachricht,'" 43.
61. Schultz, *Roggenpreis*, 83.
62. Wilke, "'Umstände Nachricht,'" 40.
63. Anonymous, "Kurzgefasste Nachricht von der ab Seiten der Russisch-Österreich und Sächsischen Troupen auf eine unerhörte Art geschehenen Verheerung der Mark Brandenburg, und von denen Grausamkeiten, welche sie bey der im Monath October 1760 auf die Stadt Berlin gemachten Unternehmung darinnen ausgeübet haben," in [Montag], *Teutsche Kriegs-Canzley*, vol. 2, x, no. 125, 772–785.

64. [George Whitefield], *Russian Cruelty: Being the Substance of Several Letters from Sundry Clergymen in the New-Marck of Brandenburgh* (London, 1760); on this, see Häberlein and Schmölz-Häberlein, "Kommunikationsnetz des Halleschen Pietismus."
65. For more detail, see Füssel, "Zwischen Schauspiel, Information und Strafgericht," 311–313.
66. Volker Jakobs, "Wittenberg im Siebenjährigen Krieg (1756–1763)," *Heimatkalender* 6 (2003).
67. See von Imhof, *Historischer Bilder-Saal*, 612–613.
68. Christian Siegismund Georgi, *Wittenbergische Klage-Geschichte* (Wittenberg: Ahlfeld und Weinmannische, 1760; repr., Siener, 1993), iv. All citations refer to Siener edition.
69. Georgi, *Klage-Geschichte*, iii.
70. Georgi, *Klage-Geschichte*, 2f.
71. Georgi, *Klage-Geschichte*, 6f.
72. Füssel, "Zwischen Schauspiel, Information und Strafgericht," 312 and n56.
73. Georgi, *Klage-Geschichte*, 31.
74. Duffy, *By Force of Arms*, 284–305; Kessel, *Das Ende des Siebenjährigen Krieges*, 23–42; Ulf-Joachim Friese, ed., *Die Schlacht bei Torgau am 3. November 1760: Und die Tage davor und danach in preußischer und österreichischer Darstellung*, 3 vols. (LTR, 2008–2011).
75. Kunisch, *Friedrich der Große*, 420.
76. Archenholz, *History of the Seven Years War*, 390.
77. Archenholz, *History of the Seven Years War*, 391.
78. Flashar, *Memoiren der Eleonore Juliane von Rehdiger*, 138.
79. Kessel, *Das Ende des Siebenjährigen Krieges*, 40–41.
80. See Daun's letter to Maria Theresa, in Arneth, *Maria Theresias*, 2:457–459.
81. Kunisch, *Friedrich der Große*, 422.
82. Letter to Prince Henri de Prusse Dittmannsdorf, September 30, 1760, in Friedrich II, *Politische Correspondenz*, vol. 19, no. 12,394, 605.
83. Hein, *Briefe Friedrichs*, 2. The text is available online at http://friedrich.uni-trier.de/de/oeuvres/18/166/text/.
84. Mediger, *Herzog Ferdinand von Braunschweig-Lüneburg*, 478.
85. Mediger, *Herzog Ferdinand von Braunschweig-Lüneburg*, 477. On the finances of the French and Allied armies, see Szabo, *Seven Years War*, 299–300.
86. Cormack and Jones, *Journal of Corporal Todd*, 121.
87. Füssel and Petersen, *Grotehenn Briefe*, 88.
88. Frearson, *Letters of Richard Davenport*, 75.
89. Frearson, *Letters of Richard Davenport*, 84.
90. On the battle of Warburg, see Hans von Geisau, "Zur Schlacht bei Warburg am 31. Juli 1760," *Westfälische Zeitschrift* 111 (1961); Landkreis Warburg, ed.,

Gedenkschrift anlässlich des 200. Jahrestages der Schlacht bei Warburg am 31. Juli 1760: Quellen und Studien zur Geschichte des Siebenjährigen Krieges in Warburg und Umgebung (Junfermann, 1960); Füssel and Petersen, *Grotehenn Briefe*, 90–93.

91. Frearson, *Letters of Richard Davenport*, 85
92. Jakob Mauvillon, *Geschichte Ferdinands Herzogs von Braunschweig-Lüneburg*, pt. 2 (Leipzig: Dyk, 1794), 113–114.
93. Mediger, *Herzog Ferdinand von Braunschweig-Lüneburg*, 520–521.
94. Mediger, *Herzog Ferdinand von Braunschweig-Lüneburg*, 537–538; Karl von Berckefeldt, "Wesel im siebenjährigen Kriege, insbesondere das Gefecht bei Mehr 1758 und die Belagerung Wesels 1760," *Annalen des Historischen Vereins für den Niederrhein* 90 (1911).
95. Mediger, *Herzog Ferdinand von Braunschweig-Lüneburg*, 543–548. On this, see also Besenval, *Mémoires*, 126–158; Van Meegen, ed., "Bericht des Camper Mönches A. Conrad Brands, Pfarrers in Camp und seit 1761 in Rheinberg über die Kriegsereignisse in Camp in den Jahren 1758 und 1760," *Der Niederrhein: Wochenblatt für niederrheinische Geschichte und Althertumskunde*, no. 38, September 21, 1878, 149–150, and no. 39, September 28, 1878, 154–155; and "Zweiter Bericht eines damaligen Camper Mönches über die Schlacht im Camperbruch," *Der Niederrhein: Wochenblatt für niederrheinische Geschichte und Althertumskunde*, no. 42, October 19, 1878, 165–166, 174.
96. Wähner, *Tagebuch aus dem Siebenjährigen Krieg*, 159–164; Szabo, *Seven Years War*, 307; Mediger, *Herzog Ferdinand von Braunschweig-Lüneburg*, 552–558.
97. On the distribution of winter quarters, see Mediger, *Herzog Ferdinand von Braunschweig-Lüneburg*, 558; Füssel and Petersen, *Grotehenn Briefe*, 96–97.
98. Ferdinand to Frederick, Uslar, December 13, 1760, in Ernst J. G. von dem Knesebeck, ed., *Ferdinand, Herzog zu Braunschweig u. Lüneburg, während des siebenjährigen Krieges*, 2 vols. (Hanover: Helwing, 1857–1858), 2:186; on the rivalry between the two men, see Klingebiel, *Feldherrn der Aufklärung*; Lindner, *Die Peripetie des Siebenjährigen Krieges*, 151; Mediger, *Herzog Ferdinand von Braunschweig-Lüneburg*, 549–550.
99. Schlenke, *England und das friderizianische Preussen*, 253–265; Szabo, *Seven Years War*, 308–309.
100. Anderson, *Crucible*, 391–396.
101. Casgrain, *Voyage au Canada*, 184–186.
102. Knox, *Historical Journal of the Campaigns in North America*, 2:415.
103. Knox, *Historical Journal of the Campaigns in North America*, 2:416.
104. Knox, *Historical Journal of the Campaigns in North America*, 2:419f.
105. Gertrude Selwyn Kimball, ed., *Correspondence of William Pitt When Secretary of State with Colonial Governors and Military and Naval Commissioners in America*, 2 vols. (Kraus, 1906), 2:231–242.
106. Wellenreuther, *Ausbildung und Neubildung*, 292.

107. J. Clarence Webster, ed., *The Journal of Jeffery Amherst, Recording the Military Career of General Amherst in America from 1758 to 1763* (Ryerson, 1931), 204.
108. Casgrain, *Voyage au Canada*, 187–189.
109. Casgrain, *Voyage au Canada*, 189–209.
110. Chapman and Macpherson, *Memoirs of a Black Watch Officer*, 147.
111. Anderson, *Crucible*, 406.
112. Chapman and Macpherson, *Memoirs of a Black Watch Officer*, 147. (The plural form *Canadas* referred to upper and lower Canada or to eastern and western Canada.)
113. Casgrain, *Lévis*, 1:316–335. A German translation of the text appeared in the omnibus edition of the *Berlinische Nachrichten*, no. 123–127, October 11–21, 1760, 501–509.
114. Webster, *Journal of Jefferey Amherst*, 247.
115. Vaisey, *Diary of Thomas Turner*, 212.
116. *Berlinische Nachrichten*, no. 123–127, October 11–21, 1760, 501.
117. Buschbell, *Tagebuch des Abraham ter Meer*, 121; Füssel and Petersen, *Grotehenn Briefe*, 95.
118. Casgrain, *Voyage au Canada*, 198.
119. John Francis Bosher, "The French Government's Motives in the Affaire du Canada, 1761–1763," *English Historical Review* 96, no. 378 (1981); Crouch, *Nobility Lost*, 128–136; André Côté, "L'affaire du Canada (1761–1763)," *Cap-aux-Diamants* 83 (2005). Vaudreuil was released from the Bastille on May 22, 1762; Bigot on December 18, 1763; Cadet on March 28, 1764; and Péan on June 30, 1764.
120. Anonymous, *Jugement rendu souverainement et en dernier ressort, dans l'affaire du Canada [. . .]* (Paris: Boudet, 1763).
121. On the fate of French officers from Canada after the war, see Crouch, *Nobility Lost*, 126–177, on Pouchot, 142–144.
122. Pierre Pouchot, *Memoires sur la derniere guerre de l'Amerique septentrionale, entre la France et l'Angleterre*, 3 vols. (Yverdon, 1781).
123. Casgrain, *Voyage au Canada*, 209–212.
124. Casgrain, *Voyage au Canada*, 213.
125. See Gary B. Nash, *The Urban Crucible: Social Change, Political Consciousness, and the Origins of the American Revolution* (Harvard University Press, 1979), 233–263.
126. Nash, *Urban Crucible*, 238.
127. See tables in Nash, *Urban Crucible*, 408–409.
128. Nash, *Urban Crucible*, 248.
129. On the concept of confraternities of violence, see Winfried Speitkamp, ed., *Gewaltgemeinschaften in der Geschichte: Entstehung, Kohäsionskraft und Zerfall* (Vandenhoeck & Ruprecht, 2017); on irregulars as a "practical corrective," see Michael Hochedlinger's preface to Theodor Horstmann, *Generallieutenant*

*Johann Nicolaus von Luckner und seine Husaren im Siebenjährigen Krieg*e (Biblio, 1977), 2; on the untamed Bellona, see Jutta Nowosadtko, "'Gehegter Krieg'— 'Gezähmte Bellona'? Kombattanten, Partheygänger, Privatiers und Zivilbevölkerung im sogenannten Kleinen Krieg der Frühen Neuzeit," in *Zivilisten und Soldaten: Entgrenzte Gewalt in der Geschichte*, ed. Frank Becker (Klartext, 2015).

130. Anonymous, *Zwey Abhandlungen von der Kriegs-Zucht*, 10.
131. Horstmann, *Generallieutenant Johann Nicolaus von Luckner*; Asbrand von Porbeck, "Der Streifzug des Königlich Preussischen Oberstlieutenants Jh. von Meyer im Jahre 1757 nach der Oberpfalz und Franken," *Jahrbücher für die deutsche Armee und Marine* 19 (1876); Gotthard Kästner, *Generalmayor von Mayr und sein Freikorps in Kursachsen* (Schlimpert, 1904); Andreas Leipold, "Der erste preussische Einfall in die Residenzstadt Bamberg im Siebenjaehrigen Krieg vom 30. Mai bis zum 10. Juni 1758," *Berichte des Historischen Vereins Bamberg* 143 (2006).
132. See Edouard de Ribaucourt, *La vie militaire et les exploits de J.-C. Fischer: Brigadier des Armées du Roy Louis XV, Fondateur et Commandant le Corps des Chasseurs (1743–1761), Chef du Service des Renseignements [. . .]* (Librairie Universelle, 1928).
133. R. Ostermann, "Das Leiden unserer bäuerlichen Vorfahren: Das Kirchenbuch zu Ovenstädt verrät, was kein Bericht zu melden weiß," *Mindener Heimatblätter* 31, no. 7/8 (1959): 72.
134. Teggers, "Der 7jährige Krieg," 85.
135. Fülling, *Chronik des Pfarrers Johann Georg Fülling*, 19–20; Mastnak and Tänzer, *Tagebuch des Garnisonsauditeurs Johann Philipp Schowart*, 167; Abelmann, *Hannover im Siebenjährigen Krieg*, 121–124; Mediger, *Herzog Ferdinand von Braunschweig-Lüneburg*, 288–290.
136. Brunner, "Aufzeichnungen des Pfarrers Johann Christoph Cuntz," 164–166.
137. G. R. Hartmann, ed., "Aufzeichnungen des Bürgermeisters Geiß von Felda über die Kriegsjahre 1759–63," *Mitteilungen des Geschichts und Alterthumsvereins der Stadt Alsfeld* 4 (1913): 25; Brunner, "Aufzeichnungen des Pfarrers Johann Christoph Cuntz," 203.
138. Quoted in Carl, *Okkupation und Regionalismus*, 235.
139. Carl Spannagel, "Barmen im siebenjährigen Krieg: Eine Beckmannsche Chronik," *Zeitschrift des Bergischen Geschichtsvereins* 26 (1890); Jürgen Olmes, "Johann Christian Fischer, sein Korps und die Überfälle auf Ruhrort im Jahre 1760," *Duisburger Forschungen* 4 (1961); Martin Stücher, *Ausfouragiert und Heimgesucht: Freudenberg im Siebenjährigen Krieg* (Arbeitsgemeinschaft der Heimatvereine und des SGV, 2006), 42, 47.
140. Vogeler, "Beiträge zur Geschichte von Soest," 17 (1899/1900): 4ff.
141. Olmes, "Fischer," 91.
142. Hammann, *Die Bottendorfer Chronik des Johann Daniel Geitz*, 39.
143. See Carl, *Okkupation und Regionalismus*, 232–237; Burghardt Schmidt, "Regionalgeschichte im Spannungsfeld von europäischer Hegemonialpolitik und

militärischer Okkupation: Die Stadt Emden im Siebenjährigen Krieg (1756–1763)," *Emder Jahrbuch* 80 (2000): 111ff.
144. Tileman Dothias Wiarda, *Ostfriesische Geschichte*, vol. 9 (Aurich: Winter, 1798), 34f.
145. Carl, *Okkupation und Regionalismus*, 235.
146. Wiarda, *Ostfriesische Geschichte*, 32.
147. Lemoine, *Sous Louis le Bien-aimé*, 371.
148. On the media impact, see Carl, *Okkupation und Regionalismus*, 237; Wiarda, *Ostfriesische Geschichte*, 63.
149. Vogeler, "Beiträge zur Geschichte von Soest," 9 (1891–92): 69.
150. See the essential article by Daniel Hohrath, "'In Cartellen wird der Wert eines Feindes bestimmet': Kriegsgefangenschaft als Teil der Kriegspraxis des Ancien Régime," in *In der Hand des Feindes: Kriegsgefangenschaft von der Antike bis zum Zweiten Weltkrieg*, ed. Rüdiger Overmanns (Böhlau, 1999). See also Renaud Morieux, *The Society of Prisoners: Anglo-French Wars and Incarceration in the Eighteenth Century* (Oxford University Press, 2019).
151. Hohrath, "Kriegsgefangenschaft," 149–152.
152. Salisch, *Treue Deserteure*.
153. Ian K. Steele, *Setting All the Captives Free: Capture, Adjustment, and Recollection in Allegheny Country* (McGill-Queen's University Press, 2013).
154. Steele, *Setting All the Captives Free*, 430; for an example, see 175–176. On Amherst, see White, *Middle Ground*, 288.
155. Hohrath, "Kriegsgefangenschaft," 163–169. On the archival situation with regard to Prussia, see Kloosterhuis et al., *Militär und Gesellschaft*, 181–184.
156. On Sluys (known in France as Écluse), see Reginald Savory, "The Convention of Écluse, 1759–1762: The Treatment of the Sick and Wounded, Prisoners of War, and Deserters, of the British and French Armies During the Seven Years War," *Journal of the Society for Army Historical Research* 42, no. 170 (1964). For the reference to Dorsten, I am grateful to Leonard Dorn (Bonn), who is working on a dissertation on French-British prisoners of war during the Seven Years' War.
157. Hohrath, "Kriegsgefangenschaft," 166.
158. See Duffy, *Armee Maria Theresias*, 233–236.
159. Hohrath, "Kriegsgefangenschaft," 167.
160. For a selection of witness accounts and other ego-documents, see Lutz Voigtländer, *Vom Leben und Überleben in Gefangenschaft: Selbstzeugnisse von Kriegsgefangenen 1757 bis 1814* (Rombach, 2005), 21–69; see also Lutz Voigtländer, *Die preußischen Kriegsgefangenen der Reichsarmee 1760/63* (Gilles & Francke, 1995).
161. Hohrath, "Kriegsgefangenschaft," 148.
162. On French POWs in Britain, see Francis Abell, *Prisoners of War in Britain, 1756 to 1815: A Record of Their Lives, Their Romance and Their Sufferings* (Oxford University Press, 1914); Charters, *Disease*, 172–190; Renaud Morieux, "French

Prisoners of War, Conflicts of Honour, and Social Inversions in England, 1744–1783," *Historical Journal* 56, no. 1 (2013).

163. Abell, *Prisoners of War in Britain*, 115; Charters, *Disease*, 172.
164. See Charters, *Disease*, 172–190.
165. For an overview of this extensive genre, see Pauline Turner Strong, *Captive Selves, Captivating Others: The Politics and Poetics of Colonial American Captivity Narratives* (Westview Press, 1999); Ian K. Steele, "The Shawnees and the English: Captives and War, 1753–1765," in *The Boundaries Between Us: Natives and Newcomers Along the Frontiers of the Old Northwest Territory, 1750–1850*, ed. Daniel P. Barr (Kent State University Press, 2006).
166. Johann Ludwig Wagner, *Schicksale während seiner unter den Russen erlittenen Staatsgefangenschaft in den Jahren 1759 bis 1763: Im Anhange einige Auszüge aus den besten Reisebeschreibungen über diese Länder, nebst eignen Bemerkungen* (Berlin: Maurer, 1789).
167. Abell, *Prisoners of War in Britain*.
168. William Henry Foster, *The Captor's Narrative: Catholic Women and Their Puritan Men on the Early American Frontier* (Cornell University Press, 2003), 91–106, 151–155.
169. Hohrath, "Kriegsgefangenschaft," 152–154.
170. Mediger, *Herzog Ferdinand von Braunschweig-Lüneburg*, 274–275.
171. See Duffy, *Armee Maria Theresias*, 233.
172. Marian Füssel, "'Als Gefangener in ein ganz fremdes, abergläubisches Land gebracht zu werden, stimmte meine Seele trübe': Kriegsgefangene in fremdkonfessionellem Umfeld und militärische Migration während des Siebenjährigen Krieges," *Religion und Mobilität. Zum Verhältnis von raumbezogener Mobilität und religiöser Identitätsbildung im frühneuzeitlichen Europa*, ed. Henning P. Jürgens and Thomas Weller (Vandenhoeck & Ruprecht, 2010).
173. Voigtländer, *Die preußischen Kriegsgefangenen*.
174. Hans-Walter Voigtländer, *Preußische Kriegsgefangene in Memmingen: Ein Beitrag zur Geschichte der reichsfreien Stadt während des Siebenjährigen Krieges (1756–1763)* (Memminger Zeitung, 2000).
175. "Fortsetzung der Nachrichten von der Königl. Preußischen Armee," *Danziger Beyträge*, vols. 51–54, pt. 1759, 620.
176. Volz, *Friedrich der Große im Spiegel*, 128–129 (incorrectly gives a figure of twelve thousand prisoners); see also Anonymous, "Ueber Friedrich den Großen, dessen Hof, und den Einfluß von beyden auf dem Zustand der deutschen Litteratur unter seiner Regierung," *Isis: Eine Monatsschrift von Deutschen und Schweizerischen Gelehrten* 3 (1807): 184.
177. Wilhelm Engelmann, *Daniel Chodowiecki's sämmtliche Kupferstich* (Leipzig: Engelmann, 1857), 11 and n8; Elisabeth Wormsbächer, *Daniel Nikolaus Chodowiecki: Erklärungen und Erläuterungen zu seinen Radierungen* (Galerie J. H. Bauer, 1988), 2.

178. Anonymous, "Ueber Friedrich den Großen, dessen Hof, und den Einfluß von beyden," 185.
179. Gorani, *Mémoires*, 129–169.
180. Gorani, *Mémoires*, 132.
181. Gorani, *Mémoires*, 137.
182. Vogel, *Die Blutbibel*.
183. Johann Christoph Adelung and Johann Christian Hörning, *Denckwürdigkeiten Friedrichs des Großen jetztregierenden Königs in Preußen*, vol. 7 ([Danzig], 1761), 120. Gorani also reports a figure of sixteen thousand prisoners; see Gorani, *Mémoires*, 146.
184. Önnerfors, "Freimaurerei und Offiziertum im 18. Jahrhundert," 238.
185. Friedrich Eberhard Boysen, *Eigene Lebensbeschreibung*, 2 vols. (Quedlinburg: Ernst, 1795), vol. 2.
186. Boysen, *Eigene Lebensbeschreibung*, 2:254.
187. Boysen, *Eigene Lebensbeschreibung*, 2:255.
188. Boysen, *Eigene Lebensbeschreibung*, 2:250–251.
189. Boysen, *Eigene Lebensbeschreibung*, 2:215–220.
190. Adelung and Hörning, *Denckwürdigkeiten*, 120–121.
191. Adelung and Hörning, *Denckwürdigkeiten*, 121.
192. Archenholz, *History of the Seven Years War*, 405–406.
193. Lutz Voigtländer, "Kontributionen, Freikorps und Douceurs: Duisburg im Siebenjährigen Krieg, 1756–1763," *Duisburger Forschungen* 47 (2001): 104; Jakobs, "Wittenberg im Siebenjährigen Krieg"; Edmund Lange, "Die Besetzung Greifswalds durch die Preußen 1758 und die Universität," *Pommersche Jahrbücher* 2 (1901); Hermann Wolfgang Bener, "Greifswald im siebenjährigen Kriege nach dem Dekanatsbuche der Theologischen Fakultät," *Baltische Studien*, n.s., vol. 33 (1931); Beyer, *Neue Chronik von Erfurt*, 33–119.
194. Ernst Kroker, "Leipzig im Siebenjährigen Kriege," in *Quellen zur Geschichte der Stadt Leipzig*, ed. Gustav Wustmann (ed.), vol. 2 (Leipzig: Duncker & Humblot, 1895), 399–401; Christoph Zeumer, "Zwischen Preußen und Sachsen: Leipzig im Siebenjährigen Krieg 1756–1763," in *Stadt und Krieg: Leipzig in militärischen Konflikten vom Mittelalter bis ins 20. Jh.*, ed. Ulrich von Hehl (Leipziger Universitätsverlag, 2014).
195. Walz, "Kriegs- und Friedensbilder aus den Jahren 1754–1759," 23.
196. Kroker, "Leipzig im Siebenjährigen Kriege," 413–416.
197. Kroker, "Leipzig im Siebenjährigen Kriege," 406.
198. Kroker, "Leipzig im Siebenjährigen Kriege," 411–412.
199. [Luise Gottsched], *Briefe der Frau Louise Adelgunde Victorie Gottsched gebohren Kulmus*, vol. 3 (Dresden: Harpeterischen Schriften, 1772), 122; Luise Gottsched, *"Mit Der Feder in Der Hand": Briefe aus Den Jahren 1730–1762*, ed. Inka Kording (Wissenschaftliche Buchgesellschaft, 1999), 296; on the wider context, see Kroker, "Leipzig im Siebenjährigen Kriege," 420–421.

200. Kroker, "Leipzig im Siebenjährigen Kriege," 466–467; for the figures, see 489–490.
201. Schepkowski, *Johann Ernst Gotzkowsky*, 268.
202. Horst Schlechte, ed., *Die Staatsreform in Kursachsen 1762–1763: Quellen zum kursächsischen Rétablissement nach dem Siebenjährigen Krieg* (Rütten & Loening, 1958), 23.
203. Jakobs, "Wittenberg im Siebenjährigen Krieg," 34.
204. Trautzschen, *Militärische und literarische Briefe des Herrn von T.*, nos. 12 and 13, 49–57.
205. Trautzschen, *Militärische und literarische Briefe des Herrn von T.*, no. 13, 56.
206. Jakobs, "Wittenberg im Siebenjährigen Krieg," 41.
207. Voigtländer, "Kontributionen, Freikorps und Douceurs," 109.
208. Voigtländer, "Kontributionen, Freikorps und Douceurs," 128–132, 149, 161–166, 181–187.
209. Voigtländer, "Kontributionen, Freikorps und Douceurs," 185.
210. Marian Füssel, "'Die besten Feinde, welche man nur haben kann'? Göttingen unter französischer Besatzung im Siebenjährigen Krieg," *Göttinger Jahrbuch* 60 (2012): 137; Rainer Bolle, "Der Göttinger Magistrat im Siebenjährigen Krieg," *Göttinger Jahrbuch* 38 (1990); Samuel Christian Hollmann, *Die Universität Göttingen im siebenjährigen Kriege*, ed. Alfred Schöne (Leipzig: Hirzel, 1887).
211. Johann David Michaelis, *Lebensbeschreibung von ihm selbst abgefasst* (Leipzig: Barth, 1793), 44.
212. Füssel, "Göttingen unter französischer Besatzung," 141.
213. See Yair Mintzker, *The Defortification of the German City, 1689–1866* (Cambridge University Press, 2012).
214. Franz Knauth, *Drangsale und Leiden der Stadt Halle und des Saalkreises während des 7jähr. Krieges: Gleichzeitigen Aufzeichnungen nacherzählt und als Festgabe zur Jahrhundertfeier des Hubertusburger Friedensschlusses* (Halle: Buchhandlung des Waisenhauses, 1863), 7–12.
215. Knauth, *Drangsale und Leiden*, 34; Anonymous, *Zuverläßige Nachrichten von dem traurigen Schicksale der Stadt und Universität Halle [. . .] vom 1sten bis 29sten Aug. 1759 [. . .]* (Amsterdam, 1759).
216. Andreas Elias Büchner to Christoph Jacob Trew, Halle, October 8, 1760, in *Briefnetz Leopoldina: Die Korrespondenz der Deutschen Akademie der Naturforscher um 1700*, ed. Marion Mücke and Thomas Schnalke (De Gruyter, 2009), no. 18, 538–539.
217. On the rumors, see Häberlein and Schmölz-Häberlein, *Kommunikationsnetz*.
218. Alexei N. Krouglov, "Kant und der Siebenjährige Krieg," *Studies in East European Thought* 68, no. 2–3 (2016): 150; [Bock], "Occupation Königsbergs," [pt. 1], vol. 1 (1858), 176–177.
219. [Bock], "Occupation Königsbergs," [pt. 2], vol. 1 (1858), 204–205.

220. Bolotov, *Leben und Abenteuer*, 1: 358. See also Walter Schmidt, "Ein junger Russe erlebt Ostpreußen—Andrej Bolotovs Erinnerungen an den Siebenjährigen Krieg," in *West-östliche Spiegelungen*, vol. 2, *Deutsche und Deutschland aus russischer Sicht: 18. Jahrhundert: Aufklärung*, ed. Dagmar Herrmann and Karl-Heinz Korn (Fink, 1992), 190–208.
221. [Bock], "Occupation Königsbergs."
222. Krouglov, "Kant und der Siebenjährige Krieg," 154; Bolotov, *Leben und Abenteuer*, 1:324–326, 1:330.
223. [Bock], "Occupation Königsbergs," [pt. 2], vol. 1 (1858), 203; for the second quotation, see [pt. 3], vol. 2 (1859), 60.
224. On the censorship of newspaper reports, see [Bock], "Occupation Königsbergs," [pt. 2], vol. 1 (1858), 211.
225. Dirk Alvermann, ed., *Im Hause des Herrn immerdar: Die Lebensgeschichte des Augustin von Balthasar (1701–1786) von ihm selbst erzählt* (Lehrstuhls für Nordische Geschichte, 2003), 144.
226. Füssel, "Göttingen unter französischer Besatzung," 150.

10. 1761: New Alliances, Missed Opportunities

1. Zellmann, "Tagebuch des Johann Philipp Zellmann," 52.
2. Baugh, *Global War*, 501–510.
3. Szabo, *Seven Years War*, 344, 378.
4. Szabo, *Seven Years War*, 328–373; Edmond Dziembowski, "Les négociations franco-britanniques de 1761 devant le tribunal de l'opinion: Le duc de Choiseul et la publicité de la diplomatie française," in *Le négoce de la paix: Les nations et les traités franco-britanniques (1713–1802)*, ed. Jean-Pierre Jessene et al. (Société des Études Robespierristes, 2008).
5. Vicente Palacio Atard, *El tercer pacto de familia* (Consejo Superior De Investigaciones Cientificas, 1945); Emile Appolis, "Les motifs idéologiques du Pacte de Famille," *Revue d'histoire diplomatique* 75 (1961); Didier Ozanam, "Les origines du troisième Pacte de famille (1761)," *Revue d'histoire diplomatique* 75 (1961).
6. Allan Christelow, "Economic Background of the Anglo-Spanish War of 1762," *Journal of Modern History* 18, no. 1 (1946); Paul W. Mapp, *The Elusive West and the Contest for Empire, 1713–1763* (University of North Carolina Press, 2011), 413–427.
7. Baugh, *Global War*, 550–558.
8. Quoted in Baugh, *Global War*, 554.
9. Middleton, *Bells of Victory*, 198.
10. Schumann and Schweizer, *Seven Years War*, 204; Szabo, *Seven Years War*, 368. See also Karl W. Schweizer, "Lord Bute and William Pitt's Resignation in 1761," *Canadian Journal of History* 8, no. 2 (1973).

11. Karl W. Schweizer, "The Non-Renewal of the Anglo-Prussian Subsidy Treaty, 1761–1762: A Historical Revision," *Canadian Journal of History* 13, no. 3 (1976); Karl W. Schweizer, "Lord Bute, Newcastle, Prussia and the Hague Overtures: A Re-Examination," *Albion* 9, no. 1 (1977).
12. Francis J. Hebbert, "The Belle-Ile Expedition of 1761," *Journal of the Society for Army Historical Research* 64 (1986); Baugh, *Global War*, 526–532.
13. Equiano, *The Interesting Narrative*, 57.
14. Barbier, *Journal historique et anecdotique*, 4:402–403.
15. Szabo, *Seven Years War*, 348–349.
16. Menneking, *Victoria by Vellinghausen 1761*; Besenval, *Mémoires*, 1:94–125.
17. Middleton, *Bells of Victory*, 148.
18. Cardwell, *Arts and Arms*, 246.
19. Jürgen Nolte, *Die Schlacht bei Wilhelmsthal: Der Siebenjährige Krieg in Nordhessen* (Wartberg, 2012).
20. See his letter to Pitt of July 3, 1761, in Friedrich II, *Politische Correspondenz*, vol. 20, no. 13,018, 507–509; Otto Bardong, ed., *Friedrich der Grosse* (Wissenschaftliche Buchgesellschaft, 1982), 410–412.
21. Schumann, *Briefwechsel mit Jean-Baptiste d'Argens*, 292.
22. Buxbaum, "Das Tagebuch des Feldpredigers Balke," 4, no. 2 (1886): 156.
23. Duffy, *By Force of Arms*, 319–323; Eberhard Kessel, "Friedrich der Grosse im Lager von Bunzelwitz," *Die Welt als Geschichte* 3 (1937).
24. Duffy, *Military Life of Frederick the Great*, 207.
25. Kunisch, *Friedrich der Grosse*, 424; [Charles Emmanuel Warnery], *Des Herrn Generalmajor von Warnery sämtliche Schriften*, ed. Gerhard J. D. von Scharnhorst, vol. 8, *Feldzüge Friedrichs des Zweyten, Königs von Preußen, seit 1756 bis 1762* (Hanover: Helwieg, 1789), 183–184.
26. Tempelhof, *Geschichte des siebenjährigen Krieges*, 5:169.
27. Duffy, *Military Life of Frederick the Great*, 224.
28. Walter, *Maria Theresia*, 159.
29. Duffy, *By Force of Arms*, 323–327; Franz Wachter, ed., *Akten des Kriegsgerichts von 1763 wegen der Eroberung von Glatz 1760 und Schweidnitz 1761* (Breslau: Max, 1897).
30. Hohrath, "Von der wunderbahren Würkung der Bomben," 312; Masslowski, *Der siebenjährige Krieg nach russischer Darstellung*, 3:331–367.
31. Hans von Held, *Geschichte der drei Belagerungen Kolbergs im siebenjährigen Kriege* (Berlin: Duncker, 1847).
32. Hermann Klaje, *Die Russen vor Kolberg: Zur Erinnerung an die Belagerung der Stadt vor hundertfünfzig Jahren (1760)* (C. F. Post, 1911).
33. Hohrath, "Von der wunderbahren Würkung der Bomben," 312.
34. On the fortified camp, see Masslowski, *Der siebenjährige Krieg nach russischer Darstellung*, 3:340–342.

35. All three accounts were published separately but also printed in the *Teutsche Kriegs-Canzley*. Kneisel, *Denkwürdigkeiten der zweyten Rußischen Belagerung*; Johann Christian Kneisel, *Denkwürdigkeiten der drey Belagerungen Colbergs durch die Russen in den Jahren 1758, 1760 und 1761* (Frankfurt, 1763); [Montag], *Teutsche Kriegs-Canzley*, 2:139–239, 1:75–284.
36. Kneisel, *Denkwürdigkeiten der drey Belagerungen Colbergs*, 3.
37. Kneisel, *Denkwürdigkeiten der drey Belagerungen Colbergs*, 266.
38. Kneisel, *Denkwürdigkeiten der drey Belagerungen Colbergs*, 279–282.
39. Kneisel, *Denkwürdigkeiten der drey Belagerungen Colbergs*, 330–331.
40. Kneisel, *Denkwürdigkeiten der drey Belagerungen Colbergs*, 304.
41. Kneisel, *Denkwürdigkeiten der drey Belagerungen Colbergs*, 309.
42. Kneisel, *Denkwürdigkeiten der drey Belagerungen Colbergs*, 332–333.
43. Voltaire to Luise Dorothée, Schloss Ferney, November 9, 1761, in Raschke, *Briefwechsel*, 206.
44. Luise Dorothée to Voltaire, Gotha, November 21, 1761, in Raschke, *Briefwechsel*, 207.
45. Kneisel, *Denkwürdigkeiten der drey Belagerungen Colbergs*, 337.
46. For the capitulation terms, see Kneisel, *Denkwürdigkeiten der drey Belagerungen Colbergs*, 389–400.
47. Kneisel, *Denkwürdigkeiten der drey Belagerungen Colbergs*, 350.
48. Kneisel, *Denkwürdigkeiten der drey Belagerungen Colbergs*, 351.
49. Kneisel, *Denkwürdigkeiten der drey Belagerungen Colbergs*, 367.
50. See Tigerström, *Langelius*, 44.
51. Tigerström, *Langelius*, 46.
52. Tigerström, *Langelius*, 47–48.
53. Tigerström, *Langelius*, 53–54.
54. Tigerström, *Langelius*, 59.
55. Tigerström, *Langelius*, 63–64.
56. Tigerström, *Langelius*, 64; Åselius, "Sweden and the Pommeranian War," 161.
57. Sulicki, *Der Siebenjährige Krieg in Pommern*, 687.
58. Tigerström, *Langelius*, 68.
59. Tigerström, *Langelius*, 69.
60. For the figures, see Åselius, "Sweden and the Pommeranian War," 136; Oldach, *Schwedens Beteiligung am Siebenjährigen Krieg*, 52. For a detailed analysis of Sweden's war costs, see Winton, "Sweden and the Seven Years' War," 22–27; Säve, *Sveriges deltagande*, 572.
61. On this, see Baugh, *Global War*, 575–581; Gipson, *British Empire Before the American Revolution*, 8:187–196; as a source for the expedition, see also the journal of Colonel Hunt Walsh in Wilfred Yorke Baldry, ed., "The Expedition Against Martinique, 1762," *Journal of the Society for Army Historical Research* 1 (1921).
62. Herr, *Wohl und Wehe der Stadt Hameln*, unpag.

63. Theodore Calvin Pease, *Anglo-French Boundary Disputes in the West, 1749–1763* (Illinois State Historical Library, 1936), 411; Yorke, *Life and Correspondence*, 3:347.
64. See Gerald James Bryant, *The Emergence of British Power in India, 1600–1784: A Grand Strategic Interpretation* (Boydell & Brewer, 2013).
65. Harold C. Wylly, *A Life of Lieutenant-General Sir Eyre Coote, K. B.* (Clarendon, 1922).
66. See the report in the *Berlinische Nachrichten*, no. 122, October 9, 1760, 492–494.
67. Bryant, "War in the Carnatic," 99–100.
68. Francke, *Ausfuehrliche Berichte Achter Theil*, 934.
69. Voltaire to Luise Dorothèe, x, January 1, 1761, in Raschke, *Briefwechsel*, 196.
70. Price and Dodwell, *Diary of Ananda Ranga Pillai*, 12:374–408.
71. Friedrich to Finckenstein, Kunzendorf, May 29, 1761, in Friedrich II, *Politische Correspondenz*, vol. 20, 425.
72. Francke, *Ausfuehrliche Berichte Achter Theil*, 895.
73. Bryant, "War in the Carnatic," 103.
74. Over the course of the eighteenth century, white largely superseded Christian as the colonists' self-description, with Native Americans now designated red. For an ample selection of these second-hand reports, see Lucier, *French and Indian War Notices Abstracted from Colonial Newspapers*.
75. Minavavana's speech originally appeared in Alexander Henry, *Travels and Adventures in Canada and the Indian Territory Between the Years 1760 and 1776*, ed. James Bain (Edmonton: Hurtig, 1969), 43–45, and is reproduced in Penny Petrone, ed., *First People, First Voices* (University of Toronto Press, 1984), 25–26. *Minavavana* is sometimes spelled *Mihnehwehna* or *Minweweh*.
76. Minavavana cited in Henry, 44.
77. Alan David Francis, "The Campaign in Portugal, 1762," *Journal of the Society for Army Historical* Research 59 (1981); Jeremy Black, "The British Expeditionary Force to Portugal in 1762: International Conflict and Military Problems," in *British Historical Society of Portugal Annual Report and Review*, vol. 16 (British Historical Society of Portugal, 1989); António Barrento, *Guerra Fantástica, 1762: Portugal, o Conde de Lippe e a Guerra dos Sete Anos* (Tribuna, 2006); Patrick J. Speelman, "Strategic Illusions and the Iberian War of 1762," in Danley and Speelman, *Global Views*; Charles François Dumouriez, "Geschichte des portugiesischen Kriegs im Jahre 1761," *Minerva* 4 (1797); Charles Esdaile, "The Peninsular War Guerrilla and Its Antecedents: Humiliation Forgotten, Disaster Prefigured: The *Guerra Fantástica* of 1762," *Small Wars and Insurgencies* 30 (2019). On the writings of Count Wilhelm of Schaumberg-Lippe, see Curd Ochwadt, ed., *Wilhelm Graf zu Schaumburg-Lippe: Schriften und Briefe*, 3 vols. (Klostermann, 1976–1983).
78. Speelman, "Strategic Illusions and the Iberian War of 1762."
79. Speelman, "Strategic Illusions and the Iberian War of 1762," 430.

80. Speelman, "Strategic Illusions and the Iberian War of 1762," 432.
81. Speelman, "Strategic Illusions and the Iberian War of 1762," 435.
82. Speelman, "Strategic Illusions and the Iberian War of 1762," 436.
83. Christa Banaschik-Ehl, *Scharnhorsts Lehrer, Graf Wilhelm von Schaumburg-Lippe in Portugal: Die Heeresreform, 1761–1777* (Biblio, 1974), 20–77; for Wilhelm's own account of the campaign, see "Mémoire de la campagne de Portugal en 1762," in Ochwadt, *Schriften und Briefe*, vol. 2.
84. Rudolf Müller, "Graf Wilhelm von Schaumburg Lippe in Portugal," *Wehrwissenschaftliche Rundschau* 13 (April 1963).
85. On the mobilization of the Spanish army, see Agustin González Enciso, "Spain's Mobilisation of Resources for the War with Portugal in 1762," in *Mobilising Resources for War: Britain and Spain at Work During the Early Modern Period*, ed. Huw V. Bowen and Agustin González Enciso (Ediciones Universidad de Navarra, 2006).
86. Speelman, "Strategic Illusions and the Iberian War of 1762," 445.
87. Quoted in Black, "British Expeditionary Force," 72.
88. Speelman, "Strategic Illusions and the Iberian War of 1762," 458.

11. Mosquitoes and Monsoons: The Grab for Spain's Colonies

1. For important source material, see Willy de Blanck, ed., *Papeles sobre la toma de La Habana por los ingleses en 1762* (Archivo Nacional de Cuba, 1948); Emilio Roig de Leuchsenring, ed., *Como vio Jacobo de la Pezuela la toma de La Habana por los ingleses: Cuatro capítulos de su Historia de la Isla de Cuba y un fragmento de su Diccionario geográfico, estadístico, histórico de la Isla de Cuba* (Oficina del Historiador de la Ciudad de la Habana, 1962); Juan Pérez de la Riva and Juana Zurbaran, eds., *Documentos inéditos sobre la toma de la Habana por los Ingleses en 1762: El libro de Ordenes de Pago de Albemarle; La Campaña de la Escuadra de Blénac; Cartas diversas; La toma de la Habana vista por la Gazette de Hollande* (Biblioteca Nacional José Martí, 1963); Amalia A. Rodríguez and Mercedes Muriedas, eds., *Cinco diarios del sitio de la Habana* (Departamento de Colección Cubana, 1963); David Syrett, ed., *The Siege and Capture of Havana 1762* (Navy Records Society, 1970); see also Francis Russell Hart, "Spanish Documents Relating to the Siege of Havana, 1762," *Proceedings of the Massachusetts Historical Society* 64 (1932). Relevant recent Spanish accounts include Celia María Parcero Torre, *La pérdida de La Habana y las reformas borbónicas en Cuba, 1760–1773* (Junta de Castilla y León, Consejería de Educación y Cultura, 1998); Guillermo Calleja Leal and Hugo O'Donnell, *Duque de Estrada, 1762: La Habana Inglesa; La toma de La Habana por los ingleses* (Editorial de Ciencias Sociales, 1999); César García del Pino, *Toma de*

La Habana por los ingleses y sus antecedentes (Editorial de Ciencias Sociales, 2002). In English, see most recently Elena A. Schneider, *The Occupation of Havana: War, Trade, and Slavery in the Atlantic World* (University of North Carolina Press, 2018); for a concise account in German, see Thomas Weller, "Clash of Empires? Die britische Eroberung von Havanna 1762 und die Folgen," in Füssel, *Der Siebenjährige Krieg: Mikro- und Makroperspektiven*.

2. Corbett, *England in the Seven Years' War*, 2:282; Nikolaus Böttcher, *A Ship Laden with Dollars: Britische Handelsinteressen in Kuba (1762–1825)* (Vervuert, 2007), 47.
3. David F. Marley, "A Fearful Gift: The Spanish Naval Build-Up in the West Indies, 1759–1762," *Mariner's Mirror* 80 (1994).
4. Böttcher, *Britische Handelsinteressen*, 48.
5. Brown and Schweizer, *Devonshire Diary*, 154; see also Syrett, *Siege and Capture of Havana*, 3.
6. Corbett, *England in the Seven Years' War*, 2:252.
7. Sonia Keppel, *Three Brothers at Havana 1762* (Russell, 1981).
8. Tom Henderson McGuffie, "A Deputy Paymaster's Fortune: The Case of George Durant, Deputy Paymaster to the Havana Expedition, 1762," *Journal of the Society for Army Historical Research* 32 (1954).
9. On the fortifications, see Pedro Luengo, "Military Engineering in Eighteenth-Century Havana and Manila: The Experience of the Seven Years War," *War in History* 24, no. 1 (2017).
10. David F. Marley, "Havana Surprised: Prelude to the British Invasion, 1762," *Mariner's Mirror* 78, no. 3 (1992).
11. For planning for the attack on Manila, see the section titled "Looting for the Empire" later in this chapter.
12. Uhlmann, *Das abwechselnde Fortün*, 69.
13. Uhlmann, *Das abwechselnde Fortün*, 72.
14. Uhlmann, *Das abwechselnde Fortün*, 74.
15. Böttcher, *Britische Handelsinteressen*, 58.
16. Böttcher, *Britische Handelsinteressen*, 55.
17. Syrett, *Siege and Capture of Havana*, 151–158.
18. See Archibald Robertson, *His Diaries and Sketches in America 1762–1780*, ed. Harry Miller Lydenberg (New York Public Library, 1930), 52–53.
19. Robertson, *Diaries*, xxiv.
20. John Robert McNeill, *Mosquito Empires: Ecology and War in the Greater Caribbean, 1620–1914* (Cambridge University Press, 2010).
21. Uhlmann, *Das abwechselnde Fortün*, 76. For perspectives from within Havana, see Rodríguez and Muriedas, *Cinco diarios*.
22. Syrett, *Siege and Capture of Havana*, xxvi.
23. Robertson, *Diaries*, 57.
24. Robertson, *Diaries*, xxix. On Miller, see Way, "Memoirs of an Invalid," 41.

25. Way, "Memoirs of an Invalid," 28.
26. David Syrett, "American Provincials and the Havana Campaign of 1762," *New York History* 49 (1968).
27. Robertson, *Diaries*, 60.
28. Syrett, *Siege and Capture of Havana*, xxxii.
29. Pocock, *Battle for Empire*, 222.
30. Uhlmann, *Das abwechselnde Fortün*, 79.
31. Syrett, *Siege and Capture of Havana*, 283.
32. Syrett, *Siege and Capture of Havana*, 284.
33. Syrett, *Siege and Capture of Havana*, 286.
34. Syrett, *Siege and Capture of Havana*, 288.
35. Syrett, *Siege and Capture of Havana*, 290.
36. See Weller, "Clash of Empires?"
37. Charters, *Disease, War, and the Imperial State*, 65–85. The articles of surrender are reproduced in Rodríguez and Muriedas, *Cinco diarios*, 209–218.
38. McNeill, *Mosquito Empires*, 169–187.
39. Charters, *Disease, War, and the Imperial State*, 66.
40. Chapman and McCulloch, *Memoirs of a Black Watch Officer*, 199.
41. John Graham, *Extracts from the Journal of the Reverend John Graham, Chaplain of the 1st Connecticut Regiment, September 25th to October 19th 1762, at the Siege of Havana* (New York: Society of Colonial Wars in the State of New York, 1896), 10.
42. Graham, *Journal*, 10–11.
43. Graham, *Journal*, 11.
44. Böttcher, *Britische Handelsinteressen*, 58.
45. Nelson Vance Russell, "The Reaction in England and America to the Capture of Havana, 1762," *Hispanic American Historical Review* 9 (August 1929).
46. Woodforde, *The Diary of a Country Parson*, 10; Füssel and Petersen, *Grotehenn Briefe*, 131.
47. "Eine Heldenode," *Der Apotheker*, 13–194, cited in Waibel, *Nationale und patriotische Publizistik*, 317.
48. Sarah Monks, "Our Man in Havana: Representation and Reputation in Lieutenant Philip Orsbridge's Britannia's Triumph (1765)," in *Conflicting Visions: War and Visual Culture in Britain and France c. 1700–1830*, ed. John Bonehill and Geoff Quilley (Ashgate, 2005).
49. Monks, "Our Man in Havana," 89–90.
50. See Böttcher, *Britische Handelsinteressen*, 58–61; Nikolaus Böttcher, "Die britische Belagerung von Havanna im Memorandum des David Dundas," in *Lesarten eines globalen Prozesses—Quellen zur Geschichte der europäischen Expansion*, ed. Andreas Eckert and Gesine Krüger (LIT, 1998); Syrett, *Siege and Capture of Havana*, 314–328.

51. José Manuel Ximeno, "El juicio de los historiadores sobre la toma de La Habana por los ingleses," *Boletín del Archivo Nacional de Cuba* 58 (1962); Judith A. Weiss, "La Conquista de la Habana 1762: El discurso hegemonizador norteamericano," *Cuadernos hispanoamericanos* 641 (2003); Parcero Torre, *La pérdida de la Habana*, 167–171; Calleja Leal and O'Donnell, *La Habana*, 184–191; Weller, "Clash of Empires?"

52. John Huxtable Elliott, *Empires of the Atlantic World: Britain and Spain in America, 1492–1830* (Yale University Press, 2006), 292–324.

53. For a collection of documents, see Horacio de la Costa, "The Siege and Capture of Manila by the British, September-October 1762," *Philippine Studies* 10, no. 4 (1962); Nicholas P. Cushner, ed., *Documents Illustrating the British Conquest of Manila 1762–1763* (Royal Historical Society, 1971); Eduardo Navarro, ed., *Documentos indispensables para la verdadera historia de Filipinas*, 2 vols. (Imprenta del Asilo de Huésfanos, 1908); Emma Blair and James Alexander Robertson, *The Philippine Islands*, vols. 48–49 (Clark, 1907); for contemporary German documentation, see *Danziger Beyträge*, vol. 18, 1763, 175–178, 288–340, including Draper's journal (301–317) and a description of the Philippines (317–338). Of more recent accounts, see Nicholas Tracy, *Manila Ransomed: The British Assault on Manila in the Seven Years War* (University of Exeter Press, 1995); Shirley Fish, *When Britain Ruled the Philippines 1762–1764: The Story of the 18th Century British Invasion of the Philippines During the Seven Years War* (1stBooks, 2003); Carlos Vila Miranda, "Toma de Manila por los ingleses en 1762," *Anuario de Estudios Atlánticos* 53 (2007). For a closer look at Draper, see James Dreaper, *Pitt's Gallant Conqueror: The Turbulent Life of Lieutenant-General Sir William Draper K. B.* (Tauris, 2006).

54. See Füssel, "Politik der Unsicherheit."

55. Draper, *Turbulent Life*, 67.

56. Draper, *Turbulent Life*, 67–68.

57. Draper, *Turbulent Life*, 69.

58. Draper, *Turbulent Life*, 75.

59. On transnational units in South Asian theaters of war, see also Marian Füssel, "Händler, Söldner und Sepoys: Transkulturelle Kampfverbände auf den südasiatischen Schauplätzen des Siebenjährigen Krieges," in *Imperialkriege von 1500 bis heute: Strukturen—Akteure—Lernprozesse*, ed. Tanja Bührer et al. (Schöningh, 2011), 318–323.

60. Cushner, *Documents*, no. 16, 35.

61. M. E. S. Laws, "The Royal Artillery at Manila, 1762," *Journal of the Royal Artillery* 87 (Spring 1960): 19–20; Pocock, Battle for Empire, 234.

62. Cushner, *Documents*, no. 16, 34.

63. Peter Borschberg, "Chinese Merchants, Catholic Clerics and Spanish Colonists in British-Occupied Manila, 1762–1764," in *Maritime China in Transition, 1750–1850*, ed. Wang Gungwu and Ng Chin-keong (Harrassowitz, 2004).

64. William Lytle Schurz, *The Manila Galleon* (Dutton, 1939), 52.
65. Arturo Giráldez, *The Age of Trade: The Manila Galleons and the Dawn of the Global Economy* (Rowman & Littlefield, 2015), esp. 176–179.
66. Don Rojo's diary and his self-justificatory account of his actions have been published. See Blair and Robertson, *Philippine Islands*, vol. 49, 104–131 (journal), 176–261 (justification).
67. Luengo, "Military Engineering," 23–26.
68. Fish, *When Britain Ruled*, 87–104.
69. Tracy, *Manila Ransomed*, 11–12; Fish, *When Britain Ruled*, 99–101.
70. "Diario de la invasión Ynglesa e las Yslas Filipinas, 1761–1765," in Cushner, *Documents*, 89.
71. Costa, "Siege and Capture of Manila," 610–614; Cushner, *Documents*, 58–59.
72. Costa, "Siege and Capture of Manila," 614–616; Cushner, *Documents*, 59–60.
73. Costa, "Siege and Capture of Manila," 616–619; Cushner, *Documents*, 60–61.
74. Tracy, *Manila Ransomed*, 38.
75. Tracy, *Manila Ransomed*, 38–39; Costa, "Siege and Capture of Manila," 623.
76. Cushner, *Documents*, no. 35, 64.
77. Tracy, *Manila Ransomed*, 39; Costa, "Siege and Capture of Manila," 627–629.
78. Tracy, *Manila Ransomed*, 42; Fish, *When Britain Ruled*, 116–119.
79. Costa, "Siege and Capture of Manila," 638–643.
80. Cushner, *Documents*, no. 43, 69.
81. Fish, *When Britain Ruled*, 118.
82. On the supply of siege materials, see Laws, "The Royal Artillery at Manila," 23–24, 28.
83. Draper, "Journal," in Blair and Robertson, *The Philippine Islands*, 48:91.
84. Tracy, *Manila Ransomed*, 48; Giráldez, *Age of Trade*, 177.
85. Tracy, *Manila Ransomed*, 49.
86. Laws, "The Royal Artillery at Manila," 29–30.
87. Draper, "Journal," in Blair and Robertson, *The Philippine Islands*, 48:98.
88. Tracy, *Manila Ransomed*, 56; Costa, "Siege and Capture of Manila," 88.
89. Borschberg, "Chinese Merchants," 357.
90. "Diario de la invasión Ynglesa," in Cushner, *Documents*, 96; Navarro, *Documentos indispensables*, 1:370–371.
91. Cushner, *Documents*, no. 54–56, 125–127; Navarro, *Documentos indispensables*, 1:211–251.
92. Cushner, *Documents*, no. 57, 127.
93. Cushner, *Documents*, no. 53, 125.
94. Blair and Robertson, *Philippine Islands*, 49:215 and n137.
95. [William Draper], *Colonel Draper's Answer to the Spanish Arguments, Claiming the Galeon, and Refusing Payment of the Ransom Bills, for Preserving Manila from Pillage and Destruction* (London, 1764), 21–22; reproduced in Gregorio Zaide, ed.,

Documentary Sources of Philippine History (National Book Store, 1990), no. 242, 510–521.

96. Joaquín Martinez de Zuñiga, *An Historical View of the Philippine Islands*, trans. John Maver, 2 vols. (London: Asperne, 1814), 2:170.
97. See the surrender agreement in Costa, "Siege and Capture of Manila," 643–650; Cushner, *Documents*, 120–123; Fish, *When Britain Ruled*, 132–133.
98. "Conditions Offered to the City of Manila by the British Commanders, 6 October 1762," in Cushner, *Documents*, 123–124; Tracy, *Manila Ransomed*, 53.
99. Blair and Robertson, *Philippine Islands*, 49:127.
100. Blair and Robertson, *Philippine Islands*, 49:129–131.
101. Navarro, *Documentos indispensables*, 1:46–92; Stuart M. McManus, "The Pacific Theater of the Seven Years' War in a Latin Poem by an Indigenous Priest, Bartolomé Saguinsín (1766)," in *The Spanish Pacific, 1521–1815: A Reader of Primary Sources*, ed. Christina H. Lee and Ricardo Padrón (Amsterdam University Press, 2020).
102. Navarro, *Documentos indispensables*, 1:62.
103. On the British occupation regime, see also Carl, "Mikro- und Makroperspektiven auf eine standardisierte Situation."
104. Fish, *When Britain Ruled*, 140–142.
105. Tracy, *Manila Ransomed*, 60.
106. See also Fish, *When Britain Ruled*, 180ff.
107. Tracy, *Manila Ransomed*, 115–128.
108. Borschberg, "Chinese Merchants," 361–371.
109. Borschberg, "Chinese Merchants," 370–371.
110. At some point in the mid-1950s, the remains of the flags were thrown out. See Cushner, *Documents*, 87–88 and n1; Laws, "The Royal Artillery at Manila," 32.
111. Giráldez, *Age of Trade*, 177–178; Serafin D. Quiason, "The East India Company in Manila, 1762–1764," *Philippine Social Sciences and Humanities Review* 28, no. 4 (1963).
112. Quiason, "The East India Company in Manila," 439.
113. Quiason, "The East India Company in Manila," 444.
114. Kristie Patricia Flannery, "The Seven Years' War and the Globalization of Anglo-Iberian Imperial Entanglement: The View from Manila," in *Entangled Empires: The Anglo-Iberian Atlantic, 1500–1830*, ed. Jorge Canizares-Esguerra (University of Pennsylvania Press, 2018), 236–254, 315–320.
115. Diego Téllez Alarcia, "España y la Guerra de los Siete Años," in *La proyección de la monarquía hispánica en Europa: Política, guerra y diplomacia entre los siglos XVI y XVIII*, ed. María Rosario Porres Marijuán and Iñaki Reguera Acedo (Universidad del País Vasco, 2009), 226–227.
116. See the account, including terms of surrender, in *Danziger Beyträge*, vol. 18, 1763, 175–178, 260–268.

117. *London Magazine* 32 (December 1763), 650–652; Andrew Graham-Yool, *Imperial Skirmishes: War and Gunboat Diplomacy in Latin America* (Signal, 2002), 6; Speelman, "Strategic Illusions and the Iberian War of 1762," 459; Dull, *French Navy and the Seven Years War*, 224.
118. Richard Gott, *Land Without Evil: Utopian Journeys Across the South American Watershed* (Verso, 1993), 241–244.

12. A Second Miracle

1. Bolotov, *Leben und Abenteuer*, 1:379.
2. Friedrich II, "O passant! ci-gît Messaline / Du Russe et du Cosaque elle fut concubine / Et, les épuisant tous, elle quitta ces bords / Pour chercher des amants dans l'empire des morts," in *Œuvres de Frédéric le Grand*, vol. 14, *Épitaphe* (Berlin: Rodolphe Decker, 1850), 199. Anderson translates the rhyme as "The Russian Messalina, the Cossack's whore / Gone to service lovers on the Stygian shore." Anderson, *Crucible of War*, 781. See also https://friedrich.uni-trier.de/fr/oeuvres/14/199/text/.
3. Schumann, *Briefwechsel*, 325–327.
4. Volz, *Friedrich im Spiegel*, 139.
5. Cited in Hildebrandt's anecdote collection in Duffy, *Military Life of Frederick the Great*, 228.
6. Elisabeth Hausmann, ed., *Die Karschin, Friedrichs des Großen Volksdichterin: Ein Leben in Briefen* (Societäts-Verlag, 1933), 155.
7. Kneisel, *Denkwürdigkeiten der drey Belagerungen Colbergs*, 360.
8. Prittwitz, *Jugend und Kriegsleben eines preußischen Offiziers*, 47–48.
9. Stefan Hartmann, "Die Rückgabe Ostpreußens durch die Russen 1762," *Zeitschrift für Ostforschung* 36 (1987).
10. Timo Kahnert, "Der drohende Krieg gegen Russland 1761/62," in *Handbuch zur nordelbischen Militärgeschichte: Heere und Kriege in Schleswig, Holstein, Lauenburg, Eutin und Lübeck 1623–1863/67*, ed. Eva S. Fiebig and Jan Schlürmann (Husum, 2010).
11. Kahnert, "Der drohende Krieg," 410.
12. Kahnert, "Der drohende Krieg," 419.
13. Porsch, *Die Beziehungen Friedrichs des Grossen zur Türkei*, 42–45.
14. Friedrich II, *Politische Correspondenz*, vol. 19, no. 12,036, 295–299.
15. Friedrich II, *Politische Correspondenz*, vol. 19, no. 12,036, 297–298.
16. Porsch, *Die Beziehungen Friedrichs des Grossen zur Türkei*, 53.
17. Friedrich II, *Politische Correspondenz*, vol. 20, no. 12,931, 435–436.
18. Frederick to Grant, Neisse, May 25, 1761, in Friedrich II, *Politische Correspondenz*, vol. x, no. 12,912, 419.

19. Friedrich II, *Politische Correspondenz*, vol. 20, no. 12,894, 399–404.
20. Friedrich II, *Politische Correspondenz*, vol. 21, no. 13,608, 368.
21. Friedrich II, *Politische Correspondenz*, vol. 21, no. 13,452, 224–226.
22. Porsch, *Die Beziehungen Friedrichs des Grossen zur Türkei*, 76.
23. Virginia H. Aksan, *An Ottoman Statesman in War and Peace: Ahmed Resmi Efendi, 1700–1783* (Brill, 1995), 67.
24. *Wochen-Blat*, yr. 4, no. 1 January 1762, unpag. [2].
25. Georges Cerbelaud Salagnac, "La reprise de Terre-Neuve par les français en 1762," *Revue française d'histoire d'outre-mer* 63, no. 231 (1976); André de Visme, *Terre-Neuve 1762: Dernier combat aux portes de la Nouvelle-France* (André de Visme, 2005).
26. Webster, *Amherst Journal*, 294–295.
27. Alfred Schneider, "Zum Ende des Siebenjährigen Krieges im Westen des Reiches: Das Gefecht an der Brücker Mühle bei Amöneburg am 21. September 1762," *Fundamenta historiae: Geschichte im Spiegel der Numismatik und ihrer Nachbarwissenschaften*, ed. Reiner Cunz (Niedersächsisches Landesmuseum, 2004).
28. Brunner, *Kassel im siebenjährigen Kriege*, 143–182.
29. Schneider, "Zum Ende des Siebenjährigen Krieges," 458–459.
30. Füssel and Petersen, *Grotehenn Briefe*, 134.
31. Fischbacher, "Die Residenz im Kriege."
32. Claus Legal and Gert Legal, *Tragödie Hubertusburg: Der einsame Kampf des Sachsen George Samuel Götze gegen Friedrich den Großen* (Burghügel, 2014), 198.
33. See the extensive evaluation of the "Report of Your Most Obedient Servant on the Clearance and Destruction of Hubertusburg" [Unterthänig-gehorsamsten Berichts wegen Ausräumung und Zerstöhrung Hubertusburg], in Legal and Legal, *Tragödie Hubertusburg*.
34. Ernst Graf von Lehndorff, *Aus den Tagebüchern des Grafen Lehndorff*, ed. Haug von Kuenheim (Severin und Siedler, 1982), 148.
35. Bisset, *Memoirs and Papers of Sir Andrew Mitchell*, 1:366.
36. Duffy, *Military Life of Frederick the Great*, 231.
37. Duffy, *Military Life of Frederick the Great*, 234.
38. Kurt Treusch von Buttlar, "Burkersdorf," *Forschungen zur Brandenburgischen und Preußischen Geschichte* 10 (1898); Gerhard Krohn, "Friedrichs des Grossen niederschlesischer Feldzug von 1762 und die Schlacht bei Burkersdorf und Leutmannsdorf am 21. Juli 1762" (diss., University of Marburg, 1925); Achim Kloppert, "Der Schlesische Feldzug von 1762" (diss., University of Bonn, 1988), 275–336; Duffy, *By Force of Arms*, 351–362.
39. Johann Gottlieb Tielcke, "Die Drey Belagerungen und Loudonsche Ersteigung der Festung Schweidnitz in den Feldzügen von 1757 bis 1762," in *Beiträge*, vol. 4 (Freyberg: Barthel, 1781); Charlotte Schütze-Böhm, "Eine wiedergefundene Handschrift 'Journal von der Belagerung Schweidnitz im Jahr 1762,'" *Jahrbuch*

der Schlesischen Friedrich-Wilhelms-Universität zu Breslau 5 (1959); Kloppert, "Feldzug," 359–417; Kessel, *Das Ende des Siebenjährigen Krieges*, 669–717; Duffy, *By Force of Arms*, 369–375.
40. "Ach wärens Myrthen, nur den Friedenskranz zu winden / Es würden Dichter sich im Überflusse finden / So aber bleibt der Krieg, die Noth wird allgemein." Flashar, *Memoiren der Eleonore Juliane von Rehdiger*, 142–143.
41. Michael Kaiser, "Prinz Heinrich im Siebenjährigen Krieg—der Oberbefehl in Sachsen und die Schlacht bei Freiberg 1762," in *Prinz Heinrich von Preussen: Ein Europäer in Rheinsberg*, ed. Jörg Meiner (Deutscher Kunstverlag, 2002); Duffy, *By Force of Arms*, 385–391.
42. Kloppert, "Feldzug."
43. Kessel, *Das Ende des Siebenjährigen Krieges*, 802–812.
44. Kessel, *Das Ende des Siebenjährigen Krieges*, 812.

13. 1763: Peace at Last

1. Matt Schumann, "The End of the Seven Year's War in Germany," in Danley and Speelman, *Global Views*, 487–491.
2. For an overview, see Heinz Duchhardt, *Gleichgewicht der Kräfte, Convenance, europäisches Konzert: Friedenskongresse und Friedensschlüsse vom Zeitalter Ludwigs XIV. bis zum Wiener Kongreß* (Wissenschaftliche Buchgesellschaft, 1976), 90–126.
3. Rashed, *The Peace of Paris, 1763*, 159–191.
4. Baugh, *Global War*, 609–612.
5. Baugh, *Global War*, 181–183, 209; William R. Shepherd, "The Cession of Louisiana to Spain," *Political Science Quarterly* 19 (1904); Mapp, *The Elusive West*.
6. Fred Anderson, "The Peace of Paris, 1763," in *The Making of Peace: Rulers, States, and the Aftermath of War*, ed. Williamson Murray and James Lacey (Cambridge University Press, 2009), 119.
7. Baugh, *Global War*, 616–617; *Proceedings and Debates of the British Parliaments Respecting North America, 1754–1783*, ed. Richard C. Simmons and Peter David Garner Thomas, 6 vols. (Kraus, 1982–1987), 1:416–423.
8. Baugh, *Global War*, 617.
9. Jean-Pierre Bois, "Le traité de Paris de 1763," in Fonck and Veyssière, *La Chute*; Sophie Imbeault et al., eds., *1763: Le traité de Paris bouleverse l'Amérique* (Septentrion, 2013); Anderson, "Peace of Paris"; Hermann Wellenreuther, "Der Vertrag zu Paris (1763) in der atlantischen Geschichte," *Niedersächsisches Jahrbuch für Landesgeschichte* 17 (1999); Barry M. Gough, *British Mercantile Interests in the Making of the Peace of Paris, 1763: Trade, War, and Empire* (Mellen, 1992); Ronald Hyam, "Imperial Interests and the Peace of Paris, 1763," in *Reappraisals in British Imperial History*, by Ronald Hyam and Ged Martin (Macmillan, 1975); Rashed, *The Peace*

of Paris, 1763; Harold William Vazeille Temperley, "The Peace of Paris," in *The Cambridge History of the British Empire*, vol. 1, *The Old Empire from its Beginnings to 1783*, ed. John Holland Rose et al. (Cambridge University Press, 1929).

10. Anderson, "Peace of Paris," 101–106.
11. Anonymous, *The Reign of George VI, 1900–1925* (London: Niccoll, 1763).
12. Cardwell, *Arts and Arms*, 268.
13. His full name was Pablo Jerónimo Grimaldi y Pallavicini.
14. The French text of the treaty is printed in Rashed, *The Peace of Paris 1763*, 212–229. For an English translation, see Corbett, *England in the Seven Years' War*, 2:377–390. A German translation of the peace terms was published in the *Danziger Beyträge*, vol. 18, 1763, 564–590.
15. *Danziger Beyträge*, vol. 18, 1763, 569.
16. Wellenreuther, "Vertrag zu Paris," 100.
17. Wellenreuther, "Vertrag zu Paris," 101.
18. *Danziger Beyträge*, vol. 18, 1763, 571.
19. Lucy Sutherland, "The East India Company and the Peace of Paris," in *Politics and Finance in the 18th Century*, ed. Aubrey Newman (Hambledon, 1984).
20. Baugh, *Global War*, 640.
21. Parkman, *Montcalm and Wolfe*, 526; on the consequences, see Colin G. Calloway, *The Scratch of a Pen: 1763 and the Transformation of North America* (Oxford University Press, 2006).
22. Colley, *Britons*, 101–103.
23. The most extensive account remains Carl Freiherr von Beaulieu-Marconnay, *Der Hubertusburger Friede: Nach archivalischen Quellen* (Leipzig: Hirzel, 1871); Duchhardt, *Gleichgewicht*, 90–126.
24. See the documents in Otto Eduard Schmidt, "Die Meißner Vorverhandlungen zum Hubertusburger Frieden," *Mitteilungen des Vereins für Geschichte der Stadt Meissen* 6, no. 4 (1904).
25. Berger and Wassermann, *Vetternwirtschaft*, 118.
26. On the choice of location, see Jörg Ludwig, "Schloss Hubertusburg als Ort der Friedensverhandlungen von 1762/63," in *Die Königliche Jagdresidenz Hubertusburg und der Frieden von 1763*, ed. Dirk Syndram and Claudia Brink (Sächsische Zeitung, 2013).
27. See the detailed account in Legal and Legal, *Tragödie Hubertusburg*.
28. Ludwig, "Schloss Hubertusburg als Ort," 198.
29. Berger and Wassermann, *Vetternwirtschaft*, 144.
30. On the strategic significance of Glatz, see Kunisch, "Die militärische Bedeutung Schlesiens," 32–33.
31. Frederick signed the treaty on February 21, 1763, at Schloss Dahlen, where he resided from February 19 to March 13, 1763. For detail, see Legal and Legal, *Friedrich II*.

32. Beaulieu-Marconnay, *Der Hubertusburger Friede*, 186.
33. Buschbell, *Tagebuch des Abraham ter Meer*, 208–209. "Today (February 15)" refers to the date of publication of the news.
34. For an overview, see Gertrud Angermann, "'Friedenstücher' und Friedensfeiern zum Ende des siebenjährigen Krieges (1756–1763)," *Westfalen* 77 (1999); Franziska Bauer, "Iustitia, Concordia, Pax: Vermittlung, Repräsentation und Legitimation von Frieden in Dichtungen zwischen1648 und 1763" (diss., University of Göttingen, 2023), 231–346.
35. Abelmann, *Hannover im Siebenjährigen Krieg*, 231.
36. Abelmann, *Hannover im Siebenjährigen Krieg*, 233.
37. Angermann, "'Friedenstücher,'" 325; Colmar Grünhagen, *Schlesien unter Friedrich dem Großen*, 2 vols. (Breslau: Koebner, 1890–1892), 259–264.
38. Knauth, *Drangsale und Leiden der Stadt Halle*, 70–75.
39. Relevant texts include Anonymous, *Friedens-Danck-Gebett: Welches in allen Kirchen des Herzogthums Wirtemberg auf den Sonntag Exaudi 1763 . . . von den Canzlen solle gesprochen werden* (Stuttgart, 1763); Anonymous, *An das Publicum bey der Feyer das allgemeinen Friedens . . . : Hamburg, den 15ten May, 1763* ([Hamburg]: Bock, 1763); [Anonymous], *Sammlung der Feierlichkeiten welche wegen des zu Hubertsburg den 15. Febr. 1763 geschlossenen Friedens am 17. März deßelben Jahres in Magdeburg angestellet worden* ([Magdeburg]: Faber, 1763); Friedrich Wilhelm von Derschau, *Umständliche Nachrichten von der nahmens Sr. Kön. Majest. in Preussen den 10., 11. und 12. Merz 1763 vollzogenen Besitznehmung der clev-, mörs- und geldrischen Provinzen und von den darin vorgegangenen feyerlichen Freudensbezeugungen über den 15. Febr. b. J. zu Hubertsburg geschlossenen Frieden* (Cleve: Sitzmann, 1764); Johann Conrad Hake, *Volständige Nachricht von den Feierlichkeiten, welche in der Kaiserl. freien Reichsstadt Nordhausen wegen des Hubertsburgischen Friedens vom 15ten Februar 1763 angestellet worden sind* (Nordhausen: Cöler, 1763); Johann Conrad Nenny, *Kurtze Beschreibung der Friedens-Feierlichkeiten in den Städten Hanau, wie auch der allgemeinen Erleuchtung am 9. Merz 1763: Nebst einem Anhang vom Lande und einiger Poesien und Aufsätzen* ([Hanau-]Neustadt, [1763]).
40. Angermann, "'Friedenstücher,'" 331.
41. On this, with the city of Minden as an example, see Angermann, "'Friedenstücher,'" 325.
42. Voigtländer, "Kontributionen, Freikorps und Douceurs," 237–245.
43. Angermann, "'Friedenstücher.'"
44. Hake, *Volständige Nachricht*. His account of celebrations in Nordhausen appears in an appendix.
45. See Johannes Burkhardt and Stephanie Haberer, eds., *Das Friedensfest: Augsburg und die Entwicklung einer neuzeitlichen Toleranz-, Friedens- und Festkultur* (Akademie, 2000), 427.

46. Hake, *Volständige Nachricht*, 2. On celebrations in Nordhausen, see also Siegried Westphal, "Festkultur zwischen städtischer Identitätsstiftung und Reichsbekenntnis: Das Hubertusburger Friedensfest von 1763 in der Reichsstadt Nordhausen," *Beiträge zur Heimatkunde aus Stadt und Kreis Nordhausen* 22 (1997).
47. Janine Heiland, "'Harmonie durch Ungleichheit': Die Feiern zum Frieden von Hubertusburg 1763 in der Residenzstadt Weimar und der Universitätsstadt Jena als Spiegel der Ständegesellschaft," *Zeitschrift für thüringische Geschichte* 65 (2011): 130–131.
48. Angermann, "'Friedenstücher,'" 332.
49. On interpretative ambiguities of peace in musical images, see Johann Georg Scheffner, *Mein Leben, wie ich Johann Georg Scheffner es selbst beschrieben* (Königsberg: Universitäts-Buchhandlung, 1821), 106–107.
50. Buschbell, *Tagebuch des Abraham ter Meer*, 211.
51. Schultz, *Roggenpreis*, 98.
52. On Frederick's entry into Berlin, see also Anonymous, *Neueröfneter Historischer Bilder-Saal. In welchem die allgemeine Welt-Geschichte von 1761 bis 1765 [. . .] beschrieben [. . .]*, vol. 14 (Nürnberg: Jacob Seitzischen Buchhandlung, 1766), 665–667, with an idealized image of the king's arrival; Ernst Graf zur Lippe-Weißenfeld, "Friedrichs des Großen Heimkehr in Berlin 1763," *Jahrbücher für die deutsche Armee und Marine* 90 (1894).
53. Johann Ernst Gotzkowsky, *Geschichte eines patriotischen Kaufmanns* (1768–1769; repr., Berlin: Königlichen Geheimen Ober-Hofbuchbinderei, 1873), 88; on Gotzkowsky's role in the Seven Years' War, see Schepkowski, *Johann Ernst Gotzkowsky*.
54. Johann Caspar Lavater, *Tagebuch von der Studien- und Bildungsreise nach Deutschland 1763 und 1764*, ed. Horst Weigelt (Vandenhoeck & Ruprecht, 1997), 20.
55. Gotzkowsky, *Geschichte*, 88. See also "Solennitäten der Stadt Berlin bey der Ankunft des Königs," *Danziger Beyträge*, vol. 19, 1764, 64–77.
56. Schultz, *Roggenpreis*, 98.
57. Reinhold Koser, *Geschichte Friedrichs des Grossen*, vol. 3 (Cotta, 1925), 173.
58. Hausmann, *Die Karschin*, 187.
59. Friedrich Nicolai, *Anekdoten von König Friedrich II. von Preußen*, 2nd ed., 6 vols. (Berlin: Nicolai, 1788–92), 1:48.
60. Lavater, *Tagebuch*, 44.
61. Theodor Schieder, *Friedrich der Große: Ein Königtum der Widersprüche* (Bertelsmann, 1986), 213.
62. Gustav Berthold Volz, "Zur Entstehungsgeschichte der 'Histoire de la guerre de sept ans' Friedrichs des Großen," *Hohenzollern-Jahrbuch* 15 (1911).
63. Stollberg-Rilinger, *Maria Theresa*, 493.
64. *Gazette de Vienne*, no. 19, March 5, 1763.
65. *Gazette de Vienne*, no. 20, March 9, 1763.

66. *Gazette de Vienne*, no. 21, March 12, 1763.
67. Karl Graf von Zinzendorf, Aus *den Jugendtagebüchern 1747, 1752 bis 1763*, ed. Maria Breunlich and Marieluise Mader (Böhlau, 1997), 315.
68. Anonymous, *Neueröfneter Historischer Bilder-Saal*, 452–453.
69. Anonymous, *Neueröfneter Historischer Bilder-Saal*, 453.
70. James Boswell, *London Journal 1762–1763* (Penguin, 2014), 315.
71. Joseph Jérôme Le Français de Lalande, *Journal d'un voyage en Angleterre, 1763*, ed. Hélène Monod-Cassidy (Voltaire Foundation, 1980), 30.
72. Lalande, *Journal*, 59.
73. Boswell, *London Journal*, 360.
74. Vaisey, *Diary of Thomas Turner*, 270.
75. Cardwell, *Arts and Arms*, 263–273.
76. Cardwell, *Arts and Arms*, 269.
77. Alain Laberge, "Entre l'allégresse du peuple et l'amour-propre flétri du roi: Les fêtes pour la publication de la paix de juin 1763 à Paris," in Imbeault et al., *1763: Le traité de Paris bouleverse l'Amérique*; Alain-Charles Gruber, *Les grandes fêtes et leurs décors à l'époque de Louis XVI* (Droz, 1972), 19–25; Yvonne Rickert, *Herrscherbild im Widerstreit: Die Place Louis XV in Paris; Ein Königsplatz im Zeitalter der Aufklärung* (Olms, 2018).
78. Hans Pleschinski, ed., *Nie war es herrlicher zu leben: Das geheime Tagebuch des Herzogs von Croÿ 1718–1784* (Beck, 2011), 178.
79. Barbier, *Journal historique*, 4:458–464; on this, see also Laurent Turcot, "Un chroniqueur curieux de Paris et de la promenade: Edmond-Jean-François Barbier et son Journal (1718–1763)," *French Historical Studies* 33, no. 2 (2010).
80. Ménétra, *Journal of My Life*, 131.
81. Barbier, *Journal historique*, 4:460.
82. Barbier, *Journal historique*, 4:460.
83. Barbier, *Journal historique*, 4:461.
84. Barbier, *Journal historique*, 4:462.
85. Voltaire to Luise Dorothée, Ferney, July 20, 1763, in Raschke, *Briefwechsel*, 227.
86. For a relativizing approach to the end of the "middle ground" and the dominance of "biological" exclusionary criteria, see Ulrike Kirchberger, "Nordamerikanische Indianer und britische Kolonisten im Siebenjährigen Krieg," in Externbrink, *Weltkrieg*, 127–139.
87. "Copy of an Embassy Sent to the Illinois by the Indian at Detroit" [September 1763], in *The Gladwin Manuscripts*, ed. Charles Moore (Lansing: Smith, 1897), 644.
88. Wellenreuther, "Vertrag zu Paris," 97–101.
89. Richard Middleton, *Pontiac's War: Its Causes, Course, and Consequences* (Routledge, 2007); David Dixon, *Never Come to Peace Again: Pontiac's Uprising and the Fate of the British Empire in North America* (University of Oklahoma Press,

2005); Gregory Evans Dowd, *War Under Heaven: Pontiac, the Indian Nations, and the British Empire* (Johns Hopkins University Press, 2004); Howard Peckham, *Pontiac and the Indian Uprising* (Princeton University Press, 1947).

90. D. Peter MacLeod, "Microbes and Muskets: Smallpox and the Participation of the Amerindian Allies of New France in the Seven Years' War," *Ethnohistory* 39, no. 1 (1992); Adrienne Mayor, "The Nessus Shirt in the New World: Smallpox Blankets in History and Legend," *Journal of American Folklore* 108 (1995); Elizabeth A. Fenn, "Biological Warfare in Eighteenth Century North America: Beyond Jeffrey Amherst," *Journal of American History* 86 (2000); see also Füssel and Petersen, "Ananas und Kanonen," 373.
91. Fenn, "Biological Warfare," 1554.
92. Fenn, "Biological Warfare," 1564–1580.
93. Fenn, "Biological Warfare," 1565.
94. Syrett, *Siege and Capture of Havana*, xxxv.
95. Paul Edward Kopperman, "The Stoppages Mutiny of 1763," *Western Pennsylvania Historical Magazine* 69 (1986); Peter Way, "Rebellion of the Regulars: Working Soldiers and the Mutiny of 1763/64," *William and Mary Quarterly* 57 (2000).
96. Terry Fenge and Jim Aldridge, eds., *Keeping Promises: The Royal Proclamation of 1763, Aboriginal Rights, and Treaties in Canada* (McGill-Queen's University Press, 2015); for the text of the proclamation, see pages 201–206.
97. George Croghan to Thomas Gage, letter of January 16, 1767, in *The New Regime 1765–1767*, ed. Clarence W. Alvord and Clarence E. Carter, vol. 2 (Illinois State Historical Library, 1916), 487–495, esp. 490–491, originally cited in Wellenreuther, "Vertrag zu Paris," 106.
98. George Croghan to Thomas Gage, 490.
99. George Croghan to Thomas Gage, 490–491.
100. Fowler, *Empires at War*, 285–290.
101. Alain Beaulieu, "Under His Majesty's Protection: The Meaning of the Conquest for the Aboriginal Peoples of Canada," in De Bruyn and Regan, *The Culture of the Seven Years War*.
102. Mann, *Bengalen im Umbruch*, 80.

14. Outcomes of the War

1. Watts, *Cultural Work of Empire*.
2. Clive was not the only "nabob" to make himself unpopular through newfound colonial wealth and a lifestyle to match. See James Mayer Holzman, *The Nabobs in England: A Study of the Returned Anglo-Indian, 1760–1785* (Published by the author 1926); Percival Spear, *The Nabobs: A Study of the Social Life of the English in Eighteenth-Century India* (Milford, 1932; repr., Oxford University Press,

1998); Philip Lawson and Jim Philipps, "Our Execrable Banditti: Perceptions of Nabobs in Mid-Eighteenth-Century Britain," *Albion* 16 (1984); Tillman W. Nechtman, "Nabobs Revisited: A Cultural History of British Imperialism and the Indian Question in Late-Eighteenth-Century Britain," *History Compass* 4, no. 4 (2006).

3. James Greig, ed., *The Diaries of a Duchess: Extracts from the Diaries of the First Duchess of Northumberland (1716–1776)* (Hodder and Stoughton, 1926), 12.
4. Bence-Jones, *Clive of India*, 189. The fact that Clive considered building a mansion named Plassey on Montfort's undeveloped estate underlines the effort he himself put into the memorialization of his most famous victory.
5. Bence-Jones, *Clive of India*, 190.
6. Bence-Jones, *Clive of India*, 266.
7. This account of the impression Clive made in Parisian society in 1763 is left to us by Caraccioli, one of his first biographers: Charles Caraccioli, *Life of Robert, Lord Clive*, vol. 1 (London: Bell, 1777), 149f. On Clive's manner of dressing, see also John Malcolm, *The Life of Robert Lord Clive, Collected from the Family Papers Communicated by the Earl of Powis*, 3 vols. (London: Murray, 1836), 2:181–183.
8. See Bence-Jones, *Clive of India*, 207, 275.
9. Walpole, letter to Horace Mann, August 1, 1760, Strawberry Hill, in Walpole, *Walpole's Correspondence*, vol. 22, *With Sir Horace Mann*, 249.
10. See Maya Jasanoff, *Edge of Empire: Conquest and Collecting in the East 1750–1850* (Fourth Estate, 2005), 37–39.
11. Bruce Lenman and Philip Lawson, "Robert Clive, the 'Black Jagir' and British Politics," *Historical Journal* 26 (1983).
12. Walpole, letter to Horace Mann, August 1, 1760, Arlington Street, in Walpole, *Walpole's Correspondence*, vol. 21, *With Sir Horace Mann*, 429; Harvey, *Clive*, 280; Bence-Jones, *Clive of India*, 188.
13. Patrick Eyres, ed., "Hearts of Oak: Commerce, Empire and the Landscape Garden I," special issue, *New Arcadian Journal* 35/36 (1993), especially Patrick Eyres, "Neoclassicism on Active Service: Commemoration of the Seven Years' War in the English Landscape Garden"; Patrick Eyres, ed., "Sons of the Sea: Commerce, Empire and the Landscape Garden II," special issue, *New Arcadian Journal* 37/38 (1994).
14. Uwe Quilitzsch, "Fürst Franz und der 'Royal Navy Room' im Schloss Wörlitz," in *Das Leben des Fürsten: Studien zur Biografie von Leopold III. Friedrich Franz von Anhalt-Dessau (1740–1817)*, ed. Holger Zaunstöck (Mitteldeutscher, 2008), 159–172.
15. Walpole, letter to George Montagu, March 22, 1762, Arlington Street, in Walpole, *Walpole's Correspondence*, vol. 10, *With George Montague*, 22.
16. František Stellner, "Zu den Ergebnissen des Siebenjährigen Kriegs in Europa," *Prague Papers on the History of International Relations* 4 (2000): 86; Speelman,

"Father of the Modern Age," 523–527; Micheal Clodfelter, *Warfare and Armed Conflicts: A Statistical Encyclopedia of Casualty and Other Figures, 1492–2015* (McFarland, 2017), 79–86.

17. Speelman, "Father of the Modern Age," 523–524; Archenholz, *History of the Seven Years War*, 540–541.
18. Anton Friedrich Büsching, *Beschreibung seiner Reise von Berlin über Potsdam nach Rekahn unweit Brandenburg*, 2nd ed. (Frankfurt: Haude and Spener, 1780), 260.
19. Frederick II, "Histoire de la guerre de sept ans," in Volz, *Werke*, vol. 3-4, 181–182. An English translation appears in *Posthumous Works of Frederic II*, 2 vols. (London: Robinson, 1789); Junkelmann, "Militärstaat," 171.
20. Duffy, *Armee Maria Theresias*, 133.
21. Anderson, *War That Made America*, 152.
22. Wilhelm Treue, *Wirtschafts- und Technikgeschichte Preußens* (De Gruyter, 1984), 91.
23. Stellner, "Ergebnissen des Siebenjährigen Kriegs," 86; on costs and debts, see also Scott, "Seven Years' War," 430–435, for contemporary figures, see Archenholz, *History of the Seven Years War*, 536–537.
24. Luise Dorothée to Voltaire, February 19, 1763, Gotha, in Raschke, *Briefwechsel*, 222–223.
25. Burkhardt, "Wie ein verlorener Krieg," 267.
26. Schieder, *Friedrich der Grosse*, 203.
27. Jean-Pierre Poussou, "Les conséquences économiques de la guerre de Sept Ans," in Fonck and Veyssière, *La Chute*, 267–284.
28. Stellner, "Ergebnissen des Siebenjährigen Kriegs," 87–98.
29. Burkhardt, "Wie ein verlorener Krieg," 303.
30. Carl, *Okkupation und Regionalismus*, 320.
31. Carl, *Okkupation und Regionalismus*, 321.
32. Reinhold Koser, "Zur Bevölkerungsstatistik des preußischen Staates von 1756–1786," *Forschungen zur Brandenburgischen und Preußischen Geschichte* 7 (1894): 239f.
33. Hartmann, "Die Rückgabe Ostpreußens," 419–422.
34. Hartmann, "Die Rückgabe Ostpreußens," 420.
35. Carl, *Okkupation und Regionalismus*, 326–327.
36. Duffy, *Armee Maria Theresias*, 133.
37. Anonymous, "Autentische Berechnung des Schadens, welchen das Hochstift Paderborn durch die königliche französische sowohl, als königlichgroßbrittannische alliirte Truppen vom Jahr 1757 bis 1762 gelitten hat," *Deutsches Museum* 1 (1785).
38. Weerth, *Grafschaft Lippe*, 182–186.
39. Beyer, *Neue Chronik von Erfurt*, 118.
40. In general, see Fritz Redlich, *De praeda militari: Looting and booty 1500–1815* (Steiner, 1956); Horst Carl and Hans-Jürgen Bömelburg, eds., *Lohn der Gewalt: Beutepraktiken von der Antike bis zur Neuzeit* (Schöningh, 2011).

41. Treue, *Wirtschafts- und Technikgeschichte*, 97f.; Wilhelm Treue, "David Splitgerber (1683–1764): Ein Unternehmer im preußischen Merkantilstaat," *Vierteljahrschrift für Sozial- und Wirtschaftsgeschichte* 41 (1954); Christian Degn, *Die Schimmelmanns im atlantischen Dreieckshandel: Gewinn und Gewissen* (Wachholtz, 1974). For a comparison of British, French, and German profiteers, see Marian Füssel, "'Quelques malhonêtes particuliers'? Army Suppliers and War Commissaries as Profiteers of the Seven Years' War," in *Officers, Entrepreneurs, Career Migrants, and Diplomats: Military Entrepreneurs in the Early Modern Era*, ed. Philippe Rogger and André Holenstein (Brill, 2024).
42. Calleja Leal and O'Donnell, *La Habana Inglesa*, 209.
43. Böttcher, *Britische Handelsinteressen*, 64–65; Hugh Thomas, *Cuba: Or the Pursuit of Freedom* (Eyre & Spottiswoode, 1971), 3–4.
44. Thomas, *Cuba*, 1530–1531; Böttcher, *Britische Handelsinteressen*, 64–65.
45. Gerald Horne, "The Biggest Losers: Africans and the Seven Years' War," in *The Counter-Revolution of 1776: Slave Resistance and the Origins of the United States of America* (New York University Press, 2014).
46. Horne, *Counter-Revolution of 1776*; Scott A. Padeni, "Forgotten Soldiers: The Role of Blacks in New York's Northern Campaigns of the Seven Years War," *Bulletin of the Fort Ticonderoga Museum* 16, no. 2 (1999); see the essential account by Maria Alessandra Bollettino, "Slavery, War, and Britain's Atlantic Empire: Black Soldiers, Sailors, and Rebels in the Seven Years' War" (PhD diss., University of Texas, 2009).
47. See Bollettino, "Slavery," 191–256.
48. Birgfeld, *Krieg und Aufklärung*, 1:214–231, 2:856.
49. Christoph Good, *Emer de Vattel (1714–1767)—Naturrechtliche Ansätze einer Menschenrechtsidee und des humanitären Völkerrechts im Zeitalter der Aufklärung* (Dike, 2011), 20–23.
50. *Danziger Beyträge*, vol. 18, 1763, 400–401. See also Speelman, "Strategic Illusions," 457. The initial 1763 account speaks of eight cannons, but all later reports mention six. On the fate of the golden cannons, see Stefan Meyer, *Georg Wilhelm Fürst zu Schaumburg-Lippe (1784–1860): Absolutistischer Monarch und Grossunternehmer an der Schwelle zum Industriezeitalter* (Verlag für Regionalgeschichte, 2007), 36.
51. Reinhold Koser, "Die preußischen Finanzen im Siebenjährigen Krieg," *Forschungen zur Brandenburgischen und Preußischen Geschichte* 13 (1900): 513–217 and 329–375.
52. Jörg K. Hoensch, "Friedrichs II. Währungsmanipulationen im Siebenjährigen Krieg und ihre Auswirkungen auf die polnische Münzreform von 1765/66," *Jahrbuch für die Geschichte Mittel- und Ostdeutschlands* 22 (1973).
53. For a typical example, see Maria Perrefort, "'Man hörte in den tagen nichts als heulen und schreien in der stadt'—Hamm im siebenjährigen Krieg (1756–1763)," *Der Märker* 53, no. 1 (2004): 34–35.

54. Duffy, *Military Life of Frederick the Great*, 228; Archenholz, *History of the Seven Years War*, 399–400.
55. Peter Blastenbrei, "Der König und das Geld: Studien zur Finanzpolitik Friedrichs II. von Preußen," *Forschungen zur Brandenburgischen und Preußischen Geschichte* 6 (1996): 75–76; Peter-Michael Hahn, *Friedrich II. von Preußen: Feldherr, Autokrat und Selbstdarsteller* (Kohlhammer, 2013), 99.
56. Carl, *Okkupation und Regionalismus*, 341.
57. Hopkin et al., "The Experience and Culture of War," 217–218.
58. On the Oberlausitz region, for example, see Gottlieb Korschelt, "Kriegsdrangsale der Oberlausitz zur Zeit des siebenjährigen Krieges," *Neues lausitzisches Magazin* 54 (1878).
59. Hartmut Finger, *Das "Gemayne Buch" von Schmannewitz: Ein Dorf in Sachsen erlebt den Siebenjährigen Krieg 1756–1763* (Burghügel, 2013); on the broader context, see Legal and Legal, *Friedrich II*.
60. Finger, *Das "Gemayne Buch,"* 71.
61. Schlechte, *Die Staatsreform in Kursachsen*.
62. Karlheinz Blaschke, "Sachsen zwischen den Reformen 1763 bis 1831," in Schirmer, *Sachsen 1763 bis 1832*, 10.
63. Ingrid Mittenzwei, *Preussen nach dem Siebenjährigen Krieg: Auseinandersetzungen zwischen Bürgertum und Staat um die Wirtschaftspolitik* (Akademie, 1979); Ludwig Beutin, "Die Wirkungen des Siebenjährigen Krieges auf die Volkswirtschaft in Preußen," *Vierteljahresschrift für Sozial- und Wirtschaftsgeschichte* 26 (1933).
64. Mittenzwei, *Preussen*, 9; Ursula Wolf, *Preußische Anwerbung von süddeutschen Kolonisten nach dem Siebenjährigen Krieg unter dem Gesandten von Pfeil: Ihre Ansetzung in der Neumark, Schlesien, Berlin und Potsdam* (Dr. Kovač, 2013).
65. Archenholz, *History of the Seven Years War*, 537.
66. Grünhagen, *Schlesien unter Friedrich dem Grossen*, 2:264–279. On the various rules governing damage in individual Prussian territories, see Kloosterhuis et al., *Militär und Gesellschaft*, 186–187.
67. Knauth, *Drangsale und Leiden der Stadt Halle*, 75–76.
68. Blastenbrei, "Der König und das Geld," 76; Stephan Skalweit, *Die Berliner Wirtschaftskrise von 1763 und ihre Hintergründe* (Kohlhammer, 1937); Isabel Schnabel and Hyun Song Shin, "Liquidity and Contagion: The Crisis of 1763," *Journal of the European Economic Association* 2, no. 6 (2004).
69. Lehndorff, *Aus den Tagebüchern*, 148.
70. See Eckhard Schinkel, ed., *Die Helden-Maschine: Zur Aktualität und Tradition von Heldenbildern* (Klartext, 2010).
71. A Freiburg University research cluster is investigating phenomena associated with heroism, viewed in the historical long term. See Ralf van den Hoff et al., "Helden—Heroisierungen—Heroismen: Transformationen von der Antike bis zur Moderne; Konzeptionelle Ausgangspunkte des Sonderforschungsbereichs

948," *Helden. Heroes. Héros* 1, no. 1 (2013). For military heroes in the long eighteenth century, see also Kelly Minelli, *"Wo alle Herzen heldenmüthig schlugen": Heroische Leitbilder in deutschen und französischen Militärselbstzeugnissen des Siebenjährigen Krieges, der Kriege der Französischen Revolution und der Napoleonischen Kriege* (Ergon, 2024).
72. Carl Friedrich Pauli, *Leben grosser Helden des gegenwärtigen Krieges*, 9 vols. (Halle: Francke, 1758–1764); see Komander, *Der Wandel des "Sehepunckte,"* 238f.
73. Pauli, *Leben*, vol. 1, unpag. preface.
74. Füssel, "Der inszenierte Tod," 149–150.
75. Joan Coutu, "Legitimating the British Empire: The Monument to General Wolfe in Westminster Abbey," in *Conflicting Visions: War and Visual Culture in Britain and France c. 1700–1830*, ed. John Bonehill and Geoff Quilley (Ashgate, 2005).
76. Füssel, "Der inszenierte Tod," 139–142.
77. Calleja Leal and O'Donnell, *La Habana Inglesa*, 205, 211–212.
78. Calleja Leal and O'Donnell, *La Habana Inglesa*, 211.
79. McNairn, *Behold the Hero*, 152–153.
80. Abbt, "Vom Tode für das Vaterland," 589–650, 625 (on Schwerin), 649 (on Kleist); Blitz, *Aus Liebe zum Vaterland*, 223–265.
81. Schumacher, "Siebenjährige Krieg in der bildenden Kunst," 250ff.
82. Schumacher, "Siebenjährige Krieg in der bildenden Kunst," 254–255.
83. Birgfeld, *Krieg und Aufklärung*, 2:590–591.
84. Wolfgang Lotz, *Kriegsgerichtsprozesse des Siebenjährigen Krieges in Preussen. Untersuchungen zur Beurteilung militärischer Leistung durch Friedrich II.* (Haag and Herchen, 1981), 102–117.
85. Lotz, *Kriegsgerichtsprozesse*, 154–168.
86. On this, see the nuanced analyses of Birgfeld, *Krieg und Aufklärung*, 2:689–719, and Tilman Venzl, "Neues zu Minna von Barnhelm: Warum der Freikorpsoffizier Tellheim an prußischem Patriotismus verzweifelt," *Deutsche Vierteljahresschrift für Literaturwissenschaft und Geistesgeschichte* 91 (2017).
87. See Böttcher, *Britische Handelsinteressen*, 77–78; Juan José Morón García, "El juicio por la pérdida de La Habana en 1762," *Baluarte* 1 (1994).
88. Baumeister, *Annotation von meinen Lebens-Laufe Johann Conrad Lütgerts*, 39.
89. Baumeister, *Annotation von meinen Lebens-Laufe Johann Conrad Lütgerts*, 40.
90. "Dasselbe bestand größtentheils aus Deserteuren, hat keine nennenswerthe Dienste geleistet und ward nach dem Kriege wieder aufgelöst." Horstmann, *Generallieutenant Johann Nicolaus von Luckner*, 82. See also Jany, *Geschichte der Königlich Preußischen Armee bis zum Jahre 1807*, vol. 2, *Die Armee Friedrichs des Grossen*, 688. Pastor Cuntz, from Kirchditmold near Kassel also reports experiences with the "Turks" in 1762. Brunner, "Aufzeichnungen des Pfarrers Johann Christoph Cuntz," 264–265, 267.

91. Hermann Grotefend, ed., *Der Königsleutnant Graf Thoranc in Frankfurt am Main: Aktenstücke über die Besetzung der Stadt durch die Franzosen 1759–1762* (Völcker, 1904), 316.
92. Manfred Driehorst, "Merkwürdige Begebenheiten zu Meinbrexen in dem Kriege von 1756 bis zum 31. Nov. 1762," *Sollinger Heimatblätter* 1 (2013): 13.
93. Bode et al., "Chronik des Pfarrers Schatz aus Wollbrandshausen," 144.
94. Brumwell, *Redcoats*, 293.
95. Brumwell, *Redcoats*, 296–297.
96. Brumwell, *Redcoats*, 292.
97. Way, "Memoirs of an Invalid," 41–43; Syrett, *Siege and Capture of Havana*, xxxiv.
98. Guy, "George Durant's Journal," 14.
99. Boswell, *London Journal*, 106.
100. "An Address to the Public in Favour of Disbanded Soldiers," *Gentleman's Magazine*, Saturday, February 12, 1763.
101. Brumwell, *Redcoats*, 299–300.
102. Brumwell, *Redcoats*, 300–301; on the psychological consequences, see also Pichichero, *Military Enlightenment*.
103. Uhlmann, *Das abwechselnde Fortün*, 102, xi.
104. Bräker, *Poor Man of Toggenburg*, 146.
105. Kerler, *Tagebuch Dominicus*, 89.
106. Füssel and Petersen, *Grotehenn Briefe*, 137.
107. Equiano, *The Interesting Narrative*, 100–101
108. Equiano, *The Interesting Narrative*, 260–262.
109. Equiano, *The Interesting Narrative*, 264.
110. Vincent Caretta, *Equiano, the African: Biography of a Self-Made Man* (University of Georgia Press, 2005).
111. James Green, "The Publishing History of Olaudah Equiano's Interesting Narrative," *Slavery and Abolition* 16, no. 3 (1995).
112. Trautzschen, *Militärische und literarische Briefe des Herrn von T.*, 197.
113. Füssel, "Ansichten des Krieges," 107–108.
114. Barsewisch, *Tagebuchblätter eines friderizianischen Fahnenjunkers und Offiziers*, 187–188.
115. Prittwitz, *Jugend und Kriegsleben eines preußischen Offiziers*, 140ff.
116. John Pringle, *Observations on the Diseases of the Army* (London, 1752); Donald Monro, *An Account of the Diseases Which Were Most Frequent in the British Military Hospitals in Germany, from January 1761 to the Return of the Troops to England in March 1763* (London: Millar, 1764); Ernst Gottfried Baldinger, *Von den Krankheiten einer Armee aus eignen Wahrnehmungen in dem letztern preußischen Feldzuge mit practischen Anmerkungen aus den besten Schriftstellern* (Langensalza: Martini, 1765) (Latin original published in 1763); Johann Ulrich Bilguer, *Chirurgische Wahrnehmungen welche meistens während dem von 1756 bis 1763 gedauerten Krieg über in denen königlich preußischen Feldlazarethen von verschiedenen*

Wundärzten aufgezeichnet; Nebst etlichen Kupfern [. . .] (Berlin: Wever, 1763). On the broader context of British military medicine, see Charters, *Disease, War, and the Imperial State*.

117. Monro, *An Account of the Diseases*, 1–221 (diseases), 222–342 (sanitary measures).
118. Charters, *Disease, War, and the Imperial State*, 36–37; [George Monro], *An Account of the Treatment of Bilious Fevers in the Military Hospitals at Martinico in 1761 in a Letter from Dr. George Monro to Mr. Donald Monro* (London, 1777).
119. Baldinger, *Krankheiten*, 122–160 (civil population), 161–284 (soldiers in general), 285–326 (final campaign).
120. Otto Freiherr von Münchhausen, *Der Hausvater*, vol. 4 (Hanover: Helwing, 1774), 473–541.
121. Szabo, *Seven Years War*, 433–434.
122. John M. Murrin, "The French and Indian War, the American Revolution, and the Counterfactual Hypothesis: Reflections on Lawrence Henry Gipson and John Shy," *Reviews in American History* 1, no. 3 (1973); Shy, "Empire Remembered"; Jack P. Greene, "The Seven Years' War and the American Revolution: The Causal Relationship Reconsidered," *Journal of Imperial and Commonwealth History* 8, no. 2 (1980).
123. Scott, "Seven Years' War," 425.
124. See Ewald, *Abhandlung über den kleinen Krieg*.
125. Douglas Edward Leach, *Roots of Conflict: British Armed Forces and Colonial Americans, 1677–1763* (University of North Carolina Press, 1986).
126. Marshall, "Thirteen Colonies," 70–72.
127. Marshall, "Thirteen Colonies."
128. Wolfgang Schivelbusch, *The Culture of Defeat: On National Trauma, Mourning, and Recovery* (London: Granta, 2003). While Schivelbusch's challenge to conventional wisdom continues to be influential, the empirical validity of his case studies has been subject to some criticism.
129. Claudia Opitz-Belakhal, *Militärreformen zwischen Bürokratisierung und Adelsreaktion: Das französische Kriegsministerium und seine Reformen im Offizierskorps von 1760–1790* (Thorbecke, 1994).
130. Dennis E. Showalter, "Hubertusburg to Auerstädt: The Prussian Army in Decline," *German History* 12 (1994).
131. A. Wess Mitchell, *The Grand Strategy of the Habsburg Empire* (Princeton University Press, 2018), 192.
132. Daniel A. Baugh, "Withdrawing from Europe: Anglo-French Maritime Geopolitics, ca. 1750–1800," *International History Review* 20 (1998); Pernille Røge, *Economistes and the Reinvention of Empire: France in the Americas and Africa, c. 1750–1802* (Cambridge University Press, 2019).
133. Marion F. Godfroy-Tayart de Borms, "La Guerre de Sept Ans Et Ses Conséquences Atlantiques: Kourou Ou L'apparition D'un Nouveau Système

Colonial," *French Historical Studies* 32, no. 2 (2009); Marion F. Godfroy, *Kourou, 1763: Le dernier rêve de l'Amérique Française* (Vendémiaire, 2011).

134. Pernille Røge, "'La clef de commerce'—The Changing Role of Africa in France's Atlantic Empire ca. 1760–1797," *History of European Ideas* 34, no. 4 (2008).
135. See Scott, "Seven Years' War," 443–446.
136. Josep M. Fradera, "De la periferia al centro: Cuba, Puerto Rico y Filipinas en la crisis del imperio español," *Anuario de Estudios Americanos* 61 (2004).
137. Denis Vaugeois, *The Last French and Indian War: An Inquiry Into a Safe Conduct Issued in 1760 That Acquired the Value of a Treaty in 1990* (McGill-Queens University Press, 2002); Nancy Christie, *The Formal and Informal Politics of British Rule in Post-Conquest Quebec, 1760-1837: A Northern Bastille* (Oxford University Press, 2020).
138. On the historiographical debate surrounding the Murray Treaty, see Thomas Peace, "The Slow Process of Conquest: Huron-Wendat Responses to the Conquest of Québec, 1697–1791," in Buckner and Reid, *Revisiting 1759*, 121–123.

Epilogue

1. Duchhardt, *Balance of Power und Pentarchie*. For a critical take on this point, see Burkhardt, "Wie ein verlorener Krieg zum Sieg umgeschrieben wurde," 301–302.
2. Scott, *Emergence of the Eastern Powers*; Mediger, *Moskaus Weg nach Europa*.
3. Szabo, *Seven Years War*, 432.
4. Hamish M. Scott, "The Decline of France and the Transformation of the European States System, 1756–1792," in *The Transformation of European Politics, 1763–1848: Episode or Model in Modern History?*, ed. Peter Krüger et al. (LIT, 2002).
5. Baugh, *Global War*, 663.
6. Poussou, "Les conséquences économiques."
7. Frank Göse, "Der Kabinettskrieg," in *Formen des Krieges: Von der Antike bis zur Gegenwart*, ed. Dietrich Beyrau et al. (Schöningh, 2007); see also Johannes Kunisch, "Der Ausgang des Siebenjährigen Krieges: Ein Beitrag zum Verhältnis von Kabinettspolitik und Kriegführung im Zeitalter des Absolutismus," *Zeitschrift für Historische Forschung* 2 (1975): 188–189.
8. Sven Externbrink, "Die Grenzen des 'Kabinettskrieges': Der Siebenjährige Krieg 1756–1763," in *Handbuch Kriegstheorien*, ed. Thomas Jäger and Rasmus Beckmann (Verlag für Sozialwissenschaften, 2011), 357.
9. David A. Bell, *The First Total War: Napoleon's Europe and the Birth of Warfare As We Know It* (Houghton Mifflin, 2007); Jean-Yves Guiomar, *L'invention de la guerre totale: XVIIIe-XXe siècle* (Félin, 2004).

10. Christopher Duffy, "The Seven Years' War as a Limited War," in *East Central European Society and War in the Pre-Revolutionary Eighteenth Century*, ed. Gunther E. Rothenberg et al. (Columbia University Press, 1982).
11. Wrede, "'Zähmung der Bellona,'" 231; Starkey, *War in the Age of the Enlightenment*, 6; on the concept of "restraining" warfare, see also Birgfeld, *Krieg und Aufklärung*, 1:98–100.
12. A phrase based on the idea of "modernity as laboratory experiment" in Michael Salewski, "1756 und die Folgen: Einleitung in den Schwerpunkt," *Historische Mitteilungen* 18 (2005): 3. See also Füssel, *Der Siebenjährige Krieg: Ein Weltkrieg im 18. Jahrhundert*, 109–116; Langewiesche, *Der gewaltsame Lehrer*, 53–55.
13. Dziembowski, for example, regards the transformation in patriotism as one of the war's main consequences. Dziembowski, *La Guerre de Sept Ans*, 583–588.
14. Schmidtchen, "Einfluß der Technik," 135–140.
15. On logistics, see Luh, *Kriegskunst in Europa*, 77–80; of the older historiography, see [Anonymous], "Ueber das Verpflegungswesen im siebenjährigen Kriege: Seine historische Entwicklung und seine Ausübung in der Praxis," *Jahrbücher für die deutsche Armee und Marine* 12 (1874).
16. Medick, *Dreißigjährige Krieg: Zeugnisse*, 269–318.
17. See Tim Blanning, *Frederick the Great* (Allen Lane, 2015), 439–472; Baugh, *Global War*, 622–628.
18. Friedrich II, *Politische Correspondenz*, vol. 18, no. 11,403, 516.
19. Johannes Kunisch, *Das Mirakel des Hauses Brandenburg: Studien zum Verhältnis von Kabinettspolitik und Kriegführung im Zeitalter des Siebenjährigen Krieges* (Oldenbourg, 1978), 12–13; Johannes Kunisch, "Die militärische Bedeutung Schlesiens," 28–32.
20. Kunisch, *Mirakel*, 16.
21. Kunisch, *Mirakel*, 91–94; Kunisch, "Ausgang des Siebenjährigen Krieges."
22. See Kunisch, "Ausgang des Siebenjährigen Krieges," 205–208.
23. Warnke, *Logistik und friderizianische Kriegführung*, 73–75.
24. Warnke, *Logistik und friderizianische Kriegführung*, 200–204.
25. Kunisch, "Ausgang des Siebenjährigen Krieges," 195; Bangert, *Russisch-Österreichische Militärische Zusammenarbeit*.
26. For the historiographical debate on the "strategy of exhaustion," see Sven Lange, *Hans Delbrück und der "Strategiestreit": Kriegführung und Kriegsgeschichte in der Kontroverse 1879–1914* (Rombach, 1995); Raschke, *Generalstab*.
27. Kunisch, "Ausgang des Siebenjährigen Krieges," 78–79; the original is published in full in Anonymous, *Staats-Betrachtungen über den gegenwärtigen Preußischen Krieg in Teutschland [. . .]* (Vienna: Kaliwoda, 1761).
28. Kunisch, *Friedrich der Große*, 434; similarly Szabo, *Seven Years War*, 425; Schumann and Schweizer, *Seven Years War*, 228.
29. Kunisch, "Ausgang des Siebenjährigen Krieges," 210.

30. For a critical view, see Szabo, *Seven Years War*, 425–427. Szabo agrees that Frederick accumulated roles but sees this as a personal failure on the part of the king, who was saved from his own stupidity only by deus ex machina factors.
31. Marian Füssel, "Vom Dämon des Zufalls: Die Schlacht als kalkuliertes Wagnis im langen 18. Jahrhundert," in *Wagnisse: Risiken eingehen, Risiken analysieren, von Risiken erzählen*, ed. Stefan Brakensiek et al. (Campus, 2017).
32. Blanning, *Frederick the Great*, 472.
33. Ute Frevert, *Gefühlspolitik: Friedrich II. als Herr über die Herzen* (Wallstein, 2012).
34. See, above all, the arguments in Baugh, *Global War*.
35. Schumann and Schweizer, *Seven Years War*, 228.
36. Eldon, *England's Subsidy Policy*.
37. August Poniatowski, *Die Memoiren des Letzten Königs von Polen Stanislaw August Poniatowski*, vol. 1 (Müller, 1917), 270; Blastenbrei, "Der König und das Geld," 60.
38. Duffy, *Military Life of Frederick the Great*, 227–228; Hahn, *Friedrich II*, 100.
39. Füssel, "Politik der Unsicherheit"; on the concept, see Barry Buzan et al., *Security: A New Framework for Analysis* (Rienner, 1998), and the research carried out at the Deutsche Forschungsgemeinschaft Collaborative Research Centre SFB/Transregio 138, "Dynamics of Security: Types of Securitization from a Historical Perspective," at the Universities of Marburg and Gießen.
40. Anonymous, *Staats-Betrachtungen*, 63.
41. See Langewiesche, *Der gewaltsame Lehrer*, 31–32.
42. For a recent overview of the discussion, see Benjamin Madley, "Reexamining the American Genocide Debate: Meaning, Historiography, and New Methods," *American Historical Review* 120, no. 1 (2015).
43. Baugh, *Global War*, 657.
44. Keep, "Die russische Armee," 137; for exact figures, see pages 150–151.
45. See most recently Wrede, "'Zähmung der Bellona.'"
46. See Kunisch, "Friedensidee."
47. Fredy Niklowitz, "'. . . bis aufs blut ausgesogen . . .': Lünen im siebenjährigen Krieg," *Der Märker* 42, no. 3 (1993): 135.
48. See, for example, Brunner, *Aufzeichnungen des Pfarrers Johann Christoph Cuntz*; Hammann, *Die Bottendorfer Chronik des Johann Daniel Geitz*.
49. See Hammann, *Die Bottendorfer Chronik des Johann Daniel Geitz*, 10–11; Brunner, *Aufzeichnungen des Pfarrers Johann Christoph Cuntz*, 155.
50. For examples, see Stücher, *Ausfouragiert*; Weerth, *Grafschaft Lippe*.
51. Warnke, *Logistik und friderizianische Kriegführung*; Schumann and Schweizer, *Seven Years War*, 91–130; Szabo, *Seven Years War*, 426.
52. Sascha Möbius, "Kriegsgreuel," 187.
53. Warnke, *Logistik und friderizianische Kriegführung*, 657–658.
54. Baugh, *Global War*, 12–13; Daniel S. Soucier, "'We Have Done a Great Deal of Mischief—Spread the Terror of His Majesty's Arms thru the Whole Gulph':

The British Strategy of Resource Control During the Seven Years' War in North America, 1758–59," in *The Greater Gulf: Essays on the Environmental History of the Gulf of St Lawrence*, ed. Claire Elizabeth Campbell et al. (McGill-Queen's University Press, 2019).

55. Warnke, *Logistik und friderizianische Kriegführung*, 106–107.
56. Arne Karsten and Hillard von Thiessen, eds., *Normenkonkurrenz in historischer Perspektive* (Duncker & Humblot, 2015).
57. Wrede, "'Zähmung der Bellona,'" 237.
58. On the flamethrower, see Friedrich II, *Politische Correspondenz*, vol. 20, no. 12,755, 278–279, Duffy, *Military Life of Frederick the Great*, 294; on rifling, see Luh, *Kriegskunst in Europa 1650–1800*, 147–149; on Shuvalov howitzers, see Dirrheimer and Fritz, "Einhörner und Schuwalowsche Haubitzen."
59. See the argument made by James Q. Whitman, *The Verdict of Battle: The Law of Victory and the Making of Modern War* (Harvard University Press, 2012); on this, see also Füssel, "Die Krise der Schlacht," 315–316.
60. Weigley, *Age of Battles*.
61. For insightful reflections on the popularity of the term *globalization* in recent research, see Eckel, "Zur Historisierung des Globalisierungsdiskurses"; for a critical take on political and economic entanglements in the eighteenth century, see Duchhardt, *Balance of Power und Pentarchie*, 222; a differentiated and convincing argument can be found in Bley and König, "Globale Interaktion."
62. See Angelika Epple, "Doing Comparisons—Ein praxeologischer Zugang zur Geschichte der Globalisierung/en," in *Die Welt beobachten: Praktiken des Vergleichens*, ed. Angelika Epple and Walter Erhart (Campus, 2015).
63. Speelman, "Father of the Modern Age," 519–520.
64. See Ruffmann, "Der Ostseeraum im Siebenjährigen Krieg," 510–511.
65. On Frederick, see Jürgen Luh, "Frederick the Great and the First 'World' War,'" in Danley and Speelman, *Global Views*, 1–21.
66. See Hermann Wellenreuther, "Von der Interessenharmonie zur Dissoziation: Kurhannover und England in der Zeit der Personalunion," *Niedersächsisches Jahrbuch für Landesgeschichte* 67 (1995).
67. [Samuel Christian Hollmann], *Lob des Krieges: In einigen Gesprächen entwickelt*, pt. 2 (Frankfurt, 1770), 412–413, on this, see Hermann Wellenreuther, "Göttingen und England im 18. Jahrhundert," in *250 Jahre Vorlesungen an der Georgia Augusta 1734–1984*, ed. Norbert Kamp et al. (Vandenhoeck & Ruprecht, 1985), 30–63. For Hollmann's perception of the war, see also Hollmann, *Universität Göttingen*.
68. See Wellenreuther, "Die Bedeutung des Siebenjährigen Krieges," 173. On the development of the blue water policy, see Baugh, "Britain's Blue Water Policy."
69. Dziembowski, "Transparence ou désinformation?"

70. Jeremy Osborn, "India and the East India Company in the Public Sphere of Eighteenth-Century Britain," in *The Worlds of the East India Company*, ed. Huw V. Bowen et al. (Boydell, 2002).
71. Ulf Engel and Matthias Middell, "Bruchzonen der Globalisierung, globale Krisen und Territorialitätsregime, Kategorien einer Globalgeschichtsschreibung," *Comparativ* 12, no. 5/6 (2005).
72. Bremm, *Preußen bewegt die Welt*.
73. White, *Middle Ground*.
74. For example, see the documentation of intercepted correspondence in Kloosterhuis et al., *Militär und Gesellschaft*, 178–180.
75. Christina Beckers et al., "Die Prizepapers—Ein Jahrhundertfund," Prize Papers Project, University of Oldenburg/UK National Archives/German Historical Institute/VZG, accessed September 4, 2023, https://www.prizepapers.de; see also Louis Cullen et al., eds., *The Bordeaux-Dublin Letters, 1757: Correspondence of an Irish Community Abroad* (British Academy, 2014); Thomas M. Truxes, ed., *Ireland, France, and the Atlantic in a Time of War: Reflections on the Bordeaux-Dublin Letters, 1757* (Routledge, 2014).
76. Marian Füssel, "Auf der Suche nach Erinnerung: Zur Intermedialität des Schlachtengedenkens an den Siebenjährigen Krieg im 18. und 19. Jahrhundert," in *Militärische Erinnerungskulturen vom 14. bis zum 19. Jahrhundert: Träger—Medien—Deutungskonkurrenzen*, ed. Horst Carl and Ute Planert (V&R unipress, 2012).
77. Eckel, "Zur Historisierung des Globalisierungsdiskurses," 50.
78. Olaf Asbach, "Die Globalisierung Europas und die Konflikte der Moderne—Dynamiken und Widersprüche in der Theorie und Praxis der internationalen Beziehungen in der Frühen Neuzeit," in Externbrink, *Der Siebenjährige Krieg*; Bartholomé Yun Casalilla, "'Localism,' Global History and Transnational History: A Reflection from the Historian of Early Modern Europe," *Historisk Tidskrift* 127, no. 4 (2007).
79. See, for example, the diversity of German authors who wrote on the war, as analyzed in Birgfeld, *Krieg und Aufklärung*.
80. Zielsdorf, *Miliärische Erinnerungskulturen in Preußen*, 87–95.
81. Way, "Memoirs of an Invalid," 26.
82. Anklam, "Siebenjähriger Krieg," 38; With regard to the officers, see the skeptical view in: Externbrink, "Wahrnehmung von Krieg und Gewalt," 50.
83. Schwarzer, *Ästhetisierung kriegerischer Ereignisse*, 237–240.
84. Schwarzer, *Ästhetisierung kriegerischer Ereignisse*, 192–199.
85. Dinges, "Soldatenkörper in der Frühen Neuzeit."
86. Möbius, "'Von Jast und Hitze'"; Höchner, *Selbstzeugnisse von Schweizer Söldneroffizieren*, 102; Carl Daniel Küster, "Von den Schlachttagen, als sogeannten heissen Tagen," in Küster, *Officier-Lesebuch*, pt. 2, 82–85.

87. Carl Daniel Küster, "Einige psychologische Erfahrungen über Vergnügen und Misvergnügen der Krieger im Getümmel der Schlacht," in Küster, *Officier-Lesebuch*, vol. 2, 88–91; for general context, see Pichichero, *Military Enlightenment*.
88. Zielsdorf, *Miliärische Erinnerungskulturen in Preußen*, 122–124.
89. On military styles of narration, see Schwarzer, *Ästhetisierung kriegerischer Ereignisse*, 216–118.
90. Harari, "Military Memoirs," 297–298, 303–309.
91. Höchner, *Selbstzeugnisse von Schweizer Söldneroffizieren*, 102.
92. From a letter written by Montgomery after Minden, included in Thomas Charles Edwards and Brian Richardson, eds., *The Saw It Happen: An Anthology of Eyewitness's Accounts of Events in British History 1689–1897* (Macmillan, 1958), 68–69.
93. Höchner, *Selbstzeugnisse von Schweizer Söldneroffizieren*.
94. Sascha Möbius, "'Bravthun,' 'entmannende Furcht' und 'schöne Überläuferinnen': Zum Männlichkeitsbild preussischer Soldaten im siebenjährigen Krieg in Quellen aus Magdeburg, Halle und der Altmark," in *Leben in der Stadt: Eine Kultur- und Geschlechtergeschichte Magdeburgs*, ed. Eva Labouvie (Böhlau, 2004); Tylor Boulware, "'We are MEN': Native American and Euroamerican Projections of Masculinity During the Seven Years' War," in *New Men: Manliness in Early America*, ed. Thomas A. Foster (New York University Press, 2011).
95. Füssel, "Kriegsgefangene in fremdkonfessionellem Umfeld."
96. Füssel, "Kriegsgefangene in fremdkonfessionellem Umfeld."
97. Mastnak and Tänzer, *Tagebuch des Garnisonsauditeurs Johann Philipp Schowart*, 119.
98. Füssel and Petersen, *Grotehenn Briefe*, 103–104.
99. Bode et al., "Die Chronik des Pfarrers Schatz aus Wollbrandshausen," 146.
100. Lehndorff, *Aus den Tagebüchern*, 146.
101. Cited in Koser, *Geschichte Friedrichs des Großssen*, vol. 3, 165.

Bibliography

Bibliographies, Reference Works, and Other Resources

Anonymous. *Summarischer Auszug der neueren Kriegsgeschichte von 1756 bis 1763: Oder Chronologische Tabellen, darinnen die wichtigsten Kriegsbegebenheiten die zu gleicher Zeit, zwischen denen im Krieg verwickelt gewesenen Hohen Machten, der Zeit-Ordnung nach, bis zu denen erfolgten Friedensschlüssen und deren Vollziehung, kürzlich und unpartheyisch beschrieben warden.* Frankfurt, 1764.

Castex, Jean-Claude. *Dictionnaire des batailles terrestres franco-anglaises de la Guerre de Sept Ans.* Presses de l'Université Laval, 2006.

Fournier, Marcel, ed. *Combattre pour la France en Amérique: Les soldats de la Guerre de Sept Ans en Nouvelle-France, 1755–1760; Le Projet Montcalm.* Société généalogique canadienne française, 2009.

Gieraths, Günther. *Die Kampfhandlungen der Brandenburgisch-Preussischen Armee 1626–1807.* De Gruyter, 1964.

Hannings, Bud. *The French and Indian War: A Complete Chronology.* McFarland, 2011.

Henning, Herzeleide. *Bibliographie Friedrich der Große: Nachträge 1786–1986.* Geheimes Staatsarchiv Preußischer Kulturbesitz, 2015.

Henning, Herzeleide, and Eckart Henning, eds. *Bibliographie Friedrich der Große: 1786–1986.* De Gruyter, 1988.

Kloosterhuis, Jürgen, Bernhard R. Kroener, Klaus Neitmann, and Ralf Pröve, eds. *Militär und Gesellschaft in Preußen: Quellen zur Militärsozialisation 1713–1806; Archivalien in Berlin, Dessau und Leipzig*, pt. 1, vol. 1, *Geheimes Staatsarchiv Preußischer Kulturbesitz* (1. Hälfte). Geheimes Staatsarchiv Preußischer Kulturbesitz, 2015.

Kroll, Ingo. *Gefechtskalender der Alliierten Armee 1757–1762*. Books on Demand, 2013.

Lydon, John Gavin. *Struggle for Empire: A Bibliography of the French and Indian War*. Garland, 1986.

Stephens, Frederic George. *Catalogue of Prints and Drawings in the British Museum—Division 1: Political and Personal Satires*, vol. 3, pt, 2, *1751–1760*. London: British Museum, 1877.

Stoetzel, Donald E. *Encyclopedia of the French and Indian War in North America 1754–1763*. Heritage, 2008.

Primary Sources

Abbt, Thomas. *Vom Verdienste*. 2nd ed. Goslar: Hechtel, 1766.

Abelmann, Eberhard Jürgen. *Hannover im Siebenjährigen Krieg: Hannoverisches Kriegsdenkmal; Das Kriegsgeschehen in Stadt und Kurfürstentum, dokumentiert von einem Bäckermeister*, ed. Hans Hartmann. Niemeyer, 1995.

Adelung, Johann Christoph, and Johann Christian Hörning. *Denckwürdigkeiten Friedrichs des Großen jetztregierenden Königs in Preußen*. [Danzig], 1757–1766.

Aland, Kurt, ed. *Die Korrespondenz Heinrich Melchiors Mühlenbergs: Aus der Anfangszeit des deutschen Luthertums in Nordamerika*. Vol. 2, *1753–1762*. De Gruyter, 1987.

Alberti, Georg Wilhelm. "Tündersche Chronik des Pastors Alberti im Auszug zu Hastenbeck." In *Die Schlacht bei Hastenbeck*, ed. Moritz Oppermann. Niemeyer, 1957.

Almon, John. *An Impartial History of the Late War: Deduced from the Committing of Hostilities in 1749, to the Signing of the Definitive Treaty of Peace in 1763*. London: Johnson and Curtis, 1763.

Alvermann, Dirk, ed. *Im Hause des Herrn immerdar: Die Lebensgeschichte des Augustin von Balthasar (1701–1786) von ihm selbst erzählt*. Greifswald University, 2003.

Alvord, Clarence W., and Clarence E. Carter, eds. *The New Regime 1765–1767*. Vol. 2. Illinois State Historical Library, 1916.

Andrews, Robert J., ed. *The Journals of Jeffery Amherst, 1757–1763*. 2 vols. Michigan State University Press, 2015.

Am Ende, Johann Joachim Gottlob. *Christliches Denkmahl des am 19den und 20ten Jul. dieses Jahres über Dreßden gebrachten schrecklichen Feuers: In Dreyen Predigten, Welche theils in der Kirche zu Neustadt bey Dreßden, theils in der Frauen-Kirche zu Dreßden, gehalten, und nebst einer historischen Nachricht von der zugleich mit eingeäscherten Kirche zum heiligen Creuz [. . .]*. Dresden: Gerlach, 1760.

Anonymous. *Die Abbildung eines Schlacht-Feldes und die Buße eines hart bleßirten sterbenden Soldaten samt einem Anhang zum Lobe der Dreyeinigkeit Gottes*. N.p., 1758.

Anonymous. *An Answer to the Letter to Two Great Men, Containing Remarks and Observations on That Piece, and Vindicating the Character of a Noble Lord from Inactivity*. London: Henderson, 1760.

Anonymous. *An das Publicum bey der Feyer das allgemeinen Friedens . . .: Hamburg, den 15ten May, 1763.* [Hamburg]: Bock, 1763.

Anonymous. "Autentische Berechnung des Schadens, welchen das Hochstift Paderborn durch die königliche französische sowohl, als königlichgroßbritannische alliirte Truppen vom Jahr 1757. bis 1762 gelitten hat." *Deutsches Museum* 1 (1785): 316–322.

Anonymous. "Beschreibung von Neu-Orleans, welches den Franzosen im Frieden verbleibet." *Hannoverisches Magazin* 41, Monday, May 23, 1763.

Anonymous. *Besonderes Gespräch eines Rußischen und Englischen Officiers von der bisher unbekannten Lebensart und Sitten der Kalmucken und Bergschotten, von welchen sich ein Theil bey denen Rußischen und Hannöverischen Armeen im Felde efinden / aus dem Rußischen und Englischen übersetzt.* Frankfurt, 1760.

Anonymous, *Beweis daß derjenige, der schon ein Hottentotte ist, nicht erst einer werden dürfe, zur Antwort auf das Pensilvanisirten Preußen witzige Frage: Ob etwan die heutigen Europ. Völker Lust haben möchten, dereinst Menschen-Fresser, oder wenigstens Hottentotten zu werden [. . .]* (Frankfurt: Simon Hallers, 1760);

Anonymous. *A Detection of the False Reasons and Facts, Contained in the Five Letters [. . .].* London: Hope, 1761.

Anonymous. "Das erfreuliche Ungewitter." In *Münchner Bott [. . .] auf das Gnadeneiche Christ-Jahr 1757.* Munich: Merz and Mayr, 1757.

Anonymous. *Friedens-Danck-Gebett: Welches in allen Kirchen des Herzogthums Wirtemberg auf den Sonntag Exaudi 1763 . . . von den Canzlen solle gesprochen werden.* Stuttgart, 1763.

Anonymous. *Gespräch zwischen einem preuß. Schwarzen Husaren und einem Moscowitischen Cosacken über die blutige Schlacht so den 2. Augusti 1758 bey Zorndorf ohnweit Cüstrin vorgefallen.* N.p., 1758.

Anonymous. *Historisch-geographische Beschreibung der in diesem Krieg von den Engländern eroberten französischen Antillischen Inseln: Besonders von Guadaloupe und Martinique etc. zur Erläuterung der gegenwärtigen Kriegs-Staats- und Handlungs-Geschichte.* Stuttgart: Mezler, 1762.

Anonymous. *Der Hohe Geist Gustav Adolphs des Grossen, Königs in Schweden, wie Er Sr. Königl. Majestät Friedrich dem Andern, König in Preußen [et]c. [et]c. kurz vor dem Siege bey Roßbach in dem Lüzner Schlacht-Felde erschienen.* N.p., 1758.

Anonymous. "Journal der Campagne des Generallieutenant, Grafen von Dohna, gegen die Rußen und Schweden, in den Jahren 1758 und 1759." *Bellona* 11 (1783): 3–86.

Anonymous. "Journal of a Naval Surgeon 1758–1763." In *Naval Yarns: Letters and Anecdotes, Comprising Accounts of Sea Fights and Wrecks, Actions with Pirates and Privateers, from 1616 to 1831,* ed. William Henry Long. London: Gibbings, 1899.

Anonymous. *Jugement rendu souverainement et en dernier ressort, dans l'affaire du Canada [. . .].* Paris: Boudet, 1763.

Anonymous. *A Letter to the People of England, on the Necessity of Putting an Immediate End to the War, and the Means of Obtaining an Advantageous Peace.* London: Griffiths, 1760.

Anonymous. "Münsterische Chronik oder Begebenheiten im siebenjährigen Krieg in Münster." *Zeitschrift für vaterländische Geschichte und Altertumskunde* 36 (1878): 82–198 and 37 (1897): 3–112.

Anonymous. *Narratives of the French and Indian War.* 4 vols. Leonaur, 2008–2019.

Anonymous. *Neueröfneter Historischer Bilder-Saal: In welchem die allgemeine Welt-Geschichte von 1761 bis 1765 [. . .] beschrieben [. . .].*Vol. 14. Nürnberg: Jacob Seitzischen Buchhandlung, 1766.

Anonymous. *Reasons for Keeping Guadaloupe at a Peace, Preferable to Canada, Explained in Five Letters from a Gentleman in Guadaloupe to His Friend in London.* London: Cooper, 1761.

Anonymous. *The Reign of George VI, 1900–1925.* London: Niccoll, 1763.

Anonymous. *Sammlung der Feierlichkeiten welche wegen des zu Hubertsburg den 15. Febr. 1763 geschlossenen Friedens am 17. März deßelben Jahres in Magdeburg angestellet worden.* [Magdeburg]: Faber, 1763.

Anonymous. *Sammlung ungedruckter Nachrichten, so die Geschichte der Feldzüge der Preussen von 1740 bis 1779 erläutern.* 3 vols. Dresden: Walther, 1782–1785. Reprint, LTR, 1983.

Anonymous. *Siege of Quebec in 1759, Translated from the French: Narrative of the Doings During the Siege of Quebec, and the Conquest of Canada; by a Nun of the General Hospital of Quebec.* Quebec: Mercury Office, 1858.

Anonymous. *A Soldier's Journal Containing a Particular Description of the Several Descents on the Coast of France Last War: With an Entertaining Account of the Islands of Guadaloupe Dominique, &c. and Also of the Isles of Wight and Jersey; To which Are Annexed, Observations on the Present State of the Army of Great Britain.* London: Dilly, 1770.

Anonymous. *Staats-Betrachtungen über den gegenwärtigen Preußischen Krieg in Teutschland [. . .].*Vienna: Kaliwoda, 1761. Reprinted in Johannes Kunisch, *Das Mirakel des Hauses Brandenburg*, 101–104.

Anonymous. "The Treaty of Logg's Town, 1752: Commission, Instructions &c, Journal of Virginia Commissioners, and Text of Treaty." *Virginia Magazine of History and Biography* 13 (1905–1906): 148–178.

Anonymous. "Ueber Friedrich den Großen, dessen Hof, und den Einfluß von beyden auf dem Zustand der deutschen Litteratur unter seiner Regierung." *Isis: Eine Monatsschrift von Deutschen und Schweizerischen Gelehrten* 3 (1807): 178–198.

Anonymous. *Zuverläßige Lebens-Geschichte des grosbritannischen Admirals von der weissen Flagge, Johan Byng, welcher am 14. März 1757. nach Urtel und Recht am Boord des Kriegs Schiffes der Monarch erschossen worden: Nebst einem kurzen Vorbericht von der jetzigen Verfassung der grosbritannischen See Macht.* Frankfurt, 1757.

Anonymous. *Zuverläßige Nachrichten von dem traurigen Schicksale der Stadt und Universität Halle [. . .] vom 1sten bis 29sten Aug. 1759 [. . .]*. Amsterdam, 1759.

Anonymous. *Zwey Abhandlungen von der Kriegs-Zucht, und Ob es nach den Regeln der Staats-Kunst rathsam ist, den Verlust einer Schlacht zu läugnen, oder falsche Siege und Vortheile auszubreiten*. Berlin, 1760.

Archenholz, Johann Wilhelm von. *Die Engländer in Indien nach Orme*. 3 vols. Leipzig: Deutsche Bushhandlung, 1786–1788. English edition, 1763.

Archenholz, Johann Wilhelm von. "Der erste Schuß im siebenjährigen Kriege." *Minerva* 4 (1806): 132–138.

Archenholz, Johann Wilhelm von. "Geschichte des siebenjährigen Krieges in Deutschland von 1756 bis 1763." In *Aufklärung und Kriegserfahrung: Klassische Zeitzeugen zum Siebenjährigen Krieg*, ed. Johannes Kunisch. Deutscher Klassiker, 1996. Originally published in 1793.

Archenholz, Johann Wilhelm von. *The History of the Seven Years War in Germany*, transl. F. A. Catty. Frankfurt: Jugel, 1843.

Aubert, Caspar, ed. "Prag und Kolin: Ein glücklicher und ein unglücklicher Tag aus dem Kriegsleben des Grossen Königs: Nach dem Tagebuch eines norwegischen Offiziers [Georg Friedrich von Krogh] während des Feldzuges in Böhmen 1757." *Militär-Wochenblatt* 1913, supp. 6 (1913): 163–196.

Bäbler, Johann Jacob. "Aus dem Tagebuch eines württembergischen Regimentsarztes im siebenjährigen Krieg." *Euphorion: Zeitschrift für Litteraturgeschichte* 7 (1900): 150–157.

Baldinger, Ernst Gottfried. *Von den Krankheiten einer Armee aus eignen Wahrnehmungen in dem letztern preußischen Feldzuge mit practischen Anmerkungen aus den besten Schriftstellern*. Langensalza: Martini, 1765. Latin edition, 1763.

Balke, Karl Andreas Friedrich. "Materialien zur Geschichte des Siebenjährigen Krieges: Tagebuch des Feldpredigers des Kuirassier-Regiments von Seydlitz [1759–1760]." *Zeitschrift für Kunst, Wissenschaft und Geschichte des Krieges* 96 (1856): 17–45, 117–146, 191–211.

Barbier, Edmond-Jean-François. *Journal historique et anecdotique du règne de Louis XV.* 4 vols. Paris: Renouard, 1847–1856.

Bardong, Otto, ed. *Friedrich der Grosse*. Wissenschaftliche Buchgesellschaft, 1982.

Barsewisch, Ernst Friedrich Rudolf von. *Von Rossbach bis Freiberg 1757–1763: Tagebuchblätter eines friderizianischen Fahnenjunkers und Offiziers: Nach dem wortgetreuen Erstabdruck von 1863 neu herausgegeben, kommentiert und bearbeitet von Jürgen Olmes*. Rühl, 1959.

Barton, Thomas. "Journal of an Expedition to the Ohio, Commanded by His Excellency Brigadier-General Forbes: In the Year of our Lord 1758." In "Thomas Barton and the Forbes Expedition," ed. William A. Hunter, *Pennsylvania Magazine of History and Biography* 95 (1971): 431–483.

Bath, Friedrich Carl. "Die Schlacht bei Minden 1759 in der Sicht englischer Kampfteilnehmer." *Mitteilungen des Mindener Geschichtsvereins* 48 (1976): 104–114.

Baumeister, Hans Georg, ed. *Annotation von meinen Lebens-Laufe Johann Conrad Lütgerts aufgesetzet im Frühjahr 1751.* Gütersloh-Isselhorst, [2000].

Bayle, Pierre. *Dictionnaire historique et critique: Nouvelle Édition.* Vol. 15. Paris: Desoer, 1820.

[Becher, Johann Christian]. *Wahrhaftige Nachricht derer Begebenheiten so sich in den Herzogthum Weimar bey den gewaltigen Kriege Friedrichs II Königs von Preusen mit der Königin von Ungarn Marien, Theresien sammt ihren Bundsgenossen zugetragen / patriotisch aufgeschrieben von Johann Christian Becher* (handwritten manuscript), Herzogin Anna Amalia Bibliothek, Weimar, Sign. Q 419, n.d.

Behrens, Johann Heinrich. *Lebensgeschichte des 105-jährigen in Wolfenbüttel lebenden Invaliden—Unterofficiers Joh. Heinr. Behrens eines Zeitgenossen und Kriegers Friedrich's des Großen.* Wolfenbüttel: Holle, 1840.

Belach, Andreas. *Der Christ im Kriege und in der Belagerung.* Breslau: Pietsch, 1758.

Belach, Andreas. *Nachtgedanken bey einer gefährlichen Reise in Kriegszeiten: Vom Verfaßer des Christen im Krieg.* Breslau: Meyer, 1761.

Berger, Günter, and Julia Wassermann, eds. *Vetternwirtschaft: Briefwechsel zwischen Friedrich II. und Luise Dorothea von Sachsen-Gotha.* Duncker & Humblot, 2012.

Beringer, Ingo. "Ein braunschweigisches Offizierstagebuch aus dem siebenjährigen Krieg: 1. Das Tagebuch des Leutnants Cleve und die Schlacht bei Bergen," *Zeitschrift für Heereskunde* 50 (1986): 41–46, 81–87.

Bernis, François-Joachim de Pierre de. *Mémoires et lettres de François-Joachim de Pierre cardinal de Bernis (1715–1758),* ed. Frédéric Masson. 2 vols. Paris: Plon, 1878.

Bernstorff, Johann Hartwig Ernst von, and Étienne-François de Choiseul. *Correspondance entre le Comte Johan Hartwig Ernst Bernstorff et le Duc de Choiseul: 1758–1766.* Copenhagen: Gyldendal, 1871.

Besenval, Pierre-Victor de. *Mémoires de M. le Baron de Besenval écrits par lui-même, imprimés sur son manuscrit original, et publiés par son exécuteur testamentaire: Contenant beaucoup de particularités et d'anecdotes sur la Cour, sur les ministres et les règnes de Louis XV et Louis XVI, et sur les événemens du temps.* 4 vols. Paris: Buison, 1805.

Beß, George. "Aus dem Tagebuch eines Veteranen des siebenjährigen Krieges: Mitgetheilt durch den Obersten z. D. Wilhelm Beß." *Zeitschrift des Vereins für Hessische Geschichte und Landeskunde* 12 (1878): 193–241.

Beyer, Constantin. *Neue Chronik von Erfurt oder Erzählung alles dessen, was sich vom Jahr 1736 bis zum Jahr 1815 in Erfurt Denkwürdiges ereignete.* Erfurt: Comission der Keyserlichen Buchhandlung, 1821. Reprint, Rockstuhl, 2002.

Biegert, Claus, ed. *Die Wunden der Freiheit: Der Kampf der Indianer Nordamerikas gegen die weiße Eroberung und Unterdrückung; Selbstzeugnisse, Dokumente, Kommentare.* Lamuv, 1994.

Bilguer, Johann Ulrich. *Chirurgische Wahrnehmungen welche meistens während dem von 1756 bis 1763 gedauerten Krieg über in denen königlich preußischen Feldlazarethen von verschiedenen Wundärzten aufgezeichnet; Nebst etlichen Kupfern [. . .].* Berlin: Wever, 1763.

Bisset, Andrew, ed. *Memoirs and Papers of Sir Andrew Mitchell, K. B.: Envoy Extraordinary and Minister Plenipotentiary from the Court of Great Britain to the Court of Prussia, from 1756 to 1771.* 2 vols. London: Chapman & Hall, 1850.

Blair, Emma, and James Alexander Robertson. *The Philippine Islands.* Vols. 48–49. Clark, 1907.

Blanck, Willy de, ed. *Papeles sobre la toma de La Habana por los ingleses en 1762.* Archivo Nacional de Cuba, 1948.

Bleckwenn, Hans, ed. *Preußische Soldatenbriefe.* Biblio, 1982.

[Bock, Johann George]. "Die Occupation Königsbergs durch die Russen währen des siebenjährigen Krieges," [ed. F. W. Schubert]. *Neue preußische Provinzial-Blätter, dritte Folge,* [pt. 1], vol. 1, 1858, 153–178; [pt. 2], vol. 1, 1858, 201–217; [pt. 3], vol. 2, 1859, 59–78; [pt. 4], vol. 2, 1859, 140–153.

Bode, Willi, Gerhard Rexhausen, and Sabine Wehking. "Das Eichsfeld im Siebenjährigen Krieg: Die Chronik des Pfarrers Schatz aus Wollbrandshausen." *Eichsfeld-Jahrbuch* 13 (2005): 125–154.

Bolotow, Andrej. *Leben und Abenteuer des Andrej Bolotow von ihm selbst für seine Nachkommen aufgeschrieben.* 2 vols. Beck, 1990.

Bond, Beverly W., Jr., ed. "The Captivity of Charles Stuart, 1755–757." *Mississippi Valley Historical Review* 13, no. 1 (1926): 63–65.

Boswell, James. *London Journal 1762–1763.* Penguin, 2014.

Böttcher, Nikolaus. "Die britische Belagerung von Havanna im Memorandum des David Dundas." In *Lesarten eines globalen Prozesses—Quellen zur Geschichte der europäischen Expansion,* ed. Andreas Eckert and Gesine Krüger. LIT, 1998.

[Bougainville, Louis Antoine de]. *Adventure in the Wilderness: The American Journals of Louis Antoine de Bougainville, 1756–1760,* ed. Edward Pierce Hamilton. University of Oklahoma Press, 1964.

Bougainville, Louis Antoine de. *Écrits sur le Canada: Memoires–Journal–Lettres.* Septentrion, 2003.

Bouvier, Jean, ed. "Le fonctionnement d'un hôpital militaire pendant la guerre de Sept ans." *Revue d'Histoire de la Pharmacie Année* 180 (1964): 56.

Boysen, Friedrich Eberhard. *Eigene Lebensbeschreibung.* 2 vols. Quedlinburg: Ernst, 1795.

Bräker, Ulrich. *The Life Story and Real Adventures of the Poor Man of Toggenburg,* trans. David Bowman. Edinburgh University Press, 1970.

Brodrück, Karl. *Quellenstücke und Studien über den Feldzug der Reichsarmee von 1757: Ein Beitrag zur deutschen Geschichte im 18. Jahrhundert.* Leipzig: Dyk, 1858.

Broglie, Victor François, duc de. *Correspondance inédite de Victor-François, duc de Broglie, maréchal de France, avec le prince Xavier de Saxe, comte de Lusace, lieutenant général, pour servir à l'histoire de la guerre de sept ans (campagnes de 1759 à 1761),* ed. Albert de Broglie. 4 vols. Albin Michel, 1903–1905.

[Brown, Charlotte]. "The Journal of Charlotte Brown, Matron of the General Hospital with the English Forces in America, 1754–1756." In *Colonial Captivities, Marches and Journeys*, ed. Isabel M. Calder. Macmillan, 1935.

Brown, Peter D., and Karl W. Schweizer, eds. *The Devonshire Diary: William Cavendish Fourth Duke of Devonshire Memoranda of State of Affairs 1759–1762*. Royal Historical Society, 1982.

Brüggemann, Fritz, ed. *Der Siebenjährige Krieg im Spiegel der zeitgenössischen Literatur*. Reclam, 1935.

Brunner, Hugo. "Aufzeichnungen des Pfarrers Johann Christoph Cuntz zu Kirchditmold aus der Zeit des siebenjährigen Krieges (1757–1762)." *Zeitschrift des Vereins für hessische Geschichte und Landeskunde* 25 (1890): 145–268.

Buchberger, Karl, ed. "Briefe Loudon's: Beiträge zur Charakteristik Loudon's und der Geschichte des Siebenjährigen Krieges." *Archiv für österreichische Geschichte* 48 (1872): 377–420.

Bührmann, Inge, ed. *Tagebuch des letzteren Krieges von 1756 bis 1762: Insbesondere des Leib-Regiments und übrigen Hochlöbl. Truppen Sr. Durchlaucht des Regierenden Grafen zu Schaumburg-Lippe/ aufgezeichnet von Jos, Daniel Merckel, damaligen Feldprediger bei dem Hochlöblichen Schaumb.-Lippe Leib Regiment, jetzigen Prediger zu Hagenburg*. Hagenburg, 2013.

Bünau, Heinrich von. *Detail De La Guerre oder Umstaendliche Historie Des Krieges zwischen den Cronen Frankreich und Engelland Und Dero Alliirten in Teutschland*. 5 vols. Ratisbonne: Bader; Leipzig: Fritsch; Frankfurt: Fleischer; Ulm: Barholomaei, 1763–1767.

Burke, William. *Remarks on the Letter Addressed to Two Great Men, in a Letter to the Author of That Piece*. Dodsley, 1760.

Buschbell, Gottfried, ed. *Das Tagebuch des Abraham ter Meer (1758–1769)*. Zelt, 1936.

Büsching, Anton Friedrich. *Beschreibung seiner Reise von Berlin über Potsdam nach Rekahn unweit Brandenburg*. 2nd ed. Frankfurt: Haude and Spener, 1780.

Butler, George Grey, ed. *A Journal of the First Two Campaigns of the Seven Years War: Written in French by Horace St. Paul*. Cambridge University Press, 1914.

Buxbaum, Emil, ed. "Das Tagebuch des Feldpredigers Balke vom Seydlitz'schen Kürassierregiment aus den Jahren 1759–1762." *Internationale Revue über die gesamten Armeen und Flotten*, Hannover, 3, no. 2 (1885): 15–22, 142–150, 251–258; 3, no. 3 (1885): 37–43, 139–146; 3, no. 4 (1885): 29–34, 126–134, 250–255; 4, no. 2 (1886): 151–165.

Cambridge, Richard Owen. *An Account of the War in India, Between the English and French, on the Coast of Coromandel, from the Year 1750 to the Year 1760*. London: Jefferys, 1761.

Caraccioli, Charles. *Life of Robert, Lord Clive*. Vol. 1. London: Bell, 1777.

Carretta, Vincent, ed. *Unchained Voices: An Anthology of Black Authors in the English-Speaking World of the Eighteenth Century*. University Press of Kentucky, 1996.

Giacomo Casanova, *History of My Life*. Everyman, 2006.

Casgrain, Henri Raymond, ed. *Collection des manuscrits du maréchal de Lévis*. 12 vols. Montreal: Beauchemin; Quebec: Demers, 1889–1895.

Casgrain, Henri Raymond, ed. *Extraits des archives des Ministères de la marine et de la guerre à Paris: Canada, Correspondance générale, MM. Duquesne et Vaudreuil, Gouverneurs-generaux, 1755–1760*. Quebec: Demers, 1890.

Casgrain, Henri Raymond, ed. *Voyage au Canada dans le nord de l'Amerique Septentrionale, fait depuis L'An 1751 a 1761 par J.C.B.* Quebec: Brousseau, 1887.

Castelnau, Louis Joseph. *Lettres du Baron de Castelnau de 1728–1793*. Champion, 1911.

Chapman, Earl John, and Ian Macpherson McCulloch, eds. *Bard of Wolfe's Army: James Thompson, Gentleman Volunteer, 1733–1830*. Robin Brass Studio, 2010.

Chapman, Earl John, and Ian Macpherson McCulloch, eds. *Dangerous Service: Memoirs of a Black Watch Officer in the French and Indian War—John Grant, 1741–1828*. Robin Brass Studio, 2017.

Cogniazo, Jacob de. *Geständnisse eines österreichischen Veterans in politisch-militärischer Hinsicht auf die interessantesten Verhältnisse zwischen Oestreich und Preußen, während der Regierung des Großen Königs der Preußen Friedrichs des Zweyten mit historischen Anmerkungen gewidmet den königlich preußischen Veteranen von dem Verfasser des freymüthigen Beytrags zur Geschichte des östreichischen Militär-Dienstes*. 4 vols. Breslau: Löwe, 1788–1791. Reprint, LTR, 1982.

Cogswell, Neil, ed. *Horace St. Paul: Journale 1756–1760*. 8 vols. Gralene, 1996–2007.

Cogswell, Neil, ed. *Lobositz to Leuthen: Horace St. Paul and the Campaigns of the Austrian Army in the Seven Years War 1756–67*. Helion, 2017.

Cormack, Andrew, and Alan Jones, eds. *The Journal of Corporal Todd 1745–1762*. Sutton, 2001.

Corneille, John. *Journal of My Service in India*. Folio Society, 1966.

Costa, Horacio de la. "The Siege and Capture of Manila by the British, September–October 1762." *Philippine Studies* 10, no. 4 (1962): 607–653.

Croÿ, Emmanuel du de. *Journal inédit du duc de Croÿ, 1718–1784*, ed. Vicomte de Grouchy and Paul Cottin. 4 vols. Flammarion, 1906–1907.

Cubbison, Douglas R. *On Campaign Against Fort Duquesne: The Braddock and Forbes Expeditions, 1755–1758, Through the Experiences of Quartermaster Sir John St. Claire*. McFarland, 2015.

Cullen, Louis, John Shovlin, and Thomas M. Truxes, eds. *The Bordeaux-Dublin Letters, 1757: Correspondence of an Irish Community Abroad*. British Academy, 2014.

Cunitius, Christian Gottlieb. *Das höchst betrübte Schicksal der in der Oberlausiz gelegenen Churfürstl. Sächsischen Sechsstadt Zittau, Bey deren am 23. Julii dieses jetzt laufenden 1757. Jahres durch die Kayserl. Königl. Armée erfolgten Einnahme [. . .]*. Zittau, [1757].

Cushner, Nicholas P., ed. *Documents Illustrating the British Conquest of Manila 1762–1763*. Royal Historical Society, 1971.

Deneke, Johann Baptist. *Begebenheiten waehrend des siebenjaehrigen Krieges in Westfalen und den angrenzenden Landesteilen, nach d. Tagebuche e. Augenzeugen, zugl. nach andern authent. Unveraend.* Stein, 1972. Originally published in 1859.

Denis, Michael. *Poetische Bilder der meisten kriegerischen Vorgänge in Europa seit dem Jahr 1756.* Augsburg: Wagner, 1768.

Derschau, Friedrich Wilhelm von. *Umständliche Nachrichten von der nahmens Sr. Kön. Majest. in Preussen den 10., 11. und 12. Merz 1763 vollzogenen Besitznehmung der clev-, mörs- und geldrischen Provinzen und von den darin vorgegangenen feyerlichen Freudensbezeugungen über den 15. Febr. b. J. zu Hubertsburg geschlossenen Frieden.* Cleve: Sitzmann, 1764.

Dietrich, Richard, ed. *Politische Testamente der Hohenzollern.* dtv, 1981.

Dittmann, Klaus. "Notizen des Pfarrers im Weiterstädter Kirchenbuch während der Schlesischen Kriege und dem 7jährigen Krieg." *Hessische Familienkunde* 27, no. 1 (2004): 39–51.

Doughty, Arthur George, and George William Parmelee, eds. *The Siege of Québec and the Battle of the Plains of Abraham.* 6 vols. Dussault & Proulx, 1901.

[Draper, William]. *Colonel Draper's Answer to the Spanish Arguments, Claiming the Galeon, and Refusing Payment of the Ransom Bills, for Preserving Manila from Pillage and Destruction.* London, 1764.

Dresemann, Otto. "Aus einer Chronik des Karthäuserklosters Vogelsang bei Jülich." *Annalen des Historischen Vereins für den Niederrhein inbesondere das Alte Erzbistum Köln* 61 (1895): 79–94.

Dreyer, Joseph Ferdinand. *Leben und Taten eines preußischen Regiments-Tambours.* Breslau: Korn, 1810. Reprint, Biblio, 1975.

Driehorst, Manfred. "Merkwürdige Begebenheiten zu Meinbrexen in dem Kriege von 1756 bis zum 31. Nov. 1762." *Sollinger Heimatblätter* 1 (2013): 9–15.

Dubois-Cattin, Dominique-Hubert-Joseph. "Correspondance du capitaine Dominique-Hubert-Joseph Dubois-Cattin pendant la Guerre de Sept–Ans." In *Soldats Suisses au Service Etranger.* Huitième Série. Jullien, 1919.

Dumouriez, Charles François. "Geschichte des portugiesischen Kriegs im Jahre 1761." *Minerva* 4 (1797): 461–476.

Edwards, Thomas Charles, and Brian Richardson, eds. *They Saw It Happen: An Anthology of Eyewitness's Accounts of Events in British History 1689–1897.* Macmillan, 1958.

Engel, Johann Jakob. *Rede zum Beschlus der auf der Bützowischen Akademie bisher angestellten Friedens-Feier in der Stadtkirche: Bützow, d. 25. Aug. 1763 gehalten von Johann Jacob Engel. Mit einer Nachbemerkung,* ed. Matthias Wehrhahn. Revonnah, 1996.

Entick, John. *The General History of the Late War: Containing It's Rise, Progress, and Event in Europe, Asia, Africa, and America [. . .].* 5 vols. London: Dilly, 1763–1764.

Olaudah Equiano, *The Interesting Narrative of the Life of Olaudah Equiano,* ed. Brycchan Carey. Oxford World Classics, 1990.

Ewald, Johann von. *Abhandlung über den kleinen Krieg*. Kassel: Cramer, 1785.

Flashar, Paul-Ulrich, ed. *Familienbuch Michaelis von Tschirschky*. Vol. 2, *Memoiren der Eleonore Juliane von Rehdiger verw. Freifrau von Lüttwitz geb. von Falkenhayn 1713– 1784; Das Tagebuch der Urahne; ein Lebensbild aus dem 18. Jahrhundert*. Self-published by Gottfried Michaelis, 1996.

Flucke, Christoph, ed. *Die litterae annuae: Die Jahresberichte der Gesellschaft Jesu aus Altona und Hamburg (1598–1781)—Zweiter Halbband: 18. Jahrhundert*. Aschendorff, 2015.

Förster, [Theodor]. "Mitteilungen eines sächsischen Feldpredigers aus dem siebenjährigen Kriege." *Beiträge zur sächsischen Kirchengeschichte* 11 (1896): 20–26.

Francke, Gotthilf August, ed. *Der Koeniglich-Daenischen Missionarien aus Ost-Indien eingesandter Ausfuehrlichen Berichte Achter Theil, Von der LXXXV bis LCVIsten Continuation: Darinnen die Fortsetzung des Missionswercks bis auf das Jahr 1761 umstaendlich beschrieben wird [. . .]*. Halle: Waysenhaus, 1765.

Franklin, Benjamin, *Autobiography*. Boston: Houghton Mifflin, 1906 [1791].

Franklin, Benjamin. *The Interest of Great Britain Considered with Regard to Her Colonies and the Acquisitions of Canada and Guadeloupe: To Which Are Added, Observations Concerning the Increase of Mankind, Peopling of Countries, Etc*. London: Becket, 1760.

Fraser, Malcolm. "The Capture of Quebec: A Manuscript Journal Relating to the Operations Before Quebec from 8th May, 1759 to 17th May, 1760." *Journal of the Society for Army Historical Research* 18 (1939): 135–168.

Frearson, Charles Walter, ed. *"To Mr. Davenport": Being Letters of Richard Davenport (1719–1760) to His Brother During Service in the 4th Troop of Horse Guards and 10th Dragoons, 1742–1760*. Gale & Polden, 1968.

Friedrich II. *Œuvres de Frédéric le Grand*. 31 vols. Berlin: Decker, 1846–1857.

Friedrich II. *Politische Correspondenz Friedrich's des Großen*, ed. Johann Gustav Droysen et al. 48 vols. Berlin: Duncker & Humblot, 1879–2015.

Friedrich II. "Political Testament" (1752), in C. A. Macartney, ed., *The Habsburg and Hohenzollern Dynasties in the Seventeenth and Eighteenth Centuries*. Harper & Row, 1970.

Friedrich der Große. *Die politischen Testamente Friedrich's des Grossen*, trans. Friedrich von Oppeln-Bronikowski. Hobbing, 1920.

Fülling, Johann Georg. *Die Isthaer Chronik des Pfarrers Johann Georg Fülling: Zur Geschichte Niederhessens im siebenjährigen Kriege*, ed. Gerhard Bätzing. Bärenreiter, 1957.

Füssel, Marian. "Stehende Söldner-Heere? Europäische Rekrutierungspraktiken im Vergleich (1648–1815)." In *Soldgeschäfte, Klientelismus, Korruption in der Frühen Neuzeit: Zum Soldunternehmertum der Familie Zurlauben im schweizerischen und europäischen Kontext*, ed. Kaspar von Greyerz, André Holstein, and Andreas Würgler. V&R Unipress, 2018.

Füssel, Marian, and Sven Petersen with the assistance of Gerald Scholz, eds. *Johann Heinrich Ludewig Grotehenn, Briefe aus dem Siebenjährigen Krieg: Lebensbeschreibung und Tagebuch*. Militärgeschichtliches Forschungsamt, 2012.

Gallup, Andrew, ed. *Memoir of a French and Indian War Soldier Jolicoeur Charles Bonin.* Heritage, 2007.

Gardiner, Richard. *An Account of the Expedition to the West Indies, Against Martinico: With the Reduction of Guadelupe, and Other the Leeward Islands, Subject to the French King, 1759.* London: Baskerville, 1759.

Gaudi, Friedrich Wilhelm Ernst. *Journal vom Siebenjährigen Kriege*, ed. Jürgen Ziechmann. Vols. 1–10. LTR, 1996–2012.

Georgi, Christian Siegismund. *Wittenbergische Klage-Geschichte.* Wittenberg: Ahlfeld and Weinmannische, 1760. Reprint, Siener, 1993.

Gibbon, Edward. *Gibbon's Journal to January 28th, 1763: My Journal I, II & III and Ephemerides.* Norton, 1929.

Gibson, Donald, ed. *A Parson in the Vale of White Horse: George Woodward's Letters from East Hendred, 1753–1761.* Sutton, 1982.

[Gilsa, Georg Ernst von und zu]. *Adliges Leben am Ausgang des Ancien Régime: Die Tagebuchaufzeichnungen (1754–1798) des Georg Ernst von und zu Gilsa*, ed. Holger Th. Gräf, Lena Haunert, and Christoph Kampmann. Hessisches Landesamt für geschichtliche Landeskunde, 2010.

Goethe, Johann Wolfgang von. *The Auto-Biography of Goethe: Truth and Poetry—From My Own Life*, transl. John Oxenford. London: Bohn, 1848.

Gorani, Giuseppe. *Mémoires de Gorani.* Gallimard, 1944.

[Gottsched, Luise]. *Briefe der Frau Louise Adelgunde Victorie Gottsched gebohren Kulmus.* 3 vols. Dresden: Harpeter, 1771–1772.

Gottsched, Luise. *"Mit Der Feder in Der Hand": Briefe aus den Jahren 1730–1762*, ed. Inka Kording. Wissenschaftliche Buchgesellschaft, 1999.

Gottwald, Gottfried. *Kurtz gefaßte Nachrichten von den Begebenheiten in Schlesien besonders zu Hirschberg von 1740 bis 1763.* Hirschberg 1763 digital file is available at https://jbc.jelenia-gora.pl/dlibra/show-content/publication/edition/10948?id=10948.

Gotzkowsky, Johann Ernst. *Geschichte eines patriotischen Kaufmanns.* 1768–1769. Reprint, Berlin: Königlichen Geheimen Ober-Hofbuchbinderei, 1873.

Gräf, Holger Th. "Vom Hirtenjungen um Grossbrit: Capitaine—George Schneider und seine Tagebuchnotizen zu den Jahren 1744–1764." *Archiv für hessische Geschichte und Altertumskunde* 73 (2015): 61–95.

Graham, John. *Extracts from the Journal of the Reverend John Graham, Chaplain of the 1st Connecticut Regiment, September 25th to October 19th 1762, at the Siege of Havana.* New York: Society of Colonial Wars in the State of New York, 1896.

Grancsay, Stephen V. *American Engraved Powder Horns: A Study Based on the J. H. Grenville Gilbert Collection.* Metropolitan Museum of Art, 1945. Exhibition catalog.

Greig, James, ed. *The Diaries of a Duchess: Extracts from the Diaries of the First Duchess of Northumberland (1716–1776).* Hodder and Stoughton, 1926.

Grenier, Fernand, ed. *Papiers contrecoeur et autres documents concernant le conflit anglo–français sur l'Ohio de 1745 à 1756.* Presses de l'Université Laval, 1952.

Griesheim, Christian Ludwig von, ed. *Verbesserte und vermehrte Auflage des Tractats: Die Stadt Hamburg in ihrem politischen, öconomischen und sittlichen Zustande.* 2 vols. Hamburg: Drese, 1760.

Gröben, Georg Dietrich von der. "Versuch von der Kriegs-Zucht." In *Kriegs-Bibliothek oder gesammelte Beyträge zur Kriegs-Wissenschaft: Erster Versuch*, ed. Georg Dietrich von der Gröben. Breslau: Korn, 1755.

Grotefend, Hermann, ed. *Der Königsleutnant Graf Thoranc in Frankfurt am Main: Aktenstücke über die Besetzung der Stadt durch die Franzosen 1759–1762.* Völcker, 1904.

Grünhagen, Colmar, ed. "Journal bey Belagerung der Vestung Schweidnitz Anno 1757." *Zeitschrift für Geschichte und Alterthum Schlesiens* 7, no. 1 (1866): 57–69.

Grünhagen, Colmar, ed. "Journal bey Belagerung der Vestung Schweidnitz Anno 1758." *Zeitschrift für Geschichte und Alterthum Schlesiens* 7, no. 2 (1866): 260–279.

Grünhagen, Colmar, and Franz Wachter, eds. *Akten des Kriegsgerichts von 1758 wegen der Kapitulation von Breslau am 24. November 1757.* Breslau: Max, 1895.

Guy, Alan J., ed. *Colonel Samuel Bagshawe and the Army of George II, 1731–1762.* Bodley Head, 1990.

Guy, Alan J. "George Durant's Journal of the Expedition to Martinique and Guadeloupe, October 1758–May 1759," in *Military Miscellany I. Manuscripts from the Seven Years War, the First and Second Sikh Wars and the First World War*, ed. Alan J. Guy, Gerard J. De Groot, and R. N. W. Thomas. Sutton, 1996.

Haasis, Hellmut G. *Spuren der Besiegten.* Vol. 2, *Von der Erhebung gegen den Absolutismus bis zu den republikanischen Freischärlern 1848/49.* Rowohlt, 1984.

Hake, Johann Conrad. *Volständige Nachricht von den Feierlichkeiten, welche in der Kaiserl. freien Reichsstadt Nordhausen wegen des Hubertsburgischen Friedens vom 15ten Februar 1763 angestellet worden sind.* Nordhausen: Cöler, 1763.

Hamilton, Charles, ed. *Braddock's Defeat: The Journal of Captain Robert Cholmley's Batman, the Journal of a British Officer [and] Halkett's Orderly Book.* University of Oklahoma Press, 1959.

Hammann, Gustav, ed. *Die Bottendorfer Chronik des Johann Daniel Geitz: Der Siebenjährige Krieg von 1756–763 im Frankenberger Land.* Evang.-Luth. Pfarramt, 1974.

Hartmann, Stefan. "Eine neue Quelle zur Schlacht von Kunersdorf." *Jahrbuch für brandenburgische Landesgeschichte* 42 (1991): 78–101.

Hartmann, Stefan. "Eine unbekannte Quelle zur Schlacht bei Zorndorf." *Zeitschrift für Ostmitteleuropa-Forschung* 34, no. 2 (1985): 176–210.

Hausmann, Elisabeth, ed. *Die Karschin: Friedrichs des Großen Volksdichterin; Ein Leben in Briefen.* Societäts-Verlag, 1933.

Hayter, Tony, ed. *An Eighteenth Century Secretary at War: The Papers of William, Viscount Barrington.* Bodley Head, 1988.

Hegel, Georg Wilhelm Friedrich. *Lectures on the Philosophy of World History*, trans. J. Sibree. Bell, 1902.

Hein, Max, ed. *Briefe Friedrichs des Großen.* Vol. 2. Hobbing, 1914.

Heinecker, Manfred, and Heiner Wajemann, eds. *Ein Leben zwischen Schule und Pfarre: Die Memoiren des Schneverdinger Pastoren Johann Christian Meier 1732–1815.* Ludwig-Harms-Haus, 2011.

Henry, Alexander. *Travels and Adventures in Canada and the Indian Territory Between the Years 1760 and 1776,* ed. James Bain. Hurtig, 1969.

Herr, Johann Daniel Gottlieb. *Wohl und Wehe der Stadt Hameln während des Krieges von 1757 bis 1763 zusammengestellt von Manfred Börsch.* Stadtarchiv, 1986.

Heydenreich, Eduard. "Ein Volkslied des Siebenjährigen Krieges." In *Archiv für Litteraturgeschichte.* Vol. 11. Leipzig: Teubner, 1882.

Hill, Samuel Charles, ed. *Indian Records Series: Bengal in 1756–1757: A Selection of Public and Private Papers Dealing with the Affairs of the British in Bengal During the Reign of Siraj-Uddaula.* 3 vols. Murray, 1905.

[Hollmann, Samuel Christian]. *Lob des Krieges: In einigen Gesprächen entwickelt.* Pt. 2. Frankfurt, 1770.

Hollmann, Samuel Christian. *Die Universität Göttingen im siebenjährigen Kriege,* ed. Alfred Schöne. Leipzig: Hirzel, 1887.

Holtze, Friedrich, ed. "Chronistische Aufzeichnungen eines Berliners von 1704 bis 1758." *Schriften des Vereins für die Geschichte Berlins* 36 (1899): 55–114.

Holwell, John Zephaniah. *A Genuine Narrative of the Deplorable Deaths of the English Gentlemen and Others Who Were Suffocated in the Black Hole.* London: Millar, 1758.

Holwell, John Zephaniah. "Zuverlässige Nachricht von den Drangsalen, so diejenigen Personen erlitten haben, welche in dem Gefängnisse, das schwarze Loch genannt, im Fort William zu Calcutta im Königreiche Bengalen eingesperret worden [. . .] aus einem Briefe von J. Z. Holwell and William Davis." *Bremisches Magazin zur Ausbreitung der Wissenschaften, Künste und Tugend* 3 (1759): 492–523.

Hoppe, [?]. "Wahrhafte Schilderung der blutigen Schlacht bei Zorndorf, von einem alten preußischen Soldaten, welcher 34 Jahr gedient und jetzt (1793) noch lebt." In *Officier-Lesebuch historisch militairischen Inhalts,* ed. Carl Daniel Küster. 3 vols. Berlin: Carl Matzdorffs Buchhandlung, 1793.

[Hotham, Charles]. *The Operations of the Allied Army Under the Command of His Serene Highness Prince Ferdinand, . . . During the Greatest Part of Six Campaigns, Beginning in the Year 1757, and Ending in the Year 1762: By an Officer, Who Served in the British Forces.* London: Jefferys, 1764.

Hülsen, Carl Wilhelm von. *Unter Friedrich dem Großen: Aus den Memoiren des Aeltervaters 1752–1773,* ed. Helene von Hülsen. Berlin, 1890. Reprint, Biblio, 1974.

Ives, Edward. *Reisen nach Indien und Persien /in einer freyen Übers. aus dem englischen Orig. geliefert, mit historisch-geographischen Anm. . . . Welcher die Reise nach Indien, und einen Theil der Zusätze des Uebersetzers enthält.* 2 vols. Leipzig: Weidmann, 1774–1775.

Ives, Edward. *A Voyage from England to India, in the Year MDCCLIV: And an Historical Narrative of the Operations of the Squadron and Army in India, [. . .].* London: Edward and Charles Dilly, 1773.

Jacobi, Christoph Gottfried. "Anmerkungen bey dem jetzigen Kriege." In *Nützliche Samlungen*. Pt. 4. 1758.

Janssen, Johannes. "Die historischen Notizen des Bürgermeisterei-Dieners Johannes Janssen." In *Beiträge und Material zur Geschichte der Aachener Patrizier-Familien*, ed. Hermann Ariovist von Fürth, vol. 3. Aachen, 1890.

Jany, Curt. "Aus den Erinnerungen eines Leibpagen des Großen Königs (Puttlitz)," *Hohenzollern-Jahrbuch* 16 (1912): 73–85.

Jessen, Hans, ed. *Friedrich der Große und Maria Theresia in Augenzeugenberichten*. Rauch, 1965.

Justi, Johann Heinrich Gottlob von. *Die Chimäre des Gleichgewichts von Europa: Eine Abhandlung, worinnen die Nichtigkeit und Ungerechtigkeit dieses zeitherigen Lehrgebäudes der Staatskunst deutlich vor Augen gelegt*. Altona: Iverson, 1758.

Justi, Johann Heinrich Gottlob von. *Deutsche Memoires, oder Sammlung verschiedener Anmerkungen, die Staatsklugheit, das Kriegswesen, die Justiz, Morale, Oeconomie, Commercium, Cammer- und Polizey-auch andere merkwürdige Sachen betreffend, welche im menschlichen Leben vorkommen, von einigen Civil- und Militairbedienten, auch von andern gelehrten und erfahrnen Personen aufgezeichnet und hinterlassen worden*. Leipzig, 1741–1744.

Justi, Johann Heinrich Gottlob von. *Gesammelte politische und Finanz-Schriften: Über wichtige Gegenstände der Staatskunst, der Kriegswissenschaften und des Kameral- und Finanzwesens*. 3 vols. Copenhagen, 1761–1764. Reprint, Scientia, 1970.

[Justi, Johann Heinrich Gottlob von]. *Wohlgemeynte Vorschläge eines die jetzigen unglücklichen Zeiten beseufzenden Menschenfreundes auf was vor Bedingungen die jetzo in Krieg befangenen Mächte zu einem dauerhaften und ihrem allerseitigen Interesse gemäßen Frieden gelangen könnten zur Aufmunterung gantz Deutschlands*. Friedensnah, 1759.

Kerler, Dietrich. *Aus dem siebenjährigen Krieg: Tagebuch des preußischen Musketiers Dominicus*. Munich: Beck, 1891. Reprint, Biblio, 1972.

Khevenhüller-Metsch, Johann Joseph. *Aus der Zeit Maria Theresias: Tagebuch des Fürsten Johann Joseph Khevenhüller-Metsch; Kaiserlichen Oberhofmeisters*, ed. Rudolf Khevenhüller-Metsch and Hanns Schlitter. 8 vols. Holzhausen. vol. 3: 1752–1755 (1910); vol. 4: 1756–1757 (1914); vol. 5: 1758–1759 (1911); vol. 6: 1764–1767 (1917).

Kiefer, Renate, and Lenelotte Möller, eds. *Die großen Reden der Indianer*. Marix, 2016.

Kimball, Gertrude Selwyn, ed. *Correspondence of William Pitt When Secretary of State with Colonial Governors and Military and Naval Commanders in America*. 2 vols. Kraus, 1906.

Kneisel, Johann Christian. *Denkwürdigkeiten der drey Belagerungen Colbergs durch die Russen in den Jahren 1758, 1760 und 1761*. Frankfurt, 1763.

Kneisel, Johann Christian. *Denkwürdigkeiten der zweyten Rußischen Belagerung von Colberg im Jahr 1760*. Berlin: Real-Schule, 1761.

Knesebeck, Ernst J. G. von dem, ed. *Ferdinand, Herzog zu Braunschweig u. Lüneburg, während des siebenjährigen Krieges*. 2 vols. Hanover: Helwing, 1857–1858.

Knox, John. *An Historical Journal of the Campaigns in North America: For the Years 1757, 1758, 1759 and 1760*, ed. Arthur G. Doughty. 3 vols. Champlain Society 1914 (repr. Books for Library Press, 1970).

Koch, Barthold. *Kurze Kriegsgeschichte des siebenjährigen deutschen, des achtjährigen englisch-amerikanischen, die Begebenheiten zwischen Hessen und Bückeburg nebst anderen Vorfällen in Hessen und zuletzt des französisch-russischen Krieges (1758–1815)*. Verein für hessische Geschichte und Landeskunde e.V., 2007.

Kohl, Rolf Dieter. "Ein Brief des Wiblingwerder Bauernsohnes Johann Hermann Dresel aus dem Siebenjährigen Krieg." *Der Märker* 28 (1979): 82–84.

Köhler, J.[ohann] T.[obias]. "Beschreibung des Landes Florida in dem nördlichen Amerika, welches durch den neulichen glorreichen Frieden von Spanien an Großbritannien abgetreten worden." *Hannoverisches Magazin* 27, Monday, April 4, 1763.

Köhler, J.[ohann] T.[obias]. "Beschreibung der philippinischen oder manilischen Eylande in Ostindien, besonders aber von Manila, der vornehmsten unter denselben und ihrer Hauptstadt, wie auch von dem reichen Handel, der von daraus mit den Gallionen nach Acapulco getrieben wird," *Hannoverisches Magazin* 46, Friday, June 10, 1763.

Köhler, J.[ohann] T.[obias]. "Kurze Beschreibung der von der Großbrittanischen Seemacht in America ohnlängst eroberten Inseln Grenada, St. Vincent und St. Lucia," *Hannoverische Beyträge* 52, Monday, June 28, 1762, and 53, Friday, July 2, 1762.

Könnecke, Max. "Ein Soldatenbrief aus der Zeit des siebenjährigen Krieges," *Mansfelder Blätter: Mitteilungen des Vereins für Geschichte und Altertümer der Graffschaft Mansfeld zu Eisleben* 9 (1895): 74–78.

Korobkow, Nikolai, ed. *Semiletnjaja woina: Materialy o Dejstvijach russkoj armii I flota v 1756–1762.* Voennoe Izdatel'stvo Ministerstva Vooružennych Sil Sojuza SSR, 1948.

Krauske, Otto, ed. *Preussische Staatsschriften aus der Regierungszeit König Friedrichs II*. Vol. 3, *Der Beginn des Siebenjährigen Krieges*. Berlin: Ducker, 1892.

Kriele, Johann Ludwig. *Ausführliche und zuverlässige historisch-militärische Beschreibung der Schlacht bei Kunersdorf und Frankfurt am 12ten August 1759: Mit beigefügtem genauen Situations-Plane nebst verschiedenen Nachrichten der Schicksale Frankfurts und der umliegenden Gegend in damaliger Zeit.* Berlin: Maurer, 1801. Reprint, LTR, 2001.

Kunisch, Johannes, ed. *Aufklärung und Kriegserfahrung: Klassische Zeitzeugen zum Siebenjährigen Krieg.* : Deutscher Klassiker, 1996.

Küster, Carl Daniel. *Bruchstück seines Campagnelebens im siebenjährigen Krieg.* 2nd ed. Berlin: Matzdorff, 1791. Reprint, Archiv, 1998.

Küster, Carl Daniel, ed. *Officier-Lesebuch historisch-militairischen Inhalts, mit untermischten interessanten Anekdoten.* Berlin: Matzdorff, 1793–1797. Reprint, LTR, 1988.

Lacoursière, Jacques, and Hélène Quimper, eds. *Québec ville assiégée 1759–1760: D'après les acteurs et les témoins.* Septentrion 2009.

Lalande, Joseph Jérôme Le Français de. *Journal d'un voyage en Angleterre, 1763*. 13th ed.Voltaire Foundation, 1980.

Lamontagne, Roland, ed. *Aperçu structural du Canada au XVIIIe siècle*. Leméac, 1964.

Lauriston, Jean Law de. *Mémoire sur quelques affaires de l'Empire Mogol 1756–1761*, ed. Alfred Martineau. Champion, 1913. English edition: *A Memoir of the Mughal Empire: Events of 1757–1761*. Gyan, 2018.

Lavater, Johann Caspar. *Tagebuch von der Studien- und Bildungsreise nach Deutschland 1763 und 1764*, ed. Horst Weigelt.Vandenhoeck & Ruprecht, 1997.

Lehmann, Max. "Urkundliche Beiträge zur Geschichte des Jahres 1756." *Mitteilungen des Instituts für österreichische Geschichtsforschung* 16, no. 3 (1895): 480–491.

Lehndorff, Ernst Graf von. *Aus den Tagebüchern des Grafen Lehndorff*, ed. Haug von Kuenheim. Severin and Siedler, 1982.

Lemoine, Jean, ed. *Sous Louis le Bien-aimé: Correspondance amoureuse et militaire d'un officier (Antoine-Rigobert Mopinot de la Chapotte) pendant la guerre de sept-ans 1757–1763*. Calmann-Lévy, 1905.

Lentzen, Johann Peter. *Geschichte des Kirchspiels Lank im Kriese Crefeld*. Fischeln, 1881. [Priest Jakob on the war]. Reprint, Heimatkreis Lank, 1985.

[Léry, Joseph-Gaspard Chaussegros de]. "Journal de Joseph-Gaspard Chaussegros de Léry, lieutenant des troupes, 1754–1755," *Rapport de l'archiviste de la province de Québec pour 1927–1928)*. L.-Amable Proulx, 1928.

Ligne, Charles-Joseph de, *Mélanges militaires, littéraires et sentimentaires*, vol. 1. Dresden: Walther, 1795.

Ligne, Charles Joseph de. *Mon journal de la guerre de sept ans: Textes inédits introduits, établis et annotés par Jeroom Vercruysse et Bruno Colson*. Champion, 2008.

Lindner, Ferdinand Gustav. "Eine handschriftliche Chronik von Hirschberg." In *Königliches Gymnasium zu Hirschberg*. Hirschberg 1874.

Lippert,Woldemar, ed. *Kaiserin Maria Theresia und Kurfürstin Maria Antonia von Sachsen: Briefwechsel 1747–1772; Mit einem Anhang ergänzender Briefe*. Teubner. 1908.

Loen, Johann Michael von. *Der Soldat oder Abhandlung vom Kriegs-Stand*. 3rd ed. Frankfurt: Fleischer, 1752. Originally published in 1738.

Lucier, Armand Francis, ed. *French and Indian War Notices Abstracted from Colonial Newspapers*. 5 vols. Heritage, 1999.

[Luynes, Charles Philippe d'Albert de]. *Mémoires du duc de Luynes*.Vols. 14–17. Paris: Didot, 1864–1865.

Lynar, Rochus Friedrich von. *Hinterlassene Staatsschriften und Andere Aufsätze Vermischten Inhalts*. 2 vols. Hamburg: Hoffmann, 1793–1797.

Marcus, Hans. "Friedrichs des Großen literarische Propaganda in England: Eine Sammlung bisher unveröffentlichten Archivmaterials." *Archiv für das Studium der Neueren Sprachen und Literaturen* 151, vol. 81, 3/4 (1927): 161–243.

Mastnak, Jens, and Michael-Andreas Tänzer, eds. *Celle im Siebenjährigen Krieg: Das Tagebuch des Garnisonsauditeurs Johann Philipp Schowart*. Bomann-Museum, 2010.

Matasovic, Josip, ed. *Die Briefe des Grafen [Peter Troyllus] Sermage aus dem Siebenjährigen Kriege*. Narodna Starina, 1923.

Maurès de Malartic, Anne Joseph Hippolyte. *Journal des Campagnes au Canada de 1755 à 1760 par Le comte de Maurès de Malartic, (1730–1800) publié par son arrière petit-neveu le comte Gabriel de Maurès de Malartic et par Paul Gaffarel*. Dijon: Damidot, 1890.

Mauvillon, Jakob. *Geschichte Ferdinands Herzogs von Braunschweig-Lüneburg*. Pt. 2. Leipzig: Dyk, 1794.

Mayer, Franz Martin. "Zur Geschichte des siebenjährigen Krieges." *Mitteilungen des Instituts für Österreichische Geschichtsforschung* 7 (1886): 378–435.

McCulloch, Ian, and Timothy Todish, eds. *Through So Many Dangers: The Memoirs and Adventures of Robert Kirk, Late of the Royal Highland Regiment*. Purple Mountain Press, 2004.

McDowell, William L., Jr., ed. *Colonial Records of South Carolina: Documents Relating to Indian Affairs, 1754–1765*. University of South Carolina Press, 1970.

McManus, Stuart M. "The Pacific Theater of the Seven Years' War in a Latin Poem by an Indigenous Priest, Bartolomé Saguinsín (1766)." In *The Spanish Pacific, 1521–1815: A Reader of Primary Sources*, ed. Christina Lee and Ricardo Padrón. Amsterdam University Press, 2020.

Mendelssohn, Moses. "Rhapsodie oder Zusätze zu den Briefen über die Empfindungen." In *Schriften zur Philosophie, Aesthetik und Apologetik*, ed. Moritz Brasch. Leipzig: Voss, 1880. Reprint, Olms, 1968.

Ménétra, Jacques-Louis. *Journal of My Life*, ed. Daniel Roche. Columbia University Press, 1986.

Michaelis, Johann David. *Lebensbeschreibung von ihm selbst abgefasst*. Rinteln: Barth, 1793.

[Michaelis, Johann David]. Review of "History of the Origin and Progress of the Present War," from *London Magazine* (June 1761). *Göttingische Anzeigen von gelehrten Sachen* 1 (1761/1762): 170–172.

Middleton, Richard, ed. *Amherst and the Conquest of Canada: Selected Papers from the Correspondence of Major-General Jeffrey Amherst While Commander-in-Chief in North America from September 1758 to December 1760*. Sutton, 2003.

Mohr, Erich. *Quellen zur Schlacht von Roßbach*. Moritz Diesterweg, 1937.

Möller, Johann Anton Arnold. *Special Geschichte von Lippstadt eine nunmehro geschlossene periodische Schrift unter der Rubrik alte Nachrichten von Lippstadt und deren Gegenden . . . mit sechs Kupfern*. Lippstadt: Müller, 1785–1788.

Monro, Donald. *An Account on the Diseases Which Were Most Frequent in the British Military Hospitals in Germany, from January 1761 to the Return of the Troops to England in March 1763*. London: Millar, 1764. German edition: *Beschreibung der Krankheiten, welche in den brittischen Feldlazarethen in Deutschland vom Januar 1761 bis zu der Rueckkehr der Truppen nach Engelland im Maerz 1763 am haeufigsten gewesen*. Altenburg: Richter, 1766. Reprint, Bad Honnef, 1982.

[Montag, Leopold]. ed. *Teutsche Kriegs-Canzley*. 18 vols. Frankfurt, 1757–1763.

Montalegre, Johann Daniel de. *Die vormahls in ihrem Flor stehende nunmehro aber in Ruin und Asche liegende Königl. Pohlnische und Churfürstl. Sächsische Sechs-Stadt Zittau in der Ober-Lausitz*. Zittau, 1758. Reprint, Neisse, 2000.

[Montcalm, Louis Joseph de]. *Journal du marquis de Montcalm Durant ses campagnes au Canada de 1756 à 1759, Québec 1895.*"Vol. 7 of *Collection des manuscrits du maréchal de Lévis*, ed. Henri Raymond Casgrain. 12 vols. Montreal: Beauchemin (vols. 1–2); Quebec: Demers (vols. 3–12), 1889–1895.

Moore, Charles, ed. *The Gladwin Manuscripts*. Lansing: Robert Smith, 1897.

Moreau, Jacob Nicolas, ed. *Mémoire contenant le Precis des faits, avec leurs pieces justificatives, Pour server de Réponse aux Observations envoyées par les Minstres d'Angleterre dans les Cours de l'Europe*. Paris: Imprimerie royale, 1756.

Moreau, Jacob Nicolas, ed. *L' observateur hollandois [. . .]*. The Hague: François, 1755.

Mücke, Marion, and Thomas Schnalke, eds. *Briefnetz Leopoldina: Die Korrespondenz der Deutschen Akademie der Naturforscher um 1700*. De Gruyter, 2009.

Mühlenberg, Heinrich Melchior. *The Correspondence of Heinrich Melchior Mühlenberg*. Vol. 3, *1753–1756*; Vol. 4, *1757–1762*, ed. Timothy J. Wengert and Wolfgang Splitter. Picton, 2009–2010.

Müller, Johann Christian. *Meines Lebens Vorfälle und Neben-Umstände*. Pt. 3, *Pastor in Stralsund (1755–1766)*, ed. Katrin Löffler. Lehmstedt, 2020.

Müller-Brauel, Hans. "Alte niedersächsische Feldbriefe," *Niedersachsen* 20, no. 9 (1914–1915): 140–142.

Münchhausen, Otto Freiherr von. *Der Hausvater*. Vol. 4. Hanover: Helwing, 1774.

Naudé, Albert. "Berichte des Prinzen Moritz von Anhalt-Dessau über die Schlachten bei Prag, Kolin, Roßbach, Leuthen und Zorndorf." *Forschungen zur Brandenburgischen und Preußischen Geschichte* 5 (1892): 232–245.

Naudé, Albert. "Friedrich der Große vor dem Ausbruch des Siebenjährigen Krieges," *Historische Zeitschrift* 55 (1886): 425–468 and 56 (1886): 404–462;

Naumann, Gottlob, and Karl Friedrich Wernich, eds. *Beyträge zur neuern Staats- und Kriegesgeschichte*. 19 vols. Danzig: Schuster, 1756–1764.

Navarro, Eduardo, ed. *Documentos indispensables para la verdadera historia de Filipinas*. 2 vols. Imprenta del Asilo de Huérfanos, 1908.

Nenny, Johann Conrad. *Kurtze Beschreibung der Friedens-Feierlichkeiten in den Städten Hanau, wie auch der allgemeinen Erleuchtung am 9. Merz 1763: Nebst einem Anhang vom Lande und einiger Poesien und Aufsätzen*. [Hanau-]Neustadt, [1763].

Nicolai, Friedrich. *Anekdoten von König Friedrich II. von Preußen*. 6 vols. Berlin: Nicolai, 1788–1792.

O'Callaghan, Edmund Bailey, and Berthold Fernow, eds. *Documents Relative to the Colonial History of the State of New York*. 15 vols. Albany: Weed, Parsons, 1853–1887.

Ochwadt, Curd, ed. *Wilhelm Graf zu Schaumburg-Lippe: Schriften und Briefe*. 3 vols. Klostermann, 1976–1983.

Oldach, Robert, ed. *Schwedens Beteiligung am Siebenjährigen Krieg im Spiegel des Tageregisters der Stadt Loitz 1757–1759*. Ernst-Moritz-Arndt-Universität Greifswald, 2014.

Oldach, Robert. *Schwedens Krieg gegen Friedrich den Großen 1757–1762: Kriegsgegner berichten*. LIT, 2023.

Orme, Robert. *A History of the Military Transactions of the British Nation in Indostan, from the Year 1745 to Which Is Prefixed a Dissertation on the Establishments Made by Mahomedan Conquerors in Indostan*. London: Nourse, 1763.

Ortmann, Adolph Dietrich. *Patriotische Briefe zur Vermahnung und zum Troste bey dem jetzigen Kriege*. 3 pts. Berlin: Voß, 1758.

Osten, Wilhelm August von der, ed. *Feldzüge der alliierten Armee in den Jahren 1757 bis 1762 nach dem Tagebuche des Generaldjutanten, nachmaligen Feldmarschalls von Reden*. Hamburg: Hoffmann, 1805–1806. Reprint, LTR, 2005.

Oughton, James Adolphus. *. . . By Dint of Labour and Perseverance . . .: A Journal Recording Two Months in Northern Germany Kept by Lieutenant Colonel James Adolphus Oughton, Commanding 1st Battalion, 37th Regiment of Foot, 1758*, transcribed by Stephen Wood. Special Pub. no. 14. Society for Army Historical Research, 1997.

Pannenborg, Albert. *Des Göttinger Universitäts-Professors und Gymnasial-Direktors Rudolf Wedekind Tagregister von dem gegenwärtigen Kriege: Als Beitrag zur Geschichte Göttingens im siebenjährigen Kriege*. Göttingen: Dietrich, 1896.

Pargellis, Stanley McCrory, ed. *Military Affairs in North America, 1748–1765: Selected Documents from the Cumberland (William Augustus, Duke of) Papers in Windsor Castle*. Archon, 1969.

Pastenaci, Friedrich. "Fragmente aus dem Tagebuch des Hospital Predigers Pastenaci über die im Jahr 1757 vorgefallene Invasion des russischen Heeres ins Königreich Preußen, die Stadt Gumbinen betreffend." *Neue preußische provinzial Blätter*. Vol. 11. Königsberg, 1866.

Pauli, Carl Friedrich. *Leben grosser Helden des gegenwärtigen Krieges*. 9 vols. Halle: Francke, 1758–1764.

Petrone, Penny, ed. *First People, First Voices*. University of Toronto Press, 1984.

Philippi, Friedrich. "Gleichzeitige Aufzeichnungen über die Belagerung Münsters durch die Alliierten 1759." *Zeitschrift für vaterländische Geschichte und Altherthumskunde* 61 (1903): 23–51.

[Pleißner, Johann Georg]. *Ausführlicher und wahrhafter Bericht von dem Feldzuge und Kriegshändeln welche zwischen der Reichs-Executions- und Französischen combinirten Armee, imgleichen der Königl. Preußischen Kriegsmacht vorgefallen | insonderheit, was die Stadt und das Fürstenthum Gotha hiebey an Durchzügen und Einquartierungen betroffen, aus was sich bey dieser Gelegenheit merkwürdiges ereignet, in Form eines Diarii verfasset von einem in Gotha sich aufgehaltenen Passagiere*. Erfurt, 1759.

Pleißner, Johann Georg. *Kriegs-Geschichte von Thüringen von Anno 1756 bis 1763: Besonders, was unser Hertzogthum Residentz Stadt Gotha dabey merkwürdiges betroffen als ein Diarium verfasset* (handwritten manuscript). Gotha Forschungsbibliothek, Chart. B Nr. 1127, 1763.

Pleschinski, Hans, ed. *Nie war es herrlicher zu leben: Das geheime Tagebuch des Herzogs von Croÿ 1718–1784.* Beck, 2011.

Pommerin, Reiner, and Lothar Schilling. "Denkschrift des Grafen Kaunitz zur mächtepolitischen Konstellation nach dem Aachener Frieden von 1748," in *Expansion und Gleichgewicht: Studien zur europäischen Mächtepolitik des Ancien Régime*, ed. Johannes Kunisch. Duncker & Humblot, 1986.

Poniatowski, August. *Die Memoiren des Letzten Königs von Polen Stanislaw August Poniatowski.* Vol. 1. Müller, 1917.

Porter, John. "An Account by an Eye-Witness of the Expedition Against St. Malo in May and June, 1758." *Royal United Services Institute Journal* 58 (1914): 755–763.

Pouchot, Pierre. *Memoires sur la derniere guerre de l'Amerique septentrionale, entre la France et l'Angleterre.* 3 vols. Yverdon, 1781.

[Pratje, Johann Hinrich]. "Nachricht von der Insel Goree, und von dem derselben abhängenden Handel." *Hannoverische Beyträge* 36, Friday, May 4, 1759.

Pratje, J.[ohann] H.[inrich]. "Nachricht von Kap-Breton und Louisbourg, und von dem Stockfischfange daselbst." In *Nützliche Samlungen* 1758.

Price, John Frederic, and Henry Dodwell, eds. *The Private Diary of Ananda Ranga Pillai, Dubash to Joseph François Dupleix . . . : A Record of Matters Political, Historical, Social, and Personal from 1736 to 1761.* 12 vols. Government Press of Madras, 1904–1928.

Pringle, John. *Beobachtungen über die Krankheiten der Armee.* Altenburg: Richter 1772. English edition, 1752.

Pringle, John. *Observations on the Diseases of the Army by Sir John Pringle, Baronet, President of the Royal Society, and Physician to Their Majesties.* 6th ed., corrected. London: Millar, Cadell, Wilson, Durham, and Payne, 1768. [Online edition].

Prittwitz, Christian Wilhelm von. *"Ich bin ein Preuße . . .": Jugend und Kriegsleben eines preußischen Offiziers im Siebenjährigen Krieg.* Hüttemann, 1989.

Puiseux, M. Abbé. "M. de Prilly: Un soldat de la guerre de Sept ans. D'après ses lettres." *Memoires de la Société d'Agriculture, Commerce, Science et Arts du Departement de la Marne,* January 1888, 37–51.

Raffle, William, ed. *Glories to Useless Heroism: The Seven Years War in North America from the French Journals of Comte Maurès de Malartic, 1755–1760.* Helion, 2017.

Raschke, Bärbel, ed. *Der Briefwechsel zwischen Luise Dorothée von Sachsen-Gotha und Voltaire (1751–1767).* Leipzig University Press, 1998.

Raynal, Guillaume-Thomas. *Histoire philosophique et politique des établissemens & du commerce des les deux Indes.* Vol. 6. Amsterdam, 1770. German edition: *Philosophische und politische Geschichte der europäischen Handlung und Pflanzörter in beiden Indien* Vol. 7. Copenhagen: Heineck and Faber, 1778.

[Resmi, Ahmed]. *Des Türkischen Gesandten Resmi Ahmet Efendi Gesandtschaftliche Berichte von seinen Gesandtschaften in Wien im Jahre 1757, und in Berlin im Jahre 1763.* Berlin: Nicolai, 1809.

Retzow, Friedrich August von. *Charakteristik der wichtigsten Ereignisse des Siebenjährigen Krieges.* 2 vols. Berlin: Himburg, 1802.

Richmond, Herbert W., ed. *Papers Relating to the Loss of "Minorca" in 1756.* Navy Records Society, 1913.

[Richter, Christoph Gottlieb]. *Die Historie des Kriegs zwischen den Preussen und ihren Bundsgenossen und den Österreichern und ihren Bundsgenossen von dem Einfalle in Sachsen an bis zu dem Friedensschlusse zu Hubertusburg von R. Simeon Ben Jochai.* 6 vols. Nürnberg, 1758–1763.

Ridpath, George. *The Diary of George Ridpath of Stitchel, 1755–1761*, ed. Sir James Balfour Paul. Edinburgh University Press, 1922.

Robertson, Archibald. *His Diaries and Sketches in America 1762–1780*, ed. Harry Miller Lydenberg. New York Public Library, 1930.

Rodríguez, Amalia A., and Mercedes Muriedas, eds. *Cinco diarios del sitio de la Habana.* Departamento de Colección Cubana, 1963.

Ropartz, Sigismond, ed. *Saint-Cast: Recueil de pièces officielles et de documents contemporains relatifs au combat du 11 septembre 1758.* Saint-Brieuc: Prud'homme, 1858.

Roques de Maumont, Jacques Emmanuel. *Briefe an einen Freund während des Aufenthalts der französischen Truppen in Zelle, in den Jahren 1757 und 1758: Aus dem Französischen übersetzt.* Braunschweig: Waysenhaus, 1780.

[Saint-Germain, Claude-Louis de]. *Correspondance particulière du Comte de Saint-Germain avec M. Paris Du Verney.* 2 vols. London: Buisson, 1789.

Schaefer, Arnold. "Urkundliche Beiträge zur Geschichte des siebenjährigen Krieges." *Forschungen zur deutschen Geschichte* 17 (1877): 1–106.

Scheffner, Johann Georg. *Mein Leben, wie ich Johann Georg Scheffner es selbst beschrieben.* Königsberg: Universitäts-Buchhandlung, 1821.

Schell, O. "Elberfelder Chronik des 7jährigen Krieges." *Monatsschrift des Bergischen Geschichtsvereins* 11 (1904): 70–84.

Schiller, Johann Caspar. *Meine Lebensgeschichte.* Schillerverein, 1993.

Schlechte, Horst, ed. *Das geheime politische Tagebuch des Kurprinzen Friedrich Christian 1751 bis 1757.* Böhlau, 1992.

Schlechte, Horst, ed. *Die Staatsreform in Kursachsen 1762–1763: Quellen zum kursächsischen Rétablissement nach dem Siebenjährigen Krieg.* Rütten & Loening, 1958.

Schmidt, Julius, ed. "Diarium von der ersten und zweiten Belagerung der Festung Schweidnitz, was sich unter derselbigen in der Stadt und Vorstadt zugetragen: Aus einer Handschrift mitgetheilt." *Schlesische Provinzialblätter*, n.s., vol. 6 (1867): 514–526, 598–591, 645–655.

Schüddekopf, Carl, ed. *Briefwechsel zwischen Gleim und Ramler.* 2 vols. Litterarischer Verein, 1907.

Schüddekopf, Carl, ed. *Briefwechsel zwischen Gleim und Uz.* Tübingen: Litterarischer Verein, 1899.

Schulte, Eduard. "Aus Westfälischen Feldpostbriefen des Siebenjährigen Krieges." *Westfalen* 9 (1918): 85–91.

Schultz, Helga, ed. *Der Roggenpreis und die Kriege des großen Königs: Chronik und Rezeptsammlung des Berliner Bäckermeisters Johann Friedrich Heyde 1740 bis 1786.* Siedler, 1988.

Schulze, Johann Michael Friedrich. *Von dem Gebrauch der Geschichtskarte des siebenjährigen Krieges.* Berlin: Himburg, 1792.

Schumann, Hans, ed. *Friedrich der Grosse Mein lieber Marquis! Sein Briefwechsel mit Jean-Baptiste d'Argens während des Siebenjährigen Krieges.* 2nd ed. Manesse, 1986.

Schüßler, Willy, ed. *Friedrich der Große: Gespräche mit Henri de Catt.* dtv, 1981.

Schwabach, Thomas. *Die Schwieren-Chroniken aus Zons: Bemerkenswertes aus einer niederrheinischen Kleinstadt und ihrer Umgebung 1733–1823.* Kreisheimatbund Neuss e.V., 2005.

Schwabe, Johann Joachim. *Allgemeine Historie der Reisen zu Wasser und zu Lande: Oder Sammlung aller Reisebeschreibungen [. . .].* 21 vols. Leipzig: Arkstee, Merkus, 1747–1774.

Shannon, Timothy J. *The Seven Years' War in North America: A Brief History with Documents.* St. Martin's, 2014.

Shaw, Edward P., ed. "An Episode in the Seven Years' War: A Memoir of Jacques Cazotte Concerning the Capture of Guadeloupe by the English." *Hispanic American Historical Review* 28, no. 3 (1948): 389–393.

Simmons, Richard C., and Peter David Garner Thomas, eds. *Proceedings and Debates of the British Parliaments Respecting North America, 1754–1783.* 6 vols. Kraus, 1982–1987.

Smith, William James, ed. *The Grenville Papers: Being the Correspondence of Richard Grenville Earl Temple K. G. and the Right. Hon. George Grenville, Their Friends and Contemporaries [. . .].* 4 vols. London: Murray, 1852.

Sommeregger, Major. "Die Schlacht von Prag im Jahre 1757: Nach den Erinnerungen eines Augenzeugen." *Mitteilungen des k.u.k. Kriegs-Archivs* 7 (1911): 1–22.

Sothen, Johann Philipp von. "Begebenheiten, die sich in und bei Duderstadt während des Krieges von Anno 1757 bis 1763 zugetragen haben, mitgetheilt von Johann Wolf." *Neues vaterländisches Archiv oder Beiträge zur allseitigen Kenntniß des Königreichs Hannover und des Herzogthums Braunschweig,* 2 (1831), 293–339 and 3 (1831), 62–103.

Spannagel, Carl. "Barmen im siebenjährigen Krieg: Eine Beckmannsche Chronik." *Zeitschrift des Bergischen Geschichtsvereins* 26 (1890): 85–212.

Spavens, William. *Memoirs of a Seafaring Life: The Narrative of William Spavens, Pensioner on the Naval Chest at Chatham,* ed. Nicholas Andrew Martin Rodger. Folio Society, 2000.

Stobo, Robert. *Memoirs of Major Robert Stobo, of the Virginia Regiment.* Pittsburgh: Skirven, 1854.

Syrett, David, ed. *The Rodney Papers: Selections from the Correspondence of Admiral Lord Rodney*. Vol. 1, *1742–1763*. Ashgate, 2005.

Syrett, David, ed. *The Siege and Capture of Havana 1762*. Navy Records Society, 1970.

[Täge, Christian]. *Christian Täge's ehemaligen russischen Feldpredigers Lebensgeschichte, herausgegeben vom Verfasser der Novellen von Doro Caro [i.e. August Samuel Gerber]*, Königsberg: Göbbels and Unzer, 1804. Partial English translation: "Pastor Täge's Account of the Siege of Cüstrin and the Battle of Zorndorf, 1758." In *The Changing Face of Old Regime Warfare: Essays in Honour of Christopher Duffy*, ed. Alexander S. Burns. Helion, 2022.

Targe, Jean-Baptiste. *Histoire d'Angleterre depuis le Traité d'Aix-la-Chapelle en 1748, jusqu'au Traité de Paris en 1763: Pour servir de continuation aux histoires de MM Smollett et Hume*. 5 vols. London: Desaint, 1768.

Teggers, Heribert, ed. "Der 7jährige Krieg im Klevischen: Aus dem Tagebuch eines Gocher Schlossermeisters." In *Heimatkalender für das Klever Land*. 1958.

Tempelhof, Georg Friedrich von. *Geschichte des siebenjährigen Krieges in Deutschland zwischen dem Könige von Preußen und der Kaiserin Königin mit ihren Alliierten*. 6 vols. Berlin: Unger, 1783–1801. Reprint, Bibliotheca Rerum Militarium XXIX, 1986.

Thwaites, Reuben Gold, ed. *The Jesuit Relations and Allied Documents*. Vol. 70, *All Missions: 1747–1764*, and Vol. 71, *Lower Canada, Illinois: 1759–1791—Miscellaneous Errata*. Pageant, 1959.

Tielcke, Johann Gottlieb. *Beiträge zur Kriegskunst und Geschichte des Krieges von 1756 bis 1763*. 6 vols. Freyberg: Barthel, 1775–1786.

Tiemann, Hermann, ed. *Meta Klopstock geborene Moller: Briefwechsel mit Klopstock ihren Verwandten und Freunden*. 3 vols. Maximilai-Gesellschaft, 1956.

Tory, John. *A Journal of the Allied Army's Marches from the First Arrival of the British Troops, in Germany, to the Present Time: With an Accurate Account of All the Paricular [sic] Battles and Skirmishes They Have Had with the French Army*. Osnabrück: Kisling, 1762.

Trautschen, Hans Carl Heinrich von. *Militärische und literarische Briefe des Herrn von T.: Die Feldzüge von 1756 bis 1763 betreffend*. Leipzig: Jacobäer, 1769.

Uhlmann, Markus. *Das abwechselnde Fortün oder das veränderte Schicksal eines Jünglingen: Ein Reisebericht aus der Zeit des Siebenjährigen Krieges*, ed. Jean-Pierre Bodmer. Schulthess, 1980.

Vaisey, David, ed. *The Diary of Thomas Turner 1754–1765*. Oxford University Press, 1985.

Van Meegen, ed. "Bericht des Camper Mönches A. Conrad Brands, Pfarrers in Camp und seit 1761 in Rheinberg über die Kriegsereignisse in Camp in den Jahren 1758 und 1760." *Der Niederrhein: Wochenblatt für niederrheinische Geschichte und Althertumskunde*, no. 38, September 21, 1878, 149–150, and no. 39, September 28, 1878, 154–155.

Van Meegen, ed. "Zweiter Bericht eines damaligen Camper Mönches über die Schlacht im Camperbruch." *Der Niederrhein. Wochenblatt für niederrheinische Geschichte und Althertumskunde*, no. 42, October 19, 1878, 165–166, 174.

Vattel, Emer de. *Völkerrecht; oder: Gründliche Anweisung wie die Grundsätze des natürlichen Rechts auf das Betragen und auf die Angelegenheiten der Nationen und Souveräne angewendet werden müssen*. 3 vols. Frankfurt: Schulin, 1760.

Vogel, Werner, ed. *Die Blutbibel des Friedrich Freiherr von der Trenck (1727–1794)*. Böhlau, 2014.

Voigtländer, Lutz. *Vom Leben und Überleben in Gefangenschaft: Selbstzeugnisse von Kriegsgefangenen 1757 bis 1814*. Rombach, 2005.

Voltaire. *Candide or, Optimism: The Robert M. Adams Translation, Backgrounds, Criticism*. 3rd ed. Norton, 2016.

Voltaire, *Philosophical Dictionary*. Tr. Theodore Bestermann. Penguin, 1979.

Voltaire, *A Pocket Philosophical Dictionary*, Tr. John Fletcher. Penguin, 2011.

Volz, Gustav Berthold. *Friedrich der Große im Spiegel seiner Zeit*. Vol. 2, *Siebenjähriger Krieg*. Hobbing, 1927.

Volz, Gustav Berthold, ed. *Friedrich der Große und Wilhelmine von Baireuth*. Vol. 2, *Briefe der Königszeit: 1740–1758*. Koehler, 1926.

Volz, Gustav Berthold, ed. *Die Werke Friedrichs des Großen*. 10 vols. Hobbing, 1913–1914.

Volz, Gustav Berthold, and Georg Küntzel, eds. *Preussische und Österreichische Acten zur Vorgeschichte des siebenjährigen Krieges*. Leipzig: Hirzel, 1899.

Wagner, Joh. Franz. "Nachricht von Quebek." *Hannoverische Beyträge* 6, Monday, January 21, 1760.

Wagner, Johann Ludwig. *Schicksale während seiner unter den Russen erlittenen Staatsgefangenschaft in den Jahren 1759 bis 1763: Im Anhange einige Auszüge aus den besten Reisebeschreibungen über diese Länder, nebst eignen Bemerkungen*. Berlin: Maurer, 1789.

Wähner, Andreas Georg. *Tagebuch aus dem Siebenjährigen Krieg*, ed. Sigrid Dahmen. Universitätsverlag Göttingen, 2012.

Walpole, Horace. *The Yale Edition of Horace Walpole's Correspondence*, ed. Wilmarth Sheldon Lewis. 48 vols. Yale University Press, 1937–1983.

Walter, Friedrich, ed. *Maria Theresia: Briefe und Aktenstücke in Auswahl*. 2nd ed. Wissenschaftliche Buchgesellschaft, 1982.

Walz, Reinhard. "Kriegs- und Friedensbilder aus den Jahren 1754–1759: Nach dem Tagebuch des Leutnants Jakob F. von Lemcke." *Preußische Jahrbücher* 138 (1909): 19–43.

[Warnery, Charles Emmanuel]. *Des Herrn Generalmajor von Warnery sämtliche Schriften*, ed. Gerhard J. D. von Scharnhorst. 9 vols. Hanover: Helwing, 1785–1791.

Washington, George. *The Diaries of George Washington 1748–1799*. Vol. 1, *1748–1770*, ed. John C. Fitzpatrick. Mifflin, 1925.

Wegener, Carl Friedrich. *Der Christ in Kriegszeiten*. Berlin: Birnstiel, 1758 [1759].

Westphalen, Ferdinand von, ed. *Geschichte der Feldzüge Herzog Ferdinands von Braunschweig-Lüneburg*. 5 vols. Berlin: Verl. d. Königl. Geheimen Ober-Hofbuchdr., 1859–1872.

Weymarn, Hans Heinrich von. *Über den ersten Feldzug des Russischen Kriegsheeres gegen die Preußen im Jahr 1757: Aus Archivalnachrichten, welche der unlängst verstorbene Russ. Kaiserl. General en Chef und Ritter Herr Hans Heinrich von Weymarn, auf erhaltenen Befehl der Kaiserlichen Conferenz zu St. Petersburg 1758 überreicht hat*, ed. August Wilhelm Hupel. Riga: Hartknoch, 1794.

Whinyates, Francis Arthur, ed. *The Services of Lieut.-Colonel Francis Downman, R. A. in France, North America, and the West Indies Between the Years 1758 and 1784*. Woolwich: Royal Artillery Institution, 1898.

[Whitefield, George]. *Russian Cruelty: Being the Substance of Several Letters from Sundry Clergymen in the New-Marck of Brandenburgh*. London, 1760.

Whitworth, Rex, ed. *The Diary of James Wood R. A. 1746–1765*. Cooper, 1988.

Wiarda, Tileman Dothias. *Ostfriesische Geschichte*. Vol. 9. Aurich: Winter, 1798.

Wilke, Jürgen. "'Umstände Nachricht von dem Ueberfall der Königl. Residentz, Berlin von Rußisch Kaiserl. Truppen unter dem Commando He. Generals und Graffen von Totleben': Probst Süßmilch schildert seine Erlebnisse im Herbst 1760." In *Berlin in Geschichte und Gegenwart: Jahrbuch des Landesarchivs Berlin*. Siedler, 1990.

Wilson, Charles Robert, ed. *Indian Record Series: Old Fort William in Bengal; A Selection of Official Documents Dealing with Its History*. 2 vols. Murray, 1906.

Wolfe, James. *The Life and Letters of James Wolfe*, ed. Beckless Willson. Heinemann, 1909.

Woodforde, James. *The Diary of a Country Parson 1758–1802*, ed. John Beresford. Canterbury Press, 1999.

Yorke, Philip Chesney, ed. *The Life and Correspondence of Philip Yorke, Earl of Hardwicke, Lord High Chancellor of Great Britain*. 3 vols. Cambridge University Press, 1913.

Zaide, Gregorio, ed. *Documentary Sources of Philippine History*. National Book Store, 1990.

Zander, Christian F., ed. *Fundstücke: Dokumente und Briefe einer preußischen Bauernfamilie (1747–1953)*. Kovač, 2015.

[Zellmann, Johann Philipp]. *Aus schwerer Zeit: Tagebuch des Johann Philipp Zellmann zu Herzberg am Harz aus der Zeit des siebenjährigen Krieges*. Angerstein, 1900.

Zinzendorf, Karl Graf von. *Aus den Jugendtagebüchern 1747, 1752 bis 1763*, ed. Maria Breunlich and Marieluise Mader. Böhlau, 1997.

Secondary Sources

Abell, Francis. *Prisoners of War in Britain, 1756 to 1815: A Record of Their Lives, Their Romance and Their Sufferings*. Oxford University Press, 1914.

Adam, Wolfgang, and Holger Dainat, eds. *"Krieg ist mein Lied": Der Siebenjährige Krieg in den zeitgenössischen Medien*. Wallstein, 2007.

Agostini, Thomas. "'Deserted His Majesty's Service': Military Runaways, the British-American Press, and the Problem of Desertion During the Seven Years' War." *Journal of Social History* 40, no. 4 (2007): 957–985.

Aksan, Virginia H. "The Ottoman Absence from the Battlefields of the Seven Years' War." In Danley and Speelman, *The Seven Years' War*.

Aksan, Virginia H. *An Ottoman Statesman in War and Peace: Ahmed Resmi Efendi, 1700–1783*. Brill, 1995.

Amann, Friedrich. *Die Schlacht bei Prag am 6. Mai 1757: Quellenkritische Untersuchungen*. Heidelberg: Petters, 1887.

Anderson, Fred. *Crucible of War: The Seven Years' War and the Fate of the Empire in British North America, 1754–1766*. Knopf, 2000.

Anderson, Fred. "The Peace of Paris, 1763." In *The Making of Peace: Rulers, States, and the Aftermath of War*, ed. Williamson Murray and James Lacey. Cambridge University Press, 2009.

Anderson, Fred. "1759—Year of Decision?" In De Bruyn and Regan, *The Culture of the Seven Years War*.

Anderson, Fred. *The War That Made America: A Short History of the French and Indian War*. Viking, 2005.

Anderson, Jocelyn. "Views of Political Geography in the Seven Years' War: Military Artists' Prints and British Consumers." *Oxford Art Journal* 41, no. 1 (2018): 19–38.

Andreas, Willy. "Friedrich der Große, der Siebenjährige Krieg und der Hubertusburger Friede," *Historische Zeitschrift* 158 (1938): 263–307.

Angermann, Gertrud. "'Friedenstücher' und Friedensfeiern zum Ende des siebenjährigen Krieges (1756–1763)." *Westfalen* 77 (1999): 299–337.

Anklam, Ewa. "Siebenjähriger Krieg." In *Frankreich und Deutschland im Krieg (18.-20. Jahrhundert): Zur Kulturgeschichte der europäischen "Erbfeindschaft" (chronologische Darstellung)*, ed. Ute Daniel, et al. Technische Universität Braunschweig, 2004.

Anklam, Ewa. *Wissen nach Augenmaß: Militärische Beobachtung und Berichterstattung im Siebenjährigen Kriege*. LIT, 2007.

Anonymous. *Geschichte des preußisch-schwedischen Krieges in Pommern, der Mark und Mecklenburg 1757–1762: Zugleich als Beitrag zur Geschichte des siebenjährigen Krieges; Nach gleichzeitigen Preußischen und schwedischen Berichten*. Berlin: Mittler, 1858.

Anonymous. "Ueber das Verpflegungswesen im siebenjährigen Kriege: Seine historische Entwicklung und seine Ausübung in der Praxis." *Jahrbücher für die deutsche Armee und Marine* 12 (1874): 33–55.

Appolis, Emile. "Les motifs idéologiques du Pacte de Famille." *Revue d'histoire diplomatique* 75 (1961): 341–350.

Arneth, Alfred Ritter von. *Geschichte Maria Theresias*. Vols. 5 and 6, *Maria Theresia und der siebenjährige Krieg, 1756–1763*. Vienna: Braumüller, 1875.

Arnold. "Schwedens Teilnahme am siebenjährigen Kriege." *Beihefte zum Militärwochenblatt* 12 (1908): 453–482.

Åselius, Gunnar. "Sweden and the Pommeranian War." In Danley and Speelman, *The Seven Years' War*.

Atkinson, C. T. "British Strategy and Battles in the Westphalian Campaigns of 1758–1762." *Royal United Service Institution Journal* 74 (1934): 733–740.

Axtell, James, and William C. Sturtevant. "The Unkindest Cut, or Who Invented Scalping." *William and Mary Quarterly* 37 (1980): 451–472.

Babits, Lawrence Edward, and Stephanie Gandulla, eds. *The Archaeology of French and Indian War Frontier Forts*. University Press of Florida, 2014.

Baldry, Wilfred Yorke, ed. "The Expedition Against Martinique, 1762." *Journal of the Society for Army Historical Research* 1 (1921): 244–245.

Banaschik-Ehl, Christa. *Scharnhorsts Lehrer, Graf Wilhelm von Schaumburg-Lippe in Portugal: Die Heeresreform, 1761–1777*. Biblio, 1974.

Bangert, Dieter Ernst. *Die Russisch-Österreichische Militärische Zusammenarbeit im Siebenjährigen Kriege in den Jahren 1758–59*. Boldt, 1971.

Banks, Kenneth. *Chasing Empire Across the Sea: Communications and the State in the French Atlantic, 1713–1763*. McGill-Queen's University Press, 2002.

Bannicke, Elke. "Die Wiederherstellung der allgemeinen Glückseligkeit: Kolin und Leuthen—zwei Medaillen von 1757." *Numismatisches Nachrichtenblatt* 61, no. 9 (2012): 360–365.

Barber, Noel. *The Black Hole of Calcutta: A Reconstruction*. Collins, 1965.

Barrento, António. *Guerra Fantástica: The Portuguese Army and the Seven Years War*. Helion, 2020.

Barrento, António. *Guerra Fantástica, 1762: Portugal, o Conde de Lippe e a Guerra dos Sete Anos*. Tribuna, 2006.

Barthélemy, Edouard-Marie. "La Traité des Paris entre la France et l'Angleterre (1763)." *Revue des questions historiques* 43 (1888): 420–488.

Bartlett Hornor, Elizabeth. "Besieged: British-American Forts, Families, and Communities in the Seven Years' War, 1755–1763." Diss., Stony Brook University, 2011.

Baugh, Daniel A. *The Global Seven Years War, 1754–1763: Britain and France in a Great Power Contest*. Pearson, 2011.

Baugh, Daniel A. "Great Britain's Blue Water Policy, 1689–1815." *International History Review* 10, no. 1 (1988): 35–58.

Baugh, Daniel A. "Withdrawing from Europe: Anglo-French Maritime Geopolitics, ca. 1750–1800." *International History Review* 20 (1998): 1–32.

Baumgart, Peter. "Schlesien als eigenständige Provinz im altpreussischen Staat (1740–1806)." In *Schlesien*, ed. Norbert Conrads. Siedler, 1994.

Baumgart, Peter, and Ulrich Schmilewski, eds. *Kontinuität und Wandel: Schlesien zwischen Österreich und Preussen*. Thorbecke, 1990.

Baumgart, Winfried. "Der Ausbruch des Siebenjährigen Krieges: Zum gegenwärtigen Forschungsstand." *Militärgeschichtliche Mitteilungen* 11 (1972): 157–165.

Beattie, Daniel J. "The Adaptation of the British Army to Wilderness Warfare, 1755–1763." In *Adapting to Conditions: War and Society in the Eighteenth Century*, ed. Maarten Ultee. University of Alabama Press, 1986.

Beaulieu, Alain. "Under His Majesty's Protection: The Meaning of the Conquest for the Aboriginal Peoples of Canada." In De Bruyn and Regan, *The Culture of the Seven Years War*.

Beaulieu-Marconnay, Carl Freiherr von. *Der Hubertusburger Friede: Nach archivalischen Quellen*. Leipzig: Hirzel, 1871.

Beauman, Fran. *The Pineapple: King of Fruits*. Chatto & Windus, 2005.

Becker, Konstantin. "Von Kurkölns Beziehungen zu Frankreich und seiner wirtschaftlichen Lage im Siebenjährigen Krieg 1757–1761." *Annalen des Historischen Vereins für den Niederrhein* 100 (1917): 43–119.

Beckers, Christina, Dagmar Freist, and Lucas Haasis. "Die Prizepapers—Ein Jahrhundertfund." Prize Papers Project, University of Oldenburg/UK National Archives/German Historical Institute, VZG. Accessed September 4, 2023. https://www.prizepapers.de.

Beer, Adolf. "Zur Geschichte des Jahres 1756." *Mitteilungen des Instituts für Österreichische Geschichtsforschung* 17 (1896): 109–160.

Bell, David A. *The First Total War: Napoleon's Europe and the Birth of Warfare As We Know It*. Houghton Mifflin, 2007.

Bell, David A. "Jumonville's Death: War Propaganda and National Identity in Eighteenth-Century France." In *The Age of Cultural Revolutions: Britain and France, 1750–1820*, ed. Colin Jones and Dror Wahrman. Berkeley and Los Angeles 2002: University of California Press.

Bence-Jones, Mark. *Clive of India*. Constable, 1974.

Benecke, Werner, ed. *Kunersdorf 1759, Kunowice 2009: Studien zu einer europäischen Legende, Studium pewnej europejskiej legendy*. Logos, 2010.

Benninghoven, Friedrich, Helmut Börsch-Supan, and Iselin Gundermann, eds. *Friedrich der Grosse: Ausstellung anläßlich des 200. Todestages König Friedrichs II. zu Preußen*, Geheimes Staatsarchiv Preußischer Kulturbesitz, 1986.

Bensch, Andreas. *Der Kampf um Hochkirch 1758: Ein militärhistorischer Tatsachenbericht*. 3rd ed. Bensch, 2000.

Berckefeldt, Karl von. "Wesel im siebenjährigen Kriege, insbesondere das Gefecht bei Mehr 1758 und die Belagerung Wesels 1760." *Annalen des Histoirschen Vereins für den Niederrhein* 90 (1911): 38–60.

Berger, Karl Ernst. *Hochkirch: Schicksalstage in der Oberlausitz während des siebenjährigen Krieges*. N.p., ca. 1999.

Berger, Patricia, Frank Thomas Gatter, and Hans Klusmann-Burmeister. *Ruhe süße Ruhe schwebe: Historische Friedhöfe in Nienburg*. Nienburger Stadtarchiv 1993.

Bergerhausen, Hans-Wolfgang. "Nur ein Stück Papier? Die Garantierklärungen für die österreichisch-preußischen Friedensverträge von 1742 und 1745." In *Menschen* und Strukturen in der Geschichte Alteuropas, ed. Helmut Neuhaus and Barbara Stollberg-Rilinger. Duncker & Humblot, 2002.

Beringer, Ingo. *Blutiger Karfreitag 1759: Die Schlacht bei Bergen und Vilbel*. Bad Vilbeler Verein für Geschichte und Heimatpflege, 2009.

Berkovich, Ilya. *Motivation in War: The Experience of Common Soldiers in Old-Regime Europe*. Cambridge University Press, 2017.

Bernhardi, Theodor von. *Friedrich der Große als Feldherr*. 2 vols. Berlin: Mittler, 1881.

Betz, Karl. *Der Siebenjährige Krieg in den Kirchenbüchern von Ettingshausen und Queckborn*. Heimatgeschichtliche Vereinigung Reichskirchen e.V., 1994.

Beutin, Ludwig. "Die Wirkungen des Siebenjährigen Krieges auf die Volkswirtschaft in Preußen." *Vierteljahresschrift für Sozial- und Wirtschaftsgeschichte* 26 (1933): 209–243.

Birgfeld, Johannes. *Krieg und Aufklärung: Studien zum Kriegsdiskurs in der deutschsprachigen Literatur des 18. Jahrhunderts*. 2 vols. Wehrhahn, 2012.

Birgfeld, Johannes. "Kriegspoesie für Zeitungsleser oder Der Siebenjährige Krieg aus österreichischer Sicht: Michael Denis' *Poetische Bilder der meisten kriegerischen Vorgänge in Europa seit dem Jahre 1756* im Kontext des zeitgenössischen literarischen Kriegsdiskurses." In *"Krieg ist mein Lied": Der Siebenjährige Krieg in den zeitgenössischen Medien*, ed. Wolfgang Adam and Holger Dainat. Wallstein, 2007.

Bitterauf, Theodor. *Die kurbayerische Politik im siebenjährigen Kriege*. Beck, 1901.

Black, Jeremy. "The British Expeditionary Force to Portugal in 1762: International Conflict and Military Problems." *British Historical Society of Portugal Annual Report and Review*. Vol. 16. British Historical Society of Portugal, 1989.

Black, Jeremy. *Continental Commitment: Britain, Hanover and Interventionism 1714–1793*. Routledge, 2005.

Black, Jeremy. *The English Press in the Eighteenth Century*. Croom Helm, 1987.

Blanning, Tim. *Frederick the Great: King of Prussia*, Allen Lane, 2015.

Blaufarb, Rafe. *The French Army, 1750–1820: Careers, Talent, Merit*. Manchester University Press, 2002.

Bleckwenn, Hans. "Das Laudon-Zimmer in Schloß Hainfeld." *Waffen- und Kostümkunde* 33, no. 1/2 (1991): 127–149.

Bley, Helmut, and Hans-Joachim König. "Globale Interaktion." In *Enzyklopädie der Neuzeit*. Vol. 4. Metzler, 2006.

Blitz, Hans-Martin. *Aus Liebe zum Vaterland: Die deutsche Nation im 18. Jahrhundert*. Hamburger Edition, 2000.

Böhme, Klaus-Richard. "Schwedens Teilnahme am Siebenjährigen Krieg: Innen- und außenpolitische Voraussetzungen und Rückwirkungen." In Kroener, *Europa im Zeitalter Friedrichs des Großen*.

Bohnen, Klaus. "'Was ist ein Held ohne Menschen liebe!': Zur literarischen Kriegsbewältigung in der deutschen Aufklärung." In *Lessing und die Toleranz*, ed. Peter Freimark, et al. Text und Kritik, 1986.

Bois, Jean-Pierre. *Rossbach 1757: La Prusse devient une puissance militaire.* Economica, 2021.

Bois, Jean-Pierre. "Le traité de Paris de 1763." In Fonck and Veyssière, *La Chute de la Nouvelle-France.*

Bolle, Rainer. "Der Göttinger Magistrat im Siebenjährigen Krieg." *Göttinger Jahrbuch* 38 (1990): 101–125.

Bollettino, Maria Alessandra. "Slavery, War, and Britain's Atlantic Empire: Black Soldiers, Sailors, and Rebels in the Seven Years' War." PhD diss., University of Texas, 2009.

Böning, Holger. *Periodische Presse: Kommunikation und Aufklärung; Hamburg und Altona als Beispiel.* Edition Lumière, 2002.

Borneman, Walter R. *The French and Indian War: Deciding the Fate of North America.* HarperCollins, 2006.

Borreguero Beltrán, Christina. *El reclutamientio militar por quintas en la España del siglo XVIII: Origines del servicio militar obligatorio.* Universidad de Valladolid, 1989.

Borschberg, Peter. "Chinese Merchants, Catholic Clerics and Spanish Colonists in British-Occupied Manila, 1762–1764." In *Maritime China in Transition, 1750–1850,* ed. Wang Gungwu and Ng Chin-keong. Harrassowitz, 2004.

Boscawen, Hugh. *The Capture of Louisbourg, 1758.* University of Oklahoma Press, 2011.

Bosher, John Francis. "Financing the French Navy in the Seven Years' War: Beaujon, Goosens et Compagnie in 1759." *Business History* 28 (1986): 115–133.

Bosher, John Francis. "The French Government's Motives in the Affaire du Canada, 1761–1763." *English Historical Review* 96, no. 378 (1981): 59–78.

Botein, Stephen, Jack R. Censer, and Harriet Ritvo. "The Periodical Press in Eighteenth-Century English and French Society: A Cross-Cultural Approach." *Comparative Studies in Society and History* 23, no. 3 (1981): 464–490.

Böttcher, Nikolaus, *A Ship Laden with Dollars: Britische Handelsinteressen in Kuba (1762–1825).* Vervuert, 2007.

Boulle, Pierre H. "Patterns of French Colonial Trade and the Seven Years' War." *Histoire Social* 7, no. 1 (1974): 48–86.

Boulware, Tylor. "'We Are MEN': Native American and Euroamerican Projections of Masculinity During the Seven Years' War." In *New Men: Manliness in Early America,* ed. Thomas A. Foster. New York University Press, 2011.

Bowen, Huw V. *The Business of Empire: The East India Company and Imperial Britain, 1756–1833.* Cambridge University Press, 2007.

Brändle, Fabian, et al., "Texte zwischen Erfahrung und Diskurs. Probleme der Selbstzeugnisforschung." In *Von der dargestellten Person zum erinnerten Ich: Europäische Selbstzeugnisse als historische Quelle 1500–1850,* ed. Kaspar von Greyerz, Hans Medick, and Patrice Veit. Böhlau, 2001.

Bratter, Carl Adolf. *Die preussisch-türkische Bündnispolitik Friedrichs des Grossen.* Kiepenheuer, 1915.

Braubach, Max. "Politik und Kriegführung am Niederrhein während des siebenjährigen Krieges." In *Diplomatie und geistiges Leben im 17. und 18. Jahrhundert: Gesammelte Abhandlungen.* Röhrscheid, 1969.

Brecher, Frank W. *Losing a Continent: France's North American Policy, 1753–1763.* Greenwood, 1998.

Breiholz, Mathilde. *Preußen und Dänemark während des Siebenjährigen Krieges (1756–1763).* Wachholtz, 1930.

Bremm, Klaus-Jürgen. *Preußen bewegt die Welt: Der Siebenjährige Krieg 1756–63.* Theiss, 2017.

Brewer, John. *The Sinews of Power: War, Money and the English State, 1688–1783.* Hutchinson, 1988.

Brinkman, Anna. *Balancing Strategy: Seapower, Neutrality, and Prize Law in the Seven Years' War.* Cambridge University Press, 2024.

Bronze, Jean-Yves. *Les morts de la guerre de Sept Ans au Cimetière de l'Hôpital-Général de Québec.* Presses de l'Université Laval, 2001.

Broucek, Peter. *Der Geburtstag der Monarchie: Die Schlacht bei Kolin 1757.* Österreichischer Bundesverlag, 1982.

Browning, Reed. "The Duke of Newcastle and the Financing of the Seven Years' War." *Journal of Economic History* 31, no. 2 (1971): 344–377.

Browning, Reed. "New Views on the Silesian Wars." *Journal of Military History* 69 (2005): 521–534.

Browning, Reed. *The War of the Austrian Succession.* St. Martin's, 1993.

Brumwell, Stephen. *Paths of Glory: The Life and Death of General James Wolfe.* Hambledon Continuum, 2006.

Brumwell, Stephen. *Redcoats: The British Soldier and War in the Americas, 1755– 1763.* Cambridge University Press, 2002.

Brunner, Hugo. *Kassel im siebenjährigen Kriege: Ein Beitrag zur Geschichte der Stadt.* Kassel: Hühn, 1884.

Bryant, Gerald James. *The Emergence of British Power in India, 1600–1784: A Grand Strategic Interpretation.* Boydell & Brewer, 2013.

Bryant, Gerald James. "Indigenous Mercenaries in the Service of European Imperialists: The Case of the Sepoys in the Early British Indian Army, 1750–1800." *War in History* 7 (2000): 2–28.

Bryant, Gerald James. "The War in the Carnatic." In Danley and Speelman, *The Seven Years' War.*

Büchel, Christiane. "Der Offizier im Gesellschaftsbild der Aufklärung: Die Soldatenschriften des Johann Michael von Loen." *Aufklärung* 11, no. 2 (1999): 5–23.

Buchet, Christian. *The British Navy, Economy and Society in the Seven Years War,* trans. Anita Higgie and Michael Duffy. Boydell Press, 2013.

Buchholz, Ingelore. "Leben in der Festungsstadt." In *Magdeburg: Die Geschichte der Stadt 805–2005,* ed. Matthias Puhle and Peter Petsch. Stekovics, 2005.

Buckner, Phillip, and John G. Reid, eds. *Remembering 1759: The Conquest of Canada in Historical Memory*. University of Toronto Press, 2012.

Buckner, Phillip A., and John G. Reid, eds. *Revisiting 1759: The Conquest of Canada in Historical Perspective*. University of Toronto Press, 2012.

Buddruss, Eckhard. *Die französische Deutschlandpolitik 1756–1789*. Zabern, 1995.

Buffinton, Arthur H. *The Second Hundred Years' War, 1689–1815*. Holt, 1929.

Burgdorf, Wolfgang. *Reichskonstitution und Nation: Verfassungsreformprojekte für das Heilige Römische Reich Deutscher Nation im politischen Schrifttum von 1648 bis 1806*. Zabern, 1998.

Burke, Peter. *A Social History of Knowledge: From Guttenberg to Diderot*. Polity, 2000.

Burkhardt, Johannes. *Abschied vom Religionskrieg: Der siebenjährige Krieg und die päpstliche Diplomatie*. Niemeyer, 1985.

Burkhardt, Johannes. "Die Friedlosigkeit der Frühen Neuzeit: Grundlegung einer Theorie der Bellizität in Europa." *Zeitschrift für Historische Forschung* 24 (1997): 509–574.

Burkhardt, Johannes. "Religious War or Imperial War? Views of the Seven Years' War from Germany and Rome." In Danley and Speelman, *The Seven Years' War*.

Burkhardt, Johannes. *Vollendung und Neuorientierung des frühmodernen Reiches 1648–1763*. 6th ed. Kletta-Cotta, 2006.

Burkhardt, Johannes. "Vom Debakel zum Mirakel: Zur friedensgeschichtlichen Einordnung des Siebenjährigen Krieges." In *Menschen und Strukturen in der Geschichte Alteuropas: Festschrift für Johannes Kunisch zur Vollendung seines 65. Lebensjahres*, ed. Helmut Neuhaus und Barbara Stollberg-Rilinger. Duncker & Humblot, 2002.

Burkhardt, Johannes. "Wie ein verlorener Krieg zum Sieg umgeschrieben wurde: Friedrich der Große, der Siebenjährige Krieg und der Friede von Hubertusburg." In *Sprache, Macht, Frieden: Augsburger Beiträge zur Historischen Friedens- und Konfliktforschung*, ed. Johannes Burkhardt, Kay Peter Jankrift, and Wolfgang E. J. Weber. Wißner, 2014.

Burkhardt, Johannes, and Stephanie Haberer, eds. *Das Friedensfest: Augsburg und die Entwicklung einer neuzeitlichen Toleranz-, Friedens- und Festkultur*. Akademie, 2000.

Burnard, Trevor, and John Garrigus. "The Seven Years' War in the West Indies." In *The Plantation Machine: Atlantic Capitalism in French Saint-Domingue and British Jamaica*, ed. Trevor Burnard and John Garrigus. University of Pennsylvania Press, 2016.

Burnard, Trevor, Emma Hart, and Marie Houllemare, eds. *The Oxford Handbook of the Seven Years' War*. Oxford University Press, 2024.

Buttlar, Kurt Treusch von. "Burkersdorf." *Forschungen zur Brandenburgischen und Preußischen Geschichte* 10 (1898): 337–344.

Buzan, Barry, Ole Wæver, and Jaap de Wilde. *Security: A New Framework for Analysis*. Rienner, 1998.

Calleja Leal, Guillermo, and Hugo O'Donnell. *Duque de Estrada, 1762: La Habana Inglesa; La toma de La Habana por los ingleses*. Agencia Espanola de Cooperatión Internacional, 1999.

Calloway, Colin G. *The Indian World of George Washington: The First President, the First Americans, and the Birth of the Nation*. Oxford University Press, 2018.

Calloway, Colin G. *The Scratch of a Pen: 1763 and the Transformation of North America*. Oxford University Press, 2006.

Cardwell, M. John. *Arts and Arms: Literature, Politics and Patriotism During the Seven Years War*. Manchester University Press, 2004.

Caretta, Vincent. *Equiano, the African: Biography of a Self-Made Man*. University of Georgia Press, 2005.

Carl, Horst. "Mikro- und Makroperspektiven auf eine standardisierte Situation—Okkupationserfahrungen im Siebenjährigen Krieg im Vergleich." In Füssel, *Der Siebenjährige Krieg 1756–1763: Mikro- und Makroperspektiven*.

Carl, Horst. *Okkupation und Regionalismus: Die preussischen Westprovinzen im Siebenjährigen Krieg*. Zabern, 1993.

Carl, Horst. "'Pavillon de Hanovre': Korruption im Militär im 18. Jahrhundert." In *Integration—Legitimation—Korruption: Politische Patronage in Früher Neuzeit und Moderne*, ed. Ronald Asch, Birgit Emich, and Jens Ivo Engels. Lang, 2011.

Carl, Horst. "Unter fremder Herrschaft: Invasion und Okkupation im Siebenjährigen Krieg." In Kroener and Pröve, *Krieg und Frieden*.

Carl, Horst, and Hans-Jürgen Bömelburg, eds. *Lohn der Gewalt: Beutepraktiken von der Antike bis zur Neuzeit*. Schöningh, 2011.

Carter, Alice Clare. *The Dutch Republic in Europe in the Seven Years' War*. Macmillan, 1972.

Casalilla, Bartholomé Yun. "'Localism,' Global History and Transnational History: A Reflection from the Historian of Early Modern Europe." *Historisk Tidskrift* 127, no. 4 (2007): 659–678.

Castex, Jean-Claude. *Dictionnaire des batailles terrestres franco-anglaises de la Guerre de Sept Ans*. Presses de l'Université Laval, 2006.

Cerbelaud Salagnac, Georges. "La reprise de Terre-Neuve par les français en 1762." *Revue française d'histoire d'outre-mer* 63, no. 231 (1976): 211–222.

Chakravarti, Sudeep. *Plassey: The Battle That Changed the Course of Indian History*. Aleph, 2020.

Charteris, Evan Edward. *William Augustus Duke of Cumberland and the Seven Years' War*. Hutchinson, [1925.]

Charters, Erica Michiko. "The Caring Fiscal-Military State During the Seven Years War 1756–1763." *Historical Journal* 52, no. 4 (2009): 921–941.

Charters, Erica Michiko. *Disease, War, and the Imperial State: The Welfare of the British Armed Forces During the Seven Years' War*. University of Chicago Press, 2014.

Chatterjee, Partha. *The Black Hole of Empire: History of a Global Practice of Power*. Princeton University Press, 2012.

Chaudhury, Sushil. "The Imperatives of the Empire: Private Trade, Sub-Imperialism and the British Attack on Chanderbagore, March 1757." *Studies in History* 8, no. 1 (1992): 1–12.

Chaudhury, Sushil. *The Prelude to Empire: Plassey Revolution of 1757*. Manohar, 2000.

Christelow, Allan. "Economic Background of the Anglo-Spanish War of 1762." *Journal of Modern History* 18, no. 1 (1946): 22–36.

Christie, Nancy. *The Formal and Informal Politics of British Rule in Post-Conquest Quebec, 1760–1837: A Northern Bastille*. Oxford University Press., 2020.

Churchill, Winston. *A History of the English-Speaking Peoples*. 4 vols. Cassell, 1956–1958.

Cisternes, Raoul de. *La campagne de Minorque d'après le journal du commandeur de Glandevez et de nombreuses lettres inédites*. Paris: Calmann-Lév, 1899.

Clark, Christopher. *Iron Kingdom: The Rise and Downfall of Prussia, 1600–1947*. Harvard University Press, 2009.

Clayton, T. R. "The Duke of Newcastle, the Earl of Halifax, and the American Origins of the Seven Years' War." *Historical Journal* 24 (1981): 571–603.

Clodfelter, Micheal. *Warfare and Armed Conflicts: A Statistical Encyclopedia of Casualty and Other Figures, 1492–2015*. McFarland, 2017.

Colley, Linda. *Britons: Forging the Nation 1707–1837*. Yale University Press, 1992.

Colley, Linda. *The Ordeal of Elizabeth Marsh: How a Remarkable Woman Crossed Seas and Empires to Become a Part of World History*. HarperCollins, 2007.

Conrad, Sebastian, Shalini Randeria, and Regina Römhild, eds. *Jenseits des Eurozentrismus: Postkoloniale Perspektiven in den Geschichts- und Kulturwissenschaften*. 2nd ed. Campus, 2013.

Consentius, Ernst. "Friedrich der Große und die Zeitungs-Zensur: Mit Benutzung der Akten des Geheimen Staats-Archivs." *Preußische Jahrbücher* 115 (1904): 220–249.

Conway, Stephen. "The Mobilization of Manpower for Britain's Mid-Eighteenth-Century Wars." *Historical Research* 77, no. 197 (2004): 377–404.

Conway, Stephen. "Provisioning the Combined Army in Germany, 1758–1762: Who Benefited?" In *The Contractor State and Its Implications, 1659–1815*, ed. Richard Harding and Sergio Solbes Ferri. Universidad de Las Palmas de Gran Canaria, 2012.

Conway, Stephen. *War, State, and Society in Mid-Eighteenth Century Britain and Ireland*. Oxford University Press, 2006.

Copeland, David A. *Colonial American Newspapers: Character and Content*. University of Delaware Press, 1997.

Copeland, David A. *Debating the Issues in Colonial Newspapers: Primary Documents on Events of the Period*. Greenwood, 2000.

Coquelle, Pierre. "L'espionnage en Angleterre pendant la Guerre de Sept Ans d'après les documents inédits." *Revue d'histoire diplomatique* 14 (1900): 508–533.

Coquelle, Pierre. "Les Projets de descents en Angleterre d'apres les archives des Affaires Étrangères." *Revue d'histoire diplomatique* 15 (1901): 591–624.

Corbett, Julian S. *England in the Seven Years' War: A Study in Combined Strategy*. 2 vols. Longman, Green, 1907. Reprint, Greenhill, 1992.

Corbin, Alain. *The Foul and the Fragrant: Odor and the French Social Imagination*. Harvard University Press, 1986.

Corvisier, André. "La Défense des côtes de Normandie contre les descentes anglaises pendant la guerre de Sept Ans." *Revue Internationale d'Histoire militaire* 35 (1976): 1–40.

Corvisier, André. "Les soldats de la Compagnie des Indes en 1755–1756." *Revue d'Histoire économique et sociale* 46, no. 1 (1968): 1–34.

Côté, André. "L'affaire du Canada (1761–1763)." *Cap-aux-Diamants* 83 (2005): 10–14.

Coutu, Joan. "Legitimating the British Empire: The Monument to General Wolfe in Westminster Abbey." In *Conflicting Visions: War and Visual Culture in Britain and France c. 1700–1830*, ed. John Bonehill and Geoff Quilley. Ashgate, 2005.

Cressy, David. *Saltpeter: The Mother of Gunpowder*. Oxford University Press, 2013.

Crocker, Thomas E. *Braddock's March: How the Man Sent to Seize a Continent Changed American History*. Westholme, 2009.

Crouch, Christian Ayne. *Nobility Lost: French and Canadian Martial Cultures, Indians, and the End of New France*. Cornell University Press, 2014.

Crouzet, François. *La guerre économique franco-anglaise au XVIIIe siècle*. Fayard, 2008.

Crouzet, François. "The Second Hundred Years War: Some Reflections." *French History* 10 (1996): 432–450.

Crowley, John E. "'Taken on the Spot': The Visual Appropriation of New France for the Global British Landscape." *Canadian Historical Review* 86, no. 1 (2005): 1–28.

Cubbison, Douglas R. *All Canada in the Hands of the British: General Jeffery Amherst and the 1760 Campaign to Conquer New France*. University of Oklahoma Press, 2014.

Cubbison, Douglas R. *The British Defeat of the French in Pennsylvania, 1758: A Military History of the Forbes Campaign Against Fort Duquesne*. McFarland, 2010.

Curran, Robert Emmett. "'[Catholics,] by the Very Principles of That Religion . . . Can Never Be Faithful Subjects': The Peaking of Anti-Catholicism and the Seven Years' War." In *Papist Devils: Catholics in British North America, 1574–1783*,. Catholic University of America Press, 2014.

Dade, Eva Kathrin. *Madame de Pompadour: Die Mätresse und die Diplomatie*. Böhlau, 2010.

D'Agay, Frédéric. "Un Episode naval de la guerre de Sept Ans." *Marins et Océans* 2 (1991): 143–171.

Dahmen, Sigrid. "Andreas Georg Wähner (1693–1762): Professor für morgenländische Sprachen in Göttingen." *Göttinger Jahrbuch* 60 (2012): 109–135.

Dalley, Jan. *The Black Hole: Money, Myth and Empire*. Collins, 2006.

Damiano, Sara T. "Women and Gender." In Burnard, Hart, and Houllemare, *The Oxford Handbook of the Seven Years' War*.

Danley, Mark H. "The 'Problem' of the Seven Years' War." In Danley and Speelman, *The Seven Years' War*.

Danley, Mark H., and Patrick J. Speelman, eds. *The Seven Years' War: Global Views*. Brill, 2012.

Dann, Uriel. *Hanover and Great Britain 1740–1760: Diplomacy and Survival*. Leicester University Press, 1991.

Davis, N. Darnell. "British Newspaper Accounts of Braddock's Defeat." *Pennsylvania Magazine of History and Biography* 23 (1899): 310–328.

De Bruyn, Frans, and Shaun Regan, eds. *The Culture of the Seven Years War: Empire, Identity, and the Arts in the Eighteenth-Century Atlantic World*. University of Toronto Press, 2014.

Degler, Annabell, and Max Gawlich. "Wahrnehmungen asymmetrischer Kriegsführung: Erfahrungen und Handhabungen irregulärer Taktiken in verschiedenen Gruppen, während des 'French and Indian War.'" In *Asymmetrische Konflikte im Spiegel der Zeit*, ed. Sebastian Buciak. Dr. Köster, 2008.

Degn, Christian. *Die Schimmelmanns im atlantischen Dreieckshandel: Gewinn und Gewissen*. Wachholtz, 1974.

Delbrück, Hans. "Der Ursprung des Siebenjährigen Krieges." In *Erinnerungen, Aufsätze und Reden*. Stilke, 1902.

Desbarats, Catherine, and Allan Greer. "The Seven Years' War in Canadian History and Memory." In *Cultures in Conflict: The Seven Years' War in North America*, ed. Warren R. Hofstra. Penguin, 2007.

Deupmann, Christoph. "Der Siebenjährige Krieg in der deutschsprachigen Lyrik." In *Geschichtslyrik: ein Kompendium*, ed. Heinrich Detering, et al. Vol. 2. Wallstein, 2013.

Dewar, Helen. "Canada or Guadeloupe? French and British Perceptions of Empire, 1760–1763." *Canadian Historical Review* 91, no. 4 (2010): 637–660.

Dickson, Peter George Muir. *Finance and Government Under Maria Theresia: 1740–1780*. 2 vols. Clarendon, 1987.

Dinges, Martin. "Soldatenkörper in der Frühen Neuzeit: Erfahrungen mit einem unzureichend geschützten, formierten und verletzten Körper in Selbstzeugnissen." In *Körper-Geschichten*, ed. Richard van Dülmen. Fischer, 1996.

Dirrheimer, Günter, and Friedrich Fritz. "Einhörner und Schuwalowsche Haubitzen: Russische Geschützlieferungen an die Österreicher im Siebenjährigen Krieg." In *Maria Theresia: Beiträge zur Geschichte des Heerwesens ihrer Zeit*, ed. Johann Christoph Allmayer-Beck. Hermann Böhlaus Nachfolger, 1967.

Ditfurth, Franz Wilhelm von. *Die historischen Volkslieder des siebenjährigen Krieges, nebst geschichtlichen und sonstigen Erläuterungen*. Berlin: Lipperheide, 1871.

Dixon, David. *Never Come to Peace Again: Pontiac's Uprising and the Fate of the British Empire in North America*. University of Oklahoma Press, 2005.

Donalies, Hans. "Der Anteil des Sekretärs Westphalen an den Feldzügen des Herzogs Ferdinand von Braunschweig (1758–62)." *Forschungen zur Brandenburgischen und Preußischen Geschichte* 8 (1895): 1–57.

Dopsch, Alfons. *Das Treffen bei Lobositz, sein Ausgang und seine Folgen*. Graz: Styria, 1892.

Doran, Patrick Francis. *Andrew Mitchell and Anglo-Prussian Diplomatic Relations During the Seven Years War*. Garland, 1986.

Dowd, Gregory Evans. *War Under Heaven: Pontiac, the Indian Nations, and the British Empire*. Johns Hopkins University Press, 2004.

Dreaper, James. *Pitt's Gallant Conqueror: The Turbulent Life of Lieutenant-General Sir William Draper K. B.* Tauris, 2006.

Dreyer, Alfred. "Hamburgische Stimmungsbilder aus den ersten Jahren des Siebenjährigen Krieges." *Hamburgische Geschichts- und Heimatblätter* 4 (1929): 58–67.

Dreyer, Alfred. *Johann Matthias Dreyer 1717–1769: Ein Hamburger satirischer Dichter und Holstein-Gottorper Diplomat*. Christians, 1934.

Droste, Stefan. *Offensive Engines: Projektemacher und Militärtechnik im langen 18. Jahrhundert*. Steiner, 2022.

Duchhardt, Heinz. *Balance of Power und Pentarchie: Internationale Beziehungen 1700–1785*. Schöningh, 1997.

Duchhardt, Heinz. *Gleichgewicht der Kräfte, Convenance, europäisches Konzert: Friedenskongresse und Friedensschlüsse vom Zeitalter Ludwigs XIV. bis zum Wiener Kongreß*. Wissenschaftliche Buchgesellschaft, 1976.

Duffy, Christopher. *By Force of Arms: The Austrian Army in the Seven Years War*. Vol. 2. Emperor's Press, 2008.

Duffy, Christopher. "Die Dynamik eines Weltkrieges im 18. Jahrhundert." In *Formen des Krieges: Vom Mittelalter zum "Low-Intensity-Conflict,"* ed. Manfred Rauchensteiner and Erwin A. Schmidl. Styria, 1991.

Duffy Christopher. *Friedrich der Große und seine Armee*. 2nd ed. Motorbuch, 1983.

Duffy, Christopher. "Militärische Aspekte Schlesiens im Siebenjährigen Krieg." *Jahrbuch der Schlesischen Friedrich-Wilhelms-Universität zu Breslau* 42–44 (2001–2003): 181–194.

Duffy, Christopher, *The Military Experience in the Age of Reason* (Routledge and Kegan Paul, 1987).

Duffy, Christopher. *The Military Life of Frederick the Great*. Atheneum, 1986.

Duffy, Christopher. *Prussia's Glory: Rossbach and Leuthen 1757*. Emperor's Press, 2003.

Duffy, Christopher. "The Seven Years' War as a Limited War." In *East Central European Society and War in the Pre-Revolutionary Eighteenth Century*, ed. Gunther E. Rothenberg, Béla K. Király, and Peter F. Sugar. Columbia University Press, 1982.

Duffy, Christopher. *Sieben Jahre Krieg: 1756–1763: Die Armee Maria Theresias*. öbv and hpt, 2003.

Duffy, Christopher. *Siege Warfare*. Vol. 2, *The Fortress in the Age of Vauban and Frederick the Great 1660–1789*. Routledge and Kegan Paul, 1985.

Duffy, Christopher. *The Wild Goose and the Eagle: A Life of Marshal von Browne; 1705–1757.* Chatto & Windus, 1964.

Dull, Jonathan R. *The French Navy and the Seven Years' War.* University of Nebraska Press, 2005.

Dussauge, André. *Le ministère de Belle-Isle: Études sur la guerre de sept ans.* Fournier, 1914.

Düwel, Sven. *Ad bellum Sacri Romano Germanici Imperii solenne decernendum: Die Reichskriegserklärung gegen Brandenburg-Preußen im Jahr 1757; Das Verfahren der "preußischen Befehdungssache" 1756/57 zwischen Immerwährendem Reichstag und Wiener Reichsbehörden.* 2 vols. LIT, 2016.

Dziembowski, Edmond. *La guerre de Sept Ans 1756–1763.* Septentrion, 2015.

Dziembowski, Edmond. "Les négociations franco-britanniques de 1761 devant le tribunal de l'opinion: Le duc de Choiseul et la publicité de la diplomatie française." In *Le négoce de la paix: Les nations et les traités franco-britanniques (1713–1802),* ed. Jean-Pierre Jessenne, Renaud Morieux, and Pascal Dupuy. Société des Études Robespierristes, 2008.

Dziembowski, Edmond. *Un nouveau patriotisme français, 1750–1770: La France face à la puissance anglaise à l'époque de la guerre de Sept Ans.* Voltaire Foundation, 1998.

Dziembowski, Edmond. "Transparence ou désinformation? La perte du Canada dans la presse gouvernementale française." In Fonck and Veyssière, *La Chute de la Nouvelle-France.*

Eckel, Jan. "'Alles hängt mit allem zusammen': Zur Historisierung des Globalisierungsdiskurses der 1990er und 2000er Jahre." *Historische Zeitschrift* 307 (2018): 42–78.

Eckert, Helmut. "Dominici—nicht Balke: Das Tagebuch des Feldpredigers beim Kür.-Rgt. von Seydlitz," *Zeitschrift für Heereskunde* 245 (1973): 39 ff.

Eder, Markus. *Crime and Punishment in the Royal Navy of the Seven Years' War, 1755–1763.* Ashgate, 2004.

Edwardes, Michael. *Plassey: The Founding of an Empire.* Hamish Hamilton, 1969.

Eicken, Heinrich von. "Die Reichsarmee im siebenjährigen Krieg: Dargestellt am kurtrierischen Regiment." *Preußische Jahrbücher* 41 (1878): 1–14, 113–135, 248–267.

Eldon, Carl William. "England's Subsidy Policy Towards the Continent During the Seven Years' War." Diss., University of Pennsylvania, 1938.

Eliott, John Huxtable. *Empires of the Atlantic World: Britain and Spain in America, 1492–1830.* Yale University Press, 2006.

Eloranta, Jari, and Jeremy Land. "Hollow Victory? Britain's Public Debt and the Seven Years War.'" *Essays in Economic & Business History* 29 (2011): 101–118.

Engel, Ulf, and Matthias Middell. "Bruchzonen der Globalisierung, globale Krisen und Territorialitätsregime, Kategorien einer Globalgeschichtsschreibung." *Comparativ* 12, no. 5/6 (2005): 5–38.

Engelmann, Wilhelm. *Daniel Chodowiecki's sämmtliche Kupferstiche.* Leipzig: Engelmann, 1857.

Epkenhans, Michael, Stig Förster, and Karen Hagemann, eds. *Militärische Erinnerungskultur: Soldaten im Spiegel von Biographien, Memoiren und Selbstzeugnissen.* Schöningh, 2006.

Epple, Angelika. "Doing Comparisons—Ein praxeologischer Zugang zur Geschichte der Globalisierung/en." In *Die Welt beobachten: Praktiken des Vergleichens*, ed. Angelika Epple and Walter Erhart. Campus, 2015.

Esdaile, Charles. "The Peninsular War Guerrilla and Its Antecedents: Humiliation Forgotten, Disaster Prefigured; The Guerra Fantástica of 1762." *Small Wars and Insurgencies* 30 (2019): 734–749.

Evans, Martin H., and Geoffrey Hooper. "Three Misleading Diaries: John Knyveton, MD—from Naval Surgeon's Mate to Man-Midwife." *International Journal of Maritime History* 26, no. 4 (2014): 762–788.

Externbrink, Sven. "Europäische gegen amerikanische Kriegskultur: Louis-Antoine de Bougainville und der French and Indian War (1756–1760)." In *Das ist Militärgeschichte! Probleme—Projekte—Perspektiven*, ed. Christian Th. Müller and Matthias Rogg. Schöningh, 2013.

Externbrink, Sven. *Friedrich der Große, Maria Theresia und das Alte Reich: Deutschlandbild und Diplomatie Frankreichs im Siebenjährigen Krieg.* Akademie, 2006.

Externbrink, Sven. "Die Grenzen des 'Kabinettskrieges': Der Siebenjährige Krieg 1756–1763." In *Handbuch Kriegstheorien*. ed. Thomas Jäger and Rasmus Beckmann. Verlag für Sozialwissenschaften, 2011.

Externbrink, Sven. "Der kürzeste Vormittag—Quebec 13. September 1759." In Füssel, *Der Siebenjährige Krieg 1756–1763: Mikro- und Makroperspektiven.*

Externbrink, Sven. "'Que l'homme est cruel et méchant!' Wahrnehmung von Krieg und Gewalt durch französische Offiziere im Siebenjährigen Krieg." *Historische Mitteilungen* 18 (2005): 44–57.

Externbrink, Sven, ed. *Der Siebenjährige Krieg (1756–1763): Ein europäischer Weltkrieg im Zeitalter der Aufklärung.* Akademie, 2011.

Externbrink, Sven. "Voltaire zwischen Candide und Roi-Philosophe." In Externbrink, *Der Siebenjährige Krieg (1756–1763).*

Eyres, Patrick, ed. "Hearts of Oak: Commerce, Empire and the Landscape Garden I." Special issue, *New Arcadian Journal* 35/36 (1993).

Eyres, Patrick. "Neoclassicism on Active Service: Commemoration of the Seven Years' War in the English Landscape Garden." In Eyres, "Hearts of Oak."

Eyres, Patrick, ed. "Sons of the Sea: Commerce, Empire and the Landscape Garden II." Special issue, *New Arcadian Journal* 37/38 (1994).

Faragher, John Mack. *A Great and Noble Scheme: The Tragic Story of the Expulsion of the French Acadians from Their American Homeland.* Norton, 2005.

Fatherly, Sarah. "Tending the Army: Women and the British General Hospital in North America, 1754–1763." *Early American Studies* 10 (2012): 566–599.

Felleckner, Stefan. *Kampf: Ein vernachlässigter Teil der Militärgeschichte; Augenzeugen aus dem Siebenjährigen Krieg (1756–63) und dem ersten Weltkrieg (1914–18) berichten über Gefechte.* Westarp, 2004.

Fenge, Terry, and Jim Aldridge, eds. *Keeping Promises: The Royal Proclamation of 1763, Aboriginal Rights, and Treaties in Canada.* McGill-Queen's University Press, 2015.

Fenn, Elizabeth A. "Biological Warfare in Eighteenth Century North America: Beyond Jeffrey Amherst." *Journal of American History* 86 (2000): 1552–1580.

Fester, Richard. "Die Erlanger Zeitung im siebenjährigen Krieg." *Forschungen zur Brandenburgischen und Preußischen Geschichte* 15 (1902): 180–188.

Feyel, Gilles. *L'annonce et la nouvelle: La presse d'information en France sous l'Ancien Régime (1630–1788).* Voltaire Foundation, 2000.

Finger, Hartmut. *Das "Gemayne Buch" von Schmannewitz: Ein Dorf in Sachsen erlebt den Siebenjährigen Krieg 1756–1763.* Burghügel, 2013.

Fink, Wolfgang. "Précepteur ou aumônier? Christian Fürchtegott Gellert et la guerre de Sept Ans: Les lettres à Grabowski." In *Soldats et civils au XVIIIe siècle: Échanges épistolaires et culturels*, ed. François Genton and Thomas Nicklas. Presses Universitaires Reims 2016.

Fischbacher, Thomas. "Die Residenz im Kriege: Graf Heinrich von Brühl, Friedrich II. von Preußen und König August III. von Polen und die symbolische Zerstörung von Schlössern im Siebenjährigen Krieg in Sachsen und Brandenburg." In *Zeichen und Medien des Militärischen am Fürstenhof in Europa*, ed. Peter-Michael Hahn and Matthias Müller. Lukas, 2017.

Fish, Shirley. *When Britain Ruled the Philippines 1762–1764: The Story of the 18th Century British Invasion of the Phillippines During the Seven Years War.* 1stBooks Library, 2003.

Fitte, Siegfried. *Religion und Politik vor und während des siebenjährigen Krieges.* Berlin: Gaertner, 1899.

Flannery, Kristie Patricia. "Battlefield Diplomacy and Empire-Building in the Indo-Pacific World During the Seven Years' War." *Itinerario* 40, no. 3 (2016): 467–488.

Flannery, Kristie Patricia. "The Seven Years' War and the Globalization of Anglo-Iberian Imperial Entanglement: The View from Manila." In *Entangled Empires: The Anglo-Iberian Atlantic, 1500–1830*, ed. Jorge Canizares-Esguerra. University of Pennsylvania Press, 2018.

Fogel, Michèle. *Les cérémonies de l'information dans la France du XVIe au milieu du XVIIIe siècle.* Fayard, 1989.

Fonck, Bertrand, and Laurent Veyssière, eds. *La Chute de la Nouvelle-France: De l'affaire Jumonville au traité de Paris.* Septentrion, 2015.

Fordham, Douglas. *British Art and the Seven Years War: Allegiance and Autonomy.* Philadelphia: University of Pennsylvania Press, 2010.

Forrest, George. *The Life of Lord Clive.* 2 vols. Cassell, 1918.

Foster, George M. "Peasant Society and the Image of Limited Good." *American Anthropologist* 67 (1965): 293–315.

Foster, William Henry. *The Captor's Narrative: Catholic Women and Their Puritan Men on the Early American Frontier.* Cornell University Press, 2003.

Fowler, William M. *Empires at War: The Seven Years' War and the Struggle for North America 1754–1763.* Douglas and MacIntyre, 2005.

Fradera, Josep M. "De la periferia al centro: Cuba, Puerto Rico y Filipinas en la crisis del imperio español." *Anuario de Estudios Americanos* 61 (2004): 161–199.

Francis, Alan David. "The Campaign in Portugal, 1762." *Journal of the Society for Army Historical Research* 59 (1981): 25–43.

Frantzius, Georg von. "Die Okkupation Ostpreußens durch die Russen im siebenjährigen Krieg mit besonderer Berücksichtigung der russischen Quellen." Diss., University of Berlin, 1916.

Frégault, Guy. *Canada: The War of the Conquest.* Oxford University Press, 1969. Originally published in French in 1955.

Frensdorff, Ferdinand. "Über das Leben und die Schriften des Nationalökonomen J. H. G. von Justi." *Nachrichten von der Königlichen Gesellschaft der Wissenschaften zu Göttingen, Philologisch-Historische Klasse*, no. 4 (1903): 356–503.

Frevert, Ute. *Gefühlspolitik: Friedrich II. als Herr über die Herzen.* Wallstein, 2012.

Frey, James W. "The Indian Saltpeter Trade, the Military Revolution, and the Rise of Britain as a Global Superpower." *The Historian* 71 (2009): 507–554.

Friese, Ulf-Joachim, ed. *Die Reichsarmee: Studien unter besonderer Berücksichtigung ihrer Beteiligung am Siebenjährigen Kriege 1756–1763.* LTR, 2008.

Friese, Ulf-Joachim, ed. *Die Schlacht bei Kolin am 18. Juni 1757 und die Tage davor und danach in preußischer und österreichischer Darstellung.* 2 vols. LTR, 2006.

Friese, Ulf-Joachim, ed. *Die Schlacht bei Torgau am 3. November 1760 und die Tage davor und danach in preußischer und österreichischer Darstellung.* 3 vols. LTR, 2008–2011.

Friese, Ulf-Joachim, ed. *Die Schlacht bei Zorndorf am 25./26. August 1758 und die Tage davor und danach in preußischer, russischer und österreichischer Darstellung.* 2 vols. LTR, 2010–2011.

Frisch, Ernst von. *Zur Geschichte der russischen Feldzüge im Siebenjährigen Kriege nach den Aufzeichnungen und Beobachtungen der dem russischen Hauptquartier zugeteilten österreichischen Offiziere vornehmlich in den Kriegsjahren 1757/58.* Winter, 1919.

Fuchs, Antje. "'Man suchte den Krieg zu einem Religions-Kriege zu machen': Beispiele von konfessioneller Propaganda und ihrer Wirkung im Kurfürstentum Hannover während des Siebenjährigen Krieges (1756–1763)." In *Militär und Religiosität in der Frühen Neuzeit*, ed. Michael Kaiser and Stefan Kroll. LIT, 2004.

Fuchs, Antje. "Der Siebenjährige Krieg als virtueller Religionskrieg an Beispielen aus Preußen, Österreich, Kurhannover und Großbritannien." In *Religionskriege im Alten Reich und in Alteuropa*, ed. Franz Brendle and Anton Schindling. Aschendorff, 2006.

Füssel, Marian. "Die Aasgeier des Schlachtfeldes: Kosaken und Kalmücken als russische Irreguläre während des Siebenjährigen Krieges." In *Die Rückkehr der Condottieri? Krieg und Militär zwischen staatlichem Monopol und Privatisierung: Von der Antike bis zur Gegenwart*, ed. Stig Förster, Christian Jansen, and Günther Kronenbitter. Schöningh, 2010.

Füssel, Marian. "'Als Gefangener in ein ganz fremdes, abergläubisches Land gebracht zu werden, stimmte meine Seele trübe': Kriegsgefangene in fremdkonfessionellem Umfeld und militärische Migration während des Siebenjährigen Krieges." In *Religion und Mobilität: Zum Verhältnis von raumbezogener Mobilität und religiöser Identitätsbildung im frühneuzeitlichen Europa*, ed. Henning P. Jürgens and Thomas Weller. Vandenhoeck & Ruprecht, 2010.

Füssel, Marian. "Ansichten des Krieges: Deutsche Augenzeugenberichte zum 1. August 1759." In *Die Schlacht bei Minden: Weltpolitik und Lokalgeschichte*, ed. Martin Steffen. Bruns, 2008.

Füssel, Marian. "Auf der Suche nach Erinnerung: Zur Intermedialität des Schlachtengedenkens an den Siebenjährigen Krieg im 18. und 19. Jahrhundert." In *Militärische Erinnerungskulturen vom 14. bis zum 19. Jahrhundert: Träger—Medien—Deutungskonkurrenzen*, ed. Horst Carl. Vandenhoeck & Ruprecht, 2012

Füssel, Marian. "'Die besten Feinde, welche man nur haben kann'? Göttingen unter französischer Besatzung im Siebenjährigen Krieg." *Göttinger Jahrbuch* 60 (2012): 137–160.

Füssel, Marian. "Frauen in der Schlacht? Weibliche Soldaten im 17. und 18. Jahrhundert zwischen Dissimulation und Sensation." In *Soldatinnen: Gewalt und Geschlecht im Krieg vom Mittelalter bis heute*, ed. Klaus Latzel, Franka Maubach, and Silke Sajukow. Schöningh, 2011.

Füssel, Marian. "Global Wars in the Eighteenth Century: Entanglement—Violence—Perception." In *The War of the Spanish Succession: New Perspectives*, ed. Matthias Pohlig and Michael Schaich. Oxford University Press, 2017.

Füssel, Marian. "Händler, Söldner und Sepoys: Transkulturelle Kampfverbände auf den südasiatischen Schauplätzen des Siebenjährigen Krieges." In *Imperialkriege von 1500 bis heute: Strukturen—Akteure—Lernprozesse*, ed. Tanja Bührer, Christian Stachelbeck, and Dierk Walter. Schöningh, 2011.

Füssel, Marian. "Händler und Krieger? Robert Clive, die East India Company und die Kapitalisierung des Siebenjährigen Krieges in Indien." In *Die Kapitalisierung des Krieges: Kriegsunternehmer in Spätmittelalter und in der Frühen Neuzeit*, ed. Markus Meumann and Matthias Meinhardt. LIT, 2021.

Füssel, Marian. "Der inszenierte Tod: Militärische Sterbe- und Beerdigungsrituale im Kontext des Siebenjährigen Krieges." In *Übergänge schaffen: Ritual und Performanz in der frühneuzeitlichen Militärgesellschaft*, ed. Ralf Pröve and Carmen Winkel. Vandenhoeck & Ruprecht 2012.

Füssel, Marian. "Die Krise der Schlacht: Das Problem der militärischen Entscheidung im 17. und 18. Jahrhundert." In *Die Krise in der Frühen Neuzeit*, ed. Rudolf Schlögl et al. Vandenhoeck & Ruprecht, 2016.

Füssel, Marian. "Lernen—Transfer—Aneignung: Theorien und Begriffe für eine transkulturelle Militärgeschichte." In *Waffen—Wissen—Wandel: Anpassung und Lernen in transkulturellen Erstkonflikten*, ed. Birthe Kundrus and Dierk Walter. Hamburger Edition, 2012, 34–49.

Füssel, Marian. "Panduren, Kosaken und Sepoys: Ethnische Gewaltakteure im 18. Jahrhundert zwischen Sicherheit und Stigma." In *Söldnerlandschaften: Frühneuzeitliche Gewaltmärkte im Vergleich*, ed. Philippe Rogger and Benjamin Hitz. Duncker & Humblot, 2014.

Füssel, Marian. "Die Politik der Unsicherheit: Versicherheitlichung, Gewalt und Expansion in den britischen Kolonien im Siebenjährigen Krieg." In *Sicherheit in der Frühen Neuzeit*, ed. Christoph Kampmann and Ulrich Niggemann. Böhlau, 2013.

Füssel, Marian. "'Quelques malhonêtes particuliers'? Army Suppliers and War Comissaries as Profiteers of the Seven Years War." In *Officers, Entrepreneurs, Career Migrants and Diplomats: Military Entrepreneurs in the Early Modern Era*, ed. Philippe Rogger and André Holenstein. Brill, 2024.

Füssel, Marian. *Der Siebenjährige Krieg: Ein Weltkrieg im 18. Jahrhundert*. 2nd ed. Beck, 2013.

Füssel, Marian, ed. *Der Siebenjährige Krieg 1756–1763: Mikro- und Makroperspektiven*. De Gruyter, 2021.

Füssel, Marian. "Der Siebenjährige Krieg in Nordwestdeutschland: Kulturelle Interaktion, Kriegserfahrung und -erinnerung zwischen Reich und Empire." In *Hannover, Großbritannien und Europa: Erfahrungsraum Personalunion 1714–1837*, ed. Ronald Asch. Wallstein, 2014.

Füssel, Marian. "Theatrum Belli: Der Krieg als Inszenierung und Wissensschauplatz im 17. und 18. Jahrhundert." *Metaphorik* 14 (2008): 205–230.

Füssel, Marian. "'Theresia fiel nieder und tanzt seitdem nicht wieder': Mediale Repräsentationen der 'Königin von Ungarn' während des Siebenjährigen Krieges." In *Die Repräsentation Maria Theresias: Herrschaft und Bildpolitik im Zeitalter der Aufklärung*, ed. Werner Telesko, Sandra Hertel, and Stefanie Linsboth. Böhlau, 2020.

Füssel, Marian. "Vom Dämon des Zufalls: Die Schlacht als kalkuliertes Wagnis im langen 18. Jahrhundert." In *Wagnisse: Risiken eingehen, Risiken analysieren, von Risiken erzählen*, ed. Stefan Brakensiek, Christoph Marx, and Benjamin Scheller. Campus, 2017.

Füssel, Marian. "Zwischen Empire und Reich: Zur Kommunikation des globalen Siebenjährigen Krieges im Raum der Personalunion." In *Kommunikation and Kulturtransfer im Zeitalter der Personalunion zwischen Großbritannien und Hannover:*

"To Prove That Hanover and England Are Not Entirely Synonymous," ed. Arndt Reitemeier. Universitätsverlag Göttingen 2014.

Füssel, Marian. "Zwischen Kriegserfahrung und Heldenmythos: Ewald von Kleist und die Schlacht von Kunersdorf am 12. August 1759." In *Ewald von Kleist: Zum 250. Todestag,* ed. Lothar Jordan. Königshausen & Neumann, 2010.

Füssel, Marian. "Zwischen lokalem Gedächtnis und kollektivem Vergessen: Der Siebenjährige Krieg in der Erinnerungskultur der Bundesrepublik Deutschland." In *Umwelten: Ereignisse, Räume und Erfahrungen der Frühen Neuzeit; Festschrift für Manfred Jakubowski-Tiessen,* ed. Sven Petersen, Dominik Collet, and Marian Füssel. V&R unipress, 2015.

Füssel, Marian. "Zwischen Schauspiel, Information und Strafgericht: Visualisierungen und Deutung von brennenden Städten im Siebenjährigen Krieg." In *Urbs incensa: Ästhetische Transformationen der brennenden Stadt in der Frühen Neuzeit,* ed. Vera Fionie Koppenleitner, Hole Rößler, and Michael Thimann. Deutscher Kunstverlag, 2011.

Füssel, Marian, and Sven Petersen. "Ananas und Kanonen: Zur materiellen Kultur globaler Kriege im 18. Jahrhundert." *Historische Anthropologie* 23, no. 3 (2015): 366–390.

Füssel, Marian, and Michael Sikora. "Einführung: Schlachtengeschichte als Kulturgeschichte." In *Kulturgeschichte der Schlacht,* ed. Marian Füssel and Michael Sikora. Schöningh, 2014.

Gale, Ryan R. *"A Soldier-Like Way": The Material Culture of the British Infantry 1751–1768.* Track of the Wolf, 2007.

García del Pino, César. *Toma de La Habana por los ingleses y sus antecedentes.* Editorial de Ciencias Sociales, 2002.

Geisau, Hans von. "Zur Schlacht bei Warburg am 31. Juli 1760." *Westfälische Zeitschrift* 111 (1961): 329–336.

Gerspacher, Hans. *Die badische Politik im Siebenjährigen Krieg.* Winter, 1934.

Gestrich, Andreas. *Absolutismus und Öffentlichkeit: Politische Kommunikation in Deutschland zu Beginn des 18. Jahrhunderts.* Vandenhoeck & Ruprecht, 1994.

Gestrich, Andreas. "Kriegsberichterstattung als Propaganda: Das Beispiel des 'Wienerischen Diarium' im Siebenjährigen Krieg 1756–1763." In *Augenzeugen: Kriegsberichterstattung vom 18. zum 21. Jahrhundert,* ed. Ute Daniel. Vandenhoeck & Ruprecht, 2006.

Geyso, Franz von. "Das Korps des Prinzen Johann Kasimir zu Ysenburg-Birstein unter Besonderer Berücksichtigung des Gefechts bei Sandershausen am 23. Juli 1758." *Zeitschrift für hessische Geschichte* 45 (1911): 218–274.

Ginzburg, Carlo. "Microhistory: Two or Three Things That I Know About It," trans. John Tedeschi and Anne C. Tedeschi. *Critical Inquiry* 20, no. 1 (1993): 10–35.

Gipson, Lawrence H. *The British Empire Before the American Revolution: Provincial Characteristics and Sectional Tendencies in the Era Preceding the American Crisis.* Vols. 6–8. Caxton, 1946–1954.

Giráldez, Arturo. *The Age of Trade: The Manila Galleons and the Dawn of the Global Economy.* Rowman & Littlefield, 2015.

Glück, Helmut, and Mark Häberlein, eds. *Militär und Mehrsprachigkeit im neuzeitlichen Europa.* Harrassowitz, 2014.

Godfroy-Tayart de Borms, Marion F. "La Guerre de Sept Ans et ses conséquences Atlantiques: Kourou ou l'apparition d'un nouveau système colonial." *French Historical Studies* 32, no. 2 (2009): 167–191.

González Enciso, Agustin. "Spain's Mobilisation of Resources for the War with Portugal in 1762." In *Mobilising Resources for War: Britain and Spain at Work During the Early Modern Period,* ed. Huw V. Bowen and Agustin González Enciso. Ediciones Universidad de Navarra, 2006.

Good, Christoph. *Emer de Vattel (1714–1767)—naturrechtliche Ansätze einer Menschenrechtsidee und des humanitären Völkerrechts im Zeitalter der Aufklärung.* Dike, 2011.

Göse, Frank. "Der Kabinettskrieg." In *Formen des Krieges: Von der Antike bis zur Gegenwart,* ed. Dietrich Beyrau, Dietrich Hochgeschwender, and Dieter Langewiesche. Schöningh, 2007.

Gott, Richard. *Land Without Evil: Utopian Journeys Across the South American Watershed.* Verso, 1993.

Gough, Barry M. *British Mercantile Interests in the Making of the Peace of Paris, 1763: Trade, War, and Empire.* Mellen, 1992.

Gradish, Stephen F. *The Manning of the British Navy During the Seven Years' War.* Royal Historical Society, 1980.

Graham-Yool, Andrew. *Imperial Skirmishes: War and Gunboat Diplomacy in Latin America.* Signal, 2002.

Granier, Hermann. "Die Russen und Österreicher in Berlin im Oktober 1760." *Hohenzollern-Jahrbuch* 2 (1898): 113–145.

Granier, Hermann. *Die Schlacht bei Lobositz am 1. Oktober 1756.* Diss., Berlin (1889).

Grant, William L. "Canada Versus Guadeloupe: An Episode of the Seven Years' War." *American Historical Review* 17, no. 4 (1912): 735–743.

Grant, William L. "La Mission de M. de Bussy à Londres en 1761." *Revue d'histoire diplomatique* 20 (1906): 351–366.

Gray, Edward G., ed. *The Language Encounter in the Americas, 1492–1800: A Collection of Essays.* Berghahn, 2003.

Green, James. "The Publishing History of Olaudah Equiano's Interesting Narrative." *Slavery and Abolition* 16, no. 3 (1995): 362–375.

Greene, Jack P. "The Seven Years' War and the American Revolution: The Causal Relationship Reconsidered." *Journal of Imperial and Commonwealth History* 8, no. 22 (1980): 85–105.

Gregory, Desmond, *Minorca, the Illusory Prize: A History of the British Occupations of Minorca Between 1708 and 1802.* Fairleigh Dickinson University Press, 1990.

Griffin, Patrick. "The Last War of Religion or the First War for Empire? Reconsidering the Meaning of the Seven Years' War in America." In *Multiple Reformations? The Many Faces and Legacies of the Reformation*, ed. Jan Stievermann and Randall C. Zachman. Mohr Siebeck, 2018.

Großer Generalstab, ed. *Die Kriege Friedrich des Großen: Der Siebenjährige Krieg*. 12 vols. Mittler, 1901–1913.

Gruber, Alain-Charles. *Les grandes fêtes et leurs décors à l'époque de Louis XVI*. Droz, 1972.

Grünhagen, Colmar. *Schlesien unter Friedrich dem Grossen*. 2 vols. Breslau: Koebner, 1890–1892.

Guiomar, Jean-Yves. *L' invention de la guerre totale: XVIIIe–XXe siècle*. Félin, 2004.

Güllüoglu, Abdullah. "Die Wahrnehmung des Anderen in den Berichten des osmanischen Gesandten Ahmed Resmi Efendi (1694/95–1783)." In *Orientalische Reisende in Europa—Europäische Reisende im Nahen Osten: Bilder vom Selbst und Imaginationen des Anderen*, ed. Bekim Agai and Zita Agota Pataki. EB, 2010.

Gupta, Brijen K. *Sirajuddaullah and the East India Company, 1756–1757: Background to the Foundation of British Power in India*. Brill, 1962.

Guratzsch, Herwig, ed. *William Hogarth: Der Kupferstich als moralische Schaubühne*. Hatje, 1987.

Häberlein, Mark. "Waffen, Monturen, Getreide: Geschäfte fränkischer Kaufleute im Siebenjährigen Krieg." *Jahrbuch für Regionalgeschichte* 32 (2014): 31–42.

Häberlein, Mark, and Michaela Schmölz-Häberlein. *Halles Netzwerk im Siebenjährigen Krieg: Kriegserfahrungen und Kriegsdeutungen in einer globalen Kommunikationsgemeinschaft*. Franckeschen Stiftungen, 2020.

Häberlein, Mark, and Michaela Schmölz-Häberlein. "Der Siebenjährige Krieg und das Kommunikationsnetz des Halleschen Pietismus." In Füssel, *Der Siebenjährige Krieg 1756–1763: Mikro- und Makroperspektiven*.

Habermas, Jürgen. *The Structural Transformation of the Public Sphere: An Inquiry Into a Category of Bourgeois Society*, trans. Thomas Burger. MIT Press, 1991.

Hagedorn, Nancy. "'A Friend to Go Between Them': The Interpreter as Cultural Broker During Anglo-Iroquois Councils, 1740–1770." *Ethnohistory* 35 (1988): 60–80.

Hahn, Peter-Michael. *Friedrich II. von Preußen: Feldherr, Autokrat und Selbstdarsteller*. Kohlhammer, 2013.

Hall, Richard. *Atlantic Politics, Military Strategy and the French and Indian War*. Palgrave Macmillan, 2016.

Hamacher, Wilhelm. "Die Reichsstadt Köln und der Siebenjährige Krieg." Diss., University of Bonn, 1911.

Hanke, René. *Brühl und das Renversement des alliances: Die antipreußische Außenpolitik des Dresdener Hofes 1744–1756*. LIT, 2006.

Hannings, Bud. *The French and Indian War: A Complete Chronology*. McFarland, 2011.

Harari, Yuval Noah. "Military Memoirs: A Historical Overview of the Genre from the Middle Ages to Late Modern Era." *War in History* 14, no. 3 (2007): 289–309.

Harari, Yuval Noah. *The Ultimate Experience: Battlefield Revelations and the Making of Modern War Culture, 1450–2000.* Palgrave Macmillan, 2008.

Harland-Jacobs, Jessica L. *Builders of Empire: Freemasons and British Imperialism, 1717–1927.* University of North Carolina Press, 2007.

Harris, Bob. "'American Idols': Empire, War and the Middling Ranks in Mid-Eighteenth-Century Britain." *Past & Present* 150 (1996): 111–141.

Hartmann, Stefan. "Die Rückgabe Ostpreußens durch die Russen 1762." *Zeitschrift für Ostforschung* 36 (1987): 405–433.

Hartmann, Stefan. "Zur Geschichte der Schlacht bei Prag am 6. Mai 1757." *Jahrbuch preußischer Kulturbesitz* 27 (1991): 357–380.

Hartwig, Dieter. "Maritime Aspekte im Denken und Handeln Friedrichs des Großen." In *Deutsche Marinen im Wandel: Vom Symbol nationaler Einheit zum Instrument internationaler Sicherheit*, ed. Werner Rah. Oldenbourg, 2005.

Hartwig, Theodor. *Der Uebertritt des Erbprinzen Friedrich von Hessen-Cassel zum Katholicismus: Ein Beitrag zur Geschichte der katholischen Propaganda aus der Zeit des siebenjährigen Krieges; Nach den Acten des Hessischen Staatsarchivs.* Kassel: Kay, 1870.

Harvey, Robert. *Clive: The Life and Death of a British Emperor.* Hodder & Stoughton, 1998.

Hasenkamp, Xaver von. *Ostpreußen unter dem Doppelaar: Historische Skizze der russischen Invasion in den Tagen des siebenjährigen Krieges.* 3rd ser., vols. 6–11. Königsberg: Theile, 1866.

Hassell, William von. *Die schlesischen Kriege und das kurfürstenthum Hannover Insbesondere die Katastrophe von Hastenbeck und Kloster Zeven: Mit Benutzung archivalischer Quellen.* Hanover: Hahn, 1879.

Haudrère, Philippe. *La Compagnie française des Indes aux XVIII siècle.* 2nd ed. 2 vols. Les Indes savantes, 2005.

Haudrère, Philippe, and Gérard Le Bouedec. *Les compagnies des Indes.* Édition Ouest France, 2015.

Hauschild, Wolf-Dieter. "Religion und Politik bei Friedrich dem Großen." *Saeculum* 51 (2000): 191–211.

Hayter, Tony. "England, Hannover, Preußen: Gesellschaftliche und wirtschaftliche Grundlagen der britischen Beteiligung an Operationen auf dem Kontinent während des Siebenjährigen Krieges." In Kroener, *Europa im Zeitalter Friedrichs des Großen.*

Hebbert, Francis J. "The Belle-Ile Expedition of 1761." *Journal of the Society for Army Historical Research* 64 (1986): 81–93.

Heiland, Janine. "'Harmonie durch Ungleichheit': Die Feiern zum Frieden von Hubertusburg 1763 in der Residenzstadt Weimar und der Universitätsstadt Jena als Spiegel der Ständegesellschaft." *Zeitschrift für thüringische Geschichte* 65 (2011): 109–142.

Heilmann, Johann von. *Beitrag zur Geschichte des Feldzugs von 1757*. Berlin: Mittler, 1854.

Heinrich, Guido. "Leibhaftige Ästhetisierung und mediale Endverwertung: Die Rezeption der Kriegslyrik Anna Louisa Karschs in Berlin, Halberstadt und Magdeburg." In Adam and Dainat, *Der Siebenjährige Krieg in den zeitgenössischen Medien*.

Heinze, Alfred. *Dresden im Siebenjährigen Kriege*. Dresden: Tittmann, 1885.

Helmes, Hermann. "Kurze Geschichte der Fränkischen Reichstruppen 1714–1756 und ihrer Teilnahme am Feldzuge von Rossbach 1757." *Darstellungen aus der Bayerischen Kriegs- und Heeresgeschichte* 16 (1907): 1–116.

Henrichs, Leopold. *Das Fürstentum Moers im Siebenjährigen Krieg*. Kaltenmeier & Berhuven, 1917.

Hermann, Otto. "Der Feldzugsplan Friedrichs des Grossen für das Jahr 1758." *Historische Vierteljahresschrift* 15 (1912): 13–33.

Hermann, Otto. "Olmütz (1758)." *Forschungen zur Brandenburgischen und Preußischen Geschichte* 23 (1910): 527–539.

Hertel, Sandra. "Ein Bild von Freund und Feind: Die Iserlohner Tabaksdosen im Medienkrieg zwischen Friedrich II. und Maria Theresia." *Der Märker* 67/68 (2019): 81–97.

Heydemann, Viktor. "Deutsche und Französische Broschüren aus der Zeit des Siebenjährigen Krieges." *Zeitschrift für Bücherfreunde*, n.s., vol. 20 (1928): 94–98.

Higonnet, Patrice Louis-René. "The Origins of the Seven Years War." *Journal of Modern History* 40 (1968): 57–90.

Hinderaker, Eric. *Elusive Empires: Constructing Colonialism in the Ohio Valley, 1673–1800*. Cambridge University Press, 1997.

Hirschfeld, Michael. "Ein Justizmord im Siebenjährigen Krieg: Der gewaltsame Tod des Glatzer Priesters Andreas Faulhaber (1713–1757) im Kontext der Eroberungs- und Kirchenpolitik von Friedrich II. von Preußen." *Archiv für schlesische Kirchengeschichte* 72 (2014): 141–158.

Hochedlinger, Michael. "'Bella gerant alii . . .'? On the State of Early Modern Military History in Austria." *Austrian History Yearbook* 30 (1999): 237–277

Hochedlinger, Michael. "Rekrutierung—Militarisierung—Modernisierung: Militär und ländliche Gesellschaft in der Habsburgermonarchie im Zeitalter des aufgeklärten Absolutismus." In *Militär und ländliche Gesellschaft in der Frühen Neuzeit*, ed. Stefan Kroll and Kersten Krüger. LIT, 2000.

Hochedlinger, Michael. *Thron und Gewehr: Das Problem der Heeresergänzung und die "Militarisierung" der Habsburgermonarchie im Zeitalter des Aufgeklärten Absolutismus (1740–1790)*. Steiermärkisches Landesarchiv, 2021.

Höchner, Marc. *Selbstzeugnisse von Schweizer Söldneroffizieren im 18. Jahrhundert*. V&R unipress, 2015.

Hoen, Maximilian von. "Die Schlacht von Prag am 6. Mai 1757." *Streffleurs militärische Zeitschrift* 1 (1911): 11–44, 369–404, 581–612, 773–796, 939–958.

Hoensch, Jörg K. "Friedrichs II. Währungsmanipulationen im Siebenjährigen Krieg und ihre Auswirkungen auf die polnische Münzreform von 1765/66." *Jahrbuch für die Geschichte Mittel- und Ostdeutschlands* 22 (1973): 110–175.

Hoff, Ralf van den, et al. "Helden—Heroisierungen—Heroismen: Transformationen von der Antike bis zur Moderne; Konzeptionelle Ausgangspunkte des Sonderforschungsbereichs 948." *Helden. Heroes. Héros* 1, no. 1 (2013): 7–14.

Hoffmann, Peter. *Friedrich II. und Russland: Die erste Periode seiner Regierung bis zum Hubertusburger Frieden 1763.* NORA Verlagsgemeinschaft, 2019.

Hofstra, Warren R., ed. *Cultures in Conflict: The Seven Years' War in North America.* Penguin, 2007. Hohenemser, Paul. *Kritik der Quellen zur Schlacht bei Hochkirch (14. Oktober 1758).* Frankfurt: Boch & Englert, 1899.

Hohrath, Daniel. "Bastionen statt Schlachtfelder? Die schlesischen Festungen und ihre Belagerungen im Siebenjährigen Krieg." In Füssel, *Der Siebenjährige Krieg 1756–1763: Mikro- und Makroperspektiven.*

Hohrath, Daniel. "Der Bürger im Krieg der Fürsten: Stadtbewohner und Soldaten in belagerten Städten um die Mitte des 18. Jahrhunderts." In Kroener and Pröve, *Krieg und Frieden.*

Hohrath, Daniel. "'In Cartellen wird der Wert eines Feindes bestimmet': Kriegsgefangenschaft als Teil der Kriegspraxis des Ancien Régime." In *In der Hand des Feindes: Kriegsgefangenschaft von der Antike bis zum Zweiten Weltkrieg*, ed. Rüdiger Overmanns. Böhlau, 1999.

Hohrath, Daniel. "Verwandte—Freunde—Vorbilder: Aspekte der militärischen Beziehungsgeschichte Preußens und Württembergs im 18. Jahrhundert." In *Preußen, Deutschland und Europa 1701 bis 2001*, ed. Jürgen Luh, Vincenz Czech, and Bert Becker. INOS, 2001.

Hohrath, Daniel. "'Von der wunderbahren Würkung der Bomben': Protestantische Theologen als Zeugen von Festungsbelagerungen des 18. Jahrhunderts." In Kaiser and Kroll, *Militär und Religiosität in der Frühen Neuzeit.*

Holzman, James Mayer. *The Nabobs in England: A Study of the Returned Anglo-Indian, 1760–1785.* Published by the author, 1926.

Hopkin, David, Yann Lagadec, and Stéphane Perréon. "The Experience and Culture of War in the Eighteenth Century: The British Raids on the Breton Coast, 1758." *French Historical Studies* 31, no. 2 (2008): 193–227.

Horn, Bernd. "Only for the Strong of Heart: Ranging and the Practice of la Petite Guerre During the Struggle for North America." In *Show No Fear: Daring Actions in Canadian Military History*, ed. Bernd Horn. Dundurn, 2008.

Horn, Curt. "Die patriotische Predigt zur Zeit Friedrichs des Großen." *Jahrbuch für Brandenburgische Kirchengeschichte* 19 (1924): 78–128.

Horn, David Bayne. "The Duke of Newcastle and the Origins of the Diplomatic Revolution." In *The Diversity of History: Essays in Honour of Sir Herbert Butterfield*, ed. John Huxtable Elliott and Helmut Georg Koenigsberger. Routledge & Paul, 1970.

Horne, Gerald. "The Biggest Losers: Africans and the Seven Years' War." In *The Counter-Revolution of 1776: Slave Resistance and the Origins of the United States of America*. New York University Press, 2014.

Horstmann, Theodor. *Generallieutenant Johann Nicolaus von Luckner und seine Husaren im Siebenjährigen Kriege*. Biblio, 1977.

Huppertz, Aegidius. *Münster im siebenjährigen Kriege insbesondere die beiden Belagerungen des Jahres 1759*. Coppenrath, 1908.

Hyam, Ronald. "Imperial Interests and the Peace of Paris, 1763." In *Reappraisals in British Imperial History*, by Ronald Hyam and Ged Martin. Macmillan 1975.

Imbeault, Sophie, Denis Vaugeois, and Laurent Veyssière, eds. *1763: Le traité de Paris bouleverse l'Amérique*. Septentrion, 2013.

Iseli, Andrea. *Gute Policey: Öffentliche Ordnung in der Frühen Neuzeit*. Ulmer, 2009.

Jaeger, Stephan. "Die historiographische Inszenierung nationaler Identität: Johann Wilhelm von Archenholz, 'Geschichte des siebenjährigen Krieges.'" In *Performative Geschichtsschreibung: Forster, Herder, Schiller, Archenholz und die Brüder Schlegel*. De Gruyter, 2011.

Jahn, Bernhard. "Die Medialität des Krieges: Zum Problem der Darstellbarkeit von Schlachten am Beispiel der Schlacht von Lobositz (1.10.1756) im Siebenjährigen Krieg." In Adam and Dainat, *Der Siebenjährige Krieg in den zeitgenössischen Medien*.

Jakobs, Volker. "Wittenberg im Siebenjährigen Krieg (1756–1763)." *Heimatkalender* 6 (2003): 31–42.

Jany, Curt. *Geschichte der Königlich Preußischen Armee bis zum Jahre 1807*. Vol. 2, *Die Armee Friedrichs des Grossen 1740 bis 1763*. Siegismund, 1928.

Jasanoff, Maya. *Edge of Empire: Conquest and Collecting in the East 1750–1850*. Fourth Estate, 2005.

Jennings, Francis. *Empire of Fortune: Crowns, Colonies and Tribes in the Seven Years War in America*. Norton, 1988.

Jessen, Hans. "Die Anfänge der friderizianischen Nachrichtenpolitik." *Zeitungswissenschaft* 15, no. 7 (1940): 303–321.

Jessen, Hans. "Die Nachrichtenpolitik Friedrichs des Großen im 7jährigen Krieg." *Zeitungswissenschaft* 15 (1940): nos. 11–12, 632–664.

Johnson, Daniel Morley. "Cannibalism." In *The Encyclopedia of North American Indian Wars, 1607–1890: A Political, Social, and Military History*, ed. Spencer Tucker, James R. Arnold, and Roberta Wiener. Vol. 1. ABC-CLIO, 2011.

Jore, Léonce. "Les établissements français sur la côte occidentale d'Afrique de 1758 à 1809." *Revue Française d'Histoire d'Outre-Mer* 51 (1964): 9–252, 253–478.

Junkelmann, Marcus. "Der Militärstaat in Aktion: Kriegskunst im Ancien Régime." In *Friedrich der Grosse in Europa: Geschichte einer wechselvollen Beziehung*, ed. Bernd Sösemann and Gregor Vogt-Spira. Vol. 2. Steiner, 2012.

Kahnert, Timo. "Der drohende Krieg gegen Russland 1761/62." In *Handbuch zur nordelbischen Militärgeschichte: Heere und Kriege in Schleswig, Holstein, Lauenburg,*

Eutin und Lübeck 1623–1863/67, ed. Eva S. Fiebig and Jan Schlürmann. Husum, 2010.

Kaiser, Michael. "Prinz Heinrich im Siebenjährigen Krieg—der Oberbefehl in Sachsen und die Schlacht bei Freiberg 1762." In *Prinz Heinrich von Preussen: Ein Europäer in Rheinsberg*, ed. Jörg Meiner. Deutscher Kunstverlag, 2002.

Kaiser, Michael, and Stefan Kroll, eds. *Militär und Religiosität in der Frühen Neuzeit*. LIT, 2004.

Kalipke, Andreas. *Verfahren im Konflikt: Konfessionelle Streitigkeiten und Corpus Evangelicorum im 18. Jahrhundert*. Aschendorff, 2015.

Kaplan, Herbert H. *Russia and the Outbreak of the Seven Years War*. University of California Press, 1968.

Karpinski, Tomasz. "Unknown Iconographic Sources for the History of the Russian Army: The Russian Garrison in Elblag During the Seven Years War Through the Observation of Eyewitnesses." *History of Military Affairs* 9 (2020): 197–226. http://www.milhist.info/2020/09/14/karpinski.

Karsten, Arne, and Hillard von Thiessen, eds. *Normenkonkurrenz in historischer Perspektive*. Duncker & Humblot, 2015.

Kästner, Gotthard. *Generalmayor von Mayr und sein Freikorps in Kursachsen*. Schlimpert, 1904.

Keegan, John. *The Face of Battle*. Jonathan Cape, 1976.

Keep, John L. H. "Die russische Armee im Siebenjährigen Krieg." In Kroener, *Europa im Zeitalter Friedrichs des Großen*.

Keil, Siegmar. "Der Choral von Leuthen—Ein preußisch-deutscher Mythos." *Die Tonkunst* 4 (2007): 442–449.

Kennett, Lee. *The French Armies in the Seven Years' War: A Study in Military Organization and Administration*. Duke University Press, 1967.

Kent-Hackman, William. "The British Raid on Rochefort, 1757." *Mariner's Mirror* 64 (1978): 263–275.

Kessel, Eberhard. *Das Ende des Siebenjährigen Krieges: Torgau und Bunzelwitz 1760–1763*, ed. Thomas Lindner. Schöningh, 2007.

Kessel, Eberhard. "Zur Geschichte des Feldzuges von 1761 in Pommern und der dritten Belagerung von Kolberg im Siebenjährigen Kriege." *Baltische Studien*, n.s., vol. 38 (1936): 317–342.

Kirchberger, Ulrike. "Nordamerikanische Indianer und britische Kolonisten im Siebenjährigen Krieg." In Externbrink, *Der Siebenjährige Krieg (1756–1763)*.

Klaje, Hermann. *Die Russen vor Kolberg: Zur Erinnerung an die Belagerung der Stadt vor hundertfünfzig Jahren (1760)*. Kolberg: Post, 1911.

Klein, Hans H. *Wilhelm zu Schaumburg-Lippe: Klassiker der Abschreckungstheorie und Lehrer Scharnhorsts*. Biblio, 1982.

Klemm, Gustav. *Chronik der Königlich Sächsischen Residenzstadt Dresden*. 3 vols. Dresden: Grimmer, 1837.

Klingebiel, Thomas. *Feldherrn der Aufklärung: Ferdinand von Braunschweig und Friedrich der Große*. Appelhans, 2022.

Klingebiel, Thomas. "Der Siebenjährige Krieg als Zäsur: Über militärischen, politischen und gesellschaftlichen Wandel im ersten globalen Konflikt." *Indes* 9 (2019): 53–62.

Kloosterhuis, Jürgen. "Donner, Blitz und Bräker: Der Soldatendienst des 'armen Mannes im Tockenburg' aus der Sicht des preußischen Militärsystems." In *Schreibsucht: Autobiographische Schriften des Pietisten Ulrich Bräker*, ed. Alfred Messerli and Adolf Muschg. Vandenhoeck & Ruprecht, 2004.

Kloosterhuis, Jürgen. "Der Husar aus dem Buch: Die Zietenbiographie der Frau von Blumenthal im Kontext der Pflege brandenburg-preußischer Militärtradition um 1800." *Jahrbuch für brandenburgische Landesgeschichte* 52 (2001): 139–168.

Kloosterhuis, Jürgen. *Menzel Militaris: Sein "Armeewerk" und das "Leuthen"-Bild im militärhistorischen Quellenkontext*. Geheimes Staatsarchiv Preußischer Kulturbesitz, 2015.

Kloosterhuis, Jürgen. "Zwischen Garbeck und Lobositz: Ein westfälisch-märkischer Beitrag zur militärischen Sozial- und Ereignisgeschichte in der Zeit Friedrichs des Großen." *Der Märker* 45 (1996): 84–97.

Kloppert, Achim. "Der Schlesische Feldzug von 1762." Diss., University of Bonn, 1988.

Knauth, Franz. *Drangsale und Leiden der Stadt Halle und des Saalkreises während des siebenjährigen Krieges: Gleichzeitigen Aufzeichnungen nacherzählt und als Festgabe zur Jahrhundertfeier des Hubertusburger Friedensschlusses*. Halle: Buchhandlung des Waisenhauses, 1863.

Knöbl, Wolfgang. "Jenseits des situationistischen Paradigmas der Gewaltforschung." In *Narrative der Gewalt: Interdisziplinäre Analysen*, ed. Ferdinand Sutterlüty, et al. Campus, 2019.

Kobelt-Groch, Marion. "Friedrich II. und Maria Theresia: Der Siebenjährige Krieg— Ein Kampf der Geschlechter?" *Historische Mitteilungen der Ranke-Gesellschaft* 18 (2005): 72–87.

Koch, Max. "Der deutsche Reichstag während des Siebenjährigen Krieges." Diss., University of Bonn, 1950.

Köhler, Heinrich. *Friedrichs Mährischer Feldzug 1758*. Thomas & Hubert, 1916.

Kolff, Dirk H. A. *Naukar, Rajput and Sepoy: The Ethnohistory of the Military Labour Market in Hindustan 1450–1850*. Cambridge University Press, 1990.

Komander, Gerhild H. M. *Der Wandel des "Sehepunctes": Die Geschichte Brandenburg-Preußens in der Graphik von 1648–1810*. LIT, 1995.

Könenkamp, Wolf-Dieter. *Iserlohner Tabaksdosen: Bilder einer Kriegszeit*. Westfälisches Museum, 1982.

Kopperman, Paul Edward. "An Assessment of the Cholmley's Batman and British A Journals of Braddock's Campaign." *Western Pennsylvania Historical Magazine* 62, no. 3 (1979): 197–220.

Kopperman, Paul Edward. *Braddock at the Monongahela.* University of Pittsburgh Press, 1977.

Kopperman, Paul Edward. "'The Cheapest Pay': Alcohol Abuse in the Eighteenth-Century British Army." *Journal of Military History* 60, no. 3 (1996): 445–470.

Kopperman, Paul Edward. "The Stoppages Mutiny of 1763." *Western Pennsylvania Historical Magazine* 69 (1986): 241–254.

Korschelt, Gottlieb. "Das Bombardement von Zittau." *Neues Lausitzisches Magazin* 62 (1886): 206–216.

Korschelt, Gottlieb. "Kriegsdrangsale der Oberlausitz zur Zeit des siebenjährigen Krieges." *Neues lausitzisches Magazin* 54 (1878): 224–293.

Koselleck, Reinhart. "Chance as Motivational Trace in Historical Writing." In *Futures Past: On the Semantics of Historical Time,* trans. Keith Tribe. Columbia University Press, 2004.

Koselleck, Reinhart. "Representation, Event, and Structure." In *Futures Past: On the Semantics of Historical Time,* trans. Keith Tribe. Columbia University Press, 2004.

Koser, Reinhold. *Geschichte Friedrichs des Großen.* vol. 3. Cotta, 1925. Reprint of 6. and 7. Ed. Darmstadt: Wissenschaftliche Buchgesellschaft, 1963.

Koser, Reinhold. "Die preußischen Finanzen im Siebenjährigen Krieg." *Forschungen zur Brandenburgischen und Preußischen Geschichte* 13 (1900): 157–217, 329–375.

Koser, Reinhold. "Vor und nach der Schlacht bei Leuthen: Die Parchwitzer Rede und der Abend im Lissaer Schloß." *Forschungen zur Brandenburgischen und Preußischen Geschichte* 1 (1888): 605–618.

Koser, Reinhold. "Zum Ursprung des Siebenjährigen Krieges." *Historische Zeitschrift* 74 (1895): 69–85.

Koser, Reinhold. "Zur Bevölkerungsstatistik des preußischen Staates von 1756–1786." *Forschungen zur Brandenburgischen und Preußischen Geschichte* (1894): 239–245.

Kostov, Chris. *Terror and Fear: British and American Perceptions of the French-Indian Alliances During the Seven Years' War.* PublishAmerica, 2005.

Kozakiewicz, Stefan. *Bernardo Belloto, genannt Canaletto.* 2 vols. Bongers, 1972.

Kraus, Thomas R. *"Europa sieht den Tag leuchten . . .": Der Aachener Friede von 1748.* Aachener Geschichtsverein, 1998.

Krause, Karl Ernst Hermann. "Rostock im siebenjährigen Kriege." *Beiträge zur Geschichte der Stadt Rostock* 7 (1913): 97–111.

Krauss, Werner. "Über die Konstellation der deutschen Aufklärung." In *Studien zur deutschen und französischen Aufklärung.* Rütten & Loening, 1963.

Kroener, Bernhard R., ed. *Europa im Zeitalter Friedrichs des Großen: Wirtschaft, Gesellschaft, Kriege.* Oldenbourg, 1989.

Kroener, Bernhard R. "Die Geburt eines Mythos—die 'schiefe Schlachtordnung': Leuthen, 5. Dezember." In *Schlachten der Weltgeschichte: Von Salamis bis Sinai,* ed. Stig Förster, Markus Pöhlmann, and Dierk Walter. Beck, 2001.

Kroener, Bernhard R. "Herrschaftsverdichtung als Kriegsursache: Wirtschaft und Rüstung der europäischen Großmächte im Siebenjährigen Krieg." In *Wie Kriege entstehen: Zum historischen Hintergrund von Staatskonflikten*, ed. Bernd Wegner. Schöningh, 2000.

Kroener, Bernhard R. "Krieg." In *Enzyklopädie der Neuzeit*, ed. Friedrich Jaeger. Vol. 7. Metzler, 2008.

Kroener, Bernhard R. "'Den Krieg lernen': Die Feldzüge Friedrichs des Großen in der amtlichen Geschichtsschreibung des Kaiserreiches." In *Archivarbeit für Preußen*, ed. Jürgen Kloosterhuis. Geheimes Staatsarchiv Preußischer Kulturbesitz, 2000.

Kroener, Bernhard R. "Die materiellen Grundlagen österreichischer und preußischer Kriegsanstrengungen 1756–1763." In Kroener, *Europa im Zeitalter Friedrichs des Großen*.

Kroener, Bernhard R. "'Nun danket alle Gott!' Der Choral von Leuthen und Friedrich der Große als protestantischer Held: Die Produktion politischer Mythen im 19. und 20. Jahrhundert." In *"Gott mit uns": Religion, Nation und Gewalt im 19. und 20. Jahrhundert*, ed. Hartmut Lehmann and Gerd Krumeich. V&R unipress, 2000.

Kroener, Bernhard R. "Wirtschaft und Rüstung der europäischen Großmächte im Siebenjährigen Krieg." In *Friedrich der Große und das Militärwesen seiner Zeit*, ed. Militärgeschichtliches Forschungsamt. Mittler, 1987.

Kroener, Bernhard R., and Ralf Pröve, eds. *Krieg und Frieden: Militär und Gesellschaft in der Frühen Neuzeit*. Schöningh, 1996.

Krohn, Gerhard. "Friedrichs des Grossen niederschlesischer Feldzug von 1762 und die Schlacht bei Burkersdorf und Leutmannsdorf am 21. Juli 1762." Diss., University of Marburg, 1925.

Kroker, Ernst. "Leipzig im Siebenjährigen Kriege." In *Quellen zur Geschichte der Stadt Leipzig*, ed. Gustav Wustmann. Vol. 2. Leipzig: Duncker & Humblot, 1895.

Kroll, Stefan. *Soldaten im 18. Jahrhundert zwischen Friedensalltag und Kriegserfahrung: Lebenswelten und Kultur in der kursächsischen Armee 1728–1796*. Schöningh, 2006.

Kroll, Stefan. "'Gottesfurcht' und 'Vaterlandsliebe': Zwei Triebfedern zur Motivierung und Disziplinierung im Krieg? Das Beispiel Kursachsen im 18. Jahrhundert," in Kaiser and Kroll, *Militär und Religiosität*.

Krouglov, Alexei N. "Kant und der Siebenjährige Krieg." *Studies in East European Thought* 68, no. 2–3 (2016): 149–164.

Krüger-Löwenstein, Uta. "Hessen im Siebenjährigen Krieg: Berichte französischer Offiziere." *Zeitschrift für hessische Geschichte und Landeskunde* 87 (1978/80): 269–275.

Krulder, Joseph J. *The Execution of Admiral John Byng as a Microhistory of Eighteenth-Century Britain*. Routledge, 2021.

Krusenstjern, Benigna von. "Was sind Selbstzeugnisse? Begriffskritische und quellenkundliche Überlegungen anhand von Beispielen aus dem 17. Jahrhundert." *Historische Anthropologie* 2, no. 3 (1994): 462–471.

Krusenstjern, Benigna von, and Hans Medick, eds. *Zwischen Alltag und Katastrophe: Der Dreißigjährige Krieg aus der Nähe*. Vandenhoeck & Ruprecht, 1999.

Kulke, Leopold. "Die Schlacht bei Minden 1759 und ihre Folgen aus französischer Sicht." *Mitteilungen des Mindener Geschichtsvereins* 43 (1971): 75–89.

Kunisch, Johannes. "Der Ausgang des Siebenjährigen Krieges: Ein Beitrag zum Verhältnis von Kabinettspolitik und Kriegführung im Zeitalter des Absolutismus." *Zeitschrift für Historische Forschung* 2 (1975): 173–222.

Kunisch, Johannes. "Friedensidee und Kriegshandwerk im Zeitalter der Aufklärung." In *Fürst—Gesellschaft—Krieg: Studien zur bellizistischen Disposition des absoluten Fürstenstaats*, ed. Johannes Kunisch. Böhlau, 1992.

Kunisch, Johannes. *Friedrich der Große: Der König und seine Zeit*. Beck, 2004.

Kunisch, Johannes. "Der Historikerstreit über den Ausbruch des Siebenjährigen Krieges (1756)." In *Friedrich der Große in seiner Zeit*, ed. Johannes Kunisch. Beck, 2008.

Kunisch, Johannes. *Der kleine Krieg: Studien zum Heerwesen des Absolutismus*. Steiner, 1973.

Kunisch, Johannes. "Die militärische Bedeutung Schlesiens und das Scheitern der österreichischen Rückeroberungspläne im Siebenjährigen Krieg." In *Kontinuität und Wandel: Schlesien zwischen Österreich und Preussen*, ed. Peter Baumgart and Ulrich Schmilewski. Thorbecke, 1990.

Kunisch, Johannes. *Das Mirakel des Hauses Brandenburg: Studien zum Verhältnis von Kabinettspolitik und Kriegführung im Zeitalter des Siebenjährigen Krieges*. Oldenbourg, 1978.

Küntzel, Georg. "Über die erste Anknüpfung zwischen Preußen und England im Jahr 1755." *Forschungen zur Brandenburgischen und Preußischen Geschichte* 12 (1899): 253–256.

Küntzel, Georg. "Die Westminsterkonvention." *Forschungen zur Brandenburgischen und Preußischen Geschichte* 9 (1897): 541–569.

Kurth, Karl. "Grundzüge der friderizianischen Nachrichtenpolitik im 1. und 2. Schlesischen Kriege." *Zeitungswissenschaft* 15 (1940): 606–631.

Laberge, Alain. "Entre l'allégresse du peuple et l'amour-propre flétri du roi: Les fêtes pour la publication de la paix de juin 1763 à Paris." In Imbeault, Vaugeois, and Veyssière, *1763: Le traité de Paris bouleverse l'Amérique*.

Lacher, Reimar F. *"Friedrich, unser Held"—Gleim und sein König*. Wallstein, 2017.

Lagadec, Yann, Stéphane Perréon, and David Hopkin. *La Bataille de Saint-Cast (Bretagne, 11 septembre 1758): Entre histoire et mémoire*. Presses Universitaires de Rennes, 2009.

Landkreis Warburg, ed. *Gedenkschrift anlässlich des 200. Jahrestages der Schlacht bei Warburg am 31. Juli 1760: Quellen und Studien zur Geschichte des Siebenjährigen Krieges in Warburg und Umgebung*. Junfermann, 1960.

Lange, Carsten. "Telemann und England." In *Aspekte der englisch-deutschen Musikgeschichte im 17. und 18. Jahrhundert*, ed. Friedhelm Brusniak and Annemarie Clostermann. Studio, 1997.

Lange, Sven. *Hans Delbrück und der "Strategiestreit": Kriegführung und Kriegsgeschichte in der Kontroverse 1879–1914.* Rombach, 1995.

Langewiesche, Dieter. *Der gewaltsame Lehrer: Europas Kriege in der Moderne.* Beck, 2019.

Lanitzki, Günter. *Galeeren auf dem Peenestrom: Die preußisch-schwedische Seeschlacht 1759 oder wie die Kartoffel nach Skandinavien kam.* Edition Ost, 2000.

Lapray, Olivier. *Hastenbeck 1757: The French Army and the Opening Campaign of the Seven Years War.* Helion, 2021.

Laube, Volker. *Die Katastrophe von Landeshut in Schl. am 23. Juni 1760*, ed. Alfred von Klützow. Landeshut: Ernst Rudolph 1861.

Laubert, Manfred. *Kritik der Quellen zur Schlacht bei Kunersdorf (12. August 1759).* Mittler, 1900.

Laubert, Manfred. "Die Schlacht bei Kunersdorf nach dem Generalstabswerk." *Forschungen zur Brandenburgischen und Preußischen Geschichte* 25 (1912): 91–116.

Lauer, Gerhard, and Thorsten Unger, eds. *Das Erdbeben von Lissabon und der Katastrophendiskurs im 18. Jahrhundert.* Wallstein, 2008.

Laws, M. E. S. "The Royal Artillery at Manila, 1762." *Journal of the Royal Artillery* 87 (Spring 1960): 18–34.

Lawson, Philip. *The East India Company: A History.* Longman, 1993.

Lawson, Philip, and Jim Philipps. "Our Execrable Banditti: Perceptions of Nabobs in Mid-Eighteenth-Century Britain." *Albion* 16 (1984): 225–241.

Leach, Douglas Edward. *Roots of Conflict: British Armed Forces and Colonial Americans, 1677–1763.* University of North Carolina Press, 1986.

Leblanc, Ronnie-Gilles, ed. *Du Grand Dérangement à la Déportation: Nouvelles perspectives historique.* Université de Moncton, 2005.

Legahn, Ernst A. "Preußische Partisanen." *Wehrwissenschaftliche Rundschau* 18 (1968): 159–175.

Legal, Claus, and Gert Legal. *Friedrich II. Preußens König, Sachsens Feind, Regent auf Schloss Dahlen.* Burghügel, 2011.

Legal, Claus, and Gert Legal. *Tragödie Hubertusburg: Der einsame Kampf des Sachsen George Samuel Götze gegen Friedrich den Grossen.* Burghügel, 2014.

Le Goff, Timothy J. A. "Problèmes de recrutement de la marine française pendant la Guerre des Sept ans." *Revue historique* 283 (1990): 205–233.

Lehmann, Max. *Friedrich der Große und der Ursprung des Siebenjährigen Krieges.* Leipzig: Hirzel, 1894.

Leipold, Andreas. "Der erste preussische Einfall in die Residenzstadt Bamberg im Siebenjaehrigen Krieg vom 30. Mai bis zum 10. Juni 1758." *Berichte des Historischen Vereins Bamberg* 143 (2006): 521–531.

Lenman, Bruce P. "Under Whose Flag? The Erratic Emergence of the East India Company as a Military Power 1688–1757." In *Britain's Colonial Wars 1688–1783.* Routledge, 2001.

Lenman, Bruce P., and Philip Lawson. "Robert Clive, the 'Black Jagir' and British Politics." *Historical Journal* 26 (1983): 801–829.

Leonhard, Jörn. *Bellizismus und Nation: Kriegsdeutung und Nationsbestimmung in Europa und den Vereinigten Staaten 1750–1914*. Oldenbourg, 2008.

Lesueur, Boris. "La garnison de la Guadeloupe sous l'Ancien Régime." *Bulletin de la Société d'Histoire de la Guadeloupe* 154 (2009): 29–58.

Liechtenhan, Francine-Dominique. "Sollte Ostpreußen ins russische Reich integriert werden? Zur Geschichte der deutsch-russischen Beziehungen im Siebenjährigen Krieg." In *Deutsch-Russische Beziehungen: Beiträge der Internationalen Konferenz in Prag vom 24.–25. November 2005*, ed. František Stellner, with contributions by František Bahenský and Radek Soběhart. Set Out, 2007.

Lind, Gunner. "The Making of the Neutrality Convention of 1756: France and Her Scandinavian Allies." *Scandinavian Journal of History* 8 (1983): 171–192.

Lindgren, Uta. "Schlachtenpläne und Kartographie im 18. Jh.: Das Beispiel Hastenbeck (1757)." In *Sine ira et studio: Militärhistorische Studien zur Erinnerung an Hans Schmidt*, ed. Uta Lindgren, Karl Schnith, and Jakob Seibert. Laßleben, 2001.

Lindner, Thomas. *Die Peripetie des Siebenjährigen Krieges: Der Herbstfeldzug 1760 in Sachsen und der Winterfeldzug 1760/61 in Hessen*. Duncker & Humblot, 1993.

Link, Viktor. "Geschichte in der Literatur: Drei Darstellungen der Schlacht von Minden und Herzog Ferdinands von Braunschweig und Wolfenbüttel in englischen Romanen des 18. Jahrhunderts." *Wolfenbütteler Studien zur Aufklärung* 1 (1974): 204–221.

Little, Hamish D. "The Treasury, the Commissariat and the Supply of the Combined Army in Germany During the Seven Years War (1756–1763)." Doctoral thesis, University of London, 1981.

Lippe-Weißenfeld, Ernst Graf zur. "Friedrichs des Großen Heimkehr in Berlin 1763." *Jahrbücher für die deutsche Armee und Marine* 90 (1894): 267–272.

Löffler, Fritz. *Dresden im 18. Jahrhundert: Bernardo Belloto genannt Canaletto*. Weidlich, 1985. Exhibition catalog.

Löffler, Ulrich. *Lissabons Fall—Europas Schrecken: Die Deutung des Erdbebens von Lissabon im deutschsprachigen Protestantismus des 18. Jahrhunderts*. De Gruyter, 1999.

Lotz, Wolfgang. *Kriegsgerichtsprozesse des Siebenjährigen Krieges in Preußen: Untersuchungen zur Beurteilung militärischer Leistung durch Friedrich II*. Haag und Herchen, 1981.

Lovejoy, David S. "Satanizing the American Indian." *New England Quarterly* 67, no. 4 (1994): 603–621.

Loyer, Pierre. "La Défense des côtes de Bretagne pendant la Guerre de Sept Ans: La Bataille de Saint-Cast." *Revue Maritime*, n.s., vol. 156 (1932): 721–739; 157 (1933): 75–98.

Ludwig, Jörg. "Schloss Hubertusburg als Ort der Friedensverhandlungen von 1762/63." In *Die Königliche Jagdresidenz Hubertusburg und der Frieden von 1763*, ed. Dirk Syndram and Claudia Brink. Edition Sächsische Zeitung, 2013.

Luengo, Pedro. "Military Engineering in Eighteenth-Century Havana and Manila: The Experience of the Seven Years War." *War in History* 24, no. 1 (2017): 4–27.

Luh, Jürgen. "Frederick the Great and the First 'World' War." In Danley and Speelman, *The Seven Years' War*.

Luh, Jürgen. *Der Große: Friedrich II. von Preußen*. Pantheon, 2014.

Luh, Jürgen. *Kriegskunst in Europa 1650–1800*. Böhlau, 2004.

Lynn, John A. *Battle: A History of Combat and Culture*. Westview, 2003.

Mackesy, Piers. *The Coward of Minden: The Affair of Lord George Sackville*. St. Martin's, 1979.

MacLeod, D. Peter. "Microbes and Muskets: Smallpox and the Participation of the Amerindian Allies of New France in the Seven Years' War." *Ethnohistory* 39, no. 1 (1992): 42–64.

MacLeod, D. Peter. *Northern Armageddon: The Battle of the Plains of Abraham*. Douglas & McIntyre, 2008.

Madley, Benjamin. "Reexamining the American Genocide Debate: Meaning, Historiography, and New Methods." *American Historical Review* 120, no. 1 (2015): 98–139.

Malcolm, John. *The Life of Robert Lord Clive: Collected from the Family Papers Communicated by the Earl of Powis*. 3 vols. London: Murray, 1836.

Malone, Patrick. *The Skulking Way of War: Technology and Tactics Among the New England Indians*. Johns Hopkins University Press, 1993.

Mancall, Peter C. *Deadly Medicine: Indians and Alcohol in Early America*. Cornell University Press, 1995.

Mann, Michael. *Bengalen im Umbruch: Die Herausbildung des britischen Kolonialstaates 1754–1793*. Steiner, 2000.

Mann, Michael. *Geschichte Südasiens: 1500 bis heute*. WBG, 2010.

Mann, Michael. "Der ungeliebte Krieg: Compagnie des Indes und East India Company als Kombattanten in einem globalen Konflikt, 1742–1763." In Externbrink, *Der Siebenjährige Krieg (1756–1763)*.

Mapp, Paul W. *The Elusive West and the Contest for Empire, 1713–1763*. University of North Carolina Press, 2011.

Marcus, Geoffrey. *Quiberon Bay: The Campaign in the Home Waters, 1759*. Hollis & Carter, 1960.

Marley, David F. "A Fearful Gift: The Spanish Naval Build-Up in the West Indies, 1759–1762." *Mariner's Mirror* 80 (1994): 403–417.

Marley, David F. "Havana Surprised: Prelude to the British Invasion, 1762." *Mariner's Mirror* 78, no. 3 (1992): 293–305.

Marowsky, Klaus. "Jobst Hinrich Lohrmann und die Schlacht bei Minden." In *Die Schlacht bei Minden: Ein Erinnerungsbuch zum 200. Gedenktag der Schlacht bei Minden am 1. August 1759*. Bruns, 1959.

Marsh, A. J. "The Taking of Goree, 1758." *Mariner's Mirror* 51 (1965): 117–130.

Marshall, Peter James. "The Thirteen Colonies in the Seven Years' War: The View from London." In *Britain and America Go to War: The Impact of War and Warfare in Anglo-America, 1754–1815*, ed. Julie Flavell and Stephen Conway. University Press of Florida, 2004.

Marshall, Peter James. "War and Its Transformations: India 1754–1765." In *The Making and Unmaking of Empires: Britain, India, and America c. 1750–1783*. Oxford University Press, 2005.

Marston, Daniel. *The Seven Years War*. Osprey, 2001.

Martinez de Zuñiga, Joaquín. *An Historical View of the Philippine Islands*, trans. John Maver. 2 vols. London: Asperne, 1814.

Masslowski, Dmitrij F. *Der Siebenjährige Krieg nach russischer Darstellung: Mit Autorisation des Verfassers übersetzt und mit Anmerkungen versehen von A. von Drygalski*. Vols. 1–3. Berlin: Eisenschmidt, 1888–1893.

Matar, Nabil I. *Turks, Moors and Englishmen in the Age of Discovery*. Columbia University Press, 1999.

Mathieu, Jacques. "Les rappels mémoriels de la guerre de sept ans au Canada." In *La guerre de Sept ans en Nouvelle-France*, ed. Bertrand Fonck and Laurent Veyssière. Septentrion, 2011.

Mathieu, Jacques, and Sophie Imbeault. *La Guerre des Canadiens, 1756–1763*. Septentrion, 2013.

Mattioli, Adam. *Verlorene Welten: Eine Geschichte der Indianer Nordamerikas 1700–1910*. Klett-Cotta, 2017.

Mayor, Adrienne. "The Nessus Shirt in the New World: Smallpox Blankets in History and Legend." *Journal of American Folklore* 108 (1995): 54–77.

McCormack, Matthew. "Citizenship, Nationhood, and Masculinity in the Affair of the Hannoverian Soldier, 1756." *Historical Journal* 49, no. 4 (2006): 971–993.

McCulloch, Ian M. "'Like Roaring Lions Breaking from Their Chains': The Battle of Ticonderoga, 8 July 1758." In *Fighting for Canada, Seven Battles, 1758–1945*, ed. Donald E. Graves. Robin Brass Studio, 2000.

McCulloch, Ian M. *Sons of the Mountains: The Highland Regiments in the French and Indian War, 1756–1767*. 2 vols. Purple Mountain Press, 2006.

McDonnell, Michael A. *Masters of Empire: Great Lakes Indians and the Making of America*. Hill and Wang, 2016.

McGuffie, Tom Henderson. "A Deputy Paymaster's Fortune: The Case of George Durant, Deputy Paymaster to the Havana Expedition, 1762." *Journal of the Society for Army Historical Research* 32 (1954): 144–147.

McKendrick, Neil, John Brewer, and John H. Plumb, eds. *The Birth of a Consumer Society: The Commercialization of Eighteenth-Century England*. Indiana University Press, 1982.

McLeod, A. B. *British Naval Captains of the Seven Years' War: The View from the Quarterdeck*. Boydell, 2012.

McLynn, Frank. *1759: The Year Britain Became Master of the World*. Jonathan Cape, 2004.

McNairn, Alan. *Behold the Hero: General Wolfe and The Arts in the Eighteenth Century*. Liverpool University Press, 1997.

McNeill, John Robert. *Atlantic Empires of France and Spain: Louisbourg and Havana, 1700–1763*. University of North Carolina Press, 1985.

McNeill, John Robert. *Mosquito Empires: Ecology and War in the Greater Caribbean, 1620–1914*. Cambridge University Press, 2010.

Medick, Hans. *Der Dreißigjährige Krieg: Zeugnisse vom Leben mit Gewalt*. Wallstein, 2018.

Medick, Hans. Eine Unterkunft im Schatten des Krieges, Frühjahr 1763: Mikrohistorische Betrachtungen einer Episode aus Karoline Kummerfelds "Die ganze Geschichte meines Lebens." *Historische Anthropologie* 29, no. 3 (2021): 437–446.

Mediger, Walther. "Hastenbeck und Zeven: Der Eintritt Hannovers in den Siebenjährigen Krieg." *Niedersächsisches Jahrbuch für Landesgeschichte* 56 (1984): 137–166.

Mediger, Walther. *Herzog Ferdinand von Braunschweig-Lüneburg und die alliierte Armee im Siebenjährigen Krieg (1757–1762) für die Publikation aufbereitet und vollendet von Thomas Klingebiel*. Hahnsche Buchhandlung, 2011.

Mediger, Walther. *Moskaus Weg nach Europa: Der Aufstieg Russlands zum Europäischen Machtstaat im Zeitalter Friedrichs des Großen*. Westermann, 1952.

Meißner, Erhard. "Die südwestdeutschen Reichsstände im Siebenjährigen Krieg (1756–1763)." *Ellwanger Jahrbuch* 23 (1969/70): 117–158.

Menke, Werner. *Das Vokalwerk Georg Philipp Telemann's: Überlieferung und Zeitfolge*. Noske, 1941.

Menneking, Friedrich. *Victoria by Vellinghausen 1761: Spaziergänge in die Geschichte des Siebenjährigen Krieges in Westdeutschland*. Hüttemann, 1989.

Merrell, James H. *Into the American Woods: Negotiators on the Pennsylvania Frontier*. Norton, 1999.

Merziger, Patrick. "Der öffentliche König? Herrschaft in den Medien während der drei schlesischen Kriege." In Sösemann and Vogt-Spira, *Friedrich der Große in Europa*.

Meyer, Hermann. *Der Plan eines evangelischen Fürstenbundes im Siebenjährigen Kriege*. Celle: Schweiger & Pick, 1893.

Meyer, Paul. *Zeitgenössische Beurteilung und Auswirkung des Siebenjährigen Krieges (1756–1763) in der evangelischen Schweiz*. Helbing & Lichtenhahn, 1955.

Meyer, Stefan. *Georg Wilhelm Fürst zu Schaumburg-Lippe (1784–1860): Absolutistischer Monarch und Grossunternehmer an der Schwelle zum Industriezeitalter*. Verlag für Regionalgeschichte, 2007.

Middleton, Richard. *Amherst and the Conquest of Canada*. Sutton, 2003.

Middleton, Richard. *The Bells of Victory: The Pitt-Newcastle Ministry and the Conduct of the Seven Years' War 1757–1762*. Cambridge University Press, 1985.

Middleton, Richard. "The British Coastal Expeditions to France, 1757–1758." *Journal of the Society for Army Historical Research* 71 (1993): 74–92.

Middleton, Richard. *Pontiac's War: Its Causes, Course, and Consequences.* Routledge, 2007.

Middleton, Richard. "The Recruitment of the British Army 1755–1762." *Journal of the Society for Army Historical Research* 67 (1989): 226–238.

Minelli, Kelly. *"Wo alle Herzen heldenmüthig schlugen": Heroische Leitbilder in deutschen und französischen Militärselbstzeugnissen des Siebenjährigen Krieges, der Kriege der Französischen Revolution und der Napoleonischen Kriege.* Ergon, 2024.

Mintz, Sidney. *Sweetness and Power: The Place of Sugar in Modern History.* Viking, 1985.

Mintzker, Yair. *The Defortification of the German City, 1689–1866.* Cambridge University Press, 2012.

Misencik, Paul R. *George Washington and the Half-King Chief Tanacharison: An Alliance That Began the French and Indian War.* McFarland, 2014.

Mittenzwei, Ingrid. *Preussen nach dem Siebenjährigen Krieg: Auseinandersetzungen zwischen Bürgertum und Staat um die Wirtschaftspolitik.* Akademie, 1979.

Möbius, Katrin, and Sascha Möbius. *Prussian Army Soldiers and the Seven Years' War: The Psychology of Honour.* Bloomsbury Academic, 2020.

Möbius, Sascha. "'Bravthun,' 'entmannende Furcht' und 'schöne Überläuferinnen': Zum Männlichkeitsbild preussischer Soldaten im Siebenjährigen Krieg in Quellen aus Magdeburg, Halle und der Altmark." In *Leben in der Stadt: Eine Kultur- und Geschlechtergeschichte Magdeburgs,* ed. Eva Labouvie. Böhlau, 2004.

Möbius, Sascha. "Ein 'feste Burg ist unser Gott . . .!' und das 'entsetzliche Lärmen ihrer Trommeln': Preußische Militärmusik in den Schlachten des Siebenjährigen Krieges." In *"Mars und die Musen": Das Wechselspiel von Militär, Krieg und Kunst in der Frühen Neuzeit,* ed. Jutta Nowosadtko and Matthias Rogg. LIT, 2008.

Möbius, Sascha. "'Haß gegen alles, was nur den Namen eines Franzosen führet?' Die Schlacht bei Rossbach und nationale Stereotype in der deutschsprachigen Militärliteratur in der zweiten Hälfte des 18. Jahrhunderts." In *Gallophobie im 18. Jahrhundert: Akten der Fachtagung vom 2./3. Mai 2002 am Forschungszentrum Europäische Aufklärung,* ed. Jens Häseler and Albert Meier. Berliner Wissenschaftsverlag, 2005.

Möbius, Sascha. "Die Kommunikation zwischen preußischen Soldaten und Offizieren im Siebenjährigen Krieg zwischen Gewalt und Konsens." *Militärgeschichtliche Zeitschrift* 63 (2004): 325–353.

Möbius, Sascha. "Kriegsbrauch." In *Enzyklopädie der Neuzeit,* ed. Friedrich Jaeger. Vol. 2. Metzler, 2008.

Möbius, Sascha. "Kriegsgreuel in den Schlachten des Siebenjährigen Krieges in Europa." In *Kriegsgreuel: Die Entgrenzung von Gewalt in kriegerischen Konflikten vom Mittelalter bis ins 20. Jahrhundert,* ed. Sönke Neitzel and Daniel Hohrath. Schöningh, 2008.

Möbius, Sascha. *Mehr Angst vor dem Offizier als vor dem Feind? Eine mentalitätsgeschichtliche Studie zur preußischen Taktik im Siebenjährigen Krieg.* Müller, 2007.

Möbius, Sascha. "'Von Jast und Hitze wie vertaumelt': Überlegungen zur Wahrnehmung von Gewalt durch preußische Soldaten im Siebenjährigen Krieg." *Forschungen zur Brandenburgischen und Preußischen Geschichte*, n.s., vol. 12 (2002): 1–34.

Molina, Ignacio. "Las Milicias 'no Españolas' del Rio de la Plata (1762–1763): Reclutamiento, movilización, functiones en campana, privilegios et integración social." *Casus Belli* 1 (2020): 47–71.

Mollwo, Ludwig. *Die Kapitulation von Maxen*. Sömmering, 1893.

Monks, Sarah. "Our Man in Havana: Representation and Reputation in Lieutenant Philip Orsbridge's Britannia's Triumph (1765)." In *Conflicting Visions: War and Visual Culture in Britain and France c. 1700–1830*, ed. John Bonehill and Geoff Quilley. Ashgate, 2005.

Montigny, Jacinthe De. "Le Canada dans l'imaginaire colonial français (1754–1756)." *French History and Civilization* 7 (2017): 80–92.

Moon, Penderel. *The British Conquest and Dominion of India*. Duckworth, 1989.

Morieux, Renaud. "French Prisoners of War, Conflicts of Honour, and Social Inversions in England, 1744–1783." *Historical Journal* 56, no. 1 (2013): 55–88.

Morieux, Renaud. "Lettres perdues: Communautés épistolaires, guerres et liens familiaux dans le monde maritime atlantique du xviiie siècle." *Annales: Histoire, Sciences Sociales* 78, no. 2 (2023): 333–373.

Morieux, Renaud. *The Society of Prisoners: Anglo-French Wars and Incarceration in the 18th Century*. Oxford University Press, 2019.

Morón García, Juan José. "El juicio por la pérdida de La Habana en 1762." *Baluarte* 1 (1994): 19–48.

Mraz, Gerda, and Gottfried Mraz. *Maria Theresia: Ihr Leben und ihre Zeit in Bildern und Dokumenten*. Süddeutscher, 1980.

Müller, Michael G. "Russland und der Siebenjährige Krieg: Beitrag zu einer Kontroverse." *Jahrbücher für Geschichte Osteuropas* 28 (1980): 198–219.

Müller, Miriam. "On dit: Die Nachrichtenrezeption des Krefelders Abraham ter Meer im Siebenjährigen Krieg." *Annalen des Historischen Vereins für den Niederrhein insbesondere das alte Erzbistum Köln* 215 (2012): 73–96.

Müller, Rudolf. "Graf Wilhelm von Schaumburg Lippe in Portugal." *Wehrwissenschaftliche Rundschau* 13 (April 1963): 230–238.

Mullin, Michael J. "The Albany Congress and Colonial Confederation." *Mid-America* 72, no. 2 (1990): 93–105.

Münkler, Herfried. *Gewalt und Ordnung: Das Bild des Krieges im politischen Denken*. Fischer, 1992.

Münkler, Herfried. *Die neuen Kriege*. Rowohlt, 2004. English edition: *The New Wars*, trans. Patrick Camiller. Polity, 2005.

Murrin, John M. "The French and Indian War, the American Revolution, and the Counterfactual Hypothesis: Reflections on Lawrence Henry Gipson and John Shy." *Reviews in American History* 1, no. 3 (1973): 307–318.

Musil, Robert. "Das hilflose Europa (1922)." In *Gesammelte Werke*. Vol. 8. Rowohlt, 1978.

Nash, Gary B. *The Urban Crucible: Social Change, Political Consciousness, and the Origins of the American Revolution*. Harvard University Press, 1979.

Naudé, Albert. "Die Einnahme von Berlin durch die Österreicher im Oktober 1757 und die Flucht der Königlichen Familie von Berlin nach Spandau." *Märkische Forschungen* 20 (1887): 149–170.

Naudé, Albert. "Friedrich der Große vor dem Ausbruch des Siebenjährigen Krieges." *Historische Zeitschrift* 55 (1886): 404–462.

Neal, Larry. "Interpreting Power and Profit in Economic History: A Case Study of the Seven Years' War." *Journal of Economic History* 37 (1977): 20–35.

Nechtman, Tillman W. "Nabobs Revisited: A Cultural History of British Imperialism and the Indian Question in Late-Eighteenth-Century Britain." *History Compass* 4, no. 4 (2006): 645–667.

Nester, William R. *The Epic Battles for Ticonderoga, 1758*. State University of New York Press, 2008.

Nester, William R. *The First Global War: Britain, France, and the Fate of North America, 1756–1775*. Praeger, 2000.

Nester, William R. *The French and Indian War and the Conquest of New France*. University of Oklahoma Press, 2014.

Neuhaus, Helmut. "Das Reich im Kampf gegen Friedrich den Großen: Reichsarmee und Reichskriegführung im Siebenjährigen Krieg." In Kroener, *Europa im Zeitalter Friedrichs des Großen*.

Newbigging, William James. "Propaganda, Political Discourse and the Battle Over French Public Opinion in the Seven Years' War." *Proceedings of the Nineteenth Meeting of the French Colonial History Society* 19 (1994): 101–110.

Nicklas, Thomas. "Die Schlacht von Rossbach (1757) zwischen Wahrnehmung und Deutung." *Forschungen zur Brandenburgischen und Preußischen Geschichte*, n.s., vol. 12, no. 1 (2002): 35–53.

Nicolai, Martin Lathe. "A Different Kind of Courage: The French Military and the Canadian Irregular Soldier During the Seven Years' War." *Canadian Historical Review* 70, no. 1 (1989): 53–75.

Niedhart, Gottfried. *Handel und Krieg in der britischen Weltpolitik 1738–1763*. Fink, 1979.

Niemann, Gerhard. "Die Operationen im Westen während des Siebenjährigen Krieges bis zur Schlacht von Hastenbeck und die Schlacht bei Hastenbeck am 26. Juli 1757." *Wehrwissenschaftliche Rundschau* 11 (1961): 577–598.

Niklowitz, Fredy. "' . . . bis aufs blut ausgesogen . . .': Lünen im siebenjährigen Krieg." *Der Märker* 42, no. 2 (1993): 47–54; 42, no. 3 (1993): 124–135.

Nolte, Jürgen. *Die Schlacht bei Wilhelmsthal: Der Siebenjährige Krieg in Nordhessen*. Wartberg, 2012.

Nordsiek, Hans. "Immer auf der Siegerseite: Die Schlacht bei Minden 1759: Realität und Interpretation." *Mitteilungen des Mindener Geschichtsvereins* 71 (1999): 139–179.

Norrhem, Svante. *Mercenary Swedes: French Subsidies to Sweden 1631–1796*. Nordic Academic Press, 2019.

Notthoff, Thomas. "Strohfeuer oder Symbolakt? Executio in effigie im Hessen des Siebenjährigen Krieges." *Hessisches Jahrbuch für Landesgeschichte* 62 (2012): 149–167.

Nowosadtko, Jutta. "'Gehegter Krieg'—'Gezähmte Bellona'? Kombattanten, Partheygänger, Privatiers und Zivilbevölkerung im sogenannten Kleinen Krieg der Frühen Neuzeit." In *Zivilisten und Soldaten: Entgrenzte Gewalt in der Geschichte*, ed. Frank Becker. Klartext, 2015.

Nowosadtko, Jutta, Diethelm Klippel, and Kai Lohsträter, eds. *Militär und Recht vom 16. bis 19. Jahrhundert: Gelehrter Diskurs, Praxis, Transformationen*. V&R unipress, 2016.

O'Brien, Patrick Karl. "Fiscal and Financial Preconditions for the Rise of British Naval Hegemony, 1485–1815." Working Paper No. 91/05. London School of Economics, November 2005.

Oldach, Robert. *Stadt und Festung Stralsund: Die Schwedische Militärpräsenz in Schwedisch-Pommern 1721–1807*. Böhlau, 2018.

Olding, Manfred. *Die Medaillen auf Friedrich den Großen von Preußen 1712 bis 1786; Anhang: Medaillen mit Bezug auf Preußen aus der Zeit von 1740 bis 1786*. Gietl, 2003.

Oliphant, John. *John Forbes: Scotland, Flanders and the Seven Years' War, 1707–1759*. Bloomsbury, 2015.

Oliva, Lawrence Jay. *Misalliance: A Study of French Policy in Russia During the Seven Years' War*. New York University Press, 1964.

Olmes, Jürgen. "Johann Christian Fischer, sein Korps und die Überfälle auf Ruhrort im Jahre 1760." *Duisburger Forschungen* 4 (1961): 78–92.

Olson, Donald W., et al. "Perfect Tide, Ideal Moon: An Unappreciated Aspect of Wolfe's Generalship at Québec 1759." *William and Mary Quarterly* 59 (2002): 957–974.

Oncken, Wilhelm. *Das Zeitalter Friedrich des Großen: Allgemeine Geschichte in Einzeldarstellungen*. 2 vols. Berlin: Grote, 1881/1882.

Önnerfors, Andreas. "Freimaurerei und Offiziertum im 18. Jahrhundert." *Militär und Gesellschaft in der Frühen Neuzeit* 14, no. 1 (2010): 229–250.

Opitz-Belakhal, Claudia. *Militärreformen zwischen Bürokratisierung und Adelsreaktion: Das französische Kriegsministerium und seine Reformen im Offizierskorps von 1760–1790*. Thorbecke, 1994.

Oppermann, Moritz. *Die Schlacht bei Hastenbeck: Zum 250. Jahrestag am 26. Juli 2007*. Niemeyer, 2007. First edition published in 1957.

Orain, Arnaud. "Soutenir la guerre et réformer la fiscalité: Silhouette et Forbonnais au Contrôle général des finances (1759)." *French Historical Studies* 36, no. 3 (2013): 417–447.

Osborn, Jeremy. "India and the East India Company in the Public Sphere of Eighteenth-Century Britain." In *The Worlds of the East India Company*, ed. Huw V. Bowen, Margarette Lincoln, and Nigel Rigby. Boydell, 2002.

Ozanam, Didier. "Les origines du troisième Pacte de famille (1761)." *Revue d'histoire diplomatique* 75 (1961): 307–340.

Padeni, Scott A. "Forgotten Soldiers: The Role of Blacks in New York's Northern Campaigns of the Seven Years War." *Bulletin of the Fort Ticonderoga Museum* 16, no. 2 (1999): 152–169.

Palacio Atard, Vicente. *El tercer pacto de familia*. Consejo Superior De Investigaciones Cientificas, 1945.

Panissié, Florian. "La petite guerre à l'épreuve des colonies, de la théorie à la pratique: Le cas du siège de Québec en 1759." In *La France face aux crises et aux conflits des périphéries européennes et atlantiques du XVIIe au XXe siècle*, ed. Éric Schnakenbourg and Frédéric Dessberg. Presses universitaires de Rennes, 2010.

Pantel, Isabelle. *Die hamburgische Neutralität im Siebenjährigen Krieg*. LIT, 2011.

Parcero Torre, Celia María. *La pérdida de La Habana y las reformas borbónicas en Cuba, 1760–1773*. Junta de Castilla y León, Consejería de Educación y Cultura, 1998.

Pares, Richard. *War and Trade in the West Indies, 1739–1763*. Clarendon, 1936.

Pargellis, Stanley McCrory. "Braddocks Defeat." *American Historical Review* 41 (1935/1936): 253–269.

Pargellis, Stanley McCrory. *Lord Loudoun in North America*. Yale University Press, 1933.

Parkman, Francis. *Montcalm and Wolfe: The French and Indian War*. Boston: Little, Brown, 1884. Reprint, Da Capo, 1995.

Peace, Thomas. "The Slow Process of Conquest: Huron-Wendat Responses to the Conquest of Quebec, 1697–1791." In Buckner and Reid, *Revisiting 1759*.

Pease, Theodore Calvin. *Anglo-French Boundary Disputes in the West, 1749–1763*. Illinois State Historical Library, 1936.

Peball, Kurt. "Aspekte der Forschung zum Kriegswesen der Zeit Maria Theresias und Josephs II." In *Österreich im Europa der Aufklärung: Kontinuität und Zäsur in Europa zur Zeit Maria Theresias und Josephs II—Internationales Symposion in Vienna, 20–23, Oktober 1980*, ed. Richard Georg Plaschka. 2 vols. Österreicheischen Akademie der Wissenschaften, 1985.

Peckham, Howard. *Pontiac and the Indian Uprising*. Princeton University Press, 1947.

Perrefort, Maria. "'Man hörte in den tagen nichts als heulen und schreien in der stadt'—Hamm im siebenjährigen krieg (1756–1763)." *Der Märker* 53, no. 1 (2004): 26–36.

Persson, Mathias. "Mediating the Enemy: Prussian Representations of Austria, France and Sweden During the Seven Years War." *German History* 32, no. 2 (2014): 181–200.

Peters, Marie. "Early Hanoverian Consciousness: Empire or Europe?" *English Historical Review* 122, no. 497 (2007): 632–668.

Peters, Marie. "The Myth of William Pitt, Earl of Chatham, Great Imperialist, pt. 1: Pitt and Imperial Expansion 1738–1763." *Journal of Imperial and Commonwealth History* 21 (1993): 31–74.

Peters, Marie. *Pitt and Popularity: The Patriot Minister and London Opinion During the Seven Years War*. Clarendon, 1980.

Picaud-Monnerat, Sandrine. *La petite guerre au XVIIIe siècle*. Economica, 2010.

Pichichero, Christy. *The Military Enlightenment: War and Culture in the French Empire from Louis XIV to Napoleon*. Cornell University Press, 2017.

Plank, Geoffrey. *Rebellion and Savagery: The Jacobite Rising of 1745 and the British Empire*. University of Pennsylvania Press, 2006.

Plassmann, Max. "Bikonfessionelle Streitkräfte: Das Beispiel des Schwäbischen Reichskreises (1648–1803)." In Kaiser and Kroll, *Militär und Religiosität in der Frühen Neuzeit*.

Pockrandt, Mark. *Biblische Aufklärung: Biographie und Theologie der Berliner Hofprediger August Friedrich Wilhelm Sack (1703–1786) und Friedrich Samuel Gottfried Sack (1738–1817)*. De Gruyter, 2003.

Pocock, Tom. *Battle for Empire: The Very First World War 1756–63*. O'Mara, 1998.

Podruczny, Grzegorz, and Jakub Wrzosek. "Lone Grenadier: An Episode from the Battle of Kunersdorf, 12 August 1759." *Journal of Conflict Archaeology* 9, no. 1 (2014): 33–47.

Pohlig, Matthias. *Marlboroughs Geheimnis: Strukturen und Funktionen der Informationsgewinnung im Spanischen Erbfolgekrieg*. Böhlau, 2016.

Pois, Robert, and Philip Langer. "Frederick the Great at Kunersdorf, August 12, 1759." In *Command Failure in War: Psychology and Leadership*. Indiana University Press, 2004.

Polskoi, Sergei, and Claus Scharf. "Der Siebenjährige Krieg." In *Deutschland—Russland: Stationen gemeinsamer Geschichte, Orte der Erinnerung*. Vol. 1, *Das 18. Jahrhundert*, ed. Horst Möller, et al. De Gruyter, 2018.

Pompe, Hedwig. "Im Kalkül der Kommunikation: Die Politik der Nachricht." In Adam and Dainat, *Der Siebenjährige Krieg in den zeitgenössischen Medien*.

Pope, Dudley. *At Twelve Mr Byng Was Shot*. Lippincott, 1962.

Porbeck, Asbrand von. "Der Streifzug des Königlich Preussischen Oberstlieutenants Jh. von Meyer im Jahre 1757 nach der Oberpfalz und Franken." *Jahrbücher für die deutsche Armee und Marine* 19 (1876): 40–57.

Porsch, Rudolf Otto Karl. *Die Beziehungen Friedrichs des Grossen zur Türkei bis zum Beginn und während des siebenjährigen Krieges*. Marburg: Ehrhardt, 1897.

Poussou, Jean-Pierre. "Les conséquences économiques de la guerre de Sept Ans." In Fonck and Veyssière, *La Chute de la Nouvelle-France*.

Pranghofer, Sebastian. "Der Umgang mit Krankheit und Seuchengefahr im Kriegsalltag in Nordwestdeutschland, 1757–1763." In *Krank vom Krieg: Umgangsweisen und kulturelle Deutungsmuster eines Zusammenhangs von der Antike bis zur Gegenwart*, ed. Gundula Gahlen, Nikolas Funke, and Ulrike Ludwig.) Campus, 2022.

Preßler, Ernst. *Schraubtaler und Steckmedaillen: Verborgene Kostbarkeiten*. Münzen und Medaillenhandlung, 2000.

Preston, David L. *Braddock's Defeat: The Battle of the Monongahela River and the Road to Revolution*. Oxford University Press, 2015.

Pritchard, James S. *Louis XV's Navy, 1748–1762: A Study of Organization and Administration*. McGill-Queen's University Press, 1987.

Pröhl, Karl. *Die Bedeutung preußischer Politik in den Phasen der orientalischen Frage: Ein Beitrag zur Entwicklung deutsch-türkischer Beziehungen von 1606–1871*. Lang, 1986.

Pröve, Ralf. "Der delegitimierte Gegner: Kriegführung als Argument im Siebenjährigen Krieg." In Externbrink, *Der Siebenjährige Krieg (1756–1763)*.

Pröve, Ralf. "Der Soldat in der 'guten Bürgerstube': Das frühneuzeitliche Einquartierungssystem und die sozioökonomischen Folgen." In Kroener and Pröve, *Krieg und Frieden*.

Puech-Milhau, Maria Louise. "La Campagne d'allemagne (1756–1762) d'après les lettres de militaries castrais." *Revue du Tarn* 11 (1945): 25–44.

Pyta, Wolfram. "Von der Entente cordiale zur Aufkündigung der Bündnispartnerschaft: Die preußisch-britischen Allianzbeziehungen im Siebenjährigen Krieg 1758–1762." *Forschungen zur Brandenburgischen und Preußischen Geschichte* 10 (2000): 1–49.

Quandt, Franz. "Die Schlacht bei Lobositz, 1. Oktober 1756." Diss., Berlin: Pfeiffer, 1909.

Querengässer, Alexander, ed. *The Battle of Rossbach 1757: New Perspectives on the Battle and Campaign*. Helion, 2022.

Quiason, Serafin D. "The East India Company in Manila, 1762–1764." *Philippine Social Sciences and Humanities Review* 28, no. 4 (1963): 424–444.

Quilitzsch, Uwe. "Fürst Franz und der 'Royal Navy Room' im Schloss Wörlitz." In *Das Leben des Fürsten: Studien zur Biografie von Leopold III. Friedrich Franz von Anhalt-Dessau (1740–1817)*, ed. Holger Zaunstöck. Mitteldeutscher, 2008.

Ranke, Leopold von. *Geschichte von Österreich und Preußen zwischen den Friedensschlüssen von Aachen und Hubertusburg*. Leipzig: Duncker & Humblot, 1875.

Raschke, Martin. *Der politisierende Generalstab: Die friderizianischen Kriege in der amtlichen deutschen Militärgeschichtsschreibung 1890–1914*. Rombach, 1993.

Rashed, Zenab Esmat. *The Peace of Paris, 1763*. Liverpool University Press, 1951.

Rasmussen, William M. S., and Robert S. Tilton. *George Washington: The Man Behind the Myths*. University of Virginia Press, 1999.

Redlich, Fritz. *De praeda militari: Looting and Booty 1500–1815*. Steiner, 1956.

Reese, Armin. *Europäische Hegemonie und France d'outre-mer: Koloniale Fragen in der französischen Außenpolitik 1700–1763*. Steiner, 1988.

Regan, Shaun. "Oladuah Equiano and the Seven Years' War: Slavery, Service and the Sea." In De Bruyn and Regan, *The Culture of the Seven Year's War*.

Rehfeld, Paul. "Die preussische Kriegsindustrie unter Friedrich dem Grossen." Diss., University of Berlin, 1942.

Reid, Stuart. *The Battle of Minden 1759: The Impossible Victory of the Seven Years War.* Frontline, 2016.

Reid, Stuart. *The Battle of Plassey 1757: The Victory That Won an Empire.* Frontline, 2017.

Rétat, Pierre. "Aux confins de la presse: Information graphique et information écrite; Récits et plans de batailles." In *Le journalisme d'Ancien Régime: Questions et propositions*, ed. Pierre Rétat. Presses universitaires de Lyon, 1982.

Rétat, Pierre. *Gazette d'Amsterdam: Miroir de l'Europe au XVIIIe siècle.* Voltaire Foundation, 2001.

Ribaucourt, Edouard de. *La vie militaire et les exploits de J.-C. Fischer: Brigadier des Armées du Roy Louis XV, Fondateur et Commandant le Corps des Chasseurs (1743–1761), Chef du Service des Renseignements [. . .].* Librairie Universelle, 1928.

Richardson, John. "Imagining Military Conflict During the Seven Years' War." *Studies in English Literature* 48 (2008): 585–611.

Richter, Daniel K. *Facing East from Indian Country: A Native History of Early America.* Harvard University Press, 2001.

Riley, James C. "French Finances, 1727–1768.," *Journal of Modern History* 59 (1987): 209–243.

Riley, James C. *The Seven Years' War and the Old Regime in France: The Economic and Financial Toll.* Princeton University Press, 1986.

Rink, Martin. *Vom 'Partheygänger' zum Partisanen: Die Konzeption des kleinen Krieges in Preußen 1740–1813.* Lang, 1999.

Ritter, Gerhard. *The Sword and the Scepter: The Problem of Militarism in Germany.* Vol. 1, *The Prussian Tradition 1740–1890.* University of Miami Press, 1969.

Rizzi, Alberto. *Bernardo Belloto: Dresda Vienna Monaco (1747–1766).* Canal & Stamperia, 1996.

Robinson, Daniel. "Giving Peace to Europe: European Geopolitics, Colonial Political Culture, and the Hanoverian Monarchy in British North America, ca. 1740–63." *William and Mary Quarterly* 73, no. 2 (2016): 291–332.

Robitschek, Norbert. *Hochkirch: Eine Studie.* Verlag von teufens, 1905.

Robson, John. *Captain Cook's War and Peace: The Royal Navy Years, 1755–1768.* Seaforth, 2009.

Roeck, Bernd. "Fabrizio auf dem Schlachtfeld von Waterloo oder zur Entstehung der 'Schrecken des Krieges' als Thema der Kunst." In *Die Schrecken des Krieges: Kriegs- und Revolutionsdarstellungen aus fünf Jahrhunderten* (Ausstellungskatalog). Galerie Mäder, 1987.

Røge, Pernille. "'La clef de commerce'—The Changing Role of Africa in France's Atlantic Empire ca. 1760–1797." *History of European Ideas* 34, no. 4 (2008): 431–443.

Røge, Pernille. *Economistes and the Reinvention of Empire: France in the Americas and Africa, c. 1750–1802.* Cambridge University Press, 2019.

Røge, Pernille. "The Seven Years' War in West Africa." In Burnard, Hart, and Houllemare, *The Oxford Handbook of the Seven Years' War.*

Rohrschneider, Michael. *Österreich und der Immerwährende Reichstag: Studien zur Klientelpolitik und Parteibildung (1745–1763)*. Vandenhoeck & Ruprecht, 2014.

Ropes, Arthur R. "The Causes of the Seven Years' War." *Transactions of the Royal Historical Society*, n.s., vol. 4 (1889): 143–170.

Rosseaux, Ulrich. "Die Belagerung Dresdens im Jahr 1760 als Medienereignis des 18. Jahrhunderts." *Dresdner Hefte* 68 (2001): 51–56.

Rothschild, Emma. *The Inner Life of Empires: An Eighteenth-Century History*. Princeton University Press, 2011.

Roy, Atul Chandra. *The Career of Mir Jafar Khan, 1757–65 A.D.* Das Gupta, 1953.

Roy, Kaushik. "The Hybrid Military Establishment of the East India Company in South Asia: 1750–1849." *Journal of Global History* 6 (2011): 195–218.

Ruffmann, Karl-Heinz. "Der Ostseeraum im Siebenjährigen Krieg." *Zeitschrift für Ostforschung* 5 (1956): 500–511.

Russell, Nelson Vance. "The Reaction in England and America to the Capture of Havana, 1762." *Hispanic American Historical Review* 9 (August 1929): 303–316.

Rustin, Jacques. "Un pamphlet romanesque contre les Anglais dans la guerre de Sept ans: Les Sauvages de l'Europe (1760) de R.-M. Lesuire." *Recherches et travaux* 49 (1995): 83–95.

Salewski, Michael. "Praevenire quam praeveniri: Zur Idee des Präventivkriegs in der Späten Neuzeit." *Historische Mitteilungen* 18 (2005): 88–100.

Salisch, Marcus von. *Treue Deserteure: Das Kursächsische Militär und der Siebenjährige Krieg*. Oldenbourg, 2008.

Salisch, Marcus von. "Zwei 'unerhörte Exempel': Die Kapitulationen von Pirna 1756 und Maxen 1759 im Vergleich." *Neues Archiv für sächsische Geschichte* 84 (2013): 97–132.

Säve, Teofran. *Sveriges deltagande i sjuåriga kriget åren 1757–1762*. Beijer, 1915.

Savory, Reginald. "The Convention of Écluse, 1759–1762: The Treatment of the Sick and Wounded; Prisoners of War; and Deserters; of the British and French Armies During the Seven Years War." *Journal of the Society for Army Historical Research* 42, no. 170 (1964): 68–77.

Savory, Reginald. *His Britannic Majesty's Army in Germany During the Seven Years War*. Oxford University Press, 1966.

Savory, Reginald. "Jefferey Amherst Conducts the Hessians to England, 1756." *Journal of the Society for Army Historical Research* 49 (1971): 152–181.

Schaefer, Arnold. *Geschichte des siebenjährigen Kriegs*. 2 vols. Berlin: Hertz, 1874.

Schaefer, Arnold. "Zur Geschichte der katholischen Propaganda in der Zeit des siebenjährigen Krieges." *Historische Zeitschrift* 25 (1871): 108–118.

Schatzki, Theodore R. "Practice Theory as Flat Ontology." In *Practice Theory and Research: Exploring the Dynamics of Social Life*, ed. Gert Spaargaren, Don Weenink, and Machiel Lamers. Routledge, 2016.

Schepkowski, Nina Simone. *Johann Ernst Gotzkowsky: Kunstagent und Gemäldesammler im friderizianischen Berlin*. Akademie, 2009.

Schieder, Theodor. *Friedrich der Grosse: Ein Königtum der Widersprüche.* Bertelsmann, 1986. English edition: *Frederick the Great.* Routledge, 1999.

Schier, Otto. "Die Kämpfe bei Gundersdorf und Domstadtl am 28. u. 30. Juni 1758." *Zeitschrift des Deutschen Vereines für die Geschichte Mährens und Schlesiens* 12 (1908): 236–277.

Schild, Georg, ed. *Kriegserfahrungen: Krieg und Gesellschaft in der Neuzeit; Neue Horizonte der Forschung.* Schöningh, 2009.

Schilling, Lothar. *Kaunitz und das Renversement des Alliances: Studien zur außenpolitischen Konzeption Wenzel Antons von Kaunitz.* Duncker & Humblot, 1994.

Schinkel, Eckhard, ed. *Die Helden-Maschine: Zur Aktualität und Tradition von Heldenbildern.* Klartext, 2010.

Schirmer, Uwe, ed. *Sachsen 1763 bis 1832: Zwischen Rétablissement und bürgerlichen Reformen.* Sax, 1996.

Schivelbusch, Wolfgang. *The Culture of Defeat: On National Trauma, Mourning, and Recovery*, trans. Jefferson Chase. Granta, 2003.

Schleinert, Dirk. "Altvorpommern im Siebenjährigen Krieg: Aus dem Tagebuch des schwedischen Regimentspfarrers Olof Langelius." In *Die Demminer Kolloquien zur Geschichte Vorpommerns: Ausgewählte Beiträge 1995–2011*, ed. Henning Rischer and Dirk Schleinert. Sardellus, 2012.

Schleinert, Dirk. "Grimmen während des Siebenjährigen Krieges im Tagebuch des schwedischen Feldpredigers Olof Langelius." In *Die Marienkirche in Grimmen und ihre Gemeinde: Beiträge zur Kirchengeschichte einer pommerschen Stadt*, ed. Norbert Buske, Haik Thomas Porada, and Wolfgang Schmidt. Ludwig, 2015.

Schleinert, Dirk. "Der Siebenjährige Krieg in Vorpommern in kulturgeschichtlicher Perspektive." *Mare Balticum: Kultur-Geschichte-Gegenwart* (2001): 67–71.

Schlenke, Manfred. *England und das friderizianische Preussen: 1740–1763; Ein Beitrag zum Verhältnis von Politik und öffentlicher Meinung im England des 18. Jahrhunderts.* Alber, 1963.

Schmid, Alois. *Max III. Joseph und die europäischen Mächte: Die Außenpolitik des Kurfürstentums Bayern von 1745–1765.* Oldenbourg, 1987.

Schmidt, Burghardt. "Die Kämpfe um die Festung Harburg im Siebenjährigen Krieg: Ein Beitrag zur Militärgeschichte des 18. Jahrhunderts." *Harburger Jahrbuch* 21 (2000): 47–77.

Schmidt, Burghardt. "Regionalgeschichte im Spannungsfeld von europäischer Hegemonialpolitik und militärischer Okkupation: Die Stadt Emden im Siebenjährigen Krieg (1756–1763)." *Emder Jahrbuch* 80 (2000): 78–123.

Schmidt, Hans. "Der Einfluss der Winterquartiere auf Strategie und Kriegführung des Ancien Régime." *Historisches Jahrbuch* 92 (1972): 77–91.

Schmidt, Otto Eduard. "Die Meißner Vorverhandlungen zum Hubertusburger Frieden." *Mitteilungen des Vereins für Geschichte der Stadt Meissen* 6, no. 4 (1904): 405–434.

Schmidt, Walter. "Ein junger Russe erlebt Ostpreußen—Andrej Bolotovs Erinnerungen an den Siebenjährigen Krieg." In *West-östliche Spiegelungen*. Vol. 2, *Deutsche und Deutschland aus russischer Sicht: 18. Jahrhundert: Aufklärung*, ed. Dagmar Herrmann and Karl-Heinz Korn. Fink, 1992.

Schmidtchen, Volker. "Der Einfluß der Technik auf die Kriegführung zur Zeit Friedrichs des Großen." In *Friedrich der Große und das Militärwesen seiner Zeit*, ed. Militärgeschichtliches Forschungsamt. Mittler, 1987.

Schmitt, Richard. *Prinz Heinrich von Preussen als Feldherr im siebenjährigen Kriege*. 2 vols. Greifswald: Abel, 1885–1897.

Schnabel, Isabel, and Hyun Song Shin. "Liquidity and Contagion: The Crisis of 1763." *Journal of the European Economic Association* 2, no. 6 (2004): 929–968.

Schneider, Alfred. "Zum Ende des Siebenjährigen Krieges im Westen des Reiches: Das Gefecht an der Brücker Mühle bei Amöneburg am 21. September 1762." In *Fundamenta historiae: Geschichte im Spiegel der Numismatik und ihrer Nachbarwissenschaften*, ed. Reiner Cunz. Niedersächsisches Landesmuseum, 2004.

Schneider, Elena A. *The Occupation of Havana: War, Trade, and Slavery in the Atlantic World*. University of North Carolina Press, 2018.

Schneider, Karl H. "Die Schlacht bei Minden—lokales Ereignis mit globaler Bedeutung." *Zeitschrift für Weltgeschichte* 14, no. 2 (2013): 31–52.

Schoch, Albert. *Siebenjähriger Krieg und Weltkrieg: Ein geschichtlicher Vergleich*. Deutscher Wille, 1922.

Schort, Manfred. *Politik und Propaganda: Der Siebenjährige Krieg in den zeitgenössischen Flugschriften*. Lang, 2006.

Schulze, Winfried, ed. *Ego-Dokumente: Annäherung an den Menschen in der Geschichte*. Akademie, 1996.

Schumacher, Doris. "Der Siebenjährige Krieg in der bildenden Kunst: Von den Anfängen durch Johann Wilhelm Ludwig Gleim und Friedrich II. bis zu den populären Illustrationsfolgen des späten 18. Jahrhunderts." In Adam and Dainat, *Der Siebenjährige Krieg in den zeitgenössischen Medien*.

Schumann, Matt, and Karl W. Schweizer. "Anglo-American War Reporting, 1749–1763: The Press and a Research Strategy." *Canadian Journal of History* 43 (2008): 265–277.

Schumann, Matt, and Karl W. Schweizer. *The Seven Years War: A Transatlantic History*. Routledge, 2008.

Schurz, William Lytle. *The Manila Galleon*. Dutton, 1939.

Schütze-Böhm, Charlotte. "Eine wiedergefundene Handschrift 'Journal von der Belagerung Schweidnitz im Jahr 1762.'" *Jahrbuch der Schlesischen Friedrich-Wilhelms-Universität zu Breslau* 5 (1959): 176–183.

Schwarze, Karl. "Gleims 'Preußische Kriegslieder von einem Grenadier' und Soldatenbriefe als ihre Quelle." *Germanisch-romanische Monatsschrift* 25 (1937): 313–317.

Schwarze, Karl. *Der siebenjährige Krieg in der zeitgenössischen deutschen Literatur: Kriegserleben und Kriegserlebnis in Schrifttum und Dichtung des 18. Jh.* Junker und Dünnhaupt, 1936.

Schwarzer, Stephanie. *Zwischen Anspruch und Wirklichkeit: Die Ästhetisierung kriegerischer Ereignisse in der Frühen Neuzeit.* Meidenbauer, 2006.

Schweizer, Karl W. *England, Prussia and the Seven Years' War: Studies in Alliance Policies and Diplomacy.* Mellen, 1989.

Schweizer, Karl W. "Foreign Policy and the 18th Century English Press: The Case of Israel Mauduit's Considerations on the Present German War." *Publishing History* 39 (1996): 45–53.

Schweizer, Karl W. "Lord Bute and William Pitt's Resignation in 1761." *Canadian Journal of History* 8, no. 2 (1973): 111–125.

Schweizer, Karl W. "Lord Bute, Newcastle, Prussia and the Hague Overtures: A Re-Examination." *Albion* 9, no. 1 (1977): 72–97.

Schweizer, Karl W. "The Non-Renewal of the Anglo-Prussian Subsidy Treaty, 1761–1762: A Historical Revision." *Canadian Journal of History* 13, no. 3 (1976): 383–393.

Schweizer, Karl W. "The Seven Years' War: A System Perspective." In *The Origins of War in Early Modern Europe*, ed. Jeremy Black. Donald, 1987.

Schweizer, Karl W. *War, Politics and Diplomacy: The Anglo-Prussian Alliance, 1756–1763.* University Press of America, 1991.

Schwerhoff, Gerd. *Köln im Ancien Régime: 1686–1794.* Greven, 2017.

Scott, Hamish M. "The Decline of France and the Transformation of the European States System, 1756–1792." In *The Transformation of European Politics, 1763–1848: Episode or Model in Modern History?*, ed. Peter Krüger, Paul W. Schröder, and Katja Wüstenbecker. LIT, 2002.

Scott, Hamish M. *The Emergence of the Eastern Powers, 1756–1775.* Cambridge University Press, 2001.

Scott, Hamish M. "The Seven Years' War and Europe's Ancien Régime." *War in History* 18, no. 4 (2011): 419–455.

Scott, Joan Wallach. "The Evidence of Experience." *Critical Inquiry* 17, no. 4 (1991): 773–797.

Sdvižkov, Denis. "Landschaft nach der Schlacht: Briefe russischer Offiziere aus dem Siebenjährigen Krieg." *Forschungen zur Brandenburgischen und Preußischen Geschichte*, n.s., vol. 22, no. 1 (2012): 33–56.

Searing, James F. "The Seven Year's War in West Africa: The End of Company Rule and the Emergence of the *Habitants.*" In Danley and Speelman, *The Seven Years' War.*

Seidel, Paul. "Schlachtendarstellungen aus der Zeit Friedrich des Großen." *Hohenzollern-Jahrbuch* 15 (1911): 297–301.

Seidel, Paul. "Vivatbänder oder Seidenbänder im Hohenzollern-Museum." *Hohenzollern-Jahrbuch* 16 (1912): 128–153.

Shannon, Timothy. *Indians and Colonists at the Crossroads of Empire: The Albany Congress of 1754*. Cornell University Press, 2000.

Shepherd, William R. "The Cession of Louisiana to Spain." *Political Science Quarterly* 19 (1904): 439–458.

Shovlin, Ian David. "Overseas Violence and the Seven Years' War: Alleged Atrocities Committed by Non-Europeans as a Subject for Public Discussion in British News Commentary, 1754–1764." PhD diss., Durham University, 2018.

Shovlin, John. "Selling American Empire on the Eve of the Seven Years War: The French Propaganda Campaign of 1755-1756." *Past & Present* 206, no. 1 (2010): 121–149.

Showalter, Dennis E. "Hubertusburg to Auerstädt: The Prussian Army in Decline." *German History* 12 (1994): 308–333.

Showalter, Dennis E. *The Wars of Frederick the Great*. Longman, 1996.

Shy, John. "The Empire Remembered: Lawrence Henry Gipson, Historian." In *A People Numerous and Armed: Reflections on the Military Struggle for American Independence*. Oxford University Press, 1976.

Sichart, Louis Heinrich Friedrich von. *Geschichte der Königlich-Hannoverschen Armee*. Vol. 3, *Vierter Zeitraum 1756–1789*. Hanover: Hahn'sche Hofbuchhandlung, 1870.

Sikora, Michael. *Disziplin und Desertion: Strukturprobleme militärischer Organisation im 18. Jahrhundert*. Duncker & Humblot, 1996.

Simányi, Tibor. *Die Österreicher in Berlin: Der Husarenstreich des Grafen Hadik anno 1757*. Amalthea, 1987.

Simmel, Georg. "The Problem of Historical Time." In *Georg Simmel: Essays on Interpretation in Social Science*, ed. and trans. Guy Oakes. Manchester University Press, 127–144.

Skalweit, Stephan. *Die Berliner Wirtschaftskrise von 1763 und ihre Hintergründe*. Kohlhammer, 1937.

Slauter, Will. "Le paragraphe mobile: Circulation et transformation des informations dans le monde atlantique du XVIIIe siècle." *Annales: Histoire, Sciences sociales* 2 (2012): 363–389.

Sloss, Janet. *A Small Affair: The French Occupation of Menorca During the Seven Years' War*. Bonaventura, 2000.

Smelser, Marshall. *The Campaign for the Sugar Islands, 1759: A Study in Amphibious Warfare*. University of North Carolina Press, 1955.

Smith Anderson, Matthew. *The War of the Austrian Succession, 1740–1748*. Longman, 1995.

Snape, Michael Francis. *The Redcoat and Religion: The Forgotten History of the British Soldier from the Age of Marlborough to the Eve of the First World War*. Routledge 2005.

Sösemann, Bernd, and Gregor Vogt-Spira, eds. *Friedrich der Große in Europa: Geschichte einer wechselvollen Beziehung*. 2 vols. Steiner, 2012.

Souchet, François. "Gazettes et journaux face à l'actualitè (été 1757)." In *Les Gazettes européennes de langue française (XVV^x-XVIIIe siècles)*, ed. Henri Duranton, Claude Labrosse, and Pierre Rétat. Université de Saint-Etienne, 1992.

Soucier, Daniel S. "'We Have Done a Great Deal of Mischief—Spread the Terror of His Majesty's Arms thru the Whole Gulph': The British Strategy of Resource Control During the Seven Years' War in North America, 1758–59." In *The Greater Gulf: Essays on the Environmental History of the Gulf of St Lawrence*, ed. Claire Elizabeth Campbell, Edward MacDonald, and Brian Payne. McGill-Queen's University Press, 2019.

Spear, Percival. *The Nabobs: A Study of the Social Life of the English in Eighteenth-Century India*. Oxford University Press, 1932. Reprint, Oxford University Press, 1998.

Spector, Egbert Donald. *English Literary Periodicals and the Climate of Opinion During the Seven Years' War*. Mouton, 1966.

Speelman, Patrick J. "Father of the Modern Age." In Danley and Speelman, *The Seven Years' War*.

Speelman, Patrick J. "Strategic Illusions and the Iberian War of 1762." In Danley and Speelman, *The Seven Years' War*.

Speitkamp, Winfried, ed. *Gewaltgemeinschaften in der Geschichte: Entstehung, Kohäsionskraft und Zerfall*. Vandenhoeck & Ruprecht, 2017.

Spivak, Gayatri Chakravorty. "Can the Subaltern Speak?" In *Marxism and the Interpretation of Culture*, ed. Cary Nelson and Lawrence Grossberg. Macmillan, 1988.

Spring, Felicitas. "Aus dem Leben des schwedischen Husaren David Ginow (um 1740–1803): Unterwegs zwischen Litauen, Schwedisch-Pommern und Mecklenburg." *Genealogie* 59, no. 2 (2010): 97–133.

Srinivasachari, Chidambaram S. *Ananda Ranga Pillai, the "Pepys" of French India*. Varadachary, 1940.

Stange, Jörg Ulrich. *Ostpreußen unter der Zarenherrschaft 1757–1762: Russlands preußische Provinz im Siebenjährigen Krieg*. Lauf, 2023.

Starkey, Armstrong. *War in the Age of the Enlightenment 1700–1789*. Praeger, 2003.

Steele, Ian K. *Betrayals: Fort William Henry and the "Massacre."* Oxford University Press, 1990.

Steele, Ian K. *Setting All the Captives Free: Capture, Adjustment, and Recollection in Allegheny Country*. McGill-Queen's University Press, 2013.

Steele, Ian K. "The Shawnees and the English: Captives and War, 1753–1765." In *The Boundaries Between Us: Natives and Newcomers Along the Frontiers of the Old Northwest Territory, 1750–1850*, ed. Daniel P. Barr. Kent State University Press, 2006.

Stellner, František. *Sedmiletá válka v Evropě*. Libri, 2000.

Stellner, František. "Zu den Ergebnissen des Siebenjährigen Kriegs in Europa." *Prague Papers on the History of International Relations* 4 (2000): 85–98.

Stephenson, R. Scott. *Clash of Empires: The British, French and Indian War 1754–1763*. Senator John Heinz Pittsburgh Regional History Center, 2005.

Stoetzel, Donald I. *Encyclopedia of the French and Indian War in North America, 1754–1763*. Heritage, 2008.

Stoffers, Alfred. "Das Hochstift Paderborn zur Zeit des siebenjährigen Krieges." *Westfälische Zeitschrift* 69 (1911): 1–90; 70 (1913): 68–182.

Stollberg-Rilinger, Barbara. *Maria Theresa: The Habsburg Empress in Her Time*. Princeton University Press, 2021.

Storring, Adam. "Subjective Practices of War: The Prussian Army and the Zorndorf Campaign, 1758." *History of Science* 60 (2022): 458–480.

Storrs, Christopher, ed. *The Fiscal-Military State in Eighteenth-Century Europe: Essays in Honour of P. G. M. Dickson*. Ashgate, 2009.

Strauß, Angela. *Freigeister und Pragmatiker: Die preußischen Feldprediger 1750–1806*. V&R unipress, 2022.

Strauß, Angela. "Kollektive Kriegserfahrung preußischer Feldprediger: Vaterlandsliebe und Nutzbarkeitsgedanken in Handbüchern." In *Geistliche im Krieg*, ed. Franz Brendle and Anton Schindling. Aschendorff, 2009.

Strong, Pauline Turner. *Captive Selves, Captivating Others: The Politics and Poetics of Colonial American Captivity Narratives*. Westview, 1999.

Stücher, Martin. *Ausfouragiert und Heimgesucht: Freudenberg im Siebenjährigen Krieg*. Arbeitsgemeinschaft der Heimatvereine und des SGV, 2006.

Subrahmanyam, Sanjay. "Connected Histories: Notes Towards a Reconfiguration of Early Modern Eurasia." *Modern Asian Studies* 31, no. 3 (1997): 735–762.

Sulicki, Karl von. *Der Siebenjährige Krieg in Pommern und in den benachbarten Marken*. Berlin: Mittler, 1867.

Suter, Andreas, and Manfred Hettling, eds. *Struktur und Ereignis*. Vandenhoeck & Ruprecht, 2001.

Sutherland, Lucy. "The East India Company and the Peace of Paris." In *Politics and Finance in the Eighteenth Century*, ed. Aubrey Newman. Hambledone, 1984.

Syrett, David. "American Colonial Governments and the Raising of Provincial Troops During the Seven Years War." *Journal of the Society for Army Historical Research* 81, no. 326 (2003): 96–113.

Syrett, David. "American Provincials and the Havana Campaign of 1762." *New York History* 49 (1968): 375–390.

Syrett, David. *Shipping and Military Power in the Seven Years War: The Sails of Victory*. University of Exeter Press, 2008.

Szabo, Franz A. J. *The Seven Years War in Europe, 1756–1763*. Pearson Longman, 2008.

Téllez Alarcia, Diego. "España y la Guerra de los Siete Años." In *La proyección de la monarquía hispánica en Europa: Política, guerra y diplomacia entre los siglos XVI y XVIII*, ed. María R. Porres Marijuán and Iñaki Reguera Acedo. Universidad del País Vasco, 2009.

Temperley, Harold William Vazeille. "The Peace of Paris." In *The Cambridge History of the British Empire*. Vol. 1, *The Old Empire from Its Beginnings to 1783*, ed. John

Holland Rose, Arthur Percival Newton, and Ernest Alfred Benians. Cambridge University Press, 1929.

Ternat, François. "Les enjeux géopolitiques intercontinentaux dans les négociations franco-britanniques entre 1760 et 1763." In Fonck and Veyssière, *La Chute de la Nouvelle-France*.

Ternat, François. *Partager le monde: Rivalités impériales franco-britanniques, 1748–1763*. Presses de l'Université Paris Sorbonne, 2015.

Thadden, Franz-Lorenz von. *Feldmarschall Daun: Maria Theresias größter Feldherr*. Herold, 1967.

Thévenin, Michel. "*Changer le système de guerre": Le siège en Nouvelle-France 1755–1760*. Presses de l'Université Laval, 2020.

Thielen, Maximilian Ritter von. "Des k.k. Feldmarschall-Lieutenants Andreas von Hadik Zug nach Berlin 1757." *Oestreichische militärische Zeitschrift* 2 (1835): 115–146.

Thomas, Hugh. *Cuba: Or the Pursuit of Freedom*. Eyre & Spottiswoode, 1971.

Thüna, Lothar Freiherr von. *Die Würzburger Hilfstruppen im Dienste Österreichs 1756–1763: Ein Beitrag zur Geschichte des Siebenjährigen Krieges; Nach archivalischen Quellen*. Würzburg: Stuber, 1893.

Tigerström, Harald, ed. *Olof Langelius drar i fält—Utdrag ur en östgötaryttares dagbok åren 1758–1762*. Tigerström, 1989.

Tischer, Anuschka. *Offizielle Kriegsbegründungen in der Frühen Neuzeit: Herrscherkommunikation in Europa zwischen Souveränität und korporativem Selbstverständnis*. LIT, 2012.

Torres Sánchez, Rafael, ed. *War, State and Development: Fiscal-Military States in the Eighteenth Century*. Ediciones Universidad de Navarra, 2007.

Tortora, Daniel J. *Carolina in Crisis: Cherokees, Colonists, and Slaves in the American Southeast, 1756–1763*. University of North Carolina Press, 2015.

Tracy, Nicholas. *The Battle of Quiberon Bay 1759: Hawke and the Defence of the French Invasion*. Pen & Sword, 2010.

Tracy, Nicholas. *Manila Ransomed: The British Assault on Manila in the Seven Years War*. University of Exeter Press, 1995.

Treue, Wilhelm. "David Splitgerber (1683–1764): Ein Unternehmer im preußischen Merkantilstaat." *Vierteljahrschrift für Sozial- und Wirtschaftsgeschichte* 41 (1954): 235–267.

Treue, Wilhelm. *Wirtschafts- und Technikgeschichte Preußens*. De Gruyter, 1984.

Truxes, Thomas M., ed. *Ireland, France, and the Atlantic in a Time of War: Reflections on the Bordeaux-Dublin Letters, 1757*. Routledge, 2014.

Tunstall, Brian. *Admiral Byng and the Loss of Minorca*. Allan, 1928.

Turcot, Laurent. "Un chroniqueur curieux de Paris et de la promenade: Edmond-Jean-François Barbier et son Journal (1718–1763)." *French Historical Studies* 33, no. 2 (2010): 201–230.

Tuxen, Ole. "Principles and Priorities: The Danish View of Neutrality During the Colonial War of 1755–63." *Scandinavian Journal of History* 13 (1988): 207–232.

Uhlig von Uhlenau, Gottfried. *Erinnerungen an die Schlacht von Kolin und die damalige Zeit: Nach authentischen Quellen bearbeitet und zur Säkular-Feier am 18. Juni 1857* Vol. 1. Vienna: Braumüller, 1857.

Ulrich, Oskar. "Die Stadt Hannover im siebenjährigen Kriege." *Zeitschrift des historischen Vereins für Niedersachsen* 59 (1894): 180–330.

van der Heyden, Ulrich. "Die erste preußische Seeschlacht auf dem Stettiner Haff im Jahre 1759." *Baltische Studien* 103 (2017): 105–135.

Vanja, Konrad, ed. *Vivat—Vivat—Vivat! Widmungs- und Gedenkbänder aus drei Jahrhunderten.* Museum für Deutsche Volkskunde, 1985.

Vaugeois, Denis. *Les juifs et la guerre de sept ans (1756–1763).* Université Laval, 1967.

Vaugeois, Denis. *The Last French and Indian War: An Inquiry Into a Safe Conduct Issued in 1760 That Acquired the Value of a Treaty in 1990.* McGill-Queen's University Press, 2002.

Venzl, Tilman. "Neues zu Minna von Barnhelm: Warum der Freikorpsoffizier Tellheim an prußischem Patriotismus verzweifelt." *Deutsche Vierteljahresschrift für Literaturwissenschaft und Geistesgeschichte* 91 (2017): 379–409.

Vernon, Christopher. "'The Inhabitants of the Province Had Been Frequently Alarmed': Fear and Rumor in the Colonial Southeastern Backcountry (1754–1765)." In Lauric Henneton and Louis H. Roper (eds.), *Fear and the Shaping of Early American Societies*, ed. Lauric Henneton and Louis H. Roper. Brill, 2016.

Veyssière, Laurent, and Bertrand Fonck, eds. *La guerre de Sept ans en Nouvelle-France.* Septentrion, 2011.

Viget, Jacques, ed. *Règne militaire au Canada ou Administration Judiciaire de ce Pays par les Anglais de 8 Septembre 1760 au 10 Aout 1764.* Montreal: La Minerve, 1872.

Vila Miranda, Carlos. "Toma de Manila por los ingleses en 1762." *Anuario de Estudios Atlánticos* 53 (2007): 167–220.

Villiers, Patrick. "Commerce coloniale, traite des noirs et cabotage dans le ports du Ponant pendant la Guerre de Sept Ans." *Centre de recherches sur l'histoire du monde Atlantique-enquêtes et documents* 17 (1990): 21–46.

Visme, André de. *Terre-Neuve 1762: Dernier combat aux portes de la Nouvelle-France.* Éditions André de Visme, 2005.

Vogeler, Eduard. "Beiträge zur Geschichte von Soest während des siebenjährigen Krieges." *Zeitschrift des Vereins für die Geschichte von Soest und der Börde* 2 (1882/83): 17–50; 7 (1889/90), 49–57; 9 (1891/92), 23–69; 17 (1899/1900), 3–30 (partially reprinted in Menneking, *Victoria by Vellinghausen 1761,* 189–245).

Voigtländer, Hans-Walter. *Preußische Kriegsgefangene in Memmingen: Ein Beitrag zur Geschichte der reichsfreien Stadt während des Siebenjährigen Krieges (1756–1763).* Memminger Zeitung, 2000.

Voigtländer, Lutz. "Kontributionen, Freikorps und Douceurs: Duisburg im Siebenjährigen Krieg, 1756–1763." *Duisburger Forschungen* 47 (2001): 79–282.

Voigtländer, Lutz. *Krieg für den "gemeinen Mann": "Der mit einem Sächsischen Bauer von jetzigem Kriege redende Französische Soldat"; Eine neue Form der Berichterstattung in einer Wochenschrift des 18. Jahrhunderts. Zugleich eine kleine Geschichte des Siebenjährigen Krieges zwischen Kolin und Zorndorf.* Lumière, 2006.

Voigtländer, Lutz. *Die preußischen Kriegsgefangenen der Reichsarmee 1760/1763.* Gilles & Francke, 1995.

Voigtländer, Lutz. "Sozialgeschichtliche Aspekte der Kriegsgefangenschaft: Die preußischen Kriegsgefangenen der Reichsarmee im Siebenjährigen Krieg." In *In der Hand des Feindes: Kriegsgefangenschaft von der Antike bis zum Zweiten Weltkrieg*, ed. Rüdiger Overmans. Böhlau, 1999.

Volz, Gustav Berthold. "Zur Entstehungsgeschichte der 'Histoire de la guerre de sept ans' Friedrichs des Großen." *Hohenzollern-Jahrbuch* 15 (1911): 76–80.

Voswinkel, Gerd. "Der nicht verstandene Vorsatz von Voltaires 'Candide' und die Schlacht von Minden." In *Die Kunst des Vernetzens: Festschrift für Wolfgang Hempel*, ed. Botho Brachmann, et al. Verlag für Berlin-Brandenburg, 2006.

Wachter, Franz, ed. *Akten des Kriegsgerichts von 1763 wegen der Eroberung von Glatz 1760 und Schweidnitz 1761.* Max, 1897.

Waddell, Louis M. "Defending the Long Perimeter: Forts on the Pennsylvania, Maryland and Virginia Frontier, 1755–1765." *Pennsylvania History* 62 (1995): 171–195.

Waddington, Richard. *La guerre des sept ans: Histoire diplomatique et militaire.* 5 vols. Paris: Firmin-Didot, 1899–1914.

Waddington, Richard. *Louis XV et le renversement des alliances: Préliminaires de la Guerre de Sept Ans 1754–1755.* Paris: Firmin-Didot, 1896.

Wagner, Ferdinand. "Die europäischen Mächte in der Beurtheilung Friedrichs des Grossen 1746–1757." *Mitteilungen des Instituts für Österreichische Geschichtsforschung* 20 (1899): 397–443.

Waibel, Nicole. *Nationale und patriotische Publizistik in der Freien Reichsstadt Augsburg: Studien zur periodischen Presse im Zeitalter der Aufklärung (1748–1770).* Lumière, 2008.

Wainwright, Valerie. "'Fellow-Citizens in Science and Brothers in Humanity': Anglo-French Rivalry and the Discursive Practices of the 'Critical Review,' 1756–1763." *Journal of European Studies* 44, no. 4 (2014): 336–361.

Walle, Heinrich. "Der Siebenjährige Krieg zwischen Anekdote und Klischee." *Historische Mitteilungen* 18 (2005): 101–133.

Waltermann, Fritz. "Mützenblech als Wandblaker." *Zeitschrift für Heereskunde* 67, no. 408 (2003): 82–83.

Ward, Matthew C. *The Battle for Quebec, 1759.* History Press, 2005.

Ward, Matthew C. *Breaking the Backcountry: The Seven Years' War in Virginia and Pennsylvania, 1754–1765.* University of Pittsburgh Press, 2003.

Ward, Matthew. "Crossing the Line? The British Army and the Application of European 'Rules of War.'" In Buckner and Reid, *Revisiting 1759*.

Ware, Chris. *Admiral Byng: His Rise and Execution.* Pen & Sword, 2009.

Warnke, Marcus. *Logistik und friderizianische Kriegführung: Eine Studie zur Verteilung, Mobilisierung und Wirkungsmächtigkeit militärisch relevanter Ressourcen im Siebenjährigen Krieg am Beispiel des Jahres 1757.* Duncker & Humblot, 2018.

Watts, Carol. *The Cultural Work of Empire: The Seven Years' War and the Imagining of the Shandean State.* Edinburgh University Press, 2007.

Way, Peter. "Class and the Common Soldier in the Seven Years' War." *Labor History* 44, no. 4 (2003): 455–483.

Way, Peter. "Memoirs of an Invalid: James Miller and the Making of the British-American Empire in the Seven Years' War." In *Rethinking U.S. Labor History: Essays on the Working-Class Experience, 1756–2009*, ed. Donna T. Haverty-Stacke and Daniel J. Walkowitz. Continuum, 2010.

Way, Peter. "Rebellion of the Regulars: Working Soldiers and the Mutiny of 1763/64." *William and Mary Quarterly* 57 (2000): 761–792.

Way, Peter. "Venus and Mars: Women and the British-American Army in the Seven Years' War." In *Britain and America Go to War: The Impact of War and Warfare in Anglo-America, 1754–1815*, ed. Julie Flavell and Peter Conway. University of Florida Press, 2004.

Weaver, Glenn. "The Germans of British North America During the French and Indian War." *Social Studies* 48 (November 1957): 227–235.

Webb, James L. A., Jr. "The Mid-Eighteenth-Century Gum Arabic Trade and the British Capture of Saint-Louis du Sénégal, 1758." *Journal of Imperial and Commonwealth History* 25 (1997): 37–58.

Weber, Nadir. *Lokale Interessen und große Strategie: Das Fürstentum Neuchâtel und die politischen Beziehungen der Könige von Preußen (1707–1806).* Böhlau, 2015.

Weddigen, Theodor. "Bielefeld und das Haus Milse im siebenjährigen Kriege." *13. Jahresbericht des Historischen Vereins für die Grafschaft Ravensberg* (1899): 26–69.

Weerth, Otto. *Die Grafschaft Lippe und der siebenjährige Krieg.* Detmold: Meyer, 1888.

Weidner, Johannes. "'Der Alte Fritz' in der deutschen Volkskunst." *Schlesien* 26 (1981): 129–134.

Weigley, Russell F. *The Age of Battles: The Quest for Decisive Warfare from Breitenfeld to Waterloo.* Vintage, 1993.

Weiss, Joseph. "Der Streit über den Ursprung des siebenjährigen Krieges." *Historisches Jahrbuch* 18 (1897): 311–321, 831–848.

Weiss, Judith A. "La Conquista de la Habana 1762: El discurso hegemonizador norteamericano." *Cuadernos hispanoamericanos* 641 (2003): 93–116.

Weißbrich, Thomas. "'Eigentliche Abbildung': Zum Verhältnis von Ereignis und Graphik in frühneuzeitlicher Bildpublizistik." In *Unvergessliche Augenblicke: Die Inszenierung von Medienereignissen*, ed. Graduiertenkolleg Transnationale Medienereignisse. Societäts, 2006.

Welke, Martin. "Die Legende vom 'unpolitischen Deutschen': Zeitungslesen im 18. Jahrhundert als Spiegel des politischen Interesses." *Jahrbuch der Wittheit zu Bremen* 25 (1981): 161–188.

Welke, Martin. "' . . . zu Österreichs Gloria durch Publicität mitzuwürcken': Zur Pressepolitik des Kaiserhofes im Reich im 18. Jahrhundert." In *Mediengeschichte: Forschung und Praxis: Festgabe für Marianne Lunzer-Lindhausen zum 65. Geburtstag*, ed. Wolfgang Duchkowitsch. Böhlau, 1985.

Wellenreuther, Hermann. *Ausbildung und Neubildung: Die Geschichte Nordamerikas vom Ausgang des 17. Jahrhunderts bis zum Ausbruch der Amerikanischen Revolution 1775*. LIT, 2001.

Wellenreuther, Hermann. "Die Bedeutung des Siebenjährigen Krieges für die englisch-hannoveranischen Beziehungen." In *England und Hannover/England and Hanover*, ed. Adolf M. Birke and Kurt Kluxen. Saur, 1986.

Wellenreuther, Hermann. "Göttingen und England im 18. Jahrhundert." In *250 Jahre Vorlesungen an der Georgia Augusta 1734–1984*, ed. Norbert Kamp, Hermann Wellenreuther, and Friedrich Hund. Vandenhoeck & Ruprecht, 1985.

Wellenreuther, Hermann. "Land, Gesellschaft und Wirtschaft in England während des Siebenjährigen Krieges." *Historische* Zeitschrift 218, no. 3 (1974): 593–634.

Wellenreuther, Hermann. "Das Spanische Reich in der englischen Diskussion während des Siebenjährigen Krieges: Überlegungen zum Habermas'schen Begriff der 'Bürgerlichen Öffentlichkeit.'" In *Iberische Welten: Festschrift zum 65. Geburtstag*, ed. Günter Kahle, et al. Böhlau, 1994.

Wellenreuther, Hermann. "Der Vertrag zu Paris (1763) in der atlantischen Geschichte." *Niedersächsisches Jahrbuch für Landesgeschichte* 17 (1999): 81–110.

Wellenreuther, Hermann. "Von der Interessenharmonie zur Dissoziation: Kurhannover und England in der Zeit der Personalunion." *Niedersächsisches Jahrbuch für Landesgeschichte* 67 (1995): 23–42.

Weller, Thomas. "Clash of Empires? Die britische Eroberung von Havanna 1762 und die Folgen." In Füssel, *Der Siebenjährige Krieg 1756–1763: Mikro- und Makroperspektiven*.

Werner, Michael, and Bénédicte Zimmermann. "Vergleich, Transfer, Verflechtung: Der Ansatz der Histoire croisée und die Herausforderung des Transnationalen." *Geschichte und Gesellschaft* 28 (2002): 607–636.

Wernitz, Frank. *Die preußischen Freitruppen im Siebenjährigen Krieg, 1756–1763: Entstehung, Einsatz, Wirkung*. Podzun-Pallas, 1994.

Wernitz, Frank. "'They Have Been Blooded and Behaved Very Well'—britische leichte Truppen in der Armee des Herzogs Ferdinand von Braunschweig 1760–63: Ein Beitrag zur Geschichte des kleinen Krieges im 18. Jahrhundert." Diss., Ludwig Maximilian University of Munich, 1993.

Westphal, Siegried. "Festkultur zwischen städtischer Identitätsstiftung und Reichsbekenntnis: Das Hubertusburger Friedensfest von 1763 in der Reichsstadt Nordhausen." *Beiträge zur Heimatkunde aus Stadt und Kreis Nordhausen* 22 (1997): 126–140.

Wette, Wolfram, ed. *Der Krieg des kleinen Mannes: Eine Militärgeschichte von unten*. Piper, 1992.

White, Richard. *The Middle Ground: Indians, Empires, and Republics in the Great Lakes Region, 1650–1815*. Cambridge University Press, 1991.

Whitman, James Q. *The Verdict of Battle: The Law of Victory and the Making of Modern War*. Harvard University Press, 2012.

Wickremesekera, Channa. *Best Black Troops in the World: British Perceptions and the Making of the Sepoy, 1746–1805*. Manohar, 2002.

Willenberg, Jennifer. *Distribution und Übersetzung englischen Schrifttums im Deutschland des 18. Jahrhunderts*. Saur, 2008.

Willis, Sam. "The Battle of Lagos, 1759." *Journal of Military History* 73 (2009): 745–765.

Wilson, Kathleen. *The Sense of the People: Politics, Culture and Imperialism in England, 1715–1785*. Cambridge University Press, 1998.

Wilson, Peter H. "Prussia as Fiscal-Military State, 1640–1806." In Storrs, *The Fiscal-Military State in Eighteenth-Century Europe*.

Wilson, Peter H. *War, State and Society in Württemberg, 1677–1793*. Cambridge University Press, 1995.

Wiltsch, Johann Elieser Theodor. *Die Schlacht von nicht bei Roßbach oder die Schlacht auf den Feldern von und bei Raichardtswerben den 5. November 1757, und was ihr voranging, und nachfolgte*. Reinhartswerben. Halle: Anton'sche Sortiments-Buchhandlung Halle, 1858.

Winter, Georg. *Die kriegsgeschichtliche Überlieferung über Friedrich den Grossen kritisch geprüft an dem Beispiel der Kapitulation von Maxen*. Berlin: Gaertner, 1888.

Winton, Patrick. "Sweden and the Seven Years' War: War, Debt, and Politics." *War in History* 19, no. 1 (2012): 5–31.

Witzel, Rudolf. *Hessen Kassels Regimenter in der Alliierten Armee 1762*. Books on Demand, 2007.

Wolf, Ursula. *Preußische Anwerbung von süddeutschen Kolonisten nach dem Siebenjährigen Krieg unter dem Gesandten von Pfeil: Ihre Ansetzung in der Neumark, Schlesien, Berlin und Potsdam*. Dr. Kovač, 2013.

Woodward, Donald. "'Swords Into Ploughshares': Recycling in Pre-Industrial England." *Economic History Review* 38, no. 2 (1985): 175–191.

Wormsbächer, Elisabeth. *Daniel Nikolaus Chodowiecki: Erklärungen und Erläuterungen zu seinen Radierungen*. Galerie J. H. Bauer, 1988.

Wrangel, Carl-Gustav von. "Der siebenjährige Krieg in Vorpommern." *Acta Wrangeliana* (1934): 58–64.

Wrede, Martin. "'Zähmung der Bellona' oder Ökonomie der Gewalt? Überlegungen zur Kultur des Krieges im Ancien régime." In *Theatrum Belli—Theatrum Pacis: Konflikte und Konfliktregelungen im frühneuzeitlichen Europa; Festschrift für Heinz Duchhardt zu seinem 75. Geburtstag*, ed. Irene Dingel, et al. Vandenhoeck & Ruprecht, 2018.

Wylly, Harold C. *A Life of Lieutenant-General Sir Eyre Coote*. Clarendon, 1922.

Ximeno, José Manuel. "El juicio de los historiadores sobre la toma de La Habana por los ingleses." *Boletín del Archivo Nacional de Cuba* 58 (1962): 93–108.

Yaple, Robert L. "Braddock's Defeat: The Theories and a Reconsideration." *Journal of the Society for Army Historical Research* 46 (1968): 194–201.

Zantop, Susanne. *Kolonialphantasien im vorkolonialen Deutschland (1770–1870)*. Schmidt, 1999.

Zeumer, Christoph. "Zwischen Preußen und Sachsen: Leipzig im Siebenjährigen Krieg 1756–1763." In *Stadt und Krieg: Leipzig in militärischen Konflikten vom Mittelalter bis ins 20. Jahrhundert*, ed. Ulrich von Hehl. Leipziger Universitätsverlag, 2014.

Ziebura, Eva. *Prinz Heinrich von Preußen*. Stapp, 1999.

Ziegert, Dieter. "Das münstersche Heer im Siebenjährigen Krieg 1756–1763." *Westfälische Zeitschrift* 137 (1987): 25–87.

Zielsdorf, Frank, *Miliärische Erinnerungskulturen in Preußen im 18. Jahrhundert: Akteure, Medien, Dynamiken* (V&R unipress, 2016), 113–117.

Zittauer Geschichts- und Museumsverein e.V., ed. *Macht und Ohnmacht: 250. Jahrestag der Zerstörung Zittaus am 23. Juli 1757*. Oettel, 2007.

Index

Abbt, Thomas, 276–277, 420
Abelmann, Eberhard Jürgen, 2, 160, 220, 294–296, 447, 451
Abercromby, James, 199, 200–201, 430
Abercromby, Robert, 430
Achenwall, Gottfried, 267
Acta Publica (Trattner), 274
Adelung, Johann Christoph, 328–329
affaire du Canada, 317, 423
Age of Enlightenment, 437. *See also* Enlightenment
Age of Extremes, 3
Age of Frederick the Great, The (Oncken), 3
Alam Conveying the Grant of the Diwani to Lord Clive (West), 407
Ali, Muhammad, 158
Alliance on the Bosporus, 384–385
All-Too-Hasty Courier, The (Will), 292–293
Almer, Georg Christian, 217
Almon, John, 5, 57
Altonaer Zeitung, 255

Ambuscade (British privateering ship), 379
Am Ende, Johann Joachim Gottlob, 302
American Revolution, 405
American War of Independence, 3, 430
Amherst, Jeffrey, 75, 199–202, 315–317, 363, 386, 450
Amherst, William, 386
Anderson, Fred, 7, 60–61, 65, 392
Anglo-French War, 296
Anglo-Maratha wars, 441
Anglophobia, 378
Anglo-Prussian Treaty of Westminster, 77
Anglo-Russian trade agreement, 433
Anhalt-Dessau, Friedrich Heinrich Eugen von, 332
Anhalt-Dessau, Moritz von, 332
Anhalt-Zerbst, Sophie Auguste Friederike von, 383
Anishinabe, 350–351, 405
annus mirabilis, 255, 264
Anson, George, 158, 194, 232, 358

Answer to the Letter, An (anonymous pamphlet), 272
Apotheker (Apothecary) journal, 55
Applied Censure, or Coup de Grace, The (printed caricature), 236–237
Apraksin, Stepan Fedorovich, 126–127, 130–131
Aprill, Matthias Joseph, 111
Archenholz, Johann Wilhelm, 6, 162, 310, 417, 483n1; cannibalism, 207; luxuries of the toilet, 288; winter of 1759–1760 in Saxony, 173
Argo, 370
armchair politicians, 289
Arouet, François-Marie, 14
asymmetric guerrilla warfare, 430
Augsburg Peace Congress, 268
August III of Poland, 416–417
Augustus III, King of Poland, 94, 107, 110, 396
Augustus II the Strong, King of Poland, 94
August Wilhelm, Duke of Brunswick-Bevern, 91, 259, 419
Austria, 2, 10, 15, 413; armed forces, 33; and Britain, 25, 28; domestic proto–armaments industry, 33–35; and France, 38, 77, 113, 115; Frederick on, 26; French subsidies, 439; Protestant prisoners in, 165; and Prussia, 27, 35, 264, 278, 297, 329; Second Versailles Treaty, 115; Treaty of Versailles, 77; war as religious conflict, 108
Austrian Armaments Commission, 33

Baldinger, Ernst Gottfried, 429
Balke, Karl Andreas Friedrich, 162, 340
Balthasar, Augustin von, 335
Barfot, George Hendrich, 12–13, 217, 260
Barrington, John, 224–225

Barsewisch, Friedrich Rudolf von, 39, 148–149, 152, 190–191, 428, 450
Bartholomäus d'O, Johann, 423
Bassecourt, Francisco González y, 420
Bassecourt, Vicente González de, 420
Battle of Bergen, 232
Battle of Hochkirch, 282
Battle of Kloster Kamp, 313, 419
Battle of Kolin, 281
Battle of Krefeld, 189, 190, 272, 279
Battle of Kunersdorf, 19, 240–241, 305
Battle of Landeshut, 329
Battle of Leuthen, 17, 18, 50, 147, 161, 163, 173, 283
Battle of Lobositz, 213, 330
Battle of Maxen, 423
Battle of Menorca, 26
Battle of Minden, 279, 452
Battle of Pharsalus, 117
Battle of Plassey, 157–158
Battle of Prague, 279, 419
Battle of Quiberon, 50
Battle of Rio San Juan de Nicaragua, 379
Battle of Rossbach, 138, 140, 170–171, 292
Battle of Saint-Cast, 196–198
Battle of the Plains of Abraham, 419
Battle of Vellinghausen, 272, 279
Battle of Waterloo, 48
Battle of Zorndorf, 18, 177, 205–208, 211, 216, 277, 285, 286
Baugh, Daniel, 21, 441
Bayle, Pierre, 209–210
Beaujeu, Daniel Liénard de, 64
Becher, Johann Christian, 12, 284–285
Belach, Andreas, 163, 279
Belle-Isle, Charles Louis Auguste Fouquet de, 187
Belle-Isle, Marshal, 189, 199, 231, 236, 313
Belling, Wilhelm Sebastian von, 344, 382

Bellotto, Bernardo, 303
Benjamin, Walter, 434
Berlin, 6, 50, 93–94, 101, 103, 133–136, 244; occupation of, 331; Russian capture of, 284; Russian prisoners of war in, 326; second raid on, 305–311; Sulzer on, 327
Berliner Zeitung, 211
Berlinische Nachrichten, 67, 74, 91, 120, 122, 205, 259, 274, 317
Bertin, Jean-Baptiste, 257
Bess, Brown, 70
Bess, Johann George, 114–115, 531n9
Bestuzhev-Ryumin, Alexey Petrovich, 36
Bigot, François, 268, 317
Bilguer, Johann Ulrich von, 429
biological weapon, 445
Bion, Johann Theobald, 279
Black Hole of Calcutta, 85–87, 325
Blakeney, William, 43, 79
Bland, Humphrey, 43
Bligh, Thomas, 193–194, 196
Blücher, Gebhart Leberecht von, 344
Bock, Johann George, 334–335
Bode, Johann Joachim, 415
Bolotov, Andrei, 16, 126–128, 130, 180–181, 209, 334, 381, 450
Bonin, Charles, 16, 41, 69, 204, 254, 314–318, 450; French withdrawal, 254; *James*, 318; North American years, 317
Boscawen, Edward, 63, 200, 260
Boston, 318–320
Boston Gazette, 155
Boston Massacre, 320
Boston Tea Party, 320
Boswell, James, 426
Bougainville, Louis Antoine de, 16, 204, 245–247, 250–251, 317–318, 430
Bouquet, Henry, 405
Boyer, Jean-Baptiste de, 162

Boysen, Friedrich Eberhard, 328
Braddock, Edward, 15, 57, 62–68
Bradstreet, John, 204, 405
Bräker, Ulrich, 14, 39–40, 43, 93–101, 427, 450
Brand, Johann Christian, 282
Braunschweig-Bevern, August Wilhelm von, 259
Brecht, Bertolt, 13
Brenkenhoff, Franz Balthasar Schönberg von, 268, 414
Brewer, John, 28
Britain, 438–439; armed forces, 31; and Austria, 25, 28; capture of Havana, 285; expansion into India, 6, 336; expeditionary forces, 405; expedition to capture Havana, 414; expedition to Guadeloupe, 220, 222, 426; expedition to Martinique, 220, 222, 285, 359–360, 363, 429; and France, 2, 22, 25, 45, 51–54, 80, 88, 219, 226, 246, 271, 346–347, 386, 436; gains and Pacte de Famille, 336–341; images of India, 86; journalism, 270–271; media-driven patriotic feeling, 273; military surgeons, 420; naval blockade, 270; and North American colonies, 431; occupation of Canada, 297; occupation of Guadeloupe, 295; occupation of Havana, 297; occupation of Manila, 297; political pamphlets, 271; and Prussia, 38–39, 189, 266; public debate in, 272; public indignation in, 76; raids on France, 192–198; religious war, 169; soldiers lost by, 412; strategic advantage, 37; supremacy in India, 347–350; territorial gains, 394; unemployment, 426; war on Spain, 352, 357, 360, 371, 378, 381

Britannia's Triumph (etchings, Orsbridge), 367
British-American hegemony, 415
British East India Company (BEIC), 23, 42, 83–84, 369, 391, 406, 408, 435; Council, 87–88, 348; *diwani* rights, 350
British Empire, 431; economic independence, 273; global successes, 280. *See also* Britain
Brodrick, Thomas, 79, 260
Broglie, Albert von, 78
Broglie, Maréchal de, 144, 235, 311–312, 339–340
Brown, Charlotte, 15, 66
Browne, Maximilian Ulysses, 95, 101–102, 106–107, 118
Brühl, Heinrich Count von, 27, 387
Brumwell, Stephen, 426
Buchenberg, Freiherr von, 109
Buckle, Matthew, 261
Buechner, Andreas Elias, 333
Buffinton, Arthur, 22
Burgholzhausen, Ernst Dietrich Marshal von, 190
Burke, Peter, 10
Burkhardt, Johannes, 28, 172, 413
burning of Zittau, 124–125
Büsching, Anton Friedrich, 411
Bussy-Castelnau, Marquis Charles de, 88–89
Buturlin, Alexander Borissovitch, 340–341
Byng, John, 78–80

Cadet, Joseph Michel, 268
Cajuns, 68
Calcutta, India, 80–89, 157, 225, 441–442
Callmucks (Kalmyks), 130, 503n107
Callot, Jacques, 280

Cambridge, Richard Owen, 296
Campbell, John, 43, 152, 355
Canada Pamphlet, 273
Canaletto, 303
Candide or, Optimism (Voltaire), 238, 280
cannibalism, 207, 487n74
Canot, Pierre, 253
Caribbean, 220–225
Carl, Horst, 416
Carnatic-Hyderabad War of Succession, 82
Carrach, Johann Tobias, 333
Carthage, 269–273
Carvalho e Mello, Sebastião José de, 352
Casanova, Giacomo, 267
Castelnau, Louis Joseph de, 176
Castex, Jean-Claude, 45
Castries, Marquis de, 313
Castro y Amuedo, Agustin Maria de, 377
Catherine the Great, 383
Catholic Church in Manila, 378
Catholicism, 167–168
"Causes Moving His Royal Majesty in Prussia" (Frederick, King of Prussia), 91
Cawm, Nabob Jaffeir, 84
Cazotte, Jacques, 220
Cevallos, Pedro de, 379
Champlain, Samuel de, 245
Chanda Sahib, 82
Charles, Duke of Brunswick-Wolfenbüttel, 142
Charles Alexander of Lorraine, 42, 147, 150
Charles de Rohan, Prince of Soubise, 113
Charles Edward Stuart, the Young Pretender, 227
Charles III of Spain, 37, 352, 356, 390, 391, 420

Charles-Joseph, Prince of Ligne, 181
Charles Wyndham, second Earl of Egremont, 390
Chernyshev, Zakhar Grigoryevich, 388
Chevotet, Jean-Michel, 298
Chodowiecki, Daniel, 280, 327, 420
Choiseul, Duc de, 21, 187, 231, 261, 336, 338, 391–392, 394, 431, 438–439
Choiseul-Praslin, César Gabriel de, 337
Cholmley, Robert, 66
Christian, Friedrich, 163, 417
Christian in Times of War, The (Wegener), 162
Christian in War and Under Siege, The (Belach), 163
Christianity, 160, 247, 384
Christine, Elisabeth, 387
Christoph II of Dohna-Schlodien, 205
Citadelle de Québec, 252
Clemens August I, archbishop of Cologne, 110
Cleve, Heinrich Urban, 531n9
Clive, Robert, 82, 87–88, 391, 406, 408, 581n7; Battle of Plassey, 157–158; and Siraj-ud-Daulah, 156–158
Cogniazo, Jacob de, 102–103, 213, 300, 450
Collenbach, Heinrich Gabriel von, 395
Colley, Linda, 9
commodity, news as, 288–294
Compagnie des Indes (CdI), 23
Congress of Vienna, 392
Considerations on the Present German War (Mauduit), 271
"consumer revolution," 283
Contades, Louis Georges, 190, 198–199, 231–232, 235–236
Containing It's Rise, Progress, and Event in Europe, Asia, Africa, and America (Entick), 5
Contest (weekly journal, London), 271

Convention of Kloster-Zeven, 132–133, 141–142
Convention of Neutrality, 74
Conversation Between a Prussian Black Hussar and a Muscovite Cossack, 211
Cook, James, 246
Cooper, Samuel, 254
Coote, Eyre, 347–348
Corbett, Julian S., 6
Cornish, Samuel, 369, 377, 378
Cornwallis, Charles, 430
Cornwallis, Edward, 43
corruption/cooperation in occupied cities, 297–299
Cossacks, 16, 49, 70, 129–131, 306–309; auxiliaries, 180; Bolotov's on behavior of, 127; raping of women, 503n107
Council of Three Fires, 351
Count Christian Ernst zu Stolberg-Wernigerode, 276
courts-martial, 422–424
Crimean Tatars, 385
Critical Review (journal), 272
Croghan, George, 405
Cross, William, 194
culture: aristocratic, 435; Baroque, 108; Catholic, 326; and European society, 408–411; material, 16, 288; memory, 47, 119, 195; Native American communication, 23; political, of colonies, 73; sociable, 45; war's impact on, 430–432
Cummings, Thomas, 218
Cuntz, Johann Christoph, 145, 171, 174, 177, 321

d'Aiguillon, Duc, 196, 416
Danziger Beyträge, 274, 415
d'Argens, Marquis, 256, 266, 275
Das, Krishna, 84

Daun, Johann Benedikt, 122
Daun, Leopold Joseph von, 42, 110, 121, 145, 162, 212, 310–311; Austrian army under, 240, 245; battle representations, 282
Davenport, Richard, 179, 312–313
de Araña, Martin, 360
Death of Field Marshal Schwerin, The (Johann Christoph Frisch), 421
Death of General Wolfe, The (West), 280, 420–421
Death of the Marquis de Montcalm, The, 421
Decadas de la Guerra (Rustant), 5
"Declaration of the Reasons Which Have Moved His Majesty to Advance Into Saxony" (Frederick, King of Prussia), 91
Decline and Fall of the Roman Empire (Gibbon), 272
Deduced from the Committing of Hostilities in 1749 (Almon), 57
de la Pegna, Hyacinth, 265, 281–282
Delbrück, Hans, 26
Denis, Michael, 278
de Pascalis de Sainte-Croix, Gaetan Xavier Guilhelm, 338
Der Apotheker, 367
der Trenck, Friedrich Freiherr von, 13, 327
descents, 192–198
De Silhouette, Etienne, 257
d'Estrées, Marshal, 115, 132–133, 340, 386
Dettloff, Anna Sophia, 15
d'Haussonville, Comte Louis Joseph, 386
Dictionnaire (Bayle), 209
Diligence (British ship), 230
Diplomatic Revolution, 74–78
disease and violence, 441–446

Dominicans, 371, 375
Dominicus, Johann Jacob, 13, 102, 151–152, 242, 265, 427
Donalitius, Georg Albrecht, 129
Dopsch, Alfons, 101
Dorothée, Luise, 396
Douglas, John, 272
Douglas, Sir James, 359
Downman, Francis, 220, 225
Drake, Dawsonne, 377
Draper, William, 369, 378
Dresden, 301–304
Dreyer, Johann Matthias, 290, 294
Dreyer, Joseph Ferdinand, 164
Dubois-Cattin, Dominique, 162–163, 174, 176
Duchhardt, Heinz, 29
Duff, Robert, 261
Duffy, Christopher, 96, 412
Duisburg Intelligenz-Zettel (Duisburg intelligence notes), 398
Dumouriez, Antoine-François, 298
Dundas, David, 368
Dupleix, Joseph François, 82
du Plessis, Louis François Armand de Vignerot, 78
Duquesne, Marquis, 58
Durant, George, 220–225, 358, 426
dustucks, 84

East India Company, 377–378, 440
economies of war, 414–418
Efendi, Ahmed Resmi, 160, 183
ego-documents, 9–11, 40, 302
Egremont, Lord, 358, 369
Ehrensvärd, Augustin, 344–345
Ehrlich, Hanss George, 416
Eichel, August Friedrich von, 305
eighteenth-century wars, 9, 31, 202, 298, 453; characteristics of, 435; figures for, 411

Elizabeth (British warship), 374
England in the Seven Years' War (Corbett), 6
Enlightenment, 257, 273; image of "limited" warfare, 323
entanglements and disentanglements, 446–450
Entick, John, 5
Ephramiten, 416
episodic images of moments, 19
Equiano, Olaudah, 14, 202, 204, 261, 338, 428, 450
Erlangener Zeitung, 294
Erlangische Öffentliche Nachrichten, 124
"essay journals," 271
Etenhueber, Mathias, 293
Euler, Leonhard, 208
European society and culture: empire at home, 408–411; repercussions for, 408–411
Europe and peace, 396–403
Ewald, Johann, 430

Falmouth (British warship), 374
Fantastic War, 351–356, 454
Fatherland, Russian concept of (*Otečestvo*), 273
Faulhaber, Andreas, 301
Ferdinand, Duke of Brunswick, 91, 142, 186; 1758 Campaign, 186–192
Ferdinand of Brunswick, 231, 256, 325, 339, 447
Ferdinand VI, King of Spain, 357
Fermor, Wilhelm Graf von, 127–128, 180, 206
Finck, Friedrich August von, 264, 266, 282, 423
Finck Lays His Sword Before Daun After the Battle of Maxen (painting, Hyacinth de La Pegna), 265
Findenigg, Franz Paul, 282

First Carnatic War, 25
fiscal-military state, 28–29, 32
Fischer, Jean Chrétien, 320
Fischer Corps, 320–323
Fladderminen (flying mines), 340
flat ontology, 5
Flörcke, Johann Ernst von, 333
Folard, Jean-Charles de, 279
Fontainebleau: and path to peace, 390–391; preliminary peace of, 356, 386, 390–391, 397
Forbes, John, 199–200, 204
Forbes Road, 204
Formey, Samuel, 327
Fort Oswego, 270
Fort Pitt, 205, 404–405
Fort Ticonderoga, 199–205
Fort William Henry, 152–156, 204–205
Fouqué, Heinrich August de la Motte, 151
Fowke, Thomas, 78–79
France: and Austria, 38; ban on king of Prussia, 112; and Britain, 2, 22, 25, 45, 51–54, 80, 88, 219, 226, 246, 271, 346–347, 386, 436; British raids on, 192–198; colonies, 433; contemporary military theory, 30; financial crisis, 257; Louisbourg's loss, 204; Martinique restored to, 393; media-driven patriotic feeling, 273; military presence in Bengal, 393; most powerful country in Europe, 26; and Native Americans, 155, 270; occupation of Hanover, 297; postwar construction of war heroes, 419; and Prussia, 22; and Spain, 37, 337, 391–392, 397
Franciscans, 371, 374
Francke Foundations, 334
Franco-British war, 57, 294, 349, 444

François-Louis-Joseph Watteau the Younger, 420
Franco-Spanish Pacte de Famille (Family Pact), 21–22
Fränkel, David Hirschel, 161
Frankfurter Zeitung, 151, 255
Franklin, Benjamin, 61, 273
Franz, Maximilian, 106
Franz Xaver, Prince of Saxony, 198, 313
Frederick, Adolf, 216
Frederick II, King of Prussia, 2, 6, 13–14, 17–18, 21, 91, 285, 298; Battle of Leuthen, 147; decree of Reichsexekution against, 115; Hochkirch, 212–215; ideology of preventive war, 26; invasion of Saxony, 107–108; Kolin, 117–123; Ottoman alliance, 182–183; Parchwitz Address, 146–147, 149; Prague, 117–123; relationship with religion, 108–109; religious repression, 171; siege warfare, 46; victory at Rossbach, 139, 141; writings, 91–93
freedom of expression, 271
Frégault, Guy, 7
Freikorps, 49–50
French and Indian War, 2–3, 7, 16, 30, 61, 285, 318, 386, 403, 431, 442; and colonists, 431; North America, 449; personal accounts of, 318; white settlers and Native Americans, 403
French military operations, 298
French pamphleteering, 270
French Soldier Speaks with a Saxon Peasant About the Current War, A, 288
Friedrich Eugen, Duke of Württemberg, 36
Frisch, Johann Christoph, 420, 421
Fritsch, Thomas Freiherr von, 389, 395, 417

Fritzen Wiese, 144
Fülling, Johann Georg, 53–54, 219, 321

Gage, Thomas, 405
Gazette de Berlin, 103
Gazette de Cologne, 103, 274
Gazette de France, 269, 338
Gazette de Leipzig, 103
Gazette de Vienne, 401
Gazette Extraordinary, 255
Gazettes d'Utrecht, de Cologne, d'Amsterdam, and de Bruxelles, 270
Geitz, Johann Daniel, 90, 174–175, 299, 322
Gellert, Christian Fürchtegott, 276, 278
Gemayne Buch (Common Book of the village of Schmannewitz), 416
Gentleman's Magazine, The, 427
geopolitics: aims and interests, 25–28; armies and other resources, 28–39; between Reich and Empire, 21–56; war and globalization, 21–25; war making, 43–51
George, third Earl of Albemarle, 358–359, 364–366
George I, King of England, 227
George II, King of England, 15, 61, 227, 336, 409
George III, King of England, 336, 391
George VI, King of England, 392
Georgi, Christian Siegismund, 309
Georg of Hesse-Darmstadt, 137
German Enlightenment, 275
Gibbon, Edward, 272
Gilsa, Georg Ernst von und zu, 75, 114–115
Gipson, Lawrence H., 6
Gleim, Johann Wilhelm Ludwig, 105, 135, 276, 422
Gleim, Ludwig, 276, 382; "Battlesong at the Launch of the 1757 Campaign,"

277; "Victory Song After the Battle of Prague," 277
global circumnavigation, 246
globalization, 4, 20, 446, 450, 591n61; historical, 449; and war, 21–25
global lives, 9
global war as media event, 294–296
Gloria (British privateering ship), 379
Goethe, Johann Wolfgang von, 104–105, 117, 231
Gorani, Giuseppe, 146, 191–192, 242, 327, 329
Göttingische Anzeigen von gelehrten Sachen, 295
Gottsched, Luise, 331
Götze, George Samuel, 387
Gotzkowsky, Johann Ernst, 307, 331–332, 399
Goubler, Marguerite, 15
Grande Dérangement, 68
Grant, Johann von, 384
Grant, John, 16, 42, 175, 316, 366
Graun, Carl Heinrich, 123
Great Alliance, 257
Great Britain. *See* Britain
Greiffenheim, Johann August, 183
"Grenadier to the Muse of War, Written After the Victory at Zorndorf on August 25, 1758, The" (Gleim), 277
Grenville, George, 405
Griesheim, Christian Ludwig von, 290
Grimaldi, Marqués de, 424
Grotehenn, Johann Heinrich Ludewig, 16, 40–41, 113, 142, 186–187, 233, 367, 427–428, 450, 453
Guadeloupe, 50, 358; Britain's occupation of, 295; British expedition to, 220, 222, 426; and Menorca, 338; in peace agreement, 272; population of, 220; restored to France, 393; unconditional retention of, 272
guerra de religione, 172
guerre universelle, 5
guerrilla fighting, 320, 436
Gupta, Brijen K., 85

Hadik, András, 134–136
Hallesche Berichte, 226
Hamburgische Correspondent, 268
Hamburgische unpartheyische Correspondent, 274
Hamilton, Gustav David, 216–217
Hampshire militia, 272
Hannoverische Beyträge zum Nutzen und zum Vergnügen, 294–295
Hannoverisches Kriegesdenkmal, 294
Hannoverisches Magazin, 294
Hanoverian Guards Regiment, 233
Hanoverrische Beyträge, 220
Harlem Gazette, 256
Harris, Christopher, 75
Hastenbeck, 132–133
Haude, Gottfried Fabian, 182
Haude-Spenersche Zeitung, 307
Havana: in 1762, 357–369; key to the New World, 357–369
Haviland, William, 316
Hawke, Edward, 79, 261–262
Hayman, Francis, 280
Hecht, Johann Julius, 289
Hegel, Georg Wilhelm Friedrich, 161–162
Henry, Alexander, 350
Herder, Johann Gottfried, 415
heroes/heroism, 199, 278, 418–422, 584n71
Herr, Johann Gottlob, 90
Hertzberg, Ewald Friedrich von, 395
Hevia, Gutierre de, 359
Heyde, Johann Friedrich, 134, 308, 400

Hildesheim, 287, 297, 312, 333, 386; 1759 siege of, 388; ecclesiastical territories of, 297; Ferdinand of Brunswick, 353; Hanoverian Troups, 424
Himburg, Christian Friedrich, 6
Histoire de la Guerre de Sept Ans (Frederick II of Prussia), 401
Historical Chart of the Seven Years' War (Schulze), 6
Historischer Bilder-Saal, 294
History of the English-Speaking Peoples (Churchill), 3
History of the Military Transactions of the British Nation in Indostan, A (Orme), 295
History of the Seven Years War (Archenholz), 207, 241
History of the Seven Years' War (Tempelhof), 5, 411
History of the Two Indies, The (Raynal), 5
History of the War in Thuringia, 289
HMS *Sutherland*, 248
Hobsbawm, Eric, 3
Hochkirch, 212–215
Hogarth, William, 55, 167, 280
Holberg, Ludvig, 289
Holburne, Sir Francis, 153
Hollmann, Samuel Christian, 448
Holwell, John Zephaniah, 85–86
Holy Roman Empire, 258, 269, 274, 278, 285, 337, 413, 442, 447
Hopson, Peregrine Thomas, 220
Houghton (British ship), 378
Howe, William, 248
Hubert de Brienne, the Comte de Conflans, 260
Hughes, Philip, 64
Hülsen, Carl Wilhelm von, 264, 266
humanitarianism, 274
humiliation, 85, 150, 232

Hundred Years' War, 73
hussar's coup, 49

Iberian Peninsula, 351, 357
Imhoff, Philipp von, 41
Immaculata Concepción, 379
Impartial History of the Late War, An (Almon), 5
Imperial Diet (Reichstag), 107–112
Index of Prohibited Books, 238
India, 3, 80, 82, 156, 225–229; Anglo-French rivalries in, 83; British expansion into, 6, 336; British images of, 86; British supremacy in, 347–350; France claims in, 338; Mughal Empire in, 29; postcolonial research, 22; road to British supremacy in, 347–350; sepoy regiments in, 440
Indigenous Canadians, 432
individual testimonies, 414
Ingersoll, Franz Rudolf Moll, 122
In Praise of the War (Hollmann), 448
Invasion, The (Hogarth), 167
Investigation Into Whether Today's European Nations Have the Wish Some Day to Become Cannibals, or at Least Hottentots, An, 54
Isaac, Moses, 416
Isenburg, Johann Casimir von, 198
itio-in-partes option, 112
Itzig, Daniel, 416
Ives, Edward, 295

Jacobi, Christoph Gottfried, 292
Jang, Muzaffar, 82
Jean François Bertet, Comte de la Clue, 260
Jerónimo Grimaldi, the first Duke of Grimaldi, 392
Jesuit College of San Ignacio, 375

Johann Hartwig Ernst, Count von Bernstorff, 267
Johann Wilhelm of Archenholz, 6
John Manners, the Marquess of Granby, 313
John Russell, the fourth Duke of Bedford, 390
Johnson, Sir William, 63, 405
José, Iñigo, 420
José de Herrera y Sotomayor, 379
Joseph, Prince of Saxe-Hildburghausen, 136
Joseph I, King of Portugal, 353
Joseph Michel Cadet, 318
Journal de ma vie (Ménétra), 196
Journal encyclopédique (French journal), 269
Journal historique et anecdotique (Jean François Barbier), 402
Juan de Aguilar y Santa Cruz, 379
Juliane von Rehdiger, Eleonore, 15, 311, 388
Jumonville, Joseph Coulun de Villiers de, 57–68
Jung, Nasir, 82
Jung, Salabat, 88
Justi, Johann Heinrich Gottlob von, 27, 54–55, 210

Kaninguen, Denis, 60
Karl Adolf von Rexin, 384
Karl Eugen von Württemberg, 35
Karl Graf von Zinzendorf, 401
Karl Joseph Graf Raab zu Rauenberg, 289
Karl Theophil Guichard, 387
Karl Wilhelm Ramler, 284
Karsch, Anna Louise, 15, 278, 382, 400
Kaunitz-Rietberg, Wenzel Anton von, 27, 340
Keegan, John, 47

Keith, James, 190
Keith, James Francis Edward, 419–420
Keith, Robert, 271
Kennion, John, 414
Keppel, Augustus, 218, 358, 430
Keppel, William, 358
Khan, Alivardi, 84
Khan, Muhammad Ali, 82
Khevenhüller-Metsch, Johann Joseph Fürst von, 14, 151, 451
Kielmannsegg, Georg Ludwig Graf von, 75
"King of Press-ia" and the newspaper war, 273–275
Kirkwood, Robert, 11
Kleist, Ewald Christian von, 105, 242, 276, 420, 422
Klemm, Gustav, 301
Klopstock, Friedrich Gottlieb, 104–105
Klopstock, Meta, 103–105, 289
Kneisel, Johann Christian, 342
knowledge, 294–296
Knowles, Charles, 358
Knox, John, 16, 169, 203, 251, 315
Knyphausen, Dodo Heinrich zu, 267
Knyveton, John, 13
Koch, Barthold, 233–234, 430
Kolberg, 177, 260, 300, 341–343
Köller, Ernst Mathias von, 259
König, Christian, 425
Koselleck, Reinhart, 3, 17
Koser, Reinhold, 26
Krauss, Werner, 6–7
Kroener, Bernhard, 44
Krogh, Georg Friedrich von, 117
Kroker, Ernst, 331
Krome, Theophilus Arnold, 67, 230
Kuhgrund, 241–242
Kunisch, Johannes, 106, 437
Küntzel, Georg, 22
Küster, Carl Daniel, 212, 450

Lacy, Franz Moritz von, 299
Lalande, Jérôme, 402
Lancey, James De, 61
Lange, Christian Hemming Von, 135
Lange, Simon Moritz von, 213
Langelius, Olof, 258, 343, 450
Langewiesche, Dieter, 4
language and languages in the war, 178–181
Lantingshausen, Jacob Albrecht von, 217, 344
Laudon, Ernst Gideon von, 191, 299–300
Lauriston, Jean Law de, 84
Lavater, Johann Kaspar, 399
Law, John, 84
Lawrence, Stringer, 228, 370
Lehmann, Max, 26
Lehndorff, Ernst Ahasuerus Heinrich von, 387
Lehwaldt, Johann von, 67, 130
Leipzig, 91, 146, 269, 311, 319, 330–333, 395–397
Lemcke, Jakob Friedrich von, 99, 330
Leopold III Frederick Franz, the Duke of Anhalt-Dessau, 410
Les Grandes Misères de la Guerre (Callot), 280
Leslie, Matthew, 64
Les sauvages de l'Europe (Lesuire), 270
Lesser Antilles, 346
Lessing, Gotthold Ephraim, 276, 280, 423
Lesuire, Robert-Martin, 270
Letter Addressed to Two Great Men, 272
*Letter from Herr von *** to Herr von N. N, A* (anonymous pamphlet), 109
Letters on Recent Literature (Nicolai), 278
Letter to the People of England, A (anonymous pamphlet), 272–273
Lévis, Chevalier de, 252, 314

Life of Great Heroes of the Current War, The (Pauli), 418
Life Story (Täge), 212
light troops, 49, 115, 130, 321, 437
linear tactics, 47–48, 65, 451
Lisbon earthquake, 269
Lobkowicz, Leopold, 266
Lobositz, 95–102, 104–106, 109, 282
L'observateur hollandois (Moreau), 51, 52
Loën, Johann Michael von, 44–45
Logejus, Jakob Friedrich Anton Logan, 13
Lohrmann, Jobst Hinrich, 235
London Board of Trade, 61
London Gazette, 271, 272
London Magazine, 295
Lord Clive (British privateering ship), 379
Los Desastres de la Guerra (Goya), 280
Louisa Ulrika of Prussia, 439
Louisbourg, Nova Scotia, 141, 153, 199–205
Louis de Bourbon, Count of Clermont, 187
Louis Ernest of Brunswick-Lüneburg, 266
Louis XIV, King of France, 31, 430
Louis XV, King of France, 257
Louis XVI, King of France, 430
Luckner, Johann Nicolas von, 320
Ludwig Eugen, Duke of Württemberg, 35–36
Luise Dorothée of Saxe-Meiningen, 14, 51, 113, 209, 257, 270, 342, 403, 412
Luise Ulrike of Prussia, 345
Luis Vicente de Velasco e Isla, 420
Lütgert, Johann Conrad, 178, 424–425
Lutheran Court Chapel in London, 309
Lybecker, Erik, 345
Lynar, Rochus Friedrich zu, 133
Lynn, John, 250

Mackellar, Patrick, 360
Madame de Pompadour, 15, 140–141
Magdeburg civilians, 328
Magdeburgische Zeitung, 274, 278
Maidstone Affair, 75
Mancini-Mazarini, Louis-Jules, 390
Manila, 369–380
Mann, Michael, 23–24
Mann, Thomas, 436
Manteuffel, Heinrich von, 343
Maria Anna Viktoria, 356
Maria Antonia of Saxony, 214
Maria Theresa, Roman Empress, 15, 26, 33, 106, 108, 122, 123, 125, 150, 190, 214, 267, 282, 285, 341
Marin de la Malque, Paul, 58
Mark of Brandenburg, 6, 217, 411
Marquis Louis-Henri-Gabriel de Conflans d'Armentières, 321
Mars and the Muses, 329–335
Marsh, Elizabeth, 9
Martin, Abraham, 245
Martinez de Zuñiga, Joaquín, 376
Martinique: British expedition to, 220, 222, 285, 359–360, 363, 429; French forces on, 346; restored to France, 393
material culture, 16, 288
Mauduit, Israel, 271
Mauvillon, Jakob, 313
Maxen, 282; Finck's Capture at, 282, 327; Prussian surrender of arms at, 282
Maximilian III Joseph, Duke of Bavaria, 110–111
Mayer, Tobias, 218
Mayr, Johann von, 320, 430
McLean, John, 349
McNamara, John, 379
media-driven patriotic feeling, 273
media war, 269–296; Carthage, 269–273; consuming/remembering the war, 283–288; global war as media event, 294–296; "King of Press-ia" fighting newspaper war, 273–275; knowledge of the world, 294–296; news as commodity, 288–294; war of images, 280–283; writers' war, 275–280
Medick, Hans, 5
Meerheim, Christian Ernst, 310
Mehl, Johann Gottfried, 217
Meier, Georg Friedrich, 281
Meier, Johann Christian, 138–139
Memoir of the Reign of Our Current King Frederick II (Adelung), 328–329
Memoirs of the Recent War in North America (Pouchot), 318
"Memorandum on the Capture of Havana" (Dundas), 368
Memories for My Children and My Children's Children's Children's Children (Verhoeven), 11
memory culture, 47, 119, 195
Mendelssohn, Moses, 276
Ménétra, Jacques-Louis, 196
Menorca, 78–80
merchandising of war, 435
Mercou, Louis d'Assas du, 419
Michaelis, Johann David, 333
Michell, Abraham Louis, 26, 267
Michels, Franz Goswin von, 180
microhistory, 18–20
Middleton, Richard, 339
Miklós Esterházy de Galántha, 52–53
Miller, James, 42, 363, 426, 450
Minavavana, Anishinabe (Chippeway) chief, 350–351
Minden Lodge, 238
Minna von Barnhelm (Lessing), 423
Mir Jafar, 156–157, 410
Mir Quasim, 406
Mitchell, Sir Andrew, 245, 271, 400

modern nationalism, 435
Mollinger, Franz Rudolf, 137–138
Monro, Donald, 429
Monro, George, 153, 429
Montag, Leopold, 274
Montagu, George, 255, 411
Montagu, Lady Elizabeth, 355
Montalegre, Johann Daniel de, 124–125
Montcalm, Louis Joseph de, 152–156, 200–201, 246–251, 255–256, 420
Montcalm, Marquis de, 247
Montgomery, Henry, 452
Montreal, 314–318
Mopinot de la Chapotte, Antoine Rigobert, 16
"moral weeklies," 271
Mordaunt, Sir John, 192
Moreau, Jacob Nicolas, 51
Morris, Robert Hunter, 72
mosquitoes and monsoons, 357–380
Mühlenberg, Heinrich Melchior, 15, 53, 64–65, 68, 70–73, 230
Münchener Bott, 91
Münchhausen, Otto von, 429
Münchnerisches Wochen-Blat in Versen, 293
Munro, Hector, 406
Münster, 113, 115, 297; chronicles, 178; ecclesiastical territories of, 297; population of, 169; smallholders, 178
Murray, James, 314, 432
Murray, Lord John, 427
Murray Treaty, 432
Musil, Robert, 4–5
Mustafa III, Sultan of the Ottoman Empire, 22, 182
My Experiences as a Cavalry Officer Under the Great King in the Years 1741 to 1759 (Logejus), 13
Mysore conflict, 441

Nachtgedanken bey einer gefährlichen Reise in Kriegszeiten (Belach), 279
Nádasdy, Franz Leopold von, 121, 145
Nadau du Treil, Charles François Emmanuel, 220, 223–225
Namur (British warship), 261
Napoleonic Wars, 3, 164, 434
Native Americans, 58, 60, 68–70, 73, 270, 275, 300, 404, 406, 415, 452; and alcohol, 178; and Fort Pitt, 404; and France, 155; and Montcalm's troops, 154; nations, 393; no peace for, 350–351; and Pontiac Rebellion, 406; religious antagonisms, 161; tribes, 246–247, 393, 441; veritable canaille, 203; violent expulsions of, 441; and white settlers, 403
Naudé, Albert, 26
Naumann, Gottlob, 274
Nazi war propaganda, 277
Neubauer, Heinrich Georg, 109
Neueröfnete Historische Bilder-Saal (Newly published historic hall of images), 125, 294, 401
New France, 317, 318
news as commodity, 288–294
New York, 318–320
New-York Gazette, 244
Nichols, Joseph, 200
Nicolai, Ferdinand Friedrich von, 147
Nicolai, Friedrich, 278
Nicolai, Gottlob Samuel, 242
Nikolaus Friedrich von Korff, 297
Nine Years' War, 236
North American colonies, 369
Northwestern Germany, 311–314
Nouvelle-France, 3, 205, 247, 314, 316, 318, 442, 446
Nützliche Sammlungen (German newspaper), 295

Observations on the Diseases of the Army (Pringle), 429
Oelsnitz, Anton Leopold von, 279
Oelsnitz, Wilhelm Ludwig von, 279
O'Hara, James, 352–353
"olfactory revolution," 452
Oncken, Wilhelm, 3
"On Dying for the Fatherland" (Abbt), 278
Onomatopoeia, 453
On the Diseases of an Army, Written on the Basis of Direct Observations (Baldinger), 429
ordre de bataille, 47
O'Reilly, Alejandro, 424
Oriental despot, 84
Orlov, Grigory, 383
Orme, Robert, 6, 295
Orsbridge, Philip, 367
Ortmann, Adolph Dietrich, 130, 277
Osborne, Sir Danvers, 61
Osman III, Sultan of the Ottoman Empire, 22, 182
Ostfriesische Geschichte, 322
Oswald, Richard, 268
Ottoman Empire, 22, 29, 182–183

Pacte de Famille (Family Pact), 21, 336–341
Palmstierna, Nils, 260
Parchwitz Address, 146–147
Parkman, Francis, 394
Patriotic Letters (Ortmann), 129–130, 277
patriotism, 8, 17, 30, 42, 193, 273, 435, 448
Pauli, Carl Friedrich, 418
peace: agreement, 272; Europe celebrating, 396–403; Fontainebleau and path to, 390–391; precarious promises, 403–407

Peace of Aachen, 25, 26, 396
Peace of Dresden, 2
Peace of Hubertusburg, 394–396, 397, 401
Peace of Montréal, 30
Peace of Paris, 392–394, 402, 410
Peace of Utrecht, 78
Peace of Westphalia, 392, 398
Péan, Michel-Jean-Hugues, 69, 318
Pécaudy de Contrecoeur, Claude-Pierre, 59
Pedro de Pablo Abarca Bolea, the Conde de Aranda, 355
Pelham-Holles, Thomas, 21
Pennsylvania Gazette, 275
Peter III of Russia, 381, 388
Philadelphia, 318–320
Philipp, Johann, 133
Philosophical Dictionary (Voltaire), 239
Pigot, George, 349
Pillai, Ananda Ranga, 13, 14–15, 80, 156, 226–229, 349, 451
pitched battle, 47, 101, 247
Pitt, William, 55–56, 199, 232, 246, 256, 267, 280
Plains of Abraham, 247, 255
Plank, Geoffrey, 43
Pleissner, Johann Georg, 289
Plotho, Christoph Edler Herr und Freiherr von, 91, 109, 111
Pocock, Sir George, 228–229, 358, 359, 362, 366
Poetic Images of Most Warlike Events in Europe Since the Year 1756 (Denis), 278
Political Tinker/The Pewterer Turned Politician, The (Holberg), 289
politics: legitimation, 273; security-driven, 439–441; War's impact on, 430–432
Polybios (Greek historian), 279

Pomeranian War, 3, 183–186, 258, 343–347
Poniatowski, Stanislaus II August, 439
Pontiac Rebellion, 405, 406
Pontiac War, 22, 324, 404
Poor Clares, 371
Porter, John, 194
Potawatomi, 351, 405
Pouchot, Pierre, 316, 318
Prado, Juan de, 359, 424
precarious promises, 403–407
Précis du siècle de Louis XV (Outline of the century of Louis XV) (Voltaire), 419
primogeniture, 83
Pringle, John, 429
prisoners of war, 323–329
Prittwitz, Christian Wilhelm von, 16, 39, 119, 121, 165–167, 177, 206–208, 242, 258, 382, 428, 450
prize papers, 449
"Problem of Historical Time, The" (Simmel), 18
Proclamation of Proclamations, The, 402
Prussia, 151, 160, 183–184, 330–334, 412–413, 418–419, 438–439; and Austria, 27, 35, 264, 278, 297, 329; bombardment of Prague, 120; and Britain, 189; capture of Dresden, 93; combat operations, 46; conquest of Quebec, 272; Corpus Evangelicorum, 108; defense investment, 33; and France, 22; invasion of Saxony, 2, 91, 94, 110, 297; invasion of Silesia, 32, 91; "Old Testament victories," 276; and Ottoman Empire, 384; *rétablissement*, 417; and Russia, 26, 126, 205, 297, 299, 382; sectarian scandal, 172; and Sweden, 38; system of military cantons, 37, 39; victory at Rossbach, 272; War of the Austrian Succession, 26
Prussia Moves the World, 449
Prussian Renaissance, 7
Prussian Soldiers' Letters, 13
Prussian War Songs by a Grenadier in the Campaigns of 1756 and 1757 (Gleim), 276
public celebrations, 271–272
Putlitz, Georg Karl Gans Edler zu, 101, 136–137, 147

Quebec militia, 250
Querfurt, August, 281
"Questions from a Worker Who Reads" (Brecht), 13

Raab zu Rauenberg, Karl Joseph Graf, 289
Rabener, Gottlieb Wilhelm, 303
Rafaela de Herrera y Torreynosa, 379
Ragib Pasha, Koca, 183
Ramler, Karl Wilhelm, 135
Ranke, Leopold von, 26
Rau, Johannes, 342
Raynal, Abbé, 5
Rebentisch, Johann Karl von, 423
Reformed Anglicans, 289
Rehdiger, Juliane von, 145, 210
Reichardt, Johann Friedrich, 415
Reichs Post-Reuter (Hamburg newspaper), 274
Reign of George VI, 1900–1925, The, 392
Reiss, Frantz, 97
religious pamphlets, 280
religious war, 160–173; British soldiers, 169; Catholicism, 167–168, 170; confessionalization, 165; sieges, 162–163

Remarks on the Letter (William Burke), 272
restricted space, 299–301
Retzow, Friedrich August von, 241–243
Retzow, Wolf Dietrich von, 212
Revolutionary War, 430
Richelieu, Duc de, 78–79, 133, 142, 144, 186–187, 297–298
Richelieu scandal, 298
Richter, Christoph Gottlieb, 101–102, 288
Ritter, Gerhard, 274
Robertson, Archibald, 360
Rochefort, 192–193
Rode, Bernhard, 420
Rogers, Robert, 72, 430
Rojo del Rio, Don Manuel Antonio, 371, 372
Rolland Michel Barrin, the Comte de la Galissonière, 52
Roman-Carthaginian conflict, 270
Roman Catholicism, 254
Roques de Maumont, Jacques Emmanuel, 144
Rosen, Gustaf Fredrick von, 216
Rossbach, 136–139
Rothschild, Emma, 9
Roubaud, Pierre, 155
Royal American Regiment, 74
Ruins in Destroyed Québec, in the Center the Church of Notre Dame de la Victoire (Antoine Benoist), 253
Ruins of the Kreuzkirche in Dresden (Bernardo Bellotto), 303
Rumyantsev-Zadunaisky, Pyotr Alexandrovich, 343
Russia: capture of Berlin, 284; patriotism, 273; peace agreement with Sweden, 382; prisoners of war in Berlin, 326; and Prussia, 26, 126, 205, 297, 299, 382; soldiers lost by, 412
Rustant, Joseph Vicente de, 5
Rutensparre, Karl, 259
Rutowski, Friedrich Augustus Graf, 94

Sack, August Friedrich Wilhelm, 276
Sackville, George, 234
Sainte-Croix, Gaetan Xavier Guilhelm de Pascalis de, 338
Saltykov, Pyotr, 240
Sarriá, Nicolás de Carvajal y Lancaster Marqués de, 353, 355
Saunders, Charles, 246
Saxon army, 106–107
Schatz, Georg, 53, 454
Schaumburg-Lippe, Wilhelm Friedrich Ernst Count von, 353
Schiller, Friedrich, 9, 173
Schiller, Johann Caspar, 164
Schimmelmann, Heinrich Carl von, 175, 268, 414
Schivelbusch, Wolfgang, 431
Schneider, George, 69, 153–154, 201
Schowart, Johann Philipp, 256
Schröder, Christoph Wilhelm, 75, 77
Schulze, Johann Michael Friedrich, 6
Schuman, Matt, 8
Schweizer, Karl, 8
Schwerin, Kurt Christoph Graf von, 117–119, 419–420
Schwoart, Johann Philipp, 201
Scott, Joan Wallach, 462n48
second Berlin surprise, 304–311
Second Carnatic War. *See* Carnatic-Hyderabad War of Succession
"Second Hundred Years' War," 22
Second Versailles Treaty, 115

securitization, 439–440
security-driven politics, 439–441
segmentary state formation, 23
Seidlitz, Friedrich Wilhelm, 137
Senckenberg, Johann Christian, 425
sensory war, 452–454
Serres, Dominic, 253, 367
Shah Alam II, Mughal Emperor, 406
Shaw, John, 60
Shirley, William, 62–63, 152
Short, Richard, 252–253
Shuvalov, Peter Ivanovich, 36, 114
Shuvalov howitzers, 36
siege: of Louisbourg in 1758, 286; of Quebec, 1759, 249; warfare, 46
Simmel, Georg, 17–19
Simón de Anda y Salazar, 377
Siraj-ud-Daulah, 84–85, 87; Battle of Plassey, 157–158; and Clive, 156–158
Smith, Joseph, 158
Smollett, Tobias, 272
Society of Jesus, 23
Songs of a Prussian Grenadier (Gleim), 281
Sorokin, Pitirim, 411
Soubisiades, 139–141
Southsea Castle (British warship), 374
Spain, 354; colonies of, 357–380; and France, 37, 337, 391–392, 397; soldiers lost by, 412
Spavens, William, 261
Splitgerber, David, 268, 414
Springer, Ivan, 120
Staats- und Gelehrten Neuigkeiten, 294
Stamp Act of 1765, 319
Starhemberg, Georg Adam Graf von, 77
Steuben, Friedrich Wilhelm von, 430
St. George (British warship), 222

St. James Chronicle, 370
Stobo, Robert, 63, 247
St. Paul, Horace, 15, 42
Striebritz, Johann Friedrich, 333
Stuart, Charles Edward, 42, 68–69
Stutterheim, Joachim Friedrich von, 344
Sugar Act of 1764, 319
Sullivan, Laurence, 410
Sulzer, Johann Georg, 326, 382
Surgeon's Mate— The Diary of John Knyveton, Surgeon in the British Fleet During the Seven Years War 1756– 1762, 13
Sussex Weekly Advertiser, 272
Süssmilch, Johann Peter, 305–309
Sweden, 28–29, 37–38, 110, 112, 183–184; peace agreement with Russia, 382; Pomeranian War, 345; and Prussia, 259, 345; soldiers lost by, 412
Swedish Pomerania, 38
Szabo, Franz A. J., 7

Tacky's War, 415
Taege, Christian, 145–146
Täge, Christian, 180, 212, 450
tamed Bellona, 43–44
Taylor, Peter, 268
"Te-Deum-ing," 108
Telemann, Georg Philipp, 279
Tempelhof, Georg Friedrich von, 5–6, 147, 234
ter Meer, Abraham, 210, 219, 256, 292, 296, 317, 396, 451
Ternay, Chevalier de, 386
territorial patriotism, 435
Test (British journal), 271
Teutsche Kriegs-Canzley (Montag), 274
Theodor, Karl, 110

Thieriot, Nicolas-Claude, 51
Third Silesian War, 2, 21, 139, 387
Thirty Years' War, 5, 48–49, 53, 160, 268, 274, 280, 398, 417, 435, 445–446
Thomas Arthur, the Comte de Lally-Tollendal, 228
Thompson, John, 256
three sieges of Kolberg, 341–343
Thurel, Jean, 430
Tilliers, Johann Anton von, 288
Todd, William, 16, 178, 192, 195–196, 312, 450
Tottleben, Gottlob Curt Heinrich von, 305
Townshend, George, 251
Traces of the Vanquished (Haasis), 14
Trattner, Johann Thomas, 274
Trautzschen, Hans Carl Heinrich von, 95, 176, 232, 332, 428, 450
Treaty of Aix-la-Chapelle, 57
Treaty of Allahabad, 406
Treaty of Hubertusburg, 394
Treaty of Lancaster, 58
Treaty of Versailles, 53, 77
Treaty of Westminster, 271
Treaty of Westphalia, 38
Trembling, Joints, 367
Trew, Christoph Jacob, 333
"tribute money," 271
True Presentation of the Current Times, A, 291
Tsarina Elisabeth of Russia, 345, 381, 417
Turner, Thomas, 141, 255, 272, 317, 402
Twelve Views of the Principal Buildings in Québec (Richard Short), 252
Twenty-One Copperplate Engravings (Montalegre), 124

Uhlmann, Markus, 40, 177, 359, 427, 446, 450
Ungern-Sternberg, Matthias Alexander von, 38, 184, 215
"Uniform Notebook" (Becher), 284
University of Greifswald, 335
urban life: Boston, New York, Philadelphia, 318–320; corruption/cooperation in occupied cities, 297–299; Dresden in flames, 301–304; fighting in Northwestern Germany, 311–314; Fischer Corps on rampage, 320–323; Mars and the Muses, 329–335; Montreal, 314–318; prisoners of war, 323–329; restricted space, 299–301; second Berlin surprise, 304–311; in state of exception, 297–335; universities at war, 329–335
Ursuline Chapel in Quebec, 251
Uz, Johann Peter, 277

Valori, Louis Guy Henry de, 93
Vattel, Emer de, 415
Vaudreuil, Pierre de Rigaud de, 246, 250, 252, 268, 316–317, 557n119
Vaugeois, Denis, 432
Vauxhall Gardens, 280
Veitel Heine Ephraim, 416
Velasco, José Antonio Manso de, 359, 364, 424
Vengeance (British warship), 261
Verhoeven, Antonius, 11
Viana, Fiskal, 377
Viana, Francisco Leandro, 375
"Victory of the King at Torgau" (Karsch), 278
Vivat! ribbons, 284, 285, 286, 290, 382, 398, 435

Volontaires auxiliaires, 425
Voltaire, 238–239, 267, 270, 273, 280, 342, 403, 412, 419
"Vom Tode für das Vaterland" (Abbt), 420
Vom Verdienste (Abbt), 276
von der Trenck, Friedrich Freiherr, 13
Vorontsova, Elizaweta Romanova, 383
Vossische Zeitung, 307
Voyage Among the Indian Seas Guillaume le Gentil), 349
Voyage from England to India, in the Year 1754, A (Ives), 295
Vrouw Clara Magdalena (Dutch ship), 359

Waddington, Richard, 6
Wagner, Johann Ludwig, 325
Wähner, Andreas Georg, 14, 133, 201, 255, 258, 292, 296, 451
Wall, Ricardo, 355
Walpole, Horace, 14, 255, 409
war: consuming, 283–288; everyday life during, 159–181; and globalization, 21–25; hunger and thirst, 175–178; of images, 280–283; impact on politics and culture, 430–432; of miracles, 436–439; outcomes of, 408–432; portents of, 90–95; religious, 160–173; remembering, 283–288; reporting, 269; of state formation, 28–29; universities at war, 329–335. *See also specific wars*
War of Jenkins' Ear, 25
War of the Austrian Succession, 26, 320, 429, 430
War of the Bavarian Succession, 431
War of the Spanish Succession, 28, 37, 78, 357, 392
Wars of Frederick the Great, The (Showalter), 6

Washington, George, 59
Watteau, François-Louis-Joseph, 421
Watts, John, 319
Wedel, Carl Heinrich von, 216
Wegener, Carl Friedrich, 162
Wellenreuther, Hermann, 393, 448
Werner, Hans Paul von, 342
Werner, Theodor, 129
West, Benjamin, 280, 407, 420, 421
West, Temple, 79
West Africa, 218–220
Westminster Convention, 74–78
Whether It Is Advisable, by the Rules of Statecraft, to Deny the Loss of a Battle, or to Spread False Victories and Advantages, 210
Whitefield, George, 309
Wiarda, Tileman Dothias, 322
Wickrath, Friedrich Wilhelm Quadt zu, 423
Wied-Runkel, Friedrich Georg zu, 121, 125
Wiener Diarium, 122, 274
Wienerisches Diarium, 101–102
Wilhelm of Prittwitz, 16
Will, Johann Martin, 292, 293
William Pitt the Elder, 21, 75–76
Williams, Hanbury, 271
Williamson, Peter, 11
winners and losers, 411–413
Winterfeldt, Hans Karl von, 106, 387, 419–420
Wittenberg, 309, 330
Wittenberg Castle, 309
"Wittenberg Taberah, The" (Meerheim), 310
Wochen-Blat in Versen (Weekly news-paper in verse), 385
Wolfe, James, 43, 66, 75, 105, 192, 199, 202–203, 246, 247, 410, 419, 420

Wood, James, 227, 230
Woodforde, James, 255, 367
Wrede, Carl Friedrich von, 423
writers' war, 275–280
Württemberg, Friedrich Eugen von, 36, 242, 306, 344
Wyandot, 405

Xaver, Franz, 198–199

Young, John, 153

Zahn, Gottfried, 94–95, 107
Zander, Johann Heinrich, 183
Zellmann, Johann Philipp, 179, 287, 336
Zieten, Hans Joachim von, 118, 121
Zittau fire of 1757, 163
Zweybrücken, Friedrich Herzog von, 265

GPSR Authorized Representative: Easy Access System Europe, Mustamäe tee 50, 10621 Tallinn, Estonia, gpsr.requests@easproject.com

www.ingramcontent.com/pod-product-compliance
Lightning Source LLC
Chambersburg PA
CBHW022023290426
44109CB00014B/726